ENCYCLOPEDIA OF
Consumer Brands

ENCYCLOPEDIA OF CONSUMER BRANDS

VOLUME I
CONSUMABLE PRODUCTS

VOLUME II
PERSONAL PRODUCTS

VOLUME III
DURABLE GOODS

ENCYCLOPEDIA OF

Consumer Brands

VOLUME 3

Durable Goods

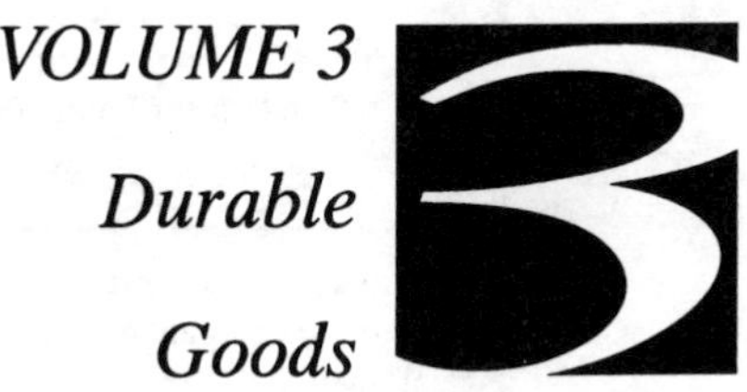

Editor JANICE JORGENSEN

St James Press
Detroit London Washington D.C.

STAFF

Janice Jorgensen, *Editor*

David Collins, Nicolet V. Elert, L. Mpho Mabunda, Mary Ruby, *Associate Editors*
Barbara Carlisle Bigelow, Suzanne M. Bourgoin, Kevin Hillstrom, Paula Kepos,
Michael L. LaBlanc, Julia M. Rubiner, *Contributing Editors*
Marilyn Allen, *Editorial Associate*

Peter M. Gareffa, *Senior Editor*

Mary Beth Trimper, *Production Director*
Shanna Heilveil, *Production Assistant*
Cynthia Baldwin, *Art Director*
Mark C. Howell, *Graphic Designer*
C. J. Jonik, *Desktop Publisher*

Victoria B. Cariappa, *Research Manager*
Jeanne Gough, *Permissions Manager*

∞™ This book is printed on acid-free paper that meets the minimum requirements of American National Standard for Information Sciences—Permanence Paper for Printed Library Materials, ANSI Z39.48-1984.

Library of Congress Catalog Card Number 93-37940
ISBN 1-55862-338-8
Printed in the United States of America
Published simultaneously in the United Kingdom

I(T)P™

The trademark **ITP** is used under license.
10 9 8 7 6 5 4 3 2 1

ADVISERS

Martin Boddy
Information Officer
ICI Group Headquarters, London, England

Linda Golden
Professor of Marketing
University of Texas, Austin

Pamela K. Jenkins
Librarian/Business Specialist
Kansas City Public Library, Kansas City, Missouri

Paul Kirner
Vice President/Executive Art Director
J. Walter Thompson, Detroit, Michigan

Jeanette M. Mueller-Alexander
Reference Librarian/Business Subject Specialist
Hayden Library, Arizona State University, Tempe

BRAND CATEGORIES COVERED IN THE ENCYCLOPEDIA

VOLUME I: CONSUMABLE PRODUCTS

Food
Pet Food
Non-Alcoholic Beverages
Alcoholic Beverages
Tobacco

VOLUME II: PERSONAL PRODUCTS

Apparel and Accessories
Cosmetics and Fragrances
Health and Beauty Aids
Household Cleaning and Paper Products
Miscellaneous Household Products
Over-the-Counter Drugs
Stationery and Office Supply

VOLUME III: DURABLE GOODS

Appliances
Automobiles and Related Products
Computers, Electronics, and Office Equipment
Home Furnishings and Building Supplies
Musical Instruments
Photographic Equipment
Sporting Goods
Toys and Games

CONTENTS

Volume III: Durable Goods

PREFACE

Encyclopedia of Consumer Brands provides substantive information on products that have been leaders in their respective brand categories and have had decided impact on American business or popular culture. Often considered "household words," the featured products have become integral parts of the lives of American consumers, and many have gone on to achieve international recognition.

The *Encyclopedia*'s three volumes highlight approximately 600 of the most popular brands in America. Coverage in each book emphasizes brands that have been prominent since 1950 and are now on the market, with a few inclusions of instructive debacles such as the Edsel. Younger products that have experienced profound success or have notably influenced their industry are also included. With thousands of new products being introduced to the market each year—and only a handful of them still in existence five years after their launch—much can be learned from the stories behind prominent brands, whose success depends on an elusive combination of careful research, quality development, market savvy, advertising prowess, and precise timing. The *Encyclopedia* is intended for use by students, librarians, job seekers, advertising and business people, and others who want to learn more about the historical and modern development of brands most significant to American culture.

Inclusion Criteria

Brands included in the series were selected by the editor and advisory board members, who chose brands possessing a combination of elements: top sales and leading market share in their field, strong public recognition, and longevity. Many top selling brands and market share leaders were discovered through listings found in trade journals, advertising periodicals, and industry and business publications; Gale Research's *Market Share Reporter* and *Business Rankings Annual* also aided in identifying leading brands. The editor and advisory panel selected brands from a wide range of categories, but because of the increasingly vast number of brand names on the market, some significant products inevitably were left out.

St. James Press does not endorse any of the brand names or companies mentioned in this book. Brands that appear in the *Encyclopedia* were selected without reference to the wishes of their parent companies, who have in no way endorsed their brands' entries. Parent companies were given the opportunity to participate in the compilation of the articles by providing first-hand research and reading their entries for factual inaccuracies. We are indebted to many of these companies for their comments and corrections; we also thank many of the companies for providing logos and other art work for identification purposes. All brand names mentioned in the *Encyclopedia* are trademarks or registered trademarks of their respective parent companies.

Focus

The focus regarding a particular brand name varies from entry to entry. When an individual *product* has found significant success in the market place, that one product is featured in its own entry (e.g. Twinkies, Scotch Tape, or Mustang). When a *brand name* or *trademark* is placed on a wide range of products in different brand categories (e.g. Pillsbury, Calvin Klein, or Sony), that brand name or trademark is the focus of the entry, and discussion of most or all of the products on which that brand name appears will ensue.

Because companies choose to market their products using a variety of tactics—which can include capitalizing on an existing brand name by placing it on new products, or creating new brand names while still emphasizing the company name—a consistent rule of thumb for determining the focus of each of the *Encyclopedia*'s entries was sometimes challenging to establish. The responsibility of deciding the focus of each article rested with the editor, advisory board members, and writers and researchers. Please refer to the Index to Brand Names to identify products that have been either historically chronicled in full or merely mentioned within the series.

Entry Format

An array of special features is included in the entries, which have been designed for quick research and interesting reading.

- **Attractive page design** incorporates textual subheads, making it easy to pinpoint specific information.

- **Easy-to-locate data sections** provide an "At a Glance" overview of brand history, sales and market share (when available), major competitors to the brand, advertising information, and the address and phone number of the brand's parent company.

- **Informative essays** trace how a product originated and was first marketed, how it evolved as a product and developed commercially, and how it fares today compared with its competitors and its own past history. Current coverage encompasses today's changing markets and marketing strategies, the impact of a global economy, and future projections, as well as any controversies associated with the product such as trade name disputes, false advertising claims, and safety, ethical, and environmental issues.

- **Current brand logos or photos** have been included with most entries to further enhance your appreciation of the brand; some entries include historical illustrations as well.

- **Sources for additional information** provide the reader with suggested further reading on the brand; these sources, also used to compile the entries, are publicly accessible materials such as magazines, general and academic periodicals, books, and annual reports, as well as material supplied by the brands' companies.

Helpful Indexes

Encyclopedia of Consumer Brands includes cumulative indexes to Brand Names, Companies and Persons, Advertising Agencies, and Brand Categories that make it easy to locate not only featured brand names but pertinent brand names, companies, people, and advertising agencies mentioned within each article.

ENCYCLOPEDIA OF Consumer Brands

ACURA®

The 1986 introduction of American Honda Motor Co., Inc.'s Acura automobiles revolutionized the U.S. luxury car market. Acura automobiles were the first Japanese luxury cars sold in the United States, and the Acura Automobile Division was the first division of a Japanese automaker to set up a separate dealership network. "Like General Motors, whose offerings range from entry-level Chevrolets to upscale Cadillacs, Honda is embracing the cradle-to-grave credo and attempting to market automobiles for every lifestyle and pocketbook," Cleveland Horton wrote in *Advertising Age.* Creating the Acura brand allowed Honda to broaden its customer base without diluting its identity; Honda dealerships could continue to be associated with reliable, economical cars, while Acura dealerships, catering to a more affluent clientele, could benefit from Honda's reputation for quality.

Despite intense competition in the early 1990s, Acura remained the leader in import luxury car sales. Acura sales peaked at more than 143,000 in 1991, but competition from Japanese luxury car brands Lexus and Infiniti caused Acura sales to slump. By 1993, when the Acura Legend was the top-selling luxury imported car, total Acura sales had declined ten percent from the previous year to 108,291 cars, and sales projections for 1994 were estimated at 120,000 cars. Together, Honda and Acura made up 8.4 percent of total U.S. car sales in 1993, making Honda the fifth-largest car manufacturer in the United States. Sometime in 1994, Acura planned to sell its one millionth car, a feat Acura claimed no luxury brand has reached so rapidly.

Success from the Start

American Honda conceived of the Acura line during the recession of the early 1980s, when the luxury car market was one of the few to report continued healthy sales, thanks to wealthy consumers untouched by the economic downturn. In addition, automotive marketing consultant J. David Power predicted in *Business Week* in 1986 that "sales of cars costing more than $18,000 should rise 28 percent to 1.5 million units by 1990, while total auto sales should increase only 12 percent." American Honda wanted to tap the growing luxury car market but thought its name was tied too closely to family and economy cars. "When you thought about Honda, you wouldn't necessarily think about luxury," noted James Higgins in the *Detroit News.* Stewart Toy wrote in *Business Week* that American Honda decided to market Acuras separately to "build the snob appeal needed to sell luxury performance cars in the United States." In the rest of the world, the cars would be marketed under the Honda name.

Acura automobiles were designed to be an extension of Honda's sporty image, with more attention paid to performance and luxury. The Legend sedan, selling for $20,000 in 1986, was intended to compete with cars made by German automakers BMW and Mercedes Benz. Two less expensive models, the three- and five-door versions of the Integra sports sedan, gave customers a powerful engine but less elbow room and sold for between $9,300 and $11,800. With 60 dealerships, Acura almost met its first year sales goal of 55,000 cars, selling 52,869 cars. Of that number, 53 percent were the lower-priced Integras.

Though European cars made up the majority of the U.S. luxury car market in 1986, American Honda, noted *Advertising Age,* was not "interested in conquest sales, or convincing a Porsche or BMW owner to give up that marque in favor of an Acura." Instead, the company sought to appeal to first-time luxury car buyers. A 1987 *Detroit News* article pointed out that the competitors felt they "haven't been hurt by the newcomer." But Acura quickly became the highest volume seller of imported luxury cars. By 1987 Acura surpassed its sales goal of 105,000, selling 109,470 cars. That year Acura sold more cars than BMW, Mercedes Benz, Volvo, or Audi. In addition, *Motor Trend* ranked Acura's new introduction, the Legend Coupe, the 1987 Import Car of the Year. Acura's sales proved that Americans were willing to pay premium prices for Japanese cars.

With superior customer service, Acura quickly climbed to the coveted top position of the J. D. Power and Associates Customer Satisfaction Study (CSI), the Holy Grail of the luxury automobile industry. Acura debuted in the CSI top position in 1987 and held it for four consecutive years. In addition, for three years, Acura ranked first in the J.D. Power and Associates Vehicle Performance Study (VPI), which rates cars according to customer satisfaction and operational and functional performance after three years of ownership.

National Marketing

Acura launched a $20 million advertising campaign to enter the luxury car market. The introductory television commercial's theme, "A matter of time," showed a clock, an American getting a phone call, and a shot of the Acura Legend, with the tagline

AT A GLANCE

Acura brand of automobiles introduced in 1986 by the Acura Division of American Honda Motor Company, Inc.; brand marketed at low end of luxury car market for most of the 1980s; in the 1990s Acura moved into the upscale segments of the car market; Acura cars made in Japan and imported to the United States; 1996 model scheduled to be produced in East Liberty, OH.

Performance: *Market share*—(Honda and Acura brands) 8.4% of total U.S. car segment (1993). *Sales*—108,291 cars (1993).

Major competitor: Toyota Motor Corp.'s Lexus; also Nissan Motor Corp.'s Infiniti.

Advertising: *Agency*—Ketchum Advertising, 1986—. *Major campaign*—Acura Integra commercials featuring Leonard the Talking Dog, who sarcastically says to dogs in other vehicles, "Adios, kibble breath" and "Hey, man, don't drool on my Integra."

Addresses: *Parent company*—American Honda Motor Co., Inc., Acura Division, 1919 Torrance Boulevard, Torrance, CA 90501-2746; phone: 310-783-2000; fax: 310-783-3900.

"precision crafted automobiles." In another early TV spot all three Acura models were shown driving down a winding road.

Since there had never been a Japanese luxury car marketed in the United States, Acura had to start from scratch. It established an association with existing symbols of quality, European cars. By using frequent comparisons between European cars and Acuras in the first few years of advertising, Acura became known as a luxury import. When the Legend coupe was introduced in 1987, the accompanying ad campaign stated that "the finest sports coupes no longer have to come from Europe." Ads in 1988 claimed the Legend sedan was "the performance sedan that's making European automakers uncomfortable." Acura needed "to use the Europeans as a point of reference. But [Acura's] intent is not to start an advertising war with [the competition]," noted Ketchum Advertising executive Ron Buckhammer in *Advertising Age.*

Throughout the late 1980s, Acura focused on the theme of performance in its commercials, switching its tagline to "precision crafted performance." Ads for the Integra highlighted the company's background in developing Formula One race cars and noted that "most automakers will tell you they don't rely on formulas. Maybe that's because they just haven't found the right one." Extensive copy followed, highlighting Acura's engineers' ability to design winning Formula One engines and the skill required to build a sports sedan with an engine as peppy and precise as Integra's. A similar television spot showed an Integra alongside a Formula One car as a voice-over says, "Formula One technology—and it's street legal." Other 1980s ads featured the Integra's 16-valve fuel-injected double overhead cam (DOHC) aluminum alloy engine, the Legend's 24-valve V-6 engine, the Legend Coupe's anti-lock brakes, and the cars' rear double wishbone suspension.

In 1990 Acura switched gears and began promoting their cars with a $100 million campaign highlighting the lifestyle of the Acura driver. Instead of featuring technical aspects, the 1990 ads were softer, placing the cars in real life situations. Ketchum Advertising dubbed the technique "slice of car" advertising, according to *Automotive News. Advertising Age* noted that the car would be promoted as more of a "fashion accessory." One lifestyle spot showed a father trying to quiet a crying baby. The baby falls peacefully to sleep when strapped into its car seat in the backseat of daddy's Legend. The only sales pitch noticeable in the commercials is a voice that announces Acura's three years of being ranked as the most satisfying car to own in the United States.

Although lifestyle spots were used for both the Legend and Integra, TV ads for the Integra continued to focus more on performance. One 1989 commercial featured the Integra's anti-lock brakes and showed the car stopping nose-to-nose with a fighter jet. Explaining the disparity in advertising techniques, Ketchum president Craig Mathiesen told *Automotive News* that the campaign is "evolutionary—we're not walking away from something that's broken." Integra sales seemed to benefit from ads that highlighted performance.

Japanese Competition

Acura had a three-and-a-half year lead on other Japanese automakers in the luxury car market when Nissan Motor Corp. and Toyota Motor Corp. announced they would both enter upscale cars into the market in 1989. Acura's lead in the market made introducing the two new cars expensive. Both Toyota's Lexus and Nissan's Infiniti expected to spend $60 million on introductory advertising campaigns to penetrate the market. The cost of advertising would be ten times the regular advertising-to-sales ratio, according to *Automotive News,* and the amount would probably have to be sustained to maintain exposure for the cars.

In addition to having to spend more on advertising, noted *Automotive News,* "neither Toyota nor Nissan can lay claim to what analysts call Honda's 'mystique.' The aura of superior customer satisfaction, warranted or not, helped pave the way for Acura's successful launch." Although the parent companies of Lexus and Infiniti did not have outstanding customer relations, both new brands pledged to topple Acura from its reigning CSI position. Infiniti planned to start a "Total Ownership Experience" program to win customer loyalty to dealerships; part of the program involved an eight-day training program in which dealership employees would learn how to appease irritated customers who complain about waiting too long. Lexus planned to have dealers loan new Lexus models to service customers.

Neither the Lexus nor Infiniti hoped to reach Acura's volume of sales, however. Both cars would focus instead on the high-end of the luxury car market, where volume was lower and profits higher. Toyota's first-year sales goal was 30,000 cars, and Nissan told *Automotive News* that its Infiniti "was not a volume-oriented division." For the first ten months of 1990, sales of the Lexus LS 400 and the Infiniti Q45 were 33,869 and 9,501, respectively, whereas sales of the Acura Legend were 45,610.

Competed for Customer Satisfaction

Customer satisfaction has been one of Acura's most renowned traits. In 1990 one-fifth of Acura's $50 million advertising budget was used to promote its customer satisfaction rating. Lexus and Infiniti put Acura on the defensive when both competitors announced their intent to win the top CSI rating.

To secure the top position, at least one Acura dealership, Cerritos Acura in California, instituted a specialist delivery program in 1990. The program has a specialist walk the customer through the various service departments, explain the warranty, guarantees, and owner's manual, take a Polaroid picture of the customer, and do a follow-up call to gather information about customer satisfaction, which is then shared with Acura headquarters. Cerritos Acura felt that having someone other than the salesperson show the customer their final product would build loyalty to the dealership and not the salesperson.

Not every aspect of customer service, however, was being bolstered to protect against the competition. Even though both Lexus and Infiniti announced they would provide free loaner cars to customers, Cerritos Acura cut back its free loaners to include only "major service, if you bought your car here," the service manager told *Automotive News.* In addition, the loaners were not like the new models Lexus and Infiniti passed out; they were subcompacts that the dealership rented for $20 per day.

Regardless of customer relations policies, the real test of Acura's customer satisfaction is the actual car. A customer at Cerritos Acura told *Automotive News,* "The main reason I'm here is that they have a good car. It doesn't make any difference how well you treat me if the car doesn't work." One salesman at the dealership said, "The car sells itself. . . . I just try to treat my customers the way I'd like to be treated and know the advantages of our cars vs. our competitors'."

Efforts to improve Acura's customer service were not enough to ward off competitors. Acura slipped from its top position in the CSI rating in 1991. After being the most satisfying car to own from 1987 through 1990, Acura dropped to the fourth position in 1991 and 1992 and plummeted to eighth in the 1993 rating.

Broadened Market Appeal

Acura felt confident that it would be difficult for its competitors to experience the same sweeping success Acura had enjoyed when it entered the market in 1986. Acura secured its leading sales position with the introduction of the second-generation Integra, which had trim options that would broaden its 1990 price range from $11,950 to $16,675. The Integra was nevertheless not a direct competitor of the soon-to-be-introduced, more expensive luxury cars Lexus and Infiniti.

Even though Acura felt it had secured itself at the low end of the luxury car market, where, according to *Advertising Age,* "89 percent of cars priced at $20,000 or more are sold," the introduction of the Lexus and Infiniti caused the first dip in Acura sales, as Legend revenues dropped 8.7 percent from the previous year. Although the competitors did not come close to selling as many cars as Acura, the automaker took notice. To compete more effectively with new luxury vehicles, Acura planned the introduction of two new models, an updated Legend in 1990 and a mid-engine exotic car in 1991. Also in 1991, Acura hoped to recapture the limelight with the new Legend. "If they had the second-generation Legend last fall, sales would not have dropped," a J.D. Power and Associates executive told *Advertising Age.*

The second-generation Legend was completely redesigned to be larger and less angular. The body panels were made thicker, which made the Legend's chassis rigidity comparable to the Mercedes 300E and BMW 535i. The more powerful 200 horsepower, 3.2 liter six-cylinder engine was placed longitudinally to improve the car's handling. The Legend adopted the use of an "A" logo, following the lead of the Lexus and Infiniti, which were both introduced with unique hood and trunk ornaments. In keeping with Acura's desire to win back consumer attention from its Japanese competitors, advertising focused on the newness of the product rather than the CSI rating.

To capture more of the upscale car market and boost brand prestige, Acura introduced an exotic car called the NSX. The 1990 introduction of the NSX won great praise from critics and much attention from car enthusiasts. The NSX was completely handmade except for some of the welding. The 3,000-pound car featured an all-aluminum body, the ability to reach 60 mph in under six seconds, and an audio system by Bose. Production was limited to about 6,000 cars per year, and only 3,000 NSXes were scheduled for shipment to the United States annually; the remaining 3,000 would supply Japanese and European markets. Though the sticker price for the NSX was $60,000, the highest of all Japanese cars, bids as high as $125,000 were made at some dealerships before customers even saw it. The exotic NSX, receiving praise for its superior engine and exceptionally comfortable interior, boosted the image of the entire Acura line.

To broaden sales, Acura developed a model between the Integra and the Legend called the Vigor. The five-cylinder Vigor was positioned in the near-luxury car market to capture consumers who wanted a more luxurious sports sedan but not the plushness of the Legend. The Vigor was the first car to offer digital sound processing, an eight-speaker system that can simulate six different environments, including a concert hall and a cathedral. Because the sound system of a car was thought to be influential to the purchase, "Acura is monitoring consumer reaction to see if the system should be offered on other Honda and Acura models," as noted in *Automotive News.* Sales of the Vigor did not meet expectations in 1991; although one California dealer liked the Vigor, he thought it was priced too high at $23,665. In 1994 the Vigor still had not reached Acura's expectations, and the company planned a new model with a V-6 engine and a roomier interior for the 1995 model year.

Target Marketing for the 1990s

Of Acura's 1994 models, the Integra was expected to receive the most advertising support. Acura planned to spend $25 million on a two-pronged campaign to capture both Baby Boomers, aged 32 to 44, and Generation Xers, aged 18 to 31. The campaign design was more elaborate than the one that launched the entire Acura Division in 1986 and was aimed at stopping the division's two-year sales decline.

Acura used targeted media buys to launch two very different commercials promoting the Integra. The first, which debuted on July 12, 1993, showed the Integra zooming around a large Hot Wheels track with a voiceover saying, "Not since Hot Wheels has a car been this much fun," and after the Acura logo filled the screen, the announcer added, "Track sold separately." The ad, targeting the Baby Boomers, was shown during such television shows as *Seinfeld, Home Improvement,* and *Northern Exposure.* The second ad was aimed at Generation Xers and featured a sarcastic dog named Leonard. Leonard leaned out of the car's window and said things like, "Finally, a car I'm not embarrassed to stick my head out of" and "Hey, man, don't drool on my Integra." The ads with Leonard were made for the younger audiences of *In Living Color* and MTV.

With so much of Acura's advertising budget being spent on the Integra, ads for the Legend appeared through Acura's local dealer ad councils, which were orchestrated by Ketchum Advertising. The slogan for the Legend, "Some things are worth the price," left out the "precision crafted performance" tagline. Although it is difficult to maintain an upscale image when the Acura line starts at $14,000, American Honda did not think that Legend buyers would feel that their cars lost integrity with all the attention focused on the Integra. As Acura executive Rich Thomas explained to *Automotive News,* "the upscale luxury buyer doesn't watch MTV and Nick at Nite."

Future Prospects

Although Acura was still the leading imported luxury car in 1993, one dealer told *Automotive News* that he felt Acura had lost "its image and momentum." For the second half of the 1990s, Acura planned to focus on finding a more successful niche for its models, moving the Legend up in the market and introducing a new model priced between the Vigor and the Integra in the near-luxury market. In addition to marketing strategies that will reposition the car, the Acura Division repositioned itself within American Honda. In 1993 the Acura Division carved out its own niche within the Honda company. It set up its own separate staff and distribution system and planned to use its newfound efficiency to boost its sales satisfaction rating and give more voice to its nearly 300 dealerships.

Acura announced in 1994 that it will move part of its production processes into the United States. Acura's 1996 model introduction, as reported in *Automotive News,* will be manufactured in East Liberty, Ohio. The new car's design and engineering will all be done in the United States as well. Acura expects to export some of the new line.

Further Reading:

"Acura Dealers Drive for High-Powered Image: SRH Ads Shed 'Canned Car Footage' for Polished, Big-Budget Look," *Adweek* (Western Edition), August 3, 1992, p. 4.

"Acura Nears Sales Milestone," *Ward's Automotive International,* October 1993, p. 2.

Armstrong, Larry, "Light, But No Lightweight: The Acura NSX," *Business Week,* August 20, 1990, p. 102.

Breese, Kristine Stiven, "Gains by Rival Make Acura Dealers Restless," *Automotive News,* May 11, 1992, p. 6; " 'We Can Do It,' Acura's New Leader Says," *Automotive News,* February 8, 1993, p. 3.

Dinkel, John, "Acura NSX: Birth of an Exotic," *Road & Track,* September 1989, pp. 42–50.

Higgins, James V., "Honda Says Upscale Line May Be Built in U.S.," *Detroit News,* March 18, 1987; "Acura Learns an Expensive Lesson by Landing in U.S.," *Detroit News,* March 22, 1987.

Horton, Cleveland, "Honda Accelerates into Luxury Sales with Acura," *Advertising Age,* June 16, 1986, pp. S35–S36; "Acura: A Tough Act for Lexus & Infiniti to Follow," *Automotive News,* March 14, 1988, p. E30; "Acura Shifts Gears," *Advertising Age,* September 11, 1989, pp. 1, 116; "Keeping a Legend-ary Lead," *Advertising Age,* November 26, 1990, pp. 3, 61; "Acura Integra Ads Swerve to Avoid Conventional: Young Boomers, Xers Are Targeted," *Advertising Age,* July 12, 1993, p. 3.

Pinto, Liz, "Selling Price of Acura NSX Is a lot More Than Sticker," *Automotive News,* October 22, 1990, pp. 1, 42; "Acura, Ford First to Offer Digital Sound Processing," *Automotive News,* November 4, 1991, p. 49.

Rechtin, Mark, "Tough Guy at Acura Comes Out Swinging," *Automotive News,* July 5, 1993, p. 1; "Acura Spends $25 Million to Launch Integra," *Automotive News,* July 12, 1993, p. 9; "New Acura Ads Aim to Add Prestige," *Automotive News,* November 8, 1993, p. 3.

Snyder, Jesse, "It's Integra No. 2," *Automotive News,* May 8, 1989, p. 7; "Cerritos Deal Typifies Acura Efforts to Keep Top CSI Spot," *Automotive News,* January 15, 1990, pp. 3, 11.

Stroud, Ruth, "The Acura Gambit Pays Off for Honda," *Advertising Age,* February 29, 1988, p. S2.

Thomas, Charles M., and Lindsay Chappell, "Acura Plans to Build Car in U.S.," *Automotive News,* January 10, 1994, pp. 3, 51.

Toy, Stewart, "The Selling of Acura—A Honda That's Not a Honda," *Business Week,* March 17, 1986, p. 93.

—Sara Pendergast

AMANA®

Founded in 1943, the Amana brand includes a variety of finely crafted appliances, including refrigerators, freezers, ranges, ovens, cooktops, air conditioners, furnaces, and central heating and cooling units. It was perhaps best known for its line of Radarange microwave ovens. Although Amana Refrigeration has been a maker of home appliances since the 1930s, it did not come into prominence until the 1960s, when it was the first company to successfully market microwave ovens to the public. The company also introduced quartz halogen cooking products in 1988, the first manufactured in the United States.

Brand Origins

The company that became Amana Refrigeration, Inc., began in 1934, when a young Iowa man, George Foerstner, decided to make beverage coolers and to sell them to taverns that were just opening up again after the repeal of Prohibition. Foerstner grew up in one of the seven Iowa villages that comprised the Amana Colonies. The colonies traced their roots to an 18th century Germanic religious sect called the Community of True Inspiration. The sect emigrated from Germany beginning in 1842, when they settled on land just outside Buffalo, New York. They moved to Iowa County, Iowa, 12 years later in order to buy more land and to escape from the encroachment of the rapidly growing Buffalo. The sect lived communally, with members working and farming together to promote the welfare of the entire community. The colonies operated what was for many years the largest farm in Iowa and had a prosperous woolens business, as well as many small craft shops. Though the Inspirationists maintained their distinct way of life for almost a hundred years, eventually the changes that affected the rest of the country would also overwhelm the Amana Colonies. In 1932, in the midst of the Great Depression, the community, which was greatly in debt, voted to disband its communal way of life. Individual members were free to find work wherever they could.

Foerstner had been a full-time salesperson since the age of fifteen, selling the colonies' woolen goods. In his spare time he began making beverage coolers out of spare parts left over from a defunct Amana automobile-accessory business. In 1934 he decided to leave his woolens job and go into business for himself with $3,500 he had saved. By 1936 his business was doing so well that the Amana Society, now reorganized as a corporation, wanted to buy him out. Foerstner agreed to sell his business, though he remained manager, and the company continued to prosper. During World War II Amana Refrigeration made walk-in coolers for the U.S. Army, and after the war the company manufactured deep freezers for home use. Amana began making home refrigerators with a freezer on top in 1949 and then side-by-side refrigerator/freezers.

The company grew bigger than the Amana Society had envisioned. The managers decided they would prefer to sell the business for a profit rather than risk running into trouble later. The Amana Society asked Foerstner to find a buyer who would pay $1 million for the company. Foerstner conferred with Howard Hall, a prominent Cedar Rapids businessman, and formed a syndicate with him and a few others. The new owners paid the Amana Society $1.5 million, considerably more than they had asked, and in 1950 the company was incorporated as Amana Refrigeration, Inc. Foerstner continued at the helm.

Commercial Success

Though Amana Refrigeration, Inc., was no longer controlled by the Amana Society, the company's products retained the reputation of craftsmanship and quality that had long been associated with the colonies. Foerstner himself was fastidious about quality control. Rather than run random spot checks, he insisted that every single item out of Amana's factories be inspected. Part of the Foerstner legend was that he had once found a pinhole-sized spot of bad paint on an appliance and ordered the whole thing sandblasted and repainted because he believed that even a tiny retouching was sloppy workmanship. Amana's sales went up and up, and by 1965 they stood at $25 million.

At that point Amana began looking to merge with a larger company. A few of the major stockholders had died, and it had no easy way to pay the survivors a fair price for their stock. Amana did not want to go public, so it arranged a deal with the Massachusetts-based Raytheon Company to be taken on as a subsidiary. Raytheon had developed many products in radio and radar, almost all for military use. The company had tremendous technical expertise but no experience marketing to consumers. In exchange for 447,328 shares of Raytheon common stock, the company took over Amana on January 1, 1965. Amana retained its name and most of its autonomy, and Foerstner continued as general manager. After the merger Amana took on the task of selling one of Raytheon's latest inventions, the microwave oven.

AT A GLANCE

Amana brand of appliances first manufactured in 1934 by George Foerstner of Amana, IA; parent company incorporated in 1950 as Amana Refrigeration, Inc., and acquired in 1965 by Massachusetts-based Raytheon Company; Amana Radarange introduced in 1967.

Major competitor: General Electric; also Maytag, Whirlpool, and Frigidaire.

Advertising: *Agency*—Grey Advertising, Inc., New York, NY, 1992—. *Major campaign*—"What You've Been Missing."

Addresses: *Parent company*—Amana Refrigeration, Inc., Amana, IA 52204; phone: (319) 622-2142. *Ultimate parent company*—Raytheon Company, 141 Spring Street, Lexington, MA 02173; phone: (617) 862-6600.

Breakthrough Marketing

Raytheon's scientists had been working on the microwave oven since the early 1940s. The company, however, had continually failed at marketing consumer products, and its Raytheon transistor radio, record player, and television set were all notable flops. Its Radarange microwave oven came on the market in 1953, and the technology was also licensed to two appliance makers, Tappan and Litton. The early model was made by hand, was a cumbersome five feet high, and needed installation by an electrician and service by a plumber. The price, too, was a forbidding $1,200. The awkward machines were sold mostly to institutions, and by the 1960s Raytheon had lost $5 million on them.

When Amana joined Raytheon, Foerstner set his mind to selling the Radarange. He decided that the unit had to be about the size of an air conditioner, plug in to regular household current, and retail for around $500. He asked Raytheon to retool the microwave to his specifications, and Amana began selling them for $450, though that price meant taking a $100 loss on each one. Starting with a lavish promotion in Chicago in 1967, Amana engaged dozens of demonstrators to show how speedily the Radarange could cook. Foerstner rented a train to run through the Chicago area and invited the press and women's clubs to come on board and pop popcorn. The demonstrators moved on to more complex foods, and the public was soon enamored with the ease of microwave cooking. Each purchaser of an Amana Radarange got a visit from a home economist, who would help with the installation and assist with the customer's first microwave meal. In 1967 Amana spent $1 million in advertising to sell not just a new machine but a new way of cooking.

By 1973 sales of microwave ovens were close to 800,000 units a year, with Amana the leading manufacturer by a wide margin. Amana was producing 12,000 Radaranges a month. Its top-selling models were the top-of-the-line Touchmatic ovens, which had built-in computer "brains" and retailed for around $600. Sales in 1974 were a record $166 million, a 100 percent increase over the previous year, and in 1975 they hit $196 million. Amana's advertising budget was up to $12 million, and orders for Amana appliances kept coming. Consumers, however, had voiced fears of radiation leaks from microwaves, especially after an unfavorable article appeared in a 1973 issue of *Consumer Reports.* Not only did Amana publish a brochure on microwave safety endorsed by a University of Iowa physicist but the company subjected its ovens to a strenuous "torture test." This earned Amana an exemption from the warning tag that the federal government required every other manufacturer to place on microwaves.

Marketing Strategy

Though the Radarange was Amana's biggest seller, the company continued to improve its other appliance lines and to promote them with national advertising. One early Amana innovation was a special meat drawer inside its refrigerators, touted as a "refrigerator within a refrigerator." Amana introduced a flatter back on its refrigerator models, and it endorsed the line with magazine ads claiming "Amana is turning its back on the public." Amana also advertised with spots on the popular Arthur Godfrey radio program. By the mid-1970s Amana was the largest advertiser in the appliance industry, spending more than $15 million a year. Amana advertising appeared on network radio and television and in national magazines, and Amana appliances were given away as prizes on dozens of television game shows. Amana paid for local advertising as well and distributed a calendar to its dealers and distributors so they could keep up with the dates of advertised sales.

To foster good relations with its dealers, Amana sponsored a long-running annual VIP golf tournament. Many appliance dealers were avid golfers, and it was a thrill for them to be invited to Iowa to play with the pros. Some professional golfers were paid to wear the Amana name, and this also translated into consumer advertising, as, for example, when a 1975 U.S. Open champion was pictured on the cover of *Sports Illustrated* in his Amana cap. Amana also had distributors in 100 countries outside the United States. In 1977 Amana brought these dealers to the United States for a tour of Amana's plants, a trip to Nashville, and, finally, a visit to President Gerald Ford in the Rose Garden of the White House. Ensuring that dealers made a profit was essential to good business at Amana, and the company worked hard to promote dealer loyalty.

Consumer advertising in the 1980s often acknowledged the brand's ties to the Amana Colonies. One slogan was "in the tradition of fine craftsmanship," referring to Amana's German artisan heritage. A major print advertisement in 1980 showed an Amana smoothtop range against a background of barns and silos, though these were not, in fact, Amana barns. Another advertisement spoke more directly of Amana's past. A photograph showed a well-stocked refrigerator sitting by a lake and was accompanied by the following text: "Wastefulness. The folks who settled Amana, Iowa loathed it. So do the folks who build refrigerators today. So it didn't surprise us any when U.S. Government figures proved that Amana refrigerators have the lowest estimated yearly operating costs in five different size categories." Though only a fraction of Amana Refrigeration's employees were actually members of the Amana Society, the aura of the earlier Amana still clung to the Raytheon subsidiary's refrigerators and ranges.

Performance Appraisal

In 1989 Amana became the headquarters for all of Raytheon's appliance subsidiaries, which included Caloric and Speed Queen. The group operated at an $8 million loss in 1990, despite profits at Amana, though the next year saw a $5 million gain. In 1993 Caloric reorganized and consolidated under the Amana name. At least one long-time Amana distributor claimed that Raytheon, as it struggled to cut costs and increase efficiency, gradually pushed out the family feeling that Amana dealers had in the days of Foerstner.

Perhaps Amana would become a different type of company in the future, but it would always be able to look at its history proudly.

Though nothing in the Amana line was as revolutionary as the Radarange, the brand had several other firsts in its past. In 1947 Amana was the first company to nationally market upright freezers for home use. The touch-control system on its microwave ovens was the first in the industry, and Amana also offered the first complete line of low-energy refrigerators to the public beginning in 1975. Amana purchased the range line of the Corning company in 1976 and then began to market a unique line of smoothtop stoves. In 1988 Amana became the first U.S. manufacturer of a new cooking technology, the quartz halogen range. The quartz halogen element gave virtually instantaneous heat and light when turned on and so provided quicker cooking than any previous smoothtop range.

Despite these many innovative accomplishments, the Amana brand still projected a conservative image. Amana products were marketed as exceptionally safe, finely crafted, energy saving appliances. Amana quietly trumpeted its singular heritage but at the same time offered consumers real guarantees in the form of exceptional quality control and five-year service contracts. Part of Amana's reputation stemmed from the business style of its founder, George Foerstner, who in the 1970s still answered calls at his home from customers across the country. Foerstner explained in an interview with *Nation's Business* in 1977 how a customer who had unwittingly bought what was apparently a stolen Amana air conditioner called him at home to complain that he could not get his unit repaired. Foerstner persuaded the customer's local dealer to service the air conditioner. Though Foerstner claimed not to pay attention to what the competition was doing, he had an extraordinary sense for the appliance market. His assessment of the potential market for the Radarange was based not on calculated research but on his personal expertise and instinct. He not only imagined what the microwave should be in terms of its countertop size and reasonable price but also promoted it with flair and acumen and in the process changed the shape of the appliance industry.

Further Reading:

''Amana Brochure to Dispel Consumer Radiation Fears,'' *Merchandising Week,* April 13, 1970, p. 20.

''Amana Highlights Radaranges and Refrigerators in New Line,'' *Merchandising Week,* February 10, 1975, p. 9.

''Amana Makes Waves,'' *Dun's Review,* April 1976, pp. 12–13.

''Amana Plans Consumer Tests of Radarange,'' *Advertising Age,* April 13, 1967, p. 27.

''Amana Puts the Heat on the Oven Critics,'' *Business Week,* June 16, 1973, p. 30.

''Amana Refrigeration: Turning Up the Heat in the Kitchen,'' *Sales & Marketing Management,* January 17, 1977, pp. 18–19.

''Amana Stays on Course,'' *Sales & Marketing Management,* September 13, 1976, p. 26.

Barthel, Diane L., *Amana: From Pietist Sect to American Community,* Lincoln, Nebraska: University of Nebraska Press, 1984.

''Figuring Out What Consumers Want,'' *Nation's Business,* February 1977, pp. 46–53.

Giges, Nancy, ''Amana Ads Heat Up Panasonic Charges,'' *Advertising Age,* December 10, 1979, p. 28.

Gershman, Michael, *Getting It Right the Second Time,* New York: Addison-Wesley, 1990, pp. 50–55.

Jones, William H., ''From Rags to Raytheon: Socialism Cools Off at Amana,'' *Business & Society Review,* no. 21, spring 1977, pp. 70–73.

Miller, Martin R., ''How Amana and Caloric Fit Into the Raytheon Family,'' *Merchandising Week,* April 13, 1967, p. 11.

Scott, Otto J., *The Creative Ordeal: The Story of Raytheon,* New York: Atheneum, 1974.

Tannenbaum, Jeffrey A., ''Cold War: Amana Refrigeration Fights Tiny Distributor,'' *Wall Street Journal,* February 26, 1992, p. B2.

''The Raytheon-Amana Marriage: Where to Go on the Honeymoon?'' *Merchandising Week,* February 1, 1965, p. 7.

''What Foerstner Plans for Amana's Microwave Oven,'' *Merchandising Week,* January 30, 1967, p. 11.

—Angela Woodward

AMERICAN TOURISTER®

LUGGAGE THAT COOPERATES.®

Born during the Depression era, American Tourister is a brand long familiar with the school of hard knocks—knocks of the accidental or gorilla variety, that is, which have made it number two in the industry and a favorite among value-conscious consumers. Durability and affordability are the areas in which Tourister continues to dominate, as much as possible, in a $3.2 billion luggage industry that is now highly fragmented. Samsonite, another venerable and somewhat pricier luggage brand, is Tourister's chief rival. However, the picture has altered significantly with Hillenbrand Industries' 1993 sale of American Tourister, Inc., to Astrum International Corp., the owner of Samsonite. The two brands now compete under the same corporate roof, albeit within companies that operate independently of each other. American Tourister produces softside and hardside luggage and business cases for a variety of American Tourister collections, including Genesis, Courier, Spectrum, and Ambiance II, which it markets primarily through such mass merchandisers as Wal-Mart and Montgomery Ward.

Sol Koffler: The Man Who Reinvented the Luggage Industry

During the first decades of the century, luggage was either relatively cheap and made of cloth or coated paper, or relatively expensive and made of leather. In both cases, the interior form was the same: thin strips of wood and plywood joined by glue. Durable luggage, not surprisingly, was an oxymoron at the time. Sol Koffler, an immigrant who had worked during the 1920s in a steamer trunk factory and in a plant that manufactured pocketbooks, was determined to make luggage of a different kind.

In 1933 he opened a shop in a vacant grocery store in Providence, Rhode Island. He succeeded in producing a suitcase that he believed would outlast that of any competitor within its price range, which was then one dollar per case. Amazingly, Koffler grossed $5,000 during his first year as sole owner and employee of American Luggage Works, during the depths of the Great Depression. As a 1973 company advertisement/retrospective stated, "The business was only a year old, but the standards that would govern Sol Koffler's future were firmly set: unsurpassed quality, value, and style." By 1935 the company had expanded to half a dozen employees. American Luggage Works suitcases were now available in two sizes, two colors (black or brown), and two prices (two or three dollars). Koffler oversaw the firm's designs as well as sales, which were made to retailers throughout the Providence-Boston corridor.

Ever the innovator, Koffler decided to rethink the shape and structure of the suitcase, which was then squat and bulky, composed of numerous pieces, and prone to splitting, cracking, and other signs of wear. Adapting machinery used to make plywood radio cases, Koffler developed his most valuable piece of plant equipment to date, an apparatus for bending materials that would help him achieve his goals of simplifying design while producing more durable luggage. So unique was the new, slim, round-cornered, and markedly roomier luggage—replete with linings and zippered pockets—that Koffler christened it with a new name, American Tourister.

The Innovations Continue

Years later the company praised this initial line as "a total industry first and a decade ahead of the pack. Some of those early improved cases are still in service, a tribute to the guiding principle of the company: American Tourister makes the case for quality." By World War II, revenues for American Luggage Works surpassed $100,000, and American Tourister customers now had their choice of four colors, four styles, and eight sizes. In 1945, following its devotion to the war effort, the company returned to the luggage industry with its sights set high. This year Koffler began propelling his regional business into a national concern by authorizing the company's first ever national advertising budget. Here again, Koffler led the industry by designating the then extraordinary sum of $12,000, a figure that grew substantially in the years to come.

Following the introduction of all-vinyl cases and other industry firsts, Koffler produced a new line of cases molded from plywood veneers that were the smoothest and sleekest available. According to the company, the full year's production of both its American Tourister leather and vinyl lines were sold out in the first two hours of that year's national trade show. During the show, Don Hawley of Hawley Products requested a meeting with Koffler. Hawley had been attempting, unsuccessfully, to interest luggage manufacturers in an aqueous plastic composition he had first produced during the war, for use in shell casings and pith helmets. The composition had several promising characteristics, including its lightness, malleability, and tensile strength. Although realizing that he would have to retool virtually every aspect of his company in order to use

AT A GLANCE

American Tourister brand founded c. 1936 in Providence, RI, by American Luggage Works owner Sol Koffler; American Luggage Works renamed American Tourister, Inc., and acquired in 1978 by Hillenbrand Industries; in 1993 American Tourister became a subsidiary of Astrum International Corp.

Performance: *Market share*—Number two luggage maker in the country (less than 5% of U.S. luggage sales). *Sales*—$100 million.

Major competitor: Samsonite (both Samsonite and American Tourister are owned by Astrum International, but the two operate as independent companies).

Advertising: *Agency*—Leo Burnett, 1993—. *Major campaign*—"Luggage that cooperates."

Addresses: *Parent company*—American Tourister, Inc., 91 Main St., Warren, RI 02885; phone: (401) 245-2100. *Ultimate parent company*—Astrum International Corp., 40301 Fisher Island Dr., Fisher Island, FL 33109.

the product, Koffler decided to take the plunge into plastics. Two years and hundreds of thousands of dollars later (Koffler at one stage mortgaged his house to see the project through), American Luggage Works could claim rights to the first molded plastic luggage ever produced.

The Rise of Brand Awareness and Gorilla Advertising

From the start, the new American Tourister suitcases sold well. In 1954 the chemical composition was further improved, giving the customer a virtually indestructible, low-cost product. (Modern hardside American Tourister luggage is still produced through a process called Aqua-Glass molding that uses fiberglass, cellulose, resins, and binder.) Interestingly enough, this same year (according to a 1969 ad in *Ebony*) a 3,800 pound car overturned and pinned a piece of American Tourister luggage for some ten hours. Two small areas of the luggage were damaged, but everything inside the suitcase was unscathed. This was to be the first in a long series of true-life accounts testifying to the durability of Koffler's products. One of the most dramatic occurred in 1964, when an American Tourister suitcase fell off a car traveling 60 miles per hour and was then overrun by another car. Scuff-marks on the outer surface were the only signs of damage. Needless to say, American Luggage Works, a company already committed to big ad budgets, capitalized on such stories and created a durability campaign that still persists.

The print and TV campaign was handled by the Doyle Dane Bernbach agency and combined customer testimonials with shots of a menacing-looking gorilla flinging an American Tourister case around his cage. The gorilla became an instant hit with the American public, as did recreations of potential luggage mishaps, including suitcases dropped from an airplane and a speeding train. Such ads came at an especially opportune time, when consumers were becoming more brand conscious about all of their purchases. American Tourister responded to the trend not only through its ads but also through continual refinement of its line, which was quite arguably the most popular name in middle-priced luggage. The little red, white, and blue tag on American Tourister bags became the symbol of what Koffler had fought for from the start: quality luggage at an affordable price. The tag, called a "whatzit," even received its own ad space for a time, with explanatory copy reading: "It's what holds your name and address. What helps you spot your bag. What tags you as someone who knows what's what about travel . . . from what's the best luggage to carry . . . to what's the best place to go."

Highs, Lows, and New Ownership

American Tourister rode a crest of prosperity during the 1970s as travel habits and luggage-buying habits changed dramatically. More rapid turnover among luggage owners and more leisure time spent traveling spelled rising revenues for the brand. The company was also quick to fill the rising need for carry-ons by business travelers. Although Koffler still kept his hands in the business, by 1978 the time had come to turn over the brand to a new owner. The purchaser was Hillenbrand Industries, an Indiana-based furniture firm that was seeking to expand by acquiring companies with strong market positions. American Tourister certainly fit the bill; together with Samsonite, it accounted for more than 70 percent of sales in the luggage retail industry, then totaling $600 million.

In its first full year with Hillenbrand, American Tourister posted record sales of $83.8 million and operating profits of $16.2 million. In the words of an *Industry Week* report, luggage manufacturers were "enjoying a banner year," despite inflation and fuel supply concerns. However, the report also noted that luggage imports over the last five years had risen significantly. The year may well have been the high point for the brand, for in the recession-year 1980 sales shrank by 7 percent and operating profits plummeted by 60 percent.

In 1981 the company rededicated itself with ads to retailers that read: "Our best salesman's back. And he's going to be working overtime helping you sell our new Spectrum line. Your customers will see him in our latest television commercial banging Spectrum into walls, dropping it down stairs and jumping unceremoniously up and down on it. . . . But don't get the idea that Spectrum is all brawn and no beauty. Our new soft-sided 8-piece set is as beautiful as it is durable." And two years later the company grabbed major media attention with the celebration of its 50th anniversary. The public relations campaign was highlighted by prime time TV commercials; print ads in *Reader's Digest, People,* and *Better Homes and Gardens;* and special appearances by Gorilla impersonator Don McLeod, including an interview with host Jane Pauley on the *Today* show. But it was apparent during this decade that the American Tourister brand was struggling as the luggage industry became increasingly fragmented.

A Rebirth in the Making

Since its inception, American Tourister has aligned itself with innovation. From springless locks and zippered pockets to molded cases and lightweight frames, American Tourister luggage has helped to define the industry. If the brand has perhaps lost some of its luster since the 1980s, it has certainly lost none of its strong reputation. Years ago the Institute of Design of the Illinois Institute of Technology conducted a survey of 100 design professionals who were asked to list the best designed mass-produced products of the modern era. "The much-publicized list," according to company literature, "included an American Tourister suitcase—the only luggage entry."

Weakened by a sluggish economy in the early 1990s, American Tourister was finally sold by Hillenbrand to Astrum International, formerly E-II Holdings Inc., for approximately $70 million. The deal was interesting for a number of reasons, not least of which was Astrum's emergence from Chapter 11. Strengthened by the leadership of CEO Steven J. Green, Astrum is seen as a potential blue chip company with bright international marketing prospects for its brands, which in addition to Samsonite and American Tourister include Culligan and Botany 500. Indeed, American Tourister may reasonably expect to follow Samsonite's lead in tapping overseas markets. According to Stephanie Strom, around 60 percent of Samsonite's sales are currently made outside the United States, versus just 2 percent for Tourister. In addition, to better service its domestic customers, American Tourister relocated its manufacturing and distribution operations from Rhode Island to Jacksonville, Florida.

Although there no doubt will be major changes ahead for American Tourister, a 1994 corporate press release offered reassurance to brand and company followers. Announcing the appointment of Frank Steed, former vice president of sales and marketing at Samsonite, as president of American Tourister, the release continued: ''With Steed at the helm—one of the people who was involved in the decision to acquire American Tourister—the two companies can establish product plans, marketing and advertising programs that will enhance both the American Tourister and Samsonite brand names. The combination of Samsonite's vast global resources and American Tourister's quality products will insure success as American Tourister enters the international marketplace, while enhancing the value of its name here in the United States.''

Further Reading:

''The American Tourister Story,'' Batesville, Indiana: Hillenbrand Industries, 1983.

''E-II Goes Ahead with Reorganization,'' *Star Tribune,* June 9, 1993, p. 3D.

Hales, Linda (*Washington Post*), ''Paris Design Exhibit Is Celebration of the Art of the Everyday,'' *Star Tribune,* June 6, 1993, p. 4F.

Hiday, Jeffrey L., ''Rival Will Purchase American Tourister,'' *Journal Bulletin,* 1993.

Hillenbrand Industries Annual Reports, Batesville, Indiana: Hillenbrand Industries, 1979, 1980, 1992.

''Increased Air Travel Boosts Luggage Sales,'' *Industry Week,* December 10, 1979, pp. 118–19.

''John Pulichino Resigns as President of American Tourister; Frank Steed Appointed as New President,'' Astrum International Corp. Press Release, January 11, 1994.

Khalaf, Roula, ''Senior Beats Junior,'' *Forbes,* January 4, 1993, pp. 41–42.

''Samsonite's Parent to Buy American Tourister,'' *New York Times,* August 4, 1993, p. 3D.

''Sol Koffler: Legendary Innovator of the Luggage Industry,'' ''Bending the Industry Forward,'' ''Get on the Brand Wagon,'' American Luggage Works Special Advertisements (retrospectives commemorating the company's 40th anniversary), *Newsweek,* 1973.

Strom, Stephanie, ''New Name, New Life, for Astrum,'' *New York Times,* September 26, 1993, p. 13.

—Jay P. Pederson

ANDERSEN®

Andersen has long been the world's top-selling brand of wooden windows and patio doors. Its products were built in a single, 63-acre plant in Bayport, Minnesota, not far from the place where the Andersen Lumber Company was founded in 1903. When Hans Jacob Andersen, a 49-year-old Danish immigrant, established the business with his two sons, no other company on the market was producing standardized window frames. The company became successful by manufacturing a standardized, high-quality, durable product that could be mass-produced. The company name was changed to the Andersen Frame Corporation in 1929 and the Andersen Corporation in 1937.

Originally the manufacturer of only wooden window frames, the company has since expanded the brand to include an immense line of complete windows made from wood, glass, vinyl, and aerospace materials. Andersen has been able ensure high quality control through its rigorous product research and development, as well as through progressive employment practices implemented by the management. Andersen windows have remained the top-seller in the marketplace because of meticulous quality control, constant product innovation, and integrated direct-response advertising.

Brand Origins

In 1870, at the age of just 16, the company's founder, Hans Jacob Andersen, traveled from Denmark to Portland, Maine. From there he decided to go to the Midwest, finding work on the way with employers who spoke only English so he would have to master the new language quickly. While working with a team at clearing tree stumps, he learned his first English words: "All together boys." These words eventually became the motto of his life and the guiding principle for his future business.

Hans Andersen and his sons, Fred and Herbert, founded Andersen Lumber Company in 1903 and began producing window frames made of white pine. Following another one of his firmly held business principles, Hans Andersen was determined to make a product that would be "different and better." This determination propelled him and his sons to create a product that revolutionized the window and window-frame manufacturing industry. At the time, no one was making standardized window frames with interchangeable parts. By creating a standard window design, the Andersen Lumber Company was able to mass-produce their window frames and gain a substantial edge over other manufacturers. The standardized Andersen products offered superior quality and greater precision than any other window frame on the market. With this first substantial innovation, the founders paved the way for many more improvements in the window and patio-door industry.

Brand Development

Andersen continued to stay at the forefront of the industry, and the company introduced several products and improvements that soon became industrywide standards. Thanks to the original idea of manufacturing a standardized product, Andersen Lumber Company was able to capitalize on the advantages of mass production and pull ahead of the competition. By 1913 the company had expanded enough to move to a new facility in South Stillwater, Minnesota (later named Bayport), which became its permanent home. The company was able to hold its own during the economic upheaval of the 1930s and continued to win market share through constant innovation. In addition to introducing the concept of standardized windows, Andersen developed a modular window design, a complete window casement unit, a vinyl coating system, and other products.

To push the concept of standardized window frames even farther, Hans Andersen developed the "two bundle" method of packaging. He packaged sets of vertical and horizontal units separately, allowing the builder to assemble them in numerous different ways. The precut units were designed to fit perfectly in a variety of combinations without having to be trimmed. Because of additional innovations, Andersen products fared remarkably well in the 1930s. In 1932 the company introduced the Andersen Master Casement, a complete window unit consisting of the sash, frame, and hardware. This new product not only allowed Andersen to grow during the Depression but also changed forever the way Americans bought windows.

Andersen continued to stay on the cutting edge of the industry with such products as the Gliding Window in 1940 and the Flexivent awning window in 1952. Within two years of introducing the Flexivent window, Andersen experienced its most dramatic growth—a twofold increase in its market share. An uncommonly successful product, Flexivent sold more than one million units, accounting for half of all Andersen sales. Other important Andersen products included the revolutionary Perma-Shield vinyl cladding system, introduced in 1966, which set a new industry

AT A GLANCE

Andersen brand of windows founded in 1903 by Andersen Lumber Company, headed by Hans Jacob Andersen and his sons, Herbert and Fred; first became a registered trademark in 1917 under the name Andersen White Pine Frames; company name changed to Andersen Frame Corporation in 1929 and to Andersen Corporation in 1937.

Performance: *Market share*—15% (top share) of window category. *Sales*—$1 billion.

Major competitor: Pella; also Marvin.

Advertising: *Agency*—Campbell-Mithun-Esty, Minneapolis, MN, 1933—. *Major campaign*—"The experience of light," an integrated, direct-response television and print campaign.

Addresses: *Parent company*—Andersen Corporation, 100 Fourth Avenue North, Bayport, MN, 55003-1096; phone: (612) 439-5150; fax: (612) 430-7246.

standard; and the energy-efficient Andersen High-Performance glass, first sold in the 1980s. The company—started by a Danish immigrant committed to building products that were "different and better"—had thus blossomed into the top window manufacturer in the United States and owner of the most respected brand name in the window and patio-door market.

Marketing and Advertising Strategy

Andersen window products owe a great deal of their popularity to the company's persistent marketing efforts. Especially important have been direct-marketing methods and the cultivation of strong relationships with suppliers, prospective buyers, and others.

The first step in marketing Andersen windows has been to create brand awareness. To do this, the company has used distinctive, elegant ads that feature Andersen window products as centerpieces in elegant home interiors. A central theme has been "the experience of light." The ads' sun-splashed photographs were rounded out with enticing descriptions that attempted to capture the readers' interest and admiration for the product. Andersen also used the direct-response approach; both print and television ads encouraged potential customers to contact the company by telephone or by filling out a coupon enclosed in magazine ads. The responses allowed Andersen to determine the prospects' interest in the products. All respondents then received additional product information, but the most serious prospects received issues of *Come Home,* Andersen's proprietary publication, handled by Meredith Publishing Services. This magazine was another venue through which the company was able to showcase its windows. Moreover, through the use of surveys and coupons, the magazine allowed the company to communicate with prospective customers and to assess their needs and interests. Joe Arndt, Andersen's former manager of marketing communications, told *Direct Marketing* magazine that "*Come Home* gives us the opportunity to establish a relationship with the consumer."

The advertisements were designed to draw consumers to retail outlets. Once there, consumers received additional publications or video cassettes. All promotional materials were visually integrated and stunning in appearance, increasing, the company hoped, customer awareness of and admiration for the brand. In the 1990s Andersen augmented its promotional efforts with multimedia and interactive technology in a program known as Andersen Window of Knowledge. It was a point-of-purchase program that retailers could use to help customers visualize Andersen products in their homes. Steve Sherod, Andersen's manager of public relations, told *Business Marketing* magazine that "the system can configure different sizes, shapes and colors right on the screen." This integrated, direct-response approach to advertising allowed Andersen to communicate and build relationships with prospects throughout the buying cycle and to respond quickly to marketplace demands.

In addition to emphasizing product innovation and responding to market trends, the company has been committed to building solid relationships with its advertising agency, suppliers, and distributors, as well as with its own work force. Employees, for example, owned 27 percent of the company's stock, and, in hiring, preference was given to their family members. Because employee compensation was based directly on work, Andersen was able to maintain excellent productivity standards and to monitor closely the quality of its products. The company's focus on innovation, its emphasis on building relationships, and the "look" captured in its advertisements together created a brand image that was up-to-date but also dependable, fashionable, and rich with tradition.

Product Changes

Initially Hans Andersen and his sons manufactured standardized window frames out of durable white pine. Almost a century later, in the 1990s, their company offered more than 1,100

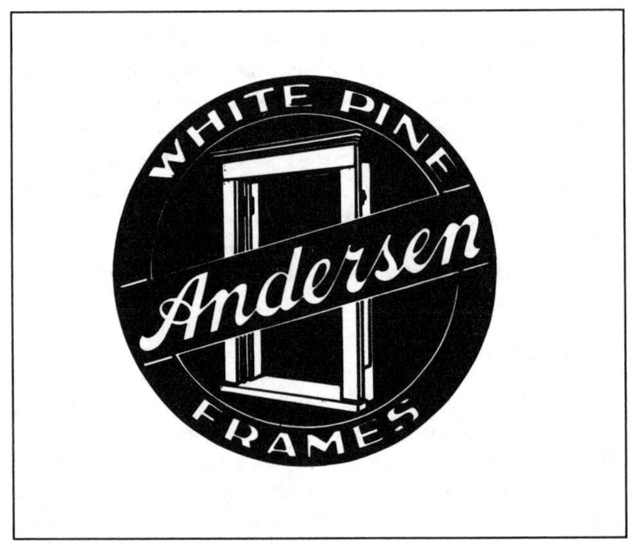

An early logo for Andersen windows also advertises their white pine frames.

assorted sizes of vinyl-clad window products. Although home owners still liked the way natural wood insulated against the elements and enhanced a home's interior, wood was very susceptible to the effects of weather. To provide windows that would last 40 to 50 years with minimum maintenance, Andersen introduced in 1966 a low-maintenance vinyl cladding known as Perma-Shield, which protected all exposed parts of its windows against the harmful effects of weather. Perma-Shield was soon used across the entire line of Andersen windows and was so successful that it became the new industry standard.

Andersen has tried to create energy-efficient products. Because Andersen windows conformed to standard measurements, they ensured a more precise fit and thus better insulation. In 1952 Andersen added a welded glass unit, which significantly increased energy efficiency. Andersen windows, morerover, were fitted with specially insulated glass made to the company's specifications. In the 1980s the company introduced Andersen High Performance glass, a Low-E glass that further enhanced the energy performance of the company's product line. The double window panes in Andersen windows were filled with argon, an inert gas that provided a better insulating barrier than air. Additionally, the exterior surfaces of windows were covered with a metallic coating that reflected heat from the sun's rays.

Andersen window products were tested in the company's research facilities, where wind tunnels and electron microscopes were used to check for weather tightness and integrity of the materials and adhesives. Rigorous testing and research allowed Anderson to constantly improve their products and stay ahead of the competition.

Brand Outlook

The company's efforts to educate consumers and create brand awareness have paid off. In the early 1990s Andersen led the industry with a 15 percent market share, and its annual sales of about $1 billion were more than those of its three largest competitors combined. Andersen windows were distributed by 122 wholesale suppliers to some 15,000 retailers. Andersen products were sold across the United States, as well as in Canada, the United Kingdom, and Japan.

While many companies floundered during the recession of the early 1990s, Andersen had the second most successful year in its history in 1992. Unlike many other companies, Andersen was able to respond quickly to changes in the marketplace. Its direct-response marketing efforts and proprietary research helped Andersen establish buying patterns and assess what consumers wanted. ''It's a consumer-driven marketplace,'' Arndt told *Direct Marketing.* The future of the Andersen brand would likely depend on the company's continued monitoring of consumer preferences, as well as the introduction of high-quality, innovative products.

Further Reading:

''Andersen Windows: Panes—and Gains—for an Old-Line Outfit,'' *U.S. News & World Report,* August 24, 1992, pp. 53–54.

Lawler, Edmund O., ''Andersen: $4.75 million,'' *Business Marketing,* October, 1993, p. 90.

Neal, Mollie, ''Andersen Takes Great 'Panes' To Build Relationships,'' *Direct Marketing,* April 1993, pp. 28–30, 68.

1903–1993: 90 Years of Innovation, Bayport, Minnesota: Andersen Corporation, 1993.

Ruble, Kenneth D., *Magic Circle,* Bayport, Minnesota: Andersen Corporation.

Santosus, Megan, ''No Pane, No Gain,'' *CIO,* November 1, 1993.

—Justyna Frank

APPLE®/MACINTOSH®

The Apple/Macintosh brand of personal computer systems, marketed by Apple Computer, Inc., of California, is the top-selling line of personal computers in the United States. Apple/Macintosh computer systems have been offering consumers reliability, performance, and technical support for nearly two decades, as they evolved from the 1976 preassembled circuit board of the Apple I to the sleek, sophisticated PowerBook 180 of 1993. Apple/Macintosh computer systems have remained a market share leader due to years of astute advertising, friendly technical support, and constant improvement through continuous product innovation.

A Computer Is Born

As the United States celebrated its Bicentennial in 1976, 26-year-old Steven Wozniak and 21-year-old Steven Jobs were building a personal computer that would radically alter the course of computer history. Frustrated with the difficulties of programming in the arcane computer languages available for personal computers, exasperated with the punched holes in Hollerith cards, and upset by the accidental errors in syntax which could render a program inexecutable, they desired to make computers easier for nontechnical people to use.

Wozniak, who worked for Hewlett-Packard, was the brilliant hardware engineer who focused on the core design of the computer. Jobs, who worked for Atari, was the marketing genius who worried about which parts the computer would use and about how nontechnical people were going to buy the parts to put the computer together. Neither man had any intention of starting a company; their sole motivation was to build a personal computer that they could show off at the Home Brew Club, a computer enthusiasts' group which gathered to display members' home-made computers.

As soon as Wozniak built the computer, Jobs began coming up with ideas to market it to the general public. Because the two inventors had little business experience, they sought the advice of Michael Markkula, a retired Intel executive who liked helping young entrepreneurs. When Markkula saw the computer, he realized that it could become the first affordable and useful computer for nontechnical people. Markkula agreed to help the two inventors start a company to market their computer. The computers were named Apple and displayed the trademark multi-colored apple with a "byte" out of it.

Start-up costs for the company were relatively low. To finance production of their Apple I preassembled circuit boards, Jobs sold his Volkswagon van and Wozniak sold his Hewlett-Packard programmable calculator in May 1976. Fifty Apple I circuit boards were ordered by The Byte Shop Computer Store that month, and Jobs leveraged the order to get credit so that he and Wozniak could build the machines in the garage of Jobs' parents. The seed Wozniak and Jobs had planted grew quickly into a microcomputer industry. Contrary to the expectations of many, people wanted to own their own computers. Some people used them for games; later, scientific and business applications were found.

So Easy a Child Could Use It

While many start-up computer companies folded in the turbulent market, Apple prospered under Markkula's careful management, and soon became the fastest-growing company in history. Wozniak, Jobs, and Markkula became rich beyond their loftiest expectations, each ending up with more than $100 million. When Apple went public in 1980, more than 40 Apple employees became instant millionaires. Never before had one company made so many people so rich so quickly.

Even though Apple computers were easier to use than their competitors, computers in general were still infuriatingly difficult to use. What Apple Computer needed was software that made the computer easy enough for a child to use. Xerox Corporation had invented such software, called Altair, a decade earlier but had failed to commercialize its great vision. After visiting Xerox's laboratories in 1979, Jobs was astonished by the software's capabilities. Returning to Apple, he realized that the company's future had just changed; the company would now focus on building a computer which was not only small and affordable but so intuitive a child could use it. Such a computer might not only change the course of computing but might also prevent IBM from taking over the personal computer industry.

When the new computer, the Macintosh, entered the market in 1984, it was supported by a stunning advertising campaign. Jobs invoked George Orwell by airing a daring and controversial commercial. Named "1984," the commercial that introduced the new Macintosh computer attracted the attention of news media all over the world. Creating an image of desperate computer users being brainwashed by Big Brother, a veiled reference to IBM, the

AT A GLANCE

Apple/Macintosh brand of computer systems founded on April 1, 1976, in Palo Alto, CA, by Steven Wozniak and Steven Jobs; incorporated in January 1977 by Wozniak, Jobs, and new partner and chairman Michael Markkula; Apple II introduced, 1977; Macintosh introduced, 1984; Powerbook introduced, 1991; Newton personal digital assistant introduced, 1992.

Performance: *Market share*—13% (top share) of personal computer category. *Sales*—$9 billion.

Major competitor: IBM; also Dell and Compaq.

Advertising: *Agency*—BBDO, Los Angeles, CA. *Major campaign*—"Apple. The easy way."

Addresses: *Parent company*—Apple Computer, Inc., One Infinite Loop, Cupertino, CA 95014; phone: (408) 996-1010; fax: (408) 252-8447.

commercial depicted computer-user lemmings about to be awakened from their slumber by the wind of personal, interactive computing. This commercial would be followed by others, the most notable of which was "Lemmings" in 1985.

In January 1984, the month the controversial commercial "1984" aired, Apple inserted a 20-page Macintosh ad in major magazines and set new records for readership and recall scores. In November, Apple bought every advertising page in a special post-election issue of *Newsweek*; the issue's final fold-out ad was used to launch the "Test Drive a Macintosh" promotion. Approximately 25,000 people took a Macintosh home for a free 24-hour trial. *Advertising Age* named "Test Drive" one of the ten best promotions of 1984.

Computers for the Masses

From the company's inception, Apple believed in computer education for the masses, and it especially encouraged young people to learn how to use computers. In December 1980, the company founded Apple Seed, a computer literacy program which would provide elementary and high school students with computer course materials. The "Kids Can't Wait" Program was announced in 1983, which gave approximately 10,000 Apple II computers to California schools. And Apple's sponsorship of a nationwide computer club competition for high school and K-12 students began that year as well. Apple also supported teachers. In 1986, educators were offered special rebates on computers for their personal use through a six-month program called "An Apple for the Teacher."

To get the attention of the general public, Apple used creative marketing techniques. Apple covered Stanford Stadium with apple-embossed seat cushions in 1985 for Super Bowl XIV. In 1986, Apple staged Open House events in shopping malls across the country in which hands-on demonstrations of computers and software attracted thousands of first-time buyers. In August 1991, the Macintosh "Right Now Rebate" was implemented, an innovative program which offered immediate savings on selected Apple/Macintosh computers and printers.

The company supported its appeal to nontechnical customers with superior customer relations. To help novice computer users, the company set up friendly technical support telephone lines, over which skilled Apple troubleshooters helped customers with their hardware and software problems. In addition, it formed a support program to promote communication between the company and nearly 600 Apple user groups nationwide in 1986.

Constant Improvement

Apple/Macintosh computers have gone through many transformations since the first Apple I preassembled board was released for sale to hobbyists and electronics enthusiasts in July 1976. By December of that year, Apple I computer boards were being retailed through ten stores in the United States. In April 1977, the Apple II, the first personal computer able to generate color graphics and to include a keyboard, power supply, and attractive case, was unveiled at the first West Coast Computer Fair. By June of that year, the Apple II had become available to the general public. Fully assembled and pretested, it included 4K of standard memory, came equipped with two game paddles and a demo cassette, and was priced at $1,298. A customer could use his own TV set as a monitor and could store programs on an audio cassette recorder. Various interface cards for connecting to most computers were introduced in March 1978, and in June of that year, the Apple Disk II was launched at the Consumer Electronics Show. The Apple II Plus was introduced in 1979 with 48K of memory and a new autostart ROM for easier startup and screen editing.

By December 1979, the Apple II sales rate was at 35,000 units, up 400 percent from 1978. Apple soon became a household name, with public awareness rising from 10 to 80 percent in 1981. In addition, in 1982, Apple became the first computer company in history to reach $1 billion in sales. The popular Apple II computers were frequently updated, and new models replaced the old. The Apple III, Apple IIc, Apple IIe, Apple IIGS are only a sample of the numerous new models that followed the Apple II. Each updated version was faster, more powerful, or easier to use than its predecessor.

The Macintosh computer marked the beginning of a new era of computing. Gone were arcane keyboard functions; instead, the computer screen, with its pictures and icons, depicted a familiar world that even a child could understand. The computer screen was made to look like a desktop. The Macintosh, launched on January 24, 1984, started selling for $2,495. During that same month, a new factory, designed and built for the production of Macintosh computers, was opened in Fremont, California. One of the nation's most automated plants, the facility used many modern manufacturing methods: robotics, just-in-time materials delivery, a linear assembly line, and improved quality of life for workers.

Enhancements to the Macintosh kept pace with the updated versions of the other Apple computers. In 1986, to speed new product development, the company purchased a Cray X-MP/48 supercomputer, valued at about $15.5 million, which would be used to simulate future hardware and software architectures. The first updated Macintosh, the Macintosh Plus, debuted in January 1986 at the AppleWorld Conference in San Francisco. In 1987, a new generation of Macintosh PC's was unveiled: the Macintosh SE (an expandable Macintosh computer), and the Macintosh II (with open architecture).

An addition to the Macintosh II family, the Macintosh IIx computer was designed to serve a variety of applications and was the first Macintosh II computer to use Motorola's 68030 microprocessor and its 68882 math coprocessor. It was also the first Macintosh to incorporate Floppy Drive High Density (FDHD), Apple's new 1.44 MB floppy disk drive that could read and write to MS-DOS, OS/2, and ProDos formats. Further innovations came in the high-performance Macintosh SE/30, which provided users with MS/DOS and OS/2 disk compatibility.

In 1989 the company introduced two new Macintosh computers: the Macintosh Portable, a full-function Macintosh in a portable design, and the Macintosh IIci, a high-performance version of the Macintosh IIcx, running at 25 MHz and featuring built-in video. In March 1990, the 40 MHz, 68030 Macintosh IIfx rolled out, becoming the fastest system Apple had ever developed.

In 1990, new low-cost Macintosh personal computers which premiered included the Macintosh Classic, the Macintosh LC, and the Macintosh IIsi. The Classic, in particular, met with stellar initial acceptance. In 1991, Apple launched the largest product introduction in history with the Macintosh Classic II, the Macintosh Quadra 700 and 900, and a new line of notebook-sized computers, the Macintosh PowerBook 100, 140, and 170. In 1992, the Macintosh Performa line, a new family of computers designed for the consumer marketplace, was launched. In October 1992, the portable and mid-range Macintosh lines were strengthened with the introduction of the PowerBook 160 and 180, the Macintosh Duo System, the Macintosh IIvx and IIvi, and the Macintosh 14″ Color Display.

Apple's revolutionary Newton technology was unveiled in 1992. The Newton technology would form the basis for new products in the personal digital assistant (PDA) category. Apple began to aggressively market its Newton technology, which integrated advanced handwriting recognition, communication, and data management technologies in 1993.

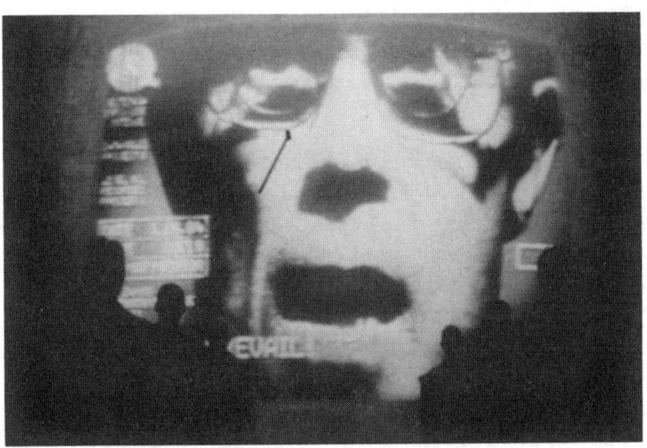

The 1984 ad campaign introducing the Apple Macintosh capitalized on George Orwell's 1984.

International Growth

Apple was thinking globally as early as 1980, when it opened a regional support center in Toronto, Canada, followed by a plant in Cork, Ireland, and a European support center in Zeist, The Netherlands. All told, Apple facilities occupied more than 500,000 square feet of floor space in the United States and Europe in that year. By the end of 1980, Apple's distribution network had become the largest in the industry, with 800 independent retailers in the United States and Canada, and 1,000 outlets abroad.

In April 1981, European headquarters opened in Paris, France, and Slough, England; in July of that year, a manufacturing plant opened in Singapore. Expanding marketing, Apple's European offices and distributors staged major events in 12 cities to launch new products. London, Paris, Zurich, Munich, Milan, Stockholm, Amsterdam, Helsinki, Brussels, Tel Aviv, Madrid, and Dublin all participated in Apple exhibitions in January 1983. Then, in May 1984, Apple's manufacturing facility in Cork, Ireland, began producing custom-made Macintosh computers for Germany, Italy, and the United Kingdom.

By 1986, Apple was selling into more than 80 countries worldwide. To accommodate its extensive sales networks, Apple's worldwide sales and marketing were restructured in 1988 into three discrete units: Apple USA, Apple Europe, and Apple Pacific. Apple had created four internal operating divisions, each to function as independent operating units headed by an operating unit president: Apple Pacific, Apple Products, Apple USA, and Apple Europe.

In 1992, net sales for Apple's European and Pacific operations increased 13 percent, representing 45 percent of total sales. Apple's personal computer business in Japan grew dramatically, generating more than $500 million in net sales. In Europe, Apple experienced strong growth in its largest markets. And Apple continued to lay the groundwork for successful operations in emerging markets like India, China, the Far East, and Eastern Europe.

Performance Appraisal

Apple's rise to the top of the personal computer industry was meteoric, as brand recognition and sales experienced almost continual growth. Apple computers and LaserWriter printers were found to rank highest in J. D. Power and Associates Business User Satisfaction Studies, and Apple topped the PC satisfaction index for the second straight year in 1991. In the first half of calendar year 1992, Apple sold more personal computers than did any other vendor, according to InfoCorp. In fiscal year 1992, Apple sold more than 2.5 million Macintosh personal computers, with unit shipments of Macintosh computers rising 20 percent over 1991, largely because of strong sales of Macintosh PowerBooks (400,000 in fiscal 1992, representing $1 billion in net sales). Boasting innovative system software, powerful hardware, and award winning product design, the PowerBook set the industry standard for notebook computing.

A major reason for Apple's sustained market dominance was its unique approach to personal computing. The company developed every element of the Macintosh computer platform: personal computers, system software, and system extensions. Therefore, the company could integrate hardware and software to create new personal computing systems which would allow users to do things they could not do before. In addition, lowered prices as well as value added to the products themselves during 1992 helped Apple/Macintosh computer systems continued to attract new customers even in recessionary times.

In an independent benchmark study completed by Ingram Laboratories in March 1992, Macintosh computers consistently outperformed other windows-based systems. In the desktop systems category, all Macintosh computers but the LC II and the Classic II outperformed their window-based counterparts. In the notebook systems category, the PowerBook 170 and 140 computers consistently outperformed their rival notebook computers, but the Macintosh PowerBook 100 lost the lead to one 80386SX-based notebook computer.

Future Predictions

The Apple/Macintosh brand humanized computing. By focusing on innovation rather than on price, Apple/Macintosh computers consistently continued to attract new customers. With value added to the computers, Apple/Macintosh computers consistently outperformed nearly every competitor. Believing that Apple's success should be heightened by new technologies, new solutions, and new businesses, the company in 1992 invested in the future by spending $602 million—8.5 percent of net sales—on research and development. In 1991 and 1992, Apple invested more than $1 billion in developing new products and technologies. Unique in the personal computer industry of the 1990s—both in construction and interface—Apple/Macintosh computer systems set the standard for the products of the Digital Information Age.

Further Reading:

Apple Computer, Inc., *Annual Report,* Cupertino, CA: Apple Computer, Inc., 1992.

"Apple Computer, Inc., Corporate Timeline," Cupertino, CA: Apple Computer, Inc., January 1993.

Bunnell, David, "Separated at Birth?," *Upside,* October 1992, pp. 54–62.

Halfhill, Tom R., and Tom Thompson, "Apple Revamps Its Lineup—Again," *Byte,* December 1993, pp. 23–26.

"An Introduction to Macintosh: Who Do So Many People Choose Macintosh?" Cupertino, CA: Apple Computer, Inc., 1993.

"Introduction to VITAL: Designing Information Systems for the 1990s," Cupertino, CA: Apple Computer, Inc., 1992.

Kawasaki, Guy, *The Macintosh Way,* New York: HarperPerennial, 1990.

March, Richard, "Apple Loses Favor on Wall Street as Its Gross Margins Decline in Last Quarter," *PC Week,* January 23, 1989, p. 62.

McWilliams, Gary, "Users Are Applauding the Apple-DEC Pairing," *Datamation,* March 1, 1988, p. 19.

Moritz, Michael, *The Little Kingdom: The Private Story of Apple Computers,* New York: William Morrow, 1984.

Pancucci, Dom, "Software Eyes Health Concerns," *Byte,* November 1993, p. 44.

"A Performance Comparison: Apple Macintosh Computers vs. Competitive Windows-Based Systems," Cupertino, CA: Apple Computer, Inc., 1992.

Pitta, Julie, "Apple Continues to Slash Mac Prices; Discounts Offered to High-End Users Buying in Volume, Through Resellers," *Computerworld,* February 27, 1989, p. 35.

Prescott, Carter A., "EMF: The Controversy," *Management Quarterly,* Summer 1993, pp. 3–9.

Rose, Frank, *West of Eden: The End of Innocence at Apple Computer,* New York: Viking Press, 1989.

Siegmann, Ken, "Alarmed Apple, IBM Target Crackdown of Gray Market," *PC Week,* March 1, 1988, p. 121.

Sustar, Lee, "Changes in Macintosh Recharge Mac-to-Mainframe Links," *PC Week,* May 24, 1988, p. C19.

Strom, David, "New Options Are on the Way for the Mac-LAN Links," *PC Week,* August 29, 1988, p. C21.

White, Thomas, "Is Apple a Serious Player?" *Computerworld,* June 6, 1988, p. 43.

Willis, Jerry, *How to Use the Macintosh,* Beaverton, OR: Dilithium Press, 1984.

Young, Jeffrey S., *Steven Jobs: The Journey Is the Reward,* New York: Scott, Foresman, Inc., 1988.

—*Virginia Barnstorff*

ARMSTRONG®

Throughout this century, Armstrong has been one of the most recognizable brand names for floor coverings, especially linoleum. While Armstrong did not invent linoleum, the company was the first in the world to mass-market it successfully. Linoleum has long since been eclipsed by other, far superior floor coverings, and Armstrong products span a very wide range beyond floor coverings—from insulation to home furnishings and ceilings, to automotive products and more. Nonetheless, the Armstrong brand name is to this day one of the oldest and most famous in the flooring and ceramic tile industries, with number one domestic market shares in both.

Brand Origins

Armstrong was the name of the cofounder of the present-day Armstrong World Industries, Inc. Thomas Armstrong was a young man in his twenties when he was approached in 1860 by his future partner, John Glass, who asked him for a loan to buy out the owner of a small cork cutting business.

Throughout the 19th century, until superior means were developed, cork was the universal raw material with which to seal or plug bottles. The main exporters of cork were Spain and Portugal. Most cork reaching this country was imported by American businessmen located near seaports. In the 1850s, William King was the biggest cork manufacturer in the United States. His employee and assistant, Harry Overington, had set up a small cork cutting branch in Pittsburgh, which he was willing to sell to John Glass for $300. Virtually penniless, Glass would have to raise the money somehow—but the year was 1860, civil war was brewing, and bankers were increasingly reluctant to give loans in such uncertain times.

Thomas Morton Armstrong was merely a clerk in a bottling concern in Pittsburgh, but he was also a highly ambitious young man who was familiar enough with the bottling business to ascertain the potential of cork cutting in one of the fastest growing, most prosperous cities in the United States. As the son of two very frugal Irish immigrant parents, Thomas Armstrong knew the value of money. Even on his small salary of $50 a month, he had saved enough to lend to Glass with the provision that Glass make him an equal partner in the cork cutting firm. Thus with Armstrong's financial backing, Glass bought out Overington and established the John D. Glass & Co.

The company foundered at the start, and Armstrong felt compelled to resign as shipping clerk in the bottling factory and devote his full energies to cork cutting. Each cork had to be cut and shaped by hand. This was a slow and cumbersome business, which also led to complaints from customers about the uneven quality of the corks they were getting. In 1862, Armstrong persuaded Glass to invest the very considerable sum of $1,000 in a cork cutting machine. The purchase was timely: the U.S. Sanitary Commission, in charge of Union battlefield wounded, placed a huge order for corks with the firm which, thanks to the new machine, could be met. Just when the company was digging out of its financial doldrums, John Glass died in 1864. Armstrong assumed full ownership of the firm and hired his brother as partner, renaming the company Armstrong, Brother & Co. The company continued to manufacture corks for bottling and other products, such as corkboard, for the next half century.

Early Commercial Successes

Even after the Civil War, Armstrong was able to find new customers, thanks to the mechanization of his cork business. There were many uses for cork in those days. Beer and other alcoholic beverages required cork bottle stoppers, as did virtually all pharmaceuticals; by the end of the 1870s, Armstrong was the biggest brand name for cork in the United States. The advent of bicycles, which required cork grips on handle bars, became one of the biggest markets for Armstrong cork.

While cork was a strong-selling product of great utility, by the turn of the century the Armstrong Cork Company (as it was then called) believed it was imperative to diversify. Cork was a raw material obtainable only in distant Europe. Cork harvesting was a very seasonal industry, leading to fluctuations in prices and profits in the United States. Even after Armstrong eliminated the middleman and the company embarked on the purchase of cork directly from Spain and Portugal, company management was well-aware of the growing public sentiment in favor of prohibition, which could eliminate in one blow one of the biggest Armstrong markets—the liquor industry.

In 1907, Armstrong had made the fateful decision to embark on a new product—linoleum—while still manufacturing cork. Linoleum required cork dust as a basic ingredient, of which there was plenty in Armstrong plants; there were linoleum manufacturers in

AT A GLANCE

Armstrong brand of floor covering originated in Pittsburgh, PA, in 1860 with the establishment of the John D. Glass and Company (John Glass and Thomas Armstrong were co-founders), which changed its name in 1864, upon the death of Glass, to the Armstrong, Brother & Co.; initially and for the remainder of the 19th century, cork bottle stoppers were the main product to bear the Armstrong brand name; 1895, company incorporated as the Armstrong Cork Company; 1907, first linoleum plant built; linoleum became main product of company (discontinued in 1974 in favor of newer, more resilient floor coverings); 1980, company changed its name to Armstrong World Industries, Inc.; headquarters in Lancaster, Pennsylvania.

Performance: *Sales*—$1.9 billion (floor coverings). *Market share*—55% of vinyl tile (flooring) industry.

Major competitor: Amtico.

Advertising: *Agency*—BBDO, Inc., New York, NY; since 1917. *Major campaign*—"Armstrong puts the height of fashion right at your feet"; "Armstrong, so nice to come home to."

Addresses: *Parent company*—Armstrong World Industries, Inc., P.O. Box 3001, Lancaster, PA 17604-3001; phone (717) 397-0611; fax (717) 396-2126.

the United States, but the market potential for linoleum had barely been tapped.

Even with the establishment of Armstrong's first linoleum factory outside of Lancaster, Pennsylvania, starting up the new venture was difficult; it did not show a profit for at least ten years. What changed the fortunes of the new product in 1917 was effective advertising. Armstrong in fact would be the first company in the world that would successfully mass-market linoleum. By the mid-1920s, Armstrong linoleum was the mainstay of the company's sales.

Early Marketing Strategy

The head of Armstrong's small publicity department, Henning W. Prentis, Jr., realized that the future linoleum market would be comprised of housewives, who had to be convinced that linoleum was practical (easy to clean), attractive, and useful for every room in the house. To get this message across, Prentis in 1917 persuaded management to commit to a three-year, $500,000 advertising campaign. The first ad splashed across an entire page of the *Saturday Evening Post*, at a cost of $5,000. Prentis even hit on the idea of hiring an interior decorator who could explain linoleum and suggest useful, attractive decorating ideas to prospective consumers. The campaign was so successful that, even as it achieved its principal goal of launching Armstrong linoleum on the U.S. mass market, it also marked the beginning of the Armstrong brand's dominance in the interior furnishings industry.

Advertising

The "Armstrong floor" message would not be limited, as it was in 1917, to the print media—the advent of radio provided an ideal opportunity to get that message to the public. In 1928, the Armstrong Quakers, a vocal and instrumental group, launched a regular radio program that eventually was carried on more than thirty stations. During World War II, movie stars like Helen Hayes and Vincent Price appeared in Armstrong radio dramas, which were introduced by the "Armstrong Quaker Girl." As early as 1950, Armstrong entered the new realm of television, far earlier than most companies; the half-hour weekly program "Armstrong Circle Theatre" featured many famous Hollywood stars in dramatic roles. Commercials aired during the program displayed Armstrong's new acoustical ceilings as well as floor coverings. With color television came the opportunity to display the beautiful colorings of Armstrong products.

Product Development

First identified with cork and cork products, the Armstrong brand became almost wholly identified with linoleum floor coverings in the 20th century; when the company stopped producing linoleum in 1974, acoustical ceilings and walls, ceramic tiles, and furniture carried the Armstrong name.

Ironically, Armstrong's break from its roots as a cork cutter was made possible by the tremendous amount of cork dust—a key ingredient in linoleum—the company had cluttering up its factory

An early advertisement for Armstrong linoleum appeared in the Saturday Evening Post.

floor. The key to the company's success in linoleum was aggressive marketing—and a superior product. Armstrong linoleum was a significant improvement over the colorless, lackluster linoleum competitors sold, mainly to institutions. The advertising blitz surrounding Armstrong linoleum succeeded because the product itself was innovative and eyecatching, superior in quality and design.

Since 1917, when Armstrong linoleum first reached national prominence, the product was continuously improved. When consumers complained that Armstrong linoleum often buckled and even ruined the flooring underneath, Armstrong developed a felt backing for the linoleum that corrected the problem. The new felt product, produced in a new plant in Fulton, New York, turned out to be useful to the auto industry as well. To the present day, specialty products for cars have evolved into an important Armstrong sideline.

In 1931 Armstrong became the first manufacturer to develop vinyl tiles. The end of World War II, the tremendous housing demands it brought, and Armstrong's expertise with felt backing led to an important business in industrial adhesives—at first for Armstrong floors and then eventually for many other industrial uses.

Cork continued to be manufactured in Armstrong's Pittsburgh plant. By 1930, corkboard for insulating purposes (which was made from the waste from cork production) was used for residential and roof insulation. Armstrong's cork division continued to find new uses for cork; one of these innovations, an acoustical material that absorbs noise, was first developed in the 1920s for the motion picture and radio broadcasting industries. In 1960, 100 years after Armstrong's beginnings as a cork producing firm, cork production was stopped. The manufacture of acoustics materials, however, to this day has remained a very important specialty of Armstrong, and although cork manufacture was discarded in 1960, the company still retained "cork" in its name until 1980, when Armstrong Cork Company became Armstrong World Industries, Inc.

International Growth

The 1980 name change to Armstrong World Industries, Inc. underscored the fact that Armstrong had indeed become a global enterprise. The brand could be found in more than 80 countries worldwide. As early as the 1930s, Armstrong had an export division at its Lancaster headquarters, and a new European headquarters was established in 1974.

As far back as the late nineteenth century, Armstrong had an office in Spain. In the 1920s, Armstrong branches were established in Canada and England, and new offices opened in Germany, India, and Australia in the 1960s. With the growing importance of Armstrong acoustical and fireproof ceilings, ceiling plants were added in Canada, France, Belgium and the Netherlands, and insulation plants in Switzerland and Italy.

Traditionally centered in Europe, Canada, and Australia, Armstrong manufacturing centers are being established in the Indian subcontinent and Asia. Through tenacious effort, Armstrong is well established in Japan, particularly in the floor tile market, where Armstrong tiles are the featured brand in the Tokyo area DO IT retail chain stores. Further product penetration into Asia is Armstrong's goal in the 21st century, thanks to the end of trade barriers in that region of the world, and to the strengthening of private enterprise economies, as on the Indian subcontinent. Currently, one-fourth of Armstrong's annual revenue derives from its international sales, a figure that the company expects to rise into the 21st century.

Future Growth

Armstrong is one of the oldest continuously operating companies in the United States and a recognizable brand name throughout the world. Strong brand recognition is an important asset for future growth and expansion, as are favorable economic climates. The recently approved North American Free Trade Agreement (NAFTA) augurs well for Armstrong in North America, where it enjoys number one market shares in such product lines as vinyl tiles, ceiling manufactures, and vinyl sheet floors, and a strong market share in furniture. The fall of communism in Russia and Eastern Europe and the rise of free market economies in China and India also bode well for a brand name that has been multinational for at least three decades.

Further Reading:

Annual Report: Armstrong World Industries, Inc., 1992.

"Armstrong, A Global Growth Company," Armstrong World Industries, 1993.

Cleary, David Powers, *Great American Brands: The Success Formulas that Made Them Famous,* New York, Fairchild Publications, 1981.

Huhn, Mary, "Armstrong Floors Plans Cuts in Print Spending," *Mediaweek,* May 10, 1993, p. 5.

Mehler, William A., Jr., *Let the Buyer Have Faith: The Story of Armstrong,* Lancaster, PA, Armstrong World Industries Inc., 1987.

Ramirez, Anthony, "Battle Gets Hot in Floor Coverings (Armstrong World Industries)," *New York Times,* September 18, 1990, p. C16(N), p. D20 (L).

Sraeel, Holly A., "Product Testing Begins at Home; Armstrong World Industries, Inc. Uses Its Own Interior Products to Define Space," *Buildings,* July, 1988, p. 42.

—Sina Dubovoj

ATARI®

Founded in 1972, Atari is one of the best-known brands of video games, video-game systems, and computers. Its trademark is shared by two firms—the Atari Corporation (a maker of personal computers and home video-game systems) and the Atari Games Corp. (a maker of coin-operated video games). Both companies began in 1972 as Atari, Inc., which introduced the first successful coin-operated video game and became the fastest-growing company in the United States during the home video-game craze of the early 1980s. For millions of parents and their children, the name Atari became synonymous with video games.

Atari's fortunes, however, plummeted in 1983 with a downturn in the video-game industry. Warner Communications, which acquired the company in 1976, broke up Atari in 1984, selling the home video-game and computer businesses, which became the Atari Corporation, to a group of investors led by Jack Tramiel, the founder of Commodore computers. The following year, Warner sold majority interest in the remaining coin-operated games division, which became Atari Games Corp., to Namco America, a subsidiary of Nakamura Manufacturing Co. of Japan. Atari Games was permitted to use the Atari trademark only on coin-operated games. Time-Warner, Inc., repurchased Namco's share of Atari Games in 1990.

The Atari Corporation concentrated on home computers and achieved some market success in Europe, but it struggled in the United States, in part because the Atari name was so strongly identified with video games. In 1993 Atari's share of the market for personal computers was less than one percent. Meanwhile, Atari virtually conceded the home video-game market to Nintendo in the late 1980s. Atari reentered the market with a new video-game system in 1993, but its market share in video-game systems was also less than one percent.

Brand Origins

Atari was founded by Nolan Bushnell, who grew up watching *Mr. Wizard* on television and entered science fairs in high school. After graduating from the University of Utah in 1968 with a degree in electrical engineering, he moved to California's Silicon Valley and became a research engineer in the graphics department of the Ampex Corporation. He also tinkered with building computer games at home.

By 1970 Bushnell had developed a game he called "Computer Space," which pitted rocket ships against flying saucers. He licensed Computer Space to Nutting Associates, a small manufacturer of arcade games, which produced about 1,500 coin-operated game units. Bushnell also went to work for Nutting. Unfortunately, Computer Space did not sell well in an industry still dominated by pinball and other mechanical games. Bushnell blamed Nutting's management for the failure and left the company in 1972. He also realized, however, that Computer Space was too complicated. Bushnell later conceded, "People didn't want to read instructions. To be successful, I had to come up with a game people already knew how to play; something so simple that any drunk in any bar could play."

Bushnell decided to start his own computer-game company and recruited two friends from Ampex, Ted Dabney and Larry Bryan, who each agreed to pitch in $100 in start-up money (Bryan later backed out when it came time to come up with the money). The three engineers considered several names for their new company before deciding on "syzygy," an astrological term for when the Sun, Earth, and Moon are aligned. "Syzygy," however, had already been registered as a trademark by a California roofing company.

Bushnell then decided to pick one of several terms used in the Japanese game "Go"—either "sente" (the equivalent of "checkmate" in chess), "atari" (roughly translated as "prepare to be attacked"), or "hanne" (used to acknowledge a good move). According to Scott Cohen in *Zap! The Rise and Fall of Atari,* a clerk in the California Secretary of State's office liked "atari" and made the final selection. Atari was incorporated on June 27, 1972.

Atari's First Game: Pong

Atari set to work on developing a computer game so simple that, in Bushnell's words, "people knew the rules immediately" and "it could be played with one hand, so people could hold a beer in the other." The result was "Pong," an electronic Ping-Pong game in which a square dot of light was batted back and forth across a television screen with "paddles" that players moved up or down by twisting a pair of knobs. Bushnell later boasted, "I made [Pong] with my own two hands and a soldering iron." Cohen, however, credits the concept to Bushnell but most of the engineering to Allen Alcorn, who had been recruited from Ampex. Alcorn also came up with the distinctive "pong" sound (which

AT A GLANCE

Atari brand of coin-operated video games founded in 1972 by Atari, Inc., of California, headed by Nolan Bushnell; its first home video game introduced in 1975; company purchased by Warner Communications in 1976; Atari personal computers first sold in the early 1980s; home video-games and computer division (Atari Corporation) sold to Jack Tramiel in 1984; majority share of coin-operated games division (Atari Games Corp.) sold to Namco America, subsidiary of Nakamura Manufacturing Co. of Japan, in 1985; Atari Games reacquired by Time-Warner, Inc., in 1990.

Performance: *Market share*—Less than 1% of personal computer category; less than 1% of home video-game systems category. *Sales*—$127 million (personal computers and home video-game systems); $75 million (coin-operated video games).

Major competitor: In computers, IBM, Macintosh (Apple Computer Inc.); in home video games, Nintendo; in coin-operated games, Sega.

Advertising: *Agency*—For personal computers and home video-game systems, Hoffman & Lewis, Inc., San Francisco, CA, 1994--; no agency for Atari Games Corp.'s coin-operated video games.

Addresses: *Parent company*—Atari Corporation (personal computers and home video-game systems), 1196 Borregas Ave., Sunnyvale, CA 94089-1302; phone: (408) 745-2000; fax: (408) 745-4306. *Parent company*—Atari Games Corp. (coin-operated video games), 675 Sycamore Dr., Milpitas, CA 95035; phone (408) 434-3700. *Ultimate parent company*—Time Warner, Inc. (80% share of Atari Games Corp.), 75 Rockefeller Plz., New York, NY 10019; phone: (212) 484-8000.

provided the game's name) after Bushnell demonstrated what he wanted by putting a thumb inside his cheek and making a popping noise.

The first Pong game was set up in Andy Capp's Tavern, a bar in Sunnyvale, California, in the fall of 1972. The only instructions were "Avoid missing ball for high score." Before long there was a line of people waiting to play the game. There was also a line of people the next day, right up until about 10 p.m., when the game suddenly stopped working. A quick inspection revealed the problem; the plastic milk carton inside the game that was supposed to catch the quarters was full, and the overflow had short-circuited the machinery. The carton was replaced with a casserole dish that could hold about 1,200 quarters, or about a week's worth of play. While the Pong game was raking in about $300 a week, a pinball game sitting next to it was bringing in about $30.

At first Atari tried to interest Nutting and other pinball-game companies in a licensing agreement to manufacture and distribute Pong games. After being turned down, Atari rented an empty roller rink in Santa Clara, hired an assortment of hippies and college students, and began assembling Pong games itself. Atari shipped its first Pong game in November 1972, relying on a network of pinball-game middlemen for distribution. Atari sold more than 8,000 Pong games in 1973, and in 1974 it sold the rights to Midway Manufacturing Co. Midway subsequently sold more than 10,000 Pong games. Atari went on to create other successful coin-operated video games, including Tanks, Breakout, Asteroids, and Gran Trak, the first video car race.

Home Video Games

Magnavox introduced "Odyssey," the first home video game, in 1972. Odyssey was similar to Pong but came with dice, cards, play money, a cardboard scorekeeper, and plastic overlays that could be taped to a television screen to create different game boards. Magnavox sold more than 100,000 Odyssey games in the first year, but sales fell off rapidly in 1973, in part because commercials gave the mistaken impression that Odyssey games could be played only on Magnavox televisions.

Atari joined the home video-game market in 1975 with "Home Pong," and Sears, Roebuck & Co., which had negotiated the exclusive distribution rights, sold 150,000 in the first year. The following year, however, Fairchild Camera and Instruments introduced Channel F, the first full-color home video-game system with changeable game cartridges. Channel F came with hockey and tennis built in, while other games, including blackjack, baseball, and tank warfare, were sold separately. Home Pong was immediately obsolete.

Atari responded by developing the VCS (Video Computer System), which was later renamed the Atari 2600. The Atari 2600 was far more sophisticated than anything else on the market. The company had been poorly managed, however, and despite its success in coin-operated games, Atari needed financial help in putting the home video-game system into production. In 1976 Warner Communications, a movie maker and entertainment conglomerate, purchased Atari for $28 million.

The following year Atari produced more than 800,000 video-game systems in time for Christmas, but the holiday shopping season came and went, and neither Atari nor any of its competitors sold many games. In retrospect, there were more than a dozen home video-game systems on the market in 1977, and consumers, apparently confused by all the hype, spent their money elsewhere. Only Atari and Coleco Industries survived the shakeout that came in 1978. Many observers believed that home video games had been nothing more than a fad.

Then in 1979 Atari acquired the home video-game rights to "Space Invaders," a wildly popular arcade game created by the Japanese Taito Corporation and distributed in the United States by Midway. Space Invaders was the first coin-operated video game licensed for the home video-game market, and sales of the Atari 2600 skyrocketed. Atari followed up with home video-game versions of Asteroids and Pac-Man, and by the end of 1982 Atari 2600 had sold more than 20 million home video-game systems.

The Fall of Atari

Almost overnight the home video-game industry had become a $3-billion-a-year bonanza, and Atari, which controlled 75 percent of the market, had become the fastest growing company in the United States, but boom quickly turned to bust in 1983. In 1981 both Mattel and Coleco introduced second-generation home video-game systems, Intellivision and ColecoVision, that generated much better graphics than the Atari 2600. Atari, however, ignored the competition and consequently badly overestimated the demand for its own game system in 1982. As a result, the market was flooded with home video-game systems (from all three companies) that had to be sold at steep discounts. Even then, most stores were left with large inventories of merchandise. "It was," *Newsweek* said, "as though Santa Claus had suddenly turned his sleigh in mid-flight and headed back to the North Pole."

Compounding the problem was a rash of boring video games that failed to generate any excitement with game players. Two of the worst—"ET, The Extra Terrestrial" and "Raiders of the Lost Ark," the first video games to be based on hit movies—came from Atari. Many other companies also churned out games and cartridges that were meant to sell for $30 but were dumped on the market for $5 or less. Even good games failed; incredibly, Atari licensed the home video-game rights to Pac-Man, then the most popular coin-operated computer game ever, and proceeded to manufacture more game cartridges than there were game systems.

Late in 1982 the second-generation Atari 5200 was introduced to compete with Intellivision and ColecoVision. In another marketing blunder the new Atari system was incompatible with most of the popular game cartridges available for the Atari 2600. Parents who purchased the new system discovered that the Atari 5200 would not play the games their children already owned or wanted most. Meanwhile, both Mattel and Coleco introduced expansion modules that allowed games made for Atari to be played on their systems.

The cumulative effect sent sales at Atari into a nosedive in the fall of 1982 that continued in 1983, when the company lost more than $530 million. Atari's market share slipped to 20 percent. James Morgan—a marketing executive from Philip Morris brought in by Warner to replace Raymond Kassar as chairman of Atari—told *Time,* "There was an incredible arrogance at Atari. It was a rigid, unchallenged and unchecked giant, and it has paid every penalty imaginable for its mistakes." Morgan was given a five-year contract in 1993 to turn Atari around, but Warner lost patience and sold the company to Jack Tramiel in 1984. Tramiel, former president of Commodore International Ltd., then the leading maker of home computers in the United States, paid no money for Atari but assumed more than $240 million in liabilities.

Atari Games Corp.

Tramiel's interest was in home computers, so Warner retained the coin-operated games division, which became Atari Games Corp. Warner, which also retained a minority interest in Atari Corporation, agreed not to use the Atari trademark for any consumer products. In 1985 Warner sold a majority interest in Atari Games to Namco America, a subsidiary of Nakamura Manufacturing Co., a Japanese maker of amusement rides. Time-Warner reacquired Namco's share of Atari Games in 1990.

Atari Games considered itself the "true" Atari since the original company started with Pong and other coin-operated video games. Several game designers who worked for Atari during the heyday of the 1970s still worked for Atari Games in the mid-1990s. Atari Games, however, did not aggressively promote the brand name. As Mary Fujihara, director of marketing in 1994, explained, coin-operated game players are not brand conscious, electing to play the most popular games regardless of the manufacturer. "It's like the movie industry," Fujihara said. "Our share of the market depends on how hot our current release is." She estimated that the share of Atari Games fluctuated between 5 and 30 percent of the market, which was divided among about a dozen major game companies. Among the more popular coin-operated video games from Atari Games Corp. were several versions of "Hard Drivin'," a 3-D driving simulation first released in 1989. Other games included "Pit Fighter," "Road Riot," and "Steel Talons." Atari Games also produced video games for home video-game systems under the Tengen brand name.

Atari Corporation and Personal Computers

During his ten months at Atari, Morgan cut the total number of employees from 9,800 to 3,500, leaving about 1,000 in the United States. He also delayed plans to introduce a home computer and consented on developing games for the Atari 5200. Morgan told *Business Week,* "We are going to re-ignite the consumer's love affair with video games." When Tramiel took over, he continued downsizing, eventually paring the U.S. work force to a mere 200 employees, but Tramiel, ousted as chairman of Commodore a few months before buying Atari, believed the future was in home computers. He revived plans for the home computer and stopped development of a new video-game system.

Atari Corporation entered the home-computer market in the early 1980s with the 600XL and 800XL computers, which competed with two computers from Commodore—the Commodore 64 and VIC 20—in the under-$500 market. Atari sold 250,000 computers in 1983, compared with one million for Commodore. In 1985 Atari Corporation unveiled the 520ST, which was based on the same microchip used in the Apple Macintosh. The 520ST duplicated many of the easy-to-use Macintosh features, including a mouse, and was dubbed the Jackintosh by industry insiders. The 520ST sold for $399, less than half what the Macintosh cost, though a disk drive ($150) and a color monitor ($350) were extra. James Copeland, then marketing vice president, explained the strategy to *Fortune:* "The average credit card limit is $500. We don't force the consumer to go broke buying the whole system." Atari Corporation sold about 100,000 520ST computers in 1985. The following year Atari Corporation added to its line of computers the 1040ST, which sold about 300,000 units. Sales, however, were strongest in Europe. *Business Week* noted, "Atari's video game image puts off consumers [in the United States] looking for a serious computer." Sales were also hurt in the United States because Atari ST computers could not run IBM-compatible software, and many U.S. retailers refused to carry them.

In 1987 Atari Corporation introduced its MEGA series of computers. Like the ST series, MEGA computers featured a Musical Instrument Digital Interface for composing and added desktop-publishing capabilities for printing musical scores. Atari introduced a hand-held computer, Portfolio, in 1989 and a laptop computer, Stacy, in 1990. In 1992 Atari Corporation launched the Falcon, which it described as a "personal integrated media system." Falcon featured a musical interface, plus full-color graphics and video capabilities. Falcon would also run software developed for IBM-compatible computers.

Atari Corporation and Home Video Games

Atari Corporation introduced a new home video-game system, the Atari 7800, in 1986. In 1987 Atari followed up with the XE system, which doubled as both a home video-game system and a low-cost personal computer. Nintendo of North America, however, a subsidiary of Nintendo Company, Ltd., of Japan, had introduced in 1985 the Nintendo Entertainment System, which quickly dominated the home video-game industry. By 1990 Nintendo had sold more than 30 million home video-game systems and controlled 90 percent of the market. Ironically, Nintendo had approached Atari, Inc., in 1984 about distributing its home video-game system in the United States, but talks were called off shortly before the company was sold to Tramiel.

In 1989 Atari Corporation introduced Lynx, a hand-held video-game player designed to compete with Game Boy from Nintendo.

Although Lynx was considered technologically superior to Game Boy and had a color-display screen, it was not promoted aggressively, and Game Boy, which came with the hit game "Tetris," captured virtually the entire market for hand-held video-game players. A $160 million lawsuit brought by the Atari Corporation alleging Nintendo of illegally monopolizing the home video-game market was dismissed by U.S. District Judge Fern Smith in 1992.

Brand Outlook

In 1993 Atari Corporation upstaged Nintendo by introducing Jaguar, the first 64-bit home video-game system. Nintendo's latest game system was then the 16-bit Super NES (Nintendo Entertainment System), introduced in 1991. Sega Enterprises, Ltd., a Japanese video arcade-game company, introduced the first 16-bit home video-game system, Genesis, in 1989. Genesis was the second-best-selling brand of home video-game systems behind Nintendo.

The initial response to Jaguar from industry analysts was that the Atari Corporation may have priced the game system too high ($249). Even so, Jaguar was evidence that the Atari Corporation was again serious about the home video-game market. Although the trademark had almost vanished from the industry it virtually created in the 1970s, it was possible that the Atari brand name would survive in consumer products.

Further Reading:

Atari Computer . . . Providing Performance without the Price in the Computer, Video Game Industry, Sunnyvale, California: Atari Computer Corporation, 1993.

"Atari: The Problem Child That Warner Can't Get Rid Of," *Business Week,* September 24, 1984, p. 110.

"Atari Refuses to Let the Video Game Fad Die," *Business Week,* May 21, 1984, p. 46.

"Atari Turns to a Marketing Magician," *Business Week,* July 25, 1983, p. 26.

"Atari's Struggle to Stay Ahead," *Business Week,* September 13, 1982, p. 59.

Bagamery, Anne, "The Second Time Around," *Forbes,* October 8, 1984, p. 42.

Cohen, Scott, *Zap! The Rise and Fall of Atari,* New York: McGraw-Hill Book Company, 1984.

DeMott, John S., "A New Pac-Man; Jack Tramiel Gobbles Atari," *Time,* July 16, 1984, p. 50.

"A Game Plan for Survival at Atari," *Business Week,* April 9, 1984, p. 32.

Hafner, Katherine M., "Father Knows Best—Just Ask the Tramiel Boys," *Business Week,* December 15, 1986, p. 106.

"How Steve Ross's Hands-Off Approach Is Backfiring at Warner," *Business Week,* August 8, 1983, p. 70.

"Jim Morgan's Unhappy 10 Months at Atari," *Business Week,* July 23, 1984, p. 90.

Nash, Jim, "Atari on the Way Back, or on the Way Out?" *Business Journal* (San Jose), June 14, 1993, p. 1.

Pauly, David, "The Video-Game Shakeout," *Newsweek,* December 20, 1982, p. 75.

Petre, Peter, "Jack Tramiel Is Back on the Warpath," *Fortune,* March 4, 1985, p. 46.

Shao, Maria, "Jack Tramiel Has Atari Turned Around—Halfway," *Business Week,* June 20, 1988, p. 50.

Sullivan, George, *Screen Play: The Story of Video Games,* New York: Frederick Warne & Co., 1983.

Wise, Deborah, "Tramiel's Atari: The Long Shot That's Coming In," *Business Week,* December 9, 1985, p. 39.

"The Zinger of Silicon Valley," *Time,* February 6, 1984, p. 50.

—Dean Boyer

BACCARAT®

Baccarat

Baccarat, a trademark of the Compagnie des Cristalleries de Baccarat in Baccarat, France, is one of the most prestigious names in crystal glassware. Baccarat crystal is sold in fine gift shops and department stores around the world and in company stores in New York, Paris, and Tokyo.

Brand Origins

In 1764 Monseigneur de Montmorency-Laval, bishop of Metz, petitioned Louis XV of France on behalf of Antoine Renaut for permission to found a glassworks in the village of Baccarat in the province of Lorraine. A succession of wars—including the Seven Years' War, which ended in 1763—had devastated the French economy, and the bishop hoped the glassworks would provide jobs for his parishioners. With the king's approval, Renaut established Verreris Renaut et Cie. (Renaut and Co. Glassworks), the first French glassworks not managed by nobility.

The glassworks operated under several names until 1823, when it became known as Compagnie des Cristalleries de Baccarat (Crystal Company of Baccarat). The village of Baccarat had taken its name from an ancient temple to Bacchus, the Roman god of wine, that was built during Julius Caesar's conquest of Gaul in 58 B.C. Bacchi Ara, Latin for ''altar of Bacchus,'' became Baccarat.

Baccarat produced flat glass for mirrors and windowpanes until 1816, when the glassworks were purchased by crystal-maker Aime-Gabriel D'Artigues. D'Artigues was a Frenchman who operated Cristallerie de Voneche in Belgium. When Belgium won its independence from France (with the defeat of Napoleon Bonaparte at the Battle of Waterloo in 1815), D'Artigues was forced to move his glassworks to France. He renamed the glassworks at Baccarat the Verreries de Vonche a Baccarat and received a license from Louis VIII to begin producing crystal. The company acquired its current name in 1823 when D'Artigues sold the glassworks to his associates.

During the nineteenth century Baccarat also became a model for social innovation. Housing for the artisans was provided within the confines of the glassworks, and in 1827 Baccarat opened a school for the children of its workers. Baccarat was also among the first companies to create a pension fund (1850) and establish an unemployment benefits fund (1890).

Lead Crystal

Lead crystal can be considered a relatively new discovery, in light of the fact that glass-making is at least 4,500 years old. Soda-lime glass, the most common type, is made with approximately 72% silica (sand), 15% sodium oxide (soda), and 9% calcium oxide (lime). During the 1500s, Venetian craftsmen modified the formula for soda-lime glass to create a nearly colorless glass they called Cristallo.

Then in 1676, an Englishman, George Ravenscroft, discovered that he could produce a glass that was softer, clearer, and more refractive than soda-lime glass by replacing the calcium oxide and some of the silica with lead oxide. This new glass melted at lower temperatures, and was easier to cut and engrave. Lead crystal soon replaced Venetian Cristallo for fine glassware.

Crystal is categorized by the amount of lead oxide it contains. Fine glass with up to 12% lead oxide can be labelled crystal. Lead crystal contains 13% to 23% lead oxide, while full-lead crystal contains at least 24% lead oxide. Compagnie des Cristalleries de Baccarat has produced only full-lead crystal since 1817. Baccarat crystal was still being produced by hand in the 1990s, by artisans who apprenticed for eight years to learn their trade.

Brand Development

After 1816 the Baccarat glassworks began producing fine tableware and simple art objects from crystal. It also produced sought-after glassware from opaline, a slightly translucent glass, and agate, an opaque glass colored to simulate semi-precious stones, in what was known as the Biedermeier style. In 1819, Baccarat and a Paris design studio collaborated to create elegant glass furniture mounted in bronze for the queen of Spain.

In 1839 the Baccarat glassworks began to produce colored glassware, sometimes adding two or three layers of color to the crystal. Colored crystal is produced by adding metal-bearing salts to the crystal formula. In 1843 Baccarat introduced a new crystal, ''cristal dichroide,'' which appeared to have either a yellow or green tint, depending on the light. The strange, shifting color was achieved by adding uranium to the glass formula. Baccarat also may have been the first glassmaker to produce Chrysoprase, a green opaque crystal.

AT A GLANCE

Verreries Renaut et Cie. founded by Antoine Renaut in Baccarat, France, 1764, under patronage of Louis XV; renamed Verreries de Baccarat 1768; renamed Verreries de Sainte-Anne in 1773; renamed Verreries de Voneche a Baccarat and began producing crystal glassware in 1816; renamed Cristalleries de Baccarat in 1823.

Performance: *Market share*—40% of French crystal. *Sales*—$110 million.

Major competitor: Compagnie des Cristalleries de St. Louis's St. Louis brand.

Advertising: *Agency*—Bozell (Europe). *Major campaign:* Tradition of Innovation (U.S.).

Addresses: *Parent company*—Cristalleries de Baccarat, 54120 Baccarat (Meurthe-et-Moselle), France; *phone:* (83) 75-10-01.

Baccarat began producing paperweights in 1846. Initially, Baccarat paperweights were made in the millefiori (thousand flowers) style, by imbedding thin slices of colored glass in a ball of clear glass to create a flower-like design. By 1848, Baccarat also was producing sulfure paperweights, encasing real flowers, fruits, and insects in glass. Sulphide paperweights with porcelain medallions and cameos of famous people were introduced in the late 1800s.

In the mid-1800s, Baccarat also began producing elaborate chandeliers, candelabra, and other interior furnishings, as the ornate fashions of the Louis XIV period came back into style. Baccarat astounded visitors to the World's Fair in Paris in 1855 with towering, 17-foot-tall candelabra, immense crystal vases, and a 23-foot water fountain made of glass. At around the same time Baccarat introduced simple, elegant balloon-style wine glasses, which contrasted sharply with the ornateness of the Louis XIV style.

Another glassware style developed by Baccarat and still fashionable in the late 20th century was the Harcourt pattern. Introduced around 1842, it featured six ovoid facets cut into the goblets and a hexagonal stem and foot. St. Remy, an unadorned, tulip-shaped Baccarat pattern, was introduced in 1878. The stem and bowl of the champagne flutes were created from a single piece of crystal rather than two separate pieces.

By 1925 and the Exposition des Arts Decoratifs in Paris, which gave the world the term Art Deco, simplicity and elegance of form had returned to most artistic endeavors, including the crystal glassware and art objects produced by Baccarat. Many Baccarat designs were created by French artist Georges Chevalier, including the famous ''Stag Head'' produced in 1952. Stag Head figurines were presented to Charles de Gaulle, Leonid Brezhnev, and other heads of state.

In 1967 Baccarat constructed the first continuous-melting tank, which allowed artisans to make larger and more elaborate objects from single pieces of crystal. In 1972 Baccarat created the De la Terre a la Lune, a 200-pound crystalline sculpture of the earth and moon unveiled at the Lisbon International Fair. It was the largest decorative piece ever made of lead crystal and won the International Design Competition Grand Prix award. In 1979, Baccarat received the Fashion Award presented by the Neiman-Marcus Co. In 1985 Baccarat became one of the first crystal companies to use computer-aided design and manufacturing techniques. However, most of the work, including blowing, shaping, cutting, and engraving the glass was still done by hand.

The Baccarat Museum in Paris displays crystal goblets, paperweights, perfume bottles, and some of the most spectacular Baccarat creations spanning nearly two centuries of glassmaking. France has honored 38 artists who have created designs for Baccarat since 1924 as ''Meilleurs Ouvriers de France.'' However, Baccarat likes to believe that its most creative and beautiful work lies ahead.

Further Reading:

Baccarat, Compagnie des Cristalleries de Baccarat: Baccarat, France, 1987.

The History of Baccarat, Baccarat, Inc.: New York, n.d.

Newman, Harold, *An Illustrated Dictionary of Glass,* London: Thames and Hudson, Ltd., 1977.

Phillips, Phoebe, ed., *The Encyclopedia of Glass,* New York: Crown Publishers, Inc., 1981.

—Dean Boyer

BARBIE®

Barbie®

Perhaps no American toy is better known than Barbie, Mattel, Inc.'s eleven-and-a-half-inch molded-plastic doll. Originally produced with blonde hair, blue eyes, and hourglass figure, Barbie has become an icon of American culture. She is the best-selling toy of all time, with over 700 million sold since her introduction in 1959. In 1993 Barbie was the leading product in the toy industry, with sales in more than 100 countries and worldwide revenues exceeding $1 billion. The average American girl owns eight versions of Barbie or companion dolls (plus clothing and accessories); the average Italian girl owns seven; and the average French or German girl owns five. Mattel also sells "Barbie for Girls" licensed products, which include girls' shoes, clothing, skates, backpacks, cosmetics, and furniture. Barbie dolls and costumes, however, make up the bulk of revenues.

Brand Origins

Barbie's origins can be traced to a comic strip called "Lili," introduced in 1952 by the German daily newspaper *Bild-Zeitung*. The strip depicted the antics of an attractive and fashionably dressed young woman named Lili. It became so popular that it eventually inspired a three-dimensional doll bearing the same name. Designed by Max Weissbrodt and produced by Greiner and Hauser GmbH, the seven-inch Lili debuted in 1955 as a slim fashion-model-type doll. Her appearance greatly resembled that of French movie star Brigitte Bardot, who wore a blond ponytail and seductive, fashionable clothing. The Lili doll was exported worldwide, but her popularity was short-lived, and eventually she was sold to Mattel.

The decision to market the doll was made by Mattel founders Ruth and Elliot Handler, who were inspired by their daughter Barbara's desire for an adult doll with adult-style clothing. With the assistance of Mattel executive Jack Ryan, the Handlers remade Lili's image into that of Barbie. Visually the two dolls were quite similar, although Barbie's eyes and mouth were softened, and her hair was made more pliable. The primary difference between Lili and Barbie, however, lay in the image Mattel created around its new product.

Early Marketing

Billed as a "teenage fashion model," Barbie, complete with a wardrobe based on haute-couture design of the era, was introduced in 1959 at the New York Toy Fair. She was originally created "to project every little girl's dream of the future," and, as designer Billy Boy said in *Barbie: Her Life and Times,* "at that time, before the advent of women's liberation, little girls believed that they would grow up to be either mothers or high-fashion models, and they generally were not encouraged to aspire to much else."

Buyers at the Toy Fair were only mildly interested in the new doll. Mattel, however, had researched the market and was convinced that "children were desperate for a role model like Barbie." Four years earlier Mattel had made toy-industry history when it had signed on as a sponsor of *The Mickey Mouse Club* in 1955. Never before had a toy company purchased a year-round sponsorship of a television show. Confident in their product, Mattel ignored the buyers and began advertising on television.

Mattel sold over 351,000 dolls in 1959 and more than one million costumes. Demand for the new doll was so high that Mattel was required to double its manufacturing capacity twice within the first two years of its introduction. Mattel also offered a variety of Paris fashions, party dresses, school sportswear, swimsuits, accessories, and even undergarments for Barbie. Barbie's early wardrobes were made with real silk linings, hand-finished seams and hems, and tiny operable buttons and zippers—all produced by cottage industry in Japan. They also reflected interests of the times. A pink "Barbie-Q" ensemble came with an apron and a complete set of miniature barbecue tools, and numerous sleeping ensembles responded to the popularity of slumber parties.

The World of Barbie

Shortly after the doll's introduction Mattel created an idealized world around Barbie, complete with family, friends, and boyfriend. She had a host of likes, interests, and experiences that fed little girls' fantasies of teenage life. Wardrobe names, such as "Resort Set," "Open Road," and "Senior Prom," hinted at Barbie's life-style. Each ensemble also came with a small booklet that further illustrated Barbie's life.

When Mattel introduced Barbie's boyfriend, Ken, in 1961, he was referred to as her "handsome steady." The first television commercial for Ken fed children's imagination with a ministory in which an animated Barbie doll, dressed in a pink satin gown called "Enchanted Evening," noticed Ken from across a ballroom. "It all started at the dance," a sultry female voice narrated. "She met

AT A GLANCE

Barbie brand of dolls and accessories founded in 1959 by Ruth and Elliot Handler, vice-president and president, respectively, of Mattel, Inc., of El Segundo, California; Barbie became a registered trademark in 1959.

Performance: *Market share*—75% (top share) of fashion doll category. *Sales*—$1 billion (1993 estimate).

Major competitor: Hasbro, Inc.'s Sindy fashion doll.

Advertising: *Agency*—Ogilvy & Mather, Los Angeles, CA. *Major campaign*—"Barbie, Come Along With Me."

Addresses: *Parent company*—Mattel, Inc., 333 Continental Blvd., El Segundo, CA 90245; phone: (310) 524-2000; fax: (310) 524-2179.

Ken! . . . Somehow Barbie knew she and Ken would be going together.'' The commercial then went on to explain that Ken was Barbie's new boyfriend and that they had numerous coordinated outfits for going to the beach and fraternity dances and for after-school sodas. It ended with the tag line, ''Get Barbie and Ken and see where the romance may lead.''

Also in 1961 Mattel introduced the first ''Barbie Sings!'' record, with songs such as ''My First Date'' and ''The Busy Buzz'' illustrating innocent fantasies of teenage romance. Early books about Barbie appeared with titles such as *Barbie's Fashion Success, Barbie's Hawaiian Holiday,* and *Barbie Solves a Mystery.* By the early 1960s Dell had produced collections of *Barbie and Ken* comic books, and Random House was publishing a *Barbie* series of teenage novels.

Included in all these Barbie stories were Barbie's family and friends. Mattel introduced Midge as Barbie's best friend in 1963 and Skipper, Barbie's little sister, a year later. Over the years Mattel has introduced more than 40 of Barbie's friends and family—including Black, Hispanic, and Asian dolls—and over 15 different pets for Barbie. These dolls could be purchased separately but could share Barbie's, Skipper's, or Ken's wardrobes.

Barbie's continued success has been due to Mattel's ability to transform the doll's image in keeping with societal changes and the roles little girls emulate. ''We have a responsibility to have Barbie represent values we feel good about,'' Mattel president Jill Elikann Barad told *Financial World* in 1992. ''We want girls to know there are no limits to their aspirations.'' Approximately 90 different Barbie dolls (including companion dolls and customized versions for retailers) were being created every year. Since 1959 Barbie has had 47 different careers (and corresponding wardrobes), including surgeon, olympic athlete, business executive, rock star, presidential candidate, and Radio City Music Hall Rockette.

Brand extensions such as these have kept Barbie sales growing by at least 10 percent annually between 1968 and 1991. In the period 1988 to 1991—thanks to a continued focus on brand extension that kept on top of children's desires—Barbie sales doubled to $840 million.

Updating Barbie

In 1967 Mattel came out with its first of three major changes to Barbie's form. The new version had a ''twist and turn'' waist (so she could dance in the latest style), bendable legs, long eyelashes, and paler skin. The new product received heavy advertising, including an ad starring Maureen McCormick of the popular *Brady Bunch* television sitcom. Borrowing a trick from auto dealers, Mattel offered a trade-in deal in which customers could purchase the new Barbie for $1.50 if they traded in their old doll. The regular retail price for Barbie was around $4. The campaign was highly successful; in May 1967 alone more than 1.2 million Barbie dolls were traded in for new ones. In 1967 Mattel also introduced New Talking Barbie.

The next major change to Barbie's body came three years later, in 1970, with the advent of Dramatic New Living Barbie—the most poseable Barbie doll ever made. The ad sought to capture the lively images of women that were appearing across the pages of fashion and sports magazines at that time. Again it starred McCormick, who ran, jumped, and twirled around her Dramatic New Living Barbie, implying that Barbie had much of the ease of movement of a young girl. The following year Malibu Barbie and friends were introduced, complete with bathing suits and golden sun tans. Barbie's image grew more sporty during the early 1970s. It culminated in 1975 with the introduction of Free Moving Barbie, Ken, and P.J., each of whom could swing a tennis racket or golf club when a tab on the doll's back was pushed.

In the early 1980s International Barbie dolls (hailing from such places as Iceland, Sweden, Switzerland, Peru, Alaska, and South Pacific Islands) were introduced. Also around that time Barbie's face underwent another makeover, giving her sparkling eyes and a sweet, teeth-revealing smile. Mattel had been producing black Barbie dolls since 1968, and in 1981 the company introduced a new series of black, Hispanic, and Asian dolls, each with new, smiling faces and separate names and identities.

Barbie as she has appeared from 1959 to 1989.

Barbie's hairstyles changed continuously to keep up with the whims of fashion. No hairstyle change was as successful, however, as the introduction of Totally Hair Barbie in 1992. Totally Hair Barbie came with blond or brunet hair that reached to her feet and with a package of gel that allowed girls to style Barbie's hair as they pleased. Totally Hair Barbie generated worldwide sales of more than $100 million in 1992, making it the most successful Barbie to date.

International Markets

Barbie has been marketed outside the United States almost since her introduction, but it wasn't until the 1980s that Mattel began heavily promoting Barbie sales in Europe. In 1980 Barbie sales led the way in Mattel's $135 million international market. By 1990 Mattel's overseas revenues had grown to more than $700 million, and Barbie sales worldwide lept to over $500 million. Much of Barbie's growth during this time was attributable to heavy marketing efforts in Europe, where, in 1991, Mattel spent over $2.3 million just in advertising Barbie.

In 1991 Mattel began an extensive new strategy for marketing Barbie in Japan after its contract with Bandai, Japan's top toy manufacturer, expired. Under Bandai's direction Barbie had made her debut in Japan eight years earlier as Moba Barbie, with facial features and a girlish figure designed especially for the Japanese market. Moba Barbie was designed to resemble Takara Co.'s Jenny doll, which held about 75 percent of the Japanese market, yet Barbie never captured more than 6 percent of the market share.

Japan was the only market in which Mattel deviated from traditional Barbie design. When the licensing agreement with Bandai ended, Mattel gave Barbie a more western look and began promoting her full range of clothing and accessories. Television advertising capitalized on her accessories, which were not available for rival dolls. Ads also showed girls how to play with the doll—a new concept in Japan, where traditionally fashion dolls had been more for display. Although it declined to give exact figures, Mattel announced in a 1991 issue of *Marketing* that results of this new effort had been good.

Competition

Since 1959 competition against Barbie has been about as slim as her tiny waist. In the early 1960s a slew of competitors were introduced but made no more than a dent in Barbie's growing market. Mattel's largest competition in the toy industry, Hasbro, Inc., has made numerous attempts at capturing a share of the Barbie market. In 1986 Hasbro introduced Jem, a doll slightly bigger than Barbie and not as pretty. Jem flopped and was pulled from the market after only one year. In 1988, however, Hasbro introduced Maxie, incorporating the knowledge they gained from the Jem failure. Maxie was the same size as Barbie. She could even wear Barbie's clothes and play with her accessories, although she also came with her own. Hasbro sought to position Maxie as a seventeen-year-old girl who likes pizza, the beach, shopping malls, and her hunk of a boyfriend, Rob. Initial sales of Maxie (which retailed for $7, far lower than most Barbies) were promising but not enough to pose a threat to Barbie's dominance. Mattel filed suit against Hasbro in 1991, charging that Hasbro's new Sindy doll, marketed in Europe, resembled Barbie's facial features too closely. Hasbro settled out of court and agreed to change the doll's face. A 1992 *Advertising Age* story on the two companies conjectured that Hasbro had basically given up trying to compete with Barbie and was instead challenging Mattel in the baby-doll and board-game markets.

Brand Outlook

As one Mattel marketing executive told *Advertising Age,* Barbie was "not just a fashion doll. She gives little girls the chance to pretend, to build a fantasy world completely. We believe that this part of our weaponry separates us from the competition." Much of Barbie's success was due to Mattel's strategy of constantly updating the doll with an infinite number of potential fantasies. Coupled with Mattel's strong worldwide distribution and advertising networks, this marketing strategy has generated tremendous growth in Barbie sales—from 485 million in 1988 to 965 million in 1992. International sales accounted for almost half of all Barbie profits in 1992.

Mattel saw tremendous potential for continued growth in international markets, noting that the child population in Europe was double that of the United States, and the child population in Latin America and Asia was even higher. With little genuine competition, Barbie's future seemed quite rosy. The opening of markets in the former Soviet Union and the introduction of toy superstores, such as Toys "R" Us, in Japan and other wealthy Asian countries presented tremendous opportunities for further growth. Mattel's success in overseas markets would be due, in part, to its ability to keep the fantasy world of Barbie alive in the minds of young consumers.

Further Reading:

Beauchamp, Marc, "Barbie at 30," *Forbes,* November 14, 1988, p. 248.

Boy, Billy, *Barbie: Her Life and Times,* New York: Crown Publishers, Inc., 1987.

Brown, Paul B., "Eternally Yours, Barbie," *Financial World,* September 1, 1992, p. 36.

"It's Not the Doll, It's the Clothes," *Business Week,* December 16, 1961, p. 48.

Kilburn, David, and Julie Skur Hill, "Western Barbie," *Advertising Age,* October 7, 1991, p. 40.

—Maura Troester

BFGOODRICH®

BFGoodrich is one of the oldest and best-known tire brands in North America. The BFGoodrich Company, in existence since 1870, did not begin producing car tires until the late 1890s, well after the death of its founder, Dr. Benjamin Franklin Goodrich. Since the introduction of its first tire in 1896, the brand has made many original contributions to the evolution of the automobile tire, from tires made of synthetic rubber, first sold in the United States by BFGoodrich in 1940, to the first tubeless tire, produced by BFGoodrich in 1947, to the first American-made radial tire, which BFGoodrich put on the market in 1965 (followed two years later by the "run flat" tire—a tire that can operate even when damaged). While BFGoodrich tires are identified in the public perception with cars, they are also sold to the aircraft industry. Owned by the Uniroyal Goodrich Tire Co.—a subsidiary of Compagnie Générale des Établissements Michelin—since 1990, BFGoodrich continues to be an innovator in the worldwide tire business.

Brand Origins

The BFGoodrich tire brand bears the name of the founder of the company, Benjamin Franklin Goodrich, who never lived to see an automobile or automobile tire. Goodrich started off his working life as a doctor, with no inclination toward business. Following his graduation from medical school at age 20 he enlisted as a doctor in the Union army during the Civil War. After the war, Goodrich returned to Jamestown, New York, to resume his practice. Impatient to marry, but unable to support a wife on his meager earnings, he gave up medicine to enter a more financially rewarding career—real estate.

Goodrich's association with rubber was accidental. In 1869, the year he made up his mind to leave medicine, he received some stock in the Hudson River Rubber Company from a patient unable to come up with cash to pay his bill. The company was hardly surviving, but the good-natured and tolerant Goodrich accepted the substitute, and he soon found himself deeply involved in the fate of the ailing firm. Goodrich's earnings from the real estate business allowed him to marry and rear a rapidly growing family, and also enabled him to invest in the company, along with a partner. Soon they were full owners and Goodrich became president.

For a variety of reasons, Goodrich decided to relocate his company to the economically expanding Midwest, which to him meant Chicago. However, on a train ride west from New York, he met a man who extolled the virtues of Akron, Ohio, with its new railway terminals and bustling economy. Goodrich made up his mind then and there to relocate to Akron. The city met all of his expectations, especially when Akron businessmen extended him a generous loan to cover the start-up costs of his relocation. On December 31, 1870, the Goodrich, Tew & Company opened its doors for business along the Ohio Canal.

First Commercial Success

For ten years, despite ongoing tuberculosis, Goodrich labored side-by-side with his workers to make his company a success. The first Goodrich brand products were fire hoses, household rubber products such as bottle stoppers and rubber rings for canning jars, wringer rolls, and billiard cue tips. There were markets for these items and excellent transportation to get them quickly to their markets, but still the company barely broke even. A turnabout occurred in 1879. Goodrich hired a new manager who quickly streamlined and cut costs; the name of the company was changed to BFGoodrich Company, and it became publicly owned.

The Goodrich name was a success long before it was associated with tires, an association that began in 1896. Because of its reputation in the rubber business, the company was asked to produce the first U.S.-made pneumatic, or compressed air, tires for the first American automobile, the Winton. A dozen years later, the BFGoodrich brand established a name for itself when its tires were mounted on the Golden Flyer, the biplane that won the prestigious International Flying competition in Rheims, France.

Early Marketing Strategy

Before Goodrich died at age 46, his marketing strategy was summarized in the oft quoted "Let us make goods destined for service." Accordingly, when he saw a friend's house burn down because the fireman's hose had frozen, he was determined to make a better hose that could withstand the freezing cold temperatures. This turned out to be the cotton covered rubber fire hose, greeted at first with skepticism, but an eventual success.

One of Goodrich's sons was instrumental in establishing the company's first research lab in 1895, making it the only rubber company and one of the few companies in the United States in those days to have research facilities. This research arm would further the marketing strategies of the company, systematically

AT A GLANCE

BFGoodrich brand of tires originated with Goodrich, Tew & Company, a rubber company founded by Dr. Benjamin Franklin Goodrich in Akron, OH, in 1870; company changed its name to BFGoodrich Company, 1880; manufactured tires for the first U.S.-made automobile, the Winton, 1896; BFGoodrich established joint venture with Uniroyal, 1986; Uniroyal Goodrich Tire Co. acquired by Compagnie Générale des Établissements Michelin, 1990; BFGoodrich tires manufactured and marketed by Michelin subsidiary, Michelin North America, Inc., with headquarters in Greenville, SC.

Performance: *Market share*—3.5% of North American replacement tire market.

Major competitor: Goodyear; also Firestone.

Advertising: *Agency*—W. B. Doner & Company Advertising, Southfield, MI; 1990—. *Major campaign*—"BF Goodrich T/A Tires: When You're Ready to Get Serious."

Addresses: *Parent company*—Uniroyal Goodrich Tire Company, 600 S. Main Street, Akron, OH 44397-0001; phone: (216) 374-3000; fax: (216) 374-4092. *Ultimate parent company*—Michelin North America, Inc., 1 Parkway South, Greenville, SC 29615; phone: (803) 458-5000; fax: (803) 458-6359. *Ultimate ultimate parent company*—Compagnie Générale des Établissements Michelin.

improving existing rubber products and developing new ones. An intrinsic part of the marketing strategy then and now, of course, was advertising.

Goodrich himself was serious about spreading the word of his company's products. Accordingly, he asked his young stenographer, Henry Corson, to begin a direct mail campaign in 1881 to prospective customers. Some years after Goodrich's death, Corson hit on the idea of including attractive young women in BFGoodrich advertising. The first model to grace a BFGoodrich ad was "Kate," a raven haired, elegantly attired, dark-eyed beauty. Corson made sure he had copies of her picture for customers. The portraits later became collectors' items.

In the decade prior to the outbreak of World War I, BFGoodrich produced a colorful and popular calendar which contributed to marketing its products to a broad public. The First World War itself brought a series of patriotic BFGoodrich ads to the print media of the day—featuring, for instance, Goodrich workers laboring in the shadows of the Statue of Liberty. These ads let patriotic consumers know that BFGoodrich tires and transmission belts were vital to the war effort.

A notable coup for the BFGoodrich tire brand occurred in 1927, when Charles Lindbergh selected it for his *Spirit of St. Louis*. Motor sporting events also were and still are important advertising venues, as are television, print ads, and radio.

Product Development

Ever since Goodrich's first product innovation, the cotton covered fire hose, came on the market, the company forged ahead in the development of rubber commodities and byproducts. Innovation was a necessity. Akron became the "rubber capital" of North America, and by the turn of the century BFGoodrich faced intense competition from hundreds of small and large rubber and tire firms, including Firestone, Goodyear, Kelly-Springfield, and General Tire.

The production by Goodrich of America's first pneumatic car tire in 1896 was a historic development. This would be followed in 1899 by an alkali process for reclaiming rubber, discovered by scientists in BFGoodrich's new research lab, followed in 1906 and 1910 by other discoveries leading to improvements in tire performance and abrasion resistance. These were important contributions to America's still infant automobile industry. In the early days of the automobile, car tires, which were little more than extra-strong bicycle tires, gave out frequently, and it was necessary for a motorist before World War I to carry upwards of a half-dozen spares, which made driving a luxury reserved for the wealthy. Only after World War I, thanks to the mass production of cars and BFGoodrich's contributions to product development, did a car become affordable for working people.

Another important product innovation was the adaptation of corded tires to automobiles, which previously were only used on bicycles. Corded tires gave cars easier maneuverability and a smooth ride. While not a Goodrich invention, the company bought the rights to this process and in 1912 developed the Silvertown cord tire, named after the town in England where cord tires first came on the world market. It was the first cord tire made in the United States.

A crucial contribution to the aviation industry was the invention by BFGoodrich engineers of a de-icing mechanism on planes to enable them to take off and land safely in winter weather. This occurred in 1930, and was without doubt the single most important contribution to airline safety in the history of commercial flying. BFGoodrich also went on to have an impact on the space industry decades later, designing and manufacturing the first space suits for American astronauts.

Tires for cars, trucks, tractors and airplanes were the business for which BFGoodrich was best known, however. The 1940s were a decade of profound innovation in tires. In 1940, BFGoodrich developed and marketed the first automobile tires made of synthetic substances. During World War II, when Japan controlled most of the world's rubber production, BFGoodrich became a pioneer in the development of durable, all-synthetic rubber. It was not until 1954, however, that BFGoodrich scientists duplicated the true rubber molecule in a test tube and developed a genuine synthetic substitute for rubber. As a result of this discovery, BFGoodrich became the biggest producer of synthetic rubber, called Ameripol SN, in the world. This led to the growth of BFGoodrich's rubber-based chemical division, which is today a separate company.

BFGoodrich had developed the first tire without an inner tube in 1947, and it followed with the collapsible spare tire for cars, called the Space Saver, in 1967, and the first pneumatic run flat tire that could operate even when punctured. The BFGoodrich T/A performance radial tire came out in 1970, followed by the advent of the first light truck performance radial tire in 1976. BFGoodrich developed the world's first performance mud terrain tire in 1980 and the tallest light-truck radial tire in 1984. Two years later, BFGoodrich formed a joint venture with Uniroyal to form Uniroyal Goodrich. In 1990, Uniroyal Goodrich was purchased by the European tire giant Compagnie Générale des Établissements Michelin.

International Growth

As early as 1902, the BFGoodrich company established an export department, and distributors were sent around the world to market BFGoodrich tires. Not long afterwards, BFGoodrich's first manufacturing facility overseas opened in France. Following the Second World War, BFGoodrich was the first major American tire manufacturer to aggressively market and manufacture abroad. By 1957, BFGoodrich products were made or sold in over twenty countries. By 1970, BFGoodrich tires were marketed in over one hundred countries, and the firm was building new tire plants at a rate of one per year.

The Future

As part of the Michelin Group, BFGoodrich continues to focus on the car enthusiasts who constitute a special market niche for BFGoodrich tires, and future advertising and promotional campaigns will focus particularly on this segment. The passage of the North American Free Trade Agreement (NAFTA) in 1993 will boost BFGoodrich tire sales in the twenty-first century. Along with its worldwide reputation, this will assure BFGoodrich a strong market presence well into the next century.

Further Reading:

BFGoodrich T/A in Competition (The History of BFGoodrich Tires in Motorsports), Akron, OH: BFGoodrich Tires, 1993.

BFGoodrich Co., *BFGoodrich 100th Anniversary,* Akron, OH: BFGoodrich Co., 1970.

Collyer, John L., *The BFGoodrich Story of Creative Enterprise, 1870–1952,* New York: Newcomen Society, 1952.

"Cutbacks Set by Tire Maker," *New York Times,* June 21, 1991, p. C3.

Firestone, Jr., Harvey S., *Man on the Move:The Story of Transportation,* New York: Putnam, 1967.

"Groupe Michelin U.S. Unit Recycles Tires in Pavement," *Wall Street Journal,* June 25, 1992, p. B4.

Hicks, Jonathan P., "Tire Company's Uphill Struggle," *New York Times,* June 13, 1989, p. C1.

"It's the Michelin Man," *Time,* October 2, 1989, p. 83.

Mufson, Steven, "Justice Approves Michelin's Purchase of Uniroyal BFGoodrich," *Washington Post,* April 25, 1990, p. G3.

—Sina Dubovoj

BISSELL®

The Bissell name is synonymous with mechanical carpet cleaners, a unique product whose origin predates electrical vacuum cleaners and continues to defy obsolescence. In fact, Bissell, Inc., the brand's parent company, views the carpet sweeper as a product entirely different from vacuum cleaners. It may easily be used daily, like a broom, to sweep up small messes before they are stepped on and ground into the carpet. By contrast, vacuums are bulky and noisy, they must be plugged in, and their use is considered a greater household chore.

Brand Origins

The Bissell carpet sweeper was developed in 1876 by Melville R. Bissell, the proprietor of a crockery store in Grand Rapids, Michigan. Bissell and his wife, Anna, received most of their fragile glass and china shipments in crates packed with sawdust, which inevitably spilled out onto the floors in their shop. Each day Bissell would sweep up the mess, but inevitably some of the dust would land on his rugs. Several carpet sweeper models had been on the market since 1858, designed specifically to achieve what no broom could: brushing dirt out of a rug. Melville Bissell purchased one of these models, called the "Welcome," for his wife. But Bissell noted several deficiencies in the design, and set out to develop a better model.

Bissell's model used floor wheels to drive a rotating brush on an improved reduction gear. The bristles bent slightly as they brushed through the carpet. When they rotated off the floor, they sprung straight again, flinging whatever debris was in their path up into a compartment. The dirt could be emptied simply by opening the top of the box and shaking it over a garbage can. One day, a patron of the shop saw the carpet sweeper in action and asked where she could get one of her own. When several more people inquired about the device, Bissell began to wonder if his carpet sweeper was a marketable product.

Early Marketing Strategy

Anna Bissell argued that because Americans were clean in mind and body, the carpet sweeper would serve the cause of responsible living while reducing the strain and drudgery of housekeeping. That was enough for Melville Bissell, who now had a much grander vision of his little invention: the carpet sweeper was a revolution in living. The Bissells converted the second floor of their crockery store into a carpet sweeper assembly shop. While Melville supervised operations in the shop, his wife visited the small army of homemakers who painstakingly assembled the brushes.

Initially, the Bissells conducted their own sales visits, choosing to distribute their product through housewares retailers rather than with door-to-door salesmen. However, convincing skeptical store owners to handle the merchandise was difficult. After several months, and with great persistence, Anna Bissell finally succeeded in getting shopkeepers to purchase and display the carpet sweeper. The device performed so well in demonstrations that word of mouth quickly established a strong demand for it. Soon the Bissells were turning out 30 carpet sweepers a day and shipping them to retailers throughout Michigan, the Midwest, and the East.

Advertising

A young Bissell bookkeeper named Claude Hopkins suggested that schematic diagrams and other mechanical details be dropped from the carpet sweeper's sales brochures because the audience, homemakers, considered the information superfluous. Instead, he pointed out that the literature should focus on aspects that were more likely to appeal to women. Talk of gear ratios was replaced with references to the "golden maple, opulent walnut, and rich mahogany" used to make the carpet sweeper. The company's male directors were appalled at the notion but couldn't deny that brochures bearing this language produced dramatically higher sales of the carpet sweeper.

Hopkins later drew up a pamphlet promoting a limited edition of the device made from vermilion, a rare and exotic wood culled from the jungles of India by elephant trains. The stunt produced more sales in six weeks than the company had been able to muster in a year. Hopkins also ran a highly successful promotion of the carpet sweeper as a Christmas gift. He subsequently left Bissell and began a celebrated career in Chicago, becoming one of the first advertising gurus.

Brand Development

In 1883 the Bissells incorporated their company and built a new factory specifically for manufacturing carpet sweepers. They also bought out the Michigan Carpet Sweeper Company and the Grand Rapids Carpet Sweeper Company, not to eliminate competition but to raid them of their managerial talent. Soon after the

AT A GLANCE

Bissell brand of carpet sweeper created in 1867 by Melville R. Bissell and patented that same year; company incorporated in 1883; presidency assumed by Anna Bissell upon her husband's death in 1889. Electric vacuum cleaner introduced in 1920s; wet extraction carpet cleaner introduced in 1952; "Stick Vac" introduced in 1960.

Major competitor: Royal; also Regina, Hoover, and Eureka.

Advertising: *Agency*—In-house. *Major campaign*—A 30-second commercial with tagline, "For All Those Times"; Big Green Clean Machine and Little Green Clean Machine infomercials.

Addresses: *Parent company*—Bissell, Inc., 2345 Walker Road NW, Grand Rapids, MI 55426; phone: (616) 453-4451; fax: (616) 453-1383.

five-story brick Bissell plant was completed, it was gutted by a devastating fire. Melville Bissell mortgaged his entire personal fortune, including his home and his horses, to finance a reconstruction. Shortly after production resumed, it was discovered that the factory's entire output was defective. In order to protect the brand name, Bissell ordered the recall of every defective model, representing a loss of more than $35,000.

The company's carpet sweepers were thoroughly patented, and Bissell vigorously sued those who infringed on his design. When he encountered a patent for a superior design held by a competitor, he simply purchased it. By 1889 the Bissell name had become so well established, and had such a strong reputation for quality, that few competitors dared to challenge it.

In March of that year, Melville caught a cold while on a trip to Kentucky. After his conditioned deteriorated into pneumonia, he died at the age of 45. Anna Bissell took control of the company and became one of America's first female executives. She remained head of the company into the 1920s, when an ominous new threat emerged to the family business.

The proliferation of household electrification led to the invention of several new appliances, including the vacuum cleaner. Anna Bissell remained committed to the mechanical carpet sweeper, confident that it would take years for the public to overcome its irrational fear of electricity. Electric vacuum cleaners were unforgiving monstrosities that were prone to destroy frail carpets and expensive Oriental rugs. Perhaps most importantly, Bissell carpet sweepers were well established in the retail network, whereas vacuum cleaner sales were dependent on often unscrupulous door-to-door salesman. However, electric vacuum cleaners were hindered by these deficiencies only temporarily. Indeed, better vacuum cleaners were developed, and their manufacturers gradually eased their way into retail channels. Bissell was obliged to introduce its own electric vacuum cleaner merely to stay in the market.

Bissell also continued to make improvements to its product line. Earlier innovations included better bearings and a handle that adjusted the sweeping pressure on the brushes. In 1928 a new design automatically adjusted the height of the brushes to different surfaces.

By the late 1920s Melville Bissell, Jr., was in charge of the company, and the Great Depression had set in. Few people had money to spend on an expensive electric vacuum, causing many of their manufacturers to go out of business. The carpet sweeper won one last respite in the battle against electricity.

The younger Bissell decided that the company had no place in the vacuum cleaner market and discontinued building electric models. He reasoned that the carpet sweeper had its own place in the home. Electric vacuums could be used for heavy duty cleaning, whereas the carpet sweeper would be favored for quick touch-ups, in the same way one might use a broom to sweep up a bit of dirt. Marketing of the product emphasized the ease and convenience of using the carpet sweeper *instead* of a vacuum cleaner for maintaining the appearance of the home, the patio, the pool, and the cottage. The company maintained that there was a place in every home for the lightweight, inexpensive, and easily portable carpet sweeper.

International Growth

After taking over for her husband, Anna Bissell set out to make Bissell an international name. The company already had agencies in 20 foreign countries, but Anna considered their market penetration to be shallow.

Bissell salesmen in England repeated the public demonstrations of the product that had proven so effective in America. The product could gently but effectively clean even the most delicate rugs, which won the brand a priceless endorsement from Queen Victoria, who allowed the Bissell sweeper to be used in her palace. Soon thousands of English homemakers were ordering the affordable device, and the practice of carpet sweeping became known as "Bisselling." However, with the rise of home electrification, vacuum cleaners gained a more dominant position in the homes of the English, and the practice of carpet cleaning soon became known as "Hoovering."

International sales were interrupted by World War II. The company reestablished its international business after the war by building factories in Britain, France, Germany, Ireland, and Switzerland, in addition to Canada and Australia. Bissell has since taken strong advantage of the fact that carpet sweepers are more popular in Europe than in the United States.

Brand Expansion

Melville R. Bissell III succeeded his uncle as president of the company in 1953. It was he who determined that the Bissell name should stand for more than just mechanical carpet sweepers. The business of the company, he reasoned, should be expanded to floor care and, later, to something much broader: complete home care. He noted that the carpet sweeper was effective only for topical dirt and that conventional vacuum cleaners were capable only of brushing up dirt in the top quarter inch of a carpet. More thorough cleaning, down to the nap of a carpet, would require shampooing. He ordered the development of a new product called the Shampoomaster.

The Shampoomaster, a nonelectric device, required the use of water and a detergent. The company described it as more than just a lightweight carpet scrubber: it was a cleaning system. The new product was manufactured from 1957 to 1967 and was promoted ahead of Bissell's carpet sweeper. Although overall revenue grew five-fold in this period, sales of the Shampoomaster were limited.

Few homes were large or consistently dirty enough to warrant the regular use of the Bissell system. The Shampoomaster was discontinued, and the company concentrated on its traditional carpet sweeper line and a lightweight "stick vac" it had introduced in 1960 in competition with models from Regina and General Electric.

John M. Bissell, a cousin to Melville III, assumed leadership of the enterprise with the belief that the carpet sweeper remained a viable product, practical for daily use in every home, even those without rugs or carpets. Indeed, the Bissell sweeper was just as effective as a broom, and more convenient because it did not require a dust pan. Because Bissell had already established itself as a leader in floor care products, the company continued to manufacture an array of floor fabric treatments, including cleaning sprays and detergents, and another line of vacuum cleaners.

In 1980, Bissell introduced a household wet cleaning device called the "Carpet Machine," followed by another model in 1981 called "It's Magic." The product signaled Bissell's desire to expand in the home care field, without degenerating into pitched battles with the vacuum cleaner makers Hoover and Eureka. It's Magic contained no pump, but drew its water pressure from a sink faucet, and was therefore less prone to breaking down. Even so, the product performed below expectations and was discontinued. In 1985 Bissell introduced a lightweight vacuum cleaner intended for use on stairs and on the second level of homes, where a heavy vacuum cleaner would be less practical or more cumbersome.

Product Image

Bissell's advertising practices sought to establish product differentiation and quality. The company clearly defined the role of its carpet sweeper as an essential complement to the vacuum cleaner. Bissell's little sweeper was perfect for the homemaker who, having just vacuumed, was confronted with an isolated spill of dirt or ash, a clump of dried mud, crumpled leaves, or any other insult to a clean carpet. In promoting the appearance of the carpet sweeper, from its wooden models, to metal, and later to plastic, Bissell targeted its market of women aged 25 to 55. The company intended to convince women that the carpet sweeper was more than a mechanical broom; it was a status symbol. It encouraged the impression that the home with a carpet sweeper was maintained by a woman with the highest standards of cleanliness.

Bissell's reputation for quality was firmly established with its first costly product recall and was maintained through vigorous protection of its patents. The company chose to invest heavily in the integrity of its design: it had to work better than any potential competitor. Over the years, Bissell held on to its position in the market, accounting for about 70 percent of domestic carpet sweeper sales and about 40 percent of the international market.

Future Growth

Bissell bolstered its position in the deep cleaning market in 1974 when it acquired the Penn Champ company, a packager of aerosol cleaners and shampoos. In 1982 it acquired Chicago-based Maxi Vac, Inc., a maker of wet/dry vacuum cleaners. These highly strategic acquisitions enabled Bissell to reenter the carpet shampoo market in 1992, with a line of multipurpose wet vacuums called the Promax and Promax Plus (since renamed the Powerlifter, due to a trademark battle with Hoover). The product was promoted in 30-second television ads with a warning that "sensitive viewers may be disturbed by the following filth," and continued with a shot of the dirt pulled from a freshly vacuumed carpet by the Promax.

A companion product, the Big Green Clean Machine, was first seen in an "infomercial," a controversial television format. Although often frowned upon as exceedingly pedestrian, the infomercial has proven to be an extremely effective form of promotion for certain types of products, including Bissell's wet cleaning system. The company risked diluting its good name in such a medium; to compensate, the execution of the ad was uncommonly tasteful and believable. As a result, the infomercial produced a successful launch for the new product, a multifunction floor-cleaning machine with many attachments and applications, and enabled Bissell to more firmly establish its family of home care products, which includes sweepers, small vacuums, deep cleaners, and cleaning chemicals. In fact, Bissell was so pleased with the success of its infomercial it launched the smaller Little Green Clean Machine in October 1993 using the same format.

Further Reading:

Bissell Carpet Sweeper, Grand Rapids, MI: Bissell, Inc.

"Bissell, Inc., Finds Niches—and Grows," *Grand Rapids Press,* June 2, 1985, p. G1.

"The Bustling Business of Bissell," *Michigan Business,* September 1984, pp. 40–42.

"More 'Filth' on TV," *Advertising Age,* February 3, 1992, p. 10.

Powers, David Cleary, *Great American Brands,* New York: Fairchild Publications, 1981.

—*John Simley*

BLACK & DECKER®

Black & Decker is the world's leading brand of power tools in the industrial and do-it-yourself markets. In the United States it is also the market leader in household appliances. Black & Decker is the principal trademark of the Black & Decker Corporation, and its products are marketed in more than 100 countries. Other Black & Decker trademarks include Dustbuster, Spacemaker, Kwikset, Workmate, and DeWalt.

Brand Origins

Duncan Black and Alonzo G. Decker, both in their early 20s, left the Rowland Telegraph Company in 1910 to open a small machine shop in Baltimore, Maryland. They named the business The Black & Decker Manufacturing Co., and in 1912 they adopted a hexagonal logo that, in various forms, would symbolize the company for more than 80 years. Among Black & Decker's first products, manufactured under contract to other companies, were a milk-bottle capping machine, a vest-pocket adding machine, a candy dipper, an automobile shock absorber, and a cotton picker. The company also made specialized machinery for the U.S. Mint.

In 1914 Black & Decker filed its first patent application for a portable power drill with a pistol-type grip and a trigger instead of a switch. The drill was a revolutionary development in tool design—industrial drills weighed as much as 50 pounds and took two people to operate—and laid the groundwork for the modern power-tool industry. The company introduced the drill in 1916, along with the Lectroflater, a portable electric air compressor. They were the first two products with the Black & Decker brand name. Black & Decker received a patent on its drill design in 1917.

Early Marketing

Black & Decker also proved to be adept at marketing. In 1918 the company opened product-demonstration centers in Boston and New York. Black & Decker also placed notices in *American Exporter* magazine announcing the appointment of company representatives in England, Canada, Russia, Australia, and Japan. By 1919 annual sales exceeded $1 million. In 1921 Black & Decker launched its first general media advertising with full-page ads in *The Saturday Evening Post.* The company issued its first product catalog in 1922 and three years later began organizing clinics to teach distributors how to demonstrate its power tools. Black & Decker also converted a pair of buses into mobile demonstration centers that toured the country. In 1929 the company outfitted an airplane as a flying showroom for power tools used in reconditioning aircraft engines.

Do-It-Yourself Market

Until 1923 Black & Decker sold power tools only for industrial use. It moved into consumer products that year with the introduction of a half-inch power drill advertised as "the first all sleeve-bearing power tool at a popular price." Unfortunately, the price was too steep for most consumers, and the drill was not a commercial success. The company retrenched and again focused on the industrial market. Then in 1942 Black & Decker organized a committee to develop a marketing strategy to put into effect after World War II. According to David Powers Cleary in *Great American Brands,* a committee member mentioned a news account about defense-plant workers stealing portable power tools in order to use them at home. With that rudimentary piece of market research, the Post-War Planning Committee began formulating the strategy that would eventually make Black & Decker the number one brand name in the home power-tool market.

According to Cleary, the committee came to five basic conclusions: (1) thousands of consumers were being introduced to power tools by working in U.S. defense plants; (2) with the right promotion, a home market for power tools would develop after the war; (3) Black & Decker was becoming a well-known brand name with widespread exposure in the defense plants; (4) other companies would probably manufacture power tools similar to Black & Decker's; and (5) sales leadership would depend on cost leadership. Black & Decker's experience with its half-inch drill in 1921 suggested that cost leadership would not be easy. Alonzo G. Decker Jr., who headed the committee, said later, "No idea is worth having unless you have the guts to back it up."

In 1946 Black & Decker introduced its Home Utility power drill and line of accessories designed for the home market. The drill was an incredible success, and more than a million were sold in the first four years. By 1953 the company had added a portable circular saw, a finishing sander, and a jig saw to its Home Utility line. The first television commercials for Black & Decker power tools debuted in 1955.

Black & Decker continually improved its products, which ensured a steady stream of customers moving up to more sophisticated tools. Black & Decker also sustained demand for its con-

AT A GLANCE

Black & Decker brand of power tools and appliances founded in 1916 by Duncan Black and Alonzo G. Decker, owners of Black & Decker Manufacturing Co.; the brand's first product was a portable electric drill; company named changed to Black & Decker Corporation in 1984.

Performance: *Sales*—(Power tools) $1.36 billion; (small appliances) $674 million.

Major competitor: (Professional power tools) Makita; (consumer power tools) Sears, Roebuck & Co.'s Craftsman; (small appliances) Sunbeam, Hamilton Beach, Proctor-Silex, and Oster.

Advertising: *Agency*—(Consumer power tools) Leo Burnett Company, Inc., New York, NY; (household appliances) McCann Erickson, New York, NY. *Major campaign*—"Serious tools for serious projects," for the Black & Decker Quantum line of power tools.

Addresses: *Parent company*—Black & Decker Corporation, 701 East Joppa Road, Towson, MD 21286; phone: (410) 716-3900.

sumer power tools by maintaining price leadership. The basic, one-speed drill that cost $16.95 in 1946 sold for $7.99 in 1970. Alonzo G. Decker Jr., then president and chairman of the company, told *Business Week,* "The bulk of our market is lower and middle income. Every time we lower the price, our market base expands tremendously."

Cordless Power Tools

In 1961 Black & Decker introduced the world's first cordless electric drill, powered by nickel-cadmium batteries, and again revolutionized the power-tool industry. A cordless hedge trimmer and four professional-model drills were introduced the following year. (Black & Decker had entered the market for lawn and garden tools in 1957 with a line of lawn edgers and hedge trimmers. In 1969 Black & Decker Ltd., a British subsidiary, would introduce an electric lawn mower, the Lawnderette.)

In 1964 Black & Decker's cordless power tools reached their ultimate—literally—when the company developed special minimum-torque tools for use in space by Project Gemini astronauts. The company later developed the Apollo Lunar Surface Drill, a battery-operated power drill designed to take samples of the moon's surface, which saw its first use in 1971 on the Apollo 15 mission. Black & Decker was inducted into the U.S. Space Foundation's Space Technology Hall of Fame for its contributions to the U.S. space program. In the mid-1970s Black & Decker introduced a cordless "power handle" that came with a drill, a flashlight, a hedge trimmer, and vacuum attachments. The multiuse tool, however, was a commercial failure, apparently because buyers forgot to recharge the batteries.

Then in 1979 Black & Decker introduced the Dustbuster, a rechargeable, hand-held vacuum cleaner. Supported by a $3 million advertising campaign, the Dustbuster was a tremendous success. It was also copied by other manufacturers, which touched off several patent-infringement lawsuits. (Black & Decker was occasionally sued as well. In 1992 the company was ordered to pay $2.35 million to National Presto Industries, Inc., which claimed that Black & Decker's Handy Slice 'N' Shred infringed on patents for its hot-selling Saladshooter.) The Dustbuster was followed in 1981 by the Spotlite, a rechargeable flashlight. The Black & Decker rechargeable screw driver, introduced in 1987, was the most successful product launch in company history and gave rise to an entire line of related battery-powered hand tools. In 1990 Black & Decker introduced the Power Pro Dustbuster, with twice the power of the original Dustbuster.

Small Appliances

Black & Decker's first foray into the household appliance market came in 1930 with the introduction of the Cinderella washing machine. Unfortunately, the washing machine, introduced just as the Depression was beginning, was a commercial failure. The company's next attempt to move out of the workshop and into the house was the Dustbuster. More than ten million were sold in the first four years, prompting Stephen Britt, then a vice president at Black & Decker, to tell *Business Week,* "Dustbuster got us out of the basement and upstairs." Retailers, however, stocked the Dustbuster in the hardware section, and consumers continued to view Black & Decker as a power-tool company.

Then in 1984 the biggest name in power tools suddenly became the biggest company in small appliances when Black & Decker purchased the General Electric (GE) small-appliance division for $300 million. The company also introduced a new logo—a bright orange hexagon—that Black & Decker described as a "contemporary statement of the company's momentum and strength." General Electric was then the market leader in small appliances with more than 150 products, but the deal gave Black & Decker the right to use the GE brand name for only three years. Black & Decker was forced to undertake an unprecedented effort to transfer a new brand name onto a leading line of consumer products, including hair dryers, irons, toasters, and blenders. *Fortune* observed, "In renaming the GE appliances, Black & Decker is doing for its competitors something they could not possibly have accomplished themselves—eliminating the best-known name in the small-appliance business." *Forbes* asked the question that was on many minds: "Can the brand name that means so much in the basement command respect in the kitchen?"

In 1985 Black & Decker introduced three small appliances under its own brand name—a three-speed cordless mixer, a cordless electric knife, and an iron that shut itself off if left unattended. Two years later, however, the Federal Trade Commission (FTC) forced Black & Decker to withdraw ads for the Automatic Shut-Off iron that carried an endorsement from the National Fire Safety Council, but only because the FTC said the private council was not qualified to make a judgment on fire safety. Black & Decker also launched a two-year, $100 million advertising campaign to change its image from a power-tool company to a consumer-products company.

More new products followed, and by 1987, when the last holdovers were weaned from the GE brand name, Black & Decker was still the leading maker of small appliances. Sales of toaster ovens had slipped slightly, but coffee makers had held their own, and Black & Decker had scored big in toasters. Market research showed that U.S. consumers generally were comfortable with the change, although the initial response was less favorable in England, where the Black & Decker name was even more closely identified with power tools. (In England a person spending time in a workshop was said to be "Black & Deckering.") John A. Quelch, then an associate professor at Harvard University, told

Business Week that the changeover was "almost a textbook example of how to manage a brand transition in the future."

DeWalt Power Tools

While the GE brand conversion was successful, expanding the Black & Decker trademark to encompass small appliances hurt the company's reputation in professional power tools, where it was already losing market share to Makita Electric Works Ltd. of Japan. Professional power-tool users felt rejected. Ellen Foreman, then an advertising manager for Black & Decker, told *Advertising Age,* "You'll hear [professional power-tool users] say, 'You used to be good. Now you're making corn poppers and toasters.' "

Makita entered the market in the late 1950s, concentrating on high-end professional tools and leaving the consumer market to Black & Decker. By the early 1980s Black & Decker, with about 20 percent of the worldwide market for industrial power tools, was just barely ahead of Makita. Any further loss of market share would cause Black & Decker to lose its lead position. Black & Decker's first response was to shore up its image with an advertising campaign called "Nothing beats a Black & Decker." Television spots featured macho men carrying Black & Decker power tools, but Black & Decker realized that more drastic measures were needed.

By 1992 Black & Decker had overhauled its entire line of professional power tools, engineering each to meet or beat its counterpart from Makita in head-to-head consumer testing. Any tool that failed the test was sent back to be reworked. The tools were also molded in bright-yellow, high-impact plastic to set them apart from the black-plastic consumer line. The most shocking move, however, was the decision to drop Black & Decker as the brand name.

In 1960 Black & Decker had acquired DeWalt, Inc., a manufacturer of radial arms saws, and market research showed that professional power-tool users associated the name DeWalt with quality. DeWalt became the brand name for the new line of professional power tools, and "Black & Decker" was relegated to a single line in small type: "Serviced by the industrial tool division of Black & Decker." When the new power tools were introduced, James Inglis, then executive vice president of Home Depot, a leading hardware merchandiser, told *Fortune,* "DeWalt rivals anything the Japanese or Germans have come up with."

Quantum

Black & Decker's efforts to differentiate its professional power tools from the do-it-yourself market in the early 1990s also led to the development of a midpriced line of tools known as Black & Decker Quantum. Joseph Galli, then head of the Black & Decker power-tool division for the United States, told *Fortune,* "We were finding in our research that a lot of nonprofessional consumers were really price sensitive when it came to power tools. Sure, we knew that some DIYers were going to pay up and buy DeWalt. But others would just go elsewhere, and we're not a company that likes to leave business on the table for our competitors."

The Quantum line of power tools offered special features suggested by consumers during market research—for example, a more powerful cordless drill with a battery pack that recharged in an hour instead of overnight. Black & Decker also introduced a circular saw and sander that came with its own built-in minivacuums to suck up sawdust. An automatic braking system on the saw stopped the blade from spinning within two seconds after being turned off. Nolan Archibald, then chief executive officer at Black & Decker, told *Fortune,* "The whole point behind this product line was to have it driven by what the consumers really wanted."

Black & Decker chose a deep green to distinguish Quantum power tools from the professional DeWalt line in bright yellow and the lower-priced consumer line in black. Quantum was originally a code name for the project but did so well in market studies that the name stuck. Since Quantum was positioned as a step-up from the lower-price line for nonprofessionals, the company decided to emphasize its Black & Decker heritage. The Black & Decker Quantum line of power tools was introduced in 1993 with the advertising slogan "Serious tools for serious projects."

Brand Outlook

In 1987 worldwide sales exceeded $2 billion for the first time, placing Black & Decker among the 200 largest industrial companies in the United States. Five years later sales had more than doubled to $4.8 billion. The company, however, posted a $333 million loss for 1992, due primarily to its purchase of the Emhart Corp. in 1989. Black & Decker paid $2.8 billion for Emhart, maker of Kwikset locks and Price Pfister plumbing products, and hoped to sell some of Emhart's other businesses to reduce its debt. As of 1994 many of the assets remained to be sold.

Perhaps more important for the future, however, was the continued strength of the Black & Decker brand name, which was consistently among the most recognized trademarks in consumer surveys. The company had also repaired its reputation among professional craftsmen with its DeWalt line, and industry analysts were enthusiastic about the new Black & Decker Quantum power tools for the consumer market—*Fortune* headlined its article "A Star Is Born"—and the steady stream of new Black & Decker household appliances, such as the Steamworks wallpaper stripper, introduced in 1989.

Further Reading:

"Black & Decker Buys a Place on the Kitchen Counter," *Business Week,* January 9, 1984, p. 29.

Blyskal, Jeff, "Splinters," *Forbes,* June 6, 1983, p. 161.

Caminiti, Susan, "A Star Is Born," *Fortune,* Autumn/Winter 1993, p. 44.

Cleary, David Powers, *Great American Brands,* New York: Fairchild Publications, 1981.

"Design: Everyone's Concern," *Appliance Manufacturer,* April 1989, p. 41.

Eklund, Christopher S., "How Black & Decker Got Back in the Black," *Business Week,* July 13, 1987, p. 86.

Eklund, Christopher S., "Why Black & Decker Is Cutting Itself Down to Size," *Business Week,* November 25, 1985, p. 42.

Highlights of Progress, Towson, Maryland: The Black & Decker Corporation, 1992.

Huey, John, "The New Power In Black & Decker," *Fortune,* January 2, 1989, p. 89.

Meyers, Janet, "Black & Decker Ups Share in Hardware," *Advertising Age,* July 24, 1989, p. 28.

Black & Decker Corporation 1992 Annual Report, Towson, MD: Black & Decker Corporation, 1993.

Saporito, Bill, "Black & Decker's Gamble On 'Globalization,' " *Fortune,* May 14, 1984, p. 40.

Saporito, Bill, "Ganging up on Black & Decker," *Fortune,* December 23, 1985, p. 63.

Sellers, Patricia, ''New Selling Tool: The Acura Concept,'' *Fortune,* February 24, 1992, p. 88.

Strum, Paul W., ''Keep 'Em Coming,'' *Forbes,* February 5, 1979, p. 54.

—Dean Boyer

BMW®

BMW brand cars have become synonymous with engineering excellence, performance, reliability, and innovation in automotive design and technology. While BMW cars do not hold the leading market share for the luxury car market, the cars are highly praised by critics and prized by their owners. Based in Munich, Bayerische Motoren Werke AG (BMW) is the fifteenth-largest producer of cars in the world. BMW is a global company, operating ten plants in Germany, Austria, and South Africa. It has 12 subsidiaries in Germany, as well as subsidiaries in 15 other countries. BMW conducts business in 20 countries around the world. In Germany, the BMW car is viewed as a high quality domestic product, but in the United States, BMW cars are prestigious luxury imports.

In the early 1990s, there were four BMW series of cars available to American drivers, each having its own line of models. The 3-series, made up of sedans, coupes, and convertibles, had the smallest cars and was the most affordable. The 5-series was the middle line and included larger sedans and sports wagons. The 7-series featured the largest, most luxurious sedans. In 1991, BMW entered the exotic car market with the 8-series, introducing an exotic sports coupe known as the 850Ci. Large luxury sedan models followed in the 8-series. The cars ranged in price from about $25,000 for the 3-series to $85,000 for the 8-series.

Brand Origins

BMW, a maker of aircraft engines since 1913, made its first cars in 1929. The small, two-door, 15-horsepower sedan was adapted from a car that the company had acquired when it bought Fahrzeugwerke Eisenach, a struggling company that made a small car under license from Austin of the United Kingdom. In 1933, BMW began making larger, sportier cars. That year, the company introduced the six-cylinder 303, the first model in the 3-series. In 1935, BMW introduced its first sports car, a roadster, and two years later the BMW 327 coupe debuted. Later, the 328 sports convertible was introduced, and later became one of the most sought-after collector cars in the world.

Auto production ceased during World War II, as the company was forced to build aircraft engines for the Luftwaffe, the German Air Force. BMW had operated plants in occupied countries but with Germany's defeat in the war they were dismantled. The company then began to manufacture kitchen and garden equipment, resuming auto production only in the 1950s. The postwar BMW cars were too large and costly for many German citizens, and they did not sell well.

When BMW introduced the Isetta, a seven-and-one-half-foot long "bubble car" in the late 1950s, the company was on its way to commercial success. From 1956 to 1959, BMW made sports cars. After Herbert Quandt took control of the company in 1959, the company focused on sports sedans and the first of the "New Range" models which appeared in 1961 as the 1500. The 1500 embodied a completely new automotive concept called the sports sedan, which combined the handling characteristics of a sports car with the practicality of a sedan.

Developing an Identity

In 1967, BMW introduced the sport sedan to American drivers with the 1600, a two-door sedan dubbed the "Bubbletop." In addition to its unique styling, the car had a roomy interior, quick acceleration, and superior handling. Moreover, its price tag was comparable to many models made by leading domestic competitors. American drivers quickly became fans of this type of driving experience, and exports to the United States increased dramatically during the 1970s.

In 1972, the 2002tii was introduced. This car was actually the 1600 sports sedan fitted with a 2.0 liter engine and smog equipment to fit U.S. clean air standards. From 1971 to 1975, the 3.0 CS coupe was marketed, offering luxury performance and smooth six-cylinder engines. In 1975, BMW introduced a midsize four-door sports sedan known as the 5301 with a powerful six-cylinder engine. *Road & Track* magazine called it "everything a luxury sports sedan should be." In 1976, the 3-series was debuted as a compact sports sedan. It, too, was acclaimed by auto critics; according to *Car and Driver,* the car had "a zest for the road that's not available anywhere else."

During the 1980s and early 1990s, new models were added to each series. In 1982, a new model was added to the 3-series; in 1986 there were additions to the luxury 7-series; and in 1988 models were added to the 5-series. In 1991, a new model was added to the 3-series, and an 8-series coupe entered the market. In 1992, new models were added to the 7-series, and the third generation 3-series began with a 325i sedan.

AT A GLANCE

BMW cars first produced by Bayerische Motoren Werke AG, (Bavarian Motors Works), in 1928; BMW founded by Karl Rapp when he opened an aircraft engine design shop near a Munich, Germany, airfield in 1913; named Bayerische Motoren Werke, 1917; Herbert Quandt bought BMW for $1 million, 1959; established BMW of North America Inc., a subsidiary of BMW, 1975.

Performance: *Market share*—1% of world auto market. *Sales*—594,895 units sold worldwide; 65,690 sold in the United States (1992).

Advertising: *Agency*—Mullen Advertising, Beverly, MA, 1993—. *Major campaign*—"The ultimate driving machine."

Major competitor: Mercedes-Benz; also Cadillac, Lincoln, Lexus, Infiniti, Acura, and Peugeot.

Addresses: *Parent company*—Bayerische Motoren Werke AG, P.O. Box 40 02 40, Petuelring 130, D-8000, Munich 40, Germany; phone: (+49) 89-38-95-0; fax (+49) 89-3-59-36-22; (North American subsidiary) BMW of North America, Inc., Chestnut Ridge Road, Woodcliff Lake, NJ 07675; phone: (201) 307-4000; fax: (201) 307-4095.

As new models were introduced, new styling and engineering changes, as well as safety features were added. In 1992, for example, the new four-seat convertible developed on the basis of the 3-series coupe had a driver-side airbag, anti-lock braking system, belt tensioners, and side impact protection. Beginning in 1992, all cars were fitted with standard driver-side airbags, and the seven and 8-series had passenger airbags as well. Also in 1992, new 8-cylinder engines were added to the 5-series, a 3-liter engine was added to the 530i, and a 4-liter engine to the 540i.

In 1993, BMW added styling, safety, and environmental innovations. The saloon and touring cars were added to the 5-series as 525td models, and the 840CI and 850CSI were added as large BMW coupes. Dual-airbag Supplementary Restraint Systems were used for all models, and All Season Traction systems were available on V-8 5-, 7- and 8-series in 1993. The traction system was either fully integrated with the anti-lock braking system or configured as a separate control unit using the wheel-speed sensors. The traction system enhanced the driver's ability to control the car by limiting wheelspin, especially under challenging driving conditions where traction is reduced.

The 1994 models had further additions and improvements. New models for the 3-series included sports coupes, sedans, and the all new 325i convertibles. A new touring car was added to the 5-series, and the 525 midsize sedan and sports wagon models got new V-8 engines for more power and higher fuel efficiency. Adaptive transmission control, which increased the number of driving modes from three to nine and made mode selections automatically, enhanced fuel economy, quietness, and smoothness in the 5-series. Two additions were made in the 7-series: a sports coupe and a sports car. These models had V-8 engines and luxury features, including standard cellular phone, standard 6-disc CD changer, and remote keyless-entry security system.

The continual changes to BMW models has enhanced the brand's reputation. BMW cars' quality reputation is grounded in the company's philosophy that the driver is an integral part of the car itself. BMW engineers believe in improving the driver's ability, awareness, and security through technical innovations that improve performance, handling, and safety. Their assumption is that a better car makes a better, more confident driver.

Each model is built with the driver in mind and takes seven years in development. The company tests all technological innovations used in luxury cars on the Nurburgring race track. The lessons learned about the cars' handling and performance are then transferred to the production of the sedans, convertibles, and coupes. Many of the design breakthroughs gleaned in this process have set new standards for the automotive industry. An example of the engineering innovations can be seen in the cars' wraparound console, which forms a cockpit around the driver, making access to all controls and instruments easy.

Advertising and Marketing

During the 1980s, BMW cars inadvertently gained a "yuppie" image because they were favored by young, urban professionals. The company sought to make its image more conservative in the early 1990s. Company officials sought to have the image reflect the cars' quality and value to owners. Karl Gerlinger, president and chief executive officer of BMW of North America, said, "We've changed the image from trendy, high-priced yuppie automobiles to products that are worth the money and generate a certain excitement." In order to help change consumer perceptions, the advertising strategy emphasized that a better car made a better driver. To convey the message of superior performance, the tagline used in print ads and TV commercials was, "The ultimate driving machine."

BMW also promoted its cars as being environmentally friendly, emphasizing its efforts to conserve energy, avoid air pollution, and recycle. In 1993, BMW introduced E2, an experimental electric car specifically designed for U.S. traffic conditions and driving habits of American owners. The electric car was a response to expected tightening of laws on exhaust emissions. E2 was a four-seat city car with a range of over 100 miles. BMW was also developing an experimental car with hydrogen power.

BMW received the 1992 Best Recycling Innovation Award from the National Recycling Coalition Inc. for the high proportion of recyclable materials used in the 3-series car. In addition, in 1992 the first recycling plants for scrapped BMW cars were opened in the United States as well in several European nations. The 1993 3-series was designed to be over 80 percent recyclable by weight when scrapped. By 1993, BMW of North America had created three U.S. recycling centers at Hunts Point, New York, Santa Fe Springs, California, and Orlando, Florida. BMW owners who returned their cars to any of the centers received a $500 incentive toward the purchase of a new or approved used car.

Performance Appraisal

Since their introduction to American drivers, BMW cars have received high commercial and critical success. In 1975, when the North American subsidiary opened, 14,000 BMW cars were sold. By 1992, sales had more than quadrupled to 65,700. In addition, every tenth car registered worldwide in the top luxury segment was a BMW in 1992.

In 1993, BMW became the best-selling German car in the United States. During the economic recession of the late 1980s and early 1990s, U.S. sales for BMW, along with other luxury car makers, dropped. By 1992, however, U.S. sales for BMW had picked up by 23 percent from the previous year.

Consumer and auto publications alike continued to praise BMW. For both 1992 and 1993, *Consumer Reports* recommended the performance, reliability, and safety of the BMW 325i for compact cars, and the 535i for midsize cars. In September 1992, *Car and Driver* awarded first place to the 325i, saying the car was "a stunning example of what a great driver's car should be." *Car and Driver* awarded first place to the new BMW 740i in a comparison of luxury cars, calling it, "a car to fall in love with" in 1993.

Future Cars

BMW management maintains that their cars of the future will continue to be technologically advanced, environmentally friendly, and affordable. For example, electronic traffic guidance systems are appearing on test routes in the United States and BMW is showing interest in car technology that interacts with the traffic guidance systems. Also, there are plans for developing more fuel-efficient, smaller cars.

In June 1992, BMW announced plans to build an assembly factory in Spartanburg, South Carolina, in part to avoid the high cost of German labor. It was expected that, beginning in 1995, the plant would produce up to 400 BMW cars per day for the United States and world markets. The company said that the car produced at the new plant would be a two-seat sports car targeted at single people and couples without children. According to Wolfgang Reitzle, head of research and design, "The style on the new model will be dramatically different than the BMWs of recent years but will have touches from BMWs roadsters of the late 1930s." The new model was expected to debut at the Detroit Auto show in January 1995. BMW was also planning to enter the luxury small car market in 1996 with a subcompact model. This car would be less expensive and meant for less affluent buyers.

Further Reading:

BMW of North America, Inc., Annual Report, Woodcliff Lake, NJ: BMW of North America, Inc., 1992.

"BMW Describes Car to Be Made at South Carolina Plant," *New York Times,* November 17, 1993, p. D5.

Schmid, John, "Mercedes and BMW Set Their Sights on a Niche in the Subcompact Market," *Wall Street Journal,* August 27, 1993, p. B5A.

Taylor, Alex, "BMW Roars Back from Yuppie Hell," *Fortune,* May 3, 1992, p. 12.

West, Ted, "'72–74 BMW 2002tii,'' *Motor Trend,* August, 1993, pp. 94–95.

—Dorothy Kroll

BRAUN®

BRAUN

The phrase "form follows function" has been a hallmark of Braun appliance design and a corporate credo for more than 50 years. Americans have equated the brand's "Eurostyle" appliances with sophistication and quality for a generation. Braun's heritage of performance-oriented design has been expressed in trendsetting ergonomics and aesthetics, making it an icon of European style. Many of the trademarked utensils have become collectors' items: more than 40 Braun appliances are held by New York's Museum of Modern Art, and a vintage Braun coffeemaker was auctioned at Christy's in Amsterdam in 1988.

In the early 1990s Braun was the leading small appliance manufacturer in Europe and one of the largest marketers of small appliances in the world. The brand was the top seller of foil shavers and handheld blenders worldwide, and its dental care and food preparation appliances occupied leading positions as well. The line also included coffeemakers, juicers, hair care devices, irons, and clocks.

Brand Origins

Braun started out as a cottage industry when Max Braun began manufacturing electronic components in his Frankfurt, Germany, apartment in 1921. It was there, according to corporate folklore, that the founder began years of work on his first consumer product, an electric foil shaver. The entrepreneur apparently carried a prototype of the grooming tool in his pocket and worked continuously on it until he had fine-tuned it to his exacting satisfaction.

Braun introduced the world's first electric foil shaver, the S50 model, in 1949. The razor was later credited with the worldwide popularization of electric shaving. The founder's sons, Artur and Erwin, succeeded him after his unexpected death just two years after the launch of the razor. In 1952 the new leaders broadened their namesake line with a product that anticipated the 1990s "juicing" craze: Braun's first multipress centrifugal juicer.

The "Braun Look"

In 1955 the "Father of Euro-design," Dieter Rams, joined Braun as an architect and interior designer. Rams would refine the Braun style, and would guide the brand's product development for the next four decades. Rams was trained as an architect, and spent two years designing U.S. consulate buildings in West Germany with Skidmore, Owings & Merrill. But he was more interested in product design. As an ardent proponent of Germany's Bauhaus movement, Rams aimed to bring simple, well-designed consumer products to the working class. His guiding principles dictated that products be inconspicuous, "like a butler," as he told *Business Week* in 1990. They should have no superfluous decoration. And of course, "form follows function." The no-nonsense design chief dedicated his career at Braun to these principles, creating the sparse, clean "Braun look."

Even the features of Braun appliances that looked like decoration were functional. For example, Braun's electric razor (the world's number one seller in its class by the 1960s) had small plastic knobs that added visual interest but, more importantly, kept the razor from slipping when put down on a wet sink. Even the Braun coffeemaker's vertical surface lines that mimicked a fluted Greek column had a purpose: they added strength and hid imperfections, allowing the company to use a cheaper plastic. The "un-decorations" reduced Braun's plastic costs by nearly 70 percent.

In 1991 Rams told *Fortune* magazine that "decoration lasts only for a short time. Bauhaus makes products that are long-lasting." He and Braun had already proven that point many times over. The KM32 kitchen machine and juicer, introduced in 1957, was just one example of the enduring quality of the brand's designs: in 1978, Longlife Award recognized it with a prestigious design prize. Both the KM32 food processor and the MP3 juicer also remained essentially unchanged into the 1990s, earning them high praise as some of "the most beautiful consumer products of modern times."

Market and Product Development

Braun was able to expand its foreign distribution network and broaden its product line after becoming a joint stock company in 1962. One of its more successful new products was the Sixtant shaver. The Sixtant sold millions worldwide and firmly established Braun as an electric shaver leader.

That same year Braun brought out the world's first handheld blender. With the cooperation of a Spanish designer, the brand devised a new blending concept, wherein the machine went into the food, rather than vice versa. The shapely appliance was designed to hang on the wall, and unlike standard blenders, could be rinsed off under running water. The unique appliance was an

AT A GLANCE

Braun brand established in 1921 in Frankfurt, Germany, and named for founder Max Braun; Braun AG converted to a joint stock company, 1962; The Gillette Company purchased controlling interest in Braun, 1967.

Major competitor: Norelco; also Krups and Black & Decker.

Advertising: *Agency*—Ingalls, Quinn & Johnson, 1988—. *Major campaign*—Slogan: "Designed to perform better."

Addresses: *Parent company*—Braun, Inc., 66 Broadway, Route 1, Lynnfield, MA 01940; (617) 596-7300; fax (617) 596-7333. *Ultimate parent company*—Braun AG, Frankfurter Strab E 1456242 Kronberg TS, Germany. *Ultimate ultimate parent company*—The Gillette Co., Prudential Tower Building, Boston, MA 02199; (617) 421-7000.

immediate success: in its first year on the British market, it sold 240,000 units and sold out within six months in Canada.

In 1967 The Gillette Company, the dominant U.S. marketer of disposable blade razors, acquired a controlling stake in Braun AG. At the time, Braun was primarily a German company with limited export business. Braun had marketed its handheld mixers, clocks, coffee grinders, food processors, and other small appliances in the United States before this time. But after the merger, the two brands were prohibited by the Federal Trade Commission from cooperating in America for at least 15 years. With help from its new parent, the company concentrated on expanding its product line and European market penetration. Braun's sales more than doubled from 1967 to the mid-1970s as the brand's marketing and distribution network expanded dramatically.

Braun launched its first coffeemaker, the KF20, in 1972. The appliance, the world's first cylindrical coffeemaker, followed in the footsteps of its illustrious predecessors and was acclaimed for its insightful design and advanced electronics. The KF20 went on to win numerous design awards worldwide.

In 1984 Braun introduced its KF40, the first "Euro-style" coffeemaker, featuring a single, "L-shaped" tower later emulated by virtually all competitors. The design incorporated a water tank and coffee carafe in one cylindrical unit, as opposed to the traditional two-tower appliance. The KF40 was applauded by the Design Management Institute and Harvard Business School as an example of the world's best industrial projects—an innovative solution to a marketing challenge. The academic case study it inspired remained a part of Harvard's undergraduate curriculum and that of several other colleges and universities into the 1990s.

By the mid-1980s, Braun was a leader of the European electric shaver market, with 40 percent of continental sales, and enjoyed a better than 30 percent stake in the Canadian shaver category. Having garnered high market shares around the world through operations in Germany, Ireland, Spain, Mexico, and Latin America, Braun made its move on the United States.

American Market

Braun appliances were distributed on a very limited basis in the United States beginning in 1981. Although the consent agreement inked by Gillette and Braun expired the following year, the two brands continued to operate separately, and the German nameplate's distribution was handled by Schawbell Corp. Despite narrow merchandising in exclusive gourmet shops and essentially no advertising, Braun's American sales grew tenfold, from $3 million in 1981 to $30 million by 1985.

Still a virtual nonentity to most Americans in 1985, Braun embarked on an ambitious marketing program to back the expanded distribution of three principal products in the United States: electric shavers, handheld blenders, and butane curling irons. The debut of Braun's unique handheld blender created a new category in the United States. Black & Decker took the concept and ran with it, creating a whole line of wall- or cabinet-mounted Spacemaker appliances. Even Braun's curling iron was a trend-setter: originally introduced in 1980, it was the first portable curling iron powered by butane gas. The nameplate broadened its range of retail outlets to include everything from high-end specialty shops to drug chains, and budgeted over $10 million for brand-boosting television advertising created by Lowe Marschalk, New York. Even as the upscale brand "lowered" itself to television advertising, its spots strived to retain a classy image: copy from Braun's debut commercial illustrates: "Fade in string quartet music. Voice-over as man shaves: 'At Braun, we believe simple is better than complicated. Order is better than confusion. Quiet is better than loud. Only through superior design can one achieve superior performance.' "

Braun's price positioning was also broadened, from the top 3 to 5 percent to the top 50 percent. Yet the brand hoped to avoid the "class-goes-mass" characterization, still planning to be a "trade up" nameplate. To accomplish this, Braun tailored products to each market—one for Nieman-Marcus customers, another with fewer features for mail-order catalogers, and "stripped-down" models for Kmart shoppers. In each case, the design fit the customer's need and price range while showcasing Braun's distinctive styling.

Shavers were an important component of the introductory program, and one of Braun's historically strongest suits: it was the second-largest manufacturer of electric shavers in the world. Competitors were predictably skeptical that the newcomer could carve out a share of the hotly contested small appliance market. For example, market surveys indicated that up to 95 percent of American electric shaver users were loyal to their brand. Luckily, Braun arrived on the U.S. market just in time for a burgeoning consumer trend toward high-tech, higher-priced "quality" merchandise.

Using the slogan "Designed to perform better," Braun snagged 10 percent of the shaver category in its introductory year, and its overall U.S. sales more than doubled, to about $80 million. By 1991, in spite of all projections to the contrary, the brand's reputation for high quality, fine design and superior technology ranked it among America's top three electric shaver marketers—and the only one gaining share.

Braun and Dieter Rams were even involved in Gillette's 1990 revival, designing the parent's wildly popular Sensor wet shaving system. Protected by 17 patents, the Sensor featured twin blades that floated on tiny springs. Introduced in the United States, Europe, and Japan in 1990, the system outsold projections by 33 percent.

Future Growth

In the early 1990s Braun chose to concentrate its growth prospects on under-exploited markets like Japan, instead of launching a torrent of new gadgets. But that did not prevent the brand and its perennial designer from refining its existing appliances. In 1990 Rams designed the world's first double-sided, pivoting foil shaver head. Dubbed Flex Control, it eliminated the need to move your wrist at awkward angles to get a close shave. According to *Fortune* magazine, demand soared so high in Europe and Japan that the company delayed the razor's U.S. launch until 1992 for lack of production capacity.

Another innovation, Braun's line of FlavorSelect coffeemakers, introduced in 1993, featured a brewing system that filtered out bitter oils and acids. The appliance's FlavorSelector feature allowed users to adjust the intensity of the coffee flavor from mild to robust by varying the amount of water that circulated around the outside of the filter. Braun also introduced a 5-in-1 Food Preparation Center, featuring a kitchen machine, food processor, blender, chopper, and ice crusher, that same year.

Braun also hitched its wagon to infomercials, 30-minute commercials that were long eschewed by mainstream marketers as lowbrow. The brand and its U.S. advertising agency determined that the longer format gave them time to explain the intricacies of gadgets like the handheld blenders and food processors while capturing consumers' interest. The infomercial's direct response feature helped offset media costs and boosted retail sales and brand awareness. Braun continued to employ traditional television advertisements, spending a record $20 million in 1992. Although some industry observers have noted the ascendancy of more fanciful designs from California and Japan, it seems clear that, for functionality and elegance, the Bauhaus aesthetic embodied in all Braun appliances will endure for the foreseeable future.

Further Reading:

Chakravarty, Subrata N., "'We Had to Change the Playing Field'," *Forbes,* February 4, 1991, pp. 82–86.

"Drive for Braun Appliances Opens," *Advertising Age,* July 18, 1966, p. 136.

Dumaine, Brian, "Design That Sells and Sells and . . . ," *Fortune,* March 11, 1991, pp. 86–94.

Fitzgerald, Kate, "Infomercials Light Up Holidays' Hottest Gifts," *Advertising Age,* December 7, 1992, p. 16.

Hall, Carol, "Braun Builds Its Brawn," *Marketing & Media Decisions,* pp. 58–60, 112.

McConville, Daniel J., "From Bauhaus to Your House," *World Trade,* December 1992, pp. 52–55.

Magrath, Allan, "Sales & Marketing Management: Differentiate by Design," *Marketing News,* November 12, 1990, pp. 19–20.

Nussbaum, Bruce, Larry Armstrong, Joan O'C. Hamilton, Stewart Toy, and Robert Neff, "California Design: Funk Is In," *Business Week,* June 15, 1990, pp. 170–180.

Phillips, Lisa E., "Braun Plugs Product Awareness," *Advertising Age,* October 5, 1987, p. 89.

Radding, Alan, "Braun Broadens Market Approach," *Advertising Age,* November 3, 1986, p. 65.

Toy, Stewart, "His Spartan Look Is the Essence of Braun," *Business Week,* June 15, 1990, p. 178.

Trachtenberg, Jeffrey A., "Styling for the Masses," *Forbes,* March 10, 1986, pp. 152–153.

—April S. Dougal

BROTHER®

Brother Industries, Ltd., a worldwide manufacturer of electronic typewriters, word processors, color copiers, facsimile machines, knitting machines, microwave ovens, appliances, and machine tools, began as a Japanese sewing machine company. A household name in Japan, Brother reached beyond the country's borders to build a network of offices and manufacturing facilities that spans 27 countries. Brother is also well known for its activities as an official Olympic Sponsor.

Brother was originally named the Yasui Sewing Machine Company. Founded in 1908, the company repaired sewing machines and manufactured parts. Almost nine decades later, Brother net sales revenues are $1,296,782 billion. Its technological progress has been hard won and so have its American sales. Indeed, Brother has fought a long battle with its chief typewriter and word processing competitor in the United States, Smith-Corona. In 1993, Brother was the largest manufacturer of portable electronic typewriters and personal word processors in the United States.

Brand History

The Yasui Sewing Machine Company produced its first sewing machine in 1920, an industrial model called the Brother. It was the first sewing machine produced in Japan. In 1932, the company successfully produced the first sewing machine marketed for use in the home. Yasui incorporated in 1934 and continued expanding its product lines. In 1941, Yasui became Brother Sales, Ltd. In 1961 the company entered the business machine field and began selling its first portable typewriter. The next year the corporation changed its name to Brother Industries, Ltd.

From its relatively recent entry into the world of business machines, Brother has helped push the humble typewriter into the future. "The simple typewriter—a machine that merely puts characters on paper as you pound keys—is all but extinct," stated *Consumer Reports* in 1991. In defiance of such conventional wisdom, that year Brother launched the Brother WP-760D, which came with a screen, an on-line tutorial, computer diskettes that hold about 120 pages of double-spaced text, and a punctuation check.

Brother opened its first overseas office in 1954: the Brother International Corporation, in New Jersey. The opening of the first marketing base in Europe followed three years later. Today Brother products are sold in over 100 countries. Overseas production began in 1978 in Taiwan with the establishment of a sewing machine factory. Since then Brother has opened manufacturing plants in the United Kingdom, the United States, Malaysia, and Ireland. The newest location is a third home sewing machine factory in Zhuhai, the People's Republic of China.

Brother's progress has been based on its ability to adapt new technologies to its products. From 1927 to 1940 it developed the precision manufacturing, motor, and technological skills necessary to produce sewing machines. Then, in 1961, the company marketed its first portable typewriter. 30 years later Brother Industries, Ltd. had produced its 20 millionth domestically made typewriter. Also in 1961, the company started manufacturing a small lathe for technical school use. In all these developments, Brother sought to build a foundation of slow but steady technological advance.

The company marketed its first knitting machine and entered the home electric appliance field in 1954. During the 1960s and 1970s it added electronics technology to its mechanical base to produce such products as the world's first high-speed dot matrix printer. The company also acquired the technology for manufacturing computer terminals and developing software and applications. In short order, Brother typewriters went from electric to electronic. By 1983 Brother's sales of information processing and office equipment had exceeded its sewing machine sales. By 1993, its technological goals involved fusing imaging and audio and optics in new products.

Despite these advances, though, the global recession of the early 1990s caused Brother's net sales to slip in 1992 below the previous year's mark—from $1,332,185 billion to $1,296,782 billion. Overseas, however, primarily in North America, exports of business machines were up, supported by strong sales of electronic stationery products and facsimile machines. In 1992, home and industrial sewing machines and knitting machines experienced a decline representing 10.7 percent of Brother's fashion-related products, but sales of business machines and equipment rose 7.3 percent from the previous year. Brother's strong showing in North America came despite the strenuous and persistent opposition of its main American rival, Smith-Corona.

AT A GLANCE

Brother Industries, Ltd. began as the Yasui Sewing Machine Company. The Japanese company sold sewing machine parts and did repairs. In 1934 it became incorporated, and in 1941 it established itself as Brother Sales, Ltd. The company's first overseas subsidiary, Brother International Corporation, was started in 1954 in New Jersey. In 1962 Brother Sales, Ltd. was renamed Brother Industries, Ltd. Brother Industries, Inc. (U.S.) was founded in Bartlett, Tennessee, in 1985 to manufacture electronic typewriters. Two financial subsidiaries, Brother Finance and PLC (U.K.) and Brother Finance, B.V. (Netherlands), were established in 1990.

Performance: *Sales*—$1,296,782 (1992; companywide).

Major competitor: Smith-Corona.

Advertising: *Agency*—Milton Samuels Inc., New York, NY.

Addresses: *Parent company*—Brother International Corporation, 200 Cottontail Lane, Somerset, NJ 08875-6714; phone: (908) 356-8880. *Ultimate parent company*—Brother Industries, Ltd., 15-1 Naeshiro-cho, Mizuho-ku, Nagoya 467, Japan; phone: (052) 824-2511.

Dumping Charges

Starting in 1974, Smith-Corona charged that Brother was "dumping" low-cost typewriters on the American market, allegedly cutting into Smith-Corona's profits. Citing the Antidumping Act of 1921, Smith-Corona filed a complaint with the federal government. Five years later import fees were imposed on Brother typewriters. In the following years, as newer, more advanced Brother typewriters and word processors arrived to market, Smith-Corona sought to have duties imposed on them as well.

The tables were turned, however, when Smith-Corona moved its factories to Singapore and began shipping cheap portables back home. Then it was Brother's turn to charge Smith-Corona with dumping. Brother's charges came at a time when its U.S. subsidiary was producing the typewriters and word processors it marketed in America strictly in American factories.

Brother first filed a dumping complaint in 1991. But the Department of Commerce ruled that Brother was not a U.S. producer and dropped the case. The Commerce Department reopened the case in 1992 after being overruled by the United States Court of International Trade. The Court stated that Brother's U.S. subsidiary was a U.S. firm. That year imports of Smith-Corona portables were valued at $82 million. In September of 1993 the United States International Trade Commission found in favor of Brother, supporting its charges by a 4-2 margin. It ruled that domestic industries were harmed by the sale of Singapore-made portable electric typewriters at less than fair value. The commission threatened to impose fines on Smith-Corona unless the unfair trade practices stopped.

Despite the earlier charges against Brother that it was able to sell more business machines than its competitors because it reduced its prices unfairly, Brother's profits held steadily. Its popularity in the United States and elsewhere, as was made clear in *Consumer Reports,* can be accounted for by the fact that its word processors and word processing typewriters have often received the highest ratings.

Today Brother is focusing its development efforts on laser and other nonimpact printers, as well as on devices that produce information in increasingly sophisticated visual forms such as color copiers and facsimile machines. The company has also been trying its hand at new communications technology. It launched JOYSOUND, a multimedia network karaoke system. With the help of advanced integrated services digital network (ISDN) communications and database processing search technologies, patrons in nightclubs become performers, crooning solos over full instrumental renditions of well-known songs. Brother has also developed and commercialized vending system software using ISDN and database technology. Program data is stored in a host computer and transmitted via a communications network to a terminal installed in personal computer shops using the same technology.

The apparel side of Brother's business has benefitted from advanced electronics as well. The company is developing computer-integrated manufacturing for the apparel industry, in addition to an on-line system that integrates processes that were once completed separately—pattern making, stretching and cutting, sewing, finishing, and shipping. And the tools that Brother originally developed for use in its own manufacturing the company now markets, offering a full line of machine tools, from compact milling machines to ultrasonic scrubbers. Its wire electric discharge machines are designed to process small precision components and are capable of machining 300 square millimeters per minute.

Vision for a New Century

Developing a more "people-oriented" outlook is part of what the company calls its "2lst Century Vision." Brother's people-oriented involvements are as diverse and widespread as its product line. They include support of the Olympic Games; the Brother Cup International Young Fashion Designer Contest in Beijing; the Halle Orchestra and the Manchester City Football Club in the United Kingdom; and the New Jersey Nets in the United States. Another special undertaking is the company's patronage of a group that repairs used sewing machines—of all brands—and donates and delivers them to Vietnam and Kenya. In terms of products and services, the new vision translates to helping customers enjoy more creative lifestyles through Brother's extensive research and development. These activities have continued, though a depressed global economy, slagging private investment, and slackened personal consumption in Japan has hurt Brother's economic performance in recent years.

Among the ways Brother hopes to improve the 2.7 percent slippage of it net sales from 1991 to 1992 is streamlining its operations and strengthening its corporate structure. Brother executives hope to accomplish this by establishing industrial sewing machine service centers in Shanghai and Indonesia and a sales subsidiary with offices in Mexico and Europe; by increasing the efficiency of operations through review of product lineup and making more effective use of personnel; and by increasing in-house production of vital components and undertaking global parts procurement. "While difficult conditions are expected to persist for the present, we view this period as another stage in our development and believe that now more than ever we must work to polish our skills in preparation for the challenges that lie ahead," stated Brother president Yoshihiro Yasui in the company's 1992 annual report.

The future is also likely to see Brother tightening its belt and discontinuing production of unprofitable products, perfecting new technological applications, continuing its efforts to develop state-of-the-art printing technology and apparel integration systems, and supporting athletic and cultural activities.

Further Reading:

''Brother World'' (promotional brochure), 1993.

''Court Clears Way for Typewriter Dumping Probe of Smith-Corona,'' *Journal of Commerce,* September 8, 1992, p. 2A.

Eng, Paul M., ''In Japan, It's Dial-a-Tune on the Karaoke Line,'' *Business Week* (industrial edition), July 20, 1992, p. 84.

Reich, Robert B., ''Dumpsters,'' *New Republic,* June 10, 1991, pp. 9–10.

''Typewriters and Word Processors,'' *Consumer Reports,* November 1991, pp. 763–767.

''Typewriter Case Ruling,'' *New York Times,* September 21, 1993, p. D20.

World's Greatest Brands: An International Review/Interbrand, New York: John Wiley & Sons, 1992.

—Margo Nash

BUICK®

Founded nearly a century ago, the Buick brand of automobile has been associated throughout its long history with high performance, reliability and innovation. Buick was the first car in the early 20th century to feature the ''valve-in-head'' engine, a more efficient and powerful type of motor than the L-head engine in general use at the time. The valve-in-head had a more compact combustion chamber and a faster fuel-burn rate, which translated into more horsepower than other engines of the same size.

The additional power of Buick enabled the car to win hill climbing contests and numerous races. In his memoirs, William C. ''Billy'' Durant, the founder of General Motors and the man who made Buick the number-one selling car in America by 1908, wrote: ''Power . . . became synonymous with Buick. . . . With Buick we sold the assurance that the power to perform was there. Power sold Buick and made it what it is today.''

Buick was so successful that it became the financial cornerstone upon which the world's largest automaker, General Motors, was built in 1908. The Buick division of General Motors has been a consistent leader in market share through the years. Buick even gained market share during the recession of the early 1990s, when its parent company and the auto industry overall suffered significant losses.

Brand Origins

The first automobile called a Buick was built in 1900 by plumbing inventor and manufacturer David Dunbar Buick and an engineer named Walter L. Marr. David Buick, a native of Scotland who had settled in Detroit, had been building gasoline engines since 1899. He started several companies around the turn of the century, including Buick Auto-Vim and Power Co. (1899), Buick Manufacturing Co. (1902), and Buick Motor Co. (incorporated in 1903).

In addition to engines for power boats and farm equipment, the Buick companies produced a ''horseless carriage'' by 1901. Buick, Marr, and Eugene Richard, another engineer, collaborated to produce the valve-in-head two-cylinder engine, an invention that would revolutionize the automobile industry. The valve-in-head was lighter and more dependable than other engines, and boasted 22 to 29 horsepower—an incredibly powerful engine for that era.

The company was incorporated in 1903 and relocated from Detroit to Flint, Michigan, and the first Flint Buick was built. Flint was the center of horse-drawn carriage production and was known as ''Vehicle City.'' By the end of 1904, Buick had produced 37 Model B cars. Unfortunately, the Buick Motor Co. wasn't nearly as strong as its powerful valve-in-head engine. The fledgling company was nearly bankrupt and lacked the capital to continue developing the innovative Buick engine.

Flint's horse-drawn carriage ''king,'' Billy Durant, stepped in and changed the course of Buick's history. Durant was impressed by the Buick's ability to climb steep hills and navigate muddy roads, and decided to focus his considerable energy and money-raising abilities on cars. He used his existing carriage outlets to promote Buicks throughout the country, and put together enough funding to build a huge Buick assembly factory in Flint.

In 1906 Buick completed a 1,000-mile relay race from Chicago to New York. Buicks won hill-climb contests and endurance races nationwide, year after year. A Buick engine powered a race car to victory at the Indianapolis Motor Speedway in 1909, two years before the inception of the Indy 500, now among the most celebrated auto races in the world. The first car to travel across South America, from Buenos Aires, Argentina, to Santiago, Chile, was a Buick.

Thanks to Durant's efforts, Buick was the leader in the United States in production and sales by 1908. By that time, production totaled 8,000 Buicks. Durant was confident enough in Buick's future to create a holding company, General Motors. From 1908 until 1910, Durant pulled more than 30 companies under the GM umbrella, including Buick, Oldsmobile, Cadillac and Oakland (later named Pontiac).

Durant lost, then regained control of GM, while Buick maintained its reputation and strong financial position. By 1926, Buick production had surpassed 260,000 autos. Buick's reliability was recognized around the world by that time, and the car was still winning races and endurance runs. In the 1920s, the car dominated the market and captured the world's attention through such events as a hill-climb in Africa, a tug-of-war with an elephant, and a jaunt through New Zealand.

AT A GLANCE

Buick Motor Division brand of General Motors Corp. founded in 1903 by David Dunbar Buick, president of Buick Motor Co. of Detroit, MI, and his engineer, Walter L. Marr; company was bought in 1903 by the Flint Wagon works and moved to Flint, MI, where it became Buick Motor Co. of Flint; first Flint Buick was built in 1904; company became part of General Motors (a holding company) in 1908.

Performance: *Market share*—5.8% of U.S. car market. *Sales*—$523 million.

Major competitor: Honda Acura; also Chrysler Concorde and New Yorker, Toyota Lexus.

Advertising: *Agency*—McCann-Erickson, Troy, MI, 1958—. *Major campaign*—"The New Symbol for Quality in America"; "Now . . . Wouldn't You Really Rather Have a Buick?"

Addresses: *Parent company*—General Motors Corp., Buick Motor Division, 902 E. Hamilton Avenue, Flint, MI, 48550; phone: (810) 236-5000; fax: (810) 236-6270. *Ultimate parent company*—General Motors Corp., 3044 W. Grand Boulevard, Detroit, MI, 48202; phone: (810) 556-2044; fax: (810) 556-1955.

Early Marketing Strategy

The marketing strategy at Buick from the outset was to capitalize on the car's power and reliability. One of the first 37 Buicks built set a record in a major hill climb in 1904. From there, Buick went on to dominate other hill climbs, races and cross-country runs. With a top speed of 35 to 40 miles per hour, a Buick could outrun and outperform competitors.

In 1904, *Motor Age Magazine* called Buick "a little machine that has attracted an immense amount of attention in the past few weeks owing to its high power and low price." By 1907, Buick was referred to as "the doctor's car," thanks to its reliability.

The Buick was taken on a worldwide tour in 1925 in which the car was exhibited briefly in England, the Netherlands, Belgium, France, Egypt, Damascus, Baghdad, India, Ceylon and Australia; the trip ended with a San Francisco-to-New York crossing of America. The point of the tour was to show that GM's service organization was so strong that a Buick could be sent anywhere without a specific driver or mechanic.

The new medium of radio made waves in the early part of the century, and in 1928 Buick created a hook-up to dealers across the country. Buick dealerships installed radio receivers, and potential car buyers could enjoy the music of Arthur Pryor's band while looking at the new line of Buick cars.

Brand Development and Innovations

Because it was a premium automobile, Buick was hit hard by the Great Depression. By 1933, production had sunk to 40,000 cars. But the division rebounded and was soon thriving once again. In 1931, Buick continued its tradition of innovation in the industry by becoming the first large auto manufacturer to use eight-cylinder engines exclusively. And, in 1934, power and speed made a comeback in the form of the new Buick Series 40 vehicle, which cost $865.

The venerable Roadmaster model made its debut in the 1936 line, along with such instant successes as the Special, Super, Century and Limited. Production was brisk that year—200,000 cars rolled off the Buick assembly line.

Buick made headlines again in 1939, when it introduced turn signals as standard equipment—an industry first. The signal was a red plastic lens in the Buick emblem, which was mounted on the car's trunk. Also in 1939, the Buick Y Job, GM's first "dream car," appeared. The oblong Y Job had a futuristic shape and sported headlamps that disappeared, electrically operated windows, a convertible top and door handles that were flush with the body.

After World War II began, Buick focused on military production, as it had during the First World War. The motor company built aircraft engines, Hellcat tank destroyers, and other military equipment.

Once the war ended, Buick entered a vigorous period of styling and engineering—a postwar golden age for the automaker. In 1948, Buick introduced Dynaflow, and the Roadmaster became the first American-built car to use a torque converter automatic transmission. Buick expanded its facilities and, under the leadership of GM designer Ned Nickles, developed famous design features such as hard-top convertible styling (in which the center side pillar was eliminated), massive, toothy "carnivorous" grilles and the renowned VentiPorts or portholes.

The sweepspear side decoration first appeared on the 1949 Roadmaster Riviera. The sweepspear, destined to become as widely recognized as the Buick logo, was a metal decoration that swept from the front fender in a downward curve, along the doors and up over the rear wheels.

Sales of all Buick models were robust, rising to 550,000 in 1950 and hitting 745,000 just five years later. Innovations were not limited to styling details. True to its long-standing reputation for building powerful automobiles, Buick introduced the high-compression V-8 engine in 1953. Buicks in the 1950s were sleek, smooth, powerful machines that sported staggering amounts of chrome and satisfied affluent postwar consumers.

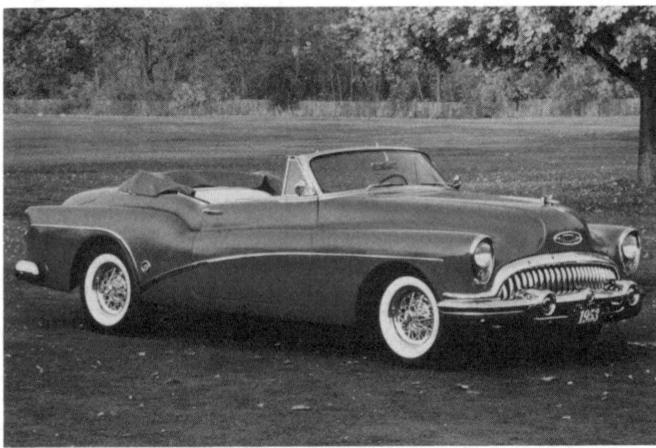

The limited edition 1953 Skylark was a special model for Buick's 50th anniversary.

But by the late 1950s, Buick's fortunes had taken a turn for the worse. A recession made small cars popular, and the giant, muscle-bound design of Buick cars fell out of style. By 1959, sales had dropped to less than 250,000 units. In an effort to regroup, Buick changed the names of its line, scrapping Special, Century, Limited and Roadmaster for LeSabre, Invicta and Electra.

The revamping of the Buick line went beyond cosmetic changes. In 1962, Buick reintroduced the Special—with an important difference. The new Special was a compact car with a V-6 engine. Buick had once again created an innovative engine design that would go on to become one of the most popular in the industry. As a result of the new V-6, the 1962 Buick Special won *Motor Trend* magazine's "Car of the Year" award for "pure progress in design, originative engineering excellence and the power concept for the future expressed in America's only V-6 automobile engine."

Buick was off the ropes and once again riding high. In 1963, the Riviera, considered a "modern classic" today, was introduced. Overall sales soared during the remainder of the 1960s and early 1970s, peaking with a record 821,165 cars during the 1973 model year. America's love affair with the automobile was in full swing, and Buick returned to making powerful V-8 engines.

The oil embargo and subsequent fuel crisis in 1974 caused the bottom to fall out of the automobile market, and Buick was no exception. Sales in 1974 and 1975 were less than 500,000 cars. To recover, Buick reintroduced the V-6 engine, made lighter car bodies and began improvements that led to highly responsive, fuel-efficient engines.

In 1979, Buick introduced its first front-wheel-drive car, the Riviera S Type. This Riviera, which had a turbocharged V-6 engine, won the "Car of the Year" award from *Motor Trend* magazine.

Buick entered the 1980s on a high note, breaking sales records and hitting the million mark for the first and, thus far, only time in its history in 1985 with more than one million cars sold worldwide. The front-wheel-drive LeSabre was a featured car in the 1986 line. The car was built at "Buick City," a state-of-the-art design and production facility that cost more than $350 million to build.

Product Changes

By the mid-1980s, Buick lost popularity among car buyers. Models were downsized and their design too closely resembled that of some Oldsmobile products. Without the distinctive features that had characterized Buick cars in the 1950s and 1960s, marketing efforts became scattered. "It was like a supermarket of cars," reflected Edward H. Mertz, Buick general manager, in a 1991 *Industry Week* article. "People didn't know exactly what to expect from Buick."

As the 1980s came to a close, the Buick line was comprised of small front-wheel-drive cars and large rear-wheel-drive cars. There were economy cars with four-cylinder engines and mid-sized models with turbocharged V-6 engines. The Toyota Lexus, the Nissan Infiniti, and the Honda Acura were targeting the luxury-car market that Buick had once dominated.

Future Growth

By returning to its roots—the smooth power/high performance formula that was a proven success—Buick entered the 1990s with confidence. The smallest cars and engines were eliminated and Buick concentrated on compact- to full-size luxury cars with V-6 and V-8 engines. Edward H. Mertz, Buick's general manager, summarized Buick's course for the future: the Buick was to be a premium automobile that was substantial, distinctive, powerful and mature, just like the buyers the division targeted. In creating advertising and marketing plans, Buick decided to concentrate on upper-middle-income consumers in their 50s and 60s who longed for "traditional American elegance." Models like the Park Avenue, Park Avenue Ultra and the resurrected and revamped Roadmaster embodied the new focus and direction.

The recession of the early 1990s crippled the U.S. automobile industry and caused General Motors to lose market share. But Buick rallied and thrived, despite the recession. During the first half of 1991, Buick's sales rose by 6.6 percent while overall American car sales fell 8.8 percent. That year, Buick led all domestic and import automakers in U.S. market share improvement and sales volume improvement.

In 1989 the Buick LeSabre was surprisingly ranked number two on the well-known and respected Power's List of the top-ten trouble-free cars worldwide, and continued to rank near the top in the early 1990s. It seemed that Buick was positioned for its ninth decade of success and leadership in the industry. But the industry-wide sales slump eventually caught up with Buick. After faring better than any other brand of automobile for most of the year, Buick sales fell toward the end of 1991.

This downturn was shortlived. The elegant 1992 Park Avenue, with a super-charged, V-6 engine, was selected as the "Best American Car Value" by an independent market research firm. In its first full year on the market, the redesigned Roadmaster hit 40,000 sales. Near the end of 1992, the LeSabre was chosen as the "Domestic Family Car of the Year" by *Family Circle* magazine.

Buick sales, while not approaching the levels of the 1980s, continued to recover as the division entered the mid-1990s. In 1993, Buick's 90th anniversary year, the division did not introduce new vehicles, but instead put extra touches, such as driver-side airbags, on existing models. To sell its most popular models—which included the number-one LeSabre and the number-two Century—Buick continued to build ads around "The New Symbol for Quality in America" theme introduced in 1989.

In an effort to appeal to younger car buyers, Buick launched a major campaign that included ads aired during the *Tonight* show and the NCAA Final Four basketball championships. The ads were designed to appeal to the 45-year-olds whom Buick wanted to woo away from rival imports. According to an article in *Automotive News,* the message was that Buick could be mature without being old.

Further Reading:

"90 Years Young: Buick Stops Acting Its Age to Court New Buyers," *Automotive News,* May 17, 1993, p. 3, 33.

"Buick Ad Couple Continue Romance with Park Avenue," *Automotive News,* September 6, 1993, p. 37.

"Buick Motor to Run Ads based on Buick Park Avenue Award," *Adweek,* June 15, 1992, p. 3.

Connelly, Mary, "Buick Seasons Lineup with Just a Pinch of Value-Priced Models," *Automotive News,* September 6, 1993, pp. 3, 37.

Dunham, Terry B. and Lawrence R. Gustin, *The Buick: A Complete History,* Automobile Quarterly, 4th ed., 1993.

Frame, Phil, "Buick Tosses a Curve with New Skylark," *Automotive News,* September 9, 1991.

General Motors Corp. Annual Reports, Detroit: General Motors Corporation, 1987–1992.

"GM Pounds Imports in New Ads," *Brandweek,* September 14, 1992, p. 1.

Gustin, Lawrence R., *Billy Durant: Creator of General Motors,* Eerdmans, 1973.

Henry, Jim, "Buick Finally Hits Sales Skids after Product Shortfall," *Automotive News,* October 28, 1991, p. 8.

Keebler, Jack, "Buick Concentrates on Safety, Performance," *Automotive News,* September 6, 1993, p. 9.

Kiley, David, "Buick Ads Adopt European Flavor," *Adweek,* September 14, 1992, p. 9.

"Making Them Like They Used To," *The Economist,* April 27, 1991, p. 70.

Moskal, Brian S., "Buick Rediscovers Its Roots," *Industry Week,* June 3, 1991, pp. 49–50.

Warner, Fara, "Buick Motor to Concentrate on Younger Consumers," *Brandweek,* March 8, 1993, p. 4.

—Marinell James

CABBAGE PATCH KIDS®

Cabbage Patch Kids are the top-selling brand of large doll in the United States. Under an exclusive licensing agreement, the dolls, a product of Original Appalachian Artworks, Inc., are produced and marketed by Hasbro, Inc. First created by Xavier Roberts in 1976, the lifelike baby dolls were made of hand-sculpted fabric. Then known as Little People, the dolls were not sold, but were ''adopted'' for a certain fee. The already popular dolls became a market sensation when the licensing agreement to produce the dolls was awarded in 1982 to Coleco Industries. Coleco mass marketed three million dolls that year but still could not keep up with the demand. The Cabbage Patch Kids set the record for the most successful new doll ever introduced. In just ten years, over 75 million dolls had been adopted.

Brand Origins

While studying art at Truett-McConnell College in Cleveland, Georgia, 21-year-old Xavier Roberts began working with a nineteenth-century German technique of fabric sculpture. He began using the technique to make dolls in 1976, combining his interests in hand-crafted sculpture and quilting. In 1977 Roberts began developing the idea of marketing the fabric sculptures as adoptable baby dolls. While working at a gift shop near Helen, Georgia, Roberts expanded the concept to include birth certificates for each doll. Roberts began calling his dolls Little People and dressing them in clothing he found at yard sales. Each of the dolls came with adoption papers and an individual name taken from a 1937 baby book.

By 1978 Roberts was selling the dolls at craft fairs and arts shows in the Southeast. He began by charging buyers a $40 ''adoption'' fee. Inspired by a first place prize at a fair in Florida, Roberts and five friends incorporated the business as Original Appalachian Artworks, Inc. (OAA). In response to the growing popularity of the dolls, the group purchased a former medical facility, which it renovated in 1978 and renamed the Babyland General Hospital. OAA began to manufacture the dolls, still known as Little People, on a larger scale at the Cleveland, Georgia, facility.

Part of the fantasy for children is the origin of the Cabbage Patch Kids dolls. An elaborate history and terminology has been created for the Cabbage Patch world. According to OAA, the dolls come from a magical Cabbage Patch located somewhere in the mountains of Northeast Georgia. The baby dolls are born in the Cabbage Patch to a mother cabbage when she is ten leaves dilated. A procedure called an easyotonomy helps the Mother Cabbage deliver the doll. After delivery, the dolls are cared for by an LPN (Licensed Patch Nurse), and administered the medications imagacillin and TLC. Each of the dolls comes with a birthmark that authenticates it as an original Cabbage Patch doll. The birthmark known as ''the Signature'' is the autograph, stamp, or screen of Xavier Roberts' signature. The company promotes this legend about the dolls: ''Many years ago a young boy named Xavier happened upon an enchanted Cabbage Patch where he found very special Little People who called themselves Cabbage Patch Kids. To help fulfill the Cabbage Patch Kids' dream of having families with whom to share their love, Xavier set out in search of parents to adopt them—a search that will continue as long as there are children looking for love.'' According to OAA, encouraging this type of nurturing behavior in children has been the key to the success of the Cabbage Patch Kids dolls.

In 1979 the dolls started becoming popular as collector's items. A limited edition ''E Bronze'' doll, signed by Xavier Roberts, was issued by the company. These hand-signed dolls immediately became valuable as collectibles. In 1980 the dolls received national attention when they appeared on NBC's ''Real People'' television program. The company was soon inundated with requests for the ''thousand dollar baby'' mentioned on the show. In response to the demand, OAA issued a diamond studded ''Grand Edition'' priced at $1000.

Change in Licensee

In the early 1980s the popularity of the dolls continued to grow. The demand for the adoptable dolls prompted articles in such publications as *Newsweek* and the *New York Times.* In 1982 Original Appalachian Artworks Inc. negotiated a long-term agreement with Coleco Industries of West Hartford, Connecticut. A major toy manufacturer, Coleco had been founded in 1932 as the Connecticut Leather Company. The company also produced video games and board games, including Scrabble and Parcheesi. When Coleco began manufacturing the dolls their name was changed from Little People to the Cabbage Patch Kids. The mass-marketed doll featured a vinyl head and a soft cloth body, as opposed to the hand-made sculpted fabric of the original version. The name ''Cabbage Patch Kid'' was registered and protected for future products.

AT A GLANCE

Cabbage Patch Kids brand of large doll founded as Little People in 1978 by Xavier Roberts, chief executive officer of Appalachian Original Artworks, Inc.; became a registered trademark, 1978; license to market brand transferred to Coleco Industries, 1982; name of brand changed to the Cabbage Patch Kids, 1982; license to market brand transferred to Hasbro, Inc., 1989.

Performance: *Market share*—66% of households with girls between the ages of 5 and 10.

Major competitor: Mattel, Inc.'s large dolls; also Tyco's large dolls.

Advertising: *Agency*—Jordan, Mcgrath, Case and Taylor. *Major campaign*—"Dear Mr. Cabbage Patch."

Addresses: *Parent company*—Original Appalachian Artworks, Inc., P.O. Box 714, Highway 75 South, Cleveland, GA 30528; phone: (706) 865-2171. *Ultimate parent company*—Hasbro, Inc.; 1027 Newport Avenue, Pawtucket, RI 02862; phone: (401) 726-4100; fax: (401) 727-5901.

While Coleco mass produced the dolls, Original Appalachian Artworks continued to make the dolls by hand at their Georgia headquarters. In 1983 the demand for the handmade dolls exceeded production. The following year, consumers continued to purchase the Cabbage Patch Kids dolls at an ever-increasing rate. Responding to corporate growth, Xavier Roberts moved out of his home and converted the structure into the headquarters for OAA. Thousands of parents and children in search of Cabbage Patch babies made visits to the Babyland General Hospital. The following year a BabyLand store was opened on Fifth Avenue in Manhattan. Similar to the Georgia facility, the Manhattan store held demonstrations of Cabbage Patch Kids being born to Mother Cabbages in labor.

In 1982 when the licensing agreement was reached, Coleco Industries had grown into one of the nation's largest toy manufacturers. Coleco had lost money on video games in the late 1970s, and again with its Adam home computer in the early 1980s. Coleco experienced a wild swing of fortune with the Cabbage Patch Kids. The company produced close to three million dolls in 1983 and could not keep up with the demand. Stories about parents and grandparents waiting in long lines to purchase one of the dolls were commonplace. It is generally recognized that Cabbage Patch Kids set the toy industry record as the most successful new doll ever produced.

Coleco Assets Sold to Hasbro

According to the *New York Times,* Cabbage Patch Kids sales by Coleco reached a peak of $600 million in 1985. Cabbage Patch Kids sales tailed off to $250 million for Coleco in 1986, when the company lost a reported $111 million. In July 1988 Coleco Industries filed for protection from its creditors under Chapter 11 of the Federal Bankruptcy Code. The company listed debts at $540.3 million at the time it filed for bankruptcy. Coleco had trouble dealing with the effects of the huge success of Cabbage Patch Kids in the early 1980s. When demand for the dolls dropped off in 1986, Coleco failed to make up for lost sales.

In April 1989 Hasbro, Inc., the world's largest toy company, proposed a purchase of Coleco's assets. The buyout offer from Hasbro included $85 million in cash for almost all of Coleco. Also offered by Hasbro were warrants for the purchase of one million shares of Hasbro stock. Hasbro's products at the time included Milton Bradley games and Playskool toys. In June of 1989 Coleco Industries accepted rival Hasbro's offer. The agreement allowed Hasbro to buy out certain accounts receivable and inventories belonging to Coleco. The deal was also subject to approval by Original Appalachian Artworks, Inc., the creators of the Cabbage Patch Kids dolls. In an April 1989 *New York Times* article detailing the buyout bid, John O'Neill, a company spokesperson for Hasbro, said: "We think there is life to Cabbage Patch Kids and that our marketing people can add more life to it."

Hasbro, Inc., holds the exclusive rights to produce Cabbage Patch Kids dolls. Original Appalachian Artworks retains the ownership and creative control of the product. Hasbro is a giant toy manufacturer with revenues totaling over $2.7 billion. Based in Rhode Island, Hasbro markets a diverse line of toy products and related items around the world. Since 1989 Hasbro has made several changes to the product. The clothing styles of the dolls were re-designed in keeping with current fashion trends. New sculpting methods were employed to give children a larger variety of facial expressions from which to choose. In 1992 the Cabbage Patch Kids were adopted as the official mascot to the U.S. Olympic Team in Barcelona, Spain.

By 1989, when Hasbro began marketing the dolls, a number of new dolls and features were added to the Cabbage Patch line of toys. New additions included the Crimp 'n Curl Kids from different ethnic groups and the following new "Kids": Dental Chair, Potty Chair, Teeny Tiny Preemies, Peek 'n Play, Ruff 'n Tuff, Check-Up Center, and My First Cabbage Patch. The company reports that an estimated 66 percent of U.S. households with children between the ages of five and ten are home to a Cabbage Patch Kids doll. According to the company's 1992 Annual Report, Hasbro plans to continue its aggressive marketing strategy for the Cabbage Patch Kids.

In October 1993 Hasbro and OAA celebrated the tenth anniversary of mass-marketing Cabbage Patch Kids. A large birthday party was held at the FAO Schwarz toy store in Manhattan. A tenth anniversary edition Cabbage Patch Kid doll was introduced. Limited in quantity to 93,000, each doll was individually numbered for collectible purposes. The tenth anniversary doll, Zora Mae, comes with a fabric covered face and is available in either blond hair or African American. During the tenth birthday party, 40,000 Cabbage Patch Kids were donated to the 1993 Marine Corps Reserve Toys For Tots Foundation.

According to Original Appalachian Artworks 1993 news release, the Cabbage Patch Kids collectors club has over 4,000 members. Beginning in 1988 the Xavier Roberts collectors convention was held in Cleveland, Georgia. The convention lasted five days and drew collectors from all over the United States. The activities ranged from demonstrations and seminars to displays showing the gradual changes that have reshaped the original Cabbage Patch Kids. Many of the original Little People dolls are worth thousands of dollars to collectors.

Future Considerations

According to a Hasbro news release, Cabbage Patch Kids have been the number one selling large doll in the United States since 1983. Starting in the late 1970s, when the Little People were first created, the success of the product has come from innovative marketing and promotion. The trouble Coleco experienced when sales fell off in 1986 seems unlikely to recur. The Cabbage Patch Kids are an important core brand for Hasbro. However, unlike Coleco, whose fortunes were tied to the success of the Cabbage Patch Kids, Hasbro has no single product category that is responsible for more than 5 percent of the company's revenue.

Other acquisitions in recent years by Hasbro include Kenner, Tonka, Parker Brothers, and Playskool. In 1993 the company secured the license for the purple dinosaur Barney, probably the hottest product in the preschool market since the arrival of the Cabbage Patch Kids. Hasbro, Inc., also markets toys and related products in Europe and Asia, and plans to expand into the Latin and South American markets. Net revenues rose to $2.541 billion in 1992, up from $2.141 billion in 1991. The company seems to be headed to continued high earnings for the foreseeable future. The combination of Hasbro's management and Original Appalachian Artworks creative input should keep the Cabbage Patch Kids at the top of the large doll market.

Further Reading:

''Coleco Agrees to Sell Its Assets to Hasbro,'' *New York Times,* June 16, 1989, p. D4.

Cantu, Marie-Christine, ''A Doll's Clothing and a Kid's Suit,'' *The National Law Journal,* May 19, 1986, p. 43.

Cuff, Daniel, ''New Head of Coleco on a Salvage Mission,'' *New York Times,* May 6, 1988, p. D4.

Hasbro, Inc., Annual Report, Pawtucket, RI: Hasbro, Inc., 1992.

McGill, Douglas, ''Hasbro to Join Creditors of Coleco in Buyout Bid,'' *New York Times,* April 20, 1989, p. D2.

''Cabbage Patch Kids 10th Anniversary—News Release,'' Original Appalachian Artworks, Inc., 1993.

Wise, Stuart, ''The Seeds of Discontent,'' *National Law Journal,* December 31, 1984, p. 67; ''Child Custody for Kids,'' *National Law Journal,* June 24, 1985, p. 39.

—*William Tivenan*

CADILLAC®

Throughout most of its history, the name Cadillac has been synonymous with style, performance, innovation, and luxury in the automotive industry. First built in 1902 by the fledgling Cadillac Motor Car Company, a joint venture of the Leland & Faulconer Manufacturing Company and the Detroit Automobile Company, Cadillac quickly became famous for its state-of-the art automobile engines and design. Over the years Cadillac has pioneered such innovations as the electric starter, the overhead-valve engine, and that automotive styling signature of the 1950s, the notorious tail fin. As Packard, Peerless, and Pierce-Arrow, Cadillac's early rivals in the luxury car market, folded one by one, Cadillac continued its ascendancy as the top luxury automobile in the United States. Cadillac held the number-one luxury car position for decades in the American market.

Cadillac sales declined in the early 1970s, followed by an eroding market share as government regulation, rising fuel prices, and competition from European and Japanese luxury brands began to play heavily against Cadillac. Not content to rest on its past laurels, the marque in the early 1990s began an aggressive campaign to reclaim its place of prominence in automaking circles. The award-winning Seville STS and the Northstar System—a fully integrated system of computer-controlled powertrain and suspension components—put the industry on notice that Cadillac's glory days were far from over.

Brand Origins

The first Model A Cadillac rolled out in Detroit in October 1902. At that time, Leland & Faulconer was a highly respected industrial manufacturing company. Its founder, Henry Martyn Leland, possessed a national reputation as a master manufacturer of precision-built interchangeable machine parts, the concept of which was still relatively new at the beginning of the twentieth century. Such parts were an American invention that hadn't caught on in England and the other industrialized nations of Europe, where new machine parts required extensive reworking to fit an older machine. This technological advancement helped the United States overtake European manufacturing, and made Cadillac cars famous as the world-wide standard for quality in the burgeoning automotive industry.

The Cadillac Motor Car Company was formed because Leland knew he had developed a superior engine design. Three years before Leland & Faulconer's (L&F) joint venture with Detroit Automobile Co., Leland had decided to move into motive power, both steam and internal combustion. In 1901, the Oldsmobile Motor Car Company awarded a contract to the firm to produce 2,000 gasoline engines, while a similar contract was awarded to the Dodge brothers. Components in both the Dodge and L&F engines were intended to be identical. That year, however, Henry Leland realized his firm could manufacture a better engine.

While attending Detroit's first automobile show, Leland and his son Wilfred witnessed an exhibit of the Dodge and L&F engines running side-by-side at identical speeds. A stranger pointed out that a cheat break had been applied to keep the speed of the L&F engine down to the same speed as the Dodge. The superiority of the L&F engine, Wilfred concluded, "was solely due to the higher craftsmanship embodied in our motor." That difference made Leland determined to make further improvements to his motor. He set a team of his best engineers to the task of redesigning the Olds engine.

The end product was a finely tuned, efficient engine capable of three times the power of standard Olds engines at that time. Leland took his new engine to the Olds plant, expecting to be welcomed. However, Olds management rejected the idea. The cost of production was too high, and management decided they were doing well enough already: demands for their cars were far outstripping capacity, and installing a new engine would only slow production.

Several months later, Leland was approached by the Detroit Automobile Co. After three unsuccessful years, the fledgling company was filing for bankruptcy and asked that Leland appraise the value of their assets. Leland examined the plant, began his calculations, then came up with an idea. Strapping the engine he had offered to Olds to the back of his car, he drove to the Detroit Automobile Co. plant. He placed both his appraisal figures and his engine on the table and made an offer, stating "I have brought you a motor we worked on at Leland & Faulconer. It has three times the power of the Olds motor. Its parts are interchangeable, and I can make these motors for you at less cost than the others for the Olds works." Then he made a claim which drew genuine laughter from his audience: "It's not temperamental."

As all car engines were temperamental at that time, such a claim seemed absurd. But Leland's argument was convincing, and so the owners decided to remain open and build cars using Leland's motor. On August 22, 1902, the firm reorganized under

AT A GLANCE

Cadillac brand founded in 1902 by Cadillac Motor Car Co., a joint venture between Leland & Faulconer Manufacturing Company and the Detroit Automobile Company; Cadillac Motor Car Company purchased by General Motors Corp. in 1909; reorganized under General Motors Buick Oldsmobile Cadillac group in early 1960s; reorganized under General Motors North American Operations, 1993.

Performance: *Market share*—2.3% of industry. *Sales*—204,159 units (1993).

Major competitor: Lincoln; also Chrysler New Yorker, Acura, Lexus, Infiniti, Mercedes-Benz.

Advertising: *Agency*—D'Arcy, Masius, Benton and Bowles, Bloomfield Hills, MI. *Major campaign*—"Creating a Higher Standard," 1994.

Addresses: *Parent company*—Cadillac Motor Car Division, 30009 Van Dyke, P.O. Box 9025, Warren, MI 48090-9025; phone: (800) 458-8006. *Ultimate parent company*—General Motors Corp., 3044 W. Grand Blvd., Detroit, MI 48202.

the name Cadillac Motor Co. (named after the French explorer and founder of Detroit, Le Sieur Antoine de la Mothe Cadillac). L&F produced the engines, transmissions, and steering gear; the former Detroit Automobile Co. built the chassis and bodies and assembled the final product. Two month later, the Cadillac Model A was unveiled.

Early Marketing

The Model A made its major U.S. debut in 1903 at the New York Automobile Show, where Marketing Director William Metzger conducted an "astonishingly successful sales drive." Accepting deposits as low as $10, he racked up orders for 2,283 cars by midweek, then announced to all other potential buyers that Cadillac had "sold out." Between March 1903 and March 1904, a total of 1,895 cars were built—a considerable achievement for the era.

Cadillac offered some major advantages over its competitors. The Model A Cadillac traveled ten miles per hour faster than Olds autos—an increase of 50 percent. The Cadillac also climbed steeper grades and ran more smoothly than all its competitors. In 1904, after Leland had reorganized production and redesigned the engine, Cadillac introduced the Model B, a single cylinder car (popularly known as a one-lunger), with the tag line, "When you buy it, you buy a round trip." It was a bold statement to make at that time, but one that Cadillac believed it could back up.

In its earliest years, Cadillac set manufacturing standards that would not be surpassed in the automobile industry for decades. The Cadillac became known across the United States as an automobile that could travel anywhere and withstand a number of adverse circumstances. But its worldwide fame was ignited by the marketing achievements of a young English automobile enthusiast named Frederick Bennett.

Hoping to market the car in Great Britain, Bennett purchased a one-lunger and entered the Thousand Miles Trail, one of the most difficult auto races in England at that time. Bennett and his American car won first place in their class—and the surprised admiration of the judges and observers. Despite this highly publicized success, Bennett had a hard time selling the Cadillac in England. British engineers were unimpressed with the gasoline powered automobile, believing steam powered auto engines to be superior. Furthermore, they had a disdain for American products. Although Bennett demonstrated the superior quality of the Cadillac, they argued that "The car may be good, but how do you get replacement parts with no factory near you and a dearth of mechanics in the country to do any fitting work on the car?"

Bennett's response that Cadillac parts went together without hand-fitting or special selection was met with strong disbelief. The American process of manufacturing interchangeable machine parts was considered by Europeans to be impractical and unfeasible. Bennett gave demonstrations, but observers were slow to accept what they saw, contending that such demonstrations could easily be rigged.

Bennett finally got his break in March 1908, when the Royal Automobile Club (R.A.C.) agreed to supervise a public test of Cadillac's interchangeability claim. Three identical Cadillacs were driven for 50 miles at an average speed of 34 miles per hour. The cars were then dismantled with no tools other than wrenches, screwdrivers, hammers, and pliers. Parts from each car were exchanged; others were replaced by stock parts sent from Detroit. By March 6, the cars were completely reassembled, and when mechanics prepared the first car and swung the crank handle, the Cadillac engine started up, running smoothly and easily. The second engine started in the same manner. And the third required no more than two turns to the crank handle.

The press and auto aficionados were amazed. The London papers treated the event as a news story of the highest magnitude. Wires were sent to the United States, and the story spread around the European papers. In 1909, Cadillac was awarded the Dewar Trophy, the automobile industry's equivalent of the Nobel Prize. In the minds of automobile enthusiasts worldwide, Cadillac was among the world's finest automobiles. Also that year, Cadillac Motor Car Company was purchased by William Durant's General Motors Corp. for $5.6 million.

Cadillac Engineering

In 1906, Cadillac was the highest volume producer of cars in the United States. That year, however, Leland and his management team decided to move away from mass market production and focus on producing automobiles of the highest quality. This fortuitous decision led Cadillac to institute several engineering innovations, which firmly established the brand as a leader in the luxury car market. In 1908, the year of Bennett's famed standardization test, the sticker price of a Cadillac was half that of the national average. As the company focused on greater quality and luxury, prices eventually rose to four times the national average.

One key development was the pioneer use of "Jo-block" gages, developed by Swedish-American Carl Edward Johansson, which greatly improved production of Cadillac's standardized parts. In 1912, Cadillac introduced the Delco system, an electric lighting and ignition system, which earned a second Dewars Trophy and revolutionized the industry. This was soon followed by the development of Cadillac's first V-8 engine, a water-cooled, eight-cylinder engine that revolutionized the automotive industry and paved the way for the development of high-speed, high-compression automotive engines.

Early Advertising

From 1903 to 1906, Cadillac was the third-largest selling car, following Oldsmobile and the newly established Ford. Of the three, Cadillac was considered the toughest and most reliable, and Cadillac owners enjoyed testing the car's limits by doing such things as driving it up the steps of the Wayne County Building in Detroit. Early advertisements capitalized on such exploits. One early ad bragged about a man who drove four passengers in his single cylinder Cadillac 93 miles from New York to Waterbury, Connecticut, in seven hours. Another told of a Cadillac customer who drew two truckloads of railroad irons weighing over eight tons up a four percent grade. "A two-cylinder opposed engine, rated at 8 [horsepower] tried it and failed to move it forward one inch," the ad claimed. "Remodel the Cadillac engine? Certainly not!"

That year, Cadillac adopted the slogan "Standard of the World," which began appearing in catalogs, advertisements, and even on the hubcaps of cars. Sixty years later, the slogan was still in use. Early Cadillac ads sold a lot of cars, but as David Holls in *Cadillac: the Complete History* suggested, they "hardly represented the ultimate in sophistication." This changed in 1915. Cadillac had made several technological and styling advancements that placed it alongside Packard and Pierce-Arrow as America's finest luxury cars, and the time arrived for Cadillac's advertising to focus less on its durability and more on its status as a luxury automobile.

Under the suggestion of Wilfred Leland, Cadillac's advertising director Theodore F. MacManus (founder of D'Arcy MacManus advertising firm), created "The Penalty of Leadership," an ad that was to change the face of advertising forever. Like earlier ads, "The Penalty of Leadership" contained long paragraphs of copy, in keeping with the "fireside chat" style of its time. Unlike earlier ads, however, this one offered no performance comparisons, blocks of data, or news items. Instead, it discussed the adverse circumstances faced by leaders in any given field, be it arts, politics, or science. At no time was the Cadillac car mentioned, but throughout, the implication was that Cadillac was the undisputed leader in automotive design. This ad appeared only once, yet its reputation lingers, and leaders in the advertising field consider it one of the greatest advertisements of all time.

The Roaring Twenties and the Golden Age of Cadillac

By the end of World War I in 1918, motorists had come to expect the latest technological advancements from Cadillac. In fact, Cadillac had become the standard mode of transportation for officers in the U.S. armed forces and also supplied the Army with V-8 artillery tractor engines. Cadillac's numerous technological advancements ushered in a new era of prosperity for the company. Annual production in 1922 rose over 20,000. Exports to Buenos Aires rose 213 percent, while those to London rose 135 percent, to Sidney 420 percent, and 651 percent in Utrecht. "The volume of Cadillac output was a constant source of amazement to European automotive authorities. They could not understand and in many cases flatly refused to believe that a car built in such large quantities . . . could equal in quality their finest automobiles," reported Holls.

In 1924, Cadillac introduced the V-8 engine, ushering in an era of mechanical advancement that, again, revolutionized the U.S. auto industry. Competition, however, was intensifying in the form of Packard's Single Eight and Single Six models, which sold a total of 22,366 between 1923 and 1925. By 1927, Packard was outselling Cadillac by more than two to one in the over $2,500 category. Leland had created a corporate climate that cared more about performance than appearance, and Cadillacs were found lacking in style. While it rivaled Packard in engineering, Cadillac's image had grown stodgy. Packard had grown to become "the most elegant automobile ever to take to the road up to that time." Cadillac learned the hard way that styling had become a factor in the sales of luxury cars.

In 1927, Cadillac introduced the LaSalle—a practically all-new model, from its engineering to its slick appearance. Designed to combat Packard's growing popularity, the LaSalle's key factor was its design by Harley Earl, the General Motors stylist who was to usher in the golden age of Cadillac cars. With Earl's input, Cadillac became known as both a designer's and an engineer's automobile. Earl's designs were dynamic, elegant, somewhat flamboyant, and impressive enough to compete with Packard, slowly stealing Packard's market share. Total sales for the years 1927 through 1929 were 118,879 for Packard and 101,833 for Cadillac and its new LaSalle.

Furthermore, Cadillac's 1929 introduction of the V-16 engine, a highly refined 16-cylinder, 175-horsepower engine, pushed Cadillac to the top of its class once again. Within the first six months of its introduction, sales reached $13.5 million, a total far beyond management expectations. Rivals Packard, Lincoln, and Pierce-Arrow introduced their own V-12 engines in response to the V-16, but their arrival was slow in coming and had only a minor effect on Cadillac's growing market share.

Cadillac styling evolved through the 1930s, establishing the brand as the permanent leader in the luxury automobile market. Key years in its development were 1934, when Earl created a streamlined, aero-dynamic style with rounded fenders and a long, lean body. This style evolved over the years until 1941, the year the United States entered World War II. For Cadillac this was another watershed year in which Earl developed the "egg crate" style with its horizontal emphasis and brought about through the elimination of the vertical grille. In February 1942, Cadillac discontinued car production and devoted all its resources to producing military trucks and other combat vehicles.

Postwar Boom

After World War II, Cadillac immediately returned to producing cars. The 1946 Cadillac was essentially a variation of the 1942 model, with the V-type engine used in Cadillac war vehicles. Within two years, new car production had reached 97 percent of its pre-war peak. Demand was so great that one journalist exclaimed that "Cadillac fever is of epidemic proportions," describing how groups of people would pool their money for the purpose of jointly buying a Cadillac, which they would then share according to agreed-upon terms. "As far as can be discovered, only Cadillac enjoys this unusual tribute," he noted.

Again Cadillac set about to improve its products. "When the 1948 Cadillac appeared in the showroom," according to *Motor Trend,* "it panicked the competition. The tail fin had arrived. . . . " Harley Earl had once again instituted a style that would control the industry for a decade. Inspired by the twin tails on the Lockheed P-38 Lightning fighter plane of World War II, the tail fin was highly controversial among stylists. But it caught on immediately with the public.

Cadillac supported its new fin style with engineering advances, introducing the revolutionary overhead-valve engine in 1949. The reconfigured engine was capable of producing higher compression (and much more horsepower) than the less efficient old "flathead" design. During this time, the United States was riding a wave of economic prosperity, and Cadillac was at the forefront. By 1950, annual production topped 100,000 units. By 1955, annual owner demand exceeded 150,000 units. Throughout the 1950s, as engineers focused on power and handling, Cadillacs grew bigger and heavier and also rode more smoothly and quietly. The 1954 Cadillac weighed 5,100 pounds and could go from zero to 60 miles per hour in 11 seconds. Interiors were furnished with luxuries such as Florentine leather, comfort control air conditioning, power windows, power steering, tilt-wheel steering, and technologically advanced hi-fi stereo sound systems.

An article in *Science and Mechanics* commented, "In the public mind, a Cadillac represents—with good reason—just about everything a motor car should be." As Cadillac sales steadily grew, the last of its old rivals slowly went under. In 1955, Packard introduced a long-awaited luxury model designed to compete with the best Cadillacs. Despite its high quality craftsmanship, the Packard fell short in acceleration and top speed. Soon thereafter, the Packard company folded.

However, competition came from other quarters. Possibly its greatest nemesis was its own fame. In 1959, the total volume of Cadillac sales was more than double the volume sold by all other luxury cars combined, including imports. Cadillac enjoyed a seemingly unchallenged domination of the luxury car market. But as *Science and Mechanics* put it, "The only trouble with staking a claim to the title of 'the finest' is that you have to start competing with perfection itself." If competition with perfection itself wasn't enough, by 1960, Cadillac was experiencing some uncomfortably close competition from Lincoln and Chrysler. Although Cadillac sales far exceeded others, auto journals were beginning to concede that there was "little to choose" between Cadillac, Lincoln, and Chrysler. Others believed that Cadillacs were no more than "enlarged, better trimmed, and more expensive Chevrolets." And Rolls-Royce advertising at that time began stressing its Old World craftsmanship, a subtle knock at Cadillac's mass production techniques, which had hovered around the 130,000 mark through the late 1950s.

Public Perception Turns

In the early 1960s, General Motors reorganized its top three luxury car makers into the Buick, Oldsmobile, Cadillac Group. Engineering and manufacturing for all three divisions were combined with other divisions, and the Cadillac branch became little more than a marketing arm. This move had tremendously adverse effects on Cadillac's status in the decades to come.

Cadillac sales continued to climb, necessitating a major expansion at the Cadillac plant in 1962. The following year, Cadillac embarked on a major overhaul of its engines. The new engines performed "contemptuously well" at speeds above 100 mph, but drivers complained that some of the new engines were less economical, others had weak pistons, and still others were troublesome when raced. While auto experts praised such details as the precision and sensitivity of the 1964 Coupe DeVille's power steering, they noted deficiencies in the car's suspension and body finish.

1964 also saw a major restyling of the Cadillac body. Gone were the famous fins, replaced by a low, long body with a broader front grille and completely new rear treatment. However, while 11 new styles were offered, they were all variations on the same shell used by the Buick Electra—a factor which contributed greatly to the growing public perception that Cadillacs were losing their distinction as a luxury automobile. Another factor that contributed to Cadillac's diminishing "elite" image was the sheer volume of its output. Cadillac production in 1965 totaled 181,435, making it the most massively produced of all luxury cars.

Around the same time, the automotive press began praising several European luxury cars. Cadillac responded through its advertising, downplaying the brand's image as a status symbol and including small bits of technical information. In 1966, Oldsmobile introduced the Tornado, incorporating a new front-wheel drive system developed by General Motors Central Research, generating a tremendous amount of enthusiasm in the automotive press

A 1994 Cadillac Seville Touring Sedan.

and selling 50,000 units in its first year. The following year, Cadillac responded with the Eldorado, a "personal car" with the same General Motors front wheel drive system and the "E" body shell used for Tornado and the Buick Riviera. The press's response was less enthusiastic, having seen a very similar introduction a year earlier. But the Eldorado did manage to steal some of the market from the Tornado. By 1969, Eldorado sales surpassed 26,000, while Tornado sales had slipped by 50 percent to 25,000.

Another threat to Cadillac's supremacy over the luxury car market came in the form of a small body import: Mercedes-Benz. In 1968, only 22,500 Mercedes were sold in the United States; by 1973 the number had doubled, while the total number of luxury car sales had increased by only 43 percent. Mercedes had created its own marketing niche, attracting a young, largely female, well-educated, and sophisticated clientele. Cadillac management disagreed on how to best handle this new competition. One camp insisted that building a quality small car was essential to the line's survival. The other group believed that small cars were perceived as the antithesis of luxury and would never sell. Sales figures supported the latter: Cadillac sales continued to climb, totaling a record 289,233 cars for 1973.

When the energy crisis hit in late 1973, however, the large-bodied, low fuel-efficiency Cadillacs suffered an enormous amount of adverse publicity. The need for smaller Cadillacs became even more acute. Extensive research and development went into Cadillac's smaller, four-door answer to Mercedes Benz. Word got out to the general public and orders were being taken for the new Seville before the car even hit the showroom. On May 1, 1975 the new Seville was unveiled with much fanfare from the American auto press, and more moderate praise among the British. However, the annual import quota of 100 cars sold out before the Seville's delivery in England.

By April 1976, Seville sales in the United States surpassed those of the entire Mercedes line. The successful launch of Seville seemed to suggest that Cadillac might be ending its economic woes. But the company made a styling error in subsequent models, adding an unusual rear treatment that sent Seville's target market of younger, more affluent customers back to European imports.

Cadillac's second foray into the small-car market came with the 1982 introduction of the Cimmaron, a luxury-appointed version of the Chevrolet Cavalier, which failed to live up to management expectations. The second oil shortage in 1979 again sent Cadillac's image plummeting. Complicating the situation was a host of government-mandated fuel and emissions standards whose implementation deadlines necessitated retrofitting existing designs or rushing new designs into production. The decision was made to equip Cadillacs with fuel efficient diesel engines, which failed to perform up to Cadillac standards after the first 50,000 miles.

Following on the heels of the Cadillac diesel fiasco was the development of the 4-8-6 modified gasoline engine. The engine was considered no more than a "clever novelty" by the automotive press. Worse yet, it suffered from numerous mechanical failures. By 1986, a year in which Cadillac redesigned the Seville and Eldorado in hopes of regaining its reputation, sales had plummeted 60 percent. Critics complained that Cadillac's quality had diminished and in appearance resembled too strongly their less expensive cars offered by other General Motors divisions. From 1983 through 1988, Cadillac's share of the U.S. car market fell from 3.3 to 2.7 percent.

Quality, the one factor on which Cadillac's reputation had been built, was slipping, and it was showing in sales. In 1985, GM updated Cadillac's Hamtramck assembly plant, making it the centerpiece of its mission to improve quality. In January 1987, Cadillac reorganized, regaining control over the design and assembly of its cars. The goal was a return to Cadillac's roots: quality and style. Cadillacs of the mid-1980s were larger and more powerful than recent Cadillacs, with styling that borrowed from classic Cadillacs rather than other GM makes. Within five years, the plant had produced the award-winning Seville STS and won the highly coveted Malcolm Baldrige National Quality Award. Despite these improvements, management and Cadillac owners found several deficiencies in the car's overall quality.

In 1987, Cadillac launched the sleek Allante, a joint venture with the stylish Italian auto firm Pinifarina. Designed to give Cadillac a slick new image and capture some of the market from the Europeans, the Allante was a low-volume, high-tech "niche" vehicle that was intended to serve as a platform to introduce the Northstar System engine and transmission. The car sold well below expectations, however. Less than 3,800 Allantes sold in model years 1987 and 1988, and in 1993 the model was discontinued.

Sales began climbing in 1988, but by 1990, as the influx of European luxury cars began to stabilize, Cadillac faced unexpected competition from new Asian luxury brands such as Acura, Lexus, and Infiniti. Despite this threat, Cadillac continued to hold 27.3 percent of the luxury car market. Lincoln, its closest competitor trailed with a 20 percent share. Market analysts contended that, despite negative public perception, Cadillac was doing reasonably well and expected to fare better in the years to come.

Cadillac revamped its line in 1992 with newly designed Seville, Eldorado, and Fleetwood models. The Seville STS was named 1992 "Car of the Year" by *Motor Trend*, "Automobile of the Year" by *Automobile* magazine, and one of *Car and Driver*'s "Ten Best." In 1993 Cadillac made its Northstar System available on select Seville and Eldorado models. At the heart of the series of components that make up the integrated powertrain-suspension system is the Northstar engine. A dual-overhead cam, 32-valve, 4.6-liter 295 horsepower V-8, the computer controlled Northstar is capable of producing speeds of 160 miles per hour and only requires a tune-up (which consists of changing the platinum-tipped spark plugs) every 100,000 miles. The Northstar System met with wide critical acclaim in the automotive press, winning 15 editorial awards.

The successful redesign effort also resulted in a 6.6 percent increase in retail sales in 1992. The following year was soft for luxury car sales and Cadillac reflected that industry trend with sales that were off 4.7 percent. Despite the drop in overall sales, Cadillac improved its retail sales performance by 7.4 percent and retained its position as the best-selling American luxury car for the 45th consecutive year.

Further Reading:

Gawronski, Frank, "Detroit's Oldest Auto Manufacturer," *Automotive News, GM 75th Anniversary Issue,* September 16, 1993, p. 97.

Gross, Ken, "What Went Wrong with Allante?" *Automotive Industries,* June 1988, p. 27.

Holls, David, *Cadillac, Standard of the World: The Complete History,* Hong Kong: Automobile Quarterly Inc., 1990.

Keller, Maryann N., "Can Cadillac Come Back?," *Motor Trend,* May 1987, p. 146.

—Maura Troester

CARRIER®

Carrier Corporation, a subsidiary of United Technologies Corporation since 1979, is one of the leading manufacturers of air conditioners and heating systems in the world. Founded in 1915 by Willis Haviland Carrier and six associates, the firm provides imaginative answers to atmospheric problems for public buildings, factories, hospitals, retail outlets, and private homes from the Sistine Chapel in the Vatican to the U.S. House of Representatives in Washington, D.C., and from the suburban homes of Levittown, New York, to numerous other towns in the United States.

Early History

Carrier Engineering Company was founded in 1915 by Willis Carrier and some of his associates from the Buffalo Forge Company in Buffalo, New York. The fledgling business developed humidity control systems that were used by companies building airplanes and weapons during World War I. Originally Carrier and his associates worked not as manufacturers but as inventors and engineers who purchased such elements as coils, fans, and refrigeration units from outside suppliers and assembled them into air-conditioning systems. One of Carrier's inventions was a nonflammable, nonexplosive coolant and a new kind of cooling machine to use it. In 1922 Carrier opened a plant in Newark, New Jersey, specifically to manufacture products using this new development in refrigeration, the first innovation since the invention of the ammonia compressor in 1872.

The initial benefactor of Carrier's new air-conditioning system was Madison Square Gardens, which awarded Carrier a contract to freeze the ice for its skating rink in 1925. Before the first hockey game was played in the new arena on December 15, 1925—with the New York Rangers facing off against the Montreal Canadiens—Willis Carrier took an inaugural spin around the ice and judged it to skate as well as it looked.

During the Great Depression, Carrier established a progressive partial payment plan that allowed companies to pay for air-conditioning equipment and service out of future profits. The reward for such progressive thinking was a contract to provide the air-conditioning for the new head office of the Metropolitan Life Insurance Company in New York City.

First Commercial Success

Carrier's earliest customers were those in the world of manufacturing. Atmospheric control in industrial plants is essential; air that is either too humid or too dry can wreak havoc with machines and materials. Carrier understood this when, in the 1920s, he began providing air-conditioning for factories. His systems were used by manufacturers of textiles, including the Huguet Silk Mills in Wayland New York, the first company to utilize Carrier's automatic humidity control system.

Also in the 1920s, the Carrier began to market and install automatic sprinkler systems for fire protection in factories throughout the United States and Canada. Another innovation was the development of air-conditioning systems for theaters and other public buildings. The Rivoli Theatre, on New York City's Broadway, was one of the first to offer continuous shows "cooled by refrigeration." At the same time, the Olympia Theatre in Miami, Florida, boasted another of Carrier's early inventions, a "draft-free" air-conditioning system, instead of the usual fan ventilation system. Carrier became an even more visible presence when its system was installed in government buildings in Washington, D.C., providing air-conditioning the U.S. House of Representatives in 1928 and the U.S. Senate in 1929.

In the 1930s, Carrier developed an air-conditioning system designed especially for skyscrapers. In 1938 the Weathermaster was introduced. The system's main attraction to architects working on high rise designs was its ability to provide atmospheric control on a room-by-room basis; designers no longer had to allow for cross-ventilation for the cooling to take place. Among the earliest recipients of this technology was New York's Rockefeller Center and the RCA Building, both constructed in the 1930s.

Carrier air conditioners were also to be found in retail centers. The J.L. Hudson Department Store in Detroit, Michigan, was one of the first to install Carrier machines to cool its basement levels during the summer shopping season. In addition, air-conditioning was no longer restricted to buildings. By the 1930s, railroad cars and ships were outfitted with Carrier units, and by the end of the 1940s, airplanes were also climate-controlled by Carrier.

Food production, shipping, and storage processes also profited from Willis Carrier's innovations in cooling. His studies on food storage in the early 1940s were a boon to growers, retailers, and

AT A GLANCE

Carrier brand of air-conditioning units and systems founded by Farmington, CT-based Carrier Engineering Company, which was incorporated as Carrier Corporation by Willis Haviland Carrier in 1915 as the first-ever independent air conditioner company; company originally based in Newark, NJ; relocated to Syracuse, NY, in 1936, where it maintains a number of facilities.

Major competitor: Trane; also York.

Advertising: *Agency*—DDB Needham, Chicago, IL.

Addresses: *Parent company*—Carrier Corporation, One Carrier Place, Farmington, CT 06034-4015; phone: (203) 674-3134 *Ultimate parent company*—United Technologies Corporation, United Technologies Building, Hartford, CT 06101; phone: (203) 728-7000.

food store customers. Not only did Carrier develop air-conditioning systems for warehouses and food stores, he also entered the world of frozen foods by developing large-scale industrial freezer units.

Among the other areas in which Carrier air-conditioning systems were adapted to solve specific problems was the health care arena. By the 1930s, the American Hospital Association pointed to the very real need for air-conditioning in hospitals. The special needs of such institutions were addressed by Carrier with his development of an air-conditioning unit for a premature baby ward at Allegheny General Hospital in Pittsburgh in the early 1930s. Since then, air-conditioning systems for other vital and occasionally problematic areas of the hospital—including operating rooms and sterile storage areas—have been provided by Carrier.

Finally, Carrier introduced residential air-conditioning units in 1928. The first model, called the Weathermaker, heated, humidified, cleaned, and circulated air during the winter, and provided additional cooling during the summer. It was also large enough for a person to sit on; by the 1930s, the overly large household air conditioners were designed to look like furniture to blend in with room decor.

Innovations During World War II

During World War II, most of the developments in air-conditioning, as in other industries, were driven by the needs of the military, and Carrier, like so many other industrial plants, produced not only equipment, but munitions as well. Besides producing refrigeration units for military food storage, Carrier was the exclusive manufacturer of Hedge Hog depth charges, which sank more than 300 German submarines. Carrier also produced air-conditioning for ordnance plants, refrigeration units for U.S. Navy walk-in coolers, and dehumidifiers for the blast furnaces used in steel plants. Atmosphere control units were developed for nylon factories, allowing for the production of nylon yarns, used for, among other things, nylon hosiery—a new product designed to replace silk stockings, which were unavailable during wartime.

The Postwar Era

The return of service personnel after the armistice in Europe and Japan was a boon for industry and for residential growth. Carrier, which had relocated to Syracuse, New York, from Newark, New Jersey, in 1936, was a major employer of World War II veterans. In 1946 the company boasted that fully one-third of its work force was made up of former soldiers.

During the 1950s, Carrier air conditioners were featured in factories, public buildings, trains, boats, airplanes, trucks, and eventually in private homes and vehicles. In 1955 430,000 American homes were air-conditioned; by the early 1990s, according to an American Housing survey, nearly 70 percent of homes were equipped with this feature. Carrier, which offered residential air-conditioning units since the 1930s, also pioneered portable room air conditioners in 1958. Air-conditioning for trailers and mobile residences debuted in 1941, and developments throughout the 1950s made the units smaller and more efficient.

In the 1960s Carrier air-conditioning units were placed in a number of innovative structures. In 1965, the Houston Astrodome—dubbed the world's largest room, with 41 million cubic feet of unbroken space—was air-conditioned by four Carrier refrigerating machines. Carrier units were used to power everything from nuclear submarines to cruise ships and subway systems.

Carrier was one of the first companies to realize that the oil crisis of 1973 posed a serious threat to the long-term future of U.S. energy sources. Accordingly, it was a pioneer in the development of such fuel-conserving devices as the heat pump, which Carrier had originally begun to work on in the 1930s, when the idea of energy conservation was unheard of. The company also designed electronic sensing controls, high efficiency air conditioners, and other energy-saving devices.

International Market

Carrier air-conditioning units came to be prevalent in almost every country around the world. Willis Carrier was an early pioneer in global communications; in 1907, he was approached by the Fugi Silk Spinning Company to develop a humidity control system and built an air-conditioning system for a Tokyo research laboratory that same year.

Carrier marketed its products overseas during the Depression. Japan, South America, Russia, South Africa, Egypt, and India were among the countries in which the company was able to secure lucrative contacts. Carrier came to have branch units in Latin America, Europe, and Asia. Except in Japan, which boasts a successful air-conditioning industry of its own, Carrier is the leader in air-conditioning in 130 countries around the world.

Future Prospects

In the early 1990s, Carrier systems were used in a number of growing industries. Air-conditioning is essential to maintain a constant atmosphere in the manufacturing of miniaturized high-precision parts such as disk drives and bearings for sensitive gyroscopes, and Carrier, with its sterling reputation, is the air-conditioning system of choice for a number of high-tech industries.

Among the most high-profile projects in which Carrier has been involved was the computer-operated environmental control system that was installed in the Sistine Chapel during the late 1980s and early 1990s. Built within the confines of a fifteenth-century structure in Vatican City, the system controls the environment to provide the best atmosphere for the preservation of Michelangelo's priceless ceiling frescoes. It was developed with the use of computer modeling in Carrier's Syracuse, New York, Corporate Engineering laboratories and tracks and monitors the chapel's microclimate constantly, providing immediate information concerning the condition of the paintings. After painstaking restoration of the masterpiece in the 1980s, the system ensures that the quality of Michelangelo's work is not compromised.

Although Carrier Corporation was acquired by United Technologies in a hostile takeover in 1979, it is still a strong company, nearly 40 percent larger than its nearest competitor. It is well positioned to be a major force within the European Economic Community and has a foothold in China. The company is also interested in expanding to new markets in India, Argentina, and other countries. Carrier's strength and reputation in the United States remain second to none in the air-conditioning industry.

Further Reading:

Carrier Corporation records, 1875–1964, Kroch Library Archives, Cornell University, Ithaca, NY.

''Carrier Corporation; 75 Years: Building on Tradition,'' *WeatherMakers*, No. 1, 1991.

Conservation of the Frescoes. The Sistine Chapel, Carrier Corporation.

Ingels, Margaret, *Willis Haviland Carrier, Father of Air-Conditioning*, Garden City, NY: Country Life Press, 1952.

Wampler, Cloud, *Dr. Willis H. Carrier, Father of Air-Conditioning*, New York: Newcomen Society of England (American Branch), 1949.

—*Marcia K. Mogelonsky*

CASIO®

Since pioneering mass-market electronic calculators in the 1950s and 1960s, the Casio brand has combined creative engineering with careful niche marketing to expand into timepieces, electronic musical instruments, electronic office machinery, and audiovisual equipment. The Tokyo, Japan-based Casio Computer Co., Ltd., was founded in 1946 and by 1994 was generating sales of more than $3 billion, of which its U.S. subsidiary, Casio Inc., accounted for a growing share. Though the four Kashio brothers created ''Casio'' as a brand name to be put on calculators that they had engineered as early as 1946, they could never have predicted the degree of success, or diversity, that the brand would enjoy during the brothers' lifetimes.

Brand Origins

The Casio brand emerged from the inventive engineering collaboration of the four Kashio brothers, who founded Kashio Seisakujo (Casio Computer Co., Ltd.) in Tokyo in 1946. With its breakthrough relay calculator leading the way, the brothers' firm enjoyed rapid growth and continued development of the product line. The invention of Toshio Kashio's electronic calculator prompted a 1957 reorganization in which the company became Japan's only manufacturer specializing in electronic calculators. Increased product development and distribution accelerated the use of the Casio brand name, a graphic and phonetic simplification of the founders' surname. Subsequent advances in semiconductor technology introduced greater power potential and smaller size, offering unprecedented flexibility in calculator design. By 1965 Casio had developed a landmark electronic desktop model with memory, a feature that made the brand's earlier lines seem obsolete.

The new Casio lines, however, became entrenched in a price war for pocket calculators that raged throughout the 1960s and 1970s, and in which Casio triumphed. According to the *Nikkei Weekly,* the average price of calculators plunged from ¥157,000 in 1968 to ¥4,570 in 1976, while shipments soared from 163,000 units to 40.3 million over the same period. Looking back from the 1990s, Casio Computer Co. President Kazuo Kashio explained that the key to survival depended on two strategies: remaining a price leader instead of methodically following the price trends set by the whole industry; and combining price cuts with new features to lure more converts to the Casio brand. Casio had no alternative but to survive the calculator price wars, since the core of its existence was exclusively calculator products. The company quite simply had to fight tooth and nail or perish.

Kashio Philosophy Brought Casio Success

The success of Casio, however, was never primarily a result of brute strength or gut survival; from its earliest years the brand was infused with a Kashio family philosophy that combined true commitment to innovation with a knack for flexibility. The result was a brand of products distinguished by their engineering and manufacturing originality and by their proprietors' almost uncanny ability to fit the products into niche markets or develop niche markets around the products. ''We've always approached the market with a different philosophy than most competitors,'' explained John McDonald, president of U.S. operations, in a 1989 article in *HFD—The Weekly Home Furnishings Newspaper.* ''Casio provides its retail accounts and their customers with products that they can't get anywhere else.'' Indeed, when Tadao Kashio, Casio's key founder, died on March 4, 1993, most obituaries mentioned his firm belief that creativity itself was a contribution to society.

Even held up to cold, academic analysis, the Casio brand exemplified unusually creative and flexible forces. In a 1991 *Journal of Marketing* article, Raavi S. Achrol, associate professor of marketing at the University of Notre Dame, credited Casio's adaptability in the ''Evolution of the Marketing Organization: New Forms for Turbulent Environments.'' Achrol identified the need for ''an ambidextrous organization, simultaneously demanding efficiency, innovation, and flexibility.'' He described Casio's unique flexibility as a ''functional strategy to integrate design and development into marketing so that consumer preferences are analyzed by persons closest to the market and quickly converted into products.''

Similar flexibility marked pricing and distribution, and Casio developed unique products that filled specific niche markets while simultaneously maintaining a wide price range for different segments of those markets. In 1989, for example, the brand introduced seven different digital diaries in different price segments. ''We can protect a department store or a Sharper Image [store] with a high-end model and still have low-end models for mass merchants, catalog showrooms and warehouse clubs without getting in each other's way,'' McDonald told *HFD.* Bypassing traditional distribution methods, the brand spurned office supply out-

AT A GLANCE

Casio brand of electronics founded by the four Kashio brothers, who established Kashio Seisakujo (Casio Computer Co., Ltd.) in 1946 in Tokyo; "Casio" is Anglicized version of "Kashio." Brand became a market leader in electronic calculators, introducing the first desktop model with memory in 1965; implemented new technologies to develop other electronic products, including electronic calculators, electronic timepieces, musical instruments, liquid crystal display (LCD) pocket televisions, office equipment, and personal information processors. Casio Inc. is the U.S. subsidiary of Casio Computer Co., Ltd.

Performance: *Market share*—1% of electronics category; leader in electronic calculators category and multifunction wristwatches category. *Sales*—¥431.7 billion (US$3.72 billion).

Major competitor: Sony; also, Sharp; (portable keyboards) Yamaha; (wristwatches) Seiko and Citizen.

Advertising: *Agency*—Merkley, Newman & Harty (formerly Doremus & Company), New York, NY, 1993—. *Major campaign*—"My Magic Diary," an electronic organizer for children aged eight and up; a campaign highlighting the Secret Sender 6000, a digital diary that lets kids send messages from one unit to another via infrared technology.

Addresses: *Parent company*—Casio, Inc., 570 Mount Pleasant Avenue, Dover, NJ 07801; phone: (201) 361-5400; fax: (201) 361-3819. *Ultimate parent company*—Casio Computer Co., Ltd., 6-1, Nishi-Shinjuku 2-chome, Shinjuku-ku, Tokyo 163-02, Japan; phone: (03) 3347-4803.

lets and offered its product line to consumer electronics outlets, mass merchants, drugstore chains, and other places where shoppers with diverse needs could find products to suit their wildest fancies.

Combining innovation and flexibility at the retail end, Casio also adapted to the scourge of customer-returned merchandise that plagued the entire retail industry since the advent of superstores in the 1980s. To help mitigate losses for both the manufacturer and retailers, the brand initiated a toll-free phone service in the early 1990s to support its wide variety of products. Receiving more than 7,000 queries each month, the service, Casio hoped, would satisfy unsure users or at least provide one less excuse for them to return undamaged merchandise.

Brand Development

With its calculator success established by the 1970s, and its solid foundation of innovation and flexibility, Casio moved into new and untapped markets, often drawing doubts from analysts but seldom faltering. As McDonald pointed out in a 1989 *Consumer Electronics* article, calculators were not considered very market-ready items when they first reached the mass market in the 1970s: "People said . . . that a standard yellow pencil with a red eraser on the top was an inexpensive and reliable calculator," he mused. And just as Casio had capitalized on a perceived need for calculators as a replacement for pencils, it moved into a wide range of other electronic products that had equally positive chances of storming the market. With rapid technological progress, especially in the domain of IC (integrated circuit) and LCI (large-scale integration), the brand was able to develop sophisticated products ranging from even more versatile calculators to electronic timepieces packed with auxiliary features; electronic musical instruments; office equipment; and LCD (liquid crystal display) televisions.

In its development of truly innovative niche products, Casio took unexpected turns, some more promising than others. The 1992 acquisition of Asahi Corp., a manufacturer of answering devices for PhoneMate and an OEM supplier of audio products, was prompted by the rising importance of communication capabilities in the development of information equipment, including computers and pocket electronic diaries. In addition to offering a whole new line of audio stereo systems, the Casio brand would benefit from joint product development between its parent and Asahi, with an eye on sophisticated communications devices and interactive devices to be used on the much-publicized "information superhighway" of the twenty-first century.

Even though Casio's success rate was not perfectly consistent, its innovation persisted. Intent on developing a large worldwide market for easy-to-use lettering and labeling systems—including color combinations and iron-on tapes without the need of font cards—Casio introduced a label maker in May of 1992. Taking innovation a step further, in August of 1993 the brand came out with its prayer compass—a clock device (in both handheld and wrist models) that indicated the direction to the Muslim religious center of Mecca and signaled prayer times five times a day. Attempts to develop product lines in the more conventional areas of typewriters and word processors, however, met with flat resistance and were discontinued.

Music and the 1980s

Just as easily as the Casio brand fell out of flat market niches like typewriters and word processors, it steered its way into such key, untapped markets as electronic music, almost without missing a beat. When the Casio brand unveiled two portable keyboards in 1980, the market was essentially empty. John McDonald's forecasts of sales topping $100 million in the category by 1985 were shrugged off by the industry majority. (A decade earlier, the Hammond Organ had incurred severe losses in low-end keyboard sales to mass retailers.) With suspicious retailers and music dealers disinterested in such products directed toward a mass market, Casio's electronic keyboards started on a low note. Nevertheless, technological improvements and aggressive marketing and advertising efforts from 1983 to 1987 resulted in exponential growth; by 1987 portable sales exceeded $150 million with industrywide sales surpassing $550 million.

In 1988 and 1989 growth dwindled under the downward, albeit unexpected, decline that one executive referred to as a "temporary hiccup" in consumer interest. Rather than idly waiting for the "hiccup" to pass, Casio took measures to cure it, including more research and development than ever before and a wide selection of new features, user-friendly add-ons, and electronic musical instruments beyond keyboards. The overhaul was marketed as "A whole new way to play" and a means of introducing the fun of playing instruments to all levels and all ages, thereby "increasing the music population." Targeting the insatiable children's market (kids aged 7 to 15) in 1990, the brand introduced its Rap-10 instrument, featuring ten built-in patterns to help the user create rap songs. And in an attempt to lure more trained musicians, in the early 1990s Casio introduced the CELVIANO series of digital pianos with large-scale integration (LSI) technology to render subtle key variations and better approximate the conventional musical touch.

Watches Ahead of Their Time

Realizing that the wristwatch market had essentially reached maturity by the 1990s, Casio applied its knack for identifying niches and positioned itself as the leader of a new movement in multifunction watches, or so-called "wrist products," combining conventional time functions with a wide range of professional, health care, leisure, and athletic applications. Such products, which made up 45 percent of Casio's 1992 watch sales and were projected to be 60 percent for 1994, included digital watches that could monitor blood pressure and take a pulse, record telephone numbers, store and transfer data, and count calories.

Some Casio watch designs bordered on the unbelievable. A fishing watch introduced in 1989, for example, could track the lunar cycles controlling the tides to determine the best time to fish. And a model designed for the ski slopes could function at -20 degrees Celsius and time intervals of .01 seconds, and featured a built-in temperature sensor. On the more controversial end, a series of Wrist Controller watches were introduced in 1993 and were equipped with universal remote controllers that could be used to operate VCRs, TVs, audio systems, and cable boxes. In January of 1994 Zenith Electronics Corp. filed a patent infringement petition with the U.S. International Trade Commission charging that Casio's Wrist Controller watches infringed on its patent rights; a final decision on the case was to be made in 1995.

PIPs, Z-7000, PDAs, and LCDs

Casio's innovations for a given line of products continually overlapped with other lines, joining calculator breakthroughs to new concepts in watches, portable televisions, and personal information products (PIPs). Late 1980s advancements in calculators, such as the first graphics calculator, introduced in 1985, led to the technology for a line of electronic diaries and calendar organizers that grew dramatically into the 1990s. By 1989 40 percent of the brand's calculator business was in diaries. By the early 1990s, though, diaries were beginning to be seen as archaic; market demands and new technological advances spawned a new generation of palm-held computers and PIPs.

Going one step further, Casio introduced its Z-7000, a Personal Digital Assistant (PDA) developed in a joint venture with Tandy Corp. and capable of deciphering limited handwritten notes and incorporating them in a multifunction system combining organization, calculation, and communication applications. Rated as the number one PDA by *HFD,* Casio's Z-7000 nevertheless faced growing competition from Apple Computer's heavily advertised Newton, Amstrad's Penpad, a Sharp version, and numerous other entrants to the market.

The Casio brand also invested in its future plans, allocating large sums—$291 million in 1993, down 8.9 percent from 1992—on sophisticated liquid crystal displays (LCDs). It set its sights on eventually replacing the cathode-ray tube (CRT) technology used on conventional televisions and monitors and developing new display possibilities for the multimedia, interactive communications age. As early as 1992, Casio had introduced the world's thinnest flexible LCD, at 0.5 millimeter, about one-quarter the thickness of most LCDs and one-tenth the weight. This technology accounted for Casio's market edge in handheld LCD televisions.

In 1993 Casio, Inc., entered the toy business and established the Casio Cool Division. Casio Cool offers an array of digital diaries for children, cassette players, drum synthesizers, and a Learning Talk Telephone that teaches children ages two and up musical notes, numbers, colors, and people/animal recognition. When the first "My Magic Diary" for children was introduced in 1993, more than 200,000 units were completely sold out in the three months prior to Christmas.

Bold Advertising and Promotion

While Casio's innovative products often spoke for themselves, bold moves in advertising and promotion added to their appeal. Beginning in 1989, for example, the brand signed jazz star Herbie Hancock to do a series of network television commercials to promote its new line of electronic instruments. After playing phrases on Casio's Tone Bank keyboard, the musician turns into an animated figure and mingles with colors springing from the instrument, suggesting that the brand exudes not only color, but jazzy creativity and imagination. A print ad showed Albert Einstein's face with Casio calculators revealed in a cross-section of his brain. The only copy was the word "Casio."

In addition to running print and television advertisements, Casio held various promotional events around the world. An almost comical misunderstanding complicated the brand's 1991 sponsorship of the annual Warsaw Jazz Jamboree organized by the Polish Jazz Society in alliance with Florida-based Festiva Productions. A conflict over sponsorship resulted in two simultaneous festivals, one sponsored by Casio and PJS and the other by Festiva and Pepsi. After some frustration on the part of all participants—and the Warsaw police department, which had twice the anticipated amount of work—all parties planned to succeed in a unified effort in subsequent years. Casio also cosponsored the June 26, 1993, pay-per-view boxing match between Evander Holyfield and Alex Stewart.

International Growth

By the early 1990s, the Casio brand was supported by divisions and units in the United States, Mexico, Canada, the United Kingdom, Germany, Taiwan, Hong Kong, South Korea, and Malaysia. Due to the stronger Japanese yen, the parent company made aggressive efforts at shifting production to sites outside of Japan, with a projected goal of 50 percent of manufacturing operations to be located in Malaysia, Thailand, Korea, and other Asian regions by 1995.

The Casio brand also moved to extend its presence throughout the world. In China, for example, it launched the production of wristwatches in Guangdong province in 1994. Two years earlier digital diaries were being distributed in Budapest, Hungary, a cooperative effort with Tomen Trading House. Other hot spots included the rest of Europe, Central and South America, the Middle East, and Africa.

Future Predictions

Describing a playful dream to *HFD* on October 14, 1991, Casio Inc. President John McDonald said, "Once before I die, I'd like to have products so hot that retailers are lined up outside my door with fistfuls of cash, ready to genuflect and kiss my ring." While the details of that fantasy remain less than likely, the Casio brand was in a favorable position to continue to lead enough niche markets to sustain enthusiasm on the part of retailers and consumers.

Further Reading:

Battaglio, Stephen, ''The 1989 Creative Media Awards,'' *Adweek,* November 20, 1989, p. 40.

''Casio Announces Flexible LCD,'' *Yomiuri News Service,* June 22, 1992.

''Casio and Sharp Calculate Electronic Notebook Strategies,'' *Japan Economic Journal,* September 23, 1989.

''Casio Zoomer PDA,'' *HFD—The Weekly Home Furnishings Newspaper,* June 28, 1993, p. 62.

Cooper, Ann, ''Siimple Siimon,'' *Advertising Age,* June 5, 1989, p. 46.

Greenberg, Manning, ''Casio's Big Plans to Spur Keyboard Sales this Fall,'' *HFD,* October 23, 1989, p. 162; ''Rapping Up Sales; Casio's Business Strategy,'' *HFD,* October 14, 1991, p. 133; ''Casio's Calculating Ways,'' *HFD,* July 20, 1992, p. 74; ''Rejection Blues: Customers Returns Mean Big Problems for Retailers and Vendors Alike,'' *HFD,* June 14, 1993, p. 65.

''How Portables Put the Industry in Its Place,'' *Music Trades,* January 1990, p. 114.

''Interview: Casio's John McDonald,'' *Consumer Electronics,* June 1989, p. 106.

''Jazz Jamboree '91: Divided Loyalties,'' *Warsaw Voice,* November 10, 1991.

''Newest Watches Tell More Than Just Time,'' *Nikkei Weekly,* November 22, 1993, p. 18.

Smith, Sid, ''The Writing Is Still on the Wall; Casio Is Zooming Ahead of the PDA Field,'' *The Guardian,* January 20, 1994, p. 17.

Unstead, R. Thomas, ''Main Events Unveils Media Plan,'' *Multichannel News,* June 14, 1993, p. 34.

Veilleux, C. Thomas, ''Organizing the Future: Today's Personal Information Products,'' *HFD,* February 22, 1993, p. 67.

''Zenith Files Patent Suit Against Casio,'' *Jiji Press Ticker Service,* January 14, 1994.

—Kerstan Cohen

CHEVROLET®

CHEVROLET

Chevrolet, manufactured by the General Motors Corporation, was the top-selling automobile brand in the United States from 1931 to the early 1990s more often than any other brand. Chevrolet's marketing strategy stressed value, economy, and close association with American values, conjuring images of baseball, hot dogs, and apple pie to present Chevy as a quintessentially American product.

Brand Origins

Louis Chevrolet designed the first Chevrolet automobile, the Classic Six, in Detroit in 1911, with the financial backing of a founder of the General Motors Corporation, William C. Durant. The Chevrolet Motor Car Company was incorporated on November 3, 1911.

The Classic Six was a five-passenger touring sedan with an extensive list of features for its time: four doors, electric lights, a folding top, side curtains, a windshield, and a tool box. The engine, with six cylinders, had a potential top speed of 65 miles per hour and the ability to accelerate from zero to 50 miles per hour in 15 seconds. The car, with a price of $2,150, was affordable only for the wealthy. In its first production year, 1912, the Classic Six reached sales of 2,999.

In 1913, William Durant more than doubled production of the model, moving Chevrolet manufacturing from Detroit to Flint, Michigan, where Durant had created the Little Motor Car Company and the Mason Motor Company to help expand capacity. The Mason Company built engines for both Chevrolets and Littles; Durant later dropped the name Little and called all the cars Chevrolets. Louis Chevrolet left the Chevrolet Motor Car Company soon after it was founded because of disagreements with Durant. General Motors bought Chevrolet in 1918.

Brand Development

The well-known bowtie-shaped Chevrolet logo appeared for the first time on Chevrolet cars in 1914. The 1914 models included the Model L or "Light Six" and the H-Series Chevrolet Fours, with four-cylinder engines. The H-Series, with the Royal Mail roadster listed at $750 and the Baby Grand touring car at $875, allowed Chevrolet to penetrate the low-priced market segment. Innovations on these models were their valve-in-head engine design, still used by many cars in the 1990s, and a starter and lighting system that greatly improved on the acetylene lamps needed at night by other models.

Ford Model T's still dominated the low-priced market. William Durant decided to compete with the 490 (Four Ninety), named in reference to its price tag. Appearing in both touring and roadster styles, painted black, with the extras of self-starter and electric lights as options, the 490 never matched the Model T in popularity, but it did contribute to a large increase in Chevrolet sales; sales jumped from about 62,500 in 1916 to over 125,000 in 1917, allowing Chevrolet to attain fourth place in overall automobile sales in the United States.

Chevrolet retailers, opening in many large cities, aided in making the cars more available to the general public. In 1918, Chevrolet produced its first truck, based on an expanded 490 platform. By 1919, Chevrolet outproduced and outranked Buick and Willys Overland for second place in overall sales; by 1920, sales were over 150,000, or 39 percent of the GM total.

Early Marketing Strategy

In 1920, after William Durant left General Motors, management considered liquidating the Chevrolet division because of Ford's dominance in low-priced cars. Ford had 60 percent of the market; Chevrolet, only 4 percent. Alfred P. Sloan, Jr., assistant to GM President Pierre S. duPont, set out to prove despite all the odds that Chevrolet could outdo Ford. The company adopted the policy of making Chevrolet its "value leader." Instead of attempting to rival the untouchable Model T, company management came up with the strategy of targeting the segment slightly above that of the Model T in price, equipment, and value. In 1923 the company replaced the 490 with the Superior. Sloan's strategy was overwhelmingly successful; sales that year reached 480,737.

The Superior introduced the "body style" selling concept. The car came in the varieties of coupe, roadster, touring car, sedan, or sedanette (two-door with a small trunk). The highly original option of a radio installed in the car cost $200, or about one-fourth the total cost for the vehicle. Another Chevrolet marketing innovation, developed by Sloan into a business canon, was the practice of updating the models annually. This policy helped Chevrolet outrank Ford in both 1927 and 1928.

AT A GLANCE

Chevrolet brand of automobile created by the Swiss racing car driver and engineer Louis Chevrolet in Detroit in 1911; the Chevrolet Motor Car Company was incorporated on November 3, 1911; William C. Durant, one of the founders of the General Motors Corporation, had provided Mr. Chevrolet with financing in 1909; General Motors purchased the Chevrolet company in 1918; making it the Chevrolet Motor Division of the General Motors Corporation.

Performance: *Market share*—16.72% of car and truck category.

Major competitor: Ford Motor Company.

Advertising: *Agency*—Lintas Campbell-Ewald, Warren, MI, 1922-1993. *Major campaign*—For GEO (Chevrolet's imports), the theme is "Get to know GEO." For Chevrolet trucks, the theme is "Most dependable, longest-lasting trucks." The tag for Chevrolet's new Camaro is "Coming soon. From the country that invented rock 'n' roll." In contrast, the theme for the Chevrolet Lumina stresses family values. Finally, the general Chevrolet "Heartbeat of America" campaign was being replaced by a new theme in the spring of 1994.

Addresses: *Parent company*—General Motors Corporation, 3044 W. Grand Boulevard, Detroit, MI 48202-3091; phone: (313) 556-2044.

Product Changes

In 1924 Chevrolet added details, such as outside door handles and front and rear bumpers, that made the vehicles look less like horseless buggies. Blue, aquamarine, and green became the major car colors, replacing black altogether. Chevrolet produced a six-cylinder, 46-horsepower, valve-in-head engine for a new model known as the Stovebolt Six. Originally mocked because of the use of iron when other manufacturers were turning to aluminum, the model won respect for its durability and the fact that while it was more powerful than the Chevy four-cylinders, the 1929 models were sold in the same price range. Chevy also offered four-wheel brakes, the first rumble seat in low-priced cars, and the first electric gasoline gauge, appearing in 1930.

The 1927 Capitol Series had a longer sloping hood and a more flowing, aesthetically pleasing shape. The 1928 National and the 1929 International Series continued the trend of attractive design, helping Chevrolet once again outrank Ford after 1930. Chevrolet held its place as the top-selling American automobile in all but four of the 55 years that followed.

Chevrolet entered the 1930s ranking second to Ford; as the decade continued, it consolidated its place as the most consistent top car and truck manufacturer in the world for that decade. The Great Depression caused countless small manufacturers to close their doors; Chevrolet, however, expanded manufacturing and strengthened production and assembly capabilities. Although sales dropped as the depression deepened, Chevrolet's very survival allowed it to outpace its competitors.

Advertising efforts during that period included sponsorship of the "Chevrolet Chronicles" radio program hosted by Eddie Rickenbacker; programs featured well-known American war veterans who narrated their experiences. Chevrolet also sponsored the Soap Box Derby in Dayton, Ohio, for the first time in 1934, continuing their sponsorship until 1973. More important than these advertising vehicles, however, was the fact that Chevrolet priced its cars for a depressed economy; the Roadster, for example, sold for $475, the lowest price for any Chevrolet automobile.

Product improvements in the 1930s included the "synchromesh," a device that synchronized the speed of the transmission gears before they meshed and greatly improved the ease with which drivers could shift gears. Independent front suspension and Chevrolet's first built-in trunk appeared in 1934. Chevrolet presented the Blue Flame Six in 1934, with an engine that generated 15 times more horsepower than previous six-cylinder engines but without more engine displacement. Chevrolet trucks in the 1930s also advanced considerably: in 1936, Chevrolet introduced the Coupe Pickup, with a standard coupe body but a pickup bed in back instead of a trunk. Chevrolet also offered its first production station wagon in 1939.

The last year of full-force civilian production before the interruption of munitions manufacturing for World War II was 1941; that year Chevrolet produced a record for the time of over 1.6 million cars and trucks. Chevrolet was first in sales, with the advertising theme "Bigger Is Better." Americans continued to crave the prestige of ever bigger cars, and Chevy continued to feed the national craving until the 1960s, when the American mindset underwent a radical change. High fuel costs in the 1970s suppressed the American big-car appetite even further.

Post-World War II

Car designs immediately after the war showed no innovations; Chevrolet, and the rest of the automobile industry, refurbished cars produced earlier to replenish stock. Chevrolet offered a new truck design in 1948 with the Thriftmaster pickup. In 1949, responding to the popularity of station wagons, Chevrolet produced its first all-steel wagon. Chevrolets that year, with their rounded, aesthetically appealing looks, outsold the rival Ford and Plymouth models. For the first time since 1927, Chevrolet sales were over one million.

Ford and Chevrolet entered the 1950s racing neck and neck to come out ahead in a textbook-case price war. Each manufacturer increased production dramatically to beat the other with lower unit pricing. Chevrolet remained first in sales.

The Chevrolet Powerglide models of 1950 were the first of their class to offer automatic transmission; sales for the enormously popular model were 300,000 the first year. The Chevrolet Bel Air, the first model with a "convertible hardtop," featured frame reinforcements that supported the top and improved on the draftiness of conventional convertibles.

In 1953, Chevrolet offered a passenger car lineup of three series for the first time since 1940. The first series featured standard sedans with two or four doors, a coupe, and a station wagon; the second series included a mid-level Two-Ten with extras such as armrests and ashtrays; the third series was the stylish Bel Air line. Also in 1953, Chevrolet showcased its first Corvette at Motorama in response to the growing American taste for European sports cars. The designer, Harley Earl, used a body of reinforced fiberglass on a conventional frame. The first Corvettes featured bucket seats, a hand-operated convertible soft-top that folded into a behind-seat compartment, and 150 horsepower at 4500 rpm.

Chevy trucks in the 1950s offered the greater power produced by the new Turbo-Fire V8 engine, introduced by Chevrolet in

1955 after a hiatus of 36 years in eight-cylinder engine production. Versions of the engine, also used in Chevy's cars, ranged from 162 to 180 brake horsepower; later in the decade, fuel injection improvements increased the rating to 290 brake horsepower. The late fifties saw steadily climbing sales for trucks and four-wheel-drive pickups.

The 1957 Chevrolet auto, with its tail fins and innovative front-end design, was later to become one of the most highly prized collectors' models Chevrolet produced. In 1958, the famous Impala nameplate first appeared, with a design that was to offer a "Cadillac big car look at a Chevy price." In the late 1950s, however, Americans surprised the Big Three domestic auto manufacturers (Ford, GM, and Chrysler) by buying compact, economical Volkswagens from Germany. Chevrolet responded with its own compact model, the Corvair, in 1960.

The Sixties and Beyond

Chevrolet's 1961 Impala lacked the big showy fins that characterized the cars of the 1950s; this design was replaced with sleeker, full-length bodyside moldings and a "thin pillar" slantback roof. In 1962, Chevrolet introduced the compact Chevy II, the forerunner of the Chevy Nova that was to become popular in the 1970s. Chevrolet achieved the versatility in its lineup that helped it clinch number-one ranking throughout the 1960s by offering V8 power engines for the sports- and performance-minded and six-cylinder engines for more conservative drivers, with both engine types usually available in the same body styles.

The 1964 Chevelle introduced a midsize sedan, hardtop, wagon, and convertible series. The high-power Turbo-Jet 396 engine appeared in 1965, as well as the Caprice nameplate, later to become Chevrolet's premier luxury model. The Corvette in the early 1960s added a stylishly tapered "ducktail" rear. The Corvette Sting Ray, a 300-horsepower performance machine, made its splash on the sports car scene in 1963. On the trucking scene, Chevrolet introduced independent front suspension, a first in the industry, and entered the diesel market. The year 1966 produced another Chevrolet classic, the Camaro, the first new GM design produced from wind tunnel testing.

In the late 1960s, responding to government regulations and emission standards, Chevrolet developed emission control systems for all 1968 engines and steered away from emphasizing performance. Chevelle designs became more compact, beginning the transformation to the Malibu nameplate. The Blazer, a four-wheel-drive sporty pickup, debuted in 1969. Finally, Chevrolet introduced the luxury Monte Carlo two-door coupe in 1970, earning the "Car of the Year" award from *Motor Trend* magazine.

The 1973 oil embargo doubled prices for fuel within two years. Catering to energy conservation awareness, power ratings in the 1970s began to be displayed as net horsepower rather than brake horsepower to distinguish fuel performance ability. Chevrolet's lineup changed drastically. It featured the Vega, Chevy's first subcompact car; Light Utility Vehicles or LUVs, the first Chevrolet compact trucks; the 1976 two-door hatch-back Chevette; and the 1979 compact Citation model, Chevy's first front-wheel drive auto.

Recent Performance and Outlook

The 1980s began with ominous signs for the U.S. automobile industry. Another oil embargo in 1979 ushered in the new decade. Market share held by imports was consolidated from 1979 to 1982.

Chevrolet responded with the subcompact Cavalier in 1982; the model became the top-selling car in the country in 1984 and 1985. Chevrolet also produced the technologically groundbreaking 1984 Corvette, again winning *Motor Trend*'s award for "Car of the Year." Three additional small cars, Sprint, Spectrum, and the revived Chevy Nova, allowed Chevrolet to offer the broadest array of choices available from any automobile manufacturer. The Nova was reborn through a joint venture between General Motors and Toyota that created a company called New United Motor Manufacturing, Inc.

Chevrolet models debuting in 1988 were the four-door Corsica sedan, the sporty Beretta coupe, and the Chevy Full-Size Pickup. From the late 1980s to the early 1990s, Chevrolet's main advertising campaign used the theme "Heartbeat of America." The theme for Chevrolet's imports and cars built through joint ventures, given the nameplate Geo in 1989, was "Get to know Geo." The Chevy Nova took the name Geo Prizm in 1989. Also that year, Lumina appeared on the scene as Chevrolet's major mid-size vehicle line.

In the early 1990s, economic necessity dictated downsizing and reversed the trend of offering broad consumer choices. In 1992, General Motors reported plans to cut some big-car models and consolidate mid-sized models. In spring 1993, in a move that continued a trend of product portfolio reduction, General Motors management decided to cut 11 models from its automobile lineup for the 1994 model year. The divisions affected were Chevrolet, Pontiac, Buick, Oldsmobile, and Cadillac. At Chevrolet, a basic Corsica replaced a deluxe Corsica sedan, the Corsica LT.

At the same time, with the intention of making Chevrolet the dominant vehicle retailer in the United States, General Motors launched a new Camaro on March 29, 1993. The tagline in the teaser advertising was, "Coming soon. From the country that invented rock 'n' roll." Chevrolet donated a Camaro, autographed by numerous rock stars, to the Rock and Roll Hall of Fame and Museum in Cleveland, Ohio, to promote the launch.

Downsized or rightsized, bigger or subcompact, Chevrolet has proved its ability to gauge the heartbeat of American market demands. While General Motors looked for a way to return its North American operations to profitability in the 1990s, Chevrolet remained at the core of the marketing strategy. It will continue to remain at the core of the United States automotive industry for the foreseeable future.

Further Reading:

"'93 Camaro Advertising Arrives with a Rock 'n' Roll Beat," PR Newswire, March 29, 1993.

"The Chevrolet Story," Detroit: Chevrolet Media Productions, June 1987.

Connelly, Mary, "Camaro Joins Bid for Chevy Sales Lead," *Automotive News,* March 29, 1993, p. 3.

Frame, Phil, "GM to Trim Model Count for 1994," *Automotive News,* May 10, 1993, p. 1.

General Motors Annual Report, Detroit: General Motors Corporation, 1992.

Hurlbert, Jeffrey P., "Automotive News Insight," *Automotive News,* October 15, 1990, p. 29i.

Keebler, Jack, and Phil Frame, "GM Sharpens Platform Ax; Nothing Sacred in Downsizing," *Automotive News,* May 4, 1992, p. 1.

—by Dorothy Walton

CHEVROLET CORVETTE®

The Corvette, a high-performance, distinctly American sports car, has been igniting the passion of car enthusiasts since 1953. Over the years more than a million of these fiberglass two-seaters have been produced, making it the world's best-selling "true" sports car. Built by Chevrolet Motor Division, a division of General Motors Corporation (GM), the Corvette has been redesigned numerous times and has been available in both convertible (1953-75 and 1986—) and coupe (1963—) body styles. Although demand for two-seat sports cars had diminished by the mid-1990s, the Corvette remained the ultimate "dream machine" for many car lovers.

Brand Origins

The story of the Corvette truly begins during World War II, when many American GIs stationed in Europe first became acquainted with European cars. The European sports car, intended as much for pleasure as for transportation, was particularly exciting to American soldiers, and after the war some would even ship sports cars back to the United States. By 1950 a handful of small American companies were attempting to imitate the European sports car. The major American automakers, however, were in no hurry to produce their own, and General Motors was no exception.

The father of the Corvette is generally considered to be Harley J. Earl, founder and head of GM's Art and Colour Section, the company's in-house styling department. Earl had been thinking seriously about a low-priced sports car as early as 1951, working privately with a personal crew on his pet project. By mid-1952 Earl's staff had completed the basic design of the car that would soon be called the Corvette. Its name came from the sleek, fast submarine chaser and convoy-escort vehicle of World War II.

Richard Langworth, who wrote *The Complete Book of Corvette* with the auto editors of *Consumer Guide,* reported that Edward Cole, chief engineer of Chevrolet, literally "jumped up and down" upon seeing Earl's masterpiece for the first time. The company quickly came up with a prototype, which was unveiled for the public at the first Motorama of 1953, held at New York's Waldorf-Astoria hotel. "The gleaming Polo White show car, with its bright Sportsman Red interior, was a hands-down success at the 1953 Motorama," wrote Langworth. "Chevrolet was soon being pressured by inquiries from all over the country. When would it be produced, and how much would it cost?"

Production began in Flint, Michigan, on June 30, 1953. The suggested retail price was $3,513. "It was a grand accomplishment," wrote Langworth. "Corvette had made the transition from dream car to road car with remarkably few alterations and in an amazingly short time." The Corvette was one of the only show cars that went into production with its styling virtually intact—a fact that would continue to endear it to car enthusiasts.

While the 1953 Corvette was the darling of many enthusiasts, it was not without its critics. Some thought the design—with its rocketlike rear fins, dazzling vertical grille, and sunken headlights—was too gimmicky. Others complained that true sports cars did not have automatic transmission. The clip-in side windows were awkward to handle, and the only way to open the door from the outside was to reach inside for the release. "The first Corvette was a mixed bag indeed," Langworth wrote. Initial production was limited to a maximum of 300 for the balance of 1953. This policy gave Chevrolet time to address the various quality problems that surfaced, particularly as they related to its fiberglass-body construction.

Early Marketing Strategy

GM's early marketing plan for the Corvette was to restrict sales to VIPs, including mayors, celebrities, and business leaders. Movie star John Wayne drove a 1953 Corvette, as did singer Dinah Shore. Each of the eight Chevrolet wholesale regions was assigned a car to send from dealer to dealer for one- to two-day showings. Dealers were instructed to accept no firm orders for delivery of a Corvette in 1953.

This look-but-don't-touch attitude would prove to be a mistake. "VIPs and beautiful people didn't like the Corvette as much as Chevrolet had hoped and the suspicion that GM wasn't really serious about it likely deterred some prospects even in 1954 when the cars were available," according to *Corvette: America's Dream Machine,* a *Consumer Guide* special issue. The discontent was reflected in poor sales. Chevrolet had anticipated a 1954 sales volume of 12,000, but the year-end tally came to a mere 3,640. Rumors began circulating that the car's days were numbered.

The introduction of the Ford Thunderbird on September 23, 1954, changed all that. The Thunderbird—Ford's answer to GM's Corvette—fueled the rivalry between the two companies and helped to ensure the future of the sporty two-seater. In *The Com-*

AT A GLANCE

Chevrolet Corvette brand of automobile introduced in 1953 by Chevrolet, a division of General Motors Corporation; first models had a convertible body style (with removable hardtop); first coupe introduced in 1963; more than a million Corvettes were sold from 1953 to 1993.

Performance: *Sales*—20,639 units (1991).

Major competitor: Ferrari North America's Ferrari; also Jaguar Cars Inc.'s Jaguar, Porsche Cars North America Inc.'s Porsche, Chrysler Corp.'s Lamborghini, Maserati Automobiles Inc.'s Maserati.

Advertising: *Agency*—McCann-Erickson, New York, NY.

Addresses: *Parent company*—Chevrolet Motor Division, 30007 Van Dyke Avenue, Warren, MI 48090; phone: (313) 492-8841; fax: (313) 492-8855. *Ultimate parent company*—General Motors Corporation, 3044 W. Grand Boulevard, Detroit, MI 48202-3091; phone: (313) 556-1508; fax: (313) 556-9394.

plete Book of Corvette, Zora Arkus-Duntov, a Belgian-born engineer with GM's research and development staff who had been tinkering with the Corvette in his spare time, recalled the mind-set of the company at the time: "There were conversations . . . about the Corvette being dropped. Then the Thunderbird came out and all of a sudden GM was keeping the Corvette. I think Ford brought out the competitive spirit in Ed Cole."

The Thunderbird presented a big challenge for GM. For one thing, it outsold Corvette for model year 1955 by a ratio of 23 to 1. It also had greater appeal as a "personal" car. Langworth, in *The Complete Book of Corvette,* described the 1955 Thunderbird as "a handsome, comfortable, steel-bodied boulevardier with amenities like roll-up windows and a V-8 engine." A team that included Earl, Cole, and Arkus-Duntov went to work immediately on transforming the awkward two-seater into a serious sports car.

Brand Development

The second-generation Corvette (1956-57) was a vast improvement over the original and was considered by many to be the epitome of Corvette styling. "Compared to its slab-sided, 'plastic bathtub' predecessor, the '56 Corvette was stunning," wrote the auto editors of *Consumer Guide* in *Great Cars of the Fifties.* "GM design director Harley Earl came up with a fresh new styling that was tasteful in an age of garishness, yet sexy, low-slung and distinctly American." The '56 got new seats, standard roll-up glass, an optional lift-off hardtop, and distinctive body-side concavities called coves. Duntov reworked the chassis, improving steering response and handling, and added Chevrolet's powerful 265-cubic-inch V-8. Designed by Cole and offered as an option on '55 models, the engine was now standard. The '56 Corvette could reach 60 m.p.h. in 7.5 seconds and a top speed of 120 m.p.h.

The car received overwhelmingly favorable reviews in auto-enthusiast magazines. Karl Ludvigsen, writing in *Sports Car Illustrated,* compared the Corvette to the Jaguar and the Austin-Healey. "It is in the handling department that the Corvette proves itself the only true American production sports car," he wrote.

Corvette styling did not change in 1957, but the engine was made even more powerful. The car could now go from 0-60 miles per hour in 5.7 seconds and reach a maximum of 135 mph. Production rose from just 700 units in 1955 to 3,467 in 1956 and 6,339 in 1957. Still, the Corvette was not making money for GM.

Duntov believed that the car's race-winning ability was the key to improving sales. A specially prepped '56 Corvette had made an impressive run of 150.583 mph at Daytona Speed Weeks. Another finished 9th in the 1956 Sebring 12-Hours. At Sebring '57 Corvettes finished 12th and 15th overall, and Corvettes took the 1st and 4th places at the '57 Nassau Speed Weeks. Corvette was finally being taken seriously by the sports-car industry. "Before Sebring," said one European writer who was quoted in *Corvette: America's Dream Machine,* "it was regarded as a plastic toy. After Sebring, even the most biased was forced to admit that the Americans had one of the world's finest sports cars—as capable on the track as it was on the road."

The 1958-62 Corvette has long been criticized for its gaudy, overblown design. "For years, the third generation Corvette was hooted at for being a hokier, heftier version of the glorious 1956-57 design—which in essence it was," according to *Corvette: America's Dream Machine.* "Lately, though, the 1958-62 models have deservedly gained in stature, not the least for accomplishing the shift from all-out sports car to civilized gran turismo, which was the only way Corvette could become a lasting commercial success." The car sported simulated hood louvers, dummy air scoops flanking the grille, and lots of chrome, including chrome "windsplits in the body coves and chrome bars down the trunklid." Writer Karl Ludvigsen noted, "If the objective was, as one designer said at the time, to make the Corvette look like a Cadillac, that aim was certainly achieved." There were, however, some definite improvements in the third generation Corvette. A new dash, for example, put nearly every instrument right before the driver, and the car was a top performer, with a rerun of its '57 engine lineup. "Again topping the list was the high-compression, Duntov-cam 283 'fuelie' with a now official 290 horsepower at 6200 rpm [revolutions per minute]," according to *Corvette: America's Dream Machine.* Production for the 1958 model year hit 9,168 units, making the Corvette profitable for the first time.

One of the first 300 Chevrolet Corvettes, all of which were polo white with red vinyl interiors and built by hand in Flint, Michigan.

By 1963 Chevrolet was ready to introduce an all-new Corvette—the so-called Sting Ray. Based on GM design chief Bill Mitchell's Stingray Special racer, it was a huge success. "The

Sting Ray hit the American sports car market like a thunderclap, reminiscent of the knock-'em-dead debut of the Jaguar E-Type two years previously,'' wrote Langworth. ''For the first time in its history, the Corvette was a sell-out success—so much so that the St. Louis factory had to hire a second shift and it still couldn't begin to supply cars rapidly enough.'' Production for model year 1963 was 21,513—50 percent higher than the year before. The car—part of the fourth generation Corvette, which spanned four model years—had distinctive styling, speed, and agility. Many enthusiasts consider it to be the best Corvette ever produced. With its humped fenders, sleek hood design, and concealed headlamps, the car's design owed little to the cars that came before. In 1963 a coupe was introduced, featuring a controversial split rear window. Duntov, among others, did not like it because it hindered rear visibility. Highly prized by collectors, it lasted only one year.

For its fifth generation (1968-77) Corvette got a radical redesign based on the styling of the Mako Shark II show car. Like the 1958 Corvette that followed the highly respected second-generation design, the 1968 car was something of a disappointment to Corvette lovers. ''After the lean and lovely Sting Ray, it hardly seemed to be the great leap forward that had been expected,'' according to *Corvette: America's Dream Machine.* The book characterized the car as a compromise: ''The graceful Sting Ray rebodied into a hulky 'Shark'—not a smooth, sporty GT but a begadgeted boulevard blaster.'' The new headlamps had a pop-up design, and the coupe featured T-top removable roof panels. The battery was moved from the engine compartment to a separate compartment behind the seats. The chassis and powerteams were essentially the same as those of the last Sting Ray, except for the addition of three-speed Turbo Hydra-Matic transmission. While the fifth-generation Corvette was not without its critics, the car continued to prosper. Production climbed to a record 49,213 units in 1977.

In 1978 Corvette celebrated its 25th anniversary with the historic rollout of the Silver Anniversary 1978 models. Since Chevrolet did not have an all-new Corvette ready for the occasion, it modified the existing car with a fastback roofline and a wide, wraparound rear backlight. A silver anniversary badge replaced the traditional crossed-flags emblem, and a special Indianapolis-500-pace-car replica was offered. Wide, low-profile 60-series tires were offered for the first time. Overall, the fifth-generation design changed little.

The sixth-generation Corvette, introduced in 1984, was eagerly anticipated because it was the first truly new Corvette in 15 years. The car received rave reviews in the media. *Consumer Guide* called the '84 Corvette ''a world class sports car with few rivals in performance.'' Compared with the 1982 model, the new car was 1.1 inches lower and 8.8 inches shorter overall. Its wind-tunnel-tuned shape carried a drag coefficient of 0.34—24 percent more aerodynamic than its predecessor. A 5.7-liter V-8 provided the power. Even so, Corvette sales dropped under 40,000 units in 1985, in part because of a $3,000 price increase, and sales dipped even further the following year to about 35,000. While the motoring press praised the '88 Corvette, the sales downturn continued with production dropping to 22,789.

Model year 1990 saw the introduction of the much-awaited RPO ZR-1, conceived by Corvette as the world's fastest production car. Originally announced for 1989, it was delayed a year because of last-minute engine problems. ''When it did hit, this new SuperVette quickly became one of America's most sought-after possessions,'' according to *Corvette: America's Dream Machine.* Available only for coupes, the ZR-1 option featured an all-aluminum, 32-valve, 5.7-liter V-8 engine that developed 375 horsepower at 5,800 RPM. The all-new engine had dual overhead camshafts for each cylinder bank and a unique dual-power mode that allowed the driver to limit the power output with a valet key in the cockpit.

In 1991 Corvette got its first major restyling since 1984. All Corvettes received the convex tail panel and square tail lamps previously reserved for the ZR-1. New side ''gills,'' wider body-color side moldings, and updated emblems were also featured. Despite the many advancements, sales continued to slide as they had since 1985. According to *Corvette: America's Dream Machine,* the decline did not signify that America had lost interest in its dream car: ''This testifies less to discontent in the sixth generation's innate quality than to the diminishing demand for the two-seaters in general plus price pressure that has forced the relatively old-fashioned Corvette to compete against newer, more exotic machinery.''

The one-millionth Corvette, a white convertible with red interior to match the first Corvette, was produced on July 2, 1992, at Corvette's assembly plant in Bowling Green, Kentucky. The technology that set the 1992 Corvette apart from other sports cars was its 350-cubic-inch V-8, a sophisticated traction-control system, and new high-performance Goodyear tires.

International Appeal

While the Corvette has always been best known and most widely revered in the United States, it has gained the respect of enthusiasts everywhere. ''Corvette has been called the American dream machine, but its appeal is international,'' Chevrolet general manager Jim Perkins was quoted as saying in a Chevrolet press release. ''For every American kid who grew up aspiring to own and drive a Corvette, there's another with the same aspirations in Zurich or Frankfort or Osaka.''

More Corvettes have been built than any other single sports car in automotive history. They have been sold throughout North America, Europe, the Middle East, and Japan, and there are more than 600 Corvette owner clubs around the world. Corvette's Bowling Green assembly plant has become an international magnet for Corvette enthusiasts. More than 60,000 visitors are welcomed for tours each year.

The car has a colorful racing history dating back to 1955, when Arkus-Duntov averaged 150.583 mph at the Daytona Flying Mile Speed Trials. By the late 1950s America's sports car, with big wins at several important motor sports events, had won the respect of competitors on the international racing circuit.

Brand Outlook

After more than four decades—and production of more than one million cars—the Corvette remained a dream car for thousands of enthusiasts. *Corvette: America's Dream Machine* predicted the car would have a vigorous future and continue to be a symbol of advanced automotive technology. ''America's sports car has always stood for change: change that advances the state of automotive art, change that's exciting and enriching for everyone who loves to drive. We suspect this will be no less true of the next Corvette and the ones to follow than it's been for all the Corvettes that have come before—and that's as it should be.''

Further Reading:

"All Wheels to Steer Running Prototype," *Machine Design,* March 20, 1986, pp. 2–4.

Auto editors of *Consumer Guide, Great Cars of the Fifties,* Skokie, Illinois: Publications International, Ltd, 1985.

Auto editors of *Consumer Guide, Corvette: America's Dream Machine,* Skokie, Illinois: Publications International, Ltd, 1991.

Auto editors of *Consumer Guide* and Richard M. Langworth, *The Complete Book of Corvette,* New York: Beekman House, 1987.

Bergstrom, Robin P., "Everybody Knows It's Coming," *Production,* December, 1989, p. 62.

Brooke, Lindsay, "Callaway Engineering: The Rapid Deployment Yankees," *Automotive Industries,* September 1986, pp. 76–77.

Brooke, Lindsay, "Mercury Builds a Chevy," *Automotive Industries,* January 1989, pp. 41–44.

"Corvette Debuts Experimental Paint," *Machine Design,* August 21, 1986, p. 2.

Falconer, Thomas, *Chevrolet Corvette,* London: Osprey Publishing Limited, 1983.

Flax, Arthur, "Innovations Speed New Vette V-8 Into Production," *Automotive News,* November 14, 1988, p. 24.

General Motors Annual Report 1992, Detroit: General Motors Corporation.

Johnson, Richard, "ZF Has Vette 6-Speed, Seeks More U.S. Work," *Automotive News,* June 13, 1988, p. 31.

Marshall, Stuart, "Corvette Flies Like an Eagle," *Modern Tire Dealer,* May 1989, pp. 49–50.

McElroy, John, "GM's First Lotus Blossom Active Suspension Corvette," *Automotive Industries,* September 1986, pp. 106–110.

McElroy, John, "Killing the Performance Comeback," *Automotive Industries,* October 1988, p. 6.

World's Greatest Brands, New York: Wiley & Sons, 1992.

—Pam Berry

CHRIS-CRAFT®

Chris-Craft, marketed by OMC Recreational Boat Group, is the most venerable name in the powerboating industry, synonymous with quality and craftsmanship. Christopher Columbus Smith, who built the first Chris-Craft boats in the late nineteenth century, was a pioneer in the development of motorboats and motorboating. His company became the foremost innovator and leader in the motorboat industry, developing leisure boating to the point where many Americans could afford to buy a boat and explore the beautiful waterways of the United States and the world, a pleasure formerly reserved for the wealthy.

Brand Origins

The brand name Chris-Craft originated along the wooded shore of the Great Lakes, fifty miles northeast of Detroit, Michigan. Christopher Columbus Smith was one of six children, born at the onset of the Civil War into a family whose livelihood depended on hunting and fishing. The future genius of boatbuilding received little formal education, and early on in life took to hunting and fishing with his brother in the Michigan wilderness. His first foray into building boats was constructing simple duck boats with his brother. Duck hunting was an important source of income, and the two usually sold between 700 and 800 ducks per week on the Detroit market.

In addition to hunting, another important sideline was serving as guides to wealthy businessmen, who arrived in the backwoods from Detroit and even farther off to hunt and fish. Some of these men so admired the simple duckboats of the Smith brothers that they started buying them. By 1884, Christopher Columbus Smith, together with his brother, had established the first boathouse in the town of Algonac, on the St. Clair River. The name "Chris-Craft," taken from Christopher Smith's first name, would not become official until the mid-1920s, some forty years later.

First Commercial Success

Hunting, fishing, and guide activities increasingly were relegated to second place as Chris Smith's boathouse enterprise took off. While he and his brother were partners, it was Chris Smith who showed both entrepreneurial talent and an innate gift for craftsmanship. The Detroit market for his boats—from duck boats to canoes, sailboats, and heavy launches (the utility boats of the day)—could barely be satisfied. By the turn of the century, naphtha engines were powering small boats, and with the development of the carburetor, gasoline motors theoretically could do the same. Chris Smith would develop the lightest gas engine in the world.

By the early 1900s, Chris Smith was solely in charge of his bustling boat business. In 1910, a fateful meeting with the gambler John Ryan turned into an unusual partnership. Encouraged by his flamboyant partner, Chris Smith set forth to develop the fastest motor boat in the country, to satisfy Ryan's yearning to have the raciest speedboats in the country. In that same year, Smith launched the *Reliance I,* a gasoline powered motorboat that could speed across the water at the unheard of rate of 31 miles per hour. It was followed by the even faster *Reliance II.* Word quickly spread of these powerful new speedboats and soon Chris Smith's renamed company, the Smith Ryan Boat Company, could not turn them out fast enough. The market had spread by then far beyond Michigan.

Early Marketing Strategy

Chris Smith capitalized on his success by entering major boat shows all over the country, as well important boat races. By 1915, Smith-made boats had won Gold Cup trophies three years in a row. This gave Chris Smith's newest motorboat models high visibility, enabling him to sell them all over the country. Soon the Algonac boathouse was churning out one motorboat every five weeks, and employing fifty men.

The unlettered Chris Smith did not shy away from the printed word; in fact, he introduced one innovation, the printed brochure, complete with the advertising slogan, "They're boats to be proud of!" For decades thereafter, brochures explained the latest product innovations, at the same time spreading the word about new Chris-Craft models.

Perhaps because of his proximity to Detroit and the auto manufacturing industry, Chris Smith was much impressed with the assembly line method of production. His was the only boat company in the business that adopted this method successfully, right before World War I, instead of following the time honored method of handcrafting each boat. As a result of this innovative production strategy, Smith's company could keep up with the demand for motorboats by turning out the unheard of quantity of one boat every other day. In the 1920s, after winning the most prestigious boat racing award in the world, the British Harmsworth cup, in 1919, Chris Smith's renamed Chris Smith &

AT A GLANCE

Chris-Craft boats first made in 1874 by hunter and woodsman Christopher Columbus Smith, who went on to found his own boathouse in 1884 in Algonac, MI; became the Smith Ryan Boat Company, c. 1912; renamed Chris Smith & Sons Boat Company, 1919; renamed Chris-Craft Corporation, 1930; in 1961 Chris-Craft boat building assets passed out of the Smith family's ownership to NAFI Corporation, which in turn sold Chris-Craft to Florida investor G. Dale Murray in 1981; renamed Murray Chris-Craft; Outboard Marine Corporation of Waukegan, IL, purchased certain of the Chris-Craft boat building assets in a bankruptcy proceeding in Florida; Chris-Craft is a registered trademark of Chris Craft Industries, Inc., and is licensed to Outboard Marine Corporation.

Performance: *Market share*—5% of U.S. powerboat category (1992). *Sales*—$45 million (1992).

Major competitor: Brunswick Corp.'s brand of boats.

Advertising: *Agency*—In-house. *Major campaign*—"Created to Raise Your Expectations As Well As Your Heartbeat."

Addresses: *Parent company*—OMC Recreational Boat Group, 8161 15 St. E., Sarasota, FL 34243; phone: (813) 351-4900; fax: (813) 351-8974. *Ultimate parent company*—Outboard Marine Corporation, 100 Sea Horse Drive, Waukegan, IL 60085; phone: (708) 689-6200; fax: (708) 689-5789.

Sons Boat Company took off: from only 24 boats in 1922, the company produced 946 by 1929.

By 1927, the boat company did not hesitate running full-page ads in magazines and had engaged a full time director of marketing, John E. Clifford. Quitting his job in the auto industry, Clifford utilized his first-hand knowledge of the car business to the advantage of the Chris-Craft brand (as the boats were then called) by greatly expanding the number of Chris-Craft dealerships, as though they were car agencies. One of the catchiest advertising slogans in the late 1920s was Clifford's "Anyone who can drive a car can drive a Chris-Craft." During the tough Depression years, this slogan changed to "Driving a Chris-Craft is easier than driving a car." Finally, it was under Clifford that the company introduced payment by credit, or "12-month deferred credit," as one ad trumpeted. These stratagems worked so well that by 1930, Chris-Craft boats were the best-selling motorboats in the world.

A unique marketing strategy during the 1950s was the introduction of Chris-Craft Boat Kits. Selling for as low as $39, any boy could assemble his own rowboat in 8 to 10 hours. So popular were these kits that fifteen years after they stopped selling them in 1958, the company was still receiving inquiries about them. Not only did this encourage the future consumer of boats, but such kits (many were more elaborate than mere rowboats) could be sold in a variety of stores, as in a hardware or lumber store, and not only in boat dealerships.

Advertising

Despite the beautiful craftsmanship of Chris Smith's mahogany boats, he could not have built up from scratch a boating empire without heavy reliance on advertising, beginning with displaying his boats at boat shows and entering them into boat races. Slogans were important in imprinting the brand's name on people's memories. Under sales manager Clifford, ads not only became more professional, they stopped being limited just to boating magazines. Clifford realized that the market for boats was the increasingly large and affluent middle class, who tended to read such publications as *Harper's Bazaar, Town & Country, Vanity Fair, The Saturday Evening Post,* and even *Literary Digest.* When credit buying was introduced in the 1920s, Clifford's ads rammed home the fact that now anyone with any income could afford his own Chris-Craft. Under him, Chris-Craft's advertising budget reached a quarter of a million dollars, huge for that era.

Chris-Craft boats were marketed to men, but women were not entirely discounted in Chris-Craft advertising before and after World War I. Ads emphasized the "amenities of home" found on Chris-Craft cruisers, some of which came with bedding, furniture, and dishes. Photographs featuring celebrities in Chris-Craft boats, such as Thomas Edison and Harvey Firestone in the 1920s, and Franklin Roosevelt in the 1930s, became an important advertising ploy. During World War II, when there was no lack of government contracts, ads cleverly linked Chris-Craft with doing one's duty to one's country: "Buy U.S. War Bonds Today—Tomorrow Command Your Own Chris-Craft!" Chris-Craft continues to be advertised in magazines, the primary advertising venue for all Chris-Craft boats, along with the time-honored racing events and boat shows.

Product Development

The fertile genius of Chris Smith would never rest content with only one or two products. His creativity found expression in innovative boating products, from the lightest gasoline engines to the hydroplane, that would make his company the world leader in the leisure boat industry. As long ago as 1940, a year after his death, there were 98 different models of Chris-Craft boats, including luxury cruisers ranging from 25 to 48 feet in length, utility runabouts, small motorboats, and motor yachts.

Even before Chris Smith and his brother established their boathouse on the St. Clair River in Algonac, they built a variety of different boats, but Chris Smith's real contribution to the boating world was the perfection of the motor boat and the development of the hydroplane. Without any knowledge of the theory of hydroplaning, Chris Smith designed and produced a hydroplane boat, inspired in part by his observation of water bugs skidding on water, rather than swimming in it. The world's first viable hydroplane boat, the *Reliance III,* emanated from his boat house before World War I, as did the *Reliance II* (at fifty miles an hour, the world's fastest motorboat), and the world's lightest gasoline engine. In 1920, the *Miss America I* became the fastest motorboat in the world, averaging nearly 77 miles per hour.

Chris-Craft yachts became ever more luxurious, sporting furnished sleeping cabins and—a Chris-Craft innovation—a private lavatory on board. In the mid-1930s, houseboats appeared, touted as the alternative to the weekend home in the country. Chris-Craft responded to the Depression by coming out with the "utility boat," which was a cheaper, smaller version of the runabout which never sold up to company expectations. During World War II, Chris-Craft manufactured a variety of products for the war effort, especially engines and landing boats; in fact, the first landing boat to hit the beach in Normandy on D-Day in 1944 was manufactured by Chris-Craft. At the same time, limited production of civilian pleasure boats was maintained.

During the 1950s, the company decided to manufacture mahogany skis, furniture, small, land-based mobile homes, and the famous Chris-Craft Kits, primarily aimed at young boys, although as these kits grew more elaborate, adults also were targeted. Manufacturing outboard motors became a new endeavor, as were specialty boats for the U.S. Navy during the Korean War. The most innovative step taken during the 1950s was the decision to begin the manufacture of fiberglass boats. By 1957, Chris-Craft had turned out the first all-fiberglass boat in the world. Chris-Craft discontinued the manufacture of the famous all-mahogany boats in 1968; just a few years later, they had become collector's items. At the same time that Chris-Craft turned to the manufacture of fiberglass boats, new and inexpensive plywood runabouts came on the market, and proved very popular.

With the sale of Chris-Craft to the NAFI Corporation in 1960, the largest small boat manufacturing concern in the world was, for the first time in its history, no longer run by the Smith family. While product developments in sporting, fishing, racing and recreational vehicles continued apace, Chris-Craft declined financially for several years. Nonetheless, an entirely new line of Chris-Craft fiberglass sailboats came out in the early 1960s, followed in 1964 by the first all-fiberglass cruisers, and in 1969 by the world's largest fiberglass yacht, the 60-foot Chris-Craft Commander Motor Yacht. In the late 1970s, Chris-Craft began installing the world's most up-to-date, sophisticated electronic displays in its large motorboats.

Despite rising fuel costs and interest rates, Chris-Craft remained the pacesetter in the boating world into the 1980s. Chris-Craft changed hands again in 1981, when in was purchased by Florida investor G. Dale Murray and renamed Murray Chris-Craft Co. The Outboard Marine Corporation (OMC), a leading manufacturer of outboard engines and boats based in Waukegan, Illinois, purchased Chris-Craft in 1989 for $58 million.

Entering a Second Century of Growth

Chris-Craft boats are sold in the United States and around the world, especially in Western Europe, Canada, the Far East, and Latin America. As far back as 1929, Chris-Craft's reputation for speed and craftsmanship was so widespread that the boats were being sold to thirty countries, and 15 percent of the sales of Chris-Craft came from abroad.

After Chris-Craft was sold to NAFI in 1961, the new management established a Chris-Craft subsidiary in Lausanne, Switzerland, an Italian subsidiary, and a Canadian subsidiary. By 1965, Chris-Craft boats were being manufactured in eleven facilities in three countries.

The leisure boat industry felt the effects of an international recession in the late 1980s and early 1990s, as consumers curtailed luxury spending and some governments increased revenues by placing a 10 percent luxury tax on boats over $100,000. Long term trends point to a healthy growth in the leisure boat industry in the twenty-first century, however, especially considering that the most important market for recreational boats, 35- to 55-year-old people, is the fastest growing in the United States. With an excellent distribution system worldwide, Chris-Craft can only benefit from the fall of international trade barriers, economic growth in Russia and Eastern Europe, and the worldwide trend toward consumer spending.

Further Reading:

Burns, Susan, "Outboard Marine: The Marine Giant That Bought Donzi and Chris-Craft," *Sarasota Magazine,* April, 1989, p. 101.

DeGeorge, Gail, "Did Irv Jacobs Sandbag Outboard Marine? It Won a Wild Auction for Chris-Craft—With a $58 Million Bid," *Business Week,* February 20, 1989, p. 38.

Egger, B. D., "Outboard Marine Corporation—Company Report," *First Boston Corporation,* February 22, 1993.

Henschen, Doug, "OMC Ousts Winn, Appoints Keim as Boat Group President," *Boating Industry,* June, 1993, p. 9.

Klaus, Krista Martin, "Boating Manufacturers Stay Afloat," *Tribune Business Weekly,* April 14, 1993, Sec. 1, p. 1.

Outboard Marine Corp., *Annual Report,* Waukegan, IL: Outboard Marine Corp., 1992.

Rodengen, Jeffrey L., *The Legend of Chris-Craft,* Fort Lauderdale: Write Stuff Syndicate, 1988.

Taylor, John, "Scrambling to Win His Biggest Gamble," *Florida Trend,* June, 1987, p. 54.

Unger, Michael, "Grumman Corporation Sells Boat-Building Division," *Newsday,* March 21, 1990, p. 49.

—Sina Dubovoj

COLEMAN®

The Coleman name, held by Coleman Company, Inc., has dominated the recreational products market for more than half a century. For many consumers, the red Coleman label is a symbol of quality and sturdy reliability, a reputation that has been carefully cultivated since the first Coleman products appeared at the beginning of the twentieth century. Early in its history, the Coleman corporate credo was ''Every product sold must be the best of its kind,'' and Coleman products have consistently been rated at or near the top in consumer surveys.

W. C. Coleman Saw the Light

William Coffin (W. C.) Coleman was a nearsighted typewriter salesman who, while passing through Brockton, Alabama, saw a brilliant light coming from a drugstore window. He appreciated the bright light emanating from the lamp, under which he could see clearly enough to read. W. C. quickly contacted the owner of the Efficient lamp, which turned out to be the Irby-Gilliand Company of Memphis, Tennessee. He bought samples of the Efficient lamp and traveled to Kingfisher, in the Oklahoma Territory, arriving there on January 1, 1900. At that time, many parts of the United States, especially rural areas, were not yet serviced by electricity. Lamps and lanterns had to be used, and they were virtually all fueled with coal oil.

The Efficient lamp, manufactured by the Edward Miller Company, of Meridien, Connecticut, was different from other lamps: it burned gasoline. Air was pumped into its reservoir, and after a valve was opened, air pressure forced the fuel into the generator. The fuel was vaporized after the generator was heated with a small alcohol torch, and the vapor passed through a tiny opening into the burner, where it mixed with air and ignited. The heat thus produced caused the mantles to glow. Mantles, part of the secret of the lamp's bright light, were made of a loosely woven fabric that was saturated with mineral salts.

W. C. Coleman encountered stiff resistance to the newfangled lamp. He soon discovered that a traveling lamp salesman had passed through Kingfisher some months before, leaving many nonfunctioning lamps and dissatisfied customers in his wake. Coleman, his small savings invested in the lamps he could not sell, came upon a novel solution: he decided that since he could not sell the lamps, he would sell the light they produced. He leased the lamps for $1 a week. Coleman serviced them himself, and if the lamps did not work, the customer would not be obliged to pay. The tactic worked, and business flourished. Within a month, Coleman had formed the Hydro-Carbon Light Company and soon expanded his service into nearby towns. Moving the business in 1901 to Wichita, Kansas, he purchased the patent for the Efficient lamp, altered the design, and renamed it the Coleman Arc Lamp.

From the beginning, W. C. Coleman stressed the importance of customer satisfaction and promoting a quality product. It is said that his business credos were ''Every Coleman product must be the best of its kind'' and ''Nothing is really sold until it is delivering satisfactory service for the user.'' To advertise his lamps, Coleman strung them up at fairs and carnivals, water festivals, and reunions. An early promotional ploy carried out on October 6, 1905, involved Coleman Arc Lamps being hung from tall poles, providing light for the first night football game. The winning team was Fairmount College, now Wichita State University.

In 1908, after tinkering with the Arc Lamp, W. C. Coleman created the Coleman table lamp and received a patent for it the following year. The table lamp, known as the Coleman Model R (for reading), had many advantages over the Arc Lamp. It was portable, and the fact that it had bug screens meant it was practical for taking outside, an especially useful feature in rural areas.

In 1912 the Hydro-Carbon Light Company became the Coleman Lamp Company. Coleman continued to expand his service, which became known as Coleman System Lighting. A central supply tank fed fuel to the light fixtures of service subscribers—mainly commercial enterprises, churches, and meeting halls. The fixtures, hung from the ceiling or attached to a wall, were fed fuel via a small copper tube. Coleman System Lighting continued until 1927, when the spread of electricity service supplanted the need for it.

The First Coleman Lantern

In 1914 W. C. Coleman introduced the Coleman lantern, one of the most enduringly popular products in the United States. After the country entered World War I, the Coleman lantern was listed as an essential product, and over a period of four years, more than one million lanterns were produced and distributed to farmers. Coleman continued to revise and update his two basic products, the lamp and the lantern.

AT A GLANCE

Coleman brand of camping and outdoor equipment founded in 1900 by William Coffin (W. C.) Coleman, owner of the Hydro-Carbon Light Company of Kingfisher, Oklahoma Territory; renamed Coleman Lamp Company, 1912; became Coleman Company, Inc., 1945; company was privately held between March, 1989, and February, 1992.

Performance: *Sales*—(Recreation goods) $394.7 million.

Major competitor: In coolers: Igloo; also, Thermos.

Advertising: *Agency*—Sullivan Higdon & Sink, Wichita, KS. *Major campaign*—True stories highlighting Coleman's durability and the tag line "Unbelievably tough."

Addresses: *Parent company*—Coleman Company, Inc., 250 N. St. Francis St., Wichita, KS 67202; phone: (316) 261-3485.

Coleman also persisted with expansion and diversification, multiplying his line of products and broadening his market. In 1920 Coleman opened a manufacturing facility in Toronto, Canada, and used the capital city as the base for his international operations, taking advantage of the tariffs and duties that Canada enjoyed as a member of the British Commonwealth. In addition, as the steady progress of rural electrification slowly changed the nature of Coleman's business, he introduced in 1920 a line of housewares, including electric irons, coffee percolators, toasters, and waffle irons. The company, however, proved ill-prepared to compete with such powerhouses as General Electric and Westinghouse, and the housewares were eventually discontinued. It was in 1923 that Coleman introduced its first camp stove.

As the grip of the Great Depression took hold in the early 1930s, the rural market upon which Coleman depended withered. Also, President Franklin Roosevelt's rural electrification program greatly expanded the reach of electricity. Coleman began to seek still other products to fill the gap. The company began to produce oil space heaters—which were seen as replacements for the wood and coal heaters then used—and gas floor furnaces—which were powered with natural gas. By the end of the decade, the company was the largest manufacturer of oil heaters and gas floor furnaces

The War Effort

After the U.S. entered World War II, production of civilian goods ceased, and the Coleman Lamp Company contributed to the war effort by producing a lantern as well as bomber parts, projectiles, and other items. But the Coleman product that gained the most fame was the GI pocket stove. The army had requested that Coleman design a compact stove that could survive battle conditions. After two months of around-the-clock trials, the company produced a stove smaller than a quart milk bottle and weighing three-and-a-half pounds. It operated at temperatures ranging from -60 degrees to 150 degrees Fahrenheit. Wartime correspondent Ernie Pyle wrote 15 articles for his syndicated newspaper column hailing the Coleman pocket stove.

The Coleman Lamp Company—which had been taken over in 1941 by Sheldon Coleman, W. C.'s son—became the Coleman Co., Inc., in 1945 and resumed its civilian business after the war. By the early 1950s, the business was divided between oil space heaters and gas floor furnaces (each 30 percent of total sales), military contracts (20 percent), and gas lanterns and camp stoves (20 percent). Due to a rapidly changing market, by 1960 oil heater and gas floor furnace demand had dropped by 85 percent. By that time Coleman had largely discontinued defense production. Over the space of a decade, Coleman had seen its markets shrink by 70 percent.

Coleman Changed Focus

Coleman urgently set about finding new markets, deciding to plunge headlong into the recreational goods business and produce portable insulated coolers and jugs. By 1963 coolers, camp stoves, lanterns, and jugs accounted for 40 percent of sales. Coleman also started manufacturing gas, oil, and electric furnaces as well as air conditioners for mobile homes. Its strength, however, was the outdoor goods market, and by 1966 over half of the company's $53.8 million in sales were from those products.

As more and more families spent their vacations outdoors, the recreational products market continued to expand. Beginning in the early 1960s, Coleman started to acquire manufacturers of such items as sleeping bags and tents (1965) and camping trailers (1966). As the company grew, its sales climbed from $38 million in 1960 to $134 million in 1970, with net profit rising from $278,000 to over $7 million.

Coleman continued its expansion throughout the 1970s. By 1976 sales had reached $235 million, and the company produced from 20,000 to 23,000 recreational products daily. Although it completely dominated the market in gasoline lanterns and stoves (more than 50 percent of the propane-burning stoves in use in 1977 were Coleman's), it faced stiffer competition in the insulated cooler and jug market, as well with the newer products it manufactured. In 1976 Coleman Company, Inc., began making canoes; the next year it started to produce backpacking equipment.

Coleman acquired the makers of Hobie-Cat sailboats and O'Brien water skis in 1976. The company decided to stay away from the golf market since most golfing items were sold in pro shops and Coleman depended on the mass merchandisers. Also, citing a fragmented and unprofitable market, the company steered away from fishing equipment, seeking only to enter markets where it could play a major role. "If we can't win leadership, we get out or extend the line or come up with a new product," Sheldon Coleman remarked in *Advertising Age*.

The consumer Coleman targeted was between 18 and 49 years old, with an income of $12,000 to $25,000—"high blue collar." Most of the outdoor goods that Coleman produced were sold by mass merchandisers, with 40 percent of its business from discount stores (Kmart was its largest account), 30 percent from such stores as Sears and J.C. Penney, and 30 percent from sporting goods stores. Television commercials sold camping as much as Coleman products. One spot featured a mother on a camping trip saying, "Go camping? 'Not this gal,' I used to say," and then, "I'm glad they talked me into it."

By 1983 the outing goods segment of Coleman Company, Inc., accounted for 73 percent of sales. Its lanterns and stoves were number one in their markets, and the Coleman name led the pack in canoes, camping trailers, coolers, and jugs. Continuing to acquire recreational goods manufacturers, in the early 1980s, the company bought makers of ski boats, archery equipment, diving equipment, and other goods. By 1985, though, a lull in camping goods sales led to a difficult year and the decision to reorganize. In 1987 Coleman sold its Alpha International wind surfing segment and put its Hobie-Cat, Holder sailboat, and Golden Eagle Archery units up for sale. The company, also deciding to discontinue the manufacture of tents, reorganized, closing at least one factory and restructuring administration.

Wall Street Invades Wichita

While still serving as co-chairman of Coleman Company, Sheldon Coleman died in 1988 and was succeeded by his son Sheldon. In early 1989, Sheldon C. Coleman put forth the idea of taking Coleman private for a price of $64 a share. About a month later the company was acquired by Wall Street financier Ronald O. Perelman for $74 a share, a purchase that set back Perelman's firm of MacAndrews & Forbes Holdings, Inc., $545 million. Sheldon Coleman left the company in June of 1989.

Under Perelman, Coleman Company, Inc., ceased its production of camping trailers, sailboats, and other assorted items but continued to produce the outdoor equipment for which it was famous, including the distribution once again of tents. Administrative costs were cut, more factories were shut down, and new equipment was installed. Advertising and marketing expenditures were increased, climbing from $10.7 million in 1988 to $21.6 million in 1992. Coleman saw its international sales grow 56 percent to $74 million between 1989 and 1991.

In February of 1992 Coleman went public again, and the sale had investors eager to purchase shares. Some saw the 1990s as a time when more people than ever before would partake in outdoor activities such as camping. "People are getting into camping, and that's a trend that Wall Street can relate to, because just about everybody here has a Coleman product in their basement," a New York market analyst was quoted as saying in the *Wall Street Journal.* Earnings from the stock offering went toward alleviating the debt associated with the leveraged buyout of 1989. Coleman's revenues in 1992 were $491.9 million.

Further Reading:

"A Brief History of the Origin and Use of Coleman Lamps and Lanterns," Wichita, KS: Coleman Company, Inc., 1980.

"Coleman, Fishing Brands Gain Prominence," *Discount Store News,* October 7, 1991, p. 77.

Coleman, Sheldon, and Lawrence M. Jones, *The Coleman Story: The Ability to Cope with Change,* New York: Newcomen Society, 1976.

Coleman Company, Inc., Annual Reports, Wichita: Coleman Company, Inc., 1987, 1992.

"Coleman Reaps Mounting Benefits from Massive Corporate Overhaul," *Barron's,* March 11, 1963, p. 20.

"Coleman Turns the Corner," *Financial World,* April 3, 1963, p. 9.

"Damn the Mosquitoes—Full Speed Ahead," *Forbes,* September 4, 1978, p. 59.

Helliker, Kevin, "Coleman Moves to Offer Public a Stake of 16%," *Wall Street Journal,* February 26, 1992, p. A4.

Marshall, Christy, "Coleman Thrives on Outdoor Life," *Advertising Age,* June 27, 1977, p. 3.

Merchandising the Outdoors," *Business Week,* May 22, 1971, p. 69.

Rubin, Lauren R., "Coleman Co.," *Barron's,* July 25, 1988, p. 42.

Sanger, Elizabeth, "Coleman's Lantern: Lighting the Way to Higher Profits," *Barron's,* November 28, 1983, p. 13.

Selz, Michael, "Coleman's Familiar Name Is Both Help and Hindrance," *Wall Street Journal,* May, 17, 1990, p. B2.

"What Sparked the Fire Under Coleman Co.," *Business Week,* August 13, 1966, p. 86.

—C. L. Collins

COLT®

Colt is one the best-known names in American firearms. The Colt .44 calibre revolver of 1872, popularly known throughout the Old West as the Peacemaker, was perhaps the most famous six-shooter in history, while the Colt .45 automatic was the standard issue U.S. Army sidearm from 1911 until 1985. The brand was named for Samuel Colt, who patented the first practical design for repeating firearms in 1836.

Since 1990, the Colt trademark has been owned by CF Intellectual Property, a London-based limited partnership, which licensed use of the brand name to Colt's Manufacturing Co. in Hartford, Connecticut. In 1992, Colt's filed for protection under Chapter 11 of the federal bankruptcy code; proceedings on that action were under way in 1994.

Samuel Colt

Samuel Colt was born in Hartford, Connecticut, in 1814, and displayed an interest in firearms and explosives even as a child. He obtained and studied the inner workings of several firearms between the ages of 7 and 14. When he was 15, Colt was forced to leave Amherst Academy in Massachusetts after a Fourth of July demonstration of an underwater mine he built went awry and covered spectators with muck instead of blowing up a raft as advertised.

For a while after leaving Amherst, Colt worked in his father's silk mill in Ware, Massachusetts. In August 1830 Colt secured a position aboard a merchant ship bound for India. On the return trip, although he later denied it, Colt probably saw several early designs for repeating firearms then on display in London. Colt also may have been inspired by the pawl and rachet mechanism used to control the capstan aboard ship. Regardless, during the voyage home, the 16-year-old whittled a crude wooden model of a multi-barreled, repeating pistol. Upon his return to the United States in 1831, Colt hired Anson Chase, a Hartford gunsmith, to build a pistol and a rifle based on his carving and a number of drawings. He financed the effort by billing himself as "the celebrated Dr. S. Coult of London and Calcutta" and giving public demonstrations of nitrous oxide, popularly known as "laughing gas."

The first pistol built by Chase exploded when it was fired. The second refused to fire at all. But Colt made several changes and soon settled on the design that he would later patent: a single-barreled firearm with a multi-chambered breech that rotated when the hammer was cocked. In 1832, Colt left a pistol and rifle with the U.S. Patent Office in Washington, D.C. However, Henry Ellsworth, then U.S. Commissioner of Patents and a friend of Colt's family, recommended against filing for a patent until Colt made more refinements in the design.

At some point, Colt ended his association with Chase, and in 1834, he hired a Baltimore gunsmith, John Pearson, to continue the work. In 1835, Colt sailed to Europe, where he applied for French and English patents. He then returned to the United States and completed the American patents, which were granted on February 25, 1836.

Patent Arms Manufacturing Co.

In March 1836 Colt and several backers formed the Patent Arms Manufacturing Co. in Paterson, New Jersey. Colt, then 22, assigned his patents to the company in return for a salary plus a royalty on every firearm sold. He also became the company's chief salesman. The Patent Arms Manufacturing Co. produced rifles, carbines, shotguns, and even a few muskets, all with revolving cylinders. However, most of the firearms made at Paterson were five-shot repeating pistols whose cylinders were inscribed with the word "Colt."

In 1837, Colt demonstrated a repeating musket for the U.S. Army, but the Ordnance Department was not impressed. Colt then went to Florida, where U.S. troops were fighting the Seminole Indians in what was then the only active military operation. The commanding officer at Camp Jupiter, Gen. Thomas Jesup, authorized the purchase of 50 repeating rifles, which were issued in March 1838. Colt also sold a few repeating pistols to individual officers. Within a few days, a board of officers reported on their effectiveness and recommended purchase of another 100 rifles. Col. William Harney later wrote Colt, "[The rifles] have surpassed my expectations, which were great. . . . It is my honest opinion that no other guns than those of your invention will be used in a few years."

However, despite the enthusiastic acceptance by the men in the field, the Army still refused to award a contract to the Patent Arms Manufacturing Co., probably because of corruption within the Ordnance Department. The company did sell several hundred pistols and rifles to the Texas Rangers and private sales went well, but poor management, the depression of 1837 and the lack of a

AT A GLANCE

Patent Arms Manufacturing Company established in Paterson, NJ, in 1836; bankruptcy declared in 1842; Colt's Patent Fire Arms Manufacturing Company established in Hartford, CT, in 1846; company purchased by Penn-Texas Corporation in 1955; Penn-Texas renamed Fairbanks Whitney Company in 1959; Fairbanks Whitney renamed Colt Industries in 1962; firearms division sold in 1990 and reorganized as Colt's Manufacturing Company. Colt trademark acquired by CF Intellectual Property in 1990; use of trademark licensed to Colt's Manufacturing Co.

Major competitor: Sturm, Ruger; also Smith & Wesson.

Advertising: *Agency*—Freebairn, Atlanta, GA.

Addresses: *Parent company*—Colt's Manufacturing Co., Inc., P.O. Box 1868, Hartford, CT 06144-1868; phone: (203) 236-6311. (Trademark licensed by CF Intellectual Property.)

government contract forced the Patent Arms Manufacturing Co. into bankruptcy in 1842.

The Mexican War

After the Patent Arms Manufacturing Co. folded, Colt again turned his attention to building underwater explosive mines, receiving a grant of $15,000 from Congress. Congress even adjourned in 1844 to watch Colt blow up a ship of 500 tons. At that point, the Colt name might have become a footnote in the development of modern firearms. But in 1846, war broke out between the United States and Mexico. Gen. Zachary Taylor, who had served in Florida and was in charge of the western Army, dispatched Capt. Samuel Walker to ask Colt for 1,000 repeating pistols. Walker, a former Texas Ranger, was also an enthusiastic believer in Colt's repeating pistols.

Colt and Walker negotiated a contract, but there were problems. Colt still owned the basic patents, but he no longer had a factory. Nor did he have any firearms even to use as a model. Taylor, in fact, had purchased the remaining Patent Arms Manufacturing Co. inventory of about 150 pistols and rifles from an arms dealer in 1845. Colt had sold or given away his own guns. He advertised in New York newspapers for one of his earlier pistols, but eventually had to recreate the design from memory, with some changes suggested by Walker, who wanted a larger calibre pistol that would fire six shots instead of five.

Colt subcontracted the manufacturing to Eli Whitney, Jr., who was then running Whitneyville, the armory his father founded in 1798. Colt personally supervised the manufacturing of the pistols, .44-calibre revolvers that came to be known as the Walker Colt, which were delivered to Taylor in 1847. Tragically, Walker was killed in action four days after receiving a set of pistols as a gift from Colt. Even before the pistols were delivered, the Army ordered 1,000 more.

Colt's Patent Fire-Arms Manufacturing Co.

Under his agreement with Whitney, Colt acquired ownership of the machinery to manufacture the revolvers when the initial contract was completed. With the second order for 1,000 pistols in hand, Colt set up his own factory in Hartford, which he named Colt's Patent Fire Arms Manufacturing Co. The Army eventually ordered 6,000 Walker-type revolvers between 1847 and 1851, although those made at Hartford were known as Dragoon Colts. Colt also manufactured several small calibre pistols.

In 1851, Colt went to London to display his revolvers at the Crystal Palace Exhibition. He was well received, and in 1853 became the first American manufacturer to establish a foreign branch when he opened an armory in London. In 1851, Colt also filed a patent lawsuit against the Massachusetts Arms Co., which had begun making repeating firearms with a rotating cylinder. Colt won the lawsuit, thus ensuring that no other U.S. company could make repeating firearms based on his design until the patents expired in 1856. His business flourished, and Colt soon became known as gunmaker to the world, selling firearms to most of the armies in Europe as well as to the U.S. military.

When he died in 1862, the sprawling compound Colt built at Hartford was the largest private armory in the world, and Colt was one of the wealthiest men in America, with an estate valued at $15 million.

The Civil War

When the Civil War began, Colt volunteered to raise and equip a regiment of riflemen at his own expense, and was commissioned a colonel of the First Connecticut Revolving Rifles. However, the commission was later withdrawn, and Colt focused his energies on manufacturing weapons for the Union army. From 1861 to 1865, Colt's Patent Arms Manufacturing Co. turned out nearly 400,000 revolvers, most of them the New Model Holster Pistol, also known as the Model of 1860 Army Pistol.

Colt's also manufactured about 7,000 repeating rifles with revolving chambers that were popular with sharpshooters organized by Col. Hiram Berdan. However, the rifles were expensive to produce, which probably accounted for the low number. Surprisingly, Colt's also made about 115,000 single-shot Springfield-model muskets, which were still in use at the start of the war. In 1864, a fire, probably set by a Confederate sympathizer, nearly destroyed the Hartford factory.

The facility, including the famous onion-shaped dome, was rebuilt after the war, when Colt's entered an unprecedented period of diversification. By 1880, the company was producing single-shot derringers, the first Colt pistols to use self-exploding, metal-cartridge bullets; pocket, belt, and holster-model pistols; a single-shot military rifle; and shotguns. Colt's also manufactured printing presses, sewing machines, a conductor's ticket punch, and the world-famous Gatling gun, the world's first practical machine gun, patented by Richard J. Gatling in 1862 and adopted by the Army in 1866. The first Colt repeating rifle to use cartridges was the lever-action Burgess rifle, introduced in 1883 and patterned after the famous Winchester of 1873.

The Peacemaker

The most fabled Colt revolver ever made was the New Model Army Metallic Cartridge Revolving Pistol, also known as "the gun that won the West." The .44-calibre Peacemaker was the first large-calibre revolver made by Colt's to use metal cartridges instead of ball and charge. It was tested by the Ordnance Department in 1872, and the Army ordered 8,000 for use by the cavalry in 1873. The Army eventually ordered more than 37,000.

The single-action six-shooter, also known as the Frontier Colt, quickly became the most popular gun in the Old West with the military and civilians alike. In *A History of the Colt Revolver,*

Charles Haven and Frank Belden wrote, "History, fiction, and ballad have made it the paramount symbol of a battlefield between the forces of the law and banditry in all its forms that stretched from the Mississippi to the coast, from Canada to the Rio Grande. Cowpuncher, rustler, gold miner, gambler, sheriff, outlaw, preacher, murderer, Indian, and cavalryman all wrote this lurid page in our history with the spurting flame and jarring crash of the old 'Peacemaker.' "

Among those Westerners who carried Peacemakers were Gen. George Armstrong Custer, Buffalo Bill Cody, Judge Roy Bean, Wild Bill Hickok, Calamity Jane, Jesse James, and William Bonney, better known as Billy the Kid. Ned Buntline, a pulp writer who chronicled the Old West, presented Peacemakers with 12-inch barrels, known as Buntline Specials, to Bat Masterson, Wyatt Earp and other frontier legends. The widespread popularity of the weapon—estimates are that more than 600,000 Colt Peacemakers were produced—inspired the axiom that "the Good Lord may have created all men, but it took Col. Colt to make them all equal." President Theodore Roosevelt carried a Peacemaker during the Spanish American War, and Gen. George S. Patton wore an ivory-handled Colt Peacemaker in both World Wars. Colt's manufactured the Peacemaker continuously until 1941. Commemorative models have been introduced periodically since then.

Colt .45 Automatic

The second-most famous Colt firearm was probably the Government Model .45 Calibre Automatic, the official sidearm for U.S. military personnel for more than 70 years. (Actually, the pistol was a semi-automatic, since each round was chambered automatically, but the trigger needed to be pulled for each shot fired.)

Colt introduced the first semi-automatic pistol made in the United States, a seven-shot, .38 calibre model designed by Jonathon M. Browning, in 1900. Browning was probably the most successful American gun designer in history, and often sold or licensed his patents to Colt. Browning also designed the Colt Machine Gun Model 1895, the world's first fully automatic machine gun, which led to the development of the Colt-manufactured Maxim and Vickers machine guns, and the Browning Automatic Rifle (BAR), which was used in both World Wars.

In 1905 Colt introduced the first Military Model .45-calibre automatic. The self-loading Military Model came with a heavy leather holster with a steel frame that locked into the butt of the pistol to form a shoulder stock. The Military Model led to the development of the Government Model of 1911, which was adopted as standard issue by the U.S. armed forces. A War Department report on the 1911 Colt .45 called the eight-shot semi-automatic "the most powerful, accurate and rapid firing pistol that has yet been produced."

Between 1911 and 1985—when the military replaced the Colt .45 with a Beretta 9mm semi-automatic—Colt produced more than 3 million Colt .45 automatics, with only minor changes in design. During both World Wars, other companies also manufactured the Government Model automatic under license from Colt. The Colt .45 was also the standard issue sidearm during the Korean and Vietnam wars. Print ads for civilian models in 1993 continued to stress the .45's military heritage with pictures of U.S. soldiers and medals set against a map of Europe.

Ownership Changes

The Colt family owned Colt's Patent Fire Arms Manufacturing Co. until 1901, when it was sold to a group of New York investors. The company did well under its new ownership up through World War I, but suffered several setbacks in the 1920s and 1930s. In 1921, the company introduced the Thompson Submachine Gun, but stopped production after making just 15,000 when the "tommy gun" became popular with gangsters. That turned out to be a poor business decision when other manufacturers stepped in and later made nearly 2 million Thompson submachine guns for World War II.

In the early 1930s, Colt, like most firearms companies, was hit hard by the Depression. In 1935 low morale and a slowdown in production led to a violent strike, during which the home of Colt president Sam Stone was firebombed. Then, in 1936, a hurricane and flood caused more than $1 million worth of damage to the Hartford factory, and the company nearly went bankrupt. The company seemingly rebounded during World War II, but mismanagement uncovered later led to another financial crisis, and manufacturing stopped altogether between 1945 and 1947.

In 1955 Colt was purchased by the Penn-Texas Corporation, one of the first conglomerates (originally founded in 1911 as the Pennsylvania Coal & Coke Corp.). Penn-Texas became known as the Fairbanks Whitney Co. in 1959 and reorganized as Colt Industries in 1962. In 1963, the firearms division of Colt Industries became the sole contractor for the U.S. Army's new M-16 automatic assault rifle. Over the next two decades, Colt Industries became a broadly diversified, billion-dollar corporation.

However, the firearms division—which accounted for less than five percent of Colt Industries' revenues—suffered several setbacks beginning in the late 1970s. In 1977, the Justice Department accused Colt, along with the Winchester Group at the Olin Corporation, of illegally selling firearms and ammunition to South Africa, which was under an embargo because of its policy of apartheid. Colt admitted the violation and fired several employees.

Then in 1985, the U.S. government dropped the Colt .45 as the standard military sidearm and adopted the 9mm Beretta semi-automatic. Less than a year later, the United Auto Workers struck the firearms factory in Hartford. Although replacement workers were hired, the lingering strike, and concerns about quality, were considered instrumental in Colt losing the government M-16 contract in 1988. Several police departments also refused to buy from Colt during the strike, which lasted until 1990.

In 1990, an investment group paid about $50 million to purchase the Colt Industries firearms division, which was reorganized as Colt's Manufacturing Co. The union ended its four-year-old strike in exchange for rehiring striking workers and an 11 percent share of the company. In the restructuring, the Colt trademark was transferred to CF Intellectual Property, a limited partnership that included many of the same investors.

Almost immediately, Colt's Manufacturing became embroiled in controversy when the company announced plans to a market the Sporter, a semi-automatic version of the AR-15. As part of the buyout, the Connecticut treasurer had invested $25 million of state pension funds in Colt's. But at the same time, the Connecticut state legislature was considering a ban on assault-style rifles. The ban passed in 1993, even though the Sporter had become Colt's best-selling firearm.

Colt stopped making the AR-15 Sporter under political pressure from President George Bush to ''do something'' about violence among drug dealers. In fact, the AR-15 was never a weapon of choice among drug dealers, who prefer smaller, more easily concealed weapons, such as the Uzi machine pistol; the AR-15 was also expensive and not readily available on the black market. An examination of official New York City crime reports shows that the AR-15 was used in less than a fraction of one percent of all violent crimes, drug-related or not.

Outlook

When Colt's Manufacturing filed for bankruptcy in 1992, industry analysts blamed two decades of management that seemed out of touch with the market, beginning with a decision in the 1970s to discontinue making .22 calibre rifles, and culminating with the failure to update its domestic product line when Colt lost the M-16 contract. However, there were many other factors as well. Sales of all small arms in the United States fell sharply in the early 1980s because of rising anti-gun sentiment, especially after the failed assassination attempt on the life of President Ronald Reagan.

Rising crime also led to renewed efforts to ban or restrict gun ownership, particularly handguns and semi-automatic rifles. Many retail outlets discontinued selling guns altogether. The market may also have been saturated, with more than 255 million small arms registered in the United States in the late 1980s—roughly one gun for every American citizen. There were also fewer recreational hunters in the United States because of environmental concerns and changing lifestyles, but offsetting that decline was a threefold increase in target shooters. Two other famous names in American gunmaking, Winchester and Smith & Wesson, were also sold in the 1980s to avoid bankruptcy.

However, the Colt brand name was expected to survive even if Colt's Manufacturing Co. failed to emerge from bankruptcy proceedings. Since the trademark was owned separately by CF Intellectual Properties, the brand could be sold or licensed to another arms company. However, the fact that Colt's Manufacturing Co. did not own the trademark was affecting efforts to find a buyer for the beleaguered company. In 1993, the Connecticut Development Authority offered CF Intellectual Property $12 million for the trademark in an attempt to attract a buyer for Colt's Manufacturing, but the plan fell through when prospective investors withdrew their bid. At the time, there was also discussion of using the Colt brand name to market additional products ranging from blue jeans to cologne.

Further Reading:

Bryant, Adam, ''Colt's in Bankruptcy Court Filing,'' *New York Times,* March 20, 1992, p. D1.

Grant, Ellsworth S., ''Gunmaker to the World,'' *American Heritage,* June 1968.

Haven, Charles T. and Frank A. Belden, *A History of The Colt Revolver,* Bonanza Books, 1940.

Holusha, John, ''Colt to Sell Unit That Won the West,'' *New York Times,* April 29, 1989, p. 33.

Isikoff, Michael, ''New Colt Assault Rifle Revives Debate,'' *Washington Post,* April 19, 1990, p. A3.

Johnson, Kirk, ''Crying Betrayal in Hartford, Colt Faces Uncertain Future,'' *New York Times,* June 12, 1993, p. 1.

Johnson, Kirk, ''Emotions and History Tied to Colt Abandonment of Semiautomatics,'' *New York Times,* March 17, 1989, p. A18.

Johnson, Kirk, ''Connecticut Debates Stake in Gun Maker It Saved,'' *New York Times,* April 26, 1990, p. A1.

Lockett, Bob, ''Colt: What Went Wrong in Hartford?'' *Shooting Industry,* July 1992, p. 34.

Sobel, Robert, and David B. Sicilia, *The Entrepreneurs: An American Adventure,* Houghton Mifflin, 1986.

Wilson, R. L., *The Colt Heritage,* Simon and Schuster, 1979.

Wyman, Stephen H., ''Colt Loses Firepower in Weapons Industry,'' *Washington Post,* March 17, 1989, p. B12.

—Dean Boyer

COMPAQ®

Compaq burst onto the computer market in the early 1980s, initially marketing a high-end product that was purchased by large companies. The few Compaq computers people had in their homes were provided by their employers. However, new promotional strategies and product development efforts in the early 1990s yielded a line of lower-priced machines that appealed more readily to smaller businesses and home users. Commensurate with this strategy, the Compaq Computer Corporation widened the scope of its advertising, hoping to appeal to a broader audience. After ten years in the market, Compaq has developed a complete line of computer products, including desktops and portables, files servers, and printers.

Brand Origins

Compaq was created in 1982 as an entrepreneurial outlet for three senior managers at Texas Instruments. At first Rod Canion, Jim Harris, and Bill Murto weren't sure whether to manage Mexican restaurants, build computer drives, or make beepers. The trio developed a business plan for a portable computer—sketched on a pie shop placemat—and, with only $3000 in capital, presented their idea to Bill Rosen, a millionaire venture capitalist.

The product was highly novel and deceptively logical. IBM had spent billions of dollars developing mainframe and personal computer systems, but neglected to evaluate the market for standalone models—computers that did most of what an IBM did, but without the mainframe and at a lower price. The heart of the product was the microprocessor, a tiny arrangement of semiconductors that miniaturized hundreds of pounds of circuitry into a lightweight computer card.

Dozens of rival manufacturers had entered the market on the strength of good engineering and marketing, but were soon blown out of the business by poor management and inconsistent customer support. By contrast, Canion, Harris, and Murto were experienced managers with a solid understanding of the market and its technology. Confident of its prospects, Rosen capitalized the venture. The company was called "Compaq," in reference to the compact size of the product, but with a distinctive spelling that could be copyrighted.

One aspect of the new company's organization that immediately distinguished it from its competitors, and which had a great influence on the company's ability to quickly develop new products, was its consensus management. Companies like IBM, Digital, and Wang were set up in a top-down style that tended to stifle creativity. Due to the company's small size, Compaq managers were able to work in close association with one another, enabling market forecasters and financial analysts to consistently consult with product developers and participate in their decisions. Thus Compaq was able to quickly respond to new conditions and was flexible enough to adapt the enterprise as necessary.

Brand Development

The first results of this approach were the Compaq Portable and Compaq Plus, briefcase-size PCs that established a new standard in small, powerful computers. During 1983, the company's first full year of operations, more than 53,000 of these models were shipped, yielding sales of $111.2 million. This was an astonishing accomplishment for Compaq—no other company had achieved such growth in such a short time.

With a solid position in the market and rapidly gaining attention, Compaq desperately needed a follow-up product. In 1984 IBM announced that it had begun development of a new desktop computer and, in a misguided effort to spur interest, explained its features in detail. Compaq marshalled all of its resources in an effort to introduce an improved model before IBM's version was launched. The result was the Deskpro, Compaq's first desktop computer and the first to have a modular design to better accommodate hardware expansion and upgrades.

Compaq established an important alliance with Intel Corporation that year. Intel, a manufacturer of microprocessors, was searching for applications for its new 80386 chip. Noting the speed with which Compaq could enter the market, and the scale of its production, Intel decided to develop a new product line around the chip in conjunction with Compaq.

There were several problems to overcome in working with Intel, but Compaq won changes in the chip design that met its own product specifications. The Deskpro 386 arrived in 1987, three times faster than comparable models from IBM. In fact, IBM wasn't able to muster a competing product for another 15 months. By that time Compaq had begun work on a portable model, a notebook PC called the Compaq LTE.

AT A GLANCE

Compaq brand of computers founded in 1982 by Rod Canion, Jim Harris, and Bill Murto, with financing provided by Bill Rosen, in Houston, TX; Compaq Portable and Compaq Plus introduced in 1983; Deskpro, Compaq's first desktop computer, launched in 1984; "It Simply Works Better" advertising theme initiated in 1984; Compaq Deskpro 386 developed in 1987; Compaq LTE notebook computer, Systempro server, and Deskpro 486 introduced in 1989; international sales exceed North American sales in 1990; operations restructured and new distribution channels opened in 1991; Concerto pen-based laptop introduced in 1993.

Performance: *Market share*—19% (third-largest-selling brand after IBM and Apple). *Sales*—$ 4.10 billion (company-wide).

Major competitor: IBM; also Apple.

Advertising: *Agency*—Ammirati & Puris, New York, NY, 1991—. *Major campaign*—"It Simply Works Better."

Addresses: *Parent company*—Compaq Computer Corp., P.O. Box 69-2000, 20555 SH 249, Houston, TX 77070; phone: (713) 370-0670.

Compaq sold 149,000 computers in 1984—outselling IBM four to one—and nearly tripled its sales over the previous year. By 1985, however, the industry was overpopulated and had become ripe for consolidation. IBM, Sun Microsystems, Apple, and AT&T instituted price cuts in an effort to shake off rivals like Compaq. This caused some problems for Compaq, whose products were expensively engineered and unable to compete on price. Nevertheless, the company continued to gain popularity with customers for whom quality was the primary criteria.

Compaq joined 60 other companies in an industry-wide effort to establish an Extended Industry Standard Architecture that would ensure compatibility between computers built by different manufacturers. This did much to promote competition in the industry by freeing consumers from captive technologies. Customers were no longer bound by proprietary operating architectures and could easily upgrade their systems with Compaq products—or anyone else's.

The EISA standards allowed Compaq to develop the Deskpro 486 to challenge the Microchannel system on IBM's new PS/2 line. In fact, EISA enabled Compaq to set new industry standards, for the first time, independently of IBM.

Compaq encountered numerous difficulties in 1989, including a disagreement with the BusinessLand chain that resulted in the company's 14-month de-authorization of the retailer. In addition, Dell Computer, a mail order assembler of PCs from the component market, launched a mean-spirited ad campaign that depicted a Dell machine with the statement, "Top of the mark," and a Compaq machine with the line, "Top of the mark-up." The ad purported to put Dell in the same league as Compaq, but was quickly dropped in light of a lawsuit.

By 1990, desktop PC models comprised 85 percent of Compaq's sales. But the company had earlier introduced its Systempro network server, a processor unit designed to run several computers at once. This mini-mainframe design was intended to steal away IBM's market for small integrated office systems, while filling out Compaq's presence in the wider market.

Advertising

Compaq's most notable campaign was in 1984, when the company resolved to utilize advertising in establishing itself as a leader in the market. To this end promotional budgets were tripled over the year before, to $20 million. The main theme of the campaign was, "Compaq—It Simply Works Better." This tagline communicated the superior quality equity Compaq had earned, while suggesting that Compaq PCs were easier to use.

In employing the popular comedic actor John Cleese as its spokesperson, the company borrowed Cleese's substantial reputation for the unconventional. Stiff and dapper, Cleese was capable of goofy facial expressions and wildly slapstick bodily contortions. The comedian's spots—largely designed by Cleese himself—poked fun at the complexity of computers, suggesting that Compaq had so simplified the device that there was now nothing to fear.

This approach played itself out by 1988, as computer makers shifted from promotion of their brand image to trumping up their technological superiority to simply selling on price. These shifts revealed the rising dominance of clones and customers' growing realization that no matter who made them, computers were all pretty much the same; "Computers are like toasters," *Adweek* aptly noted.

Although a price-only advertising strategy is not suited to an established brand with a strong quality equity, Compaq established limited "value brand" campaigns to launch new low-end products and "move product." By and large, however, the company returned to the image-building themes with which it started out. The first campaigns were aimed at business markets, with ads running in the *Wall Street Journal* and similar financial publications. The ads squarely promoted Compaq's most valuable equity, declaring, "No one scored higher on what counts most: quality." The pieces cited a *Fortune* survey in which Compaq was rated first in product quality and service.

In December of 1991, after putting its advertising account up for review, Compaq switched its agency from Ogilvy & Mather to Ammirati & Puris. This agency continued to build the Compaq name along its traditional lines and even recommended dropping slogans when there was nothing to say. But following a reorganization of the business, the company adopted the phrase "A passion to do things right," to emphasize the company's continued attention to quality.

International Growth

Given the international nature of computer technologies, and the proliferation of the IBM operating standards, Compaq had no difficulty entering overseas markets. The first Compaq models shipped to Europe arrived in April of 1984. Four years later international sales had increased to 40 percent of the company's total sales. Compaq expanded its operations overseas in 1986, when the company opened a circuit board plant in Singapore and a manufacturing facility in Scotland.

By 1989, Compaq had overtaken Apple and Olivetti to become the second-largest selling brand in Europe, after IBM. In support of the company's growing European franchise, Compaq established an Eastern European sales office in Berlin in 1990, and built a distribution center in Holland. Additional channels were opened in Austria and Finland, as well as Hong Kong and Argentina. In

1990 Compaq's international sales surpassed North American sales for the first time, comprising 54 percent of total revenues.

Compaq entered the Japanese market in July of 1991, opening sales channels in competition with IBM, Fujitsu, and NEC. The following year the company targeted Latin American markets. Compaq developed special keyboards for 17 separate languages.

Brand Development

Much of the company's early growth may be attributed to the fact that Compaq did not engage in direct sales, but sold its products exclusively through dealers. Compaq also supported dealers' training and advertising, providing them with greater incentives to display and recommend Compaq products.

The company's greatest growth had come from targeted institutional markets—large corporations with the cash to spend on high-end computing hardware. But that changed in 1991, when the company was overcome by management difficulties. In addition to a lingering recession that cut corporate demand, Compaq's ten dealer networks merged into six. Worse yet, competitors had made great progress in edging out Compaq in corporate markets, just as Compaq had done five years before with IBM.

The most serious problem was that Compaq products were over-engineered; they were built to last far longer than they were needed, and their price reflected it. Unable to compete on price, Compaq switched its attention to building less robust machines that cost less, but retained a level of quality more appropriate to the market. This approach was welcomed by loyal, but price weary, Compaq customers.

In the midst of an organizational crisis, Compaq was forced to reduce its staff, restructure its operations, reduce earnings distributions, and replace Rod Canion as CEO. Canion, an experienced product engineer but inept marketer, was succeeded by Eckhard Pfeiffer, also a former Texas Instruments manager, who had built up Compaq's formidable European operations.

To broaden it distribution and bolster customer service, Compaq abandoned its dealer-only sales channel philosophy and instituted a value-added reseller (VAR) program with TechData and Merisel. In addition to representing the Compaq line as a sales agent, these and other members of the VAR program were authorized to provide technical and other forms of support to customers.

The one enduring, and perhaps most powerful, sales tool belonging to Compaq was its support organization. Customers with problems could easily reach a specialist who could help resolve them over the phone. This did much to drive sales of Compaq products and instill confidence in the company's products. It was so effective that other companies quickly copied the concept. This concept also gave rise to an 800-number ordering system called Direct Plus, established in 1993. In addition to dealers and retail outlets, customers now could simply place equipment orders by telephone.

In 1992, Compaq introduced 45 newly re-engineered models, including 16 new personal computers, as part of its new strategy to gain a leadership position in every segment of the market. In order to support this effort, the company established four operating divisions, each charged with a specific area of the market. To counter cut-price competitors in the low end of the market, Compaq introduced the ProLinea and Contura PCs and the ProSignia server. The company also established a peripherals group, and a new printer product, the Compaq Pagemarq.

After affecting a second workforce reduction, Compaq bolstered its sales channels by designating official retailers, including ComputerCity, CompUSA, Circuit City and Service Merchandise. The company also authorized direct response resellers, including PC Connection. By chopping production costs and overheads, and opening new distribution and promotion lines, Compaq effectively leveraged its positive reputation for quality, performance, and durability in the market.

Performance Evaluation

One of Compaq's greatest assets from a marketing standpoint, as well as a technological view, was its ability to beat its competitors in getting a design off the drawing board and onto store shelves. This was accomplished by simultaneously preparing production lines, inventory controls, shipping and distribution channels and advertising campaigns, rather than waiting for one step to lead into the next. All these groups remained nimble enough to change at a moment's notice. As a result, Compaq has recorded product cycles of six to nine months, while competitors take twice as long.

Another of Compaq's most powerful equities has been its reputation for quality manufacture. The company turned this into a marketing attribute in 1992 by offering a three-year warranty and 24-hour service support. This convinced many who remained suspicious of the reliability of computers to place their trust in Compaq.

Compaq has a well-earned and unfailingly consistent reputation for product quality. But until the arrival of Eckhard Pfeiffer, it was nearly knocked out of the market by poor engineering and promotional strategies. These areas have now become great strengths for the brand and are likely to keep Compaq at the top of the market.

With about a fifth of the market under its control, Compaq is not likely to resume the fantastic growth it once enjoyed. The company must continue to protect its place in the market by defending the business markets where it has engendered the greatest loyalty, and do that by maintaining high standards of product and service support quality. This will be necessary to avoid alienating the company's most loyal customer base while it pursues increased sales in the consumer market.

Further Reading:

"Big-Business Power in Affordable Small-Business Servers," *New York Times,* October 25, 1992, p. F9.

"Brand Loyalty No Longer Name of the Game in PCs," *ComputerWorld,* September 28, 1992, p. 1.

"The Branding of the PC Business," *Computer Industry Report,* February 12, 1993, p. 1.

"Comeback-minded Compaq Launches New Products, Ad Campaign," *Business Marketing,* July 1992, p. 10.

"Compaq Aims to Battle Back with Ad Blitz," *PC Week,* May 11, 1992, p. 121.

"Compaq Background," Houston: Compaq Computer Corporation.

"Compaq is Hoping to Get Bigger by Thinking Smaller," *Wall Street Journal,* January 7, 1993, p. B4.

"Compaq Proves Road to Japan is Rocky," *PC Week,* June 24, 1991, p. 175.

"Compaq Regroups," *Advertising Age,* December 2, 1991, p. 4.

"Compaq Seeks Broader Base," *Advertising Age,* August 5, 1991, p. 37.

"Compaq: Turning the Tables on Dell?," *Business Week,* March 22, 1993, p. 87.

"IBM, Compaq Reshape PC Field of Battle with New Branding Initiative," *PC Week,* May 17, 1993, p. 3.

"IBM, Others Vie for Japanese PC Market," *Byte,* January 1993, p. 40.

"No More Cloning Around," *Advertising Age,* November 11, 1991, p. S9.

"A Role Model for Big Blue?," *Brandweek,* April 5, 1993, p. 16.

"Women are the Focus of a PC Maker," *Wall Street Journal,* October 7, 1993, p. B1.

—John Simley

CORNING WARE®

CORNING WARE®

Corning Inc. has a long tradition of technological innovation in glassmaking. The company dates from 1868 when the Brooklyn Flint Glass Works moved to Corning, New York, and became Corning Glass Works in 1875. It was not until 1989 that the company dropped the words *Glass Works* from its name. The Corning Glass Works produced specialty glass and, at the turn of the century, it manufactured such sophisticated items as thermometer tubing and pharmaceutical ware.

Brand Origins

Egyptian or Mesopotamian potters probably discovered the process for glassmaking by accident at least 6,000 years ago. Although the basic raw materials for making glass—silica in the form of sand, alkali in the form of soda or ashes, and, sometimes, lime—were readily available, glass was expensive to make. For fifteen centuries glass was a luxury item used only to hold the costliest unguents and perfumes. A milestone occurred in the first century B.C. when glassblowing was invented. Another occurred in 1825 in the United States with the invention of a method of pressing hot glass in a metal mold. By 1850 mass production of glass enabled common people to buy glass items.

Corning grew and thrived as it continued to perfect these new technologies; the company's research resulted in a collection of over 65,000 different formulas by 1958. Each formula had different properties of clarity, strength, hardness, smoothness, uniformity, and resistance to heat, electricity, radiation, and corrosion. Corning developed a heat resistant Pyrex brand borosilicate glass for use, by 1908, in the lanterns of railroad signalmen, the globes of which tended to shatter in rain and snow. The success of that application led to the introduction of Pyrex brand glass for laboratory glass and ovenware in 1915.

In the mid-1950s, a Corning scientist took glass a step further with the discovery of what became known as Pyroceram, glass ceramics impervious to thermal shock. In 1958, Corning launched its Corning Ware cookware, made from a Pyroceram composition. It came to have a 98% brand awareness by the American public.

Style and Marketing

The famous blue cornflower motif adorned the original white Corning Ware in 1958, making the pieces attractive serving dishes as well as being functional cookware. Corning has continued to expand and improve its product line over the years, adding many decorative patterns, a great variety of shapes, and trendy colors—such as beige and obsidian black, since the launch of that original cookware. More important to the success of Corning ware, however, is its usefulness and versatility in the kitchen. The various Corning Ware shapes helped homemakers prepare, serve, and store meals. The pieces could be used in conventional ovens as well as in the increasingly popular microwave and convection ovens. In fact, users discovered Corning Ware could be used for microcooking even *before* Corning began to advertise in 1975 that the pieces could be used in the microwave oven. With the addition of snap-on plastic lids, Corning Ware could be used to store food in the refrigerator or freezer. The result has been an enduring, popular line of cookware that the marketplace has devoured—by 1993 Corning had sold over 400 million pieces of Corning Ware.

As it had done in its advertising for the Pyrex brand, Corning was highly demonstrative with its early advertising for Corning Ware. To illustrate how Corning Ware could withstand extreme temperature changes, for instance, one campaign featured an image of a Corning Ware skillet half buried in a block of ice—while being blasted by a blowtorch.

Corning introduced Corelle dinnerware, composed of a unique sandwich-type glass body, in 1970. With the same simple elegance as Corning Ware, Corelle at first was available in basic white plus three patterns. Eventually, Corning added numerous patterns and several shapes to the Corelle line. As of 1993, Corelle

AT A GLANCE

Corning Ware brand of cookware introduced in 1958 by Corning Glass Works; company name changed to Corning Incorporated, 1989.

Performance: *Sales*—$3.751 billion. *Market share*—21% in cookware/ovenware category (1993).

Advertising: *Agency*—DMB&B, New York, NY, 1983. *Major campaign*—"Nothing goes from hot to cold faster than Corning Ware . . . except your average relationship."

Addresses: *Parent company*—Corning Inc., Corning, NY 14831; phone: (607) 974-9000; fax: (607) 974-8897.

was the largest-selling brand of dinnerware in the world and estimated to be in use in 40% of American homes. The billionth piece of Corelle came out of the factory door in early 1984, about the same time a television ad dramatized the dinnerware's resistance to breakage. The campaign told the story of a set of used Corelle that survived a journey from the United States to—and across—the Australian Outback, without any dishes breaking.

Sales volumes fell off in 1982 for Corning consumer products, including Corning Ware, Pyrex, and Corelle dinnerware. After the decline, Corning introduced Visions cookware, a glass-ceramic that, like Corning Ware, had the transparency of glass.

Meanwhile, Corning's French operation manufactured and introduced Visions cookware in 1980 and marketed it in Europe. Three years after the 1983 launch of Visions in the United States, the line was number one in sales in the U.S. rangetop cookware market—and by 1992 100 million pieces of the Visions line had been sold.

Corning ran a controversial television commercial for Visions in 1985. The ad showed a Visions saucepan, fired by a burner at 850 degrees Celsius, turning a metal saucepan "into sauce." The veracity of this commercial was proven in an independent laboratory test on David Horowitz's syndicated television program Fight Back in May 1985.

Outlook

The beauty, versatility, and utility of Corning Ware, as well as its adaptability to use in both traditional and new generation cooking appliances should assure that demand for the brand's cookware products will continue.

Further Reading:

Ankli, Robert E., "Corning Incorporated," *International Directory of Company Histories,* edited by Adele Hast, St. James Press, 1991, pp. 683–85.

"Corning Updates Name; Corning Glass Works Is Now Corning Inc.," *Gifts & Decorative Accessories,* June 1989, p. 10.

The Corning Glass Center, Corning Glass Works, 1958.

Duff, Mike, "Microwave Cookware Can Heat Up Other Sales," *Supermarket Business,* March 1991, pp. 96–99.

Labich, Kenneth and H. John Steinbreder, "The Innovators; America's Most Imaginative Companies Are Turning New Ideas into Big Dollars," *Fortune,* June 6, 1988, p. 50–7.

"Recognition, Not Price, Shapes Brand Popularity," *Discount Store News,* October 1, 1990, pp. 70–71.

—Doris Morris Maxfield

CUISINART®

Cuisinart®

When Cuisinarts, Inc. (now Cuisinarts Corp.) introduced the Cuisinart food processor in 1973, founder Carl Sontheimer might not have guessed that he was setting the groundwork for a highly competitive, multi-million dollar segment of the home appliance market. The Cuisinart brand food processor is a multi-purpose kitchen machine that slices, shreds, blends, grinds, mixes, dices, and kneads anything from bread, cake, and cookie dough to carrots and tomatoes. Sales began to take off in 1975; soon top appliance manufacturers such as Hamilton Beach, General Electric, and Sunbeam introduced their own lines of food processors, thereby capturing a good percentage of the market Cuisinart created. Although Cuisinart food processors are available in a variety of price ranges, the brand image is one of superior quality and craftmanship for the busy home cook.

Brand Origins

Cuisinarts was the brainchild of Carl Sontheimer, an engineer, physicist, entrepreneur, corporate executive, and self-proclaimed cooking fanatic. In 1967, he sold Amzac Electronics, the company he owned at the time; then only 53 years old, he found himself contemplating the possibility of an early retirement. Instead, Sontheimer considered several business options and decided to combine his expertise in electronics with cooking, his favorite hobby.

In 1971, Sontheimer formed Cuisinarts, Inc. While attending a housewares show in France, he and his wife, Shirley, had been intrigued by a demonstration of a restaurant food preparation machine made by Robot-Coupe, France's largest restaurant kitchen equipment manufacturer. The Sontheimers met with Pierre Verdun, the machine's inventor, who informed them that Robot-Coupe was planning to create a food processor for home use. Convinced that there would be a market for such a product in the United States, the Sontheimers purchased three prototypes of the machine and obtained sole U.S. distribution rights.

Sontheimer tinkered with the Robot-Coupe food processor for a year and a half, bending blades, lengthening the feed tube, and adapting safety features to fit American standards. Experimenting with the machine in his own kitchen, he found he could make complicated foods such as pâté, duxelles, and puff pastry dough in far less time than they took to make by other methods. Sontheimer commissioned Robot-Coupe to manufacture the new processor to his specifications and, in 1973, introduced it to the American consumer market at the National Housewares Manufacturing Association trade show under the name Cuisinart.

The Cuisinart food processor's debut was disappointing. Sales seemed so uncertain that two representatives hired to demonstrate it resigned rather than risk their reputations. To retailers, the food processor resembled little more than a jazzed-up blender, which sold for a fraction of the Cuisinart's lowest suggested retail price of $140; needless to say, they weren't very interested.

A New Market

Sales through 1973 and 1974 were practically nonexistent. But Sontheimer remained persistent, pitching his product to reigning culinary experts such as Julia Child, Craig Claiborne, James Beard, Pierre Franey, and Helen McCully. In 1975, his determination paid off in the form of a laudatory article in *Gourmet* magazine, followed by praise from Claiborne, who reportedly stated that "[the Cuisinart's] invention, in the minds of serious cooks, ranks with that of the printing press, cotton gin, steamboat, paper clips, [and] Kleenex."

According to Dale Chaney in *Appliance Manufacturer,* virtually overnight Cuisinarts "found itself in an enviable position: Alone in a burgeoning market of its own creation." Although Cuisinarts, Inc. didn't release figures, analysts estimate sales jumped to somewhere between 150,000 and 250,000 units in 1976. The food processor market segment seemed so promising that a number of imitators quickly introduced their own versions of the Cuisinart within the year. By October of 1977, there were 11 other food processors on the market, most priced far below Cuisinart's retail tag of $225 for the CFP-5 and $160 for the CFP-9. Many were produced by well-known manufacturers such as Farberware, Hamilton Beach, and Sunbeam, whose established names helped to capture 50 percent of the estimated 500,000 units sold that year. Cuisinart brand food processor sales for 1977 totaled around $50 million.

Competition Intensifies

During its early years, Cuisinarts, Inc. spent very little to advertise its new food processor, relying only on ads in trade magazines to reach retailers. Knowledge of the Cuisinart food processor's capabilities spread via word-of-mouth, assisted by positive publicity generated by prominent chefs and food journal-

AT A GLANCE

Cuisinart brand food processors introduced in 1973, two years after Carl Sontheimer founded Cuisinarts, Inc., to import high quality stainless steel cookware from France. Cuisinarts, Inc. was sold to an investment group including Robert M. Fomon & Co., Greenwich Investment Co., and George K. Barnes in January of 1988; Conair Corp. acquired the company in 1989, changing its name to Cuisinarts Corp.

Performance: *Market share*—15% of food processor category. *Sales*—$50 million.

Major competitor: Black & Decker; also Sunbeam and Hamilton Beach brand food processors.

Advertising: *Agency*—In house, ConAd.

Addresses: *Parent company*—Cuisinarts Corp., 1 Cummings Point Road, Stamford CT 06904; phone:(203) 975-4600; fax: (203) 975-4660. *Ultimate Parent Company*—Conair Corp., 1 Cummings Point Road, Stamford, CT 06904; phone: (203) 351-9000; fax: (203) 351-9180.

ists. However, Cuisinarts kicked off major print advertising campaigns—created by the Kurtz & Tarlow ad agency—in the late 1970s and '80s in an effort to stave off the growing competition that threatened to erode its 50 percent (number one) share of the food processor market.

Doubling its 1979 advertising budget to $2 million, Cuisinarts launched its first television campaign in New York City. The ads promoted five food processors with the Cuisinart name, priced from $140 to $600, and featured Sontheimer—"the father of the Cuisinart food processor"—touting Cuisinart as a "versatile quality appliance." Each advertisement ended with the tagline, "We haven't compromised. Neither should you." At the same time, Cuisinarts, Inc. kicked off a print campaign in major publications such as *Gourmet, Ladies' Home Journal, New York,* and the *New Yorker,* announcing the introduction of a new, enlarged tube system and accessory blade that would "make all other food processors obsolete."

After developing its own line of processors, Cuisinarts, Inc. discontinued marketing all but one of the Robot-Coupe models and contracted with Japanese manufacturers to make the majority of its products. In 1978, Robot-Coupe dropped its long-standing distribution agreement with Cuisinarts and introduced three of its own home food processor models, entering into a head-on battle against the Cuisinart brand for a share of the home food preparation market.

Robot-Coupe formed a U.S. subsidiary, Robot-Coupe U.S.A., which began marketing food processors in the United States. The company also launched advertisements in trade and gourmet magazines that printed the phonetic pronunciation of its brand name, followed by the sentence, "It used to be pronounced Cuisinart." Cuisinarts officials downplayed Robot-Coupe's entry into the market; however, they did intensify television advertising, again more than doubling the Cuisinart line's total ad budget. In addition, Cuisinarts printed brochures stating that the rift with Robot-Coupe was primarily caused by alleged poor craftsmanship on the part of Robot-Coupe. As documented in *Advertising Age,* the advertising battle intensified, and in March of 1981, Cuisinarts took out a full-page ad in the *New York Times* captioned: "Are you as easily fooled as they hope you are?" This was followed by a Robot-Coupe full-page ad in the same newspaper asking, "Who's fooling whom?"

Cuisinarts, Inc. filed suit against Robot-Coupe demanding that the company stop using the tag, "It used to be called Cuisinart." A U.S. district court judge ruled in favor of Cuisinarts' demand and Robot-Coupe was barred from printing advertisements that implied that the Cuisinart brand either changed its name, went out of business, or that all Cuisinart food processors were made by Robot-Coupe.

By the early 1980s there were more than 30 contenders in the food processor market. Cuisinarts continued to lead the market in terms of dollar volume, with $40 million in sales (25 percent of the market), built largely on the strength of its more expensive models. However, in terms of unit volume, Cuisinarts trailed Hamilton Beach, General Electric, and Sunbeam.

In 1983 appliance giant KitchenAid introduced its first food processor aimed at capturing a share of the Cuisinart line's high-price market. Ironically, KitchenAid's food processors were manufactured by Robot-Coupe, who also continued selling its own high-end machines in the United States. In addition, Sunbeam made efforts to capture some of Cuisinarts' high-end market after realizing that its lower-priced models were not selling as well as its more expensive ones. Cuisinarts, Inc. responded to these challenges by offering a trade-in allowance of up to $66 for old food processors, an unusual marketing ploy for the home appliance industry. Initially, the trade-up was only for Cuisinart owners who wished to purchase the more expensive Cuisinart DLC-7 Pro or DLC-X, but the company soon expanded the deal to include any brand or model of food processor. This strategy captured a greater share of the high-end market for the Cuisinart brand and stole customers from low-end competitors.

Antitrust Charges

In addition to intensified competition, the early 1980s brought legal problems for Cuisinarts, Inc. In September of 1980, a federal grand jury charged the company and a number of unidentified retailers with conspiring to fix prices on its food processors. According to the indictment, during the period from 1974 to 1979, Cuisinarts set "suggested" retail prices for its processors. Retailers who undersold the product were either threatened with a reduction in supplies or simply had their supplies cut. As a result, the indictment said, "consumers [had] to pay fixed and artificially high prices" for Cuisinart brand merchandise. In December, Cuisinarts was fined $250,000. In addition to agreeing not to contest the charges, the company had to refrain from suggesting retail prices for one year and make clear to retailers that adherence to all further suggested retail prices would be completely voluntary.

Chapter 11

In January of 1988, Sontheimer sold Cuisinarts, Inc. to an investment group headed by Robert M. Fomon & Company, Greenwich Investment Company, and George K. Barnes for a reported $60 million. By August of 1989, the highly leveraged company had filed for Chapter 11 bankruptcy protection. Cuisinarts, Inc. had a good cash flow and potential for brand extensions when Sontheimer sold it. But as a result of the buyout, the company was saddled with $43 million in debt and assets totaling less than $35 million, primarily in inventory.

A 1989 report in *Forbes* indicated that Cuisinart sales had already begun to slide by the time Sontheimer sold the business. Cuisinart's market share had fallen from 20 percent in 1984 to 12 percent by 1989, and revenues hovered around $50 million, down from $80 million in 1979. Analysts attributed declining sales to the company's inability to adapt to changing consumer needs. Cuisinart food processors seemed too heavy, complicated, and expensive next to the more lightweight, simple, moderately priced versions developed by Sunbeam, Black & Decker, and Hamilton Beach. As competition was snatching away market share, Sontheimer held tightly to the brand's image as a high-end product for the serious amateur cook. He "didn't see the appeal of selling to cooks who didn't want to make three pounds of puff pastry, but rather [wanted] to chop one onion to throw into some chili," a Black & Decker marketing director told *Forbes.*

Change in Name and Marketing Strategy

Banking on the strong appeal the Cuisinart name held in the minds of consumers, Conair Corporation acquired Cuisinarts, Inc. in December of 1989, changing the company's name to Cuisinarts Corp. Conair, one of the nation's leading producers of personal care appliances, began an intensive marketing program for Cuisinarts, improving its relations with department stores, increasing its presence in the bridal market, and launching a national print advertising and demonstrations campaign designed to reaffirm the Cuisinart brand's upscale status. Cuisinarts Corp. also introduced a number of brand extensions in 1991, including a juicer, Mini Prep food processor, espresso/cappuccino machines, and a sandwich maker, as well as a newsletter/coupon incentive to buyers of Cuisinart products.

The new organization also began an effort to open new accounts with gourmet specialty stores—among the first retailers to introduce the Cuisinart products—and averaged 50 new accounts per month in 1991. Retailers were in favor of Cuisinarts' decision to remain upscale, and most reported increased sales.

Analysis and Future Predictions

Although the Cuisinart image was tarnished slightly in the 1980s due to weak marketing efforts, heavy debt, and a change in consumer interest in cooking, the brand seemed to gain status after the Conair purchase. Under Conair, Cuisinarts Corp. continued to introduce a variety of high quality, upscale cooking products, such as a series of power blenders, a coffeemaker, a pasta machine, and the Cuisinart Food Preparation Center, a $350 food processor/ mixer that included all the standard equipment found in a food processor plus a whisk attachment, as well as optional blades, a citrus juicer, and strainer attachments. These new products served to reassert Cuisinart's image as an upscale brand for home cooks. Combined with Conair's intensive marketing strategy, the brand seemed well poised for future profitability.

Further Reading:

Chaney, Dale, "Has the Cuisinart Bitten Off More Than It Can Chew, er . . . Process?" *Appliance Manufacturer,* October 1977, pp. 64–69.

Cook, James, "Carl Sontheimer's Better Mousetrap," *Forbes,* March 6, 1978, pp. 65–66.

Hannon, Kerry, "Diced and Sliced," *Forbes,* October 2, 1989, pp. 68–72.

Harper, Sam, "Cuisinarts Tries TV for 1st Time," *Advertising Age,* November 12, 1979, p. 32.

Purpura, Linda, "Cuisinarts Reasserts Upscale Status," *HFD,* May 6, 1991, p. 96.

Sloan, Pat, "Cuisinarts Whips the Competition Handily," *Advertising Age,* May 7, 1984, p. 4.

—Maura Troester

DELTA®

Through perseverance and ingenuity, Alex Manoogian turned a small contract to make faucet parts into the world's largest faucet manufacturer. Beginning with a few styles in the 1950s, the Delta Faucet Company now has nearly 1,000 residential and commercial model variations in kitchen, lavatory, bar, tub, and shower faucets—the largest line in the industry.

Brand Origins

Alex Manoogian, an Armenian immigrant who had fled the extermination of his people in Turkey, arrived in the United States in 1920. Just nine years later, at the beginning of the Great Depression, he founded Masco Screw Products Company, a machine shop based in Detroit. Masco survived and prospered, and until 1954 its success was built on supplying automobile manufacturers with parts. That year, however, despite having no experience in making plumbing fixtures, Manoogian accepted a contract to make parts for a California manufacturer that was producing a new type of single-handled faucet. This new faucet design conveniently controlled both hot and cold water flow, but it was not perfect. Plumbers cursed it as "the one-armed bandit," and orders for the faucet declined dramatically. When Manoogian stepped in and modified the design after recognizing several flaws, the concept of a single handle faucet became viable.

Manoogian paid the California company royalties for the right to manufacture the fixture, forming a company separate from Masco to ensure that, if the venture failed, Masco would be free from risk. Although plumbing manufacturers were not interested in the new invention, claiming there was no market for single handle fixtures, the product's superiority soon became obvious. At that point Manoogian made the Delta Faucet Company a division of Masco and transferred the licensing rights. In the next year, Delta Faucet became the first to develop the single handle ball valve "washerless" faucet. Markets began to open up, and by 1958 sales of Delta faucets exceeded $1 million. Masco built a separate plant in Greensburg, Indiana, to manufacture Delta faucets because it could no longer accommodate the burgeoning Delta operations.

Marketing Strategy

The 1960s marked a period of company expansion and diversification under the leadership of Alex's son Richard Manoogian, who had taken over Delta's operations in 1959, after his graduation from Yale. In 1964 Masco purchased the Nile Faucet Corporation and in the next few years acquired several metalworking companies. By 1968 the company had achieved sales of $5.5 million from its kitchen and bathroom plumbing operations.

In 1970 Delta Faucet introduced a two-handle "washerless" faucet called Delex at a time when the housing industry was weakened by a worldwide recession. But plumbing products, especially for the do-it-yourself home improvement market, flourished for Masco, and to reinforce this the company launched a national broadcast advertising campaign, making it the first plumbing products company to do so for the consumer market. Masco's share of the faucet market had reached 22 percent and was still increasing.

In 1978, the company introduced affordable special finish faucets and two years later, high-rise "waterfall" kitchen spout faucets, both of which appear to have been good business moves. Masco maintained its dominance in the faucet industry by acquiring the Berglen group of companies, which distributed faucets in the United Kingdom, and 25 percent of Hans Grohe, a top European manufacturer of plumbing fixtures. Delta became the top selling brand of faucets, and Masco fought dearly for its name. In 1986 the corporation sued Waxman Industries, Keystone Franklin, and Radiator Specialty Company for trademark infringement—the first of several cases involving Delta's name. Competitors eventually agreed to label their plumbing fixtures according to strict trademark guidelines.

Other than appealing to do-it-yourselfers, especially those building new homes, Masco Corporation also targeted their marketing to contractors and plumbers. In the early 1990s Delta Faucet, with Ferguson Enterprises, launched a series of seminars aimed at contractors to help them build their businesses. "It's all part of our ongoing commitment to the plumbing contractor," Delta Faucet's Ralph Herbach explained in *Contractor* magazine in 1990. "If a contractor is a better businessman, we'll be more successful and the wholesaler will be more successful. Everybody wins."

In addition, in 1993 Masco began offering incentives to home builders who used its building products in new model homes. By this time, Masco Corporation manufactured Merillat cabinets, Fieldstone cabinets, Drexel Heritage, Henredon and Lexington furnishings, Aqua Glass bathroom fittings, and Baldwin Hard-

AT A GLANCE

Delta brand of faucets founded in 1954 by Alex Manoogian in Detroit, MI; Manoogian formed the Delta Faucet Company, which later became a division of his Masco Screw Products Company; Delta Faucet developed the first single handle ball valve "washerless" faucet in 1955; Masco acquired Nile Faucet Corporation in 1964; Delta Faucet sales exceeded $1 million in 1958; company name changed to Masco Corporation, 1961; introduced a two-handle "washerless" faucet in 1970; first plumbing products company to initiate national broadcast consumer advertising in 1975; developed high-rise "waterfall" kitchen spout faucets, 1980; during the 1980s Masco purchased 25 percent of Hans Grohe plumbing fixtures and acquired the Berglen group, distributors of faucets in the United Kingdom.

Performance: *Market share*—40% of faucet category; 74% total brand awareness among consumers. *Sales*—$585 million (1993).

Major competitor: Black & Decker's Price Pfister; also Moen, Kohler, American Standard, and Chicago Faucets.

Advertising: *Agency*—Lintas Campbell Ewald, Detroit, MI. *Major campaign*—"The Way Water is Brought to Life."

Addresses: *Parent company*—Delta Faucet Company, 55 East 111th St., P.O. Box 40980, Indianapolis, IN 46280; phone: (317) 848-1812; fax: (317) 573-3485. *Ultimate parent company*—Masco Corporation, 21001 Van Born Rd., Taylor, MI 48180; phone: (313) 274-7400; fax: (313) 374-6786.

ware. Participating home builders would be granted discounts off retail prices for Delta faucets and other Masco products, but would be required to work with local retailers and not sell Masco merchandise directly to consumers.

Advertising Innovations

Even though the advertising industry of the 1970s didn't believe faucets were "sexy" enough for full-scale advertising, that did not deter Masco corporate officials. Instead, they bucked the trend and launched the largest television advertising campaign ever for faucets. *Forbes* magazine quoted Richard Manoogian as saying, "Everybody thought we were crazy . . . They told us that the only time you buy a faucet is when your old one leaks."

In 1989 Masco spent $4 million to roll out a rebate program to entice consumers to make multiple faucet purchases. The promotions, called "Get a Grip," featured a toll-free number consumers could call to get rebate coupons and special product catalogs describing 43 Delta faucets. Masco targeted plumbing contractors with toll-free numbers, samples, advertising funds, and a referral program. This ad campaign also included more than 100 commercials on network television and cable, two-page ads in *USA Today,* and talk show appearances with certified designers in major markets discussing bathroom redecorating.

Advertising has featured the elegance and practicality of Delta/Delex faucets for every home use, making it one of the most recognized faucet brands among consumers. Masco claims that Delta faucets can be found in more than 30 million American homes, and that the brand has 74 percent total awareness among its customers.

Lead Weight

In 1993 Masco and 20 other faucet manufacturers were sued by the California Attorney General for leaching too much lead into drinking water. Lead accumulates in the body over time and can cause brain damage as well as impaired development in children. Although the Environmental Protection Agency requires that plumbing manufacturers use no more than 8 percent lead in their fixtures, there is no federal standard for the amount of lead allowed to leach from faucets. California's Proposition 65, however, bans the discharge of toxic substances into drinking water.

According to lab tests, Chicago Faucet's products produced the most lead, followed by Price Pfister Faucets. Delta Faucet had the third lowest amount of lead leaching. Both Price Pfister and Chicago Faucet use what some analysts considered an old fashioned sand casting method that requires twice as much lead to make a fixture than modern mold and machining techniques. Although Masco used molding and casting techniques that produced far less leaching of lead, company officials said they would consider setting their own standards for Masco products.

Future Growth

Masco was planning to roll out several new Delta products in the 1990s that would help meet consumer demands for safety features, water conservation, and barrier-free fixtures for the elderly and others with physical disabilities. "People with disabilities don't want to be singled out as the user of the institutional looking odd-ball fixture in the corner of the room," Delta Faucet's Peter Warshaw pointed out in *Contractor* magazine. "If all our products meet the standard, a contractor doesn't have to worry about meeting a barrier-free percentage in a building."

Further opportunity for growth comes from a resurgence in housing construction, where Delta faucets figure prominently—faucet sales have accounted for a 15 percent increase in revenues. According to Jagannath Dubashi in *Financial World,* housing starts rose 18 percent in 1992 after decreasing for five consecutive years. "When builders build, they buy lots of Masco products, [including] Delta faucets." In terms of faucets, Masco has been steadily gaining market share for the past 30 years and currently holds 40 percent of the faucet market. Masco's growth amid the recessionary 1990s also has made it a top stock pick. And according to Joshua Mendes in *Fortune,* Masco's target market—aging baby-boomers—will grow by 40 percent by the year 2000. Masco's growth, attributed primarily to Delta Faucet, low-cost production, and marketing and acquisitions, positions it as a market leader for the 1990s. Or as one analyst said, "This is one of the truly great companies of American industry, at a great price."

Further Reading:

Amrein, Diana L., "Delta reveals plans for national advertising blitz in May," *Contractor,* March 1989, p. 26.

"Bathroom Products Keep Pace With Consumer Trends," *Professional Builder & Remodeler,* March 1992, p. 61.

Donaton, Scott, *Advertising Age,* March 8, 1993, p. 33.

Dubashi, Jagannath. "Masco: Contrarian Delight," *Financial World,* Sept. 1, 1993, p. 27.

Frankenstein, Diane Waxer, and George, Frankenstein, *Brandnames: Who Owns What,* New York: Facts On File Publications, 1986, p. 256.

Hooper, Larry R., "Ferguson, Delta sponsor contractor cost, pricing seminars," *Contractor,* Oct. 1990, p. 52; "Barrier Free Plumbing," *Contractor,* January, 1991, p. 34.

Lee, Don, "Price Pfister May Feel Sting of Suit Filed by State," *Los Angeles Times,* Feb. 1, 1993, p. 2D.

Masco Company Report, Thomson Financial Networks, Inc., 1993.

Milne, George, R.A., "Plumbing may be coming back to copper," *American Metal Market,* April 6, 1993.

Mendes, Joshua, "A Spigot Maker Whose Earnings Keep On Pouring," *Fortune,* Oct. 10, 1988, p. 26.

Reid, Robin, "City Spotlight Greensburg," *Indiana Business Magazine,* February 1991, p. 39.

Steinke, Rene, *International Directory of Company Histories,* Vol. 3, Chicago: St. James Press, 1991, p. 508.

—Evelyn S. Dorman

DIGITAL®

The personal computer that adorns virtually every modern office desk traces origin not to Univac, IBM, or Burroughs, as many would expect, but to a series of models developed by the Digital Equipment Corporation, or Digital, as it is commonly known. The company was the first to market fully interactive devices that did not require intimate programming knowledge on the part of its users. DEC was the first manufacturer to marry a display screen, the most basic instrument of user interaction, to a computer. Prior to this, computer output was observed only on cardboard punched cards, schematic diagrams, and printouts. These innovations led Digital into a strong position in the market early in the computer era and enabled the company to maintain leadership in the industry even after competitors adopted its best ideas.

But like other computer brands, Digital for years remained a brand for business markets, rather than a consumer product. This began to change during the late 1980s, when corporations encouraged their employees to establish home offices and self-employed workers began equipping themselves with computer products. Primarily tools for business, Digital products are slowly making the transition to home appliances but still have very low profiles as consumer products.

Brand Origins

Digital Equipment was established in the summer of 1957 by Kenneth Olsen and Harlan Anderson, both graduates of Massachusetts Institute of Technology. Olsen and Anderson were convinced that an enormous market existed for computers and applications. Olsen sought funding from a venture capital firm, American Research & Development, whose president was a Harvard Business School professor named General George Doriot.

Existing computers were expensive, error-prone and had extremely limited applications. Mindful that RCA and General Electric's efforts to break into the industry had resulted in failure, Doriot suggested that Olsen and Anderson devise a business plan for their firm, but cautioned them to avoid using the much maligned word "computer." Olsen and Anderson settled on "Digital Equipment," a name that merely described a computer but which was unlikely to alarm jittery financiers.

The proposal described Digital Equipment as a manufacturer of printed circuit modules—the building blocks of computers—and guaranteed a profit in the first year of operation. Despite their youth (Olsen was 28 and Anderson was 31), the pair was granted $70,000 to start their firm. Digital Equipment, headquartered in the rural Massachusetts town of Maynard, delivered its first products in early 1958. The Digital Laboratory Module and Digital Systems Module were sold primarily to research facilities, generating a first-year operating profit of $94,000.

Having mastered production of processing devices, engineering a complete computer was a relatively simple task and a logical next step for the company. Olsen and Anderson drew heavily on their experience at MIT, where engineers had developed computers whose abilities were not limited only to performing complex mathematical equations, but which administered flight simulators and monitored radar networks. The duo regarded the million-dollar computers built by IBM and others as overpriced tabulators that could only be operated by company-trained programmers. These machines were rarely touched at MIT. Instead, students lined up to use the TX-O, a simpler model engineered at the school that required no special training.

The key concept was accessibility—what today we would call "user-friendliness." No computer was practical unless someone could use it. Olsen and Anderson immediately made this approach the core of their product development and marketing strategies.

Brand Development

One of the first innovations Digital brought to the market was the cathode ray tube, a simple computer monitor that literally enabled users to see what they were doing. This deceptively simple idea was revolutionary only because no other manufacturer had thought to make it a standard, integral part of a computer. The monitor enabled users to detect entry errors as they occurred and correct them before they accidentally became part of a computer program. This was the primary selling feature of Digital's first computer, the PDP-1 (the acronym stood for Programmed Data Processor). And unlike other computers of the day that occupied entire rooms, the PDP-1 was no larger than a small refrigerator. Accordingly, the device cost only $120,000, an eighth as much as comparable models from the market leader IBM and others.

The PDP-1 established Digital as a respected name in computers, but only within a narrow range of the market. In an effort to present a wider range of computers with more specialized functions, the company began development of the PDP-5, a more

AT A GLANCE

Company established in 1957; printed circuit modules marketed in 1958; PDP-1 computer introduced in 1960; PDP-5 and PDP-6 computer products introduced in 1963; PDP-8 minicomputer developed in 1965; PDP-11 introduced in 1970; VAX network system developed in 1979; DECMate II, Rainbow 100, and Professional personal computer series introduced in 1982; VAX 9000 and additional PCs lines introduced in 1990; Alpha series servers and work stations introduced in 1991.

Performance: *Sales*—$13,931,000,000.

Major competitor: IBM; also, Compaq, Apple, and Dell.

Advertising: *Agency*—Young & Rubicam, New York, NY, 1994—. *Major campaign*—"Digital Has It Now," "Putting Imagination to Work," and "Digital PC, Beyond the Box."

Addresses: *Parent company*—Digital Equipment Corporation, 146 Main St., Maynard, MA 01754; phone: (713) 370-0670.

powerful version of the original product, and the PDP-6, a full-sized mainframe device intended to compete with IBM's high-margin product line. Both models, designed by Digital's chief engineer Gordon Bell, were marketed in 1963 and, while they succeeded in winning only a fraction of IBM's market share, they further established Digital as a reliable, capable and cost-effective alternative to IBM. Also, Digital computers held a distinct cost advantage while still matching the performance of competing models. Now, in addition to ease of operation, Digital computers also competed effectively on the basis of price.

The key to Digital's price advantage lay in its marketing efforts. Unable to manufacture in huge volumes like IBM, Digital studied IBM's marketing strategies and discovered that IBM leased, rather than sold, its computers. And because its customers were system operators rather than scientists, it locked them into ongoing support agreements. Digital believed that these practices enslaved customers to IBM with rigid limitations. The technology enabled IBM to perpetuate a relationship of co-dependency with its customers that kept depreciation schedules behind rates of obsolescence and retarded the speedy introduction of new technologies.

Digital's customer base, concentrated in the scientific community, did not use computers as business machines, but as research instruments. They had no need for software or support because they wrote their own programs, and they had no use for long-term contracts that bound them to lease payments long after the computers were obsolete. As a result, Digital had no product support or software development expenses, and could be assured of selling the same customer an improved computer in half the time of the average IBM lease.

In 1965, Digital introduced the PDP-8, a minicomputer based on the PDP-5. Priced at only $18,000, the PDP-8 was highly popular with customers who integrated the small machine into their existing computer applications, opening new markets for the computer. The PDP-8 was most responsible for building Digital into a major manufacturer, providing more than a third of the company's sales revenue for the next 15 years.

Amid this tremendous growth, Ken Olsen recognized that Digital required a formal management structure, something its small, entrepreneurial nature had not previously necessitated. He established separate product development teams that would, in effect, compete for access to the company's manufacturing and marketing resources. This restructuring succeeded in substantially expanding the number of products Digital had under development, but the concept of internal competition was, in the long term, counterproductive. Savvy managers often promoted their own cases at the expense of others that may have been at least as promising. The troublesome system inspired Harlan Anderson to leave the company in 1966.

Digital computers were extremely flexible devices that could be made to work with virtually any other type of system—at a time before inter-operability standards existed. Therefore, a market emerged for Digital products in which other manufacturers would modify the machines and create specialized software for them. They were sold under names other than Digital, but provided a huge second market for the company's production. As an original equipment manufacturer, or OEM, Digital benefited from more favorable production economies while continuing to skirt customization and software development costs. Digital computers were used for an ever widening number of applications, from scientific uses to electronic scoreboards.

Advertising

Digital's advertising is aimed exclusively at people with authority to make corporate purchasing decisions, such as executives and MIS directors. As a result, virtually all the company's campaigns have appeared in business and trade publications.

During the mid-1980s, Digital ran a campaign under the theme, "Digital has it now." Originally, the company's ad agency developed a different tagline, "You want it now," ostensibly appealing to the concept of immediate gratification in vogue during the period. However, Digital tweaked the concept slightly to focus attention on the brand name. The campaign was clever because the "*it*" referred to in the ad could involve whatever product the company chose to feature. The ads were printed on a brilliant silvery paper and featured testimonials from respected corporations. This enabled Digital to demonstrate the confidence shown in its product line by leading companies, an indirect form of endorsement by companies whose public image was perhaps more favorable than Digital's.

In May of 1993 Digital launched two parallel themes, "Putting imagination to work" and "Putting technology to work." Like earlier campaigns, this one was intended to build brand identification with top managers and technical personnel. But unlike earlier themes, this was a global campaign aimed at establishing a standardized identity for Digital throughout the world. In January of 1994, Digital made Young & Rubicam its lead agency for PC products. The firm developed a new campaign, "Digital PC, Beyond the Box," intended to promote the company's support services.

International Growth

Digital's international expansion followed a fairly common route. The company's products became known in overseas markets initially through American affiliates of foreign companies. Conversely, American companies operating overseas extended their installed base of Digital machines to foreign offices. In time, demand in these markets made it possible to establish foreign marketing organizations in Europe, Asia and India.

One area in which Digital was especially popular was behind the Iron Curtain. A wide range of Digital products was restricted from export to the former Soviet Bloc because of the machines' potential military applications. Nonetheless, the Soviets succeeded in smuggling thousands of machines into the East through front companies. After the collapse of Communist governments throughout the Eastern Bloc, Digital found itself with a substantial and previously unknown base in Eastern Europe, where awareness of the Digital brand is very high. This has given the company a great lead over competitors for market development in these countries.

Marketing Innovations

Digital had proven that its entrepreneurial approach to the market could beat the military-style development processes at IBM and other companies. But it also spawned dozens of new competitors who learned, *from* Digital, that a management bureaucracy was an obstacle to development. In fact, Edson de Castro, the engineer most responsible for the PDP-8, left Digital in 1968 to start his own company, Data General.

This new competitor boldly announced plans for a computer even faster and cheaper than the PDP-8. It shocked Digital into speeding up development of its own successor to the PDP-8, a model called the PDP-11. In an attempt to stem growing interest in Data General, Digital announced details of its new product a year before it was available. When the PDP-11 was unveiled in 1970, it was heralded as a breakthrough in the computer industry. Priced at only $10,800, the PDP-11 was a fully versatile device, appropriate for thousands of applications, from payroll administration, accounting, and billing to a variety of scientific uses. The PDP-11 was a tremendous success, selling in numbers ten times greater than the PDP-8. It was solely responsible for powering Digital back into the lead in the minicomputer market, ahead of Data General.

During the 1970s, more than 50 new competitors entered the computer market. But many of the systems developed by these companies were incompatible with other makes. Aware of the opportunities this might present for Digital, Gordon Bell began development of a universal network system called VAX that would accommodate a variety of computer brands. The VAX extended the size and compatability with the PDP-11, and became the company's standard architecture of the 1980s. Ultimately, the VAX enabled Digital computers to interact with those made by IBM, Wang and others. But before the VAX could be marketed successfully, Ken Olsen realized, Digital would require a complete reorganization of its sales organization. The matrix that took the place of a managerial hierarchy was no longer an efficient form of organization.

This became apparent in 1982, when Digital attempted to market a series of personal computer products, including the DECMate, Rainbow 100 and Professional 325 and 350. The teams behind these models worked in competition with each other, creating quasi-independent enterprises within the company. Unable to work together, these teams left few resources to market the VAX. In fact, Digital quickly lost the small gains it had achieved in the personal computer market and was gradually squeezed out.

Olsen acted to eliminate the distractions faced by Digital's sales force by unifying the organization under a standard hierarchy and identifying key products, target markets and strict sales territories. The reorganization was completed in 1984, but not before Digital lost considerable ground in the PC market to upstarts such as Apple and Compaq.

Nonetheless, the VAX system was a very successful product in the scientific and industrial markets where Digital had always been strongest. Using a software fix, PCs of virtually any make could be linked into a unified network with VAX. This strengthened Digital's position in the network server market and provided added sales impetus for its PC products, which were marketed as components to the VAX system. Although Olsen's marketing reorganization caused dozens of experienced managers used to the entrepreneurial matrix organization to leave Digital for other companies, the plan seemed to work and, at least for a short time, Digital registered positive growth rates in an industry that had temporarily stagnated.

In another venture, Digital spent $1 billion developing a new mainframe product, the VAX 9000, in the 1980s—at a time when the industry had shunned mainframe architectures in favor of PC networks connected by LANs. But design problems delayed introduction of these systems until 1990, and sales never reached the billion-dollar goal set by the company. Digital also tried to break into the PC market again with a line of machines based on Intel's 80486 chip. But, as before, the company failed to win a viable share of the market.

The company also experienced more trouble in circumventing the massive competitive roadblock posed by ''Big Blue'': Digital was unable to establish a new operating system with other competitors that would challenge the IBM standard. Turning instead to integrated work stations, Digital designed a system based on its Alpha reduced instruction set computing (RISC) chip. But even this product had difficulty getting off the ground.

Competitive Analysis

Competitors that had survived industry consolidations during the 1980s entered the market on the basis of price competition, and used high production volumes to justify quality improvements. Companies such as Compaq and Dell that had merely been manufacturers of IBM ''clones'' maintained their price competitiveness while moving incrementally up-market. This caused Digital, and even IBM, to gradually lose their traditional marketing advantages.

As technologies and product quality rendered brands increasingly generic, new markets emerged in software—one area where Digital had always been weak. The company belatedly attempted to mount a recovery in this area by launching a software services unit. In addition, Olsen undertook a confusing series of reorganizations that succeeded only in breaking down the company's existing organizational advantages. This created a firestorm of controversy that caused considerable damage to Digital's reputation and resulted in Olsen's resignation.

Olsen was succeeded by Robert Palmer, a semiconductor expert formerly in charge of Digital's worldwide manufacturing and logistic operations. Palmer attempted to revive the company by focusing efforts on the company's most promising core operations. This had the effect of considerably reducing Digital's exposure in the market, but left it with a more competitive position in its strongest areas.

Performance Evaluation

With the PDP-8, Digital established a new market for cheap, versatile minicomputers while competitors blindly continued to turn out larger, more expensive models. This gave Digital the break it needed to establish production and marketing economies for products such as the PDP-11, a line of PCs, the VAX, and computer networks. Despite attempts to expand boldly into new office application areas, however, Digital remained a leading player only in the multivendor network environment. The typical Digital customer maintained a DEC server, a series of PCs and network printers, but also a large number of Apple, Compaq and IBM PCs.

Digital was unable to equip more desks with its own equipment precisely because one of its earlier strengths had become a huge liability. The company had elected not to concentrate on software program development, preferring to leave that to third parties. But as computer technology evolved, hardware grew increasingly generic; a processor was a processor. Meanwhile, companies such as Apple stormed the market with computers using a proprietary software so simple that almost anyone could use it to generate reports and letters and startling graphics. One Apple ad made the point brilliantly, asking, ''Why buy a computer that no one will actually use?''

To remedy this situation, Digital ''opened'' the VMS platform, allowing other manufacturers to design products for the previously proprietary VAX system. In retrospect, Digital may have waited too long to take this action.

Future Predictions

Of the 50 or so companies that entered the computer market during the 1980s, only Apple and Compaq have mastered the transition to consumer markets. Like Digital, they were established in corporate environments (an exception, Dell first gained prominence among college students). Unlike Digital, they all developed a line of PCs appropriate for home offices and tapped into a huge consumer products market. Digital missed several opportunities to develop this low-margin, but high-volume segment of the market—particularly as office computing environments grew more competitive. Under Robert Palmer, however, the company has moved forcefully into the PC market with a line of products based on its Alpha AXP RISC chip. The new effort evolves from PDP and VAX. The company continues to promote VAX as well as Alpha.

It is a formidable challenge for Digital to overcome these accidents in timing. A successful entry into the PC market at this stage would depend heavily on the development of advanced software programs and low prices. More likely is an evolution of the Digital product line to established standards. But the company's greatest task may lay in retention of its installed base—by giving established customers a good enough reason not to upgrade systems to those manufactured by its competitors.

Further Reading:

''Ad Blitz Recasts Corporate Image,'' *Business Marketing*, August 1993.

''Alpha Imperatives,'' *Computerworld,* June 21, 1993.

''America's Most Successful Entrepreneur,'' *Fortune,* October 27, 1986.

''Computers By Mail,'' *Business Week,* May 11, 1992.

''Crunch Time at DEC,'' *Business Week,* May 4, 1992.

''DEC Must Work to Rival Pentium,'' *PC Week,* March 1, 1993.

''Did DEC Move Too Late?,'' *Business Week,* August 3, 1992.

''Digital's Ads Push Sales Rejuvenation,'' *Advertising Age,* April 26, 1993.

Olsen, Kenneth H., *Digital Equipment Corporation: The First 25 Years,* New York: Newcomen Society in North America, 1983.

Pearson, Jamie, *Digital at Work: Snapshots from the First 35 Years,* Burlington, MA: Digital Press, 1992.

Rifkin, Glenn and George Harrar, *The Ultimate Entrepreneur,* Chicago: Contemporary Books, 1988.

''Where Is DEC Going?,'' *Forbes,* January 7, 1991.

—John Simley

DIRT DEVIL®

Dirt Devil is the newest and most popular brand produced by the United States' oldest vacuum manufacturer, Royal Appliance Manufacturing Co. Royal designs, assembles, and markets a full line of vacuum cleaners for home and commercial use under the Dirt Devil and Royal trade names. The Dirt Devil Hand Vac was introduced in 1984, and the successful brand was extended to include upright, stick, canister, car, and nonelectric push-sweeper models by the early 1990s.

Brand Origins

When John Balch and a group of Cleveland investors took Royal private in 1981, they worked immediately to transform the languishing, 75-year-old company into a modern vacuum marketer. One of the most significant aspects of that process was the transformation of Royal's hand-held metal vacuum. They redesigned it in red plastic, making it both cheaper and more noticeable, and dubbed it the Dirt Devil. The vacuum's old-fashioned styling made it seem like a well-established brand, but it was actually a latecomer to the hand-held vacuum segment.

The hand-held category had been created in 1979, when Black & Decker brought out its first cordless DustBuster. The Dirt Devil hand vac came out just in time to capitalize on a burgeoning replacement market for hand vacuums. The new brand featured three strong selling points: a revolving brush, large capacity, and unique, eye-catching styling. Unlike its cordless competitors, the Dirt Devil corded model offered an inexhaustible power supply. The small model's low price, under $30, made it a popular Christmas gift as well.

Marketing Strategies

Royal used aggressive new marketing and distribution strategies and focused on customer satisfaction to catapult the Dirt Devil brand to virtually immediate success. Rather than selling through "mom-and-pop" vacuum shops, as it had in the past, Royal marketed the Dirt Devil vacuums through nationwide retail outlets like K Mart, Wal-Mart and Target. Good customer relations were fostered through a customer satisfaction computer network, an unconditional 30-day return policy, and a toll-free telephone number imprinted right on each vacuum that generated thousands of customer calls each month.

The Dirt Devil hand-held quickly overtook Black & Decker's market leader and other competitors. 50,000 Dirt Devil vacuums were sold in 1984, and within a couple of years, the brand captured two-thirds of the hand-held vacuum market, selling more than all of its competitors combined. By 1992, over 4 million Dirt Devil vacuums had been sold.

John Balch, president of Royal and a "star" of Dirt Devil television ads, recognized the importance of point-of-sale displays, signs, and cooperative advertising with retailers. As the vacuum market grew more crowded in the 1980s and early 1990s, only the most distinctive and highest-selling brands survived. The unique bright red color of the Dirt Devil product made displays especially attractive.

In 1991, Royal spent $1 million to join one of its largest retail customers, K Mart Corp., in sponsorship of the Mario and Michael Andretti Championship Auto Racing team. Balch proudly noted that the expenditure paid for itself because the Dirt Devil trademark graced the front of Michael Andretti's car as he led the first 85 laps of the Indianapolis 500 that year. This marketing tool helped Royal maintain its good relationship with the large retailer. Balch hoped to use cooperative advertising to expand the quantity, visibility, and volume of Dirt Devil products sold by retailers and boost the number of major retailers carrying its products.

Brand Extensions

Royal worked to parlay the popularity of the Dirt Devil hand-held vacuum into a market-share coup in the other vacuum segments. The parent company followed a low-risk strategy that utilized outside sources for the manufacture of its vacuum components. This scheme allowed Royal more flexibility than other vertically integrated manufacturers and enabled it to respond more quickly to shifts in product demand.

The Dirt Devil Broom Vac, a lightweight model popular with smaller households, was introduced in 1987, followed by a canister model the next year. The Dirt Devil brand infiltrated the upright segment, which constituted 70 percent of total vacuum sales, in 1990. The brand's upright model featured convenient new on-board attachments that simplified "above-the-floor" cleaning of upholstery, drapes, and stairs. Royal's attempts to extend the Dirt Devil name into the upright market put the relatively young brand up against such "entrenched" competitors as Hoover, Regina, and

AT A GLANCE

Dirt Devil brand of vacuum cleaners founded in 1984 by John Balch, president and CEO of Royal Appliance Manufacturing Co.

Performance: *Market share*—63% (top share) of hand-held segment of vacuums; 7% of upright segment. *Sales*—$394.98 million (total of Dirt Devil and Royal).

Major competitor: Black & Decker in the hand-held category and Hoover in the upright category

Advertising: *Major campaign*—Royal president John Balch and "Sam the Dirt Devil Dog." Also used the tagline: "Puts the power of an upright in the palm of your hand."

Addresses: *Parent company*—Royal Appliance Manufacturing Co., 650 Alpha Dr., Cleveland, Ohio 44143; phone: (216) 449-6150; fax: (216) 449-7806.

Electrolux. Hoover still dominated the segment in 1992 with a 37 percent share, but Dirt Devil had garnered 7 percent of the market by that time, up from 2 percent in 1990.

During the early 1990s, Royal switched from an old-fashioned, two-dimensional, hand-drawn design process to computer-aided design using advanced three-dimensional solid modeling techniques. This ''next generation technology'' enabled the parent company's engineers to evaluate design concepts and engineering solutions before a prototype was made. The new technology allowed Royal to bring 1992's Dirt Devil Upright Plus, which featured a unique triangular head, from the ''drafting screen'' to market in record time, just over a year.

Royal's eagerness to rush upright models to market to capitalize on Dirt Devil's popular image backfired when one model wouldn't pick up dirt on certain types of carpet because of a design flaw. Although the problem was fixed, returned merchandise continued to accumulate in 1993, and Royal's combined share of the upright market dropped precipitously, from 24.3 percent to 17.2 percent from 1992 to 1993.

A ''Battle Royal''

Royal and Hoover's battle for the upright market erupted in the courtroom in 1993, when Royal sued Hoover Co. over what the plaintiff called ''misleading advertising.'' Royal's suit charged that Hoover's ''Cleaning Efficiency Rating,'' which measured the effectiveness of each amp of electrical power employed by Hoover's vacuums, confused consumers accustomed to seeing amperage ratings. Royal even claimed that Hoover executives had conducted, then destroyed, a marketing survey that proved the new ratings were deceptive. Royal asked for a court injunction to compel Hoover to recall all its advertising and promotional materials related to the effectiveness rating and to remove the designation from its cleaners. A U.S. District Court judge denied the request.

Hoover returned fire in mid-1993 with a lawsuit that accused Royal of false advertising, defamation, and interference with business relations. The countersuit alleged that Royal was the false advertiser: Dirt Devil's prominently displayed amperage ratings ''intentionally'' and erroneously led consumers to believe that amperage correlated to cleaning effectiveness. Late in 1993, Royal responded that it had expected such a ''delaying tactic'' from Hoover as the battle continued.

''Guaranteed Sales'' Controversy

In the meantime, Royal faced other problems related to its Dirt Devil brand. The parent company reported that its 1991 sales increased 128 percent over the previous year, largely on the strength of fourth-quarter Christmas sales of Dirt Devil Hand Vacs and uprights. By mid-1992, however, an investor-led lawsuit charged that Dirt Devil's sales figures had been inflated.

The suit alleged that the brand's parent had sold large quantities of merchandise with the understanding that it would accept retailers' returns of unsold merchandise for credit or refunds. The suit claimed that Royal had wrongly accounted those ''guaranteed'' sales as final. The lawsuit alleged that the guaranteed sales program convinced retailers to ''greatly overstock products, thereby inflating [Royal's] sales and earnings numbers disseminated to the investing community,'' according to coverage in the Cleveland *Plain Dealer.* The claim went on to assert that Royal did not create a reserve for returned merchandise. Three other class-action suits were filed by Royal stockholders in August 1992, ''alleging company officials had misled them about the company's financial health.'' Goldman Sachs analyst Dan Carasso defended Royal in *Business Week* magazine, saying that Wal-Mart had indeed sent $5 million to $10 million in merchandise back to Royal, but that the returns ''had been fully expensed in the fourth quarter of 1991.''

Advertising

For largely undisclosed reasons, the Dirt Devil advertising account was something of a ''hot potato'': at least five agencies prepared campaigns for the brand from its introduction in 1984 to the spring of 1993. Wyse Advertising in Cleveland handled the brand until the account was awarded to Pittsburgh's Marc Advertising. The Dirt Devil went without an agency for the first two months of 1989 after it dropped Marc. Griswold Inc. picked up the brand that March, but some time between then and 1993, the agency lost the account to Dix & Eaton Inc., a public relations company. Dix & Eaton, in turn, resigned in March 1993, citing philosophical differences with Dirt Devil's parent company. On May 19 of that year, Royal hired Edward Howard & Co. The firm announced that it had ''a nice relationship'' with Royal that morning, but abruptly and inexplicably dropped the account that afternoon. The highly unusual turn of events could not have reflected well on Royal or its leading brand.

Ironically, despite Dirt Devil's revolving agencies, the brand's television ads have remained very consistent. The spots primarily featured white-haired, mustachioed Royal president John Balch, Sam the Golden Retriever, and later, Sam's progeny. The ads capitalized on the dogs as attention-getting devices while deftly demonstrating the Dirt Devil Hand Vac's ''powerful rotating bristles'' and their ability to pick up pet hair. In one ad, Sam dug at the carpet to demonstrate the way the Dirt Devil Stick Vac Plus' triangular nozzle ''dug'' dirt out of hard-to-reach corners and crevices. Sam's five puppies were introduced by Balch as ''five more reasons to use a Dirt Devil.'' The dogs inspired so many letters that Balch planned to keep them in the ads indefinitely.

An early 1993 Dirt Devil ad promoted the brand's Can Vac on cable television with a woman struggling to manuever a giant upright vacuum around her house. She was emancipated from the huge appliance by the small but powerful Dirt Devil appliance.

Royal's advertising expenditures for the Dirt Devil brand, estimated at about $6 million or $7 million in 1989, increased dramatically to $21 million in 1990, then doubled to $40 million in 1991. The budget allowed the purchase of national television and print ads, as well as radio spots on the syndicated Paul Harvey show. The account nearly doubled again, to $79.3 million, in 1992. Some industry observers credited Dirt Devil's dominance of the hand-held market to its extraordinarily high advertising budget.

After almost a century of selling exclusively in the United States, Royal created a European marketing subsidiary in 1989. But it has been hard to establish Dirt Devil vacuums overseas, where there is little mass marketing. By 1991, European sales only amounted to 3 percent of total revenues ($4 million of $120 million), but Balch hoped that "beefed up advertising in Europe" would bring international sales up to par with domestic revenues during the 1990s.

Competition

In the early 1990s, rival vacuum brands brought out imitations that competed with the Dirt Devil Hand Vac on features or price. For example, Black & Decker introduced its own corded, revolving brush model in 1991. Trendata Inc., a market research firm in Norwalk, Connecticut, reported that Royal's market share for hand-held vacuums and uprights (garnered primarily by the Dirt Devil brand) slipped early that year. Dirt Devil's share of the hand-held segment fell from 63 percent in the fourth quarter of 1992 to 61.7 percent in the first quarter of 1993. Third-placed Hoover captured business from both Dirt Devil and Black & Decker, as its share rose form 2.2 percent to 3.8 percent over the same period.

Although the Dirt Devil brand maintained a leading share of the hand-held vacuum segment, its sales during the first half of 1993 continued to lag, and its parent company reported that its "profit margins were hurt by fewer sales of higher-priced products, low production levels, and more returns." Royal hoped to regain its momentum with the late 1993 introduction of the Dirt Devil Car Vac, which featured the rotating brush and could be plugged into a car's lighter.

Performance Appraisal

The Dirt Devil concept and brand have clearly brought Royal Appliance Manufacturing Co. out of obscurity and into the heat of the vacuum market. The brand's market share skyrocketed from nothing in 1984 to over 60 percent in the early 1990s in correspondence to an advertising budget that grew from $6 million to $80 million in just four years, and distribution that expanded from scattered, independent outlets to three of the largest mass retailers in the United States.

However, these successes were tempered with problems. Some analysts observed that the extravagant advertising budget was disproportionate to sales: in 1991, advertising cost $40 million, 33 percent of sales. An eagerness to extend the product line resulted in flawed designs. Challenging the "vacuum establishment" brought conflict within the industry, resulting in lawsuits that can only have distracted Royal from its main pursuit of selling vacuums. While some industry observers asserted that Dirt Devil's growth would inevitably slow, others pointed out that innovative new products could revitalize the brand's fortunes.

Further Reading:

Canedy, Dana, "Dirt Devil Maker Cites Slow Sales for Losses," *Plain Dealer,* July 27, 1993, p. 1F; "Devilish Success," *Plain Dealer,* November 19, 1991, pp. 1D, 6D; "Hoover Countersues Royal over Ad Claims," *Plain Dealer,* June 10, 1993, p. 1F; "PR Companies Drop Royal Manufacturing," *Plain Dealer,* May 20, 1993, p. 1F; "Royal Appliance Sales and Income Soar, *Plain Dealer,* February 19, 1992, p. 2H; "Royal Sues Hoover, Calls Ads Misleading," *Plain Dealer,* May 18, 1993, p. 7F.

Chanil, Debra, "Vacuums Clean Up," *Discount Merchandiser,* January 1992, pp. 48–51, 61.

Flory, Stephanie, "Select Market Seen for Corded Hand-Held Vacs" *Merchandising,* January 1985, p. 84.

Freeh, John, "Griswold Picks up a Royal Account," *Plain Dealer,* March 5, 1989, p. 3E.

Gerdel, Thomas W, "Investor Says Royal Overstated," *Plain Dealer,* August 15, 1992, pp. 1F–2F.

Holstein, William J, "Little Companies, Big Exports," *Business Week,* April 13, 1992, pp. 70–72.

Mallory, Maria, "The Dirt Devil Made Royal Do It," *Business Week,* August 26, 1991, pp. 30–31; "Royal Is Having a Devil of a Time," *Business Week,* August 10, 1992, p. 28.

Marcial, Gene G., "A Tug-of War over the Maker of Dirt Devil," *Business Week,* June 1, 1992, p. 110.

Milbank, Dana, "One Thing They Just Won't Do Is Sweep It All Under the Carpet," *Wall Street Journal,* June 22, 1993, p. B1.

Ringer, Richard, "Dirt Devil Disappoints Investors," *New York Times,* August 12, 1993, p. D1.

"Royal Creates a Devil of a Product," *Machine Design,* October 22, 1992, p. 149.

—April S. Dougal

DODGE®

THE NEW DODGE
A DIVISION OF THE CHRYSLER CORPORATION

In many respects the Dodge brand, a line of automobiles owned by Chrysler Corporation, has come full circle. Early in its eight-decade history, the brand's progressive, yet affordable engineering earned it the respect of competitors and customers alike. And in the early 1990s, after decades of declining interest, sales, and market share, Dodge has recaptured that positive image.

Brand Origins

The Dodge nameplate was founded in 1913, but the Dodge brothers, John and Horace, started making transmissions for the United States' oldest auto manufacturer, Oldsmobile, in 1901. The redheaded machinists' consistent production methods helped Olds rack up its first success, the Curved Dash Oldsmobile Runabout, and established the brothers' reputation for precision machining.

The siblings, who arrived in Detroit, Michigan, in the mid-1880s, were famously close. Neither would accept regular employment unless a job was also offered the other. Notorious for his temper, John Francis was the brawn of the partnership. Horace Elsin, the brains, would go down in history as the engineer of the Ford Motor Company's first production vehicle, the Model A. In 1963 David Wilkie wrote in *Esquire's American Autos and Their Makers,* "Few of the industry's pioneers contributed more in brawn and energy and none crowded as much achievement into so relatively a short span of life as did the Dodge brothers."

Henry Ford was just beginning to line up financial backing for his auto venture in 1902 when he approached the Dodges with his own car design. Although the brothers were very busy with their Olds contract, Ford convinced them to help him bring his plans to life. A prototype was produced, with significant revisions by Horace Dodge (the car did not function properly in its Ford-designed form), by the end of the year.

In 1903 the Dodge brothers gave up their lucrative contract with Oldsmobile to ink an agreement with Ford for 650 cars at more than $160,000. When Ford was unable to pay the first installment on the contract, the Dodges forced the incorporation of the Ford Motor Company and collected 100 shares of stock. Their combined stake in the company would eventually grow to 2,000 shares as the venture began to succeed.

After the Dodges helped Ford force his longtime partner, Alexander Malcomson, out of the company, they began to realize that Ford could soon turn on them as well, despite their vital contributions to the venture. They also became aware of the name recognition their well-built components had earned. Using the proceeds from their stake in Ford, the Dodges built a new 5.1 million-square-foot assembly plant. They continued to manufacture transmissions for Ford while firming up plans for their own vehicle.

Canceling their contract with Ford in July of 1913, Horace and John founded Dodge Brothers, Inc., in 1914. An eccentricity of the brothers' business dealings was their refusal to respond to mail addressed to Dodge Brothers if the writer did not capitalize the "B" in "Brothers." They felt that this distinction emphasized the permanence and closeness of their partnership. Henry Ford resented their use of what he considered to be his profits to build a competing venture, and the three would be embroiled in legal disputes over Ford dividends until 1919, when the Dodges won $2 million and finally sold their stake in the Ford Motor Company for $25 million.

The Dodges had to make their car stand out from Ford's and the 140 others being produced in 1914. They decided to carve out a market niche in the low- to mid-price range with a light-weight but rugged car that could be easily and inexpensively repaired or updated with the latest Dodge improvements. The car would thus be a good investment with a high resale value. In order to build a gasoline-powered car that both women and men could manage, Horace experimented with various self-starter systems before adopting a 12-volt "silent starter" that functioned through a non-stalling chain drive.

Horace eventually developed the reliable, efficient, and powerful, four-cylinder engine of Dodge's first "plain-Jane" cars. Dodges were the first automobiles to have all-steel bodies and were a success from the very start, manufactured with few major changes until the end of 1928. The Dodge brothers were among the first to set up a trial track to test each car before it was shipped from the factory. They examined speed, climbing and descending, as well as engine and brake performance on a circular wooden track outside the main plant.

Early Marketing Strategy

At a time when most advertising copy was lengthy, the Dodges used brief messages to pique the curiosity of prospective customers. First, two words appeared on billboards: Dodge Brothers.

AT A GLANCE

Dodge brand of automobiles founded in 1913 in Detroit, MI, by John Francis and Horace Elsin Dodge; brand known as Dodge Brothers through the 1930s; sold to Dillon, Read and Company in 1925, then to Chrysler Corporation in 1928.

Performance: *Market share*—Number four in the auto category. *Sales*—836,965 units.

Major competitor: Ford; also Honda and Chevrolet.

Advertising: *Agency*—BBDO, Southfield, MI, 1982—. *Major campaign*—"We're changing everything."

Addresses: *Parent company*—Chrysler Corporation, 12000 Chrysler Drive, Highland Park, MI 48288; phone: (313) 956-5741; fax: (313) 956-1462.

After the public's curiosity was aroused, two more words were added: Motor Car. Then came the words that would characterize the brand for decades of customers: reliable, dependable, sound. The formal introduction of the car was made in a half-page advertisement published in the August 19, 1914, *Saturday Evening Post.* "Dodge Brothers, Detroit, who have manufactured the vital parts for more than 500,000 motor cars, will this fall market a car bearing their own name."

The Dodges' reputation preceded them: many entrepreneurs applied to them for dealerships, and the auto-buying public enthusiastically greeted what would be known as "The Dependability Car," boosting it into third place in the production race by 1915. The first Dodge came off the factory line November 10, 1914, and by May of 1915, production exceeded 10,000 units. The black touring car was plain, but popular. In the summer of 1915, the nameplate introduced its second model, a two-passenger roadster with a price tag of $785—about $100 more than a comparable Ford. The new brand sold $35 million in its first year and reached the number four spot in terms of national sales by the fall of 1916.

John and Horace died within eleven months of each other during the influenza epidemic of 1920. Ironically, the Dodge company achieved the number two sales rank that year, its best performance ever. Valued at $52 million, the company was administered for the next five years by Frederick J. Haynes, a longtime friend and business associate of the Dodge brothers. During this interim period, Dodge became affiliated with Graham Brothers trucks. The trucks had Dodge engines, and their exclusive marketers were Dodge dealers. Graham Brothers provided the genesis of Dodge's passenger truck line after the truck manufacturer was purchased outright in 1924. The Dodge Brothers name was applied to the truck segment in 1930.

In 1925 the Dodge brothers' widows turned a generous profit by selling their husbands' legacy to banker Dillon, Read and Company for $146 million. The new owners tried to glamorize the Dodge with expensive accoutrements and raised the price to three times as much as a Model A Ford by 1928; the brand subsequently plunged to thirteenth place. Motivated seller Clarence Dillon found an equally eager buyer in Walter Chrysler, a latecomer to the auto industry who hoped to acquire the state-of-the-art Dodge Brothers plants. After five consecutive days of negotiations in a suite at the Ritz-Carlton Hotel in New York, the contract was settled and teams of men nailed large canvas signs announcing "Chrysler Corporation, Dodge Division" on the Hamtramck plant. The $170 million acquisition multiplied Chrysler sixfold, making it the third-largest automobile company in America. The Dodge purchase offered the prospect of lower costs, greater production, and a broader line of models. Dodge would do most of Chrysler's manufacturing until after World War II.

Chrysler changed some aspects of the Dodge car line, eliminating the four-cylinder engine in favor of the increasingly popular six- and eight-cylinder models. But the new parent continued to use the Dodge Brothers brand name in advertising until the late 1930s, a salute to the powerful influence of the dynamic pair in the history of the U.S. auto industry. Though Dodge's buyer loyalty declined during the uncertain period between the brothers' deaths and Chrysler's 1928 takeover, the brand rebounded slightly to seventh place in annual sales in 1929. Its manufacturing and distribution facilities would be the key to Chrysler's survival during the Great Depression.

By the 1930s the automobile market was approaching saturation. The 3.6 million unit sales plateau established in 1923 remained unchanged until the Depression, when the market was reduced by 75 percent. Market growth did not resume until 1949. Since practically every car on the market was mechanically sound and reasonably reliable, speed, comfort, options, and styling became prime selling points. Walter Chrysler tried to increase the size of the market by encouraging the purchase of a second car for each family. Installment buying and the annual model change helped bring planned obsolescence to the auto industry. Celebrity endorsements and its value-oriented reputation put Dodge in fourth place in 1935. Chrysler phased out the "Brothers" part of the name and the original triangle trademark in favor of the "Ram" hood ornament, in time for Dodge's 25th anniversary in 1939.

During World War II, all civilian auto production was curtailed, and Dodge built military vehicles and equipment. The first postwar Dodge hit the market in 1946 and was met with pent up demand. The brand offered the uninspired DeLuxe, Custom, and special nameplates, featuring integrated fenders and headlights, fastback styling, and a long, curvaceous line.

During the 1950s, Dodge adopted the theme "New, Bigger Value Dodges," emphasizing styling with more sweeping chrome and a prominent crest above "DODGE," which appeared in block letters. The cars were sleeker than their 1940s predecessors, with a one-piece windshield, wraparound rear windows, and new interior styling. The cars were promoted as "Elegance in Action." Small fins emerged in the mid-1950s and continued to grow through the rest of the decade, inspiring the "Forward Look." Unfortunately, Dodge and parent Chrysler were more concerned with making cars that were bigger, but not necessarily better, than the competition. Customers soon realized this, and Dodge plummeted to tenth place in 1958.

The 1960s were characterized by intense market segmentation. Whereas there were three clearly defined markets in 1959—low-, medium- and high-priced cars—by the end of the 1960s, there were seven segments—compact, intermediate, standard, medium, luxury, plus high- and low-priced specialty cars. Dodge introduced its compact Dart, which featured the angular, boxy styling that characterized the brand's entire 1960 lineup. Dodge tried to entice a younger market with its "Dodge Rebellion" and "Dodge Fever" promotions during the decade, but it really only succeeded in alienating the brand's traditionally older, conservative customer base.

Dodge also invested a record $50 million and almost four years of planning, engineering, and testing in the 1972 introduction of an all-new line of light-duty trucks in an effort to capture part of this burgeoning market, which had doubled over the previous decade to 1.2 million units in 1971. The brand's 1973 Club Cab, which provided an extra 34 cubic feet of protected cargo or passenger space, was copied by many competitors. Dodge also joined the growing sport utility segment during the 1970s, with the launch of the ''Ram Tough'' Ramcharger. Trucks—and increasingly popular vans—would become a mainstay of the brand, comprising more than half of unit sales by the mid-1980s. Dodge, however, continued to lag behind Ford and Chevy in the truck and van category as well.

By 1968 imports had captured one-tenth of the entire market, and the U.S. auto industry began to recognize that there was a demand for small cars. American manufacturers were even more motivated to make smaller cars by the oil crisis of the 1970s and subsequent Federal Corporate Average Fuel Economy (CAFE) standards requiring a balance between each automaker's least and most fuel efficient cars. Dodge entered the subcompact marketplace in 1972 in cooperation with Chrysler affiliate Mitsubishi.

The Japanese giant Mitsubishi's fuel-efficient Colt was imported under the Dodge nameplate. Chrysler met the ''downsizing'' challenge with the Dodge Omni (and its Plymouth twin, the Horizon), the first small front-wheel-drive car built in the United States. Lower production costs and a head start gave Japan a decided advantage, but American carmakers also suffered from bad timing; fickle U.S consumers began to turn back to big cars and, as the manufacturers followed, along came the second oil crisis of 1979-1980. The miserable conditions were compounded by an economic recession and an accompanying ebb of demand, resulting in huge losses for American car manufacturers, especially Chrysler.

A Decade of ''Change''

In the early 1980s, when Chrysler Corporation's very existence was threatened, the parent concentrated on reassuring customers that it was still in business, and the individual brands' identities blurred. BBDO advertising agency had handled the Dodge account from 1941 until 1979, when Kenyon & Eckhardt was awarded all of Chrysler's business in what was then the largest account move in history. The money-saving shift was reversed just three years later, when the parent had recovered enough to resume the quest for a unique Dodge brand identity.

In the mid-1980s, marketers began to position the brand as a youthful, performance-oriented, yet affordable line, in contrast to Plymouth's reliable, basic-transportation image. A turning point for Dodge was the 1984 model year, when it launched the Caravan minivan, the sporty Daytona, and the Shelby Charger. The Caravan (and its Plymouth Voyager counterpart) caught the competition off-guard and created a new segment. The minivan's car-like handling combined with the carrying capacity of a van reshaped the way American families thought about their transportation needs.

To emphasize changes in the brand, Dodge introduced the ''An American Revolution'' advertising campaign. The brand also successfully targeted young men with a locally oriented ''Dodge boys have more fun'' theme. The average age of Dodge customers declined from 43 to 39 between 1982 and 1986, despite the strong older appeal of the brand's best-selling auto, the Aries K-car. Dodge advanced to fourth place in the mid-1980s and emphasized its transformation from a ''stodgy'' nameplate to a ''hot young company'' with a commercial that showed the metamorphosis of a 1963 Dart into a 1986 Shadow.

When the American car market went soft again in the early 1990s, Chrysler diverted funds from its divisions to support the ''Advantage Chrysler'' campaign. But with more than 600 models competing for fewer buyers and a host of look-alike advertisements, it was very difficult for a specific name to get people's attention and consideration. Dodge responded to this challenge with low-volume niche products that fashioned an image of affordable performance, starting with the Stealth and Viper sports cars and the Intrepid.

The Viper helped boost Dodge's image as 1991's Indianapolis 500 pace car and the ''star'' of a 1993 network television crime drama series. The Intrepid was Dodge's version of the Chrysler's LH line, which targeted the midsize family-sedan market dominated by the three top-selling cars in the United States: Ford Taurus, Honda Accord, and Toyota Camry. The Intrepid enticed import buyers back into newly renovated Dodge showrooms, where they would soon find other pleasant surprises that helped round out the brand's line.

The completely—and startlingly—revamped Ram pickup series reestablished Dodge's presence in the full-sized truck market, which had grown to $22 billion. The 1994 Ram's designers gave it a bold grill and prominent front fenders that made it resemble the big rigs. The new model garnered *Motor Trend*'s ''Truck of the Year'' award, and was praised for its combination of car-like ride, interior room and comfort, state-of-the art safety features, performance, durability, and reliability, not to mention over 50 important product features that ranked as industry firsts, Dodge exclusives, or best-in-class.

Beginning in 1993, Dodge was promoted with a blunt theme that acknowledged its previously dull reputation as well as its transformation: ''We're changing everything.'' The brand's ram emblem, adopted in 1992, touted ''The New Dodge.'' Also that year, auto shoppers were invited to ''Say Hello to Neon,'' a subcompact praised by *Car & Driver* for its ''Great performance, great spaciousness, great fun, [and] great price.'' The car featured standard driver and front passenger airbags, a roomy interior (due to Chrysler's cab-forward design), and highly touted styling.

Performance Appraisal

When it was first introduced, the Dodge Brothers brand benefited from John and Horace Dodge's excellent reputation for quality and dependability. The nameplate reached an apex of second place in U.S. sales in 1920, ironically the same year that both brothers died. Dodge plummeted to a low of tenth during that decade as a result of uncertainty and mismanagement. Languishing in the bottom half of the top ten for much of its history, it had gained a following of mostly conservative, older, generally blue-collar customers.

But when Dodge tried recklessly to shake its boring image in the 1960s and 1970s, it merely alienated its loyal core. After a decade of declining quality that ended with Chrysler's well-publicized near miss with bankruptcy, the parent undertook a slower, more deliberate rejuvenation of Dodge that carried it to a secure fourth-place standing. And led by Dodge, Chrysler Corporation was expected to shake its underdog status to take its place as a leader in the industry in 1994.

Further Reading:

"1994 Dodge Ram Is the Pickup of the Future . . . Here Now," *Fleet Equipment,* September 1993, p. 8.

Bedard, Patrick, "Dodge Neon: A Little Car with a Big Motor and a Big Grin," *Car & Driver,* April 1994, p. 55.

Cooper, Ann, "Domestic Autos: Detroit's Long Road to Change," *Adweek,* January 4, 1993, pp. 26–32.

"Dodge Account Heading Back to BBDO," *Advertising Age,* October 11, 1982, pp. 1, 78.

"In for Major Service," *The Economist,* October 15, 1988, pp. 10, 19.

Pattern, Jean Madder, and Joan Potter Elwart, *The Dodges: The Auto Family, Fortune and Misfortune,* South Bend, IN: Icarus Press, 1981.

McPherson, Thomas A., *The Dodge Story,* Glen Ellyn, IL: Crestline Publishing Co., 1975.

Mortise, Michael, and Barrett Seaman, *Going for Broke: The Chrysler Story,* Garden City, NY: Doubleday, 1981.

Sears, Stephen W., *The American Heritage History of the Automobile in America,* New York: American Heritage Publishing, 1977.

Serafin, Raymond, "Performance Image Incites Dodge Revolution," *Advertising Age,* June 16, 1986, pp. S–2.

Serafin, Raymond, and Patricia Strnad, "Chrysler Readies for Van Fight," *Advertising Age,* February 6, 1989, p. 50.

Strnad, Patricia, "Dodge Commercial Casts a Long Shadow," *Advertising Age,* September 29, 1986, p. 36.

Warner, Fara, and Lisa Marie Petersen, "Blissful Domestic Resurgence," *Superbrands,* October 18, 1993, pp. 54–61.

Wilkie, David J., *Esquire's American Autos and Their Makers,* New York: Esquire Inc., 1963.

Woodruff, David, "Chrysler May Actually Be Turning the Corner," *Business Week,* February 10, 1992, 32.

—April S. Dougal

DODGE CARAVAN®

The Dodge Caravan minivan was introduced in November of 1983 by the Chrysler Corporation along with its twin the Plymouth Voyager and the Dodge Mini Ram Van. At the time of their debut Chrysler Chairman Lee Iacocca predicted that "the Voyager and Caravan will be to the 80s what the Mustang was to the 60s—vehicles that create extraordinary excitement and buyer interest and force other manufacturers to come up with copycat versions." While Iacocca has since retired, the Caravan has more than lived up to his advance billing and continues into the 1990s as a jewel in Chrysler's crown.

Brand Origins

The Caravan's story begins in 1977, when the people at Chrysler wondered how they might capitalize on the industry-leading performance of their full-sized Dodge Ram Van. Father of all the minivans that would follow, the Dodge Ram controlled 45 percent of the full-size passenger van market at that time, leading both Ford and General Motors.

Chrysler executives attributed this success to their strategy of providing car-like amenities in large vans, and they rightly supposed that a smaller, more economical version might appeal to a younger segment of the market. Featuring power windows and locks, rear window defrosters, power seats, and superior audio systems, the Ram Van became the departure point for a fuel- and space-efficient alternative in the traditional station wagon market. The fuel crisis of the late 1970s, coupled with a general economic downturn, had initiated a trend towards more compact and inexpensive vehicles, and Chrysler believed consumers who missed the space and comfort of their previous autos would see a solution in minivans.

Research indicated the continued attractiveness of the comforts a station wagon could offer, but it seemed too stodgy for the younger market. With the minivans, said a key player in their development at the time, "We think we'll be the first on the block to attract that younger mentality." And Joseph Campana, then Chrysler's Vice-President of Marketing, said "There's no question in my mind that it's the station wagon of the future."

In moving from the full-size van to the minivan, the first and most important consideration was the downsizing of the vehicle. The popularity of large vans had always been limited because they did not fit in the average garage; drawing on extensive market research, Chrysler officials realized that a vehicle that could both accomodate a family and offer space for cargo was a sure winner. Setting their sights on a "garageable" product, the engineers went to work, and by 1978 Chrysler had earmarked the minivan as an "Investigate" item in its long-range product plan. It would be five more years before the Caravan and its fellow minivans appeared, however; Chrysler's widely-publicized financial problems in the late 1970s and early 1980s stalled development on the new line, while its commitment to the K-car program, which was to issue in the Dodge Aries and Plymouth Reliant, monopolized what cash reserves there were.

One important boost for the minivan program was the arrival at Chrysler of Iacocca, who came over from Ford in 1978. Ironically, Iacocca and others at Ford had been the first people to realize the immense sales potential in a minivan, and for several years during the mid-1970s they had presented plans for what they called a "Mini/max" to Henry Ford, the company's chairman. "We were looking at a market of eight hundred thousand a year," Iacocca remembered in his autobiography. "Naturally, I went to see the king right away. . . . 'Forget it,' said Henry. 'I don't want to experiment'. . . . 'Experiment?' I said. 'The Mustang was an experiment. The Mark III was an experiment. This car is another winner'. . . . But Henry wouldn't buy it."

Ford's missed opportunity became Chrysler's windfall when Iacocca and Hal Sperlich, another Ford exile, put their weight behind the minivan at their new company and got it off the ground. Soon after his arrival, Iacocca procured $500 million for the vehicles' completion, an enormous commitment for a company in fiscal crisis. And although the final bill would come to $700 million, $40 million of which went towards the reconstruction of a manufacturing plant in Windsor, Ontario, to build the new vehicles, this commitment was the turning point in the Caravan's fortunes.

For Iacocca, as for the hundreds of thousands of satisfied customers in the coming decade, the risk had resulted in substantial dividends. "I still remember the first time I drove the minivan at our proving grounds," writes Iacocca. "They couldn't get me off the track. I just kept going around and around. I loved what the engineers had done to the handling and the ride. This car was really fun to drive."

AT A GLANCE

The Dodge Caravan brand of minivan debuted in November of 1983 with twin Plymouth Voyager at Chrysler Corporation's Windsor, Ontario, plant; brand introduced by Lee Iacocca, who along with Hal Sperlich, another ex-Ford executive, was instrumental in its development; brand joined in 1987 by extended version called Dodge Grand Caravan; in 1988 the Dodge Mini Ram Van was revamped and rechristened Caravan C/V, a cargo-oriented version.

Performance: *Market share*—24.5% of minivan segment (top share). *Sales*—262,838 units (1993).

Major competitor: Ford Aerostar; also, Chevrolet Lumina.

Advertising: *Agency*—BBDO, Southfield, MI; Bozell Worldwide, Southfield, MI. *Major campaign*—"Ask the People Who Own One."

Addresses: *Parent company*—Chrysler Corporation, 12000 Chrysler Dr., Highland Park, MI 48288; phone: (313) 956-5741; fax: (313) 956-1462.

Another crucial event in the ongoing development of the minivan line was the approval in the spring of 1980 of $1.5 billion in guaranteed loans from the federal Chrysler Loan Guarantee Board. This allowed the cash-poor company to forge ahead with its future product plans, and provided the necessary impetus for the completion of the first models. Even with such momentum, however, the Caravan had to wait three more years before it could hit the streets. Initially proposed as a 1983 model to be introduced in the fall of 1982, delays in development and funding pushed its appearance back another full year.

Widely advertised and featured in the media in the months before they arrived, the minivans were finally unveiled in November of 1983. They were hailed in *Car and Driver* as "a wonderful addition to the automotive firmament" and in *Road and Track* as "the most innovative vehicles to come out of Detroit in decades." Virtually creating a new market, the new vehicles soon justified the years of planning and development with impressive financial returns.

Market Performance

Priced at around $10,000, the Caravan sold only 4,260 units in the final days of 1983, but gained a solid foothold in its first full year, when almost 86,000 were sold. One year later, sales passed the 100,000 mark for the first time, and by 1988 over 200,000 were being sold per year. In 1993, the sales high-watermark for Caravan thus far, Chrysler sold 262,838 vehicles and commanded a market share of 24.5 percent.

One reason for the Caravan's decade of success was the jump it got on competitors, who were seen by some consumers as opportunists with inferior products. The Chrysler minivan line made its debut nine full months before GMC's Safari and Ford's Aerostar, and it has remained the leader ever since. Chrysler's market share of the minivan segment has always hovered near 50 percent, with Caravan accounting for approximately half of that share each year. Caravan and its companion vehicles have truly been what one automotive commentator called "Chrysler's financial lifeline," and some industry experts wonder whether there would be a Chrysler at all had the minivan concept not been developed.

Original Design and Subsequent Evolution

In 1993, on the occasion of the tenth anniversary of its minivan line, Chrysler Chairman and CEO Robert Eaton addressed an audience at the Windsor, Ontario plant and tried to account for the minivans' continued success. "While the minivan's original package put it on top, it's not the reason that it has stayed on top," he said. "I think the key to the minivan's longevity can be summed up in two words: continuous improvement. Over the first ten-year run of the minivan, we've never stopped improving the vehicle, its quality, or the process by which we build them."

The "original package" he referred to was good enough to draw rave reviews from trade journals when it first appeared under its code name the "T-115," but the Caravan has evolved considerably in its ten-year existence. Hyped as "A Van for All Seasons" and featured on the cover of *Car and Driver* months before it was available in showrooms, the Caravan was basically a "Blessed Box" on wheels and as such enjoyed "the most perfect storage bin yet devised by man."

At the time of its introduction to the market, the only competitors for the Caravan were both imports—the Volkswagen Vanagon and the Toyota Van Wagen—and neither had what seemed essential to Chrysler engineers and market researchers: the magic of front-wheel drive. Without front-wheel drive, the engines on these vehicles tunneled into the cabin, and research had shown that customers felt uncomfortable with that layout. A front-wheel design also allowed for a lower step-up height, important to women who were still likely to be wearing skirts, and with the engine up front, it gave the minivan a "nose" which could absorb the crush in case of an accident. "The key," said Hal Sperlich at the time, "is to get the vehicles friendly enough so the housewife feels like she's driving a car."

Since its makers were convinced the minivan of the future should be more like a car than a truck, size, flexibility, and easy handling were other main factors considered in its design. Conceived from the inside out, the success of the T-115 depended on what Sperlich, Chrysler's President of North American Automotive Operations, called "package efficiency—the concept of how to get the most usable space inside the smallest real estate." To achieve all of its goals, Chrysler engineers settled on a 112-inch wheelbase with exterior specs of 175.9 inches long, 72.4 inches wide and 64.2 inches high. This made for a van that was three inches shorter, 10 inches narrower and 15 inches lower from the roof to the road than the popular full-size Dodge Ram Van.

The chief exterior feature was a sliding door on the passenger side, which was selected after market research indicated a preference for it among people who already owned vehicles Chrysler hoped to supplant with the minivan—larger vans and station wagons. The rear featured a one-piece lift gate instead of a two-piece lift up/fold down device. Side moldings were minimal, and the front and rear bumpers were aluminum face bars. The interior, meanwhile, offered families seating for five or seven passengers, with bucket seats up front and back seats which could be removed or reconfigured. And 48 inches from wheel-well to wheel-well was hit upon as the cargo space dimension—just enough room for a standard sheet of plywood.

The front-wheel drive engine in these first models came with two power options: a 2.2-liter four-cylinder engine standard, with a 2.6-liter four-cylinder engine optional. In the passenger Caravan a five-speed transaxle transmission was standard, while the cargo model—originally called the Mini Ram Van and rechristened in 1987 as the Caravan C/V—featured a four-speed manual transmission. Another option available in both models was a three-speed automatic transaxle. The original decision to go with the four-cylinder engine instead of a V-6 caused some apprehension, as market researchers reported a preference for the larger motor and engineers worried that the Caravan might seem underpowered to buyers. This "weak link" however, did not prove too severe a deterrent to customers. In any event, by 1987 a model with a V-6 engine was available.

Among the first important changes in the basic design was a convert-a-bed option in 1985 and an eight-passenger seating option in the premium models of 1986. And in 1987 extended versions of both the Caravan and Voyager—the Dodge Grand Caravan and the Plymouth Grand Voyager—premiered. These larger vehicles featured seven more inches of wheelbase, an innovation devised to offer more space for families on vacation, and were manufactured at a second plant, in St. Louis, Missouri, which was converted for the purpose. Since their arrival in 1987, the sales mix has been about 50/50 between the shorter and extended models of the Caravan and Voyager. In 1990 the line was expanded again with the luxury Chrysler Town & Country. 1987 also saw the first electronically fuel-injected engines standard in the Caravan, and the option of a 3.0-liter EFI V-6. In 1990 this was expanded further into a 3.3-liter option.

Once the Caravan had been launched, Chrysler kept very close tabs on customers' feedback, and many of the changes over the years have come in response to specific requests by buyers. In 1984, the company surveyed thousands of Caravan purchasers by mail to gauge their response to the then-novel vehicles, and since then it has followed up every minivan purchase with a questionnaire. According to David Bostwick, manager of Chrysler's business planning and research, this is "a good five times the average concentration" on market response and it has allowed Chrysler to gear the changes in the vehicles over the years to customers' real concerns rather than imagined improvements. Many of these requests were for added conveniences in the interior like drink holders, a glovebox and a more intelligible dashboard. Very few had suggestions for the exterior, although one Vermont man was succinct in his wishes: "MORE CHROME" he wrote.

By 1990 this strategy of heeding customer feedback had won the minivans a very high loyalty rate of 86 percent and gained the admiration of other automakers. The ideas generated from customer surveys helped Chrysler make the most extensive overhaul in the Caravan make-up to date. For the 1991 model, $650 million was spent to recast the front suspension and steering systems, and an all-wheel drive alternative was added.

There was at least one phase of the continuing evolution of the minivan, however, when the dangers of fixing what isn't broken were impressed on Chrysler. This began in 1988, when a newfangled electronic transmission called Ultradrive failed to live up to its predicted potential. Given an award by The Society of Automotive Engineers and meant to respond in specific ways to individual driving styles, this sophisticated device was installed in the six-cylinder minivans as well as in some passenger cars. But leaky seals on the transmission were soon discovered, which allowed fluid into the wrong areas and resulted in burned-out clutches. Of the 1 million 1989 and 1990 model vehicles that featured the new transmissions, 19,000 had to be replaced; and in January of 1990, 53,000 vehicles were recalled for another problem with the circulation of transmission oil. Always proud of the loyalty of its buyers, Caravan lost at least one customer's business forever because of the problems: "I feel like [the transmission] is being field tested at my expense" said a Des Moines industrial components salesman, and he vowed he would not buy another Caravan. A lesser hitch in the overall extraordinary success of the brand came in 1991, when 640,000 of the 1989 and 1990 models were recalled for repairs to a front passenger seat belt buckle.

In 1992 Chrysler became the first company to make a driver's side air bag standard in its minivans, and an integrated child seat was also made available that year. Innovation continued in 1993 with the introduction of R134A, an ozone-friendly air conditioning refrigerant, and the inclusion of a quieter, higher capacity heater and air conditioning fan. Also new for the 1994 model year vehicle were a sports suspension package, a quad seating tilt feature, a full stainless steel exhaust system, a redesigned instrument panel inside, and front and rear bumper fascia outside. This fairly-comprehensive facelift came in response to over 1,000 customer product change notices, and once again affirmed Chrysler's commitment to its buyers.

Far from resting on its laurels, Chrysler has in the past two years made waves in the auto industry with the introduction of two alternative-fuel Caravans. The first of these was an electric-powered minivan, which made its debut in April of 1993 and is currently being bought by power utility companies and by companies with fleets that operate over a limited area. This Caravan, which is capable of accelerating from 0 to 50 mph in 27 seconds and has a top speed of 65 miles per hour is still prohibitively expensive, however, and isn't likely to have the impact the second alternative-energy vehicle is. Manufactured by Chrysler under a cooperative agreement with the Gas Research Institute of Chicago, this minivan, which runs on compressed natural gas, was introduced in February of 1994 and is cause for high hopes indeed. Described by one of its engineers as possessing "the cleanest running internal combustion engine in the world," the CNG Caravan is slated in particular for those states with pollution control mandates, like California, and should make major inroads by the turn of the century. It emits no hydrocarbons, no nitrogen oxide and extremely low carbon monoxide—the three chief elements of smog—and at present costs only $5000 more than the conventional gasoline minivan.

Advertising and Incentives

Apart from the jump Chrysler got on its minivan competition, other major factors in the Caravan's continued success have been wide exposure, aggressive advertising, and sophisticated marketing strategies. During the Caravan's final design stages it was featured in periodicals ranging from industry journals like *Car and Driver* and *Road & Track* to wider-circulation magazines like *Connoisseur* and *Fortune*, and the latter selected it as one of the most beautiful cars ever designed. The original ad campaign for Caravan stressed the genius and novelty of the concept with the tag line "There hasn't been anything like it before."

The runaway success of the minivans led to a long line of competing vehicles in the years following their appearance. Chrysler has met this challenge by stressing the remarkable loyalty of their products' buyers. Drawing on letters from customers that have numbered as many as 3,000 a month, the company has shown a sensitivity to the wishes of its target market, and the empowerment felt by the customers has in turn guaranteed their continued loyalty.

In a 1990 campaign, Iacocca himself appeared in television spots and challenged viewers to "Ask the people who own them" before making their minivan purchase, a slogan which had first appeared as "Ask the man who owns one" in a 1940s advertising campaign for the Packard. The print advertising for the Caravan picked up on this motif with such variations as "Ask the mom who owns one," "Ask the dog who vacations in one," and, during the Christmas season, "Ask the reindeer who was replaced by one." There was even an ad placed in the F.A.O. Schwarz toy catalog which read "Ask the toy store that fills one."

Chrysler's understanding of their target market, "young marrieds with children," has also been key to the minivan's continued success. Produced by Batten, Barton, Durstine and Osborn, the 1988 print campaign referred to the Caravan as a "family wagon" and showed a busy mother helping children into the capacious vehicle after their dancing class. And in 1990 this same theme was sounded in the TV advertising, where a home-movie like spot showed an improbable number of children coming out of the minivan and mugging for the camera. Meanwhile the voice-over said, "As long as people keep making kids, we'll keep making Dodge Caravans."

In 1992, with new minivans from Nissan and Mercury set to enter the field, Chrysler asserted its preeminence once again by mounting a combined-brand campaign as "The Minivan Company." Highlights included the appearance of an actual family that had discovered the Caravan in 1988, one year after they were named The Honda Family of the Year, and had bought six more Chrysler minivans in the ensuing years. Estimated costs for this campaign, which ran for over a year, were 75–100 million dollars and evidenced a strong desire on Chrysler's part to carry the standard for the minivan industry.

Outside of advertising, Chrysler has also had occasion during the Caravan's ten-year existence to offer such sales incentives as rebates and special guarantees. One such offer, which ran for a 45-day period at the end of 1989 and returned $1,000 to buyers of Caravans and Voyagers or provided alternative low-interest financing, resulted in record sales for many dealerships. And when it was thought cash-back incentives were becoming too costly a promotion, Chrysler introduced the "Ultimate Guarantee" program, which gave minivan buyers a resale value guarantee, a selection of warranties, a roadside assistance plan and even a free car phone.

Outlook

With the addition of the electric and natural gas-powered Caravans in the last two years and the continued strength of the standard Caravan, Caravan C/V, and Grand Caravan, Chrysler should occupy the top of this market segment for some time. As an index of the importance of these vehicles to the corporation, one need only recall the prediction by a Chrysler executive in 1988 that by the year 2000 the minivans might even be outselling four-door sedans.

Further Reading:

Bohn, Joseph, "Chrysler Minivan Rebate Ends with a Roar," *Automotive News,* February 5, 1990.

"Chrysler Develops Natural Gas Minivans," *Mechanical Engineering,* June 1993.

Connelly, Mary, "Chrysler Unveils 'Ultimate Guarantee' for '92 Minivans," *Automotive News,* August 26, 1991.

Halberstam, David, *The Reckoning,* New York: William Morrow and Company, Inc., 1986.

Gray, Ralph, "Van-Wagons Straddle Market Segments," *Advertising Age,* October 10, 1983.

Iacocca, Lee, with William Novak, *An Autobiography,* New York: Bantam, 1984.

Kiley, David, "Chrysler Brands Minivans Together," *Adweek,* September 14, 1992.

Serafin, Raymond, "Mighty Minis Roll into Fray," *Advertising Age,* November 20, 1989.

Treece, James B., "The Streetwise Makeover of Chrysler's Minivans," *Business Week,* September 24, 1990.

Yates, Brock, "A Van for All Seasons," *Car and Driver,* May 1983.

—Sean Francis

DUNCAN® YO-YO

Like the ball, the bat, and the hoop, the yo-yo has always been one of the most basic mechanical toys. In one form or another, the yo-yo has been played with by children in some part of the world for the past 2,500 years. Modern American yo-yoing, however, is the product of one man, Donald F. Duncan, who introduced the Duncan Yo-Yo to Americans in 1929. Duncan, founder of the Duncan Toys Company, borrowed the concept and the name "yo-yo" from the Philippines, where it had been a favorite pastime for hundreds of years. Thanks in large part to Duncan's promotional genius, Duncan Yo-Yos quickly became first a national fad and then a national staple, eventually occupying a permanent place in American popular culture. Performer Bob Hope entertained U.S. troops with yo-yo tricks during World War II, and entertainer Tommy Smothers of the Smothers Brothers duo brought the yo-yo to the counter-culture in the 1960s. Duncan lost the exclusive rights to the trademark "Yo-Yo" in 1965, but remained the top-selling brand of the toy. Owned by Flambeau Products Corporation since 1968, Duncan Toys controlled 85 percent of the yo-yo market in the early 1990s.

Brand Origins

While Donald F. Duncan is responsible for the first mass production of yo-yos in the United States, the history of the toy itself stretches back to early antiquity. Wolfgang Burger, a physicist who specializes in the study of physical toys, described the yo-yo in *American Scientist* as "a mechanical device that stores kinetic energy in a rotating mass—a toy flywheel." The principle of the flywheel probably dates back to the Stone Age, when toolmakers discovered that attaching a heavy stone to their drill would increase its inertia. No one, though, knows when or how the "fun" aspect of this principle evolved. The earliest evidence for the existence of a toy flywheel is found on an Ancient Greek bowl dating to 450 B.C., which depicts a figure of a boy playing with a disk on the end of a string.

The yo-yo first appeared in the modern era in eighteenth-century England, where it had been imported from China. Known as the "bandalore" or "emigrette," the idea for the simple toy traveled to Paris. There, the first of a long series of yo-yo crazes took hold. French nobles became inordinately fond of the toy and had them crafted in glass and ivory. One French nobleman even had himself painted with his yo-yo in hand. The Duke of Wellington is said to have been a yo-yo fan, and French ruler Napoleon's soldiers passed the time between battles by playing with the popular toy. The bandalore found its way to the United States from Europe in the nineteenth century, but the real source of the American yo-yo craze of the twentieth century was not the sophisticated courts of Europe, but the jungles of the Philippines.

The origin of the Philippine yo-yo is a matter of debate. Some suggest that, like the European bandalore, the toy yo-yo reached the Philippines by way of China. A more fanciful account holds that the yo-yo was independently invented by Filipino hunters who would perch in trees and throw a stone disc at passing prey, retrieving the disc with an attached thong if it missed its mark. Physicist Wolfgang Burger suggests that if the yo-yo was really used as a hunting tool there must have been many hungry Filipinos, since a yo-yo quickly loses force as it descends and would have been extremely inefficient as a weapon. Whatever its origins, by the nineteenth century the yo-yo was a standard children's toy in the Philippines. The term "yo-yo," in fact, derives from the Philippine Tagalog language and describes both the sound and the action of the yo-yo.

At some point in its evolution among young boys in the Philippines, the classic yo-yo developed a crucial twist. Instead of a single string tied to an axle in the manner of the European bandalore, the Philippine yo-yo's string was looped around the axle with the two branches of the loop twisted tautly together. While the classic single-string bandalore disc returned immediately upon reaching the end of its string, the Philippine yo-yo paused for a few seconds before returning, thus allowing it to "sleep." This feature has prompted the execution of a repertoire of tricks for which the yo-yo was to become famous.

It was the twisted-string, Philippine yo-yo that first caught the attention of Donald F. Duncan in the late 1920s. Introduced to the United States by Filipino immigrants at least a decade earlier, the yo-yo's popularity had remained restricted to immigrant neighborhoods. Pedro Flores, a Filipino hotel worker and yo-yo aficionado, was the first person to realize the commercial potential of the toy. Flores registered his "Flores Yo-Yo" with the U.S. Patent Office in the late 1920s.

Entrepreneur Duncan apparently saw one of Flores's yo-yos or a homemade version in action and decided that with the proper promotion the toy could become a very big seller. He started manufacturing the toy in 1929 and shortly thereafter applied to the

AT A GLANCE

Duncan yo-yo brand founded in 1929 by Donald F. Duncan, owner of Duncan Toys Company; company acquired by Flambeau Products Corporation and operated as a subsidiary, 1968.

Performance: *Market share*—85% of yo-yo category.

Major competitor: Spectra Star; also Marchon.

Advertising: *Agency*—Goldberg, Fossa, Seid, New York, NY, 1994—.

Addresses: *Parent company*—Duncan Toys Co., 15891 Valplast Rd., Box 97, Middlefield, OH 44062; phone: (800) 356-8396; fax: (216) 632-1581. *Ultimate parent company*—Flambeau Products Corporation (address same as above).

patent office for the registration of the "Genuine Duncan Yo-Yo" as a trademark for a toy described in the application as "a bandalore type spinning top." His trademark application was turned down on the grounds that Flores had the prior claim to the name. Undeterred, Duncan contacted Flores and arranged to buy the rights for the yo-yo from him for an undisclosed sum. Duncan reapplied for trademark registration and in 1932 was granted trademark registration not only for "Genuine Duncan Yo-Yo" but for the general term "Yo-Yo" as well. The Philippine toy thus became the Duncan Yo-Yo.

Brand Development

The physical properties of the yo-yo demanded that it be of a size to fit into the palm of the hand and that the axle radius be small enough to allow the yo-yo to return. These basic design requirements have meant relatively few major changes in yo-yo design over the years. Small variations in shape, however, have been introduced by Duncan Toys. In 1993, for example, Duncan Yo-Yos were produced in five basic shape categories: the Professional (slim and flat), the Imperial (rounded dome), and the Butterfly (inverted dome).

The original Duncan Yo-Yo was carved from hardwoods such as maple, ash, and beechwood. In 1957 the Flambeau Plastics Company, which would later purchase Duncan Toys, began to manufacture plastic yo-yos for Duncan in its plant in Baraboo, Wisconsin. The first and all-time best-selling plastic yo-yo, the Duncan Imperial, was modeled after the original wooden Duncan Model 77. Throughout their history, Duncan Yo-Yos have also been available in a range of colors. In the 1980s and 1990s, fluorescent colors, glow in the dark, and a "cracked ice" rainbow hologram were added to the Duncan line.

Promotion and Advertising

The genius of Donald Duncan lay in his flair for promotion. He maintained from the start that a yo-yo could not be appreciated unless it was seen in action. The print advertisements of the 1920s and 1930s could not possibly do justice to the small, unpretentious looking toy, and therefore it was essential that Duncan concoct an original promotional vehicle. Duncan had seen teens yo-yoing on the playgrounds of Filipino neighborhoods and realized that there could be no better promotional tool than to see these youths in action.

Duncan hired dozens of Filipino men to tour the United States, promoting the Duncan Yo-Yo with dazzling displays of skill. Duncan Yo-Yo displays soon became an annual tradition; every April groups of Duncan demonstrators would show up outside local candy stores and movie theaters to perform their newest gravity-defying yo-yo tricks. A native New Yorker recalled this springtime ritual in a 1991 *New York Times* article: "It was incredible. There we would be on the handball court and suddenly out of nowhere, the Filipino grand-master would appear. Word would get out, and we would all rush to watch him. It was charming, a real rite of spring."

Duncan's most successful single promotion—and the one that essentially began the twentieth-century yo-yo craze—was a cooperative effort with newspaper magnate William Randolph Hearst. Hearst agreed to advertise Duncan Yo-Yo contests with the condition that anyone who wanted to enter would have to sell three subscriptions to a Hearst newspaper. Introducing this restriction seemed to fuel excitement for the highly publicized contests, which now carried an aura of exclusivity as well as fun. One 1931 promotion in Philadelphia lasted 30 days and resulted in the sale of three million yo-yos.

The yo-yo craze, started during the Great Depression, had faded by the end of World War II. Although Duncan Yo-Yos were still popular, sales had dropped, and Duncan Toys found themselves in need of a new promotional vehicle. Network television

Duncan Yo-Yo's popular Butterfly model.

advertising presented the perfect opportunity to once again drum up excitement about the simple toy. Television was ideal for a product like a yo-yo, which had to be shown in action. A commercial could reach more kids in a single half hour than Duncan's roving band of demonstrators could do in a month. Duncan began to advertise heavily on network television—spending $1 million on advertising per year in 1962 and 1963—and achieved spectacular results. By the late 1950s, the second yo-yo craze was in full swing. It reached its peak in 1963, when a record 33 million Duncan Yo-Yos were sold.

As network advertising became prohibitively expensive in the 1970s and 1980s, Duncan all but abandoned its television campaign. Sales had dropped dramatically, and the company simply could not afford its previous advertising budgets. Faced with ever diminishing sales, Duncan's parent company, Flambeau Products Corp., realized that something had to be done if the Duncan Yo-Yo was to be saved from extinction.

Clyde Mortensen, marketing director for Duncan Toys during the yo-yo's heyday in the 1950s and 1960s, was brought out of retirement to try to revive the fading classic. Mortensen decided that cable television advertising was not only affordable, it would more effectively reach Duncan's target audience. He began an intensive campaign of 30-second action-filled spots on five child-oriented cable stations. "A kid watching cartoons after school could not avoid seeing a Duncan commercial," a Duncan marketing executive was quoted as saying in a 1991 *New York Times* article. Sales immediately began to rebound, and the Duncan Yo-Yo was back.

Trademark Disputes

Obtaining the exclusive rights to the term "Yo-Yo" might well have been Donald Duncan's single most important business coup. But, as recounted by Sidney Diamond in *Advertising Age,* Duncan encountered problems with the registration of the Duncan Yo-Yo trademark from the very start. His first application for registration was delayed, because Pedro Flores had already registered the "Flores Yo-Yo." It was only after acquiring the rights from Flores that the 1932 registration of the "Duncan Yo-Yo" was granted. It was in the following year that Duncan obtained a second registration covering the term "Yo-Yo" by itself, even though later court decisions revealed that, according to U.S. patent law, this second trademark registration should never have been approved.

Controlling the rights to the term "Yo-Yo" meant that competitors were severely constrained, since there was little doubt that "yo-yo" had always been the common generic term for the toy. Diamond described how later testimony clearly indicated that the toy had been known in the Philippine Islands for hundreds of years—always under the generic name "yo-yo." Trademark law had already established that "a word commonly used in other countries to identify a kind of product as a generic name may not be appropriated here as a trademark."

According to Diamond, Duncan Toys was aware of its tenuous claim on the trademark and Duncan consequently began a concerted campaign to solidify "Yo-Yo" as a brand name. The first step was to establish an alternative generic name for the toy so that the brand and generic names could be distinguished. The company began to refer to the toy as the "Yo-Yo return top," but the public refused to accept the new appellation and continued to refer to the toy generically as a yo-yo. Duncan also began to use the slogan "If it isn't a Duncan, it isn't a Yo-Yo" in the hopes that this would strengthen the association between Duncan and the term "Yo-Yo." This ploy also backfired, however, as the grammatical structure of the phrase merely reinforced the usage of "yo-yo" as the generic name and "Duncan" as the brand.

Although it had previously avoided testing its rights to the "Yo-Yo" trademark in court, in 1963, at the height of the 1960s yo-yo craze, Duncan decided that it could no longer permit encroachment on its market share by competitors. The company sued Royal Tops Mfg. Co. for trademark infringement for use of the term "yo-yo." The case was finally decided in 1965 by the Federal Court of Appeals in Chicago, which ruled that the trademark was invalid because "yo-yo" was the generic name of the toy. Duncan had lost the rights to its most famous trademark, and the Duncan Yo-Yo became once more a simple yo-yo.

Performance, Competition, and Future Growth

Like the action of the yo-yo itself, yo-yo sales have been a series of ups and downs. From the first bandalore craze in the Napoleonic era to the 1990s yo-yo revival, the yo-yo has been a toy of fashion and fad. The first Duncan Yo-Yo peak came in the late 1930s, when kids of the Depression years were willing to shell out the necessary half dollar for the little toy. Even though sales began to drop during World War II, the yo-yo remained a part of Americana, thanks to Bob Hope performing yo-yo tricks for the troops.

The 1950s saw the birth of television and the revival of the Duncan Yo-Yo mainly because of advertisements on the new medium. By that time, Duncan Yo-Yos had been around for almost 40 years and were an established part of American popular culture. In 1963, at the height of the second twentieth-century yo-yo craze, Duncan sold more than 33 million of the toys. After that amazing peak, and with the loss of their exclusive rights to the term "yo-yo" in 1965, Duncan Yo-Yo sales dropped. During a mid-1980s period of turmoil for the toy industry in general, annual sales of Duncan Yo-Yos reached a nadir of less than 500,000. Duncan Toys responded with a new advertising campaign on cable television. The new campaign, in conjunction with an overall consumer return to traditional toys, saw sales rebound. Roughly 12 million of the classic toys were sold in 1990. The early 1990s also saw Duncan moving into the international market.

Duncan Toys has dominated the yo-yo market in the United States since its creation in 1929. With exclusive rights to the very word "Yo-Yo" for over 30 years, Duncan made it difficult for any company to begin to compete with their brand. Duncan's control of the yo-yo market began to dwindle as the 1960s yo-yo craze died and as other companies found their own niches in the yo-yo market. In the late 1980s, for instance, Imperial Toy's Spectra Star brand began appearing on yo-yos depicting licensed cartoon characters that have been very popular with the under ten set. A yo-yo with a wide tape instead of a string as well as a padded yo-yo were introduced by the Marchon Company in the early 1990s and have seen some success.

Despite encroachments by smaller producers, more Duncan Yo-Yos have been sold in the United States than any other brand. In 1991 Duncan still controlled an impressive 85 percent of the yo-yo market. From the perspective of the mid-1990s, it seemed certain that the Duncan Yo-Yo would remain a perennial favorite of American children.

Further Reading:

Bahringer, D., and K. W. Du Four, *Duncan Yo-Yo Trick Book,* Baraboo, WI: Flambeau Products Corporation, 1979.

Berg, Eric N., "In World of Space-Age Toys, a Return of String and Spool," *New York Times,* April 14, 1991, pp. 1, 22.

"A Bunch of Yo-Yos from Columbus," *Indiana Business Magazine,* July 1991, p. 4.

Burger, Wolfgang, "The Yo-Yo: A Toy Flywheel," *American Scientist,* March/April 1984, pp. 137–142.

Diamond, Sidney A., "Court Ruling Invalidates 'Yo-Yo' Trademark," *Advertising Age,* April 12, 1965, pp. 105–106.

—Hilary Gopnik

DUNLOP®

A venerable name in the sporting goods industry, the Dunlop brand has been emblazoned across tennis racquets, tennis balls, golf clubs, and golf balls for generations, making the Dunlop logo a trusted and familiar symbol for many sports enthusiasts. As a pioneer in the manufacture of sports equipment, the company behind the Dunlop brand name, Dunlop Slazenger Corporation, has contributed to the evolution of the sporting goods industry from its fledgling years early in the twentieth century, to the booming, multibillion dollar business that was flourishing in the 1990s. During the course of this transformation, products bearing the Dunlop name have undergone significant technological advancements to keep pace with the more sophisticated demands of both the professional and amateur consumer. Aluminum, graphite, and other high-technology alloys used to construct tennis racquet frames have supplanted the once ubiquitous wood racquet, while golf clubs and golf balls have experienced similar revolutionary advances in construction.

To succeed in the modern sporting goods industry, manufacturers must consistently develop innovative products to meet the frequently capricious needs of consumers searching for equipment to help improve their play. At the same time, marketers must support the introduction of a product, preferably by securing the endorsement of a renowned professional athlete, by articulating the product's advantages, and by decorating the product with alluring graphics. Adhering to these fundamental marketing principles, Dunlop Slazenger Corporation has ascended into the upper echelon of the sporting goods industry, and the Dunlop brand has become one of the perennial leaders in the sporting goods market.

Brand Origins

The Dunlop brand name first appeared in Great Britain in the early twentieth century, soon after J. B. Dunlop formed The Pneumatic Tyre and Booth Cycle Agency in 1888 to market and produce his air-inflated automobile tires. The company, which would eventually become the Dunlop Corporation, achieved considerable success selling tires in Europe, enough to warrant an expansion into the U.S. tire market in the 1920s. Intent on capturing a share of the robust automobile market centered in Detroit, Dunlop established manufacturing facilities in Buffalo, New York. The company's foray into the United States, however, met with only a modicum of success. Existing U.S. tire manufacturers, such as Firestone, held a firm grip on the domestic market and were able to withstand the foreign competition, restricting Dunlop to a small percentage of the higher-priced market.

Beaten, but not ready to withdraw entirely from the United States, Dunlop's management decided to carry the company's brand name to America through a line of products it had first manufactured more than 20 years earlier—sporting goods. In 1910 Dunlop entered the sports business as a producer of golf balls, then seven years later as a maker of a line of tennis racquets. Accordingly, sporting goods seemed the logical solution to Dunlop's desire to expand into the United States.

In 1928 the subsidiary Dunlop Sports Company was formed to begin the production of sporting goods in earnest. Within three years Dunlop introduced the first multi-ply, or compositely constructed, tennis racquet, called "The Maxply," a name that in various forms would accompany the Dunlop brand name in the years to come. Following The Maxply, Dunlop's next signal product, the Dunlop 65 golf ball, emerged in 1934 and represented one of the first successful golf balls manufactured by Dunlop in the United States.

By the late 1930s Dunlop's expansion into the United States had proven to be a welcome addition to the European-based parent company's operations. The success of the company's tire business in Great Britain and in other parts of Europe had been predicated on the development of rubber molding technology, a process that was equally well suited to the production of golf balls. After the introduction of the Dunlop 65 ball, the U.S. subsidiary utilized this rubber molding process in the development of a rubber core golf ball, the Dunlop Red Eye, which entered the market toward the end of the 1930s. Before Dunlop could realize the full sales potential of the Red Eye, however, the bulk of the company's rubber supply was requisitioned by the War Department when the onset of World War II severely limited all production deemed nonessential to the prosecution of the war.

First Major Success

Although the Red Eye fell victim to the more pressing concerns of the early 1940s, Dunlop did not, reverting instead to the production of tires for war vehicles to generate revenue during World War II. When the war concluded, Dunlop resumed production of its rubber core golf ball, this time under the Maxfli name. Regarded as an "active" ball—one that responded well to a golf

AT A GLANCE

Dunlop brand of sporting goods founded in 1910 by J. B. Dunlop; Dunlop Sports Company formed in 1928; acquired Slazenger brand name, 1959; company sold to British Tire & Rubber Co. (BTR PLC), 1986; in 1987, company became Dunlop Slazenger Corporation, a subsidiary of BTR's Dunlop Slazenger International Ltd.

Performance: *Market share*—Ranked third in golf ball category. *Sales*—(Golf balls) $58.5 million (1990 estimate).

Major competitor: (Tennis equipment) Wilson Sporting Goods' Wilson; (golf equipment) Titleist.

Advertising: *Agency*—(Golf) BBDO South, 1993—; (tennis) Abbott Mead Vickers/BBDO South, 1993—. *Major campaign*—(Golf) Ads in consumer and trade sports magazines and on television featuring the "Maxfli—Go for the Max" theme; (tennis) television and print ads using the "Get Control, Get Dunlop" theme and featuring John McEnroe.

Addresses: *Parent company*—Dunlop Slazenger Corporation, P.O. Box 3070, Greenville, SC 29602; phone: 803-241-2200; fax: 803-241-2290. *Ultimate parent company*—Dunlop Slazenger Intl. Limited, Challenge Court, Barnett Wood Ln., Leatherhead, KT22 7LW, United Kingdom; phone: 0372 362222; fax: 0372 362082. *Ultimate ultimate parent company*—BTR PLC.

club's swing—the Maxfli sold well, but not well enough to launch the Dunlop name toward the level of recognition the brand would eventually command.

The reputation of a golf ball to be active, or ''hot,'' essentially meant the ball travelled a farther distance than other balls from an equally powerful stroke, obviously a desirable attribute for a golf ball to possess. The Maxfli's popularity, though, suffered from its propensity to become lopsided when the inner rubber windings snapped, causing it to react erratically while in flight, perhaps the worst attribute for a golf ball to possess.

To fix the Maxfli's inadequacies, in the late 1940s Dunlop engineers made several adjustments to the manufacturing machinery that wound the ball's rubber thread around its rubber centers and, as the legend goes, unwittingly created one of the ''hottest'' balls ever made. The United States Golf Association (USGA) tested the new Maxfli and found that its liveliness exceeded all golf ball performance parameters, making the ball ''illegal'' in USGA sanctioned tournament play. But before the USGA handed down its ruling, thousands of Maxfli's were sold, as word spread about the tremendous distances that could be reached with Dunlop's Maxfli ball. Illegal or not, the mistake was a marketing boon that significantly increased the public's awareness of the Dunlop name.

Product Development

Corrections were made in the manufacturing process of the Maxfli, and the USGA eventually sanctioned its use in tournament play. Dunlop sales continued to climb, as golfers latched on to the latest trend in the golf market. Encouraged by the success of the Maxfli golf ball, Dunlop broadened its product line in the early 1950s to include a complete selection of Maxfli golf clubs, which were initially manufactured by the John Letters Golf Company in Great Britain and by Wright & Ditson in the United States. The clubs, marketed under the Dunlop Maxfli name, sold briskly in Europe, where both the Dunlop and John Letters Golf Company names had earned the respect of consumers. But U.S. sales were comparatively flat. Dunlop's management decided a more widely recognized golf manufacturer was needed to stimulate U.S. sales, so in 1957 the Pedersen Golf Company, known for its high quality merchandise, was contracted to manufacture Dunlop's nationally distributed line of Maxfli golf clubs.

Concurrent with recruiting a new manufacturer, Dunlop began to promote Maxfli golf clubs more aggressively by launching an advertising campaign that enabled the company to carve an appreciable niche in the golf club market. Further strengthening its position, Dunlop hired Eric Jackson, a club maker from Pedersen Golf Company, to steward Dunlop's own club-making venture. A golf club manufacturing facility was constructed in Westminster, South Carolina, in 1963 to complement the company's golf ball factory, which had opened at the same location three years earlier. With these two production facilities and the increasing awareness of the Dunlop Maxfli name, the company was able to widen its profit margin and secure a larger share of the golf equipment market, leaving it well positioned to capitalize on the enormous growth of the sporting goods industry in the 1970s.

In 1971 Dunlop added its Maxpower line of golf clubs, which featured a greatly improved balanced shaft, to supplement its existing Maxfli line and enable the company to penetrate the golf market further. But the most significant boost to the company's sales came from Dunlop's original Maxfli line of golf clubs and underscored the importance of incorporating professional athletes into marketing strategies for sporting goods. Dunlop benefitted when, fortuitously, a group of U.S. touring professionals were playing in Australia during the southern hemisphere's summer season in 1975. In Australia, several Asian professionals were using a Maxfli iron manufactured by Dunlop's Australian division that differed from the type of club manufactured in the United States.

U.S. professionals liked the Australian club and began using it in U.S. tournaments, which sparked public interest in what was then being referred to as the ''new Australian Blade.'' As with the ''hot'' Maxfli ball of the late 1940s, American golfers clamored for the presumed extra edge the Australian Maxfli iron afforded professionals and inundated Dunlop with requests for the club. After considerable effort, Dunlop manufacturing facilities in the United states were able to replicate the Australian manufacturing process by importing raw forgings from Australia. Supply finally met demand in the late 1970s with the unveiling of the Dunlop Maxfli Australian Blade.

As developments were unfolding in Dunlop's golf segment, the popularity of tennis was mushrooming, reaching its zenith in the mid-1970s, when 30 million tennis players spent $182.5 million in one year on racquets alone. Dunlop, however, stood on the sidelines throughout much of the sports growth during the decade, largely because the company had grown complacent about its involvement in the tennis equipment business.

During the 1970s metal racquets were the rage, and leading tennis equipment manufacturers quickly responded to the burgeoning trend by developing new types of racquets to replace the traditional wood frames that had been the industry norm for roughly a century. While Dunlop stuck by its wooden Maxply Fort, such market leaders as Head, Wilson, and Prince began producing aluminum, graphite, and fiberglass racquets in various sizes, invigorating sales in an already robust market. Dunlop rapidly lost market share to its key competitors during the decade, dropping from an enviable 35 percent in the early 1970s to a disheartening eight percent by 1980 and leaving Wilson and Head with roughly 50 percent of the tennis market.

Accordingly, several management changes were made and market share objectives were established to effect a recovery. Five new racquet models were added to Dunlop's line, but the company and the brand name continued to suffer from a poor image. To make matters worse, Dunlop's unfavorable image, which some characterized as "stuffy," was beginning to negatively affect the company's other business segments, namely its line of golf equipment. As conditions soured, Dunlop's management responded by increasing the company's overall advertising budget 45 percent, and by signing an endorsement contract with a rising star in the professional tennis ranks, John McEnroe.

Took a Chance on John McEnroe

Though he was signed by Wilson Sporting Goods for five years for a reported $2.5 million, an unprecedented figure for its time, McEnroe's tennis career had not yet reached its peak when his contract with Dunlop's major competitor expired. Wilson's management decided against continuing its relationship with McEnroe, concluding that the risk involved made such an enormous investment too much of a gamble. As Wilson's senior vice president of marketing succinctly stated at the time, "[Dunlop is] making the basic assumption that John McEnroe will be No. 1 in five years."

For Dunlop, the gamble paid off. At the 1981 Wimbledon tournament, with Dunlop officials sitting in the McEnroe family booth, John McEnroe defeated six-time champion Bjorn Borg to become the top-ranked tennis player in the world, and the bulk of Dunlop's image problems were quickly swept away. McEnroe's win ameliorated nearly every line of tennis equipment wearing the Dunlop name, including the company's wooden Maxply Fort, the symbol of the company's exigencies during the 1970s. In the six months following McEnroe's victory, sales of the Maxply Fort increased 170 percent, evidence that Dunlop Maxply racquets, including the newly introduced Maxply McEnroe, had shaken their antiquated image and stood in the early 1980s as the preferred choice of many aspiring tennis players.

Golf Segment Boosted by Dunlop DDH

Dunlop's turnaround in the early 1980s, however, would not be complete without an equally invigorating boost to its golf equipment segment, a component of the company's business that was suffering losses imputable to the declining sales generated by its former mainstay product—golf balls. The popularity of the Dunlop Maxfli Australian Blade had helped to increase the company's golf club business, but the market representation of Dunlop golf balls had slipped behind Titleist, the market leader, and second- and third-ranked Spalding and Wilson, to occupy the fourth slot.

To bring about a resurgence, Dunlop needed to introduce an innovative product, the secrets of which had been hidden in the company's research archives since 1975. Finally, in 1979, a prototype of the company's new golf ball, the Dunlop DDH, rolled across a boardroom table surrounded by optimistic company officials encouraged by the unique dimple pattern on the ball's surface that purportedly affected its wind resistance, distance, and accuracy. Tests supported the claims of the product's early proponents, inducing Dunlop executives to allocate in 1981 $1.55 million to promote the company's golf balls. With much of the money funnelled toward supporting the introduction of the DDH, the Dunlop name once again gained prominence in golfing circles. The design of the DDH, which consisted of dimples in four different sizes, predicated the design of future Dunlop balls throughout the 1980s and into the 1990s.

Changes in Ownership

For roughly a century, the Dunlop brand name lived a dual existence as a symbol for both automobile tires and sporting goods under the Dunlop Corporation umbrella, but following the resurgence of the brand name in the early 1980s, this long-lived union ended in 1986, when British Tire & Rubber Co. (BTR PLC) purchased Dunlop and all of its divisions. BTR quickly sold the Dunlop Tire division to a group of investors and organized the sporting goods segments into a subsidiary called Dunlop Sports. Later renamed Dunlop Slazenger Corporation to reflect the inclusion of sporting goods marketed under the Slazenger name, which Dunlop had acquired in 1959, the U.S. subsidiary during the early 1990s fell under the purview of Dunlop Slazenger International Ltd., the direct, Great Britain-based subsidiary of BTR.

Future Growth

Following its acquisition by BTR, the Dunlop brand reached an increasingly greater number of consumers, particularly through the sale of the company's golf equipment and accessories. From the mid- to late 1980s, Dunlop tripled the size of its golf distribution area, which, coupled with the vast array of other sports products marketed under the Dunlop name, secured the company's position as a leading marketer in the sporting goods industry. In the early 1990s Dunlop distributed golf bags and luggage, golf gloves, golf hats, club head covers, rainwear, tennis shoes, strings, tennis balls, golf balls, golf clubs, and tennis racquets, making the Dunlop name a nearly inescapable sight on tennis courts and golf courses throughout the United States.

As Dunlop charted its course into the mid-1990s, such prominent professional golfers as Seve Ballesteros, Jeff Sluman, Larry Mize, Greg Norman, and JoAnne Carner were contracted to promote and use Dunlop products, while the company's strong seller in the early 1980s, the DDH golf ball, emerged in 1993 as the improved DDH IV. Dunlop's tennis products were also supported by notable professional athletes, particularly the Dunlop Max 200G, used by two of the game's most successful players, Steffi Graf and John McEnroe. For 1994, Dunlop re-signed McEnroe to endorse its Revelation series of tennis rackets. The company hoped that its promotional campaigns, coupled with an intense effort to communicate Dunlop's points of difference to American consumers, would raise the Dunlop brand in the United States to the level that it enjoys throughout the world.

Further Reading:

Gooding, Judson, "The Tennis Industry," *Fortune,* June 1973, p. 124.

Harper, Sam, "Tennis Racquet Marketers Court Serious Players," *Advertising Age,* September 24, 1979, p. 58.

McDaniel, Jo Beth, "Sporting Goods Makers Gear Up," *Advertising Age,* March 21, 1988, p. 79.

Raissman, Robert, "Dunlop Sports Bouncing Back," *Advertising Age,* February 22, 1982, p. 4.

—Jeffrey L. Covell

DUTCH BOY®

"The Look That Lasts"

With his blonde hair, blue eyes, and overalls, the highly recognizable Dutch Boy has symbolized hard work and good looks since 1907. After decades as a "stepchild" of National Lead, Dutch Boy went through a mercifully brief stint with a small, troubled paint company, then was acquired by paint industry leader Sherwin-Williams.

Owned by Sherwin-Williams Company since 1980, Dutch Boy paints are marketed under several different labels. The flagship brand, with its Dirt Fighter and Confidence labels, is sold through home-improvement centers and, since 1990, Sears stores. Performer and Fresh Look, two labels made exclusively for Kmart by Dutch Boy, feature the trade name and logo on the label. Dutch Boy's Chemtone is sold through discount merchandisers.

Dutch Boy introduced two new, carefully targeted labels, Renaissance and Kid's Room Paint, in 1993. The Renaissance launch capped off nearly a decade of premium positioning for the brand; Kid's Room Paint was a consumer-inspired, durable, decorative product that created a new category in the industry.

Brand Origins

In 1891 National Lead Company was formed through the merger of 25 manufacturers of white and red leads, then essential paint ingredients. The member companies were scattered from Boston to St. Louis, and the new company needed an overall brand for national marketing. Ad manager O. C. Harn devised the Dutch boy character, representing both the whitewashed reputation of the Dutch and their early leadership in the development of paint ingredients.

The original Dutch Boy was actually a nine-year-old Irish neighbor of portrait painter Lawrence Carmichael Earle. Corporate folklore recounts that the boy, Michael E. Brady, was so impressed with his pay for the sitting that he set his sights on an art career, and grew up to become a political cartoonist. The Dutch Boy underwent nine face-lifts over the years, keeping his overalls, cap, and perky hairstyle, but changing with advertising and printing styles. The original 1907 painting was revived in 1987.

Over the years, National Lead diversified into over 200 categories of products, including construction, aviation, petroleum, railroads, and steel. Dutch Boy remained the best-known component of the parent company, but its contribution to annual revenues dwindled to between 10 percent and 15 percent. Under National Lead, Dutch Boy always seemed to be following trends, rather than leading them, perhaps because the parent was so thoroughly involved in supplying paint ingredients, instead of developing them. And while Dutch Boy became more and more marginalized at National Lead, competition within the paint market intensified.

Competition

During the postwar era, mass merchandisers began to use paint as a "loss leader" to establish their competitive pricing position and lure customers. Sears, Roebuck & Co. used this technique to great advantage with its Weatherbeater line of paint. At the same time, alternative building products like aluminum siding, redwood, and glass began a period of intense competition with paint. These two external forces converged with the saturation of the paint market to simultaneously restrict volume and margin.

Dutch Boy joined its competitors in marketing fast-drying, odorless all-weather paints during this period, but it ranked seventh out of eight competitors in a 1966 *Advertising Age* listing. The brand's endurance was buttressed more by its parent's extensive raw materials reserves than its promotional support. National Lead recognized the importance of the Dutch Boy name, which still ranked among the world's top trademarks, but by 1975, the brand's sales constituted less than four percent of the conglomerate's total.

The following year, National Lead responded by raising Dutch Boy's advertising budget ten percent, to over $2 million. The print-oriented campaign emphasized "high quality ingredients and superior results," and appeared in such general circulation periodicals as *Time, Better Homes & Gardens, Life, Look, Readers Digest,* and the *Saturday Evening Post.*

With sales that had stagnated at about $45 million, Dutch Boy was acquired by ELT, Inc., a nine-year-old company that hoped to use the brand for a marketing blitz, in 1977. ELT adopted the Dutch Boy name and planned to emblazon it on everything from promotional items that included umbrellas, bumper stickers, T-shirts, and caps to such products as light bulbs, paint brushes, and drop cloths, according to a 1977 article in *Chemical Week.* At this time Dutch Boy was promoting its Dirt Fighter paint, which featured an electrostatic, dust repellent charge built into the surface of the dried paint film. ELT hoped to develop a chain of

AT A GLANCE

Dutch Boy brand of paint founded circa 1891 by O. C. Harn, advertising manager of National Lead Company; original portrait of the Dutch Boy character painted by Lawrence Carmichael Earle in 1907; company name later changed to NL Industries; NL Industries' paint operations acquired by ELT, Inc. (which subsequently changed its name to Dutch Boy, Inc.) in 1976; Dutch Boy purchased by Sherwin Williams Co. in 1980.

Performance: *Market share*—6.6% (fourth-highest share, 1991). *Sales*—$561 million (est., 1991).

Major competitor: Pittsburgh Paints; also Glidden, Weatherbeater.

Advertising: *Agency*—Griswold & Company, Cleveland. *Major campaign*—"The look that lasts."

Addresses: *Parent company*—Sherwin-Williams Co., 101 Prospect Avenue, NW, Cleveland, Ohio 44115; phone: (216) 566-2000.

"extremely large Dutch Boy (home improvement) centers," but the company lost $599,000 that year as consolidation expenses ran higher than expected.

Dutch Boy could very well have faded from the paint picture entirely in the late 1970s, as paint producers continued to be pinched between mass marketers' low price strategies and higher petrochemical prices resulting from the decade's oil embargo. Dutch Boy lost $3.17 million in 1978 and $1.56 million in 1979.

The brand was rescued from its plunge by the industry leader, Sherwin-Williams, which purchased Dutch Boy for about $6 million in 1980. The acquisition united two of the best-known trademarks in the U.S.: the Dutch Boy and Sherwin-Williams's globe-and-paint-can "cover the world" trademark.

Repositioning

Under the management of Sherwin-Williams, Dutch Boy undertook a five-year repositioning that began in 1984. The plan targeted 18- to 34-year-olds and assumed an upscale, customer-driven approach. Since overall paint sales had matured and growth had stagnated at about 2 percent annually, Dutch Boy's marketers knew that they had to capture sales from competitors without cannibalizing sales from the Sherwin-Williams brand.

Dutch Boy first changed packaging and color systems, then worked on retailer promotions like sweepstakes. In 1988 the marketers introduced a television image campaign entitled "The Look." According to Charles Cerankosky, an analyst with Prescott Ball & Turben, Sherwin-Williams's team "gave a rather boring product a fashion image rather than try to sell it based on a chemistry lesson."

With the focal theme "The Look that Gets the Looks" as a tie-in for all advertising, merchandising, and point-of-purchase materials, Dutch Boy was able to accomplish a relatively unique feat in the paint industry: a "sexy" product that held its price points. Dutch Boy's marketers found that consumers had come to expect characteristics like one-coat coverage, and were more interested in the end result—the finished wall—than in the chemical composition of a can of paint. Consumer research that indicated strong brand loyalty in the paint market led the marketers to target an age category that was younger than normal. They hoped to generate trial use and thereby capture a generation of paint users who would continue to use the brand throughout their lives.

These conclusions convinced Dutch Boy and its advertising agency, Griswold & Company in Cleveland, to reexamine the brand's advertising placements. Dutch Boy moved its television ads from traditional slots aimed at a broad demographic range, for example the evening news, to much more youthful programming, including MTV, VH1, and *Late Night with David Letterman.* Prime-time spots on programs such as the *Wonder Years* and *thirtysomething* were also purchased. To compete for consumers' attention during these key advertising periods, Dutch Boy also raised the production values of its commercials.

Paint marketers have long acknowledged the relationship between weather and paint sales: people are more inclined to paint during temperate spring and summer months than winter. But

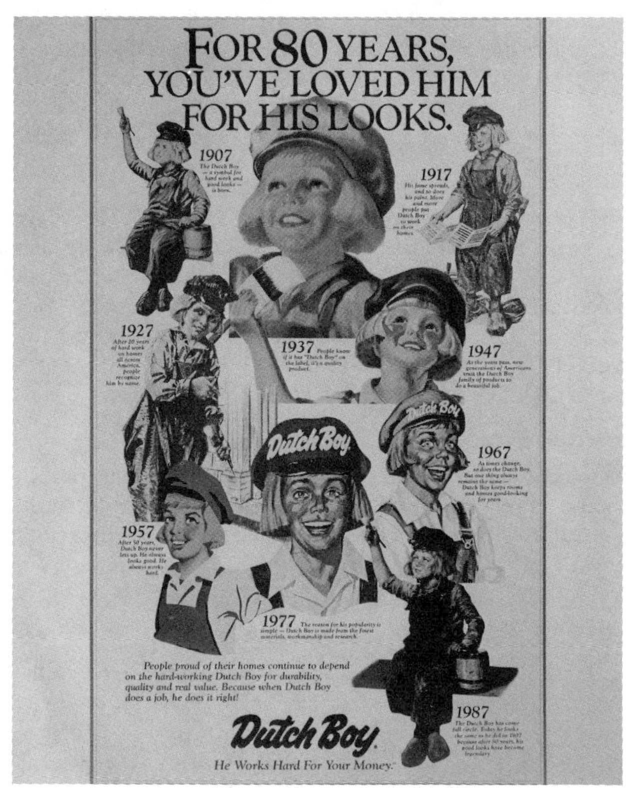

The Dutch Boy logo has changed many times through the years, but in 1987 he began appearing as he first did in 1907.

Dutch Boy put a new twist on the traditional spring paint sales. Dutch Boy found that consumers have trouble pinpointing a weekend to do a particular project, so the brand sponsored a "Weekend Weather Outlook" on the Weather Channel to encourage purchases. The cable network also produced infomercials offering painting tips to do-it-yourselfers in a segment called "The Weather and Your House."

Dutch Boy's print campaign, which cost about $700,000 in 1989, moved into three basic categories of magazines—lifestyle, life stage, and home fashion. Placements in such unlikely settings as *Cosmopolitan, Modern Bride, Parents, Country Living,* and *Metropolitan Home* set the brand apart from its competitors, which stuck primarily to the hardware and do-it-yourself periodicals, and placed it in the living (and bath) rooms of its young targets. Sponsorship on the Championship Auto Racing Teams (CART) Indy Car circuit also put Dutch Boy in upscale company with such sponsors as Benetton, Porsche, and BOSS Men's Fashions.

The brand gained 2.8 percentage points over the course of the image overhaul, from 3 percent in 1984 to 5.8 percent in 1989. The brand doubled its media expenditures to about $15 million to publicize the increased distribution and move from spot to network placements. In 1991 Dutch Boy unveiled its first outdoor ad campaign ever, using a combination of serious and whimsical ads with the slogan ''Give your house a little character.''

New Products

The success of this image campaign culminated in the 1993 introduction of the Renaissance line of premium paints. The line catered to the premium market Dutch Boy had cultivated during the previous decade, which had nearly doubled from 1986 to 1993, and constituted about 30 percent of do-it-yourself paint sales. Renaissance targeted young, fashion-conscious consumers who expected high performance, decorator colors, and a long-wearing, satin finish, and were willing to pay a premium price for those characteristics. Richly designed packaging and point-of-sale materials conveyed an upscale look and featured a gold ''satisfaction guaranteed'' seal.

That same year, Dutch Boy rolled out Kid's Room Paint, a satin-finish coating that was formulated to hold up in children's bedrooms, nurseries, playrooms, and other high traffic areas like rec rooms and hallways. The new paint was developed from consumer focus groups indicating that parents wanted a durable, washable paint, but with a flat, satin finish, rather than the shiny semi-gloss often applied in high-use areas. The line also appealed to kids themselves, with bright, friendly packaging and the colors of the National Basketball Association. Kid's Room Paint was launched with a $5 million cable TV campaign. It created a new paint segment and quickly became Sherwin-Williams's most successful new product ever.

Although Rauch Associates, an industry analyst, predicted growth of the paint market to slow to 1.2 percent in the 1990s, Dutch Boy's upscale, consumer-oriented positioning ensured that its margins and segment would grow.

Further Reading:

Bagot, Brian, ''Lookin' Good,'' *Marketing & Media Decisions,* v. 25, March 1990, 67–69.

Barach, Arnold B., *Famous American Trademarks,* Washington, D.C.: Public Affairs Press, 1971.

''Building Downturn Hasn't Hurt the Paint Companies,'' *Financial World,* v. 114, December 7, 1960, 4, 30.

Dickstein, George, ''Paint Industry Is Using Spruced up Ad Approach to Dispel Odorous Image,'' *Advertising Age,* v. 37, June 6, 1966, 4, 98.

''Dutch Boy Goes to Work for New Owner,'' *Chemical Week,* v. 120, June 15, 1977, 99–100.

''Dutch Boy Sells Its Namesake Coatings,'' *Chemical Week,* v. 127, August 13, 1980, 14–15.

Finseth, Gary, ''Kid's Room Paint,'' *Advertising Age,* v. 64, July 5, 1993, SS1–SS30.

Fitzgerald, Kate, ''Flat Sales Spur High-Gloss Plans,'' *Advertising Age,* v. 62, May 6, 1991, 12.

McCauley, Lucy A., ''The Face of Advertising,'' *Harvard Business Review,* November/December 1989, 155–59.

''More Than Just Paint Stores,'' *Chain Store Age Executive,* v. 52, November 1976, 32B, 32D.

''National Lead—Market Laggard,'' *Financial World,* v. 125, April 27, 1966, 7.

''National Lead Operations Enjoy Bright New Luster,'' *Barron's,* v. 46, June 20, 1966, 22.

''National Lead to Increase Spending 10% for Dutch Boy,'' *Advertising Age,* v. 38, March 13, 1967, 2.

''The Paint Makers,'' *Financial World,* v. 124, August 25, 1965, 11, 23.

'' 'Sales' Buy Trouble for Paint Makers,'' *Chemical Week,* v. 122, April 26, 1978, 23–24.

Winters, Patricia, et. al., ''Advertising Age Marketing 100,'' *Advertising Age,* v. 64, July 5, 1993, SS1.

—April S. Dougal

EDSEL®

In 1957, after great expense and with much fanfare, the Ford Motor Company unveiled the new Edsel as its car of the future. Two years and $250 million later the car was discontinued completely, and the Edsel became part of popular American mythology as one of the great business flops of all time.

Birth of the Edsel

The Edsel began appearing on Ford drawing boards in 1955. At that time the Ford Motor Company had three makes of automobile that it offered to the public: Ford, Mercury, and Lincoln. Its Ford line was moderately priced and often seen as a family's first car. The Mercury was a mid-priced car, and in the upper tier sat the Lincoln. However, the automaker had a problem. It seemed that when those who owned lower-priced Ford models wished to "trade up" and buy a more expensive, higher-status car—often when their annual incomes reached about $5,000—they did not buy the only mid-priced car that the company offered, the Mercury. Instead, they generally bought cars made by General Motors, which dominated the mid-priced field with Oldsmobiles, Buicks, and Pontiacs, or they turned to Chrysler, which offered the Dodge and DeSoto. Summing up the attitude at Ford that led directly to the Edsel, a vice president for Ford noted ruefully: "We've been growing customers for General Motors."

Ford's weakness in the mid-priced car market had been apparent for some time. The plans for a new automobile had gone back to 1948, when Henry Ford II, the new president of the company, called for studies to look at the possibility of putting a new mid-priced car on the market. The onset of the Korean War in 1950, however, put plans for a new car on the shelf until 1952, when the research was taken up by the company's Forward Product Planning Committee. Two years later, in December 1954, that group delivered its six-volume report to Ford's executive committee.

The Forward Product Planning Committee envisioned a future U.S. economy in which incomes would rise on an upward curve, so that by 1965 more than half of the families in the United States would be earning incomes of more than $5,000. Further, it predicted that there would be 20 million more cars on the roads than there were in 1955, for a total of 70 million, and the committee believed that over 40 percent of those cars would be in the mid-priced range or higher. The report concluded that Ford would lose significant overall market share if it did not react quickly with a new, middle-priced automobile.

The Ford executive committee endorsed the findings of the Forward Product Planning Committee. To put words into deeds, Ford formed a new Special Products Division and Richard E. Krafve, who had most recently worked as the assistant general manager of the Lincoln-Mercury division, was chosen to head the new venture. Its mission was to create a car from the ground up, an astounding challenge. That car, while in the design stages, was referred to as the E-Car ("E" for "Experimental").

An Experiment in Design

The responsibility for the design of the car was given to Roy Brown, an industrial designer who had previously worked on Oldsmobiles for Chevrolet and Lincolns for Ford. Brown decided to create a car with both recognizable, conservative elements and novel, distinctive aspects. He later related to author John Brooks: "We went to the extent of making photographic studies from some distance of all nineteen [of the car models which were on the road at the time], and it became obvious that at a distance of a few hundred feet the similarity was so great that it was practically impossible to distinguish one make from the others . . . They were all 'peas in a pod.' We decided to select [a style that] would be 'new' in the sense that it was unique, and yet at the same time be familiar."

For Krafve, the best way to achieve the optimum car design would be by breaking down the decision-making process into a series of separate choices and then making the best choice for each; thus, choosing the shape of the headlights was separate from the choice for the hood shape, which was separate from the grill design. Krafve later calculated that there were more 4,000 different design decisions made regarding the Edsel. The car's design was largely decided upon by mid-1955; an E-Car model was unveiled to Ford executives on August 15 of that year.

Personality Sells

Once the car had been designed (save for later minor modifications), it was handed over to the director of planning for market research, David Wallace, who was to ascertain what the car's "personality" would be. Wallace felt that a vehicle's personality—the certain something that defined it—was what really sold a car; after all, especially during the 1950s, cars from automaker to automaker that fell within similar price ranges were basically the same. To determine what the personalities of the E-Car's competitors were, Wallace hired the Bureau of Applied Social Research at Columbia University to interview 800 recent car-buyers in Peoria, Illinois, and 800 others in San Bernadino, California. The purpose of the study was to find out what mental images different automobiles conjured up in people. As *Consumer Reports* noted later, the respondents were asked almost everything about their impressions of the cars except such nuts-and-bolts issues as cost, safety, and performance. Instead, subjects were asked about their images of the owners of various cars, including social status, age, and sex, among other things.

The responses from the study showed that in general people thought of Ford cars as fast and masculine; Buicks were considered the cars of middle-aged females; and Chevrolets were viewed as older and slower. The Mercury, Ford's lone existing mid-priced model, was seen as a car for the young, fast-moving, lower-income crowd—which seemed to point to why Ford owners were not trading up to buy it.

Wallace sent a report to the executives at the Special Projects Division which encapsulated his department's work. The report,

AT A GLANCE

The Edsel line of cars was introduced September 4, 1957, by the Ford Motor Company; it was discontinued in November, 1959.

Performance: *Sales*—109,466 total units.

Major competitor: Various models from General Motors Corporation's Pontiac, Buick, and Oldsmobile divisions.

Advertising: *Agency*—Foote, Cone, & Belding, New York, 1956-58. *Major campaign*—"Everyone who has seen it knows—with us—that the Edsel is a success," "They'll know you've *arrived* when you drive up in an Edsel," "The one that's really new is lowest-priced one, too."

Addresses: *Parent company*—Ford Motor Company, The American Rd., Dearborn, MI, 48121; phone: (313) 322-3000.

"The Market and Personality Objectives of the E-Car," urged Ford to define the car as neither too young nor too old; not so specific and well-defined as to drive away the greatest number of people, or so generic to deny the car an identity of its own. Wallace's report stated: "The most advantageous personality of the E-Car might well be THE SMART CAR FOR THE YOUNGER EXECUTIVE OR PROFESSIONAL FAMILY ON ITS WAY UP."

Anything For a Name

The E-Car's personality had been generally defined—now it needed a name. Krafve had, at the start of the E-Car's development, actually suggested the name "Edsel," in honor of president Henry Ford II's father, who had himself served as president of the Ford Motor Company from 1918 to 1943. Edsel Ford's sons, Henry, Benson, and William Clay, disliked the idea and thought their father would not have appreciated the gesture. The Special Products Division, then, set out to find a name for the E-Car.

In mid-1955, Wallace engaged several research companies to conduct sidewalk interviews to discover respondents' images of a series of names, including Mars, Jupiter, Ovation, Dart, Ariel, Rover, and Arrow. The results of the polling were deemed inconclusive. Wallace next sought the assistance of the poet Marianne Moore, whom a friend had heard speak at a university lecture, in naming the E-Car. Wallace wrote to her that "we should like this name . . . to convey, through association or other conjuration, some visceral feeling of elegance, advanced features, and design." Moore responded with such suggestions as Utopian Turtletop, Bullet Cloissoné, Pastelogram, Mongoose Civique, and Intelligent Bullet.

Unhappy with those rather unique monikers, and still without a name, the Special Products Division hired the New York-based advertising agency of Foote, Cone & Belding, which sponsored a competition among the employees in its offices in New York, Chicago, and London. The prize for the new name of the E-car? A new E-Car, naturally. The ensuing 18,000 suggestions included Henry, Benson, Apollo, Mars, Jupiter, Cavalier, Zoom, Zip, and Drof ("Ford" backward). The initial response was trimmed to 6,000, and the list was handed over to Ford. With time running short, Krafve explained that what the company needed was not 6,000 names, but *one* name—and quickly. Directors at the agency then asked its offices in New York and Chicago to each come up with a list of ten names, separately, over the coming weekend. By a profound coincidence, the two lists were found to share four names: Ranger, Corsair, Pacer, and Citation. Corsair was the favorite.

The short list was handed to the company's executive committee and Chairman of the Board Ernest Breech in early 1956. Unhappy with all of the names presented to him, Breech eventually settled on one that had been rejected a while back: Edsel. The three Ford brothers were, coincidentally, all out of town.

On November 19, 1956, Ford publicly released the new name of the E-Car, and what had been known as the Special Products Division became the Edsel Division. Earlier that month, Richard Krafve had become a Ford vice-president while he continued to head the Edsel Division.

The Drive For Dealers

With the Edsel, Ford was essentially creating a new car with its own division and sales force. The last time Ford had tried such a feat was in 1938, when it introduced the Mercury. As Ford was creating the Edsel to stand alone (not manufactured under the aegis of another division), the car was to have its own dealer organization. Krafve's goal was to have 1,200 dealers in place by the time the car was to be introduced on September 4, 1957 (what the company began to refer to as Introduction Day). To reach the goal, it was necessary to convert, or "steal" the dealerships of other car manufacturers, and to convince some of the 9,000 Ford, Lincoln, or Mercury dealers to take on the new car. A sales team traveled around the country in an effort to coax dealers to switch over and sell Edsels. By the time Introduction Day arrived, the Edsel had about 1,160 dealers.

Other preparations were in the works. In June, 1957 a television commercial was filmed in California after an Edsel was smuggled cross-country and the actors were sworn to secrecy. During the summer, print advertisements appeared to build up the interest and excitement for Introduction Day. Images of the car were not used, of course. A two-page spread in *Life* magazine pictured a blurred image of a car traveling down a country highway with the tag-line: "Lately, some mysterious automobiles have been seen on the roads." Several weeks later, another ad pictured a car covered in a white sheet and read: "A man in your town recently made a decision that will change his life."

An Economic Downturn

Although the income projections for American consumers posited by the Forward Product Planning Committee (which helped make the case for the necessity of the Edsel) were of an ever-rising curve, by mid-1957 the U.S. economy was failing to move along that upward slope. The stock market had fallen steeply, and the country was considered to be in a recession. Ominously, medium-priced car sales started to fall by the end of the summer, and the Mercury Rambler, the only U.S.-made small car in production, grew in popularity. Mercury even announced it was going to advance a $1 million advertising campaign emphasizing the car's affordability.

The Edsel Meets the Press

In bombastic fashion, the Edsel was introduced to 250 reporters during an extended press preview in Detroit on August 26, 27, and 28. Press dignitaries from around the country and the world were shown the 18 different models of the car from four lines (Corsair, Citation, Pacer, and Ranger), treated to a hair-raising display of precision driving by a team of stunt drivers, pampered with a fashion show for their wives, and invited to a final social gala that, forebodingly, featured a former band of Glenn Miller's that still had "GM" displayed across its music stands. The spectacle cost Ford $90,000.

The 1959 model-year Edsels were unveiled at local dealerships on September 4, 1958, about a month before other new models hit the showrooms. Pre-publicity had worked well to heighten the excitement and curiosity about the new car. A print advertisement that appeared that day featured Ford president Henry Ford, chairman Breech, an Edsel, and copy that informed the reader that Edsel's creation was "based on what we knew, guessed, felt, believed, suspected—about you. YOU are the reason behind the Edsel." By the end of the day, approximately 2,850,000 people had traveled to dealerships to see the Edsel.

The car's design did elicit comment. Its most distinctive feature was its front grill; whereas the fashion of the day in car design called for a wide, horizontal front end, the Edsel's grill sat upright like a shield in the middle of more traditional grillwork. The car was filled with gadgets—levers, lights, and buttons, including push-button automatic transmission controls that sat on top of the steering column. The cars were large, heavy, powerful, and gaudy.

If the mixed and lukewarm reviews the Edsel received from the press were the first signs of trouble, more serious was the fact that many of the Edsels that were sold and delivered failed to function properly. Close inspection and a short time on the road revealed that the cars were afflicted with inferior paint, low-grade sheet metal, and nonfunctioning accessories. The Consumers Union, which publishes *Consumer Reports*, bought an Edsel for evaluation and discovered that the vehicle had a leaky power-steering pump, noisy rear axle gears, the wrong axle ratio, and a heater that, once turned on, could not be turned off.

Within several days of its introduction, Edsel sales began to fall—and they continued to fall throughout the year. It was reported that 11,544 Edsels were delivered to dealers in September, 7,601 in October, and still fewer in October. Meanwhile, Ford had calculated that it would need to sell 200,000 Edsels a year to break even.

In December company president Henry Ford II delivered a speech to Edsel dealers via closed-circuit television in which he pronounced, "The Edsel is here to stay." Soon thereafter, 1.5 million letters were sent out to medium-priced car owners asking them to visit an Edsel dealership for a test drive, and it promised an eight-inch plastic replica of the Edsel for their trouble. The expense of this promotion was picked up by the company, rather than the dealers—a departure from long-standing practice and perhaps the first sign of panic.

The First Casualties

It was announced on January 14, 1958, that Ford was consolidating the Edsel Division with the Lincoln-Mercury Division into the Mercury-Edsel-Lincoln Division. 6,000 white-collar workers lost their jobs in the reorganization. Thereafter, the Edsel received scant attention from both the company *and* the public. In November of 1958 the Edsel's second-year models came out. The car had quickly become lighter, shorter, streamlined, less powerful, and less expensive, dropping from $800 to $500 in price. Sales picked up, and by mid-1959 about 4,000 Edsels were sold a month. In July of that year (one and a half years after its introduction), the total number of Edsels on the road was tallied at 83,849. By the time the third-year models were introduced in October 1959, the Edsel looked almost nothing like its original version; it was smaller still with even leaner lines—and almost nobody bought one.

Acknowledging Disaster

On November 19, 1959, the Ford Foundation sent forth a prospectus that detailed its plan to sell a large block of Ford Motor Company stock. In a footnote it mentioned that the Edsel had been "introduced in September 1957 and discontinued in November 1959." The Ford Motor Company, which had held off from announcing the car's demise so that dealers could clear off their inventories, admitted that "Retail sales have been particularly disappointing, and continued production of the Edsel is not justified, especially in view of the shortage of steel." The 1960 Edsel, released to showrooms just prior to the car's death knell, could find only 2,846 buyers.

Post-mortems were swift in coming. Many pointed to the fact that the car was designed for a different time—specifically, 1955. In that year the economy was growing, more than 7 million cars were sold (more than any other year up to that time), and Americans wanted cars that were large and powerful—automobiles that the historian Lewis Mumford described as "those fantastic and insolent chariots with which American motor-car manufacturers now burden our streets and parking lots." The two-year lag time between the car's design and its introduction brought the car into a future for which it was ill-prepared—1957, when the trend was for smaller, more fuel-efficient cars. Also, the car was introduced one month earlier than other 1958 model cars, at a time when almost all dealers were selling their 1957 models at clearance prices to make way for new inventory. The Edsel, contrasted against such bargains, seemed like a high-priced car. Many commentators also saw the Edsel's failure as the proof of the limitations of so-called motivational research that had largely influenced the car's design and marketing. As *Time* magazine summarized: "The Edsel was a classic case of the wrong car for the wrong market at the wrong time."

Further Reading:

Barmash, Isadore, *Great Business Disasters: Swindlers, Bunglers, and Frauds in American Industry,* Chicago: Playboy Press, 1969, pp. 87–146.

Collier, Peter, and David Horowitz, *The Fords: An American Epic,* New York: Summit Books, 1987.

Deutsch, Jan G., *Selling the People's Cadillac: The Edsel and Corporate Responsibility,* New Haven: Yale University Press, 1976.

—C. L. Collins

EMERSON®

Emerson entered the 1990s as a major brand name in mass-market consumer electronics goods, continuing a tradition of affordability and quality that dated back to the 1930s, when the brand established itself as an innovator in affordable, quality tabletop radios. In the early 1980s Emerson expanded its scope from the audio past of radio to the emerging audiovisual market for television and video cassette recorders (VCRs), where the brand once again applied marketing innovation and affordable quality to enjoy rapid growth. Anticipating a veritable revolution in audiovisual technology at the turn of the millennium, the brand positioned itself for its customary mid-price, mass-market success.

Emerson's success was dampened by a combination of the saturated consumer electronic goods market, a lingering world recession, and forays into less-than-successful product lines, such as computers and home air conditioners. In September of 1993 Emerson Radio Corp. filed for bankruptcy relief, commencing a major reorganization of the company and vigorous attempts to restore the veteran brand to a position of eminence in the consumer electronics market it had helped shape.

Brand Origins

As an emblem of innovation for the early twentieth century's new vehicle of mass communication, the radio, the Emerson brand made itself heard loud and clear, not only throughout the country but throughout subsequent decades. Innovators in radio technology since 1912, the Abrams family introduced a small, inexpensive table radio in 1933. Considerable demand and efficient production kept prices low, so that by 1939-1940 the units sold for under $10, encouraging families to purchase more than one set. By 1941 the Abrams's Emerson brand had cornered four-fifths of the table radio market, setting the stage for the 1947 incorporation of Emerson Radio and Phonograph Co.

Following World War II, the Emerson brand began to appear on television, riding the crest of American TV culture from its infancy. The brand shifted parentage when National Union Electric Co. acquired Emerson Radio and Phonograph Co. in 1966. With a success record spanning more than 30 years and an impetus for growth as powerful as the television media, the Emerson brand expanded rapidly in both television and radio into the 1970s. A small Brooklyn, New York-based audio company called Major Electronics acquired the Emerson company in 1973 and changed its name to Emerson Radio Corp. to capitalize on the strong brand identity. At the helm of Major Electronics, Bill and Steven Lane decided to optimize Emerson's reputation by paying special attention to marketing strategies that would back up new products carrying the brand name. They hired marketing veteran Sonny Knazick, whose combination of business savvy and retail contacts spurred a period of almost unbelievable expansion into the 1980s.

Mass-Market Success

Emerson's growth was largely attributable to an early 1980s marketing strategy aimed exclusively at mass merchandisers and catalog showrooms. Emerson found a unique niche as a well-known and highly respected brand name in a market where other big brands had not yet penetrated and where unknown brands offered substandard quality and features. "We satisfied the need of mass merchandisers for brand-name goods at a reasonable price," explained Senior Vice-President Marino Andriani in a 1987 article in *HFD—The Home Furnishing Newspaper.* "At the time, there were famous brands at the top of the price range and the off-brands at the bottom. We satisfied the need for a national brand at a good price," he added.

In meeting this need, Emerson more than satisfied its projected rate of growth; whereas the brand was associated with the relatively small audio sales of $88 million in 1982, by the end of fiscal 1986, it was generating $810 million and boasted a much more varied product line. Such growth prompted plans to continue maximizing product diversity but to adhere to the marketing strategy that had catapulted the brand to success. "Whatever new-product category we enter," insisted Andriani, "it will be distributed through mass-market channels."

After experiencing stunning growth in the early to mid-1980s, Emerson ran into serious problems in the latter part of the decade. Based on record sales of TVs and VCRs in 1986, retailers anticipated a virtual explosion in demand for the upcoming year. From under 20 vendors of Emerson VCRs, for example, the number jumped to over 80 in 1986. These vendors not only double-ordered from Emerson, but requested unprecedented stocks from other vendors as well. By 1987 market supply so far exceeded demand that prices plummeted, retailers stopped ordering, and many manufacturers reduced and even stopped production. Emerson, like several other brands, sustained damaging losses.

AT A GLANCE

Emerson brand of electronics founded in 1947 by the Abrams family, who incorporated Emerson Radio and Phonograph Co.; brand acquired by National Union Electric Co., 1966; sold to Major Electronics Co., 1973; in the 1980s, moved from primarily audio equipment into video and company name changed to Emerson Radio Corp.; Emerson Radio Corp. acquired by Fidenas Investment Ltd., 1992.

Performance: *Market share*—3.5% of color television category (1989). *Sales*—$102.67 million (1992).

Major competitor: Sony; also Thomson Co.'s RCA, Zenith, Philips Co.'s Magnavox, Thomson Co.'s GE, Sears, Sharp, and Mitsubishi.

Advertising: *Agency*—Towne, Silverstein, Rotter, Inc., New York, NY. *Major campaign*—Print ads in major electronics magazines reminding consumers and vendors, "It's Not Just Business as Usual" at Emerson.

Addresses: *Parent company*—Emerson Radio Corp., 9 Entin Road, P.O. Box 430, Parsippany, NJ 07054-0430; phone: (201) 428-2024; fax: (201) 428-2022. *Ultimate parent company*—Fidenas Investment Ltd., Talacher 42, Zurich, CH-8001, Switzerland.

Retailer Relations

In addition to attracting mass-market retailers with brand features like design and price, Emerson provided extensive services to hold the favor of its vendors. It was one of the pioneers in electronic data interchange (EDI)—a technique by which the computers of retailers and vendors continuously communicate to control order processing, delivery scheduling, inventory replenishment, and other interactive business functions. Among other features, the system enabled both vendor and retailer to make projections of needs over time and to more efficiently plan in advance. "We don't take an order that we can't deliver. For a mass merchandiser making plans months in advance, this is an invaluable help," Andriani told *HFD*.

The interactive computer system also offered another retail-oriented service that helped strengthen the brand: direct import. The retailer was able to take ownership of merchandise directly from the point of manufacture in Asia, with shipments made directly to the retailer's warehouse. Although Emerson was not unique in offering this service to both manufacturers and retailers, it was instrumental in pioneering it and putting it to greater use than other brands. While Emerson derived approximately 50 percent of its sales to retailers by direct import in the early 1990s, the company president and chief executive officer at that time, Martin J. Holleran, estimated the industry average at 10 to 15 percent. "Our aim is to shorten the gap between the assembly line and the cash register," he commented *HFD* in 1993.

In addition to emphasizing such high-tech services as EDI, Holleran stressed the importance of basic credibility in an increasingly chaotic consumer electronics market. According to the CEO, Emerson's appeal to mass retailers largely stemmed from repeated examples of credibility. When a market glut prompted higher prices throughout the industry in 1988, for example, Holleran claimed that Emerson's price schedule was in place before other brands, facilitating planning for retailers even while risking their initial approbation. In addition, EDI coordination of the brand's order activity in proportion to market demand helped avoid high inventories and dumping practices that could affect industrywide prices.

Packaging—The Silent Salesperson

In addition to carefully servicing accounts with mass retailers, Emerson's advertising people designed packaging for the brand that would serve as point-of-purchase promotion in the store, reducing display time for vendors while drawing in as much business as possible. In 1987 the brand began packaging portable merchandise, including radios and stereo-cassette players, in clamshell containers that brought the products out from under glass and onto merchandising end caps where consumers could get a clearer look.

The success of portable packaging design prompted a bold new packaging initiative for the brand's entire product line in the early 1990s. Color became the cornerstone of the 1990s packaging concept, which featured strong product photography and brand identification enlivened by color. All cartons had a bright color band next to the product features, directing the consumer's eyes to key information about product functions. More detailed descriptions of product capabilities and features were clearly listed on the back panel. The design, by Group Four Design of Avon, Connecticut, appeared on the shelves of Emerson retailers during the second quarter of 1994.

Product Changes

Since its first success in mass-market radios, the Emerson brand continued to expand to offer ever-new products in the consumer electronics market, always distinguishing itself as a leader in the mass-retailer niche. Just as the brand tapped into the revolutionary rise of radio in the 1930s, television in the 1950s, and VCRs in the 1980s, it was positioned at the approach of the twenty-first century to expand its product lines and tap into new trends in portability, multimedia, multipurpose design, and interactive capabilities.

With varying degrees of success, Emerson continued to expand its product line in an effort to maintain its stature in the mass market. In 1985 the brand greatly enhanced its audio line by acquiring H.H. Scott and, after completing engineering and design work, investing the product line with the Emerson brand name for distribution starting in 1989. The new line was positioned in a market niche abandoned by large Japanese hi-fi brands that had moved upscale. "Our line is priced under theirs, but we believe the quality and performance are on par," explained Executive Vice-President Harvey Schneider in *HFD*.

In 1989 the Emerson brand also moved into two new markets that quickly proved unsuccessful: computers and air conditioning. The Emerson brand of personal computers, developed by Commerce, California-based Emerson Computer Co., was conceived as a complement to the brand's proven strength in audio and video equipment. "Just as there was a marriage of audio and video, there is a coming marriage between video and computers. There will be important innovations in computers that are directly related to video," explained CEO Bill Lane. While Lane's assessment was correct in principle, it would be other leading brands in computers—IBM, Compaq, Apple, and Tandy—that would steal the mass multimedia computer market of the early 1990s, forcing Emerson out of the scene before it even took solid steps.

Likewise, Emerson's foray into the home air conditioner and dehumidifier market, under the Emerson Quiet Kool name, proved as ethereal as the air being conditioned. The brand's lower-end competitor, Fedders Corp.'s Fedder brand, bought and consolidated the Emerson brand in the summer of 1990, barely two years after it was introduced. Despite its problems in the computer and air conditioner markets, Emerson's successful appearance on five models of countertop microwave ovens in 1994 proved that it could indeed carry its name from audio and video equipment to other categories.

Continuing in its long tradition of audio innovation, Emerson brought a more promising range of choices to the mass retailers of 1994. Tuning in to consumer preferences for portability, Emerson introduced a portable compact disc (CD) player and five new personal stereo designs. Catering to the increasing demands of mobile consumers, the designs incorporated such features as rounded edges for comfortable carrying, two-tone color schemes, auto-reverse cassette players with a bass boost functions, three-band equalizers, and lightweight stereo headphones. Combining trends in fitness with portability, Emerson also introduced a water-resistant bicycle radio that was easy to mount on handlebars and featured AM/FM reception as well as a safety reflector and horn.

For consumers demanding feature-packed, high-quality, and affordable audio products for their homes, Emerson also introduced a new line of clock radios and mini component systems suitable for table tops, bookshelves, and other limited spaces. Harkening back to the success of Emerson tabletop radio sets of the 1930s, the "select series" clock radios were uniquely designed to resemble tabletop audio systems; all models featured dual speakers, FM stereo reception, snooze and sleep functions, and battery back-up, while the higher models incorporated a CD player and auto-stop cassette deck. The brand's four models of bookshelf-size mini component systems also combined all popular audio systems in one integrated, contemporary, and competitively priced unit.

Capitalizing on the video market, in which Emerson accelerated as a marketing innovator and leader throughout the 1980s, the brand moved into the 1990s with a diverse and design-oriented selection. The Emerson name distinguished a new selection of small-screen color televisions, in nine- and thirteen-inch sizes and featuring distinctive, sculptured cabinets. "These new models were developed to reflect the contemporary lifestyle of today's consumer," remarked Product Manager Michael L. Strange in a company press release. "Both offer outstanding television performance and viewing enjoyment at affordable prices." In addition to the portability of both units, the larger model offered a trilingual (French, English, and Spanish) on-screen display of television functions, as well as CaptionVision, a feature enabling transmission and display of full pages of text on the screen. The new Emerson products anticipated the interactive "information superhighway" expected to change television usage dramatically by the twenty-first century.

Emerson also forged ahead in VCR development and a relatively new category that it was instrumental in defining: combination television/VCR units, or COMBIs. One of the most convenient features of these units was their simple set-up and portability; consumers no longer had to deal with cumbersome connections required by separate TV/VCR installations. For those who preferred the latter, however, Emerson also introduced a two- and four-head VCR model, as well as a portable video cassette player designed as a secondary household unit or for cars, boats, and recreational vehicles.

Company Changes

Since the Abrams family first used the Emerson brand name to sell their innovative radios as early as 1912, the brand has shifted to several parents but retained its high level of recognition from years of exposure. Emerson moved from Emerson Radio and Phonograph Co. (1947), to National Union Electric Co. (1966), to Major Electronics Co. (1973), and to Emerson Radio Corp. in the early 1990s, when the brand's parent company faced industrywide pressures that forced the most radical changes to date.

In June of 1992 Fidenas Investment Ltd. won a proxy battle with Emerson's management that gave it control of the company and replaced Bill Lane with Martin J. Holleran as president and CEO. Then in August of 1993, the company announced the formation of a new management structure to better compete in the consumer electronics marketplace. Among the sweeping changes, Geoffrey P. Jurick replaced Holleran as CEO, and the revamped marketing and sales division was headed by new Vice-President Gerald S. Calabrese. Before the dust had settled, the company filed for bankruptcy relief on September 29, 1993, asking the court to approve a prenegotiated plan of reorganization agreed upon by Emerson, Fidenas, and its senior bank creditors, who held $169 million in claims against Emerson.

Despite the magnitude of such changes in its parent company, the Emerson brand still maintained the momentum of roughly 50 successful years. The company tapped into that momentum by offering a dynamic new line of products and by running a four-color ad in key trade publications. With the theme "It's Not Just Business As Usual," the ad reassured consumer electronics dealers that the Emerson brand and products were as secure as ever. "Take a new look," the ad challenged its readers, as the brand continued to face the challenges of an unusually competitive market.

International Growth

Part of Emerson's strategy for success as it confronted the rigors of the 1990s and beyond was expansion into international markets. The search for mass-merchandising opportunities overseas developed at the tail end of spectacular growth in the 1980s. Though Emerson had no more than five chains that generated more than $1 million in 1982, by 1987 it had 72, according to Andriani, vice-president at the time. With the roster of mass-merchandisers nearly exhausted in the United States, the search moved abroad. A branch opened in Canada in 1985 and showed rapid growth by the late 1980s. In addition to subsidiaries in Canada and Hong Kong, the company had subsidiary branch offices in Korea, Thailand, and Spain, with plans for an office in Mexico and aggressive expansion into Central and South America and the European Community in the 1990s.

In January of 1993 Emerson announced a joint venture between Robeson Industries Corp., Extech Corp., and Emerson Radio Corp. to sell and distribute small appliances under the Emerson name. In a January 11, 1993, *HFD* article, Martin Holleran expressed the belief that Robeson's quality programs would combine with Emerson's brand recognition to yield "favorable reception in the marketplace for such small kitchen and household appliances."

Power Brand Vs. Brand Power

As early as 1987, before Emerson Radio Corp. suspected that bankruptcy proceedings were just six years away, Andriani spoke of a desire to expand the brand into power retailer channels in addition to its traditional mass merchandiser base. ''We're looking for a slot,'' he stated in *HFD.* ''But we have to do it cautiously and to hammer out a good relationship. We might do it through derivative models, but that decision has not been made yet.'' By 1993, still reeling from the pressures of a major company reorganization, the brand required increased market exposure. But a Top Brands study researched by Leo J. Shapiro & Associates showed that the Sony brand continued to dominate the consumer electronics market for discount shoppers. Emerson, General Electric, and RCA just missed being named a Power Brand, defined in the study as a brand that performs strongly with both discount store managers and consumers. Emerson fell short on the shoppers end.

Describing the Emerson brand's rigorous efforts to regain lost profitability and market share, Martin Holleran used the seasoned football aphorism: ''Progress in business is three yards and a cloud of dust.'' Even before the problems of the early 1990s were resolved, the brand power of Emerson was confirmed: It had conquered the playing field through radio in the 1930s, television in the 1950s, and VCR marketing in the 1980s. Whether Emerson's eminent stature in the electronics market would make it a power brand into the twenty-first century remained an issue charged with doubt.

Further Reading:

Emerson News and Information, New York: Geltzer & Company, Inc., 1994.

''Emerson Plans to Assure Future Growth; Company Wants to Repeat Successes of '80s and '90s,'' *HFD—The Home Furnishings Newspaper,* April 17, 1989, p. 89.

''Emerson Plans Fuji Brand—But Not That Fuji,'' *Communications Daily,* February 27, 1990.

''Emerson Radio Corp. Wins Approval for Payment to Trade Creditors,'' *Business Wire,* October 7, 1993.

''Emerson Radio Creates New Organizational Structure; Executive Management Group Formed,'' *Business Wire,* August 2, 1993.

''Emerson Radio Enters into Agreement in Principle for World-Wide Distribution of Emerson Household Appliances,'' *Business Wire,* December 30, 1992.

''Emerson Radio May File Chapter 11,'' *HFD,* September 20, 1993, p. 6.

''Emerson Seen Surviving: Rivals; Brand Name Key in Pending Fedders' Buy,'' *HFD,* July 23, 1990, p. 113.

''Holleran's End Run: Emerson Radio's President Aims to Restore Profitability by Stressing Commodity Items and Cutting Costs,'' *HFD,* March 22, 1993, p. 73.

''IBM Bolt to Top 10; Sony Reigns in CE; Discount House Consumers' Preferences for Brand Name Consumer Electronic Products,'' *Discount Store News,* October 18, 1993, p. 50.

Manning, Greenberg, ''Emerson Radio: Looking for Room at the Top; Product Announcement,'' *HFD,* July 27, 1987, p. 110.

''New Emerson M'Wave Units,'' *HFD,* January 11, 1993, p. 192.

''Robeson to Join Emerson, Extech Venture,'' *HFD,* January 11, 1993, p. 6.

—Kerstan Cohen

ETCH A SKETCH®

The bright red nine-and-a-half-by-eight-inch frame of the Etch A Sketch drawing toy is a familiar sight to most American parents. Chances are that either their children own the toy or they played with it themselves when they were kids. Introduced in 1960 by the Ohio Art Company, Etch A Sketch has been on the market for more than 30 years and has sold nearly 100 million units. With that kind of history, it's safe to assume that few Americans have never fiddled with an Etch A Sketch's bright white knobs and watched a black squiggly line appear on the screen.

Perhaps few people ever really create a drawing on an Etch A Sketch; that privilege is reserved for the some half dozen professional artists for whom Etch A Sketch is the medium of choice. Most people, however, have doodled on one, maybe etching a house, a bus, a set of stairs, or a tree. The makers of the Etch A Sketch have capitalized on the simple premise that doodling can be addictive: About two million units a year are sold in 65 countries around the world. Etch A Sketch has sold more units than any other drawing toy ever.

Brand Origins

Little is known about the invention of the Etch A Sketch drawing toy. A French machinist, the late Paul Chaze, first appeared with a prototype for the toy at an annual European toy festival in Nürnberg, Germany, in 1959. The toy consisted of a glass screen enclosed by a plastic frame with two knobs on it. When the knobs were moved, a stylus inside the frame etched a line in aluminum powder, which in turn showed up as a black line on the glass screen.

Chaze's rather intricate device for making what were little more than straight lines apparently seemed somewhat arcane to the European toy manufacturers at Nürnberg. None were interested in his idea for a drawing toy. The Ohio Art Company, a successful American toy manufacturer since the 1920s, was at the fair looking for new ideas to expand its line of lithographed metal playthings. Chaze demonstrated his toy to the U.S. firm's representatives without success. Ohio Art's line of traditional metal sand toys, tea sets, and toy instruments were a far cry from the glass and plastic Etch A Sketch, and the company felt that the French inventor was asking too high a licensing fee for such a risky venture.

Chaze persisted, however, and later that year he managed to convince Ohio Art that with some modifications to its assembly line, it could manufacture the toy in its Bryan, Ohio, factory. Ohio Art had been looking for a way to expand its production of plastic toys, which had begun to dominate the toy industry in the 1950s. After initial reluctance, the company conceded that Chaze's toy might sell, at least as a novelty item. Chaze and Ohio Art reached a licensing agreement, and manufacture of the Etch A Sketch began on July 12, 1960.

Early production of the Etch A Sketch was fraught with difficulties. In the first few months of 1960, almost one out of every four units was defective. The rejects were tossed in a dump outside Bryan, until Ohio Art executives discovered that local residents were picking up the defective units and returning them to department stores for refunds. Fortunately, Ohio Art quickly gained plenty of experience in manufacturing its new toy. Sales immediately took off when the company introduced Etch A Sketch to the American public with a television campaign for the 1960 Christmas season.

Etch A Sketch became the newest craze in the toy industry, and Ohio Art scrambled to meet the growing demand. Orders poured into the Ohio factory at such a pace that manufacture and shipping continued until noon on Christmas Eve so that Americans from coast to coast would be able to purchase the toy for Christmas day. Revamping its assembly line to incorporate both hand assembly and automation, Ohio Art created the manufacturing system that would be used for Etch A Sketch for the next 33 years and greatly reduced its percentage of defective units. The final step of production, in which each Etch A Sketch is ''spanked'' to distribute the aluminum in the case, become a characteristic feature of the Ohio Art assembly plant.

Brand Development

The Etch A Sketch drawing toy has remained essentially unchanged in the 33 years since its introduction. The pulleys controlling movement of the stylus have been improved, and following a series of allegations about the potential hazards of the toy's glass screen, the screen was enclosed by a Mylar overlay. Otherwise, the Etch A Sketch of the 1990s remains identical to that of the 1960s.

Travel Etch A Sketch and Pocket Etch A Sketch, simply smaller versions of the 9.5 x 8-inch original, were added to the line in the 1980s and 1990s. As part of a campaign to rejuvenate sales of Etch A Sketch in the early 1980s, Etch A Sketch games and puzzles were introduced. Featuring plastic overlays that fit over

AT A GLANCE

Etch A Sketch brand of drawing toy invented in France by Paul Chaze; licensed to Ohio Art Company of Bryan, OH, 1960.

Advertising: *Agency*—Lou Beres & Associates, Inc., Chicago, IL, 1982—. *Major campaign*—Television commercials entitled "Remember," with the tagline "Etch A Sketch. Now it's your child's turn."

Addresses: *Parent company*—Ohio Art Company, One Toy Street, Bryan, OH 43506; phone: (419) 636-3141; fax:(419) 636-7614.

the Etch A Sketch screen, these accessories were designed for various age ranges and intended to encourage additional purchases of Etch A Sketch products by the millions of households who already owned the toy. Various licensed children's characters, including Bugs Bunny and the Dukes of Hazard, have been featured in the games and puzzles over the years. In 1992 Ohio Art reached a licensing agreement with the Walt Disney Company and introduced an Etch A Sketch in the shape of Mickey Mouse.

The Etch A Sketch name has also been extended to Ohio Art products with less direct connection to the original design. The Etch A Sketch Animator was an electronic toy introduced to great fanfare in 1986. By storing drawings made on the screen in its electronic memory, the Animator could produce a sequence of up to 12 pictures and then play them back to create a 96-frame "cartoon." The Animator was a tremendous success in its first two years, selling more than 350,000 units during the 1986 Christmas season alone and contributing to a 50 percent increase in Ohio Art sales that year. The toy's relatively high price ($60-$80 retail), however, became a liability in the late 1980s. As consumers began to spend more money on such high-priced electronic systems as Nintendo, they had less to spend on single unit toys like the Animator. Sales of the Animator fizzled and the product was discontinued in 1991.

A color Etch A Sketch was introduced at the 1993 New York Toy Fair. Designed to resemble the original Etch A Sketch, the color Etch A Sketch is really more of a conventional drawing toy, using color markers on paper instead of the stylus and aluminum powder of the original. These color drawings are removable, but not erasable, and children must insert each marker into the stylus manually when they want to change colors. It remains to be seen whether, once the novelty of the toy wears off, children will prefer the awkward movement of the Etch A Sketch knobs to simply removing the markers and drawing freehand on the paper.

Advertising

An integral element in Etch A Sketch's early success was its use of television advertising to introduce the product to American children. While television had been popular since the 1950s, it was only in the latter part of that decade and early 1960s that network television advertising aimed specifically at children became a major marketing tool. Launched in 1960, Etch A Sketch was able to ride the crest of this new phenomenon while escaping the increasingly restrictive advertising regulations that were enacted later in that decade. The focus of the ad campaign was on the magical nature of the drawing toy, which was touted as being "as new as 1960." An animated character named Pernella demonstrated how lines "magically" appear on the screen and are then erased with a simple shake of the box. While animation was later banned in children's advertising, it was used effectively in the early Etch A Sketch ads, which included animated astronauts, to emphasize the magical, other-worldliness of the toy.

By the 1970s, Etch A Sketch had gone from being a toy craze to a toy staple, and its advertising changed accordingly. Television spots, run predominately during times with a high portion of female viewers, were designed to extol the durability and play value of the toy to moms, the prime purchasers of all children's toys. Kid-oriented ads were also used, but they stressed the "fun" of the Etch A Sketch drawing toy and were accompanied by a folksy jingle, proclaiming, "You can draw most anything."

The late 1970s and early 1980s were a time of reorganization for a then beleaguered Ohio Art. Deciding that the dispersed television campaign was not maximizing advertising dollars, the company dropped virtually all television advertising. Taking its

An ad announcing the 1960 introduction of the Ohio Art Company's Etch A Sketch.

place was a $1 million print campaign run exclusively in such women's magazines as *Better Homes and Gardens, Woman's Day,* and *Family Circle.* The ads delivered a consistent message of creativity, durability and play value to a generation of moms who had themselves grown up with the classic toy.

In the early 1990s the "second generation" effect was clearly drawn in a television spot by Lou Beres & Associates entitled "Remember." A series of vignettes showcases a little girl of the 1960s enjoying her Etch A Sketch. The spot then switches to the present as the little girl, now a mom, watches her child play with an Etch A Sketch and closes with the tagline "Etch A Sketch. Now it's your child's turn." The campaign took full advantage of

Etch A Sketch's main asset, its position as a "classic" of the toy industry.

Public Relations and Promotions

As Etch A Sketch moved from a fad to a classic, its marketers began to rely more and more on the toy's reputation for durability and reliability, a reputation that was jeopardized in the early 1970s during a period of turmoil for the toy industry in general. The late 1960s and early 1970s witnessed the growth of the consumer movement, and the toy industry was not exempt from its sweep. In 1972 the Consumer Product Safety Act established the Consumer Product Safety Commission, which was given the power to regulate the toy industry. Hearings were held by the commission, and Etch A Sketch became the subject of public debate.

According to toy historian Marvin Kaye, a letter was sent to the commission by a Minneapolis lawyer claiming that 22 parents were suing Ohio Art for injuries to their children incurred from the broken glass of Etch A Sketch screens. The letter was incorporated into the commission's findings, despite the fact that Ohio Art executives demonstrated that the supposed lawsuits were really complaints filed with the company and that only 13 of them involved broken glass screens. Most of the complaints were closed with settlements of less than $30. To add to Ohio Art's public relations headache, false reports were circulated that claimed the aluminum powder in the drawing toy contained mercury and was poisonous.

Ohio Art executives scrambled to restore the reputation of Etch A Sketch. They set up demonstrations in which the toy was dropped 1,051 times from a second-story window onto a sidewalk without the glass screen breaking. The company quoted letters from parents recounting various misadventures in which the toy emerged unscathed. *Parent's* magazine fed the aluminum powder to rats with no apparent ill effects.

In spite of efforts to prove the safety of Etch A Sketch, consumer perception of the toy as dangerous remained. According to Kaye, Ohio Art lost nearly $2.5 million in sales as a result of the fray. Ohio Art finally decided to place a mylar overlay on the glass screen to ensure that if the screen should break the glass would remain enclosed. The company also added a statement on the plastic toy that advised that Etch A Sketch should be "used with care." Such precautionary measures, along with the passage of time, all but eliminated consumer concerns over Etch A Sketch.

In a more proactive public relations campaign, Ohio Art initiated a college scholarship program in conjunction with its 25th and 30th birthdays in 1985 and 1990. The sweepstakes, promoted via major women's magazines, awarded ten college scholarships worth a total of $250,000 to winning applicants. Distributed in Etch A Sketch boxes, applications were received from 350,000 applicants in the 1985 campaign. The scholarship campaign allowed Ohio Art to reinforce its role as a reliable mainstay of the toy industry, while reminding at least 350,000 kids and their parents of the longevity of the Etch A Sketch toy.

While Etch A Sketch is normally regarded as a children's toy, some professional artists take the aluminum filled frame much more seriously. As described in a 1986 article in the *Wall Street Journal,* a group of nearly a half dozen artists who use the toy as their medium has emerged over the past decade. A great deal of nostalgia is associated with Etch A Sketch for the baby boom generation, some of whom are willing to pay up to $150 for an original Etch A Sketch drawing. The Ohio Art Company has actively encouraged and promoted Etch A Sketch art by arranging regional shows and national television appearances for the nontraditional artists. A fruitful relationship for Ohio Art, an association with the artists provides a high level of exposure for Etch A Sketch at a comparatively low cost and, even more importantly, strengthens Etch A Sketch's position as an integral part of Americana.

Performance and Future Growth

Etch A Sketch was an immediate success after its introduction in 1960. Almost one million units were sold during the Christmas season that year. By 1961 sales of the toy had reached fad proportions. It seemed as though every kid just had to own an Etch A Sketch and, at a relatively inexpensive $2.50, parents were willing to oblige. Four million Etch A Sketch units were sold in 1961, an all time record for the popular drawing toy. Sales leveled off through the 1960s, but, according to company reports, Etch A Sketch still sold an impressive 1.75 million units a year. In the late 1980s and early 1990s, following a major reorganization of Ohio Art in 1984, annual sales of Etch A Sketch hovered consistently near the two million mark. In a 1985 article in *Chain Store Age,* Lowell T. Wilson, then vice-president of product development for Ohio Art, claimed that Etch A Sketch is insulated from major sales declines because the product is a classic. The introduction of video games, for instance, was disastrous to many in the toy industry as they gobbled up consumer spending. Sales of Etch A Sketch, however, actually grew during this tumultuous period.

Etch a Sketch is sold in 65 countries around the world through Ohio Art's international marketing department and a series of distribution agreements with foreign toy companies. Requiring virtually no instructions or verbal cues, the Etch A Sketch is a natural for garnering international sales.

The Ohio Art Company underwent some very lean years in the late 1980s, losing almost $3 million in large part because of dwindling sales of the Etch A Sketch Animator. The original Etch A Sketch, however, maintained steady sales throughout the end of the decade and, as Ohio Art emerged from its decline in 1992 with an impressive 157 percent gain on its stock, company executives decided to invest more heavily in the classic, dependable Etch A Sketch. With sales of video games beginning to wane in the 1990s, consumers were once again choosing such less expensive and time-tested traditional toys as Etch A Sketch. A return to basics could only benefit the 30-year-old drawing toy, which was likely to continue its steady but impressive sales into the twenty-first century.

Further Reading:

Brown, Paul B., "Staying Power," *Forbes,* March 26, 1984, p. 188.

Cropper, Carol, "Etch a Mickey," *Forbes,* March 30, 1992, p. 14.

Freedman, Alix M., "If You're Talented You Can Create Art with a Mere Toy," *Wall Street Journal,* March 26, 1986, p. 1.

Hartnett, Michael, "Etch A Sketch Traces Product's Success," *Chain Store Age General Merchandise Edition,* March 1985, pp. 86–87.

Kaye, Marvin, *The Story of Monopoly, Silly Putty, Bingo, Twister, Scrabble, Frisbee etc.,* New York: Stein and Day, 1973, pp. 176–179.

Slutsker, Gary, "Etch a Future," *Forbes,* March 23, 1987, p. 72.

Weiss, Gary, "Mid-Year Investment Outlook: The Best of 1992 So Far—Ohio Art Best Amex Stock," *Business Week,* June 22, 1992, pp. 106.

—Hilary Gopnik

EUREKA®

Eureka is one of America's leading vacuum cleaner brands, with sales and service operations in the United States, Canada, Mexico, and many other countries. The branded product line includes more than 100 different models, representing the extreme segmentation of the market including uprights, canisters, hand-helds, built-in home systems, home cleaning systems (canisters with power heads), battery-powered vacuums, and wet-dry vacs. Eureka vacuums are sold under several nameplates, including Boss, Powerline, Corvette (licensed from the Chevrolet Motor Division of General Motors Corporation), Mighty Mite, and others. The appliances are marketed through department stores, warehouse clubs, discount stores, hardware stores, auto centers, vacuum cleaner shops, and other retail outlets. The company's vacuums are sold under the brand "Euroclean " in Canada and Europe, and the Eureka Company manufactures commercial vacuums under the Eureka Commercial and Sanitaire brand names. Ranked among the top vacuum cleaner brands since the 1920s, Eureka was purchased by AB Electrolux, a Swedish vacuum manufacturer and global leader in the field, in 1974.

Brand Origins

First invented in 1902, vacuum cleaners are among the oldest household appliances. Corporate folklore relates that Fred Wardell of Detroit, Michigan, felt that the Greek word "Eureka"—meaning "I have found it!"—expressed his feeling of accomplishment at founding his vacuum cleaner company in Detroit in 1909. He may have also hoped that consumers would use the exclamation upon seeing his sleek, lightweight vacuums in stores. By 1913, the brand came in six different models and included attachments for bare floors, walls, upholstery, and crevices. The versatile appliance could even be used as a hairdryer. Within its first decade, Eureka established itself as an industry leader, and in 1915 it earned fame and the Grand Prize for vacuum cleaners at that year's San Francisco International Exposition. By 1919, Eureka was headquartered in the first volume production factory devoted exclusively to vacuum cleaners. And by 1927, Eureka had captured one-third of all U.S. vacuum sales.

After merging with the Williams Oil-O-Matic Company in 1945, Eureka's headquarters were moved to Bloomington, Illinois, and the company briefly diversified into oil burners and even a battery-powered car called the "Henney Kilowatt." Vacuum cleaner production was curtailed during World War II due to material shortages, but after the war Eureka overtook rival Hoover in the sales of its canister models, which were efficient cleaners of the tiled floors that were popular during the postwar era.

The vacuum cleaner market was saturated by the 1960s: more than 80 percent of U.S. households had at least one. The trend toward multi-ownership began in the affluent postwar era, when the industry aggressively promoted the idea that one cleaner was not enough for the average homemaker. Vacuum marketers convinced consumers that they needed an "arsenal" of cleaners for their "war against dust and dirt": a canister for hard surface floors, an upright for carpets, and a portable for furniture and drapes.

The campaign was very successful: at least 30 percent of annual sales was created by multi-vacuum owners. An electric broom, introduced by Eureka in the 1960s, was developed especially for this second-vacuum market. This lightweight model for small jobs enjoyed relatively high popularity during the 1960s. Vacuum manufacturers also drove for "planned obsolescence" by adding new features and improved performance on new models. Eureka's 800 series, introduced in the late 1960s, was an example of this concept. The new line featured storage space on the machine for the hose and attachments.

In addition to innovative design, advertising played a key role in boosting sales of Eureka vacuum cleaners. Eureka made humor a hallmark of its television advertising campaigns, using its "Carpet Critters" and, to mark its 75th anniversary in 1984, the fictitious "Emilia J. Gretz," supposedly the first woman to ever buy a Eureka.

Market Segmentation

As competition in the U.S. vacuum market continued to increase in the last half of the twentieth century, manufacturers sought ways to expand the market through new product introductions. Rather than wait for the formation of new households or the slow replacement market, vacuum marketers worked to create even more new models for specific uses.

The hand-held category was created in 1979, when Black & Decker brought out its first cordless Dustbuster. This small, inexpensive vacuum created an entirely new segment of the vacuum industry, and manufacturers hurried to capture a share. In 1984

AT A GLANCE

Eureka brand founded in Detroit, MI, by Fred Wardell, 1909; company moved to Bloomington, IL, merged with Williams Oil-O-Matic, and renamed Eureka-Williams, 1945; merged with National Union Electric Corp., 1960; name reverted to The Eureka Company, 1974, upon acquisition by AB Electrolux of Sweden.

Performance: *Market share*—Number two in vacuum market. *Sales*—$390 million.

Major competitor: Hoover; also, Bissell and Royal Appliance Manufacturing Company's Dirt Devil.

Advertising: *Major campaign*—Slogan, "Performance You Expect. Quality You Demand."

Addresses: *Parent company*—The Eureka Company, 1201 East Bell St., Bloomington, IL 61701-6902; phone: (309) 828-2367. *Ultimate parent company*—White Consolidated Industries Inc., 11760 Berea Rd., Cleveland, OH 44111; phone: (216) 252-3700. *Ultimate ultimate parent company*—AB Electrolux, Sweden.

Eureka became the first major vacuum brand to enter the rechargeable hand-held vac market. The Mini Mite featured a telescoping crevice nozzle and slip-in holster recharger. Eureka was also among the first to offer electronic vacuums in the early 1980s. Eureka's Vactronic Quiet Kleen Power Team incorporated electronic controls and indicator lights. Eureka captured 28 percent of the upright market by 1987, but its share declined as the 1990s approached.

Cleaning Efficiency Rating

In 1993 Hoover began promoting a new "Cleaning Efficiency Rating," which measured the effectiveness of each amp of electrical power employed by the branded vacuums. Royal Appliance Manufacturing Company, maker of the Dirt Devil vacuum line, sued Hoover that year, charging that the new measurement confused consumers accustomed to seeing amperage ratings.

Eureka sidestepped the legal imbroglio, but publicly denounced Hoover's efforts to set industry standards on the grounds that: industry standards should not be established unilaterally; cleaning effectiveness standards already existed; the "CE" rating misleadingly implied extraordinary energy savings; and that the new standard was unfair to canister-principle uprights. Eureka also appealed to the Council of Better Business Bureaus' National Advertising Division for a ruling on the controversial rating. In the fall of 1993 the consumer protection agency convinced Hoover to revise its point-of-sale information, saying that it was "potentially confusing to the consumer" because its rating system differed from the industry standard amperage rating. Hoover's tactic was just one manifestation of the intense competition that characterized the vacuum market in the 1990s.

Cause Marketing

Eureka employed a much less combative strategy in its fight for share, combining the 1990s affinity for eco-friendliness and social awareness in a record-setting national advertising program that launched the World Vac line in 1993. This series of uprights, canisters, and home cleaning systems featured a new global logo that resembled a "seal of approval." Eye-catching packaging utilized color photos of such well-known national landmarks as the Washington Monument and the Grand Canyon. The company contributed a portion of the purchase price of each World Vac to the National Park Foundation for preservation of national parks and monuments and to programs of the American Heart Association directed against heart disease and stroke.

Although Eureka took the competitive "high road," it was clearly out to increase sales: the brand's consumer media expenditures nearly tripled from 1991 to 1994. Its 1994 media budget funded "World Vac " placements in consumer and trade magazines, including *First For Women, Good Housekeeping, Ladies' Home Journal, Better Homes & Gardens,* and *Canadian Living.* Television ads appeared on all major broadcast and cable networks. Eureka's popular Bravo! Boss line, which featured onboard tools, was emphasized in the campaign. Eureka sold over one million Bravo! Boss models within its first year alone.

Further Reading:

Chanil, Debra, "Vacuums Clean Up," *Discount Merchandiser,* January 1992, pp. 48–51.

Dorsey, Gilbert L., "Eureka Responds to Hoover 'Standard Setting,' " *Appliance Manufacturer,* September 1993, p. 10.

"The Eureka Company: A Proud Heritage, an Exceptional Future," Bloomington, IL: The Eureka Company, 1994.

Remich, Norman C., Jr., "World Vac More Than Floor Care," *Appliance Manufacturer,* June 1993, p. 55.

Willatt, Norris, "Sweeping Ahead: Sales of Vacuum Cleaners Are Picking Up Fresh Momentum," *Barron's,* January 8, 1968, pp. 11, 28–29.

—April S. Dougal

EVINRUDE®

EVINRUDE® OUTBOARDS

Founded in 1911, Evinrude was the oldest name in outboard motors in the early 1990s. Along with its sister brand, Johnson, it accounted for about half of all outboard motors sold worldwide. The brand was owned by Outboard Marine Corporation of Waukegan, Illinois, which was created in 1929 after its original owner, Evinrude Motor Co., merged with two other makers of outboard motors. Between about 1950 and 1970 the company also produced motorboats, snowmobiles, lawn mowers, campers, and camping equipment under the Evinrude brand name.

Brand Origins

Ole Evinrude, the brand's founder, was born in Norway in 1877 but raised in the United States. He left school after the third grade to work on the family farm in south-central Wisconsin. When he was 16, Evinrude headed to Madison, where he found work in a shop making farm machinery and taught himself mathematics at the library. Over the next few years Evinrude also worked for companies making electric motors and gasoline engines, as well as in a steel mill in Pittsburgh.

In 1900 Evinrude took a job in Milwaukee as a patternmaker. By then several American industrialists, including Henry Ford and Ranson Eli Olds, had introduced their first automobiles, and in his spare time Evinrude built a horseless carriage of his own. He formed several partnerships, first with the idea of making engines for other automobile makers and later to manufacture an automobile to be called the Eclipse. Evinrude's early business ventures failed, however, when he was unable to get along with his partners.

Reluctantly Evinrude returned to patternmaking but continued to tinker, and in 1908 he built an engine that could be clamped on the stern of a rowboat. Later Evinrude would say that his inspiration had been a hot summer day when he and Bess Cary, his future wife, were picnicking with friends on an island about two miles from shore. When Bess decided she wanted ice cream, Evinrude rowed back to town, but the ice cream had melted by the time he got back. Evinrude was struck by the obvious thought that someone should invent a motor for a rowboat.

Others, of course, had been struck by the same thought. A Frenchman, Gustave Troube, invented an electric outboard motor in 1881, and in 1892 his countryman, Alfred Seguin, developed a gasoline inboard engine with a stern drive. In the United States the American Motors Company in Long Island City, New York, offered a "portable boat motor with a reversible propeller" as early as 1896, and Cameron B. Waterman, who coined the term "outboard motor," sold more than 12,000 "Porto Motors" between 1907 and 1909. Evinrude's outboard motor, however, would soon outsell all the others.

When Evinrude unveiled his outboard motor, Bess said it looked like a coffee grinder, but the next day Evinrude and his brother-in-law, Russ Cary, tried it out on the Kinnikinnic River and returned more enthusiastic than ever. Evinrude made some improvements, including the addition of a muffler, and loaned it to a friend to use over the weekend. When the friend returned on Monday, he had sales orders for 10 of Evinrude's outboard motors. Evinrude filled the orders and built an additional 15 outboard motors. Meanwhile, Bess placed in the Milwaukee newspapers an ad that said, "Don't Row! Throw the oars away! Use an Evinrude motor." The extra 15 outboard motors were sold in a few days. (The first outboard motors, which developed 1½ horsepower, weighed 62 pounds, and Evinrude priced them at a dollar a pound.) Encouraged by the response, Bess Evinrude, who later become her husband's business and advertising manager, placed the same notice in a national magazine. A few days after the magazine came out, the orders started flowing in. Evinrude sold more than a thousand motors in 1910.

Evinrude Motor Co.

In 1911 Evinrude founded the Evinrude Detachable Row Boat Motor Co. Needing start-up capital, Evinrude also took a partner, Chris J. Meyer, then president of a local tugboat company, who put up $5,000 for half interest in the business. Effective marketing soon made Evinrude the leading outboard motor in the United States. Waterman had used the intimidating line "Don't be afraid of it" to sell his outboard motors, but Bess Evinrude emphasized convenience. Bess Evinrude also negotiated a deal to sell Evinrude outboard motors to fishermen in Scandinavia. After selling 2,000 outboard motors in 1911, sales increased to more than 4,600 in 1912 and 9,400 in 1913.

By 1914 the Evinrude outboard motor had become internationally famous. Bess Evinrude fell ill, however, and Ole began bickering with his partner. Finally, Evinrude sold his share of the company—which had changed its name to the Evinrude Motor Co. in 1912—to Meyer for $137,500. The Evinrudes and their

AT A GLANCE

Evinrude brand of outboard motor founded in 1911 by Ole Evinrude, owner of Evinrude Detachable Row Boat Motor Co.; business renamed Evinrude Motor Co. in 1912; company acquired in 1928 by Briggs & Stratton, Inc., a Milwaukee-based manufacturer of automobile parts; company sold again in 1929 and merged with Elto Outboard Motor Co. and Lockwood Motors Co. to form Outboard Motors Corporation; company name changed to Outboard, Marine and Manufacturing Co. in 1936 and to Outboard Marine Corporation in 1956.

Performance: *Market share*—50% of the world's outboard motor category (Evinrude and Johnson brands combined).

Major competitor: Brunswick Corp.'s Mercury/Mariner.

Advertising: *Agency*—LKH&S, Chicago, IL, 1991—. *Major campaign*—"Evinrude, Leading the Way."

Addresses: *Parent company*—Outboard Marine Corporation, 100 Sea-Horse Drive, Waukegan, IL 60085; phone: (708) 689-5438.

son, Ralph, spent the next several years traveling around the United States, while the Evinrude Motor Co. continued to prosper and even expanded into boatbuilding.

Elto Outboard Motor Co.

When Evinrude left in 1914, he agreed not to compete with his former partner for five years. He continued to tinker, however, and by the time the clause expired in 1919, Evinrude had designed an outboard motor made partly of aluminum that was lighter and 50 percent more powerful than his original model. He offered to sell the design to the Evinrude Motor Co., but Meyer turned him down. In 1920 Evinrude formed the Elto Outboard Motor Co. The name was Bess's idea—"Elto" stood for the Evinrude Light Twin Outboard.

The Elto outboard motor was introduced in 1921 with only moderate success. About 3,500 were sold in 1922, but that was fewer than half the number sold by Evinrude, which was still the industry leader. In 1922, however, another competitor, Johnson Motor Company, joined the increasingly crowded market and introduced a still more powerful, lightweight aluminum engine. The Johnson Light Twin, also known as the Waterbug, was an instant success. Faced with aggressive competition and an outdated product, Meyer sold the Evinrude Motor Co. to an investment group.

Johnson quickly became the industry leader, while Evinrude fell to third place behind Elto. Johnson's success was the result of a solid product, which it continually improved, and innovative marketing. In magazine advertisements actor Walter Beery boasted that Johnson outboard motors gave him his "greatest vacation," and explorer Richard E. Byrd said Johnson outboard motors "were invaluable" during an expedition to the North Pole in 1926. Johnson also set world speed records in 1925 and 1926.

In 1928 Elto introduced the Super Elto Quad—the first four-cylinder, two-cycle outboard motor—and the seven-horsepower Speedster, which kept it competitive. The same year Evinrude was sold to Briggs & Stratton, Inc., the Milwaukee-based manufacturer of automotive parts.

Outboard Motors Corporation

Briggs & Stratton paid more than $400,000 to buy Evinrude and modernize the manufacturing facilities. Even so, Harry Stratton, cofounder of the company, became convinced that Evinrude would never be able to compete with Johnson. His partner, Stephen Briggs, felt otherwise. In 1929 Briggs arranged to buy Evinrude from Briggs & Stratton and engineered a merger with Elto to create the Outboard Motors Corporation. A third company, the Lockwood Motors Co. of Jackson, Michigan, was also included in the merger. Ole Evinrude became president of the company that now owned his namesake brand, while Briggs became chairman of the board.

The new Outboard Motors Corporation was poised to challenge Johnson for leadership in the industry. The previous year the companies involved in the merger had combined sales of more than 25,000 outboard motors—about equal to Johnson. Both companies did well the summer of 1929, with Johnson maintaining a slight edge thanks to a new Seahorse line of outboard motors and an unprecedented $600,000 advertising campaign. The stock market collapsed in October, however, sending the United States into the Great Depression and destroying the market for outboard motors.

After struggling through 1930, Outboard Motors sold its entire remaining inventory of 10,000 Evinrude and Elto outboard motors at fire-sale prices in 1931. Ole Evinrude also gave up his salary and later loaned the company $50,000 of his own money to keep the business afloat. In 1932 Evinrude and Elto combined their production lines and sold virtually the same outboard motors under their own brand names, although Evinrude was positioned as the premium brand. Evinrude also expanded into camp stoves and bicycle motors and introduced the Evinrude Lawn Boy lawn mower and the Evinrude Water Boy lawn sprinkler. (Outboard sold Lawn Boy in 1989 to the Toro Company.)

Meanwhile, the situation was even worse at Johnson Motor, which was struggling with an enormous debt as a result of a new factory built in 1927, the massive advertising campaign of 1929, and an ill-timed decision to enter the boatbuilding industry. In 1931 Hayden, Stone & Co., an investment banking firm that had underwritten a stock offering, assumed control of Johnson and eventually decided to sell what was left of the company to the highest bidder. After almost negotiating a deal with the Stewart-Warner Co., Hayden, Stone & Co. accepted a personal bid of $800,000 from Stephen Briggs and Ralph Evinrude. Johnson officially merged with Outboard Motors Corporation in 1936, bringing the three leading brands of outboard motors under a single ownership. The corporate name was changed to Outboard, Marine and Manufacturing Co.

"Consolidated Competition"

The Elto brand name was phased out between 1936 and 1938, but Johnson and Evinrude continued to operate as separate companies in what Outboard, Marine and Manufacturing described as "consolidated competition." In 1938 *Fortune* reported that "Chief Engineer [Finn] Irgens of Evinrude and Chief Engineer J.G. Rayniak of Johnson get together for a shop talk once a week. If one of them has made some flabbergasting discovery he will tell the other, but mostly Irgens is trying to outsmart Rayniak, and vice versa."

Johnson and Evinrude also went separate ways during World War II. Evinrude manufactured the Evinrude 4-60, used to power the Army's speedy river craft known as "Storm Boats," and the Lightfour, which was dropped with inflatable rubber rafts to rescue pilots whose planes went down at sea. Johnson, on the other hand, made airplane parts and motors for the Army's pontoon bridges. Johnson also designed the portable Handy Billy pump, based on the Evinrude 4-60, that was used to fight fires aboard Navy ships.

After the war it was Johnson, not Evinrude, that was first in the market with an all-new outboard motor. Introduced in 1948, the Seahorse QD was the first outboard motor with a separate fuel tank and a shift lever that allowed the operator to select forward, reverse, or neutral. The separate 5.5-gallon fuel tank had several advantages: the capacity was twice what built-in tanks held, it was easier to fill, and it had a fairly accurate fuel gauge. The outboard motor was also lighter and easier to handle. The shift lever allowed boaters to warm up the motors at the dock and gave them added maneuverability. The innovative QD vaulted Johnson into brand leadership.

Consolidated competition, however, was coming to an end. In 1950 Outboard, Marine and Manufacturing created a single research department for Johnson, Evinrude, and its Gale Products division, which manufactured Buccaneer brand and private-label outboard motors. The Evinrude 25 and Johnson 25, introduced in 1951, were essentially the same outboard motor with different housings. The two lines were fully integrated by 1956, when Evinrude sold 153,000 outboard motors to Johnson's 166,000. (More than 640,000 outboard motors were sold in the United States in 1956, the industry's best year ever.) The corporate name was also changed to Outboard Marine Corporation in 1956.

Leisure Market

The market for outboard motors also changed dramatically after the war. Before World War II most outboard motors were sold to hunters and fishermen, but boating became a family activity in the 1950s. Women were also playing an important role in deciding which outboard motor to buy, and Outboard Marine began advertising Evinrude and Johnson in general circulation magazines, such as *Life, Look,* and *The Saturday Evening Post.* Outdoor Marine also began manufacturing fiberglass motorboats under both the Evinrude and Johnson brand names. One particularly innovative model was the Evinrude Dream Boat, a saucer-shaped boat that came with two outboard motors encased in plastic bubbles. The boats were sold through the same network of dealers and distributors that handled Evinrude and Johnson motors.

The company diversified further in 1964, when it introduced the Evinrude Skeeter snowmobile. The Evinrude division also produced an identical snowmobile, called the Skee-Horse, that was sold under the Johnson brand. Another innovation introduced in 1966 was the Evinrude Aquanaut (also sold as the Johnson Air-Buoy), a floating, gasoline-powered compressor that could pump fresh air to divers below. Outboard Motor, however, stopped making Evinrude and Johnson diving compressors in 1970, its boats in 1971, and its snowmobiles in 1976. At the time, the Evinrude line included the original Skeeter and the popular Bobcat snowmobile models. Evinrude tent campers were phased out in 1971.

Boat and Motor Packages

Japanese outboard-motor manufacturers, most notably Yamaha, began testing the U.S. market in the early 1980s just as the industry began to recover from its worst slump since the Depression. (Sales fell by 50 percent between 1973 and 1982.) Outboard Marine responded by cutting the prices on its Evinrude and Johnson outboard motors and by streamlining operations. The company also began negotiating with boatbuilders to "pre-rig" their motorboats to accommodate Evinrude or Johnson outboard motors. Dealers could then sell boats and motors as a matched package. (As outboard motors became bigger and more complex, buying a motor boat had become equally complicated, much like buying an automobile and then deciding what engine to have installed. "Clamp-on" motors were still sold individually for smaller boats.)

In late 1986 and early 1987 Outboard Marine took its strategy—designed to "lock-in" market share—a step further by acquiring five boat manufacturers in a span of two months. In 1989 it added Murray Industries, Inc., makers of Chris-Craft. Charles Strang, then chairman of Outboard Marine, explained: "Our Japanese competitors watched this sudden move to the marketing of factory-packaged boats, motors and trailers first with skepticism, then puzzlement, and now concern. If their market share in the U.S. is to grow—or even hold still—they will have to move into boat manufacturing in the U.S. At this point, they are far, far behind in responding to this fundamental change in marine marketing, and the top U.S. boat companies have already been acquired."

Outboard Marine's principal domestic competitor, the Brunswick Corporation, maker of Mercury and Mariner outboard motors, also pursued a strategy of boat and motor packages. In 1992 Brunswick controlled about 30 percent of the U.S. market for boats, compared with 20 percent for Outboard Marine.

Brand Outlook

In 1990 the company also introduced the Evinrude Spitfire (Johnson Silverstar), a 150-horsepower outboard motor that *Boating Industry* called "so dramatic that it's sure to become an . . . industry milestone." The Spitfire was 30 percent smaller than comparable outboard motors. Many of the usual hoses and gaskets were eliminated by molding pathways directly into the engine block, making the outboard much easier to install and service.

According to *Boating Industry,* Americans owned more than 8 million outboard-motor boats in 1992. There were also another 4.5 million rowboats, canoes, dinghies, and inflatables that could be powered by clamp-on outboard motors. The recreational boating industry, however, has been extremely sensitive to economic conditions. It had several strong years in the late 1980s, but sales for the industry fell in the early 1990s to their lowest levels since World War II because of a lingering recession. About 272,000 outboard motors were sold in the United States in 1992.

In its 1993 annual report Outboard Marine, which suffered a $282 million loss, acknowledged the serious problems facing the industry but noted, "Very importantly, we bring to the competition the best-selling outboards in the United States and in the world." The company was counting on its new saltwater Evinrude OceanPro V-6 outboard motor (also sold as the Johnson OceanRunner) to boost sales in 1994.

Further Reading:

DeGaspari, John, ''Masters of Their Destiny,'' *Boating Industry,* February 1988, p. 52.

Fahs, John, ''A Yen for Outboards,'' *Boating Industry,* March 1990, p. 35.

Henschen, Douglas, ''Are the Conglomerates on a Power Trip?'' *Boating Industry,* June 1990, p. 43.

Rodengen, Jeffrey L., *Evinrude-Johnson and the Legend of OMC,* Ft. Lauderdale, Florida: Write Stuff Syndicate, Inc., 1993.

Skorupa, Joe, ''A Radical Outboard for the '90s,'' *Boating Industry,* September 1990, p. 152.

Scott, Robert H., ''The Birth of a Notion,'' *Nation's Business,* February 1972, p. 92.

—Dean Boyer

FARBERWARE®

FARBERWARE

Farberware is one of the oldest, most recognizable brand names in the United States. The Farberware company is the country's largest manufacturer of stainless steel cookware and is a major producer of small kitchen appliances. In fact, the Farberware brand is considered synonymous with stainless steel cookware. In the 1920s, S.W. Farber, Inc. was the first company in the world to introduce lustrous, chrome-plated cooking accessories. Now, the company's stainless steel ware is the top-selling brand in the United States. Owned by a British-American conglomerate since 1987, all Farberware stainless steel commodities are American-made.

Brand Origins

In 1900, a 21-year old Jewish immigrant from the Russian Empire, Simon W. Farber, arrived in New York via Ellis Island. He had not done badly in the old country, where he had been manager of a copper cookware factory, but anti-Semitism was legal and official policy in his native land, and so, like millions of Jews, he left for America. He stayed in New York, living on the lower East Side of Manhattan, where far more Yiddish was spoken than English. It took only a year for Farber to learn sufficient English to set up a copper cookware business of his own. In a rented basement, Farber, along with the five men he had hired, worked on turning out brass (a mixture of copper and zinc) vases and bowls. While each was hand made, Farber was not a traditionalist who disdained machinery—he simply was too poor to afford any. Surprisingly, there was a ready market for his products—in the past, Farber discovered, cookware of such high quality had always been imported.

It took only a few years for his business to prosper. By then Farber had moved the company into sizeable quarters in the Bronx. His new wife, a former business teacher, became his partner, and the Farbers purchased machinery that enabled them to mass-produce for a national market and implement new product ideas.

Commercial Successes

In 1910, the "Farberware" line of giftware—beautiful nickel and silver plated items such as cooking crocks—appeared on the market for the first time. This proved to be so popular that the Farbers stepped up production of the existing line while working to design new products to satisfy consumer demand. In 1914, a whole line of nickel plated casserole frames (for holding the earthenware or glass inserts of the day) were introduced and became an instant success. As World War I began, business was booming.

An indication of the inventive genius and business acumen of Simon Farber was his invention of the instantly popular "Adjusto-Lite," marketed for the first time in 1919. Farber had always been bothered by the fact that lighting for such nighttime tasks as reading or sewing was never adequate because it was too difficult to adjust light to suit one's needs. One day he was inspired to create a portable light that could, when affixed with a clamp that Farber had created, be placed anywhere. Coming home one day to find his unique lamp missing, Farber became exasperated—until he realized that he probably would not be the only person who would feel so dependent on a portable lamp. No sooner had he reached that conclusion than he was determined to manufacture and market his lamp, a product quite unrelated to his metal plates and pots, but a popular item with consumers when it hit the marketplace.

In the 1920s, American women began to demand labor-saving devices that could help them finish mundane household tasks more quickly. Around the same time, the wealthy, in response to the strains of the new federal income tax, were cutting back on domestic help and finding themselves doing chores they had always paid others to do. One of these chores—polishing silver plated utensils and serving dishes—was a particularly difficult and time-consuming task. To solve this problem, in 1925 the S.W. Farber Company was the first in the world to come out with a complete product line of high quality, chrome plated serving accessories that were, like silver plated utensils, beautiful and lustrous, but required no polishing. This set the stage for other chrome plated products, on which the company built its reputation.

Product Development

Despite the severity of the Depression, the 1930s turned out to be highly innovative years for the Farberware product line. In 1930, as the economic effects of the Depression were beginning to become apparent, the first Farberware electric percolator came on the market. This was the world's first chrome plated (inside and out) percolator that came with a built-in fuse, which could be replaced, if necessary, up to eight times. This was the unique "8 in

AT A GLANCE

Farberware brand of cookware and kitchen utensils founded in 1900 with the establishment of S.W. Farber, Inc., in New York, NY, by founder Simon W. Farber; 1910, company introduced "Farberware" nickel and silver plated giftware and serving accessories; 1925, Farber introduced first chrome plated cookware; 1946, company moved to the Bronx, where it established a reputation for stainless steel cookware; 1966, Walter Kidde & Co. acquired Farberware; 1987, Farberware sold to British-American Hanson Industries, Inc.

Performance: *Market share*—72% of nonstick, stainless steel cookware market; 28% of electric coffee percolator market. *Sales*—$125 million.

Major competitor: Revere Ware

Advertising: *Agency*—Warner, Bicking, Morris, New York, NY. *Major campaign*—"Millennium Not Only Takes the Heat, It Burns the Competition."

Addresses: *Parent company*—Farberware, Inc.; 1500 Bassett Ave., Bronx, NY 10461; phone: (718) 863-8000; fax: (708) 409-0354. *Ultimate parent company*—Hanson Industries, Inc.; 99 Wood Ave.S.; Iselin, NJ 08830; phone: (908) 603-6600; fax: (908) 603-6878; *Ultimate ultimate parent company*—Hanson, PLC

1'' fuse, an innovative concept that also was incorporated in 1935 into the chrome plated Farberware coffee urn that came with matching tray, sugar bowl, and creamer. Two years later, the Farberware ''Coffee Robot,'' the first automatic electric coffee pot with a preset thermostat to keep coffee warm after brewing, was introduced. In 1938 Farber introduced the famous Farberware ''Broiler Robot,'' the first broiler that could cook food at the dinner table and another time-saving helper for busy homemakers.

The intervening war years essentially turned all manufacturing at Farber to military projects. Nonetheless, in 1942 Farberware introduced its ''hot water plate,'' which, when filled with hot water, could keep food warm. An attractive appliance, the plate featured a chrome base with walnut handles.

With the war over, the S.W. Farber Company moved to new quarters in the south Bronx, and turned its attention to the manufacture of high quality, stainless steel cookware that had its antecedents in the chrome plated accessories of pre-war days. In 1949 the famous stainless steel, aluminum-clad Farberware, the first of its kind, became an instant success. Consumers enjoyed the new Farberware's attractive appearance, the way it conducted heat evenly and quickly, and especially the way it cleaned up afterwards. Farberware's (and the world's) first electric, stainless steel frying pan came out in 1954, as did the ''super fast'' stainless steel electric percolator. Farberware's ''Open Hearth'' broiler, which eliminated smoke produced by cooking food (by heating from underneath), arrived in 1962.

After the acquisition of the S.W. Farber Company by Walter Kidde & Co. in 1966, new products continued to be added to the Farberware line: in 1973, the first counter-top convection oven; in 1975, the first crock pot with a removable ''pot;'' in 1979, the first ''Solid State Food Processor'' that could be set at different speeds; and in 1986 came the first Farberware scratch- and stain-resistant microwave cookware line. This line was augmented in 1989 with the arrival of the Farberware MicroBrew, a drip coffeemaker uniquely designed for the microwave oven. Stainless steel cutlery (Farberware had previously produced only cookware), first introduced in 1990, was a logical expansion of the Farberware array of products.

In the 1990s, Farberware is expanding for the first time into electric houseware products such as toasters, blenders, mixers and irons. It also introduced its most important new product line of cookware, the extremely popular Millennium Never-Stick stainless steel cookware. The first cookware of its kind, the Millennium line combines durable stainless steel with a revolutionary nonstick cooking surface. Millenium cookware is so durable, the company guarantees it will last 70 years—even if metal utensils are used on it.

Advertising/Marketing

From its beginnings, the Farberware brand has been advertised extensively in the print media. Since becoming a division of the conglomerate Hanson, PLC, in 1987, strenuous efforts have been made to revitalize certain traditional Farberware products, such as electric percolators, and to market on television; the company also intends to expand into international markets and establish a reputation among professionals. Farberware began sponsoring popular cooking programs on public television (most recently, ''Cooking with Master Chefs'' on PBS), and engaging famous chefs and popular food personalities to give food demonstrations using the latest line of Farberware cookware. In 1992, Farberware also began sponsoring a ''Farberware Millennium Chef of the Year'' award with the James Beard Foundation.

Much of the focus of Farberware's marketing strategy has been to broaden its consumer base by entering franchise agreements with other companies, provided they meet high criteria. In 1990, for example, Farberware entered into a license agreement with Excep Associates to market flatware and glassware, and Lifetime Hoan Corporation to market flatware and kitchen gadgets. And in 1993 Farberware and Frye International together marketed a popular boxed set package containing five pieces of Farberware's famous stainless steel cookware along with a food storage set containing five attractive plastic containers; this helps broaden market reach beyond traditional Farberware product lines. With its strong brand recognition, aggressive marketing and a new franchise program underway, there is little doubt among industry experts that Farberware will remain a dominant market brand in the U.S. in the future.

International Markets

Broadening the scope of Farberware products beyond the United States, with its saturated housewares market, is becoming an important and quite recent strategy. In 1992, an International Sales division was established, which is effectively marketing the Farberware brand name in the Western Hemisphere, buoyed especially by the recent acceptance of the North American Free Trade Accord (NAFTA). Currently, Canada constitutes the biggest foreign market for Farberware products, with Mexico the next biggest potential foreign market; Farberware is making strong inroads into several Central American and South American countries as well.

Outside of the Western Hemisphere, the Philippines, perhaps because of the strong American legacy in that country, is a growing market for Farberware. Japanese bureaucracy and distrust of foreign companies have made that country's market difficult to penetrate, although Farberware does have a distributor there. Europe, with its own distinctive cooking traditions and strong housewares brands, is far less of a field for Farberware expansion than North America, but nonetheless, efforts are being made to establish a future joint venture with a European company. Thanks to distributorships in Hungary and Romania, Farberware products have sold well in these former Eastern bloc countries. Efforts to duplicate this success in Russia are currently underway. These ambitious pursuits of international markets are only a few years old and appear to be effective. In that brief period, international sales of Farberware products have increased an average of 30 percent annually.

Future Growth

Farberware's greatest asset in the United States is its strong brand name and prestige. That advantage, coupled with an aggressive marketing strategy and new product developments, will no doubt result in Farberware's retaining its strong position in the marketplace. The international market will also present challenges to Farberware. Outside of the United States and Canada, Farberware has little, if any, brand recognition. To achieve abroad what it has accomplished at home probably will take decades. However, Farberware is being helped by the NAFTA trade agreement, which has greatly increased the marketing potential of the brand outside of the U.S. Quality is another key element; among quality-conscious consumers abroad, Farberware has been a success, despite the relatively high cost of the products. This can be attributed at least in part to the company's 90-year pursuit of high product standards.

Further Reading:

''Farberware's Cookware Survey,'' *HFD—The Weekly Home Furnishings Newspaper,* February 22, 1993, p. 45.

''Farberware Enters Stainless Flatware Arena,'' *HFD—The Weekly Home Furnishings Newspaper,* May 17, 1993, p. 51.

Fitzgerald, Kate, ''Marketer Heats New Coffee Pot (Farberware),'' *Advertising Age,* October 9, 1989, p. 56.

Garbato, Debby, ''Cookbook Author Lorna Sass to Spice Farberware Pressure Cooker Campaign,'' *HFD—The Weekly Home Furnishings Newspaper,* Septembe 21, 1992, p. 51.

''Hunter's Return: Hanson (Conglomerate Corporation Hanson PLC),'' *The Economist,* October 10, 1992, p. 84.

Lambert, Bruce, ''Milton Farber, 81, Retired Head of Farberware Company, Is Dead,'' *New York Times,* November 15, 1991, p. C19(N), p. D18(L).

Ramey, Joanna, ''Du Pont-Farberware Ad War (I.E. Du Pont de Nemours and Company, Inc. Challenges 'Never-Stick' Advertising Claim,'' *HFD—The Weekly Home Furnishings Newspaper,* March 16, 1992, p. 93.

Ratliff, Duke, ''Farberware's Bid at Full-Line Vending,'' *HFD—The Weekly Home Furnishings Newspaper,* December 13, 1993, p. 71.

Weiss, Lisa Casey, ''Polishing Its Image (Farberware's New Licensing Program and Product Line),'' *HFD—The Weekly Home Furnishings Newspaper,* May 4, 1992, p. 41.

—Sina Dubovoj

FENDER®

While many of the top electric guitar companies began as acoustic guitar makers, Fender *began* by making electric guitars and later delved into the manufacture of acoustic instruments. Interest in the unique sound of steel-stringed instruments caught fire when Americans became enamored with Hawaii and all things Hawaiian in the 1920s. A surge of interest in the Hawaiian steel guitar prompted the Rickenbacker company of guitar makers to introduce a hollow-bodied electric lap guitar that became known as "the pancake." A few years later, Leo Fender invented the first solid body electric guitar, which became popular among musicians almost immediately. Since that time, the name Fender has become practically synonymous with the electric guitar.

Brand Origin and History

Leo Fender always loved to tinker. He built a radio when he was twelve, and an acoustic guitar when he was nineteen. During college and for a few years afterwards, he built amplifiers and sound equipment for dance bands. In the early 1930s, he turned hobby into profession and opened a radio repair shop. He kept experimenting with amplified guitars and in 1943 designed a solid-body guitar with an electrical pickup: the first electric guitar. Even while his design was only a prototype, rumors about the new instrument spread, and musicians traveled great distances to his shop to try it out. He told *Music Trades:* "Guitarists from all over were coming into the shop to see and try the new guitar. I began renting it out, and it was so popular you had to reserve it a month in advance."

In 1945, Fender teamed up with guitarist Clayton "Doc" Kaufman, formed the K&F company, and began producing electric Hawaiian-style lap guitars. After Kaufman left the company in 1946, Fender formed the Fender Electric Instrument company. In 1948, he began to manufacture the first commercially-available solid body guitar, the Broadcaster, later to be renamed the Telecaster guitar.

In the early 1950s, others joined the firm and the company began to grow. First Don Randall established Fender Sales to market and distribute the guitars, and then Forrest White became plant manager in charge of production. This left Leo time to do what he did best—experiment in his shop to improve his guitars. In 1951, the company introduced the first electric bass guitar, the Fender Precision Bass, and in 1954 they launched their second electric guitar model, the Stratocaster, which was to become the single most influential electric guitar design and remain the staple of the firm for decades.

Over the next ten years, Fender Electrical Instruments continued to grow in size and complexity as new instruments were introduced and larger manufacturing space was acquired. In 1964, Leo Fender decided to sell his company; a year later he completed the sale with CBS for $13 million. For a short while, Leo remained a design consultant, but eventually left to set up a series of smaller instrument manufacturing firms. The brand name Fender, however, remained with CBS.

Under the management of CBS, the Fender brand received indifferent treatment at best. As Richard Smith of *Guitar Player* later wrote, "Back in the CBS days, Fender was a stepping stone for the career-minded executives with their own shortsighted agenda—make a profit this year and move up to another branch of the corporation." This large-firm mentality resulted in what Smith referred to as CBS's "moribund management." Slow to respond to market trends, CBS lost the cutting-edge advantage Fender had always maintained. Quality suffered when they moved their manufacturing outside the United States. When the guitar market slumped in the early 1980s, Fender suffered greatly; by 1985, CBS was ready to sell.

In 1986, Fender found a buyer among CBS employees. William Schultz, who had been hired by CBS to be Fender's chief executive officer in 1981, led a group of investors that bought the guitar firm from CBS. In buying the company, Schultz brought Fender back to its original structure of a small, private firm on the theory that the small company mentality worked much better for a guitar company. Managers, engineers, and builders, Schultz believed, would be more concerned with making guitars than upwardly-mobile career moves. Schultz swiftly instituted quality controls, increased U.S. production, and brought the company back from the brink of economic disaster. Within a decade, Schultz completed the revitalization of Fender. In 1993, the Phoenix, Arizona, magazine *Business Journal* reported that Fender was once again the world's leading electric guitar manufacturer.

Brand Product Development

Leo Fender always believed that developing new instruments was better than updating older models. Even in the post-Leo Fender years, the company has continuously developed and produced innovative instruments. After marketing his original guitar, the Telecaster, for a few years, Fender realized that it had several serious flaws which he set out to correct; for instance, the Telecaster had no vibrato unit, which a new electric guitar would need to stay competitive within the quickly-growing market. Fender also added an additional electrical pickup to his new guitar—for a total of three—to insure a more balanced sound production, and a new bridge to make tuning adjustments much easier. Because the new instrument needed a new shape for better weight distribution and balance, Fender then designed the smooth, rounded body shape and cut-away horns that have become an industry standard. Fender's second guitar, the Stratocaster, made its debut in 1954 to rave reviews, and has remained popular since. Thirty years after its introduction, *Guitar Player* called the Stratocaster's popularity a mania, and labeled it "a guitar phenomenon unparalleled in range and diversity. Never before has a single design so utterly dominated the electric guitar field."

Even before producing the Stratocaster, Fender enlarged the electric guitar field by inventing and introducing a new instrument, the electric bass, a marriage of the bass viol and the guitar. As he told *Music Trades:* "My concept of an electric bass arose in response to some important needs. First, it was impossible to get a

AT A GLANCE

Fender brand of electric guitars founded in 1948 by Leo Fender in Santa Ana, CA; sold to CBS in 1965; sold to a group of investors headed by William Schultz in 1986.

Performance: *Sales*—$100 million (1992).

Major competitor: Gibson; also Martin guitars.

Addresses: *Parent company*—Fender Musical Instruments, 7975 N. Hayden Rd., Scottsdale, AZ 85258; phone: (602) 596-9690.

[stand-up] ''Dog House'' bass around. Second, the bass player had to sing, and it was hell to try and get the bass up to center stage to the microphone. There was a screaming need for a portable bass that could be amplified and with frets so that the guitarist wouldn't have to struggle to stay in tune.'' Fender introduced the Precision Bass in 1951.

Fender has continued to introduce guitars and basses with trend-setting design features, notable among them the Jaguar, the Jazzmaster, the Jazz bass, the Esquire, the Mustang, and the Duosonic. The Fender brand name has also, right from the beginning, included not only electric instruments, but the accessories needed to make them usable. The year after the company introduced its first guitar, it began manufacturing its first electric amplifier, the DeLuxe Amp. Two years later, in 1954, they introduced the Super, which was the first amplifier to incorporate two speakers. A few years later, they began to produce a completely new design, The Fender Twin Reverb, which has become one of the most popular and most widely copied amplifiers ever.

Today, the research and development team of Fender Musical Instruments continues to work on improvements and new designs. In the early 1980s, in response to an increasingly individual demand for personalized guitars, CBS—Fender opened up the Custom Shop, where anyone who could afford the instruments' high price tags could request a guitar made to order. Soon after Schultz bought the firm and started reorganizing, he combined the Custom Shop with the Research and Development unit into a single department that has kept Fender at the forefront of innovation. Successful ideas and features first seen in the Custom Shop soon find their way into new design models. Through the Custom Shop, builders and designers can work closely with musicians to solve their musical needs and implement their ideas. As John Page, the manager of the combined R&D and Custom Shop department, told *Guitar Player* in 1991, ''Trends change, and we want to be able to address them. The Custom Shop is leading the way to get Fender to make any kind of guitar you could possibly want.''

Marketing

While Leo Fender may have been more of an inventor than a businessman, he had a talent for finding and surrounding himself with savvy business people. In his radio-repair days, he met a young salesman named Don Randall. After Fender started his own guitar business, Randall became curious and stopped by to look at the operation. Impressed with the potential of the company, Randall became Fender's distributor. A few years later, in 1955, Randall and Fender set up Fender Sales, an independent distribution company.

For years, Randall successfully handled Fender's marketing along several different avenues. Advertising focused on magazines geared towards professional musicians; the first Stratocaster ads appeared in the newspaper of the musicians union, *International Musician.* Randall also spent much of his time on the road, visiting dealers and helping them get started at selling Fender instruments. Understanding the power of celebrity endorsements, Randall solicited professional musicians to try out Fender's instruments.

Throughout the years, musicians who have helped popularize Fender instruments have included the popular sixties group, The Beach Boys, who played the Jazzmaster and Jaguar models, and guitarists Eric Clapton and Jimi Hendrix, who played Stratocasters. The company has expanded the celebrity endorsement concept into an entire line of guitars, The Signature Series, which sport an artists signature right on the instrument. The advent of MTV in the 1980s afforded a new forum for advertising. In 1993 Fender hired guitarist Vinnie Moore to promote their Heartfield Series guitar in 30-second ads that the company made available to retailers for local MTV promotions.

As the music industry grew larger over the years, the customary style of doing business—by establishing and maintaining sales contacts with individual dealers—became more difficult; this method was replaced by the trade show, a yearly convention that attracts manufacturers and dealers from all over the world. New lines of instruments and amplifiers are announced and introduced at these events that frequently feature performances by professional musicians. Fender executives took this convention a step further—and made an industry-wide pronouncement that the company was fully back in the game—at a special show for dealers just before the 1988 convention. The live demonstration of new Fender products featured Fender vice president for marketing Bruce Bolen on guitar, accompanied by pro-sound product manager Steve Grom on bass and vice president for guitar marketing Dan Smith on guitar.

After the industry slump of the early and mid-1980s, Fender bounced back to fiscal health with several new marketing strategies, including a new emphasis on designing products for specific markets. For instance, in the late 1980s they began to develop instruments and accessories geared specifically for fans of heavy metal music. This strategy led to the development of the new Power Stratocaster guitar. As marketing vice president Dan Smith told *Music Trades*, ''The new Power Strats have all the options demanded by heavy metal musicians. The instrument's flat, extra long neck has an oil finish for super-fast playability. . . . The instrument has a slightly smaller body with sharper edges, no pickguard, and specially contoured heel cutaways for easy access to all frets.'' Other new models in the same line included the Stratocaster XII twelve-string guitar with a new bridge set-up designed to eliminate intonation problems usually associated with twelve-strings. Fender introduced a new Power Jazz bass and two new amplifiers at the same time.

To cash in on other pop-culture icons, in 1993 Fender produced a new high-priced guitar in an innovative marketing link with the motorcycle company Harley-Davidson. The 90th Anniversary Commemorative Stratocaster, crafted from chromed-aluminum, became a collector's item and sold well, despite it's $10,000 price tag. Bill Schultz, president of Fender, told *Music Trades* that the special Harley-Davidson Stratocaster ''was built for the enjoyment of people with a passion for Americana. This uniquely artistic instrument celebrates the essence of the American Free Spirit.'' The Harley-Davidson guitar was the first in a proposed series of ''special-interest'' guitars Fender expected to build in limited quantities in the coming years.

Another marketing device introduced in the late 1980s was the addition of a Guitar Clinic Program. In 1988, Fender began to sponsor clinics, workshops, and product seminars at dealerships and trade shows. They hired guitarist Beau MacDougall to conduct workshops teaching guitar techniques, demonstrate instruments, answer questions, and advise dealers and consumers alike about future products.

International Market

As American-born rock music has been internationally popular, American-invented electric guitars are international products. Fender has plants inside and outside the United States, and they sell their products worldwide. Their least expensive guitars are made in Korea and sold under the Fender name, although Fender does not produce them. Middle-priced instruments are made in a Fender-controlled plant in Mexico. Because of lower labor costs in Mexico, the company is able to produce a high-quality product at a reasonable price. Higher priced guitars and custom-ordered instruments are all made in the United States. Producing instruments in several different countries is also a sound long-term strategy. As company president Bill Schultz explained to *Music Trades* in 1992: ''Given the volatile nature of currency and labor markets, we don't want to be overly dependent on any one country for our production. That's why we build guitars in the U.S., Japan, Korea, and now Mexico. The fact that our manufacturing base is so spread out goes beyond just larger economic factors. No manufacturing base in any single country is capable of producing our broad product line in the volume we need. The only way we can consistently supply our dealer network is to [manufacture] products all over the globe.''

Fender guitars also sell well across the globe. As *Music Trades* reported in 1991, ''Rock and roll remains a U.S. creation, and the rest of the world thinks it sounds better with American-made guitars.'' Fender, a world leader in electric guitars, continues to expand its international market. In 1993, they opened a new subsidiary in Germany specifically to target European dealers.

Performance Appraisal and Future Growth

In the early 1980s, many popular music experts thought the electric guitar was on its way out, to be replaced by MIDI-produced computer music. At that time, guitar sales had been consistently dropping for several years running. Ten years later, guitar sales are once again booming and Fender is riding high as both a market leader and manufacturer of a popular product. Since its comeback after the CBS sale, Fender has remained strongly profitable. Sales rose from $20 million in 1985 to new heights of $100 million in 1992. Cutting-edge innovation and new marketing strategies, such as the development of special-interest and collectible guitars, should help Fender continue to flourish—and experts, including *Guitar World* editor Brad Tolinski, will continue to consider them the best in the industry.

Further Reading:

''American Renaissance,'' *Music Trades,* October 1993, p. 70.

Chadwell, Teena, ''Fender Musical Instruments Launches German Subsidiary,'' *The Business Journal—Phoenix & The Valley of the Sun,* November 12, 1993, p. 28.

''Clarence Leo Fender (1909–1991),'' *Music Trades,* May 1991, p. 62

Cox, Tony, ''Returning a Legend: Back from the Brink, Fender Again a Leader in Guitars,'' *Orange County Business Journal,* January 21, 1991, p. 1.

''Fender Adds Guitar Clinic Program,'' *Music Trades,* January 1988, p. 151.

''Fender and Harley-Davidson,'' *Music Trades,* October 1993, p. 96.

''Fender Goes Global With Mexican Guitar Plant,'' *Music Trades,* January 1992, p. 130.

''Fender MTV Spots Hype Heartfield Line,'' *Music Trades,* January 1993, p. 53.

''Fender Opens Joint Venture Plant in Mexico,'' *Music Trades,* August 1989, p. 24.

''Fender Pursues Metal Market With New Strat,'' *Music Trades,* February 1988, p. 103.

''Fender Ramps Up U.S. Guitar Output,'' *Music Trades,* January 1988, p. 70.

Smith, Richard R., ''The Further Innovations of Leo Fender,'' *Guitar Player,* July 1990, p. 54; ''Have It Your Way,'' *Guitar Player,* February 1991, p. 85; ''Strat Mania: A History, 1954–1964,'' *Guitar Player,* August 1987, p. 90.

Wheeler, Tom, ''The Legacy of Leo Fender,'' *Guitar Player,* August 1991, p. 87; September 1991, p 88; ''Strat Mania: A '50s Design Takes the 80s by Storm,'' *Guitar Player,* August 1987, p. 85.

—Robin Armstrong

FERRARI®

Ferrari was one of the most exclusive automobile marques in the world and probably the most famous brand name in Formula One racing. Fewer than 55,000 automobiles bearing the Ferrari marque were produced between 1946, when founder Enzo Ferrari built the first Type 125, and 1993, when the $122,000 Ferrari Spider convertible made its debut. In the mid-1990s the top-of-the-line Ferrari 512 TR (Testarossa) sold for about $195,000. In racing, Ferrari's blood-red sports cars and Formula One racers, with their yellow and black prancing-horse emblem, were legendary for both their raw power and radical styling.

Fiat SpA, Italy's largest automaker, purchased a 50 percent share of Ferrari SpA in 1969. Its share increased to 90 percent after Enzo Ferrari's death in 1988. That year *Automotive News* saluted Enzo Ferrari as "the last of a breed"—that is, the last of the early automotive pioneers whose names became synonymous with the industry and whose automobiles became legendary.

Enzo Ferrari's Early Career

Enzo Ferrari was born in northern Italy in 1898 and saw his first automobile race when he was ten. He decided then to become a race-car driver. After World War I, which he spent shoeing mules for the Italian army, Ferrari was hired as a test driver for Costruzioni Meccaniche Nazionale (CMN). In those days test drivers also raced their companies' cars, and in 1919 Ferrari drove in the 32-mile Parma-Poggia de Berceto hill climb. He finished fourth. Later that year Ferrari drove in the Targa Florio road race, but he was delayed by a roadblock along the route because the president of Italy was delivering a speech and finished long after the timekeeper had gone home.

In 1920 Ferrari was recruited by Alfa Romeo, which was on its way to becoming Italy's national racing team, and put in charge of assembling the team of engineers, designers, and mechanics that would build the next Alfa Romeo racer. He also continued to race and won at the Circuit of Savio in 1923. It was a relatively minor race, but afterward the Countess Paolina Baracca, for reasons never entirely clear, offered Ferrari a prancing-horse crest that had decorated on it the airplane flown by her son, Francesco Baracca, a flying ace who died in World War I. One story was that Ferrari's brother, Alfredo Jr., who also died during the war, was a mechanic in Baracca's squadron. Ferrari began painting the prancing-horse, or *Cavallino Rampante,* emblem on his race cars using a canary yellow background, the heraldic color of his native Modena.

Ferrari's most important victory as a driver came in 1924, when he upset the favored Mercedes team at the Coppa Acerbo. The Italian government rewarded him with the title *cavaliere,* or "knight." In 1928 Benito Mussolini awarded Ferrari the title *commendatore,* which literally meant that he was "commended" for his accomplishments. The title lost any official significance after World War II, and Ferrari himself said, "I prefer to be called simply Ferrari." Even so, he would often be referred to as *commendatore* the rest of his life.

In 1932, following the birth of his son Alfredo, Ferrari officially retired from racing. He later wrote of his career as a driver: "I was beset by doubts. I had one big fault: I drove always with consideration for the car, whereas to be successful, one must on occasion be prepared to mistreat it."

Scuderia Ferrari

Ferrari left Alfa Romeo in 1929 and returned to his hometown of Modena, where he formed Scuderia Ferrari, or Ferrari "Stable." Initially, Scuderia Ferrari performed mechanical work for several of Ferrari's wealthy friends who enjoyed amateur racing, but Ferrari soon began hiring drivers and entering Alfa Romeos in Grand Prix events. In 1932 Alfa Romeo appointed Scuderia Ferrari as its official racing team, and Ferrari's prancing horse replaced Alfa Romeo's green-and-white cloverleaf on factory cars.

In 1933 Scuderia Ferrari won 27 of the 39 races it entered, including nine Grand Prix events. The following year the German firm Daimler-Benz A.G. unleashed the Mercedes-Benz W-25 racer, also known as the Silver Arrow. The Mercedes W-25 had been commissioned by Adolph Hitler, who wanted to demonstrate Germany's technological superiority to the rest of the world. Daimler-Benz would dominate road racing until the outbreak of World War II. Alfa Romeo resumed control of its racing operations in 1938, and Ferrari stayed as team manager for one season before again returning to Modena.

Whether Ferrari had been fired or left voluntarily was never clear, but he did agree not to revive Scuderia Ferrari or to compete in racing for four years. In 1939 Ferrari founded Auto Avio Costruzioni di Ferrari Enzo, an automotive design and manufacturing firm. On the side he also began building sports cars from spare Fiat parts. In 1940, despite his agreement with Alfa Romeo, Ferrari entered two racers in the last prewar Mille Miglia. As a

AT A GLANCE

Ferrari brand of automobile founded in 1946 by Enzo Ferrari, by then a well-known automobile designer; his first model, the Type 125C, was a two-seat race car powered by a V-12 engine; introduced two years later was the first Ferrari street car, the Type 166MM; 50% of Ferrari purchased by the Italian automaker Fiat SpA in 1969; Fiat's share rose to 90% in 1988, the year Enzo Ferrari died; from 1946 to 1993 total production of Ferrari automobiles was fewer than 55,000 cars.

Major competitor: Porsche; also, Jaguar.

Addresses: *Parent company*—Ferrari SpA, Via Abetone Inferiore, #4, 41053 Maranello, MO, Italy; phone: 011-39-53-6949. *Ultimate parent company*—Fiat SpA.

concession, however, neither the Ferrari name nor the prancing horse appeared on the cars. Neither car finished the race.

The Ferrari Marque

During World War II Ferrari's company made machinery for the Italian government, and in 1943 the factory was moved to Maranello, about ten miles south of Modena, in an effort to avoid Allied bombing. Nevertheless, the factory was hit by bombing runs in late 1944 and early 1945. When the war ended, Ferrari, almost 50 years old, finally launched the business that earned him a place in automobile history. Later he wrote, "The end of the war did not find me altogether unprepared. I had always continued to work on designs for racing cars." In 1946 *Inter Auto* announced that Scuderia Ferrari had been revived and would soon introduce three new models—a sports car, a competition version of the sports car, and a single-seat Grand Prix racer.

The first automobile to carry the Ferrari marque was the Type 125C ("C" meaning competition), an open two-seater designed by Gioacchino Colombo and powered by a V-12 engine. The body was styled by Carrozzeria Superleggera Touring. Although it was completed in 1946, the Type 125C did not race until May 1947 at the Circuit of Piacena. Driven by Franco Cortese, the Type 125C was leading the race with only a few laps to go when the fuel pump broke. Ferrari observed, "It was at least a promising failure." Two weeks later Cortese claimed the first victory in a Ferrari at the Circuit of Caracalla in Rome.

In 1948 Ferrari introduced the Type 166C (known as a *Barchetta*, or "little boat," because of its distinctive Touring body style), which powered the Ferrari marque into racing's limelight. In its first season the Ferrari Type 166C captured both the Targa Florio and the Mille Miglia, two of the most prestigious races in Italy. Then in 1949 Luigi Chenetti drove a Type 166C to victory at the 24 Hours of Le Mans, the most famous road race in the world. Chenetti's victory was even more dramatic because he drove almost the entire race himself after his codriver, done in by either bad food or good wine, completed only three laps before becoming ill. In 1984 Warren Weith, a columnist for *Car and Driver*, described Chenetti as "the man who invented Ferrari, and he did the job in just one day. . . . To put it bluntly, it was one hell of a drive." Over the next 40 years Ferrari would win more than 5,000 races.

Production Cars

The first Ferrari street car was the Type 166MM, introduced in the fall of 1948 and named for its predecessor's victory at the Mille Miglia. Only a few were ever sold. Ferrari went on to introduce a bewildering array of cars in the 1950s, often making less than a dozen of any one model. Among the best known was the America Type 340, introduced in 1952, which was the first in the America series that eventually gave way to the Superamerica in 1956. A particularly gaudy model in the Superamerica series was the Superfast, one of the first body styles created for Ferrari by the famous Pininfarina and featuring extremely high tail fins and protruding front fenders. In 1957 *Road & Track* called the $18,000 Superfast "one of the most beautiful cars in the world, with a performance which is so fantastic as to be almost beyond comprehension. . . . Driving a car such as this is a relief from boredom, a challenge to one's driving skill and a never ending source of satisfaction through pride of ownership."

While many car makers participated in racing to help market their cars, Ferrari sold cars to pay for its racing program. Consequently, it wasn't until after Fiat purchased control of the company in 1969 that Ferrari began stepping up production. (For example, the 250 GTO—for Gran Turismo Omologato—was considered one of Ferrari's finest sports cars, but only 39 were ever made.) The first Ferrari with a significant production run was the 365 GTB Daytona, with 1,300 produced between 1968 and 1973.

Ferrari also produced more than 4,000 Dino 246 GT and Dino 246 GTS Spyders between 1969 and 1974. The Dino was named for Enzo Ferrari's son Alfredo, who designed the car and who died of leukemia shortly before it was introduced. As a tribute, the name Ferrari did not appear on the Dino except on a metal tag on the doorpost, where it was required by law. Instead, "Dino" was inscribed on a yellow disk in the center of the steering wheel and on each hub. Dino also appeared on all official factory literature.

As Ferrari grew weaker in the years preceding his death, the demand for the Ferrari marque increased dramatically for both new and older production models. New Ferraris were snapped up by speculators, while classics fetched multimillion-dollar prices. In 1987, the year before Ferrari died, a 1963 model was sold for an estimated $11 million. John Steinbreder, writing in *Sports Illustrated,* lamented, "Unfortunately, the automobile buffs who enjoyed driving Enzo Ferrari's magnificent creations are being elbowed out of the market by the new breed of owner—the deep-pocketed investor who doesn't know a crankshaft from brake calipers but can quote you the latest record-breaking prices. Even the true Ferrari lover who can resist the temptation to peddle his car for a big profit dares not drive the car on the street. . . . An automobile famous for its performance, its power, its racing victories has become too valuable to drive."

Testarossa

The car most people in the United States probably associated with Ferrari was the 12-cylinder Testarossa, which became the company's flagship model in 1984 and was driven by actor Tom Selleck in the hit television show *Magnum P.I.* One of the most glamorous production cars in the world, the Testarossa owed its futuristic styling to Pininfarina and the earlier Ferrari Boxers, but the name came straight from racing legend. The original Testa Rossa—literally "Red Head"—was a 2.0 liter, four-cylinder competition sports car introduced in 1956. It was called Testa Rossa because engineers at Ferrari finished off the camshaft covers with a red paint. Phil Hill, who was the first American to win the World Sports Car Championship, later wrote that Testa Rossa was "a nickname we considered a bit hokey at the time," although they "were delightful little sports racers."

The first Testa Rossas were raced on tight sports-car circuits, where brute power was not important. After 1958, when the Federation Internationale de Automobile (FIA) limited the size of competition engines, the Testa Rossa was fitted with a 3.0 liter V-12 and became Ferrari's flagship racer, winning at Le Mans in its first outing. In 1960 Ferrari Testa Rossa took seven of the first eight spots at Le Mans, including first. Paul Frere, one of the winning drivers in 1960, tested the new version when it was introduced in 1984 and declared, "the Testarossa deserves its glorious name." In 1993 Ferrari introduced the 512 TR, the newest in the Testarossa line.

Ford-Ferrari

In the early 1960s the Ferrari marque was very nearly sold to the Ford Motor Company. At the time, Ford was looking for a racing partner to enhance its reputation in Europe. Meanwhile, Ferrari had been dominating in both Formula One and sports-car racing but was looking for someone to assume responsibility for its production cars.

Ferrari made the first overture to Ford early in 1963 after being unable to generate any interest among Italy's major auto makers, although executives at Ford had been discussing the possibility of acquiring Ferrari for more than a year. The two sides arrived at a tentative agreement after two weeks of negotiations. Ford would acquire 90 percent of Ferrari, and both the company and the marque would become Ford-Ferrari. Enzo Ferrari would own the remaining 10 percent. A second company would be created, to be called Ferrari-Ford, that would focus on the design, development, and construction of race cars. Enzo Ferrari would own 90 percent of Ferrari-Ford. The plan would have cost Ford $10 million.

The agreement, however, began to fall apart over who would actually direct the racing program. Enzo Ferrari was interested in Grand Prix or Formula One racing, but Ford was more interested in sports cars. When Ford suggested that Ferrari drop out of Formula One racing, Enzo Ferrari countered by demanding that Ford sever its relationship with Shelby American, Inc., maker of the Ford-powered Cobra sports car that was in direct competition with Ferrari. The deal collapsed altogether when Ferrari learned that Ford executives in Detroit would need to authorize any division expenditure greater than $10,000.

Ferrari later wrote: "My surprise, and I will say my anger, exploded, because the fundamental pre-assumption of the entire bargain had been . . . that I would have had to be completely free and independent in my field. . . . I obviously couldn't be a suitable man in that grandiose and wonderful apparatus where everything moved according to predetermined schemes." According to Don Frey, a Ford executive involved in the discussions, Ferrari told negotiators: "My rights, my integrity, my very being as a manufacturer, as an entrepreneur, as the leader of the Ferrari works, cannot work under the enormous machine, the suffocating bureaucracy of the Ford Motor Company." Ferrari ended all negotiations the next day.

Three years later Ferrari apparently tried to revive negotiations with Ford, but by then Ford had hired a British firm, Lola Cars Ltd., and spent millions of dollars to develop its own racing program. In 1966 Ford GTs finished first, second, and third at Le Mans, and Ford went on to win the World Sports Car Championship. Ferrari regained the sports car championship in 1967 but did not compete in 1968. In 1969 Fiat purchased 50 percent of Ferrari in an arrangement very similar to the one discussed with Ford. Fiat managed the production cars, while Enzo Ferrari focused on the racing program. Fiat, however, allowed Ferrari to reinvest 100 percent of its profits in the business. Fiat increased its share to 90 percent at Ferrari's death.

Brand Outlook

Ferrari's death in 1988 raised questions about the future of the marque and its involvement in racing. Although Fiat had managed the production side of the business since 1969, Enzo Ferrari continued to provide input. According to *Automotive News,* it was Ferrari who squashed plans to produce a four-door model in 1986. In addition, while Ferrari was alive, production never exceeded 4,000 cars a year. Ferrari once wrote, "There are those who wonder why I have never tried to turn my factory into a major industry. I don't know why. I have never thought of myself in terms of being an industrialist. I have always thought I should be an engineer and a builder, because industry has requirements which I could not assimilate, inasmuch as they are opposed to my temperament as a promoter of research."

Ferrari also continued to run the racing program almost until the end. Only a few months before his death, Ferrari overruled his son Piero Lardi Ferrari, which caused the younger Ferrari to quit the racing team and take a job on the production side of the company. With Enzo Ferrari gone, would Fiat remain as committed to Formula One racing? Ferrari would certainly have wanted the marque to remain in racing. "The person who comes after me will have to take on a very simple inheritance—to keep alive that desire for progress which has been pursued in the past, even if it has involved the sacrifice of some of the noblest of human beings."

Although a recession in the early 1990s held down the market for luxury automobiles, the indications were that Fiat planned to continue Ferrari as an exclusive, limited-production marque. Gian Luigi Longinotti, president of Ferrari North America, told *Automotive News* in 1993 that Fiat planned to produce between 3,300 and 3,500 Ferraris per year.

Only about 500 Ferraris were sold in the United States in 1993. It was obvious, however, that Fiat was beginning to pay more attention to the U.S. market. The Ferrari Spider convertible introduced in the United States in 1993 was the first Ferrari to debut outside of Europe, and other Ferraris were being built to meet U.S. safety and air-pollution standards.

Ferrari North America was also beginning to sponsor race-track events where Ferrari owners could run their automobiles at top speed. According to Longinotti, "Ferrari has had to realize that in America, you can't drive 180 mph or you're in jail. That's why we organize track events. We build cars for the race track that can be used on the street, not vice versa."

Further Reading:

Blumenthal, Ralph, "The Ferrari Mystique," *New York Times Magazine,* July 1, 1984, p. 19.

Burgess-Wise, David, "Ferrari: Carbuilder, Racer Was Last of Breed," *Automotive News,* August 22, 1988, p. 1.

Christy, John, "Ferrari Dino Spyder," *Motor Trend,* December 1972, p. 108.

Clinard, John, "The Day Ford-Ferrari Became Ford Versus Ferrari," *Car and Driver,* June 1974, p. 64.

Daley, Robert, "That Blood-Red Ferrari Mystique," *New York Times Magazine,* July 25, 1965.

Henry, Jim, "Speculators Desert Ferrari Showrooms," *Automotive News,* September 9, 1992, p. 9.

Hill, Phil, "Ferrari's Fantastic Redheads," *Road & Track,* June 1992, p. 63.

Johnson, Richard, "Fiat Ready to Take Full Control of Ferrari Works," *Automotive News,* August 22, 1988, p. 52.

Kettlewell, Michael, "The Prancing Horse of Maranello," *The World of Automobiles,* New York: Columbia House, 1974.

Lyons, Pete, "Ferrari: The Man and His Machines," Lincolnwood, Illinois: Publications International, Ltd., 1989.

Steinbreder, John, "Pssst! Want a Hot Car?" *Sports Illustrated,*

Weir, David, "Pride, Passion & Prototypes," *Road & Track,* April 1988, p. 152.

Weith, Warren, "The Man Who Invented Ferrari," *Car and Driver,* November 1984, p. 26.

—Dean Boyer

FIELDCREST®

Fieldcrest is one of the oldest and best-known brand names in sheets and towels in the United States. The brand, which owes its name to one-time owner Marshall Field of the department store fame, is owned by Fieldcrest Cannon, Inc., the dominant force in the home-textile industry.

Brand Origins

The story of Fieldcrest starts with Benjamin Franklin Mebane, an industrialist who hoped to build a business empire. Mebane had a plan to open one mill a year in the area of Spray, North Carolina, where he had purchased 600 acres of land in 1893. His first was built in 1898, and by 1905 Mebane owned six mills in and around the town that had been renamed Eden (after a surveyor's comment that it resembled the Garden of Eden). Mebane had gone to wealthy Chicago retailer Marshall Field for help in financing his ambitious master plan, but when Mebane started to have difficulty repaying his debt, Field decided to protect his investment and take over. Despite resistance, by 1910 Field had gained voting control of Mebane's Spray Water & Land Co.; by 1912 the takeover was complete and the company had become a subsidiary of Marshall Field & Company. Field invested in improvements and installed new managers at the subsidiary, renamed the Thread Mills Company. The company's mills produced ginghams, cotton and wool blankets, hosiery yarns, tickings, and other assorted fabrics. In 1916 Mebane's mill in Draper, North Carolina, the German-American Company, was purchased by Field. Its facilities were expanded, and a sheeting mill was built there.

That year the Thread Mills Company acquired a 1,600-acre site near Martinsville, Virginia, exclusively for the construction of a huck (flat weave) and terry towel plant and employee housing. The new community, named Fieldale, began operations in 1919 with 330 employees, 19,200 spindles, and 500 looms. The plant continued to operate into the 1990s. The towels and sheets bore the Fieldcrest brand name and were distributed nationwide at both retail and wholesale levels.

Field's mills were organized under its wholesale division until 1935, when the company began selling off many of its mills. In 1937 the remaining facilities in North Carolina and Virginia as well as a lace mill in Zion, Illinois, were formed into Marshall Field & Co.'s manufacturing division.

During World War II shortages hampered the mills' ability to meet consumer demand, but the Fieldcrest mills did produce material for the armed services, including silk cartridge cloth, camouflage net, parachute cloth, blankets, hosiery (for women in the armed forces), sheets and towels, and mosquito netting. In 1947 the division's name was changed to Fieldcrest Mills to clearly identify it with the nationally advertised products that it manufactured. That year the Fieldcrest Thermostatic blanket was unveiled.

Marshall Field Leaves Eden

By 1953 Field was eager to expand his retail stores into the growing suburban landscape, but he needed to raise capital to do so. He decided to sell his mill operations (including the carpet mills, which manufactured the well-respected Karastan brand of carpets) to Amoskeag Company, an investment trust based in Boston. Fieldcrest Mills, Co. was incorporated in September of 1953; its sales for that year were $39 million.

Amoskeag, which also owned the Bangor & Aroostoock Railroad in Maine and assorted real estate and mining interests, was itself controlled by the Dumaine Trust, a family trust organized by F. C. Dumaine, Sr., a textile mill baron who had become the head of Amoskeag in 1905. Upon his death in 1951, stewardship for the trust passed to his son F. C. Dumaine, Jr., and the company remained privately held until 1962.

Fieldcrest grew throughout the 1950s and 1960s by a series of acquisitions and improvements, and by 1967 those costs had totaled $82.3 million. At that time the Fieldcrest division, which produced blankets, bedspreads, sheets, and towels, comprised 65 percent of the company's sales. Sales that year were $175.3 million. Fieldcrest produced goods under its own name as well as for private labels; such customers as Sears Roebuck and J.C. Penney accounted for almost 15 percent of total sales. Fieldcrest's strength, however, came from its medium- and upper-priced lines, which made up almost two-thirds of total sales. Those lines, which carried the Fieldcrest label, appeared primarily in department stores. Fieldcrest's Royal Velvet line of towels, introduced in 1954, were synonymous with luxury. The lower-priced St. Marys brand was sold through mass merchandisers.

Sales and profits generally continued to grow. By the time of Fieldcrest Mills' twentieth anniversary, sales had reached $290

AT A GLANCE

Fieldcrest brand of towels and sheets introduced circa 1916 by the Thread Mills Company, a subsidiary of Marshall Field & Company, in Fieldale, VA; the subsidiary was sold to Amoskeag Company in 1953, becoming Fieldcrest Mills, Co.; in 1986 Fieldcrest acquired Cannon Mills and became Fieldcrest Cannon, Inc.; in 1993 Fieldcrest Cannon bought out its shares held by Amoskeag Company.

Performance: *Market share*—Top share of the towel market; approximately 20% of the linens market.

Major competitor: Spring Industries; also WestPoint Stevens.

Advertising: *Agency*—Chillingworth/Radding, New York, NY, 1987—.

Addresses: *Parent company*—Fieldcrest Cannon, Inc., 326 E. Stadium Drive, Eden, North Carolina, 27288; phone: (919) 627-3000, fax: (919) 627-3109.

million, and they had grown every year since 1961. However, profits crested in 1979 on sales of $517.7 million. Thereafter sales began to slide. The recession had affected the company's performance in the early 1980s, but other mills proved able to sustain earnings during that period. Market analysts pointed to ill-conceived and expensive expansion attempts. For example, Fieldcrest had responded to a surge in blanket sales in 1977 and 1978 due to unusually cold winters and high energy costs by modernizing its blanket mill in Eden at a cost of $40 million, but blanket sales began to decline after 1978.

Fieldcrest Mills had also had an unhappy experience when it tried to penetrate the European market. In 1977 the company formed Fieldcrest Ireland, Ltd., a joint venture with the Bank of Ireland and P.J. Carroll & Co., Ltd., to build and operate a Fieldcrest towel plant in Kilkenny, Ireland. In 1982 the plant was closed after high inflation in that country priced the towels out of the European market. Fieldcrest lost $8 million.

Most troubling for Fieldcrest were attempts by other manufacturers to encroach upon its ensconced (and lucrative) position at the head of the premium towel market. Fieldcrest had decided to aggressively expand its St. Marys brand, and this triggered attempts by J.P. Stevens, West Point-Pepperell, and, notably, Cannon Mills to move into the upper end of the market. Cannon added a Royal Family line that directly competed with Fieldcrest's Royal Velvet. Fieldcrest had also jumped into the designer sweepstakes, along with many of the other mills. It introduced its first designer line, the Halston collection, in 1976, and the following year a Geoffrey Beene collection was unveiled. The company found itself defending its territory at the top, where the profits were highest (and the sales on which it had sailed for years), while trying to advance farther at the other end of the market. While the recession took hold, the rounds of discounting began as inventory was reduced. Amoskeag, whose earnings were largely sustained by those of Fieldcrest, grew concerned, and in 1982 the chief executive of Amoskeag, Joseph Ely II, was brought in to head the company.

A Change in Strategy

Soon thereafter, Fieldcrest shifted its marketing strategy. Instead of trying to increase profits through turning over a high volume of its lower-end products, Fieldcrest sought to broaden the range of items built around the Fieldcrest name. By reemphasizing the Fieldcrest lines, which it neglected to update while the effort had been on designer lines in the 1970s, the company chose to retain profits and avoid price cuts at the expense of expanding its market share. Fieldcrest was the only towelmaker that continued to use its name solely with its premium products; Cannon Mills, for example, sewed its name into all of its products, regardless of the price category. Fieldcrest promised department stores that carried its line that they had the protected use of its name, meaning the company would not sell Fieldcrest products through other retail outlets. It was hoped that this would seal the stores' loyalty and expand Fieldcrest's carriage trade as well as take advantage of the retailers' increased promotion and display prowess. The company planned to sell more branded products at more price levels. "It's our strategy to have family groupings built around the Royal Velvet brand, which is widely known for its color leadership, broad department store exposure, and quality," stated the president of Fieldcrest Mills, Francis Larkin. However, the share of the towel market that the department stores held was 25 percent, compared with 45 percent for the mass merchandisers.

Fieldcrest Meets Cannon

In 1986 Fieldcrest took the bold step of acquiring Cannon Mills, which it purchased for $321 million (after borrowing $250 million). With that acquisition, Fieldcrest, which became Fieldcrest Cannon, Inc. in July of that year, gained 12,900 employees, 12 plants, and 14 sales offices, thus doubling its size and becoming the country's fifth-largest publicly held textile company. Cannon Mills was purchased from California financier and takeover artist David Murdock, who had acquired the moribund company in 1982. While he owned Cannon, Murdock had tried to update the brand by hiring designer names, discontinuing virtually all of its existing patterns, and spending lavishly on an aggressive marketing campaign. Despite Murdock's attempts to invigorate Cannon with splashy designs and heavy advertising, Cannon continued to lose money, and he decided to sell the company.

The acquisition of Cannon by Fieldcrest catapulted the company to the number one position in the towel and blanket market and the number three spot in the sheet market, where it had always been weakest. Observers wondered how Fieldcrest and Cannon, two textile powerhouses with very different marketing strategies, would work together, especially on the retail floor. Its various brands seemed poised to fight against each other for market share and counter space. Fieldcrest's flagship brand still prevailed in the department stores, where Cannon's Royal Family competed against it. Fieldcrest had chosen not to expand its market share to avoid price cuts, while Cannon had elected to lower prices to generate sales. Fieldcrest executives felt that it was best to keep the lines separate in order to hold on to precious counter space as the retail industry consolidated. Fieldcrest's department store lines, sold under the Fieldcrest label, held 25 percent of that market, while Cannon held 24 percent. By contrast, at the time of the merger Fieldcrest commanded a mere 9 percent of the mass merchandisers, while Cannon dominated with 32 percent.

In 1990 the economic downturn exacerbated internal problems, and Fieldcrest Cannon posted a record $38-million loss, after a series of disappointing years. The company's stock value, which had peaked at 43 in 1986, dropped to six. A number of analysts pointed to Ely as directly responsible for Fieldcrest's problems. They saw a too-rapid expansion financed with heavy debt commitments, a too-high price paid for Cannon, ill-timed cotton purchases (cotton had hit a ten-year high in 1991) as well as difficulties with Bigelow-Sanford, the carpeting company that it had purchased in December of 1986. Ely was seen as owing his longevity at Fieldcrest to his position as chief executive of the Dumaine trust, holding ultimate power over an elderly board on which remained several members from F. C. Dumaine, Sr.'s time.

Fieldcrest underwent a series of cost-cutting measures when a new chairman, James Fitzgibbons, took control in 1990. The workforce was reduced, the unprofitable automatic blanket operations were discontinued, and inventory was unloaded. By the early 1990s, Fieldcrest Cannon held over half of the towel market and about 20 percent of the bed and linen market. The company experienced lowered sales from 1988 to 1992, largely because of a decline in carpet and rug sales. In July of 1993 Fieldcrest sold its carpet and rug division to Mohawk Industries for approximately $140 million.

In January of 1993 Amoskeag announced that it was considering selling off its share of Fieldcrest. In May, Fieldcrest Cannon competitor Spring Industries made a tender offer of about $345 million for Fieldcrest Cannon and Amoskeag. To counter that takeover attempt, Fieldcrest offered to buy all of its shares from Amoskeag in a deal valued at $145 million, and the subsequent buyout was announced in November. Control of Fieldcrest was thus shifted from Amoskeag to the shareholders of Fieldcrest.

Further Reading:

Coletti, Richard J., "Fieldcrest: Stains on the Carpet," *Financial World,* October 18, 1988, p. 16.

Feldman, Amy, "Changing the Sheets," *Forbes,* February 3, 1992, p. 16.

"Fieldcrest: Saving Its Name for a Luxury Image," *Business Week,* January 9, 1984, p. 112.

Jaffe, Thomas, "One Rude Awakening," *Forbes,* October 25, 1982, p. 116.

Lappen, Alyssa A., "Thank You, Mr. Ely," *Forbes,* December 12, 1988, p. 100.

Troy, Colleen, "Leading Separate Lives," *Home Furnishings Daily,* November 16, 1987, p. 1.

—C. L. Collins

FIRESTONE®

Firestone

Firestone tires are widely regarded as the most venerable brand of American tire on the market. Automobile, truck, and tractor tires owe their evolution in large part to the founder of the Firestone Tire & Rubber Company, Harvey S. Firestone. Firestone tires graced the world's first mass-produced car, the Ford; advertisements and promotions for Firestone truck tires were largely responsible for the nation's deemphasis of railroad freight hauling in favor of hauling by truck, indirectly giving impetus to highway construction and road improvements; and Firestone led the switch to rubber tires on tractors, which improved fuel efficiency and were more durable than the ubiquitous steel tractor tire. The Firestone Tire & Rubber Company continued to innovate after Harvey Firestone's death: Firestone was the first to make tires of synthetic rubber and the first to produce synthetic latex, crucial developments that expanded the use of rubber and improved the quality and safety of tires worldwide.

Brand Origins

Although Harvey S. Firestone was born in 1868 into a family of prosperous Ohio farmers, farming was not to be his chosen career. After receiving a typical country education, the young Harvey Firestone gravitated toward sales, first as a salesman for patent medicine, a failed enterprise, and later as a seller of horse-drawn buggies for his uncle's carriage firm in Detroit. Firestone was attracted his entire life to new products and innovations, and demonstrated this inclination, for instance, by sporting the first rubber carriage wheels in Detroit in 1893, foreshadowing his future career as the king of rubber tires in America.

Rubber (named by British scientist Joseph Priestly in the early nineteenth century because it "rubbed out" pencil marks) was in the young Firestone's day still relatively new, especially vulcanized rubber. Vulcanization was a process invented by Charles Goodyear and patented in 1844 that enabled rubber to stay firm under heat. Goodyear's invention made a whole host of rubber products possible, and consumer demand for such rubber items as galoshes, raincoats, and bicycle tires kept escalating. Bikes were the first vehicles to use solid rubber tires, followed by the carriage. In fact, nineteenth century carriage rides before the rubber wheel were uncomfortable, slow, and often unsafe. Hence one of the first applications of vulcanized rubber was to cushion wheels.

Rubber wheels on carriages were still considered a novelty and were greeted with skepticism when Firestone went to work for his uncle's buggy firm in Detroit. Quite predictably, he became the first person in the city to ride around in a buggy with rubber wheels. Firestone was doubly ahead of his time as the first owner of rubber buggy wheels in Detroit because his were not the garden variety solid rubber wheels, but newfangled pneumatic ones (filled with compressed air) developed in Europe. Pneumatic tires caught on slowly in this country, and by the turn of the century, solid rubber tires were still the rule. With the appearance of the horseless carriage in the late nineteenth century, the market for rubber in America was big and growing; by the time Harvey S. Firestone invested in his first commercial tire venture in 1900, several hundred tire companies were already vying with each other.

Investing all he had—$1000—Harvey Firestone set up a tire manufacturing firm to sell solid tires. When more established businessmen in the tire industry offered to buy out his business for $45,000, he gladly accepted. $20,000 of this he invested in a bigger and better enterprise—the Firestone Tire & Rubber Company in Akron, Ohio, established in 1900, when Firestone himself was only thirty-two. It was not until 1903 that Firestone had amassed enough capital to purchase an old foundry and buy secondhand equipment to begin manufacturing his own solid rubber tires.

Early Commercial Successes

What made the lot of the small tire businessman so difficult at the turn of the century was the necessity of stocking thousands of different tire sizes in order to have the right size in stock when the need arose. Firestone's creative genius was at work when he came up with the idea of producing tires in reels, which could be bought in bulk and cut to size. This approach was extremely successful, eliminating the need for all of those thousands of tire sizes, and, in the process, making the Firestone brand name known among all tire dealers and makers, small and large.

Although this innovation was Firestone's first real success, it quickly would be overshadowed by an even greater one. The pneumatic tire was gaining market share over the now traditional solid tire. An American firm with a patent for the pneumatic tire and a monopoly on its sale refused to grant Firestone a license to manufacture it. Firestone was fortunate enough to meet someone who had a patent on a pneumatic tire that was straight-sided (side rings were bolted together), as opposed to the clincher variety

AT A GLANCE

Firestone brand of tires introduced in 1900 in Akron, Ohio, by Harvey S. Firestone, founder of the Firestone Tire & Rubber Company; 1906, Firestone supplied tires to the first mass-produced cars in America, the Ford; Firestone went on to develop the first low pressure tire, the first truck tires, and the first farm tractor tires; in 1988, Firestone Tire & Rubber was acquired by the Tokyo-based Bridgestone Corp.; in 1990, the new company incorporated as Bridgestone/Firestone, Inc.

Performance: *Market share*—(Bridgestone Corp.) 17.5% of worldwide tire market. *Sales*—(Bridgestone Corp.) $14.3 billion (1993 consolidated).

Major competitor: Michelin; also Goodyear.

Advertising: *Agency*—TBWA Advertising, New York, NY, 1992—. *Major campaign*—Print ads with a series of photographs showing milestones in Firestone's history, accompanied by the slogan, "America's Tire Since 1900'; television and print ads publicizing brand's re-entry in Indianapolis 500 car racing in 1995.

Addresses: *Parent company*—Bridgestone/Firestone Inc., 50 Century Blvd., Nashville, TN 37214; phone: (615) 872-5000; fax: (615) 872-1414. *Ultimate parent company*—Bridgestone Corp., 10-1 Kyobashi 1-chome; Chuo-ku Tokyo, Japan; phone: (81) 3 3567 0111; fax: (81) 3 3535 2553.

made by his relentless competitor. Entering into a partnership with this inventor, Firestone began manufacturing the unique, straight-sided pneumatic tire. Around that time, 1906, Henry Ford had finished tinkering with the "working man's" car, and was planning to produce 2,000 of them, which would sell at the affordable rate of $500 apiece. Ford and Firestone were already acquainted with each other; when Firestone offered to make tires for this first mass-produced car, at a rate lower than his chief competitor, Ford accepted. Firestone scarcely had the means and machinery to produce so many thousands of tires on time; when he did a year later, he would score a major commercial victory. That year, his company paid out its first dividends and grossed sales of over one million dollars, after only six years in existence.

Early Marketing Strategy

Firestone was first and foremost a salesman, which he had to be in order to survive in a business that had so many hundreds of competitors. He entered the tire industry because of what he sensed would be the eventual predominance of the automobile. Despite stockholder pressure at the outset for early dividends, he invested every spare dollar in the expansion of the company and the acquisition of new machinery. The company's earliest sales slogan, "Extra Quality at no Extra Cost," was his idea—a stratagem to convince the consumer that he was getting more than his money's worth. It worked. Even before the first huge Ford contract, Firestone sales had doubled the year before.

Impressed by Henry Ford's concept of mass production, Firestone inaugurated the same method in his new tire factory in 1910. When World War I demonstrated the growing importance of trucks rather than trains to carry freight, Firestone started a nationwide campaign, dubbed "Ship by Truck," that caught both the government's and the public's imagination. A fleet of trucks advertising freight hauling traveled coast to coast, over the poor roads of the day; Firestone also sponsored "truck parades" all over the country. Although the railroads sought unsuccessfully to put an end to the campaign, Firestone tires soon graced most of the trucks coming out of Detroit.

An extremely important part of Firestone's sales strategy was to sponsor auto races, ensuring that Firestone tires were mounted on every racing car. No automobile race was more popular and important than the Indianapolis 500. Each Memorial Day weekend, from 1911 until his death in 1938, Harvey Firestone attended the Indy 500 races, which provided excellent advertising for Firestone tires. From 1911 until 1966, Firestone tires were on every racing car—it was immaterial who finished first. If auto racers trusted Firestone tires, the thinking went, the average motorist would do well to do so; to put it in Firestone language: "Safety Proved on the Speedway for Your Protection on the Highway."

One of the most important marketing strategies in the tire industry was developed by Firestone in the early 1920s. Firestone established the "One Stop Service Store," which would offer the motorist not only tires, but other products and car repair service as well. These shops, the first automobile service stations, enabled Firestone to branch out into nontire-related business and to offer Firestone tires and related products across the country. Thirty years later, Firestone tires and other products were being sold in over 700 of these outlets; by the 1990s, that number had doubled.

So convinced was Firestone of the importance of good sales strategy that he alone in the industry started a "school" for the training of his company's salesmen. The school opened its doors in Akron in 1926, and only male college graduates were accepted. To graduate from this program, the students would have to become experts on tires: from the rubber they came from to the final tire product. Well-educated experts would carry the Firestone message from dealership to dealership, coast to coast.

Advertising

As a born salesman, Firestone believed in advertising. In the early days of Firestone tires, he advertised heavily in the popular magazines and trade journals of the day, as well as through store displays and direct mailing to prospective customers. From 1928 onwards, Firestone advertising was conducted on radio, and, with the advent of television, the company sponsored its own musical concert show. In 1991, when car sales and, consequently, tire sales plummeted drastically, in part because of the Persian Gulf War, the Firestone brand was advertised in *USA Today,* offering free car service to those military who had done duty in the Gulf. Whether this sales pitch was made out of a sense of patriotism or self-interest, it worked to boost sales during one of the most difficult years in Firestone's history.

Product Development

Harvey Firestone was a technical innovator from the start—producing solid tire reels that could be sold in bulk, developing and marketing the straight side pneumatic tire, as well as inventing the nonskid tire. While the United States was involved in the First World War, Firestone Tire & Rubber produced not only millions of tires and inner tubes for military vehicles, but also other war materials. After the war, Harvey Firestone turned his attention once again to improving the performance of his tires. Roads were not what they are today—mostly they were unpaved, rough, and bumpy, resulting in much wear and tear on tires. In 1923 Firestone introduced the balloon, or low-pressure, tire, a shock-resistant tire that was impervious to rough road conditions. It was an instant success.

Business boomed in the 1920s—the number of cars rose from nearly two million in 1919 to two-and-a-half times that in 1929. Competition among the major American tiremakers was nonetheless fierce. When the British cartel that controlled 75 percent of the world's supply of rubber suddenly raised prices in 1923, Harvey Firestone's business became seriously threatened. Typically, he met the threat head on, sending his eldest son, Harvey Jr., to the African country of Liberia to lease one million acres of prime rubber-growing land. In a few years, Firestone would become self-sufficient in raw rubber.

During the Depression, Firestone Tire & Rubber Company stayed in business by cutting costs, slashing prices, and reducing salaries (including Harvey Firestone's). The newest Firestone innovation—the rubber tractor tire—had arrived on the market at the onset of the Depression. Despite desperate economic times, by the end of the 1930s, virtually all tractors in the United States had converted from clumsy, uncomfortable steel tires to modern Firestone tractor tires.

During World War II, as in the First World War, Firestone Tire & Rubber's manufacturing was concentrated on war needs. A highly significant advance occurred at Firestone at that time—the development of synthetic rubber. A dire shortage of raw natural rubber had resulted from the war in southeast Asia. Although Firestone scientists did not invent synthetic rubber—German scientists had experimented with this much earlier—they evolved a practical, low-cost method of producing it. This advance was a decisive breakthrough that hastened the development of many other synthetic materials. After the war, pent-up civilian demand for tires of all kinds created a boom for Firestone Tire & Rubber.

Harvey Firestone had begun exporting his tires to Havana in 1903. By the 1950s, Firestone had an international division with manufacturing facilities in Brazil, Venezuela, Canada, Sweden, Spain, Switzerland, India, and New Zealand. Technical innovations continued to pour out of the research and development labs—tubeless tires in the 1950s, the large variety of plastic products and resins, foam rubber mattresses and paddings for cars and furniture, and shock and skid-resistant airplane tires. Radial tires, invented by Michelin in the late 1960s, lasted twice as long as their traditional counterpart. The emphasis of development therefore shifted to high-performance tires, specialty tires, and "all weather" tires.

The Japanese "Take-Over"

In the 1970s the oil shortage sent the cost of producing tires soaring (one tire requires at least six gallons of oil to make) Competition abroad stiffened, especially from Michelin in France and Bridgestone in Japan. Costly environmental regulations made Firestone's position even more difficult. In 1978, an embarrassing recall of Firestone tires cost the company over $100 million. Unless a radical solution was found, Firestone tires faced losing their competitive edge for good. Globalization of the Firestone tire business seemed to be the only feasible alternative to volatile oil prices, fickle consumer demand at home, and sophisticated foreign competition. In 1984, Firestone chair John J. Nevin approached the second largest tire firm in the world—Japan's Bridgestone, Inc. (founded by Shojiro Ishibashi, whose name means "stone brigde")—with an offer of partnership. In 1987 Firestone management proposed an outright sale of the company. Bridgestone was selected because at least 40 percent of its tire sales already came from the international marketplace.

Although Bridgestone demurred at first, it did not take long for the Japanese tire firm to come around, thanks to some disturbing developments: the German tire maker Continental had made partnership deals with two other Japanese tire companies, and the Italian tire manufacturer, Pirelli, was eyeing the purchase of Firestone. In 1988, Bridgestone agreed to pay $2.6 billion for Firestone's entire business. The deal included 20 Firestone tire factories and 20 factories producing plastics and fibers, as well as 53,000 employees worldwide—the largest purchase of an American firm by a foreign company up to that time. The company name was changed to Bridgestone/Firestone, Inc., in 1989.

Bridgestone poured an additional billion and a half dollars into Bridgestone/Firestone in the following years; the sale seemed to be the shot in the arm that Firestone needed—sales and productivity increased, and the Firestone brand could look to a future.

By the mid-1990s Firestone tires were made in a dozen countries and sold in at least 150 countries worldwide, and the Bridgestone Corp. was the only tire company in the world that had research and development facilities on three continents—North America, Europe, and Asia. More than half of the huge company's $14.3 billion 1993 sales revenues were derived from overseas, including the $5.1 billion in sales of its largest subsidiary, Bridgestone/Firestone, Inc.

The Future

After a terrible year of sales decline in 1991, Bridgestone/Firestone was returning to profitability. In the mid-1990s, the company's U.S. original equipment passenger tire market share stood at a sizable 17.5 percent for Firestone and 3.5 percent for Bridgestone. The Firestone brand was the third-largest brand in the United States, after Goodyear and Michelin. Bridgestone/Firestone has started marketing a revolutionary Run-Flat tire, which can run for at least 50 miles even on a puncture, the latest major innovation in tires to date. The tire industry has historically been volatile and extremely sensitive to economic trends and downturns. The globalization of Bridgestone, however, enables the company to deal with these problems more efficiently and was the logical step in the evolution of Firestone Tire & Rubber company, ensuring the further development and expansion of Firestone tires.

Further Reading:

"Bridgestone Corp. Sees Recovery for Firestone Unit," *The Wall Street Journal,* April 13, 1992, p. B10D (E).

"Bridgestone/Firestone Introduces Two New Lines," *Aftermarket Business,* June 1, 1993, p. 10(1).

"Bridgestone to Pour $1.4 Billion into U.S. Unit," *Los Angeles Times,* May 17, 1991, p. D2.

Eisenstein, Paul, A., "Running Flat Out," *The Detroit News,* October 15, 1992, p. E1.

Firestone, Harvey S., Jr., Man *on the Move: The Story of Transportation,* New York: Putnam, 1967.

Hicks, Jonathan P., "Firestone to Sell 75 percent of its Tire Unit in $1 Billion Deal with Japanese," *The New York Times,* February 17, 1988, p. 1(N), p. A1(L).

Lipman, Joanne, "New Account (Bridgestone/Firestone Inc. Advertising Account to TBWA Advertising)," *The Wall Street Journal,* August 14, 1992, p. B6(W), p. B4(E).

Morris, Kathleen, ''A Bridge Far Enough (Bridgestone Tire),'' *Financial World,* June 9, 1992, p. 52.

Nevin, John J., ''The Bridgestone/Firestone Story,'' *California Management Review,* Summer 1990, p. 11.

Peterson, Jonathan, and James Risen, ''Firestone Wasn't Pushed Out of Tires—It Jumped,'' *Los Angeles Times,* March 19, 1988, p. 1.

Pioneer and Pacemaker, The Story of Firestone, Akron, OH: Firestone Tire & Rubber Co., 1953.

Troyer, Bob, ''Firestone Stores Offer Free Oil Change Service to Returning Persian Gulf Military Personnel,'' *Business Wire,* March 7, 1991, p. 1.

''When the Bridge Caught Fire,'' *The Economist,* September 7, 1991, p. 72.

Wiener, Daniel P., ''Time to Re-Tire: Another American Firm Goes Japanese,'' *US News & World Report,* February 29, 1988, p. 54.

—Sina Dubovoj

FISHER-PRICE®

Fisher-Price®

A leading manufacturer of preschool toys, ready-to-assemble furniture, and infant and child equipment and clothing, Fisher-Price, Inc., was founded in 1930 and is headquartered in East Aurora, New York. Best-known for its infant and preschool learning toys—including Corn Popper, Chatter Telephone, Rock-a-Stack, and Play Desk—Fisher-Price is also a leader in the juvenile product industry—car seats, nursery monitors, high chairs, and travel tenders, among others.

Fisher-Price was acquired by Quaker Oats Company in 1969 and spun off from its parent company in 1991. It merged with the California-based toy giant Mattel, Inc., in 1993 to form the second-largest toy and juvenile products manufacturer in the United States, trailing only slightly behind the leader, Pawtucket, Rhode Island-based Hasbro, Inc.

Fisher-Price Toys

Comprising nearly 80 percent of the brand's sales in 1992, Fisher-Price toys are some of the most favored playthings of the infant and preschool set. The well-designed and safe toys include such perennial favorites as a set of multicolor stacking rings (Rock-a-Stack) and the Fisher-Price play desk. Equally popular with older preschoolers are the Fisher-Price playsets, which include a farm with animals, people, and farm vehicles; a school bus with working doors and a variety of child figures; and an airport, complete with control tower and airplane.

Fisher-Price was profiting from a ''baby boomlet'' that was underway in the early 1990s in the United States. Although 1990s families are much smaller than those of the past, the number of newborns was at an all-time high, according to the National Center for Health Statistics. Since 1989, there were an average of four million babies born per year in the United States, as baby-boom parents reproduced.

Another factor contributing to the increase in toy sales was the fact that more women were having children later in life. The older parent, usually well established in the working community, was able to spend more on toys, clothes, and juvenile products than a young couple with few assets. Also, wealthier parents were ''doubling up'' on favorite products, buying multiple numbers of the same toy so as to avoid having to transport such items from city to country home or from parents' home to home-care situations (in-home day-care or grandparents' homes). Grandparents were also spending more on toys for their grandchildren than ever before. Smaller families meant that grandparents and other relatives were able to spend much more money per child than they used to.

Some Fisher-Price toys are new and improved versions of products that baby boomers themselves used when they were children. The nostalgia factor has provided a great number of sales for Fisher-Price products that bring back memories: the crib activity center, stacking rings, and cash register, for example, were some of the most popular offerings. At the same time, new product lines—the Fun Park, Activity Table, and Mini Basketball set, all introduced in 1993—were helping to increase Fisher-Price's profitability. Although competition in all segments of the toy industry was strong, Fisher-Price relied on its sterling reputation and its broad product selection to keep its top position.

Toy industry stocks were very strong in the early 1990s, increasing about 90 percent in 1991. As boomer parents and well-heeled grandparents continued to buy large quantities of toys for all their little Jennifers and Jasons, Fisher-Price remained a major player.

Fisher-Price Juvenile Products and Clothing

Nearly 20 percent of Fisher-Price's product line is made up of juvenile products, including car seats, walkers, nursery monitors, high chairs, and table and chair sets. The company began to manufacture these types of products in 1984 as an extension of its toy lines, and was the top seller of juvenile products in the early 1990s, with sales of about $145 million in 1991.

Juvenile products are subject to intense scrutiny from a number of government agencies, including the U.S. National Highway Safety Regulation Association (NHSRA) and the U.S. Consumer Product Safety Commission (CPSC). Product safety is the number one concern of parents, and anything that could alter consumers' perception of safety—such as legal procedures or government inquiries—is a major threat to the survival of the manufacturer.

For baby boom parents concerned about the safety of their children, price was not as much a determining factor in the purchase of juvenile products as safety. No matter how low the price may be, customers were not likely to buy if they had any doubts about the safety of a product. Although Fisher-Price has had to

AT A GLANCE

Fisher-Price brand of infant and preschool toys, furniture, clothing, and car seats founded in 1930; Fisher-Price, Inc., acquired by Quaker Oats Company in 1969 and spun off by its parent in 1991; merged with California-based toy giant Mattel, Inc., in 1993.

Performance: *Sales*—$694 million (1992).

Major competitor: Hasbro, Inc.'s Playskool; also Rubbermaid, Inc.'s Little Tykes, Gerry, and Century.

Advertising: *Agency*—Ogilvy & Mather Worldwide and Foote, Cone & Belding, 1993—.

Addresses: *Parent company*—Fisher-Price, Inc., 636 Girard Avenue, East Aurora, NY 14052; phone: (716) 687-3000. *Ultimate parent company*—Mattel, Inc., 333 Continental Blvd., El Segundo, CA 90245; phone: (213) 524-2000.

recall its child safety seats at least once for design reevaluation, the product line and the company's reputation have not been harmed.

Fisher-Price infant and children's clothes—sold primarily in such discount stores as Kmart and Wal Mart—were also popular. The sales performance of children's wear is affected by parental preference as much as by changing fashions. According to a 1992 survey of discount store managers, Fisher-Price was ranked number one in sales performance from a field of 40 brands.

International Market

Fisher-Price is one of the strongest American toy manufacturers in the European market, and in 1992, foreign sales accounted for 27 percent of Fisher-Price revenues. But the weak economies of many European countries, combined with the previously inconsistent manner in which Fisher-Price entered the European market, have taken their toll on international performance.

Historically, Fisher-Price would launch products in Europe a year after they were introduced in the United States, selling only those products that had been successful in its home country. In 1992 the brand's foreign product line was the 1991 U.S. line, which had been developed in 1989 and 1990. Because of the lag between development and foreign launch, especially at a time when the company was undergoing management changes, the 1992 foreign product line was less than full and was not as economically successful as the company would have liked. The following year, Fisher-Price began to launch new products simultaneously in domestic and foreign markets. Therefore, the 1993 foreign product line represented nearly two years worth of new products. Analysts predicted that the company would be able to reestablish a strong presence overseas with this strategy.

Advertising

In the area of juvenile products, advertising does not seem to have a major impact on purchasing decisions. Instead, people usually rely more on advice from friends. But advertisements, especially print and television spots, are an effective way of launching new products, and Fisher-Price uses both media consistently.

Selling a product that is meant to appeal to both adults (the purchasers) and children (the users) can be challenging. The large baby boom segment, anxious to pass on its favorites to its children, is a powerful buying force. Grandparents, too, were buying toys for their grandchildren, and according to Frank Reysen, editor of *Playthings,* a trade magazine for the toy industry, grandparents were likely to buy the same type of toys for their grandchildren that they bought for their own children. ''This trend is contributing to the strength of basic and traditional toys,'' noted Reysen. The nostalgia factor has helped Fisher-Price, a mature brand with several well-established products, to prosper.

Further Reading:

Brunelli, Richard, ''Mattel's Purchase of Fisher-Price Would Lead to Media Consolidation,'' *Mediaweek,* August 30, 1993, p. 3.

''Mattel/Fisher-Price Link to Grow Toddler Market,'' *Marketing,* August 26 1993, p. 7.

''Mattel/Fisher-Price Merger Creates Toy Giant, Hasbro Rival,'' *Discount Store News,* September 6 1993, p. 4.

Mehlman, William, '' Revived Baby Boom Attending Fisher-Price Return to Basics,'' *The Insiders' Chronicle,* February 24, 1992, p. 1.

Sellers, Patricia, ''New Vroom in Toy Stocks,'' *Fortune,* June 1, 1992, p. 28.

''Top Performer Fisher-Price Inches to No. 1 Spot in Children's Wear,'' *Discount Store News,* October 4, 1993, p. 35.

Waldrop, Judith, with Marcia Mogelonsky, *The Seasons of Business: The Marketer's Guide to Consumer Behavior,* Ithaca, NY: American Demographics Press, 1992.

—Marcia K. Mogelonsky

FORD ESCORT®

The top-selling American car throughout much of the 1980s, the Escort was the Ford Motor Company's answer to the small, fuel-efficient cars of its foreign competitors. It was introduced in 1980, and over the next ten years Ford sold more than seven million of these subcompacts worldwide. The Escort retailed at an affordable price, and it was the most fuel-efficient car in Ford's American car line.

Large sales of this gas-conscious vehicle allowed Ford to meet the U.S. government's corporate average fuel-efficiency (CAFE) standards (requiring a minimum average fuel efficiency for its entire fleet), which gave the company room to sell its more profitable, larger cars. Thus, even though the Escort was a modest little car, its success was crucial to Ford. It also represented a new direction in Ford's business. It was the company's first car designed to suit both foreign and domestic markets and built at sites across the globe. The Escort represented another departure for Ford when the car was redesigned in 1990, as this was Ford's first joint venture with Japan's Mazda Motor Corp.

Brand Origins

Ford managers and designers had been working on the development of the Escort for almost ten years before the car reached the public. By the early 1970s it was clear to Ford executives that the company would need to produce much smaller cars in order to stay competitive. Ford began to experiment with small-engine designs in 1972 under a project code-named "Erika." The Erika project took on added urgency in the mid-1970s, when the energy crisis boosted demand for fuel-efficient cars, helping Japanese imports to eat away at Ford's market share. Ford needed a small domestic car to succeed its Pinto, which had become notorious for a design flaw that could set it afire in a rear-end collision. Ford of Europe was also looking into a small front-wheel-drive car to follow its successful Fiesta. Thus, in 1977 Ford and Ford of Europe decided to work together on the Erika project, building an engine that would suit both an American and European Ford car.

Up to that time Ford's European and American models had little in common. The idea of a standardized car had been broached before, but in practice different cars were built for different markets. Ford's advertising agency, J. Walter Thompson, claimed credit for persuading Ford executives to use the Erika project to produce an inexpensive car that could compete with cheaper imports. J. Walter Thompson argued that Ford could modernize its image. The new jointly designed car would be touted for bringing together the best engineering from around the world, and it would be advertised as a car ready to take on its overseas competitors, at last matching them for technological excellence. The car would be built and sold in many different countries, hooking Ford into a global economy.

On behalf of its car, Ford carried out 23 advertising research projects, mostly in North America, as well as 26 different product studies in seven countries. The company poured $3 billion into the Erika project, because at stake was not only the new model but the reputation of Ford itself. In the hoopla preceding the car's introduction, Ford chairman Philip Caldwell claimed to be ushering in "the most massive and profound industrial revolution in peacetime history." The result of all this research and planning debuted in late 1980 as the Escort.

Commercial Success

In 1980 market conditions were gloomy for the American auto industry. While recession slowed sales, inflation pushed up prices and interest rates. Ford's domestic market share sank to a record low of 16.5 percent, and the company was hundreds of millions of dollars in the red. Nevertheless, the Escort immediately showed signs of winning consumer confidence. The basic model, a three-door hatchback, sold for as low as $5,158, while the five-door wagon went for $5,731, making it one of the more affordable cars in the United States. The new car was narrower, shorter, and lighter than the discontinued Pinto, but it had more room inside, more cargo space, and more glass area. It was the highest-quality subcompact car yet built by an American manufacturer, and sales for the last three months of 1980 were 60,000 units. Over the entire 1981 model year Ford sold more than 320,000 Escorts, a sales figure second only to the Chevrolet Chevette. Sales climbed only slightly in the 1982 model year but enough to make Escort the best-selling domestic car.

Escorts were built at nine plants around the world, and enormous volume kept the price low. By 1984 plants in the United States, Mexico, Brazil, England, and elsewhere churned out 827,000 Escorts, and for three years in a row the Escort had the biggest production volume of any model in the world. The car was popular with people who could afford only an inexpensive car, but price was not its only advantage. Ford had tinkered with the car's handling after some initial consumer feedback, and improvements

AT A GLANCE

Ford Escort brand of automobile introduced by the Ford Motor Company in 1980; it was built both in the United States and abroad and was sold in more than 60 countries; it was the best-selling American car throughout much of the 1980s; a major redesign, developed in a joint venture with the Japanese automaker Mazda, was introduced in 1991.

Major competitor: Honda Civic; also Chevrolet Cavalier.

Advertising: *Agency*—J. Walter Thompson, Detroit, MI, 1980—. *Major campaign*—A television spot showing junked cars of other makes and explaining how many Escorts are still on the road.

Addresses: *Parent company*—Ford Motor Company, P.O. Box 1899, The American Road, Dearborn, MI 48121; phone: (313) 322-1300; fax: (313) 446-7011.

in handling were made year by year. Ford Motor Company had also made a comeback, both financially and in consumer confidence. By the mid-1980s industry surveys showed that consumers generally rated Ford vehicles the best made in the domestic market. Much of the Ford line was doing well, from the Escort to the midsize Taurus to its trucks and vans. With the Escort consistently the top-seller in the United States, Ford gained close to a 25 percent share of the domestic market for small cars.

The small-car market, however, was not especially profitable. In spite of the Escort's brisk sales, Ford made little money on it. A *Wall Street Journal* report in 1986 estimated that Ford actually lost about $1,000 for every Escort sold. The development costs had been high, and Japanese carmakers had a substantial manufacturing cost advantage. Even so, the Escort was still a good investment for Ford. American car companies were subject to the U.S. government's CAFE standards, which set the minimum average fuel efficiency for a company's entire line of cars; therefore, a fuel-efficient model at one end could balance out a gas guzzler. Ford had to keep selling its inexpensive Escorts in order to continue to sell its profitable, gas-hungry large cars. As a result, Ford's prosperity hinged on its Escort sales, whether the Escort itself made money or not.

Joint Venture

The Escort continued to top the car market both in the United States and in the world throughout the 1980s. Sales worldwide exceeded 900,000 units per year from 1986 through 1989, as the Escort was sold in more than 60 countries. By 1990 around four million had been sold in Europe, where England was a particularly strong market. In the United States the Escort had proved quite popular with female buyers. More than half of all Escorts sold during the 1988 model year were to women, and more women bought the Escort than any other single model. One selling point of the domestic Escort was that it was an American car, thus satisfying many customers' patriotic urge to "buy American." Yet beginning in 1985 Ford laid plans to produce the next generation Escort as a joint venture with the Japanese carmaker Mazda Motors.

Ford had bought 25 percent of Mazda in 1979, and since 1987 Ford had marketed several Mazda-designed subcompact cars in the United States. In revamping the Escort, Ford asked Mazda to do as much as 70 percent of the engineering. This was a concession to Japanese expertise in making small cars, but it had sound financial advantages as well. Engineering a new car cost roughly the same whether the vehicle was a low-cost model like the Escort or a profitable luxury car. Since Mazda's engineers worked for approximately one-third the salary of their American counterparts, it was clearly much cheaper to let the Japanese do the work. So for the new Escort line, which was to come out in the 1991 model year, Ford set the general specifications, built the engine, and styled the exterior, while Mazda did the rest. Ford remodeled its Escort plants in Wayne, Michigan, and Hermosillo, Mexico, after Mazda's plant in Hiroshima, Japan. The Hiroshima plant had itself been originally modeled after the Ford Rouge factory. To make the new line of Escorts, Ford fitted its factories with Japanese-made robots and stamping presses. The Escort that emerged was quite similar to Mazda's 323 and cost Ford close to $2 billion to develop.

New Marketing Strategy

Just as ten years earlier the first Escort had been announced with much fanfare and declarations of the car's ground-breaking importance, the new Escort was declared the most important new car in Ford's history, or perhaps the most significant in two decades. Ford's chairman Donald E. Peterson symbolically handed over his job to his successor, Harold A. Poling, by driving a 1991 Escort off the assembly line and then passing Poling the keys. A Michigan dealer blasted off the new model year by having NASA's Michigan Space Center carry off an old Escort by helicopter. Other dealers covered their display windows with paper to build the excitement before unveiling the new Escort. The first purchaser of a 1991 Escort in New Orleans was treated to having the car delivered by the Mississippi River aircraft carrier Cabot. Ford spent most of its advertising budget on the new subcompact at an estimated cost of $100 million. This surpassed a record set five years earlier in the introduction of the company's successful Taurus.

Advertising focused on improvements in the new car model. A lavish spread in the May 1990 *Road & Track* trumpeted the new Escort's "advanced design," "world-class" performance, better feel, extra passenger room, and "new levels of precision." Piling slogan upon slogan, the ad read, "Introducing a car that changes the idea that the only world-class small cars are imports. . . . It changes the idea that serious engineering can only be enjoyed by serious engineers. . . . The Next Escort. A new line of thought. A new line of cars." Ford management reaffirmed that the Escort was crucial to the company's continued competitiveness. With the highest mile-per-gallon rating of any car in the Ford line, Escort sales were necessary for meeting the increasingly stringent federal CAFE requirements.

In spite of the marketing splurge, sales of the new Escort were initially disappointing. Production problems held up delivery of the top-of-the-line GT model, as well as the Escort station wagon, and many buyers preferred the old Escort where it was still available because it cost less. Ford increased the Escort's marketing budget and began to offer customers cash rebates. When the 1992 model Escorts came on the market, Ford tested another marketing technique. A one-price program was introduced in several markets, where the LX model sold for $9,999 with manual transmission and $10,999 with automatic. The cars came equipped with a standard package of air-conditioning, power steering, rear defroster, and radio, and the single price meant there was no haggling with the dealer. This strategy seemed to help Escort's lagging sales, and the next year Ford instituted the one-price program nationwide. The Escort station wagon sold particularly well, passing up the Taurus to become the best-selling station wagon in the United States in 1992. The Escort held 20 percent of the U.S. station wagon market in that year; when its sales were combined with those of the Taurus wagon, Ford had almost 40 percent of the station wagon market. Despite this, sales of the new Escort fell behind the records set by its predecessor. In 1993 Ford sold 84,173 Escorts in the United States.

Performance Appraisal

In 1994 Ford could still refer to the Escort as one of the world's best-selling cars. The car remained popular with first-time buyers because of its low price. According to Ford surveys, Escort drivers liked the car's good gas mileage and the fact that it did not require frequent repair. In fact, the Escort had one of the lowest power-train repair frequencies of any car its size. Advertising in the mid-1990s began to make claims about the Escort's durability based on how many Escorts were still on the road.

The Escort has had great significance for the Ford Motor Company. It helped Ford turn around during the recession of the early 1980s, when the company was suffering record losses and seemed to be floundering. The enormous popularity of the Escort proved that Ford could compete against the imports. The Escort's brisk sales were key to the company's prosperity, as Ford was able to offset the Escort's excellent fuel-economy rating against those of its luxury cars. The Escort sold well in many parts of the globe. The high quality of Ford's best-seller also helped the company rebuild its reputation as the best American carmaker.

With the new model Escort introduced in 1991, Ford brought out the last American subcompact. The other American car companies had discontinued theirs for imports. The joint venture with Mazda represented a new direction for Ford, which it followed up by building minivans with Nissan and working on other vehicles in the Mazda line. Though some Ford employees and industry analysts felt the joint ventures jeopardized Ford's independence, working more closely with its foreign competitors seemed all in all a rational decision. The Escort was an important car for Ford because of its strong sales, but perhaps the car has even greater symbolic significance. The Escort embodied the great changes Ford Motor Company underwent as it struggled to adapt to a truly global auto market.

Further Reading:

Anderson, Steve, "Second-Generation Winner," *Hot Rod,* January 1991, p. 84.

Buss, Dale D. and Masayoshi Kanarayashi, "Wrong Road? Critics Fault Ford Plan to Produce Small Cars with Mazda of Japan," *Wall Street Journal,* June 23, 1986, p. 1.

Clark, Laura, "New Escort a Ford-Mazda Project," *Automotive News,* January 8, 1990, p. 61.

Fisher, Anne B., "Ford Is Back on Track," *Fortune,* December 23, 1985, pp. 18–22.

"Ford Says Escort No. 1 Worldwide," *Journal of Commerce,* May 1, 1989, p. 5A.

Guiles, Melinda Grenier, "Ford's 1991 Escort Symbolizes Future: Car is Engineered by Japan's Mazda," *Wall Street Journal,* February 27, 1990, p. A7.

Healey, James R., "Big Three Close Strong Year," *USA Today,* October 5, 1989, p. 6B.

Jackson, Kathy, "3-door Escort Lure Tested," *Automotive News,* September 21, 1992, p. 32.

Jackson, Kathy, "Ford Dealers Refine Pricing of Escort for their Markets," *Automotive News,* February 1, 1993, p. 6.

Jackson, Kathy, "Ford May Add Incentives to Boost U.S.-made Escort," *Automotive News,* August 10, 1992, p. 6.

Jackson, Kathy, "Ford Weighs 1-price Program," *Automotive News,* March 2, 1992, p. 4.

Jackson, Kathy, "Success of One-Price Escort Hurts Mich. Plant," *Automotive News,* August 3, 1992, p. 3.

Lamm, John, "1990 Ford Escort: Subcompacts' Success Will Secure Company Prosperity," *Road & Track,* May 1990, p. 87.

Mitchell, Jacqueline, "Ford Will Boost Marketing Spending to Aid Sales, Plans Hungarian Facility," *Wall Street Journal,* July 17, 1990, p. A4.

Schuon, Marshall, "Escort Evolves Into Mainstay," *New York Times,* May 20, 1990, p. S4.

Schuon, Marshall, "Ownership, Through the Looking Glass," *New York Times,* March 24, 1991, p. S12.

Serafin, Raymond, "Ford Puts $100M Into Small Cars," *Advertising Age,* January 8, 1990, p. 3.

Stertz, Bradley A., "Ford Pulls Out Stops in Launch of New Escort," *Wall Street Journal,* April 26, 1990, p. B1.

Templin, Neal, "Ford Expands 'One-Price' Plan for Its Escorts," *Wall Street Journal,* March 12, 1992, p. B1.

"Women Increase Share," *Automotive News,* January 30, 1989, p. 214.

—A. Woodward

FORD EXPLORER®

The Explorer is the Ford Motor Company's representative in the increasingly popular area of compact sport utility trucks. From the perspective of its competitors, the introduction was disastrous. In the eight months following its initial release in 1990, Ford sold 71,000 Explorers and was already anticipating sales of 200,000 by the end of the year; at the end of those first eight months, Ford Explorer had outsold the reigning competitor, Chrysler Jeep Cherokee, by a two-to-one margin. Achieving a 25 percent market share from the start, Ford Explorer hasn't looked back.

Product Origins

The 1980s saw the sudden expansion of the previously underdeveloped automotive segment of sport utility vehicles, reflecting the public's growing desire for versatile, comfortable, and stylish trucks. Ford created a two-door vehicle, the Bronco II, to compete with Chevy's Blazer and Jeep's Cherokee. Both Ford and General Motors were left behind, however, as Jeep and an assortment of Japanese competitors introduced four-door models that included some car-like comforts. Chevrolet compensated by stretching the Blazer frame far enough so that two more doors could be accommodated. Ford reasoned that customers would recognize such shortcuts and be turned off; at the same time, they also saw an opportunity to gain an edge on Chevy in their continuing struggle for overall industry leadership. So instead of employing Chevrolet's tactic of frame displacement, Ford shelved the Bronco II and started over.

Design

In an important break from tradition, Ford included its marketing people on the Explorer's development team, and Ford engineers and designers worked throughout 1986 on a prototype that would effectively redefine the standard for the sport utility segment. Their designs were firmly based on focus group research, which demonstrated that what people really wanted was a sport utility vehicle with amenities much more like those of a traditional passenger car. High, car-like safety standards, ease of operation, comfort, versatility, smooth road response, and style became the focal points for Ford's designers.

For the two-door market, Ford planned work in conjunction with Mazda to bring out the Navajo. Mazda's engineers maintained only a consulting role in the process, resulting in the first American-made vehicle to be sold under the guise of being a Japanese product.

Ford made Explorer rugged enough to climb a steep two-track, but the driver could do so by merely pressing a button on the dash to switch into four-wheel drive, while reclining in a contour adjustable leather seat with an air conditioner and JBL stereo. An independent front suspension system, combined with the longest wheel base in its class, made Explorer the quietest ride in the sport utility field. A 4.0 liter V6 engine and optional five-speed manual or four-speed automatic transmission gave Explorer more than ample power for most drivers. Determined not to be outdone by Japanese competitors, who already offered numerous amenities, Ford turned to focus groups for ideas about additional features. The results: front seat head restraints, rear shoulder belts, and childproof rear door locks for added safety; spare tire attached to the undercarriage instead of hanging on the back door; a divided pull down/lift up rear gate; folding rear seats (a 60/40 split in the four-door version) for added storage capacity; plastic coated lower body panels for extra scratch and rust resistance; modern styling with leather seats (adjustable bucket seats up front with the control buttons set on an angle in the driver's door armrest); and the stereo mounted above the air conditioner controls. This combination of options proved to be so persuasive that Explorer's 1990 sales surprised even Ford. Eighty-five percent of their buyers went for the four-door model, which was almost double initial expectations.

Competitors

In December 1989 Nissan Motor Corp. USA presented its four-door Pathfinder sport utility truck to the public. American Isuzu Motors was readying its four-door Rodeo for release in August 1991. Isuzu and Mitsubishi Motor Sales, as well as Toyota Motor Sales USA, already had four-door contenders in the United States. In 1987 Chrysler Corp. bought American Motors Corp. Already leading in the minivan segment, they hoped to capitalize on Jeep Cherokee's nearly ten-year reign in its class, so they entered into a program of heavy investment for new product development. Minivan sales also softened, and Chrysler lacked the ready capital to upgrade both the minivan and Jeep categories at the same time. Forced to choose, Chrysler opted to funnel money into its minivan program first. In 1988 the company initiated a five-year process of revamping its minivan line while postponing introduction of a new

AT A GLANCE

Ford Explorer brand of sport utility truck introduced nationwide by Ford Motor Company in April 1990; became the top-selling vehicle in its class its first year and has maintained the top position ever since.

Performance: *Market share*—30% of the sport utility truck category. *Sales*—More than 300,000 units annually.

Major competitor: Chrysler Jeep Cherokee; also Chevy Blazer, Nissan Pathfinder, and Isuzu Trooper.

Advertising: *Agency*—J. Walter Thompson, Detroit, MI, 1989—. *Major campaign*—"Have You Driven a Ford . . . Lately?"; "The World's Just too Big to Be Left Unexplored."

Addresses: *Parent company*—Ford Motor Co., P.O. Box 1899, The American Road, Dearborn, MI 48121; phone: (313) 322-3000; fax: (313) 446-5899.

Grand Cherokee until 1992; Jeep's dated styling had not seen an upgrade since 1984. This delay was key in allowing Ford time to build its image while capitalizing on the fading brand loyalty of Jeep customers. Chevrolet introduced into the fray a four-door Blazer, but once Explorer was introduced, the Blazer quickly lost market share.

Advertising

"Built Ford Tough" was Ford's truck slogan, and "Have you driven a Ford . . . Lately?" was the company's car jingle. Ford introduced its new product on network television to the latter tune, in keeping with Explorer's intended image as an all-around personal use and family vehicle. Viewers saw the Explorer attacking those steep two-tracks in style and being loaded up with ski and camping gear. At the same time, they also saw children piling in and buckling up for a family outing, and, most surprisingly, a couple in formal evening wear pictured in their Explorer, out for a night on the town. The appeal worked.

In January 1991, *Adweek's Marketing Week* reported that Ford did a survey of 2,300 Explorer buyers who had owned the vehicle for at least six weeks. The Explorer received the highest initial satisfaction rating of any Ford product of the previous decade. Such high marks from satisfied customers made for a tremendous word-of-mouth campaign. Solid consumer support enabled Ford to maintain a simple and consistent (though by no means inexpensive) ad campaign, without resorting to slashing prices, offering rebates, or otherwise succumbing to market pressure. In 1991 it placed seventh on the list of top-selling cars and trucks in America, marking the first time that a sport utility vehicle found a spot on the list. In 1992 it placed fifth.

Ford offered a few variations on the theme to capture a broader customer base. The two-door sport was basically the same as Mazda's Navajo and offered the same options as the four-door, though its rear seats were split 50/50 rather than 60/40. But the real star for style and luxury was the Eddie Bauer model. First priced at $22,000 dollars, or $4,500 less than Jeep's top model, this Explorer was a two-tone version with the added amenities of power rear view mirror, windows, and locks, rear window wiper, better tires, and a custom leather interior made a bit more charming by the addition of limited edition garment and duffel bags, compliments of Eddie Bauer, a maker of outdoor apparel.

Product Changes

In January of 1992 Ford's board approved plans for a revised Explorer to appear in 1995. This version was expected to be outfitted with four-wheel anti-lock brakes and driver's side air bag like the 1992 Grand Cherokee. The most significant potential upgrade entailed the addition of a front and rear air spring suspension system. This would make the smoothness of ride so car-like as to be unparalleled by any previous sport utility vehicle. Manufacturing was scheduled to begin in January 1995. In the meantime Ford compensated by adding four-wheel anti-lock brakes into its 1994 model package. In 1993 Ford also introduced a new model called the Explorer Limited. This vehicle, priced about $2,000 higher than the Eddie Bauer model, featured an overhead console with compass, temperature, reading, lamps, and storage for garage door opener; remote unlocking/keyless entry and anti-theft system; and heated outside mirrors.

Performance Evaluation

For Explorer, 1992 was an overwhelming success. In 1993, however, competition began to heat up. Chevrolet made modest improvements to its Blazer, smoothing out the ride, then cut the price of the Blazer to about $4,000 less than that of the Explorer. Combined with an attractive leasing arrangement, these innovations boosted Blazer's sales for the first time since Explorer's introduction. The Grand Cherokee's competitive prices and expanded amenities were also catching on. A recall of 344,000 1991 Explorers to install a battery cover (preventing acid from dripping onto the wiring harness and causing starting problems) gave the impression the Explorer might be slipping up. There had been earlier recalls for a reported throttle problem and a transmission that wouldn't always hold the truck in park, but these were resolved while Explorer sales were still climbing.

The first quarter of 1993 showed an 8.3 percent decline in sales. In the first quarter of 1993 the entire sport utility truck segment grew by 21.7 percent. Ford's plant in Louisville, Kentucky—still the sole producer of Explorers—had been working overtime since the model's introduction just to keep pace with the original market, and the sudden expansion left Ford unable to produce Explorers fast enough to keep up with demand. Though industry watchers speculated about Ford's possible response, it proved less than dramatic. Ford simply retooled their Louisville plant, which in December 1993 began producing an additional 500 units a week. No discounting sticker prices, no special incentives, and no rebates, just business as usual.

In a February 1994 interview, Dan Taylor, Advertising Manager for Ford's truck division, stated simply, "We continue to sell all that we can make." A company striving to set the standard in a product area could hardly hope for more. The 1995 Explorer, if it meets expectations, could redefine the standard already set by its predecessor, and should easily maintain its position at the top of the sport utility truck segment.

Further Reading:

Antoine, Arthur, "Update: Sport Utility Vehicles," *U.S. News & World Report,* May 13, 1991, p. 12.

Bloomberg Business News, "Ford Plant Will Build Popular Sport Utility Vehicle," *New York Times,* June 6, 1992, sec. N, p. 19.

Brunelli, Richard, "Ford Will Heavy up in 4x4 Ad Battle," *Mediaweek,* April 20, 1992, p. 4.

Connelly, Mary, "Price of New Jeep to Match Explorer," *Automotive News,* January 20, 1992, p. 1.

''Ford, Mazda Announce Vehicle Recalls,'' *Los Angeles Times,* June 8, 1993, p. 2.

''Ford, Mazda Warn of Transmission Glitch,'' *Los Angeles Times,* October 25, 1991, p. 2.

''Ford Plans to Boost Production Capacity for Explorer Vehicle,'' *Wall Street Journal,* January 6, 1993, p. B4.

Gates, Max, ''NHTSA Takes Closer Look at Integra, Explorer,'' *Automotive News,* September 9, 1991, p. 41.

Gray, Madison J., ''Explorer Grows at Louisville,'' *Automotive News,* June 28, 1993, p. 37.

Jackson, Kathy, *Automotive News,* ''Ford Wants Happy Explorer, Capri Owners,'' June 17, 1991, p. 4; '''95 Explorer Remake Gets Board's OK,'' January 27, 1992, p. 8; ''Ford May Add Explorer to St. Louis; Workers Worry over Future of Aerostar,'' April 27, 1992, p. 4; ''Ford Explorer a Big Star in California,'' October 12, 1992, p. 1, 2; ''Ford Readies Luxury Explorer to Woo Women,'' November 30, 1992, p. 1, 2; ''Residual on Explorer Hurts Ford,'' March 22, 1993; ''Tight Supply Chokes Sales of Explorer,'' April 26, 1993, p. 3.

Kiley, David, ''Striking Gold with Explorer,'' *Adweek's Marketing Week,* June 10, 1991, p. 20, 21.

Maloney, Lawrence D., ''Explorer Charts New Driving Frontiers,'' *Design News,* June 8, 1992, p. 40, 41.

Trachenberg, Jeffrey A., ''St. Louis Plant to Become Production Site for Explorers,'' *Wall Street Journal,* February 2, 1993, p. 59.

Treece, James B., *Business Week,* ''Beep, Beep a There Goes Ford's Explorer,'' January 28, 1991; ''Does Chrysler Finally Have the Jeep that It Needs?'' January 20, 1992, p. 84, 85.

—Timothy P. Johnson

FORD MUSTANG®

A symbol of power and performance, the Ford Mustang is one of the best-selling "sports cars" in the United States. More than six million have been sold since its introduction in 1964. Available as a two-door sedan, "fastback," or convertible, the early Mustang was distinguished by its long front hood, short rear deck, and sporty looks. Major restyling occurred in model years 1969, 1974, 1979, and 1994. Impressed with the most recent changes, *Motor Trend* magazine named it 1994 "Car of the Year."

The Ford Motor Company, headquartered in Dearborn, Michigan, was in the mid-1990s the world's second-largest automaker, surpassed only by General Motors. Production and sales were handled by its Ford and Lincoln-Mercury divisions. Ford, moreover, controlled 23.9 percent of the Japanese automaker Mazda, and in 1989 it bought Jaguar, a British car manufacturer. Among the Ford models are the Escort, Probe, Taurus, Tempo, and Thunderbird.

Brand Origins

Various social and commercial trends in the early 1960s influenced the Mustang's development. Foreign cars, long negligible on the U.S. market, were beginning to show their muscle, with sales reaching some 280,000 units by 1961. Unlike those produced in the United States, foreign cars were generally small and emphasized performance and handling. Suspension was stiff, and most were equipped with a manual stick shift. Responding to the new challenge, Chevrolet, for example, introduced the Corvair, a small, sporty-looking car with a rear-mounted, air-cooled engine similar to that on a Volkswagen Beetle, at the time the best-selling U.S. import.

Demographics were also changing. During the 1960s the 15-to-29 age group was expected to increase by 40 percent and, because of a growing economy, to become wealthier as well. Market studies suggested that, compared with their parents, they would more likely want "four-on-the-floor" transmission, bucket (as opposed to bench) seats, and other features common on foreign cars. A growing economy also meant that more women would be looking to purchase an automobile.

Although many people were involved in the Mustang's development, credit usually has been given to a single man, Lee (Lido Anthony) Iacocca, who in the late 1940s became an engineer at the Ford Motor Company. Soon transferred to sales, Iacocca rose quickly through the company's ranks and by 1960 became vice-president and general manager of the Ford division. Well aware of the changing car market, Iacocca insisted on "thinking young" and became preoccupied with developing a small, sporty, young-persons car—one combining the performance of a foreign car with distinctly American bodywork—which he hoped could be sold for some $2,500, or about a thousand dollars less than the average American car.

Donald Frey, the product planning manager, also played a significant role in the car's development. According to Frey, the idea of the Mustang began with "watching registrations of the Corvair, which was a dog. I guess in desperation they put bucket seats and a floor console in the thing, called it the Monza, and it started to sell. We got the idea that there must be something to it." Ford designers quickly began work on a two-seat sports car, and at the 1962 Grand Prix in Watkins Glen, New York, the company introduced a prototype, the Mustang I, named after the legendary P-51 Mustang fighter planes. Although its exceptional performance and small, fiberglass body were praised by car enthusiasts, Iacocca reportedly said, "That's not the car we want to build, because it can't be a volume car. It's too far out." Iacocca, in fact, would insist the car have four seats, thus expanding its potential market, and before long Ford built a new prototype, styled under the direction of Joe Oros, L. David Ash, and Gail Halderman. Their design—with its long front hood, short rear deck, and squared-off styling—set the classic Mustang shape. Although the car was called the Mustang throughout its development, there were thoughts of changing the name to Special Falcon, T-Bird II, or Thunderbird II—all referring to other Ford vehicles—but Ford advertising man John Conley finally settled on the name Mustang, which, he hoped, would bring to mind images of cowboys and prairies.

The car's official launch was on April 17, 1964, at the New York World's Fair, though Americans were given a preview the night of the 16th, when Ford bought the 9:30 PM time slot on all three networks. An estimated 27 million Americans watched the Ford program, setting off one of the greatest consumer stampedes for an automobile. Ford, which hoped to sell 100,000 of its sporty Mustangs in the first year, was swamped with 22,000 orders on the first day alone. The 100,000 mark was hit just four months later, and the 12-month total of some 417,000 set a record for a new American car. This rush, exacerbated by a shortage of Mustangs,

AT A GLANCE

Ford Mustang brand of automobile introduced on April 17, 1964, by Ford Motor Company; Lee Iacocca, then general manager of the Ford division, largely responsible for the car's development; major redesigns in model years 1969, 1974, 1979, and 1994.

Performance: *Market share*—Top share of the small-specialty category. *Sales*—98,648 vehicles sold (1993).

Major competitor: Chevrolet Camaro; also, Mazda Miata, Pontiac Firebird, and Toyota Celica.

Advertising: *Agency*—J. Walter Thompson, Detroit, MI. *Major campaign*—"It is what it was and more."

Addresses: *Parent company*—Ford Motor Company, P.O. Box 1899, The American Road, Dearborn, MI 48121; phone: (313) 322-3000; fax: (303) 446-5899.

has since become legend. In Chicago the police were called when eager Mustang customers stormed a dealership. In Garland, Texas, 15 customers wanted the same Mustang, so the dealer set up an auction; the winner, fearing the car would be sold to someone else before his check cleared the next day, refused to leave the dealership and slept that night in the Mustang. During the 1964 Christmas season, some 93,000 pedal-powered toy Mustangs were sold.

Sales and Model Changes

The early Mustangs came in three body styles: a two-door sedan, a convertible, and a fastback (with a sloping back end). The sedan weighed 2,583 pounds and cost $2,372; the price of the convertible was $2,614. Body details would change little during the first few years, and Ford factories worked overtime to keep up with demand. By March 1966 the one millionth Mustang was sold.

The car came with an exceptionally long list of options. Few people, in fact, selected the most economical base model, choosing instead to customize their Mustang into a higher performance or more luxurious car. The standard six-cylinder engine of the 1964 Mustang had a rating of just 101 horsepower—not much for a ''sports car''—but soon the engine was modified to boost horsepower to 120. Larger eight-cylinder (V-8) engines were also available, including one with a rating of 271 horsepower, which cost $327.92 extra. Other choices included a four-speed manual and three-speed automatic (Cruise-O-Matic) transmission, styled wheels, power steering, power brakes, deluxe seat belts, air-conditioning, tinted glass, a push-button radio, a luggage rack, and special handling suspension. By choosing various options a customer could place traditional American luxuries into a car with European-style performance. The V-8, in fact, transformed the Mustang into a muscle car, and the Shelby GT 350, a special Mustang designed by Carroll Shelby, was an all-out race car capable of going from 0 to 60 mph in just six seconds.

Competing brands, led by the Chevrolet Camaro, Pontiac Firebird, and the AMC Javeline, would send the Mustang into an engine war, and horsepower options were boosted to 320 in 1967 and 390 in 1968. The following year the body style became lower, longer, and wider, with a more spacious and upgraded interior. Beginning in 1969 there were also three new Mustang models. The Boss 302 fastback coupe, later followed by other Boss Mustangs, weighed 3,210 pounds and was advertised as a race car; only 1,934 were produced in 1969 and 6,319 in 1970. The Mach 1, a much more popular vehicle, came with stiffer suspension, as well as with numerous cosmetic features, such as reflective side and tail stripes. The Grande, sold as a luxurious Mustang, included extra sound-deadening material. Despite the new models, the Mustang would suffer declining sales, from the high of 549,436 in 1966 to 323,552 in 1968; 158,915 in 1970; and just 120,589 in 1972.

Iacocca, president of Ford from 1970 to 1978, ordered a rehaul of the Mustang in the early 1970s. What he got was the Mustang II, introduced on September 21, 1973, which, though sporty looking, seemed to be a small, underpowered version of the old car. The wheel base was 13 inches shorter, and the weight decreased some 400 pounds. Most surprising was the standard four-cylinder, 88-horsepower engine, which could hardly carry the Mustang tradition of high performance. The V-8 was no longer an option, nor was the convertible, and even the available six-cylinder engine was rated just 105 horsepower. Although Mustang purists would complain, the new model, in fact, came at the perfect moment. Stricter U.S. government regulations on emissions, increased insurance costs, and the Middle East oil embargo had all helped deflate the high-performance car market, and customers who were worried about gas prices flocked to the Mustang II, which boasted a highway fuel efficiency of 34 miles per gallon. Sales, previously on a decline, hit 277,846 in 1974, and *Motor Trend* magazine named the Mustang II the 1974 ''Car of the Year.'' Although the V-8 option returned in 1975, it would produce only 122 horsepower, raised to 134 the next year. In 1977 Ford introduced the new T-bar Mustang II, which had removable overhead panels.

The car was restyled again for the 1979 model year, and its name reverted to Mustang (without a roman numeral). Although the wheel base increased to 104 inches, the car's weight actually decreased some 200 pounds, and its aerodynamic design helped improve performance. The base car still had only a four-cylinder, 88-horsepower engine, but a turbocharged version was available at 140 horsepower (discontinued in 1981 because of poor reliability). The car could also be equipped with a 140-horsepower, V-8 engine, downgraded to 118 horsepower in 1980. Noticeably lacking on the front grille was the traditional galloping Mustang.

Throughout the 1980s body style changed little. But mechanically the car greatly improved, and increased horsepower would return the Mustang to its reputation as a performance car. A five-liter, 157-horsepower (V-8) engine was introduced in 1982, followed by ratings of 175-horsepower in 1983 and 210 in 1985. By 1991 even the four-cylinder engine had been boosted to 105 horsepower, thanks in part to what was called a ''twin-plug head.'' Suspension and brakes also received an upgrade, and the convertible, closely tied to the Mustang's image as a fun car, returned in 1983. Even so, sales throughout the decade hovered between 100,000 and 175,000 units, a figure barely enough to keep the Mustang going. At one point, in fact, Ford considered discontinuing the brand, though there was also discussion of giving its name to the company's new sports car, which in 1991 was instead introduced as the Probe. By this time the Chevrolet Camaro and the Pontiac Firebird were still major competitors, though it also faced challenges from a host of other brands, such as the Mazda Miata and the Toyota Celica.

When Ford finally decided to go ahead with a new Mustang, it did so with the help of Mustang owners and enthusiasts. According to Ross H. Roberts, general manager of the Ford division, "they didn't want a car that looked Japanese or European. They wanted a car that made a statement about being American." Ford toyed with several designs, including those nicknamed Bruce Jenner (lean and aerodynamic) and Rambo (warriorlike). Although both were seen as suitably American, they were eventually

A 1966 Ford Mustang fastback.

rejected in favor of a compromise model, which came to be known as the Arnold Schwarzenegger version (rugged but cultured). The actual styling was strongly reminiscent of the 1964 Mustang, though with rounded, not squared-off, edges. Even the galloping pony returned to the front grille. Also like the original model, there was an emphasis on power. The V-8 version, with a horsepower rating of 215, shot from 0 to 60 mph in just 6.9 seconds. With the six-cylinder, 145-horsepower engine, the car hit the same speed in a respectable 8.9 seconds. Introduced on December 9, 1993, the car was praised for its technological advancements, including improved handling, greater body rigidity, anti-lock brakes, and dual airbags. *Motor Trend* named it the 1994 "Car of the Year."

Advertising

The Mustang was designed as a fun, affordable, young persons car, and early advertising highlighted this theme. The car even transformed lives, the ads claimed. Hyperbole knew no bounds in a 1964 *Readers Digest* ad, which stated, "Two weeks ago this man was a bashful schoolteacher in a small midwestern city. Add Mustang. Now he has three steady girls, is on first name terms with the best headwaiter in town, is society's darling. All of the above came with his Mustang. So did buckets [seats], full wheel covers, wall-to-wall carpeting, padded dash, vinyl upholstery, and more. Join the Mustangers! Enjoy a lot of dolce vita at a low, low price." Women, seen as an important target for the Mustang, were not excluded from the car's life-transforming miracle. "Life was just one diaper after another until Sarah got her new Mustang. Somehow Mustang's sensational sophisticated looks, its standard-equipment luxuries (bucket seats, full carpeting, vinyl interior, chiffon-smooth, floor mounted transmission) made everyday cares fade far, far into the background. Suddenly there was a new gleam in her husband's eye (For the car? For Sarah? Both?) Now Sarah knows for sure: Mustangers have more fun!" In 1966, when V-8 engines were in short supply, a campaign called "Six and the Single Girl" encouraged women to consider the Mustang's "practical" and "economical" six-cylinder option.

In the late 1960s, as the Mustang and its competitors waged a war of ever greater horsepower engines, Mustang advertisements emphasized performance. In a 1969 issue of *Life* magazine, an ad announced, "1969 Mustangs shatter 295 speed and endurance records." Of course, these "Mustangs" were not the same as those bought from a dealer, but the point was clear: the Mustang was a powerful car. The country, however, would soon grow weary of muscle cars, and performance would subsequently take a back seat in Mustang promotion. By 1972 Mustang ads focused on "control, balance, and style," and sailing and surfing were popular backdrops. During this time Ford also began shifting its advertising dollars from print to television.

With the introduction of the smaller Mustang II, advertisements moved even farther away from performance and power. The focus instead was on the car's gas mileage (34 highway mpg) and low price tag, themes that worked well with a public worried about the new gas rate hikes. Sales nearly doubled in 1974, and by the following year "a little gas and a lot of class" became the Mustang's message. This theme would not last long, however, as high-performance messages crept back into Mustang promotion as early as 1976, and they were back in the front seat for the redesigned 1979 Mustang, which was advertised as traveling from 0 to 50 mph in just 7.1 seconds. "A Sports Car for the 80s," the Mustang was also advertised for its exceptional handling, which derived, Ford said, from its front disc brakes, MacPherson struts, rack-and-pinion steering, and other features. Other tactics would be used in the 1980s. In 1985 the car's low base price ($6,885) again became an important addition to the performance and handling theme, and, in a print ad for the convertible, a woman was shown sunbathing at a "Mustang swimming pool."

By this time, with more than two decades of sales, the Mustang had become a classic. A 1964 convertible, for example, was worth more than $20,000 in showroom condition, as was a 1970 Boss 302. The 1970 Boss 429 could fetch as much as $50,000. Trying to take advantage of its past glory, Ford ran a special advertisement in 1989 commemorating the Mustang's 25th anniversary. With a picture of a 1989 and a 1964 convertible sitting side by side, the ad proclaimed, "Something Great to Look Forward To; Something Great to Look Back On." This nostalgic theme would also carry the initial promotion for the fourth generation Mustang, introduced in the 1994 model year. "It is what it was and more," the campaign's new tag line, was not without irony, however, as half the potential customers were expected to be under 30 years old, too young to remember the launching of the first Mustang.

Brand Outlook

Mustang is one of the best-known brands in American automaking, with a recognition almost as high as the Ford name itself. Power, performance, and carefree fun are words that naturally flow from the Mustang's reputation. John Coletti, manager of Mustang business planning, said, "If you go to a man in the deepest part of Tennessee and ask him what a Jaguar is, he might tell you it's a cat. But if you ask him what a Mustang is, he'll tell you it's a Ford."

Although the Mustang faced possible extinction in the late 1980s, its prospects have greatly improved. Restyling and upgraded equipment have brought the car up-to-date, and there has continued to be a band of devoted followers. More than 400 Mustang clubs, together having some 35,000 members, existed in the mid-1990s. Popularity of the car was also reflected in the many celebrity Mustang owners, including actor Kevin Costner, baseball star Reggie Jackson, and President Bill Clinton.

Further Reading:

Heasley, Jerry, *Twenty-Five Years of Mustang Advertising,* La Puente, California, 1989.

Hicks, Roger W., *Mustang: America's Legend,* Philadelphia: Running Press, 1991.

Jefferson, David J., "The Mustang Is Big in Hollywood Among Sporty 'Unpretentious' Types," *Wall Street Journal,* September 21, 1993, p. A12.

Mitchell, Jacqueline, "New Ford Mustang Priced to Compete with GM's Camaro," *Wall Street Journal,* October 7, 1993, p. A6.

"Motor Trend's '94 Car of the Year: Ford Mustang," *Motor Trend,* January 1994, pp. 46–52.

"New Mustang Ads," *Wall Street Journal,* November 17, 1993, p. B10.

Ross, Daniel Charles, "'94 Ford Mustang GT," *Motor Trend,* November 1993, pp. 32–37.

Van Tune, C., "Ford Mustang 1964–1993: Mr. Iacocca Helps Create the Camaro," *Motor Trend,* November 1993, pp. 40–43.

White, Joseph B. and Oscar Suris, "New Pony: How a 'Skunk Works' Kept Mustang Alive—On a Tight Budget," *Wall Street Journal,* September 21, 1993, pp. A1, A12.

—Thomas Riggs

FORD TAURUS®

First sold in the 1986 model year, the Taurus was one of Ford's most successful models. The company spent five years and $3 billion to develop the Taurus, and when it was introduced, the car's advanced engineering and aerodynamic design drew widespread praise. By 1992 the Taurus had become the best-selling car in the United States, barely beating out the Honda Accord, which had held that position since 1989. With this honor Ford Motor Company hoped to convince American car buyers that the quality and value of its models matched those of the Japanese.

Brand Origins

The Taurus originally came in two midsized models. One was a four-door sedan that could seat six passengers (or five if there were bucket seats), while the other was a four-door station wagon that could seat eight passengers (or seven with an optional third seat). Introduced in December 1985, both were considered part of the 1986 model year. These models were designated as L and GL and priced from $9,645 to $13,860.

Brand Development

Over the years Ford has made various changes to the Taurus, both in its body design and in its mechanical systems. Features for improved safety, comfort, and luxury were also added. In the second model year, 1987, the changes were relatively minor. A 2.5-liter CLC power train became standard for both L and GL sedans, and an optional power "moonroof" was introduced. The 1988 models made rear-seat shoulder belts standard, and the 3.8-liter EFI V-6 engine was made optional. The MT-5 wagon models were discontinued in this year.

Introduced in the 1989 model year was the first new model, Super High Output, which was referred to as the SHO. This midsize model was promoted as a near-luxury performance sedan and had unusual exterior, interior, and functional features. Important among these were a 3.0-liter SEFI DOHC 24-valve engine with 220 horsepower, a new grille, new headlamps and tail lamp lenses, and a standard antilock braking system (ABS) with four-wheel disc brakes. A Ford JBL Audio System was offered as an option.

The 1990 models introduced various safety and performance features. Included were a driver-side air bag; a police package on the L sedan; speed-sensitive, variable-assist power steering; and a sequential multiport EFI added to 3.8-liter engine. Made optional was an ABS with four-wheel disc brakes on sedan models.

The first major redesign of the Taurus came in 1992. Ford spent six years and $600 million to update the car. The 2.5-liter EFI motor was dropped, and replacing it was a sequential multi-port EFI 3.0-liter engine. An electronic automatic overdrive transaxle replaced AXOD on all models except the SHO, and ABS became standard on the LX model. Among other notable changes were a sleeker interior, passenger-side air bag, and powder-window switches angled and lit for easier use. Exterior changes included slightly different headlights and taillights.

The 1992 Taurus also included numerous changes. The car received all new exterior sheet metal except on the doors; a new driver-oriented instrument panel with remote radio controls; new wheels and wheel covers; an express-down power window on the driver's side; new seat and door trim; a brake shift interlock; and improved visual differentiation for SHO, particularly on the front end. Made optional was a right-front passenger-side air bag. For the GL model this was the first major redesign since its introduction eight years before. Changes included a 3.0-liter V-6 engine and dual air bags.

In model year 1993 a driver-side air bag became standard on the SHO, though it remained optional on the passenger's side. Cast aluminum wheels were made unidirectional, a 3.2-liter AXOD engine was introduced, and the car featured a functional deck lid spoiler with an integrated LEDE stop lamp as standard equipment. Variable-assist, speed-sensitive power steering was also made standard on the SHO and was included in the GL decor/equipment group. The GL series incorporated LX body-color bumpers and bodyside molding and got new seat trim. A new floor console became standard for the LX and SHO and optional for the GL. The L series was dropped, and a flexible fuel vehicle was offered but only in the state of California.

The 1994 models were given added safety features, including a standard dual air bag and an optional ABS with enhanced functional changes in the disc brakes for quieter, smoother stops. The SHO had speed-rated tires available on the manual transaxle version. The new tire-tread design dissipated heat faster to allow better control when turning. Ford Taurus models were due for redesigns in 1995.

AT A GLANCE

Ford Taurus brand of automobile introduced in the 1986 model year by Ford Motor Company of Detroit, MI; model praised for its advanced engineering and aerodynamic design; it was the best-selling car in the United States in 1992.

Performance: *Market share*—38% of midsize sedan category (1991 estimate). *Sales*—$7-10 billion (1992 estimate).

Major competitor: Honda Accord; also Toyota Camry.

Advertising: *Agency*—J. Walter Thompson, Detroit, MI, 1985—.

Addresses: *Parent company*—Ford Motor Company, P.O. Box 1899, The American Road, Dearborn, MI 48121-1899; phone: (313) 322-3000; fax: (313) 446-5899.

Environmental Features

Ford was one of the first automakers to use recycled materials, offer a flexible fuel system, and introduce air conditioners free of chlorofluorocarbons (CFCs). Ford cars built in North America had parts made from recycled plastic soft-drink bottles. In the Taurus plastic resin was molded into various components, such as the grille-opening reinforcement that supported the grille and headlights. Ford was the world's largest automotive user of recycled plastic bottles in such structural applications. The 1993 Taurus became the first vehicle to use recycled plastic in its bumpers (in the taillight housings).

A new green leaf and road symbol was used to identify Ford products with special ''environmentally friendly'' features, and the leaf appeared on some alternative fuel models. The Taurus Flexible Fuel system could run on gasoline or a blend of methanol and gasoline. In a 1992 pilot program that was later expanded in 1993, the Taurus became the first production vehicle in the United States to have air conditioners free of CFCs, which were thought to deplete the Earth's protective ozone layer. All 1994 models had this system.

Advertising and Marketing

As 1992 drew to a close, the Taurus and the Honda Accord were the best-selling cars in the United States. In an effort to make the Taurus the year's top-seller, Ford reportedly spent $100 million in marketing efforts. These marketing strategies included rebate programs and low-cost offers to dealers to buy cars for their rental fleets. Rebates were said to be as high as $1,750 a car in some places, and $1,500 discounts were available to dealers if they bought up to half a dozen cars.

These strategies apparently paid off. As of December there were actually 15,000 fewer Taurus models sold than Honda Accords, but the generous rebates and sales incentives from Ford turned the tide for Taurus. The company reportedly delivered 65,324 Taurus models to dealers, twice as many as in November and more than double the number sold in December 1991. The total number of Taurus models sold by the year's end was 409,751, compared with 393,447 Accords. Ford celebrated the breakthrough with a parade in Detroit and earned the right to advertise the Taurus as the best-selling car in United States for 1992.

Automotive observers cited Ford's leasing plan as another contributing factor to high sales for the Taurus in 1992. Ford was among the earliest participants in the automotive industry's trend toward leasing. With this program consumers did not have to buy the car, and their monthly payment was lower than it would have been if a conventional loan had been taken for the purchase of the car. There was a 24- to 36-month trade-in cycle, compared with 48 to 60 months for a car bought with a loan. Because of the cost savings, the consumer could feel that he was getting ''more'' car for his money.

Performance Appraisal

Taurus pushed Ford's U.S. market share for midsize sedans from 14 percent in 1985 to 38 percent in 1991 and added $7 billion in both 1988 and 1989 to Ford's revenues. In addition, Taurus gave a new image and status to Ford's engineering capabilities. A 1993 survey by *Machine Design* magazine asked engineering readers which domestic cars had the finest engineering. A total of 32.7 percent of the respondents designating a specific model gave top honors to the Taurus.

The marketing and engineering success of the Taurus notwithstanding, its sales in the United States were heavily influenced by the economy. The recession of the late 1980s and early 1990s caused overall car sales to fall. By the end of 1993, however, sales started to pick up, and automotive insiders thought the trend would continue. One reason was that there was a sizable proportion of older cars on the road that would have to be replaced. An estimated 37 percent of U.S. cars and trucks were at least ten years old at that time.

Further Reading:

Braham, James, ''Ford Taurus is No. 1 in Engineering,'' *Machine Design,* April 23, 1993, pp. 36–42.

Ford Motor Company Annual Report 1992, Detroit, Michigan: Ford Motor Company.

Levin, Doron P., ''With Money No Object, Ford Beats Honda,'' *New York Times,* January 7, 1993, p. D1.

Treece, James B., ''New Taurus, New Sable, Old Blueprint,'' *Business Week,* September 9, 1991, p. 43.

Warner, Fara, ''Ford Mulls $199 Lease for Escort,'' *Brandweek,* January 18, 1993, p. 3.

—Dorothy Kroll

FORD THUNDERBIRD®

The Thunderbird, Ford Motor Company's response to the Corvette, was introduced in 1954 as a sports car with "personal" appeal. Ford captured the public's fancy by offering a car with sporty styling, a potent V-8 engine, and comfort features unavailable on most cars of its type. By 1958 the sporty two-seater had given way to the so-called Squarebird, a four-seat Thunderbird that was the pioneer of the personal luxury car. While the "Bird" has undergone many changes over the years, it has retained its personal luxury image and its popularity with car lovers.

Brand Origins

The evolution of the Thunderbird grew out of the postwar buying public's desire for a different, highly efficient, sensitive automobile. American GIs who had spent time in Europe had grown to appreciate the European "sports car." Back home, they wanted something similar.

In 1953 Chevrolet, a division of General Motors Corporation, announced its answer to the demand for an American sports car: the Corvette. Ford knew it was time to respond in kind. "Dearborn designers had been doodling two-seaters since about 1950 but it wasn't until the Corvette arrived that the firm decided to get serious about one," wrote the auto editors of *Consumer Guide* in *Great Cars of the Fifties.* "Ford Division general manager Lewis D. Crusoe, already smitten by the exotic Europeans, now gave the go-ahead to a 'personal' car with sports car overtones. The result was one of the first Fifties cars recognized as an all-time great: the 1955–57 Thunderbird."

The car, 52.1 inches high, had a 102-inch wheelbase and curb weight of 2,833 pounds. Its standard power train was a modified V-8 that put out 160 horsepower, and it was teamed with a three-speed manual transmission. An unusual feature was its separate tops—a canvas one for fair and sunny weather and a detachable plastic hardtop for foul weather.

The 1956 Thunderbird, rarest of all with a production total of just 15,631, incorporated Ford's new safety concept of "packaging the passengers." Standard equipment included energy-absorbing instrument panel padding, a concave safety steering wheel, safety door latches, and a shatter-resistant wheel. Distinctive portholes were added that year, as was a "continental" exterior-mount spare tire. The latter was a last-minute addition made less for safety reasons than for opening up more trunk space. The following year the Thunderbird got a shiny new bumper/grille, modest blade fins, and an extended rear deck to house the spare.

When the Thunderbird was first shown at the Detroit Auto Show in February 1954, the car had it all—the looks, the performance, the promise. Missing was just one important ingredient—the name. Its name came from a Ford car stylist who won a suit of clothes for entering Thunderbird in a "name that car" contest. The first production car bearing the Thunderbird name and emblem rolled off the line at Ford's Dearborn, Michigan, assembly plant on September 9, 1954. The first one was sold on October 22 of that year, almost a month before the public introduction.

Marketing Strategy

In what has been called a classic example of preview marketing, Ford introduced the Thunderbird in prototype form in early 1954—nearly seven months before the production lines were set to roll. The Bird was an overnight success. The publicity that followed the introduction of this small, advanced-looking car caused problems for dealerships everywhere. "Dealers were swamped with orders, inquiries and then complaints over non-delivery," wrote Ray Miller in *Thunderbird! An Illustrated History of the Ford T-Bird.* "Everywhere it was shown, the prototype excited an interest."

The ad campaign coinciding with the public announcement in the fall of 1954 was fairly low-key, according to Dwight F. Davis, a former executive with J. Walter Thompson, Ford's advertising agency. "Looking back at the 'quiet campaign,' it was perhaps a little tame in light of what Thunderbird advertising was to become, but it sufficed to bring the car into public attention," he wrote in a chapter of William P. Boyer's book, *Thunderbird: An Odyssey in Automotive Design.* "We used words like, 'enchantment,' and 'distinguished' and 'personal' to describe the car, and the Thunderbird name itself was pure magic and highly memorable."

The central advertising theme was that the Thunderbird was a distinctive and personal car. The advertising was aimed at upscale buyers who appreciated performance, style, and dependability. Davis described the target audience as buyers who "might be said to be leading a lifestyle as dashing as the car they thought to drive." That approach has remained fairly consistent over the years, right up to the personal luxury Thunderbirds of today.

AT A GLANCE

Ford Thunderbird brand of automobile introduced in 1954 (for the 1955 model year) by Ford Motor Company; originally a two-seat sports car, it became a four-seat "personal luxury car" in the 1958 model year; total sales from model years 1955 to 1993 reached 3,294,391 units.

Performance: *Sales*—118,107 units (model year 1989).

Major competitor: Acura Legend; also, Buick LeSabre, Pontiac Grand Prix, Chevrolet Monte Carlo.

Advertising: *Agency*—J. Walter Thompson, Detroit, MI.

Addresses: *Parent company*—Ford Motor Company, P.O. Box 1899, The American Road, Dearborn, Michigan 48121-1899; phone: (313) 322-3000; fax: (313) 446-5899.

Despite the car's allure, it did not sell in sufficient numbers at first to impress company management. "The Thunderbird that was placed into production in 1954 was doomed to be a limited segment of the American market," wrote Miller. "For while it did, in fact, provide everything that it set out to, it lacked the one thing that would have made it acceptable to the American market. That was room for the kids." Those very same GIs, whose high interest in the European sports car had ignited the project were, by 1955, the parents of growing families, and this new car that they wanted had to have room for these families, not be merely a two-seated vehicle." So, even as the first of the two-seaters was rolling off the assemble line, designers were looking at ways to stretch the little car to make room for additional passengers.

Brand Development

The Thunderbird went through many changes over the years. Some of those changes, wrote Davis, "were shocking compared to the original little 'Bird.' " Perhaps the most dramatic change of all was the car's transformation from a little two-seater in its first generation to the second-generation four-seat "Squarebird"—so-called because of its squarish body style. It was a change bemoaned by sports car enthusiasts, who saw the move as a crass attempt to sell more Birds at the expense of style. In time, however, the 1958 Thunderbird has become recognized as a great car in its own right. As Richard M. Langworth noted in *The Thunderbird Story: Personal Luxury,* "All that stuff about forsaking the sports car [and] adding the hated back seat . . . misses the point. . . . The 1958 Thunderbird was [perhaps] the outstanding automotive breakthrough of the decade."

Standing 52.5 inches high and 205 inches long on a 113-inch wheelbase, it was bigger, faster, and more plush than its predecessor. The advantages of the move to four passengers was immediately obvious. Retail deliveries of 48,482 in 1958 almost matched the number of two-seaters sold during the entire three years they were on the market. The 1958 Thunderbird was *Motor Trend* magazine's "Car of the Year."

One unique feature of the 1958-60 Thunderbird was the use of stainless steel components, including glass moldings, wheel discs, rocker panels, and side trim. To highlight this revolutionary—and expensive—approach, Allegheny-Ludlum Steel Company made a 1960 Thunderbird entirely of stainless steel and put it in a time vault to be removed on the car's 40th anniversary. Also, the first sliding sunroof on a post-World War II American car was introduced on the 1960 Thunderbird.

Over the next three decades the Thunderbird would undergo equally significant changes, keeping the model in line with contemporary tastes and advancements in technology. For the 1961 model year a "projectile" look was introduced. Inside, the theme was carried out with a dual-cockpit dash panel. Innovations included the first swing-away steering wheel and a 30,000-mile fuel filter. The standard 390-cubic-inch Sports V-8 engine, equipped with a trio of twin-barreled Holley carburetors, pumped out 340 horsepower.

On the 1964 model the body partially reverted to a "square" design theme, and wall-to-wall tail lamps added elegance. These were the first American cars to offer a windows-closed, flow-through ventilation system. The 1966 convertible was the last of the open-air Thunderbirds.

A jet-aircraft-like design, featuring a long thrusting hood and a short rear deck, was introduced in 1967, as was the first four-door model. Abercrombie and Fitch, a New York store, offered a 1967 Landau-based Apollo Special, which was equipped with custom lighting, an electric sunroof, gold nameplates, and a custom interior that included a desk and television for rear-seat passengers. Only five were built.

From 1970 through 1976 Ford gave the Thunderbird a prominent sharp nose complemented by an egg-crate grille. Other distinctive features were opera windows and a stand-up hood ornament. Special among this group of Thunderbirds were several limited edition models, the rarest being a 1976 commemorative Thunderbird featuring black metal flake paint, a spare-tire bulge in the trunk lid, and a "moonroof" as standard equipment. Only 32 were produced. The 1976 version was the last of the "big Birds."

A Ford Thunderbird as it first appeared in 1954.

Mainly the result of federally mandated fuel-economy standards, the 1977 model year marked the first time in the history of the line that a Thunderbird was smaller than in its previous year. The 1977 car, featuring a wrapover-roof treatment and beveled opera windows in the center pillars, was 216 inches long, compared with the 1976 Thunderbird's overall length of 215.7 inches, but the new wheelbase was 114 inches, more than 6 inches shorter. The curb weight, moreover, was reduced from 4,808 pounds to 3,007 pounds. Further downsizing in 1980 produced a 108.4-inch wheelbase and an overall length of 200.4 inches, but this model retained such Thunderbird hallmarks as wraparound parking lights, a prominent "B" pillar, and sculptured bodyside character lines.

In February 1983 the new model Thunderbird gave the public its first look at the innovative aerodynamic styling that was to become Ford's signature for the rest of the decade. For Thunderbird's 30th anniversary in 1985, a limited edition anniversary model was created with top-of-the-line features. In 1989 the Thunderbird got an even sleeker new shape—honed by more than 700 hours of wind-tunnel testing—reducing its air-drag coefficient to just .31 for the standard and LX models. That year the Thunderbird Super Coupe was named *Motor Trend* magazine's "Car of the Year." In 1990 Thunderbird celebrated its 35th Anniversary with a limited edition Super Coupe. It featured two-tone paint with blue accent striping, black road wheels, commemorative badges on the fenders, and Thunderbird emblems on the taillights and the hood.

International Growth

From the start the Thunderbird has been part of Ford Motor Company's international automotive operations. Ford's sales outside the United States—particularly in Europe—were down in 1992. Foreign operations incurred a loss of $909 million in 1992, compared with a loss of $206 million in 1991. "The recession in Britain has been particularly hard on us because the United Kingdom is our largest European market," wrote Harold A. Poling, Ford's chairman of the board, in the company's 1992 annual report.

Ford remained dedicated to its role as a global company and to taking advantage of opportunities around the world. The company was laying the foundation to become a key player in eastern Europe and had 100 franchised dealers. In the Asia-Pacific region Ford remained strong in Taiwan and had restructured operations in Australia and New Zealand.

Performance Appraisal

Although Ford's marketing group anticipated sales of 10,000 Thunderbirds a year when the car was introduced, the Bird actually did much better. A total of 16,155 Thunderbirds were produced for the 1955 model year, compared with only 674 Corvettes, its major competitor. The cost of the car was $2,944, about $200 more than the Corvette.

List price was increased to $3,151 for 1956, and production totaled 15,631. For the 1957 model year, production was the best yet, at 21,380 units. This figure was influenced by the unusually long model year, necessitated by the delay in releasing the four-seat 1958 Thunderbird. The newly designed car was a great success, as the sales figures showed. "Buyers loved its sporty luxury and snapped up close to 40,000 of the '58s, nearly twice as many as the last of the two-seaters," according to *Great Cars of the Fifties*. With minimal modifications, the "Squarebird" continued to sell well—more than 67,000 in 1959 and nearly 91,000 in 1960. The latter was a T-Bird record until 1977, when more than 300,000 units were sold. The Thunderbird experienced additional ups and downs over the years. For the 1989 model year, for example, 118,107 units were sold. Sales between 1955 and 1989 totaled 3,294,391 units.

Brand Outlook

The Thunderbird has evolved from an American sports car, competing with the Corvette, to a personal luxury car, competing with the likes of the Buick Riviera, Oldsmobile Toronado, Cadillac Eldorado, Pontiac Grand Prix, and Chevrolet Monte Carlo. Despite the model changes over the years, Ford has remained committed to producing an advanced car with many unique features. In fact, the old slogan "Unique in all the world," may well be the definitive comment on the Thunderbird, according to author Langworth. He believed the biggest challenge the car faced as it approached the year 2000 was the need to retain its aura of individuality. "Now more than ever it must be 'unique in all the world,' he wrote in *The Thunderbird Story*. "It has become harder to make it so, with all cars now evolving toward a common dimension. But Ford's designers and engineers have a good chance to succeed. And the record of their predecessors has given them something to shoot for."

Further Reading:

Auto editors of *Consumer Guide, Great Cars of the Fifties*, Skokie: Illinois: Publications International, Ltd., 1985.

Boyer, William P., *Thunderbird: An Odyssey in Automotive Design*, Dallas: Taylor Publishing, 1986.

Ford Motor Company Annual Report 1992, Dearborn, Michigan: Ford Motor Company.

Langworth, Richard M., *The Thunderbird Story: Personal Luxury*, Osceola, Wisconsin: Motorbooks International, 1980.

Miller, Ray, *Thunderbird! An Illustrated History of the Ford T-Bird*, Oceanside, California: The Evergreen Press, 1973.

Wilkinson, Tom, "Touring Coupes," *Popular Science*, September 1987, pp. 27–30.

—Pam Berry

FORMICA®

"Durable," "modern," and "versatile" aptly describe Formica plastic laminate, one of the most well-known home furnishing brands for the past 80 years. The Formica brand is so well known that it has virtually become a household name for decorative surfaces covering every part of the home from kitchen and bathroom counters to furniture and floors, making the Formica Corporation one of the world's largest manufacturers of high pressure laminate surfaces.

Brand Origins

Herbert A. Faber and Daniel J. O'Conor were budding engineers in the early 1900s. They joined Westinghouse in Pittsburgh as part of a dream team of scientists working on insulating material and phenolic laminate resins, inspired by the invention of Bakelite resin, the first synthetic plastic. After hours, the two talked of jointly owning a business. Meanwhile, O'Conor had produced the first laminate sheet by using layers of paper mixed with plastic resins and bonding the sheets under pressure and heat. In 1913 he applied for a patent that was to be assigned to Westinghouse, but it was not granted until 1918. The apparent reluctance on Westinghouse's part to market the new material provided the impetus for O'Conor and Faber to finally start their own firm.

On October 15, 1913, O'Conor and Faber founded the Formica Insulating Company with a tiny investment of $7,500. Based in Cincinnati, Ohio, the company was named after the term Faber coined to identify the new plastic material: "for" (rather than of) and "mica" (a mineral used as electrical insulation material). The resulting substance exhibited "greater versatility in application."

First Commercial Success

In its first year, Formica's sole products were insulating rings and tubes, but by 1914, Faber and O'Conor were churning out flat laminate sheets. Using resin they bought from the Baekeland (Bakelite) Company, Formica only made laminate when an order was placed, usually by Westinghouse or Bakelite. Both companies would later terminate all their orders as they entered the plastic laminate business themselves. To keep Formica in production as the market expanded, O'Conor turned to chemist L. V. Redman who developed Redmanol resin.

By 1915 Formica laminate was regularly used for radio sets in commercial shipping and naval vessels to insulate coils, tuners, and other parts. But Formica was becoming a decorative property as well because its flawless, uniform character formed the perfect radio exterior. During World War I, military demand took manufacturing priority. The addition of Allis-Chalmers Manufacturing and Cutler-Hammer to the client list helped Formica Insulating earn $75,000 from the sale of electrical insulation, radio parts, and cabinets by 1917.

Just as Formica Insulating was really getting off the ground—total sales for 1919 totaled $175,000—it became a target of lawsuits involving Westinghouse, Continental Fibre, and Baekeland for patent infringements. At issue was whether the patent for phenolic laminate was viable; Cincinnati's District Court ruled in favor of Formica, stating that Westinghouse's patent was "invalid because of prior art." Westinghouse sued Formica again, this time for patents assigned to them when O'Conor was an employee. Formica won that case too, as well as other suits filed against it. As a result of mergers and changes within the Baekeland Company—which became Bakelite Corporation and eventually a part of Union Carbide—Formica eventually gained access to more plastic resins.

Brand Development

Formica Insulating began focusing more on its laminate sheet business than on insulation and gears. Radios remained an important product-base for Formica, whose laminate was integrated into the manufacture of home radios in 1921, when Formica commenced offering radio panels in brown and standard black to blend with traditional home furnishings. Additionally, hobbyists were now able to assemble radios from kits and were credited with helping boost Formica's fortunes to $3 million in annual sales by the mid-1920s. Laminate-based timing gears comprised the other side of the business during this time. Increasing success led to the company's introduction of Gyro-Tex bobbins and more decorative laminates.

Formica salesmen seized the opportunity to sell the material on its ornamentive uses. In 1927 Faber and O'Conor had discovered that by putting decorative paper through a lithographic printing process, Formica laminates had extra appeal. That year, according to Susan Grant Lewin in *Formica & Design,* Formica gained patents for "lithographed wood grains of light color, employing an opaque barrier sheet to block out the dark interior of the laminate sheet." They experimented with patterns that simulated wood grains and marble; later more solid colors and other patterns

AT A GLANCE

Formica brand of laminated plastic invented in 1913 by Westinghouse engineers Herbert A. Faber and Daniel J. O'Conor in Pittsburgh, PA; Formica granted U.S. patent in 1918; Faber and O'Conor formed Formica Insulating Company in Cincinnati in 1913; became Formica Company in 1948; as a wholly-owned subsidiary of American Cyanamid Company, became Formica Corporation in 1956; Formica Corporation Design Center formed in 1969; became Formica Corporation, an independent, privately held company through a management-led leveraged buyout in 1985; listed on New York Stock Exchange in 1987; became privately held when Vincent P. Langone, Formica Corporation Chairman, President and CEO organized a team of investors in 1989.

Performance: *Market share*—32% of the plastic laminates market.

Major competitor: Premark International's Ralph Wilson Plastics; also DuPont's Corian.

Advertising: *Agency*—Chillingworth/Radding, New York, NY.

Addresses: *Parent company*—Formica Corporation, 1680 Route 23 N, Wayne, NJ 07474-0980; phone: (201) 305-9400, fax: (201) 305-1095.

and textures were added. Marble patterns were used to replace metal strips on soda fountains for Liquid Carbonic Corporation. Lighter colors of Formica would grace surfaces in the Library of Congress and the luxury liner Queen Mary. And Formica brand laminate was combined with aluminum to create Art Deco furniture for New York's Radio City Music Hall. Yet most popular was black laminate, in vogue due to the burgeoning influence of Bauhaus architectural design, which emphasized "synthesized" technology and dark colors.

As Formica was granted more plastic laminate patents, new uses for the surfacing material unfolded. In 1931 Formica rolled out the first all-paper-based laminate, and by adding a layer of aluminum foil between the core and the surface, Formica was made cigarette proof. Formica's Realwood was introduced in the late 1930s as a laminate with genuine wood veneer mounted on a paper lamination with heat-reactive binder. A switch to melamine resin enabled Formica products to be more attractive, colorful, and resistant; these product improvements spurred kitchen furniture and dinette manufacturers to use Formica laminate for table tops.

Throughout World War II, Formica produced plastic laminate sheets. Sales quadrupled to $15.7 million by 1943, as the company sold such brand extensions as Pregwood, a laminated plastic made of wood veneers and resin that replaced aluminum in airplanes. For example, the P-51 fighter plane contained 88 separate Formica laminate pieces. But it would be the postwar construction boom that fueled Formica's development as a popular home furnishing brand.

Plastics modernized every facet of American life, from drinking cups to hair brushes to walls. O'Conor, who had changed his enterprise's name to The Formica Company in 1948, was credited for much of the marketing strategy that launched Formica on an even grander scale. He targeted homes, schools, and public buildings as potential customers.

Evolving Marketing Strategies

Formica had increased its advertising, engineering, and research budgets during the Great Depression years and also instituted a key management policy that everything be produced one order at a time and that all items be inspected and delivered on schedule. In the late 1940s though, Formica distributors began stocking the brand to keep up with the intense housing demand that opened up markets for Formica laminates.

In 1949 Formica offered the "Color Range"—a spectrum of six patterns presented in several "colorways" and ten solid pastels or muted brights available in satin or polished finishes. Moonglo, Pearl, Arabesque, and Batik were just some of the Formica brand laminate colors and textures. Then in 1951, the company opened a new one million-square-foot plant in Evendale, Ohio, outside of Cincinnati, for producing decorative laminate sheets. Five years later, Formica became Formica Corporation after being purchased by American Cyanamid, long a producer of plastics and one of Formica's plastic resin suppliers.

O'Conor and Faber had based their vision for Formica on providing a material that would improve people's lives. During the 1950s, Formica—synonymous with the era's emphasis on upward mobility, convenience, and modernism—experienced phenomenal popularity, due in great part to designers Raymond Loewy and

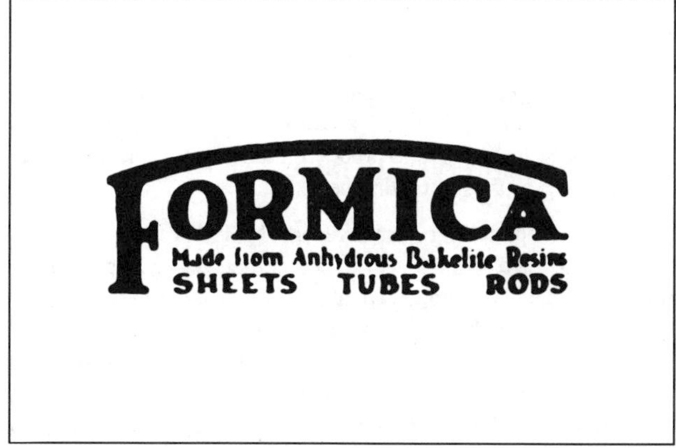

The familiar Formica Corporation "F" first appeared in the 1920s, when the company manufactured industrial parts.

Brooke Stevens. But Formica's founders would not live to witness the corporation's coup in Flushing Meadow, New York: in 1964 the World's Fair House was constructed entirely of Formica laminates, serving as a magnificent showcase of the material.

Hoping to be more in synch with the appliance industry, the Formica Corporation formed its own Design Center in 1969. The center explored the coordination of new and existing laminate colors with those of home appliances. The new Citation Series of colors, including Grape, Raspberry, Signal Red, and Caribbean Blue won an International Design Award. And an expanded pallet of wood grain patterns and faux marbles was brought forth at the end of the 1960s. Formica's Design Center, responsible for further developing the decorative laminate end of the company, met with so much success that the Formica Corporation completely ceased producing industrial grade laminate.

As greater emphasis was placed on design, Formica management strongly promoted the idea of generating a "solid-color-throughout laminate,'' which it did by 1982. The new seamless laminate, ColorCore, was revolutionary. (A sheet of ColorCore is the same color throughout its entirety and one can no longer distinguish the lines of paper that were visible in other laminate patterns.) The rollout of ColorCore in 115 colors brought Formica into the ''1980s design world,'' and a Yankelovich, Skelly & White survey claimed that ColorCore was recognized by 80 percent of architects and designers making it the laminate of choice.

Advertising Innovations

Ever since its introduction as a key home furnishing in the 1940s, women, mainly housewives, were used to help promote Formica on its utility and convenience in the cleaning of kitchen surfaces. Advertisements emphasized how easy Formica made a woman's life. Sue Lewin described how Formica laminate ''transformed the traditional woman's space into the most streamlined, modern room in the house.'' Formica colors and patterns were even created with fashion consciousness in mind. Formica didn't stop with the kitchen. It also promoted the way its laminate could transform bathrooms from ceramic tiles to modern plastic surfaces with its ''Vanitory,'' a built-in cabinet under the sink where ''Mom could apply makeup and generally pamper herself.''

Advertisements featuring the Formica Girl, a happy homemaker demonstrating the versatility of Formica, appeared in the 1960s. She was a departure from the model of the previous decade, when Formica Freddy, the young son of a Formica company employee dressed in bow tie and suspenders—and looking a little like *Little Rascals'* ''Alfalfa''—appeared in promotional materials. Then the great American diner helped immortalize the uses of Formica. The uniform, clean look of smooth Formica surfaces coupled with its ''cigarette-proof'' qualities made the substance very alluring to those building new diners.

Women kept selling Formica from the 1940s until the 1970s when the women's movement forced companies to stop feminizing its products. Men appeared rather infrequently unless it was to demonstrate do-it-yourself Formica applications or in ads with Formica wood grains. By 1975 ads featuring women espousing how Formica made them ''real women,'' disappeared and future advertisements focused on the product rather than people. Kitchen surface ads often just showed physical spaces.

As the 1970s waned though, so did the country's fascination for man-made synthetics; environmental trends eroded interest in anything plastic. The Formica Corporation decided to reposition its product by working with designers and architects. The company also started using water-based resins and metal based pigments to reduce toxic emissions. A virtual renaissance of the material as art resulted.

To further promote its product as an essential architectural material, Formica Corporation sponsored several design exhibitions and experiments during the 1980s. Among its award-winning exhibitions of furniture and conceptual objects were ''Surface & Ornament,'' ''Material Evidence,'' and ''From Table To Tablescape,'' which have traveled to major museums throughout the world. Other famous design uses were New York City's 57th Street McDonald's and United Airlines' ''Terminal for Tomorrow'' at O'Hare International Airport in Chicago. The company also worked with Italian competitor Abet Laminati to market laminates worldwide, aiding Formica in becoming internationally known for use in home furnishing, art, and jewelry. Changes were ahead for the company, however.

Transition and Future Growth

Formica Corporation underwent a management-led leveraged buyout in 1985. Two years later it was listed on the New York Stock Exchange only to become privately held again in 1989, when Vincent P. Langone, Formica Corporation Chairman, President, and CEO organized a team of investors to take the company private. Today Formica Corporation still maintains Departments of Design in Cincinnati, the United Kingdom, and Greater Europe.

Industry experts rank Formica second to Texas-based Premark, manufacturer of Ralph Wilson Plastics. According to Barnaby J. Feder in the *New York Times,* Premark has 45 percent of the market share compared to Formica's 32 percent. While not a household name, Premark has surpassed Formica because of its marketing strategy that enables the company to deliver products within 10 days rather than 25 days for Formica and other competitors. Feder wrote that during the 1950s heyday of plastic laminates, Formica actually declined in sales because American Cyanamid management neglected the brand.

Formica officials have disputed this and say they are improving service and support, as well as promoting their strong brand lines of Colorcore and newest arrival Surell, a solid surfacing material resembling stone that competes against DuPont's more expensive Corian. ''DuPont has 90 percent of the market in this country so we are shooting for second place here, but we think we have the distribution to beat Corian overseas,'' Formica's CEO Langone told Feder in the *New York Times.*

Today more than 50 percent of the company's sales come from international markets. Formica is the largest laminate producer in the world, with factories in the United States, England, France, Spain, Canada, and Taiwan. Company records indicate that Formica brand products are used by people in more than 150 countries. Europe's demand for the popular surfaces has also spurred 15 new designs that were slated for market in 1993—a good indicator of Formica's global status.

What will keep the brand strong in the United States is the renewed interest in home remodeling and preservation. Formica has long established its name recognition as a popular brand and has withstood a Federal Trade Commission attempt to disrobe it of trademark status. Brand extensions are also up to date with the latest home furnishing designs. The 1990s have marked a new period for Formica Corporation with the introduction of new products, including Granulon spray-on surfacing and Nuvel surfacing material. Such qualities are likely to carry the brand into the next decade.

Further Reading:

Alexander, Jack, ''What's in a Name? Too Much, Said the FCC,'' *Sales & Marketing Management,* January 1989, p. 75.

Barach, Arnold B., *Famous American Trademarks,* Public Affairs Press: Washington, D.C. 1971.

Feder, Baranaby J., ''Formica: When a Household Name Becomes an 'Also-Ran,' '' *New York Times,* August 12, 1990, p. 12.

Lewin, Susan Grant, *Formica & Design From the Counter Top to High Art,* Rizzoli International Publications, New York, 1991.

—Evelyn S. Dorman

FRIGIDAIRE®

FRIGIDAIRE
BUILT FOR GENERATIONS

Frigidaire, founded in 1918, has long been one of the leading brands of refrigerators and other appliances in the United States. So successful were its early refrigerators that the Frigidaire name became virtually synonymous with the product itself. Frigidaire Company—since 1986 a subsidiary of Swedish-owned AB Electrolux—marketed more than 100 Frigidaire products.

Brand Origins

Frigidaire's humble beginnings date back to the year 1913, when Fred W. Wolf invented the first electric refrigeration unit, which he named the ''Domelre.'' The product featured an air-cooled refrigeration unit designed for mounting on top of an old-fashioned ice box. Wolf found few fans for his new product, and consequently the first refrigerator was little more than a curiosity. Few people were willing to give up their old-fashioned ice boxes—then a symbol of fine American living. Two years later, in 1915, engineer Alfred Mellowes created a redesigned electric refrigerating unit, which he installed in the base of a wooden cabinet. It was in Mellowes's modest little backyard washhouse in Fort Wayne, Indiana, that the first self-contained refrigerator was born.

In 1916 Mellowes joined forces with several partners to create the Guardian Refrigerator Company, which was to manufacture and sell his invention. The company's operations began on a modest scale in the small, rented loft of an organ factory equipped with just two lathes, a drill press, a shaper, a power saw, and some hand tools. Through painstaking and laborious work, the small group of employees produced the first Guardian refrigerator on August 17, 1916. Several years later the company purchased the rights to Wolf's ''Domelre.''

The slow manual labor and lack of state-of-the-art equipment soon began to take its toll on the young company. Though Guardian refrigerators were operating satisfactorily, the company could not produce enough units to push itself over the break-even point. By 1918 the Guardian Refrigerator Company had produced fewer than 40 units and lost $34,000. The company hovered on the brink of complete failure.

An unlikely savior soon came to Guardian's rescue when W. C. Durant, then president of General Motors Corp., purchased Guardian. Durant coined the name ''Frigidaire'' and made the young company a subsidiary of General Motors. That year the first refrigerator bearing the Frigidaire nameplate entered the marketplace. The General Motors acquisition marked a turning point in the history of Frigidaire and in the appliance industry. The automobile company was a pioneer of mass production, and Durant immediately began applying the same techniques to refrigerator production. The new entity upgraded and moved its production facilities to Detroit and opened several sales offices. Soon the new electric refrigerator hit the American marketplace at full throttle. Still, however, the young refrigerator company was far from a profitable venture.

The company produced Frigidaire refrigerators in Detroit until 1921, when General Motors turned the operation over to one of its subsidiaries, the Delco-Light Company. Delco-Light, a manufacturer of individual electric lights for farm homes, moved Frigidaire operations to its home base of Dayton, Ohio. The young company soon began to prosper under the skillful engineering leadership of Charles F. Kettering and the sales leadership of Richard H. Grant.

When General Motors was producing Frigidaire refrigerators in Detroit, the price of a nine-cubic-foot unit was $775. By the time Delco-Light was producing the products in Dayton, the price per unit had dropped to $714. By 1926 mass production was running smoothly, and the price had dropped to $468. The Frigidaire refrigerator was on its way to the mass-consumer market. Soon Frigidaire's success began to overshadow Delco-Light, and the two entities separated in 1926. Frigidaire Corporation became a new General Motors subsidiary, with Elmer G. Biechler appointed president and general manager.

New Product Developments

While Frigidaire was on its way to becoming America's refrigerator of choice, the company was busy breaking new ground in nearly every area of the refrigeration business. In 1923 Frigidaire began marketing an ice-cream cabinet, and over the next three years it introduced refrigeration equipment for soda fountains, milk coolers, and drinking-water fountains. The company produced the first room air conditioner in 1929. Also in 1929 Frigidaire developed the first combination display and storage cabinet for frozen foods and marketed a low-temperature cabinet designed for sportsmen who needed to store game and fish. This evolved into the world's first food freezer.

AT A GLANCE

Frigidaire brand of refrigerators and other appliances founded in 1918 by General Motors Corp. of Detroit, Michigan; the rights to its first product, a refrigerator, were acquired that year with the purchase of Guardian Frigerator Company; General Motors' Frigidaire division purchased by White Consolidated Industries in 1979 to become part of its WCI Major Appliances Group; WCI Major Appliances Group purchased by AB Electrolux in 1986; Frigidaire operations renamed Frigidaire Company in 1991.

Performance: *Market share*—Less than 10% of the major appliance category.

Major competitor: Whirlpool; also, General Electric, Electrolux, Maytag.

Advertising: *Agency*—Shelly Berman Communicators, Westerville, OH. *Major campaign*—"Frigidaire: Built for generations."

Addresses: *Parent company*—Frigidaire Company, 6000 Perimeter Drive, Dublin, OH 43017; phone: (614) 792-4100. *Ultimate parent company*—AB Electrolux, Luxbachen 1, S-105 45, Stockholm, Sweden.

Frigidaire was also busy developing new features for its refrigerators. In the early 1920s the company introduced the first one-piece metal food-compartment lining that sealed the product's cork insulation. The products' interiors were chilled by a water-cooled compressor concealed under the cabinet bases. Soon Frigidaire researchers developed an air-cooled condenser that eliminated the need for a water connection. By 1926 the company replaced the old-fashioned wooden-ice-box-type cabinet with a steel refrigerator cabinet, and the modern-day refrigerator was born.

The late 1920s witnessed the development of the first porcelain-on-steel cabinets, all-porcelain cabinets with two-tone finishes, and all-porcelain enamel cabinets. By 1929 the company had invented the first customer-adjustable refrigerator cold-control function. It was also in 1929 that the one-millionth Frigidaire refrigerator rolled off the assembly line. To mark the occasion, the company flew the refrigerator to an Atlantic City exposition in an early trimotored transport plane. Although the United States population was suffering through the ravages of the Great Depression, Frigidaire refrigerator sales continued to climb. By 1932 the company had produced its 2,500,000th Frigidaire. To promote its growth, the company sent this refrigerator around the world on the ship *President Pierce.* By the end of 1941 Frigidaire had produced more than six million units.

Frigidaire supported its sales success with a nationwide organization of distributors and factory branch offices, which supplied Frigidaire products to dealers in every trading center in the country. The company made sure that reliable, factory-trained servicemen were available to customers wherever Frigidaire products were sold. This was the beginning of Frigidaire's effort to build tremendous customer satisfaction and goodwill.

While Frigidaire was the undisputed leader in the refrigerator business, corporate officials recognized the need to diversify their business. In 1937 Frigidaire introduced its first products outside the refrigeration area: a range with a porcelain enamel finish and a large oven with fibrous-glass insulation. To this the company added its first line of laundry products, including an all-porcelain clothes washer, the first vertical pump agitator washer, and the "Rapidry 1000" clothes dryer with "the fastest spin for the driest clothes."

During World War II all nonessential civilian production halted, and Frigidaire, like most other manufacturers, turned its energy and resources toward the war effort. The company began producing .50 caliber Browning machine guns, aircraft propellers and parts, hydraulic controls for airplanes, and various other military equipment. In a specially built factory in Moraine City, Ohio, Frigidaire produced nearly a million major components for a revolutionary hollow-steel propeller for fighter planes. In addition, the company produced more than 500,000 aircraft control valves.

Postwar Production

In 1943, under the direction of General Manager Edward R. Godfrey, Frigidaire was one of nine manufacturers authorized to resume production of household refrigerators. The company became the first to deliver these much needed family appliances when the first postwar unit rolled off the assembly line in July of 1945.

During this early postwar period, Frigidaire expanded its appliance line to include household laundry products, and it added large-size refrigerators and refrigerated cases to its commercial product line. The Frigidaire washer was the first all-porcelain model in the industry, and it provided improved washing and rinsing, in addition to rapid damp-dry spinning action. The company also pioneered the first dryer with a lifetime-guaranteed porcelain finish on the interior and exterior, as well as a new "Filtra-matic" system, which eliminated the need to vent the dryer to remove excess moisture and lint.

In June 1948 the company completed its 10-millionth refrigerator unit and in 1949 its 11 millionth. The company introduced the appliance industry's first 30-inch electric range in 1950. By June 1950 Frigidaire management announced a large expansion of its Moraine City factory buildings, which would increase the company's production by some 40 percent.

Engineering Leadership

By 1952 Frigidaire celebrated the sale of its 12-millionth refrigerator. The company also acknowledged its employees' leadership in engineering technology. By that year Frigidaire had offered its first automatic ice maker for sale and introduced its first air-conditioning system for automobiles. Also in 1952 Frigidaire announced its novel "Cycla-matic" feature for automatically defrosting its refrigerators and its "Refrig-O-Plate," a separate section within its refrigerators for cooling fresh food. In 1953 Frigidaire announced the production of the first year-round air conditioner for both heating and cooling an entire residence.

With the production of its 1954 appliance models, Frigidaire became the first manufacturer to offer matching colored sets of household appliances. That fall the company further expanded its extensive line by offering an "ice-ejector" storage bin (with a built-in ice cube storage release) and a refrigerator with a "flowing cold" bottom freezer. This model included an ice-ejector storage bin, a roll-bonded aluminum evaporator, "picture window" hydrators, a foot-pedal door opener, and decorator panels.

The "Sheer Look"

In 1956 Herman F. Lehman took over the Frigidaire helm as general manager. Under his leadership the company continued to pioneer. In the fall of his first year as general manager, Lehman scored a major customer-satisfaction coup when he led Frigidaire to introduce its new design concept called the "Sheer Look." Soon this new straight-line styling became all the rage in the appliance market. The design concept merged slim, sleek styling with everyday household appliances, and it marked the first major appliance redesign in more than a generation.

In 1958 Frigidaire introduced "Frigi-Foam" insulation in its household refrigerators, and it marketed the first frost-proof refrigerator freezer. Not long afterward it created "drop-leaf door" wall ovens and the "Pull 'N Clean" oven that pulled out for easy stand-up cleaning. By 1960 the company introduced "Flair" ranges with the first "roll-to-you" cooking top and featuring an automatically closing cover and glide-top oven doors. Frigidaire soon added to its bevy of inventions the "Roller-matic" washer mechanism with no belts, pulleys, or gears and the "Tender-matic" automatic meat-tenderizing control.

The WCI Acquisition

In 1979 Frigidaire was acquired by White Consolidated Industries and became part of its parent company's Major Appliance Group. Other brands in this group included White-Westinghouse, Tappan, and Kelvinator. The company invested more than a half billion dollars in improving plants and equipment for the Frigidaire brand during a four-year period in the late 1980s. The investment included such capital improvements as expansions and updates of existing facilities and the addition of a refrigerator facility in Anderson, South Carolina, and a dishwasher factory in Kinston, North Carolina. Under WCI's direction, the brand's slogan became "Frigidaire: Here today, here tomorrow."

Frigidaire's ownership changed yet again in 1986 when WCI Major Appliance Group was purchased by Swedish-owned AB Electrolux. The company was renamed the Frigidaire Company in May 1991.

Frigidaire Promotional Campaigns

When Frigidaire adopted its new name, it also adopted a new logo and slogan. The slogan, "Creating a Better Tomorrow," conveyed Frigidaire Company's commitment to product breakthroughs and engineering leadership. Under new management, Frigidaire's leaders voiced their intent to maintain the company's multibrand strategy and market-driven responsiveness.

In 1993 Frigidaire added the "UltraStyle" line of appliances to its arsenal. This full line of major household appliances included more than 100 products with gently rounded shapes that were intended to create distinctive, perfectly coordinated styling for all kitchens. The UltraStyle line was the result of a $500 million redesign program begun in 1988. In addition to its sleek styling, the line also included easy-to-clean, energy-efficient products. Company engineers received their inspiration from the 1990s lifestyle—people spent more time in the kitchen, and they were in the market for more user-friendly, energy-efficient products.

Upon its introduction, Frigidaire initiated a $20 million television and print campaign, using the theme "Built for generations," which premiered in May 1993. The theme ran alongside two family-oriented spots. One featured a family unloading food in the kitchen after an outing to the farmer's market; the other showed a mother and baby going to the refrigerator for the night's feeding. According to Dan Heimbrock—a spokesman for Shelly Berman Communicators (SBC) of Westerville, Ohio, which handled the Frigidaire account—much of the campaign's $20 million budget was spent on print ads, while television commercials, aired during network news and information shows, were used to improve the brand's image and to raise consumer awareness. Heimbrock said, "It's not likely that you'll remember Frigidaire is the washing machine that handles unbalanced loads, but you might remember that it's the brand that gave you a warm, fuzzy feeling, lasts a long time and is really cool-looking."

Further Reading:

"A Brief History of Frigidaire," Dublin, OH: Frigidaire Company, 1966.

Cortez, John P., "Appliance Ads Get 'Warm, Fuzzy,' " *Advertising Age,* May 3, 1993, p. 44.

Fitzgerald, Kate, "Appliance Ads Try to Put Spin Back into Sales," *Advertising Age,* July 29, 1991, p. 4.

"Frigidaire History," Dublin, OH: Frigidaire Company, 1990.

"Frigidaire History & Home Appliance Firsts," Dublin, OH: Frigidaire Company, 1993.

"History of Frigidaire, Dublin, OH: Frigidaire Company, 1993.

—*Wendy Johnson Bilas*

FRISBEE®

Wham-O Manufacturing Company's Frisbee brand of flying disc became virtually synonymous with the product itself. Made of durable plastic, the Frisbee was a lightweight, circular object with curved edges. With a flick of the wrist, it gently soared over a distance up to 200 feet and could be easily caught with the hands. Although the product dated back to college campuses during the first half of the twentieth century, Frisbee was officially introduced and marketed under the name Pluto Platter in 1957 by Wham-O of San Gabriel, California (manufacturer of the Hula Hoop and Super Ball). One year later, Wham-O changed the name of its plastic disc to Frisbee.

Frisbee quickly became a fad among college students. Many predicted that, like Hula Hoop, the Frisbee fad would fade. However, through savvy promotional activities Wham-O was able to transform Frisbee from a fad into an internationally recognized sport. Over 1,000 teams competed on the college and professional level in Ultimate Frisbee, and over 30 different periodicals were published on the sport. Although no sales or market share figures were calculated for the flying disc segment, Wham-O claimed that more Frisbee discs were sold annually than basketballs, footballs, and baseballs combined. Frisbee gained a brand recognition factor of 99 percent, and over 90 percent of Americans claimed to have played with one.

Brand Origins

No one can honestly discern when a person threw a round disc into the air and watched it soar for the first time, although several conflicting stories arose as to what was the direct predecessor of Frisbee discs. One claim was that Hollywood camera crews instigated the fad in the 1930s and 1940s by tossing about film can lids during down times on the set. Another had it that youngsters in California were "nearly addicted" to tossing plastic coffee can lids in the air. Still a third claim came from a Frisbee fan who remembered throwing lids from Frisbie Sugar Cookie tins in Connecticut.

This most commonly held theory concerning the origins of the Frisbee fad dated back to the 1920s, when students at Yale University began amusing themselves by throwing pie tins from the Frisbie Baking Company of Bridgeport, Connecticut. Legend had it that, in order to alert pedestrians to the flying pie plates, students would yell "Frisbie!"—and thus the name was derived. The enjoyment of whirling a disc through space slowly caught on throughout the United States. During the years following World War II, an official from the Frisbie Baking Company estimated that the company lost over 5,000 returnable pie tins to disc-throwing fanatics.

It was not until 1948 that a California carpenter named Fred Morrison first conceived of the commercial possibilities of this fascination. He began experimenting with plastic (then a newly developed substance) and made his first disc by hand that year. In 1955, Morrison patented his creation and sold it to the Wham-O Manufacturing Company, an upstart novelty and toy company. Wham-O introduced the disc in 1957 under the name "Pluto Platter," hoping to capitalize on the nation's preoccupation with unidentified flying objects. The disc, which sold for a mere 59 cents, became an instant hit on college campuses. By summer it was the rage on beaches everywhere. Vacationing college students stowed their discs in their backpacks as they travelled through Europe and Africa, and within a year orders were placed from such places as Norway, New Zealand, and Africa. The Frisbee had become a full-fledged fad. Soon, other manufacturers were introducing copies of the Pluto Platter under names such as "Space Saucer," "Scalo," and "Flying Saucer."

By that time, the name Frisbie had become the generic term for plastic discs among Ivy League students, where the sport was the most popular. (Legend had it that over $1,500 worth of discs were sold at a Princeton alumnae gathering during one weekend.) In 1959, Wham-O fortuitously acquired and trademarked the name Frisbee for all its discs. Despite their popularity among college students, Frisbee discs were initially viewed as a novelty whose popularity would wear off quickly. But there was something in the aerodynamic play of Frisbee that caught the attention of men and women across the country and insured that Frisbee would be more than just a passing fancy.

Promotional Activities

Wham-O did little to advertise Frisbee, perhaps because its popularity was overshadowed by the 1958 introduction of Wham-O's Hula Hoop, which ignited a craze that swept the world. Frisbee was doing quite well on its own, however. Disc fans were taking the inscription on the underside of Frisbees seriously. "Play catch. Invent games," it said. Ed Headrick, former vice president of Wham-O, was the first to note the Frisbee disc's potential as more than just a toy. In 1964, he began actively promoting Frisbee as a sport, introducing the Professional Model Frisbee and the Frisbee disc flight rings (later named the Lines of Headrick). Three years later, he founded the International Frisbee Association as a means of providing support for Frisbee players and officially sanctioning Frisbee games and competitions.

One of the first team sports using the Frisbee was a game called Guts, in which a disc was thrown from one team to another at such a speed that the other team was prevented from catching it. The development of Guts shed further light on the role of student participation in the growth of the Frisbee disc's popularity. Some accounts stated that the first Guts game was played using cookie tins at Dartmouth in 1954. Another account claimed that the name Guts came from a Princeton pastime in which students threw a rusty, six-inch circular saw between teams. Either way, it seemed that Frisbee filled a market need by providing a standard, well-balanced disc to replace old pie and cookie tins. In 1958, Guts was "officially" sanctioned as a sport at the first annual International Frisbee Tournament in Escanaba, Michigan. Headrick also helped organize the California Guts Masters Team in the late 1960s, and by 1972 Guts's popularity grew to such a point that 36 teams from a number of countries participated in the World Guts Frisbee Championships in Copper Harbor, Michigan.

AT A GLANCE

Frisbee brand of flying discs introduced as the Pluto Platter in 1957 by Wham-O Manufacturing Company; name changed in 1958 to Frisbee; Wham-O purchased by Kransco Group Companies in 1982.

Performance: *Market share*—75% (top share) of recreational disc category.

Major competitor: Imperial Toy's brand of flying discs.

Advertising: *Agency*—Gardner Communications, San Francisco, CA.

Addresses: *Parent company*—Wham-O Manufacturing Company, Kransco Group Companies, 160 Pacific Ave., San Francisco, CA, 94111; phone: (415) 433-9350; fax: (415) 989-2345.

With little marketing effort on the part of Wham-O, Frisbee became a mainstay of the burgeoning counter-culture movement in the 1960s. This gave the disc an aura associated with hippies, be-ins, and peace-niks. In 1969, the game of Ultimate was invented in the parking lot at Columbia High School in Maplewood, New Jersey, by a group of high school students interested in a low-key, "non-jock" sport. Using two seven-person teams, Ultimate combined aspects of football, basketball, and soccer. The Frisbee could only be moved in the air; whoever caught it was allowed only three steps before passing the disc off again. When a player had the disc, only one opponent at a time was allowed to block the pass. A goal was scored when a person caught a Frisbee in the end zone. The players formed a varsity Ultimate team at their school and founded an Ultimate league in their school district. In 1972, Ultimate was officially introduced on a college level when the first intercollegiate game was played between Rutgers and Princeton universities. In many ways, Ultimate's popularity stemmed from its anarchistic spirit, which spoofed big-time college sports and allowed anyone who could throw a disc, male or female, to participate.

During these years, professional-class Frisbees were considered the only official disc for serious sporting events. To market the Frisbee brand, Wham-O had little more to do than support the games that had organized spontaneously around the product. Headrick's International Frisbee Association grew at a rapid pace. By 1974, the World Frisbee Disc Championships had grown to such an extent they were held in the Rose Bowl in Pasadena, California. The first book on Frisbee, *The Official Frisbee Handbook,* was written by Goldy Norton in 1973; one year later *Flying Disc World,* a bi-monthly magazine, was introduced, followed by the 1975 publication of *Frisbee: A Practitioner's Manual and Definitive Treatise,* by Dr. Stancil Johnson.

There were other games that grew up around the disc and were promoted through the International Frisbee Association. In 1957, A. K. "Spud" Merlin, one of the founders of Wham-O, invented the game of Frisbee Golf, laying out the first course in a park in Thousand Oaks, California. Frisbee Golf was closely related to the traditional game, with drives and puts aimed at hitting special poles placed at intervals around a course. The game did not catch on as quickly as Guts. The first major Frisbee Golf competition was not held until 1969 at the International Frisbee Association meet in Pasadena, California. Through the promotions of the International Frisbee Association, Frisbee Golf became much more popular in the 1970s. The number of officially designated disc golf courses grew to over 500 in the United States, and Frisbee Golf became a major event at IFA meets. Other versions of Frisbee games introduced during the 1970s included an all-dog flying disc competition, with such events as Freestyle, Throw, Run, Catch, Maximum Times Aloft, and Distance.

Wham-O's efforts to legitimize Frisbee sports paid off well. No longer associated with students and the hippie movement, Frisbee sports gained national recognition and respect. By 1991, over 1,000 Ultimate teams competed at the college level and over 50,000 men and women played the sport on a regular basis. More important to the Frisbee disc's success was the fact that through the 1980s, Wham-O held about 90 percent of the disc market. "We're at a point where we feel we don't have to educate people about the existence of our discs," said Wham-O promotional manager Dan Roddick in 1991. "It's more a matter of raising consciousness about the ways the disc can be used. In our view, a marketing success would be for someone to watch the Freestyle championship on television and say to himself, 'I have a Frisbee myself, but I never realized I could get such good exercise with it.' "

Competition

Serious competition to sales of Frisbee discs did not occur until well into the 1980s, when a new game called Hacky Sack became the hit on college campuses. As one Rutgers University student told *Forbes* magazine in 1984, "Not that many people play Frisbee around here anymore. Frisbees have too much philosophical baggage. Everyone hacks." To play Hacky Sack, a group of people stood in a tight circle and kicked around a small bag filled with plastic pellets. The objective was to keep the bag in motion using only legs and feet. The rules were that players could not use arms or hands to keep the bag aloft, nor could anyone apologize for missing a kick. In the first three years of after its introduction, Kencorp Sports sold over 1.2 million Hacky Sacks, primarily to Frisbee players. Wham-O's response to the competition was to acquire the U.S. and Canadian rights to Hacky Sack for $1.5 million. Kencorp kept world distribution rights and also was able to tap into Wham-O's marketing expertise. Wham-O's approach to marketing Hacky Sack was to legitimize it in much the same way it legitimized Frisbee.

Other competition began to crop up in the early 1990s from within the disc segment. Young Frisbee fanatics had grown up and founded their own disc companies, providing serious competition to Frisbee discs in organized sports. The Frisbee brand's market share dropped about 15 points to 70 percent by 1991 due to competition from a number of small companies. Innova and Discraft both developed highly refined discs that flew farther and responded more adroitly than traditional Frisbees. Innova developed a golf disc that captured about 75 percent of that market segment. And in 1991, Discraft presented some alarming competition when the World Club Ultimate Championship chose the Discraft Ultra-Star over Wham-O's 80 series, the traditional choice of Ultimate players.

Performance Analysis

Ironically, Wham-O's competition in the professional disc category stemmed from its own success at nurturing Frisbee sporting events. Competition from upstart, specialized disc manufacturers could provide a serious challenge to the Frisbee brand's future supremacy in this category. However, while the popularity of disc sports long supported Frisbee sales, Wham-O believed its greatest strength was in the mass recreational market, where the name Frisbee was still synonymous with flying discs.

To maintain its mass-market position, Wham-O began actively promoting other uses of Frisbee discs in the early 1990s by providing school athletics teachers with training packages and demonstrations of ways to use the disc. The company estimated it reached around a million fourth- to sixth-graders a year with this program. Wham-O's major competition in the mass market came from Imperial Toy of Los Angeles, which sold a variety of lightweight discs at many of the same outlets as Wham-O.

Despite a growing variety of competition, Frisbee discs still reigned supreme over the market the product created. And with a name that was commonly used to describe any flying disc, the Frisbee brand's descent from its lofty market position did not seem imminent at any time in the near future.

Further Reading:

''After the Frisbee,'' *Forbes,* June 4, 1984, p. 167.

Griswold, Wesley S., ''Can You Invent a Million-Dollar Fad?'' *Popular Science,* January 1966, p. 78.

O'Rourke, P. J., ''Play It Where It Lays,'' *New York Times Magazine,* June 12, 1977, p. 25.

Schwartz, Judith, ''Frisbee Fights an Air War,'' *Adweek's Marketing Week,* September 16, 1991, p. 20.

''Ultimate Frisbee,'' *Time,* May 26, 1975, p. 44.

—Maura Troester

FUJI®

Fuji Photo Film Co., Ltd., along with its subsidiary Fuji Photo Film U.S.A., Inc., is the world's second-largest and Japan's largest producer of photosensitized materials, which include photographic film and paper. Fuji categorizes its products into four broad imaging and information (I&I) categories targeted to different end-use markets—for consumers, professionals, and commercial/diagnostic users. Fuji's consumer products are characterized as Amusement I&I, because they provide "image capturing and viewing pleasures." The products encompass various photographic and audiovisual experiences, such as cameras, color photographic film, black and white film, audiocassette tapes, videotapes, floppy disks, computer cartridge tapes, and 8mm camcorders. Consumers can also use some of the products classified for the commercial market, such as color copiers.

Throughout the years, Fuji has used its technical expertise to develop innovative consumer products. By upgrading products as technology evolves, Fuji has produced products that offer better performance than that offered by competitors, including films that are faster and provide better, sharper color and cameras that are easier and more convenient to use. The company's experience with the chemical technology, which is the basis of photographic science, has enabled it to develop other types of information recording systems as well, including videotapes and audiotapes.

The Fuji name has also been associated with highly developed marketing strategies, reflected by corporate divisions created to handle sales and marketing for specific types of products. The first direct sales and marketing division of the company was formed in the United States in 1971 and called the Consumer Products Division. In 1974, the Magnetic Products Division was formed to market magnetic tape products. In 1983, the Computer Media Division was formed to market floppy disks. In addition, Fuji maintains a Technical Communications Center in Hollywood to display new products, coordinate market research, and offer follow-up services such as training in the use of the company's products.

More than anything else, Fuji's sponsorship of sports events has made the Fuji brand name familiar to millions of TV viewers around the world. The company's photo films and/or videotapes were officially designated for use at such events as the Summer and Winter Olympics, track and swimming meets, and tennis, soccer, baseball, and football matches.

Brand Development

The Fuji Photo Film Co. began operations in Japan in 1934 with the manufacture of a 35mm motion picture film meant for use by professionals. Its first consumer product was a black-and-white still film introduced two years later. In 1948, the company introduced its first color film. Many Fuji brand products were first marketed in Japan and then introduced in the United States. Fuji introduced some 10 new products in the decade of the 1960s alone. In 1960, Fuji introduced its first magnetic tape product, the audiocassette tape. In this period, an amateur film system compatible with the C-22 processing system, then in use for Kodak films, was developed. Prior to that time, Fuji sold its own, noncompatible film, chemicals, and equipment in Japan.

Fuji's product development quickened in the 1970s, when the company introduced more than 40 new products. In 1970, Fuji debuted its first completely compatible color print film in the U.S. market, called Fujicolor N-100, and its first single-lens reflex (SLR) camera, the ST-701. In 1972, Fuji Color Paper was first marketed. Also in the 1970s, Fuji introduced the world's first SLR with LED exposure readout, the ST-801. A later model was called the ST-901. During this period, Fuji also marketed the AZ-1 SLR camera with standard zoom lens. In 1974, Fuji became the first film company to follow Kodak's new C-41 color print film process by introducing Fujicolor F-11 film. In 1976, the company introduced the world's first high speed color print film, Fujicolor F-11 400. In 1977, Japan's first 8-inch floppy disk was developed, and in 1978, Fuji VHS and beta videocassettes debuted.

It was during the decade of the 1980s, however, that Fuji's pace of product development quickened even further and the company introduced a total of 246 products, almost triple the production of the previous decade. In the photographic market, Fuji launched a new AX line of SLR cameras, the world's first drop-in-load 35mm cameras, the DL-20 and DL-100 (1983), and the first dual lens autofocus camera (1985), which was later ranked number one by Consumer Reports. The company also introduced several new audiocassette and videocassette products: L-750 videocassettes (1981), Super HG videocassettes and FR audiocassettes (1982), Super XG, Super HG and Super HG Hi-Fi videocassettes (1984), Super Metallix 8mm videotape (1985), and improved Super HG and Super HG Hi-Fi videocassettes and FRI Super and FRII Super audiocassettes (1986).

AT A GLANCE

Fuji brand of photographic film and cameras trace their origin to the Fuji Photo Film Co., Ltd., founded by Mokichi Morita in Japan in 1934; first U.S. office established, 1958; Fuji Photo Film U.S.A., Inc., formed as the North American subsidiary of Tokyo, Japan-based Fuji Photo Film Co., Ltd., 1965.

Performance: *Market share*—25% of 35mm film category; 20% of single-use camera category. *Sales*—$10.16 billion worldwide consolidated sales (1993).

Major competitor: Cameras: Kodak, Minolta, Polaroid, and Vivitar; film: Kodak.

Advertising: *Agency*—Riney, Angotti & Hedge, New York, NY, 1989—. *Major campaign*—"Why are you taking pictures with the same old film? Try Fujicolor Super G film, because your pictures should be nostalgic. Your film shouldn't."

Addresses: *Parent company*—Fuji Photo Film U.S.A., Inc., 555 Taxter Road, Elmsford, NY 10523; phone: (914) 789-8100; fax: (914) 682-4955. *Ultimate parent company*—Fuji Photo Film Co., Ltd., 26-30 Nishiazabu 2-chrome, Minato-ku, Tokyo 26, Japan; phone: (03) 3406-2111.

Also in 1986, Fuji introduced a revolutionary new product, a single-use camera called Fujicolor QuickSnap. The Fuji innovation ushered in a new era of "film with lens" which provided consumers with optimum convenience and ease of use. Fuji followed its Quicksnap camera with the world's first 35mm one-time use camera. The next year in 1988, Fuji provided this camera with a flash. In 1987, the company introduced MD2HD colored floppy disks.

More film, camera, and disk introductions followed in the latter part of the decade. In 1989, Fujicolor Reala became the first film to reproduce colors as they are seen by the human eye. In this year, Super HG 200 and 400, high speed films with the clarity of a 100 speed film, were first marketed. New cameras, from the top-of-the-line Discovery 2000 to the base model FZ-5, debuted. The world's first 2-inch floppy disk and metal 3 1/2-inch floppy disk were introduced. The three-and-a-half-inch floppy disks were manufactured in a joint partnership with BASF Corp. at a factory in Bedford, Massachussets.

Fuji continued to introduce new and upgraded products in the 1990s. A total of eight cameras were introduced in 1990. One model had the capability to take both standard and panoramic shots on the same roll of film when a switch was flicked, while later models had a multifunctional unit with a zoom lens.

Upgraded color print films in the Fujicolor Super G series of ISO 100, 200, and 400 films were launched in 1993. The Super G series incorporated three proprietary technologies that produced very high quality film. Super Fine Grain technology enabled Fuji to reduce the grain volume by 50 percent compared with previous Fujicolor print films. The result was that very fine-textured images were possible even with the high-speed ISO 200 and 400 films. A second technique, SuperConcerted technology, facilitated delicate control of the many chemical reactions taking place within the film, thereby producing considerably sharper images. The third technology was Super Composite Coupler that enhanced color saturation.

Fuji applied its technological expertise to videotapes as well. Hi8 Super DC 8mm videotape was developed by applying an advanced metal super-thin coating technique which offered high output, fine picture quality, and consistently high performance through an extended life. Innovations were also added to the Quicksnap line, which included built-in flash, a panoramic lens, a telephoto lens, and waterproofing.

In 1993, Fuji brought out two more compact models, the Discovery 80 Plus and DL-25 Plus line, which featured drop-in loading capability. Fuji also added the Plus 3 Series to the QuickSnap film-with-lens single-use cameras. The series was able to take three extra shots per standard-length roll of film. This new series, which replaced the original QuickSnap series, was lighter, smaller and used more reusable and recyclable parts than other film-with-lens units. The Plus 3 series was 20 percent smaller in volume than the original Quicksnap line.

Advertising and Marketing

Fuji utilized several strategies to help consumers become acquainted with the Fuji brand name. In 1980, Fuji changed its logo from the Fuji Film ellipse to a stylized Fuji arrow. To make the brand even more recognizable, the company introduced the Fuji blimp in 1984. Two years later, Fuji debuted its worldwide corporate slogan, "Imaging & Information," which was meant to symbolize the company's commitment to the future of the imaging industry.

Shifting product emphasis has been another marketing strategy. From July 1990 to January 1992, Fuji ran a promotion, "Quality Above the Rest," which was meant to remind consumers that Fuji made photo film, floppy disks, blank audio and video tapes, cameras, color copiers, and photofinishing supplies. In addition, a high quality blank audiotape, called Extraslim, sported new packaging that took up nearly 20 percent less space than conventional blank tapes. Advertising for audiotape was targeted to 18- to 24-year-olds.

Fuji and Sports Events

Sports lovers around the world know the Fuji name from the company's sponsorship and promotions of national and international sports events. In 1981, Fuji became the "Official Film" of the NBA. In the same year, the company received designation as an Official Sponsor of the 1984 Los Angeles Olympics as well as for the U.S. Olympic Team. The first Olympians to become members of the Fuji Sales Team were track stars Wilma Rudolph and Frank Shorter.

In 1983, Fuji became the "Official Tape" of the NBA, and Olympic stars Don Schollander, Ann Meyers, and Jim Ryun were added to the sales team. In 1986, Fuji became "Official Sponsor" of major league baseball. The next year baseball giant Mickey Mantle became a spokesman for Fuji's Baseball Sponsorship. In 1988, Fuji videotape was selected by ABC-TV for use on broadcasts of the National Political Conventions and Winter Olympics.

Sports promotions continued in the 1990s with Fuji's sponsorship of International Amateur Athletic Federation World Athletic Series, which led up to the ultimate track and field event, the IAAF World Championships in Athletics. Fuji also sponsored the U.S. Swimming Federation and U.S. Track and Field Team and signed tennis stars Stefan Edberg and Gabriela Sabatini as spokespersons.

Further recognition for the quality of Fuji products occurred when Fuji became the "Official Film, Magnetic Tape, and Computer Media" of the U.S. Open Tennis Championships, the "Official Film" of U.S. Space Camp and The Space & Rocket Center, and the "Official Videotape" of the National Football League. At the Barcelona Olympic Games in 1992, Fuji provided a full range of high-quality photofinishing services for the press.

Fuji was to be a cosponsor of the 1994 World Cup USA soccer tournament, and in the summer of 1993, the company began to promote the event with a multilevel campaign. Called "Kids in Gear," the program allowed individual children or a team to redeem proofs-of-purchase from Fuji products for various soccer-related items. The program was supported by ads in soccer publications.

Since clean air and water are necessary elements in the manufacture of photosensitive materials, Fuji's stated mission is to protect the natural environment. The corporate slogan embodied its philosophy, "Green Fujifilm Treasures the Green Earth." Fuji's goal is to protect the environment from the earliest product development stages. For example, there is a network among photofinishing labs for the recycling of the Quicksnap products. In addition, the company develops processing chemicals that can be used with lower rates of replenishment and disposal.

Performance and the Economy

Fuji's global sales and distribution network includes 32 consolidated subsidiaries for manufacture and distribution. They are located in the United States, Canada, Brazil, in eight European countries, in seven Asian nations besides Japan, and in Australia. In addition, Fuji has seven principal factories and six research labs in Japan. There are also Technical Communications Centers based in Tokyo, Dusseldorf, and Singapore.

In addition to photographic products for consumers, Fuji makes products for professional and commercial photography, electronic imaging, cinematography, micrographics, reprographics, graphic arts, medical diagnosis, broadcasting, and office automation. Fuji won many citations and awards in Japan and the United States for its imaging products, including an Academy Award for its motion picture film and an Emmy for its videotape. Fuji also operates 17 wholesale photofinishing labs located across the United States.

Many of Fuji's products are so-called entertainment or luxury products, and thus experience diminished sales during slow economic times. Such was the case during the recession of the late 1980s and early 1990s, when the company reported slower demand for its products, and slow or negative growth in sales. Fuji's history of quality, innovative products is expected to continue, however, as it uses existing and new technology to develop products that consumers find creative and convenient.

Further Reading:

Davis, Riccardo A., "Kodak, Fuji Focus on Summertime Promos for Kids," *Advertising Age,* March 15, 1993, p. 36.

Fuji Photo Film Co., Ltd., Annual Report, Tokyo, Japan: Fuji Photo Film Co., Ltd., 1992.

"Fuji: Products and Promos Lead to Success," *Dealerscope Merchandising,* January 1991, pp. 100–102.

Additional information provided by Fuji Photo Film U.S.A., Inc.

—Dorothy Kroll

G.I. JOE®

G.I. Joe is the most successful action figure of all time. Introduced in 1964 by Hassenfeld Brothers—later to become Hasbro, Inc.—it became the best-selling toy in the United States in the mid-1960s. The popularity of the military-style action figure waned in the late 1960s, however, as the American public grew disenchanted with the Vietnam War, but it grew popular again in the 1970s. The rising cost of plastic finally forced Hasbro to drop G.I. Joe in 1979. The action figure was revived with an expanded line of paramilitary accessories three years later, and G.I. Joe again became one of the most popular toys in the United States. According to Hasbro, more than 230 million G.I. Joe action figures and 110 million G.I. Joe vehicles were sold between 1964 and 1993.

A Doll for Boys

In 1962 independent toy designer Stanley Weston approached Hassenfeld Brothers, a Pawtucket, Rhode Island-based manufacturer of pencils and toys, and suggested an action figure based on "The Lieutenant," a television show about a marine. Mattel Inc. had introduced the highly successful Barbie doll in 1959, and Weston believed that an action figure for boys could also tap into the market for accessories that made Barbie so profitable.

Don Levine, then director of product development at Hassenfeld, liked the concept, but he hesitated to base the figure on a television show that could be canceled at any time. He was even more uncertain after watching clips of the show and realizing that it was not an action/adventure program for children but a drama for adults. Then in 1963 Levine spotted a sculptor's mannequin in the window of an art supply store. The wooden figure had fully articulated joints so it could be posed realistically. Levine purchased a dozen mannequins and had designers at Hassenfeld dress them in military uniforms, giving birth to the basic concept of G.I. Joe.

Levine set about convincing Hassenfeld executives that he could sell a doll for boys. He recalled later, "Everyone kept telling us, 'You guys are crazy; a boy will never play with a doll.' " Levine persisted and was eventually authorized to spend $30,000 to develop a prototype. Weston was paid $100,000 for the original idea.

Naming G.I. Joe

Levine had Hassenfeld's creative department design figures made of high-impact polystyrene plastic. Ball joints and connector studs allowed the figures to be posed like the sculptor's mannequin. The figures—which stood 11½ inches tall, the same as Barbie—were held together with elastic bands. The heads were made of a polyvinyl chloride (PVC) plastic. The public relations department at Hassenfeld would later claim that the face was a composite of 26 Congressional Medal of Honor winners, but that was pure fantasy. The face was the work of Phil Krackowski, an artist with Hassenfeld. Levine suggested the scar because "there was no other way to trademark the human body."

Levine planned to introduce four action figures, one for each branch of the military—Army, Navy, Air Force, and Marines. He also planned to give them names: Salty the Sailor, Ace the Pilot, Rocky the Marine, and a fourth that he later forgot. The advertising agency, Fred Bruns, convinced him otherwise. Levine recalled, "They told me that it was like shooting buckshot to use that many names. They said, 'You guys need a target and one direct hit.' " Sometime later Levine turned on the television to watch the 1945 movie *The Story of G.I. Joe.* The action figure had a name.

G.I. Joe was then the name of a candy bar and had been the name of a comic book series published by Ziff Davis Company from 1951 through 1956, but it had not been registered by anyone in the toy industry. Levine said, "It was as if the gods were looking down on us." Hassenfeld eventually registered the name in more than 30 countries.

Product Launch

Levine then invited ten major buyers to New York to preview the action figure, which almost ended G.I. Joe's career before it began. Fredric C. Behling, then associate marketing director for Hassenfeld, recalled, "They said that we were trying to make a doll for boys, and everybody knew that boys do not play with dolls. We figured that boys do play with soldiers, but the buyers balked at that, too." Despite the response, Merrill Hassenfeld, then president of the company founded by his father and two uncles in 1923, decided to proceed with the project. He would later be inducted into the Toy Manufacturers Hall of Fame for the creation of G.I. Joe.

The next hurdle was the annual American International Toy Fair in February 1964. To head off complaints that it was a "doll for boys," Hassenfeld spent $25,000 to create a sales film that portrayed G.I. Joe as a "fighting man." Again the response was less than enthusiastic, but buyers at the toy show agreed to pur-

AT A GLANCE

G.I. Joe brand of action figure introduced in 1964 by Hassenfeld Brothers, Inc.; company name changed to Hasbro Industries, Inc., in 1968; brand discontinued in 1978 but revived in 1982; company name changed to Hasbro Bradley, Inc., with the purchase of Milton Bradley, Inc., in 1984; name changed to Hasbro, Inc., in 1985.

Advertising: *Agency*—Griffin Bacal, Inc., New York, NY.

Addresses: *Parent company*—Hasbro, Inc., 1027 Newport Avenue, Pawtucket, R.I. 02862; phone: (401) 431-8697.

chase a small supply of the figures. Salesmen were instructed never to refer to G.I. Joe as a doll. It was an "action figure."

The first G.I. Joe action figures went on sale in New York that August. Hassenfeld supported the product launch with an award-winning commercial on a local television channel that included a catchy jingle sung to the tune of "The Caissons Go Rolling Along"—"G.I. Joe, G.I. Joe, fighting man from head to toe. On the land, on the sea, in the air." The figures sold out within a week.

Hassenfeld then shifted its commercials to the NBC network, and the success was repeated nationwide. According to Marvin Kaye, author of *A Toy Is Born,* "Soon everywhere the doll appeared, little boys welcomed it with outstretched arms." Jeff Kilian and Charles Griffith, authors of *Tomart's Price Guide to G.I. Joe Collectibles,* noted, however, that sales were weaker in the South, where feelings about boys playing with dolls were apparently stronger. Nevertheless, the entire 1964 production run was sold out. Sales totaled nearly $17 million.

By the end of 1965 more than 100,000 children had paid 50 cents to enroll in the G.I. Joe Club, organized by Hassenfeld in December 1964. They received a membership certificate, an iron-on G.I. Joe patch, a dog tag and chain, and a subscription to *Command Post News,* a newsletter that kept them informed about G.I. Joe's activities and all the new accessories. Sales in 1965 topped $36 million, helped along by the introduction of an African-American Action Soldier (at first available only in Northern cities) and a jeep scaled to fit G.I. Joe. The jeep came with a battery-operated searchlight and spring-activated recoilless rifle that fired miniature rocket shells.

Over the next three years Hassenfeld sold nearly $100 million worth of G.I. Joe paraphernalia, making it the best-selling toy in the United States. Merrill Hassenfeld told *Time* in 1966, "Once a kid gets Joe his parents are hooked."

Original G.I. Joe

Most collectors considered the original action figures, in production from 1964 to 1976, to be the real G.I. Joe. The Action Marine sold best, followed by the Action Soldier. Behling later recalled, "It was evident that the most popular G.I. Joes were the more militant ones." It was also easier for young boys to engage the marines and soldiers in imaginary battles. As Kilian and Griffith noted, "The Action Sailor . . . was kind of landlocked unless Mom gave you permission to make a big mess in the bathroom."

In 1966 Hassenfeld introduced a Special Forces action figure dressed in the same type of jungle uniform worn by John Wayne in the movie "The Green Beret." They company also introduced the "Action Soldiers of the World," a series of World War II soldiers equipped with uniforms and weapons representing six different nationalities: German Storm Trooper, Russian Infantryman, French Resistance Fighter, British Commando, Australian Jungle Fighter, and Imperial Japanese Soldier. (Hassenfeld's Canadian subsidiary produced a Mountie and a Canadian Commando.) Technically, these were not G.I. Joes since the trademark was not expanded to encompass the entire line of action figures until 1969, but they used the same size body with different heads. The European, Canadian, and Australian soldiers had a thinner head without the characteristic G.I. Joe scar. The Japanese soldier had a more rounded head with slanted eyes.

In 1967 the company, by then known as Hasbro Industries, added a talking doll to its line of G.I. Joe action figures. Pulling a tiny "dog tag" in the figure's chest would elicit commands, such as "Man the machine guns," "Hit the dirt," or "Scramble the fighter pilots." Merrill Hassenfeld told *Newsweek* the talking figures were "a toy soldier grown up and made more true to life." That same year Hassenfeld unveiled a G.I. Nurse, which came with crutches, plasma, and splints to tend to the wounded G.I. Joes. The nurse, however, was a flop.

G.I. Joe Adventure Team

When G.I. Joe was introduced in 1964, there were about 16,000 American "advisers" in Vietnam. Less than a year later President Lyndon B. Johnson had committed more than 60,000 American ground troops to Vietnam, and by 1969 there were more than half a million Americans fighting in Southeast Asia. As American involvement in Vietnam deepened, there was an antiwar backlash that virtually destroyed the market for war toys in the United States. Author Kaye says Vietnam was "probably the first war in history which caused large numbers of children to be denied war toys by their parents."

Sales of G.I. Joe action figures and accessories, which accounted for as much as 65 percent of Hasbro's revenues, plummeted in the late 1960s, and inventory began to pile up in Hasbro's Pawtucket warehouse. Merrill Hassenfeld remembered: "In marketing terms, G.I. Joe desperately needed repositioning. Parents had to view him as something more than a military figure, or else we'd face the inevitable—his retirement from the line."

To rescue G.I. Joe, Hasbro repackaged the action figures in 1970 as "The Adventures of G.I. Joe" and later as the "G.I. Joe Adventure Team." Instead of soldiers, the G.I. Joe action figures were outfitted as adventurers in search of fame and fortune and included a frogman, test pilot, jungle explorer, fire fighter, deep-sea diver, and astronaut. Hasbro also packaged various adventures for its decommissioned hero. Each G.I. Joe Adventures kit—with such titles as "Peril of the Raging Inferno," "Secret Mission to Spy Island," and "Capture of the Pygmy Gorilla"—came with a full-color G.I. Joe comic book and all the paraphernalia children would need to recreate the comic-book adventure using their own G.I. Joe action figures.

According to Behling, "At first, the idea was only moderately successful. We had to work through the old inventory, altering it to fit the new look of the toy, [and] image is a hard thing to change. Part of the problem was the military sounding name. But we could not change that, because some buyers would not have bought the new toy without the old name." By 1972 G.I. Joe was again one of the best-selling toys in the United States. More than a million G.I. Joe adventure figures were sold in 1975. That year Hasbro added two superhuman characters to the G.I. Joe Action Team—the bionic "Mike Power, Atomic Man" and "Bullet Man"—which came with their own adventure kits. "The Intruders," aliens from another world and the G.I. Joe Adventure Team's arch enemies, were introduced in 1976.

Super Joe

In 1977 the rising cost of petroleum, used in making plastic, forced Hasbro to discontinue the elaborate 12-inch G.I. Joe action figures. They were replaced by "Super Joe" 8-inch molded adventure figures and otherworldly creatures, such as "GOR, King of the Terrons." Kilian and Griffith suggested, "The line was more fantasy oriented, a good sign the toy designers were out of ideas. When famous characters lower themselves to battling dinosaurs, extinction is never far behind." Super Joe also faced the onslaught of Star Wars action figures from Kenner Products. Super Joe was discontinued in 1978.

G.I. Joe, A Real American Hero

When Super Joe died an ignominious death after just one year on the market, it apparently marked the end of the G.I. Joe trademark. You can't keep a good man down, however, and G.I. Joe was back by 1982.

The new G.I. Joe was again a military man, but this time he was defending the United States against the forces of "Cobra," a paramilitary terrorist organization. Cobra troops all wore masks to conceal their nationality and ethnic origin. It was acceptable to fight Russians, German storm troopers, and Imperial Japanese soldiers in the 1960s but not in the 1990s. Other than being in the military, "G.I. Joe, A Real American Hero" action figures bore little resemblance to the original G.I. Joe doll. The new G.I. Joe action figure was less than four inches tall and came with molded plastic uniforms instead of cloth. It also came with more accessories than ever before, including futuristic military vehicles and weapons.

The idea of bringing back G.I. Joe was credited to Bob Prupis, who was vice president of boy's toys for Hasbro. Prupis had played with the idea of bringing back G.I. Joe in 1979 but shelved the idea during the Iranian hostage crisis. Then in 1980 Prupis watched on television as the U.S. Olympic hockey team came from behind to upset the heavily favored Russians in the semifinals. Two days later the United States won the gold medal by beating Finland. Prupis recalled: "Everybody was cheering and hugging and congratulating each other . . . total strangers, for the most part, united in patriotism. That was the spirit I needed to capture to bring back G.I. Joe."

Prupis also wanted to create a line of toys that would be forever changing with new characters and new accessories. Kirk Bozigian, then a copywriter for Hasbro, suggested naming each new G.I. Joe action figure and creating a military-style dossier. By 1986 G.I. Joe was again the best-selling toy in the United States. By 1993 Hasbro had introduced more than 150 G.I. Joe figures and more than 200 vehicles, adventure kits, and accessory packs, making "G.I. Joe, A Real American Hero" the most extensive line of action figures ever produced.

Among the more unusual G.I. Joe figures was "The Fridge," a military look-alike to real-life football player William "The Refrigerator" Perry of the Chicago Bears. In 1991 Hasbro introduced the G.I. Joe Eco-Warriors to battle attempts by Cobra to destroy the Earth's environment, and in 1992 the company created the G.I. Joe Drug Elimination Force to fight drug dealers. Hasbro also licensed the G.I. Joe name for use on other children's products.

"G.I. Joe, A Real American Hero" was promoted by a cartoon show, action-packed commercials, and in the mid-1980s with its own G.I. Joe Action Stars cereal. Between 1988 and 1991 Hasbro sponsored the "G.I. Joe Search for Real American Heros," which recognized schoolchildren for heroic action. In 1993 Hasbro agreed to pay a $175,000 fine levied by the Federal Trade Commission, which said two of its G.I. Joe commercials were misleading.

G.I. Joe Hall of Fame

In 1991 Hasbro reintroduced the original G.I. Joe in an exclusive marketing arrangement with Target Stores. The 12-inch doll—named "Duke" after one of the early "G.I. Joe, An American Hero" characters—was outfitted in a cloth camouflage suit and armed with an electronic weapon that emitted light and sound. Duke was a resounding success. Most stores sold out of their original consignment within hours. Target eventually sold more than 107,000 of these Hall of Fame G.I. Joe figures. "Duke" was followed by "Stalker," "Cobra Commander," and "Snake Eyes" as Hasbro expanded the Hall of Fame series in 1992.

In 1993 a group calling itself the Barbie Liberation Organization made headlines by switching the voice boxes on about 300 talking Barbie dolls with those on G.I. Joe Hall of Fame figures. Boys unwrapping G.I. Joe figures on Christmas morning were shocked to hear the military men saying things like, "Want to go shopping?" The Barbie Liberation Organization said its goal was "to reveal and correct the problem of gender-based stereotyping in children's toys." A spokesman for Hasbro said the vandalism "will move us to have a good laugh and go on making more G.I. Joes. Barbie dolls and G.I. Joes are part of the American culture."

Further Reading:

Barmash, Isadore, "G.I. Joe Goes High-Tech," *New York Times*, March 19, 1987, p. D2.

"G.I. Joe Doll: Back in Action," *Newsweek*, February 1, 1982, p. 11.

"G.I. Joe Talks," *Newsweek*, March 13, 1967, p. 99.

Greenburg, Brigitte, "Barbie Gets Tough, Joe Goes Shopping: Gender Guerrillas Switch Dolls' Voices," *Seattle Times*, December 29, 1993, p. 1.

Javna, John, and Gordon Javna, *'60s!* New York: St. Martin's Press, 1988.

Kaye, Marvin, *A Toy Is Born*, New York: Stein and Day, 1973.

Kilian, Jeff, and Charles Griffith, *Tomart's Price Guide to G.I. Joe Collectibles*, Dayton, Ohio: Tomart Publications, 1993.

Pereira, Joseph, and Francine Schwadel, "Early G.I. Joe Is Called Back To Active Duty," *Wall Street Journal*, September 30, 1991, p. B1.

Rosenkrantz, Linda, "The Story of G.I. Joe," *Antiques & Collecting*, December 1989, p. 21.

Santelmo, Vincent, *The Complete Encyclopedia to G.I. Joe*, Iola, Wisconsin: Krause Publications, 1993.

"Toys: Front & Center," *Time*, December 23, 1966.

Walsh, Sharon, "Hasbro Settles Complaints with FTC on Toy Advertising," *Washington Post*, April 16, 1993, p. F1.

—Dean Boyer

GENERAL ELECTRIC® APPLIANCES

Manufactured by the research- and technology-oriented, multi-billion-dollar General Electric Company, General Electric (GE) appliances hold the top share of the market in refrigerators, dishwashers, and electric ranges; in washers and dryers, where Whirlpool is the leader, GE maintains a second-place market share in dryers and a third-place in washers. GE manufactures a host of other consumer and industrial products, including GE aircraft engines, GE industrial and power systems, GE lighting products, and GE plastics.

Brand Origins

General Electric founded the first industrial research laboratory in the United States in 1900. Located in Schenectady, New York, the GE Research Laboratory recruited Dr. Willis R. Whitney from the Massachusetts Institute of Technology as its director. Dr. Whitney worked with the German-born electrical engineer Charles P. Steinmetz to produce new materials, technologies, and products, including Steinmetz's mathematical systems for predicting the efficiency and power of alternating current equipment.

By 1907, General Electric marketed a line of heating and cooking devices to the general consumer. GE also sold these early appliances to specialty markets, such as ocean vessels. In 1922, Gerard Swope became president of GE and established the GE appliance and merchandise department. The company offered the first hermetically sealed refrigerator, the GE Monitor Top, in 1927. By 1928, there were 1.25 million refrigerators in households in the United States, whereas they did not even exist ten years prior to that. General Electric began manufacturing automatic washers in 1933. By 1934, electric ranges and refrigerators were popular items for American families; the Great Depression, however, made them scarce in American homes.

After World War II, GE implemented a large-scale expansion program to redirect the company's production and technological facilities to a peace-time economy and to respond to the enormous demand for consumer goods that had been cut short during the war. In 1946, the first post-war refrigerator was finished in Erie, Pennsylvania. The same year, a designer created a clay model for a new washing machine in Bridgeport, Connecticut. In order to decentralize the company's operations and hone in on the large home appliance market, in 1950 GE decided to construct Appliance Park, devoted exclusively to the manufacture of appliances, in Louisville, Kentucky.

Brand Development: Refrigerators

French technology developed the first small refrigerator marketed in the United States, the Audiffren machine invented by Abbé Audiffren, a French monk. General Electric marketed these refrigerators from 1911 to 1928. The machines used sulfur dioxide as a refrigerant; the chemical worked by cooling a salt brine that circulated in the refrigerator's system. GE's Fort Wayne Electric Works built the refrigerators, which sold for approximately $1,000 each, or twice the price of an automobile.

The GE Monitor Top was the first commercially successful refrigerator sold for residential use. In 1924 and 1925, a hermetically sealed refrigeration system had been introduced in GE's OC-2 model, but the model never rid itself of troublesome operational kinks. The engineer Christian Steenstrup redesigned this model by adding a new oscillating cylinder; the model then became the Monitor Top, featuring the first sealed compressor unit with forced feed lubrication and a coil mounted on top, allowing the unit to benefit from cooling by a natural draft. It was also the first all-steel-cabinet refrigerator, with improved durability that enabled GE to offer warranties of five years. In 1929, Steenstrup built a combination refrigerator featuring a frozen food storage space with its own evaporator and door, as well as a fresh food space with a separate cooling system and its own door.

A General Motors scientist, Thomas Midgely, Jr., discovered Freon 12 in 1928; the entire refrigeration industry made use of the refrigerant in the 1930s. In 1931 GE developed and produced "Thermocraft" insulation, a material that reduced the weight of insulators used in refrigerators from 12 pounds per cubic-foot to two and one-half pounds. In addition, it reduced heat leakage in refrigerator cabinets by 15 percent.

The GE "Shelvador" model, featuring the first adjustable shelves on a refrigerator, made its debut in 1933. The first real two-door refrigerator appeared in 1947, produced by the GE Erie factory, with a freezer compartment that maintained a temperature range of 0 to 10 degrees Fahrenheit, and a refrigerator section with a temperature of approximately 38 degrees Fahrenheit.

The refrigerator soon became the most popular household appliance in America, with over 90 percent of American homes featuring them by 1950. The 1950 GE "Spacemaker" fit in an area 64 inches high and 33 inches wide. The freezer was actually

AT A GLANCE

General Electric (GE) brand of appliances are marketed by the General Electric Company, formed in 1892 by the merger of Thomas Edison's Edison General Electric Company and the Thomson-Houston Company, led by Charles A. Coffin; General Electric marketed a line of consumer heating and cooking devices by 1907; Gerard Swope became president of GE in 1922 and established the GE appliance and merchandise department the same year.

Performance: *Market share*—25% of appliance category (as estimated by *Appliance Magazine,* 1991). *Sales*—$5.3 billion.

Major competitor: Whirlpool Corporation.

Advertising: *Agency*—BBDO, New York, NY, 1979-1993. *Major campaign*—Family-oriented television ads with a humorous tone that vary according to the product. The advertising theme umbrella for 13 GE divisions, including GE appliances, is "GE. We bring good things to life."

Addresses: *Parent company*—General Electric Company, 3135 Easton Turnpike, Fairfield, CT 06431; phone: (203) 373-2211.

an evaporator that maintained a temperature only slightly colder than that of the refrigerator section. In 1955, GE introduced its first wall refrigerators, as well as the first two-door, bottom-mount freezer-refrigerator combination.

In 1957, the most important product innovation was the functional, straight-line refrigerator—flat and square, rather than rounded and difficult to fit into kitchen spaces. Thanks to a forced draft refrigeration system, GE units no longer needed the condensers previously attached to the backs of the refrigerators, so they could be placed directly against walls. The early 1970s saw a major appliance industry boom, with 1973 as the best year for the industry up to that date. In 1974, GE produced a top-mount refrigerator with a dispenser for ice cubes and crushed ice. GE unveiled an extensive line of new refrigerators in 1985; one star product was a deluxe side-by-side model called "The Refreshment Center."

GE introduced a new refrigerator compressor in the mid-1980s without first completing extensive field testing. The compressors failed under heavy use, and the company was forced to implement a recall campaign that resulted in a $450-million pre-tax charge in 1988.

Brand Development: GE Ranges

In the early 1900s, several companies, including GE, were manufacturing small electrical cooking devices that usually consisted of a series of plugs or individual accessories. George A. Hughes invented the forerunner of the modern range in 1907; to convince American homemakers that the device actually worked, Hughes relied on cooking demonstrations first presented in electric utility offices all over Iowa. In 1918, the Edison Electric Appliance Company was formed from a merger of the Hughes Electric Heating Company, the Hotpoint Company, and the Heating Device Section of the General Electric Company. GE ranges, the Hotpoint-Hughes line, made use of the most desirable features of all three previous company lines.

In 1922, a Raleigh, North Carolina, utility executive ordered an as-yet unavailable and unheard-of range in the color white. Hotpoint quoted a price high enough, so management reasoned, to relieve the company from the burden of producing a new technology for a product it did not have. But the executive promptly agreed to pay the price, and Hotpoint soon thereafter delivered a white range. The newly developed technology involved ridding the metal of stress before applying the enamel.

In 1927, many gas ranges had already been converted to electricity. In 1928 and 1929, Hotpoint presented the first Calrod heating elements. Electric ranges had previously heated very slowly and the heating elements had a tendency to lose their effectiveness quickly. Calrod elements featured a protective sheathing for the resistance wire, allowing the elements to reach hotter temperatures and at the same time have a longer life. In 1934, the first Hotpoint cabinet model came on-line. In 1935, the ratio of gas to electric ranges was 13 to 1; by 1945, the ratio was 3 to 1.

In 1950, GE electric ranges had double ovens and "back splashers," featuring control panels and rotary switches. The names of the GE range lines, such as Stewardess, Airliner, and Stratoliner, reflected the newfound American fascination with air travel. In 1963, GE introduced the first self-cleaning oven, which heated to approximately 880 degrees during the cleaning cycle. The GE Americana range of 1964 featured both conventional and electronic microwave ovens.

By 1980, GE's range line emphasized energy efficiency. The "TimeMaker Range" offered both conventional and microwave cooking capabilities; the "Energy Saver" was a 30-inch free-standing range with a specially insulated oven to achieve a high degree of energy efficiency. Modern GE gas ranges did not appear until 1987, when the General Electric Company bought Roper Corporation in order to enter that market.

Brand Development: GE Laundry Equipment

The Hurley Machine Company of Chicago produced the first electrical washing machine, driven by chains, recognized as dangerous, and named "Thor," in 1906. In 1930, GE purchased laundry appliances from the Hurley Company to enter the market. By 1933, GE manufactured its own full line of electrical washing machines; GE also produced gasoline-engine-powered wringer-washers. Although GE added the Judelson clothes dryer to its line in 1934, because of the inadequacies of the model, the company sold only token numbers.

Washing machine technology advanced considerably in 1935 with the advent of a device invented by John W. Chamberlain that washed, rinsed, and extracted water from laundry in one operation. GE designed and manufactured the first completely automatic washing machine soon after World War II. By 1950, GE produced its own clothes dryers.

Washing machines in 1950 had limited flexibility and could hold only 10 pounds of clothes; the dryers of the time often left the clothes slightly wet. GE's 1962 washer offered considerably improved flexibility with the advent of the "Mini-Basket," a removable tub for small loads and delicate fabrics. In 1966, GE's 12-pound Filter-Flo washers had stainless steel wash trays with hot and cold water faucets on top for use in pre-treating clothes.

Brand Development: GE Dishwashers

In 1913, the first electric dishwasher was sold by its inventors, the Walker Brothers, for $120. GE bought out the Walker Brother's Company in 1930 and moved manufacturing operations to the Chicago Hotpoint factory, which produced the first GE dishwasher in 1932. Hotpoint presented the first front-loading, single-rack dishwasher in 1936. The 1939 model featured wash and rinse cycles, as well as a flush pre-rinse cycle. GE produced a dishwasher with a pump to remove water more efficiently in 1948.

Dishwashers gained acceptance in American households, however, only very slowly. Without company approval, a Louisville production manager implemented manufacture of the greatly improved Mobile Maid Portable Dishwasher in 1954 on the Appliance Park factory floor. The product was highly successful, soon winning public as well as company approval.

The GE Potscrubber dishwasher of 1974 promoted the Power Scrub Cycle, said to rid dishes of even heavily encrusted food. The models also featured the first GE Perma Tuf molded thermoplastics dishwasher tubs; because these one-piece tubs used fewer fabricated parts, they gave the machines longer life. In 1983, GE poured $39 million into Appliance Park's dishwasher factory, adding robotics technology to improve manufacturing efficiency.

GE Appliances introduced the Profile dishwasher in 1993. The model featured a SmartWash System with a large number of water paths for powerful, three-level wash action. It also offered increased loading flexibility, QuickClean controls, and a 25-percent reduction in water consumption over previous models, enabling it to meet 1994 federal government energy consumption standards.

Nineties Technological Requirements

According to Ric Manning, writing in a January 1993 Louisville *Courier-Journal,* the design of the washing machine remained basically the same from 1926, when the spinning tub replaced the wringer, to the early 1990s. Whereas ranges and refrigerators underwent constant technological advances, most manufacturers ignored their washing machines, relegating them to the basement of their priority lists, just as many customers relegated the machines to the basements in their homes and buildings.

Federal energy efficiency requirements for 1994 made technological improvements imperative in order to produce washers, dryers, and dishwashers that consumed less water and electricity. According to the Energy Department, in 1993 dishwashers, clothes washers, and dryers consumed almost 2 percent of the energy used in the United States. General Electric's laundry and dishwashing appliances needed few changes to meet the 1994 energy consumption requirements. Instead, the company's main challenge was to reduce its manufacturing costs, which were higher than those of its competitors.

Refrigerators also faced more stringent energy consumption requirements in 1993. Refrigerators and freezers were reported to use as much as 20 percent of some households' electricity in the early 1990s. The 1993 federal standards required 18 cubic-foot refrigerators to consume no more than 690 kilowatt hours of electricity per year, or an average electrical consumption no greater than that of a continuously operating 75-watt light bulb.

Refrigerators were also the subject of a hotly contested environmental debate that resulted in additional requirements for technological change. In the early 1990s, all refrigerator manufacturers used the efficient, long-lasting chemical chlorofluorocarbon 12, or CFC 12, as a refrigerant. The chemical worked by moving through a maze of tubes in vapor form, absorbing heat as it went. Compressors then condensed the vapor to make it hotter so that it would flow to cooler, outside air. Another chemical, chlorofluorocarbon 11, acted as the agent that puffed up the plastic foam insulating refrigerator walls. Both forms of CFC, however, were shown to cause damage to the earth's ozone layer. International agreements called for a stop to the manufacture of CFCs by the year 2000. Former United States President George Bush asked for a halt in their production by 1995.

In 1992, the chemical hydrofluorocarbon 134a, shown to have less effect on the ozone layer, was seen by chemical suppliers as a possible replacement. The question of whether or not suppliers could develop lubricants for refrigeration systems that would be compatible with the chemical, however, remained unsolved. A proposed substitute for CFC 11 was the insulator hydrochlorofluorocarbon 141, less effective and reported to have a tendency to corrode plastic refrigerator interiors. The possibility of using different plastics was under exploration.

Recent Performance and Future Growth

The highly competitive major appliance industry entered the 1980s on a downhill slide. Sales declined due to depressed housing starts, high mortgage rates, and inflation; in 1981, most retailers scaled back their inventories. In 1982, housing starts in the United States were at their lowest since World War II. Whereas most American manufacturers began to see declining sales in foreign markets, General Electric bucked the trend: GE exports increased from $1.9 billion in 1976 to approximately $4 billion in 1981. The company formed the General Electric Trading Company to market manufactured products for GE components.

In the early 1990s, appliance manufacturers in the United States faced the possibility of still more restrictive energy consumption standards. Although North American customers continued to prefer top-loading clothes washers, for example, in 1993 a proposal was already on the table that by 1999 manufacturers produce only front-loading, horizontal-axis washers that use less energy. If such proposals succeed, domestic appliance makers will have to overhaul their factories; an estimate by the Association of Home Appliance Manufacturers put the total costs of an overhaul of U.S. appliance factories at more than $1 billion.

Because GE Appliances is only one division of the global, technologically cutting-edge, financially powerful GE Company, the division could absorb the high costs of a manufacturing overhaul and new technological and environmental requirements much more easily than smaller competitors. GE itself might swallow some of its competitors before they bite the dust; in any case, GE should "bring good things to life" well beyond the twentieth century.

Further Reading:

Cortez, John P., "Appliances Set Emotional Appeals," *Advertising Age,* May 3, 1993, p. 44.

GE 1994 Calendar, Fairfield, CT: General Electric Company, 1994.

General Electric Company 1992 Annual Report, Fairfield, CT: General Electric Company, 1992.

Holusha, John, "The Refrigerator of the Future, for Better or Worse," *The New York Times,* August 30, 1992, sec. 3, p. 3.

Manning, Ric, "Appliance Math," *The Courier-Journal,* September 7, 1992, p. 1E.

Manning, "Energy Efficiency Retooling May Give Washer Makers Bath," *The Courier-Journal,* January 26, 1993.

Schiller, Zachary, "GE's Appliance Park: Rewire, or Pull the Plug?" *Business Week,* February 8, 1993, p. 30.

Ward, Joe, and Ric Manning, "1,500 Jobs at Risk as GE, Union Aim to Reverse Losses," *The Courier-Journal,* January 16, 1993, p. 1A.

A Walk Through the Park: The History of GE Appliances and Appliance Park, Louisville, KY: Elfun Historical Society, 1987.

—Dorothy Walton

GEO®

Like its more celebrated cousin Saturn, the Geo brand has come to represent the rediscovered flexibility in manufacturing and marketing of General Motors Corp. (GM). Created in 1988 and positioned in the subcompact and compact segments, Geo was a marque of GM's Chevrolet Motor Division. In the mid-1990s the brand encompassed four nameplates: Metro, Prizm, Storm, and Tracker. All featured "import-inspired" styling, were manufactured through cooperative ventures with Japanese automakers, and were categorized as subcompacts until the 1993 model year, when the remodeled Prizm grew into the compact segment.

Brand Origins

In 1987 Chevrolet held only 6.5 percent of the compact car category, and its primary entry, the Chevette, was getting clobbered by imports. While such Japanese carmakers as Honda Motor Co. and Toyota Motor Corporation had been earning a reputation for manufacturing high-quality small cars, Chevrolet had rushed its substandard Monza and Vega to the market. This shortcoming reflected badly on Chevrolet's overall sales; in 1987 the division relinquished its unit-sales leadership in passenger cars to Ford. The division realized that it could not allow its entry-level segment to languish because first-time buyers had the potential to trade up to bigger, more profitable Chevrolets.

In order to capitalize on the Japanese reputation for small-car design and manufacture, Chevrolet joined a growing number of American carmakers in joint ventures with importers. Ford had already started building Escorts in Mexico, Pontiac was manufacturing its LeMans in Korea, and General Motors itself already held substantial interests in Isuzu Motors and Suzuki Motor Co.

Chevrolet's first joint venture was with New United Motor Manufacturing Inc. (NUMMI), a division of Toyota Motor Corporation, to build the Nova in North America. A joint venture with Isuzu Motors to make the Spectrum overseas followed shortly thereafter, and Suzuki joined General Motors in a cooperative known as CAMI to build the Sprint. These collaborative cars, however, were undermined by Chevrolet's poor reputation for small-car manufacture, and the division's share of the subcompact segment slipped another point, to 5.4 percent, in 1988.

Chevrolet developed the Geo umbrella brand as a distinct identity for its entry-level offerings. The "worldly" Geo name and global logo represented the line's import-inspired styling, which had sleek, curved lines and a unified body. During the 1989 model year Chevrolet changed the names of the three models that initially constituted Geo's family of vehicles in order to disassociate them from their ill-fated predecessors. Thus, Nova became Prizm, Sprint became Metro, and Spectrum became Storm. NUMMI manufactured the Prizm in Fremont, California, the Storm was built by Isuzu in Japan, and the Metro was made by Suzuki in Japan and Canada.

Brand Target

Chevrolet described Geo's overall "import intender" or "uncommitted" target as first-time new-car buyers aged 18 to 34 years, mostly women, and regionally focused on the West Coast, in the Northeast, and in Chicago (all areas of high import ownership). The line's colors—ranging from an elegant Champagne for the Prizm to tropical-green metallic for the Metro, Storm, and Tracker—expressed Geo's "fun" side.

Each car in the Geo line was designed to appeal to a particular consumer. The Prizm sedan was aimed at the practical buyer and soon became Geo's best-selling car. It was targeted especially at women and came with an ergonomic interior and driver's side air bag. The sporty Storm coupe was the brand's second-best-seller. It was aimed at young singles or married couples who were looking for a sporty car with style and performance. The Metro subcompact (sometimes derisively called an "econobox") was designed for the economy-minded buyer. It became a fuel-economy leader for Chevrolet and all cars sold in the United States—from 1990 to 1993 the subcompact Metro XFi beat Honda's Civic VX hatchback for highest miles per gallon (mpg). In 1993 the Metro was rated at 53 mpg in the city and 58 mpg on the highway. The Tracker—a compact, four-wheel-drive, all-purpose vehicle—was introduced in 1989. Based on the Suzuki Samurai, the Tracker was two feet shorter than Chevrolet's S-10 Blazer but had more head and hip room and a lower base sticker price. Designers made sure to leave room for the custom graphics that were fleetingly popular in the early 1990s.

Overall, Geos were successfully targeted at single young women. Market research showed that by mid-1990 a whopping 80 percent of Geo Storm buyers were female, and in 1991 more than 70 percent of Prizms were sold to women.

AT A GLANCE

Geo brand of automobile launched in 1988 by General Motors' Chevrolet Motor Division in a joint venture with United Motor Manufacturing Inc. (NUMMI), Isuzu Motors, and Suzuki Motor Co.; the Geo nameplates were the Metro, Prizm, Storm, and Tracker; in 1993 the Metro's fuel-economy rating (53 mpg in the city, 58 mpg on the highway) was the highest of any car sold in the United States.

Major competitor: Ford Escort; also, Honda Civic, Toyota Corolla, Jeep Wrangler.

Advertising: *Agency*—Lintas Campbell Ewald, Warren, MI, 1988—. *Major campaign*—"Get to know Geo."

Addresses: *Parent company*—General Motors Corp., 30007 Van Dyke Avenue, Warren, MI 48090; phone: (313) 492-9188.

Advertising and Promotion

Geo promotion by Chevrolet's advertising agency—Lintas: Campbell-Ewald (Warren, Michigan)—incorporated both umbrella brand campaigns and targeted model strategies. Early print ads linked Geo with the dominant small-car manufacturers of the previous two decades, Toyota in the 1970s and Honda in the 1980s. Described as a "leveraged pull up," the ads encouraged prospective customers to "Get to Know Geo" in the 1990s just as they had gotten to know the Japanese automakers in previous decades. The ads appeared in newsweeklies and in such lifestyle-oriented magazines as *Rolling Stone*, *People*, *Cosmopolitan*, *Elle*, *Spin*, *Outside*, *Premiere*, and *Ski*.

Geo also utilized innovative incentive programs, including matching down payments to encourage its young customers. These inducements both stimulated sales and put equity in the vehicles at the time of purchase, thereby shortening the length of the purchase agreement and getting customers back into the showroom more quickly.

Television advertisements sought to position Geo as a fun line of cars, using the song "Getting to Know You" from "The King and I" in the 1991 model-year campaign. The ads aired with age-appropriate shows like *Roseanne*, *The Wonder Years*, *Friday Night Videos*, and *Saturday Night Live*, as well as Fox network shows, MTV, Nick at Night, and the USA network.

Commercial Success

During 1989, its first full model year, more than 165,000 Geos were sold. The brand "blew the doors off just about everybody else in the segment," according to a 1990 article in *Marketing & Media Decisions*. In calendar year 1990 Geo gained more than five percentage points in its small-car market share, capturing 12.8 percent of the segment. Sales increased 50 percent in the first eight months of 1990 alone. The brand racked up more than 270,000 unit sales during that model year, "exceeding most industry watchers' expectations" and boosting Chevrolet's share of the American passenger-car market to 15.4 percent.

"Green" Promotions

As a resurgence of environmental awareness took hold of the auto industry in the late 1980s and early 1990s, car manufacturers sought to ally themselves with the movement. In 1989 Geo marketers linked the brand to several tree-planting groups in California, including TreePeople. In a purported effort to help offset the air pollution produced by its cars, Geo started planting trees on the East Coast and in the West and Southwest for each car sold in 24 markets in those regions. Perhaps more important (in terms of promotion), the marketers sent their customers packets that included Geo tree-logo lapel pins and certificates from the U.S. Forest Service acknowledging that trees were planted in their names. According to Dan Pearlman, president and CEO of the Pearlman Group, the Los Angeles "cause marketing" agency that created the program, "This type of cause marketing not only boosts brand awareness and consideration but also added a perceived, tangible value to the product in the mind of consumers—in this case anywhere from $400 to $500." About 150,000 trees were planted in Geo's cooperative program with TreePeople from 1989 to 1993.

Some environmental groups, however, disparaged Geo's efforts as merely "cosmetic." In 1993 a representative of Greenpeace told the *Los Angeles Times* that it was "the ultimate green-wash." According to an estimate by Earth Island Institute, "to counteract the amount of carbon dioxide produced by a single Geo Metro, GM would have to plant 734 trees over the 10-year life of each Geo."

Even so, Geo continued to rely on its gas-sipping Metros as evidence of its environmental concern. The brand also worked with nonprofit environmental groups, providing advice and literature for community education, school programs, workshops, seminars, and conferences. Even the Sierra Club accepted ads touting the tree-planting program for publication in its national magazine, *Sierra*. In 1993 Geo announced that R134a refrigerant, a non-ozone-depleting CFC (chlorofluorocarbon) substitute, would be used in the air conditioners of all its models.

Product Development

The flagship Prizm was redesigned for the 1993 model year. Based on the Toyota Sprinter (a car offered in Japan but not in the United States), the Prizm's mechanics were identical to the Toyota Corolla, but the two cars did not share a single body panel. The 1993 Prizm was promoted to the compact segment by virtue of its longer wheelbase, which was translated into more head and leg room than either the Honda Civic or the Ford Escort. Engine, wind, and road noise were reduced through the use of new sound-deadening material. The Prizm also featured a standard driver's side air bag and optional antilock brakes.

Brand Outlook

Several factors would influence the future of GM's youngest brand. One was, simply, taste. Although the Geo Metro's sales rose about ten percent in 1993, one 1990s observer characterized the subcompact segment as "notoriously fickle." Popular models have disappeared from the top of the sales charts within a few months. "Cannibalism" was another unsavory possibility. In 1993 GM's Saturn pushed Prizm out of the ranks of the top five subcompacts, despite the latter's price advantage. Even so, as awareness of the Geo line in general and the Prizm in particular was anticipated to grow, many auto analysts expressed confidence that the new brand would endure.

Further Reading:

Bott, Jennifer, "'93 Prizm Targets Women," *Ward's Auto World*, August 1992, p. 58.

Bagot, Brian, ''Golly Geo,'' *Marketing & Media Decisions,* October 1990, pp. 47–51.

Bowens, Greg, ''Stickers That Won't Stick in Your Craw,'' *Business Week,* January 11, 1993, p. 134.

''Chevy Pulls Out Stops to Market Geo; Matches Down Payments to Woo Young,'' *Ward's Auto World,* May 1990, pp. 19, 21.

Cortez, John P., ''Geo Feeds Tree Program,'' *Advertising Age,* July 5, 1993, p. 12.

''The Heartbeat of America Is Imported,'' *The Economist,* September 8, 1990, p. 81.

Horovitz, Bruce, ''Honk If You Love the Environment,'' *Los Angeles Times,* March 23, 1993, pp. D1, D6.

Schuon, Marshall, ''From Geo, a Second-Generation Prizm,'' *The New York Times,* November 29, 1992, section 8, p. 12.

Serafin, Raymond, ''Cars to Get Green Light: Environmental Concerns Grow in Detroit,'' *Advertising Age,* September 3, 1990, pp. 3, 54.

Serafin, Raymond, ''Ford, Chevrolet Raise the Ad Ante in Race for No. 1,'' *Advertising Age,* September 24, 1990, pp. 3, 60.

—April S. Dougal

GIBSON®

For a century the Gibson brand name has denoted quality fretted string instruments. Orville Gibson, the company founder, first made Gibson mandolins and acoustic guitars; later, the firm expanded into electric guitars and guitar accessories. Gibson Guitar Corporation also manufactures and distributes bass guitars, synthesizers, drums, and amplifiers. In the early 1990s, the company began planning a centennial celebration to highlight 100 years of achievement.

Brand Origin and History

Orville H. Gibson began making fretted string instruments as a young man in the 1870s. By the turn of the century his innovative designs, including applying construction techniques and features from violins to mandolins and guitars, had become so well known that his name had become synonymous with excellence. In 1902 Gibson and a group of five businessmen joined together to capitalize on the name, forming the Gibson Mandolin-Guitar Manufacturing Co., Ltd., later named Gibson, Inc.

While mandolins dominated Gibson's production before 1920, and banjos predominated in the 1920s, guitars soon became their most important instrument. When the Chicago Musical Instrument Company (CMI) acquired Gibson in 1944, the Gibson name was already widely respected. CMI applied all of its business acumen and marketing skills to produce one of the largest fretted-instrument firms in the world.

Though Gibson had manufactured their first electric instruments in the 1930s, namely the Hawaiian steel string guitar, they did not come to emphasize or specialize in electric guitars for two more decades. As Paul Verna wrote in a special *Billboard* and *Musician* article about Gibson's anniversary, "The company's breakthrough came in 1952, when it cut a deal with guitarist extraordinaire and inventor Les Paul to mass-produce a solid-body electric guitar. Guitarist Paul had tried to sell the company the idea years before, but had been unceremoniously rebuffed. After Fender solid-body guitars began to become enormously popular, however, Gibson changed their mind and contacted the guitarist. The resulting model, the Les Paul, quickly became and has remained one of the company's best-selling guitars.

In 1969 CMI was taken over by ECL, an Ecuadorian company, and the Norlin Corporation was formed in 1970. Norlin's music division included not only Gibson guitars, but also Moog synthesizers and Lowrey organs and pianos. Norlin management was not terribly conducive to running a profitable music unit, and the division's profits fell continuously. In 1979 they were nearly one million dollars in the red. The U.S. economic recession of the early 1980s was particularly hard on the musical instrument industry. Norlin Chairman Norton Stevens told *Music Trades* in 1980 that "the impact of current forces on our music business is devastating. Unexpectedly higher interest rates and credit restrictions make it expensive for music dealers to stock instruments and hard for players to get the instruments they want." Corporate restructuring over the next few years, including the divestment of Norlin's Ecuadorian beer subsidiary and its electronics division, did not solve the problems. After Rooney Pace and Piezo Electric Products, Inc.'s hostile takeover in 1983, the new owners placed the Gibson music division up for sale. Finally in 1986, three entrepreneurs led by Henry Juszkiewicz bought Gibson and began turning the company's fate around.

Juszkiewicz brought to Gibson a unique balance of musical knowledge and business sense. He had spent much of his youth playing in a variety of garage bands and played guitar professionally in high school and college. In addition, he brought an MBA from Harvard and previous experience turning red accounts black. He applied his belief in product excellence, customer concern, and lean management to the company and started planning its future. He explained in *Music Trades* shortly after the sale that "with some basic restructuring, this will be a profitable operation within a very short time. After taking care of [some] internal areas, we plan to aggressively address the market."

Juszkiewicz's restructuring included centralizing management in the firm's Nashville plant; establishing a custom division; and in conjunction with the newly acquired Flatron Mandolin Company, forming a new flat-top acoustic division in Bozeman, Montana. Other acquisitions included the Original Musical Instrument Company of Huntington Beach, California, makers of the Dobro guitar, and the Oberheim Corporation, which manufactures synthesizers. Their successful new marketing strategies would include high-profile endorsements and an extensive reissue program as well as emphasis on product development.

Product Development

Gibson has a long history of innovation and experimentation. In the beginning, Orville Gibson spent much of his energy on new

AT A GLANCE

Gibson brand of fretted instruments founded in 1894 by Orville Gibson; incorporated in 1902; sold to Chicago Musical Instrument Company in 1944; taken over by ECL in 1969; name changed to Norlin Corporation in 1970; acquired by Rooney Pace and Piezo Electric Products, Inc. in 1983; sold to Henry Juszkiewicz et al. in 1986.

Performance: *Sales*—$29 million (1991).

Major competitor: Fender guitars; also, Martin guitars.

Advertising: *Agency*—Dera & Associates, Inc., New York, NY, and Laister Dickson Limited, London, England hired to help plan 1994 centennial celebration.

Addresses: *Parent company*—Gibson Guitar Corporation, 1818 Elm Hill Pike, Nashville, TN 37210; phone: (615) 871-4500.

designs. His early designs of differently fretted instruments incorporated structural elements from violin construction, such as carved tops and backs. He changed the shape of his mandolin bodies from almond-shaped to circular. Around the turn of the century, he began incorporating Art Nouveau principles of asymmetrical designs. He was constantly changing his instrumental designs to produce better looking and finer sounding instruments.

In 1922 Gibson introduced a guitar using the F-holes characteristic of violins; they also invented the truss rod to strengthen the neck of steel-string guitars. In 1926 they began production of a flat-top instrument and in 1935, the company's first electric Hawaiian steel guitar was added to the family. During the 1950s, under the management of the Chicago Musical Instrument Company, Gibson greatly expanded production of electric guitars. Beginning with the Les Paul model, they marketed several new instruments, including the Flying V, Explorer, and Firebird, all of which had unusual solid body shapes.

Gibson continued experimenting under Norlin's management, but sometimes had questionable results. When Norlin top brass wanted an instrument made out of plastic, a cheap construction material, designers made a guitar out of a refrigerator drawer. The current owner of the guitar, Buck Munger, proclaimed in *Guitar Player* that the instrument ''sounds like a dobro and is surely the strangest guitar Gibson ever built.''

When Juszkiewicz acquired Gibson in 1986, he made product development a high priority. He asserted in *Music Trades* that ''this is a company that was built on innovation. Features that are commonplace on guitars today, like the F-hole, the truss-rod, and the humbucking pickup, and renowned designs like the Les Paul, the ES Series, the Explorer, and the Flying V, to name a few, all represent Gibson innovations. My plan for this company is to create an environment that fosters this type of innovation.'' He added that ''Gibson has a unique heritage and very unique products. Our challenge is to offer the highest quality at reasonable prices and advance our heritage through innovation.''

One of the first things Juszkiewicz did as the new CEO, was to borrow expertise from his other company, Phi-Technologies. He explained to *Music Trades,* ''At Phi-Tech, our strength was in manufacturing devices that had unmatched reliability. The disciplines necessary for achieving this reliability are the same disciplines required to build a premium guitar of superior quality.'' Although he was going to keep the companies separate entities, he did believe that ''this factor makes for some interesting synergy between the two companies.'' One of the first developments under Juszkiewicz was the use of chromyte (balsa), a wood substance that is very light, but at the same time has excellent acoustical properties. One of the first instruments to be produced under his directorship was the 20/20 Bass, a uniquely shaped instrument with special features such as an adjustable brass nut to space the strings at the top of the neck.

While Gibson's name has long been most associated with guitars, they have, since the early years, also produced accessories, such as strings and straps. Under Juskiewicz's management, the brand has been slowly broadening their range of instruments and accessories. ''We have some very exciting new string products under development,'' he announced in *Music Trades,* ''and our accessory program will soon consist of a lot more than just guitar straps.''

Juszkiewicz has always seen product development as one part of his marketing strategy. ''Input from the market has to guide the product development effort,'' he affirmed in *Music Trades.* Following this principle, many of the new product lines were instituted to cover the price spectrum. Towards this end, they brought back the earlier Asian-made, low-price line of Epiphone guitars. ''Epiphone by Gibson'' offered a wide variety of styles and shapes in affordable price ranges. ''One of our primary goals,'' Juszkiewicz further theorized, ''is to ensure that all Gibson products are extremely profitable.''

Marketing

Juskiewicz's new marketing strategies took effect immediately upon his arrival, and all of the company's trademark guitars enjoyed a new life under him. Besides product development and reissue, he was committed to U.S.-based manufacturing, understanding the American preference for American products. The Gibson product line will always be manufactured in the United States,'' he declared in *Music Trades.* ''With the proper manufacturing approach and the commitment to succeed over the long term, we can effectively compete with any other guitar maker in the world.'' Customer service is also an important part of marketing. ''We exist to serve our customers, and I think that in the months to come Gibson dealers will benefit from a management that is more decisive and concerned with their special requirements.''

Artist endorsement has always played a vital role in musical instrument marketing strategy; in the late 1980s, Gibson embarked on an aggressive artist endorsement campaign. The variety of famous guitarists who have played Gibson instruments run the gamut from country musician Emmylou Harris to rock star Angus Young of the heavy-metal group AC/DC. Rock legend Chuck Berry played an ES-350T that is now on display in a collection of Berry memorabilia at the famed St. Louis restaurant, Blueberry Hill. Blues impresario B.B. King's Gibson Guitar, Lucille, spawned several offshoots including the B.B. King Standard and the B.B. King Custom. In fact, since Gibson began manufacturing guitars based on the designs of guitarist Les Paul, more than 50 different models have boasted the Les Paul name. Other artists using Gibson guitars include Chet Atkins, whose name appears on several guitar models, Travis Tritt, Johnny Cash, Stephen Stills, Pam Tillis, Pete Townshend, Neil Young, Peter Frampton, Paul McCartney, and Slash. Periodically Gibson creates a new guitar in honor of a well-known guitarist and presents it to the artist in a special ceremony. In 1990 Juszkiewicz handed jazz guitarist Herb Ellis the prototype for the new ES-175 hollow-body model.

1994 saw Gibson initiating a major international promotion. The year-long anniversary campaign, planned in part by the New York-based Dera & Associates, Inc. and Laister Dickson Limited in London, includes a wide variety of events and productions. The series of national and international concerts will be kicked off with an MTV special featuring heavy-metal favorites the Scorpions in Tokyo and will include a White House salute to be hosted by President Bill Clinton and First Lady Hilary Rodham Clinton; all proceeds will benefit the Nordoff-Robbins Music Therapy Foundation. Other plans include an historical film documentary, an interactive rock and roll museum to tour college campuses, syndicated radio shows and promotions, and the publication of a new book, *100 Years of Gibson.* The event, like the company, is international in scope.

Gibson and the World

Since the early 1900s Gibson has been global-minded; Norlin too, marketed products through their own international division. When Henry Juszkiewicz acquired the company, he turned a great deal of his energy towards improving Gibson's international connections and reputation. ''In competing internationally,'' he told *Music Trades,* ''we have to organize around our strengths and work to compensate for our weaknesses. We compete with companies from all over the world in a market that is very volatile. We have to be fast on our feet to meet the challenge.''

Gibson guitars can be found all over the world, and have distributors in Austria, Belgium, Denmark, England, Finland, France, Germany, Greece, Holland, Ireland, Italy, Norway, Portugal, Spain, Sweden, and Switzerland. The company also has operations in London, Hamburg, Tokyo, and Russia. Juszkiewicz told *Billboard's* Paul Verna that the company will always continue to expand and seek growth opportunities abroad.

Performance Appraisal and Future Growth

During the 1980s' economic recession in the United States, many music experts believed that MIDI computer music hardware and software would replace the electric guitar in consumer popularity; this view was somewhat substantiated by the drop in guitar sales during the late 1970s and early 1980s. The forecast proved erroneous, however, for guitar sales revived in the late 1980s and remained strong into the early 1990s. In that period, as market research showed acoustic guitars becoming more popular, Gibson enlarged its acoustic production, opening the Bozeman, Montana, plant dedicated to acoustic instruments with much success.

Gibson's financial security has rested on Juskiewicz's ability to read the market and judge new trends, which he seems to be able to do admirably. Juskiewicz's management and the changes he initiated when he took over have apparently been right on target. In his first two years as Gibson CEO, the company's revenues increased by approximately 75 percent each year. By fiscal year 1991, the company was making $29 million.

The 1994 centennial celebration demonstrates Gibson's belief in a strong financial outlook. ''Gibson finds its inspiration for the future in its 100-year-old tradition,'' stated a Gibson press release. ''As one of the prime forces on the international scene, Gibson still maintains the spirit of Orville Gibson—searching for improvements and innovations, striving to uphold the highest standard of quality.'' Hoping to become the ''largest musical purveyor in the world,'' Juszkiewicz summed it up best in a *Billboard* Music Group Advertising Supplement: ''Being around for 100 years and still kickin' butt is pretty cool.''

Further Reading:

''Gibson and Guild Merge,'' *Music Trades,* February 1988, p. 22.

''Gibson Celebrates Les Paul's 40th,'' *Music Trades,* October 1992, p. 73.

''Gibson Introduces 20/20 Bass,'' *Music Trades,* March 1987, p. 89.

Gibson: 100 Years, Billboard Music Group, 1994.

''Gibson Plans Acquisition of Financially Ailing Oberheim Corp,'' *Music Trades,* April 1990, p. 21.

''Gibson Returns to Private Ownership,'' *Music Trades,* February 1986, p. 28.

''Gibson to Handle Mapex, Ends Pat with Pearl,'' *Music Trades,* May 1992, p. 24.

Gruhn, George, ''Gibson's Amazing 'Florentine',,'' *Guitar Player,* February 1987, p. 52.

''The Guitar That Shook the World,'' *Guitar Player,* March 1988, p. 59.

''Innovation and Quality: Gibson's Manufacturing Strategy,'' *Music Trades,* August 1986.

Miller, Bryan, ''Saving Gibson Guitars From the Musical Scrap Heap,'' *New York Times,* March 13, 1994, p. 7.

''Norlin Reports Earning Decline in First Quarter,'' *Music Trades,* May 1980, p. 14.

''The Sale of Gibson,'' *Guitar Player,* April 1986, p. 8.

Wheeler, Tom, ''Experimental Gibson Unearthed,'' *Guitar Player,* January 1987, p. 12.

Additional information for this profile was supplied by Gibson Guitar Corporation.

—Robin Armstrong

GLIDDEN®

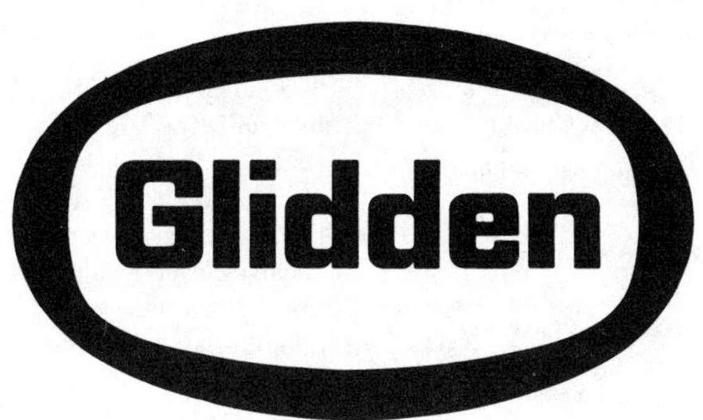

Glidden branded paints lead the American household consumer market, and as a subsidiary of the world's leading paint manufacturer, ICI, The Glidden Company is the United States' third-largest paint company. Glidden was responsible for bringing two of the paint industry's most important developments of the twentieth century to the consumer market.

In 1949 Glidden introduced Spred Satin, the first water-based paint that reduced the use of petroleum-based solvent in paint by 90 percent. In 1994 Glidden's new paint technology removed all petroleum solvent from paint and launched Spred 2000, the no-VOC (volatile organic compounds) paint. When VOCs enter the air, they can interact with nitrogen oxides (from sources like auto exhaust) in sunlight to form ground-level ozone, polluted air commonly called smog. Glidden branded paints are distributed through home improvement centers, leading retail chains, and traditional dealers. Much of the brand's success can be attributed to a combination of groundbreaking technological improvements and strong promotion and advertising.

Brand Origins

The brand was named for one of the company's founders, Francis Harrington Glidden. In 1875 Glidden founded a Cleveland varnish-making business with Levi Brackett and Thomas Bolles named Glidden, Brackett & Co. The business produced 1,000 gallons of varnish each week and made deliveries via horse and wagon. As partners retired over the years, the company's name went through several changes, settling in 1894 as The Glidden Varnish Company. By that time, the company produced a variety of industrial finishes for furniture, pianos, carriages, and wagons.

Before 1895, Glidden had concentrated on industrial finishes, but that year the company introduced Jap-A-Lac, a varnish for the consumer market that came in an array of 16 colors, from "dead black" to "malachite green." Despite competition within Cleveland from the formidable Sherwin-Williams, Jap-A-Lac became one of the better-known varnish brands when Glidden established a remarkable $60,000 advertising account for the product in 1903. The investment paid off: a 1904 ad reported that Jap-A-Lac had already sold $250,000.

Early advertisements focused on the economy and the "satisfaction of doing it yourself." Recognizing that women were the primary caretakers of home interiors, Glidden's Jap-A-Lac ads targeted them with depictions of homemakers finishing chairs, window casings, and other furnishings in *Ladies' Home Journal, Housekeeping Magazine,* and the *Delineator.* Varnish cans proclaimed that Jap-A-Lac "wears like iron" and was suitable for "everything of wood or metal." Ads warned against dealer substitutions, wherein paint salesmen would stock a limited amount of the branded product, but encouraged customers to buy a cheaper (and therefore higher margin) alternative.

In the early years of the twentieth century, Glidden expanded geographically into New York, Chicago, and St. Louis, then made its first international acquisition with the purchase of Toronto's Blackwell Varnish Company in 1910.

At 85 years-old, Francis Glidden sold the company to a former Sherwin-Williams director, Adrian D. Joyce, and his associates. Joyce became executive president of The Glidden Company and incorporated it in 1917, when it had annual sales of about $2 million. He dropped the "Varnish" from the company name in the hopes of broadening its product line to include, among other things, paint. Joyce was a master salesman, and his team of young executives expanded Glidden westward to San Francisco and southward to New Orleans, opening retail outlets in 40 cities. Soon, Jap-A-Lac "became the most famous paint trademark in the country," (if not the highest-selling) according to a 1959 *Printer's Ink* article.

Product Innovations

The Glidden name often dominated print advertisements, but the family of brands included Speed-Wall, Ripolin, Florenamel, Endurance House Paint, and Glidden Spar Varnish by 1932. By World War II, Glidden and its family of brands had clearly broken away from the plethora of small, local paint brands, but still sought a blockbuster product. In 1949, the introduction of Glidden Spred Satin, the first commercially successful latex paint, launched a new industry category.

Glidden's postwar development of water-based latex paint was based on decades of research into alternatives for petroleum solvents. The development began when The Glidden Company branched out into the soybean field in the 1930s, building a soybean oil extraction plant in Chicago in 1934. Soybean oil was used in the production of paint and linoleum. Glidden was one of only two American companies licensed to use a German process

AT A GLANCE

Glidden brand of paints founded in 1875 in Cleveland, Ohio, by Francis Harrington Glidden of Glidden, Brackett & Company; first consumer product was called Jap-A-Lac; company incorporated as The Glidden Company in 1917; merged with SCM Corporation in 1967; purchased by Hanson Trust PLC, then sold to ICI (Imperial Chemical Industries PLC) in 1986.

Performance: *Market share*—13.6% (top share) of consumer paint category (early 1990s).

Major competitor: The Sherwin-Williams Company's Sherwin-Williams and Dutch Boy brands.

Advertising: *Agency*—Meldrum & Fewsmith, Cleveland, OH, 1948—. *Major campaign*—Glidden Spred 2000 no-VOC paint, promoted in 1992-93 as "The Clean Air Choice."

Addresses: *Parent company*—The Glidden Company, 925 Euclid Avenue Cleveland, OH 44115; phone: (216) 344-8140; fax: (216) 344-8150. *Ultimate parent company*—ICI (Imperial Chemical Industries PLC), London, England.

for producing lecithin, a soybean oil byproduct used by paint manufacturers. By the mid-1940s, Glidden had developed a full line of soy-protein and water-based paints.

During the war, many manufacturers substituted casein, a milk derivative, for traditional oil-based solvents. But this inferior replacement gave alternative paints a bad reputation—they were easy to use, but had limited colors and poor durability. When traditional resources were restocked after the war, customers reverted to oil-based paints, but Glidden continued to work on a latex alternative. Researchers tried such newly-developed synthetic polymers as vinyl chloride, vinyl acetate, and acrylics, finally settling on butadiene-styrene. Glidden developed a gloss-finish enamel in 1946 and made the first batch of Spred Satin flat paint the following year.

Advertising Innovations

Spred Satin was field tested in major metropolitan markets like Cleveland, Detroit, and Buffalo in 1948, during Dwight Page Joyce's first year as president after succeeding his father. The new product was launched nationally in 1949 with a two-page color spread in the September issue of *Life* magazine headlined, "A new Wonder Paint almost beyond belief." The ad campaign included half-page coverage in *American Home, Better Homes & Gardens,* and *The Saturday Evening Post* extolling the virtues of Spred Satin: a quick-drying, waterproof finish that was both washable and durable.

In its first year of national distribution, 100,000 gallons of Spred Satin were sold. Sales of Spred Satin drove Glidden's sales to $188.61 million in 1950. The brand had launched a "latex revolution": Glidden alone sold 3.5 million gallons of the paint annually by 1951, and latex coatings went from only about 10 percent of paint industry volume to over 75 percent in the early 1990s.

In the early 1950s, Dwight Joyce suggested and led another unique promotional campaign for the new product. Top Glidden executives made department, hardware, and specialty store counter demonstrations, where they spread the paint, let it dry for 20 minutes while they extolled its virtues, and then wiped clean spilled mustard, ketchup, lipstick, and crayon to show it would do everything it was advertised to do. These "executive demonstration days" continued into the 1950s and turned customers into "impulse purchasers," according to accounts of the promotion programs.

Glidden spent $250,000 on another distinctive ad campaign in the late 1950s. The five-page gatefold insert was the largest paint ad ever carried in a national magazine, *The Saturday Evening Post.* It featured a half-page that was actually coated with the branded paint. consumers were invited to "Mark this page with smudges, even lipstick, and see how easily they wipe off with a few light strokes of a damp soapy cloth—even though the Spred Satin film on this paper is less than one-third as thick as a single coat applied on your walls." This campaign was coordinated with more "executive demonstration days."

After tackling the development and commercial introduction of this revolutionary product, Dwight Joyce set to work on Glidden's retail distribution. He expanded the Glidden brand's network of stores from 40 to 260, which helped boost its market share to about 5 percent, or $119 million annually. Joyce also shored up Glidden's retail distribution network in the 1950s with the purchase of

An early Glidden advertisement with the slogan "Everywhere on Everything."

several sales outlets and paint plants. In 1950, the company acquired general sales agent E. W. Colledge G.S.A., Inc., of Jacksonville, Florida. Mound City Paint & Color Co. in St. Louis, the Zapon industrial finishes business of Atlas Powder Co., and the domestic paint business of General Paint Corp. followed in close order. The General Paint acquisition included 21 retail branches and plants in Tulsa and Portland.

Glidden launched a new television campaign in 1965 in an effort to boost its fourth-place, 5-percent share of the paint market. The $500,000 television budget bought 55 spots on the NBC network's *Today* morning news and information program and *Tonight* evening talk show. The ads incorporated a money-back guarantee in the hopes that it would inspire customers to try Spred Satin.

Competition

During the post-war era, mass merchandisers started to use paint as a ''loss leader'' to establish their pricing position and lure customers. Sears, Roebuck & Co. used this technique to great advantage with its Weatherbeater line of paint. At the same time, alternative building products like aluminum siding, redwood, and glass, began a period of intense competition with paint. These two external forces converged with the saturation of the paint market to simultaneously restrict volume and margin. By the end of the 1960s, the Glidden Company had diversified into spices and chemicals to stabilize profits battered by market forces—although the brand still maintained its 5-percent share of the market, paint accounted for less than half of Glidden's sales.

The Glidden Company merged with SCM Corporation (formerly Smith-Corona Company) in 1967 after Glidden was approached (with varying levels of hostility) by Dallas' Greatamerica Corp. and General Aniline & Film of New York for takeover. SCM had broached the subject with Glidden in the past, but was forced into the role of ''white knight'' by Greatamerica's 40 percent tender offer.

At the time of the merger, Glidden's annual sales eclipsed SCM's by almost $100 million, at $364.2 million. Glidden was reorganized as the Glidden-Durkee division of SCM. Dwight Joyce stepped down that year, and Paul W. Neidhardt (a leader of Spred Satin's original marketing campaign) served as the company's chief management officer from 1968 to 1976. William D. Kinsell, Jr., another marketing executive, became president of Glidden in 1976; John S. Dumble succeeded Kinsell upon his 1984 retirement. In 1990, John R. Danzeisen assumed responsibility for the ICI Paints business in North America, including Glidden.

International Market

Historically, overseas trade has not contributed significantly to the U.S. paint market. This trend continued into the 1990s: exports generated only $696 million in 1991, and over half of that went to Canada and Mexico. Glidden's international activities reflect this national trend.

Glidden organized a subsidiary, Glidden International C.A., in Venezuela in 1955 to license, manufacture, and distribute the company's products—especially Spred Satin—outside the United States and Canada. By the end of the decade, Glidden's international group sold a complete line of enamels, paints, and stains on every continent of the world and in almost every nation. Unfortunately, the poor economic climate of the 1970s forced Glidden to pull out of Europe mid-decade. Its French subsidiary was liquidated in 1975, the German affiliate was disposed of in 1976, and the Italian company was sold in 1977. However, the division's Central and South American businesses enjoyed increasing sales and income despite currency fluctuations and import restrictions, and the company even invested $14 million in a three-million-gallon per year paint plant in Sao Paulo, Brazil, in the late 1970s.

During the mid-1980s, Glidden became enmeshed in a series of large-scale transactions involving two of the world's largest conglomerates, Hanson Trust PLC and ICI (Imperial Chemical Industries PLC). Hanson acquired SCM, then sold Glidden's American and Canadian operations to rival ICI for $580 million in 1986. The shift in ownership made Glidden part of the world's leading paint manufacturer, and gave ICI a top competitor in the U.S. do-it-yourself paint market. The addition of Glidden to ICI's American operations more than doubled that division's annual sales to $3 billion and increased ICI's corporate presence in the United States dramatically.

Competition in a Mature Market

By the late 1970s, Glidden had captured 10 percent of the American consumer paint market despite competition from 600 rivals. The branded paints still stood fourth among leading manufacturers, behind Sears, Roebuck & Co., Sherwin-Williams, and Pittsburgh Paint & Glass, but was number three in sales to contractors. From 1982 to 1986, Glidden's paint shipments grew 7 percent annually, or twice the U.S. industry average, as the brand began to capture an increased share of the market and eventually the number-three spot.

Reduced paint and solvent consumption and economic recession slowed the paint industry to an average growth of about 2 percent annually in the late 1980s. Rauch Associates, an industry analyst, predicted short-term growth to slow even further to 1.2 percent. These dismal figures inspired increased advertising spending in the early 1990s. In 1991, Glidden doubled its media budget to $12 million in the hopes of increasing its 13.6 percent share of the consumer market. Television ads by Cleveland's Meldrum & Fewsmith agency featured witty musical references like ''Whole Lotta Shakin' Goin' On'' and ''Stormy Weather,'' as well as National Football League tie-ins. The ads won the agency an award in 1993.

Glidden hoped to spur stagnant paint sales with new paint technology that contributed to a better environment after thorough market research using focus groups in the early 1990s. The trademarked slogan, ''The Clean Air Choice'' announced Spred 2000, a virtually odorless paint with no petroleum-based solvents or volatile organic compounds (VOCs). Organic solvents, the oils that liquefy many paints, have been blamed for some air pollution. As paint dries, the liquid portion evaporates. When the liquid is an organic solvent, volatile organic compounds are released. VOCs react with sunlight to contribute to smog. Spred 2000 was the first paint of its kind to be offered in the United States.

The innovation marked an important step in the paint industry toward more environmentally sensitive paints but was not hailed as a rescue from the paint business's doldrums. Some analysts criticized its limited range of colors and reduced durability, but Glidden supported the new product with a $4 million national network and spot campaign that started in June of 1992.

To address Spred 2000's limited color range, Glidden introduced Spred 2000 no-VOC tint base. It allows for up to one ounce of colorant to be added to the base, opening the product's color dimension to more than 460 variations of pastels and off-whites. An ounce introduces only seven to ten grams per liter of VOC to the tint base. This minimal amount of solvent does not rob the consumer of the benefits of no-petroleum-solvent odor and improved air quality.

Further Reading:

Alper, Joseph. "Glidden's Antitrust Secret Is Out," *Chemical Week,* June 15, 1988, p. 10.

Cooke, Stephanie. "ICI Wants to Be a Household Name in the U.S.," *Business Week,* September 1, 1986, p. 40.

Dunn, Don. "Color this Paint Green," *Business Week,* June 29, 1992, p. 130.

"Everybody Wants Glidden," *Chemical Week,* May 27, 1967, p. 22.

"Expand or Die," *Forbes,* November 15, 1967, p. 23.

Fitzgerald, Kate. "Flat Sales Spur High-Gloss Ad Plans," *Advertising Age,* May 6, 1991, p. 12.

Gibson, David W., "ICI Americas: Sales Up 100 percent in Three Years, with More Acquisitions to Come," *Chemical Week,* November 5, 1986, pp. 22–25.

"The Glidden Company," Cleveland: ICI Paints—North America, 1993.

"Glidden Paints 'Post' Inserts to Prove Point," *Advertising Age,* September 5, 1960, p. 10.

"Glidden's Flying Dwight Joyce: Paint and Spices for a World Market," *Printers' Ink,* March 27, 1959, pp. 48, 50, 52.

"Glidden's Golden Offer," *Sponsor,* March 29, 1965, pp. 44–45.

Kemizis, Paul, "Wait-and-See Stance Taken on Zero-VOC Architectural Paints," *Chemical Week,* October 14, 1992, pp. 52–53.

"Promise Redeemed?" *Forbes,* February 15, 1966, pp. 46–47.

Schulenburg, Fred, "Part IV: The House of Francis H. Glidden," *American Paint & Coatings Journal,* February 16, 1987, pp. 41–49.

"Strange Bedfellows?" *Financial World,* October 11, 1967, pp. 5, 22–23.

"Streamlining the Management at SCM," *Business Week,* February 21, 1977, pp. 96, 98.

"U.S. Paint Industry Faces Reduced Growth," *Modern Paint & Coatings,* May 1991, pp. 10–16.

Wical, Noel, "Exec Recalls Humble Start of Latex Revolution," *Advertising Age,* May 8, 1978, p. 62.

—April S. Dougal

GOODYEAR®

Goodyear brand tires, marketed by Goodyear Tire & Rubber Co., have dominated the global tire industry for three-quarters of a century. The Goodyear brand has remained a leader by introducing new products and using innovative marketing techniques. Goodyear lost the world market share lead to Michelin in 1990. In the early 1990s, it hovered a scant 2.5 points behind Michelin globally. Even though Goodyear tires were second to Michelin in world sales, they held 30 percent, the top share of the U.S. tire market.

Brand Origins

Frank and Charles Seiberling founded the Goodyear Tire & Rubber Co. in 1898. Although totally unrelated to the Goodyear family, they named their tires after Charles Goodyear, the Connecticut inventor who accidentally discovered the key to vulcanizing rubber in 1839 when he spilled a concoction of India rubber and sulphur onto a hot stove. Goodyear patented the process and tried to capitalize on the discovery, but he couldn't come up with any practical uses for the compound. When Goodyear's business failed, he was thrown into a Paris debtors' prison. He died, penniless, in New York in 1860.

The "Wingfoot" of the tires' trademark was added by Frank Seiberling. A statuette of Mercury was perched on a newel post in his home, and Seiberling hoped that the winged foot, like the god of trade and commerce it represented, would be the speedy harbinger of good news for Goodyear Tire & Rubber Co. But Seiberling had chosen an industry dominated by a few key patentholders who had organized a monopoly of the rubber market. Goodrich, Diamond, and United States Rubber formed the Clincher Manufacturers' Association and split up about 85 percent of the tire market amongst themselves. Goodyear was limited to 2 percent of the market.

Unhappy with such a small share of a growing market, Seiberling searched for an engineer who could give him his own patents. He found such a talent in Paul Weeks Litchfield, a member of the Massachusetts Institute of Technology's first engineering class. Although Litchfield had set his sights on a more prestigious field, the slow turn-of-the-century economy forced him to accept an offer with Goodyear. At age 24, the engineer launched a six-decade career that would propel the company and the brand to the forefront of the industry.

In 1900, Litchfield designed Goodyear's first auto tire. It took eight years for the company to turn a profit on the tires, but during that time, Litchfield worked to develop a unique product that would free Goodyear from its market share limitation. He succeeded in 1905 with the invention of the "straight side" tire and its "Universal Rim," a design that made tires easier to change and made damage from rim cutting less likely. Goodyear sales manager George M. Stadelman rushed the new tire's specifications to the era's most prominent car manufacturers: Pierce-Arrow, Packard, and Pope-Toledo. But the manufacturers refused to accommodate the small company's new design. Stadelman turned to the secondary auto manufacturers, Buick, Reo, and Oldsmobile, who agreed to give the new tire a try. The fledgling brand got a promotional boost when Louis Chevrolet agreed to drive on "straight sides" in the next Indianapolis 500 race.

In 1908, Litchfield created the first non-skid tread. Its diamond-shaped protrusions were adopted as the third element of the tires' logo, and would help catapult the brand from a 2 percent share to over 33 percent in the first decade of the twentieth century. The diamond-patterned tread provided four-way edges for traction, braking, and protection against side skids. Virtually overnight, the Goodyear diamond became the national standard for tire tread.

First Commercial Success

When Buick and Oldsmobile combined to form General Motors in 1908, Goodyear locked up sales to all the group's member companies. One Goodyear employee called the GM contract "the most important order Goodyear ever obtained. . . . It made Goodyear tires standard equipment on most General Motors cars for years thereafter." Goodyear added Henry Ford's popular Model T to the original equipment customer list that year as well.

But Frank Seiberling and sales manager Stadelman were not content to rely exclusively on the original equipment manufacturer (OEM) market for sales. By the end of the first decade of the twentieth century, there were almost one million cars on America's roads. Tires were then recognized as the single largest expense of ownership, about 25 percent of the total purchase price. Tire life was at best about 2,000 or 3,000 miles. To ensure that car owners chose Goodyear tires as replacements, management initiated an aggressive public promotion.

AT A GLANCE

Goodyear brand of tires introduced in 1900 by the Goodyear Tire & Rubber Co., which was founded by Frank and Charles Seiberling in Akron, OH, in 1898; introduction of straight side tires with Universal Rim, 1905; non-skid tread tire introduced, 1908; introduction of Tiempo all-weather, all-surface radial tire, 1977; introduction of Aquatread, 1993.

Performance: *Market share*—30% (top share) of U.S. tire market; 19% of world tire market. *Sales*—$10.9 billion.

Major competitor: Michelin; also Firestone.

Advertising: *Agency*—Young & Rubicam, Detroit, MI, and New York, NY, 1987—. *Major campaign*—"The best tires in the world have Goodyear written all over them."

Addresses: *Parent company*—Goodyear Tire & Rubber Co., 1144 East Market St., Akron, Ohio 44316; phone: (216) 796-2121.

Early Advertising

In 1908, Claude C. Hopkins, one of the United States' top advertising executives, was entrusted with Goodyear's $250,000 national advertising budget. Hopkins's full-page, copy-rich ads appeared in general circulation magazines, including *The Saturday Evening Post, Collier's, Leslie's,* and *Harper's.* The campaign enumerated the advantages of Goodyear's straight-side tire over competitors' and detailed the tires' construction for aficionados.

In 1910, Goodyear unveiled the United States' first two-page, national magazine advertisement. The precedent-setting announcement touted Goodyear's recent industry coup, listing 44 automakers that had signed original equipment contracts to give the brand 36 percent of that market. Just before World War I, sales manager Stadelman told his agents that "thanks to aggressive advertising, the name Goodyear on tires was as well-known to the public as Ivory on soap." Sales had grown from $1.8 million in 1908 to $22.4 million in 1912. By this time, the U.S. tire industry's top competitors had radically changed. Goodyear and U.S. Rubber grappled for the number one spot over the next four years. In 1916, Goodyear assumed the position of world leader in tire sales, and continued to hold it for more than seven decades. To commemorate the achievement, the brand adopted the slogan, "More People Ride On Goodyear Tires Than On Any Other Kind."

Litchfield proved he knew how to market the tires he created. He inaugurated Goodyear's "Wingfoot Express" in 1917 to demonstrate the efficacy of the brand's new pneumatic truck tires. Before this time, truck tires were usually solid rubber. The Wingfoot Express, the first organized attempt to cross the United States by truck, traversed the continent in 1918 in record time: thirteen days, five hours. Later, Litchfield organized one of the nation's first bus lines to demonstrate Goodyear's heavy-duty tires.

The Goodyear Blimp

In 1911, Litchfield developed a steel-reinforced rubber fabric for balloons and airships, launching another of Goodyear's enduring symbols, the dirigible or blimp. The company became the leader in American airship engineering and construction during World War I, and Litchfield hoped to construct a fleet of airships for commercial transportation. The engineer had long been interested in air travel, and focused his inventive efforts on the field.

In 1909, he developed the first tire made especially for airplanes, and the Goodyear brand was selected for the first U.S. airmail flight in 1911 and the first transcontinental flight, an 84-day trip with 63 landings. Goodyear's aeronautical department, organized in 1910, added to the brand's fame when it won the International Balloon Race of 1913, and was subsequently chosen to build Britain's first "kite" observation balloons and the U.S. Navy's first blimps.

With the support of the U.S. government, Litchfield attempted to develop a dirigible fleet and establish passenger service over the Atlantic and Pacific in 1925. Goodyear bought the German patents required to start production and built the Pilgrim that year. The company built two giant blimps, the USS Akron and the USS Macon, for the Navy in 1931 and 1933, respectively. But when three Goodyear blimps and the notorious Hindenburg were lost over the next few years, the commercial viability of this mode of transportation diminished.

Though Goodyear's dirigible fleet served in World War II as an effective and accident-free patrol against submarines, the fleet's most important function would be as a brand symbol. By the 1970s, Goodyear blimps were vital, unique envoys of the brand. Several airships toured the United States' major sporting events, and one cruised Europe's skyways. The biggest blimps carried 25-foot-high sign areas with nearly 4,000 night-message lights on each side, all visible for at least a mile in the dark. Goodyear allocated about 75 percent of message time to public service announcements and kept the remainder for its own promotion. The blimp was even used to introduce new advertising campaigns. "Goodyear day," January 1, combined college bowl game coverage from the namesake blimp with the launch of new ad campaigns.

Competition and Change

In the late 1910s and early 1920s, some of Goodyear's original equipment manufacturing business was siphoned off when Ford switched to Firestone and DuPont gained control of both General Motors and U.S. Rubber. In 1920, the tire industry was decimated when wide fluctuations in rubber prices revealed American manufacturers' dependence on outside suppliers of natural rubber. Almost 200 tire companies went out of business. Goodyear survived but was saddled with debt. When the company went through a fiscal reorganization, creditors forced the Seiberlings out of the company. An outsider, Edward G. Wilmer, succeeded Frank Seiberling as president, and served from 1921 to 1923. George Stadelman took office in 1923, but died three years later. After almost a quarter-century with Goodyear, Paul W. Litchfield assumed the helm, a position he would hold for the next three decades. To combat the company's financial troubles, Litchfield "reaffirmed Goodyear's determination to be the maker not only of the most tires, but of the finest quality tires" with the 1928 introduction of Goodyear's first Double Eagle passenger car tire.

Throughout the 1920s, Goodyear searched for a synthetic replacement for natural rubber so that it could free itself from the influence of suppliers. Goodyear developed rayon- and then nylon-reinforced truck and auto tires during the decade. After over ten years of research, Goodyear produced the first American synthetic rubber tires, made of patented "Chemigum," in 1938. Synthetic rubber helped alleviate World War II's chronic rubber shortages. By late 1945, 89 percent of the rubber used in U.S. industry was synthetic. This development also helped stabilize world rubber prices.

International Market

Goodyear had become the world's best-selling tire brand in 1916 by virtue of dominating the American tire market, which was the world's largest. Because the American market was so large, the brand's overseas activities were relatively small until the early 1900s. The English import firm of Daws & Allen had arranged the first export of Goodyear's proprietary straight side tires in 1901, and the brand inaugurated Canadian production in 1910. Sales agencies in Germany, Russia, the Netherlands, Austria, Sweden, Denmark, Finland, Argentina, Australia, and South Africa were established over the course of the decade.

The Goodyear brand managed to capture substantial market share even though it met competition from powerful national tire names, including Dunlop in the United Kingdom, Michelin in France, Continental in Germany, and Pirelli in Italy. Exports grew by almost 700 percent in 1922 alone and by the end of the decade Goodyear had distributors in 145 countries, capturing 18.3 percent of overseas replacement tire business. In 1952, Goodyear became the first rubber company to exceed a billion dollars in annual sales; by the mid-1960s, the brand held formidable shares of Europe's primary markets and distribution in every country outside the Communist bloc.

Racing Promotions

After a 34-year hiatus, Goodyear re-entered the prestigious field of high-performance tires in 1956 to boost its image. The brand rejoined the high-performance market by designing custom tires for drivers attempting to establish new land speed records. Using Goodyear tires in 1959, Mickey Thompson set several new records at the Bonneville Salt Flats and broke the 400 mile-per-hour (mph) barrier the following year. By the end of 1962, Goodyear racing tires were being used on more winning stock and sports cars than any other brand, out-selling Firestone, which had dominated the industry in the absence of Goodyear. In 1965, Craig Breedlove's jet-powered, Goodyear-equipped racer hiked the land speed record to 600.6 mph.

Goodyear tires helped A. J. Foyt win the Indianapolis 500 in 1967, the first racer to win using Goodyear tires since Howard Wilcox won in 1919. The next year Bobby Unser won using Goodyear tires, and Mark Donohue repeated the brand's success in 1972. In 1973, 26 of the 33 Indy cars, including that of the winner, Gordon Johncock, used Goodyear tires. By 1975, all Indy contestants used tires from Goodyear. These implicit endorsements gave Goodyear press and prestige. In addition to race track publicity, Goodyear tires were used on NASA's Apollo 14 in 1970.

The Radial Revolution

Although Goodyear had manufactured radial tires for the European market in the 1960s and 1970s, it had resisted producing them for U.S. customers for nearly two decades. The company had initially claimed, with some validity, that American-made cars were too heavy for radial tires. But economics and technology lurked behind company reticence; it would be prohibitively expensive to convert production facilities and train employees to make radial tires, even if Goodyear could catch up with Michelin's 25-year head start.

In an effort to combat Michelin's advance on the U.S. tire market, U.S. tiremakers called for a 100-percent tariff on imported tires, but got only 6.6 percent in 1973. Goodyear invested millions of dollars into polyester, fiberglass, and bias belted tires, all of which could be built on its conventional machines, but these were just stalling tactics. The company finally spent $2 billion to upgrade plant and equipment to radial technology over the course of the 1970s. Even after U.S. manufacturers made the transition to radial tires, they had a hard time maintaining the quality standards set by Michelin. Goodyear was able to stave off Michelin's competitive onslaught with the introduction of the "Tiempo" all-weather, all-surface radial tire in 1977. By the end of the 1970s, Michelin had come within a few percentage points of ending Goodyear's 60-year reign at the top of the world's tire dynasty.

Market Consolidation

As the 1970s came to a close, several factors that dramatically shrank sales volume and radically transformed the competitive structure of the global tire market converged. The oil crisis of the 1970s made it more expensive to drive, thus reducing miles driven. The development of lighter, smaller cars, combined with less driving overall, decreased tire wear. The conversion to longer-lasting radial tires also contributed to the reduction of the replacement tire market. The 1980 recession was the final blow; OEM demand plunged 30 percent and the replacement segment dropped 18.9 percent.

When competition in the shrinking market started to heat up, Michelin launched a price war. The cutthroat competition led to consolidation of the global tire industry. Over the course of the decade, a spate of mergers and acquisitions concentrated the tire business into fewer and fewer hands. Sumitomo, Japan's second largest tire company, began its acquisition of the venerable Dunlop name and properties in 1983. Continental and General Tire merged, then established a joint venture with two Japanese tire companies in 1987. That same year, BFGoodrich withdrew from tire manufacturing after a costly takeover fight with Uniroyal. In 1988, Firestone merged with Bridgestone Corporation of Japan, and Pirelli purchased America's Armstrong.

After fishing for Firestone and coming up empty, Michelin became the world's top tire company with the 1990 purchase of Uniroyal. Only Goodyear avoided the merger/acquisition blitz, but it lost its long-running dominance of the field in the process. By 1990, the top four tire companies, Michelin, Goodyear, Bridgestone, and Continental, controlled 68 percent of the global tire market, up from 48 percent in 1980.

All of the big mergers meant big debt, and the top companies continued to cut prices just to maintain their cash flow. Goodyear's strategy in this competitive new environment was to segment the tire market and concentrate on high-margin, high-performance sales. Its 1993 introduction of "Aquatread" is a good example. Since it could no longer claim sales of the most tires in the world, Goodyear instead boasted of selling "the best tires in the world."

Further Reading:

Barach, Arnold B., *Famous American Trademarks,* Washington, DC: Public Affairs Press, 1971, pp. 75–76.

Cleary, David Powers, *Great American Brands,* New York: Fairchild, 1981, pp. 128–148.

Gibson, Paul, "Goodyear Vs. Michelin," *Forbes,* August 7, 1978, pp. 62–63.

"Goodyear: Will Staying No. 1 in Tires Pump Up Profits?" *Business Week,* July 12, 1982, pp. 85–88.

O'Reilly, Maurice, *The Goodyear Story,* Elmsford, NY: Benjamin Company, 1983.

Schiller, Zachary, "After a Year of Spinning Its Wheels, Goodyear Gets a Retread," *Business Week,* March 26, 1990, pp. 56, 58.

—April S. Dougal

HAMILTON BEACH®

Hamilton Beach®

Founded in 1911, Hamilton Beach is an innovative, affordable, high-quality brand of home appliances. Its parent company, Hamilton Beach/Proctor-Silex, Inc., is headquartered in Glen Allen, Virginia. In the 1990s Hamilton Beach products were known for their sleek Euro-styling, technological advancements, and numerous features for safety, speed, and convenience.

The success of Hamilton Beach is partially the result of careful market research to determine consumer needs, preferences, and trends. For example, when women began entering the labor force in large numbers, the company developed a Hamilton Beach slow cooker, which allowed women to start cooking a meal in the morning before work, leave it unattended during the day, and arrive home to a fully cooked, ready-to-serve meal. Similarly, the trend toward healthy eating during the 1980s and 1990s saw the development of juice extractors for making fruit and vegetable juices and cooking appliances for making lowfat foods.

Brand Origins

In 1911 Chester Beach and L.H. Hamilton created their own company and built the first commercial drink mixer using their "universal fractional horsepower motor," which ran on either AC or DC electricity. At the time, druggists were prescribing malted milk as the newest strength builder, and the mixer was used in drugstore fountains. Beach was a young mechanical genius, who had left his farm to work for the Arnold Electric Company in Racine, Wisconsin, where he met Hamilton, a former steamship cashier. Their new motor was a breakthrough because at that time different areas of the country used different types of electrical currents.

Hamilton and Beach's goal, however, was to adapt the motor to products used in the home. Hamilton Beach small electric appliances began when the motor was adapted for sewing machines, which signaled the end of an era of treadle sewing. Soon the motor was incorporated into attachments to grind knives, buff silver, and mix cake batter.

Brand Development

In the ensuing years the Hamilton Beach motor was incorporated into many new types of products, enabling certain tasks to be performed more easily, quickly, and effectively. The early products were mostly concerned with food preparation and made such tasks as blending, chopping, and grinding easier. Subsequent products also focused on making cooking, steaming, and grilling food more convenient.

One of the early Hamilton Beach products was a blender. Hand-held and standard blenders for liquefying and pureeing foods and for mixing drinks were created in the company's Blender line. The hand-held models weighed only a couple of pounds and had the motor located in the handgrip. People found it convenient to use and easy to clean. The larger, standard blenders had the motor located in the mixing pitcher's base. These blenders were more powerful than the hand-held models and more versatile because they could also blend, chop, grind, or grate some solid foods. They also provided more speed choices. In the subsequent decades Hamilton Beach would develop a wide range of appliances, including drink mixers, can openers, electric knives, slow cookers (for stews or casseroles that cook for 5 to 12 hours), rice cookers/food steamers, buffet/table ranges, and roaster ovens.

During the 1980s the health and fitness trend began to take hold, and consumers wanted household products that would facilitate preparation of healthy meals. Food processors, for example, could perform such tasks as chopping vegetables, slicing and shredding foods, and crumbling crackers. Available in both compact and full-sized models, Hamilton Beach food processors were equipped with electronic controls for greater convenience. Another Hamilton Beach product line associated with the health movement was juicers and juice extractors, which were used to make fresh juice from fruits or vegetables.

In the 1990s the company introduced new updated models of many of its products. In 1994, for example, four new blenders were added to the BlendMaster line. Two of the blenders had new speed features. One was a powerful two-speed model that could crush even ice in seconds. The two speeds were high and low, providing flexibility and ease of use. Also introduced was a seven-speed model, which provided greater choice and flexibility to the user. The other two blenders had new electronic touch-pad controls, called "Easy Touch," which gave the option of manual or programmable operation. Both models offered a choice of ten speeds and could be programmed in five-second increments for a duration of 5 to 25 seconds. They also had powerful ice-crushing capabilities. The difference between the two models was size and material of the jar. One model featured a 40-ounce, extra-wide

AT A GLANCE

Hamilton Beach brand of appliances, along with the Hamilton Beach Manufacturing Company, founded in 1911 by Chester Beach and L. H. Hamilton; first product was a commercial drink mixer, though soon the company specialized in home appliances; since 1990 the brand's parent company has been Hamilton Beach/Proctor-Silex, Inc., a subsidiary of HB-PS Holding Co., Inc.

Performance: *Sales*—$350 million (1992 estimate for all company brands).

Major competitor: Oster; also, Waring, Black & Decker, Braun, Cusinart, and Sunbeam.

Advertising: *Agency*—Arian, Lowe & Travis Advertising, Inc., Louisville, KY, 1989—. *Major campaign*—Infomercials on cable TV featuring television personality Sarah Purcell and California restaurateur and radio host Piero Biondi using Hamilton Beach's products.

Addresses: *Parent company*—Hamilton Beach/Proctor-Silex, Inc., 4421 Waterfront Drive, Glen Allen, VA 23060; phone: (804) 273-9777; fax: (804) 527-7230. *Ultimate parent company*—HB-PS Holding Co., Inc.

mouth, dishwasher-safe jar, and the other had a 48-ounce, shatter-resistant plastic jar.

Another innovative product, introduced in 1993, was an indoor steam grill, which gave food a fresh-grilled taste in five minutes or less. Not only was it faster than an outdoor grill but no smoke was used, and food did not need to be turned over. A red indicator light showed when grilling was complete. The year 1994 also saw an updated version of the Hamilton Beach food steamer/rice cooker. This new version, meant for cooking whole grains and vegetables, featured stackable sections that allowed one to four family-sized food portions to be cooked at the same time. The stackable steaming baskets accommodated up to 16 cups of vegetables and 10 cups of rice.

During this time there were also three new versions of mixers. A new 5-speed hand mixer was equipped with an innovative ''bowl rest'' feature, which allowed users to rest or prop the mixer on the edge of the mixing bowl instead of the countertop. Further convenience features included a top-mounted fingertip control switch that doubled as a beater-ejector button. The two other new models, with 12 and 14 speeds, respectively, were standard mixers in the ProMix line. The mixers had a unique SensorSpeed motor, which sensed when beater speed declined as a result of increased mixing load and automatically increased the unit's power to maintain a steady mixing rate. The consumer thus got consistent mixing power without adjusting speed settings or interrupting the mixing process to hand stir.

Advertising and Marketing

In addition to using print ads in magazines, Hamilton Beach/Proctor-Silex advertised on cable television during the 1990s and used infomercials to inform consumers about the inventiveness, quality, and value of its products. One such infomercial used TV personality Sarah Purcell and Piero Biondi, restaurateur and popular host of the radio program ''Chef Piero's Food and Wine Show,'' which was featured on KIEV-Radio in Burbank, California. Biondi used the Hamilton Beach steam grill to cook various foods with his own line of barbecue sauces and salad dressings. In Chicago in January 1994, Biondi was a special guest at a trade show given by the National Housewares Manufacturing Association. There Biondi used the steam grill, the food steamer/rice cooker, and the Super Shooter.

Brand Outlook

The philosophy of developing reliable, innovative products for home use, which has served the company so well in the past, was expected to be practiced in the future. George C. Nebel, president and chief executive officer at Hamilton Beach/Proctor-Silex, said, ''Customers continue to invest in the strength of our two brand names and in our products. In turn, we continually invest in service and products to ensure our customers receive the best value for their investments.''

Further Reading:

Hamilton Beach Brand History, Glen Allen, VA: Hamilton Beach/Proctor Silex, Inc.

Additional information for this profile was obtained from Hamilton Beach/Proctor-Silex, Inc., press releases, 1994.

—*Dorothy Kroll*

HARLEY-DAVIDSON®

Harley-Davidson motorcycles are a distinctive breed of long, low, rumbling, heavyweight machines that have inspired fanatical loyalty on the part of customers and almost unparalleled brand recognition, even among non-riders. The Milwaukee-based Harley-Davidson, Inc., first incorporated in 1907 as the Harley-Davidson Motor Company, was one of the world's earliest motorcycle manufacturers and stands alone today as the sole remaining American motorcycle company.

The invention of the motorcycle dates back to the 1700s, when steam engines were first developed as a source of power. Several inventors are credited with building two-wheeled vehicles during that period, all with extremely limited success. Gottlieb Daimler of Germany is generally cited as the inventor of the gasoline-powered motorcycle, having installed an internal-combustion engine in a bicycle in 1865. But seeing little commercial potential for his machine, Daimler gave up after that first prototype and went on to pursue the development of four-wheeled gasoline vehicles, founding the firm that would someday become Mercedes-Benz. The evolution of the motorcycle proceeded slowly through the end of the 1800s, with numerous bicycle manufacturers in Europe and the United States experimenting with small engines mounted in their standard frames. None of them proved reliable enough to be used as actual transportation.

Harleys and Davidsons

Around the turn of the century, two bicycle enthusiasts dedicated themselves to the development of a practical two-wheeled motor vehicle. William S. Harley and Arthur Davidson had been friends from their elementary-school days in Milwaukee, Wisconsin, and shared an intense fascination for mechanical devices, particularly gasoline engines. Harley, a natural mechanic who had served an apprenticeship at a bicycle factory, took a job as a draftsman at the small metal shop where Davidson worked as a pattern-maker. In their spare time, the pair built three or four prototype single-cylinder engines and began testing them in bicycle frames.

The inventors realized that progress was coming too slowly, and they needed more help. Davidson's brother, Walter, was a highly skilled mechanic working at the time as a machinist for a railroad in Kansas. Arthur Davidson wrote and offered him a ride on their motorcycle, painting a rosy picture of the vehicle's state of development. According to Thomas C. Bolfert in *The Big Book of Harley-Davidson,* Walter later recalled, "Imagine my chagrin to find that the motor bicycle in question had reached the stage of blueprints, and before I could have the promised ride, I had to help finish the machine." Nevertheless, in 1902 Walter took a railroad job in Milwaukee and began working on the motorcycle project.

The team completed its first working prototype in the spring of 1903. That model featured a single-cylinder engine of 3 horsepower and achieved a top speed of 25 miles per hour. It ran well but clearly lacked sufficient power to negotiate the muddy and rutted roads of the day. Harley quickly designed a bigger, more powerful engine, with heavier castings and larger flywheels. Arthur Davidson made up the casting patterns, and the three partners worked together on the construction of the new engine.

The increased power solved one problem but created another: the bicycle frame couldn't handle the stress. In response, Harley designed a revolutionary, heavyweight loop frame. He also further increased the prototype's roadworthiness by designing heavy-duty wheels, a departure from the standard lightweight bicycle wheels offered by their competitors. Such developments helped set the tone for Harley-Davidson's future reputation for sturdiness. Finally, Harley and the Davidsons had a machine they felt could be marketed for commercial sale.

From the beginning, the partners had agreed that the name of the motorcycle would be Harley-Davidson, even though there were two Davidsons and only one Harley. They felt the names in that order sounded more harmonious than Davidson-Harley (in which case, the company's products might now be called "Davidsons" rather than "Harleys"). But the Davidson brothers also wished to recognize William Harley for his conceptual work, his creative designs, and his development of the prototypes.

Success

The inventors sold three motorcycles in 1903, all of which were bought and paid for prior to completion. Production rose steadily through 1905, when their output totaled 50 units and the firm hired its first full-time employee (neither a Harley nor a Davidson) to work in the plant, a 10-by-15-foot shed in the Davidson backyard. In 1906 the company moved to its first real factory, a 2,380-square-foot brick structure on Chestnut Street (now called Juneau Avenue), still the site of the firm's headquarters in Milwaukee.

AT A GLANCE

Harley-Davidson brand of motorcycles founded in 1903 in Milwaukee, WI, by Walter Davidson (president and general manager), William S. Harley (chief engineer and designer), and Arthur Davidson (secretary and general sales manager); joined shortly thereafter by William A. Davidson (vice-president and works manager); incorporated 1907, as Harley-Davidson Motor Company.

Performance: *Market share*—63.2% of U.S. "super-heavyweight" (850cc or larger engines) motorcycle market. *Sales*—$940 million.

Major competitor: Honda; also BMW, Kawasaki, Suzuki, and Yamaha.

Addresses: *Parent company*—Harley-Davidson, Inc., 1700 West Juneau Ave., P.O. Box 653, Milwaukee, WI 53201; phone: (414) 342-4680; fax: (414) 935-4806.

On September 22, 1907, the Harley-Davidson Motor Company was incorporated. Walter Davidson was named president and general manager, Arthur Davidson served as secretary and general sales manager, William Harley became chief engineer and designer, and another Davidson brother, William A. (with extensive knowledge of metallurgy and experience as a toolroom foreman) was brought on board as vice-president and works manager.

Production for the 1907 model year reached 152 units, with an increase to 456 by 1908. Harley-Davidson clearly had a hot product on its hands. Part of the reason for the company's success was the reliability of its vehicles compared to other motorcycles of the day. Additional factors were an aggressive advertising campaign and a carefully selected and tight-knit dealer network.

A Landmark Engine

In 1909 Harley-Davidson premiered the engine configuration that was to become its trademark: the V-Twin. This design set two cylinders at 45 degrees to each other, mounted longitudinally in the frame, and offered a significant increase in horsepower compared to the old single-cylinder power source. The V design was not a Harley original, as Harry V. Sucher points out in *Harley-Davidson: The Milwaukee Marvel:* "Most of the American [motorcycle] manufacturers of any consequence were offering V-Twin models. . . . The V-Twin engine showed remarkable torque development at very moderate engine speeds, . . . which made for a slow turning, long lasting engine." It also resulted in the characteristic low rumble from the exhaust pipes that has also become a Harley trademark.

Refinements continued at a rapid pace: mechanical intake valves arrived in 1911; an optional chain drive made its appearance in 1912, replacing the old drive belt; and in that same year Harley introduced the first clutch ever devised for a motorcycle. The next all-new model, the J, came along in 1915. This model is instantly recognizable as a motorcycle, rather than a motorized bicycle. It featured a larger 61-cubic-inch engine, a three-speed transmission, and a kickstarter in place of bicycle pedals.

The War Effort

World War I provided a major sales and publicity boost for Harley-Davidson. From the beginning, the company had pushed the commercial use of its products by such customers as police departments, the postal service, and various small businesses in need of fuel-efficient delivery vehicles. In 1916 the Harley-Davidson brand of motorcycles first saw military action by the U.S. Army in border skirmishes with Mexican revolutionary Pancho Villa. When the First World War broke out, the Harley plant was turned over to military production. One story, cited in *The Big Book of Harley-Davidson,* holds that the first American soldier to enter Germany, in 1918, was Corporal Roy Holtz, "aboard his Harley-Davidson."

The war spread the Harley-Davidson name throughout the world. By 1919 Harleys were being sold on almost every continent, by more than 2,000 dealers in 67 countries. One-sixth of the company's production was being shipped overseas. And by 1920 Harley-Davidson was the largest and best-known manufacturer of motorcycles in the world.

Although Harley continued to produce some single-cylinder models, the V-Twins had clearly taken over, both in terms of sales and engineering developments. Displacement and horsepower steadily increased. In 1921 the company introduced a 74-cubic-inch V-Twin that put out 9.5 horsepower. For the rest of the decade, the 61 and 74 Twins led the Harley product line. Then, in 1929, Harley further increased its domination of the V-Twin market with the addition of a 45-cubic-inch model, featuring the power of a big twin and the light weight and crisp handling of a single.

Surviving the Depression

The Great Depression hit the motorcycle industry hard. In the early part of the century there had been dozens of American motorcycle manufacturers; by the end of the 1930s, only Harley and Indian survived. Several factors allowed Harley-Davidson to weather the economic storm. The company had a well-established reputation for quality; it had a strong, loyal dealer network; and it had more commercial sales than most manufacturers.

In the 1930s, at the height of the Depression, Harley continued an aggressive marketing campaign. It pushed commercial sales even harder. (Motorcycles were cheaper to operate than fleets of cars or trucks.) It introduced sleeker, streamlined gas tanks; new, more vibrant color choices; and a wider selection of optional accessories. The proactive approach had its effect. Sales, which had slipped to 3,700 units in 1933, climbed to 10,000 for 1934 and remained constant through the end of the decade.

War Again Spreads the Harley Name

World War II provided another boost in sales. By 1945 Harley-Davidson had manufactured almost 100,000 motorcycles for the United States and its allies. And, as Bolfert points out in *The Big Book of Harley-Davidson,* "by producing motorcycles instead of tanks or machine guns, all the manufacturing processes were kept intact, which insured more rapid conversion to civilian production at the war's end."

The war served to introduce a whole new generation to Harley-Davidson motorcycles, and demand for the company's products increased dramatically in the late 1940s and early 1950s. Many servicemen had also come into contact with British motorcycles during the war, and they came home demanding a lighter, sportier machine similar to the Triumphs and BSAs they rode in Europe. Harley responded in 1952 by introducing its K model, which replaced the old 45. The K featured a 750cc V-Twin engine and, a first for Harley, the engine and transmission in a single unit case, with a foot-shift on the right side, like the British bikes. The K saw many improvements over the next few years, and in 1957 it became the Sportster—"a genuine superbike," according to David Johnson in *Cycle World*—which remains one of the company's most popular models to this day.

Of course, Harley-Davidson continued to produce its legendary big-twin touring machines at the same time. The major developments for the touring bikes centered around improved suspension systems. When hydraulic front forks replaced the old springer front end in 1949, the machine was named the Hydra-Glide. The addition of hydraulic rear suspension resulted in the Duo-Glide of 1958. And when electric starting was introduced in 1965, the famous Electra-Glide was born.

Competition Heats Up

Along the way, a new force had arrived in the world motorcycle market. The Japanese began producing low-cost, practical two-wheeled transportation shortly after World War II ended. Their management techniques were revolutionary, and their production methods pushed the boundaries of efficiency. By the early sixties, exports to the United States had begun to cut into Harley's sales.

Hollywood played at least a minor part in this development. Motorcycles had begun suffering from image problems during the 1950s, when a group that was later called the "outlaw" element of motorcycle riders first came to public attention. The outlaw biker image was promoted by the 1954 release of the movie *The Wild One,* starring Marlon Brando as the leader of a rebel cycle gang that terrorizes a small California town. The film was based on a true-life incident in which a gang of outlaw bikers invaded the town of Hollister, California, in 1947, and harassed the local citizens, eventually requiring 500 Highway Patrol officers to restore peace. *The Wild One* caused concern among the non-riding population and spawned a long line of movie imitators that further increased the public's mistrust of bikers.

But the Japanese motorcycles, led by Honda, were of a different breed. They were small, brightly colored, clean, and quiet, while Harley's machines were notoriously big, loud, and menacing. Hell's Angels rode Harleys; the Beach Boys rode Hondas. When the Japanese bike explosion struck the United States in the 1960s with the marketing slogan, "You meet the nicest people on a Honda," the implication was clearly that you never knew who or what you'd meet on a Harley.

The Indian company had gone out of business in 1953, leaving Harley-Davidson as the sole American motorcycle manufacturer. And so it was that Harley faced the image problem and the influx of foreign competition alone.

The AMF Years

In 1965, amid increasing sales by its foreign competitors, Harley-Davidson went public, with the two founding families giving up controlling interest in the firm for the first time since it was founded. By the end of the decade, facing a hostile takeover, Harley agreed instead to a merger under which it would become part of American Machine and Foundry (AMF), an East Coast conglomerate with a heavy concentration in leisure products. Harley-Davidson management was enthusiastic about the deal, believing it might save the company.

Whether the AMF affiliation was good for Harley or not is a hotly debated topic. As Alan Girdler explains in the *Illustrated Harley-Davidson Buyer's Guide:* "There are at least two sides to this story. The one you're most likely to hear is the one about how AMF nearly ruined Harley." The conglomerate was not familiar with motorcycle production and so had a hard time communicating with Harley management. AMF was a tightly run business and in exchange for its financial investment exacted a heavy bottom-line price from the Milwaukee firm. Additionally, as Girdler points out, "The motorcycle boom was even stronger than anyone had dared predict." Harley's production was stretched beyond capacity, rising from 25,328 units in 1965 to 75,403 in 1975.

Even with the addition of new plants, more employees, and modern equipment, quality control was difficult to maintain. As Girdler puts it: "AMF invested literally millions of dollars in Harley-Davidson. Production facilities were improved beyond description. But while some thought was given to the future and a few new models appeared, the emphasis wasn't on the product." As a result of the increased production and emphasis on the bottom line, quality did suffer for a time. Harley's reputation as the world's most durable motorcycle was seriously damaged, and customers moved to the new lines of heavyweight touring machines being marketed by the Japanese firms.

The Legendary Willie G.

One bright spot during those years was an enterprising young executive named William G. Davidson, known to Harley enthusiasts as Willie G., grandson of one of the company's founders and a Harley designer since 1963. In 1971, under the AMF banner, Willie G. created a pivotal motorcycle, the FX 1200 Super Glide. It was, essentially, a big V-Twin—stripped of windshield, saddlebags, and other touring accessories—to which had been grafted the smaller Sportster front end and a few other bits and pieces that helped it mimic the light, fast cycles being turned out by aftermarket customizers. Known as choppers (because extraneous equipment was "chopped" off), these bikes had increased in popularity with the 1969 release of the film *Easy Rider,* in which Peter Fonda rode a heavily customized Harley.

Although Harley-Davidson had previously discouraged such modifications of its vehicles, the Super Glide proved so popular that it changed the company's direction. To this day, Harley produces a wide variety of enormously popular factory-custom cycles. Explains Willie G. in *Fortune:* "Our customers really know what they want on their bikes. . . . Every little piece on a motorcycle is exposed, and it has to look just right. . . . Harley riders see their bikes as art objects, and they want them to look a certain way."

New Ownership

But the success of the Super Glide and subsequent innovative models alone was not enough to turn the company around. AMF was quickly losing patience with its subsidiary, and rumors of a possible sale abounded. In 1981 a group of thirteen Harley executives, led by Vaughn Beals, proposed to buy the firm from AMF with a $1 million cash investment. They believed in Harley-Davidson motorcycles and felt the company's problems lay not in the market, the products, or the workforce, but in AMF's management policies.

That Beals thought he could buy a $300 million company for so small a cash outlay was cause for concern among some of the other executives. But they took the proposal to Citicorp Industrial Credit, which ended up providing the additional financial backing. As one Citicorp executive, quoted by Peter C. Reid in *Well Made in America,* explained, "What hit me was that this was the only product I'd ever seen that people had tattooed on their bodies." Harley was purchased by its management group from AMF on June 16, 1981, for a total of $81.5 million. Says Girdler: "Harley-Davidson was saved (in my opinion) when it was bought by AMF, and saved again when it was bought *from* AMF by its own managers."

The Harley managers, with Willie G. in the lead and a pack of well-wishers following, celebrated with a ceremonial motorcycle ride from the AMF-built assembly plant in York, Pennsylvania, back to company headquarters in Milwaukee. Notes Reid: "Along the way they [were] greeted by Harley dealers and riders with a fervor reminiscent of the Allies' liberation of Paris."

Evolution, Marketing, and Sales of the Harley

Back in the office, the managers implemented a strategy to turn Harley-Davidson around. Techniques included such Japanese-inspired concepts as increased employee involvement in decision-making, just-in-time inventory control, quality circles, and customer-driven product focus. Rather than corporate accountants, Harley was now controlled by an enthusiastic group of managers who actually rode motorcycles. Willie G.—the spiritual leader of the newly energized company—and other executives became regular fixtures at cycle races, rallies, and other events around the country, interacting with customers and asking detailed questions about buyers' problems and preferences.

The change was dramatic. In 1984 Harley introduced the Evolution engine, a highly refined version of its venerable V-Twin. The new engine, along with a host of new models—including a series of nostalgic fifties-style bikes that remain among the company's most popular models—and a renewed emphasis on quality and customer service, resulted in throngs of Harley enthusiasts flocking back to the fold.

Harley-Davidson was listed on the New York Stock Exchange in the summer of 1987, an event that signaled the completion of its turnaround. Normally the Exchange celebrates a new listing with a quiet luncheon. Not so with the addition of Harley to its board. Explains Reid: "A Harley Heritage Softail motorcycle was displayed above the floor of the Exchange. The Harley flag flew outside. And a big motorcycle parade led by Harley executives rumbled down to Wall Street."

By 1992 Harley's sales were up to $940 million, and the company held a 63.2 percent share of the heavyweight motorcycle market in the United States (significantly ahead of its nearest competitor, Honda, with 16.2 percent). Sales continue to rise, and demand for Harley products consistently outweighs supply. Although the potential for even further sales increases is strong, executives are loathe to increase production too rapidly for fear of risking a decrease in quality.

What It's All About

Why are Harleys in such demand? In *The Iron Stallion,* author Rafael Francisco Carmona interviews Harley owners about their devotion to their bikes. Some comments: "A Harley will last forever if you take care of it." "You can pass them, but you can't outclass them." "Harley's turn people's heads. You're on a Harley and you become the center of everyone's interest." "After you experience 600 or 700 pounds of iron beneath you going down the highway, you know there's no other machine." "This is rolling art." "Once you've experienced a Harley, there are no other motorcycles." "Harley-Davidson is a motorcycle. Everything else is a sewing machine."

In *Harley-Davidson: The American Motorcycle,* a videotape celebrating Harley's 90th birthday in 1993, actor Peter Fonda cites the story of a Frenchman who criticized the United States as "a wasteland, a cultural desert. . . . The only things you have given the world are rock and roll and Harley-Davidson." Replies Fonda, "Yeah, well . . . what more do you need?"

Further Reading:

Bolfert, Thomas C., *The Big Book of Harley-Davidson,* revised edition, Milwaukee, WI: Harley-Davidson, Inc., 1991.

Carmona, Rafael Francisco, *The Iron Stallion: An American Love Story,* Los Angeles, CA: Hirshberg Publishing, 1990.

Girdler, Alan, *Illustrated Harley-Davidson Buyer's Guide,* Osceola, WI: Motorbooks International, 1992.

Harley-Davidson: The American Motorcycle (videotape), Cabin Fever Entertainment, Inc., 1993.

"How Harley Beat Back the Japanese," *Fortune,* September 25, 1989.

Johnson, David, "The Bikes That Made Milwaukee Famous," *Cycle World,* September 1993.

"Maintaining Excellence Through Change," *Target,* Spring 1989.

Reid, Peter C., *Well Made in America: Lessons from Harley-Davidson on Being the Best,* New York: McGraw-Hill, 1990.

Sucher, Harry V., *Harley-Davidson: The Milwaukee Marvel,* revised edition, Yeovil, Somerset, England: Haynes Publishing Group, 1992.

"Why Milwaukee Won't Die," *Cycle,* June 1987.

Wright, David K., *The Harley-Davidson Motor Company: An Official Ninety-Year History,* third edition, Osceola, WI: Motorbooks International, 1993.

—Peter M. Gareffa

HEAD®

The name Howard Head was virtually synonymous with innovation in the ski industry in the 1960s and the tennis industry in the 1970s. Before leaving Head Sports, Inc., and joining Prince Manufacturing, Inc., Howard Head introduced metal skis and revolutionized the ski industry before establishing Head Sports as a leading manufacturer of tennis racquets.

Origins

Head Sports, Inc., began as an innovator's dream. As a young man with a Harvard engineering degree and a wide range of job experience, Howard Head in 1946 discovered skiing during a vacation from his job as a draftsman at the Glenn L. Martin Co. Upon returning from his vacation, he theorized that the materials that had made aircraft wings lighter and stronger could also be applied to the manufacture of skis, traditionally crafted from hickory. For the next few years Howard Head lived off part-time jobs, devoting his energies to creating a workable metal ski.

After many early attempts failed due to breakages and poor maneuverability, in 1950 Howard Head introduced a workable design that would be enthusiastically received, particularly in Europe. This was at a time when European innovations in ski equipment were hurting U.S. manufacturers (Scandinavian companies led the market). For his skis, Head featured two layers of aluminum bonded around a core of plywood at 50,000 pounds pressure. This package was enveloped in an outer layer of plastic. The new skis, selling for $50 a pair, including excise tax, performed fabulously, becoming known as the most maneuverable skis in the world. Much more durable than wooden skis, Head's skis were less likely to twist and therefore were more forgiving to use. In 1952 Head introduced skis with edges made of tempered steel.

Early Performance

By 1959, Head skis were selling for $90 and more a pair, grossing more than $1.5 for the company, whose post-tax profits totalled approximately $90,000. Howard Head had gained an international reputation, becoming "the most famous name in the business" in just ten years. In order to raise capital, the company went public in the spring of 1960. The company sold 50,000 pairs of skis in 1960—not a bad increase over the 300 pairs sold the first year. Head's 1963 net income was $200,000 on sales of $4 million. In 1964 Head skis were retailing for $98.50 to $142 a pair.

It is difficult to exaggerate the impact of Head's company on the world ski market. As a commentator for *Barron's* noted in 1961, "This company single-handedly has converted the U.S. from a net importer to a net exporter of skis." The exports of the Head company alone exceeded all U.S. ski imports. In 1961 Head exported two-thirds of its total production to Europe. But it also capitalized on a postwar increase in the popularity of skiing in the United States. In the late 1950s estimates of the number of recreational skiers in the United States ranged from 2.5 million to 15 million; in 1946 the Athletic Association estimated the number of recreational skiers at only 1.4 million. Another factor aiding in the sale of Head skis was that the new metal skis (nicknamed "cheaters") reduced the learning curve for the new, affluent skiers.

Competition and Diversification

Competitors often entered the sporting goods market not by virtue of their marketing experience but rather of their manufacturing capability—much like Howard Head had entered the market because of his experience with aircraft fabrication. Head Sport's philosophy would continue to be based on technology instead of marketing. As light metal alloys had replaced wood and canvas in airframe construction, so would metal be supplanted by fiberglass, both in aviation and in skiing. At the same time that technological advances in the ski business occurred, though, ski marketing became more fashion-oriented (as one executive put it, "Skiing is a snobbish sport").

Head was unprepared for both the new technology and new marketing strategies dominating the skiing industry. "For the first four years," explained Head, "we had the market to ourselves." Not any more. In addition, many of the new competitors were more diversified and more stable than the Head Ski Company, which had often found profits, if not devotees, elusive. Although it sold 125,000 pairs of skis in 1966, the company experienced problems after diversifying into clothing as it was unable to find qualified stitchers and experiencing delays in the delivery of clothing. In 1982 Head Sports Wear was sold to Leslie Fay Companies, Inc., who in turn sold it to Odyssey International in 1991 for $60 million.

Head gained a new chief executive in 1967, Harold J. Seigle, and embarked upon a vigorous diversification program. The Head brand eventually appeared on javelins and aluminum tennis

AT A GLANCE

Head brand skis founded in Timonium, MD, by Howard Head, owner of Head Ski Company; the company, which later produced tennis racquets, was renamed Head Sports, Inc.; company acquired by AMF, Inc., 1969; AMF acquired by Minstar, 1985; Head brand sold to HTM Sports Holding B.V., 1989.

Performance: *Market share*—16.0% of tennis racquet category.

Major competitor: For tennis racquets: Prince and Wilson; for skis: Olin and Rossignol.

Advertising: *Agency*—Racquet sports: McClain Finlon Advertising, Inc., Denver, CO; winter sports: John Creel Advertising, Newport Beach, CA. *Major campaign*—"Where Technology Comes Into Play."

Addresses: *Parent company*—Head Sports, Inc., 4801 North 63rd St., Boulder, CO 80301; phone (800) 874-3234/3235, (303) 530-2000; fax (303) 530-2965. *Ultimate parent company*—HTM Sports Holding B.V. (Netherlands).

racquets (developed with the late Wimbledon champion Arthur Ashe). The costs of opening Head Austria in 1969, though, diminished profits. In 1969 Head introduced its own fiberglass (made in Europe) and fiberglass/metal skis (made in the United States), but this could not strengthen the company enough to stop its takeover in 1969 by AMF, Inc. (originally known as American Machine and Foundry) in a transaction that earned Howard Head $4 million in cash.

Hoping to capitalize on a very diversified product line, in the late 1970s AMF moved to centralize its advertising for all its various brands of leisure goods, including Head skis and tennis racquets, Harley-Davidson motorcycles, and Hatteras yachts. Benton & Bowles, Inc., was chosen to provide advertising for all 20 of AMF's leisure goods subsidiaries. AMF also hoped that buyers satisfied with one AMF product would look for another.

In 1985 AMF, Inc., was acquired for $300 million in a corporate takeover by Minstar of White Plains, New York. AMF was vulnerable at this time due to declining profits and high corporate overhead. Four years later the international investment group HTM was formed, acquiring the brands Head, Tyrolia, and Mares from Minstar. In March of 1992 Robert S. Puccini was appointed president and chief executive officer of Head Sports, Inc. Stephen Miller had resigned from the position in June of 1991.

Decline in the 1990s

After a decade of decline, industry sales for skis and ski clothing increased approximately 20 percent from 1991 to 1992. However, industry experts predicted the ski equipment industry would never again see the robust growth of the postwar years when the Head ski was introduced. By this time, Head was eclipsed in the ski market by such high-end brands as Volkl and Bogner, as well as by other popular brands, such as Rossignol Ski. Production came to be dominated by fewer, larger, and more powerful companies. The Japanese imports also had been largely edged out.

Head Tennis Racquets

In addition to its skis, Head is known for its tennis racquets. Metal racquets were a logical extension of Head's product line, as the tennis products kept production lines running during skiing's off season. After trying unsuccessfully to acquire an existing racquet company, Howard Head in 1968 formed a tennis division to develop a metal tennis racquet. Head introduced its metal tennis racquets, dubbed the Competition and the Master, at the U.S. Open in 1969.

Head was not the first company to market a metal racquet—that honor belonged to Wilson Sporting Goods and its T2000. Although Howard Head did not begin with a monopoly on metal tennis racquets as it did with metal skis, he did achieve a market share in that category of approximately 15 percent in 1972, with metal racquets costing from $36 to $56, compared to Wilson's wood and metal racquets, which ranged from $5 to $60. The move into manufacturing tennis racquets was indeed shrewd, for during the early 1970s the tennis market was growing. In 1973 there were an estimated 27 million tennis players in the United States, spending a total of $500 million on tennis equipment, $100 million of that on balls and racquets; in 1970 only $27.8 million had been spent on tennis balls and racquets.

Head racquets were produced at the Maark Corp. near Princeton, New Jersey. After Howard Head had sold his interest in Head Sports and became the chairman of Prince Manufacturing, Inc., he turned to the same plant to manufacture his legendary Prince oversized racquets: the top two high-end brands were being manufactured in the same place. In 1977 Maark Corp. was acquired by AMF.

Industry racquet sales peaked in 1976 when 8.6 million were sold. In 1980 only 3.5 million were sold, with a value of $128 million. Low-priced Taiwanese midsize racquets, namely Pro Kennex, hurt domestic racquet sales in the 1980s. With approximately 30 brands on the market in the early 1980s, though, Head Sports managed to lead the midsize racquet category with the Edge racquet in 1984.

By 1994, Head racquets included the Prestige Tour 300, a mid-sized racquet featuring Head's Suspension Grip; the Pro Tour 280, a $199 mid-size, was a part of Head's Trisys series; and the Radical Trisys 260, retailing for $169, featured what was called the Integrated Damping System. The racquets were painted in a vivid yellow, red, and green color scheme and were aimed at 14- to 24-year-olds, augmenting Head's traditional strength in the over-30 market. Head offered a number of racquets in the Trisys series, including the Trisys 250, a mid-size, mid-wide, mid-flex racquet retailing for $99.95. Head also continued to offer full wide-body racquets. Its Trisys 300, offering "classic" flexibility, was billed as its most popular racquet among pros. In the 1990s most manufacturers, including Head, were offering "classic" styles and feels—that is, for example, narrower bodies for more control. "Mid-wide"s ranged from 22mm to 26mm wide.

Endorsements

Endorsements have always played an important role in marketing Head sporting goods. Head Skis won the trust of world-class skiers early on. Out of 141 places at the 1962 International Professional Ski Race Association, Head skis won 77. Later, Olympic gold medalist Jean-Claude Killy was signed on to endorse the high-end "Killy 800" skis.

In tennis, however, the company employed a low-key strategy similar to that of Prince, sponsoring a variety of tennis professionals, most notably the late Wimbledon champion and Davis Cup coach Arthur Ashe and Argentine French Open champion Guillermo Villas. However, in 1993 Head signed a multi-million dollar deal with flamboyant tennis pro Andre Agassi to promote its Radical Trisys 260 tennis racquets.

Further Reading:

"The $4-Billion Market in Fun," *Business Week,* February 8, 1969, pp. 82–84.

Beercheck, Richard C., "Sporting Goods Win with High-Tech Materials," *Machine Design,* June 6, 1991, pp. 62–66.

Chernoff, Allan, "Short-term Profits Rise as Long-term Interest Declines," *New York Times,* September 12, 1993, p. S13.

Chirls, Stewart, "New Racquets Are Fit to Be Tried," *Tennis,* March 1994, pp. 64–97.

Dumaine, Brian, "Prince Gets into Some New Rackets," *Fortune,* October 29, 1984, p. 78.

Edmands, Michael J., "Friendly Elements: Surging Popularity of Skiing Gives Welcome Lift to Equipment Makers," *Barron's,* March 30, 1970, pp. 5, 14, 16.

Ehrlich, Elizabeth, "Behind the AMF Takeover: From Highflier to Sitting Duck," *Business Week,* August 12, 1985, pp. 50–51.

Greising, David, "Whap! Ace. Point. You Call This Tennis?," *Business Week,* September 9, 1991, p. 71.

Harper, Sam, "Sporting Good Sales Bit [sic] Flabby," *Advertising Age,* July 6, 1981, p. 10.

"The History of Head," *SportStyle,* September 24, 1990, p. 41.

Josty, Peter L., "A Tentative Model of the Innovation Process," *R&D Management,* January 1, 1990, pp. 35–45.

Kaiser, Deborah, "With Tennis Pros' Squabble Settled, Marketers Can Exploit Sport's Appeal," *Advertising Age,* June 5, 1972, pp. 10, 58.

Kreisman, Richard, "Downhill Takes on New Meaning for Ski Market," *Advertising Age,* November 23, 1981, p. 3.

Lerman, Josh, and Mike Finkel, "What's Wrong with the Industry?," *STN, Skiing Trade News,* December 1991, p. 20.

McQuade, Walter, "Prince Triumphant," *Fortune,* February 22, 1982, pp. 84–90.

Moffatt, Terence, "The SGB Tennis Market Survey," *Sporting Goods Business,* October 1992, p. 40.

"New Life for the Ski Business," *Business Week,* March 29, 1958, pp. 132–34.

Raissman, Robert, "Bigger Budgets Volley for Bigger Racquets," *Advertising Age,* July 25, 1983, pp. 20, 86.

"Royal Flush in Skis," *Fortune,* March 1959, p. 214.

Sloan, Pat, "Prince Makes a Racquet to Raise Market Share," *Advertising Age,* July 25, 1985, p. 20.

"The Sporting Life," *Forbes,* March 15, 1964, pp. 18–19.

Stone, Amey, "Getting a Grip on High-Tech Tennis," *Business Week,* June 7, 1993, p. 118.

Tanler, Bill, "Ski Production Turns to the Fewer, the Bigger," *STN,* October 1993, p. 30.

"Tennis Market Seen Topping $500 Million in '74," *Advertising Age,* October 21, 1974, p. 44.

Thomas, Dana L., "Play's the Thing: There's Profit as Well as Pleasure in All Kinds of Sports," *Barron's,* March 27, 1961, p. 3.

Willatt, Norris, "World of Sports: It Is Growing Bigger and More Sophisticated Every Year," *Barron's,* April 2, 1962, p. 5.

—Frederick C. Ingram

HEWLETT-PACKARD®

Hewlett-Packard Company (HP) operates in several different markets, manufacturing electronics and computer equipment for a variety of institutional customers. The company is best known in consumer markets for its unique line of calculators, computer systems, and printers. The company's superior product line has done much to define the Hewlett-Packard brand name. HP has a very narrow presence in consumer markets because its products occupy the high end of their segments, they have specialized uses, and they are not cheap. As an example, HP calculators work differently than standard mathematical calculators because they are designed specifically for scientific applications. They are formatted to work like computers; functions are executed with an "enter" key. Difficult to operate for the uninitiated, they make perfect sense to engineers.

Brand Origins

Hewlett-Packard's modest beginnings follow a pattern that is by now common among California's Silicon Valley firms. In 1938, Dave and Lucile Packard moved into a house in Palo Alto, California. Bill Hewlett, a friend of the Packards who, like Dave, was an electrical engineer, rented a cottage behind the house. With only $538 in start-up capital, Packard and Hewlett spent their free time manufacturing a resistance-capacity audio oscillator that could be used to test sound equipment. Hoping to market their device, the two men needed to settle on a company name, which they did by tossing a coin. To avoid sounding like a start-up firm, they grandly named their first product the HP200A. The paint on the product's shell was baked on in Mrs. Packard's kitchen oven.

Hewlett-Packard, still operating out of the garage, won an order for eight rack model HP200Bs from Walt Disney Studios, which used the devices to calibrate sound for the movie *Fantasia.* At $55 per unit, the HP200B represented a breakthrough in size, performance, and price. Packard and Hewlett formed a partnership on January 1, 1939. Sales, primarily of frequency calibration equipment, remained slow through 1940. That year, the company—with three employees and eight products—moved out of the garage and into a factory space.

The U.S. entrance into the war late in 1941 immediately created an overwhelming demand for HP measuring instruments, which the Army and Navy used to true up radio transceivers and calibrate radar systems. With the sudden deluge of orders, HP was forced to build a larger factory. By 1943, sales had mushroomed to more than $1 million.

Brand Development

After the war, HP suffered from a sudden cancellation in government orders. Spurned from reliable government work, the company elected to pursue institutional markets in the private sector, mainly because its technologies far exceeded applications for consumer markets. The company was incorporated on August 18, 1947, and sales began to recover slowly. The war had created a burgeoning electronics industry whose primary focus was in broadcast communications. Here again, HP products led the market for measuring equipment. The company developed its HP524A frequency counter in 1951. This device could accurately measure high frequencies in less than two seconds, as opposed to the ten minutes required by existing equipment. Radio stations used the HP524A to comply with FCC frequency stability requirements.

HP moved into new areas outside the measurement instrument market, not by immediately developing its own products, but by first acquiring other manufacturers in the markets it hoped to enter. The first of these acquisitions occurred in 1958, when HP took over the F.L. Moseley Company. Moseley, based in Pasadena, produced high-quality X-Y and strip-chart graphic recorders, of the type used in electric motor testing and seismic logs. In 1961, the company acquired the Massachusetts-based Sanborn Company, a manufacturer of medical monitoring and diagnostic equipment. Sanborn represented Hewlett-Packard's entrance into the medical equipment market, where HP would later become a leading supplier. By 1965, the Hewlett-Packard name was firmly established in the area of instrumentation and was regarded as operating in a market similar to Sperry, Sundstrand, and others. That year, the company expanded its presence in analytical instrumentation—that is, a measuring device connected to a computer—by acquiring the F&M Scientific Corporation.

In order to support new product development and, indeed, to develop the technological platforms for hundreds of new products, HP established a technological research facility, HP Laboratories, in 1966.

AT A GLANCE

Hewlett-Packard brand of electronics, calculators, computers, and printers founded in 1938 by David Packard and William Hewlett with their creation of an audio oscillator; company incorporated in 1947; developed its first computer in 1966; desktop scientific calculator introduced in 1968; a business computer introduced 1972; developed inkjet printing technology with HP ThinkJet in 1984; HP#95LX "palmtop" PC marketed in 1991.

Major competitor: Epson, also Texas Instruments, Canon, and Panasonic.

Advertising: *Agency*—Saatchi & Saatchi DFS/Pacific. *Major campaigns*—"Think again" for HP computer systems; ads featuring leap-frogging printers for printer products.

Addresses: *Parent company*—Hewlett-Packard Company, 3000 Hanover Street, Palo Alto, CA 94303-1185; phone: (415) 857-1501.

Extensions

HP developed a highly accurate portable clock in 1964. The HP5060A used a cesium beam to measure time. In a mission that was part practical and part advertising stunt, an HP5060A was flown around the world to standardize clocks in all 24 time zones. In 1966, Hewlett-Packard introduced its first computer, the HP2116A, designed as a controller for the company's other testing and measuring apparatus.

The first extension of the Hewlett-Packard brand name to a genuine consumer product came in 1968, when the company developed its first desktop calculator, the HP9100A. Considerably larger than the deck-of-cards-size calculators in common use several years later, the HP9100A was intended for scientific use, rather than simple mathematical functions. As a result, the product's utility to a mass market was highly limited; few people had a need to run complex logarithmic functions or perform calculus integrations.

The company continued to develop both calculators and computers, and in 1972 introduced the HP-35 handheld scientific calculator, which the company maintains rendered the slide-rule obsolete. Similarly, the computer system had been upgraded to a business model called the HP#3000. By 1980, several computer manufacturers had begun a coordinated move on IBM's flanks, developing powerful desktop computers. Hewlett-Packard participated in this movement by developing its first personal computer, the HP-85. In 1982, the company introduced a "desktop mainframe," the HP9000, using 32-bit "superchip" technology.

In 1984, Hewlett-Packard introduced a unique printer called the HP ThinkJet, which produced images with a tiny ink nozzle. The following year, the company developed an even more successful printer, the HP LaserJet. This product set a new standard in printer quality. Thousands of LaserJet printers were purchased by individual consumers who matched them to their IBMs, Compaqs, and other computers.

Advertising

Due to the nature of its product lines, HP has never used a great deal of advertising. The company produces more than 22,000 products, but the majority of these are special-use diagnostic or measuring instrumentation. Only the company's printers, computers, and calculators may be considered consumer products. As a result, HP advertising is something of a recent phenomenon. The campaigns HP has launched have been targeted mainly at managers of corporate information technology.

Among the most memorable HP advertising campaigns was the "What if . . . " campaign, which ran from 1986 to 1988. This series was designed to illustrate the 24-hour dedication of HP managers in dreaming up new solutions for customers. The ads depict an HP manager—far from the office, even on vacation—who suddenly gets a brainstorm and calls an associate from a public telephone. "Bob?" the manager says, "I was just thinking, what if we . . . " and continues to speak as a voice over announces, "At Hewlett-Packard, we never stop asking "What if." The "Think again" series followed in 1990. These ads were intended to draw customers' attention to HP products as alternatives to market mainstays. The tagline was used more as a punchline, imploring customers who thought their options were limited to IBM or DEC to "Think again."

One area in which HP has cultivated an emerging brand is in the printer segment, where the HP "LaserJet" has set a standard for quality. One campaign featured a Dalmatian to demonstrate that HP is the businessperson's best friend. A more tongue-in-cheek approach was accomplished in a series featuring competing printers playing leap frog. As they hopped out in front of each other, none was able to overtake the Hewlett-Packard LaserJet, which remained securely in the lead. These ads demonstrated HP's leading position in this market.

International Growth

As an instruments company, HP was quick to realize benefits from global expansion. The company established a marketing organization in Geneva, Switzerland, and a manufacturing facility in Boblingen, Germany, in 1959. By entering into a partnership with Tokyo-based Yokogawa Electric Works in 1963, HP used Yokogawa's existing connections to gain entry into Japan's otherwise restrictive market.

Reflecting its growth in Japanese and European markets, HP gained a listing on the Tokyo stock exchange in 1988 and listings in London, Zurich, Paris, and Frankfurt in 1989. The company also established a research facility in Tokyo, with the aim of further leveraging its presence in Japan and taking advantage of that country's collegial approach to technological development. These developments illustrate the growing importance of overseas markets to Hewlett-Packard. In the early 1990s, these markets constituted more than 50 percent of the company's total sales, and this number is expected to surpass 70 percent by the year 2000.

Brand Development

In 1986 HP undertook the creation of a new family of computer systems based on its innovative HP Precision Architecture. The five-year, $250 million project, called "Spectrum," was the most expensive and ambitious product development effort in the company's history. The result, in 1992, was a line of corporate business products, including nine HP3000 and HP9000 computing systems. These models provided mainframe performance in a desktop, at as little as 10 percent the cost of a mainframe system.

Hewlett-Packard made an important move into the workstation market in 1989, when it purchased Apollo Computer. The acquisition greatly strengthened HP's position in office-based computer networks and telecommunications interfaces and broadened the scope of its competition with companies like IBM and Apple Computer.

Technological development at HP Labs resulted in several new products in the early 1990s. Hewlett-Packard introduced an improved HP LaserJet printer in 1990. The product, again priced primarily for institutional markets, helped preserve HP's lead in printer technologies. Customers interested in the most advanced system commonly purchased an IBM or Macintosh computer, but chose HP LaserJets for their printers. In 1991 Hewlett-Packard introduced a "palmtop" personal computer called the HP95LX. This 11-ounce device provided all the power of a desktop PC in a unit only slightly larger than a conventional calculator. Again, this product was priced out of the general consumer market and was aimed primarily at the corporate market. In an extension of this application, Hewlett-Packard introduced its HP Kittyhawk Personal Storage Module, containing a 1.3-inch disk drive, the world's smallest.

Future Direction

Hewlett-Packard has performed extremely well in the business markets it has occupied since it was founded. A number of its products have made successful crossover sales in consumer markets, but only in narrow ranges where customers have highly specific or unique requirements. The company's research and development organization and progressive administrative philosophies have translated directly into a well-earned reputation for quality that may play very well in consumer markets, should the company choose to broaden its exposure to this segment. However, Hewlett-Packard would have to launch a sizable campaign to make "superstore" customers aware of its great reputation and to compete with brands that are better established in the consumer products markets.

Rather than expand its consumer sales with established products, HP may use new technologies. With the bold predictions of an "information superhighway" being proclaimed at all levels of the telecommunications and electronics industry, HP has announced its intention to be the leading supplier of what it terms "information appliances." Using the capabilities provided by optoelectronics and massively improved computing power, consumers, HP maintains, will be able to define the information they need and receive it immediately.

One example of HP's development of these technologies is its HP#95LX palmtop PC. A more ambitious and yet-to-be-realized product would marry telecommunications and television. HP has established a partnership with TV Answer, Inc., to develop interactive television technologies that would convert home televisions into a kind of visual interface for more sophisticated information appliances. These appliances would provide custom-ordered newspapers and catalogs, personal accounting systems, and online consultation and shopping services.

HP is likely to leverage the venerable name it earned in institutional markets to consumer markets. Although few households today contain a Hewlett-Packard product, many may by the year 2000. The new HP consumer product is likely to be much more than a computer or a cable box—more a full-blown server interface, complete with administration software. As Hewlett-Packard moves into this new field, it will face competition from an entirely new set of competitors, including AT&T, Sony, Scientific Atlanta, Panasonic, and Apple.

Further Reading:

Hewlett-Packard Annual Report, Palo Alto, CA: Hewlett-Packard, 1992.

"Hewlett-Packard Keeps Reinventing Itself," *Industry Week,* August 19, 1991.

Historical Highlights of Hewlett-Packard Company, Palo Alto, CA: Hewlett-Packard.

"HP Directions for the '90s," Hewlett-Packard document.

—*John Simley*

HITACHI®

HITACHI

The Consumer Products division of Hitachi, Ltd., markets a wide variety of consumer electronics under the Hitachi brand name, including color and projection TVs, VCRs, camcorders, audio systems, small and major appliances, fax machines, lighting fixtures, and home heating and cooling equipment. Hitachi, Ltd., is the twelfth-largest industrial corporation in the world, and the second-largest industrial corporation in Japan. One of Japan's "big six" electronics companies, Hitachi, Ltd., contributed almost 2 percent of Japan's total gross national product in the early 1990s. Hitachi, which means "rising sun," is Japan's top patent holder, and ranks fourth for total U.S. patents awarded since 1963. Hitachi, Ltd., held over 85,000 worldwide patents as of the early 1990s.

Hitachi's success in the highly competitive consumer electronics field has been attributed to its ability to deliver innovative, reliable, quality products that enhance the lives of consumers. One strategy has been to reach different groups of consumers by marketing the same type of product at different prices based on the range of features and level of product sophistication. Some top of the line products are for audio or videophiles while products at the middle and lower end are for less sophisticated users. Another strategy has been to develop and market products that tap into the interests and preferences of consumers at a given time and use technology to satisfy them. For example, consumer interest in fresh foods influenced the company to market a breadmaking machine for home baking, made easy and convenient to use through electronic controls.

Hitachi, Ltd.'s other divisions are involved in making commercial or industrial products and include information/communication systems and electronic devices, power systems and equipment, industrial machinery, and wire, cable, metals, and chemicals. Hitachi also plays leadership roles in some of these products, such as being the world leader in DRAM production and a major producer of IBM-compatible mainframe computers, heavy machinery, and power plants.

Brand Origins

In 1910, Namihei Odaira built five-horsepower electric motors in the engineering and repair shop of the mining company where he worked in Hitachi, Japan. His intent was to show Japanese power companies that they did not have to depend on foreign technology. During World War I, Japanese power companies had to buy electric motors from Odaira because it was difficult to import them. Fortunately for Odaira, the new Japanese buyers were so impressed with his generators that they reordered and the seeds of what became Hitachi, Ltd. were planted.

As an independent company in the 1920s, Hitachi, Ltd., produced new designs for motors, fans, generators, and electrical products. In the 1930s and 1940s, Hitachi, Ltd., developed vacuum tubes and light bulbs. During World War II, the company made radar and sonar for defense use. However, Japan's defeat in the war caused plant closures, war damage, and labor problems for Hitachi, Ltd. The company was saved from bankruptcy only through military contracts awarded from the United States, which was involved in the Korean War. In the 1950s, Hitachi, Ltd., was a supplier for Nippon Telegraph and Telephone, the state-owned communications monopoly.

Brand Development

During the 1950s, as Japan began to recover economically from the devastation of World War II, Japanese consumers began to demand more products as their earning power increased. Hitachi, Ltd., began to mass produce many of the consumer electronic products that helped to make it a world leader. Radios, televisions and home appliances were first marketed during this period, and in the 1960s the company produced its first color televisions.

In the ensuing years, Hitachi kept pace with trends. It was during the late 1980s and early 1990s, however, that technological advances allowed consumer electronic companies to incorporate features hitherto unavailable. First, television screens increased in size from 13 to 20 to 27 inches in size. In the early 1990s, on-screen menus helped guide users through features and adjustments, and the system's sound could be provided as surround or normal stereo in the 13- and 20-inch screens. The larger 27-inch screen systems had a channel blockout feature, as well as on-screen help menus.

Still larger screens were used in 1993 when several different types of projection television systems were introduced as two different lines. Consumers were moving toward the concept of home theater and projection televisions were marketed as entertainment systems that emulated the viewing and sound experiences of live theater. The UltraVision line consisted of seven new

AT A GLANCE

Hitachi brand of electronics marketed by Hitachi Home Electronics (America), Inc., the U.S. subsidiary of Hitachi, Ltd., of Japan; founded by Namihei Odaira in Hitachi, Japan, in 1920, Hitachi, Ltd., became a major manufacturer of electrical equipment and machinery; first U.S. sales office opened in New York, 1959.

Performance: *Market share*—13% (top share) of worldwide electronics market (1990). *Sales*—$9 billion in worldwide consumer electronics sales; $5 billion in total U.S. sales; $60 billion in total worldwide sales.

Major competitor: Matsushita; also Pioneer, Sharp, Sanyo, and Sony.

Advertising: *Agency*—(U.S. consumer products) Hakuhodo Advertising America, Inc., New York, NY, 1989—. *Major campaign*—Baseball giant Reggie Jackson featured in TV commercials for big screen TVs in 1993.

Addresses: *Parent company*—Hitachi, Ltd., Kabushiki Kaisha Hitachi Seisakusho, 6, Kanda-Surugadai 4-chome, Chiyodo-ku, Tokyo 101, Japan; phone: 3-3258-1111; fax: 3-3258-2375.

televisions, using the UltraBlack high-contrast dark tint screen. Two 60-inch systems, the 60SX4K and 60SX3B, contained such features as Hitachi's unique quick freeze PIP and 1,000 lines of horizontal resolution.

Another UltraVision model, the 50SX5P, was an industry first. It was the first 50-inch PIV model to use a High Definition Television (HDTV) lens system and digital convergence to get 1,000 lines of horizontal resolution. The UltraVision line, rated number one by *Consumer Reports* in March of 1993, also included two 46-inch models. The UltraVision models had the new illuminated Genius remote control as well as a second remote, the Easy Remote, to control basic functions. The Genius remote was a unique four-way controller that accessed the Easy Guide On-Screen Display for quick adjustments to sound, picture and convenience features. The UltraVision line ranged in price from $2,799 to $4,399. Hitachi's other line of televisions was called Maxus, and had projection television systems with screens ranging from 46 to 55-inches. The aim was to provide consumers with big screen enjoyment at an affordable price under $2,500.

Continual additions in features were also made in other video products. During the 1980s, VCRs contained such features as tape counter, tracking control on remote control, and search features. By 1993, technology had so advanced that Hitachi was able to develop a top-of-the-line model, the "Laser VLS", a laser-controlled videoloading system. The system was activated by an infrared sensor that automatically opened whenever a video tape was placed before it. The feature provided easy, quick and reliable tape loading. Another feature, the RM-772 illuminated LCD remote, had a door covering the upper half of the remote to protect the more involved controls while allowing the user access to the basic command functions. The remote had a jog/shuttle knob to advance or reverse/forward the tape. Another VCR model had Hitachi's exclusive Easy Guide Graphic menu system in three languages: English, Spanish, and French. Prices for these models ranged from $269 to $999.

During the 1980s, camcorders gained popularity with consumers. The early Hitachi models had stereo sound, a special control cable to help with editing, and a wind noise suppression setting. By 1993, technology had once again allowed the company to provide enhancing features. The new VM-H57A had Hitachi's exclusive advanced artificial intelligence technology which provided a program autoexposure system, advanced video focusing, advanced AI circuitry for iris and white balance adjustment, and built-in automatic wind noise filter.

Hitachi also introduced two full-size VHS camcorders with different lenses and battery packs, and artificial intelligence circuitry. The VM-2600 model had a 24x zoom lens system and two-hour battery, and was priced at $899. The VM-1600 had a 12x zoom and one-hour battery, and was priced at $799. During the early 1990s, Hitachi also first marketed three new Ultra-compact 8mm camcorders priced from $1,099 to $1,399. All three models weighed just one pound nine ounces and had a 1/3-inch CCD sensor.

Audio systems were similarly advanced and feature-laden. In 1993, Hitachi introduced two small, programmable audio systems. The AX12 had a single CD. The AXC12 system contained a built-in six-plus-one compact disc player and changer. This model had such features as continuous playing without interruption while the six-disc cartridge was being changed.

Advertising Innovations

During the early 1990s, Hitachi's print and TV advertising focused on acquainting American consumers with their products, particularly their big screen TVs. TV commercials were chosen as the chief media because the greatest number of consumers could be reached to create product awareness. Commercials often appeared during sports events such as football games.

During this period, Hitachi advertised primarily its big screen TVs and emphasized the product's superior clarity. For example, Reggie Jackson, the baseball star, was shown in one TV commercial that featured a real cheerleader inside a TV screen next to a TV picture of a cheerleader. The viewer could see that Hitachi's picture was like reality itself and would have difficulty differentiating the TV picture from the live cheerleader.

Marketing Strategies

Hitachi goes directly to its consumers to determine their interests, and some consumer electronics products have included features requested by consumers to make product usage easier and more convenient. Another marketing strategy is more broad-based and strives to encompass whole communities. Each Hitachi group company seeks to develop strong relationships with local business partners and suppliers who provide materials and support. This technique serves two purposes: Hitachi is ensured of steady deliveries of supplies, and local communities are enriched by the company's business, thereby increasing local consumer buying power for Hitachi products.

Another community outreach program was introduced in 1985, when the company established the Hitachi Foundation to develop social programs with individual communities and on a national level. The Hitachi Foundation supports education, recreation, and many different charities through employee involvement and donations. Each of the 67 Hitachi group companies in the U.S. considers itself a part of its local community, and each group tries to honor that relationship by contributing to educational support, funding for local causes, and establishing college and university scholarships. Some groups have organized employee Community Action Committees to help identify and alleviate the most important community needs, assign volunteers, and allocate appropriate funding. On a national level, the Foundation provides national grants to support projects in education, community development, and global citizenship.

Performance Appraisal

In 1991, Hitachi reported that 12 percent of its total worldwide sales came from TVs and VCRs alone. Worldwide sales for consumer electronics in 1991 were $9 billion. The company reported in 1992 that consumer products accounted for 12 percent of total revenues, while 34 percent of revenues came from information systems and electronics devices, 29 percent from power and industrial systems, and 25 percent from materials and others products.

Hitachi is a global company operating in 38 countries. The company makes more than 20,000 products at 70 different manufacturing companies guided by 23 overseas offices. Global marketing reflects the policies used in the United States. Each local market is analyzed in terms of its individual consumer needs. Then, Hitachi tailors its sales, manufacturing, and other operations to satisfy those needs.

Future Products

Recognizing that new products that excite consumers are the lifeblood of the consumer electronics industry, Hitachi spends an estimated 7 percent of its total sales each year for research and development. In the United States, Hitachi has a High Definition Advanced Research lab in Princeton, New Jersey, and the world's most automated color TV picture tube plant in Greenville, South Carolina. Though Hitachi reduced its research budget during the worldwide recession of the 1990s, the company expected to introduce future products that would match the inventiveness and quality of its current products. Some company ideas for the future were handheld video phones and palmtop supercomputers that will accept voice commands instead of typed commands or touched screens.

Further Reading:

Gross, Neil, "Inside Hitachi," *Business Week,* September 28, 1992, pp. 94–98.

Pollack, Andrew, "Big Companies in Japan Trim Research Budgets," *New York Times,* November 11, 1993, D2.

Additional information provided by Hitachi Home Electronics (America).

—*Dorothy Kroll*

HONDA ACCORD®

Since the American Honda Motor Company, Inc., introduced the Accord to the U.S. car market in 1976, the brand's rise to success was so dramatic that by the time it became the top-selling car in America in 1989, it had acquired such an aura of superiority that the Accord seemed to sell itself. However, at the very end of 1992, the Accord began to seriously stumble in sales. This was especially shocking given the Accord's historic knack for staying one step ahead of the competition. From the moment the Accord was introduced in 1976, it consistently overcame import quotas, currency exchange rates, and U.S. political resistance to set the standard for popularity in its market segment, with Honda always selling as many Accords as it could build.

Revving Up

In 1976 Honda launched the Accord in an attempt to gain a larger share of the suddenly resurgent American car market. As gasoline became more easily available, American car consumers were starting to move away from their desire for super-small cars and beginning to demand larger, more comfortable models. Although the Accord was almost a foot longer than the Honda Civic, introduced just two years earlier, the Accord was still clearly a small car. As long as gas availability remained high, it seemed likely that the Accord and Civic would be passed over for bigger cars. In 1977, though, President Jimmy Carter announced an energy-conservation package that would dramatically raise the cost of owning and operating a gas-guzzling car while rewarding buyers of gas-stingy cars with tax rebates. As a result, car customers turned back to gas-stingy cars, but this time looking to retain some of the roominess they were giving up with their big cars.

Enter the Accord. While Detroit automakers were hastily racing to cut back the size and weight of their upcoming 1978 models, the comfortable Accord already exceeded many of the standards the new Federal law demanded cars to meet by 1985, with highway mileage, for instance, close to 50-mpg. Though the Accord had attracted some interest in its introductory year, it was in 1977 when Accord sales really shot up, doubling sales of the 1976 model and forcing many customers to sign up on long waiting lists to purchase one.

Enjoying Its Special Appeal

Accord sales continued to boom even when most other Japanese-made small cars began losing market share in 1978. Because the dollar steadily fell against the yen in 1978, the Japanese opted to raise their prices rather than ship more cars to America; this latter move would risk pushing the United States—already concerned about its trade deficit with Japan—to impose import restrictions. The Accord seemed to have some kind of special appeal that its contenders did not, but the car basically offered the same advantages its imported competitors did: high fuel-efficiency, front-wheel drive, and the general sense that Japanese-made small cars were superior to their late-coming American counterparts. Somehow, though, the Accord managed to gain a reputation for high quality, a reputation so strong that the Accord continued to enjoy it throughout its history.

Just how exactly the Accord managed to develop such a singular status before it had much of a history to back it up is somewhat of a mystery. Part of the answer perhaps rested in the innovative combustion technology the Accord offered, high-quality technology that both impressed customers and saved them money. Honda originally introduced the CVCC (or compound vortex-controlled combustion) engine in 1973 with the Civic, giving the car the distinction of running on cheaper leaded fuel while still meeting all government emissions standards. Because of Honda's unusually high emphasis on research and development, the CVCC was just one of the high-quality innovative features customers could always count on every year from each new Accord. Honda was forced to give up the CVCC due to new government standards in 1980, but the loss of this early advantage was minor compared to the tougher competition the Accord was facing from American automakers who were developing higher quality subcompact cars.

Steering into the Mid-Sized Sedan Market

Honda's response to the billion-dollar efforts of U.S. automakers to produce fuel-efficient subcompacts was to steer the Accord out of this already-crowded market and into the increasingly profitable market for mid-sized sedans. Small cars had peaked in 1980, claiming a 42.9 percent share of the car market, while mid-sized cars held a 40.2 percent share. But by 1984, mid-sized cars comprised 47.8 percent of the market, overtaking small cars, whose share had dropped dramatically to 31.3 percent. Honda took its first step into the mid-sized car market in 1982 by completely re-engineering the Accord: Honda expanded the Ac-

AT A GLANCE

Honda Accord brand founded in 1976 in Tokyo, Japan, by the Honda Motor Company, Ltd.; the American Honda Motor Company, Inc., a wholly owned subsidiary, introduced the Accord to the United States as a subcompact in 1976; for the 1983 model year, the Accord was redesigned as a mid-sized sedan and became the first Japanese car manufactured in the United States; from 1989 through 1991, the Accord was the top-selling car brand in the United States.

Performance: *Market share*—2.38% of 1993 U.S. car category. *Sales*—330,030 units (1993).

Major competitor: For the sedans (DX, LX, and EX): Ford Taurus, Toyota Camry, and Chrysler LH sedans; for the wagons (LX and EX): Ford Taurus, Subaru Legacy, and Volvo 240 wagons.

Advertising: *Agency*—Rubin Postaer & Associates, Los Angeles, CA, 1974—. *Major campaign*—Television and print ads selling the Accord as "a car ahead," with some TV ads using voice-overs by actor Jack Lemmon.

Addresses: *Parent company*—American Honda Motor Company, Inc., 1919 Torrance Boulevard, Torrance, CA 90501-2746; phone: (310) 783-3170; fax: (310) 783-3622. *Ultimate parent company*—Honda Motor Company, Ltd., No. 1-1, 2-chome, Minami-Aoyama, Minato-ku, Tokyo 107, Japan; phone: (03) 3423-1111; fax: (03) 3423-0511-4.

cord's length and width and, for the first time, marketed the four-door Accord as a five-passenger sedan.

This move turned out to be favorable for Accord sales, as gasoline prices soon began to drop significantly and car buyers decided that they could afford to drive roomier and less fuel-efficient cars. Though the new Accord lost the selling points of a subcompact, it remained highly competitive because of its moderate price, sporty design, powerful yet quiet engine, and its continuing reputation for quality. And starting in 1983, the Accord had a further edge over its imported competition: it became the first Japanese car manufactured in the United States, thus avoiding import restrictions while dramatically increasing its production—and sales.

Becoming Made in America

Because Honda's Japanese plants could not build enough Accords in the late 1970s when American demand soared, and because building new plants in Japan was hindered by new environmental regulations and inflated land prices, Honda started taking a serious look at the idea of building an Accord plant in America—a bold idea that would make the Accord the first Japanese car built in the United States. Building an American plant had the added benefits of creating American jobs and of avoiding import restrictions, which would likely be imposed by import-wary U.S. politicians. Honda decided to construct a plant in Marysville, Ohio, starting construction there in 1980. Unfortunately for Honda, a year before its American plant would start producing Accords, the Japanese government gave into U.S. political pressures and imposed a quota on exports to the United States.

But operating one year under the quota restrictions would not hinder Honda all that much, especially considering that the two biggest Japanese automakers—Toyota and Nissan—were far from building their own U.S. plants. When the first American-made Accords—1983 model-year four-door sedans—were sold in December, 1982, the Accord suddenly enjoyed an advantage over its quota-restricted competitors. By mid-1984, the plant was operating at full capacity, producing 150,000 Accords annually, which more than doubled the number of Accords sold in America. By 1988, the Accord was the best-selling Japanese car in America.

Even though the Accord continued to be in high demand despite its dramatically increased supply, Honda was particularly concerned about how it could reconcile the marketing dilemma it had created for the Accord by giving it the distinction of being the first Japanese car built in America: on the one hand, Honda hoped it could give American-built Accords an advantage by advertising them as "made over here." But on the other hand, Honda knew that American-built cars carried a certain stigma of low quality. "Put two identical cars side by side—one made in the U.S. and the other made in Japan—and nine out of ten buyers will take the Japanese car," asserted John M. Hemphill, J. D. Power & Associates executive VP, in a 1983 *Industry Week* article. To ensure product quality, Honda of America Manufacturing Inc.—the subsidiary that ran the Marysville operations—"Japanized" its production by encouraging its assembly-line workers to participate in daily decision making. This departure from the status quo of American automaking practices paid off as the Accord maintained its reputation for quality—and enjoyed steadily increasing sales—throughout the 1980s.

Transforming into a Yuppie-Mobile

As the 1980s revved up, Honda was already targeting for the Accord a customer base of young, upwardly mobile professionals ("yuppies"). Honda completely re-engineered the Accord in 1982 to enter the passenger sedan market. Though this version of the Accord (1982-1985) was not a luxury sedan, its style, roominess, dependability, and handling made it increasingly attractive to many middle-class families and young professionals. By completely redesigning the Accord once again for the 1986 model year, Honda made a deliberate move to take full advantage of this interest among upwardly mobile customers, making the Accord a "yuppie-mobile" of choice. The roomier 1986 Accord was sleek and sporty, featuring a low hoodline and retractable headlights. The Accord always had a reputation for being fun to drive, and this new design managed to make a further leap in that department with a new double-wishbone suspension and a more powerful engine.

Even with all the success of the 1986-88 Accord, Honda pushed to stay ahead of the competition by redesigning the Accord for 1989. Refurbishing the Accord with more luxury-like styling paid off as the Accord began four years of incredible success, becoming the top-selling individual car model in the United States in 1989, 1990, and 1991. In 1992 the Accord was barely edged out for the top spot by the incentive-rich Ford Taurus.

To maintain the Accord's top-selling position, Honda ran a series of ads in the late 1980s and early 1990s designed not only to maintain the Accord's longtime image as an extremely reliable, unpretentious, yet classy, mid-sized car, but also to establish the image of the number one Accord as one-of-a-kind. In 1989 Honda ran a classic ad in which the Accord is displayed on an art gallery wall among original modern masterpieces. Though such a scene by itself might have appeared pretentious, Honda's longtime ad agency, Rubin Postaer & Associates of Los Angeles (hired in

1974), gave the ad a witty, and attention-grabbing, twist of special effects that portrayed the Accord as not only appealing to look at but even more irresistible to drive. In this TV spot, a man strolling through the gallery stops to admire the Accord and then actually climbs in and drives it right off the wall, leaving behind two dark tread marks. An elderly women then inches her way into the scene and stares, completely baffled, at the tread marks; she is apparently too old-fashioned to recognize what the Accord's target consumers appreciate: avant-garde artwork and the trend-setting Accord, a car so captivating it did not remain in showrooms (or galleries) for long.

Responding to Increased Competition

Ever since the Accord became the top-selling car in America, it was the clear target for an increasing number of rivals in the mid-sized car market. Honda initially planned not to respond to attacks from Accord's competitors: "We don't want to get into a big screamer; this is the price of leadership," said Eric Conn, Honda senior manager of automobile advertising, in a 1990 *Adweek* article. However, as Honda felt more and more pressure from Accord's competitors, the company spent much of its $100 million 1990 ad budget (up ten percent from the previous year) on some television spots designed to respond to the shots taken by its competitors. The most noteworthy ad begins with an Accord parked in front of a white wall while actor Jack Lemmon provides the voice-over: "Accord: what the competition is shooting for." Suddenly, three volleys of arrows shoot in from off screen and stick into the wall without striking the Accord. After a pause, a single arrow shoots in, hopelessly missing the Accord; Lemmon comments, "Nice shot."

Experiencing Car Troubles

While the Accord was sitting atop the world of domestic car sales, a significant slip occurred, not in the sale of any of the popular Accord sedans (or at least not yet) but in a new brand extension: the Accord station wagon. Introduced in the 1991 model year, the wagon produced sales running well behind what Honda had hoped for in its first year, selling about 2,000 per month instead of 3,000. Many wondered why the most successful car in America did not enjoy a successful brand extension. Although the entire car industry was suffering from a U.S. recession, the wagon's high price and limited interior space were partly to blame for struggling sales. Even though Honda increased the price only slightly the next year, and later redesigned the wagon's disappointing features for the 1994 model year, the company was still faced with the fact that the market for station wagons was steadily declining as the minivan market was experiencing rapid growth.

However, Honda was not planning to launch an Accord-based minivan until the 1995 model year. The company's slow reflexes were again exposed when it failed to redesign its 1993 mid-sized Accord sedan in response to increasing sales by such competitors as the Ford Taurus (although the increase might be attributed to fleet sales, an area in which Honda did not compete). The Accord's 1993 sales proved disappointing, dropping 16.1 percent from the previous year. Suddenly, Honda was put in the unfamiliar position of having to play catch-up. The competition expected that Honda would regain more competitiveness in 1994 by increasing the Accord's size and offering a V-6 engine, an expectation based on the astounding success of other automakers' big V-6 family sedans. However, Honda was not prepared to release a V-6 Accord until 1995. Instead, the company introduced a redesigned 1994 Accord that was named "Import Car of the Year" by *Motor Trend* magazine.

Honda marketed its 1994 Accord as a "leap year" model, intimating that the car represented a significant leap in technology from the 1993 model. In one Accord ad, Jack Lemmon discussed the car's new features: "We thought it was time to make a few changes. Like more interior space, dual airbags, better performance, and all new styling. The 1994 Accord DX." The new styling seemed to be the most important new feature: from 1988 to 1993 the average age of Accord buyers went from 40 to 45, and Honda appeared to have restyled the Accord in an effort to re-attract a younger and bigger category of car customers. It also didn't hurt that the new Accord cost an average of only 1.7 percent more than the 1993 models.

Getting Back on Track

But Honda would have to do a lot more than reshape the Accord and keep its sticker prices down if it wanted to re-interest car buyers. Gone were the days when Accord dealers simply had to sign up a long line of eager new customers on the Accord waiting list. The sudden need to convince consumers to get back into the showrooms came as quite a shock to the Accord's nonaggressive sales culture. Forced to become aggressive, Honda doubled its advertising budget to sell the 1994 Accord. Honda also considered selling only American-built Accords in the United States, a decision that would in the long run consistently allow Honda to control the pricing by reducing shipping costs and avoiding currency swings. For instance, even though 80 percent of 1993 Accords were made in the United States, the rising Japanese yen that year had forced Honda to raise Accord prices, only further driving away potential buyers from this already struggling model.

Would Honda's aggressive advertising efforts for the new Accord, its modified designs, its moderate price increases, and its increased U.S. production allow the Accord to regain the top spot? Despite the Accord's past glories, industry analysts were skeptical. Maryann Keller, auto analyst for Furman Selz, stated in a 1993 *USA Today* article: "I don't think the Accord can ever be what it once was. The competition has gotten so much stronger." Even so, based on Honda's strong record of producing quality cars, the Accord seems likely to remain a worthy contender vying for the coveted number one position in the American automobile market.

Further Reading:

"Behind the Surge in Foreign-Car Sales," *U.S. News & World Report,* June 13, 1977, p. 54.

"The Civic Is in Chronic Short Supply, the Accord Is Five Months Behind," *Business Week,* May 23, 1977, industrial edition, p. 27.

Conway, John A., "Thinking Big in Tokyo," *Forbes,* August 7, 1978, p. 8.

Dole, Charles E., "Honda Setting Its Sights on Even Higher Sales in U.S.," *Christian Science Monitor,* February 21, 1980, midwestern edition, financial sec., p. 10.

Dubrowski, Jerry, "Honda Looks to Regain Old U.S. Magic with New Accord," *Reuters,* August 31, 1993, financial report sec.

English, Carey W., "For Imported Cars, Bigger Is Better," *U.S. News & World Report,* October 19, 1981, p. 67.

"First Look at New Foreign Cars," *U.S. News & World Report,* October 31, 1977, p. 39.

"From Abroad: A Raft of New Models to Stem Slump in Sales," *U.S. News & World Report,* June 21, 1976, p. 57.

Healey, James R. and Michael Clements, "A Lot Is Riding on Accord; Restyled Honda 'Must Succeed,'" *USA Today,* September 2, 1993, p. 1B.

Healey, James R., "Demand Spurs Early Rollout for Revamped Accord," *USA Today,* May 28, 1993, p. 1B.

Henry, Jim, "Honda Accord Roars Back, Tails Ford Taurus Again," *Automotive News,* November 8, 1993, p. 4.

Hinsberg, Pat and Theodore P. Roth, "Honda Motor Turns Other Cheek to Chrysler's Broadcast Ad Slap," *Adweek Western Advertising News,* May 14, 1990, p. 2.

Hinsberg, Pat, "Honda Slings Arrows at Competitors," *Adweek Western Advertising News,* October 1, 1990, p. 1.

History of Honda, Tokyo, Japan: Honda Motor Co., Ltd., 1993.

"Honda Begins Turning Out Accords at Its Plant in Marysville, Ohio," *Japan Economic Journal,* November 9, 1982, special U.S. sec., p. 13.

"Honda Plans to Recapture Number-One Auto Spot," *National Public Radio,* September 2, 1993, morning edition.

"Honda Turns Out Its First Car Made in America," *United Press International,* November 1, 1982, AM cycle, regional news sec.

Horovitz, Bruce, "Honda Not So Simple Anymore," *Industry Week,* April 4, 1983, p. 45.

Kenzie, Jim, "Honda Hits Back with New Accord; Hot Fight for Family-Favorite Crown," *Toronto Star,* September 4, 1993, p. J1.

Levin, Doron P., "Honda Finally Has a . . . Flop? Accord Station Wagon Doesn't Catch Buyers' Interest," *Chicago Tribune,* November 10, 1991, transportation sec., p. 5.

Louis, Arthur M., "Honda's Happy Predicament," *Fortune,* July 30, 1979, p. 92.

Maynard, Micheline, "Mid-Sized Cars Take Over Auto Market," *United Press International,* August 1, 1984, financial sec.

Nulty, Peter, Geoffrey Colvin, Lisa Miller Mesdag, and Peter D. Petre, "Too Many Customers; Honda's Showroom Frustrations," *Fortune,* November 30, 1981, domestic edition, p. 7.

Oka, Takashi, "How Honda Builds Cars in Ohio to Match Its Home-Plant Quality," *Christian Science Monitor,* October 18, 1983, business sec., p. 17.

The Power Report on Automotive Marketing, Westlake Village, CA: J. D. Power & Associates, December 1993.

Rice, Faye, "America's New No. 4 Automaker—Honda," *Fortune,* October 28, 1985, domestic edition, p. 30.

"Rising Yen Drives Up Honda Prices Despite U.S. Shift; Autos: Although It Now Builds More Than 60% of Its Cars in North America, Honda Is Caught in an Exchange-Rate Squeeze," *Los Angeles Times,* April 13, 1993, business sec., p. 4.

Weinstein, Steve, "Just How Did They Do It? With a Lot of Imagination and Heavy Equipment, the Law of Gravity Is Repealed for a Honda Commercial," *Los Angeles Times,* January 14, 1990, calendar sec., p. 3.

—*Jeffrey E. Mash*

HONDA® MOTORCYCLES

Sold in more than 70 countries, Honda is the world's leading brand of motorcycles. An extremely effective advertising campaign for Honda in the early 1960s created a new market for motorcycles in the United States after all but one U.S. manufacturer had gone out of business. In the process, Honda has sold millions of motorbikes in the U.S and more than 50 million Honda motorcycles have been sold worldwide since 1948.

Brand Origins

Honda was the surname of Soichiro Honda, the son of a blacksmith, who owned and operated a piston-ring factory that was badly damaged during World War II, then destroyed by an earthquake soon after the war ended. Not to be thwarted, he founded the Honda Technical Research Institute in 1946. Located in Hamamatsu, the institute built small engines for bicycles. Since automobiles were scarce in postwar Japan, the engines were an immediate success.

Honda built its first motorcycle in 1948, a 90-cc three-wheeler with a cart mounted on the back. Reflective of their product line, the name of the company was changed to Honda Motor Co., Ltd. Honda then introduced the first in a long-running series of ''Dream'' motorcycles in 1949, and in 1950 the company moved from Hamamatsu to Tokyo, the center of Japanese finance and manufacturing after the war. By 1951 Honda was turning out more than 1,200 motorcycles a month.

In 1952 Honda brought out the Cub, a motorized bicycle with pedals and a traditional bicycle seat. Motorcycle enthusiasts laughed at the vehicle, but it was immensely popular with Japanese buyers looking for cheap transportation. The 200-cc Juno scooter, first manufactured in 1954, further solidified Honda's appeal with the masses, while the Dream series and Benly motorcycles appealed to traditional motorcycle riders. By 1954 Honda was firmly entrenched as Japan's leading maker of motorcycles. The brand's success also convinced the Japanese government to lend the company the equivalent of $1 million to purchase modern manufacturing equipment.

About the same time, Takeo Fujisawa, then Honda's director of marketing, challenged the research department to develop ''an inexpensive, safe-looking motorcycle that can be driven with one hand.'' The result was 1958's 50-cc Super Cub, promoted as being ''more like a bicycle than a motorcycle.'' Featuring a three-speed transmission, an automatic clutch, an electric starter, and a step-through design that appealed to women, the contraption looked more like a motor scooter than anything else. The Super Cub was sold in bicycle shops instead of motorcycle shops, a strategy that Honda would later duplicate in the United States. The Super Cub was so popular that Honda sold nearly 170,000 units in 1959 alone, comprising 60 percent of the company's total sales for the year.

U.S. Market

While the Super Cub was carving out a new market for small motorcycles in Japan, Honda was also considering overseas expansion. Although Honda had been exporting Juno scooters to the United States since 1954, a feasibility study advised against expanding in that declining market. Fujisawa rejected the reports' recommendation, and in 1959, Honda established a marketing subsidiary, American Honda Motor Co., Inc., in Los Angeles. Following the shut-down of the Indian Motorcycle Co. in 1953, Harley-Davidson was then the only U.S. motorcycle manufacturer and thus would be Honda's only competition.

Ironically, Kihachiro Kawashima, who led the study team that discouraged a full-scale move into the United States market, was named president of the U.S. subsidiary. His staff consisted of two assistants he brought with him from Japan. Honda had applied to the Japanese Ministry of Finance for permission to invest $1 million in the United States, but was allowed to take only $250,000 out of the country.

Attempting to maximize their resources, Kawashima and his assistants placed small advertisements in motorcycle magazines and visited motorcycle shops to establish a distribution network. However, their June arrival—past the prime motorcycle-buying ''season''—proved to be a major barrier; they managed to line up just 15 dealerships and sold fewer than 200 motorcycles the first year. Kawashima's team managed to expand the distribution network to 40 dealers in 1960, but Honda soon began receiving complaints about its motorcycles breaking down.

Honda motorcycles were built with the urban Japanese market in mind and were simply unable to withstand the harsh treatment they received on American highways. Kawashima recalled, ''We couldn't believe it. We had great confidence in our product, and here our reputation in America was practically destroyed before

AT A GLANCE

Honda Technical Research Institute founded in Japan in 1946; name changed to Honda Motor Co., Ltd., and first motorcycle produced in 1948.

Performance: *Market share*—32% of U.S. motorcycle category; 30% of worldwide motorcycle market. *Sales*—(U.S) ¥55.1 billion (US$500 million); (total) ¥569.5 billion (US$5.17 billion).

Major competitor: Yamaha motorcycles.

Advertising: *Agency (U.S)*—Dailey and Associates,, Los Angeles, CA.

Addresses: *Parent company*—Honda Motor Co. Ltd., No. 1-1, Minami-Aoyama, Minato-Ku, Tokyo 107, Japan; phone:, (03) 3423-1111.

we could get started.'' American Honda Motor Co. shipped its motorcycles to Japan for testing, which resulted in the head gaskets and clutch springs being replaced. But before the motorcycles could be shipped back to Los Angeles, a political debate developed in Japan about its continuing ties with the United States. After a student protest disrupted President Eisenhower's visit, several U.S. motorcycle dealers cancelled their orders.

Honda's big break in the United States came unexpectedly. Despite the Super Cub's huge success in Japan, Honda was pushing its bigger motorcycles in the United States to compete with Harley-Davidson. Kawashima later explained, ''We believed [Super Cub] would hurt our image in the United States because we believed Americans were in love with power and speed. Naturally we went after the big bike market. The Super Cub was not macho. We didn't want to alienate the motorcycle dealers who catered to the black-leather-jacket customers.'' Meanwhile Kawashima and his staff continued using the Super Cub for personal transportation around Los Angeles. When the motorcycles began attracting attention, Kawashima ''began to get the feeling the small bike might have some great sales potential in the country after all.''

To avoid ''offending the black-leather-jacket crowd,'' Honda began marketing the Super Cub through nontraditional outlets, including sporting goods stores, lawn mower repair shops, hardware stores, and even college bookstores. Honda would leave Super Cub motorcycles with retailers, whose only obligation was to put them on display. The Super Cubs generated so much interest that Honda had more than 500 retailers signed up by the end of 1961, and branch offices had been set up in Wisconsin and New Jersey.

The company continued selling bigger motorcycles through motorcycle shops, but as it did in Japan, Honda had also created a new market in the United States. In a 1985 retrospective on Honda, a *Cycle* writer noted: ''A Super Cub took the terror out of motorcycling. Its automatic centrifugal clutch let beginners put the bike in gear and then turn up the throttle to move forward. No mastering a hand clutch, no fear of an unpredictable death lurch. A summer zephyr had enough force to kick start the Super Cub, but the electric-start version eliminated the last shadowy fear of failure.''

"You Meet the Nicest People . . . "

Overcoming the outlaw image of motorcycle riders remained the major challenge facing Honda in the United States. In many respects the reputation was deserved: most motorcycles were noisy, intimidating, and unreliable. Riding one meant living on the edge, an image that was reinforced by Marlon Brando and company in the 1954 movie "The Wild Ones.'' In the early 1960s, ''respectable'' adults simply did not ride motorcycles, and few parents would allow their children to buy them. But Honda motorcycles had proven remarkably reliable and began changing the common notion that Japanese products were cheaply made. Marketing the Super Cub through retail stores instead of motorcycle shops was an important step toward respectability. The next was a remarkable advertising campaign launched in 1963 that made motorcycles much more socially acceptable.

The $5 million print and television advertising campaign was built around the theme ''You Meet the Nicest People on a Honda.'' Commercials featured clean-cut Americans riding Honda motorcycles, from businessmen in suits to college students with their books strapped onto the seat behind them. Instead of motorcycle magazines, print advertisements were placed in popular magazines such as *Life, Look,* and *The Saturday Evening Post.* For many people in the United States, Honda's ''Nicest People'' campaign was the first time they had ever seen an advertisement for a motorcycle. The campaign was so effective that in 1963 American Honda sold more than 87,000 motorcycles. In 1964 a *Newsweek* article acknowledged: ''thanks to the dramatic emergence in America of a Japanese-made line of motorcycles named Honda, the cyclist has become downright respectable.'' The magazine went on to say, ''Hondas, should any parent not yet know, are selling like pizza pies among well-scrubbed, perfectly sane young people in the United States, and have become the shining badge of status among high-school-age American kids.''

Amazingly, ''You Meet the Nicest People on a Honda'' was created by an advertising student at UCLA as a class assignment. The student's professor was impressed and suggested he submit the concept to Honda's Los Angeles advertising agency. The agency also liked the idea and took it to Honda, where it was nearly rejected because Kawashima felt it might offend other motorcycle riders.

Honda sales in the United States surged to 150,000 in 1964. That year Honda also announced that its motorcycles would no longer be sold on consignment—then standard for the industry—and dealers would have to pay cash on delivery. Sales reached 270,000 in 1965, making Honda the best-selling motorcycle in the United States with more than 50 percent of the market. Among the more popular models was the high-performance 305-cc Super Hawk. The Super Hawk, marketed in 1963, was the first Honda motorcycle to catch the attention of traditional motorcyclists, although they were still scoffing at its push-button starter.

Made in the U.S.A

Honda's spectacular growth slowed in 1966, which the company blamed on the U.S.'s involvement in the Vietnam conflict. Kiyohiko Okumoto, then general manager for American Honda, told *Newsweek,* ''the Vietnam war has drafted youngsters from 18 to 25, right around 50 percent of our market.'' He pointed out that banks were also reluctant to finance motorcycles for young men who might be drafted. To counter the extensive loss of consumer base, Honda stimulated sales with an advertising campaign showing women riding motorcycles alone rather than as passengers.

Honda was also being challenged in the U.S. market by new competitors from Japan, including Suzuki, Yamaha, and Kawasaki. By 1972 a glut of Japanese motorcycles had clogged the market, resulting in a price war and calls from Harley-Davidson for stiffer import quotas. In response, both Honda and Kawasaki built assembly plants in the United States. Honda's assembly plant in Marysville, Ohio, began turning out Elsinore CR250R motocrossers in 1979.

Even as late as 1969, Honda had not posed much of a threat to Harley-Davidson's 80 percent share of the U.S. market for super heavyweight motorcycles. But in the late 1960s, Honda and other Japanese cycle manufacturers began producing more powerful motorcycles that provided direct competition for Harley-Davidson. One *Cycle* reviewer affirmed that the Honda CB450, added to the Honda family in 1965, "served notice that the Japanese technological blitzkrieg would run straight up the ranks of traditional motorcycles." And in 1969, Honda put out the Dream CB750, launching the Super Bike craze of the 1970s. *Cycle* later called the CB750 "the most important motorcycle built in the modern motorcycle era." The magazine added, "In the days when the Japanese customarily played technological leapfrog, the CB750 was a space shot."

In 1975 Honda developed the Gold Wing GL1000, a super heavyweight luxury model designed specifically for U.S. highways. The bike was the genesis of "American-style" touring. According to *Cycle,* "The Wing was Honda's interpretation of the American long-hauler: size, comfort, luxury, convenience, and, piece by piece gadgetry. . . . Its mandate was the open road, four-channel stereo, and 500-mile days. . . . " In 1982 Honda shifted production of the Gold Wing to Marysville, Ohio. The Marysville plant had turned out more than 500,000 motorcycles by the early 1990s, and had a capacity of 60,000 bikes per year. Marysville was the only factory in the world making Honda Gold Wing motorcycles, which were exported to countries around the world.

Outlook

By 1982, when the United States imposed a 45 percent tariff on Japanese-built motorcycles, Harley-Davidson's share of the heavyweight market had fallen to less than 20 percent. The market for motorcycles in the United States began shrinking in the late 1980s as baby boomers, who had fueled the market in the 1960s, grew older and gave up their motorcycles. By estimates of the Motorcycle Industry Council, more than 1 million motorcycles were sold in the United States every year from 1970 to 1987. During the early 1990s, the market was cut in half.

Japanese manufacturers were particularly hurt by shifts in the exchange rate between the dollar and the yen that forced prices up in the United States. As a result, Honda's sales fell from a high of 776,000 in 1984 (60 percent of the market) to about 170,000 in 1990 (37 percent). Some dealers also blamed Honda's emphasis on heavyweight motorcycles for its loss of market share. California dealer Lee Fleming told *Cycle World* in 1990, "Honda abandoned the sportbike too soon. They wanted to sell investment bankers bikes to put in their Manhattan loft apartments. Believe me, those aren't the average motorcycle buyers."

Honda lost about 30 percent of its dealers between 1988 and 1990 as reported by *Cycle World.* However, Honda expanded its product line in the early 1990s, again offering a full range of motorcycles in the United States, from the 49-cc Z50R trail bike to the 1520-cc Gold Wing SE. Honda also marketed several scooters and all-terrain vehicles. Sales increased slightly in the early 1990s, and Honda led all other manufacturers by accounting for approximately 32 percent of the U.S. market; Honda claimed a 30 percent share of the world market in 1993.

Undoubtedly, Honda remains an important brand in a market riddled with roller coaster-type ups and downs. *Cycle* told its readers in 1987, "Most likely, neither the motorcycle you currently own nor the magazine you're reading right now would exist if it weren't for Soichiro Honda, the man who started it all. His inventiveness, his perseverance, and most of all his vision of a world on two wheels were the driving forces in the motorcycling revolution of the Sixties." Soichiro Honda died in 1990. But it was a good bet that the Honda name in motorcycles would be around for some time to come.

Further Reading:

"The Classics," *Cycle,* September 1985, p. 29.

Edwards, David, "Welcome back, Honda," *Cycle World,* 1990, p. 8.

Shook, Robert L., "Honda: An American Success Story," Prentice Hall Press, New York, 1988.

"History of Honda," Honda Motor Co., Ltd., Tokyo, Japan, 1993.

"Honda's Hang-Up," *Newsweek,* July 11, 1966, p. 66.

"How the 'Thunder Herd' Boss Brought a Honda Boom to U.S.," *Newsweek,* July 6, 1964, p. 66.

—Dean Boyer

HOOVER®

Hoover, founded in 1908, has long been a best-selling vacuum brand in the United States. Its name, in fact, is a household word around the world. Over the years Hoover's red circle logo has been placed on an ever-expanding variety of consumer and industrial floor-care products, including upright, canister, and hand-held vacuums, wet-dry utility vacs, "steam" deep cleaners, and stick vacs. It was also well-recognized in foreign markets, especially Europe, where it was a leading brand of laundry products, dishwashers, refrigerators, and freezers, in addition to floor-care appliances.

Originally a family-run business headed by its founder, W. H. Hoover, The Hoover Company was purchased by Chicago Pacific Corporation in 1985. When Chicago Pacific itself was acquired in 1989 by the giant Maytag Corporation, Hoover joined an impressive family of appliance brands, including Admiral, Jenn-Air, and Magic Chef, as well as flagship Maytag, famous for its line of long-lasting washers and dryers.

Brand Origins

Hoover vacuums came into existence in 1907 while janitor/inventor Murray Spangler was cleaning rugs in a Canton, Ohio, department store. As dust from the rugs billowed up and "aggravated" his asthma, Spangler decided to create a device that would pull the dust out of the air. Using a tin soap box, a fan, a sateen pillow case, and a broom handle, Spangler constructed a "suction sweeper." Weighing in at more than 40 pounds, the homemade machine was an improvement to earlier hand- and foot-operated suction machines. Realizing the marketing potential of his new contraption, the inventor sought financial backing from his cousin, Susan Hoover, and her husband, W. H. Hoover. After what must have been a convincing "in-home demonstration," Mr. Hoover bought Spangler's patent outright in 1908.

At first Hoover maintained the suction sweeper business as a sidelight to his leather goods shop. As it became increasingly apparent that the "horseless carriage" would soon eliminate the market for horsewhips and saddles, the vacuum business became Hoover's top priority. To create awareness about the new product and simultaneously build national distribution, Hoover offered ten days' free use of his "Electric Suction Sweeper" through an ad in the *Saturday Evening Post.* Hoover did not, however, deliver the vacuum directly to the potential customer. Instead, the "Boss," as he was called, selected a reliable retailer in each city from which requests arrived and sent the product to that store. He then asked the respective store managers to deliver the machines in exchange for a commission. If the customer agreed to purchase a vacuum after the ten-day trial, Hoover then offered the store the opportunity to become a dealer for the brand. If not, the storekeeper could opt to keep the vacuum for in-store demonstrations. This rather elaborate scheme laid the foundation of a national dealer network that would eventually become Hoover's primary distribution channel.

Early Product Innovations

Although Hoover's was not the first vacuum, the young manufacturer's engineering and design development program (established in 1909) made several improvements on the appliance that set it apart from its predecessors. In 1926 Hoover engineers introduced the "beater bar," a metal bar that gently tapped the carpet to loosen ground-in dirt. The beater bar remains a part of Hoover design into the 1990s, having evolved into the "Quadraflex agitator for double the brushing action." The beater bar popularized Hoover's most memorable advertising slogan: "It beats as it sweeps as it cleans."

Hoover designers later developed the disposable paper dust bag and the vacuum-cleaner headlight, both of which became standard features on uprights, as well as other "firsts," including the plastic motor hood and the "self-propelled" feature. The company also patented the side-mounted attached-hose feature in 1936—more than 50 years before consumer demand made it a marketable option.

Commercial Success

Although W. H. Hoover and his son H. W. Hoover, who later became the company president, had set up a network of national retailer distributors with the brand's first national advertisement, Hoover's primary sales technique for the first half of the century centered on a corps of door-to-door salesmen backed up by a local dealer. The highly trained salesmen attended daily meetings that invariably concluded with an inspirational "Hoover Song." One of the most popular was sung to the tune of the militaristic "Caisson Song": "All the dirt, all the grit; Hoover gets it every bit; For it beats as it sweeps as it cleans."

AT A GLANCE

Hoover brand of vacuum founded in 1908 in New Berlin (later North Canton), OH, by W. H. "Boss" Hoover; its parent company, Hoover Electric Suction Sweeper Co. was renamed The Hoover Company in 1922; acquired by Chicago Pacific Corporation in 1985; Chicago Pacific purchased in 1989 by Maytag Corporation.

Performance: *Market share*—37% (top share) of upright vacuum category, according to *Appliance* magazine. *Sales*—$3 billion (total for Maytag Corporation).

Major competitor: Eureka; also Royal Appliance Manufacturing Company's Dirt Devil, Regina, Singer, Sears, and Electrolux.

Advertising: *Agency*—Tatham Euro RSCG, 1989—. *Major campaign*—"Nobody gets the dirt like Hoover. Nobody."

Addresses: *Parent company*—The Hoover Company, 101 E. Maple St., North Canton, Ohio 44720; phone: (216) 499-9200; fax: (216) 966-5439. *Ultimate parent company*—Maytag Corporation, 403 W. Fourth Street N., Newton, Iowa 50208; phone: (515) 792-8000; fax: (515) 791-8102.

Hoover's troops contributed the image of the enthusiastic salesman to twentieth century Americana. With vacuum cleaner in hand and a foot in the door, the salesman emitted a stream of irresistible sales talk and carried a handful of dirt. Door-to-door sales were genuinely successful for Hoover; in the early 1940s the brand's sales reached $20 million, and its stake in the U.S. vacuum market topped 66 percent. The product had cultivated a well-established and much-envied reputation.

Because it was making such items as helmet liners, parachutes, and parts for proximity fuzes to aid in the war effort, Hoover did not manufacture vacuums during World War II. For their efforts, the company and its employees won numerous government awards, including the Army/Navy "E" five times.

Hoover introduced a canister vacuum in 1949. As competitors entered the vacuum market at that time, they eschewed door-to-door sales for more conventional distribution channels. Hoover, though, continued to employ a legion of door-to-door salespeople, while it began putting a retailer network in place in small towns.

Turnover in the door-to-door sales force was running high, and as more women began to work outside the home, it grew increasingly difficult to catch them there. Hoover reduced the work force by 50 percent (eliminating virtually all direct salesmen) in favor of larger retailers that were beginning to gain strength. The brand also reduced its prices and expanded into production of canister vacuums and "floor washers." As the U.S. vacuum market neared saturation in the late 1950s, Hoover began to concentrate more seriously on foreign markets for growth.

International Markets

"Boss" Hoover had promoted his electric suction sweeper in foreign markets from the outset, opening the brand's first Canadian operations in 1911. By 1921 Hoover products were sold "in the four corners of the world," but the brand's British division would become its most successful.

Hoover started exporting Canadian-made vacuums to Great Britain in 1919. British sales grew slowly until the 1930s, when an assembly operation (Hoover Ltd.) was built there to circumvent the exchange rate. With virtually no competition and the leadership of Sir Charles Colston, Hoover soon dominated the British market, becoming that country's biggest appliance manufacturer by the early 1940s. After World War II the British subsidiary began manufacturing washing machines (Hoover did not want to diversify in the United States), and by the early 1950s the brand had captured more than 50 percent of the washing machine market and 70 percent of the vacuum cleaner market. With this secure foothold in Great Britain, Hoover Ltd. started to expand into the Continental market in the 1960s.

The brand's growing global enterprises were organized into Hoover Worldwide in 1961. Area divisions included Hoover Canada, Hoover America Latina, Hoover Europe, Hoover Ltd., and Hoover U.S. Within a couple of years Hoover's overseas sales far exceeded those in the United States; more than 60 percent of annual sales came from Hoover Ltd., the brand's primary exporter to Europe. By 1970 Hoover appliances were sold in 100 countries. Hoover would continue to look toward the European market for future sales growth. The Continent had low market saturation, and its total population, as well as its combined gross national product, exceeded that of the United States.

Hoover's U.K. share declined in the late 1970s because of aggressive competition from inexpensive Italian imports and complacent designs. In the early 1980s the British division undertook a comprehensive reorganization and a dynamic new marketing campaign. Competition in Europe remained fierce throughout the 1980s. By 1989 Hoover had sustained its British stronghold but had not yet captured a significant portion of the robust Continental market.

Market Segmentation in the United States

In the meantime, Hoover's U.S. sales representatives concentrated more and more on contacts with such large retailers as Wal-Mart, True Value, and Kmart. While the brand continued to organize some in-store demonstrations reminiscent of the door-to-door days, Hoover relied increasingly on television and print advertisements to "pre-sell" consumers on the brand.

As competition in the U.S. vacuum market continued to increase in the last half of the twentieth century, manufacturers sought ways to expand the market through new-product introductions. Rather than wait for the formation of new households or the slow replacement market, vacuum makers worked to create new models for specific uses. Royal Appliance Manufacturing introduced its corded Dirt Devil, which featured a revolving brush, in 1983. Hoover came out with the Help-Mate that same year. These "hand vacs," used for small, quick pickups, had been preceded by "stick vacs," intended for smaller households. Eventually, wet/dry vacuums and extraction cleaners for high-traffic areas and seasonal deep cleaning were developed.

Hoover was among the first to offer electronic vacuums in 1983. The brand's Celebrity QS Quiet Series featured red and green LED displays to show the machine's setting (floor or carpet), warn of a jam or overload, and signal the need for a belt replacement. The Concept Two Cleaning System incorporated a Help-Mate hand vac that was stored in the body of an upright. Hoover supported these introductions with a million-dollar ad campaign, which featured network television spots and print advertisements in *Southern Living, Better Homes & Gardens, Sunset, Good Housekeeping,* and *Reader's Digest.*

By 1990 the upright segment still constituted 63 percent of total vacuum sales. Despite competition from such newcomers as Panasonic and Dirt Devil, Hoover in 1992 remained the leader of the upright segment with a 37 percent share, as reported by *Appliance* magazine. Buoyed by the 1989 introduction of a hand-held, wet/dry vacuum, Hoover captured an increased stake in this segment from both Dirt Devil and Black & Decker.

Cleaning Efficiency Rating

In 1993 Hoover began promoting a new "Cleaning Efficiency Rating," which measured the cleaning effectiveness of each amp of electrical power employed by the branded vacuums. The system was developed to give consumers a more meaningful method of comparing the performance of various vacuum cleaner models. Royal Appliance Manufacturing Company, maker of the Dirt Devil vacuum line, sued Hoover that year, charging that the new measurement confused consumers accustomed to seeing amperage ratings. Royal asked for a temporary restraining order and later a preliminary injunction against Hoover. A U.S. District Court judge denied both requests.

Hoover returned fire in mid-1993 with a lawsuit that accused Royal of false advertising, defamation, and interference with business relations. The countersuit alleged that Royal was the false advertiser and that Dirt Devil's prominently displayed amperage ratings "intentionally" and erroneously led consumers to believe that amperage correlated to cleaning effectiveness. Late in 1993 Royal responded that it had expected such a "delaying tactic."

Although the other major vacuum manufacturers skirted the legal battle, Regina and Eureka both voiced their opposition to the new ratings system. Their primary complaint was that Hoover did not apprise them of its new system and that it left customers unable to make comparisons among the competing brands.

Brand Outlook

Although Hoover became part of the Maytag appliance family as a result of Maytag's acquistion of Chicago Pacific in 1989, the two nameplates looked forward to taking advantage of "synergies" in the 1990s. Maytag hoped to use Hoover, the 68th most recognized brand in the world, according to an *AdScore/Brandweek* survey, to catapult into Europe. In the United States, Hoover's aggressive new product offerings and marketing strategies (i.e., wet-dry and extraction vacuums, as well as the cleaning efficiency rating) helped it maintain a top position in the vacuum industry.

Further Reading:

Bremner, Brian, "Can Maytag Clean Up around the World?" *Business Week,* January 30, 1989, pp. 86-87.

"Britain: British Hoover Is Cleaning Up," *Business Week,* August 19, 1972, pp. 35–36.

Campanella, Frank W., "Pickup in Demand Here and Abroad Spurs Profits Rebound at Hoover," *Barron's,* March 22, 1976, pp. 66–67.

"The Challenger from North Canton," *Forbes,* June 15, 1972, p. 60.

Downer, Stephen and Scott Hume, "Hoover Promo Nightmare," *Advertising Age,* April 5, 1993, p. 4.

Dreyfack, Kenneth, "Where Does Chicago Pacific Grow from Here?" *Business Week,* November 3, 1986, pp. 60, 62.

"Foresight Saga," *The Economist,* September 1, 1973, p. 72.

Gillman, R.W., "One Man's Theory Opens a New Door," *Nation's Business,* January 1970, pp. 84–85.

"How Hoover Swept into the Black," *Business Week,* September 26, 1983, p. 55.

"In the Nick of Time," *Forbes,* September 1, 1968, p. 46.

Rath, Lee, "Electronic Vacuums, Hand-Held Units Highlight Floor Care," *Merchandising,* March 1983, pp. 84, 86.

Rosenblum, Debbie. "Electronic Vacs Create Sales; Demand for Hand-Helds Grows," *Merchandising,* September 1983, pp. 25, 85.

Seikman, Philip, "Hoover's Well-Vacuumed World," *Fortune,* June 1964, pp. 143–146, 208, 210, 212.

"Who's 'oovering' Now?" *Forbes,* December 25, 1978, p. 44.

—April S. Dougal

HOT WHEELS®

For millions of Americans the Hot Wheels name conjures up images of the late 1960s: back yard barbecues, the Beatles, and the lunar landing. Introduced in 1968 by Mattel, Inc., Hot Wheels immediately captured the imagination of American kids. The cars were painted in flashy, psychedelic colors, and the style was undeniably cool. Hot wheels cars sped down a bright orange track and defied gravity when they looped the loop. Even girls liked them. An instant and encompassing success, Hot Wheels cars sold so well in their first year that their sales outnumbered those of all other toy car brands combined in the year before. What's even more remarkable, however, is that Hot Wheels endured. To the kids who played with the toy when it was first introduced, it is hard to believe that Hot Wheels is now more than 25 years old and still one of the strongest brands of the giant Mattel toy company.

The Hot Wheels brand has been extended to a number of subcategories, including Attack Pack and Top Speed Pipejammers toy vehicles, but the original concept of brightly colored die-cast metal cars with free spinning wheels remains a very strong seller. Hot Wheels have graduated from being a toy fad to a toy classic. There are thousands of Hot Wheels collectors around the United States who are willing to pay up to $600 for a very rare vehicle. After some troubled years at Mattel, the late 1980s and 1990s saw a renewal of the company's core brands, with an increased focus on proven winners like Hot Wheels.

Brand Origins

The concept for the Hot Wheels line of miniature cars is credited by Mattel literature to Elliot Handler, one of the original founders of Mattel. Mattel already had a huge hit in its Barbie fashion doll and was looking for a similar spearhead for its line of boy's toys. Handler is said to have been conducting research for new boy's products when he realized that almost all of the die-cast miniature vehicles currently on the market had static wheels. Handler reasoned that, although boys collected miniature cars for their appearance, they would be doubly enthusiastic if the cars could actually race. He felt that speed, and not just movement, would have to be the selling point for these cars. Larger scale race car sets had been on the market for years, but they were normally single purchase items rather than the collectibles that small die-cast cars had been. Handler envisioned combining the low cost and high collectability (i.e., multiple purchase) of miniature die-cast cars with a racing feature.

Mattel's research and development department went to work to develop a prototype for a speedy, gravity-powered miniature car. They used low-friction styrene wheels hung on a thin metal torsion bar to produce minimum resistance and maximum speed. Company lore has it that Handler took one look at this new, ultra-fast car and exclaimed, "Wow, those are hot wheels," thereby coining the name for the new toy.

With the mechanical prototype in hand, Handler placed an ad in a Detroit newspaper seeking an automobile designer who could help design the body of the car. Harry Bradley, a designer with General Motors, had recently designed a new custom show car whose flashy styling convinced Handler that he was the man to work on Hot Wheels. The Mattel design team determined that the new cars should be about three inches long and would be modeled after California-style customized show cars with a scale of 1/64. Their main competitor in die-cast miniature cars would be the well-established Matchbox brand, and it was important to establish points of difference with the 30-year-old classic. They decided that while Matchbox toys had prided themselves on their exact replicas of production-line vehicles, Hot Wheels would concentrate on the flashier models only, and all would sport bright paint jobs and red line tires. In addition, Mattel devised a system of flexible plastic track, later the subject of a much publicized lawsuit, on which the Hot Wheels cars could run. The track with its famous loop was to become a symbol of the Hot Wheels brand to a generation of children.

Sixteen Hot Wheels models were introduced in 1968, including one modeled on Bradley's show car and another on the 1968 Chevrolet Corvette, even though the full-size, adult version of that year's Corvette was not yet available for sale itself. Sales of the new toy cars surpassed even Mattel's expectations. Heavily advertised on network television as "the fastest metal cars in the world," the Hot Wheels line generated more than $25 million in its first year alone. Annual sales for the entire miniature car category were only $23 million before the launch of Hot Wheels. Hot Wheels permanently changed the very nature of the category itself. Production rates for Hot Wheels reached nearly 16 million cars in 1968, and Mattel was soon making more toy cars than all the life-size automakers in the world.

AT A GLANCE

Hot Wheels brand of miniature toy cars created by Elliot Handler of Mattel, Inc., in El Segundo, CA, 1968.

Performance: *Market share*—Top share of miniature toy car category. *Sales*—$150 million in worldwide die-cast car sales.

Major competitor: Matchbox miniature cars.

Advertising: *Agency*—Foote, Cone and Belding, Los Angeles, CA, 1987—. *Major campaign*—Various campaigns for different sub-categories; all are action oriented, targeted to boys three to ten years old, and emphasize speed as point of difference from other brands.

Addresses: *Parent company*—Mattel, Inc., 333 Continental Blvd., El Segundo, CA 90245-5012; phone: (310) 524-2000; fax: (310) 524-2179.

Brand Development

Mattel has capitalized on the spectacular success of Hot Wheels with many brand extensions. According to toy historian Sydney Stern, the first such venture nearly ended in bankruptcy for the huge toy company. In 1970, following two record-breaking years with Hot Wheels sales, Mattel introduced Hot Wheels Sizzlers, a motorized version of the popular cars. Toy store buyers pounced on the new product, ordering heavily after experiencing shortages of the Hot Wheels line in its first two years. But American parents and kids were not as enthusiastic. The higher priced motorized version of the toy had technical problems, according to a 1970 article in *Business Week,* and sales stalled. On top of poor sales of the Sizzlers cars, the backlog of the new toy in retailers stockrooms began to impede orders of other Mattel products. Mattel executives reportedly scrambled to cover up the loss with questionable accounting procedures. The debacle finally ended in the resignation of the company's founders, Ruth and Elliot Handler, and a restructuring of the entire Mattel corporation.

After this near disaster it was a number of years before Mattel would further extend its popular brand. The Hot Wheels cars and race sets with looping plastic track continued to be very popular, however, and newer models of the flashy cars were introduced on an ongoing basis. By 1993, 562 different Hot Wheels models had been created. Designs of Hot Wheels cars have always reflected popular culture and have changed with the fads and fashions of the times. When the cars were introduced in the late 1960s, psychedelic, wildly colored cars were all the rage. The 1980s' Reagan era saw a renewed interest in the military, with a line of camouflage vehicles, and the 1990s featured a return to California-inspired beach cars.

In 1988, following a spate of lean years for Mattel, Inc., newly appointed Mattel chairman, John Amerman, decided to concentrate once more on the company's core brands; Barbie and Hot Wheels. Amerman felt that Mattel's biggest asset was the brand equity that had built up in these popular toys over the years, and that the company should try to extend and build on that reputation.

In keeping with this decision, in 1988 Mattel introduced the Hot Wheels Color Racers, cars that change color when immersed in water. The unlikely concept was a huge hit, with Color Racers being produced at a record rate of two million vehicles per week in June, 1989. By 1994, the Hot Wheels brand had been extended to a number of new toy car products including the Top Speed Pipejammers (cars with a catapult launcher) and the Criss Cross Crash Set. One of the largest departures from the original Hot Wheels concept has been the Attack Pack series of off-road vehicles. These larger scaled vehicles can transform from monster trucks into creatures with names like Screwdriver, Terror-Dactyl, and Riptile. These fantasy-based transformable trucks seem to have more in common with action figure dolls than with toy cars, but by marketing them as a Hot Wheels segment, Mattel can both exploit and expand the popular Hot Wheels brand.

Advertising and Promotion

A large part of Mattel's early success can be attributed to its pioneering use of television advertising. The company was responsible for the first major network campaign for a toy (the Burp Gun) and had used television successfully to promote its wildly successful Barbie fashion doll. In 1969 Mattel executives decided to test the waters for a wholly new form of promotional vehicle.

As recounted by historian Stern, Mattel underwrote a 30-minute animated television show entitled *Hot Wheels* to run on the ABC television network. The cartoon featured imaginary cars performing various stunts, but avoided specific references to Hot Wheels toys. Although the original Mattel proposal to the National Association of Broadcasters specified that there would be no cross-references between the show and the company's Hot Wheels products, Mattel catalogues did tag certain models as "from the Hot Wheels TV show." The promotional experiment did not last long. Rival toy car manufacturer Topper Corp. brought a complaint to the Federal Communications Commission, which ruled that the television show was a 30-minute-long commercial and

A Hot Wheels 1968 Custom Camaro.

should be logged as commercial time by ABC. The show was dropped. Ironically, it was Mattel that would, 14 years later under a Reagan era Communications Commission, successfully introduce another product-based cartoon and thereby begin a trend that was to transform children's television advertising.

Hot Wheels advertising woes did not end with the cancellation of the *Hot Wheels* TV show. In a well-publicized pre-Christmas decision in 1970, the Federal Trade Commission, under a great deal of pressure from consumers' groups to regulate children's television advertising, announced that it would charge Mattel and its rival Topper Corp. for deceptive practices in their advertisements for Mattel's Hot Wheels and Topper's Johnny Lightning racing cars. As reported in *Advertising Age* at the time, the Commission accused both firms of using "special camera and sound techniques to convey a sense of involvement and participation which falsely represents the actual use of the toys and exaggerates their appearance or performance." A settlement was reached in July, 1971, in which both companies agreed among other terms to stop advertising "scale" speeds (actual vehicle speed multiplied by the scale of the model—a 20 mph toy is said to run at speeds "equal to" 1300 mph) and to stop using camera angles that exaggerate size or speed.

By the 1990s, regulations regarding children's television advertising have become a well established, and, more or less, accepted part of the toy industry. As part of the late 1980s Mattel campaign to build on the brand equity of their core brands, Hot Wheels received greatly increased ad expenditures in the first half of the 1990s. With agency Foote, Cone and Belding, Mattel runs an extensive television campaign for all of its Hot Wheels segments. Targeted to boys aged three to ten years, the ads feature the particular qualities of the sub categories as well as emphasizing Hot Wheels' brand identifiers: movement and speed.

The early 1990s also saw a stepped-up promotional campaign for Hot Wheels in supermarkets and fast food outlets in an attempt to broaden the exposure for Mattel's core brands. Mattel began a coupon give-away in cross-promotional campaigns with such companies as Kraft General Foods and Walt Disney. They also handed out millions of free miniature Hot Wheels cars and discount coupons with McDonald's Happy Meals. Mattel's vice-president of marketing services, Richard DeHerder, was quoted in a 1993 article in the *Wall Street Journal* as stating, "It gives us an opportunity to broaden our message and deliver it where our customers are. They go to toy stores six or seven times a year, but they go to the grocery store 60 or 70 times a year. What we're doing is creating new reasons to come into the toy department every month."

Legal Disputes

Mattel's move to build on the brand equity of Hot Wheels has been helped along by the final settlement of a 22-year legal battle with inventor Jerry Lemelson over the Hot Wheels plastic track. Lemelson brought his suit in the early 1970s claiming that he had shown his patented design for a flexible toy track to a toy company executive who later went to work for Mattel. Lemelson sued for $32.7 million, the 6 percent of total Hot Wheels sales accounted for by the track. In 1989 a Federal Jury in Chicago found in favor of Lemelson and awarded him $24.8 million plus $46 million in interest charges, the largest jury award ever given to an independent inventor. Toy industry historian Richard Levy quoted a Mattel attorney as stating, "This man is entitled to be compensated for his damage, not to be given a windfall." Mattel appealed to the Federal Court of Appeals and, in 1992, the three-judge panel overturned the earlier award, denying Lemelson's claim of patent infringement. In 1993 the final blow was struck for the inventor when the Supreme Court, notoriously leery of patent cases, refused Lemelson's request to hear his appeal. Mattel had won the long, drawn-out battle but only at the cost of millions in legal fees and considerable negative publicity.

Performance

Upon its introduction, the Hot Wheels line was an immediate and overwhelming hit. The flashy model cars not only soared to the top of the die-cast car market but reshaped the category itself. Production rates of the toy during 1968 leaped to nearly 16 million cars. Mega-hits of this scale are a rare but not unknown phenomenon in the toy industry with its reliance on fashions and fads; but parlaying this kind of fad into an enduring success can be much more difficult. After the debacle surrounding the motorized Sizzlers in the early 1970s and subsequent resignation of company founders Ruth and Elliot Handler, Mattel's sales in 1972 dropped by 30 percent. Much of that loss was due to declining sales of Hot Wheels, according to a 1973 article in *Business Week.* In spite of these serious problems with the brand, Hot Wheels continued to generate sizable sales, and Mattel, with no other hit on the horizon, stuck with the still popular brand.

The early 1980s saw a brief respite for the beleaguered toy giant as sales rose, thanks in large part to its hit He-Man action figures, but by the mid-1980s, Mattel was recording losses in the millions. According to Marc Beauchamp of *Forbes* magazine, heavy losses in the videogame market and overproduction of their Masters of the Universe line left Mattel with a 23 percent drop in overall sales and no hit product to take up the slack. John Amerman, former head of Mattel International, was appointed chairman of the company in 1987 and undertook a massive campaign to restore Mattel to profitability. After launching an intensive new marketing effort behind Hot Wheels, sales rose an astounding 80 percent in 1988, in large part thanks to the very popular Color Racers. New brand extensions such as Top Speed Pipejammers and Attack Pack further boosted Hot Wheels sales by 32 percent in 1992.

Mattel has an extensive international presence through its Mattel International division that, under Amerman's direction, increased its profitability and quadrupled its sales. By the early 1990s, more than half of Mattel's sales were overseas. Although Hot Wheels is not as popular overseas as Mattel's global "power" brands—Barbie and Disney products—the cars nonetheless do well outside the United States.

At age 26, Hot Wheels has reached a watershed in its brand life. Over the years Hot Wheels has gone from being a fad, to a staple, and from a staple to a classic of the toy industry. Hot Wheels sub-categories will undoubtedly come and go, but the brand itself has built up enough brand equity through two generations of children's play that it seems likely to remain on the toy car scene for years to come.

Further Reading:

Beauchamp, Marc, "Barbie at 30," *Forbes,* November 14, 1988, pp. 248–49.

"FTC Charges Mattel, Topper Ads for Toys Deceive Children," *Advertising Age,* November 30, 1970, pp. 3, 59.

"FTC Expected to Settle Ad Complaint with 2 Toy Makers," *Advertising Age,* July 12, 1971, p. 16.

" 'Hot Wheels' Doesn't Push Mattel Toys; Mattel Pushes 'Hot Wheels' Toys, FCC Says," *Advertising Age,* February 16, 1970, pp. 3, 64.

Jefferson, David J., "Mattel Steps Up Toy Promotions for Christmas," *Wall Street Journal,* August 17, 1993, pp. B1, B6.

Kaltenheuser, Skip, "Don't Cross This Inventor," *Across the Board,* April 1993, pp. 28–31.

Levy, Richard C. and Ronald O. Weingartner, *Inside Santa's Workshop,* New York: Henry Holt and Company, 1990, p. 179.

Mattel Annual Report, El Segundo, CA: Mattel, Inc., 1993.

"New Bosses Tackle Mattel's Troubles," *Business Week,* March 24, 1973, p. 23.

"Not Much Fun for Mattel Last Year," *Business Week,* April 8, 1972, p. 26.

Stern, Sydney and Ted Schoenhaus, *Toyland: The High Stakes Game of the Toy Industry,* Chicago: Contemporary Books, 1990.

—Hilary Gopnik

HUFFY®

Huffy bicycles are the top-selling brand of bicycles in the United States and second in the world behind the Raleigh brand. The market includes not only children and adults who buy the bikes for recreation and exercise, but also world-class riders who like Huffy's sophisticated racing bikes. Huffy is revered as an innovator in the technological design of bicycles. The company is also an aggressive user of market research and focus groups.

Brand Origins

During the Great Depression of the 1930s, Horace Huffman Sr., founder of the Huffman Manufacturing Company of Dayton, OH, noticed that bicycles were becoming more and more popular as a mode of transportation. His company was already a successful producer of automotive equipment, but Huffman decided to begin producing two-wheeled vehicles as well. The first Huffy bicycle rolled off the assembly line in 1934. Within two years, the company was able to increase its production rate from 12 bikes per day to 200. However, the company was not producing fast enough to keep up with its competition and, consequently, lost several major customers—including the Firestone Tire and Rubber Company.

Horace Huffman, Jr., who had joined his father's company in 1936, changed the production process to a straight-line, conveyerized assembly with admirable results. By 1940, bicycle production had increased by 100 percent and the company was able to regain Firestone as a customer and attract such new accounts as the Western Auto Company. After the Second World War, the Huffy Convertible bicycle met with enormous success and became the foundation on which the Huffy brand was built.

Brand Development

During the 1950s and 1960s, foreign bicycle makers controlled the U.S. market. Their prices were so low that many United States tire, chain, and brake manufacturers were driven out of business, forcing American bike makers to depend on foreign parts, which further cut into domestic profits. By 1972, foreign imports accounted for 37 percent of the U.S. market. Three factors soon changed this trend. First, the devaluation of the U.S. dollar cut the foreign manufacturers share to 15 percent. Second, new federal regulations setting stricter safety standards affected the import of foreign models. Finally, the 1970s brought an emphasis on energy conservation and physical fitness—and bicycles were suddenly a hot item with American adults as well as children.

By 1979, adults accounted for 25 percent of the bicycle market, compared with just 6 percent in 1969. To take advantage of this trend, Huffy developed its own model of the lightweight European-style 10-speed bicycle to meet the overwhelming demand. With the profits made during this period, Huffy was able to streamline its operations so that it could produce a product comparable to the foreign models—at a cheaper price.

A licensing, sales and manufacturing agreement with the British-owned Raleigh Cycle Company in 1982 allowed Huffy to enter the high-specification bike market. Even though the rights were sold in 1988, Huffy remained a leading manufacturer of racing bikes. In the 1980s, Huffy's U.S. Cycling Federation Technical Development Center began to use composites to make the lightweight, highly-aerodynamic disc wheels often preferred by racers. With composites and other refinements, Huffy engineers were able to reduce the wheel weight from 5.5 pounds to 2.5 pounds.

To generate even more recognition of the Huffy Brand, the Huffman Manufacturing Company changed its name to Huffy Corporation in 1979; by the end of the 1980s, however, Huffy was also producing infant carriers and strollers, basketball equipment, and lawn and garden tools.

Marketing Innovations

Until the 1960s, half of the bicycles sold in the United States came from small specialty shops that offered custom service. Bikes often required individual adjustment and calibration. But the proliferation of large, supermarket-sized discount stores, which offered a plethora of products at reduced prices, changed the way Americans shop. Huffy recognized a golden opportunity and developed a 10-speed bicycle with a pre-adjusted gear assembly and caliper brakes that required the bare minimum of service. By distributing the bikes to mass merchandising chains such as K-Mart, J.C. Penney and Montgomery Ward, Huffy was able to establish itself as the number one bike manufacturer in the United States.

Huffy employs intense market testing to help guide its technological innovations and designs. Huffy's Design Communications Center combines the design and engineering functions. Engineers and marketing specialists share their respective expertise. Their ultimate goal: to produce a bike that every adult and child ''has to

AT A GLANCE

Huffy brand bicycles created in 1934 in Dayton, OH, by Horace Huffman, Sr., founder of Huffman Manufacturing Company; Huffman Manufacturing Company was renamed Huffy Corporation in 1977.

Performance: *Market share*—30% (top share) of mass-produced bicycles. *Sales*—$703.3 million.

Major competitor: Murray Bicycle Company.

Advertising: *Agency*—Tatham Euro RSCG, Chicago, IL.

Addresses: *Parent company*—Huffy Corporation, 7701 Byers Road, Miamisburg, OH 45342; phone: (513) 866-251.

have.'' Test groups are held at shopping centers and schools with a carefully selected mix of adults and children.

This ongoing, hands-on assessment of the bicycle market has proven beneficial to Huffy on many occasions. Market surveys conducted in the 1970s indicated that the motorized bike, or moped, had little future in the United States. Huffy saved millions of dollars by deciding not to manufacture a moped and was able to use the money to improve production processes.

By the end of the 1970s, the bicycle market's focus shifted back to children. Huffy responded with a flashy new motocross-style bike called Thunder Trail that sported waffle handle grips and knobby tires. A girl's version, in pink and dubbed ''Sweet Thunder'' was also introduced. Huffy's focus groups showed that children wanted brighter colors, more decals and higher numerals on the number plates. Armed with that information, Huffy stepped up advertising during the hours of children's television programming—and Thunder Trail bikes were soon a roaring success.

Future Growth

Although Huffy clearly owes its success in the bicycle market to its mass-merchandising abilities, the company plans to continue its specialty bike research and development. Huffy officials believe that innovations found in these pursuits will benefit future models of its mass-produced, non-specialty bicycles. Another major task ahead is the automation of the composite production process.

Further Reading:

Bergstrom, Robin P., ''The $10,000 Bike: It Can't Be Made Any Other Way—Yet,'' *Production,* March 1992, p. 60.

Hannon, Kerry, ''Easy Rider,'' *Forbes,* November 16, 1987, pp. 304–305.

''Huffman Highlights,'' Miamisburg, Ohio: The Huffman Manufacturing Company, 1973.

''Huffy History,'' Miamisburg, Ohio: The Huffy Corporation.

''Huffy Pedals Into First Place,'' *Sales & Marketing Management,* January, 1978, p. 28.

''Huffy Puts New Spin in the Bicycle Business,'' *Business Week,* October 10, 1977, p. 134.

Kreisman, Richard, ''Huffy Rides Raleigh Into Upscale Market,'' *Advertising Age,* May 17, 1982, p. 4.

Miller, Cyndee, ''Popular Bicycles Don't Cost a Fortune—Only $3,000,'' *Marketing News,* July 20, 1992, p. 2.

''Motocross: New Type Bicycle Puts Huffman Mfg. in High Gear,'' *Barron's,* August 23, 1976, pp. 28–29.

—Mary F. McNulty

HULA HOOP®

Regarded as one of the most popular fads of the twentieth century, the plastic hoop toy known as the Hula Hoop became a nationwide craze within months of its introduction, achieved worldwide popularity within the year, and saw its sales dwindle almost as quickly. Introduced in 1958 by the Wham-O Manufacturing Company of San Gabriel, California, Hula Hoop prompted competition from rival toy manufacturers, which produced similar toys called Spin-A-Hoops, Hoop-Zings, Hooper Doopers, and Whoop-De-Dos. Nevertheless, Hula Hoop dominated its market, and the brand name became a generic term used to refer to all lightweight plastic hoop toys. While Hula Hoop sales may never again compare to those of the late 1950s, Wham-O continued producing modest numbers of the toy and remained the category leader in the 1990s.

Product Origins

The Wham-O Manufacturing Company began in the garage of one of its founders, Richard Knerr. In 1948, Knerr and his childhood friend Arthur "Spuds" Melin, both students at the University of Southern California, became interested in the hobby of raising and training falcons. To teach their falcons to dive at prey, the men constructed a slingshot, which they used to shoot meatballs towards the airborne birds. During this time, a prospective purchaser of one of Knerr's and Melin's falcons admired the slingshot and offered to buy it.

Recognizing the potential value of their product, Knerr and Merlin spent $7 for a bandsaw and began manufacturing the slingshots in Knerr's garage. They called their slingshot Wham-O, because, as Knerr later noted, "That's the sensation you felt when you hit something with one of them." Knerr and Melin began selling the slingshots door-to-door, and within two years, Wham-O slingshots were available in sporting good stores across the United States. As business grew, the company moved to larger quarters and began manufacturing such sporting equipment as throwing knives, fencing foils, and boomerangs. In 1957, Wham-O scored a national hit with their Frisbee Flying Saucer. But the Frisbee's success was soon eclipsed by the popularity of the Hula Hoop.

The idea for the Hula Hoop was suggested by a friend of Knerr and Merlin who had been traveling in Australia. There he spotted a group of schoolchildren twirling bamboo hoops around their waists as part of their gym classes. Knerr and Merlin agreed that American kids might be interested in a similar product. In 1958 they began developing prototypes out of the wood used to manufacture the Wham-O slingshot. Unsatisfied with the wooden hoop, however, they turned to plastic, still a relatively new substance at the time. With the assistance of W. R. Grace & Co., Wham-O developed a satisfactory hoop made out of a polyethylene called GREX.

Knerr and Melin called their new product Hula Hoop (after rejecting such names as Twirl-A-Hoop and Swing-A-Hoop), and in late spring of 1958, they began demonstrating it in parks and playgrounds near their offices in San Gabriel. Children who could successfully twirl the hoops around their waists, by swaying in a motion that recalled a hula dance, were given a Hula Hoop free of charge. Soon, thousands of Hula Hoops were being sold in stores across southern California.

Marketing

The Hula Hoop craze spread quickly across the country. Children using the Hula Hoop were featured on national television, while department stores staged demonstrations and offered free lessons. Hula Hoop Derbies with televised championships were organized. Children, as well as increasing numbers of adults, were purchasing the toy in large numbers. By July 1958, Wham-O could not manufacture enough hoops to meet demand, and scores of other hoop manufacturing companies emerged to cash in on the craze.

Hula Hoop had become so popular that the nation's media called on top psychologists to explain the phenomenon. Some speculated that a trend toward frequent relocations among American families during the 1950s—in 1957 alone, almost 20 percent of the U.S. population changed homes—created a condition ripe for fads, which, psychologists contended, created a "community of interest" around the product. Dr. Joyce Brothers, on the other hand, speculated that use of the Hula Hoop represented "almost a little form of rebellion against adults," who found it more difficult to keep the hoop in motion around their waists. Although the reasons for its popularity were disputed, it's success was not. Within four months of Hula Hoop's introduction, over 20 million were sold at $2.79 apiece. At its peak, Wham-O contracted with 120 plastic tube manufacturers to turn out over 150 dozen hoops a day.

International Sales

Through the considerable influence of television, the hoop craze spread around the world, and Wham-O quickly set up plants in Toronto, London, Tokyo, and Frankfurt. In London, Hula Hoop made the front page of the *Times,* and entire pages of several newspapers were devoted to articles and pictures describing the technique of Hula Hooping. In France the hoop became popular after noted author Francoise Sagan was photographed twirling a hoop around her waist. Hula Hoop also established markets in Germany and Finland. In the Soviet Union all hoops were manufactured by state-run companies, and while some government bodies praised its health benefits, others denounced it as undignified and uncultured.

News of the Hula Hoop was also transmitted via television to Japan. There, as in other parts of the world, the Hula Hoop achieved widespread popularity, and a newspaper dispatch in the fall of 1958 claimed that, "every yard, vacant lot and alley is a potential sight of demonstration and practitioners are by no means all children." However, the "huru hoopa," as it was translated in Japanese, soon suffered negative publicity in the country. A young girl was killed while chasing her hoop across the street, and adults began complaining of backaches and slipped discs. By November

AT A GLANCE

Hula Hoop brand introduced in 1958 by Richard Kerr and Arthur "Spuds" Melin, owners of the Wham-O Manufacturing Company; Wham-O purchased by Kransco Group Companies, 1982.

Advertising: *Agency*—Gardner Communications, San Francisco, CA.

Addresses: *Parent company*—Wham-O Manufacturing Company, 160 Pacific Ave., San Francisco, CA 94111; phone: (415) 433-9350; fax: (415) 989-2345. *Ultimate Parent Company*—Kransco Group Companies (same as above).

1958, all hoops had been officially banned from the streets of Tokyo.

Performance Appraisal

By late September 1958, nationwide hoops sales had peaked and a period followed in which sales declined sharply, leaving competitors to scramble for new marketing strategies. New models including hoops with bells, hoops that swung up and down while being twirled, and hoops made out of welded aluminum tubing were introduced. But the fad had ended, and as psychologists predicted, it did not return. "This is a TV generation," one psychologist told the *Wall Street Journal,* observing that "children are used to another program on the hour. They're quick to cast off one fad and look around for another."

Wham-O's October sales were down about 90 percent from their peak, although international sales were still climbing. Hoping that Hula Hoop might turn into a seasonal toy, Wham-O began developing marketing strategies for the following spring, including local and national Hula Hoop contests and other promotional activities. Although sales increased slightly as a result, Hula Hoop never generated the feverish buying spree experienced at its introduction.

During the early 1960s, Hula Hoop sales remained modest but steady. In 1967, Wham-O introduced the Shoop-Shoop Hula Hoop. This variation of the traditional hoop contained steel ball bearings inside the tube, making a "shoop-shoop" noise when twirled. The Shoop-Shoop Hula Hoop caused sales to jump slightly.

In 1982, Wham-O tried again to revive the old Hula Hoop fad, introducing the Peppermint Hula Hoop, a barber pole striped, peppermint scented hoop. Promotional events included a demonstration by Miss U.S.A. at New York City's annual toy fair, an appearance on the popular television series *The Dukes of Hazzard,* and sponsorship of hoop-based sporting events in Daytona, Florida, during the college spring break season. "We believe the nation and the world are ready for another Hula Hoop era," a Wham-O vice-president announced to the press. But the new Hula Hoop sparked only minor interest, and Wham-O discontinued production of the Peppermint Hula Hoop in 1986.

Future Growth

While Wham-O found that fads are rarely repeated, the company did create a market niche with Hula Hoop and continued to hold the top market share. In 1992, the company introduced a transparent Hula Hoop featuring the Barbie doll character, aimed specifically at the children's market. Through this and other slight variations, the company has sought to update the toy. While Hula Hoop sales may never again skyrocket, they are expected to hold steady, and may even increase slightly as the company strives to increase the product's appeal among young consumers.

Further Reading:

Bush, Thomas, and Frederick Taylor, "Hoop Fad Slips Fast Despite New Efforts to Keep It Spinning," *The Wall Street Journal,* October 28, 1958, p. 1.

"Grandson of Hula Hoop," *Time,* March 15, 1982, p. 63.

Griswold, Weseley S., "Can You Invent a Million-Dollar Fad?," *Popular Science,*-January 1966, p. 78.

Lasky, Victor, "The Hula Hoop May Be a Capitalist Fad, But It Has the Reds Jumping, Too!," *Saturday Evening Post,* July 4, 1959, p. 10.

—Maura Troester

IBM®

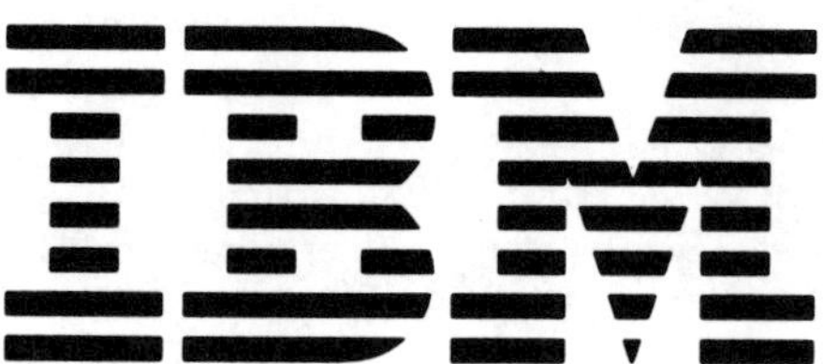

The IBM brand of computer systems is one of the top-selling lines of computers in the American business and scientific communities. Displaying the digitized, striped "IBM" logo, IBM computer systems impact our lives in some form every day as the machines record, process, communicate, store, and retrieve information in manufacturing, banking, retailing, weather forecasting, health services, and education. IBM computers have gone from the vacuum-tubed Model 701 of 1952 to the portable, pen-based ThinkPad 710T Personal Digital Assistant of 1993. Despite the emergence of the mouse-driven Apple/Macintoshes in the 1970s and 1980s, IBM computers have consistently maintained a bold share in the personal computer market. Just one product put out by The International Business Machines Corporation, which also manufactures such other popular products as Database 2 software, Pennant printers, and Pulse Viper memory chips, IBM computer systems have remained a market share leader due to years of superior salesmanship and constant improvement through technological innovation.

Brand Origins

Beginning as the Computing-Tabulating-Recording Company (C-T-R), a corporation composed of 3 companies which manufactured tabulating machines, scales, and time recorders, IBM (International Business Machines) assumed its new name in 1924. Founded in 1896 by Dr. Herman Hollerith, The Tabulating Machine Company, one of the 3 companies which formed IBM, manufactured a series of electrical machines that processed data stored on punched cards; these machines were first recognized during the tabulation of the 1890 U. S. Census, when they reduced tabulation time from 7 to 3 years. With the data capacity of a punched card increased from 45 to 80 columns of information in 1928, a new series of machines were introduced in the early 1930s which not only added and subtracted but performed full-scale accounting operations as well.

Because IBM, during the 1930s, continued to add salesmen and continued to manufacture innovative machines, the Company in 1936 was prepared to provide the machines and services to satisfy its governmental contract to process the accounting operation for the start-up Social Security Program. Forerunners of IBM's first computer included the ASCC (Automatic Sequence Controlled Calculator), completed in 1944; the Mark I, an electromechanical machine that used relays and tape-controlled programming devices; and the SSEC (Selective Sequence Electronic Calculator), the first operating computer to combine electronic computation with stored instructions. In 1952, the Company premiered its first large, vacuum-tubed, tape-driven computer, the IBM 701, which executed 17,000 instructions per second. Although the 19 IBM 701s shipped were used primarily for governmental and research work, vacuum-tube technology quickly moved computers into business applications such as billing, payroll, and inventory control. From the Company's work in developing core memories for the SAGE air defense system in 1952 in a joint project with MIT's Lincoln Lab, IBM produced the first main core memories for commercial products, the 704 and 705 computers, which were announced in 1954. Earlier, IBM had developed a small buffer core memory for the 702 computer launched in 1953.

But IBM was still not ready for commercializing its computers. Few engineers thought that any single individual would even *want* to purchase a computer. First, the early computers were powered by large numbers of vacuum tubes which were prone to burning out rather quickly. Second, the early mainframes were the size of a small house and cost, in terms of 1993 money, approximately $3,000,000 to build. Finally, the early computers were very difficult machines to use, and very few people had the expertise to program them. In the 1940s, IBM had showed little interest in computers, even in Eckert and Mauchly's UNIVAC I. IBM had seemed content to stay with the punched-card tabulating equipment it had pioneered at the turn of the century. Since that time, IBM had placed tabulating machines in every conceivable business environment, from small wholesale firms to huge data-processing centers. For half a century, IBM had grown rich on a technology that would soon be rendered obsolete by electronic computers. Yet, IBM had not recognized the approaching paradigm shift. The then-President of IBM, Thomas J. Watson, was not unaware of computers, for IBM had even built a "monstrosity" called the SSEC, a hybrid machine, part electronic, part electromechanical. Completed in 1948, the SSEC was dedicated by Watson to scientific research, thus ending the Company's foray into computers.

Like most people at the time, Watson thought that computers were purely scientific machines; he did not believe they posed any threat to his beloved tabulating equipment. But when the United States Census Bureau, an organization that used hundreds of

AT A GLANCE

Founded as The Computing-Tabulating-Recording Company in 1911; name changed to International Business Machines in 1924; name changed to IBM in the 1930s; the IBM 701, the Company's first vacuum-tube computer, completed in 1952; information products business of IBM acquired in March 1991 by The Lexmark Company, which developed, manufactured, and marketed IBM personal printers, typewriters, information processing supplies, notebook computers, and keyboards; developers included Thomas J. Watson, Sr., and Thomas J. Watson, Jr.

Performance: *Sales*—$64,523.0 million.

Major competitor: Apple; also, Compaq, Dell.

Advertising: *Agency*—Lintas, New York, NY; also, Wells, Rich, Greene BDDP, New York, NY. *Major campaign*—"We're putting the personal in personal computing."

Addresses: *Parent company*—International Business Machines Corporation, Old Orchard Rd., Armonk, NY 10504; phone: (914) 765-1900; fax: 1-800-426-4329 and 1-800-426-3395.

tabulators, ordered a UNIVAC computer from its manufacturers, Eckert and Mauchly, one IBM vice-president, Thomas J. Watson, Jr., became alarmed. Visiting the Census Bureau in Washington, D.C., young Watson felt "a great sense of panic." Returning to New York, the headquarters of IBM, he convinced his father that computers were the "beginning of the end for IBM" unless the Company recognized that computers were here to stay and unless the Company "did something."

Early Marketing Strategy

Thomas Watson, Jr., knew IBM would lose everything if the Company did not get into the computer business, but nothing was ever done at IBM without his father's permission. The elder Watson would not listen to IBM executives who were advancing their own thoughts about the coming importance of computers; however, he *would* listen to his son, who could champion the computer to his obdurate father without fear of job reprisal. Believing that IBM should be market-driven, young Watson urged his father to begin manufacturing computers in order to take the lead over UNIVAC.

IBM finally took its first steps into the computer age with a production line of 20 scientific computers. The year was 1951, only 5 years after Eckert and Mauchly had started their UNIVAC. That delay would come to haunt Thomas Watson, Jr., for while IBM was building its scientific computer, UNIVAC was slowly stealing away IBM's commercial customers. So infuriated was the younger Watson that he vowed to focus all his energy on beating UNIVAC. Because the senior Watson had decided to step aside as President of IBM after 40 years, Thomas Watson, Jr., was then free to introduce one of IBM's first business computers, in 1953.

At first glance, this new machine was no match for the UNIVAC model; the IBM 650 was slow and inefficient, but it did have one big advantage—IBM's sales force, the Company's greatest asset, the envy of IBM's competitors, and the powerful legacy of Thomas J. Watson, Sr., whose approach to sales had been ferocious, and his understanding of salesmen, superb. The salesman, in his mind, was an American hero. These "heroes" of IBM soon convinced hundreds of ordinary businessmen to buy the IBM 650 computer. Orders started pouring in, and the IBM 650 soon became known as the "Model T" of the computing industry—the first truly mass-produced computer. Within a year, IBM sold almost 1,000 units.

Relatively inexpensive, the genius of the IBM 650 was that it used punched-card readers, punches, and printers that the customer already had and with which the customer was familiar. Although tabulating equipment made the machine run much more slowly, the computer was easier for customers to use than was UNIVAC, which required its customers to give up the old equipment and to transfer punched-card data onto magnetic tape. Simply put, UNIVAC's method was a more *efficient* way of processing information, but customers were more *comfortable* with the old methods IBM had mastered.

First Commercial Success

In 1956, IBM soared past Remington Rand (which had purchased UNIVAC from bankrupt Eckert and Mauchly) as the largest computer company in the world. Thomas Watson, Jr., had won in his battle for corporate survival. The punched card business had represented most of IBM's business, so the Company by necessity was *forced* to develop computers; whereas, at Remington Rand, which owned UNIVAC, the punched-card business represented only 10 percent of the that firm's output (other products included razors and typewriters), so the incentive did not exist there to push forward with computers, even though Remington Rand had had three commercial machines installed at a time when IBM had none. As the 1950s came to a close, IBM had captured more than 75 percent of the United States computer market; the other 25 percent was shared by Remington Rand and a half-dozen other companies. With almost 10,000 computers in operation in the United States, computers proved they could be a useful and a reliable business tool.

Advertising Innovations

IBM's company-trained, blue-suited sales force (hence, the company's nickname "Big Blue") was responsible—far more than any print, radio, or television advertising—for the stellar success of the Company's computer systems. The legacy of Thomas Watson, Sr., IBM's aggressive sales force—the phalanx which sold the IBM 650—knew how to convince potential customers that only an IBM computer would satisfy their needs. Even though other companies initially had better technology than IBM and certainly a better knowledge of how to use that technology, IBM was able to zip right by them with its superior sales and service force. The elder Watson rewarded his salesmen with high commissions, pushed them with quotas, inspired them with speeches, educated them in classrooms, and punished them if they didn't perform satisfactorily. Expecting at least the moon and perhaps the galaxy, he wanted a good sales job and a lot of orders because the Company grew with orders. *After* the sale, Watson believed, was when the item was manufactured, delivered, and used. But, without a sale, none of these activities could happen.

Brand Development and Product Changes

In 1945, IBM's Selective Sequence Electronic Calculator (SSEC) became the first operating computer to combine electronic computation with stored instructions. Two hundred fifty times faster than the IBM-built Mark I, it used vacuum tubes for arithmetic and logic operations. However, most memory devices in the SSEC were still electromechanical.

Out of IBM's work with the SAGE air defense system in 1952 and MIT's Lincoln Lab came the magnetic core memory used in the 704 and 705 computers making their debuts in 1954. (Earlier, in 1953, IBM had independently developed a small buffer core memory, used in the 702 computer introduced in 1953.) Soon, through IBM's innovative manufacturing process, which made magnetic core technology inexpensive, dependable, and amenable to mass-production, data could be retrieved from core memories in millionths of a second.

The transistor, a small electric switch and amplifier invented at Bell Laboratories in 1947, gradually wove a path into everyday use in radio, television, spacecraft, and hearing aids. By 1960, the transistor had come into general use in the computer industry. That year, IBM installed the first automatic production line for transistors and was able to produce and test up to 1,800 individual transistors in one hour. With all these transistors in reserve, IBM was able to roll out the Stretch computer system in 1961. Capable of performing tens of billions of computations a day, the Stretch was the most powerful computer in the industry because it was able to overlap operations. Resembling spiders because of wire connector legs, the transistors were at first wired with other components, such as resistors, on circuit cards to form the logic and control elements of processors. When the IBM System/360 was launched in 1964, however, the circuits were closely combined on 1/2-inch ceramic modules. The 360's processors, ranging from small to large, could use most of the same peripheral equipment and programs and facilitated power upgrades. With the new Solid Logic Technology (SLT), the smallest processor of the System/360 could perform 33,000 additions per second; the largest could perform 3/4 of a million. In addition to providing a technological building block for the System/360, the SLT module solidified the Company's commitment to supplying the bulk of its own component technology.

Not only did IBM develop this technology—it also manufactured the equipment to make and test it. An industry "first" occurred in 1968 when the semiconductor cache appeared in the System/360, Model 85. Small and extremely fast, the cache, or buffer, relieved demands on the main memory by supplying data or instructions most often needed in processing. The IBM 2250, introduced with the System/360, enabled designers to perfect their work on the screen through the use of the keyboard and light pen. By this time, the wonders of computer technology were beginning to capture the imagination of the American public. In fact, IBM computers similar to the IBM 2250 appeared in the 1968 film epic *2001: A Space Odyssey.*

Although the era of microminiaturization had begun, the integrated circuit (in which all of the same elements—resistors, capacitators, transistors, and diodes—were fabricated on a single slice of silicon) had yet to be invented. With IBM's introduction of "floppy" disks in 1970, the standard for small systems was set. That same year, IBM rolled out a revolutionary 128-bit bipolar chip which was used in the industry's first all-monolithic main memory. (In monolithic architecture, circuits are fabricated on thin wafers of silicon and later diced into chips.) Premiering in the System/370, Model 145, this bipolar chip measured less than 1/8-inch square and thrust IBM headlong into a promising new technology. Requiring low power and costing little, the chip quickly became popular for main memory, where data were constantly in motion. Faster than the IBM System/360, yet operating on the same instructions, the 370 family boasted larger models which could handle up to 15 program tasks at once. In 1972, N-channel FET (field effect transistor) technology was introduced in the System/370, Model 158, becoming the basic technology for large-scale integration semiconductor memory.

Disk storage took a huge leap forward when virtual storage was introduced on a large scale in the System/370 in 1972. In this type of storage, information is exchanged automatically between main memory and disk storage so rapidly that disk storage appears to be an extension of main memory. The user benefits because he or she gets faster computing speeds; yet, the cost of the storage is comparable to that of less expensive disk storage.

Setting the industry standard for advanced technology when it made its debut in 1973, the 3340 disk storage unit (nicknamed the "Winchester") doubled the information density of IBM disks nearly to 1,700,000 bits per square inch. The "Winchester" would be only one of numerous innovations by IBM in computer systems.

During this time, IBM had been quietly watching the fledgling personal computer industry develop, but Big Blue wasn't sure how to respond to this strange new market. When IBM did make a half-hearted attempt to enter the field, it failed. In 1975, IBM put out a personal computer, the 5100, which was portable, weighed 50 pounds, was "big as a breadbox," sported a 5-inch screen, and cost $5,000 just "to open the box" and $9,000 if the user "really wanted it to *do* anything." Marketed at the Second West Coast Computer Faire by blue-suited IBM salesmen, the 5100 did not attract very many customers. Learning from this experience, IBM soon realized that while demand for mainframe and minicomputers was still strong, small, inexpensive personal computers were the machines of the future.

The System/38, rolling out in 1978, with its distinctive architecture and programming, allowed database management and virtual storage to be utilized by experienced and novice computer users alike. New software productivity functions shifted much of the applications development burden from the programmer to the system. That same year, IBM became the first company to mass-produce a memory chip storing approximately 64,000 bits of data. Only 11 years earlier, the densest chip could store only 64 bits.

First announced in 1966, more than 5,000 of the small but rugged System/4 Pi computers were delivered for a variety of missions in missiles and aircraft and space stations in 1979. Later models would be used aboard the Space Shuttle.

In 1980, the computer logic and buffer memory for the large-scale IBM 3081 computer, nearly 800,000 circuits, was contained on just Thermal Conduction Module circuit boards, with the result that processing and reliability went up while costs came down. Also introduced in 1980 was the IBM 3687 Holographic Scanner, used with the IBM 3683 supermarket terminal. One of the first major uses of holography in a commercial product, the IBM 3687 Holographic Scanner emitted light rays which "wrapped around" and easily read the product code marked on packages, thereby speeding checkout.

In 1981, IBM finally introduced a serious machine which, with the Company's superior sales network, soon dominated the personal computer industry. Called simply the Personal Computer, this machine, the smallest computer in IBM's history, made its debut in 1981 and was able to churn out calculations at the rate of 250,000 per second—15 times faster than the earliest IBM mainframes. The IBM 3084, the most powerful computer in IBM's history, rolled out in 1982, featuring 4 processors running under the same operating system and able to tap into the same data pool.

With the 1984 introduction of the 10,000-circuit chip (the product of a powerfully new automated design system developed by IBM) and the 1 MB chip (an experimental memory chip—fabricated by IBM on an existing manufacturing line—which could store more than 1,000,000 bits of information), the foundations were laid for the premiere of the IBM 3480; this new magnetic tape subsystem introduced a new generation of tape drivers that replaced the familiar reel of tape with an easy-to-handle cartridge. One-fourth the size of a standard 10.5‘ tape reel, the cartridge could store up to 20 percent more data.

Automatic banking, too, took on a technological look with the 4730 Personal Banking Machine, which could dispense exact change to the penny, cash third-party checks, and authorize personal checks for acceptance at a store's checkout counter. Also, the MVS/XA appeared—a new operating system designed to keep pace with the increasing processing power of IBM's largest computer systems. This system, which could be used by the entire 308X Series as well as the 4381, significantly expanded the available storage, increased data transfer speed, and increased the number of peripherals that could be attached to the system. Personal computer products announced that year included the IBM Portable PC, the Personal Computer Engineering/Scientific Series (which featured a graphics display using up to 256 colors simultaneously), the Personal Computer AT (IBM's most powerful computer to-date), and the Personal Computer AT/370.

In 1992, IBM computer hardware included the System/390 processor, Application Systems/400 products, PS/2 products, and RISC System/6000 workstations. Hardware available in 1993 included the ValuePoint Si PC, the ValuePoint Desktop, the ValuePoint Mini-Tower, the new PS/1 with Rapid Resume, and the ThinkPad Series of laptop PCs (''Use them wherever you think best''), which boasted the ThinkPad 710T, a Personal Digital Assistant (PDA).

International Growth

Early recognizing the importance of the global economy, IBM (as C-T-R) in 1917 entered the Canadian market under the name of International Business Machines Co., Ltd., and also opened an office in Brazil. In 1919, C-T-R entered the European market, and, in 1925, it opened sales offices in Latin America and the Far East; in 1945, they opened in the Philippines. Accounting machines were introduced in Japan that year, also. Nineteen thirty-one saw the first permanent installation of the Filene-Finlay Translator at the League of Nations in Geneva. In 1950, IBM Israel began operating in Tel Aviv. A year later, IBM United Kingdom was formed.

In 1954, the plant at Sindelfingen, Germany, was expanded. 1960 saw the World Trade Corporation completing a manufacturing plant in Argentina, plant expansion occurring in Scotland and France, and construction of new laboratory buildings beginning in France, Holland, and Germany. IBM's manufacturing plant in Japan expanded in 1961. 1965 witnessed the opening of the first IBM-sponsored computer centers in European universities in the cities of London, Copenhagen, and Pisa and the opening of a new IBM plant in Montpelier, France. By 1967, the expansion of manufacturing facilities at Mainz, Germany, Amsterdam, The Netherlands, Greenock, Scotland, and Fujisawa, Japan, had been completed. In 1971, the IBM laboratory in Zurich built transistor amplifiers and oscillators operating at 18,000,000,000 cycles per second, the highest transistor circuit frequency to-date. Also, manufacturing plants opened in Bromont, Canada; Sumare, Brazil; and Yasu, Japan.

Then, in 1972, construction of new headquarters for IBM Germany and IBM Mexico was completed, and the IBM World Trade Corporation reorganized into two operating groups: IBM/Europe and Americas/Far East. With 1974 came IBM's restructuring of its non-U.S. business into two new operating units: IBM World Trade Europe/Middle East/Africa Corporation and IBM World Trade Americas/Far East Corporation. A New Office Products manufacturing plant began operations in Guadalajara, Mexico, in 1975. In 1976, IBM Brazil dedicated Gavea Residential Educational Center, IBM's first on-site customer education facility in South America; IBM Colombia dedicated a new plant in Bogota; and the IBM Latin America Advisory Board was formed to advise the Americas/Far East management on regional issues. Because of equity requirements of the Indian government, IBM was forced to change its mode of business operations in that country in 1977. Also in that year, the Indonesian government accepted IBM's reorganization plan, thereby enabling the company to remain in operation there, and IBM Mexico celebrated its 50th anniversary. In 1979, the first IBM retail shops, called IBM Product Centers, opened in London and Buenos Aires.

IBM Japan commemorated the 55th anniversary of business in that country in 1980 and the 30th anniversary of the resumption of operations after World War II. Seven additional IBM Product Centers opened in Europe and South America. 1981 saw a realignment of the worldwide marketing structure to permit the sale and distribution of the entire product line to customers by a single marketing team. Additionally, IBM's first scientific center in South America opened in Brasilia, Brazil; IBM Taiwan celebrated its 25th anniversary; IBM Canada headquarters moved to a 74-acre site northeast of Toronto; IBM began a $2,700,000 audio-visual project in Soweto aimed at improving the quality of education for South African blacks; and IBM United Kingdom celebrated its 30th anniversary.

In 1982, an innovation was implemented at the IBM laboratory at Hursley, England, when a display terminal with audio output for sight-impaired operators was developed there. By 1983, IBM PCs were being marketed in 16 countries in Europe and the Middle and Far East. Also, a scientific center was established in Caracas, Venezuela, and IBM and major European universities announced an international computer network to exchange scientific and technical information among academic communities in Europe and the United States.

In 1992, an emphasis on market segmentation, growth businesses, greater delegation to country management, and tight control of expenses and assets helped to enhance by 4 percent the profitability of IBM's 18-country IBM Asia Pacific region. In Japan, IBM focused on services, small- and medium-sized businesses, and large customers. To keep IBM Pacific in the lead, a new, wholly owned subsidiary opened in China, and a joint venture in India was launched. Despite a disrupted economy, IBM Europe/Middle East/Africa (EMEA) accelerated a transformation through its larger country operations, becoming the largest professional services organization in Europe.

Among the fastest-growing of IBM's business units in 1992, IBM Latin America, comprising a 20-nation region of political and economic versatility, segmented markets and leveraged the skills of its people through alliances. In 1992, IBM Latin America ranked first among its competitors in the region in customer satisfaction.

Emerging as a world-class provider of computer systems and services, IBM North America in 1992 offered such specialized services as application design, consulting, and systems integration. Indeed, in 1992, IBM virtually covered the globe.

Performance Appraisal

Although IBM lost considerable ground in the mainframe category in the early 1990s because of high prices, it did make significant progress in lowering its cost base for these machines. Also, while LAN-based client/server architectures gained popularity during the time period, the need for "industrial strength" mainframes was still obvious: personal computers simply could not run a business conglomerate. Even in the recessionary 1990s, when most companies were reluctant to spend on big systems, IBM's mid-range AS/400 line did quite well and gained market share against traditional minicomputer competitors. The RS/6000 line fared just as well, carving a significant niche in the workstation market and also finding its way into broad business applications.

During the late 1980s and early 1990s, despite economic downturns, IBM's financial performance proved quite a bit better, relative to historical trends, than many analysts supposed; conventional reasoning was that the "glory days" of IBM's mainframe success (1982 to 1986) had made the years 1987 to 1991 seem bleak by comparison. Also disproportionately affecting analysts' perceptions was the fact that the conversion from lease/rental to outright sales in the early 1980s had inflated sales revenue between 1983 and 1986. As a result, IBM's overall financial performance during the latter half of the 1980s *appeared* volatile because the stabilizing conversion of lease/rental to sales had slackened. In the early 1990s, with the growing success of OS/2, IBM's operating system, IBM seemed poised for a turnaround in market influence.

Although 1992 was a difficult year for IBM computer systems, with intense price competition and skyrocketing product launches, the fourth quarter launch of IBM Personal Systems helped to regain PC market share and strengthen financial performance. Created in September 1992 to manage the Company's PC business worldwide, the IBM Personal Computer Company introduced more than 80 new products, many of which were conceived, manufactured, and introduced in fewer than 6 months.

Future Predictions

Volatility in earnings produced problems for IBM computer systems during the Recession of the late 1980s and early 1990s. However, with the combination of the U.S. economic recovery, renewed IBM mainframe demand, and IBM's reduced cost structure, pleasant upside surprises were certain to happen for IBM. IBM's positive new approach to management (an approach containing neither the bureaucratic centralization of the past nor an unplanned fragmentation into totally independent units) integrated a substantial independence and autonomy with a sensible degree of overall coordination across units, emulating Japanese corporate structures.

With more aggressive pricing, more timely innovation, broader distribution, and more effective marketing, the 1992-created IBM Personal Computer Company seemed on the road to recovering market share in personal computers and servers.

In order to forge forward technologically, corporate partnership was essential. Sharing costs, risk, and knowledge, in 1992 IBM formed a 3-way pact with Siemens and Toshiba to develop a 256,000,000-bit memory chip.

From 1982 to 1992, IBM computer systems moved from an inwardly-directed company to an enterprise seeking new ideas and strategies that would utilize its own talents and strengths. In 1992, the IBM Corporation had more than 20,000 business partnerships worldwide and more than 500 equity alliances with agents, dealers, distributors, service companies, and manufacturers.

Further Reading:

Bashe, Charles, et al., *IBM's Early Computers,* MIT Press, 1985.

Carroll, Paul, *Big Blues: The Unmaking of IBM,* Crown, 1993.

DeLamarter, Richard Thomas, *Big Blue: IBM's Use and Abuse of Power,* Dodd, Mead and Company, 1986.

Hoskins, Jim, *IBM Personal System/2: A Business Perspective,* John Wiley & Sons, Inc., 1957.

How One Company's Zest for Technological Innovation Helped Build the Computer Industry, IBM Corporation, 1984.

The IBM 1992 Annual Report, IBM Corporation, Inc., 1993.

IBM . . . Yesterday and Today, IBM Corporation, 1985.

Innovation in IBM Computer Technology, IBM Corporation, January 1984.

Katzan, Harry, Jr., *The IBM 5100 Portable Computer: A Comprehensive Guide for Users and Programmers,* Van Nostrand Reinhold, 1977.

Killen, Michael, *IBM: The Making of the Common View,* Harcourt Brace Jovanovich, 1988.

Lexmark International, Inc., Lexmark International, Inc., October 1993.

Pancucci, Dom, "Software Eyes Health Concerns," *Byte,* November 1993, p. 44.

Prescott, Carter A., "EMF: The Controversy," *Management Quarterly,* Summer 1993, pp. 3–9.

Pugh, Emerson A., *IBM's 360 and Early 370 Systems,* MIT Press, 1985; *Memories That Shaped An Industry: Decisions Leading to the IBM System/360,* Cambridge, Massachusetts: MIT Press, 1984.

Rodgers, F. G. "Buck," with Robert L.Shook, *The IBM Way: Insights Into the World's Most Successful Marketing Organizations,* Harper & Row, 1986.

Sobel, Robert, *IBM vs. Japan: The Struggle for the Future,* Harcourt Brace Jovanovich, 1988.

Watson, Thomas J., Jr., *Father, Son & Company,* Bantam, 1991.

The World's Greatest Brands, John Wiley & Sons, 1992, p. 89.

Zachmann, William F., "IBM's No Dinosaur," *Upside,* December 1992, pp. 16, 19.

—Virginia Barnstorff

JACUZZI®

Jacuzzi Whirlpool Bath is the world's largest manufacturer of whirlpool products. When Roy Jacuzzi built the first home whirlpool bath, he built a product that would prove to be enduringly popular as a symbol for a way of life—and changed the way millions of people bathed every day. For the first time, home users could participate in a form of relaxation and recreation in an environment of luxury that was previously open only to a privileged few who visited spas.

Over the years, Jacuzzi products have become so highly esteemed for their innovation, quality and reliability that the company name is now synonymous with its most famous product. However, the name Jacuzzi is the brand name and is the only registered trademark in both the Oxford and Webster's dictionaries that recognizes Jacuzzi as the inventor of the whirlpool bath.

Jacuzzi products are known for their design and inventiveness through the use of patented, cutting-edge technology. By the early 1990s, Roy Jacuzzi held more than 250 patents for his innovations in whirlpool design and technology—for pump systems, jet technology, air controls, and product design. Jacuzzi products are also valued for their safety and reliability, established through rigorous testing, and features that make bathing more comfortable and convenient.

In addition to styling and technological changes, Jacuzzi product lines have expanded in order to fit changing consumer lifestyles, needs and interests. The needs of people who wish to escape the pressures and stresses of modern life, in addition to the need for luxury items that most people can afford, have all influenced the development of products of different sizes, price ranges, shapes and colors. Jacuzzi whirlpool products have become standard amenities in a large number of new homes and hotels, and whirlpool bathing has become part of the lives of millions of consumers around the world.

Brand Origins

With a degree in industrial design and an eye for spotting social trends, Roy Jacuzzi joined his family's manufacturing company in the late 1960s and developed and marketed the first whirlpool bath that incorporated his patented hydromassage system in 1968. Noting that Americans were becoming more interested in health, fitness, and leisure and demanded highly stylized products that would enhance home design, Jacuzzi created the first completely self-contained whirlpool bathtub. The new, spa-like tub enabled the user, wherever he or she sat, to receive a relaxing, invigorating massage from water stirred by jets of air. Jacuzzi took his invention to an industry trade show and returned to the pleasantly surprised family company with many orders.

Roy Jacuzzi's invention was designed to bring relaxation and pleasure, but was actually based upon the company's previous experience in developing a system meant for medical and therapeutic use. As it happened, in 1956, a member of the Jacuzzi family had a problem that required daily hydrotherapy treatment. A team of engineers adapted one of the industrial pumps the company manufactured and created a portable pump for home use. From that serendipitous beginning, the J-300 was created as a portable pump for use in hospitals and schools and a small, niche business was built.

The company's first production model of a bathtub with a built-in whirlpool system was introduced in 1968. Called the Roman Bath, this unit eliminated the need for the portable pump to be placed *inside* the tub, allowing the bather the full space to enjoy the hydromassage experience. The whirlpool jets were located in two places in the tub, providing more and broader exposure to the aerated water. The Roman Bath was designed to fit into a standard bathroom in place of a traditional, non-whirlpool tub.

Brand Development

In the years to come, the Jacuzzi line of products expanded to include whirlpool baths, spas, and shower systems. Moreover, the products became available in larger sizes, colors, and shapes as well as becoming more luxurious and feature-laden. Most importantly, the systems got bigger, to the point where the public's image of the new spas usually involved a large group of people relaxing and socializing in their "Jacuzzi." The expansion in the size of units began in 1970 when the Roman Bath line was expanded; the new Adonis tub was large enough to accommodate two people.

The whirlpool spa was developed shortly after the Adonis because the company wanted to enhance the convenience of these new, larger units. The thinking was that it would be unrealistic to fill and drain these large systems with every use, so heating and filtration systems were added to keep the water clean and warm.

AT A GLANCE

Jacuzzi brand whirlpool baths, spas and shower systems are manufactured by Jacuzzi Inc., a private subsidiary of London-based Hanson PLC; Jacuzzi is a trademark for products made by the divisions of Jacuzzi Inc.; Jacuzzi Inc. originally founded in the early 1900s by seven brothers who emigrated from Italy to California and manufactured airplane propellers and irrigation pumps for agricultural use; in 1968, after graduating college, Roy Jacuzzi joined the family company as head of its Research Division; shortly thereafter, he developed and marketed the first whirlpool bath that incorporated his patented hydromassage system.

Performance: *Sales*—$250-300 million (1993 estimate).

Major competitors: Hesco, American Standard, Kohler.

Advertising: *Agency*—In-house. *Major campaign*—"Jacuzzi: The Ultimate Bathing Experience."

Addresses: *Parent company*—Jacuzzi Inc., 2121 North California Blvd., P.O. Drawer J, Walnut Creek, CA 94596; phone: (510) 938-7070. *Ultimate parent company*—Hanson Industries, 99 Wood Ave. South, Iselin, NJ 08830; phone: (908) 603-6600; fax: (908) 603-6878. *Ultimate parent company*—Hanson PLC, 1 Grosvenor Place, London SWIX 7JH, England; phone: 44-71-245-1245; fax: 44-71-235-3455.

The innovation resulted in the first whirlpool spa to be sold in the U.S., and once again the company succeeded in creating a whole new market for a new type of product.

Feautures that have evolved to meet various needs of consumers include PowerPro jets for massaging the whole body, special neck jets for therapy on this tense area of the body, and a number of differing seating configurations. Other features include a Water Rainbow waterfall, a multi-function timer to schedule thermostat settings on spas, and programmable controls for the jets.

In 1990, Jacuzzi also entered the shower market with the J-Dream shower system. The system included an enclosure featuring 16 hydrotherapy jets, multi-function shower heads, a steam bath and cascading waterfall—all within the dimensions of a traditional bathtub. Two years later the line was expanded and J-Dream II, built for use by two people, was introduced. Users could have a side-by-side shower, yet still have a personal set of 16 hydrotherapy jets easily programmed from the control panel. They could also sit on sculpted seats and enjoy their steam bath or cascade waterfall. Other features helped this line live up to its name: for instance, a concealed closet allowed users to store a robe or towel, and a built-in shelf held bathing accessories. Dual, adjustable, hand-held showers with eight massage settings were standard equipment on J-Dream II systems, but optional equipment included a built-in stereo sound system with CD player, AM/FM tuner and four high-fidelity speakers.

New shower systems were developed to accommodate consumers who had limited space. While the features offered were the same as the other shower systems, the new units were more compact. The Corner J-Dream was designed for corner spaces and the J-90 and J-100 models incorporated hydrotherapy, steam bath and traditional showers into one unit. Another corner unit, J-Carre, followed and was designed for maximum relaxation in a minimum amount of space.

Another combination unit was then added, J-Shower Tower, which connected the whirlpool bath with the shower in a completely new way. A full-size whirlpool bath, available in 5-foot and 6-foot lengths, was combined with a shower enclosure of transparent tempered glass. For the first time, homeowners could have the benefits of a whirlpool bath and shower in one compact unit.

The next expansion was the Custom Shower System, a new modular series that consisted of shower bases, walls and innovative features. The series allowed homeowners to create their own shower environment by choosing the exact size and features that met their needs. Nine different bases were available and components were sold separately.

In 1994, Jacuzzi Inc. introduced a "two-in-one" whirlpool product which was a combination whirlpool bath and spa. Called Delfino Bath/Spa, the unit contained an in-line heater and filter system so that it could be used as a spa or as a traditional fill and drain whirlpool bath.

Patented Technology

For all of the hedonism and luxury that Jacuzzi's varied products connote, at their core is sound engineering based on patented technology. For example, the patented PowerPro jets distribute a soothing water massage to the entire body, unlike the straight-on, conventional shower. The jets mingle air and water from all directions, creating a broad circular pattern of bubbles and high-power hydrotherapy for the whole body. Jacuzzi engineers have also developed PowerPro jets that are fully adjustable, allowing users to focus water pressure on body areas that need special attention. Electronic controls allow users to adjust the air and water mixture of the PowerPro jets. Other Jacuzzi Inc. patents include the Water Rainbow fill spout, which releases a cascading waterfall; many of Jacuzzi's safety, comfort, and luxury features derive from other technological advances and patents.

Advertising and Marketing

The distinctive Jacuzzi logo and the name Jacuzzi is registered in the U.S. Patent and Trademark Office. Most Jacuzzi advertising is done through print ads that appear in popular magazines. Jacuzzi products are marketed to, and purchased by, everyday consumers and people involved in some aspect of construction, such as architects and plumbers.

International Markets

Jacuzzi is an international company with two domestic and five overseas divisions. Each division manufactures and markets a different mix of products including whirlpool baths, whirlpool spas, the J-Dream Family of shower systems, steam systems, shower bases and enclosures, faucetry, domestic pumps and water systems, swimming pool equipment, and industrial pumps.

Jacuzzi Whirlpool Bath, located in Walnut Creek, CA, manufactures and markets products for the United States, Pacific Rim, Mexico and Puerto Rico. European divisions include Jacuzzi Europe, located in Pordenone, Italy, and Jacuzzi U.K. Ltd in London. South American divisions include Jacuzzi Chile based in Santiago, and Jacuzzi Brazil in Itu, Brazil. Other North American units are Jacuzzi Bros. in Little Rock, and Jacuzzi Canada in Toronto.

Further Reading:

''How to Use Jacuzzi Whirlpool Bath Trademarks,'' Walnut Creek, CA: Jacuzzi Inc.

Jacuzzi Inc. fact sheet and press materials.

—Dorothy Kroll

JAGUAR®

The Jaguar brand name has graced many of the world's most elegant sedans and sinuous sports cars. The name also came to symbolize unreserved speed and classic, hand-crafted British indulgence, even though the first Jaguar in 1935 was a low-cost sedan sometimes referred to as a working man's Bentley. Jaguar enjoyed its greatest popularity in the 1960s with the XKE sports car. However, in the 1970s, quality and reliability deteriorated and the name nearly went out of existence in 1980. The Ford Motor Company purchased Jaguar PLC in 1989 and planned to revive the brand with new product introductions.

Brand Origins

The name "Jaguar" was introduced to the automobile world by SS Cars Ltd. in 1935, after being chosen by the British car maker from a list of possibilities prepared by the company's publicity director, E. W. Rankin. It replaced the name "Swallow," which had been associated with the company since William Lyons and William Walmsley formed the Swallow Side Car Company Limited in Blackpool, England, in 1922.

Lyons, who turned 21 the day the company was founded, and the older Walmsley concentrated on manufacturing motorcycle sidecars until 1926, when they produced the first Austin Seven Swallow Sports, a two-seat automobile that combined Swallow's colorful two-tone coach work with a chassis from the Austin Company. Over the next several years, Lyons and Walmsley also produced cars known as the Morris Cowley Swallow, the Wolseley Swallow, and the Standard Swallow for different chassis assemblies.

In 1927, the company changed its name to the Swallow Side Car & Coach Building Company Limited. A year later, operations were moved to Coventry, then the center of the British automobile industry. Sidecars were relegated to a subsidiary in 1930, and the company became known as the Swallow Coach Building Company.

In 1931, Swallow unveiled the SS-I, a rakish, low-cost sedan with 2+2 seating, which became the first automobile to use a chassis designed by Lyons. Advertisements preceding the introduction proclaimed: "SS is the name of a new car that's going to thrill the hearts of the motoring public and the trade alike. It's something utterly new . . . different . . . better. Long, low and very FAST!"

The derivation of the "SS" name was never clear. The chassis was built to Lyons's specifications by the Standard Motor Car Co. Ltd., which apparently wanted the car to be called the Standard Special. However, Lyons wanted it to be called the Swallow Sports. Some automobile historians believe SS was a compromise that allowed Standard and Lyons to apply their own interpretations. It may also have stood for Super Sports, Super Swallow, or nothing at all.

Whatever the case, the SS-I was a hit with the motoring public. *Autocar* said the SS-I had the look of "a powerful sports coupe costing £1,000, although the actual price is less than a third of that figure." In addition, at a time when most cars came only in black, the SS-I was available in yellow, gray, blue, red, and apple green. Ironically, it was not available in black.

In 1935, the company reorganized as SS Cars Limited and Walmsley left the business to manufacture house trailers. That fall at the London Car Show, SS Cars unveiled its first full-sized automobile, a four-door sedan that resembled the more expensive Bentley. The company named it the SS Jaguar. However, Lyons's ambition was to build a sports car capable of reaching 100 MPH. That was achieved with the SS-100 Jaguar, also introduced in 1935. The SS-100 Jaguar was an open two-seater with an aluminum body built around a wooden frame.

At the outbreak of World War II, SS Cars was turning out about 12,000 SS Jaguar sedans a year. However, only 314 SS-100 Jaguars were ever produced. In 1945, the company abandoned the name SS Cars Limited—which reminded people of the Nazi SS police—and adopted the name Jaguar Cars Ltd.

American Market

When World War II ended, the British economy was in shambles, and the government adopted a policy of encouraging exports. The steel industry was nationalized and steel was allocated to car makers based on the percentage of cars that were sold abroad. In addition, a stiff tax ranging from 27 to 55 percent was imposed on automobiles sold in England. The first postwar Jaguars—only slightly modified 1940 model SS Jaguar sedans—were exported to the United States in September 1947. The company adopted the slogan "For Grace, Space, Pace." Grace referred to the styling, space to the interior, and pace to the 90 MPH top speed.

AT A GLANCE

Jaguar brand of automobiles introduced under name SS Jaguar by SS Cars Limited in 1935; SS Cars Limited was founded as Swallow Side Car Company Limited in 1922; name changed to Swallow Side Car & Coach Building Company Limited in 1927; name changed to Swallow Coach Building Company Limited in 1930; name changed to SS Cars Limited in 1935; name changed to Jaguar Cars Limited and "SS" dropped from Jaguar brand automobile in 1945; Jaguar Cars Limited merged with British Motor Corporation in 1966 to become British Motor Holdings; merged with British Leyland in 1968 to become British Leyland Motors; British Leyland reorganized in 1978 as BL Ltd.; Jaguar brand assigned to specialty car subsidiary, Jaguar Rover Triumph Ltd.; Jaguar PLC divested by Jaguar Rover Triumph in 1984; Jaguar PLC purchased by Ford Motor Company in 1989.

Performance: *Market share*—1.5% of luxury car market. *Sales*—(U.S.) 12,734 units (1993).

Major competitor: BMW; also Mercedes-Benz and Infiniti.

Advertising: *Agency*—Ogilvy & Mather, New York, NY, 1992—. *Major campaign*—"The Jaguar Moment."

Addresses: *Parent company*—Jaguar Cars Inc., 555 MacArthur Blvd., Mahwah, NJ 07430-2327; phone: (201) 818-8500; fax: (201) 818-9770. *Ultimate parent company*—Jaguar Cars Limited, Browns Lane, Coventry, England CV59DR; phone: 44-203-402-121. *Ultimate ultimate parent company*—Ford Motor Company, Dearborn, MI, 48121-1889.

The first true postwar Jaguar was the dignified Mark V, a high-performance family sedan introduced in 1948. However, it was the racy six-cylinder Jaguar XK120 roadster, also launched in 1948, that established the brand's reputation in the United States. The sleek XK120 was set apart by a long, graceful hood and teardrop fenders. The lavish interior was covered in leather from the seats to the dashboard and cockpit trim. The "XK" referred to the engine. The "X" stood for "experimental" and the "K" referred to the model. In 1949, the Royal Automobile Club of Belgium road-tested an XK120 at more than 126 MPH, which justified the company's claim that the XK120 was the fastest production car in the world. The fastest U.S.-made production car at the time was the Cadillac, with a top speed of about 100 MPH.

In 1982, automobile historian Richard Busenkell called the Jaguar XK120 possibly "the most significant automobile—certainly the most significant sports car—of the entire postwar era." An XK120 sedan was introduced in 1951, followed by a convertible in 1953. More than 12,000 XK120s were produced between 1949 and 1954, with more than 60 percent exported to the United States. The XK140 was introduced in 1954 with only a few styling changes, including heavier bumpers for the American market. The XK150, which followed in 1957, was the first production car equipped with disc brakes. The last XK150 left the Jaguar plant in 1961.

The XK120 also became the first Jaguar competition racer. Private owners had raced XK120s since the car was introduced, but Jaguar Cars Ltd. did not participate on the racing circuit until 1951, when it entered three modified XK120s at Le Mans. The racing version of the XK120 was known as the XK120C (for competition) or the Type C, and was 800 pounds lighter than the production model. Top speed was about 150 MPH. Two of the Type C Jaguars dropped out with mechanical problems, but the third took first place, having covered 2,243 miles at an average speed of 93.5 MPH. It was the first win at Le Mans for a British-made car since 1935 and a victory for Jaguar Cars Ltd. in its very first race.

In 1953, the company again took Le Mans with a Type C Jaguar. In 1954, Jaguar Cars introduced the Type D, the first Jaguar with monocoque construction. Type Ds won at Le Mans three straight years—1954 through 1957—before the company disbanded its competition division and withdrew from racing. Jaguar Cars put the XK120C into limited production, selling 43 of the racers for less than $6,000 each. The company also sold a few Type D cars, but only to recognized competition drivers or racing teams. It intended to introduce a production sports car based on the Type D racer to be called the XK-SS. However, a New Year's Day fire in 1957 destroyed 300 cars and the equipment used to build them. Jaguar Cars managed to assemble 16 cars from leftover Type D parts, but replacing the tooling fixtures would have made full production too costly and the XK-SS was dropped.

Jaguar Sedans 1948–1968

The first big Jaguar sedan was the Mark V, introduced in 1948. It was replaced in the fall of 1950 by the Jaguar Mark VII. There was never a Jaguar Mark VI, probably because that designation was used by the Bentley. The durable, five-passenger Mark VII weighed more than 4,000 pounds but used the XK engine and could easily sustain highway speeds of 100 MPH. The Mark VII also had two gas tanks—one in each rear fender. Each of the gas tanks had its own fuel line and was filled separately. The driver could change tanks with a switch mounted on the dashboard.

Upon its introduction in the United States, the Jaguar E-Type appeared at the 1961 New York Show.

The Mark VII was replaced in 1956 by the Mark VIII. Although there were few styling changes, the Mark VIII did feature a one-piece windshield and a new hood ornament—a leaping Jaguar. The Mark IX was introduced in 1958, again with only a few styling changes. Nearly 50,000 Jaguar Mark VII, VIII, and IX sedans were produced between 1950 and 1960, with the majority exported to the United States.

In 1955, Jaguar Cars introduced a smaller sedan known simply as the Jaguar 2.4 Litre, for the size of its engine. The Jaguar 2.4 Litre was less luxurious than the big sedans and was aimed at the

British market. However, in 1956 the company brought out a 3.4 Litre model, which satisfied the U.S. desire for more power. In 1959, Jaguar Cars launched a new luxury version of its small sedan that was designated as the Mark II. Thus, the Jaguar Mark II was introduced after the Mark VII, VIII, and IX. The Mark II was a high-performance sedan with a top speed of 120 mph. It was also very compact, only 3 1/2 inches longer than the XK150 sports car and 1 1/2 inches shorter than the Ford Mustang that was introduced almost a decade later.

In 1961, Jaguar Cars introduced the Mark X, which broke ranks completely with earlier sedans. The wheelbase was several inches longer than the previous big Jaguars, yet the Mark X was three inches lower than even the compact Mark II. The Mark X was also wider and appeared to bulge at the sides. The Mark X sold well in England, but not in the United States. In 1966, the Mark X was renamed the Jaguar 420G.

Jaguar XKE

Perhaps the most famous Jaguar ever built was the two-seat E-Type (popularly known as the XKE), introduced in 1961. The designation ''E'' was chosen purposefully as a reminder of the Type C and Type D Jaguar racers, and the aerodynamic XKE was capable of reaching 150 MPH. It quickly became the benchmark for all other production sports cars. The original XKE came in two body styles, an open roadster and an even more sinuous hatchback coupe. The XKE coupe was not introduced until 1966.

The wildly successful XKE remained virtually unchanged until 1967, when car makers were forced to meet tougher emissions and safety laws in the all-important U.S. market. On the outside, the glass covers were removed from the recessed headlights and the large ears on the stylish knock-off hubs were eliminated—presumably to prevent potential injury to pedestrians. The company was forced to install a different carburetor, which reduced the engine's horsepower, and to replace the airplane-style toggle switches on the dashboard.

In 1969, Jaguar Cars introduced the Series 2 XKE with more changes to meet U.S. safety requirements. At the front, the headlights were moved forward and turn signals added. At the rear, both the bumper and tail lights were made bigger. There was also a change in the axle ratio that further reduced the XKE's top speed. In 1971, the company introduced the Series 3 XKE with a V12 engine under the elongated hood. Although the XKE went out of production in 1974, it remained the car most people thought of when they heard the Jaguar name. More than 72,000 XKEs were sold, more than 49,000 of them in the United States.

Quality Problems

In 1968, company co-founder William Lyons posed for publicity photos beside the new Jaguar XJ6 sedan, the first Jaguar he had ever personally endorsed in advertising. Lyons called the XJ6—the first new full-size Jaguar in more than a decade—''the finest saloon car Jaguar has ever made and one that challenges comparison with any in the world.'' Car enthusiasts agreed. *Road & Track* called the Jaguar XJ6 ''uncannily silent and gloriously swift.'' *Car & Driver* said, ''The XJ6 has to be one of the best balanced, most enjoyable cars made.''

Unfortunately, Jaguar quality began to plummet in the 1970s. Jaguar Cars Limited had merged with the British Motor Corporation in 1966. Then, in 1968, the company joined the state-owned British Leyland to become British Leyland Motors. The merger was designed to provide the small, independent Jaguar Cars with the resources to modernize its factory and increase productivity. The company was promised ''the greatest degree of autonomy.'' However, problems at British Leyland spilled over to the new Jaguar division, where quality became a bad joke, for example: Why do Jaguar owners need two cars? So they have one to drive while the other is in the shop for repairs.

In 1978, British Leyland reorganized and became known as BL Ltd. The Jaguar brand became part of a specialty car division, Jaguar Rover Triumph Ltd. By 1980, Jaguar sales had fallen to about 14,000 cars from about 32,000 cars in 1974. Sales in the United States were down to about 3,000 cars. U.S. owners were so reluctant to talk about their cars that J. D. Powers & Associates excluded Jaguar from its annual survey on customer satisfaction. British Leyland, which had already relegated the Triumph brand name to the history books, was ready to shut down Jaguar as well. John Egan, who took over the Jaguar division in 1980, told *Road & Track,* ''I was thinking at the time that I might be the only chairman of a car company never to make a single car.'' The problems and delays were so bad that Jaguar never produced any 1981 cars, but instead skipped directly to the 1982 model year.

Amazingly, Egan was able to turn the Jaguar division around in just two years. In 1982, the company sold a record 10,349 Jaguars in the United States. As part of the turnaround, the company eliminated about half of its U.S. dealers, many of whom had become the target of complaints about poor service and dirty repair shops. In 1984, the Jaguar division was separated from British Leyland and again became a public company traded on the London stock exchange, Jaguar PLC. Egan was knighted in 1986 for saving the Jaguar brand. Lyons had also been knighted, in 1956, for his contributions to the British automobile industry.

Ford Motor Company

In 1987, Jaguar PLC introduced the ''new XJ6.'' An advertising campaign in the United States proclaimed the ''Evolution of the Species''—''It's out there waiting for you. Stronger, sleeker, smarter than any of its kind has ever been.'' In 1988, the company sold a record 52,000 Jaguar cars, including more than 20,000 in the U.S. market. However, Jaguar PLC still needed financial help to develop new models, and in 1989, the Ford Motor Company paid $2.5 billion for the company. Despite misgivings by Jaguar enthusiasts, Ford promised to preserve the brand's mystique.

Ford expected to introduce several new models of the Jaguar XJ6 sedan and XJ-S sports coupe in the mid 1990s, beginning with the high-performance XJR-S in 1993. The first totally new Jaguar developed under Ford's ownership was expected to be a sporty sedan designed to challenge the BMW. It was scheduled to be introduced in 1998. Unfortunately, the worldwide market for luxury automobiles collapsed in the early 1990s, which could delay introduction. Jaguar sales fell to about 25,000 in 1991, with about 9,000 sold in the United States. The company also continued to struggle with quality problems. In 1990, it announced the recall of more than half the Jaguars sold since 1988 because of a potentially leaky brake line.

Jaguar XJ220

The limited edition Jaguar XJ220 was the fastest production car in the world, with a top speed of 212 MPH. It also carried a price tag of more than $600,000. Yet when Jaguar Sport, Ltd., a joint venture between Jaguar and Tom Walkinshaw Racing, announced in 1989 that it would build 350 of the sleek, 500-horsepower XJ220s, more than 1,500 potential buyers submitted applications. Those lucky enough to be chosen had to put down a $76,000 deposit to ensure delivery beginning in 1992.

However, the Jaguar XJ220 fell from grace with some of its potential buyers in the early 1990s because of the worldwide recession that affected the luxury car market. In 1993, industry analysts said the value of the car had fallen by a third, and Jaguar Sport announced that about 100 buyers wanted out of their contracts. Customers were allowed to invoke an escape clause by paying another $107,000. About 150 XJ220s had been delivered in 1993.

Further Reading:

Aeppel, Timothy, ''Jaguar Chairman Must Steer Company Through New Model Plan to Boost Sales,'' *Wall Street Journal,* July 22, 1992, p. A7.

Beaulieu, Lord Montagu, *Jaguar,* London: A.S. Barnes, 1981.

Berss, Marcia, ''Jaguar Johnny,'' *Forbes,* February 27, 1984, p. 104.

Busenkell, Richard L., *Jaguar Since 1945,* New York: W.W. Norton, 1982.

''Can Mike Dale Fix Jaguar—Again?'' *Fortune,* November 5, 1990.

Dale, Michael H., ''How We Rebuilt Jaguar in the U.S.,'' *Fortune,* April 28, 1986, p. 110.

Eisenstein, Paul A., ''Jaguar's Quality Leaps Up, But New Models Needed,'' *Christian Science Monitor,* June 15, 1993, p. 9.

Elliott, Stuart, ''Ogilvy Gets Jaguar Account in Chief's First Big Victory,'' *New York Times,* July 16, 1992, p. D17.

Flint, Jerry, ''Luxury Doesn't Come Cheap,'' *Forbes,* January 22, 1990, p. 72.

Ingrassia, Paul, ''Jaguar Recalling Majority of Cars Sold Over 3 Years,'' *Wall Street Journal,* February 21, 1990, p. A11.

''The Jaguar Roars Back on Track,'' *Newsweek,* March 15, 1982, p. 61.

Kanner, Bernice, ''Jaguar Revs Up,'' *New York,* August 31, 1987, p. 23.

Lamm, John, ''Jaguar XJ220: Unleashed!'' *Road & Track,* September 1992, p. 52.

Lipman, Joanne, ''Ogilvy Snares $20 Million Jaguar Account,'' *Wall Street Journal,* July 16, 1992, p. B10.

Lubin, Joann S., ''Hayden Is Aiming to Make Jaguar Roar,'' *Wall Street Journal,* June 22, 1990, p. B1.

Maremont, Mark, ''Can Ford Make a Tiger Out of Jaguar?'' *Business Week,* October 29, 1990, p. 71.

Maremont, ''A Jaguar Buyer May Be in for a Long, Slow Drive,'' *Business Week,* November 13, 1989, p. 48.

Maremont, ''Jaguar: Pouncing on Sticker Shock,'' *Business Week,* December 12, 1988, p. 85.

Melcher, Richard, ''The Law of the Jungle Catches Up with Jaguar,'' *Business Week,* October 2, 1989, p. 54.

Miller, Krystal, ''Jaguar Pulls in Its Car-Pricing Claws,'' *Wall Street Journal,* October 14, 1992, p. B1.

Pauly, David, ''Have You Driven a Jag, Lately?'' *Newsweek,* November 13, 1989, p. 64.

Prokesch, Steven, ''Ford's Jaguar Bet: Payoff Isn't Close,'' *New York Times,* April 21, 1992, p. D1.

''A Promise from Jaguar: 212 M.P.H. for $736,000,'' *New York Times,* June 2, 1992, p. D5.

''Save the Cat,'' *Forbes,* September 16, 1991, p. 191.

Schuon, Marshall, ''Jaguar's XJ-S: Sunshine and Power,'' *New York Times,* May 5, 1991, p. I28.

Simpson, Robert L., ''Jaguar Slowly Sheds Outmoded Habits,'' *Wall Street Journal,* July 26, 1991, p. A6.

Smith, Chuck, ''Saving Jaguar from the Taxidermist: John Egan Unleashes the Cats,'' *Road & Track,* May 1985, p. 124.

''Stalking the Cat,'' *Economist,* February 25, 1989, p. 66.

Taylor III, Alex, ''Shaking Up Jaguar,'' *Fortune,* September 6, 1993, p. 65.

Wherry, Joseph, *The Jaguar Story,* Philadelphia: Chilton Book Company, 1967.

''Would You Pay $183,600 Not to Drive a Jaguar?'' *New York Times,* September 22, 1993, p. D4.

—Dean Boyer

JEEP®

After more than fifty years on (and off) the road, Jeep has evolved from the strictly utilitarian, military CJ to the luxurious, prestige-oriented Grand Cherokee. This transformation has radically expanded Jeep's target audience as well, from macho, hard-driving men to safety-conscious parents. In many respects Jeep has been able to reconcile these divergent attractions, allowing its customers to enjoy the adventurous potential of their vehicles while simultaneously appreciating the security and comfort of four-wheel-drive and leather upholstery. Since 1987 the Jeep brand has been owned by the Chrysler Corporation.

In the 1990s the Jeep Wrangler continued to dominate the open-body 4x4 category that the brand originated in World War II despite challenges from such upstarts as the Geo Tracker and Suzuki Sidekick. After years of dominating the compact sport utility segment, Jeep's Grand Cherokee, however, slipped into second place behind Ford Motor Company's newly introduced Explorer in 1990. The Explorer continued to outsell the Grand Cherokee into the 1994 model year. Some analysts questioned Jeep's heretofore celebrated brand loyalty in light of this early 1990s upset, but it would take more than a market shift to obliterate the Jeep mystique.

Product Origins

As early as 1938, with hostilities mounting in western Europe, the U.S. Army informed the nation's automobile manufacturers of its need for a light reconnaissance vehicle to replace the motorcycle and side-car used in World War I. The call launched an industrywide competition for this valuable and prestigious military contract. Ward M. Canaday, chairman of Willys-Overland Corp. of Toledo, Ohio, set the company's vice president of engineering, Delmar ''Barney'' Roos, to the task of designing a light and maneuverable, yet powerful and sturdy, military vehicle.

Willys' toughest competitor in the race to design a contract-winning entry was the American Bantam Car Company, located in Pennsylvania. In fact, Bantam won the government's first request for bids in 1940 with its ''Blitz Buggy.'' Obviously, Willys and Barney Roos did not give up; they objected to the Army's unrealistically low weight specifications and earned a second test run before Army officials in November 1940.

Willys ''Quad'' car offered a choice of two- or four-wheel-drive and a powerful engine nicknamed the ''Go-Devil,'' but it still exceeded the Army's revised weight requirements by 240 pounds. The simplest way to conform to the weight specification would have been to install a lighter, less-powerful engine, but Roos and his staff elected instead to disassemble the entire car and reevaluate the weight and composition of each part. By shortening bolts and using alternative materials, Willys' design team was able to bring the prototypical ''Quad'' to within seven ounces of the weight guideline.

The first production model was essentially a Willys-Overland design that incorporated features from Bantam's prototype, as well as from that of a third competitor, Ford. In 1941 Willys-Overland underbid Bantam and Ford for the 16,000-vehicles contract. As the United States became increasingly involved in the war, the contract negotiations assumed a sense of urgency; the Army required delivery of 125 per day. Later in the year, with demand running even higher than expected, Willys was compelled to turn its designs over to Ford so that the competitor could augment production. Over the course of the war, Willys supplied the Army with more than 368,000 ''Quads.'' By that time, however, the vehicles had a new name.

Brand Origins

Although Jeep has been a household word since World War II, the origin of the trademark has been the subject of ongoing debate. Some attribute the name to the slurring of the initials G.P.—the Army gave Willys' Quad the uninspiring appellation ''General Purpose vehicle.'' According to one Army officer, however, the term was used in Oklahoma as early as 1934 to designate a truck equipped with special equipment for drilling oil wells.

An affidavit from a Minnesota company (Minneapolis-Moline Power Implement Co.) asserted that Sergant James T. O'Brien referred to a four- or six- wheeled test vehicle as a ''Jeep'' in 1940. His frame of reference for the name was a character from E.C. Segar's 1930s ''Popeye'' comic strip. ''Eugene the Jeep'' was described as ''a small, impish-looking animal that had the power to travel back and forth between dimensions and could solve all sorts of problems.'' To the soldiers who used Jeeps in World War II as litter bearers, machine-gun firing mounts, and reconnaissance vehicles, this aptly described their ''G.P.'' as well. Most authorities credit the Segar strip as the source of the Jeep name.

AT A GLANCE

Jeep brand of automobile registered as a trademark on June 13, 1950, by Willys-Overland Corp. of Toledo, OH; the vehicle itself developed by Willys in 1940 for use by U.S. forces in World War II; Willys-Overland purchased by Henry J. Kaiser in 1953, when the company name was changed to Willys Motors Inc.; company name again changed in 1963 to Kaiser Jeep Corporation; company acquired by American Motors Corporation in 1970 and renamed Jeep Corporation; Chrysler Corporation purchased American Motors in 1987 and made the Jeep line part of its Jeep/Eagle Division.

Performance: *Market share*—Jeep: 8.2% of total U.S. automobile category; 33.6% (top share) of compact sport utility category (models Grand Cherokee and Cherokee); 53.1% (top share) of open-body 4x4 category (model Wrangler). *Sales*—408,323 units (1993).

Major competitor: Ford Explorer; Chevy S-10 Blazer; Geo Tracker; Suzuki Sidekick.

Advertising: *Agency*—CME-KHBB, Southfield, MI, 1983—. *Major campaign*—"There's Only One Jeep" and "Advantage Jeep."

Addresses: *Parent company*—Chrysler Corporation, 12000 Chrysler Drive, Highland Park, MI 48288; phone: (313) 956-2088.

Jeep was first used in the news media to describe the Willys vehicle in 1941, when a *Washington Daily News* photo and story told the public about the Army's new motorcar. Willys got more free publicity when President Franklin D. Roosevelt reviewed troops in a Jeep, and enlisted men got a taste of Jeep's sturdiness and maneuverability over rough terrain throughout the conflict. During the war Willys capitalized on its military contract with the slogan ''The sun never sets on the Willys-built Jeep.''

Recognizing the marketing potential of the Jeep name, Willys-Overland registered it in the United States and internationally on June 13, 1950, after winning the right to the trademark from both the American Bantam Car Co. and Minneapolis-Moline Power Implement Co. The two complainants had challenged Willy's right to the Jeep name before the Federal Trade Commission.

Product Development

Willys set out to make the Jeep ''the ultimate recreational vehicle for man, woman and family,'' as a company publication exulted. Willys started developing the Civilian Jeep, or ''CJ'' (a.k.a. Jeep Universal), even before the end of the war. In 1944, 22 prototypes were reviewed, and the first Jeep CJ was introduced in August 1945. Touted as one of ''America's most useful vehicles,'' it listed at $1,090 and featured such ''amenities'' as a tailgate, auto wipers, and an outside gas cap. Since Willys would be wrapped up in litigation over the Jeep name for five more years, early civilian models only carried the company name.

Willys brought out extensions of the line in 1946, the second year of commercial production. The second model became the auto industry's first all-steel station wagon/delivery sedan. These two-wheel-drive vehicles could hold seven passengers and had a top speed of 65 m.p.h. The 1949 addition of four-wheel-drive and a six-cylinder engine made the Jeep All-Steel Station Wagon the forerunner of the contemporary Jeep Cherokee. Willys continued to manufacture practical vehicles for the Army and soon garnered contracts with the U.S. Postal Service, making the compact, light Jeep an everyday sight.

The two-door, convertible Jeepster was brought out in 1948. The Jeepster name was a creative way to get around ongoing trademark litigation and still capitalize on the appealing Jeep name. The line was discontinued in 1950, when Willys won the rights to the Jeep trademark. Jeepster was briefly revived in 1966 to denote a line of pickup trucks and station wagons.

In 1953 the Willys-Overland Corp. was purchased by Henry J. Kaiser, who renamed it Willys Motors Inc. Over the course of the decade, Jeep came out with several unique vehicles, including the Forward Control series, which featured a cab-over-engine design that foreshadowed Chrylser's ''cab-forward'' design of the 1990s. New half-ton and full-ton trucks featuring the Roos-developed, high-compression ''Hurricane'' engine were introduced. In 1954 the CJ5 was brought out and grew so popular that it endured, with modifications, until 1983. The CJ5 featured softer styling lines and rounder body contours than its more angular predecessors.

Upon its acquisition of Jeep, Kaiser began almost immediately to extend the brand internationally. From 1954 to 1959 the foreign share of Jeep's sales increased from 25 to 49 percent. By the end of the 1950s, Jeep's overseas network extended from Latin America across Europe to Asia. By 1965 Jeep's worldwide sales totaled $670 million, or 257,000 vehicles.

The original Willys-Overland pilot model delivered to the U.S. Army on November 11, 1940.

In the mid-1950s Henry Kaiser launched a research and engineering program aimed at broadening the utilitarian four-wheel-drive vehicle market. This work came to fruition in 1962, when Jeep opened the model year with the new ''J'' line of Jeep Wagoneer station wagons and a full line of Jeep Gladiator pickup trucks. Advertisements called the extensions ''All New and All Jeep.'' The J line included the first Jeeps to have no roots in military design, and the Wagoneer was the first station wagon to combine passenger-car styling, comfort, and convenience; automatic transmission; and four-wheel-drive. Some analysts contend that it launched the sport utility segment of the auto industry. In 1963 Kaiser changed Willys' name to Kaiser Jeep Corporation to properly reflect company ownership and to identify more closely with its famous trademark.

Birth of the Sport Utility Segment

In the 1960s the only four-wheel-drive vehicles in the United States were Jeeps and International Harvester Scouts. These practical vehicles featured such functional options as snow plows, winches, wreckers, post-hole diggers, rotary mowers, and implement lifts. During the 1970s, however, trucks overall and sport utility vehicles in particular were restyled and repositioned to capture a more mainstream (and therefore larger) share of the U.S. auto market.

Jeep presaged the movement with the 1965 introduction of its "Super Wagoneer," which combined comfort and luxury features with the practicality of four-wheel-drive. Automatic transmission, power/tilt steering, radios, upholstery and trim packages, power brakes and windows, and cruise control—all features on top-of-the-line cars—were incorporated in these new models. While the Super Wagoneer reached into the comfort zone, it retained the traditional Jeep versatility and on- or off-road ability.

Jeep changed hands again in 1970, when the American Motors Corporation (AMC) purchased it for $70 million. AMC split military and civilian production into two subsidiaries: Jeep Corporation in Toledo for commercial vehicles and AM General Corporation in South Bend, Indiana, for military and post-office vehicle production. American Motors itself would be purchased in 1987 by Chrysler Corporation, which placed the Jeep brand under its Jeep/Eagle Division.

Several external influences converged in the 1970s to create the environment in which the sport utility segment of the auto industry was born and flourished. The trend took shape in the truck market, which then encompassed anything that was not a car—vans, pickups, and open-air 4-x-4s. This segment grew more than three times faster than the auto market during the decade, the manifestation of a fundamental life-style change for many Americans. Some were spending more time outdoors—boating, camping, and off-road motorcycling, for example—and they needed transportation that could both haul their "toys" and negotiate the path to their often remote destinations. Other Americans got involved in the burgeoning do-it-yourself trend, building additions, making their own home improvements, or renovating historic homes. Safety became a selling factor in the North, as people began to realize that four-wheel-drive (4WD) provided better handling on ice and snow. Still others who had no practical use for a truck purchased them for purely emotional reasons; trucks, and especially Jeeps, represented "daring but untried adventures" for these consumers. Jeep cornered the market on this emotional appeal by virtue of its historically rugged image. The emerging sport utility market's diverse customer base reflected these varied motivations, ranging from adventurous youths to status-conscious drivers seeking "stylish utilitarianism."

Over the course of the 1970s, truck sales rose at a compounded average annual rate of 9 percent, compared with 2.3 percent for autos. This rate would have soared even higher had manufacturers been able to keep up with surging demand. Sport utility trucks were still the smallest segment of this expanding market in the late 1970s, accounting for less than 10 percent of the 3.3 million trucks sold in 1977.

Jeep XJ Series Dominates New Segment

By the late 1970s Jeep had already carved out a 30 percent stake in the new sport utility segment, putting it ahead of its main competitors, the Ford Bronco and Chevy Blazer. In a move that would help maintain that lead, Jeep introduced its luxurious Wagoneer Limited in 1978. The Wagoneer Limited's standard features included leather upholstery, air conditioning, and AM/FM/CB stereo. Comfort options included automatic transmission, power/tilt steering, power brakes and windows, and cruise control.

Like most American cars of its day, the Wagoneer Limited was a big, flashy vehicle. Anticipating an expansion of the compact sport utility segment, Jeep introduced a shorter, narrower, lighter model, called the Cherokee, in 1984. First launched in 1974, the Cherokee became the leader of Jeep's new XJ series and brought several design exclusives to the category. As mundane as it may seem, the vehicle's four-door design would be a key to its dominance of the sport utility segment because it made the vehicle an alternative to the traditional family car.

Jeep drove this concept home with its 1980s slogan "Why buy a car when you can buy a Jeep?" The Cherokee (and later, Grand Cherokee) became the sporty new "station wagon" of the 1980s. Professor Paul Fussell, author of *Class: A Guide Through the American Status System,* described Jeep's modern appeal: "There's a lot of prestige involved in pretending that we're still on the frontier. It's the lust of most people, once they've made it, to return to a sort of cowboy status, a primitive frontier status." Ronald Reagan, a bellwether of 1980s consumerism, owned two Jeeps. With a Jeep Cherokee, mommies, daddies, and even presidents could "rough it." The Cherokee XJ series was named "4x4 of the Year" by the three major off-road magazines in 1984, and between 1983 and 1984 Jeep sales rose an astonishing 87 percent—from 82,000 to more than 150,000 units.

Competition

Not to be left out of this success story, other automakers, including the Japanese car companies, joined Chevy and Ford in the fray. This prompted Jeep marketers to establish slogans that clearly delineated the first from the rest: "Only in a Jeep" and "Easy to be a truck. Hard to be a Jeep."

Jeep's unit sales grew steadily throughout the 1980s. By the end of the decade, more than one million XJs had been sold, and in the 1989 model year Jeep Cherokee/Wagoneer was the number-one nameplate among vehicles with a median price over $20,000, placing it in a class with Cadillac DeVille, Lincoln Town Car, Mercedes-Benz, and BMW. Market research showed that these prestige cars were often garage mates of the rugged Jeeps.

Then along came the Ford Explorer. With its lower sticker price, four doors, and enticing image, this replacement for the outdated Bronco II outsold the Cherokee almost two-to-one in the second half of 1990. Beside the brand-new Explorer, the Cherokee looked passé; its most recent overhaul was in 1984. The newcomer had also incorporated features, such as push-button 4WD and better safety restraints, that were aimed at women, who by this time accounted for half the category's primary drivers.

Falling back on its brand power, Jeep introduced a new advertising slogan, "There's only one Jeep," which was a refinement of its ongoing "Only in a Jeep" tag line. It also followed Ford's lead, adding optional antilock brakes and "shift on the fly" four-wheel-drive. Chrysler even discounted Jeeps for the first time, offering stripped-down versions with price tags comparable to the Explorer. Prior to this time, Jeeps had been the automaker's profit leaders, commanding 15 percent margins. As the Explorer continued to lead the compact sport utility market throughout the early 1990s, Jeep experimented with a variety of marketing schemes (including a video game) to regain its dominant share.

Green Marketing

Jeep has employed environmentally friendly marketing since the 1970s, when the "Green Movement" became popular. That decade's "Jeep Owner's Code of Ethics," for example, encouraged customers to drive responsibly.

Jeep became a charter member of TREAD LIGHTLY! and made this program of the U.S. Forest Service part of its Jeep Jamborees and 4WD clubs in 1987. TREAD LIGHTLY! was established to teach off-road drivers to drive responsibly. Two years later, as the environmental movement continued to gain steam, Chrysler created the Jeep Marketing Environmental Advisory Council to review all its advertising and promotional programs in order to prevent "green gaffes" in its ads, which were often filmed in remote areas.

In 1993 Jeep aligned itself with John Denver's "Plant-It 2000" and pledged to plant one tree for each vehicle it sold in California. The automaker sent qualifying customers personalized tree-planting certificates informing them that trees were planted in their honor in the Sequoia National Forest. These eco-friendly efforts were disparaged, however, by groups like Greenpeace, Earth Island Institute, and the Sierra Club, who claimed that tree planting on such a relatively small scale was "a cosmetic means of addressing the problem." Carl Pope, executive director of the Sierra Club, called the tree-planting program "deceptive," noting that "Jeeps are large, not very fuel efficient and are often driven places where they do damage to the outdoors." Even so, "Plant-It 2000" staunchly supported its sponsor, maintaining that "To move ahead in the world you have to embrace almost any genuine effort a company makes."

Brand Outlook

As numerous other manufacturers—including Mercedes-Benz, American Honda Motor Co., Isuzu Motors, Toyota Motor Sales USA's Lexus, and Nissan Motor Corp. USA's Infiniti—brought sport utility vehicles to market in the early 1990s, Jeep's efforts concentrated on reinforcing the brand's rugged, scrappy image. Television advertisements continued to emphasize the outdoors and only rarely showed people.

Jeep's combined share of the sport utility market led the segment in the early 1990s, but Ford's Explorer captured the top ranking among individual models. Marketers for Jeep hoped to capitalize on this "underdog" status, choosing to emphasize the unique character of the nameplate rather than its overall dominance of the category.

Further Reading:

Gray, Ralph, "Smaller Jeeps Create Big-Size Marketing Woes," *Advertising Age,* August 22, 1983, p. 14.

Horovitz, Bruce, "Honk If You Love the Environment," *Los Angeles Times,* March 23, 1993, pp. D1, D6.

"The Jeep: Still Going Strong," *Forbes,* April 15, 1965, p. 47.

Jeep: The First Fifty Years. Highland Park, Michigan: Chrysler Corporation, [1989].

"Kaiser Hustles Overseas to Expand Its Diversified Empire," *Business Week,* August 22, 1959, pp. 52–54.

Kuntz, Mary, "Everyone's Driving Jeeps These Days," *Forbes,* May 20, 1985, pp. 224–225.

McCormick, Jay, "Jeep Gears Down for Winter XJ Ad Push," *Advertising Age,* September 20, 1982, p. 42.

Serafin, Raymond, "Jeep Line Blazed AMC's Trail to Saatchi," *Advertising Age,* September 30, 1985, p. 80.

Serafin, Raymond, "Chrysler Spreading Its Wings," *Advertising Age,* December 14, 1987, p. 6.

Serafin, Raymond, "Cars Squeeze Mileage from Awards," *Advertising Age,* June 4, 1990, p. 36.

Serafin, Raymond, "Cars to Get Green Light," *Advertising Age,* September 3, 1990, pp. 3, 54.

Treece, James B., "Beep, Beep! There Goes Ford's Explorer," *Business Week,* January 28, 1991, pp. 60–61.

"Trucks Muscle in on the Car Market," *Fortune,* February 27, 1978, pp. 62–68.

—April S. Dougal

JOHN DEERE®

With a full range of John Deere brand lawn mowers and tractors and an untarnished reputation for quality and durability, the Lawn & Grounds Care Division, which posted sales of $1.05 billion in 1993, holds a leading position in several segments of the lawn and garden equipment industry. Few American manufacturers enjoy the reputation of John Deere, which has been producing high-quality agricultural and industrial implements and machinery since 1837. Long known for their large green-and-yellow farm tractors, Deere & Company entered the lawn and garden tractor market in 1963 with the introduction of its John Deere 110 tractor, a seven-horsepower, three-speed tractor capable of mowing lawns, throwing snow, and hauling wood. By 1984 John Deere had sold its millionth lawn and garden tractor; eight years later it had sold two million.

Farm Heritage

Vermont blacksmith John Deere ventured west to Grand Detour, Illinois, in 1837 in search of economic opportunity. Within a year of his arrival Deere had developed a plow that would revolutionize American farming. When farmers in the Mississippi Valley boasted that their soil was some of the richest in the world, they also had to admit that plowing the heavy, sticky soil was enough to challenge the hardiest pioneer. Turning over the dark soil required plenty of horse power, a heavy iron plow, and the patience needed to continually scrape the plow blade clean. John Deere changed all that when he took a smooth steel saw blade, fashioned it into a gracefully sweeping curve, and attached it to a plow frame. According to legend, a local farmer tested Deere's plow and reported that it sliced through the soil without sticking; he asked Deere to make him two more. From these humble beginnings grew the largest agricultural machinery manufacturer in the world.

Deere & Company, as the family-run business came to be known, grew up alongside American agriculture, providing American farmers with a variety of equipment, including a line of tractors. Farmers developed an intense loyalty to their green-and-yellow machinery, and by the mid-1980s Deere & Company had captured 45 percent of the U.S. farm equipment market, according to *Business Week.* It was this brand loyalty that prompted Deere & Company to manufacture their first lawn and garden tractor in 1963. "Farmers who swore by John Deere tractors also had lawns," Lawn & Grounds Care Division public relations manager Bob Tracinski told *Encyclopedia of Consumer Brands* (*ECB*)," so we knew we had a market."

The first John Deere lawn and garden tractor, the model 110, was designed and developed by the same engineers who worked on the big tractors and was sold alongside the other John Deere equipment at agricultural dealers. When pilot marketing east of the Mississippi River proved successful, Deere began selling the 110 nationwide in 1964. Sales of the sturdy, compact machines boomed, as suburban Americans proudly mowed their lawns on tractors that they associated with the country's agricultural heritage. By 1969, sales of John Deere lawn and garden tractors were so strong that Deere & Company devoted its Horicon Works manufacturing facilities, located in Horicon, Wisconsin, to its new products.

Deere's Diversity

Deere & Company soon developed a wide range of products that were marketed to homeowners under the John Deere name. To a growing variety of tractors, the company added several models of rear-engine riding mowers, walk-behind snow throwers, lawn sweepers, tillers, chain saws, and a range of hand tools and accessories. "We wanted to promote the 'one-stop shopping' idea," Tracinski told *ECB,* "because John Deere's appeal was going beyond the farm customer." More and more Americans spent their leisure time taking care of their lawns and gardens, and John Deere wanted to supply them with the equipment to do it right.

John Deere gained a leading share in the lawn and garden tractor market by continually improving and updating their machines. The second generation tractors introduced in 1974 had new styling, new features, and a hydrostatic drive transmission. "Homeowners liked the automatic transmission they had in their cars," noted Tracinski, "and they wanted something similar in their lawn tractor." With a hydrostatic transmission, the driver could select the direction and adjust the tractor's speed using one lever, allowing them to mow quickly over straight stretches and then slow down around plantings without clutching or changing gears. Many of John Deere's tractors still use a version of the hydrostatic transmission, while others allow the driver to change travel speed in gear while the tractor is moving.

AT A GLANCE

John Deere brand of lawn and garden tractors introduced in 1963 by Deere & Co., which was founded in 1837 by John Deere; John Deere model 110 marketed nationally beginning in 1964; walk-behind mowers and snowthrowers introduced, 1970; Tricycler mulching technology introduced, 1991.

Performance: *Sales*—$1.05 billion (Lawn & Grounds Care Division).

Major competitor: Toro; also Snapper, Lawn-Boy.

Advertising: *Agency*—Hal Riney & Partners, Chicago, IL. *Major campaign*—"Nothing Runs Like a Deere."

Addresses: *Parent company*—Deere & Company, John Deere Road, Moline, IL 61265-8098; phone: (309) 765-8000.

Not all of Deere & Company's attempts to satisfy consumer desires in the 1970s were as successful as the tractors. In 1972 the company began to market a line of snowmobiles, believing that farmers who could not plow their fields or mow their lawns could still have fun on a John Deere. But they did not count on declining snowfall in the snow belt, which imperiled the entire U.S. snowmobile industry. In 1984 Deere & Company sold its snowmobile interests to Polaris Industries. A similar story describes Deere & Company's experience with bicycles: a nationwide biking boom prompted the company's entrance into the market, but when the market declined, Deere & Company got out. The company has been most successful with its tractors and mowers, products with which it has developed both expertise and a reputation.

Marketing and Distribution

Deere & Company entered the lawn and garden business with a well-established distribution network in place, and since the introduction of the 110 that network has grown substantially. By the mid-1980s there were approximately 3,000 servicing dealers selling John Deere lawn and garden equipment. Of these, about half were "combination" John Deere dealers that sold both farm and lawn and garden equipment; the remainder of the dealers focussed on residential customers and sold a number of brands of lawn equipment.

John Deere's initial advertising efforts involved cooperative arrangements with dealers, in which Deere & Company paid half the costs of local advertising efforts that concentrated on newspapers, radio, television, and billboards. As the company came to realize that the lawn and garden products were capable of generating substantial revenues, it began to develop national advertising campaigns for both print and television. Beginning in 1972 John Deere brand lawn and garden products began to be marketed under the slogan "Nothing Runs Like a Deere." "The slogan focuses the consumer's attention on what is best about John Deere products: quality and durability," Tracinski pointed out to *ECB.* Twenty years after the introduction of the John Deere 110, customers wrote to the company to say that, not only were they still using the same tractor, but some still used the original mower blade.

John Deere has typically marketed its products to men who are in the homebuying age bracket, but they also recognize the influence of women in homecare purchasing decisions. Their advertising typically appears in such male-oriented magazines as *Home Mechanix, Popular Mechanics,* and *Popular Science,* or on televised sports programming and news. "The first step is to get men into our stores and excited about the tractors," said Tracinski. The next step is to show wives that the tractor is equipped with safety devices to protect their families. Some dealers estimate that half of the John Deere purchase decisions are made with or by women; some say that figure is as high as 90 percent. "When a woman is comfortable with the product," noted Tracinski, "then the dealer feels confident about the sale because today lawn care is shared and either spouse will operate the mower—or a teenager." In fact, John Deere targets men and women equally when it advertises rear-engine riding mowers.

Product Development

John Deere has long prided itself on developing technically sophisticated, safe products. Long before government regulation of walk-behind mowers made consumers aware of lawn mower safety, John Deere had incorporated a number of safety features in its tractors: a seat-safety switch that shuts off the engine and blade if the operator gets off the seat when the mower deck is under power; color-coded and specially shaped controls; a triple-safety starting system to prevent children from starting the tractor; parking brakes; foot-operated drive controls that allow the operator to keep both hands on the wheel; and a return-to-neutral function that disengages the drive system when the brake is applied. Many of these features have become standard on lawn and garden tractors, due to manufacturers' cooperation in developing standards through the Outdoor Power Equipment Institute. This trade association's efforts to develop safety standards has allowed the industry to avoid government regulation concerning riding mowers.

Technological innovations in the late 1980s and 1990s have been driven primarily by environmental issues. Studies prompted by the growing concern over the state of U.S. landfills showed that nearly 20 percent of landfill materials came from lawns. As environmental regulations shut down landfills and forced cities to ban lawn waste from garbage collection, consumers looked to lawn mower manufacturers to develop mowers that allowed them to recycle grass clippings and other lawn waste. The result was the development of mulching mowers, which chop grass clippings into very fine pieces and blow them down into the turf, providing a rich source of biodegradable mulch that university studies have

The John Deere model 110 tractor was launched in 1963.

shown produces healthier, thicker lawns. Promoted as a solution to an environmental problem, mulching mowers also fostered healthy turf.

Like other lawn mower manufacturers, John Deere has sought to develop successful mulching mowers and to promote their benefits. In 1989 the company introduced a mulching plate that could be attached to existing mowers, keeping grass clippings inside the mowing chamber. Since that time, they have developed the Tricycler mowing system, which uses a specially-designed blade, an aerodynamically designed mowing chamber, and special ramps to ensure effective mulching action. ''Designing this technology for a single deck mower was difficult,'' Tracinski stated, ''but transferring it to two- and three-blade systems was even more challenging.'' The Tricycler system is convertible: it can mulch, it can discharge clippings out the side, and it comes with a bagger attachment. John Deere offers the Tricycler mowing system for walk-behind mowers, riding mowers, and lawn and garden tractors.

In 1991, John Deere furthered its mulching technology with the development of a variable plate mulching attachment for one- and two-blade decks on riding mowers. Two wing nuts allow the operator to move the plate into five different positions. In the top positions the deck mulches grass clippings; in the lower positions it mulches leaves as well, pulverizing them into a fine powder that can be blown down into the turf where they can decompose. This attachment promises the end of raking leaves.

John Deere has been active in educating the public about the benefits of mulching. In addition to advertisements and brochures that promote their mulching products, the company is involved in producing video news releases and public service announcements. John Deere has worked with the Professional Lawn Care Association of America (PLCAA) on a project called Grasscycling to educate homeowners about recycling grass clippings and leaves. The public service announcements produced by the PLCAA were sent to 300 television stations and 2000 radio stations. ''Most people want to make a contribution to alleviating the landfill crisis, and they want to know what is available to help them do that,'' claimed Tracinski. ''John Deere wants to let them know what they can do to help, and wants the consumer to associate John Deere with expertise in lawn care and mowing.''

The late 1980s and early 1990s were a time of remarkable growth and expansion for John Deere's lawn and garden products. In 1985 the division had $576 million in sales; by 1993 that figure soared to $1.05 billion. John Deere had entered the commercial market in 1984, and by 1988 they held the leading market share in wide-area front mowers. John Deere entered the golf and turf market in 1988, producing large mowing equipment for the specialized needs of golf course operators. By the late 1980s the company had the broadest line of lawn and grounds care equipment in the industry. In 1991, as a result of the rapid growth of the lawn care segment of the company, Deere & Company moved the lawn and garden products staff out of its Farm Equipment division and into a division of its own: the Lawn & Grounds Care Division. This arrangement gave the Lawn & Grounds Care Division more resources, the freedom to develop different marketing strategies, and new facilities in Raleigh, North Carolina, located closer to the majority of John Deere's lawn and grounds care dealers and customers.

The line of John Deere brand lawn and grounds care products available to homeowners reflects the division's health. John Deere offers seven walk-behind mowers for small mowing jobs; four riding mowers for larger lawns; a smaller, ''suburban'' lawn tractor, the STX 38; and a line of lawn tractors that runs from the 14-horsepower LX172 to the 22-horsepower, diesel-powered 455. The largest tractors can utilize the complete range of John Deere options and attachments, which includes a rotary broom, snow blowers, sprayers, a weather enclosure, a tiller, and many other implements. John Deere is beginning to incorporate thermoplastic technologies into many of its tractors; the parts, developed in conjunction with GE Plastics and Dow Plastics, are tougher and more resilient than sheet metals and resist rust. With a tradition of aggressive research and development efforts and a strong marketing base, John Deere products should continue to dominate the premium lawn and grounds care market.

Further Reading:

Broehl, Wayne G., Jr., *John Deere's Company: A History of Deere & Company and Its Times,* New York: Doubleday, 1984.

Deveny, Kathleen, ''As John Deere Sowed, So Shall It Reap,'' *Business Week,* June 6, 1988, pp. 84–86.

''John Deere Lawn Mowers Feature Dow, GE Resins,'' *Chemical Marketing Reporter,* August 20, 1993, p. 32.

''Lawn & Grounds Care by Introductory Year,'' John Deere & Company, 1993.

Tracinski, Robert L., interview conducted with Tom Pendergast, February 3, 1994.

Additional information provided by Deere & Company

—Tom Pendergast

K2®

Alone, the name K2 evokes images of precipitous snow and ice walls towering upward to oxygen-poor heights, but seen on a pair of alpine skis, the name represents, to generations of skiers, one of the most respected and coveted brands of skis on the market. As one of only a handful of ski manufacturers worldwide, K2 Corporation has enjoyed an enviable marketing and sales record, engendered first by its revolutionary fiberglass ski and maintained through corporate sponsorships with world champion skiers and careful attention to the fashionability of its product. As a perennial leader in the ski industry since the emergence of the K2 brand name in the mid-1960s, K2 stood atop its field in the early 1990s as the largest ski manufacturer in the United States, proof that the familiar K2 logo, although no longer surrounded by the red, white, and blue stripes that first graced the company's skis, represents, for thousands of skiers worldwide, the paradigm of alpine skis.

Encouraged by the enduring success of the company's mainstay product, K2's management diversified into other sporting good markets during the 1980s and 1990s, leading to the ubiquitous presence of the K2 logo on in-line skating equipment, snowboards, water wake boards, and recreational clothing.

Brand Origins

The roots of the K2 brand name stretch back to modest and rather obscure beginnings on a small island near Seattle, Washington, back to the Kirschner Manufacturing Co., a manufacturer of fiberglass animal splints. Owned and operated by Otto Kirschner and his two sons, Don and William (Bill), Kirschner Manufacturing enjoyed a modicum of success designing and fabricating animal splints in the years immediately following World War II, then broadened its product line to include "chew-proof" fiberglass dog cages, which the three Kirschners sold to veterinary hospitals and research facilities. Dog cages and animal splints, however, were not to be the products to launch the Kirschner name toward fame.

Fame would come, and come quickly, from another use for the fiberglass used to manufacture the splints and animal cages. In the late 1950s, after purchasing new skis for his four children, Bill Kirschner discovered "there wasn't enough money left for Dad," so he borrowed a pair of skis to use as a pattern and constructed his own pair using the fiberglass from his family's manufacturing company. Realizing that his new skis were an improvement on the then recently introduced and widely popular aluminum skis, Bill Kirschner took his idea to a Seattle-based distributor of ski equipment, Anderson & Thompson Ski Company, and the fiberglass ski began its inexorable rise to the top of the skiing industry.

Although Bill Kirschner's new fiberglass ski significantly reduced the "chatter" experienced with aluminum skis, that is, the unnerving propensity of metal skis to slip and bump on the snow, causing the skier to easily loose control, it took several years for his concept to materialize into a reality. By 1964, however, Kirschner Manufacturing was ready to add fiberglass skis to its product line, and 250 pairs entered the market. Consumer reaction was immediate: the following year 1,600 pairs of skis, still manufactured under the aegis of Kirschner Manufacturing and distributed by Anderson & Thompson, were sold, and in 1966 the production output ballooned to roughly 4,000 pairs.

Encouraged by the success of his new skis, Bill Kirschner decided to separate the ski manufacturing operations from the family company in 1967 and form a company entirely devoted to the production of fiberglass skis. Kirschner named the new company K2 Corporation in honor of the world's second-highest mountain, Mount Godwin Austen (K-2) in the Karakoram Range in Kashmir, and for the two Kirschner brothers, Bill and Don.

Early Marketing Strategy

The initial success of K2 skis was largely attributable to the technological innovation they represented. Howard Head and his Head skis had revolutionized the sport in 1950 with the introduction of aluminum skis, which quickly supplanted the wood skis that had been the only choice for skiers since recreational skiing had first become popular. Kirschner's fiberglass skis, fabricated by wrapping fiberglass around a core of tapered spruce, represented a commensurate technological leap in the evolution of alpine skis and sparked the early interest in the product. But during these early years of K2 skis, the brand name also benefitted from decorative touches on the skis, most notably, the red, white, and blue stripes that attracted skiers in droves and set the purchasers of K2 skis apart from those schussing down the slopes in Head's all black skis, the most popular skis in America during the late 1960s.

Converts to K2's colorful fiberglass skis increased exponentially in a matter of months, pushing sales up to 21,000 pairs by 1968, which persuaded Kirschner to sever his marketing and distribution ties with Anderson & Thompson and create his own

AT A GLANCE

K2 brand of skis founded in 1967 by William Kirschner; became registered trademark, 1967; brand sold to Cummins Engine Company, 1970, acquired by Sitca Corporation, 1976, and then sold to Anthony Industries, Inc., 1985; K2 Corporation also owns the rights to Pre brand skis.

Performance: *Market share*—22% of downhill skis category. *Sales*—$75 million.

Major competitor: Rossignol brand skis; also, Salomon brand skis.

Advertising: *Agency*—Wong/Doody, 1993—. *Major campaign*—"Torsion Box Construction."

Addresses: *Parent company*—K2 Corporation, 19215 Vashon Hwy. S.W., Vashon, WA 98070; phone: 206-463-3631; fax: 206-463-5463. *Ultimate parent company*—Anthony Industries, Inc., 4900 S. Eastern Ave., Ste. 200, Los Angeles, CA 90040; phone: 213-724-2800; fax: 213-724-0470.

distribution network and marketing strategy. This newfound independence eventually led to the creation of one of the three marketing pillars that would support the company into the 1990s.

At the time K2 skis were emerging as the skiing industry's product of the future, there were four million skiers in the United States, the ranks of which were increasing 25 percent annually. Spending more than $100 million annually for ski equipment, accessories, and apparel, these consumers and the significant number of skiing neophytes who would join the sport in the coming years represented the future of the then burgeoning ski industry. It was a definitive era for ski manufacturers, a time during which the importance of winning the loyalty of consumers was paramount. Accordingly, K2 and other U.S. ski manufacturers, including Head, Hart, and Lange, were fighting for market share with unprecedented intensity, perhaps cognizant of the future implications their success in the late 1960s would portend. For skiing consumers, the decision as to which skis to purchase was based essentially on the answer to the simple question: which is the best ski on the market? While enticing graphics and promotional material delineating the various attributes of a particular brand of skis frequently could influence a consumer's choice, during the late 1960s these marketing ploys were not as effective or pervasive as they would be in later years. Rather, the answer to the perennial question regarding which skis were the best was greatly determined by which type of skis professional skiers used to win their trophies and medals. These men and women were the idols of the skiing world, and their success on the slopes translated into significantly increased sales and market share for the manufacturer whose skis a winner wore.

Consequently, the decision by Kirschner to develop his own marketing direction propitiously led to the creation of a K2 world class racing ski to complement the company's existing line of intermediate skis. Quickly, a pair of prototype competition skis were developed and later that year, in a 1968 World Cup giant slalom race, K2's research investment paid dividends, as the winner crossed the line wearing a pair of K2 skis, the first World Cup victory on skis manufactured in the United States.

K2's foray into the competitive ranks of alpine skiing dramatically elevated the recognition of a brand name that already enjoyed widespread popularity. Shipments of K2 skis doubled each year between 1966 and 1970, making the company the third-largest ski manufacturer in the United States by the beginning of the decade and the only major manufacturer producing fiberglass skis. Following K2's first World Cup victory in 1968, Marilyn Cochran became the first American woman to win in World Cup competition in 1969, and, to K2's benefit, she used K2 skis to record her historic victory. Other manufacturers of skis, both domestically and abroad, were also pinning a considerable part of their marketing efforts on the exposure and increased revenue potential international competitions provided to the winning manufacturer, as the sponsorship of talented racers and affiliations with famous skiing personalities became a necessary component of any ski manufacturer's successful marketing strategy.

Marketing Boons

Toward this objective, K2's sponsorship of two World Cup winners had laid the foundation for future partnerships with competitors in the professional skiing circuit, each a major contributor to the popularity of the company's brand name. In 1973 K2's sales were bolstered by hiring famed skier Jean-Claude Killy, the winner of three gold medals in the 1968 Winter Olympics, as a consultant in the design and promotion of K2 skis, a relationship that would continue to enrich K2 in the years to come and help to increase its presence in foreign markets. But perhaps the most important relationship fostered by K2 with the ski racing world occurred several years later, when the company, as the official sponsor of the United States Ski Team, prospered from the success of two of its members, twins Phil and Steve Mahre.

The ascension of the Mahres toward the top of the international rankings list dovetailed with the windfall announcement in 1978 that K2 had been designated as the official ski of the XIII Winter Olympic Games in 1980. With two years to promote its products and Phil Mahre ranked number two in the world, K2 launched a formidable campaign to capitalize on the immense international exposure the Winter Olympics provided. K2 skis were decorated with the official Olympic logo abutting the K2 logo, fusing the popularity of both into one, while K2 promotional videos were shown throughout the world. By this time, K2 ranked as the largest ski manufacturer in the United States, eclipsing Head, Hart, and Lange, each of which had been absorbed by conglomerates. With annual sales of roughly $25 million, K2 spent $750,000 on promotional activities alone, excluding the fee paid to the Lake Placid Olympic Organizing Committee for the rights to the Olympics and the costs incurred from supporting the United States Ski Team, which totaled nearly one million dollars a year.

Although the K2 brand name received considerable exposure during the two years leading up to the XIII Olympic Games, the effectiveness of the marketing campaign essentially was predicated on the success of the Mahre twins during the Olympic alpine competition. A medal, preferably a gold medal, by either of the brothers and the promotional benefit to K2 would be enormous, but if the company's two most likely prospects for Olympic medals failed to display a strong showing, the ensuing embarrassment would taint, to a certain degree, the K2 name and reputation. Fortunately for K2, Phil Mahre took the company's image to new heights, earning a silver medal in the slalom event and, thereby, earning a commensurate victory for K2.

But the best was yet to come for K2, as the company's investment in the United States Ski Team and the Mahre twins continued to cast K2 skis in the spotlight. Following his second place finish in the Olympics, Phil Mahre reigned as the World Cup champion for three successive years, recording overall alpine titles in 1981, 1982, and 1983. K2's management decided against bidding for official sponsorship of the XIV Winter Olympic Games at Sarajevo in 1984, but, as sponsor of the United States Ski Team, the company's publicity once again focused on Phil and Steve Mahre and the hope that one or both of the racers would demonstrate to the world the superior quality of K2 skis. In this hope, the dreams of K2 marketers were realized, as Phil Mahre captured a gold medal in the slalom event, while brother Steve finished two-tenths of a second behind him, winning the silver medal.

Marketing Busts

Of course, not every marketing endeavor proved as successful as K2's relationship with the Mahre twins and the Winter Olympics. Two marketing blunders in particular, both of which occurred during the 1970s, stained what otherwise was a prolific decade for the company, and demonstrated to K2's management that there were limits to the marketability of the company's brand name.

The first of these, in skiers' argot, "face plants," occurred as a response to flagging sales during the economically recessive mid-1970s. The Eastern United States had suffered three successive skiing seasons with a shortage of snow, driving the demand for K2 skis downward. To invigorate sales, K2 decided to capitalize on the current trend on the ski slopes, "hot-dogging," or trick skiing with short skis. In 1974 K2 introduced three models of short skis called "Cheeseburgers," "Cheeseburgers Deluxe," and "K2 Briefs." The skis were an absolute failure. As Kirschner later recalled, "We dropped that crazy food and underwear line like a hot potato. . . . Professional people like doctors and lawyers weren't about to pay $185 for skis called Cheeseburgers."

In 1979 K2 once again attempted to tap into a burgeoning skiing trend by manufacturing cross country skis, a recreational activity that was becoming increasingly popular in the late 1970s. The company's management quickly discovered, however, that foreign ski manufacturers, particularly European producers, already had secured a nearly insurmountable lead in the U.S. cross country ski market. Unable to wrest control of the market away from its foreign competition, or at least garner an appreciable share of the market, K2 ceased production of cross country skis soon after operations had begun and was forced to sell its inventory at a loss.

Changes in Ownership

Against this backdrop of prodigious growth and sporadic failures, K2, as a corporate entity, had undergone several changes in ownership, although its management remained essentially autonomous throughout the various shifts in ownership. The company's initial success, during the late 1960s, came too quickly, creating a sprawling enterprise that Kirschner found difficult to manage. Consequently, he sold K2 to Cummins Engine Company in 1970, when the Indiana-based manufacturing company was in the midst of diversifying into banking, ranching, and leisure goods.

Six years later, Kirschner and five other partners regained control of K2 and formed Sitca Corporation as a holding company for K2. The creation of Sitca brought James Garrison, a vice president of employee relations at Boise Cascade Corp., into the K2 organization as president, a position he would hold until becoming K2's chairman and chief executive officer. Several seasons of low snowfall in the early 1980s drained K2's cash flow, forcing the company to seek an equity partner to ameliorate the company's financial difficulties. In 1985 a suitable arrangement was found, and K2 was sold to Anthony Industries Inc. based in City of Commerce, California, a manufacturer of Shakespeare fishing rods, Pflueger fishing tackle, Stearns flotation devices, swimming pools, and athletic apparel.

Domestic Competition

K2 skis gained an initial jump on domestic competitors with their revolutionary fiberglass/torsion box construction, which eventually enabled the company to surpass the long-time leader in the industry, Head skis. As the company's marketing efforts became more sophisticated, incorporating alluring graphics into the design of the skis, K2 outpaced other U.S. ski manufacturers, benefitting from the dramatic attrition of domestic manufacturers. In 1968 there were approximately ten U.S. ski manufacturers vying for market share, with K2's major competition coming from Head, Hart, and Lange. During the 1970s, each of these three manufacturers was acquired by conglomerates and their market shares plummeted, leaving K2 as virtually the sole U.S. competitor for the domestic and international ski market. By the early 1980s, there were only two major ski manufacturers in the United States, K2 and Olin Corp., while the other manufacturers had either exited the business or moved their manufacturing operations overseas.

At this time, K2 controlled 20 percent of the U.S. market, which accounted for roughly 40 percent of the company's total sales, and garnered 60 percent of its sales from international sales, primarily in Europe and Japan, the company's second-largest export market. In 1989 K2 bolstered its domestic presence in the U.S. market by acquiring Olin Corp. from Tristar, Olin's parent company. Although the acquisition strengthened K2's position simply by virtue of absorbing the number two U.S. competitor, an appreciable gain in the company's domestic market did not materialize, as foreign manufacturers, particularly European companies, continued to maintain a stranglehold on the global ski market. Entering the mid-1990s, K2's domestic market share remained roughly 20 percent; the company also owned the rights to Pre brand skis.

International Competition

Historically, foreign ski manufacturers have posed the greatest threat to K2's sales performance, both in the U.S. and global markets. Led by French manufacturer Rossignol, the wealth of international competitors compensates for the scarcity of U.S. manufacturers, making K2's position in the worldwide ski industry a perennial battle for market share, a battle that is primarily predicated on brand image and brand reputation.

K2's growth in the international ski market was spurred by the company's association with Jean-Claude Killy, which engendered, in the early 1970s, a line of K2 skis called "Killy Skis." Sold primarily outside of the United States, these skis exported the popularity of the K2 brand name to many European skiers, a group characteristically nationalistic in their choice of skis. Subsequent endorsements by victorious ski racers further strengthened the K2 brand image in Europe, earning K2 skis the reputation of being "boutique" skis. By the mid-1980s Japanese consumers had become a significant source of revenue for K2, purchasing 1.3 million pairs of K2 skis in 1984.

Despite the popularity of the K2 brand name overseas, the global market continued to be dominated in the early 1990s by Rossignol and the world's largest manufacturer of ski equipment, Salomon. Within the United States, K2's growth is predicated not just on racing, but also on further growth of the all-mountain, or "extreme," ski category, which has spurred sales of the top-selling ski models in the United States beginning in the late 1980s. Extreme skiing, which has been showcased and popularized in various ski films, has become synonymous with aggressive American skiing.

Future Predictions

Emerging from the recessive economic conditions of the early 1990s, K2's management entered the mid-1990s hopeful of a return to more robust sales. By adopting a management improvement program during the 1980s, called "Total Quality Management," K2 improved the quality and the speed of its manufacturing processes significantly, enabling the company to place a higher quality ski on the market and reduce the alarming rate of manufacturing defects. In 1982, 80 to 90 percent of all K2 skis manufactured were defective, while 25 percent of the company's shipments had to be scrapped entirely. By 1992, the incorporation of Total Quality Management in the supervision of K2's manufacturing processes had reduced the frequency of these defects significantly, to as low as one percent by 1992. In the all important battle to improve on quality and reputation, this dramatic improvement should help K2 skis to continue their legacy of success into the 21st century.

Further Reading:

Belanger, Herb, "Vashon Island's Growing Ski Maker," *Seattle Times*, January 31, 1971, p. 9.

"Cummins Engine Marketing Pact," *Wall Street Journal*, January 24, 1974, p. 19.

Day, Connie, "Searching for Quality," *Washington CEO*, August 1992, pp. 19–21.

Finkel, Mike, "More Grateful: The Dead and Lunatic Fringe," *Skiing Trade News*, November 1992, p. 10.

Flynn, Dan, "K2 Waxes Warm and Steps Up Ski Making in Wake of Downhill Journey," *Seattle Business Journal*, August 30, 1982, pp. 10–11.

Henderson, Paul, "Rapid Growth of a Little Giant," *Seattle Times*, March 11, 1970, p. B12.

King, Harriet, "Making Skis on a Pacific Isle," *New York Times*, November 28, 1976, p. F7.

Lee, Gordon, "Olympic Sponsorship Was Bitter Lesson for Ski Firm," *Seattle Business Journal*, December 19, 1983, p. 5; "Buyout Ends K-2's Quest for Capital Infusion," *Puget Sound Business Journal*, September 16, 1985, p. 1A.

Marple, Elliot, "K2 Tells How It Became Olympics 'Official Ski,' " *Advertising Age*, November 20, 1978, p. 34.

McInnis, Peter, "Cold War on the Slopes: Ski Makers Vie for a Slippery, If Fast-Moving, Market," *Barron's*, December 22, 1975, p. 11.

Minard, Lawrence, "Has Rossignol Lost Its Edge?," *Forbes*, March 17, 1980.

"No Business Like Snow Business," *The Economist*, March 3, 1990, p. 65.

"NW Firms Hurt by Foreign Competition Take Advantage of Government Program," *Seattle Daily Journal of Commerce*, November 7, 1985, p. 1.

Oliver, Peter, "K2 Acquires Olin Skis from Tristar," *Skiing Trade News*, October 1989, p. 3.

Williat, Norris, "Big Year for Snow Business," *Barron's*, January 25, 1965, p. 11.

—Jeffrey L. Covell

KITCHENAID®

KitchenAid®
HOME APPLIANCES

KitchenAid, owned by global superpower Whirlpool Corporation, is a leading brand of premium household appliances. The KitchenAid brand name, in fact, can be found on nearly all types of built-in and portable kitchen appliances. The renowned quality and durability of KitchenAid products have been the brand's hallmarks since its founding in 1919.

Brand Origins

Around 1910 Hobart Corporation—then the world's largest manufacturer of commercial food equipment—developed its first successful commercial mixer. During that era, testing of household products was handled by the wives of executives working on the projects. Such was the case during the early stages of the mixer's development. In a discussion around a kitchen table one evening, Hobart's executives and their wives were debating what brand name they should select for their exciting new product. According to company records, one wife said, "I don't care what you call it, but I know it's the best kitchen aid I ever had!" Thus, the KitchenAid brand name was born.

The first KitchenAid product, the home mixer, was developed and produced by a subsidiary of Hobart, Troy Metal Products of Troy, Ohio. By 1919 the first KitchenAid hand mixer hit the market. Accompanied by a large array of food preparation attachments, this early mixer drew wide acceptance among homemakers throughout the 1920s and '30s.

The sales force at the time was largely female, and most mixers and attachments were sold door-to-door. The company encouraged homemakers to host "mixer parties" at which they would invite a groups of friends into their homes. Professional salespeople would prepare food using the mixers and attachments and then take orders for the new products.

New Products

The second product developed under the KitchenAid brand name was the electric coffee mill. Like the mixer before it, the coffee mill was based on a commercial version of the same product. In the 1920s a consumer could find Hobart commercial coffee mills in any local A & P grocery store. The new KitchenAid grinder was a smaller, electric version of its predecessor. Now homemakers could grind coffee in their own kitchens.

In 1949 Hobart made its entry into the major home appliance market by developing its first home dishwasher. Again the product was based on Hobart's know-how and experience at developing a commercial dishwasher. The new product, marketed under the KitchenAid name, had a patented washing system and quickly earned a reputation as the highest-quality dishwasher of its time. From the early days KitchenAid products set standards for durability, and many of its early products were still in use some 40 to 50 years later. More product introductions followed the dishwasher—including food-waste disposals and instant hot-water dispensers in 1966—after Hobart acquired the plumbing equipment division of National Rubber Machinery Corporation. KitchenAid introduced trash compactors in 1972 and food processors in the early 1980s.

In 1983 Hobart took a major step toward creating its vision of the "total KitchenAid kitchen" concept by acquiring Chambers Corporation of Oxford, Mississippi, a major manufacturer of high-quality, premium built-in cooking equipment. This purchase allowed Hobart to broaden its KitchenAid line and introduce a full line of ovens and cooktop stoves. The early introductions included a convection/microwave and thermal oven combination. The purchase also enabled Hobart to take KitchenAid one step closer to being the leader in the high-end segment for all built-in major appliances and home appliances.

In February 1986 KitchenAid became a division of Whirlpool Corporation. In August of that year the company moved its administrative, sales, and marketing offices from Ohio, to St. Joseph, Michigan.

The Whirlpool Acquisition

In the mid-1980s the management of Whirlpool Corporation conducted a thorough study of the North American major appliance industry and of the Whirlpool brand's long-term stability within it. At the time, the brand was the global leader in many categories, and the company's executives were concerned about the success of extending the Whirlpool name into the high-profit premium segment—defined roughly as the upper 15 to 20 percent of the consumer market. The typical consumer in this segment sought high levels of styling, features, and performance and was willing to pay a premium price.

AT A GLANCE

KitchenAid brand of home appliance introduced in 1919 by Hobart Corporation of Troy, Ohio; its first product was a home mixer; KitchenAid brand purchased by Whirlpool Corporation in February 1986.

Performance: *Market share*—Less than 10% of the major home appliance category. *Sales*—$540,000,000.

Major competitor: Whirlpool; also, General Electric, Electrolux, and Maytag.

Advertising: *Agency*—N.W. Ayer, New York, NY. *Major campaign*—"A refrigerator designed from a blueprint by Mother Nature. KitchenAid: For the way it's made."

Addresses: *Parent company*—Whirlpool Corporation, 2000 M-63 North, Benton Harbor, MI 49022; phone: (616) 926-5000.

As a result of the study, Whirlpool's management decided to develop "flanker brands" to round out its major home appliance line. The new full-line brands would offset Whirlpool's leadership in the broad middle segment by positioning themselves first in the no-frills, value-oriented lower segment and second in the fancy, premium upper segment. Whirlpool knew that the quickest route to market entry was through acquisition. The company therefore purchased two of the leading brands in their respective segments: Roper, in the lower-end segment; and KitchenAid, in the premium segment.

At the time, KitchenAid was regarded throughout the appliance industry as a niche player and was especially renowned for its high-quality dishwashers and stand mixers. Competitors fought Whirlpool's bid to purchase the brand, and it was 12 full months before the courts resolved the disputes. Finally, on January 31, 1986, it was final—Whirlpool owned the KitchenAid brand.

Quality Assurance

Since KitchenAid's inception in 1919, the brand differentiated itself by its uncompromising dedication to quality. This reputation began with extensive laboratory testing of products and components long before they went into production. This policy continued after the Whirlpool acquisition. In the brand's St. Joseph headquarters, laboratory technicians conducted an intensive program of round-the-clock testing that simulated years of heavy use.

When Whirlpool purchased KitchenAid, company officials immediately began to create a long-term business plan for their new brand. Five months after the acquisition, they took a giant, risk-laden leap toward repositioning by canceling KitchenAid's entire existing distributing system. The network of wholesale independent distributors and 9,000 retailers was eliminated in favor of an exclusive KitchenAid sales force that would sell direct to dealers. Whirlpool designed the new sales force around four zones and 24 district offices.

This drastic strategy was based on the belief that KitchenAid retailers had to manage their KitchenAid business in a manner consistent with the brand's premium positioning in order for the brand to succeed. Whirlpool executives firmly believed that retailers had to display the full line of KitchenAid products and not advertise price. In return, retailers would enjoy the higher margins and profitability inherent in high-priced, highly visible products. Then KitchenAid president Glenn Olinger stated the company's strategy: "We believe that our products should have the full attention of field personnel in sales and after-the-sale service, including a concentrated and effective sales training program."

The new sales force emerged gradually throughout the end of 1986, and KitchenAid slowly built a new dealer network from the ground up. By December the company was ready for the first introduction of a full line of KitchenAid major appliances, including dishwashers, cooking products, trash compactors, washing machines, dryers, and refrigerators. The company hosted a gala introduction celebration in Dallas and unveiled the new products to the media.

Whirlpool's Reorganization

The strength of the KitchenAid hand mixer helped the new company somewhat, but KitchenAid's first year of operation under the Whirlpool umbrella was fraught with challenges as the company fought to build consumer awareness that KitchenAid produced a full line of major appliances. The problems with consumer recognition were compounded by an industrywide decline in appliance sales throughout the 1980s. With such imposing obstacles, KitchenAid management knew the brand needed an aggressive marketing plan.

The new KitchenAid president, Ken Kaminski—a marketing specialist—worked painstakingly with his team to build a solid distribution network and maintain the brand's dedication to quality. In 1987 KitchenAid set a new record for sales of stand mixers by selling 450,000 units. Still, this success could not offset the company's struggles, and the KitchenAid division recorded a first-year loss of more than $23 million.

In 1988 Whirlpool Corporation underwent major reorganization. The company established all corporate brands as stand-alone units, one competing with another in each consumer market. The move had a tremendous impact on the KitchenAid brand. Suddenly the brand was competing with the Whirlpool/Roper and Kenmore brands for resources and opportunities. Most important, however, the reorganization provided the impetus KitchenAid needed to pursue a strategy of aggressive differentiation to distinguish itself from Whirlpool's other brands, as well as from brands within the larger marketplace. By the end of the year, the groundwork for success had been laid. Each of the Whirlpool appliance brands had established a separate niche for itself, and KitchenAid was poised for future growth.

Also in 1988 was the introduction of several new major KitchenAid appliances: a freestanding refrigeration line, expansions of the existing built-in oven and laundry lines, and—the item that dominated the appliance news in 1988—built-in refrigeration. With this new product, KitchenAid entered a lucrative market previously reserved for exclusive niche players. The introduction also gave KitchenAid the ability to offer consumers one source for all their built-in appliances and for complete sales and service. Retailers, contractors, and kitchen designers quickly began to recognize KitchenAid as a new player in the high-end built-in appliance arena.

KitchenAid's reputation for quality stood on 40 years of experience in the mixer and dishwasher market. Company officials knew that the brand's long-term success depended upon its ability to spread this reputation across all categories. While retailers and consumers quickly accepted KitchenAid's new line of coordinated appliances, the rapid introduction of so many new models presented quite a few quality problems for corporate officials. By the end of the 1980s, however, the company had conquered most of the quality "bugs" in the new systems.

Soon the industry was taking note of KitchenAid. In *HFD,* an influential interiors magazine, a Merrill-Lynch analyst said, "KitchenAid has a good strategy. They've definitely got a brand that calls people in who are looking for quality and features, not price." Later that year KitchenAid's leaders received the reinforcement they needed. The end-of-year financial report revealed that KitchenAid had reduced its operating loss by 76 percent, portable appliance sales set new volume and profitability records, and unit sales for major appliances jumped to more than 550,000.

In 1989 industrywide appliance sales continued to struggle, yet KitchenAid sales flourished. The company's high-quality image drove the business to new heights and allowed it to introduce more new products, including a modular downdraft cooktop, a new glass-surface cooktop with sealed gas burners, and a new laundry line. That year unit sales topped 965,000, and its operating margin skyrocketed from a loss of $5.66 million to a profit of more than $21 million.

A New Marketing Campaign

A new television advertising campaign debuted in 1990. The commercials took the tag line from the name of its familiar theme song, "Through the Years." KitchenAid ran the commercials in key markets throughout the United States, especially during the early evening, late at night, and on cable stations. Over the next three years the campaign increased brand awareness dramatically in those markets. In addition to being popular among consumers, the commercials were very popular throughout the advertising industry. They received many industry awards, including a prestigious Clio.

KitchenAid managers added new tactical approaches to the brand's strategy in 1991. The company introduced its annual National Kitchen Design Contest for certified kitchen designers and professional interior designers. More significantly, the company began selling KitchenAid major appliances throughout Sears Brand Central locations. According to sales and distribution vice president Greg McManus, "We've grown by building on three key philosophies: maintaining product quality, differentiation and reliability; refining selective distribution; and increasing dealer yields. But to move to the next level as a major player in the high end, KitchenAid needs a larger market presence, and Brand Central gives us that presence." The year-end financial report again proved the worth of the KitchenAid strategy. Unit sales had grown to 1.54 million, and operating profit hit more than $41 million.

Despite the success of the KitchenAid brand, parent company Whirlpool decided once again to reorganize in 1992. This time the company decided to reorganize the sales and distribution functions for all of its brands under a single entity, the North American Appliance Group. The reorganization precipitated many changes in KitchenAid's management, and for quite awhile sales goals were not the top priority within the corporation. Despite the circumstances, KitchenAid continued to make headlines with the introduction of a new freestanding refrigerator line, a new Create-A-Cooktop component cooking system, a new 24-inch deep freestanding range, and a more water-and-energy efficient dishwasher line.

By the end of 1992 sales and profitability of the KitchenAid brand were flourishing despite the distraction of its parent company's reorganization. The brand entered the mid-1990s with more promise than ever.

Further Reading:

Cortez, John P., "Appliance Ads Get 'Warm, Fuzzy,'" *Advertising Age,* May 3, 1993, p. 44.

KitchenAid, Past and Present [brochure], St. Joseph, Michigan: KitchenAid, Inc., 1990.

Stuart, Don, "KitchenAid from 1986 through 1992," St. Joseph, Michigan: KitchenAid, Inc., May 1993.

Weiner, Steve, "Growing Pains," *Forbes,* October 29, 1991, pp. 40–41.

—Wendy Johnson Bilas

KODAK®

In 1888 George Eastman revolutionized photography with his invention of the compact Kodak camera—making photography more accessible to the masses. More than a century later the legacy of the founder endured as the company continued to make photography more effortless and photographs more true to life. From the earliest Brownie cameras to the Instamatic of the 1960s and the Fun Saver single-use cameras of the 1990s, the Kodak brand has been a market leader. Famous for its photographic innovations Kodak also extended its brand name to other fields, including office imaging equipment, medical diagnostic equipment, and chemical products. By the early 1990s "Kodak" was one of the world's most recognizable brands and was worth nearly $9 billion.

Brand Origins

During the 1870s George Eastman, a young bank clerk in Rochester, New York, took an avid interest in photography. Eastman learned French and German so he could keep up with the latest European photography journals. In 1877 he invested $100 in his first photographic kit, which included a portable darkroom tent, photographic plates, and various chemicals. At the suggestion of a co-worker he considered taking a trip to Santo Domingo to make photographs which he could later sell in New York. But the wet-plate photographic equipment was so bulky and unwieldy that Eastman canceled the trip. As Eastman commented in *The Story of Kodak*: "one did not 'take' a camera; one accompanied the outfit of which the camera was only a part.

Inspired to improve the picture-taking process, Eastman experimented in his mother's kitchen sink with photographic emulsion techniques for several years. Soon he was making his own dry plates and in 1879 he invented and patented a mechanical emulsion-coating device which he also manufactured. Two years later he formed the Eastman Dry Plate Company with a local businessman, Henry A. Strong, and Eastman left his clerking job to become treasurer and general manager of the company.

In 1885, after much research, Eastman finally developed a practical alternative to glass-plate photographic technology—gelatin-coated paper "film" which was used with his new patented roll holder. Eastman soon expanded beyond plates and film and began designing small cameras, called detective cameras. The first "Kodak" cameras were released to the public in 1888 at a price of twenty-five dollars. The Kodak was a revolutionary new camera because it came preloaded with a 100-exposure roll of film which was later returned to the Eastman Company for processing. Eastman had introduced a division of labor in photography, separating the mechanical process of taking a picture from the chemical process of developing the film. Thus the photographer was freed from the messy, complicated, and impractical job of developing pictures immediately after shooting them.

The brand name Kodak was another invention of George Eastman's. "K" happened to be his favorite letter and the first letter of his mother's maiden name. He also liked the name Kodak because it was short, incapable of mispronunciation, and did not resemble any other brand names in the industry. It also turned out to be an enduring world-famous trademark.

Early Marketing Strategy

Early on, the Eastman Company won a reputation for fairness in dealing with customers and for producing high-quality products. Despite a commercially competitive environment, the Kodak brand managed to thrive largely because Eastman had the foresight to pursue long-term strategies. His guiding principles were mass mechanical production, low prices, foreign distribution, and lots of advertising featuring the simplicity of the Kodak technique.

The Kodak "complete system of practical photography" was a huge success, selling more than 13,000 cameras before the end of its first year. Eastman made his cameras more accessible to consumers by offering them for sale in drugstores. He appealed to the masses of would-be amateur photographers with Kodak's simplicity, advertising the Kodak in mainstream publications with the famous slogan: "Kodak Cameras. You press the button—We do the rest." The motto became a popular source of anecdotes and punchlines among a variety of people, including journalists and even politicians. The advertisements also featured instructional drawings of the easy three-step process of taking a picture with a Kodak: pull a cord, turn a key, and press a button. "Kodaking" made photography easy and fun.

Product Development

Not long after the first Kodak cameras were introduced, improved versions appeared on the market, such as the Pocket Kodak, the Folding Kodak, and in 1897 the combination Folding Pocket Kodak Camera. Three years later Eastman designed the Brownie camera especially for children. Priced at one dollar, the

AT A GLANCE

Kodak brand of cameras founded in 1888 in Rochester, NY, by George Eastman, treasurer and general manager, and Henry A. Strong, president, of the Eastman Dry Plate and Film Company; became a registered trademark, 1888; changed name to Eastman Kodak Company, 1892.

Performance: *Market share*—70% of single-use cameras (early 1990s). *Sales*—$7.3 billion of photographic imaging products worldwide (1991); $140 million of single-use cameras, 1992)

Major competitor: Nikon; also, Minolta.

Advertising: *Agency*—J. Walter Thompson USA, New York, NY, 1930–; camera account, 1992–; Young & Rubicam, New York, NY; and UniWorld Group, New York, NY. *Major campaign*—"A Kodak Moment."

Addresses: *Parent company*—Eastman Kodak Company, 343 State Street, Rochester, NY 14650; phone: 716-724-4000; fax: 716-724-0663.

Brownie came in a box decorated with little sprites and was an instant success, selling a quarter of a million cameras in its first year. The Eastman Company promoted the Brownie by sponsoring competitions for children and creating Brownie camera clubs. For 80 years Brownie cameras continued to be a popular line. In 1923 Kodak introduced the first Kodak home-movie camera, the 16mm Cine-Kodak camera. But the Cine-Kodak outfit—with camera, projector, tripod, and screen—cost $335 and was prohibitively expensive for most families, considering that a standard camera outfit cost only a few dollars.

During World War I the Eastman Kodak Company virtually halted the manufacture of its core photographic products in order to provide the U.S. government with technological assistance. Kodak designed automatic aerial-reconnaissance cameras and trained military personnel to operate the cameras and develop the film. After the war Kodak resumed marketing photographic products for amateur and professional use and also experimented in the educational field. In 1928 the Kodak subsidiary, Eastman Teaching Films, produced over 100 educational films.

The most successful lines of Kodaks of the 1920s and 1930s were those geared toward the extended family, such as the Boy Scout Kodak and Camp Fire Girls' Kodak which came with scout logos. The Baby Brownie, like the original Brownie, cost one dollar and was highly popular. A Gift Kodak, sold in a fancy wooden box, was also a success. Kodak continued innovating and soon developed smaller film spools which led to the design of the lightweight Six-20 cameras series. During the later 1930s Kodak camera designs tended toward more sophisticated and expensive models as the popularity of serious amateur photography increased. At this time the first Kodak 8mm motion picture system for amateur photographers also came on the market.

During World War II Eastman Kodak Company again decreased its production to assist the U.S. military. Shortly thereafter Eastman Kodak re-entered the market with several new products, such as the low-priced Brownie version of the 8mm movie camera in 1951; the Cavalcade, Kodak's first fully automatic projector; and the Brownie Starflash, the brand's first camera with a built-in flash holder. In the 1950s Kodak offered more than a dozen new Brownie designs and over two dozen 35mm models.

In 1963 Kodak introduced the innovative, 35mm, cartridge-loaded Instamatic camera. This "point-and-shoot" camera was one of Eastman Kodak Company's most successful, efficient, and easy-to-use cameras, selling more than 70,000,000 worldwide. The cartridge system was later applied to a super-8 format for movie cameras, projectors, and several models of the Pocket Instamatic. In 1974 the Tele-Instamatic camera featured two lenses and the first pop-up Flipflash. With each new model the Kodak point-and-shoot cameras became simpler to use, with advanced technological features like electronic flash and film speed adjustments.

In 1982 Kodak introduced the disc camera, which recorded pictures onto a small disc and reduced the amount of room needed inside the camera for holding the film. Though more than 25 million disc cameras were sold, the demand did not live up to Kodak's expectations. The market was not ready to absorb the new technology. Moreover the enlargement quality was inferior to 35mm film and a new series of low-priced, point-and-shoot cameras were introduced by other firms. By 1988 the Kodak disc camera was discontinued.

Kodak had abandoned production of 35mm cameras in 1970 in the belief that the format would soon lose its appeal. However by 1985 Kodak realized its mistake and re-entered the 35mm camera market. In 1987 Kodak introduced the first single-use camera, the Kodak Fling, which used 110 film. In 1988 a 35mm version was marketed as the Fun Saver 35. Ironically, these innovative cameras were similar to the first Kodaks, which were pre-loaded with film and sent to the lab for developing. The Fun Saver point-and-shoot cameras, requiring no settings, were an instant success; they were easy to use, convenient, and compact. The company even boasted that the Fun Savers were nearly 100% recycled. A number of inexpensive variations, ranging in price from $8 to $15, were soon introduced. In 1989 Kodak launched the water- and dust-proof Kodak Weekend 35 camera and the Kodak Stretch 35, later called the Fun Saver panoramic, which recorded a 75-degree field of view. Other models featured a flash and a telephoto lens. In early 1993 the Fun Saver portrait 35 camera with a soft-light flash was put on the market. Kodak also marketed several special edition Fun Savers like the Aladdin and the NFL cameras.

More expensive lines in the 1990s included an 8mm camcorder and the automatic Star cameras, including the Star 1035z with an auto-focus zoom lens. At a cost of $200 it was the first camera priced over $100 that Kodak had developed in several years. In early 1993 Kodak introduced the sleek Cameo line of 110 and 35mm compact cameras designed to fit easily in the picture-taker's hands or pockets. The following year Kodak updated the Cameo to an "all-in-one" zoom, plus versions with options for standard use or panoramic, portrait, or zoom photographs.

Kodak also developed several sophisticated new photographic technologies during the 1990s. Released in 1992 the Photo CD system stored pictures on compact discs to be viewed and edited on televisions or computers. Two years later Kodak launched the filmless electronic News Camera 2000, intended for use by news photographers. At a cost of about $17,000, the camera transmitted images through a modem, bypassing film processing altogether.

Marketing Developments

From the earliest days of the Eastman Kodak Company, George Eastman was fully aware of the importance of effective advertising. He even wrote some of the first Kodak advertising copy himself. In 1901 the company designed advertisements which featured a prim woman in full afternoon dress taking photographs and demonstrating the ease and convenience of Kodak photography. Clad in a blue striped dress, the Kodak Girl became a world-famous figure known as the Blue Girl in England and Dame Kodak in France. Twenty years later the Kodak Girl endured in the form of a more stylish and spirited woman. In the 1920s Kodak set up nearly six thousand road signs along U.S. highways which read: "Picture Ahead! Kodak as you go." When Kodak received several complaints from motorists who literally expected to find photographs in the landscapes, the company modified the signs to: "There's Always a Picture Ahead!"

In the late 1920s Kodak sponsored half-hour radio shows which promoted casual weekend photography. The in-house magazine, *The Kodak Salesman*, encouraged salespeople to promote the importance of capturing special family moments with a Kodak camera. The company devised the "baby plan" of recording a child's growth with periodic pictures and advertised photo portraits, or "living walls," as a stylish way to decorate one's home. Eastman Kodak also promoted the brand name by sponsoring international amateur photography contests which attracted millions of contestants. George Eastman was always keenly aware of potential new outlets for the Kodak brand. Decades after Eastman's suicide in 1932, the Kodak company continued to expand its consumer base with innovative new products.

Kodak's television advertisements, similar to its print ads, focused on family photography. Snapshot photography remained Kodak's most important market segment for some time. In 1956 Eastman Kodak sponsored its first television program, "Ozzie and Harriet," and later partially sponsored "The Ed Sullivan Show."

In the late 1980s Kodak altered its marketing approach as sales began to decline. To expand its market, Kodak targeted professional photographers and specific age groups, especially those consumers who found high-tech photography intimidating and those outside the 25 to 40 year-old bracket who already owned photographic equipment. Eastman Kodak experimented with the infomercial form of television advertising in the early 1990s when it introduced the Cameo Zoom Lens Plus camera on a QVC telecast. The infomercial format was conducive to demonstrating the operation of the camera's special features and for testing consumer response.

During the early 1990s Kodak ranked among the top 80 megabrands in advertising spending. In 1992 Kodak invested an estimated $82 million on advertising consumer photographic products—including nearly $25 million allocated to the Photo CD system alone. That year Kodak transferred its camera account, estimated at $15 million, to J. Walter Thompson USA, consolidating its long-time photography account with that ad agency. Kodak shifted its marketing strategy towards promoting product lines in an umbrella campaign, Kodak's first global campaign, which reached over 40 countries. With their "A Kodak Moment" theme, the 1993 "lifestage marketing" ads were targeted toward parents, seniors, and children with emotional messages, such as a father and son hugging good-bye as the son prepares to move from home. Product-specific ads also included the "Kodak Moment" theme.

Legal Controversies

In the early 1970s Eastman Kodak faced several antitrust suits. In one suit, a number of smaller photographic companies argued that Kodak was monopolizing the industry and conspiring with other companies in the development of flash products. After a prolonged legal battle the case was settled for $6.8 million in 1981. In another suit, the Polaroid Corporation alleged patent infringement by Kodak with regard to Kodak's instant camera, which ejected developed photos. In 1986 the case was decided in favor of Polaroid and Kodak was forced to terminate its instant camera and film lines and offer customers trade-in options. In a third case, Kodak's Rochester, NY plant was discovered to be leaking chemicals into the groundwater. The company was fined $2 million and was required to clean up the plant and reduce chemical emissions.

Brand Extensions

Eastman Kodak began as a photographic products company, but the Kodak brand developed beyond photography. As long ago as the late 1890s, Kodak was involved in the health care industry, creating numerous diagnostic imaging and informational devices. 100 years later, the Kodak Health Group was a global leader in the medical, cardiology, dental, and industrial markets. The health segment produced diagnostic imaging and information systems, such as automated blood analyzers, as well as specialty pharmaceutical and household products.

In 1953 Eastman Chemical Products was established for marketing industrial products like plastics and fibers, and Eastman Technology was established in the 1970s to develop markets outside of photography; the recording industry was a particular target. As the recession of the late 1970s cut into the demand for Kodak photographic products, the company diverted its attention to other areas, such as business systems and chemicals. In 1975, after a couple of decades of experimentation with office copiers, Kodak successfully marketed the Ektaprint 100 Copier-Duplicator machine for large-volume business needs. The improved 1580 Copier-Printer introduced in the mid-1990s featured a high-speed scanner and a range of other finishing operations. The Office Imaging division of Kodak concentrated on improving productivity of the equipment. Kodak has manufactured a wide range of office items, including microfilm image management systems, mass storage devices, and a variety of imaging products.

The 1980s were also a difficult period for sales of Kodak photography equipment because of competition from Japanese products. As a result Eastman Kodak underwent a major reorganization, decentralizing the company into 17 autonomous operating units. Kodak also expanded overseas marketing and, because Kodak's own research and development process was historically slow, acquired several high-technology firms. Kodak experimented with marketing video cassettes and computer discs, although with little success. In 1991 after a second company reorganization in less than a decade, sales of the Kodak brand revived.

Special Distinctions

The Kodak brand has won numerous awards throughout its history. In 1992 *Petersen's Photographic* Readers' Choice Award for "Best 35mm Camera under $100" was given to the entire Fun Saver line. The Fun Saver panoramic 35mm received *Popular Science's* "The Best of What's New" award. And several awards for technological innovations were granted for a variety of Kodak products, including the Photo CD system, the DCS 200ci digital camera, and Kodak printers and scanners.

International Markets

As early as the 1880s, George Eastman had recognized the potential of foreign markets. The first Kodak store overseas was opened in London shortly after the incorporation of Eastman's company. By the late 1890s Eastman's stores were selling photographic products in Europe, Australia, and Egypt. The Kodak brand quickly became a global leader and has remained so despite stiff competition from Japanese competitors. Japanese brands like Nikon and Minolta began to produce low-priced, high-quality 35mm cameras which were superior to the Kodak disc and Instamatic cameras. In response, Kodak increased its overseas marketing in the 1990s and developed new and competitive products.

Performance Appraisal

After nearly a century as market leader in photographic equipment, the Kodak brand in the 1980s was lagging behind other firms in technological innovations. As a result the Eastman Kodak Company was restructured in 1985. After a few years of improved sales—a 15% increase in 1987 and 28% in 1988—the company again suffered losses, with a sales increase of only 3% in 1990. The following year Kodak re-consolidated into a single Imaging company. Thereafter Kodak sales improved each year, reaching a 5% increase in 1992.

Total 1992 sales of Kodak photographic imaging products worldwide reached $7.4 billion, an increase of 5% from the previous year. Photographic imaging sales in the U.S. were $3 billion and global film sales $2.7 billion. Information products such as copiers, printers, and scanners had global sales of $4 billion in 1992, up 2% from the year before, with $2.3 billion in the U.S.

The global market for single-use cameras in 1993 was more than 25 million units worth more than $200 million. Sales in the early 1990s more than doubled each year, making it the fastest-growing segment of 35mm cameras. Kodak's Fun Saver line led the market with an estimated 70% share throughout the early 1990s. Fuji Photo Film USA's Quick Snap Plus camera trailed behind Kodak with about 20% of the market. Kodak, the market leader of 35mm cameras and film, also faced some competition from Polaroid, which entered that market segment in the mid-1990s with lower-priced, point-and-shoot cameras, as well as single-use cameras. Overall, however, the Kodak brand remains universally recognized and widely popular.

Future Growth

In the 1990s, as the world continued on its high-technology wave, Kodak was poised to innovate and expand into new markets. Recognizing the potential in foreign distribution, Kodak intended to expand overseas, especially in the European and Asian markets. Kodak also planned to explore ways to make inroads into the information industry and improve the company's digital imaging technology.

Further Reading:

''AP and Kodak Announce Breakthrough Digital News Camera,'' *Business Wire,* February 8, 1994.

Collins, Douglas, *The Story of Kodak,* New York: Harry N. Abrams, Inc., 1990.

Davis, Riccardo A., ''Kodak Takes its 'Moment' Global,'' *Advertising Age,* March 29, 1993, News sec., p. 3.

Davis, Riccardo A., ''QVC Clicks For Kodak Cameras,'' *Advertising Age,* January 17, 1994, Interactive sec., p. 17.

Davis, Riccardo A., ''Single-use Cameras Put Some Snap in Market,'' *Advertising Age,* March 8, 1993, News sec., p. 16.

Endicott, R. Craig, ''The Top 200 Brands,'' *Advertising Age,* February 7, 1994, News sec., p. 23.

Holusha, John, ''Kodak Chief Offers a New Vision,'' *The New York Times,* October 29, 1993, sec. D, p. 1.

Janofsky, Michael, ''Kodak Adds 20 Products In Big Shift,'' *The New York Times,* February 11, 1993, sec. D, p. 6.

''Kodak Technology, Products and Services Voted Best in Nearly a Score of Awards,'' *PR Newswire,* Financial News Section, December 28, 1992.

—Audra Avizienis

KOHLER®

KOHLER®

Known worldwide for innovation, quality, and sophistication, Kohler Co. is generally credited with bringing high-tech fashion design to the bathroom. Kohler was the first plumbing manufacturer to suggest that bathrooms could be decorated with color-coordinated fixtures, tiles, and fabrics. The company has also gained the reputation for anticipating as well as responding to market demands for beautiful yet functional plumbing products. Although Kohler Co. also manufactures small engines and generators, owns two furniture manufacturers, and has expanded its operations to include resort and real estate management, it is the plumbing products that come to mind when the name Kohler is mentioned.

Brand Origins

John Michael Kohler, the company's founder, arrived in the United States from Austria at the age of ten. In 1871 he married a women from Sheboygan, Wisconsin, named Lillie Vollrath, whose father owned the Union Steel and Iron Foundry. Although the foundry was making a tidy profit turning out plows, horse troughs, and a variety of small casings, John Michael had a vision. After working for his father-in-law for two years, Kohler and a partner purchased the foundry. To Kohler, the steady immigration of Europeans to the midwestern region of the United States during the latter part of the 19th century represented a ready market for sophisticated, custom-made bathroom plumbing; the bathroom had achieved a certain status in Europe during the 1800s, but in the United States bathrooms were stark and unappealing.

Ironically, given Kohler's reputation for sophisticated design, the first bathtub manufactured by the company was an enameled hog scalder that, as legend has it, was sold to a farmer for the price of one cow and fourteen chickens. After the initial success of the enameled scalder, the company quickly expanded its line of plumbing products to include five lines of roll-rim bathtubs, enameled-iron water closets, and bathroom sinks. One of Kohler's first innovations was a one-piece built-in bathtub with attached apron. Previously, built-in tubs were cast as two separate pieces and had to be joined when installed by a plumber. Kohler's one-piece bathtub was not only more attractive because it eliminated all cracks and seams, but was considered more sanitary as well.

Lillie Kohler died in 1882 leaving six children, one of whom, Walter, would later expand the company and the village around it, and then serve as governor of Wisconsin. John Michael married Lillie's sister, Minneline. Their sole offspring, Herbert Vollrath Kohler, would also someday head the company, and his son, Herbert V. Kohler, Jr., was in 1994 the company's president.

In 1900, when John Michael Kohler decided to move the company to an area four miles west of Sheboygan, many thought the business would never survive, isolated as it was from its work force, utilities, and transportation. Kohler's vision, though, included more than bathrooms; he planned to create a town. Soon after the move, John Michael's partner sold his share of the company to the family, and Kohler has remained a private, family-owned firm since then.

Over the next several years the family and the business suffered a series of setbacks. John Michael died in 1901 and the factory burned down a few months later. Although the plant was rebuilt within a year, further tragedy struck when the two oldest Kohler sons, Carl and Robert, died in quick succession. John Michael's third son, Walter, became president in 1905 and held that position for the next 35 years. It was Walter who brought his father's dream of a planned community to fruition. In 1912 the small group of homes that had sprung up around the factory was incorporated as the village of Kohler. After studying European industrial communities and consulting with urban designers, Walter hired the Olmsted Brothers firm, designer of New York's Central Park, and Milwaukee architect Richard Philipp to design and direct the community's growth. In 1918 the American Club was built to house the single immigrant men who had come from Europe to work for the company.

"Though the village has been referred to as a little Camelot," noted Elaine Markoutsas in the *Chicago Tribune,* "it has its blemishes." Suffering through one labor strike in 1897, the Kohler company went on to endure two more strikes throughout its history. In 1934 employees went on strike calling for collective bargaining; the dispute was settled seven years later. Another strike, arising out of a disagreement on contract changes, began in 1954 and became, according the Markoutsas, "the longest in the nation's history, lasting until a U.S. Supreme Court ruling ended it in 1965."

Brand Development

The 1920s signaled a period of imaginative innovation and intense growth for Kohler plumbing products. A pottery was

AT A GLANCE

Kohler plumbing products were first manufactured in 1883 in Sheboygan, WI, by John Michael Kohler, who had purchased the Union Steel and Iron Foundry from his father-in-law in 1873; in 1901 the company was renamed J. M. Kohler Sons, and then renamed Kohler Co. in 1914.

Performance: *Sales*—$1.5 billion (according to the *Chicago Tribune*, February 14, 1994).

Major competitor: American Standard; also, Eljer, Jacuzzi, Delta, Moen, and Price Pfister.

Advertising: *Agency*—Grey Advertising, New York, NY (additional advertising handled by Meyer & Wallis, Milwaukee, WI, for hospitality and real estate). *Major campaign*—Tag line: "The Bold Look of Kohler"; plumbing campaign: "As I See It."

Addresses: *Parent company*—Kohler Co., 444 Highland Dr., Kohler, WI 53044; phone: (414) 457-4441; fax: (414) 459-1623.

added to the foundry so that the company could produce lightweight, durable toilets and sinks of vitreous china. A new brass plant turned out faucets, shower heads, and other fittings in brass and chrome. In 1926 Kohler designed a combination sink and dishwasher; the product's large size and prohibitive cost did not appeal to consumers, but its introduction signaled the beginning of dishwashers in American kitchens.

The following year Kohler introduced color into its plumbing fixtures and changed the look for bathrooms forever. Bathtubs, sinks, and toilets that were previously only made in white were now available in haute couture-sounding shades of autumn brown, spring green, horizon blue, old ivory, or jet black. The ultimate proof that the company was an influential voice in interior design came when Kohler fixtures were chosen for an exhibition at the Metropolitan Museum of Art in New York. For the exhibit, architect Ely Jacques Kahn used a jet black lavatory sink in a black marble counter top to complement his Art Deco setting featuring a velvet chaise and glass walls. Beauty and fashion design had been introduced into the bathroom and kitchen without sacrificing form or function.

Throughout the 1930s new colors were added to the Kohler line. Kohler responded to the growing popularity of the powder room—a smaller bathroom with a sink and toilet built in the main living area of the house as opposed to the sleeping areas—by developing the Lavette line of bathroom sinks and toilets. Technological improvements continued during this time as well. Of particular significance was the aesthetically pleasing one-piece toilet.

Another surge of creativity occurred in the 1960s when the company introduced its "Bold Look of Kohler." The bright, vibrant shades of green, blue, yellow, red, and orange that characterized the decade were now showing up in Kohler's plumbing products. Competitors began to imitate Kohler's colors, especially the ubiquitous avocado and harvest gold that graced tens of thousands of bathrooms and kitchens across the United States. Kohler's Bold Look campaign was advertised on popular television programs such as *Today* and the *Tonight Show*. New products also included sinks in different sizes to fit large homes and small apartments. Toilets were offered in round and oval shapes. Tubs featured grip rails and slip-resistant surfaces. Choices were also offered in a variety of colors for faucet handles: consumers could choose clear, amber, white, or charcoal, and they could even select interchangeable handle inserts of white, black, teak, and walnut. In *Wisconsin Trails* magazine, Susan Mahnke said, "Using a sense of timing and innovation that is the mark of manufacturing success, Kohler anticipated—and helped create—public demand for new and beautiful indoor plumbing fixtures."

Product Changes

In 1966 Kohler's engineers developed self-rimming toilets and kitchen sinks of enameled iron that were adaptable to countertop installations. Fiberglass-reinforced plastic fixtures were introduced; these included showers and tub-shower combinations in which the fixtures and walls were molded in one piece.

Throughout the 1970s Kohler continued to respond to consumers' desire for elegant and self-indulgent bathrooms. The company introduced a motorless whirlpool bath called the Hydro-Whirl, for which Kohler received the Wisconsin Governor's New Product Award. Another Governor's Award was bestowed two years later on "Treiste," a three-compartment kitchen sink. In 1975 Kohler met the growing demand for environment-friendly products when the company introduced water-saving toilets, faucets, and showerheads. Water-saving products continued to be produced in the 1990s; Kohler's 1.6-gallon toilets operate via Pressure-Clean, a patented compressed air pressure system. Other 1.6-gallon toilets feature conventional gravity flushing. Perhaps the most innovative toilet in the Kohler line was the Peacekeeper Seat-Activated Flush that Kohler marketed as the answer to the "age-old dispute over leaving the toilet seat up." By employing a battery-operated sensor, the Peacekeeper flushes automatically when the user closes the lid.

The "Environment," a shower-like enclosure that allows the user to experience the affects of the sun, steam, rain, and wind with the touch of a button, appeared in 1977. A second such enclosure, the "Habitat," received the Governor's New Product Award the following year. By the close of the decade, Kohler added three whirlpools to its line of products: the "Caribbean," the "Steeping Bath," and the "Bath Whirlpool." The company greeted the 1980s with its first entry into the spa market. The "Super Spa," a fiberglass-reinforced acrylic unit, seats four to six people. Kohler's "Infinity" whirlpool brought home the company's fourth Governor's New Product Award.

Kohler's designers focused on the issues of water conservation and accessibility in the 1990s. Inspired by consumers over the age of 65 and those with disabilities who rejected the lack of esthetics in the sterile, institutional-like products that were on the market, Kohler created a line of bathroom fixtures that both pleased the eye and provided accessibility. The Freewill products offered wheelchair-accessible showers and sinks in a variety of Kohler's famous colors and styles. The Persona shower had an adjustable shower head. A wall-mounted sink included a vitreous cover over the pipes and drain to prevent scalding or scraping. The Highline Water-Guard 28-inch-high toilet offers extra height. Precedence, a whirlpool bath with a swing-open door, won a 1992 Industrial Design Excellence Award from the Industrial Designers Society of America.

The same consumers who wanted sophisticated bathrooms were also looking for innovation and design in the kitchen, leading Kohler to expand its line of kitchen and bar sinks. In addition to a broad palette of colors, consumers could choose from a variety of options including cutting boards, drainboards, in-sink colanders, and soap/lotion dispensers.

Marketing Strategy

The Kohler philosophy has always been to produce at the highest level of quality and then market its products under its own name through independent wholesale distributors. In the early days, John Michael Kohler loaded his plumbing products into a horse and buggy and drove it around Sheboygan County calling on his customers. In the 1990s the Kohler Company's market was worldwide, but the marketing strategy remained the same. In the *Chicago Tribune* Howard Greenspan, owner of Community Home Supply Inc. in Chicago, credited Kohler with setting an industry standard for consumer-directed advertising that leads consumers who have specific model requests to the retailers who carry the product. Carrying the company's signature slogan, "The Bold Look of Kohler," four-color brochures and booklets in design showrooms and full-page advertising spreads in home decorating magazines feature beautifully photographed bathrooms and kitchens.

A prime example of the company's unique style of marketing is Kohler's American Club resort hotel. The red-brick Tudor-style structure was no longer being used as a dormitory for workers when Herbert Kohler, Jr., proposed converting it to a world-class hotel and resort in 1978. Although many of the company's board members thought the idea was foolish, Herbert persevered. The building was declared a national historic landmark, and an extensive three-year renovation turned it into a 236-room hotel. In addition to its elegant surroundings and gourmet food, the hotel is known, of course, for its bathrooms. Each guest room comes with a Kohler whirlpool. Larger suites are furnished with more elaborate bathrooms. Across the street from the hotel is the Kohler Design Center, a 36,000-square-foot exhibit hall filled with bathroom settings created by professional interior designers. Thus, hotel guests can sample Kohler plumbing fixtures in their rooms, and then shop for them at the Design Center.

Performance Appraisal and Future Growth

When John Michael Kohler first started manufacturing bathroom fixtures, the company had one factory with 65 employees. By 1914, the Kohler work force numbered 1,000 employees who were turning out five lines of bathtubs, toilets, and bathroom sinks. In 1994 Kohler, a privately owned company with approximately 200 shareholders, employed 12,500 people in 35 factories around the world. With its commitment to quality and reputation for success, it seems likely that Kohler Co. will continue to be a leader in the design and sale of plumbing fixtures. In *Wisconsin—The Milwaukee Journal Magazine,* Herbert Kohler, Jr., asserted: "My personal goal is to produce, day in and day out, a higher degree of gracious living for a broad sweep of people. . . . Make the best you can. Then it's art. And the irony is when you do that well, the buck follows."

Further Reading:

Bold Craftsmen, Kohler, WI: Kohler Company.

Kenyon, Richard., "Industry & Elegance," *Wisconsin—The Milwaukee Journal Magazine,* October 3, 1993, p. 16–25.

"Kohler Develops Products for Changing Needs and Market Demands," *Professional Builder & Remodeler,* January 15, 1992.

Mahnke, Susan, "Kohler of Kohler of Kohler," *Wisconsin Trail,* spring 1979.

Markoutsas, Elaine, "Resort's Secret: Its Bathrooms," *Chicago Tribune,* February 14, 1994, sec. 4, p. 1.

100 Years of Kohler Co. Plumbing Products, Kohler, WI: Kohler Company, 1973.

Rubin, Bonnie Miller, "Baby Boomer's Eye the Future with Style," *Chicago Tribune,* July 18, 1993, home section, p. 6.

—Mary F. McNulty

LAND ROVER®

Rover Group plc, Britain's largest car manufacturer, was co-owned by British Aerospace plc (80 percent) and Honda Motor Co., Ltd. (20 percent) until 1994, when Bayerische Motoren Werke AG (BMW) bought controlling interest of Rover. Known worldwide for ruggedness and dependability, Land Rover is the group's marque for upscale four-wheel drive utility vehicles. In 1994 Land Rover North America, Inc., a subsidiary of the Rover Group, marketed three Land Rover vehicles in the United States—the Land Rover Defender, the Land Rover Discovery, and the Range Rover County.

Brand Origins

The Rover name has a long history. In 1870, John Kemp Starley established the Coventry Machinist Co. in Coventry, England, to manufacture bicycles. The Rover bicycle came out in 1884, and was selling more than 10,000 bicycles each year by 1896. That year Starley also changed the name of the company to The Rover Cycle Co. Ltd. Rover Cycle began manufacturing motorcycles around the turn of the century, and produced its first automobile in 1904. Two years later, the company became known as the Rover Car Co. Ltd.

Soon after, Rover vehicles began earning some recognition: in 1907, a Rover automobile won the annual International Tourist Trophy road race on the Isle of Man; Rover was awarded the Dewar Trophy by the Royal Automobile Club of England in 1924; and in 1930 a Rover Light Six raced a locomotive across France, finishing 20 minutes ahead of the train. However, Rover was little known outside England until the Land Rover brand appeared in 1948. That year the Rover Car Co. Ltd. unveiled its first four-wheel drive utility vehicle—modeled after the American Motor Co. (AMC) Jeep—at the Amsterdam Motor Show.

Land Rover

After World War II, Maurice Wilks, then chairman of the Rover Co., purchased a surplus U.S. Army jeep to use on his farm near Coventry. He and his brother, Spencer, then the company's chief engineer, soon decided that Rover should build a four-wheel drive vehicle based on the same basic design, with the idea of marketing it to other English farmers. Since there was a shortage of steel in post-war England, Rover used aluminum for the body, which was then mounted on a rigid ladder-style chassis made of steel. As a result, the Land Rover, as it was called, was light, rugged, and had a low center of gravity, making it perfect for off-road use.

The Land Rover was an immediate success, with orders coming in not only from English farmers, but also police departments, the military, forestry services, and estate owners. Land Rovers also developed a foreign market, especially in Africa and the Middle East, where they were well suited for both desert and jungle terrain. Within a few years, Land Rovers were being sold in more than 30 countries, including the United States.

The first Land Rovers were equipped with permanent four-wheel drive, a canvas roof, and optional doors. A station wagon was added a few months after the Amsterdam Auto Show, and a metal hardtop was offered as an alternative to the canvas roof in 1950. Rover debuted a Land Rover with a longer wheel base in 1954, and began offering an optional diesel engine in 1957. But the first significant change in styling came the next year when the Series II Land Rover hit the production line, followed by The Series III in 1971. More than a million Land Rovers were sold between 1948 and 1977. Sales peaked in 1985, as more than 31,000 Land Rovers were sold worldwide.

Range Rover

During the mid- to late 1960s, the hard-pressed British automobile industry underwent a series of consolidations. Rover had been acquired by the Leyland Motor Corporation in 1967, then merged with the state-owned British Motor Holdings in 1968, creating the British Leyland Motor Corporation.

Under pressure to expand its market, Rover brought forth an upscale version of the Land Rover in 1970, calling it the Range Rover. Initially, Rover intended to dub the new vehicle the "Road Rover," to differentiate it from the off-road Land Rover, but the name was judged to be too boring. The Range Rover—offering a refined interior, a more cushioned ride, and a less angular body—was still quite well-suited for off-road excursions. The Range Rover quickly developed a following among heads of state, including Queen Elizabeth, who received a specially made Range Rover convertible for her Silver Jubilee in 1977. However, Rover withdrew from the American market after 1970, and Range Rovers were not available in the United States until 1987.

AT A GLANCE

Coventry Machinists Co. established in 1870; Rover bicycle introduced in 1884; company name changed to J.K. Starley and Co. Ltd. in 1886; company name changed to The Rover Cycle Co. in 1896; Rover automobile introduced in 1904; company name changed to Rover Co. Ltd. in 1906; Land Rover automobile introduced in 1948; company acquired by Leyland Motor Corporation in 1967; Leyland merged with government-owned British Motor Holdings to form British Leyland Motor Corporation in 1968; Range Rover automobile introduced in 1970; corporate name changed to British Leyland Ltd. in 1975; corporate name changed to BL Ltd. and subsidiary Land Rover Ltd. created in 1978; corporate name changed to Rover Group plc in 1986; Rover Group acquired by British Aerospace plc in 1988; 20% of Rover Group acquired by Honda Motor Co., Ltd., in 1989; Bayerische Motoren Werke AG bought controlling interest in Rover in 1994.

Performance: *Sales*—(U.S.) 4,900 vehicles.

Major competitor: Ford Explorer; also Jeep Cherokee and Isuzu Trooper.

Advertising: *Agency*—Grace & Rothschild, New York, NY, 1986—. *Major campaign*—Introduction of Land Rover Discovery.

Addresses: *Parent company*—Rover Group plc, Ivy Cottage, Canley Road, Coventry CV5 6QX, England; phone: (20) 367-0111. *Ultimate parent company*—Bayerische Motoren Werke AG.

Illustrating its unique combination of elegance and hardy dependability, Range Rover received the Dewar Trophy from the Royal Automobile Club for technical merit in 1971, and, in recognition of design excellence, became the first vehicle ever displayed at The Louvre museum of Paris. In 1976 *Car Magazine* tested Range Rover, Land Rover, AMC Jeep, and a four-wheel drive utility vehicle from Toyota and concluded, "We have still not found a vehicle to challenge the Range Rover." Eight years later, in 1984, the magazine's opinion had not changed. After comparing the Range Rover to several competitors, the magazine's reviewer advised, "Out of it all emerged the superiority of the Range Rover."

U.S. Market

In 1978 Rover Co. was reorganized into Land Rover Ltd. Land Rover announced in 1985 plans to re-enter the U.S. market with the Range Rover, and created a marketing subsidiary for that purpose, Range Rover North America, Inc., in 1986. The first Range Rovers built to meet U.S. safety and emission standards were delivered in 1987. Land Rover also loaded them with extras, like electric sun roofs, stereo systems, and deep-pile carpeting.

The product launch was backed with whimsical advertising developed by the New York agency of Grace & Rothschild that showed the vehicles either covered with mud or plowing hub-deep through a river. The advertisements, with taglines such as "We brake for fish," later won several awards for creativity, including a gold medal at the International Film & TV Festival in 1988. Of course, Land Rover also recognized that most people who bought Range Rovers never left the highway. But as Charles R. Hughes, then head of Range Rover North America, told a news conference, "How many people do you suppose take their Rolex watches 300 feet underwater?"

Land Rover also recruited dealers from among existing luxury-car dealerships, especially Mercedes, Cadillac, and Jaguar dealers, so the pricey Range Rovers would be immediately visible to car buyers who could afford luxury off-road vehicles. Despite a $30,000 sticker price, more than 3,000 Range Rovers were sold in the first six months. As *Automotive Industries* pointed out, many Jeep dealerships looked "like the 'last outpost' [while] Range Rovers are displayed in settings worthy of the Crown Jewels." Later marketing surveys showed that 68 percent of Range Rover buyers already owned three other cars and had a median household income of $200,000. Worldwide sales of Range Rover topped 20,000 in 1987. The next year, sales of Range Rover surpassed Land Rover for the first time.

So why was it popular? In 1989 *Town & Country Monthly* said of the Range Rover: "Unlike other fadmobiles that have come and gone, the Range Rover has real character, a spectacularly impressive background and a combination of utility and luxury that renders it unique . . . it can go places—muddy, sandy, snowy, rocky, flooded, impossible places—where no other luxury motor vehicle would dare try, and it effortlessly conveys its passengers there in air-conditioned, leather-wrapped, walnut-grained comfort with absolute security and dependability." The magazine added, "It's expensive, but not excessively so. It's stylish, but in its own boxy, utilitarian way. It's very well finished, but one would expect that of any $36,000 motor vehicle. It could hardly be called space efficient; it will hold five persons comfortably, but when you walk up to a Range Rover for the first time it appears to be about the size of a small house."

To promote the U.S. Forest Service's "Tread Lightly" off-road environmental awareness and safety program, Range Rover sponsored The Great Divide Expedition, the first north-south crossing of the Continental Divide, in 1989. Among the honors awarded Range Rover that year were "Best Multi-Purpose Vehicle" by the nationally syndicated *Motorweek* television program and "Four Wheeler of the Year" by *Four Wheel Magazine.* In 1991, *Motorweek* called Range Rover "the crown jewel of sport utility vehicles."

Outlook

The parent corporation, British Leyland Motor Corporation, underwent several changes in the 1970s, finally emerging in 1978 as BL Ltd; then became the Rover Group Ltd. in 1986. In 1988 the British government sold the Rover Group plc to British Aerospace, which then sold 20 percent to the Honda Motor Co., Ltd. In 1992, Range Rover North America became Land Rover North America in anticipation of the Land Rover's U.S. return. The Land Rover Defender, a European model marketed in 1990, and based on the original Land Rover, made its U.S. debut in 1993.

The Defender, then the only open-air V-8 powered sport utility vehicle available in the United States, was also backed by a humorous advertising campaign from Grace & Rothschild. The advertisements played on the legendary Land Rover reputation for taking "adventurers deep into the lush Amazon jungle. Up the Atlas Mountains of Morocco. Down into the copper mines of Zambia," but translated that to a suburban residence. In TV commercials, jungle animals were heard as a garage door was raised and a Land Rover Defender emerged, followed by a rhinoceros, an elephant, or a herd of zebras. Roy Grace, then chairman of

Grace & Rothschild, explained the concept: ''What Land Rover represents to a lot of purchasers is a sense of freedom, guts, individualism. One of the best things going for us is our heritage of adventure. . . . It really separates us from the competition, so we wanted to tie into that while keeping a sense of fun.''

In 1994 Land Rover also exported the Land Rover Discovery to the United States. The Discovery, priced between the Defender and the Range Rover County, was developed in response to competition from Japanese automakers, particularly Toyota and Isuzu. Although developed with the U.S. market in mind, the Discovery was presented first in Europe, where it quickly became popular. More than 6,500 were sold in 1989—60 percent above first year projections—and Land Rover claimed a 20 percent share of the British market for upscale utility vehicles in 1992.

Management Today labeled the Discovery ''proof that British motor manufacturers and designers still have the spirit to fight back—and win—when they put their minds to it.'' In 1994 Land Rover North America was also urging its network of U.S. dealers to switch exclusively to Land Rover dealerships. The plans called for dealers to establish Land Rover Centres in major cities and satellite facilities in smaller markets. Land Rover said this would provide ''levels of customers service and expertise previously unavailable to buyers'' of four-wheel drive vehicles.

However, Land Rover also faced stiff challenges ahead. In addition to competitors such as the Ford Explorer, Chrysler's Jeep Cherokee, and Isuzu Trooper, Mercedes-Benz planned to enter a luxury sport-utility vehicle in the United States in 1997. Early in 1994, however, Bayerische Motoren Werke AG, maker of luxury BMW automobiles, bought controlling interest of Rover Group Holding plc; BMW is expected to market BMW branded versions of the Land Rover and Range Rover sport-utility vehicles.

Further Reading:

Elliott, Stuart, ''Zebras and Elephants and Rhinoceroses, Oh My! Land Rover Aims at Those Going a Bit Off the Road,'' *New York Times,* October 27, 1993, p. D22.

''Fighting Back: How the Discovery Took Off,'' *Management Today,* October 1991, p. 64.

Gross, Ken, ''The Rover Boys Strike It Rich,'' *Automotive Industries,* April 1989, p. 39.

Henry, Jim, *Automotive News,* ''Land Rover Rolls out Defender 90,'' *Automotive News,* September 13, 1993, p. 20; ''Rover Plans Steep Climb in U.S.,'' June 28, 1993, p. 1.

''Rover Group plc,'' *International Directory of Company Histories,* volume 7, Detroit: St. James Press, 1993.

Vorderman, Don, ''Roving in the Range,'' *Town & Country Monthly,* March 1989, p. 112.

—*Dean Boyer*

LANE® CEDAR CHESTS

The Lane Company turned its line of basic, utilitarian wooden boxes into one of the world's most familiar and recognizable wood furniture brand. Over the years, the company has cultivated the association of Lane Cedar Chests with the hope and promise of youthful romance. With their moth-repelling qualities, protective locks, and decorative walnut and mahogany veneer exteriors, Lane chests are purchased by and for young brides across the nation. This single product allowed the Lane Company to establish its name to the consumer public, and, over the past eight decades, the brand has grown to include popular wood and upholstered furniture in a range of prices.

Brand Origins

In March 1912, John Edward Lane attended a public auction in Altavista, Virginia, and paid $500 for a packaging company that had gone bankrupt. In June, he ordered his twenty-one-year-old son Edward to go to Altavista and attempt to turn the factory into a chest company, which he had heard was a profitable item at the time. Edward's brothers, under the name Lane Brothers Company, had built many sections of railroads across the southeast, and when they heard the Virginian railway would cross the main line of the Southern Railway, they decided to buy 2000 acres of land at the junction. Upon those acres, the brothers founded the town of Altavista in 1907. With a father as ambitious and stern as John Lane, Edward was not surprised when he was called to duty at the new enterprise.

Although he helped manage the family's sawmills, farms, and bookkeeping, Edward Lane had no manufacturing experience and had never seen a cedar chest. Fortunately, he had taken technical courses in woodworking, foundry, forge, and machine shop during his two years at Virginia Polytechnical Institute. Purely by chance, Ed Lane ran into his woodworking instructor, Mr. Loop, on his way to Altavista from his home in Charlottesville. Lane asked Mr. Loop to accompany him to the factory and advise him on what machinery was necessary to turn the packaging company into a cedar chest company.

To their dismay, Ed Lane and Mr. Loop found a small, corrugated iron building with very little usable equipment other than two dry kilns, a boiler and a small engine. They quickly made a list of the machinery the company needed to make chests, secured financing, and placed their order. When Edward Lane reported this progress to his father one month later, "He hit the ceiling . . . and began to shout that he was ruined," Edward recalled later. With his usual youthful optimism, Ed carefully explained the credit terms to his father—a small down payment with the balance due over the next three years—and he convinced him that he would be able to produce and sell ten to fifteen chests per day. Grudgingly, the senior Lane gave his approval to the investment, but because he was skeptical of how successful the venture would be, he did not want it to carry the Lane name. The family therefore incorporated the little company as the Standard Red Cedar Chest Company, with John Lane as president and Ed Lane as vice president and general manager.

Early Production

The company hired its first employees and installed its new machinery, and soon production of cedar chests climbed to a rate of ten per day. With the production well underway, the company now faced a sales dilemma. Small factories usually relied on commissioned sales forces that represented a number of different furniture lines. This form of sales distribution, however, presented problems to the chest company. Salesmen rarely had reason to promote the cedar chests over the other furniture brands they represented, and the chest company failed to develop any of its own internal sales expertise. To learn more about why this sales program was not working, Ed frequently visited customers on his own.

On a disappointing business trip to Utica, New York, Ed was returning to his hotel discouraged with the prospect of selling his cedar chests when he began to consider the product from the dealer's point of view. He gradually began to conceive of a novel window display using cedar shavings, logs, and small cedar trees surrounding cedar chests with cards illustrating the chests' many practical uses. With the idea fresh in his mind, he hurried back to a dealer who had just turned him down. Upon hearing Ed's idea, the dealer ordered twenty-five chests. Next, he approached another dealer who had turned him down in Buffalo. That dealer ordered fifty chests. He repeated the success in several other New York cities, and, as a result, forever instructed his salesmen, "Along with making a good product, you've got to sell with an *idea.*"

Around the same time, Ed Lane made yet another fortuitous decision. He knew his chest factory was a natural outgrowth of his experience running the family sawmill. When the major cedar suppliers expressed no interest in supplying the start-up company

AT A GLANCE

Lane brand of cedar chests founded in March 1912, by John Edward Lane and his son, Edward Hudson Lane, in Altavista, Virginia; original brand name was Lane Cedar Chests (later, the brand name was changed to Lane Cedar Hope Chests, Lane Sweetheart Chests, and finally, Lane Love Chests); company name originally the Standard Red Cedar Box Company; name changed to the Lane Company in 1922; company made initial public stock offering in 1968; conglomerate INTERCO became parent company in 1980s.

Advertising: *Agency*—In-house by Lane Advertising, Inc., Altavista, VA, 1970—. *Major campaign*—"Give her the gift she'll be opening the rest of her life."

Addresses: *Parent company*—The Lane Company, Inc., East Franklin Avenue, Altavista, VA 24517; phone: (804) 369-5641.

with lumber, Ed decided to install a small sawmill of his own. The risky decision resulted in a five percent savings over his competitors using traditional lumber suppliers, and the savings was plowed into an advertising budget. The decision turned out to be one of the company's most profitable moves.

Early Marketing Strategy

As part of educating himself in the chest business, Ed learned everything he could about the history of cedar chests. He found, for example, that the chests were more than simple storage places with protection against moths and had evolved to symbolize romance. The early Egyptians discovered the protective qualities of cedarwood, and their young brides used such chests to deposit delicate garments and keepsakes that were part of their dowries. The tradition spread to Europe where artisans made their chests quite ornate. It soon became a custom for a new bride to be carried to meet her husband atop her trousseau. Many years later in the United States, "hope chests" had become a traditional gift for young, soon-to-be-married women. The romantic allure of his product was particularly interesting to Ed Lane since he had recently married. He knew that he had found his company's strategic positioning—pure romance. With this goal in mind, Ed began experimenting with decorative walnut and mahogany veneer exteriors. He wanted his cedar chests to become the treasured antiques of the future.

During World War I, the government placed embargoes on freight deemed nonessential, and Standard faced the decision of going out of business or providing something to contribute to the war effort. The company managed to win government contracts to manufacture pine ammunition boxes. Although the venture was not profitable, it did enable Standard to develop a progressive assembly line that was the first known moving conveyor system in the furniture industry.

The firm's early years were troublesome, and Ed Lane describes the corporate atmosphere as being in a constant state of crisis over financing, production, and personnel. At the end of the company's first decade in operation, a banking representative told Ed that his company was insolvent. The young man asked him what that meant. "If you don't know what that means, you probably would be better off to remain ignorant of its meaning," the banker replied. "You might muddle through somehow."

Those words proved to be foretelling. As The Standard Red Cedar Chest Company began its second decade of operation, Ed's efforts suddenly seemed effective as the company enjoyed a succession of profitable years. The year 1922 marked a turning point for Standard. The management team began advertising nationally, changed the company's name, introduced decorative walnut and mahogany exteriors, and devoted more attention to developing an exclusive sales force. Also in that year, Lane hired Arthur D. Little Commercial Chemists for an ambitious research and development program to find out how the company could reduce its wood waste and improve the "aroma-tightness" of its chests. The program allowed the company to improve its construction significantly.

Advertising

In 1920 and 1921, Edward Lane enjoyed positive responses to railway billboard advertisements between Washington and New York and planned to follow up with pre-Christmas newspaper ads in large, eastcoast cities. N.W. Ayer, one of the country's leading advertising agencies, accepted Standard as a client and convinced Ed instead to invest his advertising dollars in two half-page black and white ads in the leading national publication of the time, *The Saturday Evening Post.* The first ad carried the headline, "Every woman wants a chest of fragrant cedar wood," and directed the reader to "the young girl gliding into womanhood . . . the radiant wife swiftly fashioning a host of baby things . . . the mother of mothers fondly dreaming o'er the lace and lavender of a bygone year." The advertisement also included practical information about the product.

At the same time, the agency also recommended that the cumbersome name Standard Red Cedar Chest Company be dropped in favor of Lane Cedar Chests. Over the years, the brand name Lane Cedar Chests evolved into "Lane Cedar Hope Chests," then "Lane Sweetheart Chests," and finally, "Lane Cedar Chests" with the tagline, "The gift that starts the home." Over the years, the Ayer agency's program of national advertising took the Lane name and product to the attention of the mass public. The campaigns consistently proclaimed the romantic nature of the product and heralded its practical storage functions.

In the early 1920s, Ed Lane knew the company needed to develop its own exclusive sales force to travel consistently and secure broad distribution. A new sales manager devoted a great deal of attention to this endeavor, and by the early thirties, the Lane Company had a well-trained, promotion-minded sales force. During the Depression, the company had the unlikely accomplishment of doubling the number of its existing accounts.

Creative Promotions

Some Lane employees enjoyed an interesting hobby: they made miniature cedar chests for their girlfriends in Altavista. The women treasured their small boxes and stored small valuables, jewelry, and love letters in them. In 1925, the Lane Company began manufacturing miniature chests, and this pastime gave rise to one of Lane's most successful promotions. The sales force collected the names of girls nationwide who were graduating from high school and sent them certificates good for one free miniature cedar chest at the local Lane dealership. The response was overwhelming, and over the years it continued to grow until two out of every three girls graduating from high school received a Lane miniature. This sampling program was a stroke of genius for Lane, who managed to introduce future homemakers to dealers at the beginning of their furniture-buying years.

In 1938, Lane initiated a promotion in Phoenix, Arizona, as ambitious as the "Girl Graduate" program. Because they were popular gift items, sales for cedar chests had always been strong during the Christmas season. To pump sales during the slow season, Lane decided to offer special low prices for Valentine's Day. The promotion allowed the company to smooth the cyclic nature of the sales and production seasons. The Valentine promotion, combined with June's "Girl Graduate" program and birthday, bridal, and anniversary specials allowed Lane to forge ahead with its market-leading success.

By the early 1940s, Lane was the best-known name in the wood furniture business. Research indicated that the company's stereotypical consumer was a young woman dreaming of furnishing her first home. According to the survey, however, a surprisingly large number of chests were being purchased by young men for their sweethearts. This knowledge, plus wartime letters from servicemen who wanted to have cedar chests sent to girlfriends and wives, prompted Lane, via national advertising, to set up a special network between servicemen, dealers, and the "girls back home." Soon, the company was swamped with requests from overseas for these mail-order chests.

Moving Toward Diversification

Lane's board of directors recognized the inherent weakness of being dependent on a single product, and they began to urge the company's managers to diversify the chest company. Under the leadership of Edward Lane, Jr., the company was determined to expand the Lane name and develop new product lines. In spring of 1951, Lane introduced its first line of modern and traditional occasional tables at the High Point, North Carolina, furniture market. The company's venture proved fruitful, and the consumer public responded positively to this new collection. Lane's expertise in matching wood veneers and executing national advertising campaigns resulted in strong consumer recognition and successful first-year sales.

Soon, Lane capitalized further on its name and expanded into other furniture products, including record cabinets, upholstered furniture, rocking and recliner chairs, and bedroom and dining room furniture. In the ensuing decades, Lane acquired such notable furniture company names as Hickory Chair, the Clyde Pearson Company, Hickory Tavern, Bruington (now HTB), and Craft Associates. These careful acquisitions allowed Lane to span the furniture price range, from moderately priced pieces to the high-end reproductions of Hickory Chair.

The Lane Company was privately held for the first 56 years of its history. In 1968 officials made an initial public stock offering, and the number of outstanding common shares has since grown to more than five million.

Sixty-one years after founding the small chest company, Edward Lane died in May 1973. That year, the company's annual sales exceeded $100 million. Although the company grew significantly during his lifetime, he always made certain that the company never lost sight of his father's basic guiding principle: the first concern should be people, not production, sales, or finance. Throughout the following years, his successors emphasized at every opportunity, "Our people are our most important asset."

Further Reading:

Cleary, David Powers, "Lane Cedar Chests," *Great American Brands,* New York: Fairchild Publications, 1981, pp. 202–10.

The Lane Company, Inc., "Lane: A Brief Account of a Cedar Chest Business," Altavista, VA: The Lane Company, 1984.

—Wendy Johnson Bilas

LAWN-BOY®

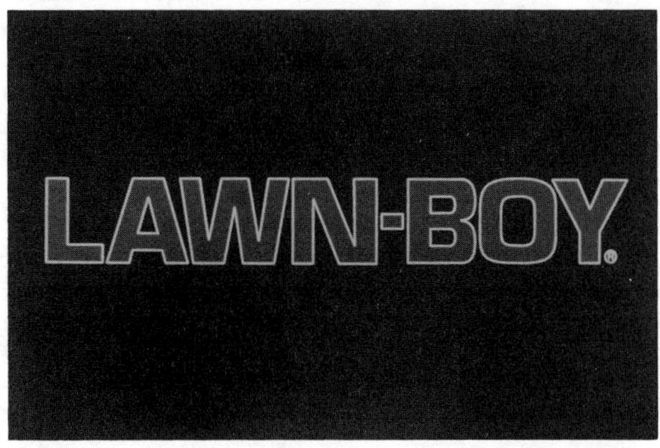

First marketed in 1952, Lawn-Boy brand walk-behind power mowers have developed a solid reputation for quality and have regularly captured close to ten percent of the lawn care market. As part of Outboard Marine Corporation (OMC), a manufacturer of outboard boat engines and recreational equipment, Lawn-Boy received years of solid corporate backing. Increased competition in the outdoor power equipment industry and OMC's desire to concentrate on its primary market compelled the company to sell the brand in 1989. Lawn-Boy was acquired by the leading U.S. manufacturer of lawn and garden equipment, the Toro Company. Toro took steps to expand its already dominant market share by marketing the Lawn-Boy brand as a medium-priced mower that makes lawn care easier. The Lawn-Boy product line features two series of walk-behind mowers, four riding mowers, a line of gas trimmers, and a number of commercial mowers. Lawn-Boy's 1990s marketing was aimed at younger buyers, women, and the elderly, behind the slogan "Lawn-Boy, Making It Easier."

An Idea Whose Time Had Come

In the years following World War II, a number of American manufacturers scanning the horizon for business opportunities recognized that the rotary power mower was "an idea whose time had come," in the words of Outboard Marine Corporation's 1983 annual report. OMC researched the market and in 1952 acquired RPM Manufacturing of Lamar, Missouri, a manufacturer of power mowers. Given the brand name Lawn-Boy, these mowers were marketed that same year and by 1957 had become the top-selling power mowers in the United States. Lawn-Boy mowers built a solid reputation for quality and durability, as OMC marketed the brand to homeowners with smaller lawns who did not need the larger riding mowers and tractors sold by competitors like Toro and John Deere.

With a staggered right front wheel and a large, side-discharge channel, Lawn-Boy mowers have been easily identifiable for years. Lawn-Boy's distinctive styling was changed for the 1983 model year, when the brand incorporated blade-braking systems required by federal regulations. Also in 1983, Lawn-Boy moved its manufacturing facilities from Galesburg, Illinois, to Sardis, Mississippi, to be closer to the geographic center of the mower market. The 261,000-square-foot plant was equipped with the latest technologies in lawn mower assembly, boasted the company's 1983 annual report, most notably a "$1 million quality assurance machine that automatically checks and double-checks the new blade stopping mechanism on each mower."

Lawn-Boy products were sold to independent distributors who then sold to authorized dealers, who in turn would provide sales and service to customers. By 1988, Lawn-Boy had 38 distributors in the United States selling to about 8,000 dealers, and 25 distributors outside the country. Overseas sales accounted for about 15 percent of Lawn-Boy's sales, which reached $153 million by 1988, according to the *Milwaukee Sentinel.*

Expansion and Acquisition

In September of 1987, Lawn-Boy took steps to radically expand its product line by purchasing Gilson Brothers Company, a manufacturer of riding mowers; lawn and garden tractors; rotary tillers; trimmers; snowthrowers; and portable, oil-fired heaters. Larry Engel noted in the *Milwaukee Sentinel* that the purchase was designed to allow Lawn-Boy to compete with Toro and John Deere, both of which offered a full range of premium lawn and garden equipment. In 1989, Lawn-Boy president Jerome M. Stumbras told Engel, "Lawn-Boy is committed to being a leader in the premium segment of the market, to growing our business through innovation in quality products and services." Lawn-Boy moved its headquarters from rented space in Memphis, Tennessee, to the 450,000-square-foot Gilson facilities in Plymouth, Wisconsin, where it manufactured all but the walk-behind mowers, which were built in plants in Oxford and Sardis, Mississippi.

Shortly after Lawn-Boy's expansion, Outboard Marine Corporation surprised industry analysts when it announced in 1989 that it was interested in selling both Lawn-Boy and another profitable subsidiary, Cushman Inc., maker of golf carts and light vehicles. Charles D. Strang, chairman and chief executive officer of Outboard Marine, announced that the company wanted to "concentrate solely on its worldwide marine business, which has grown dramatically in the past few years," according to Engel. Lawn-Boy turned down an acquisition offer by Diversified Investments Corporation of Clearwater, Florida, in August, but accepted the offer of $85 million in cash made by the Toro Company of Bloomington, Minnesota. The acquisition joined the two leading manufacturers of premium walk-behind mowers; Toro was estimated to hold eight to nine percent of the market while Lawn-Boy held seven to eight percent at the time of the deal.

AT A GLANCE

Lawn-Boy brand walk-behind power mowers introduced in 1952 by Outboard Marine Corp.; introduced riding tractors and snowthrowers in 1988, after acquiring the Gilson Brothers Co.; brand acquired by the Toro Company, November, 1989.

Performance: *Market share*—15% of walk-behind mower sales (with Toro); 14% of riding mower sales (with Toro). *Sales*—$367.9 million (includes Toro).

Major competitor: John Deere; also Snapper.

Advertising: *Agency*—Laughlin-Constable, Milwaukee, WI, 1989—. *Major campaign*—Easy Street campaign, with slogan "Lawn-Boy, Making It Easier."

Addresses: *Parent company*—The Toro Company, 8111 Lyndale Ave. S., Bloomington, MN 55420; phone: (612) 888-8100; fax: (612) 887-8258.

Remaking a Brand

"Our style is not to go in and make changes right away," Toro vice-president and treasurer Dennis P. Himan told the *Milwaukee Journal*'s John Slania in 1989. "We are really looking at this as business as usual for Lawn-Boy." For six months after the deal, Lawn-Boy did operate as usual, but in May of 1990 Toro began a substantial restructuring of Lawn-Boy production, distribution, and marketing. The late 1980s were a particularly challenging time for the lawn and garden equipment industry, as a drought in the summer of 1988 exacerbated the early effects of an industrywide recession. Moreover, mass retailers were increasing their share of lawn mower sales, challenging the tendency of premium mower manufacturers to sell their products through two-step distributor-dealer networks. If Toro and Lawn-Boy were to coexist, they would need to have distinguishable brand identities.

Toro's efforts to reshape Lawn-Boy's identity involved widespread consolidation of production and market differentiation. In 1990, the Toro Company initiated this consolidation when it closed the underutilized Plymouth, Wisconsin, manufacturing plant and discontinued the manufacture of Lawn-Boy snowblowers and tillers. Then, in January of 1992, facing a second quarter operating loss of $9.5 million, Toro announced a major restructuring: the company closed a Tennessee distribution center, offices in Plymouth and Sheboygan Falls, Wisconsin, and the Sardis manufacturing plant, moving Lawn-Boy production to existing facilities in Windom, Minnesota, and South Bend, Indiana. The restructuring resulted in 450 layoffs. Analyst Frank Rolfes of Dain Bosworth Inc. told *Minneapolis Star and Tribune* reporter Susan Peterson, "I think the key motivation [for the restructuring] is to try to have Lawn-Boy perform up to the standards of Toro mowers. If they run green [Lawn-Boys] and red [Toros] through the same plant, there's no reason why they can't make the green ones as profitably as the reds."

Of more importance to the consumer were the changes Toro was making in Lawn-Boy's distribution. The Toro Company announced in September of 1990 that it would begin selling Lawn-Boy products through Sears and Montgomery Ward. Toro chief executive officer Kendrick B. Melrose expected that these retailers would add $25 million to $30 million to Toro's sales, reported Linda Owen of the *St. Paul Pioneer Press-Dispatch.* Lawn-Boy's distribution was expanded even further in 1992 and 1993, when Toro added Target, Hechinger's, and Builders Square to its list of retailers. "This is the first time a premium-brand lawn mower has been available at mass merchandisers and home centers," Toro sales director Frank Conney told *Appliance Manufacturer* in 1993. "Traditionally, lawn mowers at these outlets have sold for $129 to $199. Our strategy is to offer a premium-branded product at retail outlets where consumers are used to shopping. Consumers are willing to move up from a $199 mower to a $249 Lawn-Boy because of the features and perceived quality."

The choice to sell Lawn-Boy products through mass merchandisers posed significant problems to the network of Lawn-Boy dealers that numbered between 4,000 and 5,000 in 1990. The Toro Company sold Lawn-Boy mowers to the retail chains directly, while dealers still had to purchase the mowers from a distributor at a higher price. Toro quieted some discontent among the Lawn-Boy dealer network when it agreed to sell directly to 1,800 of the largest dealers, but industry analysts predicted that the company was willing to lose some of its smaller dealers because chain store sales were growing faster than traditional dealer sales. By 1993, 45 percent of Lawn-Boy sales went through the direct sales channel. Lawn-Boy dealers were expected to compete with the big chains by emphasizing their strength in aftermarket service, Toro's consumer division general manager told *Appliance Manufacturer.*

Making It Easier

The biggest problem surrounding the integration of the Lawn-Boy brand into the Toro Company's overall lawn and garden product line involved brand differentiation. The Lawn-Boy and Toro brands had always competed head to head, but the Toro Company was intent on repositioning the Lawn-Boy brand to capture an untapped segment of the mower market without stealing sales from the Toro brand. "There is a middle-priced segment of the walk-behind mower market that has not been served very well," McIntosh told *Appliance Manufacturer.* Traditionally, mowers had sold for less than $200, like Murray or store brand mowers, or for between $300 and $600, like the Toro brand. "We are positioning Lawn-Boy to move into that unserved middle," noted McIntosh, who added, "We kept the Lawn-Boy name and image because of its high national recognition, strong customer loyalty and repeat sales."

By 1993, ease of use became the concept around which Lawn-Boy was marketed. "Lawn-Boy customers want simplicity and convenience, and are less interested than Toro-brand customers in the aesthetics of the lawn," Toro Company director of consumer sales and marketing Scott Barlass told *Appliance Manufacturer.* "When it comes to marketing Lawn-Boy Power Mulch mowers, the strategy is to focus on how much easier it is to mulch." Lawn-Boy mower engines use a Fresh Lube Oil System which automatically mixes oil with gas, eliminating the need for premixing. Moreover, Lawn-Boy's two-cycle engine is lighter than traditional mower engines, making it easier to push. "Market research also has shown that the Lawn-Boy name and green color suggest a high degree of user friendliness," noted *Appliance Manufacturer.*

The Toro Company's consumer research, reported by Barlass in a speech given at the 1993 Outdoor Power Equipment exposition, showed that those consumers who purchase Lawn-Boy mowers tend to be older than those who purchase Toro mowers, have lower household incomes, are more likely to live in rural areas, and have older homes with more moderate values. Moreover, 41 percent of Lawn-Boy mowers are used primarily by women, whereas only 30 percent of Toro mowers are used primarily by women. Such information has guided the Lawn-Boy marketing that targets women and older consumers.

Lawn-Boy Products

In 1994, Lawn-Boy marketed a Gold and a Silver Series of walk-behind mowers. The higher-priced Gold Series featured a lightweight aluminum mowing deck and a 3-speed, Easy Stride self-propel system with easily accessible controls. The lower-priced Silver Series had a steel deck and a 1-speed self-propel system. Both mowers could be fitted with a bagger attachment or a Mow & Feed fertilizer spreader, which discharges fertilizer evenly while the mower is operated. Both mowers were also equipped with Lawn-Boy's Easy Mulch System, which circulates grass clippings in the mowing chamber where they are cut into fine pieces before falling to the turf. (These clippings provide a biodegradable mulch that is known to enhance the health and beauty of lawns.) The operator could convert from mulching to side-discharge to bagging simply by twisting a set of plastic handles. These models also featured Lawn-Boy's unique staggered-wheel design which, according to promotional literature, allows for easy maneuverability and closer trimming capabilities.

Although walk-behind mowers are the core of Lawn-Boy's product line, consumers can also purchase Lawn-Boy gas trimmers and riding tractors, both of which are variations on Toro brand products. Lawn-Boy offered four small riding mowers in the mid-1990s, all featuring engines ranging from 8- to 13-horsepower and mower decks from 25 to 38 inches. The tractors and trimmers, however, were only available at authorized Lawn-Boy dealers.

In 1991, the last year in which Lawn-Boy and Toro sales figures were reported separately, Lawn-Boy sales reached $107.4 million—down significantly from the high of $153 million in 1988, when Lawn-Boy was still with Outboard Marine Corporation, but reflective of the overall recession affecting the industry. Lawn-Boy sales for 1991 thus represented 25 percent of the Toro Company's consumer division sales. According to Toro, Lawn-Boy sales slumped slightly in 1992 but rose sharply in 1993, contributing to 1993 worldwide consumer division sales of $367.9 million. The company expected Lawn-Boy sales to continue to rise through the mid-1990s, as more consumers take advantage of Lawn-Boy's ease of use and its attractive market positioning.

Further Reading:

Engel, Larry, "Lawn-Boy Products Cut Wider Swath in Industry," *Milwaukee Sentinel,* July 13, 1989.

Magy, Robert, "Toro's Second Season," *Corporate Report* (Minneapolis, MN), May 1, 1990.

Outboard Marine Corporation Annual Report, Waukegon, IL: Outboard Marine Corp., 1969–1983.

Owen, Linda, "Toro to Sell Its Lawn-Boy Mowers through Sears, Wards," *St. Paul Pioneer Press-Dispatch* (Minnesota), September 5, 1990.

Peterson, Susan E., *Minneapolis Star and Tribune,* "Toro Agrees to Buy Lawn-Boy," October 4, 1989; "Toro Moves to Consolidate Its Lawn-Boy Operations," May 8, 1990; "Toro Restructuring Will Shut Down Mississippi Plant, Cut 450 Workers," January 22, 1992.

Slania, John, "Toro Grabbing More of the Premium Market," *Milwaukee Journal,* October 4, 1989.

"The Toro Company," *Appliance Manufacturer,* February 1993, pp. T1–T21.

The Toro Company Annual Report, Bloomington, MN: The Toro Company, 1989–1993.

Weinberger, Betsy, *Minneapolis St. Paul Citybusiness,* "Toro Boosts Distribution," September 25, 1992; "Toro Cuts Deals to Push More Mowers in Stores," February 19, 1993.

Additional information supplied by the Toro Company and by Axiom Business Development Group.

—Tom Pendergast

LA-Z-BOY®

The La-Z-Boy Chair Company is the nation's largest manufacturer of upholstered furniture and its third-largest producer of household furnishings. From its first simple reclining lounge chair, the La-Z-Boy product line has grown to include stationary chairs, sofas and loveseats, motion chairs, recliner sofas, sleep sofas, and motion modular groups. Quality furniture stores and chains, department stores, and La-Z-Boy Furniture Galleries, La-Z-Boy Gallery Stores, and La-Z-Boy Showcase Shoppes all sell La-Z-Boy furniture. The company also manufactures office, healthcare, and hospitality furniture.

Brand Origins

Edward M. Knabusch, who made desks for Weis Manufacturing Company, introduced his cousin Edwin J. Shoemaker to the band saws, jointers, and shaping machinery he used at night to make mirrors, cabinets, and novelty furniture for friends and family. Soon the two cousins had new occupations: Knabusch became a marketer and Shoemaker an engineer. On March 14, 1927, the Kna-Shoe Manufacturing Company set up shop in Knabusch's fathers garage in the southern Michigan town of Monroe and started making doll furniture and cabinets.

Soon after Knabusch and Shoemaker formed the Kna-Shoe Manufacturing Company they realized their company had an identity problem. One day Knabusch went to pick up a freight order for the company, but the terminal operator would not release the shipment because it was incorrectly labeled the "New Shoe Company." When Knabusch finally got home with the order, he and Shoemaker renamed their business Floral City Furniture Company.

The new name, however, did not solve another of the company's problems: the banks would not give the partners a loan to build a manufacturing plant in what those conservative institutions considered the middle of nowhere. Fortunately for the company, friends and family of Knabusch and Shoemaker financed the construction of a brick building in a cornfield. A ten-horsepower electric motor powered the entire building.

In their new factory, the men began constructing novelty furniture, including the "gossiper." Designed for people talking on the telephone, the piece had a place to sit as well as storage space. Another innovative piece proved to be the genesis of the world famous La-Z-Boy trademark: an outdoor wood slat folding chair Knabusch and Shoemaker designed for "nature's way of relaxing." According to Albert B. Jannsen in *I Remember When . . . : A History of La-Z-Boy Chair Company,* the partners used orange crate mockups while refining the design so "the chair followed the contour of a person's body, both sitting up and leaning back." The reclining lounge chair was the first of its kind.

Again Knabusch' s and Shoemaker's friends and family helped back their venture and, thus, ward off industry thieves and copiers. They gave Floral City Furniture, which incorporated in April 1927, money for patents and start-up production costs for the reclining chair. Although Floral City's chair was a unique, comfortable product, it was not until the company took the advice of Arthur Richardson, a buyer for the Lion Store in Toledo, Ohio, that the chair became a hit. Richardson refused to buy the out-of-season piece and suggested the company upholster the wood slat porch chair so it could be used throughout the year. Floral City did just that, patenting the invention just before the stock market crashed. Despite the economic depression, Floral City Furniture's reclining chair and reputation for quality craftsmanship led the company to prosper. However, the company sometimes took wheat, coal, and cows in payment for its furniture instead of cash.

After they learned that retailers made twice the profits that a manufacturer did, Knabusch and Shoemaker converted Floral City Furniture Company into a retail store and joined with Michigan Chair Company in Grand Rapids to manufacture even more chairs. Within a year's time, the company tripled in size. When Knabusch and Shoemaker realized they needed a special name for their popular reclining chair, they combined promotion with necessity and held a contest. As told by Jannsen in *I Remember When . . . :* "The names people thought up! The Sit-N-Snooze. Slack-Back. Comfort Carrier. But one in particular—La-Z-Boy—was the best."

The success of the La-Z-Boy reclining chair did not escape the attention of other manufacturers. Even after the patent and trademark were established, manufacturers from Michigan to Mississippi tried to copy the design, mechanism, and even the name of the La-Z-Boy reclining chair. Competing manufacturers also complained about Floral City being both a manufacturer and retailer. In 1941, Knabusch and Shoemaker decided to separate the La-Z-Boy reclining chair factory from Floral City Furniture, thus creating the La-Z-Boy Chair Company. However, a new La-Z-Boy

AT A GLANCE

La-Z-Boy brand furniture created in 1927 by Edward M. Knabusch and Edwin J. Shoemaker, cofounders of the Kna-Shoe Manufacturing Company; company changed name to Floral City Furniture and was incorporated, 1927; company name changed to La-Z-Boy Chair Company, 1941.

Performance: *Market share*—35% (top share) of single-seat recliner category; 8.5% of upholstered furniture products. *Sales*—$684 million (total company sales).

Major competitors: Broyhill, Ethan Allen, Lane; also, Stratolounger and Barcalounger.

Advertising: *Agency*—Ross Roy Inc., Bloomfield Hills, MI, 1979—. *Major campaign*—Brand slogan, "Genuine La-Z-Boy"; consumer magazine advertising theme: "Who Built All This Beautiful Comfortable Furniture? You'll Never Guess," featuring photographs of consumers and La-Z-Boy products in "at-home" situations.

Addresses: *Parent company*—La-Z-Boy Chair Company, 1284 N. Telegraph Rd., Monroe, MI 48161-3390; phone: (313) 242-1444; fax: (313) 241-4422.

building did not produce any recliners until 1946; because of World War II, Woodall Industries manufactured specialized plane parts in the factory and La-Z-Boy made tank seats and crash pads in rented garages.

Innovative Designs

People found the way the first La-Z-boy chair opened into a recliner a welcome feature. Throughout the years, La-Z-Boy developed several enhancements to the basic recliner, but retained its use of superior hardwoods in frames and exposed components. In the 1950s and 1960s, the company added built-in ottomans and rocking and close-to-the-wall mechanisms to recliners. The Sofette was a dual reclining loveseat.

The La-Z-Boy Reclina-Rocker, introduced in 1959, both rocked and reclined. The recliner formed an unbroken line from back to footrest, unlike standard recliners that had a gap between the chair seat and footrest. The Reclina-Rocker was a big success even though there were similar chairs already on the market, some of which had electric massage motors and pop-up snack trays. The Reclina-Rocker had independent seat back and footrest mechanisms. Another innovative model, the Reclina-Way wall chair, allowed chairs to be placed close to a wall without worry about having enough clearance for reclining. And the Reclina-Rest line of reclining chairs included a chaise recliner with a multiple motor massage system that could reduce muscle tension and stress. The line also included a dual recliner sofa featuring a recliner mechanism at each end.

During the early 1980s, La-Z-Boy introduced soft-looking recliner models that contrasted with its traditional tightly upholstered lines. By 1983, customers could buy recliners in 50,000 style and fabric variations, and the company held 40 separate patents for the mechanisms that operated the chairs. In 1991, the company expanded its lines to include stationary furniture by introducing a sofa and a sleep sofa.

Advertising

The La-Z-Boy trademark benefited from promotions and advertising attuned to the times. An early product and marketing strategy Knabusch and Shoemaker created drew people from Detroit and Toledo to their Michigan factory. They pitched a circus tent in front of the Floral City building and entertained families with "Furniture Shows." While their parents shopped, children watched acrobatic circus mice perform on teeter-totters, Ferris wheels, and merry-go-rounds and fish flip and glide in a magnificent sculpted pond at the store's entryway. Floral City also gave prospective customers shrubs and fruit grown by Henrietta Knabusch.

The La-Z-Boy Chair Company fit right in with the 3-D movies and Hula Hoops of the late 1950s. In 1959, the company built a unique La-Z-Boy loveseat for a promotional auction. The piece looked like a car seat upholstered in "mink" and had horns, radio, lights, and blinkers.

In the 1960s, La-Z-Boy hired Jim Backus to record commercials as his alter ego, Mr. Magoo. Backus recorded more than 15,000 radio and television commercials for La-Z-Boy as the voice of the popular Mr. Magoo cartoon character, whose severe myopia caused hilarious situations. The large number of commercials earned Backus a spot in the *Guinness Book of World Records.* The campaign advertised the Reclina-Rocker, whose sales skyrocketed from $1.1 million to $52.7 million.

The company continued to use humor in its advertising when actor and ex-football star Alex Karras became a La-Z-Boy print and broadcast spokesperson in the 1980s. A 1983 ad showed him snoozing in a La-Z-Boy recliner under the headline "a testimonial for genuine La-Z-Boy recliners by Alex Karras." A humorous television campaign featured a dog lounging in a La-Z-Boy recliner. When the dog's owner came home, the dog leaped down from the chair without being spotted on it and was rewarded for being good.

Other La-Z-Boy advertising emphasized the company's dependability and the comfort of its furniture. During the 1980s, the company used the slogans "La-Z-Boy . . . because it was the first. And still is." and "La-Z-Boy, the name America's comfortable with." The theme for La-Z-Boy office furniture was "at home in any office."

In the early 1990s, La-Z-Boy Chair Company decided to discontinue television advertising and concentrate on advertising in magazines, especially in upscale titles targeted at women. The company also advertised in such general interest titles as *People* and *Parade,* and in special interest books on decorating and remodeling homes. The company based the decision to use print advertising on its longevity; consumers tend to keep magazines and books that gave them decorating ideas. An example of the company's new advertising was the 1994 "Surprise" national campaign, which featured the phrase, "Who built all this beautiful comfortable furniture? You'll never guess"; the print advertising campaign, which ran in conjunction with ads for the American Home Collection of living room furniture, showed an exterior photograph of a typical American home with an inset showing a room furnished with pieces from the La-Z-Boy American Home Collection. Ads included the La-Z-Boy toll-free number to direct consumers to the nearest La-Z-Boy retailer.

Brand Outlook

Over the years, the La-Z-Boy name became synonymous with reclining chairs and one of the most recognized brand names in the furniture industry. However, the company realized that the reclining chair market was maturing and that their sales growth was slowing. The company responded by making a transition from specialist to broad-based upholstery furniture manufacturer. La-Z-Boy sales of $160 million in 1980 derived entirely from recliners. By 1993, recliner sales had gone up 144 percent and La-Z-Boy still sold more motion chairs than any other manufacturer. However, the company's expansion into stationary upholstery and wood furniture resulted in the specialty chairs accounting for only 57 percent of companywide sales.

The La-Z-Boy Chair Company acquired subsidiaries to make the transition. La-Z-Boy's Kincaid Furniture Company Inc. marketed residential wood furniture, such as case goods and solid wood bedroom and dining room outfits, and its Hammary Furniture Company Inc. marketed stationary upholstered furniture, occasional tables, and entertainment centers.

In 1992, La-Z-Boy employees turned out more than 30,000 chairs and sofas a week. The company had manufacturing plants in Canada and seven U.S. cities, and had lisencees in such countries as Australia, Italy, Japan, New Zealand, and Germany. To ensure quality, the company had its own fabric processing center and continued to use kiln-dried lumber as Knabusch and Shoemaker did in the mid-1900s.

In spite of a recession that affected the furniture industry in 1992, La-Z-Boy posted its twelfth consecutive year of record sales and its consolidated sales grew to an all-time high of $684.1 million. The company's consistent sales growth was attributable to its exceptional marketplace presence and its being positioned for profitable growth in an era that promised to reward vision and preparedness. The company introduced 70 percent of its products within the five years ending 1992. La-Z-Boy targeted its new products to America's largest consumer segment, mid-life consumers, plus introduced products geared toward single people with and without dependents. The company also took into consideration cultural diversity and mobility, which affect buying decisions.

Because of unsurpassed brand recognition in their market, integrity and responsible business behavior, and the ability to diversify in response to changing consumer tastes, the La-Z-Boy brand should maintain its strong sales and reputation well into the future.

Further Reading:

Buchanan, Lee, "La-Z-Boy Transforming Itself from Chair Maker to Complete Living Room Resource," *Furniture/Today,* July 26, 1993, pp. 28–29.

Byrne, John A., "Sittin' and Rockin,'" *Forbes,* November 7, 1983, p. 124.

Cortez, John, "La-Z-Boy Cozies Up to Print," *Advertising Age,* July 22, 1991, p. 41

Jannsen, Albert B., *I Remember When . . . : A History of La-Z-Boy Chair Company,* n.d.

La-Z-Boy Chair Company 1993 Annual Report, Monroe, MI: La-Z-Boy Chair Company, 1993.

—Doris Morris Maxfield

LEGO®

Walk into any American household with children and chances are you'll see, or more likely step on, a brightly colored, knobby Lego System brick. Developed in the late 1950s by the Danish Lego Company, the Lego System construction toy has been manufactured and marketed in the United States since 1973 by Lego Systems, Inc., of Enfield, Connecticut. The versatile toy system now includes 1,500 elements, all of which can fit together to construct just about anything a child can think up. Lego products, including the Duplo line for preschoolers and the Lego Technic line for the older child, can be found in about 70 percent of American and 80 percent of European households with children. Lego Systems, Inc., now controls the top share in the American construction toy segment. Coordinated by the founding company, Lego A/S of Billund, Denmark, the Lego Group now consists of 41 companies that distribute Lego toys in 129 countries around the world. The tremendous global success of the brand can be attributed both to the ingenuity of the Lego toys and to the integrated marketing approach of this essentially one-product corporate group.

Product Origins

The Lego brand of toys traces its origins to 1934 when Ole Kirk Christiansen, a Danish carpenter, decided to extend his carpentry business by manufacturing a line of simple, hand-carved, wooden toys. He called his new toy business "Lego," a contraction of two Danish words "leg godt" meaning "play well." According to toy historian Marvin Kaye, Christiansen sold the toys door to door in the tiny farming community of Billund, Denmark, where he lived. By 1947 the Lego company had grown to a prosperous family firm run by Ole and his four sons. After World War II, when good quality plastic first became widely available for general merchandise, the Lego company added plastic toys to its toy line. In 1949 it introduced Automatic Binding Bricks, a plastic building toy in which the blocks could grip together to prevent toppling towers, always the bane of block builders. These blocks had studs on top, like today's Lego bricks, but their undersides were hollow allowing the blocks to grip only when they were placed directly on top of one another.

Company histories report that the concept for the Lego System was born in 1954 when Ole Kirk Christiansen's son Godtfred was visiting a local toy fair. One of the buyers at the fair complained to Godtfred that all of the toys being offered at the fair were alike and that no toy company offered a comprehensive toy system that would encourage creativity in children. Godtfred felt challenged by this complaint and returned to the Lego toy factory determined to come up with an original toy system. Godtfred Christiansen drew up a list of ten requirements that he felt were essential for a quality line of toys. Among the more obvious criteria, like high quality and good play value, were some particular qualities that would distinguish the future Lego brick system. These included the requirement that the toy line be enjoyable for either sex, that it span a wide age-range, that the system include a large number of components, and that compatible pieces be available for adding on to the parts already purchased. Upon reviewing the some 200 toys already being produced by the Lego toy company, Godtfred Christiansen decided that the Automatic Binding Bricks held the most promise as the basis for an integrated toy system.

The Christiansen family began to experiment with the simple plastic brick in an attempt to improve its construction capabilities. The breakthrough came in 1958 when, after experimenting with a variety of models, the company introduced the now famous Lego brick with studs on top and tubes underneath. This new design not only held the bricks together more firmly, it allowed a child to place the bricks together in any configuration. Three eight-studded bricks could now be combined in 1,060 ways. A child could build tall structures of practically any shape or size, limited only by the number of Lego bricks at his or her disposal. The new bricks, manufactured in bright red, yellow, white, and blue, were an instant success in the European toy market. Now marketed not just as a building set but as a toy "system," the new bricks were packaged with model street signs, cars, and trucks, allowing children to create whole city blocks instead of just one building. The great virtue of the Lego system was that it was infinitely expandable. From the start, a parent could purchase a set with bricks and accessories and then be encouraged to purchase limitless numbers of add-on sets. The small Billund toy factory was deluged with orders. By 1960 all other toy production at the Lego plant was dropped in favor of the small plastic brick.

Product Development

The basic Lego brick has remained virtually unchanged since its introduction in 1958. The mechanical properties of the bricks have been improved so that they fit together more easily, but a brick made in 1958 will still join with one made in 1994. Many

AT A GLANCE

Lego brand of construction toy invented in 1958 by Godtfred Christiansen of Lego Company (now Lego A/S), Billund, Denmark; brand licensed to Samsonite Corporation for U.S. and Canadian sales, 1961; Samsonite cedes license, and American sales company, Lego Systems, Inc., was founded, 1973.

Performance: *Market share*—80% of plastic construction toy category. *Sales*—$206.5 million.

Major competitor: Tyco Toys, Inc.'s Super Blocks.

Advertising: *Agency*—Lintas, New York, 1976—. *Major campaign*—For Lego System: Lego Maniac theme; for Lego Technic: "The Ultimate Building Machine"; for Duplo: "Doin' it with Duplo."

Addresses: *Parent company (USA)*—Lego Systems, Inc., 555 Taylor Rd., Enfield, CT, 06082; phone: (203) 749-2291; fax: (203) 749-9096. *Ultimate parent company*—Lego System A/S, Aastveg Dk-7190, Billund, Denmark; phone: 45-5-33-11-88.

new components have been added to the Lego system over the past 40 years, with the basic requirement that all new products be compatible with all other elements of the system. In the 1970s the Lego System sets had begun to be organized around specific themes, including trains, space, and airplanes. By the 1990s these theme sets had evolved into eight product lines: Basic, Town, Space, Castle, Pirates, Boats, Trains, and Model Team. Each product line includes many different sets with components geared to each specific theme but nonetheless compatible with the components of all the other product lines. A child could decide to have a knight play on the space shuttle, or a pirate ride a train, and all the pieces would fit together. Although these basic product lines remain relatively constant, some 30 percent to 40 percent of sets in each line are new each year. In 1994, for instance, 80 of the 203 Lego sets on the market are new. This constant renewal of the product has been important in maintaining the company's top position in the construction toy segment.

One of Godtfred Christiansen's original principles for his toy system was that it be attractive to both boys and girls. Although girls have always formed a share of the Lego market, market research conducted in the early 1990s revealed that the majority of Lego sets were being bought for boys. In 1992 Lego Systems, Inc., brought out a new, specifically girl-oriented segment of their play theme line. Called Paradisa, the main feature of the new line was color. Pink, pastel purple, and turquoise blocks were considered more attractive to girls than the traditional primary colors of the Lego bricks. According to David Lafrennie, Lego System's public relations manager, the Paradisa line was very successful and a new girls product is in place for 1994.

Another of Godtfred Christiansen's principles was that the toy system be fun for all ages. Lego toys are designed for a fairly broad age range (3-16 years), but the Christiansen's felt they could strengthen either extreme of this range by adding lines specifically developed for preschoolers and the older child. In 1969 Duplo Toys were introduced. Using the same principle of the interlocking brick as the Lego System, Duplo blocks are larger and more easily manipulated by small hands but can also be combined with the smaller Lego bricks as the child grows. Lego Technic, introduced in 1977, was designed to bolster the other end of the age range and bring Lego play into the teen years. With Lego Technic, the older child (age 7-16) can build technically realistic models using the gears, pulleys, beams, and other special pieces found in Lego Technic sets.

International and American Management

Since its humble beginnings in a small carpentry shop in Billund, Denmark, the Lego Company, later known as the Lego Group, has grown into a collection of 41 companies on 6 continents. The group includes: the coordinating company Lego A/S, still headquartered in the small town of Billund; and national sales companies in 15 European countries, the United States, Canada, Australia, Brazil, Singapore, South Korea, and Japan. The Lego System is sold in 125 countries around the world through a further series of local distributors. The production of Lego products begins in three tooling factories in Switzerland and Germany where molds with tolerances of a mere 5/1000 of an inch are produced and shipped to manufacturing plants in Denmark, the United States, South Korea, Brazil, and Switzerland.

American distribution of Lego products began in 1961 when the giant Samsonite Corporation acquired the American and Canadian license to manufacture and distribute the popular Danish construction toy. Samsonite was looking to diversify its growing company and felt that its experience in plastics and retailing would mesh with the plastic toy industry. Samsonite opened plants in Stratford, Ontario, and Loveland, Colorado, to manufacture Lego bricks and set up a separate sales force to market the product. Although they managed to sell a respectable $5 million in Lego products annually, the sales figures never matched the huge success that Lego was having in the European market. "Our managerial expertise was better suited to consumer durables than to toys, so we eased out of the toy business," a Samsonite executive was quoted as saying in a 1976 *Business Week* article. Samsonite gave up its Lego System license in 1973. The Lego Group moved in immediately, establishing an American sales company, Lego Systems, Inc., in Brookfield, Connecticut. In only two years, through heavy investment in advertising and promotion, they were able to raise sales levels by more than ten times, and in 1975 they set up a huge 14-acre site in Enfield, Connecticut, for manufacture and sales of Lego products. By 1994, U.S. production of Lego and Duplo products was able to provide almost half of all Lego products sold in the United States and Canada.

Marketing and Promotion

The marketing of Lego products is unlike any other item in the toy industry. With 70 percent of American and 80 percent of European households with children already owning a Lego set, the challenge is not to convince parents to buy Lego toys but to convince them to buy more of it. Lego Group companies are essentially single brand companies; this means that brand equity is first and foremost in their marketing plans. With Duplo, Lego System, and Lego Technic, Lego products cover the whole range of childhood from toddler-hood up to the teenage years. The Duplo and Lego Technic ends of this range receive a disproportionate amount of marketing support in an attempt to establish Lego products as an integral and continuous part of the American experience of childhood. According to company president Peter Eio in a 1991 article in *Advertising Age,* Lego Systems' marketers have tended to rely on package-goods marketing theories rather than "typical" toy marketing tactics. This includes year-round advertising campaigns (as opposed to the fourth quarter blitz used by most of the toy industry) and an avoidance of transient fads.

A crucial element in Lego Systems' campaign to build brand equity has been the Lego Road Shows. These traveling exhibits of professionally designed Lego models are displayed in department and toy stores across the country. They are designed to generate excitement about the potential of Lego toys and always include a hands-on area for kids where they can experience the fun of building with a huge variety of Lego bricks. The Lego Builders Club as well as contests have also formed an integral part of the Lego Systems marketing approach. The educational potential of Lego has been developed through the Lego Dacta division of Lego Systems, which is responsible for a program that brings Lego products to schools for use as manipulatives in problem solving.

An invaluable part of the Lego marketing campaign in Europe has been the Legoland Park in Billund, Denmark. Built from some 42 million Lego Bricks, the theme park has attracted more than 20 million visitors. A new Lego Family Park is scheduled to open outside London in 1996, and plans for an American park in Carlsbad, California, are also underway. Although part of a separate profit making company of the Lego Group, the theme parks are worth a lot of hard-sell TV commercials to the marketers of Lego toys.

Competition

Although other construction toys, such as Gabriel Industries' Erector Sets and Playskool's Lincoln Logs, had been popular for some time when Lego entered the American market, by the late 1970s Lego had amassed the lion's share of the construction toy segment. The largest threat to Lego has come not from competing construction toys but from Lego imitators. One of the great virtues of the Lego System is the simplicity of its basic building blocks, but this simplicity has also meant that Lego has been plagued by knock-offs. Compounding the problem is the fact that the patent on the design for the Lego brick expired in 1981, reducing Lego to suits involving trademark infringement on packaging, logos, and accessories but not on the brick design itself. Although any number of small companies have produced imitations of Lego bricks using names like Rego, Dalu, or even Leggo, these small-scale, unpromoted brands have been little more than an irritant to the giant Lego Group. A much greater threat has come from established toy company Tyco Toys, Inc., who in 1984 launched Super Blocks, plastic building blocks that are interchangeable with Lego bricks. Lego Systems promptly sued in both the United States and Hong Kong courts but, after four years of litigation, Lego was unsuccessful in stopping sales of Super Blocks. Tyco's copy-cat product, while never coming close to Lego Systems' sales in the United States, has nonetheless managed to garner some ten percent of U.S. sales of construction toys. Even more importantly, the lower price of Super Blocks has put pressure on Lego Systems to keep their prices at a competitive level.

Advertising

When Lego Systems took over the American distribution of Lego toys in 1973, their very first move was to launch a massive $2 million dollar advertising campaign. At an advertising-to-sales ratio of about 20 percent, this campaign was to exceed anything previously seen in the toy industry, according to *Business Week.* Advertising has since remained the cornerstone of Lego Systems' integrated marketing campaign. Assigned since the 1970s to Lintas, New York, Lego Systems' advertising has taken a double edged approach, touting the fun of the building toy system to kids and the creative value of the versatile bricks to parents. In 1987, threatened with a new competitor in Tyco's Super Blocks, Lego Systems doubled its advertising expenditure to $10 million, according to a 1991 article in *Advertising Age.* They also introduced the tremendously successful Lego Maniac campaign that featured a quintessentially cool teenage boy named Zack (later renamed Jack). The Lego Maniac has remained a key identifying feature of the kid-oriented Lego campaign into the 1990s.

Performance and Future Growth

The redesigned Lego brick system introduced in 1958 was an almost immediate success in Europe. By the early 1970s the company was earning $50 million annually and was responsible for nearly one percent of Denmark's industrial exports, according to toy historian Marvin Kaye. By the late 1980s worldwide sales had soared to about $600 million, much of the increase due to the huge gains made in the United States and Canada. When Lego Systems took over American sales of Lego products from the Samsonite Corporation in 1973, Lego products were selling at a rate of about $5 million annually. Following a massive advertising and marketing campaign accompanied by new packaging and instructions, American sales of Lego toys took off. By 1976 annual retail sales in the United States had reached $100 million, accounting for almost one third of Lego sales worldwide. Sales continued to grow at an average rate of about ten percent a year through the 1980s and early 90s in spite of overall slow growth in the toy industry during this period. This steady growth was capped by an astounding 18 percent increase in 1991, a time when overall toy industry sales rose by only 4 percent. By 1992, annual sales of Lego products in the United States were estimated at $206 million, representing about 80 percent of the plastic construction toy market, according to *Advertising Age.*

Lego Systems' marketers attribute the tremendous success of their construction system to their integrated marketing approach and their emphasis on brand building. "We put all our eggs in one basket, and we market that basket," said Dick Garvey, vice president of marketing, as quoted in a 1992 *Advertising Age* article. But according to *Advertising Age*'s Kate Fitzgerald, some observers say Lego Systems' phenomenal growth cannot last. "Lego's been allowed to grow by leaps and bounds for the past decade mainly because they had a lot of catching up to do. The construction-toy market in the U.S. was wide open." Fitzgerald quoted a toy analyst with Kidder, Peabody & Co. as stating in 1991: "Lego is only now reaching the saturation point in the U.S. and they're going to have a hard time keeping up their momentum." In spite of these predictions, Lego sales have continued to grow in the 1990s. With its very stable base and continually new product lines, it would appear that Lego Systems will continue to dominate the plastic construction toy segment into the 21st century.

Further Reading:

"A Danish Toymaker Puts It Together in the U.S.," *Business Week,* September 6, 1976, pp. 80, 83.

Fitzgerald, Kate, *Advertising Age,* "Lego Builds with Year-Round Ads," June 17, 1991, p. 17; "Lego: Dick Garvey. (The Marketing 100)," July 8, 1992, p. S–20; "Toy Marketers Bank on 'Gross' Sales," November 30, 1992, p. 14; "Toyland's Elusive Goal—Win Over Both Sexes," February 8, 1993, pp. S2, S18.

Kaye, Marvin, *The Story of Monopoly, Silly Putty, Bingo, Twister, Scrabble, Frisbee et cetera,* New York: Stein and Day, 1973, pp. 155–159.

Kestin, Hesh, "Nothing Like a Dane," *Forbes,* November 3, 1986, pp. 145, 148.

"Lego and Tyco Blocks," *New York Times,* November 15, 1988, p. D13 (L).

"Lego Systems Wins U.S. Trademark Suit Against Tyco Toys," *Wall Street Journal,* September 1, 1987, p. 45.

"Lego Taps New Markets, but Keeps an Eye on Its Image," *Brandweek,* February 8, 1993, p.28.

Meeks, Fleming, "So Sue Me," *Forbes,* November 28, 1988, pp. 72, 74.

—Hilary Gopnik

LENNOX®

Lennox is among the world's leading brands of commercial and residential heating and air-conditioning equipment. Lennox products are distributed worldwide through a network of 6,000 independent dealers in 70 different countries. This direct-to-contractor system of distribution is unique among major heating, ventilation, and air conditioning (HVAC) producers. The method has been in place for nearly all of the brand's century-long existence. Although a wide range of HVAC products bear the Lennox name, it is most closely associated with high-efficiency replacement air-conditioning equipment, an area in which it is recognized as a leader in quality. Lennox equipment is manufactured by Lennox Industries Inc., a subsidiary of Lennox International Inc. The Lennox subsidiary generates over half the parent company's revenue. Lennox International's other subsidiaries, Armstrong Air Conditioning Inc. and Heatcraft Inc., also produce well-known brands in the HVAC market.

Brand Origins

Lennox first appeared in Marshalltown, Iowa, toward the very end of the 19th century. At that time, most furnaces were made of cast iron. In 1895 two inventors, Ernest Bryant and Ezra Smith, registered a patent for a coal furnace made of riveted-steel sheet metal. The new design was much more efficient than the standard cast iron models in use. Bryant and Smith hired Dave Lennox, a machine shop operator, to build the manufacturing equipment necessary for production of the furnace. Their financing, however, was insufficient to complete the project, and they could not pay Lennox for his work. For compensation, Lennox took over the patents on the furnace. He then modified the design a bit and took on the task of marketing the furnace, assisted by local businessman W. J. Heald.

Early Marketing Strategy

The unusual and successful method by which Lennox products have always been marketed was established early in the brand's history. Dave Lennox sold the business in 1904 to a group of investors led by D. W. Norris, editor and publisher of the local newspaper. Norris incorporated the business as Lennox Furnace Company, and in its first year of operation, the company managed to sell 600 furnaces. Ownership of Lennox has remained in the hands of the Norris family ever since. Lennox enjoyed phenomenal growth in its first ten years, as Norris concentrated on expanding his customer base. Because he had unlimited access to newspaper advertising space, Norris was able to establish a direct link to dealers and develop methods of distributing, selling, and delivering products directly to authorized dealers.

Technological Advances

It quickly became clear that the Lennox sheet metal furnace was far superior to its cast iron predecessors. After years of use, cast iron furnaces would often warp and then crack, allowing smoke and coal gas to leak into living spaces. The Lennox model eliminated this problem, since it did not warp. By the 1920s, enough Lennox furnaces were being sold to justify opening a warehouse and factory in Syracuse, New York. Another plant, located in Ohio, was purchased as well.

Norris's son, John W. Norris, went to work for the company in 1927. The younger Norris, a graduate of Massachusetts Institute of Technology, proceeded to set up a research department in the back of a company warehouse. There he oversaw the development of several advances in furnace manufacturing. In the mid-1930s, Lennox began building furnaces with blowers. Gas and oil furnaces were also introduced around the same time. John Norris also worked on improving the furnaces' appearance, developing a smooth enameled cabinet in which to house the unit. This was the first time that serious consideration was ever given to a furnace's appearance. Furnaces were also made cleaner and quieter, to accommodate the increasing use of the American basement as a living area. In 1939 Lennox began producing a gas forced-air furnace designed for installation in attics and crawl spaces. These advances in both the performance and aesthetics of furnaces brought about huge changes in the furnace industry, and Lennox was at the forefront of this revolution.

Brand Development

By 1940, Lennox was providing sales support, distribution, and product service to contractors across the entire eastern half of the United States from its facilities in Marshalltown, Syracuse, and Columbus, Ohio. Lennox continued to add manufacturing and sales centers, and by the beginning of World War II, the company was a major force in the heating industry. During the war, Lennox produced heating equipment for military use. When the war ended, demand for Lennox products soared, and several new facilities were added. These included sales centers in Atlanta, Los

AT A GLANCE

Lennox furnaces were first manufactured in 1895 by Dave Lennox of Marshalltown, IA; sold to D. W. Norris and incorporated as Lennox Furnace Company, 1904; company name changed to Lennox Industries Inc., 1955.

Performance: *Sales*—$600 million (estimate).

Major competitor: Carrier; also Trane.

Advertising: *Agency*—Ross Advertising, St. Louis, 1974—. *Major campaign*—actor portraying brand founder Dave Lennox.

Addresses: *Parent company*—Lennox Industries Inc., P.O. Box 799900, Dallas, TX 75379-9900; phone: (214) 497-5000. *Ultimate parent company*—Lennox International Inc. (same address and phone).

Angeles, and Salt Lake City, reflecting the brand's increased presence in the southern and western United States.

The 1950s were a period of rapid growth for Lennox, both in its product line and its geographical scope. Lennox began making residential air conditioning systems in 1952. The first Lennox air conditioner was a water-cooled model weighing in at three tons. That year also marked the creation of a Canadian subsidiary, Lennox Industries (Canada) Ltd., through which the company's products were marketed in that country. The 1950s also brought Lennox into the commercial and industrial heating and cooling markets. The parent company's name was changed to Lennox Industries Inc. in 1955, in order to better reflect the diversity of products being offered under the Lennox name. More new product developments followed before the decade was over. Lennox soon unveiled a commercial air conditioning system that used outside air whenever possible, saving substantial amounts of energy. Modular systems, in which each floor of a high-rise building was heated and cooled independently, were also introduced.

International Market

In 1962 Lennox established an International Division. Sales offices and warehouses were opened in the Netherlands and West Germany, enabling the company to sell Lennox equipment throughout most of Western Europe. A production facility was put into operation in Basingstoke, England (outside of London), as well. The Duracurve heat exchanger, which eliminated noise and cracking in gas furnaces, and multizone rooftop units for heating and cooling were among the products added to the Lennox line during the 1960s.

Lennox Industries began to outgrow some of its facilities in the 1970s. To better accommodate its rapid expansion, a gradual migration of the Lennox operation to the Dallas, Texas, area began to take place around that time. In 1977 the company's Marshalltown Research and Development Laboratory was consolidated with its Fort Worth heat pump research facility and moved into a larger, more modern location in Carrollton, Texas. The company's corporate headquarters were relocated from Marshalltown to Dallas the following year.

Product Improvements

A number of technological innovations were developed in the 1970s. In 1978 Lennox completed LOGIC (Lennox Objective Guide to Installation Comparisons), a computer program for the analysis of HVAC designs. A computerized corporate data center was also opened that year. The increased use of computers in the design and testing of Lennox equipment helped sustain its reputation as a high-quality brand. Testing was completed in 1979 on a government contracted home-sized soar-powered air conditioning system, produced in cooperation with Honeywell.

By 1981, the network of authorized Lennox dealers in the United States and Canada had grown to 6,000. Thirty-one warehouses were serving those dealers by that time. That year, Lennox controlled 17 percent of the residential market for gas forced-air furnaces. Lennox also controlled 14 percent of the central electric heating market and 15 percent of the market for unitary air conditioners. Lennox introduced the G14 Pulse furnace in 1982, the first pulse combustion gas furnace to hit the market. The G14 Pulse was a high efficiency forced-air unit, operating with no open flame. Instead, tiny bursts of gas and air were ignited at a rate of about 60 bursts a second. Operating at over 90 percent fuel efficiency (compared with the 55 percent rate common in the industry at that time), the Pulse represented the first major breakthrough in home heating in 20 years. The Pulse furnace has remained one of the industry's more popular models since that time, and in 1992, its tenth anniversary was celebrated with a special open house in Marshalltown. The event included the dedication of the one millionth Pulse furnace built.

Lennox introduced the Power Saver air conditioner in 1984. The Power Saver was the first two-speed air conditioner to achieve a 15.0 Seasonal Energy Efficiency Ratio. In 1986 Lennox International Inc. was formed as a new parent company to Lennox Industries and Heatcraft Inc.,, which Lennox had acquired in 1973. The following year, Lennox began offering limited lifetime warranties on its Pulse furnaces, sparking a wave of comparable offers among its competitors. Aggressive research and marketing continued through the rest of the decade. In 1988 Lennox introduced the first heat pump to use a scroll-compressor. A licensing agreement with Powell Energy Products to develop and market thermal energy storage systems was also reached that year. On the marketing side, a new Lennox sales and distribution center was opened in Wilmington, Massachusetts, in 1989 to serve dealers in New England and eastern New York.

Distribution Programs

During the early 1990s Lennox instituted a Dealer Standards program in which authorized dealers were evaluated according to a list of Lennox guidelines. Consulting and advisory services and support were provided to dealers who qualified by achieving a satisfactory rating. The concept was unique in that it involved the manufacturer imposing standards on its own customers, thereby seeking a high degree of quality and image control at the risk of alienating some loyal dealers. The Dealer Marketing Advisor (DMA) program, later called the Dealer Business Consultant (DBC) program, was first launched in 1986. Dealers in the DBC program were required to make a commitment that the majority of the residential equipment they sold would be Lennox. They also participated in Lennox-sanctioned financing, inventory, and service programs. In return, DBC dealers received marketing and advertising support, as well as access to seminars and other information on how to run their businesses profitably.

In 1991 Lennox tied the DBC program in with a Five Star rating system. Under the system, dealers were evaluated in a variety of areas including customer service, marketing, productivity, financial responsibility, and manufacturer commitment. Those who achieved a five-star rating could qualify for a number of benefits, such as dealer group advertising, individual dealership advertising, truck identification packages, education programs, refrigerant recovery-recycle equipment, and incentive trips. The Five Star rating was made available to all Lennox dealers, regardless of whether they had bought into the DBC program, which cost $10,000. Five Star dealers were required to commit as much as 80 percent of their sales to Lennox, and to meet requirements in a broad range of categories covering everything from management structure to computerized billing systems.

Product Changes

Prior to the 1990s, Lennox products were geared primarily for the replacement market. As the 1990s began, an effort was made to establish more of a presence in the residential new construction market, an area that Lennox had been priced out of in the past. Toward this end, the Diplomat line of central air conditioners, heat pumps, and gas furnaces was introduced in 1993. The Diplomat line was priced considerably lower than most products bearing the Lennox name, making it more competitive for the business of large residential tract developers. Lennox also began developing its Complete Heat System, scheduled to make its debut by the end of 1994. The Complete Heat System is designed to provide both warm air and hot water, combining work usually done by two separate units into one package.

Performance and Future Growth

Because Lennox stock is held entirely by approximately 100 members of the Norris family, there has always been a willingness to invest in long-term research to a degree not possible for many publicly owned companies. This has contributed to Lennox's ability to remain at the cutting edge of HVAC research throughout most of its existence. The fact that its parent company has remained privately owned in an industry where private firms are frequently bought out by huge conglomerates has also meant a high degree of stability in the Lennox brand. The 1990s present an interesting challenge for Lennox, whose position in the replacement market for heating and air conditioning equipment is secure. Now it is entering an area in which it is not a proven contender. Lennox's performance for the remainder of the decade will be determined to a great extent by the success or failure of its attempt to penetrate into the residential new construction market on a large scale.

Further Reading:

Bas, Ed, "Lennox Touts Dealer Standards at 'Great Expectations' Meeting," *Air Conditioning, Heating and Refrigeration News,* May 25, 1992, p. 36.

Consdorf, Arnold P., and Behrens, Charles W., "A Combination of Change and Stability," *Appliance Manufacturer,* November 1977, pp. 40–47.

Duffy, Gordon, " 'Five Star' Dealer Program Evaluates Participants," *Air Conditioning, Heating and Refrigeration News,* February 18, 1991, p. 19.

Duffy, Gordon, "Lennox Gears Up for Expansion in New Home and World Markets," *Air Conditioning, Heating, and Refrigeration News,* January 25, 1993, pp. 102–04.

"Gas Furnaces: Lennox Is Hot in Ownership Now and in the Future," *Appliance Manufacturer,* July 1983, p. 38.

The History of Lennox, Dallas: Lennox International Inc., 1992.

"Lennox Contractor Evaluation Program Continues on Schedule," *Air Conditioning, Heating and Refrigeration News,* February 17, 1992, pp. 16–19.

Lennox International Inc. Profile, Dallas: Lennox International Inc., 1993.

"Lennox Link to Dealers Thrives on Direct Communication," *Appliance Manufacturer,* October 1981, p. 54.

"Lennox Moving Corporate HQ to Dallas Area," *Air Conditioning, Heating, and Refrigeration News,* March 20, 1978, p. 1.

"Lennox Reorganizes," *Air Conditioning, Heating, and Refrigeration News,* April 8, 1991, pp. 1–2.

"The Lennox Story," *Appliance,* February 1982, special section.

"Lennox Will Rate Its Dealers, Cut Those Who Don't Qualify," *Air Conditioning, Heating and Refrigeration News,* February 11, 1991, pp. 24–26.

"Lighting a Fire under Furnace Sales," *Business Week,* October 25, 1982, p. 82.

"Special Section: Lennox International," *Appliance Manufacturer,* August 1990.

"Sun-Powered Home Air Conditioner," *Machine Design,* June 21, 1979, p. 8.

—Robert R. Jacobson

LENOX®

Lenox china, manufactured in the United States for over a century, boasts the kind of handcrafted perfection seldom found in today's fast-paced world. Lenox produces bone china, vitrified china, and Lenox Chinastone, which combines the strength of stoneware with the look of fine china. Lenox, Inc., was also the first china manufacturer in the United States to manufacture fine crystal stemware, through its 1965 acquisition of Bryce Brothers, a crystal glass-blowing company based in Pennsylvania. Lenox crystal is used in U.S. embassies and consulates throughout the world, and Lenox china has graced the White House tables of four U.S. presidents.

Brand Development

Porcelain was being made in China as early as the 9th century A.D. Many centuries later, the Ohio River valley became the first china manufacturing center in the United States. There, manufacturers had easy access to kaolin, the soft, white clay that was essential to the manufacture of china and porcelain. This was one of the earliest industries in the United States.

In 1889 Walter Scott Lenox, of Trenton, New Jersey, founded the Ceramic Art Company with a partner, Jonathan Coxon, Sr. The pair sought to improve the quality of American ceramics. Lenox acquired Coxon's interest in 1894, and in 1906 he formed Lenox, Inc.

Modern technology entered the industry in the twentieth century, with electric potter's wheels for throwing pieces and jiggerblades for speedily shaping them. The glazes on the china were dried by infra-red heat, and pyrometers constantly monitored the heat and humidity levels in the kilns and heating tunnels. Nevertheless, in many ways Lenox china was made in the 1990s just as porcelain and china were made centuries ago. It was very labor-intensive, with skilled artisans working to extremely high standards of quality; in fact, about 70 percent of the cost of china was attributed to skilled labor. Closely guarded secret glaze recipes and clay mixtures, as well as methods of molding, casting, and firing, remained the same.

Lenox china is made of clays that are glazed and fired at extremely high temperatures. The temperatures cause the glaze to fuse with the clay and become non-porous. This china is both delicate and extremely durable. Lenox lines include vitrified china, bone china, and a type of advanced ceramics called Lenox Chinastone. This product is strong enough to be used in the microwave, the dishwasher, and the freezer without damage.

Marketing

In the early 20th century, salesmen traveled around the country with different patterns of china. This sales technique, based on the European system, required purchasers to buy a complete china service. Lenox found that this limited the market, so the company began to offer three-piece place settings known as buffet place settings, individual china pieces, and the traditional five-piece place settings.

The American innovation of bridal registration at department stores also proved beneficial to Lenox. Brides and grooms selected a china pattern, a crystal pattern, and a sterling pattern, leaving the information at the store for friends and relatives who wished to purchase wedding gifts. Stores kept track of the number of pieces purchased to help the couples complete their sets.

Acquisitions

Annual sales of Lenox china approached $1 million by World War II, but it became apparent in the 1960s and 1970s that the company would have to branch out to keep the business successful. In 1965 the company acquired Bryce Brothers, the oldest crystal glass-blowing company in the United States. Bryce Brothers, which was founded in Mt. Pleasant, Pennsylvania, in 1841, became Lenox Crystal.

Lenox acquired Kirk Stieff Company, a manufacturer of fine sterling that had also been used in the White House, in 1991. In the same year, the company acquired Dansk International Designs Ltd. and Gorham Silver, Dansk's wholly owned subsidiary. Gorham was a leading producer of sterling silver in the United States, and Dansk was a leader in the housewares, gift, and tabletop markets.

Responding to the Economy

The recession of the late 1980s caused changes in the buying patterns of Lenox's customers. Many consumers who would not previously have skimped on china chose less expensive patterns, or decided to hold off on purchasing china until their financial situations improved. Competition from abroad was also intense,

AT A GLANCE

Lenox china was founded in 1889 in Trenton, New Jersey, by Walter Scott Lenox; first manufactured with partner Jonathan Coxon, Sr., in the Ceramic Art Company; Walter Lenox acquired sole ownership in 1894; formed Lenox, Inc., in 1906; acquired Bryce Brothers glass-blowing company, which became Lenox Crystal, in 1965; Lenox, Inc. was acquired by Brown-Forman, Inc., in 1983.

Major competitor: Royal Doulton; also Wedgwood, Noritake.

Advertising: Agency—FCB/Leber Katz Partners, New York, NY, 1975—. *Major campaign*—"Lenox. Always Elegant."

Addresses: *Parent company*—Lenox, Inc., 100 Lenox Drive, Lawrenceville, NJ 08648; phone: (609) 896-2800, fax: (609) 896-4268. *Ultimate parent company*—Brown-Forman Inc., 850 Dixie Highway, Louisville, KY 40210; phone: (502) 585-1100.

coming especially from Japan, Taiwan, China, and England. Imports accounted for about half of the U.S. market of housewares, kitchenware, and tableware.

In the early 1990s Lenox introduced its American Home Collection, geared toward the bridal market and others interested in place settings that cost less than $100. After the introduction of this new line, Lenox's market share in the category doubled. The lingering recession and increased competition from abroad also caused Lenox and several other manufacturers to reduce prices on some lines of china. For the first time, Lenox offered a 20 percent promotion on its Classic collection. Four new patterns from its Debut collection featured five-piece place settings for under $100.

Retailing

Lenox china and crystal were sold in fine department stores, china and crystal boutiques, and also in a few retail outlets operated by Lenox, Inc. By the mid-1990s there were several branches of The Lenox Store across the United States, selling Lenox china and crystal as well as products by other company-owned manufacturers, including Gorham, Dansk, and Kirk Stieff. In 1992 Lenox executives changed the name of The Lenox Store in Danbury, Connecticut, to Samuel Kirk and Son and began selling china and crystal brands by other makers.

In the early 1990s Lenox joined many other U.S. companies who were looking for new ways to market their product to a public that was increasingly protective of its spending dollar, teaming up with other companies to experiment with cross-promotion. In one such program, Lenox joined Thomasville Furniture Industries to offer consumers free dinnerware and crystal with the purchase of a dining room set from Thomasville. Thomasville showed increased sales as a result of the promotion, and Lenox got increased advertising as well as the sale of serving pieces.

Advertising

Advertising for Lenox china and crystal has featured straightforward, simple themes, allowing the beauty of the china and crystal to speak for themselves in glossy color pictures. An advertising campaign featured in national magazines in the early 1990s showcased Lenox china's Tuscan Orchard. Underneath the photograph was the Lenox logo, and underneath that were the words "Always Elegant." Lenox had its advertising account under review in the mid-1990s after mutually agreeing to end its long relationship with FCB/Leber Katz Partners in New York City. FCB had advertised Lenox china and crystal since 1975.

Further Reading:

Bernard, Sharyn, "Lenox Builds an American Home," *HFD, The Weekly Home Furnishings Newspaper,* November 15, 1993, p. 55.

"Ceramicware Group: Makers Meet Lead Norms," *HFD, The Weekly Home Furnishings Newspaper,* March 16, 1992, p. 97.

"Gifts, Tableware, Novelties," *Hardware Age,* December 1992, p. 53.

Kehoe, Ann-Margaret, "The Price Is Right: Fine-China Industry Slashes Tags in Battle Over Market Share," *HFD, The Weekly Home Furnishings Newspaper,* June 7, 1993, p. 59.

Kelt, Deborah, "Thomasville Lenox: Double Date," *HFD, The Weekly Home Furnishings Newspaper,* April 19, 1993, p. M2.

"Lenox Fine China—The First Hundred Years," Lawrenceville, New Jersey: Lenox China, 1992.

"Lenox Gets Krafty With Cushioning," *Packaging Digest,* May 1992, p. 34.

Oliver, Brian, "The China Syndrome," *Marketing,* July 11, 1991, pp. 26–27.

"Tabletop Report 1991," *HFD, The Weekly Home Furnishings Newspaper,* September 23, 1991.

—Francine Shonfeld Sherman

LEXUS®

Lexus automobiles represent Toyota Motor Corp.'s first foray into the luxury car market. Introduced during the fall of 1990, Lexus quickly proved to be a formidable contender in the highly competitive American market. Within a year, it threatened the position of Honda Motor Co.'s Acura as the best-selling Japanese luxury car in the United States and outsold Infiniti, Nissan Motor Co.'s entry into the luxury market, two to one. The combined force of Lexus, Infinity, and Acura, all introduced within a six-year period in the later 1980s, took a large percentage of Germany's Mercedes' and BMW's American market share and severely threatened the position of American luxury cars such as Cadillac and Lincoln.

Brand Origins

Soon after Honda's 1985 introduction of its tremendously successful Acura, Toyota Motor Corp. began laying the groundwork for its Lexus Division. Toyota's reasons for moving into the luxury market were twofold: research indicated that Toyota was losing a segment of its economy-car market to luxury car makers; at the same time, rising prices for European luxury cars created an opening for more price-sensitive entries into the market. Lexus sought to create a price-sensitive luxury car that offered a value equal or superior to those produced by European manufacturers.

By 1988 Lexus had developed prototypes for its ES 250 (a front-wheel-drive, five-passenger, four-door sports-luxury sedan) and LS 400 (a larger, five-passenger luxury sedan with a fuel-efficient, 250-horsepower V8 engine capable of reaching speeds over 150 mph). In its development stage, Lexus went to great effort to ensure that its cars would provide a quiet ride, even placing microphones in its early clay prototypes to detect and eliminate any sources of wind noise. Another industry first was an "anti-aging" study aimed at determining the materials that would best allow its cars to "age gracefully and with uniformity." Engineers also created a highly aerodynamic body for the new vehicles, with a .29 drag coefficient, the best in the luxury car class.

Lexus positioned its new line as an exclusive entry into the luxury car market, with sticker prices considerably below those of other luxury car makers. "Without question," a Lexus senior vice president was quoted as saying in *Automotive Industries,* we're going to get a share of the BMW and Mercedes buyers who have been priced out of the market." Lexus sold within the $20,000 to $40,000 price range, while European makers and Cadillac were introducing cars in the over-$50,000 range. To maintain its exclusivity, Lexus planned to sell only 100,000 to 110,000 cars by the year 1992, considerably fewer than Acura's projected sales of 600,000.

Both the Lexus ES 250 and LS 400 went on sale in the United States in September of 1989, well before Japan's Nissan Motor Co. introduced its Infiniti line. (Toyota Canada, Inc.'s Lexus Division introduced the cars the following year in Canada.) Shortly after its introduction, Lexus lowered its projected sales figures for 1990 from 75,000 to 60,000 units, citing the "incredibly competitive" American market as the reason. Despite this competitive market, Lexus fared very well in its first year, outselling Infiniti four to one.

Advertising and Marketing

Following the tradition of European luxury car adverting, Lexus introduced its cars with a series of distinctive, elegant print ads. Copy was filled with exacting discussions of Lexus engineering and attention to detail—factors that assured potential buyers of Lexus's position in the luxury car class. Lexus also developed direct mail campaigns and established a solid dealership network across the United States. Lexus also made its name known among potential buyers by sponsoring a number of theater openings, golf tournaments, and classic car rallies.

In an interesting public relations move, Lexus previewed both the LS 400 and the ES 250 by racing them on the legendary German autobahns, then entering them in a race against the Mercedes-Benz 420SEL and a BMW 7-Series. Lexus won first place in every contest it entered, garnering the much-needed praise and attention of the automotive press. The almost uniformly laudatory quotes were then highlighted in later Lexus campaigns.

Lexus also won high ratings in the coveted J.D. Powers and Associates Customer Satisfaction Index with its bend-over-backwards service program. Viewing customer service as another means to distinguish Lexus from its competitors, the division instituted an educational program on customer service for all its dealers in 1991. Dealers have gone so far as to buy back certain cars from unsatisfied customers or tell others who locked their keys in their Lexuses to break in through a back window and the dealership would replace the window for free. Lexus was also

AT A GLANCE

Lexus brand of luxury automobiles was founded in 1987 by the Lexus Division of Toyota Motor Sales U.S.A., Inc., a subsidiary of Toyota Motor Corp. of Japan. The first Lexus automobile was introduced in 1989.

Performance: *Market share*—16.5% of luxury car class.

Major competitor: Nissan Motor Corp.'s Infiniti line of luxury cars; also Honda Motor Co.'s Honda Motor Co.'s Acura.

Advertising: *Agency*—Team One Advertising, Los Angeles, CA. *Major campaign*—Print ads for Lexus 1994 ES read "Improved, Revised, Refined, Embellished. In a Word, New."

Addresses: *Parent company*—Lexus, 19001 South Western Ave., Torrance, CA 90509-2991; phone: (310) 328-2075. *Ultimate parent company*—Toyota Motor Sales U.S.A., Inc. *Ultimate ultimate parent company*—Toyota Motor Corp., Japan.

rated best in two top Power surveys: the least number of problems reported during the first 90 days and for customer satisfaction after one year, a fact which brought a certain amount of uneasiness to Mercedes-Benz and BMW.

Performance Appraisal and Future Predictions

Lexus sales jumped from 71,000 units in 1991 to 92,890 units in 1992. The growing line of Lexus cars (totaling five in 1992) outsold Infiniti by a narrowed margin of two to one and gained closely on Acura's sales totals. But Lexus's volume grew by only 2.3 percent in 1993, aided by the introduction of the new GS 300 sedan, which sold 19,000 units that year. Sales of the LS 400, Lexus's original top seller, were off by 26.7 percent. Still, Lexus did manage to capture 22.5 percent of the Prestige Luxury Class. Other models, the ES 300, SC 400, and SC 300, were off between ten and 24 percent, yet each managed to capture roughly a 14 percent market share for their respective classes.

Lexus officials predicted a slow entry into the luxury car market. However, the strong performance of its cars disproved conventional wisdom that it would be next to impossible to break into the American prestige market. "We will have to earn the prestige [that European luxury auto manufacturers] enjoy," said a Lexus official in *Automotive News* in 1988, adding that it takes time to establish a prestige line of automobiles. Despite the relatively slow pace of Lexus's growth, Toyota is banking that the line will eventually establish itself as a global brand, able to compete in Europe and Asia against the best of both markets. Judging from its road performance and solid marketing efforts, Lexus seems well poised to capture an even greater market share in the years to come.

Further Reading:

Armstrong, Larry, "Who's the Most Pampered Motorist of All?," *Business Week,* June 10, 1991, p. 90.

DeLorenzo, Matt, "Toyota's Goal for Lexus Far Short of Acura Sales," *Automotive News,* September 26, 1988, p. 1.

Gross, Ken, "First Round to Lexus," *Automotive Industries,* June 1990, p. 21.

Kobe, Gerry, "Lexus," *Automotive Industries,* December 1988, p. 72.

—Maura Troester

LINCOLN®

The Lincoln automobile is manufactured by a division of Ford Motor Company. The Lincoln's image—of quality and luxury—has endured through major social and economic upheavals that affected sales and production, including economic recessions, wars, oil embargoes, and federal mandates setting various types of standards. Upon the Lincoln's introduction, about 30 domestic competitors existed in the market for luxury automobiles; four decades later the number had dwindled to three. Lincoln's success depends largely on its superior performance and comfort. Improvements and refinements in the design of Lincolns have accurately reflected changes in the industry and consumer demand.

Brand Origins

The first Lincoln was introduced in 1920 by Henry Martyn Leland and his associates and was named after Abraham Lincoln, the man whom Leland admired the most. Priced at $6,600, the Lincoln boasted a V-8 engine, but did not have the elegant styling that one day would be associated with the Lincoln name. These first L models included seven-passenger sedans, five-passenger touring cars, town cars, four-passenger coupes, and four-passenger and five-passenger Phaetons. All Lincolns featured lighted instrument boards and electrical systems that used circuit breakers rather than the traditional fuses. An automatic tire pump was driven by the transmission, the connection for which was hidden beneath the driver's seat, while the air hose was carried in the pocket of the driver's door. An emergency kit was provided as standard equipment.

The early Lincolns made their debut in the midst of a declining economy, and they sold poorly. Experiencing financial difficulties, Leland's company was purchased by Ford in 1922 for $8 million. The quality of Leland's engineering was so high, however, that Ford made few changes during the period from 1920 to 1930.

This period is noteworthy for its introduction of the Lincoln "police flyers." These cars were equipped to outpace urban gangsters, who favored luxury cars for their fast getaways during the crime-ridden Prohibition era. The flyers were standard seven-passenger touring cars, with such added features as bulletproof glass and four-wheel brakes. By 1930, the Lincoln lineup included touring cars, roadsters, coupes, sedans, limousines, broughams, town cars, Phaetons, and cabriolets. Prices ranged from $3,000 to $7,200.

Brand Development

The L series stopped production in 1930, and the K series was introduced the following year. The country was in the early stages of the Great Depression, however, and sales were at their lowest levels in a decade. The K series was praised for its improved styling, quality, and reasonable price, and by 1934 sales for Lincolns had begun to rise. While competitors were offering lower-priced models, Lincoln maintained its upscale image. In 1932, two new lines were added, the KB with a new 12-cylinder engine and the KA, a moderately priced version of the 1931 K, which was dropped shortly after its introduction.

In 1936, the Zephyr Continental was introduced as a medium-priced car. The car had a V-12 engine and was heralded chiefly for its streamlined styling. New bodies were also designed for the 1934, 1935, and 1937 models in the K series. In 1937, the last major changes in the K series took place and they were the most dramatic in styling, giving the cars a completely new look with more rounded sedan bodies. By 1939, the Lincoln line included a total of 21 body types, and the K series had been phased out.

The Zephyr Continental series became known as a specialty luxury series notable for its elegance and beautiful styling. The Continental was actually first created in 1938 for the personal use of Henry Ford's son Edsel. Inspired by a trip to Paris, Edsel wanted a car with continental flair and style. The first car was shipped to him at his vacation estate at Hobe Sound, Florida, and it became so popular with his friends that he received 200 orders for the car. The Continental was put into production and introduced in late 1939 as a 1940 model.

During this time, the Lincoln lineup included Zephyrs, Continentals, and Customs as three distinct series that were based on Zephyr lines and features. During World War II, raw materials were scarce, and Lincolns underwent several changes, including new grills made of stainless steel rather than zinc. The Lincoln plant was eventually converted to the production of tanks and jeeps needed for defense.

After the war, the Zephyr and Custom series were dropped, and two new models were added, the standard Lincoln and the Cosmopolitan. Though they differed in appearance, both models featured new V-8 engines. By 1950, however the Cosmopolitan town sedan had been dropped along with the Lincoln convertible.

AT A GLANCE

Lincoln brand of luxury automobiles founded in 1919 by Henry Martyn Leland; brand purchased by Ford Motor Company, 1922.

Performance: *Market share*—1.96% of car and truck category. *Sales*—$4.84 billion.

Major competitor: Cadillac; also BMW, Mercedes Benz, Lexus, Infiniti, and Acura.

Advertising: *Agency*—Young & Rubicam, Detroit, MI, 1979—. *Major campaign*—"Lincoln: What a Luxury Car Should Be."

Addresses: *Parent company*—Ford Motor Company, The American Road, Detroit, MI 48121-1899; phone: (313) 322-3000; fax: (313) 446-5899.

During the 1950s several styling and engineering changes and improvements occurred. In 1951, the new "fin-type" rear fenders with vertical tail lights made their debut. In 1953, Lincoln first offered power assist optional equipment such as power steering, power brakes, and power front seats. In 1955, Lincoln introduced its exclusive new automatic transmission, the Turbo-Drive. During this time, the Continental Mark I, a Lincoln with elegant lines and distinct body targeted to luxury car buyers, emerged. In 1956, Lincoln offered the Continental Mark II as well two new series, the Capri and Premiere series that had new styling, new ventilation systems, and a few engineering changes. But it was the Mark II that captured the public's attention and was heralded as an instant classic by the media. The Mark II, a sporty personal luxury car of unique coachwork, high quality, and style, was 50 percent more expensive at $10,000 than the most expensive luxury model offered by Lincoln's major competitor.

In 1957, new features included power vent windows, electric door locks, and new six-way power seats. The following year, the Continental Mark II was discontinued and a new top-of-the-line Mark III series was introduced. These new models looked larger as a result of new styling and featured completely revised instrument panels.

In 1961, the Continental again sparked a styling revolution with its sleek design that paved the way for Lincoln's increasing success in the luxury field to rival its major competitor, Cadillac. The shorter, lower model started a trend toward cleaner, more functional design with less chrome, bare sides, and simple design.

In 1970, the Continental received its first new body change in nearly ten years. The new design was more efficient to manufacture and weighed nearly 300 pounds less than the standard Lincoln. In 1971, the Lincoln Town Car, known as the "Golden Anniversary Continental" was introduced. In 1972, the new Mark IV debuted with a smooth, sleek design that helped Lincoln to reach unprecedented sales levels.

The 1973 Lincolns incorporated new federally mandated front and rear bumpers, which provided added protection in low speed collisions. During this time, a Town Car was presented as a gift by President Richard Nixon to Soviet Party Secretary Brezhnev during a state visit. Also in 1973, a special silver "moonroof" Mark IV was first marketed, featuring a special glass panel in the roof made of glass with a silver reflective surface designed to complement the car's silver exterior and interior. This was the first of the series of special decor options for which Lincoln was to become known during this decade. In addition, an anti-theft alarm system was added, because the Mark IV had earned the dubious distinction of being one of the more frequently stolen cars in the country's urban areas.

Despite the Arab oil embargo of the early 1970s, which caused economic recession and an oil crisis, Lincoln experienced its third best production year in its history in 1974. All Lincoln models were subsequently fitted with new federally mandated catalytic converters, which required the use of unleaded gasoline. In 1977, Lincoln introduced the compact Versailles and the new Mark V, both of which were offered in Designer Edition models inspired by the leading designers of the day: Givenchy, Cartier, Blass, and Pucci. This year also marked Lincoln's best year of production in history.

In 1978, the Ford Motor Company celebrated its 75th anniversary with a Diamond Jubilee Edition of the Mark V, priced at about $8,000. However, in response to continuing government regulations, economic recession, inflation, rising interest rates, and an energy crises, Lincoln's competitors were in the process of downsizing their cars. Consumers demanded smaller, more fuel-efficient transportation. Lincoln soon followed suit, discontinuing its line of full-sized luxury cars and offering a the Collector Series to commemorate the event. Nevertheless, Lincoln refused to lower its quality standards and maintained its position of producing elegant cars, now with many innovations allowed by the advent of the microchip.

In 1980, the Versailles was dropped, and smaller, lighter Lincolns were introduced. The 1980 models had the first automatic overdrive transmissions made in America, as well as some new electronic options that included an on-board computer. In this year, the first and only four-door Mark sedan was marketed in the Mark VI series. In 1982, the Continental was also downsized.

A 1994 Lincoln Town Car.

In 1984, the Mark VII luxury coupe was introduced with a cockpit-like, wraparound instrument panel, the industry's first electronic air suspension system that used air springs and was controlled by an on-board microcomputer, and the first fully integrated flush-mounted road lighting system which featured European-style halogen headlamps. The following year, a redesigned Town Car was introduced with rounder, softer body and with anti-lock brakes. Multiport electronic fuel injection was eventually added to the 5.0 liter V-8 engine, as was Ford's JBL sound system as an option. At the same time, anti-lock brakes were made standard on all Continental and Mark VII models. The 1988 Continental featured a wholly revised design and was the first front-wheel drive Lincoln. *Motor Trend* magazine called it the "best engineered, best-driving Lincoln ever built". In 1989, dual air bags were made standard equipment on Continentals, one of the first dual applications offered in any American car.

Despite the economic recession of the early 1990s, Lincoln continued to improve the comfort and handling of its cars. The 1994 Town car included dual air bags, an anti-theft alarm system, hands-free cellular phone, and programmable memory seat in the Signature Series. The 1994 Continental featured style changes in grillework and bumpers, and additional features as solar-tinted glass and CFC-free air-conditioning. The 1994 Mark VIII offered the highest level of standard equipment ever available on a Lincoln, including such features as remote keyless entry and memory outside mirrors. Options included such features as voice-activated cellular telephone, trunk-mounted CD changer, electronic traction assist, and chrome directional wheels.

Advertising and Marketing

From its earliest days, the message that Lincoln sought to convey to potential buyers was that the car was a unique part of an exciting lifestyle. From the 1920s to the 1940s, typical ads were hand drawn depictions of Lincolns in settings that represented excitement, including river views and ski slopes. Starting in the 1940s, photographs were used to convey a message of affluence and elegance. The cars were depicted in fields of green trees and grass, or parked in front of expensive homes, often with well-dressed couples standing near the car.

Until the 1970s, print ads prevailed as television commercials were relatively expensive. Promotional efforts included offering Lincoln cars free of charge as props for TV shows and films, motorsports competitions, auto shows, and showroom catalogs.

Lincoln's chief marketing strategy remained its price structure, which was aimed at high income families. In the 1920s, a Lincoln cost almost $7,000, and 70 years later a Lincoln could be purchased for $25,000 to $40,000. The Town Car remained the least expensive and most popular Lincoln, selling nearly twice as many as the Continental and Mark models combined.

Performance Appraisal

Almost since its inception, Lincoln has placed second in luxury car sales to its chief domestic rival and market leader, General Motors' Cadillac. Towards the end of the twentieth century, however, Lincoln sales began to catch up, and by the spring of 1990 Lincoln had actually tied Cadillac in sales for the first time in its history. Economic conditions again adversely affected luxury car sales in 1993, and sales of Continentals and Mark VIII were so disappointing during this time that Ford idled its luxury car assembly plant in Michigan. Despite slow economies and social conflicts, Ford expected that its Lincolns would continue to provide owners with the elegance, style, and engineering innovations that prompted and maintained its success.

Further Reading:

Bonsall, Thomas E., *The Lincoln Motorcar: The Complete History of an American Classic,* Baltimore: Stony Run Publishing, Inc., 1992.

Cook, William J., and John Walcott, "Driving in the Lap of Luxury," *U.S. News & World Report,* January 8, 1990, pp. 59–62.

Ford Motor Company Annual Report, Detroit, MI: Ford Motor Company, 1992.

"Ford Motor to Idle a Luxury-Car Plant Amid Sluggish Sales," *Wall Street Journal,* August 13, 1993, p. C16.

—Dorothy Kroll

LINCOLN LOGS®

Lincoln Logs are one of America's oldest and best known brand name toys. Like Erector sets, Tinkertoys, Legos, and other construction toy sets, Lincoln Logs were designed to provide hours of creative diversion for children from young to old. Nonetheless, they are unique in the field for their simplicity of design and ease of manipulation. There is good reason for this. Lincoln Logs were invented by architect John Lloyd Wright, whose father, famous American architect Frank Lloyd Wright, was renowned for his original designs merging form and function. Surprisingly enough, Wright's sets of notched brown- and green-colored pine lengths, instantly reminiscent of pioneer log cabins, owe more to Japanese than American or European design. Today Lincoln Logs are owned by Playskool, a subsidiary of Hasbro, Inc., the $2.5 billion world leader in toy and game manufacturing and marketing. Although the perennially popular product—recently refurbished with plastic accessory pieces—contributes only a fraction of Hasbro's overall revenues, the Lincoln Log brand is highly valued, an indisputable and irreplaceable classic of the toy industry.

Rooted in American History, Allied with Architectural Genius

Lincoln Logs belong to the "Golden Age of Toys," an era stretching from about 1860 to 1930 that produced the Flexible Flyer sled, Madame Alexander dolls, Lionel trains, Crayola crayons, Tinkertoys, Buddy L trucks, and Kingsbury airplanes. To be sure, there were basic construction toys long before Lincoln Logs, beginning with wood or stone blocks or bricks. However, Wright's wooden sets were the first to gain wide popularity; in fact, they were among the first in the entire toy industry to become a clear and sustained hit with kids.

During his childhood, John Lloyd Wright was surrounded by building blocks and mechanical toys of all sizes and shapes. Wright's parents, in fact, were strong believers in the concepts of play, learning, and analytical thinking championed by German educator and kindergarten originator Friedrich Froebel (1782-1852). In Froebel's view, play pieces that could be assembled, taken apart, and reassembled, were central to creative development in the child. As a young adult who had thrived on such an education, Wright was naturally drawn to the study of architecture and worked for his father on a variety of projects. Early on he also began to experiment with toy block construction design. The elder Wright used some of his son's early blocks for an exhibition of his own designs at the Chicago Architecture Club in 1914.

In 1917 John went to Japan and served as chief assistant to his father, who was commissioned to design Tokyo's Imperial Hotel. The earthquake-proof foundation Frank Lloyd Wright created consisted of an interlocking beam system called "floating cantilever construction." It was during this trip to Japan that John, while helping his father test the innovative design, developed the idea for Lincoln Logs. Following a disagreement, John ended his apprenticeship with his father and went back to Chicago to begin making his living designing wooden toys. Soon Marshall Field & Company was distributing his "Redsquare" toys, which included construction blocks, jigsawed birds, chess pieces, and animals. But as Sally Anderson Chapell wrote, the inventor's "most successful toy, by far, was his log cabin construction set, Lincoln Logs," which went on the market in 1918.

A Toy for the Times

Wright promoted his Lincoln Logs with the slogan "the spirit of America" and packaged his sets in colorful boxes featuring a log cabin and a prominent portrait of Lincoln on the front. His product arrived as the era of the American frontier was ending and the pastoral life was being romanticized anew. Companies such as L.L. Bean were selling outdoor and sporting goods and organizations such as the Boy Scouts of America and the Camp Fire Girls were being established. Less than a decade earlier, the nation had celebrated the 100th birthday of President Lincoln and memorialized the log cabin in which he was born. According to Erin Cho in *History Today,* the name Lincoln Logs "captures the sentiments of this period," the interest in preserving the mystique of the pioneer life along with a growing sense of prewar patriotism. Notwithstanding claims that Wright's Lincoln Logs were just a modernized version of Joel Ellis's 1866 "Log Cabin Playhouse" toy, there was an undeniable beauty and symmetry to Wright's creation. And, of course, there was the august and indelible imprint of the brand itself, Lincoln Logs.

He Had It Right the First Time

Wright returned to architecture in 1924 but continued to design and market toys as well. Years later, in 1950, he began to sell Wright Blocks using a design he had patented in 1933 and again in 1949. Rectilinear and cross-grooved, the interlocking block set

AT A GLANCE

Lincoln Logs brand founded in 1918 in Chicago, IL, by J. L. Wright Company owner John Lloyd Wright; J. L. Wright Company purchased by Playskool Manufacturing Company, 1943; Playskool acquired by Milton Bradley Company, 1968; Milton Bradley merged with Hasbro Industries, 1984; Hasbro eventually renamed Hasbro, Inc.

Performance: *Sales*—Estimated $100 million (less than 5% of Hasbro's total revenues).

Major competitor: Lego brand toys.

Advertising: *Agency*—Kidvertisers, New York, NY.

Addresses: *Parent company*—Hasbro, Inc., 1027 Newport Ave., Pawtucket, RI 02862-1059; phone: (401) 727-5000; fax: (401) 727-5779.

pushed children to be creative. According to Chapell, "The Wright Blocks were not only more abstract and modern than Lincoln Logs, but they were also more versatile and could be assembled into lighter, more open structures. Nevertheless, they failed to catch the public's fancy to the same extent as their log cabin predecessors and were not produced in any great quantity." Also in the 1950s Wright developed an even more complex interlocking construction set that included blocks and flat wood strips and allowed for the creation of everything from houses to bridges to skyscrapers. Unfortunately, he was unable to successfully launch this product, which he named the Timber Toy.

The Competition

Predating Lincoln Logs by four years were Tinkertoy construction sets. The sets consisted of colored wooden sticks, connecting pieces, moving parts, wheels, and, later, plastic pieces. By the baby boom years of 1946 to 1964, the Tinkertoy company was hailing its namesake as the "world's favorite construction set." Another construction toy competitor, Lego, came on the scene in the 1930s and has since invaded half of all American homes. However much these two rivals have succeeded over the years (actually, Tinkertoy is no longer a rival but an ally within the Hasbro fold), neither Tinkertoy nor Lego directly mimicked the unique Lincoln Logs design. One product, though, did directly imitate Lincoln Logs: Halsam's Square American Logs, first developed in 1934. "Although Halsam's Logs were marketed for years," wrote Cho, "they were always in the shadow of Lincoln Logs, children even referred to these so called 'improved' logs by their predecessor's name." Thus was the originality and appeal of Wright's product proven.

Surviving in the Age of Acquisitions and Electronics

The J. L. Wright Company merged with Playskool in 1943. Lincoln Logs fit right in and, like many of the Playskool toys, have hardly changed since they first came on the market. Playskool, the offspring of a Milwaukee lumber company that two former teachers formed as the Playskool Institute in the 1920s, was by 1935 producing 40 different toys. Two employees bought out the Institute from the lumber company and formed Playskool Manufacturing Company in the 1940s. The Chicago-based company focused on pre-school and grade school children's toys.

Milton Bradley Company, maker of toys, games, and educational teaching aids, acquired Playskool in 1968. In the late 1970s and early 1980s Milton Bradley boasted the largest research and development department in the toy industry. The company's hot sellers, however, were electronic items. Classic toys like Lincoln Logs were simply not receiving the big marketing dollars of the day. The advertising budget of $22.5 million in 1978 and $27 million in 1979 was targeted on the electronic and promotional toys. In 1984 Milton Bradley introduced Robotix, a construction toy that was motorized and operated by remote control. The same year, Milton Bradley merged with Hasbro Industries and was renamed Hasbro Bradley Inc. Lincoln Logs seemed destined for obscurity.

Obscurity, though, was not to be. With the year 1984 came heightened volatility in the toy industry. Sales of non-electronic toys, including those of Lincoln Logs, experienced some of the best gains of the decade. The early 1980s classic toy revival, according to Eugene Gilligan, was brought on in part by the country's conservative climate. But no doubt more significantly, baby boomer parents were now interested in purchasing Lincoln Logs and other classic toys that they had played with during their own childhoods. In addition to updating the look of these toys, manufacturers were using devices such as toys clubs to promote the old favorites.

Collectibility: The Sign of a Classic

Construction toys, with their numerous parts, have not been a popular collector item because of the difficulty in determining if the set is complete. But Lincoln Logs has made the leap into collectibility with citations about the toy appearing in collectors books. Joseph Doucette and C. L. Collins wrote in 1981 that "while speculating on the future collectibility of construction sets is difficult . . . some collectors are now looking for early Lincoln Logs sets in good condition." In 1990 an architectural toy exhibition in Canada featured building toys including Lincoln Logs. According to Pilar Viladas, "Architectural toys such as [Lincoln Logs, Erector sets, or Tinkertoys] have a fascinating history—one that reflects the development of modern Western architecture."

Production, Pricing, and Future Prospects

Lincoln Logs are made on a one-of-a-kind machine in Walla Walla, Washington. Each year Playskool uses 2.2 million board feet of Ponderosa pine to produce the logs, the same pine that is used to manufacture Playskool's wooden blocks.

In April of 1993 Cho wrote that "today, up to a million American consumers buy a set of Lincoln Logs for their children every year, suggesting that the values and ideals this toy represents are still important in an increasingly technological world." Even so, Hasbro decided to modernize Lincoln Logs in 1993. A company release promised that "the new Lincoln Logs will have a lighter, more contemporary wood stain for lasting durability and good looks. Also each Lincoln Logs set now includes chunky plastic accessory pieces that add color and make building structures easier and more satisfying for pre-schoolers." The four new Lincoln Logs sets—playground, house, fort, and village—contain five different log sizes. Because the interlocking system is the same, the sets can be combined with any other Lincoln set, old or new. The price ranges from $10 to $30, with additional log packs priced at four dollars. In the 1992 Hasbro Annual Report, Lincoln Logs were referred to as one of the Playskool toys that has "retained their classic appeal from generation to generation." The company expected the updated Lincoln Logs to sell as well as their

1992 update of the Tinkertoy.

Almost no one would argue with Gil Asakawa and Leland Rucker's assertion in *The Toy Book* that Lincoln Logs are "one of the most instantly identifiable young children's toys." That this has remained true year in and year out is tribute to the brilliance of the product's inventor. Although overshadowed throughout his life by the towering reputation of his father, John Lloyd Wright can nonetheless claim to have created a classic, however humble, that is no less enduring than Frank Lloyd Wright's architectural masterpieces.

Further Reading:

Asakawa, Gil and Leland Rucker, *The Toy Book,* New York: Alfred A. Knopf, 1992, pp. 17–22, 144–45.

Chapell, Sally Anderson, *John Lloyd Wright: Architecture and Design,* Chicago: Chicago Historical Society, 1982.

Cho, Erin, "Lincoln Logs: Toying with the Frontier Myth," *History Today,* April 1993, pp. 31–34.

Davis, Bob, "Hasbro Bradley Scores with Its 'Terror' Toys, Adroit Licensing Plans," *Wall Street Journal,* December 13, 1984, pp. 1, 23.

Doucette, Joseph and C. L. Collins, "Construction Sets," *Collecting Antique Toys: A Practical Guide,* New York: Macmillan Publishing Co., 1981, pp. 105–06.

Gilligan, Eugene, "Classic Toys Sport New Look," *Playthings,* July 1982, pp. 34, 36, 60.

Ketchem, William C., Jr., "Construction Toys," *Collecting Toys: For Fun and Profit,* Tucson: HP Books, 1985, p. 47.

Levy, Richard C., and Ronald O. Weingartner, "The First Megahits," *Inside Santa's Workshop: How Inventors Develop, Sell, and Cash in on Their Ideas,* New York: Henry Holt & Company, 1990, pp. 54–56.

Viladas, Pilar, "Buildings in a Box," *House & Garden,* December 1990, p. 54.

—Jay P. Pederson

LIONEL®

Lionel Trains, Inc. is the oldest manufacturer of electric model trains in the United States. The company has been providing high quality toy trains for over 90 years. The trains produced by Lionel are considered by many to be an American institution. Whether located in home basements, hobby clubs, or large public displays, Lionel trains have fascinated millions of American children and adults. Recent marketing and manufacturing strategies confirm the brand's leadership in the electric model train market.

Brand Origins

The founder of Lionel, Joshua Lionel Cowen, was born in New York City in 1877. His aptitude for electrical devices became apparent at an early age. After dropping out of Columbia University, Cowen was hired as an assembler at an electric lamp factory, where he conducted electrical experiments after hours. In 1898 Cowen developed a new kind of dry cell battery, and he also developed a fuse for igniting magnesium powder for photographers. This invention led to a contract with the U.S. Navy for production of fuses for exploding land mines. Cowen used the $12,000 from the Navy contract to open the Lionel Manufacturing Company in New York in September of 1900. The small shop produced low voltage electrical motors and other articles.

In 1901 Cowen began experimenting with small electrical motors and model scale tram cars. Although the cars were originally designed as attention-getting devices for store window displays, the train cars soon became popular with stores and individual customers. By 1903 Cowen had published the first Lionel train catalog which featured a 2 7/8-inch gauge of track. The gauge refers to the width between the rails of track. The 1903 catalog highlighted a steel reproduction of a Baltimore and Ohio R.R. locomotive, which was powered by a wet cell battery. The locomotive made by Lionel in 1903 began the demand in this country for small scale models of real trains. These first locomotives were complemented by a steel derrick car and a gondola car.

Early Marketing Strategy

Cowen soon grasped the notion of a larger market for model scale trains. He began by experimenting with smaller cars and track sizes. Cowen chose the unusual size of 2 1/8 inches for the space between the rails of the new track. Consequently he issued a train that did not fit into gauge sizes 1, 2, or 3. The 2 1/8 inches between the three rails soon became widespread in the United States, and was known as "standard gauge." In 1905 Cowen hired a young engineer named Mario Caruso, who stayed with the company for 40 years and later became director of manufacturing for Lionel. The two men worked well together: Cowen managed the marketing of the trains while Caruso strictly supervised the manufacturing plants. By 1910 the company had outgrown its New York manufacturing facilities and moved to a new factory in New Haven, Connecticut. The company changed facilities again in 1924 when it moved from New Haven to Irvington, New Jersey. Lionel trains were manufactured at the New Jersey plant until the late 1960s when the operation was moved to Mt. Clemens, Michigan.

In 1915 Lionel brought out a specialized line of "O" gauge locomotives and railcars. Lionel's largest competitor, Ives Trains, had introduced the "O" gauge train in 1910. These trains were smaller (1 1/4 inches between the rails) than the standard gauge. Within five years Lionel was manufacturing at least 17 sets of different trains in "standard gauge" (with three rails), and nine sets in the "O" gauge (two rails). In 1918 the company changed its name from the Lionel Manufacturing Company to the Lionel Corporation. The 1920s were a successful period for the firm—several lines of highly authentic trains were introduced. By the late 1920s, the company was producing an extensive assortment of model locomotives and train cars from which consumers could choose.

In 1928 Lionel, with the model train company American Flyer Trains, bought Ives Trains. During 1929 and 1930 American Flyer and Lionel supplied some parts for the Ives trains. At the end of 1930 Lionel bought American Flyer's share of Ives, becoming the exclusive producer of Ives trains. The Ives plant in Bridgeport, Connecticut, was shut down and the operations moved to Lionel's facilities in New Jersey. After producing trains under the Ives trademark in 1932 and 1933, the Ives name and product catalog were dropped in 1933. During this time Lionel's lowest priced trains were called Lionel-Ives. In 1934 these trains were given the name Lionel Jr., which ended the use of the Ives name on model railroad items.

Product Changes

Lionel was immune to the effects of the economic depression of the 1930s. In response to market demand for lower prices, Lionel sharply reduced its "standard gauge" line of trains. Instead

AT A GLANCE

Lionel brand of model trains founded in New York, NY, by Joshua Lionel Cowen, when he founded the Lionel Manufacturing Company; company name changed to The Lionel Corporation in 1918; company changed hands several times during the 1960s; brand sold to General Mills, Inc. in 1969, and production was taken over by a subsidiary, Fundimensions; Lionel became a division of Kenner-Parker Toys Inc., another General Mills subsidiary, in 1985; brand sold to group head by Richard Kughn and Lionel Trains, Inc. formed in 1969.

Performance: *Market share*—Top share of the toy train and accessories market. *Sales*—$50 million.

Advertising: *Agency*—Young & Rubicam Inc., Detroit, MI; also Goldberg, Moser, O'Neill, San Francisco, CA. *Major campaign*—"Experience the Magic," (for hobbyists, Young & Rubicam); also "The World of Little Choo Choo," (for preschool, Goldberg, Moser, O'Neill).

Addresses: *Parent company*—Lionel Trains, Inc., 50625 Richard W. Blvd., Chesterfield, MI, 48051; phone: (810) 949-4100; fax: (810) 949-3340.

the company focused on the smaller "O" gauge line. An interesting marketing development occurred in 1934 when Lionel collaborated with the Walt Disney Company to produce the Mickey Mouse hand car. The toy was a single car that was wound by hand. The item was an immediate success, selling at an affordable one dollar. The following year a Santa Claus hand car was introduced, and in 1936 the Donald Duck and Peter Rabbit "chick mobiles" were jointly marketed. Another competitively priced item was the Mickey Mouse Circus Train. The tin locomotive and three cars featured Mickey at the helm of the engine, and a crowd of Disney characters in the passenger cars. The set featured a cardboard circus as a backdrop.

In 1937, when the company held its first public stock offering, Lionel produced an estimated 40,000 model train engines, 1.2 million railcars, and well over a million sets of track. The company employed more than 1,000 people in its New Jersey facility. In 1939 Lionel stopped production of the "standard gauge" three rail train track, and produced only the "O" gauge.

In 1942 the production of trains was halted for the remainder of World War II so that Lionel could manufacture communications and navigational equipment for the war effort. When production resumed after the war, Lawrence Cowen, son of Joshua Lionel Cowen, assumed the presidency of the company. The red, yellow, and silver Santa Fe Diesel, the all-time top selling train engine, was unveiled in 1948.

By 1953 the company had celebrated fifty years in the toy business and production was at peak levels. Over 2,000 people were employed by the firm and Lionel was considered the largest toy manufacturer in the world. At the time, Lionel was the only toy company listed on the New York Stock Exchange. However, during the mid-1950s the company began to lose money, after Lawrence Cowen had unsuccessfully tried to diversify the company's holdings. A stereo camera was produced, and the Airex Corporation, makers of fishing reels, was bought; both ventures failed to raise profits. Also at this time, production at Lionel was disrupted or halted by labor disputes and strikes at the New Jersey plant. During the late 1950s the public's fascination with toy trains was starting to decrease. The country was in a deep recession, and Lionel sales figures reflected the national economy. In 1958 the company posted its first yearly loss since the depression. Sales figures that year totaled $14.5 million with a total loss of $470,000.

Lionel Changes Hands

In 1959 Joshua Cowen's great nephew, the politically active attorney Roy Cohn, headed a group that purchased control of the company. Cohn began acquiring electronics firms in hope of gaining government missile contracts. He hired a former major general, John Maderis, to head the Lionel Corporation. When sales had not increased by 1962, Maderis was replaced as president by Melvin Raney, but Cohn's scheme to obtain the missile contracts failed. In 1963 he sold the company to financier Victor Muscat. The same year Muscat sold control of the ailing firm to a group headed by A. M. Sonnabend of Hotel Corporation of America. After one year of ownership, Sonnabend died, and Robert Wolfe, a former executive in the toy industry, was named president of the company. Wolfe vowed to consolidate the company and put the focus back on toy production. For the previous ten years Lionel had cut personnel, dropped quality items, expanded into microscopes, science labs, and tape recorders.

In 1965 Joshua Lionel Cowen died at the age of 88. The company he had founded 65 years earlier was continuing to lose money, but was again producing quality model trains. Two years later Lionel purchased their main competitor, American Flyer Trains, from the A.C. Gilbert Company. In 1969 the Lionel Corporation was reorganized under a bankruptcy proceeding, during which the license to produce trains under the Lionel name and all of the manufacturing equipment was sold to the food conglomerate General Mills, Inc. The Lionel Corporation, a shell of what it once was, began evolving into a holding company for toy stores and hobby shops.

In 1970 General Mills moved all of the Lionel manufacturing equipment from New Jersey to Mt. Clemens, Michigan, and Fundimensions, a subsidiary of General Mills, assumed production of Lionel trains. During the 1970s Lionel trains experienced steady growth under Fundimensions. In 1983 General Mills decided to consolidate its toy manufacturing operations and moved Fundimensions, Kenner Toys, and Parker Brothers Games to Mexico. In 1985 Lionel became a division of Kenner-Parker Toys Inc., which was a spin-off company of General Mills non-food division. At that time General Mills moved Lionel manufacturing operations back to Mt. Clemens. In April of 1986, Richard Kughn, a Detroit-area real estate developer and avid model railroad fan, formed a corporation that purchased Lionel from General Mills. Incorporated as Lionel Trains, Inc., the operation continues to be based in Chesterfield, Michigan, where, under the direction of Richard Kughn sales figures have risen steadily.

Brand Development

Since the inception of the Lionel brand of model trains, the product has gone through a number of important changes. The selection in the 1906 company catalog consisted of a steam type locomotive with or without a tender—a car attached to the locomotive used for carrying coal and water. Other items included two electric trolley cars, two passenger cars, and seven freight cars. The freight cars consisted of an oil tank, coal car, cattle car, box car, gondola, and caboose. The expanded 1910 catalog indicated Lionel's success. Eleven different trolley cars were offered, four with twin motors to pull different passenger cars. There were several types of locomotives from which to choose, and several freight and passenger cars attached to them. Tin lithograph stations were available, and small human figures were added to the scene.

By 1920 Lionel was offering more than 25 types of locomotives in "standard gauge" and "O" gauge. For collector and model railroad enthusiasts, the 1920s are considered Lionel's classic period. The detail used on the model cars and engines was extremely authentic. Some engine and cars contained brass and nickel trim. One type of electric locomotive produced at this time was the powerful twin motored 408E engine. The locomotive ran on "standard gauge" track, had operating pantographs, six running lights, and all brass detail. Another outstanding locomotive

The Santa Fe F3A-A diesel engine set is modeled after the only two F3-Class diesel engines used by the Santa Fe Railway.

was the 381, a less expensive model than the 408E, but also less powerful. By 1929 there were eight large types of electric locomotives and a considerable assortment of passenger and freight cars. Like the locomotives, these passenger cars were extremely detailed and colorful toys. Sets from this time period are highly valuable to collectors and train enthusiasts. The most sought after sets include the "Broadway Limited," with a steam or electric type locomotive, the "Blue Comet" set with the 400E engine, or the "Transcontinental Limited" in green with the 381E or in brown with the 408E.

In 1930 Lionel began manufacturing a steam-type "O" gauge locomotive. In 1935 there were eight "O" gauge steam engines in the Lionel catalog; the top of the line was the 263W 2-4-2 with a whistle and a 12-wheel Vanderbilt tender. Also around 1935 Lionel began manufacturing streamlined passenger train engines in "O" gauge. Some of these popular items included the "Flying Yankee," the "Blue Streak," and the "Union Pacific City of San Francisco." In 1937 Lionel produced what could be considered Joshua Cowen's greatest achievement, the exact scale "O" gauge Hudson steam locomotive. The set cost $75, and came with a plaque, attached track, and a walnut display stand.

In 1938 Lionel entered the smaller "OO" gauge market with a scale model of the Hudson engine with tender and four freight cars. Lionel's entries into the smaller gauge market were immediately popular with "OO" railroading enthusiasts. When Lionel stopped toy train production in 1942 because of the war, "OO" gauge models were discontinued permanently. At that point Lionel also discontinued the production of the larger, more expensive "standard gauge" line of trains.

After the war, Lionel started using plastics in its "O" gauge line of trains and accessories. In 1950 to celebrate 50 years of train production, Lionel marketed Magne-Traction to improve the pulling power of the locomotives. The new engines had magnets placed in the driving axles to create greater attraction between the wheel and the track. In 1957 Lionel began marketing an "HO" gauge train, licensed from Rivarossi and later Athearn, but they were not successfully marketed, and the line was discontinued in 1967. "HO" gauge trains were again produced by Lionel from 1974-78, while Fundimensions held the license to produce and market the company's products.

Under the direction of Kughn a number of successful items has been added to the Lionel line of merchandise. The company still produces the "O" gauge model trains, but now sells ready-to-run "O27" gauge train sets. The "O27" is a slightly smaller railed track than the "O" gauge track. In 1987 the company began manufacturing and marketing the Lionel Large Scale line of trains. These large scale trains are approximately 1:32 scale reproductions of full-size trains, which is almost twice the size of "O" gauge. The large trains are made especially for outdoor use. Constructed of weather resistant plastic, the trains allow enthusiasts the option of operating indoors or outside.

Kughn has begun other innovative merchandising practices. In 1991 Lionel Trains joined with the Smithsonian Institution to offer the first in a collection of museum-quality "O" gauge engines. The first engine produced and issued in 1992 was a reproduction of the 1938 New York Central Dreyfuss-Hudson locomotive. Only 500 of the locomotives were produced in the initial offering. On February 19, 1992, the Lionel Trains, Inc. Visitor's Center was opened at company headquarters in Chesterfield. In it's first year of operation more than 17,000 people visited the center, which was designed by Lionel employees, many donating their time and resources after hours and on weekends. The center features a 560 square-foot layout of track and settings. Visitors can enjoy up to 15 trains operating simultaneously in the train room. Suspended from the ceiling, a large scale locomotive train and a "standard gauge" train circle the interior of the center. Other displays show memorabilia dating back to Lionel's beginnings in 1900.

Future Predictions

Lionel Trains, Inc. has experienced a revival in recent years for a number of reasons. Since Kughn purchased Lionel, the company has introduced several new items and marketing features, and the Visitor's Center has been a successful venture for the company. In addition, there has been an upswing in the public's interest in model trains: such celebrities as late-night talk show host Jay Leno and musician Neil Young have spoken publicly about their enthusiasm for model railroading. Lionel has also increased emphasis on marketing aimed at the general public, and their new catalogs provide more basic information about model railroading. With innovative marketing and manufacturing practices, Lionel Trains, Inc. continues to be the leader in the production of model trains and accessories.

Further Reading:

Drucker, Stephen, "Railroads That Carry Grown Men Away," *New York Times,* December 22, 1988, p. C1.

Hollander, Ron, *All Aboard,* New York: Workmans, 1981.

McComas, Tom, and James Tuohy, *Lionel: A Collector's Guide and History,* Wilmette (Illinois): TM Productions, 1978.

Pressland, David, *The Art of the Tin Toy,* New York: Crown, 1976.

Treece, James, "The Little Train that Could; A Turnaround at Lionel," *Business Week,* December 26, 1988, p.70.

—William Tivenan

LOTUS®

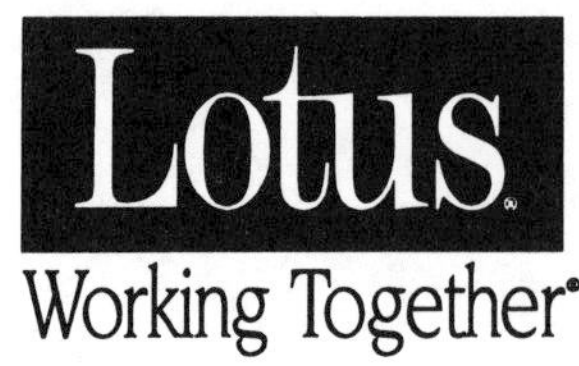

Lotus is the second-best-selling software for personal computers (PCs). A perennial leader in financial spreadsheets, the Lotus brand is most commonly associated with the original Lotus 1-2-3 program, introduced when the Lotus Development Corporation was founded in 1982. Through saturation of the market and increasing competition from other brands such as Microsoft, Lotus's position in the computer software segment quickly eroded in the late 1980s and early 1990s. Nonetheless, the most recent version of Lotus 1-2-3 remains the best-selling PC business software, and the Lotus name is associated with a diversified line of software application packages, including word processing, integrated office management systems (SmartSuite), and telecommunications and other message communication systems such as electronic mail (e-mail). The Lotus name also appears on graphics application software, produced by the Graphics Products Division.

Brand Origins

In the minds of many consumers, the Lotus name is synonymous with financial spreadsheet software, specifically the Lotus 1-2-3 spreadsheet package introduced in 1982 by Mitchell D. Kapor, founder of the Lotus Development Corporation. Kapor had been working on microcomputer applications since 1978 and began setting up programs for friends' personal needs. While a graduate student in psychology at the Massachusetts Institute of Technology, he helped write Tiny Troll, a program that produced line charts, statistics, and multiple regressions, and performed editing functions, all in an integrated software package.

Shortly after creating Tiny Troll, Kapor became involved in the development of another precursor to the financial spreadsheet; while working for VisiCorp, he conceived what would become a best-selling software called VisiTrend, which performed spreadsheet-like functions such as creating business charts. Signing with VisiCalc creator Bob Frankston, Kapor was hired to design two new programs based on Tiny Troll. Kapor's creations earned him $500,000 in royalties before VisiCorp bought him out for $1.7 million. With this capital, Kapor began looking toward an improved spreadsheet capable of translating tables into graphs and featuring a faster calculating speed.

Enlisting the services of Jonathon Sachs, a programmer experienced in spreadsheets and versed in the language of the IBM personal computer, Kapor built a strong technical team. At the time, many entrepreneurs were trying to meet the rising demand for software that would accompany the expected market growth of personal computers. In addition to his technical team, Kapor convinced a group of venture capitalists, including Ben Rosen, who contributed $600,000, to invest a total of $5 million to get the Lotus spreadsheet off the ground.

Kapor and Sachs dreamed of developing a powerful electronic spreadsheet with data processing and graphics functions. Assuming that substantial funding was necessary to secure enough press coverage for Lotus 1-2-3, Lotus spent more than $1 million on advertising for the product before it was even released. Among its advantages, Lotus 1-2-3 could run on IBM's new PCs with 256K of memory, which enabled the software to far exceed the spreadsheet capabilities of its successful predecessor, VisiCalc.

Early Marketing Strategy

Kapor and company's initial strategy was to design and market Lotus 1-2-3 as ''smart but lazy,'' that is, easy to use but very powerful, two qualities that at the time were considered incompatible in software marketing. With the 1981 introduction of the new version of the highly successful IBM PC, Lotus hoped to benefit from the growing demand for IBM-compatible software. The new IBM, with its 16-bit processor, was undoubtedly the wave of the future. At the time of the new IBM's release, all available IBM software was geared toward the old 8-bit processor, and Kapor and Sachs saw a competitive advantage in adapting their software to the more powerful PC.

With the substantial venture capital that was raised, Kapor launched a massive advertising campaign, unprecedented for the nascent PC industry of the early 1980s. The advertising blitz for the single product included full-page ads in newspapers and magazines across the country.

Three months into Kapor's ad campaign, Lotus 1-2-3 hit the market with a splash in November of 1982. Before long, Lotus 1-2-3 ranked at the top of the software charts. The first few days after its release the company received more than $1 million in orders, and during its first nine months on the market, nearly 110,000 copies of Lotus 1-2-3 were each sold at a price of $495. The company went public 18 months after its founding, with Kapor netting $5.4 million in cash from the stock sale while still holding $50 million in stock. The original venture capitalists, who had put up $5 million, increased their investment to $100 million. From

AT A GLANCE

Lotus brand of integrated computer software packages debuted in 1982, when the Lotus Development Corporation, founded by Mitchell D. Kapor, introduced Lotus 1-2-3 business spreadsheet program; company produces electronic mail, computer network software, and integrated office management programs.

Performance: *Market share*—10.9% of personal computer software category; 60% of spreadsheet category. *Sales*—$900.1 million for all Lotus products.

Major competitor: WordPerfect; also Microsoft and Borland.

Advertising: *Agency*—Leonard Monahan Lubars & Kelly, Providence, RI.

Addresses: *Parent company*—Lotus Development Corporation, 55 Cambridge Parkway, Cambridge, MA, 02142; phone: (617) 577-8500.

the time of its release until mid-1986, Lotus 1-2-3 sold more than two million copies, capturing 17.6 percent of the business sector software market.

Product Innovations

Mitchell Kapor left Lotus in July of 1986 and was replaced by Jim P. Manzi, who had been the firm's marketing director. Under Manzi's direction, Lotus 1-2-3's success continued: 750,000 copies were sold in 1986, more than three times as many copies as its nearest competitor, Microsoft's Multiplan.

With virtually 60 percent of its revenues coming from Lotus 1-2-3, the Lotus Development Corporation was being labeled a one-product company. Arguing that a company must make an effort to grow, Wall Street investors were becoming skeptical of Lotus's stability. Lotus recognized the need to diversify and expand and adopted several different strategies, including investing in software start-ups developed by former employees and in the creation of completely new programs. One of the company's most successful efforts was Symphony, a package that built on initial Lotus features by adding a word processing function, a more sophisticated data management system, and the ability to network with other computers.

Kapor and his associates focused on musical names for many of Lotus's new product lines. Symphony was introduced in the summer of 1984 amidst another multimillion dollar television advertising campaign launched during prime time coverage of the Summer Olympic Games. Sales were disappointing, though, as users seemed to feel that the program was too unwieldy and difficult to learn and preferred the greater power and simplicity afforded by such single-application packages as the original Lotus spreadsheet. New users were apparently not quite ready for the multi-application packages that would thrive a decade later.

Lotus Development Corporation acquired many other software packages by buying other firms' software and, in a major, expansive move into software for the Macintosh computer, created a graphics interface program. With a design similar to Symphony, the new Jazz program—a combination spreadsheet and word processing package—sought to attract introductory-level computer users who favored the Mac. Although it had the support of an extensive advertising campaign and an endorsement from Apple Computer, Inc., Jazz nonetheless had many troubles. Its March 1985 introduction date was delayed due to programming bugs, and after it was released, sales were disappointing. The program was criticized for being slow and difficult to learn, the same complaint that was leveled against Symphony when it hit the market.

Meanwhile, Microsoft was pushing its own spreadsheet for the Macintosh, Excel, and captured the Macintosh spreadsheet market in the same manner that Lotus had secured the IBM market. Both Excel and Lotus 1-2-3 sold for $495, and while Excel was considered more user friendly, Lotus 1-2-3 had kept its product loyalty, enabling it to maintain its market share. In order to enhance its quality, Lotus marketed a new version of 1-2-3 and, to improve its market position, entered into an agreement to develop 1-2-3 for mainframe computers. the company also launched a multimillion dollar advertising campaign in late 1986 in an attempt to capture a slice of the Japanese market. The strategy was a huge success: By mid-1987 Lotus 1-2-3 was outselling Microsoft's Multiplan five to one in Japan, and 1-2-3's share of the total spreadsheet market stood at 70 percent.

Upgrading of Lotus 1-2-3 continued in June of 1988, when the third version was released. Lotus also put on the market 26 other programs bearing the Lotus name in the year ending in June of 1989. These products' success kept Lotus Development growth rates high; the company's income rose to $68 million in 1989.

Further Brand Development

Since 1990 competition for Lotus's market has intensified, with price wars in PC hardware spreading to the software market. Lotus's toughest competitor, Microsoft, with its highly successful word processing package and Excel spreadsheet, gave Lotus a run for its money and captured 50 percent of the market. Lotus perhaps failed to capitalize on the growing market for programs that run on Microsoft's Windows, mainly because of the firm's bitter rivalry with Microsoft, but Lotus eventually decided to develope programs for Windows. The initiative got off to a rocky start when, due to many bugs, Lotus had to replace its Windows-compatible program only one month after it was released. The result was that the company reached only a 20 percent share of the Windows spreadsheet market; Lotus sold 250,000 copies by the end of 1991, while sales of Windows were about one million. In addition, troubles with the Lotus 1-2-3 program for the Macintosh led to further sales declines and the brand's market share fell from 75 percent in 1988 to 55 percent.

By late 1990 Lotus took on perennial rival Microsoft in the word processing arena. With the purchase of Samna Corporation for $65 million, Lotus Ami Pro word processing software was on the market. Lotus's word processing package, however, would remain third in market share behind Microsoft's Word and WordPerfect. Lotus's diversification, though, would eventually reap large dividends by 1992, when the revised word processing program won great praise and garnered sales of nearly $50 million.

In addition to price wars, there was a shift in the market from single application software to what would be called the "suite" market, a popular new category in multiple application software. Since about 1990, according to some industry analysts, consumers were catching on to the idea of buying all of their software in one box. The suite category took the form of all-encompassing packages that included applications for data base management, presentations programs for making slides, spreadsheet capabilities, and word processing programs. It was thought that software packages from one company would work together more seamlessly than multiple programs from multiple suppliers. Thus, Lotus and Microsoft began positioning these multiples as brands in their own right rather than as a bundle of different software programs.

Introduced in 1991 as a competitor of Microsoft's Office, Lotus's entry into the suite market was called SmartSuite. ''The 'suite' category . . . is increasingly becoming the way that people buy software,'' commented Hank Vigil, Microsoft's director of applications-software marketing, in *Advertising Age.* In the early 1990s, Office was winning the competitive battle against SmartSuite. In a move that was to have boosted sales for SmartSuite, in May of 1992 Digital Equipment began providing every buyer of its PCs with Lotus's SmartSuite for Windows, which had a list price of $295. According to Lotus, Digital provides the most Lotus software in their PC promotions, giving significant exposure to Lotus products.

Also in the early 1990s, Lotus 1-2-3 was released for the Macintosh, and in the ever-present price wars, Lotus Development began selling the software at a discount to try to win market share from Microsoft. Lotus products invaded new markets as the company released a graphics package called Freelance Graphics for Windows, OS/2, and DOS. And the company moved into electronic mail, a major new market for both Apple and IBM machines.

Lotus sought to make improvements in its electronic mail offerings and networking packages. Its X.400 software was designed to bolster the performance of forms-routing and message software on large and advanced networks. This software was offered beginning in 1993 as an option for the cc:Mail and Lotus Notes programs. By October of 1992, 200 of Notes' 800 customers had been on board since June of 1992. The Notes package surpassed sales of 1,000 by the end of 1992. When IBM chose Notes as the local area networking element of its office plan, it effectively axed its own Office Vision/2 LAN efforts. Lotus Notes, designed for such applications as e-mail and information distribution, was also being sold overseas as part of a joint marketing and research and development collaboration between Lotus and France Telecom, a telecommunications operator.

Performance Appraisal

While engaged in a continuing battle for the computer software market, Lotus brands continued to sell well in the early 1990s while expanded opportunities were emerging. Though Microsoft led in the suites category with its Office, Lotus 1-2-3 remained at the top in the overall business category. Price wars in the PC market continued to rage, but part of the competition was for an expanding pie as demand for PCs in general, and Lotus products in particular, was expanding. As always, price and quality were the keys. ''The underlying theme for software in '93 was bang for the buck,'' noted Jon Hulak, an industry analyst with market researcher BIS Strategic Decisions. ''The value for the dollar has never been like it was in 1993.''

Aside from price competition, Lotus was expanding by acquiring other brands as well as developing new products. To gain access to a data base software product, Lotus acquired Approach Software of Redwood City, California. Data base software gives users the ability to access multiple lists of information. Approach's software targeted the casual computer user and was designed to help set up data base management systems. The acquisition of Approach put Lotus products into direct competition with Microsoft and Borland International, who already had popular data base software products.

One of Lotus's packages, Freelance Graphics, was judged number one in the early 1990s in terms of quality among a group of Windows-based software packages of the same type. The program was deemed fastest and easiest to use, beating Harvard Graphics and Claris's Hollywood.

Finally, Lotus Notes, networking software designed by Iris Associates, was fast becoming Lotus Development Corporation's key product. The package, part of a new category of software called groupware, was designed to allow groups of users to collaborate from distant locations. Lotus planned to offer a whole array of software around the Notes products. 112,000 copies of Notes were sold in 1991, with major firms like General Motors and Metropolitan Life building their computer networks around it. The software boasted some 500,000 users at 2,000 companies as of mid-year 1993, up from 350,000 users at 1,400 firms only six months earlier.

Further Reading:

Ichbiah, Daniel, and Susan L. Knepper, *The Making of Microsoft,* Rocklin, CA: Prima Publishing, 1990.

Johnson, Bradley, ''Software 'Suites' Keep Original Brands Fresh,'' *Advertising Age,* February 7, 1994, p. S-10.

Levering, Robert, Michael Katz, and Milton Moskowitz, *The Computer Entrepreneurs: Who's Making It Big and How in America's Upstart Industry,* New York, NY: New American Library Books, 1984.

''Lotus Buying Approach Software and Acquiring a Data Base Program,'' *New York Times National Edition,* June 9, 1993, p. C5.

''Lotus to Augment Notes, cc:Mail With Workflow Software,'' *InfoWorld,* December 14, 1992, p. 6.

McLeod, Doug, ''Profiles and Strategies Amid the Changing Development Model,'' *Computer Industry Report,* October 18, 1991, p. 6.

''Software: It's a New Game,'' *Business Week,* June 4, 1990, pp. 102–110.

—John A. Sarich

LOUISVILLE SLUGGER®

Louisville Slugger®

The finest softball bats in the world.

"Louisville Slugger" is one of the most famous trademarks in American sports. Registered more than 100 years ago by J. F. Hillerich & Company in Louisville, Kentucky, the trademark has been branded on millions of baseball and softball bats used by players from sandlot baseball to the Major Leagues. In 1993, nearly 70 percent of all Major League players used Louisville Slugger baseball bats. Louisville Slugger was the second-leading brand of bats for amateur and recreational-league use in the United States. In 1975, Hillerich & Bradsby Co. began marketing gloves for baseball and softball and other equipment with the Louisville Slugger brand name. In 1993, Louisville Slugger was the fourth leading brand of baseball and softball gloves.

Brand Origins

The origin of the Louisville Slugger trademark is a story that has taken on mythical proportions in keeping with the legendary beginnings of the American pastime. In 1884, John Andrew "Bud" Hillerich, a young apprentice in his father's wood-turning shop, slipped away from work to watch the Louisville Eclipse team of the old American Association. During the game, Louis "Pete" Browning, the team's best hitter, who happened to be in a slump, broke his favorite bat. There were frantic efforts to repair the bat, but to no avail. After the game, young Hillerich offered to create a custom-made bat for Browning, and the two of them returned to the wood shop.

Hillerich selected a piece of white ash and began turning a bat to Browning's directions. He would stop every so often so Browning could take practice swings and suggest changes. Eventually, Browning was satisfied. The next day, Browning broke out of his slump with three hits in three at bats. His teammates on the Eclipse were soon asking Hillerich to make custom bats for them as well.

Hillerich's father, a hard-working German immigrant, apparently saw little future in making baseball bats. According to some accounts, the elder Hillerich roared at his son, "I won't allow some whim to get the best of my business judgment. There's no future in supplying an article for a mere game." But the younger Hillerich continued turning out bats after the wood shop had closed for the day. Eventually, his father relented and baseball bats became a major part of the family business.

The bats were branded with the company name—J. F. Hillerich & Company—and a trademark. Louisville was known as "Falls City" because of its location on the Ohio River, and the original brandname was "Falls City Slugger." The brand was changed to "Louisville Slugger" around 1894. The company's name was changed to J. F. Hillerich & Son in 1897, and became Hillerich & Bradsby in 1916. When Browning died, he was buried in Louisville. A new tombstone dedicated in 1983 had Browning's baseball statistics etched on the face and a crossed pair of stone Louisville Slugger baseball bats on top.

Signature Bats

Hillerich also branded the bats he sold to professional baseball players with their names in block letters. That practice, which started as a courtesy, eventually led to one of the most successful marketing promotions in history. In 1905, the legendary "Honus" Wagner, who led the National League in batting eight times during his career, agreed to allow Hillerich & Son to brand his signature on bats sold to the public. Since then, Louisville Slugger baseball bats have carried the signatures of baseball's most famous players, including Ty Cobb, Babe Ruth, Ted Williams, Mickey Mantle, Roger Maris, and Hank Aaron. One way to measure a baseball player's popularity was by the number of Louisville Slugger bats sold with his signature.

Autograph-model baseball bats lost much of their impact when high school and recreational leagues began using aluminum bats in the 1970s. Bill Williams, vice president of advertising and public relations at Hillerich & Bradsby, explained in 1993: "A 10-year-old kid just doesn't care what bat his favorite player uses anymore. The Big Leaguers use wood and the Little Leaguers use aluminum. Signatures just don't mean as much anymore. The marketing thrust is gone." Although Hillerich & Bradsby sold more than a million wooden bats annually to amateur and recreational-league players as late as 1993, the company stopped advertising wooden bats in the late 1980s.

Slugger Park

In 1974, Hillerich & Bradsby moved its manufacturing facilities across the Ohio River to a 56-acre complex in Jeffersonville, Indiana, called Slugger Park. In the late 1980s and early 1990s, Slugger Park annually attracted more than 100,000 visitors who were interested in seeing how wooden baseball bats were made. In 1992, Williams told a writer for *Antiques & Collecting* magazine: "You are truly witnessing a part of Americana here. We don't

AT A GLANCE

Louisville Slugger brand of baseball bats first made by the J.F. Hillerich Company, in Louisville, Kentucky, in 1884; original brand name "Falls City Slugger" changed to "Louisville Slugger" circa 1894; company name changed to J.F. Hillerich and Son in 1897; name changed to Hillerich & Bradsby Company in 1916; brand name extended to baseball gloves in 1975.

Performance: *Market share*—30% of aluminum bat category; 80% of wood bat category.

Major competitor: Easton Aluminium Inc.'s Easton.

Addresses: *Parent company*—Hillerich & Bradsby Company, 200 West Broadway, Louisville, KY 40202; phone: (502) 585-5226.

claim to be haunted, but many people insist that the ghosts of Ty Cobb, Babe Ruth, Lou Gehrig, Jackie Robinson, and so many other great baseball players walk the floors at Slugger Park. Their memories are all around you.'' In 1993, Hillerich & Bradsby made about 200,000 wooden bats for professional baseball.

In addition to tours, the company operated a gift shop at Slugger Park where visitors could buy replicas of the bats used by the legendary players of the game. The replicas were exact because Hillerich & Bradsby maintained records of all the orders ever filled for major league players, including notations about grains and staining. Over the years, Hillerich & Bradsby also worked with movie makers to ensure realism. In 1993, the company was asked to make bats for the movie *The Last Days of Ty Cobb.*

Aluminum Bats

Aluminum bats made their appearance in the early 1970s. They cost about five times as much as wooden bats, but they were nearly indestructible and became popular with schools and youth leagues. Hillerich & Bradsby, however, resisted breaking with tradition. Williams, who joined the company in 1971, recalled, ''We really thought aluminum bats were a fad; that they would go away.'' However, in 1974, the NCAA approved the use of aluminum bats for college play and the demand for wooden bats began to drop dramatically. Hillerich & Bradsby broke down in 1976 and began marketing aluminum bats with the Louisville Slugger trademark. Initially, the bats were produced for Hillerich & Bradsby by Alcoa Inc. at a factory in Santa Fe, California. In 1978, Hillerich & Bradsby bought the Alcoa plant and began making its own aluminum bats.

Hillerich & Bradsby insisted that it would continue making wood bats as long as they were used by the major leagues. However, from a peak of nearly 7 million bats per year in the 1960s, production at Slugger Park fell to less than one million in the late 1980s. Hillerich & Bradsby made about 1.5 million wood bats in 1993—about the same number of aluminum bats it made in California. However, worldwide, aluminum bats outsold wooden bats 19 to 1.

In an interview in 1989, J. A. ''Jack'' Hillerich III, then president of the company, predicted ''a time in the not too distant future when everyone will be using some alternative bat—aluminum, graphite, or some composite.'' Williams also lamented the likely passing of wood bats in an interview with *Sports Illustrated:* ''One day we may be playing with something that acts like wood but isn't. Is the future of baseball going to be written in laboratories and on launching pads?'' In the early 1990s, Hillerich & Bradsby introduced a Louisville Slugger bat made of a composite graphite for softball and was continuing developmental work on a composite bat for baseball.

Baseball Bat Folklore

Professional baseball players were picky customers, and their idiosyncrasies have became part of baseball lore. Ted Williams, the only Major League player to bat .400 since 1930, would go to Louisville and sort through the wood billets—or rounded forms—to pick out the ones he thought would make the best bats. He preferred a narrow grain, which he though made a stronger bat. Most hitters, however, preferred just the opposite. Hugh Duffy, whose .438 was the highest batting average ever in the Major Leagues, also liked to inspect the billets. He would bounce them on the factory's concrete floor and selected the ones he wanted by the sound they made.

Williams once sent back an entire batch of Louisville Slugger bats because the handles felt wrong. They were measured carefully and found to be 5/1000th of an inch wider than what Williams had ordered. The persnickety Babe Ruth, who liked to see tiny pin knots in the barrels of his bats, also once rejected an entire batch of Louisville Sluggers, declaring them ''not worth a damn.'' He later reconsidered and used the batch anyway. That was 1927, the year Ruth hit 60 home runs. One of the Louisville Sluggers that Ruth used that season was eventually displayed at the Hillerich & Bradsby plant in Jeffersonville, Indiana, across the river from Louisville. There were 21 notches encircling the trademark where, like a gunslinger, Ruth marked the bat for each home run. Another Louisville Slugger used by Ruth was sold in the early 1990s for $55,000.

Harry ''The Hat'' Walker, who played for the St. Louis Cardinals in the 1940s, was touring the Hillerich & Bradsby plant when he spotted a bat standing in a vat of brown stain. He tried it out and liked the feel. He also liked the two-toned look, and ordered all his bats half stained and half natural. The ''Walker finish'' soon caught on with professional and amateur players alike. In the 1970s, George Foster, who played for the Cincinnati Reds, wanted his bats stained black. Reggie Jackson, a Hall of Fame slugger who played for the New York Yankees and the Oakland A's in the 1980s, also wanted all-black bats. Jackson claimed the black bats gave him an advantage at night because outfielders had a harder time seeing the ball right after it was hit.

Yogi Berra, the Hall of Fame catcher for the New York Yankees, also holds a special place in Louisville Slugger history. Before the days of aluminum bats, even Little Leaguers were taught to hold the bat with the trademark facing up so the bat would strike the ball with the grain where the wood was strongest. Holding the bat so a fastball would hit the trademark was almost a sure way to crack the wood, which Berra did with consistency. Berra's retort to those who pointed this out was, ''I'm up there to hit, not to read.'' Hillerich & Bradsby outwitted Berra by rotating his bats a quarter turn before branding them with the Louisville Slugger trademark.

Al Simmons, a star with the Philadelphia Athletics in the 1930s, was easier to outwit. Like others before him, Simmons once rejected a batch of Louisville Slugger bats. He also rejected the replacements sent by Hillerich & Bradsby. The company then repackaged the original bats, which Simmons found acceptable. Simmons reportedly told Hillerich & Bradsby, "This is exactly what I wanted. Why couldn't you have sent them in the first place?"

George Brett of the Kansas City Royals once used the same Louisville Slugger bat during a 31-game hitting streak. When the streak ended, he returned the bat to Hillerich & Bradsby with a note explaining, "This bat has no more hits in it."

Further Reading:

Arnow, Jan, *Louisville Slugger: The Making of a Baseball Bat,* New York: Pantheon Books, 1947.

Curreri, Jow, "Romance of the Bat," *Antiques & Collecting,* May 1992, p. 26.

"Facts about Louisville Slugger Aluminium Bats," Louisville, KY: Hillerich & Bradsby Company.

"Facts about Louisville Slugger Wood Bats," Louisville, KY: Hillerich & Bradsby Company.

Gammons, Peter, "End of an Era," *Sports Illustrated,* July 24, 1989, p. 16.

Helyar, John, "The Ball and Glove May Be Imported; The Bat Is American," *The Wall Street Journal,* October 9, 1984.

Hersch, Hank, "The Good Wood," *Sports Illustrated,* April 14, 1986, p. 66.

"History," Louisville, KY: Hillerich & Bradsby Company.

"One Strike on the Slugger: Did a Bat Company Abuse Its Young?" *Newsweek,* January 15, 1990, p. 70.

"Sculpting a Louisville Slugger," *Harper's Magazine,* May 1989, p. 34.

Taylor, John H., "Make Mine Aluminum," *Forbes,* December 7, 1992, p. 150.

Watt, Richard, "Memorabilia," *Sport,* June 1993, p. 62.

Wilkinson, Francis, "Wood, That It Be True: Getting a Grip on the Louisville Slugger," *Harper's Magazine,* June 1990, p. 60.

—Dean Boyer

MACK® TRUCKS

Although not, strictly speaking, a consumer brand, the Mack nameplate and Bulldog mascot are almost universally recognized symbols of the trucking industry. Although Mack is arguably the best-known truck brand in America—as evinced by the well-known expression "built like a Mack truck"—it is not the top-ranking heavy-duty truck manufacturer. Mack's line of vehicles includes vocational vehicles for the construction, logging, mining, and other industries, as well as the more familiar over-the-road transports, also known as "tractors" in the trucking field.

Brand Origins

Mack was founded by three Mack brothers—Augustus, William, and John—in 1900. John (nicknamed Jack) Mack has been credited with most of the brand's early success. At the age of 14, this pioneer of the trucking industry ran away from home in 1878 to work as a teamster, fireman, and, finally, an engineer for steam power plants in the United States and at sea. Upon his return from overseas work, Jack joined his brothers in Brooklyn, New York, in the acquisition of a small carriage and wagon manufacturer in 1893.

The brothers soon began experimenting with motorized vehicles, executing America's first bus in 1900 after eight years of painstaking experimentation and testing. The hand-crafted vehicle had a 20-passenger capacity and was put to work carrying tourists through Brooklyn's Prospect Park. This first Mack rig established the brand's reputation for longevity: after eight years of service in the park, it was converted to a truck and was finally retired after 17 years and over 1 million miles of service.

This prototypical vehicle, dubbed "Old Number One," was so successful that orders for others followed rapidly, production increased, and the three Mack brothers incorporated their namesake company in New York City. Within a couple of years, demand outran the New York location's capacity, and the business relocated in Allentown, Pennsylvania, and was reincorporated as Mack Brothers Motor Car Company. But the name was misleading: Mack would focus on truck, not car production. At a time when trucks were often made of surplus or obsolete car parts, the Mack brothers pioneered the design and manufacture of custom-built, heavy-duty motor trucks.

Early Marketing

Mack's first advertising campaign was launched in 1903 in *Horseless Age* magazine. The brothers called their early vehicles "Manhattans" to differentiate them from the business's old horse-drawn Macks. Mack grew dramatically during the first decade of the 20th century. The nameplate continued production of buses, brought out a line of railway cars, and built its first "seat over engine" truck. The company used demonstrations to illustrate the features of its earliest trucks, and established a truck drivers' school to train men to properly operate and repair the vehicles. Mack also produced a seven-ton, five-cubic-yard dump truck developed for use in the construction of the New York City subway system. The company dropped the "Manhattan" name around 1910 and applied the script "Mack" to all its products. By that time, Mack ranked as one of the largest manufacturers of heavy-duty trucks in America, and had adopted the slogan: "The Leading Gasoline Truck in America." It was generally recognized that Mack manufactured the preeminent heavy-duty truck in the United States.

By 1911, Mack had expanded its distribution to Washington, D.C., Philadelphia, Pittsburgh, Baltimore, and Brooklyn. Despite ample demand, Mack was compelled to seek financial assistance for up-front production expenses from J.P. Morgan & Company, which merged the truck manufacturer with the Saurer Motor Company and the Hewitt Motor Company to form the International Motor Truck Corporation in 1911. In the course of the consolidation, the Mack brothers were pushed out of the top management, and they left the combine shortly thereafter.

Edward R. Hewitt, founder and former president of Hewitt Motor Company and chief engineer of Mack after the merger, designed a new, medium-duty truck in 1914 called the AB Mack. This one- to three-ton capacity vehicle was one of the first to feature distinctly truck styling, rather than looking like a "horseless wagon." The model remained in continuous production throughout World War I and long afterward, from 1914 to 1936. Over 50,000 units were produced during that time.

Over the course of the first World War, Mack delivered thousands of AC Macks (a larger, more powerful model introduced in 1916) to American, British, and French forces. Durable and reliable, the trucks endured extraordinary abuse, including rough terrain, continuous operation, inexperienced drivers, and gross

AT A GLANCE

Mack trucks founded by Mack Brothers Company in New York, NY, 1900; originally known as Manhattan vehicles; company moved and reincorporated as Mack Brothers Motor Car Company in Allentown, PA, 1905; Mack trade name used consistently after 1910; company merged with Saurer Motor Company and Hewitt Motor Company and renamed International Motor Truck Corporation, 1911; company changed its name to Mack Trucks, Inc., 1921; Bulldog trademark designed by A. F. Masury and registered in 1932; company acquired by Northeast Capital Corporation, 1959; merged with Signal Companies, 1968; sold public in 1983; acquired by Renault V.I., 1990.

Performance: *Market share*—10.9% of heavy-duty truck category.

Major competitor: Kenworth; also, Freightliner, Daimler-Benz, Peterbilt, and Volvo.

Advertising: *Major campaign*—Slogan, "Drive one and you'll know."

Addresses: *Parent company*—Mack Trucks, Inc., 2100 Mack Blvd., Box M, Allentown, PA 18105-5000; phone: (215) 439-3011; fax: (215) 439-3308. *Ultimate parent company*—Renault V.I., 40 Rue Pasteur, BP 30292156, Suresnes Cedex, France.

overloading. The rigs' "pugnacious" looks inspired its British users to nickname them "Bull Dog Macks." The name stuck, and in 1932 A. F. Masury, designer of the AC model, created and patented the Bulldog radiator mascot. The original Bulldog had a white coat, but it was later given a more lifelike Brindle coloring. Around the same time, Mack adopted the long-running and well-known slogan "Performance Counts." But an even better-known analogy made the branded trucks part of American culture. By the end of World War I, Mack was producing almost 4,000 trucks per year, and the phrase "built like a Mack truck" had come to be a compliment of the highest order.

Product Innovations

Mack received more than 270 patents for its improvements on truck design from 1919 to 1927. Innovations included improved cooling systems and a four-speed transmission. But the nameplate's most significant development was the first major breakthrough in vibration dampening since the dawn of the automotive era. The new shock system was so successful that a separate operation was set up to manufacture it for distribution to auto manufacturers. The development of improved intercity roads and pneumatic tires, the inherent flexibility of trucking versus rail transit, and Mack's superior design and manufacturing standards combined to more than double the nameplate's sales from $22 million in 1919 to $55 million in 1927.

During the late 1920s Mack introduced a new line of higher-speed, six-cylinder trucks created especially for tractor-trailer operations. Although tractor-trailers had been used for short-haul operations since World War I, their potential for direct factory to warehouse delivery of large volumes would not be recognized until the 1930s. This BJ line would serve as a transitional model between the slower, old-fashioned four-cylinder rigs and modern high-speed transports. Mack's 1920s-era AP model was stylistically similar to the earlier "Bulldog," but was specially suited to heavy-duty construction.

The Great Depression was a serious blow to Mack, but the economic crisis ironically accelerated the truck industry overall and Mack in particular. Tight finances forced businesses to seek out the most efficient distribution methods, and that meant trucks. As shippers increasingly switched to truck transport, railroaders retaliated by lobbying (in many cases successfully) for restrictive state and local laws limiting axle loading and gross vehicle weights and lengths. The regulations prompted Mack to relaunch its cab-over-engine (COE; formerly seat-over-engine) trucks as "Traffic Type" Macks in 1933. This design helped distribute the truck's weight to the best advantage and maximized the usable freight space on the chassis. The company displayed nearly every model and application of its rigs in a presentation called the "Mack Highway" at the 1934 Chicago Century of Progress exhibition.

The now-classic E series was introduced in 1936. This new, long-nosed, streamlined series boosted Mack sales dramatically, but the brand's most significant development of the decade was the diesel engine. The truck manufacturer had tested diesel engines from Mercedes-Benz over the course of the 1930s but was eager to develop its own motor. Mack became the first truck maker to achieve this coveted goal in 1938. By 1940, Mack's sales had reached $4 million, and the Bulldog graced the industry's most extensive line of commercial trucks: from small delivery vehicles, to massive dump trucks, to buses and fire trucks.

During World War II Mack manufactured troop transport vehicles for the United States and its allies. In fact, virtually all of the nameplate's facilities were dedicated to the construction of military vehicles and equipment. As a result, Mack set up extensive maintenance programs on the home front to keep its vehicles on the road while the parent company was occupied with war production. After the war, pent-up demand was met with the introduction of the L series snub-nosed truck, which came to be known as "The King of the Road."

That appellation had negative connotations for some automobile drivers who shared crowded roads with ever-larger trucks. Mack joined the American Trucking Associations, Inc., in a public relations campaign to combat anti-truck sentiment that blamed big rigs for road damage and congestion. The Mack Diesel Caravan drove around the country and taught the public and fleet owners about trucks. Mack's institutional advertising drive employed the theme, "National Security Rides On Trucks," playing on the use of Macks in World War II and Korea. A timely railroad strike further illustrated the exigency of trucking during the 1950s.

Trucking Comes of Age

The trucking industry was finally recognized as a vital national interest in the postwar era, and the recognition brought increased acceptance. The development of the interstate highway system boosted the industry, and relaxed interstate commerce laws further promoted trucking. Mack capitalized on the attention by marketing Bulldog memorabilia to the public—ash trays and cigarette lighters were among the favorite items. Around 1950, a major toy manufacturer marketed a series of large, die cast models of Mack trucks. Some of these toys were used in the nameplate's print advertising appearing in such nationally circulated magazines as *Fortune* and *Newsweek.* The slogan "They've worked their way into the language'' was used to emphasize Mack's worldwide reputation for quality built trucks.

Mack registrations increased modestly during the early 1950s, then doubled from 6,098 in 1954 to 13,190 in 1956. The completely new model B extra-heavy-duty truck, featuring a wider chassis that facilitated servicing and the larger engines that were being developed, was brought out during this period. The new line also included revolutionary safety and convenience features that soon became standard: improved ventilation and lighting, a glare-reducing windshield, and a more accessible central fuse panel. Manufactured from 1955 through 1966, the B sported styling that was more curvaceous and sleek. The 1953 launch of the ''Thermodyne'' fuel-injected engine brought more power and enhanced reliability to the Mack lineup. The nameplate introduced a high-cab series nicknamed the ''Cherrypicker'' during the decade as well.

In the early 1960s a hostile takeover—and the poor management that resulted—brought the truck nameplate to a historic low. As Mack's production facilities deteriorated, ''built like a Mack truck'' began to be less of a boast. Market penetration and sales declined accordingly: between 1959 and 1964 Mack lost one-third of its stake in the market.

Led by a new president (a ''truck man,'' Zenon C. R. Hansen), the tractor manufacturer fell back on its outstanding brand identity by producing Bulldog flags, jewelry, posters, decals, and bumper stickers to boost employee morale, quality, and public recognition. The promotional drive was backed up with a technological breakthrough, the 1966 introduction of the Maxidyne engine and Maxitorque transmission. Called ''the greatest breakthrough in diesel technology'' of the era, Maxidyne offered constant horsepower over a wider range of operation than previously achieved, and enabled the use of the five-speed Maxitorque transmission instead of the standard 10- to 15-speeds.

By the end of 1966, Mack attained record production, sales, and earnings. The company merged with Signal Oil & Gas Company and formed The Signal Companies in 1967. Mack retained its autonomy, but received vital financial backing.

International Market

Mack established a network of company-owned sales and servicing facilities with the goal of going international as early as the 1910s. During the decade, the brand did indeed go international, with large numbers of vehicles going to the United Kingdom and European continent for the war effort. In the 1920s Mack Trucks of Canada, a distribution arm, was established, but the brand's foreign operations floundered after World War II. In 1955 the brand reached an agreement with Electro Rail, S.A., a Belgian company, to distribute Mack vehicles in Europe, and the manufacturer subsequently set up an affiliate, Mack Belgium, S.A., for the same purpose.

The International division was reorganized in 1961 and emerged as Mack Trucks Worldwide, Ltd. International distribution doubled from 1961 to 1964. After many years of planning, the brand set up an authentic Canadian subsidiary in 1964, and expanded its Latin American, Australian, and French operations as well. By 1967, Mack trucks were distributed in 67 foreign countries. Canada and Australia would evolve into two of Mack's leading markets.

During the 1970s Mack consolidated its efforts on the heavy-duty portion of the truck market, which was divided into classes 7 and 8. Class 7 trucks weigh between 13 and 16.5 tons, and class 8 designates anything over 16.5 tons. At the time, the largest class offered the best prospects, with an annual growth rate averaging 30 percent from 1961 to 1971.

As the U.S. bicentennial approached, Mack advertising took on a very patriotic theme. Beginning in 1970, several models were painted in red, white, and blue, with stars and stripes. The effort earned Mack recognition for the Freedoms Foundation of Valley Forge for encouraging patriotism. Mack introduced the world's first air-to-air intercooled diesel for highway trucks in 1973. The innovative engine, which was soon on backorder, fueled a 220 percent sales increase, from $275 million in 1965 to $880 million in 1974.

Current and Future Prospects

In 1979 French tractor manufacturer Renault V.I. made its initial investment in Mack, which was sold public by Signal in 1983. Battered by declining sales, significant losses, union discord, and upper management upheavals in the late 1980s, Mack's decline became ''a textbook case of how a dismal market, overly ambitious capital spending, and management missteps can combine to humble even the best-known name in a business,'' as *Business Week* summarized the situation in 1990.

Mack's problems started with trucking deregulation in the early 1980s. Like many rivals, Mack faced the very competitive marketplace with old plants and high production costs. Mack executives' cost-cutting methods only inspired labor strife, which contributed to declining quality—in 1990, an executive admitted to *Fleet Owner* magazine that 40 percent of units produced at one plant were of ''sub-standard quality.'' This fact, in turn, eroded dealer and customer confidence: Mack's share of the shrinking heavy-duty-truck market fell from 15.2 percent in 1988 to 13.2 percent in 1989, 12.4 percent in 1990, and 11.8 percent in 1991. The company underwent a thorough restructuring in the early 1990s, after Renault made it a wholly owned subsidiary. The brand faced a formidable challenge in a shrinking market: capture share from five other North American competitors.

Mack concentrated on improving quality by instituting in-house audits. It also reduced its supplier base by 45 percent, and allowed customers to choose particular features from suppliers. To increase visibility and access, management hoped to increase the number of on-highway dealers, authorized parts stores, and service centers. And once again, Mack began to place increased emphasis on its bulldog as a symbol of the company's pride.

In the 1990s Mack also had to concentrate on several large issues in the trucking industry: safety, emissions (and alternative fuels), and long-haul comfort. The nameplate benefited from an improved truck market in 1992, with its Class 8 U.S. retail sales increasing 15 percent over 1991. The company took 60 percent more North American truck orders in 1992 than in 1991, and halted the erosion of its North American market share at 10.9 percent.

Further Reading:

Bradley, Peter, *Purchasing,* ''Will Mack Drive Out of the Rut?,'' October 10, 1991, pp. 63–67; ''Its a Buyers' Market for Heavy-Duty Trucks,'' June 6, 1991, pp. 87–89.

Cassidy, William B., *Fleet Owner,* ''Pascual Plans to Bring Mack Back,'' December 1990, p. 28; ''Mack Trucks Charts a Comeback Course,'' February 1990, pp. 8, 12.

Cullen, David and Thomas L. Moore, ''The New Models for 1991,'' *Fleet Owner,* July 1990, pp. 95–110.

Hansen, Zenon C. R., *The Legend of the Bulldog,* New York: The Newcomen Society, 1974.

''Highway Tractors: Accent on the Creature Comforts!,'' *Traffic Management,* November 1992, pp. 49–52.

Kelly, Kevin, ''Navistar Labors Up Another Hill,'' *Business Week,* July 30, 1990, pp. 40–41.

Montville, John B., *Mack,* Newfoundland, N.J.: Haessner Publishing, Inc., 1973.

''Truck Makers Feature Safety, Driver Comfort,'' *Traffic Management,* October 1991, pp. 73–77.

—April S. Dougal

MAGNAVOX®

Magnavox is one of the best-selling brands in the American consumer electronics market, occupying a leading position in the videocassette recorder (VCR) market and holding second place in televisions and compact disc (CD) players. During the 1970s, when the market was experiencing a decline that led to the demise of Admiral and the near collapse of Zenith, Magnavox was acquired by North American Philips Corporation (now Philips Electronics North America Corporation)—a subsidiary of the Dutch electronics firm N.V. Philips Gloeilampenfabriken—in 1974. The brand was later merged into Philips Consumer Electronics Company, which had been formed as a subsidiary of North American Philips. After years of careful brand building and expansion of its product line, Magnavox has emerged as one of the most valuable brand names in the industry. It operates in almost every sector of the home electronics market, including televisions, VCRs, camcorders, and CD and videodisc players.

Brand Origins

The origins of the Magnavox brand can be traced to the Commercial Wireless and Development Company, which was established in 1911 by Edwin Pridham, Peter Jensen (both of whom were engineers), and Richard O'Connor in Napa, California. The initial purpose of the company was to develop improved wireless and telephonic equipment, but the focus changed after Pridham developed an electro-dynamic principle for a speaker in 1915. Pridham's speaker produced a clearer sound than had been possible with earlier models developed by Bell and Edison. He marketed the invention under the name Magna Vox, latin for *great voice.* In search of a significant market, Pridham demonstrated the device for AT&T, but was shown no interest because the speaker weighed an unwieldy 30 pounds.

Matching the speaker system with a microphone, Pridham built the first public address system, which was used by presidents Taft and Wilson, a fact that earned tremendous publicity for the company and its product. On a lark, Pridham attached his speaker to a horn-type phonograph. By amplifying the signal from a record, the resulting sound reproduction was made louder and clearer. At last he had found a commercial application for his speaker.

Pridham filed a patent in 1916 for an electric phonograph, using an electric pick-up on the needle and his electro-dynamic loudspeaker. The following year the Commercial Wireless company was joined with the San Francisco-based Sonora Phonograph Distributing Company. The new organization, established to manufacture and market the phonograph, was established under the name of The Magnavox Company.

Due to its position of leadership in sound reproduction, Magnavox was asked to develop special communication devices for the military during World War I. These included a microphone that could carry a human voice without being drowned out by the cacophonous buzz of an airplane engine and a variety of radio transmitters and circuits for the U.S. Army and Navy.

At the close of the war, Magnavox immediately returned to commercial production of phonographs. However, with the advent of radio and the proliferation of broadcast stations, public demand for phonographs plummeted. People were far more interested in the variety offered by radio—and unlike records, radio programs were free. The company's solution was to simply build a phonograph containing a radio. From a marketing standpoint, this was something of a coup; why buy two devices when you can buy one—the one with the best speaker?

Brand Development

The speaker system firmly established Magnavox as the highest-quality brand on the market, and with such a reputation, the company could afford to price its product accordingly. This provided the firm with the financial resources to incorporate new technological developments, such as a single-dial radio tuner. Competing models required as many as four separate dials, any one of which could frustrate reception if not properly tuned or calibrated.

In one of its many promotional stunts, Magnavox was commissioned by an amusement park operator to build a 12-foot speaker horn, capable of blaring music out over a distance of 29 miles. Ostensibly shut down as a nuisance, the mighty speaker gave new meaning to the name "great voice." In addition to its profitable audio enterprise, Magnavox encountered strong institutional demand for its speaker systems from competitors, including Crosley, Zenith, and Colonial, who used Magnavox speakers in their own radio models.

In 1929 Magnavox relocated to Chicago in order to be more centrally located and closer to its Eastern markets. The company secured access to electrical components by acquiring the Mershon

AT A GLANCE

Magnavox brand of consumer electronics developed by Edwin Pridham (co-founder with Peter Jensen, and Richard O'Connor of the Commercial Wireless and Development Company) with the invention of the Magna Vox electro-dynamic speaker in 1915 in Napa, CA; The Magnavox Company established, 1917; electric phonograph pick-up developed in 1919; single-dial radio introduced, 1923; high-fidelity phonograph marketed in 1937; first television marketed, 1952; stereo phonograph introduced in 1958; videomatic television introduced, 1961; solid state stereo marketed in 1962; 82-channel remote control developed in 1967; North American Philips, a subsidiary of N.V. Philips Gloeilampenfabriken, acquires The Magnavox Company, 1974 (North American Philips changed name to Philips Electronics North America Corporation, 1993); VCR introduced in 1977; Magnavox brand becomes part of newly formed N.A.P. Consumer Electronics Corporation, 1981; N.A.P. Consumer Electronics Corporation becomes Philips Consumer Electronics Company, 1988.

Performance: *Market share*—10.25% of color television market (second behind RCA; source: *Television Digest's* 1993 Color Television Market Share Survey). *Sales*—approximately $2 billion (total electronics).

Major competitor: RCA; also Zenith, Sony.

Advertising: *Agency*—D'Arcy Masius Benton & Bowles, New York, NY. *Major campaign*—"Smart. Very Smart."

Addresses: *Parent company*—Philips Consumer Electronics Company, P.O. Box 14810, One Philips Drive, Knoxville, TN 37914; phone: (615) 521-4316. *Ultimate parent company*—Philips Electronics North America Corporation, 100 E. 42nd Street, New York, NY 10017; phone: (212) 850-5000. *Ultimate ultimate parent company*—N.V. Philips Gloeilampenfabriken.

Division of the Amrad Corporation. The following year Magnavox moved its production facilities to Fort Wayne, Indiana, to be closer to its largest parts suppliers, Phelps Dodge and Essex Wire.

The Great Depression had no negative effect on radio sales. In fact, with other forms of entertainment unaffordable to millions of people, radio became a great new source of cheap and diverse amusement. As the economy declined, demand for radios actually increased.

To bolster its position in the premium audio products market, Magnavox acquired the Electro-Acoustic Product Company and its patents for a high-fidelity phonograph. The first of these new products, which were incorporated into the Magnavox line, were marketed in 1937, and to sell them, the company organized a national sales force of six men. Despite such a small sales group, the Magnavox name was already well-established. Dealers specifically sought out the brand for the premium end of their selection.

Commercial production was interrupted in 1942 by World War II, and Magnavox factories were converted to military production. This provided the company with experience in new areas of electronics and manufacturing. Magnavox was the leading manufacturer of solenoids that were used to fire guns as small as the .30 caliber Browning machine gun, all the way up to 155-mm cannons. The company also produced a variety of communication equipment, radar and sonar systems, and navigation equipment.

After the war, Magnavox turned its attention to the next great revolution in broadcasting: television. The company developed a glare-reducing chromatic optical filter in 1949, but the first televisions had only small black and white screens mounted in huge wooden boxes. A later model, introduced in 1952, featured a large 27-inch screen. Because these huge sets crowded the average family parlor, Magnavox designed its televisions to serve as pieces of furniture, and even acquired several wood furniture manufacturers to produce TV cabinets.

Televisions were expensive and programming was sparse, but the medium held a commercially viable appeal for those who could afford it. Indeed, as demand grew, production was expanded and unit costs were reduced. The more televisions people bought, the cheaper they became. In 1954 Magnavox introduced a stately model with tuning controls located on top—and out of view. A year later, as television began to rival radio as a commercial medium, Magnavox developed its first color television. Color programming took years to catch on, but as it did, families began trading their black and white TVs for color sets.

In 1959 Magnavox decided that the television and radio/phonograph should be the centerpiece of home entertainment. It developed an all-inclusive console containing everything one may care to view or hear, a precursor to modern home entertainment systems. The company introduced solid state components in 1962 in its "space age" Astro-Sonic stereo. The technology was expanded to televisions three years later.

In 1964 Magnavox developed three new television features: an automatic fine tuning control that prevented stations from drifting in and out, a "Chromatone" control for maintaining constant color values, and a "Quick-On" picture tube that eliminated the 20-second warm-up before an image could be generated. A remote control capable of switching 82 stations was introduced in 1967. The Total Automatic Color system, which debuted in 1969, followed broadcasts through minute frequency changes and maintained constant picture quality.

Advertising

In order to capitalize on the superiority of Magnavox's earliest products, the company effectively promoted the name through prominent branding. Wherever displayed, the Magnavox name was featured in large type, often plastered across the horn or speaker box. Other brands were using mascots in their logotypes, such as RCA's dog Nipper, so Magnavox adopted the image of a striding lion. The animal was featured in advertising plaques from 1928 to 1929, but was later discontinued, possibly because it detracted from the presentation of the brand name. One great distinguishing factor of the brand was the composition of its name. Rooted in Latin, its meaning was lost upon those unfamiliar with Romance languages. But it was easy to pronounce and contained the rare letter "X," which did much to set it apart from other brands, including Packard, Belmont, and Majestic.

Magnavox brands were well-distributed and great demand was generated from print advertising. These ads featured new models and listed their features while providing ordering information. The company favored distribution through dealers, however, in the hope that customer orders would inspire retailers to stock the products.

Magnavox became a major brand shortly after World War II, when defense-related facilities provided the company with the industrial capacity to meet growing demand for radios and televisions. The focus of Magnavox advertising during this period centered on such special features as automatic fine tuning on the 1961 Videomatic TV, the "Quick-On" picture tube, push button tuning, and solid state electronics. Rather than cultivating one enduring advertising theme, Magnavox began centering promotional attention on its name, rotating taglines as the product warranted. Lines such as "Quality in every detail" and "We make staying home fun" were used to promote specific products.

During the 1980s, Magnavox retained the comedy duo of Dick and Tom Smothers as spokespersons for the brand. Using their standard formula, in which Tom played the fool and Dick the straightman, the two showed how simple it was to use a Magnavox product. The theme for these ads was, "Smart. Very Smart." The company continued the theme after taking on the British comedian John Cleese as spokesperson in 1989. Cleese was featured in several surrealistic spots in which his pitches for a portable stereo were successively interrupted by ads for a television, VCR, and camcorder. Later spots depicted Cleese demonstrating the "Smart Sound" feature that defended the viewer from the raised volume of commercials. Magnavox further leveraged public awareness of its ad campaign by extending the word "smart" to several branded technologies, including the Smart Window picture-in-picture feature and a Smart Talk voice-activated VCR control.

Growth and Development

Magnavox has remained a North American brand since the company's inception. Although some early models were exported at a time when no other brands could be obtained in less developed areas of the world, by and large there was no coordinated strategy for business development outside the continent. However, following a dismal performance in a miserable economy during 1974, The Magnavox Company placed itself on the auction block and was acquired by North American Philips. While Magnavox now had access to the financial resources it would need, any hope of expansion into international markets through the Dutch holding company was dashed when Philips elected not to employ the Magnavox brand name outside of North America. Philips already had a viable franchise under its own name, and Magnavox had no existing profile in foreign markets.

Philips did, however, provide Magnavox with the financial backing and technologies necessary to develop several new products. In addition, during the 1970s Magnavox implemented several improvements to its product line, including brighter, clearer TV picture quality, larger screens, touch-tune (rather than dial) tuning, and more robust electronics. The company had also introduced a home video game system called Odyssey in 1972, years before Nintendo.

While Sony, Matsushita, and RCA were struggling with video cassette recorder (VCR) formats during the late 1970s, Magnavox pioneered a unique new technology called the videodisc. Introduced in 1978, this system worked like the CD player that would emerge some years later and produced audio and video images superior to a VCR. Unfortunately, the "Magnavision" videodisc could not record like a VCR, and the public was more interested in recording television programs than assembling costly libraries of movie discs. The device never caught on in great numbers, and low demand prevented scales of production from affecting price decreases. The technology enjoyed a renaissance ten years later, when Pioneer, Panasonic, and Magnavox introduced systems capable of running videodiscs as well as the nearly ubiquitous audio CDs.

The company had better luck with its VHS-format VCR, which was launched in 1977 and eventually became the best-selling VCR brand in the American market. A bulky two-piece camcorder followed two years later, and in 1983 Magnavox introduced an improved single-piece device. Expanding on the 1959 home entertainment concept, Magnavox developed a large projection TV in

A Magnavox ad featuring the Super Magnasonic radio-phonograph and the Cosmopolitan television, both with concealed controls.

1978. A later model, the Superscreen, featured rear projection and stereo sound. In 1982 Philips, a co-developer of the compact disc with Sony, actively began promoting the new technology in North America under the Magnavox brand name.

Performance Evaluation

Magnavox benefited from an unusual positioning strategy under North American Philips. The company acquired the Sylvania and Philco names from GTE in 1981 and continued to operate the franchises parallel to the Magnavox and Philips brands. Despite some successes, particularly with Sylvania, it became strategically unfeasible for Philips to simultaneously support four distinct brand identities. Instead, Sylvania and Philco were migrated to the lower end of the market, where price competition is the primary competitive criteria. Magnavox, with its excellent reputation for quality, remained in the higher-margin segment of the market. Philips began phasing out Sylvania in 1994, but Philco had become a specialty brand, produced only in lots for distribution by such discount chains as Target and Kmart.

Philips's strategy has been to defend Magnavox from market failures by introducing new technologies under the Philips brand name first. Should the technologies fail to catch on in the United States, they can do only limited damage to the international Philips brand. However, if they are successful, they may be transferred into the Magnavox line.

In recent years Magnavox has begun to pay closer attention to styling. The company had long understood that televisions are furniture as well as appliances. In the past, however, Magnavox styling has concentrated on baroque wooden sculptures that, although beautiful, were appealing only to older customers. In an effort to update the appeal of its televisions, Magnavox introduced sleeker cabinets, resembling the lines of an expensive sports car. These modern designs are favored by new, younger customers. Magnavox's strategy of technological leadership accompanied by snappy promotion and styling recently earned the brand the position of North America's second-largest selling names in color TVs (RCA holds the number one spot) and the top position in VCRs.

Future Predictions

Philips's stated goal is to expand Magnavox beyond its core markets in order to double 1993 sales volume by the year 2000. One example is the company's partnership with Bell Atlantic, in which the two companies are working to develop enhanced broadband communications services. Another is high-definition television, where Philips has worked with AT&T, General Instrument, Zenith, Thomson, and two research organizations to develop an industry standard.

The Magnavox name also is likely to be extended to the accessories market, including camcorder lights, bags, and straps. In this and other new ventures, Philips will consider outsourcing production to other manufacturers, while working to improve the quality and cost characteristics of its product line. Finally, Philips has established a factory service organization, in addition to its authorized service shop arrangement—a method favored by many competitors—to maintain higher and more consistent standards of service quality and levels of consumer loyalty.

One of the company's greatest challenges will be to keep pace with the rapid consolidation of retailers. To overcome changes in the distribution of its products, the company plans to pursue more aggressively a greater commonality in Magnavox's merchandising, retail displays, and advertising. Driving this strategy, Philips has consistently devoted between six and seven percent of worldwide revenues toward research and development.

Further Reading:

"Brief History of the Magnavox Company," Fort Wayne, IN: The Magnavox Company.

"Cleese, Very Cleese," *Adweek,* October 14, 1991, p. 39.

"Magnavox Moves to No. 2," *Television Digest,* August 30, 1993, p. 10.

Magnavox: 60th Anniversary, Fort Wayne, IN: The Magnavox Company, 1971.

"North American Philips: History," Knoxville, TN: North American Philips Corporation.

"Pitchman John Cleese," *Adweek,* October 5, 1992, p. 50.

"70 Years of Excellence in Consumer Electronics," *Dealerscope,* March 1980, pp. 29–42.

—*John Simley*

MARTEX®

M A R T E X®

Martex, created by the brothers W.H. and A.E. Margerison for their terry-cloth towel business in Philadelphia in the early 20th century, is one of America's best-known and oldest brand names for towels and sheets.

Brand Origins

In 1928 the West Point Manufacturing Company bought out the Margerison brothers lock, stock, and barrel—acquiring everything from the machinery and production space of the company to the brand name "Martex" and its well-established reputation. At the time, West Point had already been an established textile manufacturer for nearly 50 years. West Point was established when two Georgia-based textile makers that specialized in the manufacture of canvas wagon tops and tents merged in 1880. As the railways opened up the West, the demand for textiles soared. The company grew impressively, adding a number of new mills. In 1916 it opened a manufacturing facility in Fairfax, Virginia, a large, new plant built with the intention of making towels. However, with the onset of World War I the plant was converted to produce army duck. It was not until 1926 that the Fairfax mill produced its last yard of duck and exclusively made towels.

West Point continued to expand throughout the 1930s and 1940s. In 1948 West Point introduced its premium-quality Luxor towel within the Martex brand, meant to occupy the upper strata of the towel market and appeal to the carriage trade. The line was intended to serve as the flagship of Martex. In 1965 West Point merged with the Pepperell Manufacturing Company of Biddeford, Maine, another textile manufacturer. Originally organized in 1850, Pepperell had expanded to produce a range of woven goods, including sheets (its Lady Pepperell line of sheets was introduced in 1926). The name of the newly merged company became West Point-Pepperell, Inc. (WPP).

Martex Gets a New Look

The new West Point-Pepperell was able to fully develop a range of lines at varying price points. Several years after the merger, the company decided to position Martex at the top of the market. Martex was to be its higher quality department-store line of sheets and towels, while its Lady Pepperell line was designed to be distributed to mass merchandisers. WPP decided to build Martex's name and image, which had previously been somewhat staid and boring, by updating its styling and creating for it a fashionable image.

By the mid-1970s, West Point-Pepperell had developed a reputation for consistent quality, a stable executiveship, and fashion innovation. Martex had gained an industry-wide reputation for its leading-edge fashion sensibility. Its premium-quality Luxor line held a strong position in the high-margin, high-profit department store business. WPP's reputation for constancy proved especially important through the 1980s, as other mills (including its main competitor, Fieldcrest) became embroiled in takeovers and buyouts. By the mid-1980s, WPP, and especially its Martex segment, was considered the fashion leader of the industry.

Although consumer spending grew substantially during the 1980s, spending on towels and sheets did not climb significantly. In this flat-growth environment, more and more textile makers, including J.P. Stevens, tried to move into the sphere that Martex had dominated—namely, highly fashionable home textiles—because the profits were greater there. Other mills took on more designer names and tried to elbow forward in the crowded field. WPP's advertising budget for 1984 was double that of 1982.

In this competitive environment, Martex tried to put an added emphasis on quality and distinguish itself from its biggest competitor—the Royal Velvet line at Fieldcrest—by introducing a pima cotton towel in its Luxor line. A company executive, speaking of the competition between Luxor and Royal Velvet, told *HFD,* "We were head to head, the towels were not that much different. We wanted a handle to separate the two." The new product did increase sales in that line, the largest share of its department store business. However, according to *HFD,* massive promotion by Fieldcrest had helped Royal Velvet consistently outsell Luxor by as much as four to one. WPP's marketing efforts continued to keep Martex (and Lady Pepperell, too, at the other end) a fashion leader without pushing the consumer's taste too far.

As other mills attempted to challenge Martex's preeminent position at the fashionable and profitable end of the spectrum, WPP held to its strategy of focusing on increasing profit, as opposed to market share. Instead of cutting the prices of its goods to generate volume, and by staying away from high-volume yet import-sensitive goods, Martex prices (as well as those of Lady Pepperell) remained steady. This strategy fueled WPP's reputation as the highest priced mill in the industry. WPP also held un-

AT A GLANCE

Martex brand of towels created by the W.H. and A.E. Margerison and Company; brand purchased by the West Point Manufacturing Company in 1928; West Point merged with another textile manufacturer to become West Point-Pepperell in 1965; became WestPoint Stevens in 1993.

Major competitor: Fieldcrest Cannon, Inc.

Advertising: *Agency*—Warwick Baker & Fiore, New York, NY.

Addresses: *Parent company*—WestPoint Stevens, Inc., 400 W. 10th St., West Point, Georgia, 31833; phone: (706) 645-4000.

waveringly to its tradition of distributing Martex only to department stores, avoiding wholesalers and linen shops. "We feel traditional department stores have the image to project fashion goods, display and advertise them, and that's what the Martex brand needs to create the fashion image," vice president of marketing Dick Williams told *HFD.*

The market was also rapidly changing. Imports had a big impact, especially at the lower end, while more and more department stores sought to shore up their own profits with private-label merchandise, which provided a wider margin. And more mass merchants pushed more aggressively for nationally recognized brand names. Consumers, also, had become much more quality- and style-conscious. WPP thus made the decision to focus on the branded, upper-end products, including Martex, where the profit margins were widest—and where it had an advantage as a recognized design and style leader. In 1985, however, the company shifted gears somewhat when it sold solid-color sheets to J.C. Penney, generating an estimated $70 to $100 million in volume. The packaging read "Made expressly for J.C. Penney by Martex," and fell into the Penney strategy of using known name brands to lure customers.

West Point also avoided using designer names too heavily. The company rejected a Ralph Lauren line because the designer wanted his name to stand alone. "When we do a designer, we do it for a purpose: The patterns are right and it fits into our whole strategy. Martex is our designer name," Williams told *HFD.* WPP spent heavily to advertise the Martex name and its image.

In 1988, WPP acquired J.P. Stevens & Company, which produced various lines that competed with Martex's, including Ralph Lauren and Laura Ashley, for $790 million. West Point-Pepperell instantly became number one in the bed-linen market, increasing its market share from 14% to 36%, and jumped to number two in the towel market behind Fieldcrest Cannon, Inc. However, the leverage incurred to finance the purchase made WPP an attractive target for acquisition.

WPP Meets FOL

In 1989, WPP was acquired by Farley Inc., after an intense and bruising takeover battle. Bill Farley had fought for five months to win WPP, eventually gaining control with a complicated deal that put him $1.5 million in debt. Farley earned his reputation after he had taken over Northwest Industries in 1985. He sold most of its assets but focused his attention on its Fruit of the Loom (FOL) segment. He cut costs, expanded lines, increased advertising, and turned Fruit of the Loom into a megabrand with tremendous sales growth.

Farley promised to apply much the same strategy at WPP. He planned to cut costs and increase profit margins at the company, just as he had done at FOL. However, it would prove a much more difficult task at WPP; the managerial staff there was already quite lean and recent capital improvements had made the company one of the most efficient in the industry. To meet Farley's lofty profit projections (made necessary by debt obligations undertaken to finance the buyout), WPP needed to double its profit margin to about 18%, approximately double the industry's five-year average. WPP's debt as a percentage of total capital was 70%.

WPP soon launched a $20 million advertising campaign—approximately 10 times the industry average. Most of the advertising dollars initially went to market Lady Pepperell. Farley's strategy centered on his conviction that, as the home textile market was not dominated by any one brand, it was ready for megabrand domination. Farley intended to create three such brands—Martex, Lady Pepperell, and the to-be-introduced Fruit of the Loom line. WPP tried to create a strong brand identity for Martex, hoping to catapult Martex, just as he had done for FOL. He hoped that these tactics would not only foster name recognition but increase overall sales as well.

Martex Sells Tassels and Trim

The new campaign marked Martex's first appearance on television. The image conveyed was one of fashionable luxury, as Martex towels and sheets were showcased in a series of well-appointed, comfortable-looking rooms. The tag line was "Martex—Extraordinary in every detail." For Martex the emphasis would be on the details that, it was hoped, would prove it different from the other department-store brands. Consumer research showed that Martex's affluent customers paid attention to the finer points, such as the color of trim or tassels. Farley intended a soft-sell approach and vowed to invest in capital improvements and to attempt to keep the products at their price points.

Under Farley's direction, Martex soon increased its involvement with designer names. Martex produced the new Esprit and Liberty of London lines, and in March 1992 Paloma Picasso launched a home-linen line. A Bloomingdales executive noted in *HFD:* "This is a very high-fashion line, geared toward a sophisticated customer who appreciates quality and who can afford to change the look of her bedroom often enough to buy more than one of the styles."

Farley Bails Out

In August 1991 Farley, unable to come up with the funds to cover the debt incurred to take control of WPP, agreed to terminate his control of 95% of WPP stock through his holding company, West Point Acquisition Corp. In September 1992 West Point Acquisition Corp. changed its name to Valley Fashions Corp., which then held 95% interest in WPP. In October 1992 Farley agreed to sell his stock back to Valley Fashions. Although WPP's sales remained fairly healthy, the burden from financial restructuring—including bankruptcy procedures—created large losses.

In October 1992 Martex dropped the price of its Luxor towels to be more competitive with Fieldcrest Cannon's industry-dominating Royal Velvet brand. Noting that "it's difficult to sell an expensive product in the nineties," a WPP marketing manager told *HFD,* ''Luxor has been around for 25 years. It's a strong name, but it was vacillating.''

In March 1993 WPP launched a strategy to position Martex as the company's premier brand. Previously, Martex had shared the same niche with Utica, a brand carried over from J.P. Stevens. The designer lines under the Utica label were to shift to Martex's area; Utica was then to come under the umbrella of Martex as well. Martex was also slated to try to broaden its appeal among a wider spectrum of lifestyles and tastes. An advertising campaign with the tag line ''created in the spirit of how we live'' was launched—more friendly and less highbrow than previous campaigns. The company continued the emphasis on brands that Farley had brought. Reasons cited by the president of the company, Thomas Ward, were that brands were important to consumers when making decisions at the point of purchase and that consumers interested in value and quality see value in a recognized name brand. It seemed that in the 1990s value had become of paramount importance to consumers.

In December 1993 Valley Fashions Corp., the holding company, and West Point-Pepperell, Inc., its operating subsidiary, merged to form WestPoint Stevens, Inc. Its capital structure continued to be highly leveraged. WestPoint Stevens, in an attempt to generate sales volume, kept its prices low.

Further Reading:

Adler, Sam. ''WestPoint Stevens Shifts Martex,'' *HFD,* March 29, 1993, p. 33.

Bershad, Lynne. ''The WestPoint Pepperell Way,'' *HFD,* May 12, 1986, p. 1.

''Department Store Towel Wars,'' *HFD,* June 4, 1986, p. 28.

Fraser, Mark. ''Farley Slates Lady Pepperell, Martex for Megabrand Status,'' *HFD,* November 6, 1989, p. 58.

Greising, David. ''Bill Farley Is on Pins and Needles,'' *Business Week,* September 18, 1989, p. 58.

Lido, Sari Botton. ''Paloma at Bloomie's; Tiffany's Prize Designer Unveils Martex Linen Line,'' *HFD,* March 30, 1992, p. 60.

Lanier, Joseph L., Jr. ''How WestPoint Pepperell Adapts to Changing Market Conditions,'' *Textile World,* October 1985, p. 59.

Paul, Cynthia A. ''Assessing Martex's Impact,'' *HFD,* August 17, 1992.

''Valley Fashions, WestPoint Pepperell to Become WestPoint Stevens,'' *Textile World,* October 1993, p. 26.

''WestPoint's Martex Unit Cuts Tags of Luxor to $9.99,'' *HFD,* August 3, 1992, p. 6.

—C.L. Collins

MATCHBOX®

Tiny Matchbox cars and trucks have delighted children in Europe, the United States, and Asia since the early 1950s. The brand's original parent company, Lesney Products, was at one time Britain's largest toy company. It was the most profitable company in the country as well, and its amazing growth even earned it a place in the Guinness Book of World Records. Lesney received a West German award in 1963 as the world's leading manufacturer of die-cast toys. Beginning in the late 1960s the company suffered declining sales, and in 1982 the brand was purchased by Hong Kong-based Universal International Ltd. Despite the financial difficulties, Matchbox remained the world's best-selling brand of die-cast toy vehicles.

Since 1992 the Matchbox brand has been owned by a leading American toy maker, Tyco Toys, Inc. Its Matchbox toys were manufactured in China and Thailand and were marketed in 120 countries. Matchbox spawned a collectors club as early as 1966, and a Matchbox museum in Massachusetts drew visitors from across the globe.

Brand Origins

Matchbox toys began as a sideline to an already existing die-casting business. Leslie Smith and Rodney Smith, two of the company's founders, met as boys and later served together in the English Royal Navy in World War II. They went into business together once the war was over, naming their company "Lesney," a compound of their first names. They called their company simply Lesney Products because they had only a general idea of what their products would be. In 1947 the two Smiths rented a condemned pub, The Rifleman, and installed some secondhand die-casting equipment. Some of the company's first orders were for string cutters and ceiling plates. The Smiths soon took on a third partner, Jack Odell, who had his own casting equipment and much technical expertise. The firm grew in a small way, producing tools and components for industrial use. By 1948 Lesney had eight employees.

At that time English businesses closed for inventory at the beginning of January, and orders at Lesney were consequently always low in December. Like other small die-casting firms, Lesney experimented with making toys during this lull. Some of the company's first toys were cars and trucks with moving wheels; others were animals, such as Jumbo the Elephant and Muffin the Mule. The tiny, low-cost toys were an immediate hit with London children. The Smiths and Odell soon realized that their toys could be more than just filler business, but the three men were engineers, not toy salesmen. Thus, they contacted an agent, Moses Kohnstam, to market the toys under the name of his company, Moko. In 1951 Lesney manufactured a model Coronation Coach that sold 33,000 units. The next year the company sold more than a million of a smaller version Coronation Coach. It seemed that vehicles were their best-sellers, and the smaller they were, the better.

Rodney Smith left Lesney Products in 1951, and it was Jack Odell who came up with the first Matchbox cars. In 1952 Odell made a little car for his daughter and put it in a matchbox so she could take it to school with her. Toys packaged in matchbox-style boxes had been made in Germany in the 1900s, and Lesney revived the idea for a new series of miniatures. In 1953 the company made scaled-down versions of seven of their earlier toys and put them in colorful yellow boxes with red lettering, designed after a Scandinavian brand of safety matches. Lesney and Moko registered the Matchbox trademark that same year. This first Matchbox series included a Cement Mixer, a Caterpillar Tractor, and a Horse-drawn Milk Float, but the big hit was the London Bus. Lesney exhibited 18 Matchbox models at next year's Harrogate Toy Fair and began advertising that children could now "buy a toy that was a complete toy" for pennies.

Commercial Success

Lesney added to its Matchbox line year by year, and by 1960 the company was making 75 different models. Matchbox cars were distinctive because of their size and packaging, but the cars were also finely crafted and extremely detailed. Some of the models depicted cars "of Yesteryear," like the 1904 Spyker touring car and the 1913 Mercer Raceabout, while others mimicked in every feature the latest Ford, Mercedes, or Ferrari. The wheels turned, the doors opened, and some sported four-wheel spring suspension. Some of the models had as many as thirteen separate parts and went through 28 different manufacturing processes. Because the cars were made in great volume, Lesney could keep the price low. In 1963 Matchbox models sold for only 49 cents in the United States (25 cents in Britain).

Lesney began to sell Matchbox cars in the United States beginning in 1954, when the company hired the Fred Bronner Corporation to manage marketing and sales there. Lesney, how-

AT A GLANCE

Matchbox brand of miniature toy car introduced in 1953 by Lesney Products, a die-casting business in London; in 1982, when Lesney went bankrupt, Matchbox bought by Universal International Ltd., a holding company in Hong Kong; the following year Universal formed Matchbox International to handle the Matchbox brand; company name changed to Universal Matchbox Group in 1988; Universal Matchbox Group acquired by Tyco Toys, Inc., of Mount Laurel, New Jersey, in 1992.

Performance: *Market share*—36% (second share) of the U.S. die-cast toy vehicle category. *Sales*—$200 million.

Major competitor: Mattel's Hot Wheels.

Advertising: *Agency*—Bozell, New York, NY, 1992—. *Major campaign*—Television spots with the slogan "Get in the fast lane."

Addresses: *Parent company*—Tyco Toys, Inc., 6000 Midlantic Drive, Mount Laurel, NJ 08054; phone: (609) 234-7400; fax: (609) 273-2885.

ever, was somewhat hampered in its efforts to expand into other markets by its arrangement with Moko. Moko owned 50 percent of the Matchbox trademark and retained broad marketing rights. Moko's manager, Moses Kohnstam's son Richard, disagreed with Lesney's Leslie Smith that Matchbox would sell well in Japan. Smith decided in 1958 that Lesney needed to buy out Moko in order to expand Matchbox internationally. An agreement was concluded the next year, and after 1960 the name Moko no longer appeared anywhere on Matchbox packaging.

Lesney Products also went public in 1960. The two remaining directors, Leslie Smith and Jack Odell, kept 1.2 million shares for themselves and sold 400,000 more for $2.80 a piece. The company was soon one of the stars of the London stock market. Share value quickly quadrupled, and annual profits at Lesney were sometimes as high as 70 percent. The company built more factories in England to keep pace with the growing clamor for Matchbox cars. Within a few years there were 14 factories together employing 6,500 people. By 1963 Lesney was exporting 70 million toy cars to 120 different countries. The company exported close to 80 percent of its output and so became one of Britain's leading foreign currency earners. In 1969 Lesney topped the London *Times* list of England's most profitable companies, and Queen Elizabeth II paid the Hackney factory a visit. Sales were $46.3 million. By the end of Lesney's first decade as a public company, profits had multiplied 20 times.

New Competition

The United States was Lesney's best market by far. At the height of Matchbox popularity in the 1960s, 40 percent of Lesney's production was sold in the United States, totaling approximately 100 million cars annually. Because Matchbox cars sold for a higher price in the United States (up to 55 cents each) than in other countries, that market provided a large portion of Lesney's profits. Matchbox cars seemed to sell themselves. Lesney spent virtually no money on promotion because there was no need. There were other model-car makers, most notably Dinky and Corgi, but these did not compete with Matchbox in terms of size and low price. The demand for Matchbox seemed unstoppable, and so Lesney was completely unprepared for the loss of its U.S. market in 1970.

Mattel, the largest American toy company, decided to enter the miniature car market in late 1968. Instead of building the kind of precisely crafted models that Lesney made, Mattel introduced tiny cars that went really fast. Their Hot Wheels were race cars. Mattel's cars were built with a low-friction axle, and they were sold along with plastic race tracks so that children could pit their toys against each other and see which was the fastest. Matchbox cars had not been designed for speed, and young American consumers soon dropped the British brand for Hot Wheels. They were prompted in the switch by Mattel's lavish television promotions. Mattel linked Hot Wheels to two prominent drag race drivers, Don (The Snake) Prudhomme and Tom (The Mongoose) McEwen. Another American toymaker, Topper Corp., also came out with a line of toy race cars, Johnny Lightning. Johnny Lightning was promoted by Indianapolis 500 winner Al Unser. Fiercely competitive ad campaigns by the two American companies eventually had to be halted by the Federal Trade Commission for exaggerating and falsely representing the toy cars.

Lesney responded to Mattel's challenge by introducing its own line of racers in mid-1969. The Matchbox Superfast had a low-friction axle like that on Hot Wheels, though Lesney had to throw out tens of thousands of pounds worth of equipment and inventory in order to get the new models on the market. Even so, Superfast came too late. In 1970 Mattel took about two-thirds of the $130 million American toy car market, and most of the other third went to Topper. Lesney's profits collapsed by 47 percent, and the company's stock skidded. Lesney's American sales had been $28 million; they sank to $6 million. Lesney still had its other export markets to fall back on, but since a predominance of the company's profits had come from the United States, the new competition was a serious blow. Lesney began to spend money in 1971 on American advertising, including television spots. The company also began to diversify its products somewhat, moving into other toy areas, and Lesney for a time regained a respectable profitability, but Matchbox was no longer the unparalleled market leader it had been.

Changing Market Conditions

In 1968 Matchbox models were donated to time capsules sealed in Texas, and in 1969 the chairman of the Smithsonian Institute selected an assortment of Matchbox cars to represent the era's vehicles to posterity. After Hot Wheels entered the market, Matchbox became more sensitive to trends in the toy world and produced some cars that were a departure from its accurate models of real vehicles. In 1977 Matchbox introduced the Adventure 2000 series, its first line of toys from imaginary designs. The 1977 catalog announced the new line: "The year—2000 A.D. Aliens attack earth! Disaster on the Antarctic! . . . action packed vehicles from 'Matchbox' to the rescue." The series included a Cosmobile, Planet Scout, Hovercraft, Rocket Striker, and Shuttle Launcher. Matchbox also debuted some cars piloted by Walt Disney characters. In 1971 Donald Duck drove a Matchbox Astrocar and Fun Bug, and Mickey Mouse had a Draggin Waggin hot rod. Introduced in 1979 were more Disney models, including a Minnie Mouse Lincoln, a Mickey Mouse Mail Jeep, Goofy's Sports Car, and Donald Duck's Ice Cream Van. This successful line inspired more toys based on comic book characters, such as the Popeye series in 1982.

Lesney began to experience financial difficulties related to its high labor and shipping. The company had opened a Matchbox plant in Moonachie, New Jersey, in 1971, but most of its other factories were concentrated around London. Its competitors, however, were taking advantage of cheap labor in Asia. Lesney Products went into receivership in early 1982, and in June the Matchbox Toy division was bought by Universal International Ltd., a Hong Kong holding company.

The new owners of Matchbox were determined to restore the brand's lost ground. In 1983 Universal formed Matchbox International to handle Matchbox worldwide. The new company moved much of its manufacturing out of Lesney's British plants and opened new die-casting operations in Macao and other locations in Asia. In spite of this move, Matchbox was still the largest domestic toy manufacturer in England. Money saved through manufacture abroad was spent on aggressive promotions. Matchbox acquired the rights to market Voltron, a toy robot inspired by Japanese television, in all English-speaking countries in 1985, a significant departure from its vehicle-bound past. When Voltron debuted on American television, Matchbox sales took off and put the company's American revenues over $100 million. Matchbox International also sought other companies to license the Matchbox name on their products. Chef Boyardee promoted Matchbox, and a New York clothier came out with a line of Matchbox Juvenile Clothing for infants and boys. Other licensees included makers of party favors and school supplies.

Matchbox International spent much more on advertising than Lesney had. The new company spent $10 million on American advertising in 1985, compared with the $4 million that Lesney had put out in its final year. Matchbox also spent advertising money in other countries where its toy cars continued to sell well. In the mid-1980s Matchbox was still the number one seller of die-cast vehicles worldwide. England, Germany, and Australia were leading markets for Matchbox's traditional products, such as the Models of Yesteryear line of antique cars. Matchbox also sold model kits that were popular in Europe, and it was the number two market leader in that area. The company, moreover, recovered much of its American market in toy cars. Hot Wheels remained in first place with 44 percent of sales, but Matchbox was close behind with 36 percent. Matchbox International changed its name to Universal Matchbox Group in 1986 and sold shares on the New York Stock Exchange. In that year Matchbox was the number one toy in Europe, and by the late 1980s the toys were again being sold in 120 countries. The bankruptcy of Lesney Products had led to more modern and competitive marketing of Matchbox, preserving what was recognized as one of the top five names in the international toy business.

Performance Appraisal

Matchbox in the 1990s continued to mix its classic sellers with new products. In 1991 Matchbox came out with cars to commemorate the 75th anniversary of the Indy 500, a set of futuristic vehicles based on magnetic levitation and superconductivity technologies, Lightning Challenge race cars with racing playset, and the Matchbox Monster in My Pocket line of miniature monsters "based on the most renowned monsters of all time." Its 1992 Graffic Traffic, a set of vehicles with decorative parts and stickers, won the number nine slot in the *Early Childhood News* top 100 toys list. That year Tyco Toys, Inc., bought Universal Matchbox for $106 million. Tyco celebrated the 40th anniversary of Matchbox cars in 1993 by recreating some of the very first Lesney Matchbox models in limited editions. Tyco continued to promote the full line of Matchbox models and introduced new trucks and racers, its Incredible Crash Dummies cars, and a complete line of Harley-Davidson model motorcycles.

Matchbox cars had inspired collectors from the brand's earliest years, and Matchbox demonstrated right away that it was not a trend toy that would boom and fade. Miniature cars seemed to appeal to children of all nations and in any generation. The enormous initial success of Matchbox indicated the toy's winning combination of high quality, detailed casting with low price. Though Lesney, the brand's originator, eventually capsized in a more competitive global toy market, the new owners of Matchbox, first Universal and then Tyco, seemed better prepared to promote what was undoubtedly a solid product. Universal and Matchbox both changed the bounds of the Matchbox line somewhat by tying it to other toys like monsters and robots. Even so, both were wise enough to maintain the core idea of accurate miniature representations of existing vehicles.

Further Reading:

Ferguson, Gerald, " 'Quality Brand Recognition Sells,' Says Marc Levine of Concept & Design," *Playthings,* February 1985, p. 266.

Fitzgerald, Kate, "U.S. Toy Marketers Hitch Their Hopes to Super-Fast Cars," *Advertising Age,* July 10, 1989, p. 25.

Force, Dr. Edward, *Matchbox and Lledo Toys,* West Chester, Pennsylvania: Schiffer Publishing Ltd., 1988.

Forkan, James P., "Matchbox Moves into Toy-Making Fast Lane," *Advertising Age,* December 15, 1985, p. 4.

Gilligan, Eugene, "Matchbox Museum: Dream to Reality," *Playthings,* January 1984, p. 70.

Gofton, Ken, "The Switchback Career of Lesney Products," *The Director,* January 1974, pp. 52–55.

"The Great Auto Race," *Forbes,* February 15, 1971, pp. 28–31.

Griffin, Larry, "Made in Moonachie," *Car & Driver,* July 1988, pp. 60–65.

"How the Mighty Have Fallen," *The Economist,* October 31, 1970, p. 80.

"Lesney Files Chapter 11 in U.S." *Playthings,* August 1982, p. 12.

"Making the Most of a Great Name: Matchbox," *Playthings,* August 1985, p. 114.

"Matchbox Line Bought by Universal International," *Playthings,* November 1982, p. 15.

"Matchbox Millions," *Newsweek,* April 29, 1963, pp. 79–81.

"Matchbox's New Line Mixes Lightning Cars, Monsters," *Playthings,* February 1991, p. 134.

Miller, Krystal, "To the Small World of Model Cars, GM Becomes a Big Bully," *Wall Street Journal,* February 15, 1991, p. A1.

"Pocket Money Profits," *The Economist,* April 20, 1963, p. 260.

Schiffer, Nancy, *Matchbox Toys,* West Chester, Pennsylvania: Schiffer Publishing Ltd., 1993.

Tyco Toys News Releases, Mount Laurel, New Jersey: Tyco Toys, Inc., 1993.

—A. Woodward

MAYTAG®

In part through the persistent and highly successful lonely Maytag repairman advertising campaign, Maytag appliances maintain a strong association in the public mind with long life and dependability. Best known as a maker of washers and dryers, the Maytag Corporation offers a full line of major appliances, including equipment for laundry, dishwashing, cooking, and refrigeration. In the high-priced market segments for laundry equipment and dishwashers, Maytag is the top-selling brand name. Although Maytag has entered the low-priced appliance market segments, its emphasis remains on the premium price segment and upscale builder market. Dependability remains its well-known brand-name mantra.

Brand Origins

Frederick Louis (F. L.) Maytag went into business with his two brothers-in-law and George W. Parsons in 1893, creating the Parsons Band Cutter and Self-Feeder Company with total capital of only $2,400. Based in Newton, Iowa, the company produced farm implements, including a threshing machine feeder that reduced accidents among farm laborers by feeding straw more safely into the threshing cylinder. In 1898, the company hired Howard Snyder, reputed to be a mechanical wizard, to improve the technology of the company's threshing machinery.

The company built its first washing machine, the Pastime Washer, in 1907, after another mechanic, George Seed, transferred the technology developed by Snyder to a simple design for a wooden-tub washer. The first Maytag washer was made of cypress because of the wood's durability and water-resistant qualities. Users turned a handle on the tub lid, rotating an internal dolly, which then rotated the clothes and produced friction between the fabric and the machine's grooved interior. The Maytag advertising read, "So simple, a child could do it." The company built and sold the clothes washers during the off-season for farm implements.

F. L. Maytag acquired full ownership of the company and renamed it the Maytag Company in 1909. The Hired Girl, the company's first power machine, appeared the same year; the washer was capable of using power from any engine commonly found on a farm, including that of a tractor. In 1911, the company created a washing machine division, headed by L. B. Maytag, one of F. L. Maytag's sons. Howard Snyder, who was by then head of the company's Experimental Department, improved on the technology of Maytag's "swinging wringer," the first movable wringer in the industry, by making it electrical.

Appearing in 1915, the next incarnation of the Maytag washer, the Multi-Motor, was the first gasoline-powered washer; its target market consisted of families in rural areas who did not yet have access to electricity. Within only six months of the product's introduction, sales and production of Maytag washing machine products doubled; the washing machine division outperformed the farm implement division for the first time in the company's history.

Brand Development

Maytag technology advanced considerably when the company produced its first aluminum washer tub in 1915. It took four more years, however, to solve the problem of casting a high-quality, rust-resistant aluminum machine in the quantities needed to make production economically feasible. After developing the technology to cast the aluminum tub in a single process in 1919, the Maytag company began manufacturing aluminum washers in 1920 in a new foundry built specifically to meet immediate market demands. The company dropped farm machinery production altogether to devote its attention exclusively to its new product.

From 1919 to 1922, the company produced the Cabinet Washer, called "the baby grand of electric washers." Users placed clothes in a cylinder that rotated them through water. The Maytag Fruit Jar Engine appeared in 1921; the "fruit jar" gas tank in the engine was designed to enhance washing convenience.

The next Maytag washer, the 1922 Gyrafoam, known as the "gray ghost" because of its aluminum exterior, was an instant success. The machine had a finned "Gyratator" agitator that forced water through the clothes inside instead of pulling the clothes through the water, resulting in less wear and tear on the fabric as well as cleaner laundry. Because the new model was in such great demand, all other Maytag models were discontinued. Maytag produced one out of every five washers in the United States by 1924. From 1922 to 1926, production of the Gyrafoam washer increased by 300 percent; by 1926, Maytag had manufactured one million washing machines.

Maytag introduced a porcelain-enamel-tub washer in 1931; the porcelain offered resistance to soaps, lyes, and other cleaning

AT A GLANCE

Maytag brand of appliances founded and registered in 1907 when George Seed transferred farm machinery technology to a design for the first Maytag wooden-tub washer, the Pastime; Frederick Louis (F. L.) Maytag, along with his two brothers-in-law and George W. Parsons, had formed the Parsons Band Cutter and Self-Feeder Company in Newton, Iowa, in 1893; all the company's early home appliances were called Maytags; F. L. Maytag acquired full ownership of the Parsons Company in 1909, rechristening it the Maytag Company; the Maytag Company became a division of the Maytag Corporation in 1986.

Performance: *Market share*—14% of major appliance category.

Major competitor: Whirlpool; also, GE.

Advertising: *Agency*—Leo Burnett, Chicago, IL, 1955—. *Major campaign*—Ol' Lonely, the idle Maytag repairman, appearing in the longest-running national network television advertising campaign to feature a real-life character, celebrated 25 years of waiting for a call to repair a Maytag appliance in 1992. In 1994, he was still waiting.

Addresses: *Parent company*—Maytag Corporation, 403 West Fourth St. N, Newton, IA 50208; phone: (515) 792-8000.

compounds. In 1939, the Maytag Master Washer, one of the first appliances to use the color white, featured 50 percent greater capacity than previous Maytag models and an insulated tub that enhanced the maintenance of hot water temperatures. On the promotion side of Maytag's development, many films in the thirties and forties featured Maytag washers, including "Blondie Meets the Boss," with Penny Singleton as Blondie and Arthur Lake as Dagwood. In 1941, Maytag produced its four-millionth washing machine; shortly thereafter, washer production ended and munitions manufacturing began as America entered World War II.

Innovations: Maytag Laundry Equipment

Maytag reconverted its munitions operations to appliance production from 1945 to 1951. Demand for washing machines was so intense in 1945 that production of Maytag washers reached an unprecedented level that remained unsurpassed into the early 1990s. In 1947, the five-millionth Maytag wringer washer was produced. The first Maytag automatic washer, the Maytag AMP (Automatic Maytag Pump) debuted in 1949. The company had rejected six prototypes and 12 different tub variations before it settled on its first automatic washer design. Maytag washers came in both automatic and wringer models thereafter. The company added an electric dryer to its appliance line in 1953.

In the early 1950s, Maytag began offering appliances in color. Maytag Supermatics, top-of-the-line washer and dryer pairs, were available in soft greens and yellows, and later in pink. Halo of Heat dryers produced by Maytag in 1953 were giveaway items on popular television game shows, such as "It Could Be You," with Bill Leyden as host. In 1954, Maytag washers featured a zinc-coated steel cabinet that protected against rust; a 1955 innovation was a delicate fabrics cycle to wash synthetics. An automatic washer with a two-speed motor, one speed for delicate fabrics, appeared in 1956.

The same year, Maytag introduced the helical drive system, which enabled washers to switch from agitation to a spinning cycle through the use of a reversible motor. The helical drive system eliminated the number of movable parts needed in the washers by one-third. By the end of the 1950s, Maytag washers had cold-water wash and rinse cycles, cycles for wool, and cycles for wash-and-wear fabrics. In 1958, the company made a successful push into the commercial laundry market with its first coin-slide washer.

In a move that was to color Maytag's image for decades to come, Maytag hired the Leo Burnett Company to handle its advertising in 1955. Research had demonstrated that Maytag appliances were longer-lasting and required fewer repairs than other brands. Relying on letters from customers that complimented the durability of Maytag machines, the television advertising campaign of 1961 used unsolicited testimony to claim that Maytag was "the best you can buy."

To instill these situations with more "inherent drama" and further reinforce the image of Maytag dependability, the company and its advertiser came up with the idea of the lonely Maytag repairman with nothing to fix. Given the name Ol' Lonely and appearing for the first time on television in 1967, the Maytag repairman was himself soon to become a fixture in Maytag history. Maytag inducted its three most famous lonely repairmen into the Loneliness Hall of Fame in 1992: Serge Christaenssens, Ol' Lonely in French-speaking Quebec; Jesse White, Ol' Lonely for the first 22 years of the ad campaign; and Gordon Jump, Ol' Lonely from 1989 into the 1990s.

Maytag washers in the late 1960s offered a choice of water levels; in 1969, Maytag washers featured a permanent-press cycle with an automatic cool-down phase. In 1974, a special cycle for knits, delicate fabrics, and hand-washables was added. From 1968 to 1983, the Maytag Porta-Pair was popular; the washer and dryer pair handled small loads and rolled from room to room. In 1983, the last Maytag wringer washer was manufactured, signaling the end of an era in washer technology. A new era began in 1985 when Maytag introduced the first full-size, stacked washer and dryer pair, which took up half the floor space of the traditional side-by-side models, or, more precisely, only 27 and one-half inches.

In the early 1990s, Maytag offered an extensive Deco-White model line, an all-white line that included a side-by-side laundry pair, a stacked washer and dryer model, and laundry equipment with built-in cooking features. In 1993, Maytag introduced a new line of laundry appliances called Dependable Care. Seeking to satisfy market demand for more energy savings, the newly designed Maytag washers recycled water between loads by storing it in a separate tub; after allowing sediment to fall to the bottom, the machines pumped most of the water back into the system. A feature called Quiet-Pak decreased the level of noise made by Dependable Care "Plus" washers and dryers. Computer touch washers featured thermostatically controlled water temperature levels, self-cleaning lint filters, vacuum fluorescent display, and one-button programming. Dryers featured reversible doors and bright white interiors to make it easy to see the clothes inside.

Maytag Dishwashers

Maytag first offered a line of built-in dishwashers in 1969. In 1992, Maytag introduced the Maytag Jetclean dishwasher manufactured in Jackson, Tennessee. With the advertising campaign tag line "No Pre-wash," the model responded to market demand for a dishwasher that could clean unrinsed dishes. Available in both Deco-White and a wide array of colors, the models also featured a 20-year warranty on the tub and door, sophisticated noise control, and new dispenser designs and styling. The 1992 dishwasher model helped Maytag triple its share of the U.S. dishwasher market from mid-1986 to 1992.

Maytag Cooking Equipment

Maytag added cooking appliances to its product line in 1981 when it acquired the Hardwick Stove Company. The line included gas and electric ranges, microwave and wall ovens, and cooktops. To continue the expansion of its product line and ensure its survival in a rapidly consolidating industry, Maytag bought Jenn-Air in 1982 and Magic Chef (Admiral and Norge brand names) in 1986.

One exclusive feature provided by Maytag's 1993 electric ranges was a plastic liner in the lower drawer to reduce rattling and provide easy lift-out for cleaning. The Maytag 1993 top-of-the-line electric range was the Deco-White, self-cleaning, ceramic glass model with touch clock and oven controls; at the other end was the standard coil-element-top model. All models featured flexible, five-position racking; upswept top for easy wipe-up of spills; thick fiberglass insulation to increase heat retention; and damage-resistant cabinets. Another feature that helped the Maytag brand stand out from other ranges was the inclusion of towel bars on all the models.

The 1993 gas range line included a self-cleaning range with Deco-White styling and sealed gas burners constructed to prevent liquids from entering the range underneath the cook-top area. Most gas ranges featured pilot-free ignition to enhance energy savings; others offered removable knobs and one-piece lift-up surfaces.

Maytag Refrigerators

The first Maytag refrigerator was on the market in 1989. Federal energy standards for 1993 dictated the redesign of Maytag refrigerators in 1992; the new design reduced energy consumption by Maytag models an average of 25 percent. All models had a foam that improved the insulation injected into the doors and cabinet walls; select models also contained a function that helped the refrigerator use less energy in cooler, less humid weather. Some models qualified for utility rebates based on their ability to exceed 1993 energy efficiency requirements.

The range of choices in 1993 included ten top-mount and five side-by-side models. All Maytag refrigerators featured the following: meat compartments that could be adjusted for temperature and humidity control, sealed vegetable crispers, removable egg cradles, and covered dairy compartments. Some models included the Maytag Thirst Aid Station, a large fountain opening with room to fill large water pitchers. Side-by-side models offered the option of an ice crusher. The redesigned refrigerators came in a choice of Deco-White or almond; some models were available in black and traditional white.

Performance Appraisal

Maytag Corporation profits dropped severely in the early 1990s. Losses in 1992 were at $315.4 million. Profit margins suffered partly because Maytag-owned Hoover operations in Europe produced steep losses. The company also faced stiff competition from the General Electric Company and the Whirlpool Corporation in its targeted high-price, luxury appliance category.

One major problem facing the appliance industry in the early 1990s was the saturation of the domestic market. Because of the need to penetrate foreign markets, in January 1989 Maytag purchased the Chicago Pacific Corporation, owner of the Hoover Company, with its Britain-based appliance business. But because Hoover was heavily dependent on the British market in Europe and Britain was mired in a deep recession in the early 1990s, the Hoover operations lost a significant amount of money. Those loses and the costs to restructure Hoover contributed to a pretax charge against earnings of $95 million for Maytag in the summer of 1992. The company restructured to face difficult market challenges, creating two marketing divisions, one for its Jenn-Air and Magic Chef products and another for its Maytag and Admiral brand names. The Maytag name continued to hold a distinct advantage over competing brands in the early nineties: one survey, conducted in 1991, listed Maytag as one of the top 15 recognized brand names in the country.

Future Growth

Maytag corporate managers expect the aging of the baby boom population in the United States to boost sales of the Maytag brand name. As the boomers increase in age and buying power, the corporation predicts, they will tend to trade up in both homes and appliances. David Leibowitz, an analyst at American Securities, supported the Maytag predictions in the *New York Times* on April 13, 1993, maintaining that Maytag would benefit greatly from a domestic economic upturn and increased housing sales.

In early 1993, Maytag's goal was to push Frigidaire from the third-place slot in the major appliance category. In the *Weekly Home Furnishings Newspaper,* May 10, 1993, Maytag CEO Leonard A. Hadley, demonstrating the tenacity of the lonely Maytag repairman himself, remarked, "We know the competitive threat is there and we are responding to it. Whirlpool will still have to deal with us." If Maytag can prove the same staying power the public has come to expect of the appliances the company makes, Hadley is probably right.

Further Reading:

Brumback, Nancy, "Maytag Pushing to Become Third Largest," *Weekly Home Furnishings Newspaper,* May 10, 1993, p. 86.

Gilpin, Kenneth N., "Maytag Sees a Profit Drop in Third Period," *New York Times,* August 25, 1992, sec. D, p. 4.

Maytag Company New Product Press Releases, Newton, Iowa, 1993.

Maytag Corporation Annual Report, Newton, Iowa, 1992.

"Maytag to Buy Its Microwaves; Sells Magic Chef Plant to Mike Davitt," *Weekly Home Furnishings Newspaper,* June 22, 1992, p. 98.

"Maytag Updates, Innovates," *Weekly Home Furnishings Newspaper,* March 8, 1993, p. 68.

Rehfeld, Barry, "Where Whirlpool Flies, and Maytag Sputters," *New York Times,* January 3, 1993, sec. 3, p. 5.

Ryberg, William, "Maytag Holds U.S. Market Share," Gannet News Service, September 8, 1992.

"The Spirit of Maytag: 100 Years of Dependability," Newton, Iowa, 1993.

Tait, Nikki, and David Waller, "Maytag and Bosch Form Business Alliance," *Financial Times,* September 15, 1992, p. 24.

Wayne, Leslie, "Market Place; Maytag Faces a Load of Problems Both at Home and in Europe," *New York Times,* April 13, 1993, sec. D, p. 8.

—Dorothy Walton

MAZDA®

Mazda is best known as the brand of automobiles that use the unusual Wankel engine. Praised at its introduction as a revolutionary advance in fuel-efficiency, Mazda encountered a spate of problems with the engine, causing tremendous consumer skepticism and even ridicule. The Wankel's poor reputation may have been well-earned, but the technological problems with the engine were quickly resolved. Mazda has sidestepped the Wankel issue, no longer touting it as a unique proprietary propulsion system, but instead working to resurrect its reputation by promoting individual models, regardless of what type of engine drives them. The most notable success in this area is the Mazda Miata, a sports car modeled after discontinued European classics.

Mazda Motor Corporation is the fourth-largest manufacturer of automobiles in Japan, behind Honda, Toyota, and Nissan. True to its founder's basic philosophy, Mazda has elected not to follow Japan's Big Three into the market for larger luxury automobiles, but to concentrate on specific niches where the Mazda brand name might achieve greater success.

Brand Origins

Mazda was established in 1920 as a small manufacturer of cork products. Located in Hiroshima, the company later diversified into a line of machinery products and tools and phased out its cork business, adopting the name Toyo Kogyo, or East Sea Manufacturing. Jugiro Matsuda, who founded the enterprise, firmly believed that Toyo Kogyo must have a unique product to separate it from the legions of competitors. Hoping to take advantage of the growing demand for small trucks, he ordered the development of a three-wheeled model called the DA. Cheap and reliable, it gave Toyo Kogyo a successful entry into the automotive market.

Toyo Kogyo remained a major manufacturer of machine tools, supplying mining companies, and later was drawn into producing military implements, including a variety of automotive parts and machinery. The company escaped bombing during World War II, but lost most of its urban-dwelling work force to an atomic bomb.

Toyo Kogyo resumed production of DA trucks in December 1945. Matsuda was succeeded by his son Tsuneji, who dreamed of building automobiles to meet the increasingly sophisticated demands of Japanese consumers. In 1954 the company established a technological agreement to use a new shell-molding method developed by the Acme Resin Company, and began laying plans for its first mass-produced automobile, the two-door R360 coupe. Matsuda named this car the ''Mazda'' after the Japanese god of light, Auda Mazda, and because it was a homonym for his own name. The R360 was a perfectly sound car, but it had no unique attribute to set it apart from the Honda, Toyota, and Datsun automobiles already on the market.

Mindful of Japan's reliance on imported oil, Matsuda hoped to develop a more efficient engine for the Mazda. He decided to pursue a radical but virtually forgotten design developed years earlier by the German inventor Felix Wankel. Wankel's engine contained no pistons, but instead used a single triangular rotor that circulated around a large combustion chamber with a gear at its axis. The rotor enclosed air and fuel on one side of the chamber. A spark plug ignited the mixture, driving the rotor into a lopsided orbit and thus providing torque to the axial drive shaft at its center. The rotor repeated a combustion every third of a revolution. The Wankel engine converted the wasted inertia of pistons directly into torque. As a result, it could run smoother and more efficiently than conventional piston engines.

Engineers in Germany were unable to develop machining accurate enough to mass produce the Wankel, and therefore they abandoned it. Matsuda was certain that Toyo Kogyo could overcome this problem and turn out Wankel engines by the thousands. He negotiated a licensing agreement from NSU/Wankel, the German patent holder, and in 1961 began development of a commercial Wankel engine.

Early Marketing Strategy

Development of the Wankel consumed years of testing and millions of yen in capital. Most of these expenditures were funded by the introduction of new car models, including the Carol 600, a four-door sedan brought out in 1962. Despite strong competition, Toyo Kogyo produced its one millionth vehicle the following year. The company developed another new model, the Mazda 800/1000 coupe, in 1965.

In a continued effort to explore new engine technologies and perhaps provide some insurance against the failure of the Wankel, Toyo Kogyo licensed a diesel engine technology from the American company Perkins. A proven design, the Perkins diesel was best suited for larger vehicles, and was eventually used to power

AT A GLANCE

Mazda brand of automobile founded in 1960 by Jugiro Matsuda, president of Toyo Kogyo; won exclusive rights to manufacture Wankel-type engines in 1961; first Wankel-powered auto, the Mazda Cosmo 110S, produced in 1967; company name changed to Mazda Motor Corp. in 1984.

Major competitor: Toyota; also Nissan and Honda.

Advertising: *Agency*—Foote, Cone & Belding, 1970—. *Major campaign*—"It Just Feels Right," illustrating ergonomic engineering philosophy.

Addresses: *Parent company*— Mazda Motor Corporation, 3-1, Fucho-cho Shinichi, Aki-gun, Hiroshima-ken 730-91, Japan; phone: (082) 282-1111.

the Mazda Proceed B-series light pickup truck, which was introduced in 1966.

However, work on the Wankel was successful, and plans were made to use the engine in the Mazda Cosmo 110S, a sports car first produced in 1967. The Cosmo marked a revolution in the automotive industry. To the chagrin of skeptics, the Wankel that powered it not only worked, but it was quiet, produced little vibration, and delivered great acceleration. As the only manufacturer licensed to build Wankel engines, Toyo Kogyo finally had the unique product its founder had labored to find. The Wankel engine became the focus of the company's marketing, as Toyo Kogyo cleverly leveraged its unique product in promotional campaigns. As large as Honda, Toyota, and Nissan had become, they had no product nearly as appealing as the revolutionary Cosmo.

Brand Development

The Wankel enabled Toyo Kogyo to make bold plans for the future. Matsuda decided that sales of Mazda cars, particularly the rotary-powered versions, would outstrip the company's capacity to build them. Unable to expand quickly enough, he established a supply arrangement with Kia Motors, an automotive subcontractor. The company also began an aggressive development program to broaden the product line and firmly establish the Mazda brand name in the market. Joining the Cosmo in 1967 was the standard engine Mazda 1000/1200, and the rotary-powered R100 Mazda Familia Coupe in 1968. Toyo Kogyo added the RX-2 Capella in 1970, the RX-3 Savanna in 1971, and the RX-4 Luce in 1972.

By 1972, Toyo Kogyo had turned out its five millionth vehicle. Nearly one million of these cars had been exported, mostly to Europe and the United States. Unlike its competitors, Toyo Kogyo's international growth strategy focused not on Third World nations, but on the growing economy car niche market in the West. In Europe particularly, huge taxes on fuel heightened consumer interest in the miserly Mazda brand.

Toyo Kogyo's strategy of building a product line around the Wankel appeared to be in the early stages of massive success. The growing worldwide popularity of the Mazda brand led Henry Ford II to inquire about licensing the rotary design from Toyo Kogyo. But Matsuda was unwilling to dilute his target market and refused to share the Wankel technology with Ford.

Notable Failure

Matsuda could not have known that hostilities in the Middle East during 1973 would result in an oil embargo led by Arab nations. The ensuing shortage of petroleum caused gasoline prices to double, and in some countries, quadruple. After years of promotional campaigns, the Mazda name was virtually synonymous with fuel economy. Under the circumstances, the brand required no identity changes to take advantage of the swelling consumer interest in fuel-efficient automobiles. The rotary engine had already been promoted as a unique solution to rising fuel prices.

However, in California, Toyo Kogyo's largest and most promising export market, the fuel-efficient rotary engine failed to meet strict antipollution standards. In fact, sales of rotary Mazda automobiles were banned until the engine could be cleaned up. Toyo Kogyo engineers quickly made adjustments for cleaner emissions, but these alterations eliminated the engine's advantages in fuel economy and performance. In fact, at ten miles per gallon of gasoline, the rotary had worse mileage than big Ford and Buick cars. Even worse, modifying the engine for cleaner air caused it to break down more often.

The Wankel engine simply had not been engineered to run cleanly. With its entire franchise on the line and its respected Mazda brand hanging in the balance, Toyo Kogyo commenced a complete re-engineering of the Wankel design. By 1974 these efforts began to bear fruit. The Wankel's rating was stretched to 16 miles per gallon, and then 20. Despite these efforts, consumers had learned to avoid the rotary models, causing the poor reputation to persist needlessly. Toyo Kogyo perfected the Wankel in 1975, giving it the fuel-efficient, environmentally friendly engine it had touted for so many years. However, the energy crisis had begun to wane, and with it went consumer interest in rotary engines.

Modern Development

Toyo Kogyo's product line remained of interest for its fuel economy, if nothing else. But the company had lost two years fixing its rotary engine—two years in which Honda, Ford, and GM developed their own fuel-efficient engines. The value of the rotary engine in itself wasn't enough to sustain the Mazda enterprise. In response, Toyo Kogyo developed several new models, hoping to stay competitive using style and quality. The company introduced the Mazda Familia and Capella 626 in 1977 and the Savanna RX-7 in 1978.

Toyo Kogyo was now in the hands of its founder's grandson, Kohei Matsuda, who greatly strengthened the company's financial position. However, these efforts fell short of goals set by the company's Wankel-weary backers. Matsuda was shuffled out in favor of Yoshiki Yamasaki, thus ending the family dynasty. To avoid layoffs, the company dispatched thousands of factory workers into the sales force. Sales rebounded in 1979, after another brief oil crisis renewed consumer interest in fuel economy. In addition, Japanese manufacturers were widely favored in the United States, where their reputation for quality had become a tremendous competitive factor.

Ford still saw great promise in Mazda as an avenue into the closed Japanese market. In 1979 the company agreed to merge its Japanese subsidiary with Mazda, leaving Ford with a 24.5 percent interest in Toyo Kogyo. Although in many ways the Japanese company conducted its business differently than American auto makers, it did incorporate one Americanism into its business practices: the auto showroom. Auto showrooms had long been common in America, but in Japan many car sales were made by door-to-door salesmen. Whereas Nissan and Toyota had huge sales forces, Toyo Kogyo established a chain of showrooms under the name Autorama.

In 1984, Toyo Kogyo adopted Mazda as its corporate name, reflecting the strength of the brand name. Between 1985 and 1987, Mazda introduced new versions of its RX-7 and 626, and introduced the MX-6, a two-door version of the 626. The company virtually abandoned its world car philosophy. Rather than build one model for all its markets, Mazda created designs specifically for target markets.

The most successful of these new models was an impressive sports car called the MX-5 Miata. Bubbling with European inspiration, the Miata was modeled after the British Lotus and Elan—which Mazda engineers had disassembled for "reference." The Miata was intended for upper-income American males, aged 35 to 50, seeking the same thrill that so powerfully drove sales of the Ford Mustang during the late 1960s. Sales of the car were brisk, giving Mazda a new reputation for reviving the great tradition of building stylish and capable sports cars. Once again, Mazda had an entirely unique product on the market, one that targeted a long-ignored but tremendously viable niche.

Mazda also developed a small car, the Proteg, in 1989 and the Mazda Navajo, a sport/utility vehicle modeled after the Ford Ranger and intended to compete with the Suzuki Samurai and Sidekick. Within the Japanese market, Mazda developed the Persona and Proceed, which joined the company's most popular domestic car, the 323 Sedan. Additionally, the MPV minivan that Mazda had targeted for the American market was introduced in Japan. In 1994, Mazda introduced the Millenia, a midsize luxury sedan aimed at a slightly sportier segment of the market than the stately, age 40-to-55 male market, at which the 929 was aimed. With this model, Mazda offered a 12-model product line, covering many more segments of the market than it had in the past.

Advertising

The first Mazda campaigns were used to establish the company's name as well as its unique engine. The "Mazda goes Hmmm" theme, launched in 1973, was created to illustrate the smooth humming sound made by the rotary engine. When the RX-7 was introduced in 1978, it was accompanied by ads that worked to establish it as the most affordable sports car and the epitome of rotary technology. But one of the company's most memorable ads featured the tag line, "The more you look the more you like." Introduced in 1980, this snappy blurb was intended to lure customers into showrooms and take a test drive, in the belief that the car would sell itself. In 1986, the company employed a trusted spokesman, the actor James Garner, whose relaxed, folksy style ensured a measure of confident curiosity in the Mazda name. The endorsements did much to sweep away the public's distrust of the rotary engine.

Hoping to establish a more philosophical identity, Mazda introduced a new series of ads in 1988 around the "Mazda Way" concept. These ads were intended to illustrate how Mazda's unique approach to car building resulted in a superior product. Unfortunately, the concept was woefully underdeveloped, leaving few viewers with any concept of what the *Mazda* way was and how it could be different from any other company's approach.

The idea, however, was not bad. Mazda automobiles were, in fact, developed around a unique design approach called *Kansei* engineering. Mazda products were developed to appeal to all of a customer's senses. As an example, the company tested more than a hundred exhaust systems for its Miata. Although all of them worked, the one chosen was the one that produced the most appealing sound. As a result, the company launched an ad campaign around the statement, "It just feels right." This quasi-testimonial dismisses the facts-and-figures approaches of competitors and highlights Kansei engineering by simply proclaiming that whatever it is about a Mazda, it just *feels* right.

When compared to the advertising of its principal rivals, Nissan, Toyota, and Honda, Mazda campaigns in the 1980s and 1990s have emphasized lifestyles to a greater extent than products. Mazda automobiles are portrayed in the situations of daily life, featuring the active lifestyles of the younger, well-educated adults who compose Mazda's target market.

Performance Evaluation

Mazda operates within a well-defined segment of the market, manufacturing a relatively narrow line of midsize cars and small trucks. The company continues to be plagued by the unfortunate reputation of the rotary engine. As an indication of this, Mazda had produced 20 million vehicles by 1987, but only 1.5 million of these were rotary powered. Possibly Mazda could have avoided some damage to its reputation by allowing other manufacturers to incorporate rotary engines in their models. By doing this, the company could have blunted the direct association of its name with the notorious engine. Instead, skeptical customers continue to ask Mazda salesmen, "It doesn't have one of those *Wankel* engines, does it?"

Through its association with Ford, Mazda has taken on the job of producing cars for a segment of the market that Ford has chosen to de-emphasize. Some American consumers consider Mazda to be a kind of small car division of Ford. The association enabled Mazda to pursue a different strategy from Nissan, Toyota, and Honda, all of which graduated into the luxury car market to maintain growth. Mazda instead concentrated on improving its existing product line and found them easier to market because the other Japanese auto makers had shifted their attention to different market segments.

Future Predictions

As a brand name, Mazda is associated only with automobiles. The company has as yet seen no opportunity to use the Mazda name in new motorized markets, such as motorcycles, boat motors, or snowmobiles. The company has avoided these markets because it would possess few competitive advantages in them, not necessarily because it lacks the ability. Instead, Mazda has concentrated on building its core business. Here, it is likely to continue to incorporate improvements in its product line, while enjoying limited cooperation with Ford and Kia Motors, another major investor.

Gradually, the unfortunate reputation of the Wankel engine will fade. Consumers unfamiliar with the Mazda line will either learn that the Wankel has been improved but is not standard—nor necessarily suitable—on all models, or they will remain unaware of the Wankel engine at all. Instead, they will be drawn by unique characteristics, such as design, performance, and quality.

Further Reading:

"Family Operation Ends in Toyo Kogyo Shuffle," *Automotive News,* January 30, 1978, pp. 15–16.

"A Ford Acquisition," *Business Week,* July 23, 1979, p. 72.

"History of Mazda Motor Corporation," Hiroshima: Mazda Motor Corp.

"Kenichi Yamamoto: Leading by Courageous Example," *Automotive Industries,* February 1986, pp. 46–49.

"Mazda's Bold New Global Strategy," *Fortune,* December 17, 1990, pp. 109–11.

"Mazda Motor Corporation," *Diamond's Japan Business Directory 1992,* pp. 852–53.

"Mazda Motor Corp.," *Moody's International Index 1992.*

"Mazda Ponders Its Route Through a Bumpy Future," *Wall Street Journal,* September 8, 1993, p. B4.

"The Rotary Turnabout," *Forbes,* March 1, 1975, p. 46.

"Toyo Kogyo Agrees to Court Settlement on Mazda Complaints," *Wall Street Journal,* February 25, 1980, p. 18.

"When I Was a Lad," *The Economist,* December 23, 1989, p. 70.

—John Simley

MERCEDES-BENZ®

Mercedes-Benz brand luxury automobiles, marketed in the United States by Mercedes-Benz of North America, Inc., are best known for their powerful engines and refined German engineering. Mercedes-Benz, often known simply as Mercedes, is one of the oldest automobile marques in the world, introduced in 1926 by Daimler-Benz A.G., which was created by the merger of Benz et Cie. and Daimler-Moteren-Gesselschaft, both pioneers in the automotive industry. The first self-propelled vehicle powered by an internal-combustion engine was a three-wheel velocipede built by Carl Benz in 1885, while the name Mercedes had been used by Daimler since 1901. For many automobile owners around the world, driving a Mercedes is the ultimate symbol of success.

Carl Benz (1844-1929)

The Mercedes-Benz story begins with Carl Benz, who operated a machine shop in Mannheim, Germany. In the late 1870s, Benz began experimenting with internal-combustion engines, and successfully demonstrated a two-cylinder engine in 1879. In 1883, Benz and two financial backers founded Benz et Cie., Rheinische Gasmotoren-Fabrik, to manufacture internal-combustion engines. Though early internal-combustion engines were designed for factory use, Benz developed a smaller engine that he mounted on a three-wheeled car. He also designed a carburetor, cooling system, electric ignition, throttle regulator, and other equipment.

In the spring of 1885, Benz rolled his velocipede out of the workshop and began puttering around the yard in the first self-propelled vehicle powered by an internal-combustion engine. A few days later, Benz assembled the townsfolk for a demonstration and promptly scored another first by crashing into a brick wall. Benz continued to work on his gas-powered velocipede, eventually achieving a consistent 10 miles per hour (mph) with a reasonable degree of mechanical reliability. He received a German patent in January 1886.

Benz's velocipede was far from an instant success. In 1888, the *German Yearbook of Natural Sciences* commented on his ''Patent Motorwagen'' exhibited at the Munich Engine Show: ''[T]his employment of the petroleum engine will probably be no more promising for the future than the use of the steam engine was for road travel.'' There was even less interest at the Paris World's Fair in 1889.

In 1893, Benz patented a steering mechanism for a four-wheeled vehicle he called the Viktoria. That fall, a Viktoria was put on display at the Astor Building in the United States. A headline in the *New York Sun* proclaimed: ''The new propelling power that has come out of poetic Germany!'' The article informed Americans that the car ''is independent of rails and can fly over country roads at 30 miles an hour.'' In 1894, Benz introduced a newer model, the Benz Velo, which became the world's first production automobile. By the end of 1901, Benz had sold more than 2,700 vehicles, and for a brief time Benz et Cie. was the leading automobile maker in the world.

Gottlieb Daimler (1834-1900)

Gottlieb Daimler, another of the principal creators of the car that was to be called Mercedes-Benz, was the first of his family in four generations not to become a baker. Instead, he studied at the Stuttgart Polytechnic Institute and became a engineer. The experienced engineer and mechanic was soon given the task of designing an internal-combustion engine for the German firm Gasmotoren-Fabrik Deutz, but he left the company when they failed to develop his ideas. In 1882, Daimler joined with Wilhelm Maybach to develop an engine small enough to drive a vehicle. Though they lived only 60 miles apart, Daimler and Benz never met.

In 1885, the same year that Benz rolled out his velocipede, Daimler and Maybach mounted an engine on a wooden bicycle, thus creating the first motorcycle. The following year, they installed an engine in a carriage, probably the first time an internal-combustion engine was used to drive a four-wheel vehicle. Soon afterward, they installed an internal-combustion engine in a boat, another first. However, since the public still considered gasoline engines dangerous, wires and insulators were mounted on the outside to make the boat look like it was battery powered. In 1888, Daimler and Maybach created an engine-driven propeller system for hot-air balloons.

A Daimler ''steel-wheeler,'' the first four-wheel vehicle driven by an internal-combustion engine, was also on display at the 1889 Paris World's Fair, but like Benz's Patent Motorwagen, it drew little notice. However, Daimler licensed the design for his engine to several manufacturers, including Panhard-Levassor in France and William Steinway's Daimler Motor Co. in the United States. The latter company built a few automobiles, called the American Mercedes, but a fire in 1913 destroyed the factory where they were

AT A GLANCE

Mercedes-Benz brand of automobiles originate with the German company Benz et Cie., founded in 1883, and Daimler-Motoren-Gesselschaft, founded in 1890; Benz self-propelled velocipede introduced, 1885; Mercedes marque introduced by Daimler-Motoren-Gesselschaft, 1901; Benz et Cie. and Daimler-Motoren-Gesselschaft merged to form Daimler-Benz A.G., 1926; Daimler-Benz introduced Mercedes-Benz marque, 1926; Mercedes-Benz A.G. formed as automotive division of Daimler-Benz A.G., 1989.

Performance: *Market share*—7% of U.S. luxury car market; 52% of U.S. ultra-luxury car market. *Sales*—$3.3 billion (U.S. sales).

Major competitor: Bayerische Motoren Werke AG's BMW.

Advertising: *Agency*—Scali, McCabe & Sloves, New York, NY, 1992—. *Major campaign*—"Sacrifice Nothing."

Addresses: *Parent company*—Mercedes-Benz of North America, Inc., One Mercedes Drive, Montvale, NJ 07645-0350; phone: (201) 573-2246. *Ultimate parent company*—Mercedes-Benz A.G., Untertuerkheim, W-7000 Struttgart, Germany. *Ultimate ultimate parent company*—Daimler-Benz A.G.

manufactured and the company went out of business. Daimler assigned patent rights in Germany to Daimler-Motoren-Gesselschaft, founded in 1890. He joined the company himself in 1895 after Daimler-Motoren-Gesselschaft licensed the engines to the Daimler Motor Company Ltd. of England.

Emile Jellinek (1853-1918)

An unlikely collaborator in the Mercedes-Benz story was Emile Jellinek, a wealthy Austrian banker and consul-general in Nice, France. In 1897, Jellinek became a member of the Daimler-Motoren-Gesselschaft managing board and a distributor of Daimler motor cars. It was Jellinek who convinced Daimler to position the engines at the front of the car ''because that was where the horse used to be.'' Jellinek also pressured Daimler to create faster, more powerful automobiles. His favorite sales technique apparently was to pass other motorists, especially on hills, and then stop to sell them the car he was driving.

In 1900, Jellinek asked Daimler to design a racer with a longer wheelbase, a lower center of gravity, and an engine capable of generating speeds of at least 30 mph. Jellinek also promised to purchase 36 of the cars—a big order in those days—in return for exclusive rights to distribute Daimler automobiles in Austria-Hungary, France, Belgium, and the United States. Jellinek had one other stipulation: he wanted the car named the ''Mercedes,'' in honor of his one-year-old daughter, Maria de las Mercedes Adrenne Manuela Ramona.

The first Mercedes was delivered to Jellinek in December 1900. When millionaire industrialist William Kissam Vanderbilt Jr. purchased a Mercedes from Jellinek the following year, the *New York Times* reported, ''The first Mercedes make of automobile built in Germany . . . is expected here in a few days.'' The newspaper described the car as ''one of the best built in Germany this year. It is very low in front, with accommodations for four persons for carriage traveling. But two seats are to be used when the machine is in racing trim.'' In 1902 Daimler-Motoren-Gesselschaft registered the name ''Mercedes'' as a trademark, and the name ''Daimler'' faded from use as a marque.

Jellinek's association with Daimler-Motoren-Gesselschaft came to an acrimonious end in 1908, although the rift had begun years before. When a Mercedes did well in competition, Jellinek, a racing enthusiast, was quick to claim credit. But he was equally quick to place blame whenever a Mercedes was bested. After a loss in 1905, Jellinek wrote, ''The only good thing which this heavy defeat may have is that the engineers of DMG will have their arrogance and overweening opinion of themselves somewhat damped.'' But when a reviewer praised a new Mercedes without mentioning Jellinek, he replied, ''The whole lot would not exist if I had not appeared on the scene. Not only the whole business, but also the whole construction of the Mercedes car, was and still is, entirely built on my plans.''

In 1906, when Daimler-Motoren-Gesselschaft stopped supplying Jellinek with free parts, he responded bitterly, ''I give up the ceaseless battle with you. If you want to ruin yourselves completely, do so. You will surely destroy yourselves with the miserable construction of your cars, but mainly it will be with your swollen heads.'' Jellinek was arrested during World War I and accused of spying for Austria. He died in prison in 1918. His daughter Mercedes died impoverished in 1929.

Racing Heritage

The introduction of the Mercedes in late 1900 spelled an end to Benz et Cie. as the largest automobile maker in the world, especially since Carl Benz believed that 30 mph was as fast as a passenger car needed to go. Benz eventually resigned from the board of directors in 1903, when others began leading the company into racing. He rejoined the board in 1904 after the Benz race car proved to be a dismal failure. He also brought aboard a new design engineer, Hans Nibel.

By 1908, Benz had turned over management of the company to his sons, Eugene and Richard. They encouraged Nibel to design a race car for the Grand Prix at Dieppe, France. The race turned out to be a fierce battle between two Benz automobiles and a Mercedes. The Mercedes won, but Benz finished second and third. Benz and Mercedes automobiles would dominate European racing for the next two decades. In 1909, a bullet-shaped Benz Blitzen was clocked at 141 mph, a record that stood until 1922. In the last Grand Prix before the outbreak of World War I, Mercedes racers took first, second, and third in 1914 at Lyon, France.

Two of the Mercedes from the 1914 Grand Prix have interesting post-race histories. One of the cars was acquired by Ralph Palma, who drove it to victory at the Indianapolis 500 in 1915. The car was then shipped to the Packard Motor Company in Detroit. The Liberty engines used in U.S. planes during World War I were based on the Daimler design. The other Mercedes was shipped to the Daimler Motor Co. in England. When the Royal Air Force appealed to Rolls-Royce Ltd. to manufacture airplane engines for the British war effort, Rolls-Royce also used the Daimler engine as its model. Daimler-Motoren-Gesselschaft also produced engines for the German air force.

Mercedes-Benz

When World War I ended in 1918, there were 86 German car makers competing in a devastated market. In 1924, Benz et Cie. and Daimler-Motoren-Gesselschaft agreed to an ''association of common interest,'' and for two years the companies shared technical and marketing information and avoided producing competing models. This informal agreement became a merger in 1926 with the formation of Daimler-Benz Aktiengesellschaft. Daimler-Benz A.G. created a logo that combined the three-pointed Daimler star and the laurel branches that symbolized Benz automobiles. Mercedes-Benz became the new marque.

The Daimler star apparently originated with Gottlieb Daimler's sons, who recalled that their father had once sketched a star to symbolize his rising fortunes. In 1909, Daimler-Motoren-Gesselschaft registered both a three-pointed star and a four-pointed star as trademarks, but only the three-pointed star was ever used. Daimler-Motoren-Gesselschaft later said the star stood for air, sea and land—the elements dominated by Daimler engines. The star became the radiator emblem in 1921. The circular emblem used by Benz began in 1903 as a gear wheel with ''Original Benz'' printed inside. It was changed to a laurel wreath in 1909.

The Mercedes-Benz passenger cars produced by Daimler-Benz A.G. between 1926 and the beginning of World War II are considered among the most magnificent automobiles ever created. Likewise, the aerodynamic ''W'' series racers were among the fastest. The supercharged Mercedes-Benz W-25 was commissioned in 1933 by German leader Adolph Hitler, who advanced the company 500,000 marks to develop a racer that would demonstrate Germany's technological superiority to the rest of the world. Originally, the racer was covered with several thick coats of white paint, Germany's official color for Grand Prix events. But when the car was weighed before its first race at Nurburgring in 1934, it was two pounds over the limit. The paint was scraped off, exposing the aluminum. The W-25 became known as the Silver Arrow, and Mercedes-Benz race cars have been painted silver ever since.

The Silver Arrow won the race at Nurburgring in 1934, and also set a world record at the Gyon road race, near Budapest, with an average speed of 117 mph. In 1935, Mercedes-Benz W-25 racers were entered in 10 events and won nine, including six Grand Prix races. A W-25 was leading in the 10th race, the German Grand Prix, until it blew a tire on the last lap. The Mercedes-Benz W-125, introduced in 1937, was even more awesome. W-125 racers again won six Grand Prix events, including a sweep at Switzerland and Monaco, and a one-two finish at Germany and Czechoslovakia. In 1938, a Mercedes-Benz W-125 driven by Rudolf Caracciola topped 271 mph on the German autobahn.

With the outbreak of World War II in 1939, Daimler-Benz turned its attention to producing airplane engines and vehicles for the German Third Reich, including the remarkable six-wheel off-road Gelandewagen. From 1930 until 1943, the company also produced the Mercedes-Benz 770K, also known as ''Der Grosser Mercedes,'' for German officials. Several of the cars were outfitted with armor plating and bulletproof glass for Hitler's personal use. They weighed more than 10,000 pounds and averaged about 3 miles per gallon. They also featured special tires, each with two dozen air chambers, to eliminate the possibility of a flat. The cars became prized by collectors after the war.

Mercedes Gullwing Coupe

Daimler-Benz factories were heavily damaged by Allied bombing runs in 1945, and the company did not introduced its first post-war passenger car until 1949, when it launched the Mercedes-Benz 170S. The 170S was followed by the Mercedes 220 and the Mercedes 300. Then, in 1952, Daimler-Benz returned to the international racing circuit with the Mercedes 300SL—the legendary gullwing coupe. The 300SL was built using a lightweight tubular frame that made conventional doors impossible. Rudolph Uhlenhaut, a race-car driver and engineer, solved the problem by designing doors cut into the roof. The door opened upward, giving the car a bird-like appearance. Powered by the same six-cylinder engine used in the Mercedes 300, 300SL racers took first place at Le Mans, the Bern Grand Prix, and the Carrera Panamericana, a rugged road race stretching the length of Mexico. In Mexico, the winning Mercedes 300SL averaged more than 100 mph for 1,993 miles. The only mishap was when the 300SL, traveling at 140 mph, collided with a low-flying condor.

From 1954 to 1957, Daimler-Benz produced 1,485 production-model gullwing coupes, most of which were sold in the United States. In 1955, Daimler-Benz also produced eight 300SLR racers, two of which were gullwing models. Daimler-Benz won every race it entered in 1955 except Le Mans, and it won the World Sports Car Championship. At Le Mans, a gullwing 300SLR driven by Pierre Levegh careened into the crowd, killing 83 people, including Levegh, in the worst accident in auto racing history. Daimler-Benz withdrew from factory-sponsored racing after the 1955 season because of the accident. The familiar Mercedes-Benz silver returned to LeMans in 1989 in a joint venture between Daimler-Benz and the Swiss-based Sauber Racing Team, finishing first, second, and fifth.

The Baby Benz

For almost two decades, beginning with the Mercedes-Benz 600 in 1963, Daimler-Benz focused on building full-size luxury sedans. Every model was bigger, more advanced, and more expensive than the last. Then, in 1982, Daimler-Benz introduced the Mercedes-Benz 190, a smaller, sleeker, less expensive automobile that was immediately dubbed the Baby Benz by automotive writers. The Mercedes 190 could average 40 miles per gallon at legal speed limits, but also claimed a top speed of 120 mph. It sold in the United States for about $25,000, which placed it in the luxury class but was half the cost of the next best Mercedes-Benz.

The Mercedes 190 also signalled another change in policy for Daimler-Benz. For years, the firm had deliberately allowed production to lag behind demand. This helped establish Mercedes-Benz as a prestige marque and kept prices up. But the 190 was the first Mercedes-Benz meant to be mass-produced, up to 200,000 cars per year. However, the Mercedes 190 was never as popular as Daimler-Benz had hoped, especially in the U.S. market. When the model was dropped in 1993, *Chicago Tribune* reporter Jim Mateja wrote: ''Psst, Mercedes owners. It's safe to come back. The compact 190 series . . ., a line that was as old as the Berlin Wall, is gone.'' The Mercedes 190 was replaced in by the mid-sized Mercedes C-class sports sedans, which were priced about the same as the smaller, less powerful Mercedes compacts.

Outlook

In the late 1980s, Daimler-Benz began offering pricier models and moved even more strongly toward the upper end of the luxury market. Some analysts interpreted this as ''fleeing'' the Japanese auto makers, who had begun making inroads into the lower luxury bracket in the United States with cars such as the Acura Legend from Honda Motor Co. Ltd., the Lexus from Toyota Motor Corp., and the Infiniti from Nissan Motor Co. Ltd. Many analysts also doubted the wisdom of the move at a time when it seemed that ultra-luxury automobiles were becoming less socially acceptable. New taxes in the United States on luxury items and gas-guzzling automobiles also cut into the market. To make matters worse, the BMW, from Bayerische Motoren Werke AG, passed Mercedes-Benz in 1989 to become the best-selling luxury car in Europe after 30 years as the runner-up. In 1992, BMW also passed Mercedes in the critical U.S. market.

Daimler-Benz denied it was abandoning the lower end of the luxury market to the Japanese, however, and fought hard to defend its U.S. market share. In 1990, Edzard Reuter, then chairman of Daimler-Benz A.G., announced that Mercedes-Benz would introduce a ''fundamentally new model'' every year for the next five years. (Mercedes-Benz A.G. was created in 1989 as a division of Daimler-Benz A.G. when the parent company expanded into electronics and aerospace technology.) The first new model, introduced in 1990, was the Mercedes-Benz 190E, a high-powered version of the Mercedes 190 compact. The Mercedes 190 model line was dropped in 1993.

In 1991, Mercedes introduced a new version of its 10-year-old, ultra-luxury S-class automobile. The new S-class sedans were marvels of engineering with 12-way power seats, disappearing trunk-lid handle, and a charcoal air-filtering system. Disappearing ''parking rods'' extended above the rear fenders whenever the car was in reverse. Unfortunately, the S-class sedans, with sticker prices ranging from $70,000 to $130,000, were widely criticized as being too big and too expensive for the changing market. Embarrassingly, the S-class Mercedes was also too wide for the popular auto trains in Europe.

In 1992, Mercedes-Benz introduced the mid-sized C-class as a replacement for the Mercedes 190. The sports sedans were generally well received by the trade press. *Automotive News* also lauded the inclusion of a cupholder in the C-class sedans as an indication that Mercedes-Benz was beginning to listen to its customers. Mercedes automobiles were often criticized for being over-engineered while simple amenities that customers wanted were neglected. At a news conference, Dieter Zetsche, a member of the Mercedes-Benz board of directors, obliquely acknowledged the shift in philosophy: ''We designed our cars for one reason: our devotion to engineering excellence. We loved to design products that outperform the competition and that outdeliver the competition, and that's still true today. But markets change. Customer requirements change.''

Mercedes-Benz of North America also launched a new advertising campaign in the early 1990s that it hoped would turn around slipping sales by focusing less on superb engineering and more on the pleasure and satisfaction of owning and driving a Mercedes-Benz. The advertising slogan ''Engineered like no other car in the world,'' which many potential buyers found intimidating, was replaced by ''Sacrifice nothing.'' Sam Scali, president of the agency that developed the theme, told *Automotive News* that it ''not only positions Mercedes-Benz, it also positions the competition too. All other cars are a compromise.'' Ads focused on Mercedes' reputation for safety, longevity, and resale value. However, the advertising campaign lost some glitter in 1993 when Mercedes-Benz of North America sent a letter to major magazines asking that ads for Mercedes-Benz automobiles not run in any issues that carried negative stories about the company or about Germany. Many magazines had tacit understandings with advertisers about sensitive materials, but Mercedes-Benz demanded that publishers sign an formal agreement and threatened not to pay for ads that were not pulled. After a barrage of negative stories in the newspapers, Mercedes-Benz rescinded its policy.

Mercedes-Benz announced in 1993 that it would build a factory in Vance, Alabama, to build a new sport-utility vehicle to be introduced in 1997. Sales of Mercedes-Benz automobiles in the United States peaked at 99,300 in 1986, before falling to about 59,000 in 1990 in a generally weak market for luxury automobiles. In 1992, Mercedes-Benz sold about 63,300 automobiles in the United States. Prices for the 1994 model line ranged from $30,000 for the Mercedes C220 sedan to $120,000 for the SL600 roadster.

Further Reading:

Ball, Robert, ''Mercedes's New Baby Benz,'' *Fortune,* December 27, 1982, p. 84.

Boesen, Victor and Wendy Grad, *The Mercedes-Benz Book,* Garden City, NJ: Doubleday, 1981.

Brown, Warren, ''Luxury Car Makers Battle for the Boomers,'' *Washington Post,* October 19, 1989, p. E1.

''Daimler-Benz A.G.,'' *International Directory of Company Histories,* Vol. 1, Chicago: St. James Press, 1988.

Donaton, Scott, ''Mercedes in Full Retreat on Ad Placement Order,'' *Advertising Age,* September 20, 1993.

Henry, Jim, *Automotive News,* ''Mercedes: We're Not Fleeing Japanese,'' October 7, 1991, p. 8; ''Mercedes Redesigns S-class Sedans,'' October 7, 1991, p. 16; ''Mercedes Ads Say You Can Have It All,'' August 31, 1992, p. 6; ''Cupholder or Creed? Mercedes C-Class: A New Attitude,'' September 27, 1993, p. B1.

''Hitler's Car,'' *Motor Trend,* June 1973, p. 88.

''In Retrospect: Mercedes 300SL Gullwing Coupe,'' *Motor Trend,* August 1971, p. 61.

Johnson, Richard, *Automotive News,* ''Mercedes-Benz Readies New Models for U.S.,'' September 26, 1988, p. 34; ''Mercedes Bets on New SL Roadster to Boost Its Image,'' March 27, 1989, p. 50.

Ludvigsen, Karl, ''Mercedes Milestones,'' *Motor Trend,* April 1977, p. 46.

Marks, John, ''Mercedes-Benz Gets Turned Upside Down,'' *U.S. News & World Report,* November 15, 1993, p. 59.

''Mercedes with a Human Face,'' *Forbes,* September 14, 1992, p. 474.

Mateja, Jim, ''Mercedes Gets Its Senses Back for '94,'' *Chicago Tribune,* November 26, 1993.

''The Origins of 'Mercedes' and the Star,'' Stuttgart, Germany: Daimler-Benz A.G., 1988.

Protzmann, Ferdinand, *New York Times,* ''BMW Gives Daimler-Benz a Race,'' May 30, 1989, p. D1; ''German Car Makers Defend Status,'' March 19, 1990, p. D1.

Rossant, John, ''Diverse Daimler Versus Brilliant BMW,'' *Economist,* June 3, 1989, p. 65.

Serafin, Raymond, ''Mercedes Will Push Product, Not Image,'' *Automotive News,* January 20, 1992, p. 43; ''New Mercedes Ads Are Humor-injected,'' *Advertising Age,* April 20, 1992, p. 43.

Steinwedel, Louis William, ''Eva Braun's Mercedes,'' *Motor Trend,* May 1974, p. 92.

Strnad, Patricia, ''Motion Emotion; Mercedes-Benz Ads Take New Turn,'' *Advertising Age,* November 16, 1987, p. 104.

Taylor III, Alex, ''BMW and Mercedes Make Their Move,'' *Fortune,* August 12, 1991, p. 56.

—Dean Boyer

MERCURY®

The Mercury brand comprises several models of automobiles sold by the Lincoln-Mercury Division of the Ford Motor Company, including the Marquis, Topaz, Sable, Capri, Cougar, and Tracer. In a joint agreement with the Nissan Motor Corporation, Lincoln-Mercury recently began producing a front-wheel drive minivan called the Mercury Villager.

Early Roots of the Mercury Name

The Mercury name was attached to many car brands long before Edsel Ford's decision to use the name in 1937. As early as 1903, the Mercury Machine Company of Philadelphia produced a one-cylinder, seven-horsepower, open-seated gasoline car with wood wheels, which sold for $925; however, the undercapitalized company failed after only one year. In 1908 a Mercury put out by the Mercury Motor Company of Hillsdale, Michigan, also failed. By 1913 another short-lived venture, the Mercury Cycle Car Company of Detroit, organized by W. J. Marshall and R. C. Albertus, boasted that it had produced the "first distinctively American cyclecar." The car had a very small wheelbase and a 9.8 horsepower engine and came in two body types, a two-seater and a monocar designed for salesmen's use. After a brief success, the company went under in 1915.

In Hollis, New York, in 1918, yet another Mercury was produced by Mercury Cars, Inc., a venture that lasted until 1921. This company's 1920 Mercury Touring car was powered by a four-cylinder, 243-cubic-inch engine set in a relatively large 114-inch wheelbase. The model was priced at $2750 to $2959 for open models and $3600 to $3900 for closed models. A luxury Mercury Model H was made by the Mercury Motor Car Company of Cleveland in 1920, with 4 cylinders and a very large 381.6-cubic-inch Rochester-Duesenberg engine. The car was priced at $6750; the company went under the same year. The last of the "pre-Ford" Mercurys was made by the Mercury Motors Company of Belfast, New York, in 1922; Mercury Motors made two closed coupe models, with four and six cylinder engines.

Brand Origins

Under the aegis of the Ford Motor Company, the name Mercury took off to reflect its namesake, the fleet-footed messenger of Roman mythology. By the 1930s Ford's sales had slipped, its market share plummeting to 22 percent in 1936, while General Motors had 43 percent and Chrysler had 25 percent. Ford's Lincoln Zephyr, a luxury car developed by Henry Ford's son Edsel, was a bright spot for the struggling company. Edsel proposed to capitalize on this success by developing a car that fell between the Ford and the Lincoln in price to compete against GM's mid-range cars. By the late 1930s, Ford had weathered the storm of the Great Depression, and in 1938 Edsel Ford convinced his father to market his new Mercury. The new series, which came in convertible, coupe, two-door sedan, and Town Sedan models, was a product of Ford's new Lincoln Division.

Early Marketing Strategy

Asking why a big car couldn't also be economical, early ads for the new Mercury dubbed the model "the car that dares to ask 'why?' " The Mercury was priced in the $1000 range, which was several hundred dollars more than the Ford V-8 and several hundred dollars less than the Lincoln Zephyr. The car was designed to compete with upper range Oldsmobiles and Dodges and lower range Buicks and Chryslers.

The new Mercury had a 95-horsepower version of the flathead Ford V-8, with body styling inspired by the Zephyr. The car got 20 miles per gallon with a good-sized wheelbase of 116 inches and an overall length of 196 inches, allowing Ford to claim that "few cars of *any* size can equal such economy." By 1941 Ford happily pronounced that "It's made 156,000 owners change cars!" The car sold so well that Ford introduced new models, including a sedan in 1940 and, in 1941, the Series 19A, which included a station wagon and Town Sedan. Production was increased in 1941 by 80,000 cars. During World War II, production was shut down or converted to support the war effort, but Mercury had already established a lasting image of high performance and good mileage. In 1945 the Lincoln-Mercury Division was established.

The Boom Years

Although the early Mercurys were essentially enlarged versions of Ford's Model 91 V-8, with a 3.9 liter 95-horsepower engine, its main selling point was the fact that its was $230 more than its predecessor but less than Buick's cheapest 4-door sedan. Thus, the car went head-to-head with its competitors' moderately priced lines, but was marketed as a higher quality product. As technology progressed, innovations included a new axle and front suspension, hydraulic brakes as standard, overhead valves, and oversquare cylinder dimension; by 1955, Mercury offered V-8

AT A GLANCE

Mercury brand introduced in 1937 by the Lincoln Division of the Ford Motor Company; Mercury markets car models including Topaz, Sable, Grand Marquis, Tracer, Capri, and Cougar, as well as the Villager minivan; division renamed Lincoln-Mercury in 1945.

Performance: *Market share*—Lincoln-Mercury has 7% of automobile category.

Major competitor: Nissan; also Pontiac, Buick, Mazda. For minivan segment, Chrysler; also Oldsmobile, Chevrolet.

Advertising: *Agency*—Young & Rubicam, Detroit, MI, 1992—. *Major campaign*—"There's a new Mercury on the streets."

Addresses: *Parent company*—Ford Motor Company, Lincoln-Mercury Division, 300 Renaissance Center, Detroit, MI, 48243; phone: (313) 446-4368.

engines of 188 or 198 horsepower. The choice of engines became larger as a new series was added throughout the late 1950s. The Mercury of the late 1950s was bigger and more expensive, in order to avoid competing with Ford's Edsel.

The Mercury division was expanding into new markets while increasing market share in its traditional medium-priced market. During the 1960s Mercury introduced the Comet, a semi-compact; the larger, pricier Monterey; the sporty Comet Cyclone; the Cougar, a coupe version of the Cyclone which featured the waterfall-type radiator grill that had been popular in the early 1950s; and the Marquis Brougham, a luxury car with concealed headlamps and a 7-liter V-8 engine with automatic transmission as standard.

In 1971 Mercury released the Comet, its own version of Ford's Maverick compact. During the 1970s Mercury had many successful lines, including the Cougar, Montego, Monterey, Colony Park, and Marquis. Lincoln-Mercury also began distributing the German Ford Capri with 2-liter or 2.6-liter engines. During the 1970s the auto industry moved toward smaller, more fuel efficient cars, due to consumer demand and federal regulations mandating smaller engines. Safety features including reinforced bumpers, and radial ply tires also became standard.

Recent Brand Development

In 1985 Ford introduced the Taurus while Mercury trotted out the Sable; both were solid sellers with the same basic design. The end of the 1980s also saw the revival of the Mercury Capri, which competed with the Mazda Miata; however, sales of both plummeted as the small car market suffered, and the Capri was plagued with quality problems in the United States. To offset domestic declines in sales of the Capri, Mercury increased exports to Hong Kong, Singapore, and Thailand.

In the 1990s Mercury introduced the subcompact Mercury Tracer, priced at $8,969. The Tracer was Mercury's version of the Ford Escort, and, like the Escort, was developed in a partnership with Mazda Motor Corporation. Commentators noted that such low-priced, low-profit cars were important to Mercury in order to attract younger buyers as well as for their fuel efficiency, which helped meet government regulations by balancing the inefficiency of Mercury's larger models.

The new Villager minivan, touted as Mercury's first "truck," was introduced in 1992 in a joint venture with Nissan Motors. The Villager was designed and engineered by Nissan and assembled at Ford's manufacturing plant in Avon Lake, Ohio, and was designed to go head-to-head with Chrysler's upscale minivans. Production began in April 1992 and the Villager was formally introduced in September 1992. The design was also sold by Nissan as the Nissan Quest.

The minivan market is projected by some observers to hit the one million unit mark by the mid-1990s as more consumers shift to minivans instead of cars. Ford had a 16.9 percent market share of the 1991 small and midsize passenger vans market, which totalled 811,565 units. Chrysler dominated the minivan market segment with a 45 percent market share in 1991, while General Motors had a 26.7 percent share.

Mercury's strategy to compete in this highly competitive market was to carve out a niche. In 1992 Lincoln-Mercury launched a $40 million promotion for the Villager, which was followed in 1993 by a $120 million ad campaign—the most expensive campaign in Lincoln-Mercury's history—touting "The Minivan that Drives like a Car."

Also in 1992, Mercury spent $615 million for product improvements on the Sable to enhance safety features; however, not much was changed because the original design had been very successful. The redesigned Sable sold for between $16,351 for the GS four-door and $18,323 for the LS wagon. The Tracer, Capri, Topaz, and Cougar also incorporated new engines and safety features for 1992. To mark the Cougar's silver anniversary, Mercury introduced a special LS model with a 5.0 liter, V-8 engine; new luxury seats on the Cougar XR7; a new LTS Sport model of the Tracer; and an all-new model of the Grand Marquis.

In a pricing change, Ford expanded its "one-price" program (used for its Escort) to include the Mercury Tracer. This meant that all sedans with automatic transmission would retail for the same price (in this case, $11,655). In some cases, Mercury offered options such as air conditioning and automatic transmission, which cost up to $1,500 for buyers in some regions. In spite of this strategy, Tracer sales declined.

Performance Appraisal

In looking ahead to the year 2000, Lincoln-Mercury and its Ford parent were testing the marketability of a "World Car." Introduced in Europe in March 1993 as the Mondeo, the World Car was designed to replace the Ford Tempo and the Mercury Topaz in the United States. However, while the average Topaz buyer was 55 years old and made $40,000 a year, the U.S. version of the World Car was directed toward a more upscale buyer, with an average age of 45 years, a college education, and an annual income of $50,000. The new World Car was about the same size as the Honda Accord and was planned to compete against the Pontiac Grand Am and the Mazda 626.

The Mercury lines were holding steady as they moved into the mid-1990s. The Villager minivan maintained a 1.3 percent share of the truck market. Overall, as of May 1993, Lincoln-Mercury dealer profits were up 20 percent from the previous year. Approximately 80 percent of the division's dealers were profitable, a slight increase over the previous year. In a minor failure, the newly redesigned Grand Marquis registered disappointing sales, which were down 5,092 units through April 1993.

Lee Miskowski, Division General Manager at Lincoln-Mercury, indicated that Ford was considering adding an all-new vehicle that would be positioned between the more luxurious Grand Marquis and the Sable. Miskowski also stated that he thought that the Lincoln-Mercury and Ford Divisions were pulling farther apart in terms of vehicle overlaps. In this strategy, the Ford Division would go after the youth market, "and then hope they upgrade to us."

Further Reading:

Bohn, Joseph, "Mercury Villager Holds Few Surprises," *Automotive News,* December 23, 1991, p. 3.

Chalsma, Jennifer K., "1993 Mercury Villager," *Machine Design,* October 8, 1992, p. 156.

Complete Encyclopedia of Motorcars 1885 to the Present, London: Ebury Press, 1968.

"Ford Motor Jointly Developed a New Generation Front-Drive Minivan with Nissan Motor," *Ward's Auto World,* April, 1992, p. 54.

"Ford to Spend $30 Million to Market New Mercury Villager Minivan in 1992," *Wall Street Journal,* December 18, 1991, p. B5.

Jackson, Kathy, *Automotive News,* "All New, Yet the Same: '92 Taurus, Sable," September 9, 1991, p. 16; "Mercury Betters Power, Safety," September 16, 1991, p. 30; "Uncertain Future: Is the End Near for the Mercury Capri?" June 29, 1992, p. 3; "Lincoln-Mercury Prepares U.S. Tests of Ford's 'World Car,' May 10, 1993, p. 8.

Kimes, Beverly Rae, *Standard Catalog of American Cars 1805–1942,* Iola, Wisconsin: Krause Publications, 1985.

"Lincoln-Mercury to Get about 75% of Production of Front-Drive Mercury Villager Minivan," *Ward's Automotive Reports,* December 23, 1991, p. 3.

Sawyer, James, "Mercury Introduces Villager Minivan with Versatile Seating Arrangement," *Automotive News,* October 12, 1992, p. 11i.

Serafin, Raymond, *Advertising Age,* "Mercury Thinks Young," May 28, 1990, p. 8; "Graying of the Minivan," June 15, 1992, p. 4.

Shook, Robert L., *Turnaround: The New Ford Motor Company,* New York: Prentice Hall Press, 1990.

—John A. Sarich

MICHELIN®

Represented by a tire man mascot known as Mr. Bib, Michelin is the oldest, most recognizable, and highest-selling tire brand in the world. Michelin's reputation for technological innovation and impeccable quality was established before competitors Goodyear and Firestone were founded, but it took a century for the French brand to surpass its American rivals.

Michelin, marketed in the United States by Michelin Tire Corporation, has dominated the global tire market since 1990, when it supplanted Goodyear as the number one brand. Unlike most of its rivals, Michelin's product line is comprised virtually exclusively of tires. The only other product offered under the Michelin name, a global series of road maps and tourist guides, has upheld and reinforced the ideals of quality and reliability imbued in the tires. François Michelin, grandson of the founders of the tire business, has managed Michelin since 1955, when he was 33 years old.

Brand Origins

In 1886, André Michelin was asked to assume control of a rubber business that his family had inherited in Clermont-Ferrand. Already occupied with an iron business in Paris, André called on his brother Edouard, an artist with a law degree, to take charge of the business they had both inherited. Edouard became the company's first general manager.

The development of the tires that would launch the Michelin name to international prominence came about during this time. In the 1880s, bicycling was an increasingly popular, but uncomfortable, pastime. Pneumatic tires, invented in 1888, were usually glued to wooden wheels, and the easily punctured tires took over 12 hours to replace. In 1889, this problem was brought to Edouard Michelin's attention when a hapless cyclist was literally carted to their rubber plant with two flat tires. The tires were repaired and the glue dried overnight, but when Edouard tried them out the next day, they punctured almost immediately. Realizing the market potential of a more easily replaceable tire, Edouard spent two months developing the first detachable bolt for a pneumatic tire. It took only 15 minutes to replace. In 1891, the Michelin brothers applied for three patents on the invention, and Michelin brand tires were born.

Early Marketing Strategy

The Michelins knew that their innovative product was vastly superior to standard tires, and they set out proving this to potential customers, primarily by staging and competing in bicycle, and later, automobile races. Their first promotional opportunity came when a Paris newspaper organized a 750-mile bicycle race in 1891. Although none of the top cyclists would gamble on Michelin's newfangled tires, the brothers convinced one of the 210 entrants to give detachables a try. The Michelin rider won by eight hours, beating the third-place finisher by a day. These margins were credited almost exclusively to reduced tire-changing time.

After a year of refinements, Michelin had shortened tire replacement time to just two minutes, and the brothers decided to stage their own bicycle race. They stacked the deck in their own favor by secretly scattering nails along the race route. Over 240 punctures were quickly and easily repaired over the course of the competition, proving that a flat was no longer a disaster with Michelins. By 1893, over 10,000 cyclists were riding on Michelin tires.

A publicity stunt at the 1895 Paris Bicycle Exposition illustrated the superior ride and maneuverability of Michelin tires to a wider audience. André, who was proving himself something of a marketing genius, set up a merry-go-round with two rolling chairs. One was equipped with Michelins, the other with metal rims. Riders had to pilot their chairs around obstacles on the track, which helped illustrate both the comfort and handling superiority of Michelins. The following year Michelin developed pneumatic carriage tires, and by the end of the year, 300 Paris cabs were riding on the branded tires.

André's 1894 participation in a 90-mile automobile race inspired the brothers to extend their line further. At the time, "horseless carriages" were equipped with solid rubber tires. Since there weren't many cars in the 1890s, Michelin built three for testing purposes and fitted them with pneumatics. In 1895, Michelin designed the prototypes, the first three cars to ride on pneumatic tires, and entered one of them, L'Eclair, in a 745-mile race. The L'Eclair's faulty steering caused it to zig-zag all over the road, rendering it hard to control. The car was so difficult to drive that only the Michelin brothers were willing to risk piloting it in the race.

AT A GLANCE

Michelin brand of tires founded in 1889 in Clermont-Ferrand, France, by André and Edouard Michelin; Monsieur Bibendum (also known as Bib), the Michelin Tire Man logo, introduced in 1898; company name changed to Manufacture de Caoutchouc Michelin, 1940; company renamed Compagnie Générale des Établissements Michelin, 1951.

Performance: *Market share*—19.7% (top share) of global tire market. *Sales*—FFr 66.8 million (1992).

Major competitor: Goodyear; also Firestone.

Advertising: *Agency*—DDB Needham, New York, NY. *Major campaign*—Television commercials featuring babies and small children with the tag line, "Because so much is riding on your tires."

Addresses: *Parent company*—Michelin Tire Corporation, P.O. Box 19001, Greenville, SC 29602-9001; phone: (803) 458-5000. *Ultimate parent company*—Compagnie Générale des Établissements Michelin, 23 Place des Carmes, 63040 Clermont-Ferrand Cedex, France; phone: 33-73-30-42-21; fax: 33-73-30-22-02.

L'Eclair was among the nine autos that finished the race. Although it came in last place, L'Eclair served its ultimate purpose; when the competition was restaged two years later, all the entrants rode on Michelin tires. "La Jamais Contente" (The Never Satisfied), an electric car, became the first auto to break 100 kilometers per hour—on Michelins, of course—in 1899.

Trademark Origins

Known in the United States as the Michelin Tire Man, Bibendum (or, Mr. Bib) is one of the world's oldest and most recognized trademarks. The man made of tires emerged virtually fully formed from the imaginations of the original Michelin brothers.

While attending France's Lyon Exhibition in 1898, Edouard remarked to his brother that a display of stacked tires curiously resembled the outline of a man. Around that time, André was involved in the development of a new advertising campaign for the company's bicycle and automotive tires. The Michelin man's first appearance mimicked a contemporary beer advertisement. The ad featured a plump beer drinker raising an overflowing mug. The copy read "Nunc est bibendum," a Latin phrase meaning "Now is the time to drink."

Working with Marius Roussillon, an artist who went by the pseudonym O'Galop, André co-opted the entire concept, but with an interesting twist: he replaced the beer drinker with a man made of tires and the stein of beer with a champagne glass full of nails and broken glass. Surrounding the Michelin tire man were other, presumably inferior, tire men, deflating and gasping. The headline still read "Nunc est bibendum," but in this context, it represented an unmet challenge to competitors. Copy continued, "To your health—The Michelin Tire Swallows Obstacles."

The ad was an instant success. A few months later Thery, a famous turn-of-the-century race car driver, saw André Michelin passing by one day and shouted, "I say, there goes Bibendum." The Michelin Tire Man was christened.

The changing images of Bib have reflected changing tire shapes, artistic styles, and even cultural mores. In his early years, Bib wore pince-nez glasses and smoked a cigar. The tires he was composed of were narrower, just like turn-of-the-century bicycle and auto tires. As tire technology progressed and balloon tires replaced narrow tires, Mr. Bib changed shape to wider and more round tires in his body and head. Around 1930, as smoking and drinking (especially while driving) went out of style, Mr. Bib lost those props, too.

As health-consciousness in general spread, Bibendum slimmed down—presumably through all the bicycling, walking, running, jumping, and even flying he has done over the decades. The "running Bib" has been popular with Michelin marketers in the 1990s because he projects a forward-moving image of the company and its products.

Bib has promoted Michelin products in many different cultures around the world. The mascot can be found in many different sizes, from the huge 50-foot inflatable Bib to the tiniest Bib figurines used as desk ornaments and key rings. He has been depicted as a pilot, leader, sportsman, gladiator, race driver, and in many other roles.

Michelin is justifiably proud and protective of its emissary, and a very limited number of artists are authorized to draw Bib, so that he looks the same all over the world and projects Michelin's corporate ideals of strength, solidarity, quality and reliability.

The Michelin Guides

World-renowned Michelin guides and maps are the only extension of the Michelin brand. These tourists' tools have made the brand a generic term for "road map" in France. The first "Guide Michelin," published in 1900 by André Michelin, was primarily a list of places that sold gas. Mr. Bib played a starring role in the booklet, which helped promote the brand's image of reliability. Although there were only 3,000 cars in all of France and a 50-mile trip was newsworthy, André declared that the manual "was born with the century and would last as long as the century." But even he could not have anticipated the influence this traveler's primer would have on France's chefs and hoteliers.

André was known as a "bon vivant" and his guide quickly became the authoritative ranking of French, and later, European, restaurants. The Michelin guide rates restaurants and hotels according to a star system. The top rating, often equated to earning France's Legion of Honor, is three stars; most sites listed in the guides don't even rate one star. By mid-century, Michelin had extended its line of "Red (food and lodging) Guides" to Benelux, Germany, Italy, Great Britain, and Spain. "Green (sightseeing) guides" covered Germany, Austria, Switzerland, Italy, and many other countries.

Product Developments

Michelin's tire innovations formed the foundation of its phenomenal success. From 1906 to 1937, detachable rims and spare tires, tubeless tires, treads, and low-profile tires were all introduced under the Michelin name. By 1930 Michelin became the first company to master the complicated techniques necessary to combine steel wire and rubber for use in an automotive tire. And in 1938, Michelin launched the "Metalic" tire. But the brand's most important development of the twentieth century came in 1946, when Michelin patented the radial-ply tire. Some of the basic ideas of the radial concept had first been patented in 1913 by two British men, but no one then had the capacity to build a radial without the risk of the components separating and the tire disintegrating.

Radials differed radically from conventional bias tires, which had ''inner plies'' wrapped around the tire at an angle to each other. Radial tire plies were wrapped perpendicular to the tire carcass with a steel or synthetic mesh belt underneath the tread. The advantages of the radial included increased durability, improved handling, and higher gas mileage.

As radial tires gained acceptance, Michelin garnered increasing shares of Europe's primary markets almost by default: the new tires rose from 30 percent of the European market in 1965 to 90 percent by 1975. Since Michelin was the premier producer of radials, it captured the bulk of this business.

European Market

By 1965, Michelin held 55 percent of France's tire market, 25 percent of Europe's tire business, and estimated total sales of $450 million. The brand still ranked second to Britain's Dunlop Rubber Company in continental sales, but held strong positions in Europe's major markets: first in Belgium with 30 percent, second to Pirelli's 50 percent of the Italian market, 12 percent of Britain's competitive market, and ten percent of Germany's equally cutthroat business. Michelin had made these impressive encroachments on national brands despite the fact that its tires cost about ten percent more than competitors' and it did little or no advertising, save for the Guides.

After faltering slightly in the late 1960s, Michelin became Europe's top tire brand in 1972, with dominant shares of the French and Belgian markets, and better than one-fourth of Italian and British sales. It was estimated that the brand held seven percent of the global market, ranking third to Goodyear and Firestone. To get to number one, Michelin would have to conquer the American market, which comprised 33 percent of world tire sales.

American Market

Michelin had first entered the United States tire market in 1908, when it began production in New Jersey. The plant was forced to close during the Great Depression, however, and the brand maintained a sales agency in New York to import small quantities of tires for industrial and agricultural equipment and foreign cars until the mid-1960s.

At that time, Michelin, now under the guidance of François Michelin, determined that it had cultivated enough American devotees to justify an increased presence in America. Sears, Roebuck & Co., then the nation's third-largest retailer of replacement tires, asked Michelin to develop a tire for the United States' larger vehicles for private-label distribution through its extensive catalog and store system.

Michelin tires often cost up to 20 percent more than the most comparable domestic tire, but many American consumers were willing to pay more for tires that carried an almost unheard of 40,000-mile money-back guarantee. Michelin was the first brand in America to make such an offer; at the time, most American-made tires had 15,000 miles of useful life. By 1969, Michelin's U.S. sales had quadrupled, to an estimated four percent of the market, and the brand had established a dozen regional sales offices of its own.

Although Goodyear and Firestone manufactured radial tires for the European market, they resisted producing them in the United States for several reasons. First, they claimed that American-made cars were too heavy for radial tires. More importantly, however, the companies realized that it would be too expensive to convert production facilities and train employees to make radials, even if they could catch up with Michelin's 25-year head start.

In an effort to check Michelin's American onslaught, U.S. tiremakers called for a 100 percent tariff on imported tires. However, they got only 6.6 percent in 1973. Goodyear then invested millions of dollars into polyester, fiberglass, and bias belted tires, all of which could be built on its conventional machines. But these were just temporary tactics. Even after U.S. manufacturers made the transition to radials, they had a hard time maintaining the quality standards set by Michelin.

Michelin began to bank on its superiority with an all-out assault on the North American market in the 1970s. From 1970 to 1975 alone, the company invested well over $1 billion in its global operations, building two plants in Nova Scotia, Canada, and two more in South Carolina. Michelin made inroads in the original equipment market (OEM) and advanced its prestigious image when Ford equipped its high-end Lincoln Continental and Mark models with the branded tires. To capture more of the replacement tire market, Michelin doubled its retail dealers from 1970 to 1975 to 3,800 outlets and increased its cooperative and national advertising in the United States. In 1976, Michelin employed its customary advertising media, publishing the official Bicentennial guide to New York, as well as guides for such popular American tourist spots as New England and Canada. In 1978, Michelin re-entered grand prix racing as another subtle promotional vehicle.

But, as in the past, most of Michelin's share increases in the United States were based on superior product reputation and conversion to radials, not advertising or promotion. In 1976, Michelin brought out the TRX, a revolutionary concept tire. The radial tire's share of the U.S. passenger car market, which included original equipment and replacement sales, grew from seven percent in 1972 to 55 percent in 1979. As in Europe, Michelin reaped the benefits of the conversion; in 1979, the brand passed Firestone to become the second-largest tire company in the world.

Market Consolidation

As the 1970s came to a close, several factors that would dramatically shrink sales volume and radically transform the competitive structure of the global tire market began to converge. The oil crisis of the 1970s made driving more expensive, thus decreasing miles driven. Furthermore, the development of lighter, smaller cars decreased tire wear. Ironically, the conversion to longer-lasting radials also contributed to the reduction of the replacement tire market. The 1980 recession was the final blow: OEM demand plunged 30 percent, and the replacement segment dropped 18.9 percent.

When competition in the shrinking market started to get fierce, Michelin abandoned its premium pricing strategy, sacrificing profits for market share. The cutthroat competition led inexorably to consolidation of the global tire industry, and over the course of the decade, a spate of mergers and acquisitions condensed the tire business. Sumitomo, Japan's second-largest tire company, began its acquisition of the venerable Dunlop name and properties in 1983. Continental and General Tire merged, then established a joint venture with two Japanese tire companies in 1987. In 1988,

Firestone merged with Bridgestone Corporation of Japan, and Pirelli purchased America's Armstrong.

After attempting to take over Firestone and coming up empty, Michelin became the world's top tire company with the 1990 acquisition of Uniroyal Goodrich Tire Company. Only Goodyear avoided the merger/acquisition blitz, but it lost its long-running dominance of the field in the process. By 1990, the top four tire companies, Michelin, Goodyear, Bridgestone/Firestone, and Continental, controlled 68 percent of the global tire market, up from 48 percent in 1980.

But these big mergers led to large debts, and the top companies continued to cut prices just to maintain their cash flow. Michelin had also realized that it could no longer rely on its travel guides to promote its products in heated, global competition. Accordingly, the company's U.S. Commercial Division was renamed the Marketing and Sales Division "to correctly reflect the aggressive market-driven company" Michelin had become. In 1985, Michelin launched its highly popular "baby ads," featuring an admittedly unusual combination, babies and tires. With the slogan, "Because so much is riding on your tires," the baby ads soon ranked among America's 20 most popular, winning international acclaim.

Michelin also jumped on the environmental bandwagon in the early 1990s, with new "green" tires. First exhibited at the 1992 Detroit and Geneva Auto shows, the tires' environmental efficacy was touted as contributing to greater fuel efficiency and cleaner air through 35 percent less rolling resistance than conventional tires. Michelin also paved a highway in Greenville, South Carolina, with 20,000 shredded scrap tires as part of a rubberized asphalt pilot project. U.S. federal law required that an increasing percentage of new pavement be made of rubberized asphalt after 1994. Such forays into advertising and promotion reflected Michelin's fervent desire to hold onto its number one position.

Further Reading:

Ball, Robert, "The Michelin Man Rolls into Akron's Backyard," *Fortune,* December 1974, pp. 138–143, 186, 188.

Gibson, Paul, "Goodyear vs. Michelin," *Forbes,* August 7, 1978, pp. 62–3.

"Guiding the Traveler a la Michelin et Cie," *Business Week,* July 17, 1965, p. 138.

Lewis, Vivian, "The Enigmatic Monsieur Michelin," *Dun's Review,* November 1969, pp. 97–100.

"Michelin Goes American," *Business Week,* July 26, 1976, pp. 56–60.

"Michelin Is Losing Its Market Grip," *Business Week,* July 12, 1992, p. 88.

"Michelin: On the Way to Global No. 1," *Barron's,* September 22, 1980, p. 5.

"Michelin Steps Up Its Radial Attack on Akron," *Business Week,* August 14, 1971, p. 40–1.

"Michelin Stretches Its Rubber Empire," *Business Week,* July 17, 1965, pp. 137–40.

"Monsieur Bib Meets the Akron Five," *Forbes,* April 15, 1973, p. 55–6.

Morgan, Hal, *Symbols of America,* New York: Penguin, 1986, p. 22.

"Tired of Tyres," *The Economist,* January 13, 1973, p. 60.

"Vaut le Voyage?," *The Economist,* November 3, 1979, p. 62–3.

—April S. Dougal

MICROSOFT®

Microsoft®

Developed in 1975 by William H. (Bill) Gates and Paul G. Allen, Microsoft has grown into one of the best-selling brands of computer products in the world. Since its founding, Microsoft Corporation's success has been unmatched by its competitors, and as a result, the company has gained a cult-like following among customers and employees alike. The goal of Microsoft products is to make it easier for people at work and at home to take advantage of the power of personal computing. The brand owes its reputation to the innovativeness and intelligence of its founders, Gates and Allen.

Product Origins

The Microsoft phenomenon began in February of 1975 in Albuquerque, New Mexico, when Bill Gates and Paul Allen completed their first product—the BASIC programming language—and sold it to the Albuquerque-based company MITS. Two months later, on April 4, 1975, Gates and Allen officially established Microsoft as a business partnership. The following year the pair encountered enormous success when they refined and enhanced BASIC and sold the improved product to such heavyweight companies as General Electric and Citibank. Soon, the partners created and began selling their second language, FORTRAN. By April of 1978 Microsoft had developed a third language product, COBOL -80 for the 8080, Z-80, and 8085 microprocessor computer systems.

In response to rising demand in the Pacific Rim, Microsoft founded Microsoft Far East in Japan in June of 1978, and the company officially named itself the exclusive sales agent for its products in Asia. By October of that year, Microsoft had licensed its BASIC language to the Radio Shack retail franchises and Apple computer manufacturer. Less than one year later, Microsoft had implemented the BASIC compiler on virtually every microcomputer available. The improved BASIC 5.0 was released in 1979.

Early in 1979 Microsoft moved its headquarters from Albuquerque to Redmond, Washington, and four months later, Microsoft 8080 BASIC became the first microprocessor product to win the ICP Million Dollar Award, which was presented to Paul Allen. Within several days of this announcement, Microsoft founded its Retail Division dedicated to retail products and end-user customers.

By 1980 Microsoft had licensed the UNIX operating system from Bell Laboratories to form the XENIX group. Not long after, Microsoft released the SoftCard system, a ground-breaking software/hardware enhancement product that allowed Apple II users to run CP/M applications. In the first two years of availability, the SoftCard system's sales topped 60,000 units.

In response to the heavy sales levels, Gates and Allen decided to form two groups to help Microsoft cope with customer needs and demands: the End-User Systems Software Group and a network of national retail sales representatives. Both groups were instrumental in helping Microsoft grow dramatically through the early 1980s.

Microsoft Corporation Is Born

In June of 1981 Microsoft was incorporated and reorganized as a privately held corporation. Bill Gates became president and chairman of the board, while Paul Allen took the title of executive vice president of what was then called Microsoft Corporation.

That same year, another event occurred that dramatically altered Microsoft's growth: IBM introduced its personal computer. At the time, no one knew how much each organization would affect the other's success, but together, Microsoft and IBM altered the way the world uses computers. IBM designed its new PC to function under Microsoft's 16-bit operating system, MS-DOS Version 1.0. In addition, the PCs would be able to use Microsoft's BASIC, COBOL, and Pascal languages and several other Microsoft products.

In April of 1982 Microsoft established Microsoft Ltd., a subsidiary headquartered in England, which became the exclusive sales agent for Microsoft products across Europe. With IBM's heralded support, Microsoft BASIC was fast becoming the world's standard programming language, and Microsoft Ltd., together with the Far East operations, was ready to take advantage of the language's international reputation.

In 1982 Microsoft received another award. *InfoWorld* magazine honored the company with its "Software Product of the Year" award for the Multiplan Electronic Worksheet, the first product from the End-User Systems Group. By September Microsoft had finished work on MILAN (Microsoft Local Area Network), which linked all of its in-house development comput-

AT A GLANCE

Microsoft brand of computer software founded in 1975 by William H. (Bill) Gates and Paul G. Allen in Albuquerque, NM, with the introduction of the BASIC programming language; Microsoft incorporated in 1981, becoming Microsoft Corporation; in 1983 Microsoft Window was introduced.

Performance: *Market share*—Top share of the computer software category. *Sales*—$3.75 billion.

Major competitor: Novell; also Lotus, Apple, WordPerfect.

Addresses: *Parent company*—Microsoft Corporation, Microsoft Way, Redmond, WA 98052-6399; phone: (206) 882-8080.

ers. This local area network was an early version of what was to become a ubiquitous part of the workplace.

In the fall of 1982 two major events further spurred the growth of Microsoft. First, the company released two powerful programming packages for the IBM PC, a fully-interactive symbolic math package and a high-level language development package. Second, the number of MS-DOS installations skyrocketed, as 50 additional microcomputer manufacturers licensed the 16-bit operating system from Microsoft during its first 16 months of availability. The following year the company introduced what was to become a household item within several years—the Microsoft ''Mouse,'' a hand-held pointing device. Later that year Microsoft introduced its first full-featured word processing program, Microsoft Word for MS-DOS. To market the new program, a demo disc of Word was included in the October issue of *PC World* magazine.

Windows Is Introduced

In November of 1983 Microsoft introduced what was to become its most successful product, Microsoft Windows. The program was an extension of the MS-DOS operating system that provided a universal operating environment for developing bit-mapped application programs. Designed to make learning new computer applications easy, the user interface used graphics to eliminate the intimidation factor many people encountered when using typical MS-DOS applications. With just a few clicks of a mouse, a user could start up an application, invoke a command, explore a list of online Help topics, or move between several documents. Even novice computer users immediately grew fond of Microsoft's new Windows product with its colorful and creative list of shapes, symbols and icons, and drop-down menus. The operating system arrived complete with a calendar, a calculator, and a clock on-screen for every user. From the point of its introduction, Windows began to change the way that people thought about computing.

By the early 1990s, Microsoft Windows could be found on over 30 million computers worldwide and was largely regarded as the standard operating system for personal computers. The Windows phenomenon was credited with contributing to substantial industry growth by creating new businesses, new jobs, and expanding opportunities for related third-parties and vendors. In 1993 approximately 2,500 independent software vendors offered more than 5,000 applications for Windows. In addition, Microsoft offered a family of Windows products to satisfy all levels of customer needs, from the single desktop machine to corporate-wide networked groups. Windows for Workgroups, introduced in 1992, combined the popular Windows operating system with networking capabilities, making it easier for people to share information and work together more effectively.

Other Powerful Products

While Windows was rapidly becoming one of the world's most successful computer programs, Microsoft was hard at work creating many other new products for the Windows, MS-DOS, and Macintosh operating systems. The company also took a leading role in developing software for the Apple Macintosh computer. Microsoft shipped its Microsoft BASIC and Microsoft Multiplan for the Macintosh simultaneously with the January 1984 introduction of the Macintosh. In May of 1984, Microsoft announced an enhanced version of Flight Simulator, which would eventually become the best-selling recreational software package for the IBM PC and compatibles. The following year Microsoft celebrated its tenth anniversary with sales of $140 million.

In October of 1987 Microsoft released Excel for Windows, a spreadsheet program that was to become the base for its ''Office'' package. Microsoft Office combined innovative technology and extensive usability features to help employees at work. The package offered seamless integration of the most commonly used desktop applications, including Microsoft Word; Microsoft Excel; PowerPoint, a presentation graphics program; Microsoft Access database management system; and Microsoft Mail, an electronic mail system for personal computer networks.

From Microsoft's founding, part of its mission was to have a computer on every desk and in every home. To further this mission, the company began a program of developing, testing, and marketing a full line of consumer products and multimedia titles. These products were specifically designed for new computer users in the home or small business environment. By 1993 the Microsoft consumer division produced 29 products available in 27 languages around the world.

Support and Information Services

As Microsoft's management celebrated the success of the company's product sales, they also recognized the responsibilities inherent in supporting the huge base of more than 30 million customers. Early in their company's life cycle, Microsoft's leaders knew that they needed quality service and user support in addition to state-of the-art products. As a result, Microsoft ensured that one of every five of its employees was dedicated to supporting existing customers. By the early 1990s, Microsoft created a number of support-based divisions.

The Microsoft Product Support Service was created to provide technical support for all Microsoft products and utilities. Customers needed only to contact this division by phone or electronic inquiry. On a typical day, Microsoft determined that this division's facilities in Washington, North Carolina, and Texas received more than 50,000 requests for assistance.

A division was also created to provide technical education and training courses on Microsoft products. Most training provided by Microsoft Education Services took place at the more than 150 Microsoft Solution Provider Authorized Training Centers in the United States and at Microsoft subsidiaries worldwide. Microsoft Education Services also developed high quality technical education and training that spanned all phases of technology adoption.

Through this division, Microsoft held seminars and hands-on, lab-based and video courses.

Microsoft Press, which was established in 1983, grew rapidly, and by the early 1990s it was publishing approximately 50 titles each year, many of which became international best-sellers in their categories. These award-winning books educated and provided product support solutions for users of Microsoft systems software, applications, and languages. By 1993, Microsoft Press titles were translated into 25 languages and were distributed to book and software stores worldwide.

The company also initiated the ''Solution Providers,'' an independent group of organizations that provide business services with Microsoft products. Named Solution Providers because they apply technology to help solve customers' real-world business problems, Microsoft offered the group a variety of programs to access and utilize information. This included software acquisition, timely information via electronic networks, training from authorized Microsoft training centers, support from Microsoft's Product Support Services, and business development referrals, leads, and opportunities.

Future Projections

In early 1994, Chairman Bill Gates addressed Microsoft's 14,000 employees in an open letter. ''Microsoft must be smart, nimble, and focused,'' he wrote. While Microsoft was still the undisputed leader in the computer software industry, Gates knew that competition from such companies as the networking leader, Novell, and ease-of-use leader, Apple, would be stiff. In light of this, Microsoft announced that it would experiment with a simpler look and feel for its Windows environment. Instead of icons, the system would use pictures of familiar scenes such as a living room.

In addition, in February of 1994 Microsoft made is second-largest acquisition ever when it purchased Montreal-based Softimage, Inc. in a stock-swap deal valued at $130 million. Softimage is one of the leading companies making software capable of creating stunning, two- and three-dimensional animation, as well as melding real life images with animation. The software was used to produce the blockbuster film *Jurassic Park,* with its life-like dinosaurs. The purchase projects Microsoft head-first into the high-end graphic design category.

This is evidence that Microsoft is planning to utilize the software to one day create images that will flow over the ''information superhighway'' of computers, televisions, and telephone services. Many expect the system will put everything from banking to video rental on demand in many homes. Microsoft pledged to spend what it takes to be part of this new technology. Therefore, through both acquisition and internally generated products, Microsoft will lead its competitors through the information age proving that it has no intention of becoming a dinosaur among software companies.

Further Reading:

''Competition breathing down our neck, Gates tells Microsoft workers,'' *Charlotte Observer,* January 22, 1994, p. 6D

Williams, Scott, ''Microsoft buys into animation to claim role in video's future,'' *Charlotte Observer,* February 16, 1994.

Additional information provided by Microsoft Corporation.

—*Wendy Johnson Bilas*

MINOLTA®

Minolta, a trademark of the Minolta Camera Co. Ltd. of Japan, is the best-selling brand of 35mm cameras in the United States and a leading brand of photocopiers, facsimile machines, and other business office equipment. Minolta also markets a line of electronic-imaging systems for data retrieval.

Brand Origins

Nichi-Doku Shashinki Shoten, which later would introduce the Minolta trademark, was founded in 1928 by Kazuo Tashima, the son of an import-export merchant. In the summer of 1928, Tashima represented his father as part of a Japanese trade mission to the Middle East and Europe. In France, the trade mission toured a company that made high-quality optics, and Tashima returned to Japan eager to start a camera company. Since neither his father nor the Japanese government approved of his plans, Tashima was forced to borrow money from the chief clerk at his father's company. He founded Nichi-Doku in November.

The firm's name, which translated as the Japanese-German Camera Co., reflected both Germany's leadership in quality optics and the fact that Tashima took on two German partners, Willy Heilemann, who operated an import business in Kobe, and Billy Neumann, an engineer with a background in optical instruments. Heilemann and Neumann arranged for Tashima to have access to the latest German technology. Nichi-Doku produced its first camera, the Nifcalette, in 1929. Both the lens and shutter came from Germany.

Tashima's company introduced several new cameras between 1929 and 1932, despite the worldwide effects of the Great Depression. In 1933 the company introduced the first camera to carry the Minolta brand name. Minolta, a word coined by Tashima, was a loose acronym for (M)achinery and (IN)struments (O)ptica(L) by (TA)shima. (A more colorful tale of the brand's origins holds that Minolta was a corruption of the Japanese word "minoru-ta," which means "a rice field of rich harvest." Tashima supposedly associated the word with a proverb his mother told him as a child to teach humility: "The ripest ears of rice bow their heads the lowest.")

In 1934 the company—which was renamed Molta Goshi Kaisha in 1931—introduced the Minolta Vest, a bellows camera. A shortage of imported sheepskins forced the company to develop a form of Bakelite as a substitute, thus creating the first rigid bellows made from a synthetic resin. The plastic bellows actually made the camera easier to focus and cheaper to produce. The Minolta Vest became the first Japanese-German Camera Co. product to become popular outside Japan. In 1937 Tashima became the first Japanese camera manufacturer to develop a twin-lens reflex camera, the Minoltaflex, based on the German Rolleiflex. The company also incorporated in 1937, and became Chiyoda Kogaku Seiko Kabushiki Kaisha (Chiyoda Optics and Fine Engineering Ltd.).

Post-War Developments

Chiyoda Optics began manufacturing high-powered binoculars and other optical instruments for the Japanese military in the late 1930s as Japan invaded China and French Indonesia. After the attack on Pearl Harbor, Japan banned the manufacture of commercial cameras, and Chiyoda Optics turned exclusively to producing instruments for the war effort. Employment increased from 1,000 to 4,000. However, massive Allied bombing in 1945 destroyed the company's factories in Osaka.

Tashima managed to salvage some manufacturing equipment and moved his business into the Kyuhoji National School, one of the few buildings in Osaka not leveled by the bombing. The war ended in September 1945, and Chiyoda Optics returned to making cameras. The Minolta Semi III, the first camera made in Japan after the war, appeared in 1946. It was modeled after the German Leica, with one notable improvement. Instead of loading from the bottom, the back of the Semi III opened to allow easier handling. The Semi III also became the first Japanese camera exported after the war, when 170 cameras were shipped to South Africa in 1947.

Japanese camera makers also received help after the war from General Douglas MacArthur, who headed the Allied occupation forces. MacArthur, who implemented several political and economic reforms, arranged loans from the U.S. government and issued special import licenses so watchmakers and camera companies could obtain precision tools from Europe. In return, the companies committed 80 percent of their watches and cameras for sale on U.S. military bases in Japan, allegedly because MacArthur wanted servicemen to have something to spend their money on other than alcohol and women. In effect, 80 percent of all Japanese cameras were "exported." MacArthur also ordered Japanese companies to design their cameras to use Kodak film, so servicemen could use the cameras after returning to the United States.

AT A GLANCE

Minolta brand introduced in 1933 by the Molta Goshi Kaisha company; company name changed to Chiyoda Kogaku Seiko Kabushiki Kaisha (Chiyoda Optics and Fine Engineering Ltd.) in 1937; company named changed to Minolta Camera Co., Ltd., in 1962.

Performance: *Market share*—30% U.S. market for 35-mm cameras; 7% U.S. market for copiers. *Sales*—$800 million (U.S.); $2 billion (global).

Major competitor: Canon.

Advertising: *Agency*—(U.S., cameras) William Esty, New York, 1983—. *Major campaign*—"Only from the Mind of Minolta."

Addresses: *Parent company*—Minolta Camera Co., Ltd., 3-13, Azuchi-machi 2-chome, Chuo-ku, Osaka 541, Japan; phone: (06) 271-2251.

Although the Allied occupation officially ended in 1952, the outbreak of the Korean War in 1950, with thousands of troops passing through Japan, ensured a steady market for Japanese cameras.

U.S. Market

Early in 1954, Tashima sent Sadahei "Sam" Kusumoto to the United States with a suitcase full of cameras and instructions to create an American foothold for the Minolta brand. Kusumoto's first stop was the Master Photo Dealers and Finishers Association trade show in Chicago. However, the cameras attracted little attention, and Kusumoto went on to New York without lining up a distributor or selling a single camera. Later that year, Tashima also traveled to the United States, and Kusumoto arranged several magazines interviews. At a reception given by *Photo Dealer,* Tashima and Kusumoto met Larry Fink, then president of FR Corporation, a manufacturer of darkroom chemicals for amateur photographers. Fink agreed to distribute Minolta cameras, but he wanted to market them under the FR Corporation name. When Tashima objected, Fink compromised by including a "dual warranty" from both companies in Minolta advertising.

Also in 1954, the Japanese government created the Japan Camera Inspection Institute, which was given the power to regulate exports. There were then more than 40 Japanese camera companies, and in an effort to bolster Japan's reputation in foreign markets, the institute denied export licenses to those companies making cheap, toy-like cameras. In 1955 the institute set up the Japan Camera Information Center in New York, and sponsored the first Japan Camera Show in December.

Chiyoda Optics introduced two cameras in 1955, the Minolta Autocord and the Minolta A. The Minolta Autocord was a twin-lens reflex camera with an X-sync shutter for use with electronic flash, designed specifically for the U.S. market. Chiyoda Optics planned to sell the Autocord for $100, but in another nod to the U.S. market, the camera was priced at $99.95. The lighter weight Minolta A was priced at $49.95. In 1956 Chiyoda Optics began advertising in popular American magazines, including *Life* and the recently introduced *Playboy.* Ads in other magazines began carrying the tag line, "As advertised in *Life.*" In 1957 New York's Peerless Cameras, the highest volume camera store in the United States, ran full-page ads in the *New York Times* maintaining that Minolta cameras were as good as German brands.

However, the biggest boost for the Minolta trademark may have come in 1958, when Kusumoto persuaded Sears, Roebuck & Co. to drop a small German camera, the Minox, from its mail-order catalog and replace it with the Minolta 16 "spy camera." In his book *My Bridge to America,* Kusumoto wrote, "Just being in the Sears catalog was an excellent form of advertising for us, getting the Minolta name before more consumers than any advertising we could have afforded on our own at the time. And beating out a German-made camera helped our reputation in the industry." Chiyoda Optics also introduced its first single-lens reflex (SLR) camera, the Minolta SR-2, and introduced the first Japanese-built planetarium in 1958. In 1959 Chiyoda Optics' U.S. subsidiary became known as the Minolta Corporation.

Minolta Camera Co.

In 1960 Chiyoda Optics introduced its first copier, the Minolta Copymaster, based on a diazo process licensed from a Dutch company, Van der Grinten. However, the copier was never successful, in part because the process smelled bad. That same year, Chiyoda Optics introduced the Minolta Uniomat, the first Japanese camera with a programmed shutter. Triggered by a built-in selenium light meter, the Uniomat automatically selected the proper shutter speed and f-stop. The Uniomat led to the development of the Minolta Hi-matic, sold in the United States by the GAF Corporation under the name Ansco Autoset. The Hi-matic became one of the world's most famous cameras when it was carried into space by astronaut John Glenn, the first American to orbit the Earth.

Originally NASA, the U.S. space agency, did not plan for Glenn to carry a camera. However, a few days before his historic flight in February 1962, Glenn purchased seven different cameras and compared them feature by feature. He finally picked the Hi-matic as probably the easiest to adapt for use with the heavy gloves he would wear during the flight. NASA engineers drilled holes in the camera to make it lighter and attached a special handle. The focus was set permanently at infinity.

After the flight, Glenn's photographs appeared in newspapers and magazines all over the world, although the first news stories identified the camera as an Ansco. GAF notified the Minolta Corporation to set the record straight, and the price of Chiyoda Optics stock on the Tokyo exchange nearly doubled in less than a week. Later that year, Chiyoda Optics changed its name to the Minolta Camera Co., Ltd. Minolta later created the Minolta Space Meter, a light meter designed especially for the U.S. space program, which was used on all manned Apollo missions, including the first moon landing in 1969. The Hi-matic used by Glenn was put on display at the Smithsonian Institution.

In 1962 Minolta also introduced its first microfilm reader-printer, the Minolta 401S. That was followed the next year by the Minoltafax 41, the world's first reducing copier, which was sold by Graphic Communications of New Jersey. In 1966 Minolta introduced in Minolta SR-T 101, the first SLR camera with through-the-lens light metering. By the late 1960s, Minolta was one of the best-known brands in the world, and by 1973, Minolta had passed Nikon as the best-selling brand of 35-mm cameras in the United States.

Product Innovations

In 1974 Minolta introduced the EG 101, an electrographic copier that used a lightly coated paper that felt much like ordinary bond paper. The EG 101 was the first inexpensive copier that offered most of the advantages of plain-paper copiers. In its ads, which challenged readers to distinguish between a copy and a black-and-white photo of the Mona Lisa, Minolta used the term bondlike paper to describe its special stock. The EG 101 was followed in 1978 by the Electrographic 301, the first copier to use fiber-optics. The Minolta EP 710, a plain-paper copier introduced in 1980, was the first copier that was able to both reduce and enlarge document images.

However, in 1976, Canon, Inc. had introduced the Canon AE-1, the first 35-mm range-finder camera with an electronically controlled exposure system. The AE-1, with fewer mechanical parts, was smaller, lighter, less expensive, easier to use, and more reliable than previous 35-mm cameras. Canon also signed tennis start John Newcombe as its spokesman and advertised heavily during the 1976 Olympic Games. Within months, Canon replaced Minolta as the best-selling brand of 35-mm cameras in the United States. By 1985, Minolta's share had slipped from a high of 30 percent to about 20 percent, while Canon's had risen to 28 percent.

Minolta fought back in 1977 with the XG-2, an automatic-exposure SLR camera that used the latent electric current in the human finger to signal the electronic circuitry. Minolta used track and field star Bruce Jenner in several commercials for it XG cameras in 1979 and 1980.

Minolta also introduced other innovative cameras, including the 110 Zoom SLR, the world's first compact SLR camera to use 110-size cartridge film; the bright yellow Weathermatic-A, the first watertight, all-weather 110 camera; several compact cameras using Kodak's ill-fated disc-format film; and the Minolta AF-S "Talker," a 35-mm SLR camera with a computer-synthesized voice that warned photographers about common errors.

In 1982 Minolta unveiled the Minolta X-700, the first Minolta to be named "European Camera of the Year." The X-700 was also the first product from Minolta to use the tag line "Only From the Mind of Minolta," created by the William Esty advertising agency in 1983.

Maxxum

However, Minolta had nothing to challenge the Canon AE-1 until 1985, when it introduced the Maxxum, then the world's most automatic camera and the first SLR camera with an internal, auto-focusing system. Two computer chips—one in the lens and one in the camera body—and a tiny motor automatically focused the picture, adjusted the exposure, and advanced the film. All a photographer had to do was release the shutter, although there were manual overrides available for every step.

Minolta spent more than three years developing the Maxxum, which Kusumoto, then president of the Minolta Corporation, called "the biggest single project we've ever undertaken in the 55 years of Minolta's history." James D. de Merlier, then director of photographic marketing in the United States, called the Maxxum "a Yuppie camera," and told *Business Week,* "It's quality, it's expensive, it's got all the latest features." Most camera buffs were equally ecstatic. *Popular Photography* declared Maxxum "the first of what everyone will be trying to do over the next couple of years." *Modern Photography* called it "ingenious," and added, "No one else has dared try to do this." Motohiko Kimura, with the Japan Camera Industry Association, said the Maxxum was "one of those epoch-making products that come out once in a decade."

Minolta promoted the Maxxum with a massive advertising campaign, and within a year, Minolta had regained a 30 percent of the U.S. market for 35mm cameras while Canon's share fell to about 22 percent. Minolta also became the No. 1 brand of 35-mm cameras in the world. The Maxxum was sold in Japan as the Alpha 700 and in Europe as the 7000 AF. Minolta also introduced the PCW-1, its first word-processing office system, in 1985. In 1987 Canon unveiled the EOS, for "electronic optical system," to challenge Maxxum. Several other companies also introduced auto-focus cameras.

The Minolta Maxxum also faced two legal challenges in 1987. First, the National Association of State Attorneys General accused Minolta of price fixing. Kusumoto countered that all Minolta did was tell U.S. dealers they could charge the suggested retail price for Maxxum cameras, since there were no low-priced competitors on the market. However, Minolta agreed to offer rebates of $8 to $10 to customers who had purchased cameras at full price.

A more serious challenge came from Honeywell, Inc., which alleged that Minolta infringed on its patents in developing the Maxxum. Honeywell experimented with auto-focusing in the 1970s, but gave up before bringing a product to market. However, Honeywell did patent several of its developments and had allowed Minolta to review the work. After five years of legal wrangling, a jury in 1992 found that Minolta had unknowingly infringed on two of four Honeywell patents.

Minolta was ordered to pay $96 million, or about $40 for every Maxxum that had been sold to that point. Honeywell also threatened to stop sales of Maxxum and Minolta auto-focus cameras unless Minolta agreed to pay a licensing fee. Minolta ultimately paid Honeywell $127.5 million to cover the jury award and licensing fees until the patents expired in 1995. Honeywell also sued several other camera makers. Those suits were settled out of court in 1992, with Honeywell receiving $124.1 million plus royalties through 1995.

In 1988 Minolta introduced the Maxxum 7000i, the first major technological advance since the Maxxum was introduced in 1985. The Maxxum 7000i came with small "feature cards," each with its own microchip, that could be plugged into the camera to create special effects. For example, the "Fantasy Effect" programmed the camera to shift the focus slightly just as the shutter was closing to "soften" the image and create a "dream-like effect." There were also cards for portraits, strong back lighting, and other special situations. Photographers also could create their own settings and program them into a feature card.

The Maxxum 7xi, introduced in 1991, represented yet another breakthrough. The Maxxum 7xi incorporated a type of artificial intelligence called "fuzzy logic" to determine whether a picture was a landscape, portrait, or close-up. The camera's 16-bit microprocessor then made continuous decisions concerning focus, exposure, flash, and even zoom. *Business Week* called the Maxxum 7xi "the closest thing yet to a 'thinking' camera," although as *Fortune* noted, "if you get tired of using a camera that's smarter than you are, you can seize control of any or all functions."

Further Reading:

Bremner, Brian, ''From the Mind of Minolta—Oops, Make that 'Honeywell',''*Business Week,* February 24, 1992, p. 34.

''This Camera Has a Built-In Special Effects Lab,'' *Business Week,* May 30, 1988, p. 101.

''Canon Finally Challenges Minolta's Mighty Maxxum,'' *Business Week,* March 2, 1987, p. 89.

''Fuzzy Logic Puts Minolta in Sharp Focus,'' *Business Week,* June 17, 1991, p. 100.

Hart, Russel, ''Minolta's New Autofocus SLR May Be a Substitute for Photographic Experience,'' *New York Times,* June 9, 1991, Sec. 1, p. 62.

Hayes, Arthur S., ''Jury Says Minolta Owes Honeywell $96 Million for Infringing Two Patents,'' *Wall Street Journal,* February 10, 1992, p. B9.

Kusumoto, Sam, *My Bridge To America: Discovering the New World for Minolta,* New York: E. P. Dutton, 1989.

''Minolta Through Six Decades,'' *Minolta Messenger,* No. 7, 1988.

Port, Otis, ''A Camera to Shoot Minolta Back to the Top,'' *Business Week,* February 4, 1985, p. 50.

Rodriguez, Ginger G., ''Minolta Camera Co., Ltd.,'' *International Directory of Company Histories,* Vol. III, Chicago: St. James Press, pp. 574–76.

Scott, Carlee R., ''Honeywell Inc., Camera Makers Reach a Pact,'' *Wall Street Journal,* August 8, 1992, p. B2.

—Dean Boyer

MONOPOLY®

In the extremely competitive and fickle U.S. games market, Parker Brothers' board game Monopoly stands out as an enduring winner. Developed in the early 1930s by Charles B. Darrow, an unemployed engineer, Monopoly has become one of the world's most popular board games. Monopoly's initial success was unprecedented in the game industry and has seldom been matched in the 60 years since. Since its introduction in 1935, 100 million Monopoly sets have been sold worldwide and an estimated 250 million people have played the game. Monopoly sets are sold in 33 countries in 23 languages, making it the most popular proprietary board game in the world.

The Origins of Monopoly

The creation of Monopoly is generally attributed to Charles B. Darrow, although a similar game had been patented by a woman named Lizzie J. Magie in 1904. Like Monopoly, Magie's "Landlords Game" included purchasable properties, utilities, and a "Go to Jail" square. Darrow had undoubtedly seen or played Magie's game but his changed a straightforward board game into a game where negotiating properties became the key playing feature.

Like a number of toy successes, Monopoly was the product of the Depression. Darrow's successful career as a salesman for a Philadelphia engineering firm came to an abrupt halt in 1929 when the stock market crash virtually halted construction. Darrow soon turned to peddling jigsaw puzzles that he produced in his small hobbyist's workshop in his home. In 1930, he began experimenting with his version of Magie's "Landlord's Game." The notion of controlling large amounts of cash to speculate with was the perfect form of playful wish fulfillment during the Depression. Darrow made one of his first games from a piece of linoleum, lumber remnants, and cardboard and began playing it with his wife and neighbors. He based the property names on the streets of Atlantic City because he had fond memories of vacationing there with his wife in more prosperous times.

According to all accounts, Darrow never intended to produce a saleable game until friends started asking for copies of their own. He began very small scale production in his workshop, making no more than a game a day at a profit of about $1.75 each. Marvin Kaye, author of *The Story of Monopoly, Silly Putty, Bingo, Twister, Frisbee, Scrabble, et cetera,* quoted Darrow as remarking that "it was a funny thing, but almost invariably the winner wanted a copy while the loser was convinced that he could win the next game—so he'd frequently want a game, too." As more and more of his friends played the game with their friends, requests for copies began to mount up faster than Darrow could produce them. He enlisted the help of a friend in the printing business who agreed to produce the game for Darrow, who was now processing orders by the hundreds. By 1934, interest in Monopoly had reached across the country and Darrow found that he could no longer handle the number of orders pouring in. Faced with the choice of borrowing money to set up a game manufacturing business of his own or selling out to an established supplier, Darrow decided that he would attempt to sell his game. "Taking the precepts of Monopoly to heart, I did not care to speculate," Kaye quoted Darrow as saying.

Darrow approached the Parker Brothers company, which had dominated game manufacturing in America since 1888. Their response was not enthusiastic. The four page instruction booklet was considered much too complicated for a family game which, according to Parker Brothers, should be easy enough for a nine year old to learn quickly and should never take more than an hour to play. In addition, traditional board games had involved throwing a die and moving across the board towards a single end point. In Monopoly the players kept going around and around with no defined goal. Darrow's Monopoly game was rejected with the comment that it contained "fifty-two fundamental playing errors."

Darrow was not deterred, however. He knew that his game was not only playable but positively contagious. He ordered a printing run of 5000 sets and began to give personal demonstrations of Monopoly in department stores in Philadelphia. The game became so popular in that city that F.A.O. Schwarz, New York City's largest and most prestigious toy store, was persuaded to take on about two hundred sets. After these sets sold out in a matter of weeks, Parker Brothers was finally convinced that the game might have some merit and agreed to take the remaining 4800 games on consignment. Darrow watched with growing excitement as Parker Brothers sold not only this consignment but an additional 10,000 games by Christmas. Monopoly was not just marketable, it was a hit.

Traditionally the post-Christmas season is a quiet time for toy companies but not for Parker Brothers in 1935. All of the Monopoly sets bought during the 1934 Christmas season had converted

AT A GLANCE

Monopoly brand board game developed in Philadelphia, PA, by Charles B. Darrow, 1933; bought by Parker Brothers, Inc., 1935; Parker Brothers bought by General Mills and combined with Kenner Toys to create Kenner Parker Toys, 1968; Kenner Parker Toys becomes independent, 1985; bought by Tonka Corp., 1987; Tonka Corp. bought by Hasbro Inc., 1991.

Advertising: *Agency*—Grey Advertising, New York, NY, 1991—.

Addresses: *Parent company*—Parker Brothers, 50 Dunham Road, Beverly, MA 01915; phone: (508) 927-7600; fax: (508) 921-3521. *Ultimate parent company*—Hasbro Inc., 1027 Newport Avenue, P.O. Box 1059, Pawtucket, RI 02862-1059; phone: (401) 431-TOYS; fax: (401) 727-5544.

new players to the Monopoly craze, and instead of a lull in sales, requests for the game poured in by the thousands in January 1935. Orders arrived in such large quantities that laundry baskets filled with paperwork lined the halls of the Parker Brothers' Salem, Massachusetts offices. Parker Brothers company lore has it that a bookkeeping firm, brought in to sort out the chaos, took one look at the overflowing baskets and refused the job at any price.

Parker Brothers, on the verge of bankruptcy three years earlier, sold 20,000 Monopoly games a week in 1935. Charles Darrow found himself in the enviable position of owning a hit game with as yet no contract with Parker Brothers, who had originally only agreed to sell the game on a consignment basis. A deal was soon worked out giving Parker Brothers rights to the game in exchange for a hefty ongoing royalty fee for Darrow. After an unsuccessful attempt to duplicate his success with a stock market game, Darrow retired at the age of 46 to grow orchids in Pennsylvania, the first person to make over a million dollars from the invention of a game.

Promotions and Advertising

From the beginning, the popularity of Monopoly relied almost exclusively on word of mouth. News of the game had spread from state to state while Darrow was still typing up each property card by hand. By the time Parker Brothers bought the game it was already so successful that the problem was in filling existing orders, not in drumming up more. Parker Brothers changed hands a number of times in the 1980s and 1990s, but the approach to Monopoly advertising remained consistent. Monopoly advertising has always been relatively low-key, as its marketers relied on the established reputation of the game. By the early 1990s, Parker Brothers conducted a limited campaign, consisting of an animated television spot that had been used for a number of years and some limited print advertising.

Instead of conventional advertising Parker Brothers often exploited the well established reputation of Monopoly in unusual or eye-catching promotions. In 1992, the company erected a huge billboard on the actual boardwalk in Atlantic City. Sporting an oversized portion of Monopoly's familiar board, the sign included a bright red arrow pointing to the boardwalk space and the message "You Are Here."

Realizing from the start that the success of Monopoly had its roots in the almost compulsive desire of Monopoly fans to play the game, Parker Brothers has encouraged and supported Monopoly "events." Because a game of Monopoly can be stretched out almost indefinitely by the simple expedient of "bank loans" to insolvent players, Monopoly marathons have become a board game tradition. This tradition is manifest not only in the thousands of "all-nighters" pulled by college students and kids home for the holidays but also in some more remarkable Monopoly events. The Guinness Book of World Records documents the longest Monopoly game played in a moving elevator (16 days), in a bathtub (99 hours), and the longest antigravitational game (played on a ceiling for 36 hours). In 1989, the Muscular Dystrophy Association in Atlanta, Georgia sponsored a fund-raising event in which 1,500 professional divers took turns staying underwater for 50 days of continuous Monopoly play.

Parker Brothers has traditionally supported these types of events by helping to promote them as well as by providing additional Monopoly money and playing pieces, including special weighted versions for underwater games. On one notable occasion in 1961, students at the University of Pittsburgh, in the midst of a 161-hour marathon game, discovered that the bank lacked sufficient funds to continue. The players wired an urgent request to Parker Brothers for an additional one million dollars, predicting another depression if the bank were to go broke. The company, sensing a great opportunity for Monopoly publicity, immediately packed up one million dollars of Monopoly money and sent it by plane to Pittsburgh where they arranged to have it met by a Brinks armored car (and undoubtedly a number of local journalists). The money was delivered to the student's depleted bank under armed guard but in time to save the game.

An important component of Parker Brothers' approach to publicizing Monopoly has been to actively promote its role as part of Americana. In 1972, the Atlantic City Commissioner of Public Works, as part of a campaign to give the faltering city a new image, proposed to change the names of Baltic and Mediterranean

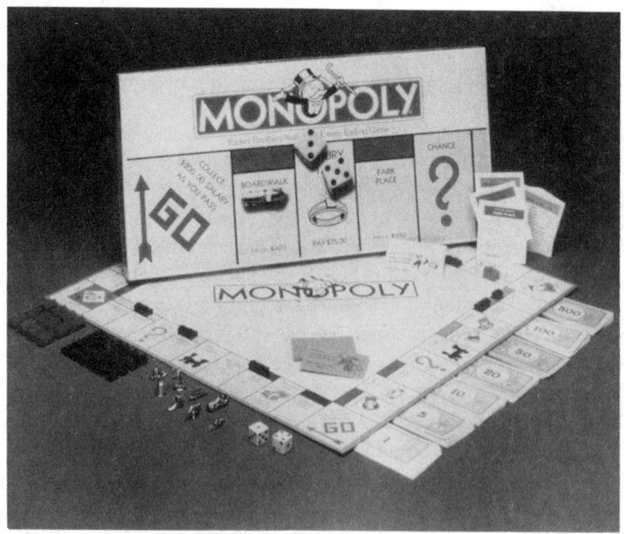

The Monopoly board game as it appears today.

Avenues to Fairmount and Melrose. Monopoly fans were outraged by the proposed desecration to the namesakes of the poorest but sentimentally favorite Monopoly properties. Hundreds of calls and letters flooded into both the Commissioner's office and the Parker Brothers headquarters in Salem, Massachusetts. Parker Brothers executives, alert to the publicity that the uproar was creating, dispatched their executive vice-president, Randolph P. Barton, to speak at a public hearing about the name change in Atlantic City. A tone of respectful satire suffused the entire meeting as one speaker after another rose in defence of the lowliest of the Monopoly properties. A letter from Edward J. Parker to the commissioners epitomized the flavor of the debate. "Would you be willing," he wrote, "to take the responsibility for an invasion by hordes of protesting Monopoly players, all demanding that you go directly to jail, without even the dignity of passing GO?" The commissioners were not willing and the proposal was dropped.

Through the 1980s and 1990s, Parker Brothers promoted its game by sponsoring Monopoly breakfasts, and regional and national championships, as well as the World Monopoly Championships, which take place every three years. To celebrate Monopoly's 50th anniversary in 1985, Parker Brothers initiated a series of events including the introduction of Deluxe versions of the game complete with original wooden houses and metal tokens. In 1991, the Franklin Mint designed a Monopoly Collector's Edition that included gold plated hotels, silver houses, and a hardwood board.

Protecting the Monopoly Name

Parker Brothers has always maintained firm control over the Monopoly name, threatening and often taking legal action whenever it was used without permission. While Parker Brothers executives sometimes took a tongue-in-cheek approach to promoting their game, they were not amused when others took liberties with the Monopoly name. In one case, a Portland area real estate firm, Northwest Mortgage, noting the similarity between one of its housing developments and a Monopoly board, decided to promote their property using a Monopoly theme. Naming the development Marvin Gardens, they painted squares on the sidewalks, set up a Free Parking space, and installed utility units decorated to look like Monopoly utilities. As reported in *Business Week* in 1971, Parker Brothers lawyers responded by threatening a lawsuit claiming that the development posed a threat to the integrity and reputation of Monopoly. The lawyer representing Northwest Mortgage replied with a satirical letter pointing out the deficiencies of the Monopoly version of Marvin Gardens, which he claimed was overpriced, badly located, and returned only half its value when mortgaged. The Portland housing development, he wrote, could only improve the reputation of such a white elephant. Parker Brothers was not amused. After further threats of legal action the real estate promotion was dropped.

In a more serious precedent setting case, Parker Brothers sued a game called Anti-Monopoly for trademark infringement. The lawyers for the creator of the game, Ralph Anspach, claimed that "Monopoly" had become a generic term for the real estate game and was not associated in the public's mind with the manufacturers of the game. Although in 1976 the San Francisco District Court ruled in favor of Parker Brothers, the Ninth Circuit Court of Appeals overturned the decision, ruling that the game's name had indeed become a generic term. The case eventually made its way to the Supreme Court which, in 1983, upheld the Appeals Court decision.

International Sales

After Monopoly's huge success in the United States in 1935, Parker Brothers quickly set up licensing deals with John Waddington Ltd. for British sales and the French Miro Co. for sales on the European continent. The Atlantic City street names upon which the American board was based were replaced with local street names and currency that would be familiar to foreign players. In England, Boardwalk was converted to London's Mayfair, in France to Paris's Rue de la Paix, and in Spain to Madrid's Paseo del Prado.

Monopoly is licensed in 33 countries and printed in 23 languages, making it the most popular proprietary board game in the world. In the United Kingdom alone it is estimated that almost 50 percent of all households own a Monopoly set. For a very long time the only boundary the game could not cross was into the communist bloc countries, where it was banned as "too capitalistic." This barrier fell in 1988 and a Russian version of Monopoly with Moscow street names was added to the Monopoly family.

Performance

After Monopoly's huge success in 1935, Parker Brothers executives felt that booming sales could not last, and the president of the company ordered a halt in production in December of 1936. Monopoly, however, steadfastly refused to follow the traditional toy industry pattern of short lived fads and sales of the game continued to spiral upwards. Monopoly soon became a guaranteed steady seller. As a spokesperson for Parker Brothers was quoted as saying in *New England Business*, "if a household had kids, then about the time the first child is 8 to 10 years old the Monopoly set would show up at the house. You could practically issue it to the kid at the hospital." To the dismay of Parker Brothers executives, Monopoly was often used as a loss leader in toy departments, as managers would advertise sale prices on the game just to get people into the store, and Monopoly sales levelled off in the 1950s and 1960s. But in the late 1960s and early 1970s, there was a mini-boom for the game as sales once again soared. A market survey in 1975 found that of households with a first child aged 8 or older, 80 percent owned the game.

Sales of all traditional games and toys including Monopoly were severely challenged in the 1980s by the advent of the electronic video game. Parker Brothers marketers responded by increasing their advertising budget and adding an optional electronic component to the game. Dubbed the "Monopoly Playmaster" this accessory spun automatic dice, auctioned off properties, and piped out electronic versions of "We're in the Money" and "I've Been Working on the Railway" at appropriate moments in the game. Selling for $60.00, some six times more than the traditional game, this gadget did little to attract kids away from the video arcade. What an electronic component could not do, time could, and by the late 1980s the saturated video game market underwent a serious slump, leaving traditional games like Monopoly to regain lost market share. By the 1990s, Monopoly, bought by Hasbro Inc. in 1991, seems poised to spend another 50 years as a standard fixture of family game cupboards.

Further Reading:

Adams, Jane Meredith, "Marketing Monopoly," *New England Business*, October 18, 1982, pp. 64–67.

"Advance to Arbat," *Time*, October 10, 1988, p. 89.

Croft, Martin, "In Pursuit of the Playing Public," *Accountancy*, January 1990, p. 65.

Elliot, Stuart, "Back to Roots for Monopoly," *New York Times*, November 23, 1982, p. D7.

Kaye, Marvin, *The Story of Monopoly, Silly Putty, Bingo, Twister, Frisbee, Scrabble, et cetera,* New York: Stein and Day, 1973, pp. 35–42.

Levy, Richard C., and Ronald O. Weingartner, *Inside Santa's Workshop,* New York: Holt, 1990, pp. 90–93.

Levy, Robert, ''Joy in Toyland,'' *Dun's Business Month,* November 1984, pp. 82–86.

''Marvin's Garden Plays Monopoly,'' *Business Week,* November 13, 1971, pp. 42–43.

''Parkers Bros. Plays the Game,'' *Chain Store Age General Merchandise Trends,* February 1985, p. 124.

Sammons, Donna, ''The Name of the Game,'' *Inc.,* September 1983, pp. 28–29.

''Where Monopoly Is Not a Dirty Word,'' *Business Week,* March 25, 1967, pp. 180–182.

—Hilary Gopnik

MR. COFFEE®

MR. COFFEE®

A household name connected with automatic drip coffee makers (ADCs), the Mr. Coffee brand name also covers teamakers, small kitchen appliances, water filtration devices, coffee filters, replacement decanters, and beverage accessories. Relying on strong brand-name recognition, Mr. Coffee is the market share leader in automatic drip coffee makers, teamakers, and branded filters.

Brand Origins

Vincent G. Marotta, Sr., a real estate developer in Cleveland, Ohio, produced the first Mr. Coffee automatic drip coffee maker in 1971. Co-founder (with Samuel Glazer) of the Cleveland-based company North American Systems, Inc., Marotta introduced the machine to the market in 1972. During the coffee shortage of 1977 and 1978, the company maintained an edge over the competition by offering an innovative coffee-saving attachment for its Mr. Coffee machines; the device was no longer viable in the market after coffee prices settled. By the late 1970s, Mr. Coffee had more than hit home: the brand had grabbed more than 50 percent of the market share for automatic drip coffee makers, with annual sales of more than $150 million. At least for some years, its place as the definitive market leader was assured.

North American Systems soon introduced a faster automatic drip coffee machine, purported in promotional materials to make two to ten cups of coffee better, faster, and easier than any other coffee maker. Two cups needed only a few seconds of brewing time; ten cups required five minutes. Cups were measured on a five-ounce-per-cup basis. Promotional descriptions of the this machine also touted a built-in warming plate that was heat-controlled so that the coffee remained at a "piping hot temperature to prevent flavor breakdown"; the controlled temperature adhered to the standards of the Coffee Brewing Center of the Pan-American Coffee Bureau. Later Mr. Coffee temperature-control mechanisms turned off the coffee maker's heater entirely when the coffee decanter was empty.

By far the leading heavyweight in market share for ADCs, the Mr. Coffee II machine, made of "shatterproof" polyprolylene and sized to fit under standard kitchen cabinets, weighed only 5.2 pounds. The metal tank and brewing system were self-cleaning. Advertised to "guarantee balanced flavor extraction" and produce "pure, rich, sediment-free coffee," Mr. Coffee filters were available in packages of 50, 100, and 200; heat-resistant Mr. Coffee replacement decanters were offered in both 10- and 12-cup sizes. Soon a Mr. Coffee machine with timing capabilities was introduced, so that owners could wake up and smell the coffee before they even got out of bed.

Early Marketing Strategy

The first and best-known spokesperson for the Mr. Coffee brand was baseball great Joe DiMaggio, who made casual, at-home appearances in television ads, coffee-cup in hand and a Mr. Coffee machine brewing that perfect cup of coffee in the background. Coffee-drinking homemakers who adored Mr. DiMaggio made their appearances to corroborate Joe's testimony. The Joe DiMaggio advertising campaign lasted from the mid-1970s to the early 1980s.

In spite of a well-known ad campaign and strong brand-name recognition, Mr. Coffee's market share skidded to 35 percent in 1981. Sales had decreased by 1982 to the $110-million to $120-million range. The competitors had descended on the automatic-drip coffee maker scene, and even using Joe DiMaggio as a spokesperson was not enough to strike them out. Marotta contemplated the brand's position in an April 1982 issue of *Forbes:* "There used to be only 4 or 5 companies making drip coffee makers. Now there are around 25. [The competition] has been eroding our market share point by point. But we still have at least double the market share of each of our nearest competitors in the field." In the early 1980s, the closest Mr. Coffee competitors were Norelco, General Electric, and Proctor-Silex.

Company Changes

In 1987, in a leveraged buyout of North American Systems, Inc., Mr. Coffee was bought by John M. Eikenberg, along with other investors led by the McKinley Allsopp, Inc., securities firm. The new owners changed the company's name to Mr. Coffee, Inc. President and CEO Eikenberg decided to make waves by introducing Mr. Coffee brand-name products that targeted upscale market segments, as opposed to the $16-to-$50 price segment targeted by Marotta. The company faced intense competition from European-imported coffee makers, such as Krups North America and Braun, Inc. Diversifying outside of the coffee maker market was another important aspect of the company's plan to increase earnings.

Strategic moves initiated by the new owners soon appeared to be working; Mr. Coffee earnings in 1989 were $1 million, com-

AT A GLANCE

Mr. Coffee brand of automatic drip coffee maker for household use introduced in 1972 by North American Systems, Inc., a company founded in Cleveland, Ohio, in 1955 by Vincent G. Marotta, Sr. and Samuel Glazer; Mr. Coffee Iced Tea Pot first marketed in 1989; Mr. Coffee Water Filter introduced in 1992; the company became Mr. Coffee, Inc., on July 27, 1987, after a leveraged buyout led by John M. Eikenberg and investors organized by the securities firm McKinley Allsopp, Inc.

Performance: *Market share*—35% (top share) of automatic drip coffee maker category; 70% (top share) of iced tea maker category; 15% of water filtration device category. *Sales*—$175 million (1993).

Major competitor: Black & Decker.

Advertising: *Agency*—Meldrum & Fewsmith Advertising, Cleveland, OH, 1986—. *Major campaign*—Intended to increase consumer awareness of Mr. Coffee as a manufacturer of innovative kitchen appliances as well as of beverage appliances, the 1992 advertising tag line for most Mr. Coffee products was, "What'll he think of next?"

Addresses: *Parent company*—Mr. Coffee, Inc., 24700 Miles Rd., Bedford Heights, OH 44146; phone: (216) 464-4000; fax: (216) 464-5629.

pared with the $1 million loss reported in 1988. Sales saw a 24 percent jump, from $103 million in 1988 to $128 million in 1989. Mr. Coffee, Inc., planned to sell a 59 percent stake of its shares in a public offering in 1990; proceeds from the offering were to be used to reduce debts acquired in the company owners' leveraged buyout. Also in 1990, Mr. Coffee launched its first major advertising campaign since the Joe DiMaggio ads.

Product Diversification

Mr. Coffee introduced the first automatic iced tea maker, the Mr. Coffee Iced Tea Pot, in 1989; the appliance's retail price was $49.99. The Mr. Coffee teamaker worked very much like the Mr. Coffee automatic drip coffee maker, with a brew basket to be loaded with a filter and either loose or bagged tea. The appliance made up to two quarts of tea in ten minutes. Users filled the pitcher with ice cubes; then they filled the appliance reservoir with water.

In the early 1990s, Mr. Coffee faced an ever widening field of competitors, including Black & Decker Corp., Proctor-Silex, Braun, Krups, Melitta, and Bunn. Mr. Coffee filters, under intense competition from private label brands and Melitta, represented about 15 percent of Mr. Coffee sales. The automatic-drip-coffee-maker revolution in America was complete, with nine out of ten readers of *Consumer Reports* in 1991 drinking coffee brewed with a drip coffee maker, usually an electric one. In 1990, Mr. Coffee presented the Expert, a model that incorporated a computer microchip. By this time, the company also had on the market a four-cup capacity Mr. Coffee Jr. and a ten-cup capacity Mr. Coffee Sr.

In 1991, Mr. Coffee's top-of-the-line, Euro-styled Accel coffee maker featured "accelerated brewing for a better tasting coffee" and became the brand name's flagship model line. The same year, in response to concerns about the possible harmful effects of trace amounts of dioxin left by the bleaching process in white coffee filters, Mr. Coffee filters advertised a "chlorine-free" bleaching process, meaning that the filters were made with a chlorinated compound, chlorine dioxide, rather than chlorine gas.

Because company management was convinced that Mr. Coffee coffee makers could not again hold much more than 40 percent of the market, a big part of the Mr. Coffee strategy of the early 1990s was to further diversify the product line. The company began producing small food appliances, all tagged with the well-known Mr. Coffee brand name to help them gain consumer acceptance.

Mr. Coffee presented three new products in 1992: the Mr. Coffee Water Filter, the Potato Perfect Quick Potato Baker, and the Mr. Coffee Juice Extractor. Developed in response to reports of dangerous levels of lead in tap water and problems with bottled water, the Mr. Coffee Water Filter purportedly removed more than 90 percent of the lead, chlorine, and copper found in household drinking water. The 1992 Potato Perfect Quick Potato Baker, a countertop appliance, was capable of baking two potatoes on metal skewers in 25 minutes, or about half the time required by a conventional oven. According to Peter Howell, CEO of Mr. Coffee, Inc., the idea came from the Tater Twister, an appliance from Presto that makes curly French fries. The ad campaign for these new appliances, with the tag line, "Mr. Coffee—What'll he think of next?," relied on the image of a personified Mr. Coffee tinkering in the tool shop after brewing away in the kitchen.

Mr. Coffee faced the problems of saturated small household appliance markets and recessionary economic pressures in the early 1990s. Overall net sales for Mr. Coffee declined from $173.2 million in 1990 to $158.8 million in 1991. The company experienced a net loss in 1991 of $1.4 million. However, the original Mr. Coffee product, the automatic drip coffee maker, continued to hit home with consumers. Mr. Coffee ADCs showed an increase in unit volume sales of 7 percent in 1991 over 1990. In 1991, Mr. Coffee ADCs held just under one-third of the market. Mr. Coffee's performance improved in 1992, with net sales increasing to $169 million; the company's net income was $3.7 million. In 1993 net sales increased four percent to $175 million, and net income was $5.5 million.

Future Growth

Mr. Coffee's 1993 plans included continued product expansion to target specialty markets. The company's strategy was to maintain its anchor product line of coffee makers, while introducing new nonbeverage product lines very gradually. The company also had a new design in the works that would replace its traditional "C-shape" coffee maker line. Even under the pressure of intense competition, Mr. Coffee seems prepared to forge ahead with new ideas for the kitchen and game plans for the Mr. Coffee team of small appliances and coffee makers.

Further Reading:

Bernstein, Aaron, "Will Mr. Pasta Help?" *Forbes,* April 12, 1982, p. 186.

"A Brief History of Brewing," Consumer Reports, January 1991, p. 42.

Cuff, Daniel F., "New Mr. Coffee Owner Has Dream Come True," *New York Times,* July 7, 1987, sec. D, p. 2.

Daniels, Jeffrey, "Mr. Coffee Hopes Initial Offering Will Prove to Be Palatable Brew," *Investor's Daily,* April 23, 1990, p. 30.

Datzman, Cynthia, "Mr. Coffee Brewing Up New Marketing Plan," *Crains Cleveland Business,* September 21, 1987, sec. 1, p. 2.

"Dioxin in Coffee Filters," *Consumer Reports,* January 1991, p. 41.

Fitzgerald, Kate, "Getting an Iron Grip; Black & Decker Worries Appliance Makers," *Advertising Age,* January 30, 1989, p. 78.

Mr. Coffee Annual Report, Bedford Heights, Ohio: Mr. Coffee, Inc., 1991, 1992.

"Some Like It Cold," *Consumer Reports,* July 1992, p. 470.

Talley, Karen, "Robeson, Mr. Coffee Brew a Deal," *LI Business News,* March 4, 1991, sec. 1, p. 3.

"This Spud's for You: Potato Baker Helps Broaden Mr. Coffee Line," *Crains Cleveland Business,* September 21, 1992.

—Dorothy Walton

NERF®

Soft, fun, and safe, Nerf Balls were originally marketed as the "first official indoor ball." The four-inch foam balls were invented and sold to Parker Brothers by toy specialist Reynolds Guyer in 1970. When Hasbro Inc. acquired Parker Brothers in 1991, Nerf items were shifted to sister company Hasbro Kenner Products. Under Kenner, Nerf brand of toys has opened new markets, expanded appeal to older age groups, and almost doubled sales in 3 years. By 1994, Nerf brand of sport and activity toys has expanded to over 40 items.

Brand Origins

The four-inch cut-foam ball, later named Nerf, was invented by Reynolds Guyer in 1970. Guyer, a toy inventor, is best known for creating the game Twister. Guyer brought the prototype ball to Parker Brothers Inc. toy company in 1970. Parker Brothers, of Beverly, Massachusetts, chose Nerf as the brand name for the foam ball. The toy was billed as "the world's first official indoor ball" by Parker Brothers. The popularity of the ball grew modestly through the next two decades. The original iridescent orange ball is usually associated with office basketball and indoor horseplay. Children and adults were attracted to the toy because it was fun and safe.

Brand Development

Three developments have kindled an outburst of Nerf brand sales since 1991: Toy giant Hasbro bought Parker Brothers and Kenner from Tonka Corp. in 1991; Parker Brothers created the successful Nerf Bow 'N' Arrow; and Hasbro transferred manufacturing and marketing of Nerf to Kenner. From the simple beginnings of a sponge basketball and utility ball, Nerf brand has expanded into a wide variety of sports and action toys. Nerf's sales have risen dramatically from $40 million in 1991 to $60 million in 1992. Estimates for the near future have Nerf sales reaching $100 million.

Kenner, based in Cincinnati, uses a team concept for toy development. Team Nerf is comprised of seven designers, six engineers, and four marketers. It is typical for marketers on team Nerf to challenge their teammates in engineering and design to devise a new sport toy or Nerf gun. The team has been responsible for expanding the line from 16 to more than 40 items. The Nerf Master Blaster was released in 1992, and is considered a highly successful new toy. According to the *Chicago Sun-Times,* Kenner engineer Dave Webber invented the toy while experimenting with a double barreled bicycle pump. Webber retooled the pump in the Kenner model shop and rigged it to eject small Nerf balls. That was the beginning of the double barrelled Master Blaster, which fires up to eight Nerf balls in rapid succession. In 1993 Nerf introduced the NB-1 Missile Blaster. The pump action toy is slightly smaller than the Blaster, and shoots two Nerf missiles instead of balls. The Nerf Slingshot was introduced in 1992. The toy can be loaded with up to three small Nerf balls for slinging. Kenner markets this toy for children ages 5 and up.

New Nerf product introductions practically doubled in 1993. A large portion of the new items are in the toy weapons category. The Nerf Arrowstorm Gatling Unit is named after the Gatling Gun first used in the American Civil War. The toy has a rapid auto-rotating magazine that fires six arrows simultaneously. New in 1993 was the Nerf Sharp Shooter, which is similar to a traditional dart gun. The hand held pistol shoots foam darts with rubber suction tips. To meet the demand for lost and wayward Nerf balls, arrows, missiles, etc., Hasbro also markets refill packages.

Acquisitions of Nerf Brand

Kenner was bought by General Mills in 1967. Parker Brothers, the original producer of Nerf, was acquired in 1968. General Mills rationalized that it could sell toys to the same kids who were eating their Wheaties, Cheerios, and other cereals. Kenner and Parker Brothers were combined by General Mills, and formed Kenner Parker Toys. Popular items for the company included the Star Wars line of toys and Strawberry Shortcake dolls. In 1985 Kenner Parker sold an estimated $40 million worth of the new Hugga Bunch Doll—but the company had manufactured dolls valued at $60 million. Kenner Parker also produced board game favorites such as Monopoly, Risk, Sorry!, and Clue, but sales figures were stagnant. Finally, General Mills divested itself, and spun off Kenner Parker to shareholders in November of 1985. New management at Kenner Parker cut overhead and developed new toys. In 1985 a loss of $123 million before taxes was reported on sales of $527 million. The following year Kenner showed earnings of $33 million on sales of $503 million.

In October 1987 Tonka Corporation purchased Kenner Parker Toys for $548 million, of which $448 million was goodwill, to be charged against earnings for 40 years. After the purchase of Kenner Parker, Tonka was saddled with a massive debt totaling

AT A GLANCE

Nerf brand of sport and activity toys invented by Irwin Guyer in 1970; brand sold to Parker Brothers Inc.. 1970; brand sold to Tonka Corp. 1987; brand sold to Hasbro Inc. 1991; brand shifted to Kenner Products 1991.

Performance: *Sales*—$60 million (1993; *Brandweek* estimate).

Major competitor: Winter Design/Manufacturing, Super Soaker.

Advertising: *Agency*—Grey Advertising, New York, NY, 1991—. *Major campaign*—"It's Nerf or Nothin'!"

Addresses: *Parent company*—Kenner Products, 615 Elsinore Pl., Cincinnati, OH, 45202; phone: (513) 579-4000. *Ultimate parent company*—Hasbro Inc., 1027 Newport Avenue, Pawtucket, RI, 02862-1059; phone: (800) 242-7276.

about $500 million in 1988. Although Tonka's operating income skyrocketed to $94 million in 1987, the company still lost $10.5 million. Over the next few years, Tonka experienced moderate success with some of its staple toys, such as Play-Doh, but was unable to make any headway against its debt. With reduced marketing strength, Tonka was sold to Hasbro in 1991 for $486 million. Hasbro divided up Kenner Parker, placing Milton Bradley and Parker Brothers together, and promoting Kenner separately.

Hasbro Inc. was started in 1923 by the brothers Henry and Hillel Hassenfeld (hence the name: Hasbro) in Pawtucket, Rhode Island. At first a fabric remnant business, the company introduced toy doctor and nurse sets in the 1940s. The company was the first toy producer to use television to promote a product when they aired ads for Mr. Potato Head in 1952. In the mid-1960s the company introduced G.I. Joe—a large soldier doll that soon became its primary toy item. In the 1980s Hasbro grew rapidly under the direction of Stephen Hassenfeld, the third generation of family members to manage the business. The company reduced the number of products by one third, and focused on developing a stable line of toys. A number of successful toys were produced or revitalized. These included a smaller scale G.I. Joe in 1982, My Little Pony in 1983, and Transformers in 1984. In 1984 Hasbro acquired a major competitor, Milton Bradley. In 1989 the license for certain items were purchased from Coleco. Among those toys were Cabbage Patch Kids, Scrabble, and Parcheesi. Stephen Hassenfeld died in 1989, and his brother Alan took over as CEO at that time.

Hasbro Kenner Rejuvenates Nerf

Nerf is a good example of Hasbro's ability to revitalize declining or languishing toy lines. The resurrection of the G.I. Joe line in the 1980s is a prime example. And when Hasbro acquired Cabbage Patch Kids, sales had fallen to about 25 million, but product development and heavy advertising helped sales to nearly triple.

Now on its own with Hasbro, Kenner started strong with the Nerf Bow 'N' Arrow, which is equipped with Nerf arrows designed to fly 35 feet in the air. Parker Brothers had introduced the Bow 'N' Arrow in 1991, six months before Nerf was switched to Kenner. With additional marketing money from Hasbro, Kenner quickly began to capitalize on Nerf's name. In a 1993 *Brandweek* spotlight, Nerf's boys' toys vice-president marketing director Tom McGrath said: "We knew we had something with dramatic growth potential, so it was just a case of classic marketing—going with trends in the market and extending the age reach." To assess buying patterns, Hasbro and Kenner check the weekly sales numbers at hundreds of U.S. stores. The company can make adjustments to supply and manufacturing plans within weeks, or change the supply of new items for the following year.

The toy industry spawns many imitations. As soon as a popular toymaker like Nerf brings out a new item, similar, and often cheaper products made by smaller manufacturers often appear. Kenner has fortified its market share with effective advertising campaigns from Grey Advertising of New York. Grey's current television spots carry the brand slogan, "It's Nerf or Nothin." The commercials show mostly pre-teen boys using Nerf toys. "To distinguish Nerf, we felt we had to give the product an attitude," Grey's account supervisor Richard Weber told *Brandweek.* "Clearly these products stem from relatively simple ideas, but Kenner had the vision to see how they could extend the niche category into many different kinds of toys."

In the toy industry, the term "promoted brand" means those brands that have traditionally been pushed by advertising and promotional activities. Nerf is one of Kenner's top promoted brands. Nerf has benefitted from an unprecedented product development and marketing support effort. In November of 1992 Hasbro set a marketing precedent when it purchased all the commercial time during a 14-hour Thanksgiving cartoon marathon on 3 Turner Broadcasting Network stations. For just over $1 million, Hasbro aired some 700 30-second spots. Many of the commercials promoted new Nerf sports and activity items.

Future Predictions

With the effective support of design and marketing, the Nerf line of sports and action toys should continue to grow. This indicates Kenner and Nerf's mastery at opening new markets and bringing out popular line extensions. As marketing director Carla Meeske told *Brandweek:* "There are very few categories I won't consider for Nerf right now."

Further Reading:

Fitzgerald, Kate, "Toy Makers Set to Soak the Market with Water Guns," *Advertising Age,* March 22, 1993, p. 4.

Gallagher, Patricia, "Team Nerf Keeps on Scoring," *Chicago Sun-Times,* April 27, 1993, p. 45.

Hammonds, Keith, "'Has-Beens' Have Been Very Good To Hasbro," *Business Week,* August 5, 1991, p. 76–77.

Hasbro Inc. Annual Report, Pawtucket, Rhode Island, 1992.

Lefton, Terry, "Turbo-Powered Toy," *Brandweek,* February 15, 1993, p. 28.

Poole, Claire and Jeffery Trachtenberg, "Bear Hug," *Forbes,* November 16, 1987, p. 186–192.

Sweitzer, Letitia, "What's Selling," *Playthings,* August, 1992, p. 16.

Weiner, Steve, "Keep On Truckin," *Forbes,* October 16, 1989, p. 220–221.

—*William Tivenan*

NINTENDO®

Nintendo, a registered trademark of Nintendo Co. Ltd. of Kyoto, Japan, is the best-selling brand of home video-game systems in the world. Introduced to the American market in 1985, more than 50 million Nintendo video game systems had been sold in the United States by the end of 1993.

Brand Origins

Fusajiro Yamauchi, an artist and craftsman in Kyoto, founded Marafuku Company Ltd. in 1889, to produce playing cards for the ancient Japanese game of Hanafuda. During the Russo-Japanese War (1904-05), Marafuku began producing Western-style playing cards for Russian prisoners. After the war Yamauchi negotiated an agreement with the Japanese tobacco monopoly to sell the cards in tobacco shops throughout the country, and Marafuku became the largest playing card company in Japan.

In 1949, Hiroshi Yamauchi, although only 21 years old, became president of the company founded by his great-grandfather. He changed the company name to Nintendo Karuta (Nintendo Playing Card) in 1951. The written Japanese characters for "Nin-ten-do" were most often translated as "Work hard, but in the end it is in heaven's hands." Among the company's most successful products was a set of Walt Disney-character playing cards introduced in 1961.

Yamauchi dropped Karuta from the company name in 1962, creating Nintendo Company Ltd. After several failed attempts to diversify—including a line of instant rice, a taxi company, and a "love hotel" that rented rooms by the hour—Yamauchi created a toy division in 1969. Gunpei Yokoi, who had a degree in electronics and was responsible for maintaining the playing-card machinery, was put in charge and told to concoct "something great" to sell for Christmas.

Yokoi created a wooden latticework contraption that could be extended like an arm to grasp small objects. The "Ultra Hand," Nintendo's first entry into the Japanese toy market, was a hit as more than 1.2 million were sold in 1970. In the early 1970s, Yokoi also dreamed up Nintendo's first electronic toy, the "Beam Gun," which came with spring-loaded targets that exploded when photoelectric cells were triggered by a light beam. Nintendo began exporting the Beam Gun to the United States in 1974.

Video Games

The video game craze was launched in the United States by Atari, Inc., responsible for introducing the first arcade Pong games in 1972. That same year Magnavox brought forth Odyssey, the first home video game system; the set-up played various Pong-type games. In 1975 Nintendo acquired the rights to manufacture and sell video game systems in Japan based on the Magnavox technology. The Nintendo Color TV Game 6, capable of playing six different "light tennis" games, was offered in 1977. Nintendo Color TV Game 15 followed the next year. Nintendo sold more than one million of each game system. Then in the early 1980s, Nintendo put out Game & Watch, a hand-held video game about the size of a pocket calculator with a digital clock in one corner. It was a phenomenal success in Japan. Nintendo also began manufacturing coin-operated arcade video games, including Hellfire, Sky Skipper, and Radarscope.

Nintendo introduced the Family Computer in 1983, dubbed the Famicom by company president Yamauchi. The Famicom, marketed as an advanced home video game system, was far more sophisticated than the Atari 2600—then the best-selling video game system from the United States—and included an expansion port that could be connected to a keyboard, disk drive, or modem. The Famicom was also affordably priced. "Forgo the big profits on the hardware," Yamauchi told a Japanese wholesalers group, "because it is really just a tool to sell software." Proving him right, Nintendo developed several high-quality games and sold more than 500,000 Famicoms in the first two months. Millions more were sold over the next several years, until Nintendo controlled more than 80 percent of the Japanese market for home video games.

The U.S. Market

In 1980 Nintendo formed a subsidiary, Nintendo of America, Inc., headed by Yamauchi's son-in-law, Minoru Arakawa. At the time, Nintendo had a limited presence in the United States through licensing of its arcade games. Arakawa's task was to carve out a bigger share of the $8 billion arcade market through direct sales. Radarscope, in which a player shot down enemy aircraft, was the game Nintendo of America chose to import. Based on American test marketing, Arakawa ordered 3,000 units. However, by the time the games arrived from Japan four months later, Radarscope had lost its luster with U.S. game players. Nintendo sold about

AT A GLANCE

Nintendo brand of video games originated with Marafuku Company Ltd., founded in 1889; Nintendo introduced as trademark in 1951; company name changed to Nintendo Karuta Company in 1951; name changed to Nintendo Company Ltd. in 1961.

Performance: *Market share*—70% of home video game market. *Sales*—$5.6 billion.

Major competitor: Sega.

Addresses: *Parent company*—Nintendo Co., Ltd., 60 Fukuine Kamitakatamatsu-cho, Higashiyama-ku, Kyoto 605, Japan; phone (075) 551-2722.

1,000 game units, but was left with a warehouse full of unwanted arcade games. Arakawa told Yamauchi that he needed a new game that could be retrofitted to the Radarscope game units, and he needed it fast. Because the U.S. market was not very important to Nintendo at the time, and the games division had no one available, Yamauchi assigned the job to Sigeru Miyamoto, a staff artist who had never before developed a video game.

Miyamoto abandoned the sports and warfare themes that usually dominated video games and originated an electronic fairy tale in which players had to overcome obstacles while rescuing a beautiful maiden who had been kidnapped by an ape. The hero of Miyamoto's fairy tale was an awkward little carpenter with a bulbous nose and a bushy mustache. When time arrived to give the video game a name, Miyamoto considered "Kong"—which since the 1933 movie *King Kong* has become Japanese slang for "ape." But the video-game ape was more comical than menacing, so Miyamoto turned to a Japanese/English dictionary that translated the Japanese word for "goofy" as "donkey" and came up with "Donkey Kong."

When the first Donkey Kong program arrived in the United States and was plugged into a Radarscope arcade game, Arakawa was disappointed with the results. However, Yamauchi refused to allow any changes. The fate of Nintendo of America would rest on the shoulders of the little carpenter. Arakawa named the video-game character "Mario" after Nintendo's landlord, who interrupted a staff meeting to announce that the rent was overdue. Nintendo test marketed Donkey Kong in The Spot, a small tavern on the south side of Seattle, Washington near the company's headquarters. Within a few days, people were lining up to play, and the tavern owner was begging for additional games. Nintendo sold all 2,000 converted Radarscopes within a couple of months.

Donkey Kong went on to become one of the most popular video games ever made. More than 62,000 Donkey Kong arcade games were sold in 1981 alone. Nintendo licensed the rights to Donkey Kong too. A flood of Donkey Kong products hit the market ranging from comic books to pajamas. Coleco purchased the rights to create a home video game version of Donkey Kong, while Atari purchased the computer rights, and Milton Bradley created a board game. Meanwhile, Mario, who became a plumber in future Mario Bros. games, also became one of the most famous cartoon characters of all time. The Mario cartoon show ran throughout the late 1980s and early 1990s, and a feature-length Mario movie was released in 1993. A 1990 survey showed that Mario was recognized by more American children than Mickey Mouse.

Nintendo Entertainment System

In 1983 Nintendo decided the time was ripe for bringing the Famicom to the United States, despite the fact that the home video game market had come crashing down. After revenues of $3 billion in 1982, the U.S. home video game industry nearly disappeared in 1983, with revenues of about $100 million. However, arcade games were still going strong, raking in nearly $6 billion in quarters annually, and the malaise in the home video game market appeared to be a rash of boring games rather than a lack of interest. Nintendo believed that with better graphics and more high-quality games the Famicom would appeal to dissatisfied home video game players.

Unlike the strategy for Japanese buyers, Nintendo also decided to market the Famicom as a home computer as a means of further distancing itself from the lackluster home video game market. Nintendo's engineers created a keyboard, music keyboard, disk drive, remote-control controllers, and a Zapper gun to work with the basic Famicom computer. Next a "lock-out" program that would stop anyone except Nintendo or its licensees from producing games for the Famicom was developed. The revamped Famicom was given a new name, the Advanced Video System, and was introduced at a consumer electronics show, instead of a toy show, in January of 1984. A colorful brochure announced: "The evolution of the species is now complete. . . . Welcome to the future of American home video entertainment." Unfortunately, nobody seemed very interested.

Hoping to cut loses, Nintendo approached Atari about acquiring the rights to the Advanced Video System in the United States. A deal was very nearly struck, but Atari was in serious financial trouble, and negotiations were called off shortly before Atari was sold by Warner Communications. According to *Game Over,* Atari's only real interest was in keeping the Advanced Video System off the market. When the truth came out years later, Arakawa remarked, "Can you believe that we almost sold the whole thing? If we had, no one outside of Japan would know about Nintendo."

With the Advanced Video System generally ignored by the consumer electronics industry and the deal with Atari dead, Nintendo began again. The computer peripherals and infrared controllers were scrapped, the game cabinet was redesigned to give it a simpler look, and a new name was chosen to emphasize fun: the Nintendo Entertainment System or NES. Although market research continued to be discouraging, Nintendo decided to unveil the NES in time for Christmas of 1985 in New York City.

The launch was supported with fast-paced television commercials that screamed "Now you're playing with power." Nintendo also created elaborate hands-on displays for stores and malls and paid professional athletes to demonstrate games. Perhaps most importantly, Nintendo told retailers they could return unsold NES units after Christmas. With a $50 million budget for promotion, Nintendo was able to place NES game systems in more than 500 New York City stores in time for holiday shopping, including FAO Schwartz. Sales were modest—approximately 50,000 units—but were enough to justify a nationwide rollout.

In 1986 Nintendo sold more than 3 million home video-game systems in the United States. Pepsi, Inc. advertised Nintendo products on the outside of 2 billion Pepsi cans and organized a $10 million giveaway shortly before Christmas of 1988. Sales that year topped 7 million video-game systems and 33 million game packs. More publicity came in 1989, when Universal Studios produced the motion picture *The Wizard* based on a fictional nationwide contest to determine the best Nintendo game player in the United States. During the final scene, hundreds of frenzied game players are introduced to the latest game from Nintendo, Super Mario Bros. 3. The film was only a mild box office success, but it created tremendous demand for Super Mario Bros. 3, which went on to become the most successful video game in history, grossing more than $500 million. That year U.S. consumers spent more than $11 billion on toys; 23 percent of those monies went to Nintendo products. By 1990 one out of every three households in the United States—about 30 million—owned a Nintendo Entertainment System. Nintendo had not only single-handedly resurrected home video games, it had taken over the toy industry.

Game Boy

In 1989 Nintendo presented Game Boy, the first hand-held video game system with replaceable game cartridges. Although Game Boy was criticized because it had a monochrome display, more than 200,000 were sold in the first two weeks in Japan, and 40,000 were sold the first day in the United States. Game Boy came with Tetris, a video game created in the former Soviet Union that was popular not only with kids, but with their parents too. Seizing the new audience, Nintendo encouraged marketing campaigns that targeted adults. A Father's Day campaign urged children, "This Father's Day treat Dad like a kid." Advertisements in airline magazines taunted, "If you're reading this, you're very bored." Game Boy video games soon appeared almost everywhere. In 1991 newspaper pictures showed then-President George Bush playing with a Game Boy while in the hospital. More than 32 million Game Boy video games were sold through 1992.

Super NES

The year of Game Boy was also the year Sega Enterprises, Ltd., another Japanese video game company, began selling the first 16-bit home video game system. Compared to Nintendo's 8-bit NES, Sega Genesis offered more colors, sharper graphics, and more realistic action. Nintendo was reluctant to introduce its own 16-bit system because the NES was still the best-selling video-game system in the United States. At first, Nintendo was able to justify its decision and defend its position in the industry because Sega failed to introduce any blockbuster games. But in 1990, Sega introduced several sports games endorsed by celebrities, such as golfer Arnold Palmer, baseball manager Tony Lasorda, football announcer John Madden, and football quarterback Joe Montana, that became popular with older video game players. Then in 1991 Sega released Sonic the Hedgehog, an action-packed video game with an appealing cartoon character that provided the first real competition for Nintendo's Mario.

Nintendo responded to the Sega threat by evolving its own 16-bit video game system. The Super Famicom, as it was called in Japan, was put forth late in 1990; meanwhile, the U.S. version, known as the Super NES, was not available until late in 1991. An immediate success, the Super NES came with a new Super Mario World game cartridge. Supported by a $25 million advertising campaign, Nintendo sold more than 6 million Super NES game systems in the United States in 1992 alone. By 1994 more than 300 Super NES video games had been designed by Nintendo and third-party licensees.

Outlook

Nintendo's share of the home video game market in the United States was close to 70 percent in 1994, down from as much as 80 percent just a few years earlier. Some of the market loss was resultant of more flexible licensing and, consequently, more independently produced game cartridges for Nintendo systems. But the Sega Genesis was also proving to be a worthy challenger in the marketplace. According to the Toy Retail Sales Tracking Service, Nintendo's Super NES and the Sega Genesis split the market for 16-bit games systems almost evenly in 1993, though Nintendo's Game Boy still dominated the market for hand-held video game systems with Sega's portable Game Gear a poor second. Nintendo also persisted in selling its original 8-bit NES video game system and supporting it with new games.

New product development continued as well. In 1993 Nintendo introduced a video game system for airlines and cruise ships. Based on the Super NES, the Nintendo Gateway system featured game units fitted into the backs of passenger seats. Technologically, though, Sega managed to press Nintendo, revealing late in 1992 a compact disc (CD) video game player that could be attached to the Sega Genesis. Nintendo apparently considered, then rejected the idea of a CD-based system, announcing in early 1994 that it would instead focus on a 64-bit video game system. Scheduled to be released in 1995, the new system was being developed in conjunction with Silicon Graphics, Inc. and would use high-capacity cartridges. Nintendo said the game cartridges would have at least 12.5 megabytes of memory, five times the storage capacity of games developed for the Super NES. The 3DO Co. and the Atari Corporation also introduced higher-performance video-game systems in the early 1990s, but initially neither had a significant impact on the market.

Although it was likely that Sega would continue to erode Nintendo's market share, Nintendo was expected to retain a firm grip on the market. But, most analysts believed the days of rapid growth were over for Nintendo and its competitors.

Further Reading:

Adler, Jerry, "The Nintendo Kid," *Newsweek,* March 6, 1989, p. 64.

Carlton, Jim, "Sega, Aided by Hedgehog, Is Gaining on Nintendo," *The Wall Street Journal,* November 5, 1993, p. B1.

"Game Over?" *The Economist,* November 20, 1993, p. 74.

Neff, Robert, "The Newest Nintendo Will Take a Slow Boat to America," *Business Week,* July 2, 1990, p. 46.

Pollack, Andrew, "Nintendo's Dominance in Games May Be Waning," *The New York Times,* April 23, 1993, p. D-1.

Richards, Bill, "Nintendo, Sega Gear Up to Battle Over Video Game Market Share," *The Wall Street Journal,* January 12, 1993, p. B12.

Sheff, David, *Game Over,* Random House, New York, 1993.

Tetzeli, Rick, "Videogames: Serious Fun," *Fortune,* December 27, 1993, p. 110.

—Dean Boyer

NISSAN®

Nissan is Japan's second-largest selling automotive brand name, and ranks fifth largest in the world. For many years, however, the company was known mainly through its Datsun brand of automobiles. The brand was associated more with low-end economy cars, rather than the high-margin midsize sedans and luxury automobiles Nissan intended to market. Therefore, the Datsun brand was discontinued in 1981 in favor of the corporate name, in keeping with Nissan's strategic shift from exports to local production during the 1980s.

Brand Origins

Nissan's origins stem from the Kwaishinsha Motor Car Works, established in Tokyo in 1911. Its founder, Masujiro Hashimoto, who studied engineering in New York for several years, hoped to build Japan's first automobile. He won funding for his effort from three backers, Kenjiro Den, Rokuro Aoyama, and Meitaro Takeuchi. Hashimoto named his 10-horsepower car the "DAT," an acronym constructed from his supporters' last names. Conveniently, *Dat* is also the Japanese word for "fast rabbit."

In 1926 the Kwaishinsha company merged with Osaka-based Jitsuyo Jidosha Seizo, established in 1919 to manufacture three-wheeled vehicles designed by an American aircraft engineer, William R. Gorham, who had moved to Japan in 1918 and became a naturalized citizen in 1941. In 1931 an improved two-seat model of the DAT was developed and wryly dubbed the "Son of DAT," or Datson. The new company continued to manufacture the Datson car, but was subsequently acquired by Tobata Casting, an automotive parts manufacturer led by Yoshiuke Aikawa.

The Datson name was clever for those familiar with English, but a poor choice for the Japanese market because *son* is Japanese for "damage" or "loss." In 1931 Tobata Casting changed the spelling to Datsun in a dual effort to lose the negative connotation of *son* and to make use of Japan's rising sun flag. A new logo based on the national symbol was also instituted.

Production and marketing of Datsun automobiles was handled by the Jidosha Seizo Company, a joint venture between the Nihon Sangyo Company—generally known as Nissan—and Tobata Casting, a business unit of Nihon Sangyo. The company took valuable direction from American production engineers and built parts for local operations run by General Motors and Ford.

In order to meet the government's need for heavy-duty military trucks, in 1936 Nissan purchased design plans and complete assembly lines from the financially troubled Graham-Paige Motors Corporation in the United States. This enabled Nissan to begin mass production of several new automobile and truck designs.

When Japanese militarists plunged the country into war in the late 1930s, Nissan's operations were requisitioned for truck and engine manufacturing. While the episode meant a complete suspension of Nissan's business activities, it did enable the company's engineers to gain experience in commercial vehicle production techniques.

Nissan escaped the war without damage and resumed truck production in 1945. Two years later the company began turning out Datsun sedans aided by William Gorham, who had become executive managing director and head of the Yokohama plant. The company became a large supplier to American occupation forces, and later established a licensing arrangement with Austin in order to jump-start its commercial operations.

Early Marketing Strategy

Sales of Datsuns were initially limited in Japan, as the nation struggled to rebuild its economy. Interestingly, Nissan found a strong market for Datsuns in the fleet market, particularly taxis, where standardization simplified maintenance and repair. The company established a good reputation in this market and has maintained a strong position as a supplier of taxi cabs ever since.

Nissan branched into several new areas during the 1950s, including machine tools, forklifts, and diesel engines. It gained recognition for its achievements in 1958, when a Datsun model won the gruelling Australian Rally. The company won further technological recognition in 1960 when it was awarded the Deming Prize for excellence in manufacturing.

During the 1960s, which was known as the period of motorization in Japan, companies like Nissan endeavored to develop an affordable car for the mass market. To this end, Nissan introduced the Bluebird in 1959 and the Cedric in 1960. In 1966 the company rolled out its Sunny, a simple model priced so that even modest wage-earners could own a car.

That year, Nissan acquired the Prince Motor Company, a commercial operation born of the wartime Nakajima and

AT A GLANCE

Nissan brand of automobile originally founded as DAT in 1916 by Masujiro Hashimoto, founder of the Kwaishinsha Motor Car Works, in Tokyo, Japan; Kwaishinsha merged with Jitsuyo Jidosha Seizo, 1926; later acquired by Tobata Casting, a business unit of Nihon Sangyo Company known as Nissan in the stock market; two-seat Datson introduced in 1931; Datsun spelling adopted, 1932; Datsun brand replaced by Nissan in 1981.

Performance: *Sales*—687,751 units (1993).

Major competitor: Toyota; also Honda and Mitsubishi.

Advertising: *Agency*—Chiat/Day/Mojo. *Major campaign*—"We're Changing Our Name to Nissan"; also "It's time to expect more from a car."

Addresses: *Parent company*—Nissan North America, Ltd., 990 West 190th St., Torrance, CA 90502; phone: (310) 768-3700. *Ultimate parent company*—Nissan Motor Company, Ltd., 17-1, Ginza, 6-chome, Chuo-ku, Tokyo, Japan 104-23; phone: (03) 3543-5523.

Tachikawa aircraft companies. Prince brought new engine technologies to Nissan, as well as two successful car models, the Gloria and Skyline. The Nissan Prince Royal, a limousine favored by Japan's Royal Family, was introduced at that time.

The "My Car" era in Japan was, quite literally, a smashing success. With so many people driving, auto accidents were common and pollution emerged as a major environmental concern. In 1975 Nissan engineered a catalytic converter system called NAPS, or Nissan Anti-Pollution System, in an effort to meet ambitious emission goals established in the United States under the Clean Air Act. Although difficult to achieve, Nissan succeeded in developing a cleaner operating car, which became an immediate marketing asset.

International Growth

The first exports of Datsuns were made to Australia in 1934. It wasn't until the 1950s, when the company took note of rising U.S. sales of small European cars—particularly the Volkswagen—that Nissan adopted a true export strategy. With improved quality steel at its disposal, the company was confident of entering the American market with a distinct cost advantage. Datsuns would have a natural appeal in the United States as a second family car. The first Datsun was displayed at the Imported Motor Car Show in Los Angeles in 1958. Like other Japanese models, however, it was dismissed as having little commercial potential in a country dominated by Edsels and Roadmasters.

The American market remained critically important to Nissan because it could greatly enhance Datsun's reputation at home, while providing necessary scales of production to substantially reduce unit costs. After failing to increase sales through distributorships, Nissan established its own American sales operation in 1960. Over the next dozen years, the Datsun brand name achieved a strong position in the American market.

Having set up a factory in Taiwan in 1959, Nissan added assembly plants in Mexico in 1961, and Australia in 1966. An American operation was tooled up in 1980, and that same year a joint venture agreement was made with Alfa Romeo to produce small cars in Italy. A plant in the United Kingdom was brought online in 1984.

Brand Development

Because they were engineered to burn fuel more cleanly, Nissan models were highly fuel-efficient. This became an important selling point in 1973 when the OPEC oil embargo caused world fuel prices to skyrocket, especially in the United States, where the cost of gasoline tripled in a period of only months.

The rising popularity of Datsun models prompted protectionist moves in the United States, when the automotive industry proved incapable of responding to market demands. This experience convinced Nissan to make long-range plans to establish factories in America, which would allow the company to circumvent any future trade restrictions.

One of the most successful Datsun models in the American market was the 240Z, a sports car introduced in 1969 that shared many attributes with the celebrated Ford Mustang. It was stylish, fast, fun to drive, and affordable. A small Datsun pick-up truck also was very successful because it was more appropriate to many consumers' needs. It was rugged, efficient, and cheap, and its popularity encouraged many dealerships to begin carrying Datsuns.

As demand for Datsuns grew in the United States, so did the nation's trade imbalance with Japan. President Nixon responded by devaluing the dollar and imposing import restrictions. These decrees increased the price of Datsuns and limited the number that could be sold in the United States. Even as the energy crisis began to wane, however, Nissan introduced a highly promising economy car called the Datsun B210 Honeybee. This car had, for the time, amazing fuel efficiency, recording 41 miles per gallon of gas.

The company made several changes in 1976 with regard to styling. Until this time Datsuns had been engineered for Japanese roads and were not completely adequate for the speedy wide open freeways of the United States. An effort was made to modify the Datsun line to include sophisticated options and complex detailing, luggage racks, and air conditioning units. The first result of these restyling efforts was the Datsun 200SX, introduced in 1980.

Advertising

Nissan's first promotional slogan, dating from before World War II, was "The Rising Sun as the Flag and the Datsun as the car of choice." When the company began an export program during the 1960s, it went without an advertising theme, choosing instead to promote its products only by their names and on their merits. This changed in 1973 when the worldwide energy crisis heightened consumer interest in fuel economy and pollution standards. Nissan used the theme "Datsun Saves" to simultaneously communicate fuel efficiency and environmental protection as well as affordability.

Unwilling to support a separate brand identity, the Datsun company decided to change its products' name in overseas markets to Nissan in 1981. This was a deceptively simple task, but it took six difficult years to accomplish. Advertisements stated that Datsun was changing its name to Nissan, but offered no explanation why. Consumers were either amused or confused by the curious ads. After six years, Nissan finally gave up the campaign, choosing to continue only with product advertisements. The public quickly forgot about Datsun and developed a new interest in the Nissan line.

Ads for Nissan models during the 1980s were typically high-budget productions with an especially pleasing aesthetic quality, featuring cars in gallery-like showrooms, rather than on roads. This approach was intended to portray Nissans as engineering marvels and works of art, rather than mere cars. In order to concentrate attention on the Nissan name, the company used no tag lines. In the early 1990s, however, Nissan began to incorporate into its ads such tag lines as "Built for the Human Race" and "It's time to expect more from a car."

The change in brand name from Datsun to Nissan provided the company with an opportunity to present a new era of more advanced, and more expensive, automobiles. The first of these was the popular Stanza, a model aimed roughly at the same market as the earlier 240Z, followed by the Quest, a minivan designed by Nissan and built by Ford. The Altima sedan was aimed at the same market as the Toyota Camry, Honda Accord, and Ford Taurus. However, when Nissan established a line of luxury cars, it decided not to market them under the Nissan name. Instead, the company created the name Infiniti for the new line.

Performance Evaluation

Despite the substantial successes enjoyed by the Datsun and Nissan brands since the 1960s, Nissan suffered strong reverses in its enterprise in the 1990s. This is due mainly to the rising competitiveness of American manufacturers and strong products from traditional rivals Toyota and Honda.

In addition, a lingering economic recession in Japan stunted market growth in that country. Sales dropped by 16 percent from 1991 to 1992, while currency valuations have increased the price of Nissan products in the United States. The company's car and truck sales fell by 30 percent in North America over the same period, leaving the brand with only a 4.7-percent share of the market.

As part of its globalization campaign, Nissan has relegated research and development, marketing, and production responsibilities in the United States and Europe to its subsidiary operations in those markets. This stems from the belief that only local knowledge can efficiently evaluate market conditions and manage labor forces and supplier networks.

As it strives to maintain technological leadership and product differentiation, Nissan is developing leading-edge technology in safety and environmental protection, which are major social concerns. Nissan hopes this strategy will position the brand among the leading automotive companies in the world.

Further Reading:

"Nissan Motor Co., Ltd.," *Diamond's Japan Business Directory,* Bristol, PA: Taylor & Francis, 1992, pp. 824–825.

"Nissan Motor Co., Ltd.," *Hoover's Handbook of World Business,* Austin, TX: Reference Press, Inc., 1993, pp. 352–353.

Additional information was provided by Nissan North America, Ltd. and Nissan Motor Company, Ltd.

—John Simley

NORDICTRACK®

NordicTrack

Advertised with the registered label "The World's Best Aerobic Exerciser," NordicTrack is both the originator and leader of the cross-country ski simulator market. The Chaska, Minnesota-based brand is owned by CML Group of Acton, Massachusetts, a company whose $378 million in annual revenues is about 60 percent dependent on sales of NordicTrack, Inc. products. Since its inception in 1975, the NordicTrack company has sold almost two million of its exercise machines—"a remarkable feat," wrote Tony Carideo, "given the typical $500 price tag on the product." The secrets to NordicTrack's success are numerous and include a hefty annual advertising budget, a sustained fitness culture in the United States, high customer satisfaction among NordicTrack users, and a unique, patented design that many say delivers the ultimate in in-home fitness.

From Specialized Training Device to Home Fitness Favorite

The inventor of NordicTrack is Edward A. Pauls, a mechanical engineer of sports equipment and a cross-country ski enthusiast. According to Cecily Patterson of *Forbes,* "Pauls was training for local races during an exceptionally cold Minnesota winter back in 1975. Running one night on a dark, ice-covered street, he was inspired to build an indoor exerciser that duplicated the motions of cross-country skiing." Pauls soon had his machine: a sturdy platform atop which rested two short wooden skis that glided back and forth by means of a clutch and flywheel system. Pauls's exerciser also featured a pulley device to replicate the upper-body motions of poling.

The name NordicTrack was soon born when friends began asking Pauls to manufacture identical machines for their use. After securing $10,000 in capital, Pauls founded PSI NordicTrack Cross Country Skiing Exerciser, Inc. During the early years, NordicTrack products were marketed primarily to other ski enthusiasts like Pauls, either through magazine ads or word of mouth. But there was another, vastly larger market just opening up, that of a burgeoning fitness crowd in the throes of a nationwide fitness craze. Pauls tapped this market through running magazines and a number of general interest publications.

During the 1980s one of his key endorsements came from his daughter, Terri Pauls, two-time national collegiate cross-country skiing champion. The ad copy read: "Scientific tests at major universities prove NordicTrack to be an extremely effective fitness builder. But Terri has confirmed the proof in one of the toughest tests of all. National competition—twice! In the sport considered the ultimate test of fitness, cross country skiing. . . . Terri's time is valuable. So is yours. 'To get the greatest workout for time spent, use the NordicTrack,' says our champ." Another prominent endorsement came from world speed record holder and Olympic medalist Bill Koch, at the time "America's Most Famous XC Skier." Koch said, "I've tried all types of indoor exercisers, including others claiming to duplicate XC skiing. Nothing even comes close to NordicTrack's effectiveness and smooth striding action." He also stressed that: "The NordicTrack is not just for athletes. It's for anyone who wants to keep physically fit." Personal endorsements continue to play an important role in NordicTrack marketing and come from NordicTrack users of all types. Typical is one from a New York physical therapist, who wrote: "The NordicTrack is simply the best piece of fitness equipment on the market. Period."

From Small Family Business to "America's Number One Fitness Company"

By 1985 Pauls's company had grown from three to around 80 employees, and the home exercise equipment market had blossomed into a billion-dollar industry, despite an earlier economic downturn. Yet NordicTrack was still only a small player in the market, with only two products to its name. The first was a standard home exerciser, weighing 58 pounds and priced at $470; the second was a deluxe model for health clubs, schools, and other institutions, weighing 63 pounds, featuring an arm resistance adjustment, and priced at $559. What the brand had going for it, of course, was not only a superior product but a growing awareness among doctors, scientists, and the public that the upper- and lower-body motions of cross-country skiing produced the best cardiovascular workout of all exercises. What was needed for NordicTrack to make the leap to superbrand status was an infusion of capital and high-powered marketing expertise.

In 1986, with Minnesota-based competitor Fitness Master a still small but growing threat, NordicTrack was ready for new ownership and Pauls was ready to sell. CML Group of Boston, a specialty retailer, purchased the company for $24 million and then hired marketing executive Jim Bostic to chart a course of accelerated growth for the company and the brand. Although 1987 brought another downturn for the industry, along with "knock-

AT A GLANCE

NordicTrack brand founded in 1975 in Minnesota by PSI NordicTrack Cross Country Skiing Exerciser, Inc., owner Edward A. Pauls; NordicTrack sold to CML Group in 1986.

Performance: *Market share*—3% penetration of a core market of 55 million households. *Sales*—$378 million.

Major competitor: Soloflex; also, Fitness Master.

Advertising: *Agency*—In-house. *Major campaign*—NordicTrack: "Fitness at Home."

Addresses: *Parent company*—NordicTrack, Inc., 104 Peavey Rd., Chaska, MN 55318-2355; phone: (612) 368-2500; *Ultimate parent company*—CML Group, 524 Main St., Acton, MA 01720; phone: (508) 264-4155.

off'' products priced well below NordicTrack or other premium brands, the company thrived under Bostic's leadership and saw sales expand 500 percent by 1990, to $86 million.

During the period from 1988 to 1990, especially, NordicTrack underwent a major transformation, expanding its line from just two to sixteen different exercise machines. The company still had the edge over Fitness Master and other ski simulators due to its patented one-way clutch, which by numerous accounts allows the exerciser to more effectively duplicate the motions of nordic skiing than any other technology on the market. And it was now boldly entering the broader home (and office) fitness market with a number of innovative products, including the $1,200 Executive Power Chair, a black leather chair with specially designed attachments for upper-body exercises.

The transformation became even more pronounced over the next two years, during which NordicTrack introduced its first strength-training machine, NordicFlex Gold, and a host of other products, from fitness bikes to videos, many under distribution agreement from outside manufacturers. Some of its newest products include the Walk-Fit, a non-motorized treadmill that gives a total-body workout; the Easy Ski, a cross-country skier with rigid poles for extra balance; and the affordable All American cross-country skier. In addition, the company entered the retail store business, growing from just one East Coast outlet in late 1990 to 65 stores in fiscal 1993. The company had plans to open another 30 stores in fiscal 1994. Finally, in late 1992 the company began its first major diversification beyond the exercise market with its introduction of Healthy Express, a food retail store featuring healthy sandwiches, yogurt smoothies, juices, and various kitchen appliances including juicers and breadmakers.

Through all of this growth, the NordicTrack brand has retained its original identity. In fact, NordicTrack ads, which now appear in more than 120 magazines and newspapers, and also take the form of catalogs, direct-mail fliers, and MTV and network TV commercials, are still largely based on the original, factory-direct marketing philosophy of Pauls: educate and inform the consumer. The ads, wrote Josephine Marcotty, ''are as simple as they come—a photo of someone using a cross-country or other machine, with a detailed copy block extolling its virtues.'' The move into retailing, then, was not an abandonment of this philosophy but seemed a logical extension of it, given that company market research found that some 50 percent of consumers prefer to ''test-drive'' and acquire additional information on an exercise machine before buying it. In a 1992 *Pioneer Press* article, NordicTrack's vice president of retail operations, Henry Barksdale, said, ''We are either No. 1 or No. 2 in sales per square foot in every mall we're in, so we must be doing something right.'' According to Barksdale, NordicTrack customers tend to be ''affluent suburban couples between 35 and 50 years old, people who want products designed for a better way of life.''

The Future

The original, specialized NordicTrack cross-country ski machine, now available in nine models (including the Aerobic Cross-Trainer, a $1,200 machine that accommodates walking, skiing, and stepping exercises), is still the company's most popular product. But as Marcotty pointed out, NordicTrack is also ''a major player in the fragmented home exercise equipment business, up there with Nautilus, Soloflex, and other manufacturers.'' Although the brand will always be identified with ski simulator machines, it may just as easily attach itself in the future to a variety of other technologies. In November of 1993, Marcotty reported that NordicTrack had signed an agreement with a Russian training center to secure the exclusive rights to inventions—many related to athletic conditioning—from some 800 Soviet scientists. The

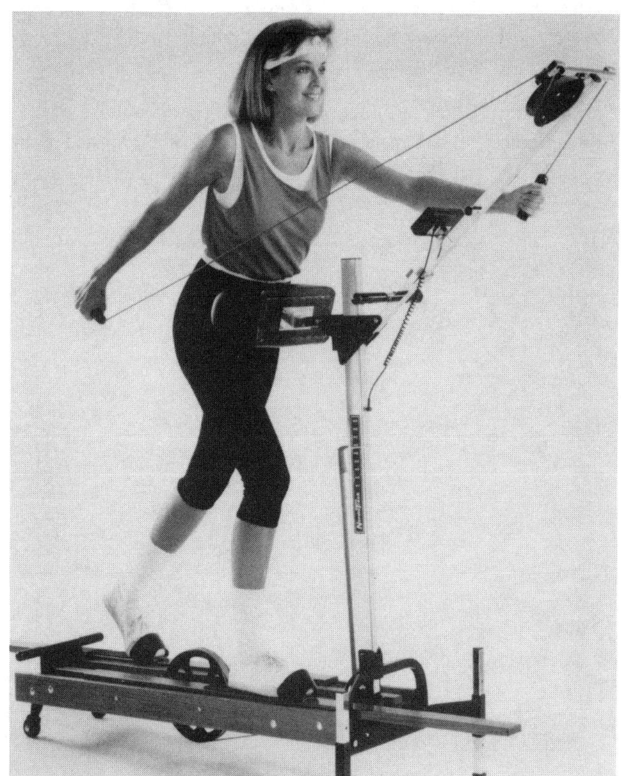

The NordicTrack exercise machine.

agreement was likely timed to help minimize the effects of the loss of NordicTrack's original patent, which expires in 1994. The company, however, has recently introduced more advanced technology for its ski machine, called MC_2. Available on its graphite-composite NordicSport ski simulators, the new patent-pending technology is based on an electromagnetic resistance principle that generates its energy from the motion of the person using it. MC_2

also can simulate different types of snow conditions—as chosen by the user—including fast, normal, slow, or even wet snow.

Fortified by independent studies that show home exercise equipment users prefer NordicTrack products over other machines, use them consistently in seven out of ten cases, and would overwhelmingly recommend them to friends and relatives, the company believes there is still a large potential for market growth. In the 1993 CML Annual Report, the NordicTrack market is divided into three categories with reference to fitness attitudes: Enthusiast (15 million households); Aware (48 million households); and Couch Potato (33 million households). NordicTrack penetration of the first two markets is just 3.3 percent and 1.8 percent, respectively. Given continued growth in retail sales and the willingness of these core consumers to convert from existing fitness strategies, NordicTrack's potential may indeed still be enormous.

And then there's the international market. The company has recently established telemarketing operations in both Germany and the United Kingdom and has high hopes for overseas expansion. Whatever the future holds, it cannot be argued that Pauls created a machine that in less than 20 years has become a classic. There is little wonder that the NordicTrack was named one of the top 25 products made in the USA by the Made in the USA Foundation, or that *Consumers Digest* rates the NordicTrack Achiever and the NordicTrack Sequoia as "best buys" in their class for their superior performance and value.

Further Reading:

Beran, George, "Ski Simulator Market Matures as Fit-Minded Baby Boom Ages," *Pioneer Press,* January 22, 1989, pp. 1–2H.

Carideo, Tony, "NordicTrack Planning Ahead for Patent Expiration," *Star Tribune,* June 19, 1993, p. 3D.

Jones, Jim, "Need for a Safer Exercise Led to Home Skiing Machine," *Star Tribune,* September 6, 1985, pp. 5–6B.

Howatt, Glenn, "NordicTrack Making Strides in Mall Sales," *Star Tribune,* February 21, 1992, p. 6D.

Kahn, Aron, "A New Track," *Pioneer Press,* March 8, 1992, pp. 1–2G.

Katayama, Frederick H., "Seat of Power," *Fortune,* August 13, 1990, p. 102.

Lloyd, Barbara, "A Home Exercise Machine for a Customized Workout," *New York Times,* April 25, 1992, p. 50.

Marcotty, Josephine, *Star Tribune,* "NordicTrack Keeps CML in Great Shape; Chaska Firm Intends to Continue Its Rapid Growth," December 7, 1992, p. 1D; "NordicTrack Wins $1 Million Settlement," May 27, 1993, p. 3D; "NordicTrack Sales Goals Are Met; A Boss Pays a Visit to Celebrate," August 4, 1993, p. 1D; "New Ski Machine Technology Doesn't Help CML Stock," October 20, 1993, p. 3D; "NordicTrack Nearing Deal with Russia for Technology from Cosmonaut Center," November 16, 1993, p. 1D; "Nordic Track Inc. and Soloflex Both Claim Victory in Court Decisions Over Their Advertising Dispute," February 16, 1994, p. 1D.

Patterson, Cecily, "Eclectic Chair," *Forbes,* December 24, 1990, pp. 112, 114.

Schwartz, Joe, "Ski for Your Life, Says Nordic Track," *American Demographics,* August 1991, p. 16.

Sprout, Alison, "Aerobic Cross-Trainer," *Fortune,* September 21, 1992, p. 115.

Williams, Monte, "People to Watch (NordicTrack President-CEO Jim Bostic)," *Advertising Age,* December 3, 1990, p. 36.

Woodward, Bob, "Skiing in Your Living Room," *Backpacker,* November 1984, pp. 24–25.

Youngblood, Dick, "NordicTrack's in Great Shape Thanks to the Fitness Boom," *Star Tribune,* June 8, 1992, p. 2D.

—Jay P. Pederson

NORELCO®

For most of the 1960s, '70s, and '80s, the animated television commercial featuring the Norelco Santa gliding over snow-covered hills atop a rotary razor was a sign that the holiday season had begun. Revived in 1993 after a seven-year hiatus, the character continued to rank among the best-known and best-loved product representatives.

The Norelco brand encompasses the widely advertised men's and women's electric shavers, travel and household irons and steamers, and clean-air machines. In 1981 Norelco purchased longtime rival Schick and relegated that brand to bladed razors. After two decades of clear-cut dominance in the field of electric shavers, Norelco faced intense competition from a revitalized Remington in the early 1990s.

The brand's parent company, Norelco Consumer Products Company (a division of Philips Electronics North America Corporation), is a subsidiary of Philips Electronics N.V. of Holland. The American business activities of this leading international conglomerate include lighting, consumer electronics (televisions, stereos, radios, razors, irons, and clean-air machines), medical systems, and electrical components (semiconductors, switches, capacitors, and resistors).

Brand Origins

Norelco electric razors were first sold in the United States in 1948. By that time the shaving market in general had gotten very competitive. Gillette, the originator of disposable blade razors, had dominated the industry for most of the 20th century. Philips had established American operations in 1933 and formed a trust to protect its assets and patents in North America prior to the start of World War II. It introduced its first razor, the Philips Philishave, to the market in 1939, and its 1948 Norelco launch introduced the industry's first single-headed rotary shaver.

As a relatively late entry in the shaver market, Norelco first focused its competitive energies on rivals within the electric segment: Remington, Schick, and Sunbeam. Like all electric shaver manufacturers, Norelco concentrated its advertising in the fourth quarter to encourage gift purchases. Market research has shown that nearly half of all shaver sales occur between mid-November and Christmas.

During the 1950s Norelco introduced its Speedshaver, a double-headed rotary razor that featured a pop-up trimmer for sideburns and moustaches and "Microgroove" shaving heads. Despite the Speedshaver's convenience, added features, and the growing potential market, sales declined in the late 1950s. Overall electric shaver sales peaked in 1956 at about $140 million annually, and by 1961 the industry had shrunk to less than $100 million. The decline was blamed primarily on Gillette, which was not only the dominant marketer of disposable razors but also one of the most effective and formidable American advertisers.

First Commercial Success

In the early 1960s Norelco, with 18 percent of the market, ranked fourth among electric shaver brands. Remington and Schick each had 30 percent, and Sunbeam had 20 percent. During the 1960s Norelco began to increase its advertising budget to build a campaign around sports programming, especially National Football League (NFL) games, which coincided neatly with the brand's fall advertising push. Norelco dedicated more than 50 percent of its $3 million in advertising monies to broadcast television. Promotions often accompanied the brand's NFL ads; they offered free footballs, a book about professional football, and even sweepstakes for trips to playoff or Super Bowl games.

In 1961 Norelco's principal ad agency, C.J. LaRoche & Co. (later known as McCaffrey & McCall), launched the brand's highly recognizable and long-running holiday campaign. The animated ads featured Santa Claus riding a shaver through a snowy scene and calling the brand "Noelco." Sales messages during the first half of the year focused on gifts for Father's Day, graduation, and, for the Lady Norelco shavers (introduced by the mid-1960s), Mother's Day.

During the decade the man who would influence Norelco's advertising and sales for nearly three decades joined the company. That man, Richard Kress, became the brand's advertising director in 1963. He held a Masters in Business Administration from Wharton and was brought to Norelco after a stint with N.W. Ayer agency. Over the years Kress would stage outlandish stunts to motivate his sales force. He rappelled down buildings, dressed up as "Norelco Man," and even went a few rounds with a professional wrestler at yearly sales conventions. The versatile executive was elected president of Norelco in 1971 and later explained away

AT A GLANCE

Norelco brand of electric shaver founded in 1948 by Consolidated Electronic Industries Corporation ("Conelectron"), the U.S. subsidiary of N.V. Philips Gloeilampenfabrieken Philips Incandescent Lamp Works Company of Holland; Conelectron renamed North American Philips Corporation in 1959 and later Philips Electronics North America Corporation; Norelco became the best-selling brand of electric shaver in the mid-1960s.

Performance: *Market share*—47% (top share) of men's electric shavers (1991). *Sales*—$30 million (1993 estimate).

Major competitor: Remington; also, Panasonic and Braun.

Advertising: *Agency*—D'Arcy Masius Benton & Bowles, New York, NY, 1987—. *Major campaign*—Animated holiday commercials featuring the Norelco Santa riding a shaver and calling the brand "Noelco." Also, the slogan "We make close comfortable."

Addresses: *Parent company*—Norelco Consumer Products Company, A Division of Philips Electronics North America Corporation, 1010 Washington Boulevard, P.O. Box 120015, Stamford, CT 06912-0015; phone: (203) 973-0200; fax: (203) 975-1812. *Ultimate parent company*—Philips Electronics N.V., Groenewoudseweg 1, 5621 BA Eindhoven, The Netherlands FF.

his wacky behavior to *Forbes* magazine: "I was a bad speaker and presenter and I started using props."

Kress's self-effacing manner belied the aggressive campaign that led to the brand's dominance of the electric razor market. By 1965 he had doubled the advertising budget to $6.2 million and supplanted Gillette as a significant sports advertiser among shaver marketers. The bladed razor maker had begun to favor placing its ads during evening television programming. In the meantime, Norelco added sponsorship of horse racing's Triple Crown—the Kentucky Derby, the Preakness, and the Belmont Stakes—to its schedule. The brand also made its concentrated fall budget count with sponsorship of such popular 1960s shows as *Smothers Brothers, Mission: Impossible, My Three Sons, Carol Burnett Show, Lost in Space, Gunsmoke, Gilligan's Island, Candid Camera, Ed Sullivan Show,* and several others.

Industry analysts credited these new marketing approaches, improved shaving technology, and greater acceptance of electric shavers by women for the industry's mid-1960s upswing. Seven million electric shavers were sold in 1965, and the Norelco name graced the top share of them.

Advertising Innovations

Several factors influenced a dramatic shift in Norelco's advertising in the late 1960s. Led by Gillette, advertising for bladed razors was three times that for electric shavers, thereby restricting the latter market. By the mid-1970s sales of electric shavers declined from 7 million units annually to 4.5 million. Dollar sales stood at just $175 million. The shrinking market heightened tensions in the already fiercely competitive segment.

Having captured the lead among electric shavers, Norelco turned from internecine competition to bigger game: blades. In 1967 the brand introduced the first Tripleheader razor, which featured three microgroove floating heads (designed to follow the contours of the face and neck) in a triangular arrangement. Each head housed 18 self-sharpening rotary blades traveling at 77 miles per hour. The design and arrangement of the heads was said to reduce shaving time by 40 percent. Armed with its new, improved shaver, Norelco took on bladed razors with the theme, "We dare any blade to match shaves with a Norelco." By the end of the decade, the brand's advertising budget had risen to $10 million, and its campaign grew ever more aggressive.

Norelco's new "We beat the blades" theme was substantiated by three comparative tests conducted by an independent research organization using the new Tripleheader. More than 100 men in the experiment shaved half of their face with a blade and half with the Tripleheader. In the subjective part of the test, 75 percent of the participants said that the Norelco side was shaved as well as or better than the blade side. Barbers (who were not told what shaving instrument was used) also judged the Norelco cheek as good as or better than the blade half, both in terms of less irritation and the closeness of the shave, in 90 percent of the cases. Finally, a photographic and microscopic test showed that whiskers shaved by the Tripleheader were 108 percent shorter than the blade shave. Norelco called the experiment "the most intensive consumer and laboratory testing ever developed for the product category." The comparative campaign helped make Norelco the first choice among electrics, and the brand vaulted to a 45.2 percent stake in the electric shaver market—its highest share up to that point—in 1972.

In the meantime, ABC and CBS had joined NBC in allowing truly competitive television advertising. For years the networks had prohibited advertisers from specifically naming competitors' products in broadcast spots. When these bans were lifted in the early 1970s, Schick became one of the first major brands to "name names." A 1972 commercial pitted Schick's electric Flexamatic against Norelco's Tripleheader and claimed that the former gave a closer shave. Since Schick refused to reveal the basis of its claim, Norelco challenged its validity. Schick was allowed to run the ads until 1974, when the National Advertising Review Board judged the commercials "false in some details" and "misleading in [their] over-all implications."

One of Norelco's most successful advertising ventures was its 1970s "Gotcha!" campaign. The brand attacked wet-shave systems by showing a man getting nicked by a blade razor punctuated with the voice-over "Gotcha!" When the campaign first broke in 1974, the brand held about 48 percent of the market. By the following year its stake had grown to 58 percent.

By 1978 Norelco alone sold over three million shavers and captured an estimated 60 percent of the segment. Longtime rival Schick dropped out of the market in 1980 after years of dismal sales. Norelco purchased the brand in 1981 and marketed men's and women's bladed razors under the brand.

Product Innovations

The highly successful "Gotcha!" campaign was extended to publicize Norelco's new Solid State Charge Rotary Razor, the first to automatically convert to any electrical current in the world. Promoted as "the Rolls-Royce of the electric shaver market," the new razor also featured a built-in eight-hour charger.

The 1980 development of the Rotatract (Lift and Cut) Rotary Razor revolutionized the American shaving industry. This system competed directly with the twin-blade razors that proliferated during the 1980s. Rotatract lifted whiskers up to cut them as close as possible without the blades actually touching the skin. Norelco continued to milk its 1970s ad campaign to promote the Rotatract, asserting "Twin-blade closeness with no 'Gotcha.' "

Norelco further segmented its market (and followed the lead of rival Remington) with the introduction of the "Black Pro" shaver in 1980. This model was especially designed with the needs of African-American men in mind. It featured a custom-engineered "razor bump" that lifted curly whiskers as it shaved.

Brand Extensions

Norelco has introduced a variety of consumer products over the years, but none received the advertising support afforded electric shavers. The electric razor line was extended to include Lady Norelco shavers, hair dryers, hot rollers, and other grooming aids in the 1960s and 1970s. The brand introduced home appliances like food mixers, electric knife and scissors sharpeners, coffeemakers, and even a deep fryer and an ice cream maker during that time as well. During the 1970s Norelco elaborated on its "Gotcha" razor campaign with the introduction of Gotcha Dry blow-dryers. In the 1980s the brand brought out a home health care line that included a digital thermometer, a scale, and an electronic analog blood pressure meter. These products were targeted toward the growing numbers of senior citizens.

Although Norelco was not a pioneer in the field of hand-held vacuums, the brand was a formidable (but fleeting) competitor in the category. Its Clean-Up Machines captured an estimated 20 percent of the market in 1984 owing to a very competitive pricing strategy. They were pushed out of the market soon after the introduction of Royal Manufacturing's fabulously popular Dirt Devil hand-held.

Renewed Competition

In 1979 Victor Kiam bought Remington and quickly revived the brand by offering a bargain-priced model and by starring in the brand's commercials. The CEO became a familiar character by asserting that he, a loyal blade shaver, liked the Remington electric so much that he "bought the company." By 1982 Remington's share doubled to 40 percent, and Norelco's slipped to 55 percent.

By 1985 Remington's pricing pressures compelled Norelco to introduce a successful new low-priced line, but reduced profit margins doomed the effort, and it was dropped in 1986. Richard Kress retired that year, and the Norelco advertising account was put on review shortly afterward as part of a major restructuring directed by the brand's ultimate parent company. D'Arcy Masius Benton & Bowles, headquartered in New York, was awarded the $9 million account in 1987, ending Norelco's 33-year relationship with McCaffrey & McCall.

Norelco still claimed over 53 percent of the $280 million shaver market in 1987, but both Remington and Braun (which had recently been licensed by Gillette) were coming on strong. Later that year Remington placed full-page ads in several newspapers, including the *New York Times,* announcing that it had "overtaken Norelco as the #1 electric shaver brand in the United States." The notice was based on a consumer survey commissioned by the rival brand. It claimed that Remington had moved into first with 43.1 percent of the market, compared with Norelco's 40.5 percent stake. Norelco quickly responded with its own retail audit that showed it held 44 percent, attributing only 30 percent to Remington. Industry analysts said the electric shaver business had grown difficult to measure because of its seasonal selling pattern—market share figures could change dramatically within just six weeks.

Brand Outlook

Electric shaver shipments in the United States peaked at 8.9 million units in 1987 but fell to 8.5 million units by 1991. The drop was attributed to the resurgent popularity of wet shaving, which moved steadily upmarket during that period and was driven by Gillette's premium "system" shaver, the Sensor.

In 1993, however, *Appliance Manufacturer* magazine predicted that electric shavers had some of the best prospects for growth during the rest of the decade. The industry organ expected this category to show a 31.1 percent gain in dollar sales for 1995 over 1990. Still, only one-third of American men, and even fewer women, used electric shavers, a figure that had remained constant for many years.

With the cooperation of its advertising agency, Norelco entered the relatively new field of "infomercials" in the early 1990s. Although these 30-minute promotions were originally used for less reputable products, mainstream advertisers had begun to note the advantages of the new medium, especially for complicated or versatile items.

According to *Appliance* magazine, competition continued to run high into the 1990s. Norelco led in men's shavers, with 47 percent of the market, followed by Remington with 25 percent, Braun with 15 percent, and Panasonic with 8 percent. Remington captured 35 percent, the top share, of the significantly smaller women's segment. Norelco and Panasonic trailed close behind with 31 percent and 29 percent, respectively, and Braun had captured only 1 percent of the category.

Norelco's parent company has consistently earmarked generous budgets for its namesake razors, and this has long been considered a deciding factor in its dominance of the electric shaver business. As Remington and Panasonic threatened the leader, a new strategy ascended: pricing. Recession-battered consumers of the 1990s would decide which company carried more clout as the marketplace grew increasingly volatile in the 1990s.

Further Reading:

"Competitors Hail NARB for Schick Shaver Ruling," *Advertising Age,* January 7, 1974, pp. 1, 6.

"Cutthroat Battle Set in Shaving Field," *Printers' Ink,* August 18, 1961, pp. 9–10.

Davis, Riccardo A., "Electric Razors Plan Aggressive Fourth-Quarter," *Advertising Age,* October 12, 1992.

"Electric Razor Sales Hurt by 'Huge Budgets' of Wet Shavers," *Advertising Age,* May 12, 1975, pp. 2, 79.

Fanelli, Louis A., "Norelco Aiming to Slice into Wet Shave Market," *Advertising Age,* June 9, 1980, p. 4.

Jervey, Gay, "State Takes Remington Side in Its Norelco Antitrust Suit," *Advertising Age,* September 6, 1982, p. 60.

McGeehan, Patrick, "Shavers Face Off," *Advertising Age,* December 28, 1987, pp. 6, 30.

"Norelco Earmarks $6.2 Million in Record-High 1965 Ad Budget," *Sponsor,* March 1, 1965, p. 16.

"Norelco Sharpens Its Newspaper Ads," *Editor & Publisher,* November 20, 1965, pp. 18, 20.

O'Connor, John J., "Norelco Challenges Schick TV Claims; Reveals Own Tests," *Advertising Age,* January 15, 1973, pp. 1, 66.

O'Connor, John J., ''Rotary Razor Leads Norelco New Product Parade,'' *Advertising Age,* December 12, 1977, p. 146.

Phillips, Lisa E., ''DMB&B Charged for Norelco Task,'' *Advertising Age,* March 16, 1987, p. 39.

''Stunt Man,'' *Forbes,* August 1, 1983, pp. 155–156.

Wells, Melanie, ''D'Arcy Joins Trend to Infomercials,'' *Advertising Age,* March 29, 1993, p. 12.

—April S. Dougal

OLDSMOBILE®

Forever memorialized in the 1905 Gus Edwards composition "In My Merry Oldsmobile," this division of General Motors Corp., the world's largest automaker, is also America's oldest car manufacturer. After a precipitous drop in popularity in the late 1980s that continued into the early 1990s, the Oldsmobile marque ranked tenth among automotive brands sold in the United States.

Brand Origins

The Oldsmobile marque was named for Ransom E. Olds, founder of the Olds Motor Vehicle Company in 1897. This was the first company organized specifically to manufacture automobiles in quantity. Until this time, cars were custom made and very expensive. The volume was small that first year, however, as just four cars were produced. Auto manufacture was very complicated, and no one had come up with a way to make standardized parts. Like 60 percent of the automotive ventures that were established at the turn of the century, the first Olds venture failed.

In 1899 the Olds Motor Vehicle Company was reorganized into the Olds Motor Works with $500,000 in capital from Detroit investors, and a new plant was built on that city's riverfront. Soon, the company began producing a light, compact vehicle, the Curved Dash Runabout. This new model was very simple, incorporating an angle frame, chain and sprocket, ball bearings, and bicycle-type wheels. Just when it appeared that Oldsmobile would take off, tragedy struck: the Olds factory burned down in March of 1901; salvaged was one completed model of the Curved Dash Runabout, along with plans, drawings, and automobile patterns for both electric and gasoline-driven vehicles.

Oldsmobile enlisted the help of the Dodge brothers, John and Horace, to avoid a production delay that threatened another business failure. The Dodges would later go on to create their own automotive enterprise, but in the meantime, they manufactured Oldsmobile transmissions. Olds also used Leland engines in the Curved Dash, along with parts from other outside suppliers. The company was able to produce 425 cars in 1901, and 2,500 in 1902. This then phenomenal rate helped rank Michigan as the source of almost half the United States' motor vehicles.

Early Marketing Strategies

Oldsmobile used publicity stunts to establish the speed and durability of its early products. In 1901 Roy Chapin (later the chief executive of Hudson Motor Car Co.) drove an Oldsmobile Curved Dash Runabout from Detroit to a national auto show in New York City. The trip, over dauntingly muddy roads and canal tow paths, took more than a week at 14 miles per hour. But this feat made the car the focal point of the show. Two years later, the Oldsmobile Pirate made headlines when it established a world's record of 5 miles in 6.5 minutes at Daytona Beach, Florida. And in 1905 two Olds Curved Dash Runabouts participated in the first transcontinental automobile race, traveling the 4,400 miles from New York City to Portland, Oregon, in 44 days.

Brand Development

Oldsmobile joined what would become the world's largest automaker, General Motors Corporation, in 1908. The division began to carve out a niche in expensive, high-quality cars, the most prominent of which was the massive Limited, equipped with 42-inch tires and a 6-cylinder, 60-horsepower 707-cubic-inch engine. Manufactured from 1910 to 1912, this behemoth carried a price tag to match: $5,000.

During World War I, automobile production was curtailed, and Oldsmobile built mobile kitchen trailers for the Army. But at war's end, the division returned quickly to auto manufacture, building 33,220 cars in 1919. Oldsmobile then turned its design attention toward the mass market. The division brought out the 6-cylinder Model 30A, which sold for just $750, in 1923. Olds staged yet another publicity stunt to draw attention to the new car, when Cannonball Baker drove one from New York to Los Angeles in 12.5 days.

Oldsmobile racked up several industry firsts before and during World War II, pioneering chrome-plated trim in 1926 and offering Hydra-Matic—the first mass-produced, fully automatic transmission system—beginning with the 1940 model year. By 1941, Olds had produced over two million vehicles. The division also became a leading designer of cars with special controls for handicapped drivers during this period. In fact, Oldsmobile built over 26,000 cars for paraplegic war veterans in the years after World War II.

Oldsmobile launched its long-running "88" series in 1949. This high performance car was selected as a pace car for that year's Indianapolis 500, and its popularity grew after the introduction in late December, 1949, of the 1950 Holiday coupe hardtop

AT A GLANCE

Oldsmobile brand cars founded in 1897 in Lansing, MI, by Ransom E. Olds as part of the Olds Motor Vehicle Company; company reorganized in 1899, becoming Olds Motor Works, with assembly operations moving to Detroit, MI; company joined General Motors Corp. in 1908, becoming the Oldsmobile Division, January 1, 1942.

Performance: *Market share*—Tenth best-selling automobile brand in the United States. *Sales*—416,126 units.

Major competitor: Other American-made car brands, including Ford, Chevrolet, Dodge, Pontiac, Buick, and Mercury; also, Japanese-made car brands, such as Toyota, Honda, and Nissan.

Advertising: *Agency*—Leo Burnett, Southfield, Michigan, 1967—. *Major campaign*—Slogan, "Demand Better."

Addresses: *Parent company*—General Motors Corp., 3044 West Grand Blvd., Detroit, MI 48202; phone: (313) 556-5000.

model. Demand for the new 88 pushed Olds production to a new peak of 293,769 cars in 1949.

Brand Positioning

Oldsmobile consistently finished among the top 10 American auto marketers, and even popped into the top five a couple of times throughout the 1950s and 1960s. The marque attained several industry firsts, exclusives, and awards throughout these years that helped it establish a reputation for innovative engineering and design. In 1955 Oldsmobile, along with several other car manufacturers, introduced a four-door hardtop sedan, the Holiday. The brand heralded the 1960s with a smaller, sleeker body styling called a ''tapering profile.''

Olds began to establish a reputation for engineering expertise that would become a hallmark of the brand during the 1960s. In 1962 it launched America's first production car equipped with a fuel-injected, turbo-charged V8 engine. Called the Jetfire, it featured a hardtop, bucket seats, and a central console. Just two years later, Olds introduced its legendary 442 sports option, featuring a 4-barrel carbuerator, 4-speed transmission, and dual exhausts. The package, available on 8-cylinder Cutlass sports coupes, hardtop coupes, convertibles, and F85 sports coupes, heralded the ''muscle car'' age. *Cars* magazine would later name the 442 ''Top Performance Car of the Year.''

Oldsmobile established yet another industry standard in 1965 with the introduction of the 1966 Toronado, the first mass-produced front-wheel drive vehicle in America. The positioning of all powertrain components under the new model's hood complemented the car's front-wheel drive, giving it superior traction and handling. The innovative Toronado was widely hailed as ''the most unique American automobile in many years''; it won *Motor Trend*'s ''Car of the Year'' and *Car Life*'s ''Engineering Excellence'' awards.

Building on the reputation it earned during the 1960s, Oldsmobile quickly ascended into the auto industry's top rankings in the 1970s. In testimony to its continuing ''muscle car'' prowess, the marque won the National Hot Rod Association's ''Manufacturer's Cup'' for 1971. The division captured third place in the sales race for the first six months of 1971, and eventually finished fourth for the year.

Oldsmobile commemorated its diamond anniversary with a special edition Ninety-Eight Regency Sedan that featured velvet upholstery and a ''Tiffany gold'' dash clock by the world-renowned jewelers. The 75th anniversary celebration was made complete when Olds placed third for the entire 1972 calendar and model year. Oldsmobile would capture the Number Three ranking six times from 1972 to 1979, and in 1976 the brand's Cutlass became America's best-selling car. The Cutlass was in such high demand that it occupied nearly half of Oldsmobile's production in 1978.

In the wake of the decade's oil crisis, the division started offering diesel as an option on some of its models. The lower grade fuel was often cheaper and more efficient than standard gasoline, which helped Olds keep up with increasingly stringent government mileage standards. The division's models also ''dieted'' during the 1980s to improve fuel efficiency. In 1982 Oldsmobile captured 32 percent of the diesel passenger car market, the top position in that category. The division had attained diesel's highest market penetration up to that time, 10.1 percent of the auto market. Diesel proved to be a short-lived fad, however, and Oldsmobile's diesel operations were discontinued after the 1985 model year.

The original Olds Motor Works emblem, which was featured on the popular 1900-07 Curved Dash Olds models.

The Cutlass Supreme continued to be the nation's best-selling nameplate in the early 1980s, and Olds held onto third place through 1985. After a full decade of unquestionable success, though, the division soon fell victim to the poor decisions of its parent.

Loss of Brand Identity—and Sales

In the mid-1980s General Motors instituted a new, automated production scheme that enabled Oldsmobile to manufacture 120 cars per hour. The division would build a single basic line, known as GM20, that was offered under the Oldsmobile, Pontiac, and Buick nameplates with cosmetic changes. The GM20, a mid-sized, five passenger car, was designed for 25- to 44-year-old consumers, a generation younger than Olds' traditional target audience. The model (in its Oldsmobile, Pontiac, and Buick interpretations) was envisioned as "everyman's car": compact owners would trade up to one, and owners of full-sized sedans would buy one as alternate transportation. General Motors hoped to increase its volume and achieve economies of scale with this manufacturing and marketing scheme, but that was not to be.

Oldsmobile's sales peaked at over one million units in 1985, the first year that GM20 models were offered. The brand's precipitous slide started the following year. By 1990, Olds' sales plummeted to 583,440, then to just over 512,000 in 1992. At one low point, the rumor that General Motors was about to drop its oldest brand circulated, further undermining Oldsmobile's credibility.

Many factors, both internal and external, were blamed for the brand's rapid downfall. Oldsmobile's brand image was diluted by its close cooperation with Buick and Pontiac—it could not claim engineering or technological primacy when the three marques' cars were fundamentally identical. Poor quality resulting from sloppy manufacturing methods reinforced the conventional wisdom that imports were built better. Even the Oldsmobile logo itself was blamed for the slump. Of course, there were some influences Oldsmobile could not control. The diversion of drivers to the burgeoning sport utility and minivan categories may have accounted for one-third of its precipitous 60 percent drop in sales.

Prompted in part by dealer complaints, a new management team led by John Rock put the division's $140 million advertising account, long held by Leo Burnett USA, into review in 1992. The agency had held the account since 1967, when it purchased D.P. Brother & Co. in Detroit, Olds' agency since 1934. During the late 1980s, Burnett worked to capture a younger audience for the marque with its "New generation of Oldsmobile" campaign, featuring the memorable slogan, "This is not your father's Oldsmobile." But when this new image put off a loyal core of older customers, the slogan was dropped. Burnett replaced the "new generation" campaign with "The power of intelligent engineering" for the 1992 model year, trying to focus on product advantages. The claim was hard to substantiate, however, since the brand's most advanced technical features were shared with other divisions.

Olds tried to dam the outward flood of customers by launching a sport utility vehicle and a minivan, the Bravada (1991) and Silhouette (1990), respectively. But here again, the Silhouette was the same basic vehicle as Pontiac's TransSport and Chevrolet's Lumina APV, perpetuating brand overlap.

Future

General Manager Rock focused on what he called "the Saturnizing of Oldsmobile"—fashioning the image of GM's oldest division after one of its newest projects, Saturn. Rock hoped to emulate Saturn's excellent customer and dealer relations, envisioning Oldsmobile as the step up from an entry-level Saturn. But drafting off the new guys would not give Olds the distinct identity it had lost in the 1980s, or the ageless appeal it needed to ensure its future. Rock predicted that it would take six years to get Olds on solid footing, and set the division's annual sales goals between 500,000 and 700,000 units.

In 1993, Leo Burnett was re-awarded the Oldsmobile account, after months of nerve-wracking meetings and presentations. Most observers pronounced the review a success, because it brought the management, the dealers, and the agency to common ground.

The agency unveiled a new campaign theme, "Demand Better." The multiple-spot strategy featured about 125 30-second commercials. The series interspersed title cards with live action and used voice-overs to keep production costs down. The seemingly ever-changing, topical ads were intended to hold viewers' attention and project an image of responsiveness. The versatile campaign was also used to take on imports, with flip lines on the price-value advantage of Olds such as, "It's the exchange rate, simpleton." The spots were adapted by many dealer ad groups, illustrating the new cooperation between the dealers and Burnett. Oldsmobile also adopted a value pricing strategy that bundled popular options and offered them on a "package deal." This value positioning appeared to appeal to recession-weary consumers—Oldsmobile's sales for 1993 stood at 416,126 units, up slightly from 1992—which seemed to indicate that the brand had reached equilibrium.

Further Reading:

Connelly, Mary, "Auto Dealers Flex Their Muscles," *Advertising Age,* March 22, 1993, p. S6.

"A History of Oldsmobile," Oldsmobile History Center: Lansing, Michigan, 1991.

Kiley, David, "A Look Back at a Strange and Stressful Automotive Year," *Adweek,* January 4, 1993, p. 38.

Krebs, Michelle, "Olds Diverts Off-Road," *Advertising Age,* January 21, 1991, pp. S5–S7.

Levin, Gary, "Study: Some Logos Hurt Image," *Advertising Age,* September 13, 1993, p. 40.

Serafin, Raymond, *Advertising Age,* "GM's Troubled Olds Unit Reviews $140 M Account," September 21, 1992, pp. 1, 54; "Olds Ad Overdrive," *Advertising Age,* August 30, 1993, p. 38.

Serafin, Raymond and Scott Hume, "Olds Win: How Burnett Rallied Back," *Advertising Age,* February 8, 1993, pp. 1, 46.

Treece, James B., "They're Still Groping," *Business Week,* July 9, 1990, p. 31.

Warner, Fara and Lisa Marie Petersen, "Automobiles: Blissful Domestic Resurgence," *Superbrands,* October 18, 1993, pp. 54–61.

—April S. Dougal

OLIVETTI®

olivetti

Olivetti typewriters and office furniture earned a reputation for high quality design that has been maintained in their award-winning computers. Ing. C. Olivetti & Co., S.p.A., is ranked among the top ten information technology companies in the world. Founded on the production of typewriters, calculating machines, and office furniture in the first half of the twentieth century, Olivetti has transformed itself into a major producer of minicomputers, specialized work stations, and personal computers.

Brand Origins

Camillo Olivetti started his company on October 29, 1908, in Ivrea, Italy. Friends and relatives bought a portion of the company's original shares and thus supplied the necessary cash for the purchase of machinery from the United States. Olivetti, however, provided most of the company's initial capital himself, establishing from the start his determination to maintain control of his own company. His son, Adriano Olivetti, as quoted in *Design Process,* explained his father's business philosophy: "His greatest ideal was independence, not being indebted to anyone, and not being subject to restrictions of any sort. Although he had powerful initiative, he was not reckless; he was extremely prudent, keeping the development of the firm in proportion to his own financial resources and organizational ability."

In the beginning, those resources dictated a modest 500-square-meter machine shop and 20 employees. However, Olivetti grew rapidly in those early decades. The company's first product, the M1 typewriter, proved so successful that employees numbered 110 by 1913. New products bearing the Olivetti name were introduced in quick succession. The rate of production was approximately 1400 machines a year in 1914; in 1926, the rate was 8000 a year; in 1929, it was 13,000 a year. The company's sales force grew in proportion, and Olivetti typewriters were soon being sold in Spain, Argentina, Holland, France, and Belgium.

This growth did not come easily in early twentieth-century Italy, a primarily agricultural country. Most of Olivetti's labor force was untrained, and few avenues for industrial export existed. Camillo Olivetti drew most of his inspiration from the United States. Although his early machines showed the concern for aesthetic design that would later become the hallmark of the company, Olivetti structured the machines following the standards set by American typewriter models.

Early Advertising

In 1928 Olivetti put his son Adriano in charge of an advertising department. The company primarily used two types of advertising that were popular in Europe at the time: publicity in newspapers and magazines, and posters. Although the company's print advertising was unremarkable, its use of posters provides early examples of art being used to promote industry. Designs for the posters were created by acclaimed artists, and many were done in the Art Nouveau style.

Early advertising promoted typing itself as much as Olivetti typewriters in particular. The images emphasized the speed, modernity, and functionalism of typewriting. In one poster, a typewriter ran on rails, outstripping a train. By equating the typewriter with the train, then a potent symbol of power and efficiency, Olivetti tried to convince businesses of their need for typewriters. Olivetti's promotion of typewriting included the promotion of the female typist, a new and at first uneasy addition to business offices.

Product Development

In the 1930s Olivetti extended its line of typewriters and moved into several new markets. The M40 typewriter was introduced at the beginning of the decade; the Studio 42, a semi-standard typewriter, was added in 1935. The Studio 42 represented the company's first attempt at conscious, planned industrial design. Around this time Olivetti staff designed new alphabets and numerals, contributing to the company's image as a producer of modern, imaginative products. Although production centered on office machines, portable typewriters contributed a significant number of sales. The company entered the office furniture market in 1930 with its Synthesis card files and in 1934 introduced Olivetti adding machines. More office furniture products and bookkeeping machines were added in the next few years.

Production rose steadily throughout the decade: in 1937, the company made over 21,000 office machines and 15,000 portable typewriters. By 1942 those numbers had risen to 37,000 office machines, 26,000 portables, and 2,500 calculating and bookkeeping machines. However, World War II disrupted the company's operation, and with the Nazi occupation of Italy production ceased. Adriano Olivetti, who had become president in 1938, was

AT A GLANCE

Olivetti brand of office equipment and personal computers founded in 1908 by Camillo Olivetti, president and major shareholder of Ing. C. Olivetti & Co., S.p.A.

Performance: *Market share*—40% of the electronic typewriter category in Europe; approximately 25% of the personal computer category in Italy. *Sales*—$6.4 billion.

Major competitor: IBM in the computer category.

Advertising: *Major campaign*—"Difference in value. Olivetti Personal Computers. Seriously built, seriously sold."

Addresses: *Parent company for U.S. office equipment*—Olivetti Office USA, 765 U.S. Highway 202, P.O. Box 6945, Bridgewater, NJ 08807-0945; phone: (908) 526-8200; fax: (908) 526-8405. *Ultimate parent company:* Olivetti S.p.A., Via G. Jervis 77, 10015 Ivrea, Italy; phone: 39.125.52 37 33; fax: 39.125.52 23 77.

forced to flee to Switzerland during the war. He returned in April 1945, and production resumed.

Olivetti continued to expand its lines of typewriters, calculating machines, and office furniture, and a line of teleprinters was added. The company also entered the field of electronic computers in 1959 with the introduction of the Elea 9000. The lack of technological and scientific expertise in Italy at the time and the vast investment required to develop large computers forced the company to withdraw from this market after only a few years.

Olivetti Design

In the years after World War II Olivetti earned a reputation for excellent design and high aesthetic standards. The company won several industry awards for design, and the New York Museum of Modern Art created an exhibition on Olivetti design. The Swiss architect Le Corbusier was quoted in a company publication as saying, "Olivetti's products seem almost to glow with the exact proportions and the love with which objects should be made, the love with which man performs his duty, the love for his work."

In the early 1950s IBM was greatly influenced by Olivetti design. In his essay *Good Design Is Good Business,* quoted in *Design Process,* Thomas J. Watson, Jr., described the impetus Olivetti gave IBM in the area of design: "One night in the early 1950s, as I was wandering along Fifth Avenue, I found myself attracted to typewriters sitting in front of a shop window. . . . They were in different colors and very attractively designed. . . . I went into the shop and also found attractive modern furniture in striking colors with a kind of collectiveness. The name plate over the door was Olivetti. . . . At the time we didn't have a design theme or any consistent color program. All we had were some very efficient machines, not too well packaged, and some competence in the new field of computers. . . . We thought it was time for the outside to match the inside. . . . We took all of the top-level people in the IBM Company to a hotel in the Pocono Mountains where we considered IBM design in contrast with that of Olivetti. . . . "

In the ensuing decades office machines proliferated, and their designs had to accommodate their new functions and surroundings. The modular requirements of integrated work stations meant machine designs could no longer be treated as sculptures, as earlier Olivetti machines were. According to *Design Process,* "especially in distributed information and information systems, these products have to be designed to relate properly to other elements, such as video, display, printing devices, and other machines." These restrictions did not prevent Olivetti from maintaining their reputation for design excellence, even after their expansion into word processors, personal computers, and data processing equipment. Four Olivetti PC models won the SMAU Industrial Design Prize, and the Metropolitan Museum of Art in New York included five typewriters, four calculators, a video terminal, and a computer, all created by Olivetti, in its permanent display of industrial design.

Brand Expansion

Competition in the office automation market intensified in the 1960s and 1970s; the new electronic machines quickly made traditional models obsolete. Olivetti scrambled to keep up. In addition to updating its traditional typewriter models, the company began developing an electronic typewriter with a daisy-type printer and display. It introduced portable electric typewriters, a line of duplicating and copying machines, and a new office furniture line. When its position as a leader in the mechanical calculating market was threatened by electronic display models from Japan and other countries, Olivetti added not only electronic display but also electronic printing to its entire line.

Olivetti's attempt to enter the age of electronics came at a cost. Investment in research and development, production changes, and sales development resulted in a hefty debt load. Despite its efforts, it had only a few competitive products. As the 1970s came to a close, Olivetti was losing approximately $8 million a month and neared bankruptcy. Relief came in the form of Carlo De Benedetti, who offered $17 million for a 20 percent stake in the company and a chance to turn the company around as its CEO. He immediately took bold steps to restore the faltering company, including drastic cuts in the staff and huge investments in the research and development of high technologies.

The company introduced the first electronic typewriter in 1979. De Benedetti's emphasis on high-tech development resulted in a plethora of new products for the company, including word processing and office automation systems, electronic teleprinters, telematics terminals, voice-data telephonic switching systems and transmission networks, and cash registers. New lines of copiers and calculators were introduced, and the office furniture line was again redesigned. Although Olivetti had returned to the field of computers in 1965 with the introduction of the Programma 101, a desk-top computer for scientific and technical calculations, the company again abandoned the market. De Benedetti recommitted Olivetti to computers in the early 1980s with the introduction of new business computers and a personal computer, the M 20.

De Benedetti's changes brought the Olivetti name back from the brink. Sales went from approximately $1 billion in 1978 to almost five times that in 1986, and net income rose from a loss of approximately $100 million in 1978 to a profit of almost $400 million in 1986. Olivetti held 40 percent of the European typewriter market in 1986 and replaced IBM as the leading seller of personal computers in Italy.

Strategic Alliances

De Benedetti's plan for Olivetti was not only to get it operating in the black again, but to make it a major international player, competing with the likes of IBM and Matsushita Electrical Industrial Co. After the company's investment in research and development paid off in competitive products in burgeoning fields, De Benedetti was ready to begin what he saw as the logical next phase: a series of alliances that would open international markets to Olivetti products. He explained his strategy to William Symonds in a 1987 *Business Week* article: "The traditional multinational approach is *depasse.* Corporations with international ambitions must turn to a new strategy of agreements, alliances, and mergers with other companies."

One of the first places De Benedetti attempted to grow through alliances was North America, where he had been unable to match his European success. The company's U.S. subsidiary had endured ten straight years of losses when De Benedetti took over Olivetti. After four years of trying to turn the subsidiary around, De Benedetti merged it with the Dallas-based bank-automation company Docutel. The strategy backfired: sales fell even further and losses skyrocketed. Olivetti bought out Docutel, closed its factory, and moved all operations from Dallas back to New Jersey. Although the enormous losses ended, Olivetti still held only 5 percent of the U.S. market in typewriters in 1986.

In the mid to late 1980s, Olivetti pinned many of its hopes on an alliance with AT&T. In 1984 AT&T bought 25 percent of Olivetti for $260 million with the understanding that they would sell Olivetti personal computers in the United States under the AT&T nameplate, and Olivetti would market AT&T products in Europe. The influx of capital and the rush of new orders at the Olivetti factory sent profits soaring. In the long run, however, the AT&T deal was disappointing. In 1987 Olivetti PCs sold through AT&T accounted for approximately 3 percent of the IBM-compatible market in the United States. By 1989 that figure was 1.1 percent. In 1989 the alliance effectively ended.

Olivetti's other mergers and acquisitions in the 1980s yielded mixed results. Olivetti sold 20 percent of its Japanese subsidiary to Toshiba, because, according to Olivetti's Vittorio Levi in the 1987 *Business Week* article, "If you want to be in Japan, you have to be Japanese." However, Koichiro Kurita, CEO of Olivetti Corp. of Japan, admitted in the same article that sales "have been somewhat weak compared to the size of the market." In 1986 Olivetti acquired the German typewriter manufacturer Triumph-Adler, which immediately raised Olivetti's share of the European typewriter market to over 50 percent and the company's U.S. market share to 11 percent. In 1987 a joint venture with Canon to produce copiers, laser printers, and facsimile receivers and transmitters promised to yield high profits.

Recent History

In the late 1980s, Olivetti's successes began to falter. The company had achieved record profits in 1986 of $403 million, but by 1988 net profits had fallen to $254 million. Olivetti personal computers, which had captured the number two spot in the European market between 1984 and 1988, fell to number four in 1989, behind IBM, Compaq Computer Corp., and Apple Computer Corp. Although Olivetti had introduced several new computers in the mid-1980s, including a portable PC, industry experts felt they were slow coming to market, causing Olivetti to fall behind the fast-rising Compaq. Quality-control problems were also cited as contributing to Olivetti's slip in the market.

In 1988 a new managing director, Vittorio Cassoni, restructured Olivetti into four operating companies: Olivetti Office, which included the company's typewriters and stand-alone personal computers; Olivetti Systems & Networks, which included minicomputers, high-end PCs, and software; Olivetti Information Services; and Olivetti Technologies Group. The restructuring may have helped the company bring out its new technology in a more timely fashion. In 1989 Olivetti was one of the first companies to introduce a PC that used Intel Corp.'s latest 80386 microchip. However, the line of minicomputers Olivetti had introduced in 1987 continued to lose ground to Digital Equipment Corp. (DEC) in Europe and were threatened by the new microcomputer technology. An entirely new PC development team was set in place in 1989.

Olivetti's sales continued to slip, and in 1991 the company reported its first losses in 13 years. Late in 1991 De Benedetti took operating control from Cassoni, restructured the operating groups, and began a series of layoffs. In 1992 the company hoped to increase its sales with the Quaderno, a two-pound portable PC that received mixed reviews. An updated version, the Quaderno 33, was slightly heavier but more powerful and retained the original's well-liked voice-recording feature. De Benedetti found a new ally in 1992 when DEC agreed to pay $300 million for 10 percent of Olivetti. In addition to the infusion of capital, Olivetti gained access to core microprocessor technology.

As of the mid-1990s, Olivetti had maintained a 40 percent share of the European typewriter market and gained ground in the U.S. typewriter market. Faced with stiff competition in the computer market, Olivetti hoped to regain ground through its alliances with DEC and other international partners. However, the company's losses in the early 1990s and its constant scramble to keep up with the latest technology made its future uncertain. De Benedetti, for one, faced that future with optimism. In a 1992 *Forbes* article he was quoted as saying, "When I look back and think of the sales mix when I joined the company—85 percent typewriters!—and I think that today typewriters are 8 percent of sales, I think we have had a fantastic evolution in the past ten years. And that's what we are looking for in the next ten."

Further Reading:

"Carlo's Formula," *The Economist,* September 12, 1992, pp. 76–77.

Design Process: Olivetti, 1908–1983, Ivrea, Italy: Ing. C. Olivetti & Co., S.p.A., 1983.

Klebnikov, Paul, "Fallen Hero," *Forbes,* April 27, 1992, pp. 110–12.

Levine, Jonathan B., "A Helping Hand for Europe's High-Tech Heavies," *Business Week,* July 13, 1992, pp. 43–44.

Olivetti S.p.A., *1982–1992: 10 Years of Olivetti PCs,* Ivrea, Italy: Olivetti S.p.A., 1992.

Rossant, John, and Jonathan B. Levine, "De Benedetti's Latest Role: Sisyphus," *Business Week,* May 4, 1992, p. 53.

Rossant, John, and Thane Peterson, "Can Cassoni Get Olivetti off the Slippery Slope?" *Business Week,* June 12, 1989, pp. 99, 102.

Rowell, Dave, "Windows Under 4 Pounds," *Byte,* November 1993, pp. 249–54.

Solomon, Steven, "More Rabbits, Please, Signor De Benedetti," *Forbes,* March 9, 1987, pp. 114–18.

Symonds, William C., "Dealmaker De Benedetti: Olivetti's CEO Doubles as an Entrepreneur," *Business Week,* August 24, 1987, pp. 42–47.

—Susan Windisch Brown

OLYMPUS®

OLYMPUS

In its position at the forefront of contemporary camera technology, the Olympus camera reflects the achievement of a global, integrated network of operations—organized under the Tokyo-based, multinational corporation Olympus Optical Co., Ltd.—linking research and development, marketing, sales, and production in a variety of video and electronic fields. Drawing on a history of contribution to new camera technologies since the 1930s, Olympus is a recognized market leader in innovation and new product development. In 1994, for instance, Olympus offered the IS power zoom series, the Stylus and SuperZoom for compact auto-zoom, the Infinity with autofocus (a technology originally by Honeywell), the ultra-compact and automated Trip line, and the OM-4T, a titanium-frame camera with precise controls over subtle details of the image for professional photographers. The company is also currently working on a new digital card camera, which it believes will revolutionize the industry when completed.

Brand Origins and Early Development

Olympus cameras arose from humble origins in the 1930s in an industry that was new to the Japanese. Japan had just suffered through the depths of a depression, but by 1935 the economy began to prosper once again. The avid Japanese consumer appetite at the time for German cameras enticed a young Japanese optics company to foray into that market. Founded in 1919 as Takachiho Manufacturing Co., Ltd., named after the mythological mountain of Japan's traditional gods, the young company had been producing microscopes since 1920. In the mid-1930s, Takachiho engineers researched and experimented with various camera lens designs.

One day in June of 1936, in Takachiho's Shibuya factory, two engineers tested a number of lens prototypes and confirmed the efficacy of the No. 1 lens, the first of what would become the Zuiko series. In a ten-square-meter darkroom, the two pored over a projector and a screen. One handled the projector, loading different lenses and adjusting the focus, while the other studied the precision of the image on the screen. When the two finally examined the clarity of the image projected from the Zuiko 75mm F4.5 lens, they knew they had discovered the centerpiece of a new camera. In 1937, Takachiho introduced its first camera, the Semi-Olympus, using the newly registered Zuiko lens and an imported Auto-Compur shutter.

The initial production run of the Semi-Olympus was small but successful. Pirate versions of German cameras flooded the Japanese market and complicated Takachiho's effort to sell a legitimate, high-quality domestic camera. Still, with the success of the initial run, Takachiho continued to refine its product and to introduce new models during the years immediately preceding World War II.

During its first year on the market, for example, in 1937 the Semi-Olympus ceased to be constructed with the imported Compur shutter and began to sport a newly developed, Japanese shutter named the ''Koho.'' Soon after, Takachiho improved the frame of the camera and introduced the Semi-Olympus II. While both used ''frontal focusing,'' a focusing method of sliding the lens forward or back on a protruding front plate, the Model II incorporated a ''body release'' button to set the front plate in place automatically. Another innovation followed in 1940 with the introduction of two versions of the Olympus Six, which utilized the superior, newly designed ''S Zuiko'' lenses. The Model I ''fold camera'' fell in popularity against the ''spring camera'' format of the new Model II and the Olympus Six.

From Wartime Devastation to International Sales

Takachiho and its development of the Olympus camera did not escape the devastation that World War II brought upon Japan. First, the ferocity of the war demanded that all Japanese production be targeted for wartime purposes. Takachiho temporarily suspended production of Olympus cameras and focused instead on weaponry optics. Next, relentless allied bombing campaigns against Japanese targets near the end of the war, including the use of nuclear weapons at Hiroshima and Nagasaki, severely crippled Japan's industrial capabilities. Takachiho's main office and factory for the earlier production of Olympus cameras was razed to the ground during an air raid on May 26, 1945. All production equipment for the Koho shutter was destroyed.

Within one year, however, the war ended and the production of Olympus cameras resumed. Despite a severe shortage of everyday necessities immediately following the war's end on August 15, 1945, Takachiho was already making preparations to begin rebuilding by September of that year. The U.S. Occupation Forces in Japan at the time served as an enthusiastic market for all brands of cameras, and despite the devastation from the war, the few cameras that made it to store shelves sold quickly. Takachiho

AT A GLANCE

Brand designed in 1936 as the Semi-Olympus (the Olympus Chrome Six Model I introduced in 1940) on the Zuiko lens invention of two engineers in the Shibuya factory of the Takachiho Manufacturing Co., Ltd., in Japan; Takachiho was renamed Olympus Optical Co., Ltd., in 1949.

Performance: *Sales*—$2,307,914,000 (1993 net sales).

Major competitors: Minolta, Canon, Kodak.

Advertising: *Major campaign*—"Never miss another O."

Addresses: *Parent company*—Olympus America Inc., 145 Crossways Park, Woodbury, NY 11797-2087; phone: (516) 364-3000; fax: (516) 677-1699. *Ultimate parent company*—Olympus Optical Co., Ltd., P.O. Box 7004, Monolith 3-1, Nishi-Shinjuku 2-chome, Shinjuku-ku, Tokyo 163, Japan.

worked quickly to meet this demand. The first shipment of the Olympus Six camera hit the market in the spring of 1946.

During the subsequent decade, Olympus cameras underwent a number of changes and began to sell internationally. First, spring cameras regained the popularity in Japan that they had enjoyed before the war. Next, ultra-miniature cameras using 10-exposure spool roll film were invented, sold widely in Japan, and passed off the market to the next innovation. Ultra-miniature models Micro, Guzzi, and Snappy, for instance, had their brief day in the sun and then deferred Olympusflex, a semi-automatic twin-lens reflex camera that allowed the photographer to observe the image as it would appear in focus.

Drawing from overseas markets for the first time, as well as from stationed U.S. military personnel and the Japanese domestic market, the boom in manufacturing twin-lens reflex cameras achieved unprecedented proportions for the Japanese camera industry. In the interest of international sales, Takachiho changed its company name to Olympus Optical Co., Ltd., in 1949 to reflect more readily its leading product, Olympus cameras. By the mid-1950s, Olympus and other Japanese camera manufacturers were selling their twin-lens reflex cameras in the United States. Minolta and Nikon led the Japanese share of the U.S. camera market, while Olympus, Pentax, Konica, and others followed.

Innovating Olympus

While the Olympusflex twin-lens reflex camera had brought significant success to the company, the future of the industry lay in yet another kind of camera, the single lens reflex 35mm. Already produced in Europe and the United States, early versions of the 35mm camera required a complicated procedure to prepare the film for loading into the camera. When Afga introduced a ready-to-load film roll for the 35mm camera in 1932, the technical benefits of the 35mm camera finally became convenient as well. The modern 35mm camera combined greater speed, maneuverability, and control over the photograph image than ever before. By the end of the fifties, the 35mm single-lens reflex camera outstepped the twin-lens reflex in popularity.

Olympus developed a prototype 35mm camera in 1949 called the Olympus 35. The Olympus 35 boasted a design unique from the dominant German model and quickly grew popular. In 1959, Olympus contributed to the dominance of the 35mm camera in the market by introducing the Pen series. In *A History of the 35mm Still Camera,* Roger Hicks praised the design of the viewfinder and the frame. Hicks described the viewfinder as "a most ingenious binocular-like system" and noted, in reference to the frame, the "pleasingly smooth top-plate without the usual pentaprism bulge."

In 1963, overall worldwide sales of the original Olympus Pen exceeded 1 million. The Olympus Optical Co. (Europa) GmbH was established in the same year, and five years later the Olympus Corporation of America (now Olympus America Inc.) came into being. The success of the Olympus Pen cameras fueled this growth. Meanwhile, Olympus had been developing related photo-imaging technologies. In 1951, Olympus introduced the world's first gastrocamera, while in 1958 a new research microscope was brought to the market. These related-product innovations have helped Olympus remain diversified as it continues to improve on its camera technologies.

The next major innovation in camera technology appeared in 1972 with the introduction of the OM System and the OM-1 single lens reflex. Olympus then assumed leadership in developing small, compact cameras. During the mid- to late-1970s, the newest trend was the smart camera, which offered the feature of automatic exposure. Minolta, Olympus, and Asahi Pentax led the way. With the new products and widespread television advertising campaigns, the overall 35mm camera market increased from 700,000 cameras per year in 1977 to over two million in 1981. Light, compact, automatic, and high-quality became the developing reputation of Olympus during the late '70s and early '80s. By 1981, Olympus had sold over 10 million Pen cameras.

Forging Ahead in a Challenging World

Between 1982 and 1994, the line of Olympus cameras expanded by some 53 models, all aiming for maximum photographing power in the most convenient, automatic, and compact form possible. Various models combined auto-exposure, auto-rewind, auto-focus, auto-zoom, and even programmable levels of background light. Olympus billed its 1994 "Superzoom 80 Wide" camera, for example, as "the smallest and lightest wide zoom in the world." Also, the Infinity Stylus Zoom represented the latest expansion in 1993 of the Olympus Stylus series, which was introduced in 1991 and sold over 2 million units through 1992. This camera offered a night-scene mode and five-function flash in addition to a 35mm-to-70mm zoom.

In the race to lead technological change, Olympus and other companies have encountered legal difficulties. In March of 1992, Honeywell Inc. sued six camera manufacturers for infringement of two patents on autofocus technology. Olympus was one of these six companies. In September of 1992 Olympus and Asahi Optical, makers of Pentax cameras, agreed to pay Honeywell $51.5 million and future royalties on the technology.

The camera market is not the only arena of challenge for Olympus during the early 1990s, however. Werner Teuffel, the executive managing director of Olympus (Europa), pointed to reducing toxins in the environment as another challenge facing the industry. In the 1993 Olympus (Europa) Annual Report, he wrote: "There is no doubt that environmental protection is more than just a social responsibility. It will in the future become an economic necessity." The production of Olympus cameras has changed as a result. In Japan, Olympus Tokyo, in conjunction with the Chemical Technology Research Company, has developed two chlorofluorocarbon (CFC)-free industrial cleaning agents. From September of 1993, all Olympus manufacturing in Japan was to cease using CFCs, chemicals that are believed to harm the protective ozone layer of the earth's atmosphere. The use of less toxins and more biodegradable and recyclable materials in packaging has also become a goal at Olympus worldwide.

Entering the mid-1990s, the Olympus camera continued to reshape itself for a changing market and a changing world. With offices, research centers, marketing, and manufacturing facilities spread across the world, the Olympus camera is a global brand. Currently the company is researching a revolutionary image-recording process that relies on electronic digital cards rather than traditional roll film. A new method of production is also being developed to help Olympus cameras maintain a major share of the world camera market.

Further Reading:

Hicks, Roger, *A History of the 35mm Still Camera,* Focal Press, 1984, pp. 8, 28–9.

Kusumoto, Sam, with Edmund P. Murray, *My Bridge to America: Discovering the New World for Minolta,* E.P. Dutton, 1989, pp. 104, 212.

New York Times, September 26, 1992, p. 18; March 7, 1992, p. 23.

Olympus Annual Report 1993, Olympus Optical Co., Ltd.

Olympus Annual Report 1991/92, Olympus Optical Co. (Europa) GmbH.

''Olympus, Minolta 35mm Units, Built-In Zoom Lens Camera Bow,'' *HFD,* February 15, 1993, p. 86.

Olympus Pocket Guide to 35mm Cameras, Binoculars and Microcassette Recorders, Olympus Optical Co., Ltd., 1994.

Sakurai, Eiichi, ''The Zuiko Story: A History of Olympus Cameras,'' VisionAge, provided by Olympus Optical Co., Ltd., 1994.

Wall Street Journal, March 5, 1992, p. B6.

—Nicholas Patti

ONEIDA®

ONEIDA®

Oneida is one of America's best-known brands of sterling, silverplated, and stainless tableware and has been supported with some of the nation's most effective and innovative advertising campaigns. From its daring full-page print ads at the turn-of-the-century to its classy, yet irreverent print campaign of the 1990s, Oneida has cultivated outstanding brand recognition and earned numerous advertising awards in the process.

Brand Origins

The Oneida name originated with the Oneida Community, a religious and social utopia founded by John Humphrey Noyes in upstate New York in 1848. The Community was founded on Noyes' theology of Perfectionism, a form of Christianity with two basic values: self-perfection and communalism. This ideal was translated into everyday life through shared property and work. Community members manufactured animal traps, chains, silk items, and silver cutlery to support themselves. The Oneida Community soon became known not only for the unconventional lifestyles of its members, but also for the quality of its goods.

The Oneida Community existed longer than most other utopias of the 19th century because of the solvency of its businesses, and its members lived and worked together in harmony from 1848 until the late 1870s. However, prosperity didn't shield the organization from conflict, and in 1879 the Community split into two factions. Although they were unable to resolve their differences, the members were disciplined enough to study, discuss, and vote on the resolution of their assembly.

They decided to transform the group and its businesses into a joint-stock company, the Oneida Community, Limited, which would be owned and operated by former members of the society. During the decade and a half following Oneida's reorganization, the company's financial standing deteriorated. A severe depression in the 1890s, inadequate leadership, and emigration from the Community plagued the new venture. In January 1894, however, 23-year-old Pierrepont Burt Noyes (P. B. Noyes), son of Oneida's founder, rejoined the company after working as an Oneida wholesaler in "The World," as many Oneidans referred to the larger society. His experience outside the Community enabled him to perceive and criticize the weaknesses that threatened the struggling company's existence.

By the time he reached the age of 30, Noyes had risen to defacto control of Oneida. The board nominated him to the newly created post of general manager with authority to oversee all of the company's divisions—tableware, traps, chains, silk thread, and canning. Noyes' rise to prominence at Oneida marked the company's emergence into the modern industrial world, just in time for the 20th century. He recognized that Oneida's diversified product lines kept it from expanding beyond regional sales. Although the silver market was dominated by several established companies, Noyes chose that field as Oneida's focus. He introduced new production and distribution methods, cut-throat competitiveness, and, perhaps most importantly, groundbreaking promotional efforts.

Early Marketing Strategy

In 1902 Noyes established Oneida's 90-year emphasis on marketing and brand recognition when he increased the company's promotion budget from $5,000 per year to $30,000 annually—an astounding figure for the era. The importance of marketing was also reflected in Oneida's administrative hierarchy. From 1902 onward, Oneida's chief advertising executive has maintained a seat on the table unit's board of directors.

Oneida's earliest advertising campaigns established many of the standards that would characterize the company's advertising for decades to come. Until the mid-1960s, Oneida's wares were promoted under the "Community" brand name. The print ads typically appeared in widely circulated women's magazines. Most ads of the period tried to cram the most copy possible into the smallest purchased space. Noyes, however, decided to use a full page, relatively little copy, and a prominent illustration of one or two pieces of silver plate, often associated visually with someone or something attractive.

The first ad, which showed a society matron holding a Community fork and spoon, appeared in *Harper's* nationally circulated magazine. It capitalized on the established reputation for quality enjoyed by all Oneida products with copy that reminded readers that the company's "canned and preserved fruits, vegetables and jellies are recognized as this country's finest." Oneida introduced its famous "lace background" campaign, which featured expensive and rare laces as a backdrop for Community silverplate, in 1905. These pricey props helped lend status to Oneida's products, which often competed with more expensive sterling silver table-

AT A GLANCE

Known as Community tableware until the mid-1960s, Oneida tableware originally was produced by the Oneida Community, Limited, established in 1880 in Oneida, NY; brand launched nationally by P. B. Noyes, 1902; company name changed to Oneida, Ltd., 1935

Performance: *Market share*—40% of the department store stainless flatware category; 60% of the department store silverplate flatware category. *Sales*—$322.5 million (fiscal 1993).

Major competitor: Gorham.

Advertising: *Agency*—Deutsch Inc., New York, NY, 1970–; Kenwood Advertising (in-house). *Major campaign*—"Large Logo" print advertisements in major national magazines feature prominent Oneida logo and usually only one tableware or giftware pattern.

Addresses: *Parent company*—Oneida, Ltd., Sherrill Road, Oneida, NY 13421; phone: (315) 361-3636.

ware. In 1907 popular artist Coles Phillips was hired to romanticize the tableware. His drawings set another advertising precedent by featuring beautiful young women instead of the matrons usually associated with tableware ads.

The Strategy Pays Off

Despite the innovations, for eight years national advertising appeared to be a huge mistake; the expenditures seemed to squander Oneida's paltry profits, giving no promise of return. Instead of cutting back, Oneida launched a daring full-page, full-color ad for Community in the *Ladies' Home Journal.* As national magazines earned more editorial authority and wider readership, the brand began to enjoy sales that far outpaced its advertising budget.

Oneida was one of the first companies to employ celebrity spokespeople to promote its products. Ten years before the practice was mainstream, Oneida commissioned Irene Castle, a famous dancer and fashion plate, to promote Community ware. Comedian Bob Hope even took a turn at silver promotion.

The company opened its first international factory, in Niagara Falls, Ontario, in 1916. By 1993, Oneida had subsidiaries in Canada, Mexico, the United Kingdom, and Italy, in addition to its American plants. In 1925, Noyes convinced Oneida's board to sell all of the company's peripheral businesses and concentrate exclusively on the manufacture of silverplate.

Advertising remained a significant item in the company's budget, even during the Great Depression. After losing $1 million in 1932 alone, the promotional budget for Community was increased by one-sixth to enable the ad department to progress from straight product advertising to colored illustrations of brides. Sales increased by 33 percent on the heels of the new ads, further cementing the company's commitment to brand promotion.

The company's name was changed to Oneida, Ltd., in 1935 to differentiate Community brand tableware from that produced by lower quality subsidiaries of the company, such as Wm. A. Rogers. The Wm. A. Rogers salesmen had been claiming that their cheaper lines were "Community" ware by virtue of being owned by Oneida Community, Limited. Noyes changed the name to preserve the reputation of Oneida products.

The "For Keeps" Campaigns

Although the production of almost all silverware was suspended during World War II, Oneida worked to maintain its high brand awareness in preparation for the postwar return to production. Ad executives spent at least $1.6 million over the course of the war to "build consumer predisposition toward Community." In 1943, it introduced the fabulously popular and long-running "Back Home For Keeps" campaign, which featured sentimental drawings by Jon Whitcomb. During the war, melodramatic copy enhanced a romantic, four-color drawing of the reunion of a serviceman and his wife or fiancee: "You see his special smile (he's been saving it for you). Your head finds its home-place on his very special shoulder. It's true—he's home for keeps!" The brand connection was made with, "Community—today's brides tell us—is the silverware girls want for keeps."

Hoping that the ads would be pin-up candidates, Oneida made up a few thousand reprints. The brand's promoters were completely unprepared for the torrent of 500,000 requests that poured in. High-school girls plastered the sentimental ads in their rooms, co-eds tacked them up on dormitory walls, and soldiers pasted them in their barracks. "Back Home For Keeps" clubs were established, and even a song by the same name got big radio play. *Life* magazine covered the phenomenon with a spread featuring the ads and a photo of a teenaged girl's room covered with the promotions in 1945.

When the G.I.s started coming home in 1945, Oneida extended the theme to "This Is For Keeps." Ad illustrations depicted the postwar marriage of young couples and copy pointed out that "It's Community you'll want for keeps." When that line grew old, Oneida stretched the "for keeps" concept still farther with a clever, timeless twist aimed at the younger girls just getting engaged: "Let's Make It For Keeps."

After the war, Oneida's "The happiest brides have Community" campaign played on the idea that silverware was second only to a wedding band as a symbol of marriage, and that it was the most important acquisition for married life. Advertising in the 1950s and 1960s began to relate the Community name more strongly with "Oneida Silversmiths" until 1965, when the Community name was dropped. Print campaigns produced during the two decades after World War II tended to showcase Oneida's pieces and patterns, focusing less on the emotional draw.

Oneida's "Tessera Hospitalis" campaign, which featured the Oneida logo on a silversmith's cube, ran from 1965 to 1971. The tessera was defined in promotional materials as "a pledge of hospitality and friendship." The concept was rooted in an ancient Roman custom, wherein a small cube was offered to guests as a sign of welcome. In 1970, Oneida moved the tessera off to the side of the logo, and the cube was dropped around 1986.

A strict media schedule rotated the Oneida name through dozens of America's most popular consumer magazines, including *Vogue, The New Yorker, Gourmet, The New York Times Magazine,* and *Seventeen,* throughout the second half of the twentieth century. Oneida followed the lead of a competitor, Lenox, in its ads for the "pre-bridal market" that *Seventeen* furnished. Oneida successfully targeted this "notoriously difficult age group" in the 1960s with posters. Both the media and the sentimental message harkened back to Oneida's "for keeps" campaign.

The brand's first poster employed one of the hippie generation's favorite subjects: love. At just 50 cents, the pin-up portrayed two long-haired "flower children" gazing into each other's eyes. A small silver spoon was pictured at the bottom. The caption read simply: "Some things you decide with your heart." The response was immediate and remained steady through several incarnations in the 1980s the early 1990s. Over 1 million posters of sixteen different Oneida ads were distributed through the program by 1988, and Oneida won its first Clio Award for an ad that had been part of the campaign.

The "Large Logo" Campaign

Oneida debuted its ongoing "Large Logo" campaign in 1979, when David Deutsch Associates (Manhattan) ushered in yet another era of innovative Oneida advertising. The nationally circulated ads featured eye-catching, full-color photographs with the tradename written in bold, easy-to-read print on a background that faded from dark to light. The whimsical ads helped increase Oneida's brand awareness by "concentrating on the human elements in situations we all can relate to," as David Deutsch noted in a 1988 *Gift Reporter* article. Adorable kittens, miniature rabbits, mischievous puppies, and well-intentioned children were juxtaposed with the inanimate silver or stainless products.

Sometimes, Oneida wares were a focal point of the composition. In one, a Norwich terrier hungrily eyed a bonbon on a silver platter, and in another, a child served his Mother a cockeyed birthday cake on holloware. But several of the advertisements featured an evocative illustration having nothing to do with tableware except a photo of a spoon in the bottom margin. Directly or indirectly, the campaign was designed to sell the "Oneida concept."

Kenwood Advertising, Oneida's in-house agency, was responsible for planning and placement, and David Deutsch Associates painstakingly executed the ads. By 1988, Deutsch had won more than 25 Clio awards and numerous other honors, including several "Andys" from the Advertising Club of New York, for "Large Logo" ads.

Television

Oneida considered using television commercials in the mid-1970s, but instead found an inexpensive yet effective vehicle for its tableware in game shows. For about $100,000 annually, the brand appeared in "fee-spots" on about a dozen game shows each year. These ten-second mentions could be a promotional consideration at the end of a show, but more often meant that donated Oneida products were awarded as prizes on the shows. Fee-spots were not only cheaper than standard spot television ads, they also carried a greater impact for viewers. A late-1980s study revealed that consumers often remembered more about the prizes won on a game show than the merchandise advertised during that same show.

Rating services conservatively estimated that game shows like *Jeopardy, Wheel of Fortune, Name That Tune,* and *Let's Make A Deal* exposed Oneida's products to more than 100 million consumers each week. Albeit limited, the brand's print and television media mix offered Oneida an estimated 3.7 billion "ad impressions" annually by 1988.

Product Changes

By 1983, the centenarian company sold over half of all flatware purchased in the United States. Management sought to capitalize on Oneida's reputation for quality by purchasing companies with expertise in related products and using the Oneida name to market the new products. Oneida purchased Buffalo China Inc., the nation's largest producer of commercial chinaware, and Webster-Wilcox, a producer of expensive holloware (silver serving platters) in 1983. In 1984 the company acquired D. J. Tableware, maker of high quality flatware, holloware, and china for the foodservice industry. Oneida also began to market a line of crystal stemware and giftware in the mid-1980s.

An early 1980s recession saw Oneida's earnings plummet 65 percent in 1982. The company's problems were exacerbated when Japanese and other importers flooded American housewares departments with inexpensive flatware. Oneida attempted to compete by taking the high road—emphasizing the superiority of its products and leaving the cheaper markets to fight among themselves. Unfortunately, the strategy backfired—Oneida's market share plummeted to 39 percent in 1986. The company laid off workers, and lost over $1 million between 1985 and 1986.

In 1986 the board of directors moved to revive Oneida using a strategy new to the company, one based not just on marketing and new products, but also on thrifty production. President John Marcellus resigned, and the company named Samuel Lanzafame, formerly of the Camden Wire subsidiary, as president. Lanzafame worked to enhance Oneida's economies of scale—when he became president, the company's two flatware plants operated at only 60 percent to 70 percent of capacity because they were concentrating on expensive flatware alone. The company began importing more inexpensive flatware to market under its name until it could bring its own factories up to speed on production of lower-quality (but higher-volume) merchandise.

Late in the decade, a new chairman of the board, William Matthews, oversaw the investment of over $26 million into plant improvements, including computer design and manufacturing systems, plant consolidation, and machinery upgrades. By the end of the 1980s, Oneida had regained its 60 percent share of the department store silverplate flatware market. The brand's recognition rate increased 20 percent from 1982 to 1988. And Oneida got all that mileage with an advertising budget of just $2.5 million per year (1993's advertising budget was boosted to $3 million).

Since 1902, when P. B. Noyes inaugurated the Oneida Community's first national advertising campaign, marketing has proven to be a vital component of the brand's success. From the mid-1930s to the late 1940s, Oneida utilized a very persuasive emotional appeal to sell tableware. Throughout the 1950s and 1960s, a more straightforward, and rather dull, campaign focused on the products themselves. Then, in 1979, the company debuted its long-running, award-winning "Large Logo" campaign, which continued to garner astounding brand recognition rates. In 1992, an independent national consumer study revealed that 87 percent of consumers name Oneida as the first company they think of when asked about stainless steel flatware—there was no close second.

Further Reading:

Carden, Maren L., *Oneida: Utopian Community to Modern Corporation,* Baltimore: The Johns Hopkins Press, 1969.

Clancy, Heather, ''A Stainless Record,'' *Gift Reporter,* February 1988, pp. 28–30, 72, 74.

''Community Silver: A Case Study,'' *Tide,* June 17, 1949, pp. 27–29.

McGough, Robert, ''Too Much of a Good Thing,'' *Forbes,* November 17, 1986, pp. 68–70.

Robertson, Constance, ''The Oneida Community,'' Oneida, Ltd. [1985].

Rosen, Daniel, ''Big-Time Plugs on Small-Company Budgets,'' *Sales & Marketing Management,* December 1990, pp. 48–54.

''Speaking of Pictures,'' *Life,* May 14, 1945, pp. 13–14.

Sutor-Terrero, Ruthanne, ''Oneida: Making Stainless Shine,'' *Financial World,* July 25, 1989, p. 14.

Taub, Stephen, ''First a Strikeout, Now a Triple Play,'' *Financial World,* August 31, 1983, pp. 34–35.

—April S. Dougal

OSTER®

Oster is the most recognizable brand name in the United States for such portable electrical appliances as blenders (the famous ''Osterizer''), hair clippers, and massagers. As part of the Sunbeam-Oster Company, Inc., Oster continues to garner number one domestic market shares for the majority of its products, and prides itself on being ''the world's largest professional clipper company.''

Brand Origins

John Oster established the John Oster Manufacturing Company in Racine, Wisconsin, in 1924 to manufacture hair clippers. Conditions were right for his product: the country was just emerging from a deep, postwar recession, and women were ''bobbing'' their hair for the first time in history. The hair clippers of the day, however, were heavy and designed to clip animal as well as human hair; they simply did not do justice to women's styles and neck contours. Working out of a basement with fifteen employees, John Oster designed hair clippers that were small, flexible, and lightweight. Barbers and beauticians liked them, and business grew so quickly that within a year he purchased a plant that employed 65 workers. Oster hair clippers faced four competitors in the market. John Oster purchased two of them, and a third went out of business. The fourth, the Wahl Clipper Company, remained Oster's major contender in the market into the 1990s.

Not content with his success, Oster was driven to improve his clippers even further. In 1928, he invented a tiny motor—no bigger than a thumb nail—and attached it to a hair clipper. While this was not the first electric hair clipper, it was the first small portable hair clipper, priced far below the average $100 for the power driven hair clippers of the day, and barbers snapped it up. At the height of the Depression, Oster once more scored a major success when he invented the first hair clipper with a detachable blade, which enabled a barber to clean and sterilize the hair clipper more efficiently. This turned out to be another best seller. Oster had established a solid reputation for his hair clipper products.

John Oster soon became intrigued with the possibility of adding a new and unique product to his product line: massagers. The massagers of his day were applied directly to the body. In 1935, Oster marketed a massager that applied Swedish massaging movements (for which he had obtained a patent) to allow the hand to do the massaging. His ''Oster massager'' was a success, and adopted by hospitals and sanitoriums alike.

Brand Expansion

World War II had a profound impact on the future direction of the Oster product line. By 1941, Oster's firm had a reputation for developing and manufacturing small horsepower motors, and the government put the Oster Company to work producing compact motors for mines and artillery. At the height of the war, Oster was making motors for radio and radar transmission. At the same time, the firm continued to manufacture hand and electric clippers for the armed forces, at a volume undreamed of before the war.

With the return to civilian production at war's end, John Oster once again sensed the need for a change of direction in his product line. America was the greatest industrial power on earth, the standard of living was high, and four years of wartime sacrifice had created a huge demand for products of all kinds, especially labor-saving devices. In 1946, the Oster Company purchased the Stevens Electric Company, which had invented the drink mixer in 1922. John Oster put his engineers to work to refine this mixer for household use. The Oster blender came on the market that year. Like the Oster hair clippers and massagers, the blender was a big hit. From now on, food for infants and the sick could be produced at home. Housewives found that the drudgery of chopping foods and vegetables was a lot easier, thanks to the ''Osterizer.'' Two years later, the Osterizer was succeeded by the ''Osterett,'' an attractive hand-held mixer that was the first of its kind. From a modest but solid reputation in hair clippers and massagers, the Oster brand name had climbed to national fame and recognition.

Product Development

Though the Oster Company again aided wartime production during the Korean conflict, the fame and fortune of the Oster brand name was inextricably linked to portable household products. Oster came out with the Oster Model 202 hair dryer in 1949, followed a year later by the Oster Model 500 knife sharpener, massage pillows, humidifiers, and ice crushers. When the Oster Company was acquired by the Sunbeam Corporation in 1960, making it a wholly owned subsidiary of Sunbeam, product refinement continued apace.

One area that grew more important over the years was pet supplies and products. Oster produced a multitude of products for pets, including Oster creme rinses for dogs, dog massagers, a variety of sophisticated clippers, and equestrian grooming prod-

AT A GLANCE

Oster brand of portable electronic appliances introduced as electric hair clippers by the John Oster Manufacturing Company, established in 1924 by John Oster in Racine, Wisconsin; introduced massage instruments, 1935; introduced the famous Oster food blender, the "Osterizer," 1946; company acquired by Sunbeam Corp. as wholly owned subsidiary, 1960; Sunbeam and Oster purchased by Allegheny International, 1981; Allegheny International dissolved, and Sunbeam and Oster emerged as the Sunbeam-Oster Company, Inc., 1989.

Performance: *Market share*—50% of domestic hair clipper market. *Sales*—$350 million.

Major competitor: (Hair clippers) Remington.

Advertising: *Agency*—In-house. *Major campaign*—"Oster Out-Cuts the Competition."

Addresses: *Parent company*—Sunbeam-Oster Company, Inc., 200 East Las Olas Blvd., Suite 2100, Fort Lauderdale, FL 33301; phone: (305) 767-2100; fax: (305) 767-2105.

ucts. Oster held several number one domestic market shares in pet products in the 1990s, as well as in barber and beauty supplies. In addition, Oster has retained its number one position in the hair clipper market, offering consumers a wide range of clippers with adjustable parts, both electric and battery-operated.

During the years when the John Oster Manufacturing Company was independent, advertising was carried on heavily in print media. With the emergence of Sunbeam-Oster Company, Inc., as an independent company in 1989, there was a renewed commitment to advertising the famous Sunbeam and Oster brands on television in addition to the customary print media, and to advertising year round. The advertising budget was increased substantially by the 1990s. A renewed effort was made to distribute traditional as well as new products to large discount stores such as Wal-Mart, K-Mart, Target, Sears, and Best Products, with strong promotional support to retailers in the form of flyer programs, point of purchase material, and promotional videos. One of the newest Oster massagers, the "Foot Massager & More," also included consumer sampling of the product before purchase.

International Markets

Playing an increasingly important role in the fortunes of Sunbeam-Oster are international markets, which the company is well-positioned to exploit. The International Division, established when the company was formed in 1989, accounts for one quarter of company sales, and while most of these sales are generated in Canada and Latin America, Sunbeam-Oster continued efforts to expand in the United Kingdom, the Middle East, Eastern Europe, and Japan. In Latin America, Oster's portable electric products held a greater than 75 percent market share. In 1993, Oster held a greater than 60 percent market share in Venezuela alone. While most of Sunbeam-Oster products are made in the United States, the company has some manufacturing facilities in Mexico, Venezuela, Peru, and several Central American countries.

Sales and distribution of Sunbeam-Oster products in Canada have been extremely strong for decades, with leading market shares in blenders, beauty products, and barber supplies. Sunbeam-Oster Company, Inc., planned to expand its international presence by building on its brand name recognition and marketing an increasing array of products that hitherto had been sold mainly in the United States and Canada, such as outdoor folding furniture and barbecue grills.

The Future

The Oster brand's greatest strengths in the future undoubtedly will remain its widespread recognition, which is synonymous with quality and durability, as well as the huge variety of products introduced by Sunbeam-Oster. New products continuously appear on Sunbeam-Oster's assembly lines; some, such as the Oster Stim-U-Lax, a "heavy duty" massager with a frame that fits the contour of the hand, require high technological proficiency. With a small, manageable company debt, integrated manufacturing, and a greatly streamlined corporate structure, Oster brand products will continue to dominate the market for small appliances well into the next century. Oster brand products should also gain a greater presence in the international market, with increasing promotion of brand recognition in parts of the world where economies are growing, and where free market economies are still evolving, as in the developed countries of Eastern Europe and Russia. The North American Free Trade Agreement, adopted by the United States Congress in 1993, also holds the promise of larger market shares for Oster products in the company's traditional stronghold, Latin America.

Further Reading:

Allegheny International: A New Global Business Enterprise, Princeton: Newcomen Society, 1983.

Farnsworth, Steve, "Sunbeam-Oster Sets Expansion; Company Plots Strategy to Bolster Sales in International Markets," *HFD,* July 6, 1992, p. 61.

"Florida Move for Sunbeam," *New York Times,* October 4, 1993, p. C2.

"Good 4th Quarter Vibrations: Features, Price, Strategies Differentiate Massagers as Makers Vie for Holiday Bounty," *HFD,* October 18, 1993, p. 92.

Purpura, Linda, *HFD,* "Determined to Dominate: Sunbeam-Oster Team Unifies Efforts to Win Market Share Across All Lines," February 15, 1993, p. 49; "Home Trims Spur Clippers," March 1, 1993, p. 54.

Ratliff, Duke, "Sunbeam Oster Shaking Up Massager Field," *HFD,* May 17, 1993, p. 54.

Sunbeam-Oster Company, Inc., Annual Report, Providence, RI: Sunbeam-Oster Co., 1992.

"Sunbeam's Net Rose 71% in 4th Quarter; Overseas Sales Cited," *Wall Street Journal,* February 4, 1993, p. B4.

Tylinski, Joh, "Oster," Oster Specialty Products.

—Sina Dubovoj

PANASONIC®

Panasonic
just slightly ahead of our time

Panasonic electronics are known for their high quality at affordable prices, as well as for their value and reliability. The original aim of Matsushita, Panasonic's parent company, was to make electronic products available to all types of consumers. The founder, Konosuke Matsushita, wanted to serve "the greater social good" by providing all households with high-quality, low-cost products." As such, he is revered as Japan's "god of business management."

Matsushita also produces consumer electronics and home appliances under the brands National, Quasar, and Technics. In addition, through a controlling interest in Victor Company of Japan, acquired in 1959, some products are marketed under the Victor and JVC brand names.

Brand Origins

During the 1920s and 1930s, the Matsushita company made inexpensive lamps, batteries, radios, and motors. During World War II, the company was consigned by the Japanese government to build laminated wood products for the military. After Japan's defeat in the war, the occupation forces wouldn't allow Konosuke Matsushita to work in his company for a period of four years. His return to the company, however, coincided with Japan's postwar economic recovery. War-weary Japanese consumers were beginning to demand products that enabled them to enjoy life. Like many other Japanese consumer electronics makers, Matsushita started to produce products that could enhance the lives of average consumers by keeping prices within their reach.

Brand Development

In 1952, Matsushita formed a joint venture with Philips of The Netherlands, another large consumer products manufacturer. By the following year, Matsushita was marketing TVs, refrigerators, and washing machines. By 1960, Matsushita had added vacuum cleaners, tape recorders, stereos, and color TVs to its product line. During the 1960s and 1970s, the company introduced air conditioners, microwave ovens, stereo components, and VCRs.

Although Panasonic has not been a technological leader, the company incorporates the latest technological developments as soon as possible into products to enhance usage. Panasonic developed many products in the late 1980s and early 1990s because of technological advances in the electronics industry, particularly the microchip. By 1992, a wide range of products carried the Panasonic name, including audio and video electronics, home appliances, and office equipment.

A successful strategy Panasonic has used in several product areas is marketing products in integrated systems. Panasonic has applied this approach particularly well to its audio products. For example, CD players were paired with tape decks. The company developed mini, shelf, and rack home entertainment systems that included CD players, tape decks, and AM/FM stereo tuners. Panasonic audio systems also offered tabletop CD players and portable CD players for personal or car use, combination stereo radio and cassette players in both tabletop and portable versions, and portable stereo radio and cassette recorders with CD players.

Panasonic also marketed audio components and related products, including power amplifiers, graphic equalizers, speaker systems, speakers, microcassette recorders, clock radios, minicassette recorders, portable cassette recorders, compact multiband radios, pocket radios, personal stereo radios, and stereo headphone radios. Related products included microcassette, digital audio, and digital compact cassette tapes.

The Panasonic line of video products was equally diverse, ranging from televisions and video cassette recorders to camcorders. Panasonic's television line included portable, table, or console models and stereo projection systems. The models introduced in the early 1990s used improved technology to create better sound systems and picture clarity and depth. Special audio/video products included a color video printer that allowed users to get color prints from their home videos in about 80 seconds. The system helped users to preserve moments that would otherwise have been difficult to catch with a still camera.

In the early 1990s Panasonic incorporated the latest advances in digital technology, marketing multilaser disc players that played up to five types of optical discs: 8- or 12-inch laser discs, 3- or 5-inch compact discs, and 5-inch compact disc videos. The company also introduced the Digital A/V Mixer, a two-source digital audio/video mixer offering digital special effects. Consumers could experiment with various operations, including A/V synchronization for pulsing video with certain levels of musical accompaniment.

AT A GLANCE

Panasonic brand of consumer electronics and home appliances established in 1975; Panasonic Company is a division of Matsushita Electric Corporation of America, which is a subsidiary of Matsushita Electric Industrial Co., Ltd., of Japan; Matsushita was started in 1918 by Konosuke Matsushita; in 1959 a Matsushita subsidiary was established in New York as the company's first step in reaching the North American market.

Performance: *Market share*—North American sales for Matsushita were $6.1 billion in 1992 and $60.8 billion worldwide.

Major competitor: Sony; also Pioneer, Sharp, Sanyo, and Hitachi.

Advertising: *Agency*—Grey Advertising, New York, NY, 1988—. *Major campaign*—1993 TV commercials and print ads for Panasonic audio systems with the message, "Shut Up and Listen," advising consumers to compare Panasonic to other audio products. Tag line was, "Dare to Compare."

Addresses: *Parent company*—Panasonic Company, One Panasonic Way, Secaucus, NJ 07094-2917; phone: (201) 348-7000; fax: (201) 348-8378. *Ultimate parent company*—Matsushita Electric Corp. of America (address same as above). *Ultimate ultimate parent company*—Matsushita Electric Industrial Co., Ltd., Osaka, Japan.

The Panasonic brand also covered such home appliances as microwave ovens, air conditioners, vacuum cleaners, bread makers, toasters, toaster ovens, juice extractors, food processors, electronic rice cookers, and irons. Personal care items, such as electric shavers, were offered under the Panasonic name. Panasonic office equipment for home use included cellular phones, digital phones, stand-alone answering machines, transcribers, word processors, personal and notebook computers, and printers. The company developed integrated systems in this product category to good effect, offering cordless phones with answering systems, combination tabletop phone and answering machines, and fax/answering systems.

In 1993, Panasonic marketed several products that were inventive, and even unique. A check writing system called Check Printing Accountant allowed users to print checks for easier bill-paying, and a new TV format used a wider and shorter picture tube. The tube, known as 16-by-9, allowed the screen to show the full, wide-screen version of cinematic movies and eliminated the squeezed look of some movies shown on regular TV. The price tag for this new TV was $4,500 to $6,000.

Panasonic's most daring new product, however, was expected to revolutionize home entertainment and education. In 1993 the REAL 3DO Interactive Multiplayer debuted as the industry's first interactive system and was called "the most hyped consumer electronics venture of the year" by *Advertising Age.* The Multiplayer turned a television into an interactive medium, running entertainment and educational software, including games and programming, wherein the viewer controlled action on the screen. The machine used special compact discs, as well as music CDs, photo CDs, and video CDs. Panasonic, actually a licensee, priced the system around $500.

Advertising Innovations

Panasonic products are advertised widely in TV commercials and print ads, and often both mediums carry the same message for a given product. The company frequently introduces new products with heavy advertising and promotional campaigns. For example, the 1993 introduction of the REAL Multiplayer was supported by one of the most extensive sales, advertising, and promotion programs in Panasonic's history. Since the multiplayer was not only a new product for Panasonic, but also a totally new type of product for the industry, the launch had to be accompanied by a consumer education effort.

To create public awareness, local and national print and TV ads were targeted to both the 12- to 17-year-old market segment and the 25- to 49-year-old segment. Television ads ran on youth-oriented cable programs and for mature viewers on network news, entertainment, and sports programs. Two-page color spreads emphasizing simulations, sports, and educational applications appeared in consumer, electronic, game, and hobbyist magazines. In addition, there were in-store promotions for retail stores. A nationwide program included in-store demonstrators, point-of-purchase materials, advertising kits with camera-ready ad slicks and ready-to-use clip art so that dealers would have the means to create local ad campaigns. Also, there was a month-long, seven-city mall tour supported by local dealer tie-ins in October 1993 and January to April 1994.

Panasonic has also identified itself with major events as a means of promotion, such as being an Official Sponsor of the 1992 U.S. Olympic Team. The team's logo was used in Panasonic advertising beginning in 1990.

Company Organization

In order for the Panasonic Company to deliver products to consumers most effectively, it has been structured into separate divisions by type of product. Restructuring began in 1982 with the Panasonic Company set up to handle consumer products and the Panasonic Industrial Company organized to handle industrial products. In 1986, both Panasonic Finance Inc. and Panasonic Broadcast Systems Company were established. In 1987, Panasonic Technologies Inc. was established. In 1992, the Computer Division was formed to market communication and computer products. In 1993, the Panasonic Company established an Interactive Media Division for the development and marketing of a new generation of consumer products based on emerging interactive technologies.

The consumer electronics industry is highly sensitive to economic conditions, and during times of poor economic activity, companies can suffer. Such was the case during the late 1980s and early 1990s when the worldwide economic recession lowered demand both in the United States and in Japan. High unemployment in the United States and shaky consumer confidence led to disappointing sales for Matsushita. Nevertheless, Matsushita was able to retain its world leadership in consumer electronics. By 1993, Matsushita operated more than 140 companies in 38 countries. The North American operations included 37 companies at 150 business locations, with 18 manufacturing operations.

Future Products

The consumer electronics industry thrives on the introduction of new products. Consumers become captivated by the new way a product allows them to use an old product or by something totally new and different. In order for Panasonic to keep pace with changes in digital technology, the company established Panasonic Advanced TV-Video Laboratories in Burlington, New Jersey, in 1990. The facility conducts research in digital transmission technologies, and Panasonic will incorporate any findings into future high-definition TVs. Another area of interest is interactive technology, which Panasonic expects to be an emerging field for the development of future products. Judging by Panasonic's history of bringing consumers products that satisfy their needs and interests, it can be expected that the company will continue to do so into the twenty-first century.

Further Reading:

Johnson, Bradley, "Philips, 3DO Prepare for Interactive Battle," *Advertising Age,* June 7, 1993, p. 6.

Grey Advertising, 1990–1993, Advertising Materials.

Matsushita in America, Secaucus, N.J.: Matsushita Electric, 1993.

Matsushita Electric Annual Report, Osaka, Japan: Matsushita, 1993.

Panasonic News, Secaucus, N.J.: Matsushita Electric, 1993.

Teinowitz, Ira, "Marketers Launch New TV Format," *Advertising Age,* January 18, 1993, pp. 13–14.

—Dorothy Kroll

PIONEER®

Pioneer, marketed in the United States by Pioneer Electronics (USA) Inc., is among the world's most popular brands of car stereo speakers and audio and video products for use in the home. The Pioneer name adorns a wide variety of audio-visual products, including compact disc (CD) players, LaserDisc (LD) players, stereo receivers, tuners, cassette players, amplifiers, speakers, digital signal processors, equalizers, headphones, and projection televisions. Much of this home equipment is also available for use in cars, as is the Pioneer brand of cellular telephone.

Pioneer has garnered a reputation for its innovations in the industry, particular in the field of car stereos. For example, the company's technical expertise enabled it to develop car stereo systems that overcame such adverse conditions as intense heat, dust, vibration, security, and space limitations. As a result, Pioneer electronics created a personal listening space for the driver similar to that of the home audio experience. Pioneer's car audio systems are featured as standard equipment in such luxury automobiles as the BMW.

Pioneer has continually worked to improve speaker designs and materials in order to achieve the best hi-fi sound reproduction. In the 1990s, digital technology was employed in Pioneer receivers; wide frequency response technology was capturing sound more effectively in Pioneer cassette decks; and digital signal processing was featured in Pioneer CD players.

Brand Origins and Development

The Pioneer name was first given to a line of high fidelity loudspeakers introduced in 1937 by Nozomu Matsumoto and his company, Fukuin Shokai Denki Seisakusho, based in Osaka and later Tokyo, Japan. The name Pioneer was thought to suggest the company's progressive spirit, and ten years later the company was renamed Pioneer Electronic Corporation, reflecting the importance of the Pioneer brand name. From its founding through the 1950s, Pioneer built a reputation in Japan as a maker of high quality speakers. During this time, the brand name was extended to include a line of turntables, amplifiers, and audio receivers.

In the 1960s, Pioneer shifted its focus from the production of audio components to audio systems. Pioneer introduced the world's first stereo with speakers separate from the control unit, called the PSC-5A, in 1962. The Pioneer S-71X, a stereo system first marketed in 1964, became the best-selling product in its market.

During the 1970s, in order to keep pace with increasing consumer interest in television, Pioneer began work on laser disc (LD) technology. Innovations early in the decade led to the optical videodisc, and later the LaserDisc (LD) videodisc system. In 1976, Pioneer introduced the first car stereo that featured the Supertuner, an automatic, high-sensitivity tuner system that allowed drivers to experience the same high quality sound in a car system as that of a home system. Later developments included the first CD player for automobiles and the first LD combination player for use with both LDs and CDs.

Over the next two decades, Pioneer products reflected the rapidly changing technologies in the industry. The multi-play format for CD players became available, allowing users to play up to six discs at a time and providing easy access to specific tracks on any one of the six discs. Furthermore, the multi-play magazines could be used on both home and car CD players, allowing consumers full compatibility between home and car systems. The magazines were later modified to accommodate up to 18 CDs. The Pioneer name was extended to the company's first 40-inch projection TV in 1985, and two years later Pioneer gave consumers the world's first combination player compatible with CDs, LDs, and CD videos.

In 1989, Pioneer car stereo systems began featuring a detachable face, which could be removed from the car, for security purposes, and this option soon became the industry standard. The following year, Pioneer introduced a line of cellular telephones—which included mobile, hand-held, and personal compact designs—as well as the first car stereo headunit with built-in digital signal processing. During the early 1990s, Pioneer focused on its "LaserActive" system, the world's first combination player to feature LD-ROM technology for consumer application and combine full motion video with sophisticated interactive capabilities.

Advertising and Marketing

Pioneer used a combination of print and television ads to inform consumers about their home and car systems. A major print campaign that ran in the early 1990s for car audio products used the slogan "Pioneer Rules." The tag line "The Art of Entertain-

AT A GLANCE

Pioneer brand of electronics founded in Japan in 1937 by Nozomu Matsumoto, owner of Fukuin Shokai Denki Seisakusho; company name changed to Pioneer Electronic Corporation, 1947; U.S. subsidiary Pioneer Electronics (USA) Inc. established in New York, 1966.

Performance: *Sales*—$5 billion (1993 estimate).

Advertising: *Agency*—BBDO, Los Angeles, CA, 1989—. *Major campaign*—"The Art of Entertainment."

Major competitors: Hitachi; also Panasonic, Sharp, Sanyo, and Sony.

Addresses: *Parent company*—Pioneer Electronics (USA) Inc., P.O. Box 1720, 2265 East 220th St., Long Beach, CA 90801-1720; phone: (213) 746-6337; fax: (310) 952-2402. *Ultimate parent company*—Pioneer Electronic Corporation, 4-1, Meguro 1-Chome, Meguro-Ku, Tokyo 153, Japan; phone: (81 03) 3494-1111; fax: (81 03) 3495-4428.

ment'' was also used during this time, and was eventually adopted as Pioneer's corporate slogan.

The marketing of Pioneer products has largely emphasized the company's ability to adapt to changing technologies. Furthermore, the brand has become environmentally friendly, using different types of recycled paper for its packaging of home and car products.

International Marketing

The Pioneer brand name has adopted an increasingly global presence. The company has subsidiaries in 19 countries, with plants in Belgium, France, Japan, Malaysia, Mexico, Singapore, Spain, Taiwan, and the United Kingdom. The United States maintained four manufacturing facilities and three marketing subsidiaries in 1993. Sensitive to the individual needs of the areas in which Pioneer electronics are marketed, the company strives to establish manufacturing facilities in a wide variety of locations, supporting local businesses by purchasing materials produced in those areas.

Performance Appraisal

The sale of consumer electronics is, of course, subject to economic conditions. During the recession of the late 1980s and early 1990s, the sales of Pioneer products experienced declines, as did those of its competitors. Nevertheless, in 1993, Pioneer floor model stereo systems, LD players, projection TVs, car stereo, and CD players experienced an increase in sales.

The company's annual report for 1993 indicated that total sales of Pioneer products could be broken down as follows: 28.5 percent for audio products, 31.4 percent for video products, 33.7 percent for car electronic products, and 6.4 percent for other types of electronic products. Broken down by region, total sales represented: 25.5 percent in North America, 38 percent in Japan, 26.1 percent in Europe, and 10.4 percent in other countries.

Future Growth

Pioneer's line of electronics is expected to continue to reflect the importance the company places on research and development. In the mid-1990s, the company was experimenting with laser-optic technologies, digital signal processing systems, and mobile information and communications. Laser optic and digital technologies are expected to open up new arenas for home entertainment products.

Further Reading:

Pioneer Electronic Corporation Annual Report, Tokyo: Pioneer Electronic Corporation, 1993.

The Art of Entertainment, Tokyo: Pioneer Electronic Corporation.

''Pioneer Electronics (USA) Inc.,'' *Corporate Backgrounder,* November 16, 1993.

—Dorothy Kroll

PITNEY BOWES®

Based in Stamford, Connecticut, Pitney Bowes, Inc. is a leading maker of business machines. In 1993 the Pitney Bowes name graced the label of more than 85 percent of the mailing machines—perhaps its most famous product—sold in the United States and appeared on copiers and fax machines. The company's solid market share has treated stockholders to strong financial growth in recent years and has earned Pitney Bowes, Inc. a position among America's corporate giants.

Brand Origins

Pitney Bowes owes its success chiefly to three leading personalities. Arthur H. Pitney, a clerk in a Chicago wallpaper store, recognized the inefficiency of sticking stamps on envelopes in bulk and decided to devise a machine to do the job, while Walter Bowes, a high-energy, personable promoter, had the salesmanship to successfully market a product as the one Pitney had invented. There was also the strong business administrator and social philosopher, Walter H. Wheeler, Jr., who exemplified the conventional pattern of a promising young executive when he joined the company in the early 1900s. These three men were responsible for building the Pitney Bowes brand.

The origins of the product can be traced to one of the most daring post office robberies. On the night of October 21, 1901, someone had removed 400 pounds of stamps through underground tunnels from the post office vault in the downtown Chicago post office. The market for stolen stamps was a large one during this era. According to the *Chicago Tribune,* a number of the "largest business houses in the city are in the habit of purchasing stamps from 'jobbers' "—stamp dealers engaged in the business of selling second-hand stamps.

The day after the robbery, the Chicago postmaster was visited by Arthur Pitney, who entered the postmaster's office carrying a large, box-like structure about a foot-and-a-half high, equipped with a crank, chain action, and printing die. He explained to the postmaster that the contraption was a postage machine that would eliminate the need for stamps. A counter could be set to the desired amount of postage, paid in advance, and as the envelopes were stamped the counter would record it in descending order. The postmaster immediately recognized the significance of Pitney's invention. Pitney's machine could handle in one hour the amount of mail it took an expert a full day to move. During the industrial revolution, machines were replacing human beings for all sorts of jobs. Certainly a machine could handle postage imprinting as well. Pitney was on his way to fame with his new invention.

Arthur Pitney's background, however, was far from glittering. A bout with polio as an infant left him with a shortened left leg and a limp, and perhaps because of this physical limitation, he developed a passion for experimenting. When he arrived in Chicago from Quincy, Illinois, Pitney secured a job as a wallpaper clerk and immediately began inventing such products as a rack for wallpaper books. In 1893 the World's Fair in Chicago captured his imagination, and he became more and more absorbed in his inventions. By 1900 Pitney was experimenting with ways of sticking postage stamps on letters.

Pitney noticed in his own wallpaper shop how laborious mailing operations were. Clerks applied postage stamps by hand to hundreds of envelopes each day. He also noticed that postage stamps had a mysterious way of disappearing from the stamp box. One idea led to another, and he realized that a machine might be built that could print stamps right on the envelope, doing away entirely with the costly, time-consuming process of buying, licking, and sticking stamps to envelopes.

In December of 1901 Pitney submitted his first application for a patent to the U.S. Patent Office. A year later, on October 14, 1902, the patent was granted. The patent allowed Pitney to set himself up in business—the Pitney Postal Machine Company. In the next several years Pitney won subsequent patents for machines that were electronically operated. Soon the Pitney postal machines were automatically sealing and stacking envelopes as well as printing the stamps or "indicias." While the machine won early support—especially from the Chicago postmaster—Pitney needed to first gain the support of the U.S. Postal Service before his machine could be used on the market. After a demonstration in late 1902, the Post Office Department in Washington, D.C. proposed that a special test period be established for the new machine.

More than nine years passed, and Pitney received no acceptance of his machine from Washington, but his dedication to the new product was permanent. Although the machine functioned flawlessly, it dawned on Pitney that the machine could be made more practical if the printing and registering mechanism could be embodied in a self-contained detachable box. This would eliminate the necessity of sending a representative from the post office every time a company needed additional postage. The change

AT A GLANCE

Pitney Bowes brand of business machines developed initially in 1909 by Arthur H. Pitney, president of the Pitney Postal Machine Company, in Chicago, IL; merged in 1920 with the Universal Stamping Machine Company, owned by Walter Bowes, to become Pitney Bowes Postage Meter Company; later renamed Pitney Bowes, Inc.

Performance: *Sales*—Approximately $3.5 billion.

Major competitor: Deluxe Corporation; also CUC International and Diebold, Inc.

Addresses: *Parent company*—Pitney Bowes, Inc., Walter H. Wheeler, Jr. Drive, Stamford, CT 06926-0700; phone: (203) 356-5000.

marked a significant improvement for the Pitney machine, and the Post Office Department responded by extending the trial period. Pitney enlisted the help of ten large Chicago companies, and during the trial period, 853,924 pieces were mailed. Postal authorities were impressed with the tremendous savings in time and money.

Walter Bowes Joins Pitney

Around the same time, Pitney heard about a New York-based company that was interested in a machine to print postage. The company's leader, Walter Bowes, had many ideas similar to Pitney's. Bowes's personality, however, differed tremendously from Pitney's. He was a natural-born salesman and promoter with great mental agility and energy. In the early 1900s, a friend of Bowes owned a company that manufactured high-speed check-endorsing machines. The inventor of the machines was talented but lacked business and sales sense and needed an energetic salesman to put the company on its feet. Bowes soon earned the job at the Universal Stamping Machine Company. When the owner offered to sell out in 1909, Bowes jumped at the opportunity, purchased the company, and moved its headquarters to Stamford, Connecticut.

Walter Bowes was always on the lookout for new fields to conquer, and he soon heard about the success of Pitney's postage machine. Bowes knew that the two companies might be able to help one another, and he immediately sent a telegram to Pitney inviting him to Stamford. Pitney accepted Bowes's invitation. Although developing an entirely new industry would be challenging, several things worked in their favor. First, the 1920s were a period of postwar expansion, and new industries were flourishing everywhere. The postal service became the largest single business in the world, employing 300,000 people and handling approximately 20 billion pieces of mail annually. The war encouraged a boom in letter writing among servicemen and their families and friends, and this surge in volume made it apparent that the postal service was lagging far behind in efficiency.

It was under these circumstances that Pitney and Bowes came to an agreement. They obtained the sanction of the boards of their respective companies to form the Pitney Bowes Postage Meter Company as soon as the necessary legislation that would allow the Postal Department to approve the machine was enacted by Congress. The new firm would absorb the assets of both the Pitney Postage Machine Company and the Universal Stamping Machine Company, primarily through an exchange of stock. On March 15, 1920, Congress dramatically approved the Act allowing the Pitney Bowes postage machine to handle mail. Later that year, 23-year-old Walter H. Wheeler, Jr., the stepson of Walter Bowes, joined the management team. Although not a trained engineer, he was mechanically gifted as well as being a talented, organized administrator. The addition of Wheeler completed the circle of leadership that would eventually carry Pitney Bowes to the top of its market.

The First Customers

The first Pitney Bowes postage meter was officially set for postage in the small Stamford post office, and on November 16, 1920, the first metered mail was dispatched. The Pitney Bowes Postage Meter Company was the first customer to receive postage from the meter. This first official mailing under the new law consisted of envelopes with newly issued stamps and pamphlets promoting the new postage meter. Items from the mailing would eventually become valuable to stamp collectors.

Pitney Bowes hired able salesmen and production supervisors, and soon the business was flourishing. Early customers included the influential Commercial Travelers Mutual Accident Association and the National City Bank in New York. England soon approved the machine, thereby opening a new market for Pitney Bowes overseas. By the end of its first year, the companies from across the nation that had contracted for the new machine read like a *Who's Who* of the corporate world.

At the start, Pitney Bowes rented both the machines and the meter, but pressed financially, the company soon approved the machine for outright sales at a price of $1,350 with the meter still available on a rental basis. Such a leasing system, however, drastically reduced the immediate cash flow of the company and sent it into financial tailspins for the next several years. The sales force lobbied for a national advertising campaign, but Pitney Bowes had no budget set aside for such an undertaking.

By 1922 Pitney Bowes had branch offices located in a dozen of the largest cities throughout the nation, from Boston to Los Angeles, and there were 404 meters in service within these markets. While everything possible was being done to speed production, it still required a long time to complete a single postage machine, with one skilled worker carrying out all operations. In the years that followed, Pitney-Bowed enhanced its production lines and designed and tested new models of machines. Although operations were running smoothly, Arthur Pitney seemed unable to find a place for himself in the organization. Untrained in management duties, he found less and less to do, and the relationship between Pitney and Bowes deteriorated. During a board meeting on June 23, 1924, Pitney resigned from the company he had helped to establish.

Not much time went by before he started a new business, Red Star Appliances, Inc., located in Stamford. Pitney approached several key Pitney Bowes employees to join him, and several accepted his offer. Arthur Pitney and his new firm began manufacturing permit machines, devices that were presenting competition for the meters Pitney himself had invented.

During this time, Bowes was also having trouble concentrating on the day-to-day operations of Pitney Bowes. His attentions were turning more and more to steeplechase racing, sailing, and other sporting activities, and he was increasingly absent from the business. The directors of the company decided to promote Walter

Wheeler to a high-level position. The promotion of Wheeler, who would later become chairman of the company, proved to be a stabilizing step for Pitney Bowes.

A World Leader

While Pitney Bowes was the world's top brand of mailing machines, the company's executives had recognized the danger in too narrow a product line and had begun diversifying into the production of other business machines. Through the late 1980s and early 1990s, Pitney Bowes's management team spent many millions of dollars on research and development. The investment paid off, and by 1992 Pitney Bowes had grown by leaps and bounds in terms of financial performance and technology. Two of its flagship fax machines, the models 9750 and 9720, were advanced enough to store data in memory if the units ran out of paper or toner. The company's Paragon mail processor, Pitney Bowes traditional market, had signified a milestone for the company in its transformation from an old-line manufacturer to a high-technology growth company. The Paragon could seal, weigh, and print postage on mail at a rate of up to 240 pieces per minute. The machine employed three kinds of microprocessors, and its development generated 75 new patents. Pitney Bowes's revenues reached $3.5 billion in 1992. The company hoped to make further strides in the high-tech business machine market.

Further Reading:

Alpert, Mark, "Pitney Bowes—Jumping Ahead by Going High Tech," *Fortune,* October 19, 1992, pp. 113–114.

Arend, Mark, "New Systems Tame Rising Postal Costs," *ABA Banking Journal,* November 1992, pp. 66–70.

Battles, Sheryl, "Pitney Bowes makes announcement," *Business Wire,* September 22, 1993.

Cahn, William, *The Story of Pitney Bowes,* New York: Harper and Brothers, Publishers, 1961.

Hartman, Mitchell, "Pitney Bowes cited for promoting diversity," *New Haven Register,* April 27, 1993.

Tangney, Scott, "Pitney Bowes introduces new flagship fax machines, super fast Models 9750/9720," *Business Wire,* September 21, 1993.

Vogel, Todd, "Search for Tomorrow at Pitney Bowes," *Business Week,* March 5, 1990, pp. 50–51.

—*Wendy Johnson Bilas*

PITTSBURGH® PAINTS

Pittsburgh Paints has been a significant product of PPG Industries, Inc., for nearly a century. Well established among professional painters as a preferred product, it also has for many years enjoyed strong brand recognition, reinforced in recent years by its colorful "rainbow P" brand mark. While not the primary business of its parent—unlike the Sherwin-Williams brand—architectural paint constitutes a major unit of PPG's Coatings and Resins Group, the largest of the global company's core business segments. Pittsburgh Paints has ranked among the top-five brands in America for much of its existence. PPG also markets Lucite paints and Olympic stains, and offers Corona branded paint in Europe.

Brand Origins

Paint had been part of the product mix at PPG since the turn of the century. The brand's parent was established near Pittsburgh, Pennsylvania, as the Pittsburgh Plate Glass Company by John Pitcairn and John B. Ford, among others, in 1883; the company began manufacturing and marketing paint with the 1900 purchase of paintmaker James E. Patton Company as an extension of its large glass distribution network. Other acquisitions followed. PPG was its own distributor, independent of middlemen. Its merchandising division would handle about 50 percent of paint sales for more than 60 years, and its outlets would be promoted as "The Store for Paint." By 1923 there were 46 such outlets between New York and San Francisco. The stores offered a complete line of paint and applicators, as well as wallpaper and, perhaps most significantly, professional expertise. PPG called its paint merchandising system "the most complete of its kind in the world."

Paint products were initially sold under the Patton's "Proof" trademark, which featured a beaming sun and its rays. PPG also sold automotive, interior, exterior, and industrial paints—as well as some varnishes—under this trademark. That every paint bore the "Proof" label was touted as an advantage and gave the line a "family" look. However, because the name was also used at one time for chemical products like insecticides and disinfectants, Pittsburgh Paints was eventually adopted to identify PPG's architectural coatings products.

PPG was vertically integrated and capitalized on this aspect of its business in paint promotions: "From raw material to finished product, the manufacture and distribution of Proof Products are under one ownership, one organization, operating through specialized manufacturing divisions . . . assuring dependability of supply and consistent maintenance of Highest Quality Standards." PPG also clung strongly to the National Paint and Varnish Association's "Save the Surface and You Save All" national promotional campaign launched in 1919. A banner on point of purchase displays appealed to the customer's vested interest in his property and attempted to transform the image of paint in consumers' minds from a "luxury beautifier" to a "necessary preservative."

After more than quadrupling in size from 1933 to 1947, it would take the paint industry 17 more years to increase its size from $1.25 billion to $2 billion in revenues. Overcapacity, increased competition, and rising expenses plagued the field. To make matters worse, paint had a generally poor reputation until after World War II and the development of latex formulations. Until about 1960, paint was perceived as a necessary but unpleasant product that was likely to peel, blister, or otherwise deteriorate in unattractive ways in anything but ideal weather. Paint manufacturers began to promote their advances more strongly in the 1960s, when Pittsburgh Paints ranked third among top brands.

During the late 1950s, Pittsburgh Paints stores began offering an increased selection of colors to consumers by shipping a white base paint to retailers with separate oil or powdered pigments. The desired paint color would be concocted at the point of sale on the customer's request. The company's Maestro Colors mixing machine, which could mix more than 1,000 hues on-site, also reduced retailers' risk of overstocking an unpopular color.

Competition

During the postwar era, mass merchandisers started to use paint as a "loss leader" to establish their pricing position and lure customers. Sears, Roebuck & Co. used this technique to great advantage with its Weatherbeater line of paint. At the same time, building products like aluminum siding, redwood, and glass began a period of intense competition with painted surfaces. Paint producers began to sacrifice their profit margins in an attempt to maintain market share. These external forces converged with rising labor, packaging, and distribution costs, as well as the saturation of the paint market to simultaneously restrict volume and margin.

In the face of this increasing competition, Pittsburgh Paints's traditional marketing scheme proved inadequate for the task at hand. The system underwent a reorganization during the mid-1960s; the merchandising division was eliminated and the chain of

AT A GLANCE

Pittsburgh Plate Glass Company acquired the James E. Patton Company of Milwaukee in 1900, and the Patton's Paint brand later became Pittsburgh Paints. The parent company's name was changed to PPG Industries, Inc. in 1968.

Performance: *Market Share*—2.4% (estimate) of the architectural paint market. *Sales*—$300 million (estimate).

Major competitor: Glidden; also Sherwin-Williams, Dutch Boy, and Sears, Roebuck & Co.'s Weatherbeater.

Advertising: *Agency*—Wyse Advertising, Cleveland, OH. *Major campaign*—The slogan "You work too hard to paint with anything less."

Addresses: *Parent company*—PPG Industries, Inc., One PPG Place, Pittsburgh, PA 15272; phone: (412) 434-3131.

distribution centers was reduced from 240 to 15, yet overnight delivery to dealers was maintained. Separate distribution systems were established for glass and paint. And from 1964 to 1968, 400 company-owned paint stores were established.

The brand launched one of its biggest print and radio campaigns in 1965. Eight-page inserts in *Reader's Digest, Popular Mechanics, Better Homes & Gardens,* and *Life* magazines outlined hints and shortcuts for interior painting. They also offered a "Pittsburgh Paints Decorating Guide" by mail, which included a $1.00 coupon to encourage store traffic.

At this time glass remained PPG's largest business, and coatings of all kinds constituted less than 20 percent of the parent company's annual sales volume. Pittsburgh Plate Glass's decision to change its name to PPG Industries, Inc., in 1968 reflected its diversification and the passing of the old plate process for making flat glass; in addition, the PPG logo was well recognized. Other major businesses included chemicals and fiber glass. Automotive coatings had become increasingly important to the paint division. In fact, PPG would soon become the world's largest supplier of automotive and industrial coatings, and in 1990 coatings would surpass glass as PPG's largest business unit in terms of sales.

Pittsburgh Paints improved consumer and professional paints during the 1960s and early 1970s with a wide variety of latex paints resistant to mildew and discoloration from air pollution. These included the premium Manor Hall line of flat latex paints; Wallhide paints, which create microvoids in the applied film to reflect light more efficiently than hiding pigments; and spray-applied paints for use in new construction and rehabilitation.

PPG was an industry leader in reformulating paints to eliminate lead and mercury compounds, and by the mid-1970s, nearly all Pittsburgh Paints products were available in water-based formulations that performed as well as solvent-based products and conformed to new federal and state regulations.

During the 1970s, paint marketers, including Pittsburgh Paints, began to establish home redecorating centers to even out cycles in the paint business. They believed that wallpaper, carpet, and home furnishings would lure customers and provide a competitive edge in the hotly contested industry. This edge became more important because as the do-it-yourself movement gained momentum, mass home improvement retailers and discount merchandisers ascended as paint outlets. Pittsburgh Paints, nonetheless, was successfully promoted as "the house paint that weathers the weather" after the historically harsh winter of 1977.

By 1984 Pittsburgh Paints had started to penetrate the home center market, which had grown to $1.4 billion in annual sales. During the decade, PPG divested its company-owned stores, removing it from competition with its dealer customers and reducing costs. Architectural finishes' share of PPG's annual coatings and resins sales declined to about 13 percent from about 25 percent as the company's automotive finishes business increased five-fold. The parent purchased the well-recognized Olympic stains and Lucite paint businesses in 1989 to boost its trade paint sales to $300 million from $200 million and raise its stake in the domestic market from about two percent to about five percent.

Current Aspects

Reduced paint and solvent consumption and economic recession slowed average paint industry growth to about two percent annually in the late 1980s. Rauch Associates, an industry analysis group, predicted near-term growth to slow even further, to 1.2 percent. These dismal figures inspired increased advertising spending in the early 1990s. The Pittsburgh brand's television spots featured the Pittsburgh Symphony Orchestra playing "Over the Rainbow" and the tag line "The colors you love for the people you love."

Pittsburgh Paints was also a sponsor of the 1992 Summer Olympics. The brand donated paint for Olympic training and administrative facilities in the United States in exchange for use of official U.S. Olympic Committee logos and sponsorship statements in advertising, packaging, and special promotions. The timing of the Games meshed well with Pittsburgh Paints's peak summer selling seasons, and in-store promotions included Olympic jackets, caps, and a sweepstakes for trips to Barcelona, Spain, the site of the Olympiad. The patriotic theme of the campaign was "PPG Salutes the American Spirit."

In 1993, Pittsburgh Paints returned to its independent paint dealer heritage, focusing particularly on the growing painter-maintenance segment, and its advertising re-adopted the "You work too hard to paint with anything less" tag line originally introduced in 1988. Its product offering has been updated and expanded to reflect premium positioning. In all applications—architectural, institutional, residential, industrial, new or repaint—Pittsburgh Paints offers quality coatings in ready-mix or custom colors in systems that comply with volatile organic compound requirements.

Further Reading:

Brady, Catherine, "PPG Tones Up Trade Paints," *Chemicalweek,* October 4, 1989, p. 9.

"Building Downturn Hasn't Hit the Paint Companies," *Financial World,* December 7, 1960, p. 4.

Dickstein, George, "Paint Industry Is Using Spruced Up Ad Approach to Dispel Odorous Image," *Advertising Age,* June 6, 1966, pp. 4, 98.

"Going for the Olympic Gold," *American Paint and Coatings Journal,* February 12, 1992, p. 43.

Kemezis, Paul, "A Disappointing Year for House Paint," *Chemicalweek,* October 13, 1993, p. 42.

"New Name, Team, and Mix at PPG," *Business Week,* October 2, 1968, pp. 68–70, 72, 74.

"The Paint Makers," *Financial World,* August 25, 1965, pp. 11–23.

"Pittsburgh Paint Drive Is Aimed at Home Painters," *Advertising Age,* January 25, 1965, p. 8.

Pittsburgh Plate Glass Company, Paints Varnishes and Brushes: Their History, Manufacture and Use, Pittsburgh: Pittsburgh Plate Glass Company, 1923.

"PPG Goes to TV to Introduce Its New All-weather Paint," *Broadcasting,* July 3, 1978, p. 12.

—April S. Dougal

PLAY-DOH®

For nearly four decades, American children have grown up with the squishy texture and sweet smell of Play-Doh brand modeling compound. Play-Doh, a product of Playskool, Inc., was introduced in 1956 when the post-World War II baby boom was in full swing and became popular in the nursery schools that began to crop up all over the country to serve this ever growing population of three- and four-year-old kids. For many adults, just one whiff of Play-Doh's distinctive scent is enough to conjure up warm memories of nursery school, afternoon naps, and milk and cookies.

Play-Doh, originally produced in a single bland off-white color, achieved almost instant success, for it filled a genuine need for good quality non-toxic preschool toys and faced virtually no competition in the preschool crafts category. Advertising also figured in the brand's early success, as Rainbow Crafts became one of the early sponsors of the extremely popular *Captain Kangaroo* show. Rainbow Crafts was bought by General Mills in 1965 and was eventually merged with Kenner, under whose management Play-Doh was produced until 1991. In 1991, Play-Doh was transferred to the Playskool, Inc., division of Hasbro, Inc., after Hasbro acquired Kenner along with its then parent company, Tonka Corp. Through the vicissitudes of its changing owners, Play-Doh managed not only to retain its dominance over the reusable modeling compound market but also to expand sales with the addition of a large number of companion playsets. It was only in the late 1980s that Tyco's Super Dough offered any serious competition to Play-Doh's hold on the under-six set.

Product Origins

Play-Doh was conceived by Joseph McVickar, a 24-year-old Cincinnati resident. As reported in Marvin Kaye's book on the toy industry, *The Story of Monopoly, Silly Putty, Bingo, Twister, Frisbee, Scrabble, et cetera,* McVickar came up with the idea after visiting his sister's nursery school and watching the young children play with traditional modeling clay. The tacky stiff clay was difficult for little hands to shape and left a messy film on tables and little fingers, not to mention carpet and clothes. McVickar decided that it must be possible to come up with a better substance to satisfy the creative instincts of kids who seemed to love kneading and shaping even this relatively unfriendly clay.

McVickar brought his idea to Tien Liu, a Chinese born chemist working for Rainbow Crafts, then a small chemical company specializing in soaps and cleaning compounds. Liu experimented with a variety of compounds for almost a year before coming up with the formula that was to become Play-Doh. In 1955, Rainbow Crafts tested the new compound in nursery schools in Cincinnati and found that both kids and teachers loved it. It was soft and pliable, easy for small fingers to manipulate, and would stay soft when enclosed in an airtight container but, when dry, was easily cleaned off furniture, clothes, or hair.

By 1956, Rainbow Crafts decided that Play-Doh was ready to be offered for general sale and set up a series of demonstrations in the toy department of the Woodward & Lothrop Department Store in Washington, D.C. Parents were impressed with the new product, in spite of the fact that it was only available in a bland off-white color and was being sold in a rather awkward one and a half pound can. Demonstrations followed at Macy's and Marshall Field department stores and soon Play-Doh was being sold and advertised nationwide. One of the only complaints about the product was its color, or lack thereof. Traditional plasticine had never been able to take bright colors but it was, at least, produced in earth reds, oranges, and dark green. By 1957, Liu had devised a way of coloring Play-Doh and produced a child-pleasing bright red, yellow, and blue version of the increasingly popular compound. The new colors also allowed Rainbow Crafts to sell Play-Doh in a three can pack format, thereby reducing the size of each individual can to a more manageable six ounces.

Rainbow Crafts could not have chosen a better time to launch their product. The late 1950s saw an explosion in the number of kindergarten and nursery schools being founded. Not only was the preschool population growing by leaps and bounds, but the threat of Soviet technological superiority created a cold war push towards better and earlier education for children. It was in the 1950s that preschool toys, invariably touted as educational, began to form a distinct category in the toy industry. The introduction of Play-Doh was very much part of this trend as arts and crafts were particularly lauded by the nursery school movement as having positive play value.

Product Development

The basic composition of Play-Doh has changed very little over the years, although a softer, less crumbly formula was introduced in the early 1990s. Many new colors have been added to the Play-Doh palette which by, 1983, had grown to an eight-color rainbow. By 1993, Special Sparkle and Glow-in-the-Dark Play-

AT A GLANCE

Play-Doh brand of modeling compound founded in 1956 in Cincinnati, OH, by Joseph McVickar and Tien Liu of Rainbow Crafts; Rainbow Crafts bought by General Mills, 1965; Rainbow Crafts merged by General Mills with Kenner-Parker Toys, 1971; Kenner-Parker Toys became independent company, 1985; Tonka Corp. purchased Kenner-Parker Toys, 1987; Hasbro, Inc., bought Tonka Corp. and transfered Play-Doh to Playskool, Inc., division, 1991.

Major competitor: Tyco's Super Dough; also Mattel's Gak.

Advertising: *Agency*—(Broadcast) Griffin Bacal, New York, NY, 1991—; (print) Kidvertisers, New York, NY, 1991—. *Major campaign*—Sparkle creations exploding from Play-Doh can with the tag line, "A million bright ideas in every can."

Addresses: *Parent company*—Playskool, Inc., 1027 Newport Avenue, P.O. Box 1059, Pawtucket, RI 02862-1059; phone: (401) 725-TOYS; fax: (401) 727-5544. *Ultimate parent company*—Hasbro, Inc. (address same as above).

Doh had also been added to the product line. The fundamental source of product innovation and renewal has been the playsets designed to accompany Play-Doh play. The first accessory sets, including the Pixie-Pak and Little Baker's Set, were introduced in 1959. During the following thirty-five years over one hundred playsets appeared in the Play-Doh line. These activity sets consist of molds, extruders, shaped cutters, crinklers, and plastic accessories, all in the playset theme. Many of these sets were based on traditional fantasy play activities, including food related themes (Bake 'N Cake Shop, Electronic Sizzlin' Skillet, Make-A-Meal, Burger and Malt Shop), career related sets (Barber & Beauty Shop, Pet Shop, Dr. Drill 'N Fill, Pumper No. 9), and creative or science themes (Shape Makers, Zoo Set, Dinosaur Playset, Bug Oozer, Jewels & Gems). Playsets based on licenses from popular kids' movies, television programs, and other toys have also formed a very important part of the Play-Doh line of products. Through the years, these have included many of the most popular children's properties such as Star Wars, Sesame Street, Strawberry Shortcake, Care Bears, the Real Ghostbusters, Beetlejuice, and Barney.

In 1990, Play-Doh, then managed by the Kenner division of Tonka, introduced a new segment to the Play-Doh line. Dubbed "Bright Starters," this new line was designed especially for younger children and was heavily advertised in woman's magazines as encouraging creative, educational, play. This segment included such perennial preschool favorites as a Schoolhouse, a Fire House, and a Farm Set. Somewhat surprisingly, the Bright Starters line performed poorly at retail. According to Linda Franzblau, brand manager of Play-Doh in 1994, study groups of moms and kids revealed that mothers preferred a more popular, playful approach to learning and the Bright Starters segment was dropped in favor of preschool-oriented licensed properties such as Barney and Sesame Street.

Advertising and Promotion

Play-Doh has relied heavily on advertising since its introduction in 1956. Taking early advantage of the phenomenon of children's television advertising, in 1957 Rainbow Crafts' Play-Doh became a sponsor of *Ding Dong School* and *Captain Kangaroo,* the only two major programs directed to preschoolers at that time. The introduction of the "Play-Doh Boy" trademark in 1960 began one of the more successful series of children's television campaigns of that decade, eventually being voted one of the top 100 commercials of 1970 by *Advertising Age.*

From very early on in its history, Play-Doh relied on a double-edged advertising strategy. Since Play-Doh was designed for preschoolers, the advertising aimed to get children interested in the product. On the other hand, decisions about the purchase of Play-Doh were clearly being made by a parent. Television advertising was therefore directed towards the children themselves and a separate series of adult oriented print advertisements appeared in such journals as *Parents Magazine* and *Grade Teacher.* This dualistic approach to advertising, introduced in the 1960s, remained in use through the 1990s. In 1994, three years after the transfer of Play-Doh to the Playskool, Inc., division of Hasbro, the Griffin Bacal agency began to run a new series of kid directed television ads featuring four- and five-year-old kids playing with Play-Doh and sporting the tag line "When you've got Play-Doh, Whooaa! Anything goes!" Print ads produced by Kidvertisers ran simultaneously in womens' magazines promoting the creative play value of Play-Doh along with the slogan "A million bright ideas in every can."

Marketers of Play-Doh have used promotional tie-ins with a variety of companies to get their product into the hands of children and into the minds of adult toy purchasers. As early as 1963, Rainbow Crafts was giving away 2-ounce mini-cans of Play-Doh as a premium with Proctor and Gamble products. In the 1980s, Tonka Corp., the new owner of Play-Doh, began a similar series of promotional giveaways with previous owner General Mills and their Lucky Charms breakfast cereal. The Playskool division of Hasbro, the newest owner of Play-Doh, also expressed interest in the development of promotional tie-ins with other companies.

International Presence

By 1964, Play-Doh had become an international phenomenon as Rainbow Crafts reached distribution deals for its product in England, France, and Italy. When General Mills bought Rainbow Crafts in 1965, European distribution of Play-Doh was expanded further and consolidated. Hasbro's purchase of Play-Doh in 1991 extended the reach of the popular modeling compound into even more distant areas through Hasbro subsidiaries in Canada, Mexico, Europe, the Far East, and India. Play-Doh has remained particularly popular in Canada and the United Kingdom, where the Bright Starters segment, a poor seller in the United States, has performed very well, according to a Playskool spokesperson. Apparently British moms—or their children—are more interested in explicitly educational toys than are their American counterparts.

Performance and Competition

Play-Doh faced no serious competition in reusable modeling compounds for over 30 years. Recipes for homemade compound abounded in parenting magazines and books but, in spite of the cheaper cost of doing it yourself, parents continued to buy the brightly colored Play-Doh brand. Play-Doh's virtual monopoly on the preschool modeling compound industry ended in 1987, when Tyco brought out a Play-Doh imitation called Super Dough. Kenner-Parker Toys, then owners of the Play-Doh brand, promptly sued Tyco. Kenner-Parker claimed that the idea for the two color extruder toy that came with Super Dough had been stolen from Kenner-Parker by a former executive of the company. As reported by William Power in the *Wall Street Journal,* the judge in the case ruled that although the two toys were indeed very similar the "simultaneous extrusion of two colors of dough does not strike us as a novel proposition. [It] seems to us that no marketing study is required to know that children, if given the choice, prefer two colors to one color." The judge also denied Kenner-Parker's request for an injunction against Tyco saying that to do so might unfairly strengthen Kenner-Parker's "monopolized domain" in the modeling compound industry.

Tyco's Super Dough, although successful itself, did not significantly diminish Play-Doh's sales. Play-Doh, successful from the start, had seen sales rise on a fairly steady basis through the 1960s and 1970s. In the 1980s, however, as part of a general downward trend in toy sales, Play-Doh sales levelled off. Annual sales appeared stuck at about $20 million. In 1987, the year Tyco introduced Super Dough, Tonka Corp. bought Kenner-Parker Toys with their Play-Doh brand. Faced with the new threat of Super Dough and determined to make the most of their new acquisition, Tonka brought out a new line of Play-Doh playsets including the very popular Make-A-Meal segment. The new fast food related playsets were supported by a series of ads announcing that with Play-Doh, "you can make a meal impossible to beat."

Sales of Play-Doh more than doubled between 1987 and 1989, reaching $60 million despite the new competition from Super Dough. When Hasbro's Playskool acquired Play-Doh in 1991, sales had once again reached a plateau, however. The Playskool marketing team decided to revamp Play-Doh packaging and logos, making the product more visible on retail shelves. They also launched a new ad campaign with the Griffin Bacal agency and Kidvertisers, reminding a generation of parents who had themselves grown up with Play-Doh how much fun they had had with the product as children. Consumers responded to the new marketing tactics and sales rose by 30 percent in 1992. Linda Franzblau, the brand manager for Play-Doh in 1994, stated that a good part of that increase came in sales of the compound itself, rather than the playsets. She believes that parents of the 1990s became increasingly concerned with getting good play value for their toy dollars and that a multi-colored variety pack of Play-Doh compound delivered just that.

By the mid-1990s, Play-Doh was a classic of the toy industry. For a generation of adults the distinctive Play-Doh scent brings back a flood of warm early childhood memories. It looks as if that scent will continue to work its magic for at least one more generation of kids.

Further Reading:

Casey, Robert W., "Toy Companies' Tidings of Joy," *New York Times,* December 24, 1989, p. F9.

Fitzgerald, Kate, "Toy Activity Is Heating Up Early," *Advertising Age,* May 3, 1993, p. 44.

Hasbro, Inc., Annual Report, Pawtucket, RI: Hasbro, Inc., 1992.

Kaye, Marvin, *The Story of Monopoly, Silly Putty, Bingo, Twister, Frisbee, Scrabble, et cetera,* New York: Stein and Day, 1973, p. 150.

Ladensohn Stern, Sydney, *Toyland: The High Stakes Game of the Toy Industry,* Chicago: Contemporary Books, 1990, p. 221.

Power, William, "U.S. Judge, in a Suit over Rival Toys, Rules Squishing Dough Is Nothing New," *Wall Street Journal,* April 22, 1987, p. 49.

Weiner, Steve, "Keep on Truckin'," *Forbes,* October 16, 1989, pp. 220–221.

—*Hilary Gopnik*

PLAYSKOOL®

Playskool is a leading brand of toys for infants and preschool children. Originally, the brand was best known for educational toys made of wood. However, since becoming a division of Hasbro, Inc.—the largest toy company in the United States—in 1984, the brand has been extended to encompass a wider range of merchandise, including stuffed animals and clothing. Since the founding of Playskool in the 1920s, many classic toys have carried the brand name, including Lincoln Logs, Tinkertoy, Mr. Potato Head, and Play-Doh.

Brand Origins

In the early 1920s, Lucille King, a teacher in Milwaukee, Wisconsin, developed several wooden toys as teaching aids for her preschool students. Later, as an employee of the John Schroeder Lumber Co., she and another former teacher formed the Playskool Institute to manufacture and market preschool toys. By 1930 Playskool, which had become a division of the lumber company, was producing more than 40 items, including wooden beads, blocks, doll houses, peg boards, and pounding benches.

A full-page ad in the December 1930 issue of *Child Life* promoted Playskool's ''Playthings With A Purpose.'' Among the featured products were the Home Kindergarten and a sandbox built into a table, known as Playskool Sandie. The ad noted that ''each Playskool Product provides valuable benefits in mental stimulation, coordination of mind and muscle, and general sense training.'' The ad also noted that ''The Playskool . . . ideal of 'Learning While Playing,' as expressed in Playskool Products, is approved by recognized authorities on child-training and preschooling.''

Company History

The Playskool Institute became a division of Chicago-based Thorncraft, Inc., in 1935 and was sold to the Joseph Lumber Co. in 1938. In 1940, two employees of Joseph Lumber, Manuel Fink and Robert Meythaler, purchased the Playskool division and formed the Playskool Manufacturing Co. Playskool continued to market brightly painted wooden blocks and toys for younger children, including the Col-O-Rol Wagon and the Walker Wagon, two pull toys filled with various wooden shapes. Another classic Playskool toy introduced in the 1940s was a wooden mailbox with slotted sides and various push-in pegs. Playskool continued to market the mailbox until the mid-1960s. Meythaler once explained, ''The postal station was just an adaptation of the IQ test, fitting a round peg into a round hole and a square peg into a square hole.''

In 1958 Playskool acquired Holgate Toys, Inc., another maker of wooden toys, many of them suggested by noted child psychologist Lawrence K. Frank and designed by Jerry Rockwell, the brother of artist Norman Rockwell. Rockwell continued to work for Playskool until 1971, creating such toys as the Playskool Tyke Bike. By 1962 Playskool was selling about $20 million worth of toys annually. *Newsweek* noted, ''Next to baby-sitting grandmothers, the stylized wooden toys made by [Playskool] may well be the greatest parent savers of the age.''

In 1962 Playskool acquired the Halsam Co., which had earlier merged with the Embossing Co. to become the only U.S. firm producing embossed wooden blocks for children. Playskool continued to manufacture wooden blocks in 1994. In 1962 Playskool also introduced the first phonograph designed for preschoolers. Magic Phono played small plastic disks that were inserted into a slot. *Newsweek* noted that Magic Phono was ''designed to withstand the whims of a child who pulls the record out before the tune is finished.'' The 1994 Playskool catalog included tape players and other musical toys manufactured by KIDdesigns, Inc., under license to Hasbro.

Another popular Playskool product in the 1960s was a set of small wooden characters known as Weebles. Weebles had rounded bottoms and were weighted so they stayed upright. They were marketed with the slogan ''Weebles wobble but they won't fall down.'' Although they were more popular in Europe than the United States, Weebles were still in the Playskool line-up in 1994.

Playskool moved into outdoor games in 1960 when it acquired the South Bend Toy Manufacturing Co. South Bend Toy was founded in 1874 as a manufacturer of croquet balls, mallets and stakes. In 1895 South Bend Toy introduced the first doll carriages made of willow and eventually became the leading maker of doll carriages in the United States. Although the line-up no longer included doll carriages or outdoor games for adults in 1994, Playskool did continue to produce outdoor games designed for preschoolers, including a set of plastic horseshoes that electronically created the clank of real horseshoes hitting a metal stake.

AT A GLANCE

Playskool brand of toys introduced in the 1920s by Lucille King in Milwaukee, WI, with the founding of the Playskool Institute; Institute became division of John Schroeder Lumber Co. by 1930; division purchased by Thorncraft, Inc., 1935; division sold to Joseph Lumber Co. in 1938; Playskool Manufacturing Co. formed in 1940; acquired by Milton Bradley, Inc., 1968; Milton Bradley acquired by Hasbro, Inc. in 1984.

Major competitor: Fisher-Price; also Mattel.

Advertising: *Agency*—Griffin Bacal, New York, NY, 1978—; also Kidvertisers, New York, NY, 1987—. *Major campaign*—"What will they think of next?"

Addresses: *Parent company*—Hasbro, Inc., 1027 Newport Avenue, Pawtucket, RI 02862; phone (401) 431-8697.

In 1968 Playskool was acquired by Milton Bradley, Inc., best known for its board games. Under Milton Bradley, Playskool again began to focus primarily on toys for preschoolers. In 1984 Hasbro, Inc. purchased Milton Bradley, and began to organize all of its infant and preschool products under the Playskool banner. However, several classic toys retained their brand identity even while being incorporated into the Playskool division.

Lincoln Logs

Lincoln Logs, the classic wooden toy that simulated pioneer construction, was the creation of John Lloyd Wright, the son of architect Frank Lloyd Wright, who apparently was inspired by watching workmen move huge timbers into place for Tokyo's Imperial Palace Hotel in 1916. Construction of the hotel, one of the few buildings to survive a devastating earthquake in 1923, was planned and supervised by Wright's father. The J. L. Wright Co. introduced Lincoln Logs at the New York Toy Fair in 1924. Playskool acquired the company and the rights to Lincoln Logs in 1943.

In 1991 Dan Owen, then president of the Playskool division, called Lincoln Logs "one of those magical toys that, year after year, unleashes a world of fantasy for youngsters. It inspires creativity and that, we believe, is the secret of its long-term success." In 1994 Lincoln Logs were still made of real ponderosa pine that was stained and waxed to withstand rough play. However, in 1994 Playskool added a variety of plastic window frames, doors, and roofs to the original play set. Although the Playskool brand was featured prominently on the package and several of the plastic parts, Lincoln Logs are not marketed under the Playskool name, but retain their original brand identity.

Play-Doh

Play-Doh, the sweet-smelling modeling compound for preschoolers, was created in 1956 by Dr. Tien Liu, then a chemist with Rainbow Crafts, a company that specialized in soaps and cleaning compounds. The idea had been suggested by Joseph McVickar after watching children play with traditional modeling clay that left a mess on hands, tables, carpets, and clothing.

Rainbow Crafts was purchased by General Mills, Inc. in 1965, when then merged the company with Kenner-Parker Toys in 1971. Kenner-Parker became an independent company in 1985, and was acquired by the Tonka Corp. in 1987. Hasbro acquired Tonka in 1991 and transferred the Play-Doh brand to its Playskool division.

Since the early 1990s, Hasbro has used Play-Doh to strengthen the Playskool brand with parents and preschool teachers. Like Lincoln Logs, Play-Doh has retained its own brand identity, although the Playskool logo also is featured prominently on the packaging. An advertising campaign launched in 1994 used the slogan "Play-Doh, what will they think of next?" This echoed a new Playskool slogan, "Playskool, what will they think of next?"

Tinkertoy

Tinkertoy, another classic construction toy under the Playskool banner in the 1990s, was introduced at the New York Toy Fair in 1913. It was created by Charles Pajeau, a stonemason in Evanston, Illinois, who was inspired by watching children play with pencils and empty spools of thread. In 1993 Playskool introduced the first major overhaul of Tinkertoy in 80 years when it replaced the wooden rods and spools with plastic parts.

Ages & Stages

The Playskool brand has stood for learning as much as playing since the days of preschool teacher Lucille King in the 1920s. The brand has also stood for durability. In 1962 Robert Meythaler, a founder of the Playskool Manufacturing Co., told *Newsweek,* "We're going to pit our best creative minds and finest technological resources against the unlimited capacity of children to break toys with incredible speed." In 1994 the Playskool division of Hasbro reaffirmed its commitment to creating long-lasting toys to stimulate young minds with the introduction of Playskool Ages & Stages, a marketing concept that provided parents with guidelines for purchasing age-appropriate toys.

As part of its Ages & Stages program, Playskool redesigned its packaging to include an icon reflecting one of four developmental stages—either Newborn, Infant, Toddler, or Preschooler. In addition, packaging included an explanation of the Ages & Stages concept and a brief description of the principal developmental benefit of the product. Playskool also introduced store displays that reflected the four developmental stages. According to Playskool, Ages & Stages "makes it easy to buy Playskool toys and childcare products whether you're a savvy parent or a long lost uncle who hasn't walked down a toy aisle in umpteen years."

Outlook

Since acquiring the Playskool brand with the purchase of Milton Bradley in 1984, Hasbro has strengthened the brand name by organizing hundreds of products for preschool children under the banner of its Playskool division. This has included such classic toys as Lincoln Logs and Play-Doh, that now carry the Playskool name as well as their own well-known brand names. It also has included newer toys either introduced or acquired by Hasbro, including a wide variety of toys based on Sesame Street characters, Jim Henson's Muppets, and Barney, the purple dinosaur.

In the early 1990s Playskool also introduced several preschool versions of active toys popular with older children, including inline skates with an adjustable "training wheel" and the Playskool 1-2-3 Bike. Playskool also moved into the baby market with such products as high chairs and baby monitors. In 1991 *Playthings* noted, "Playskool has aggressively gone after new business with a number of bold product introductions. Since toys for the older market are handled by the Hasbro and Milton Bradley divisions, Playskool is free to concentrate only on items geared for children under six.'' With its Playskool brand, Hasbro clearly intends to challenge Fisher-Price, acquired by Mattel, Inc. in 1994, for leadership in the infant and preschool markets.

Further Reading:

Botwinick, Stacy, ''Preschool products get extra credit,'' *Playthings,* September 1991, p. 38.

''Hardly Child's Play,'' *Newsweek,* Oct. 1, 1962, p. 68.

History of Playskool, Springfield, MA: Milton-Bradley, Inc., 1979.

—Dean Boyer

PLYMOUTH®

Since 1928 Plymouth has been a major brand of cars for the Chrysler Corporation. The name Plymouth, according to the company, was intended as the ''symbol of the endurance and strength, the rugged honesty, enterprise and determination of achievement, and freedom from old limitations'' as it is associated with the Pilgrims. Plymouth's reputation as the car for everyone has shown this to be true.

Brand Origins

The first Plymouth car was introduced by the Chrysler Motors in June of 1928, with a logo that featured the image of an old-time masted ship on the high seas. This first car, a four-cylinder model with a relatively modest base price of $670, offered the amenities of a more expensive car, including four-wheel hydraulic brakes and full pressure engine lubrication. The Model Q was, according to *Automobile Quarterly,* a redesigned Chrysler 52, which was based on the design of the four-cylinder Maxwell—the product of Chrysler's first automotive venture at the beginning of that decade.

Introduced during the early boom in the automotive industry, the new economy car had the products of some 30 other US companies to compete with. But the company's legendary founder, Walter P. Chrysler, attracted attention to Plymouth by signing on some of the most famous personalities of the day as spokespeople. Aviator Amelia Earhart rode in a Plymouth at the car's Madison Square Garden debut, and race car drivers Barney Oldfield and Lou Miller also promoted the car.

In its first year the car garnered about one percent of the total U.S. automotive market. As the depression era began, however, the hopes of many new automakers plummeted. Plymouth's low price allowed it to prosper and become the third-highest seller in the country, with its sales increasing 50 percent in 1929. The make would retain its number three status through the 1950s. After this initial success, consumers' apparent willingness to buy the low-priced car in the worst of times led Chrysler to erect a new plant especially for Plymouth and enfranchised all of its dealers—including Dodge and DeSoto—to sell the new cars. Plymouth, with 7,000 dealers, thus had the broadest chain of outlets of any car available. In 1930 Plymouth became a separate division of Chrysler. Within five years the Plymouth had helped propel Chrysler Corporation ahead of Ford Motor Co., to second place in total sales.

Aggressive Marketing

In the early 1930s Chrysler used aggressive marketing tactics to keep sales moving despite continued hard times. In 1931, Plymouth introduced an engine mounting system called ''Floating Power'' on its new Model PA. According to the company it was the engineering advance of the decade: by attaching the front end of the engine to a rubber mounting, the system greatly decreased the vibration that had been unavoidable in four-cylinder cars. The slogan ''Smoothness of an eight, economy of a four'' pushed Plymouth ahead of Buick in sales, which were further boosted in 1932 by an advertising campaign featuring a photograph of Walter Chrysler with the new car under the daring legend ''Look at All Three! But don't buy any low-priced car until you've driven the new Plymouth with floating power.'' Lacking the advertising budgets of some of its competitors, Plymouth launched a ''torture-testing'' promotion, in which they would run cars off cliffs, drive them hard, and otherwise abuse them for state fair audiences, while filming the stunts for future promotions.

In 1934 Plymouth sold its one-millionth car. In the latter years of the 1930s, several advances in passenger safety were made, including the elimination of projecting knobs from the interior and the introduction of safety glass as standard equipment. In honor of its efforts, Plymouth received the Eastern Safety Conference award for the cars' design in 1939 and 1940. By the end of 1941 Plymouth had produced 4 million cars.

The War Years

That year Chrysler Corporation became the first company to receive a major defense contract and was exclusively involved in the war effort until 1946. During that period, Chrysler produced Navy Corsair aircraft, aircraft guns, and tank parts. Toward the end of the war, according to the company, Plymouth was involved in the building of the atomic bomb with the production of nickel-plated steel containers, the only receptacles that could contain the scientists' work with a volatile Uranium isotope.

Plymouth resumed producing cars in 1946, but it wasn't until 1949 that the company introduced a completely new model, after spending $90 million to overhaul the whole Chrysler line. The new line quickly became popular, especially the turn-key ignition feature on all of the cars and the new Deluxe Suburban 6-passenger wagon with all-steel body construction.

AT A GLANCE

Plymouth brand of cars introduced in 1928 by Walter P. Chrysler's Chrysler Motors in Detroit, MI; Chrysler Motors name later changed to Chrysler Corporation; popular models have included the Valiant, Horizon, Reliant, and Voyager.

Performance: *Market share*—Approximately 2.3% of the auto market. *Sales*—200,136 units (1993).

Major competitor: (for Voyager minivan) Ford Explorer.

Advertising: *Agency*—Bozell, Inc., Birmingham, MI. *Major campaign*—Chrysler's "Form Follows Function."

Addresses: *Parent company*—Chrysler Corporation, 12000 Chrysler Dr., Highland Park, MI, 48288; phone: (313) 956-5741.

With the advent of the Korean War in 1950, however, Chrysler returned to defense work, using one-third of production capacity for that purpose. Even so, the cars produced between 1951 and 1953—the Concord, Cambridge, and Cranbrook—featured several engineering advances. These included oriflow shock absorbers, electric windshield wipers, optional overdrive, and a one-piece windshield.

"The Forward Look"

The 1954 line of Plymouths offered full-time power steering and automatic transmission. Advertising included the motto "bigger on the inside, smaller on the outside," in response to market surveys which indicated that consumers were looking for smaller, more practical cars. However, the actual market that year proved otherwise. The new postwar prosperity dampened consumers' taste for low priced cars. "[General Motors'] massive, slab-sided styling stole the show," observed *Business Week.*

The following year Chrysler Corporation invested $270 million in yet another retooling, this one called the "Forward Look." The new models featured longer, sleeker styling and the first hint of the fins that would distinguish the Chrysler-Plymouth silhouette in the following years. The 1955 model, according to *Business Week,* impressed customers and others within the industry, but the new styling coupled with older manufacturing techniques resulted in complaints about poor body work. A new set of high-finned clean-lined cars were introduced in 1957. Advertising used the forward-looking motto "Suddenly it's 1960" to grab style-conscious consumers. More than 600,000 of the cars were sold, helping Chrysler earn 20 percent of that year's market.

Despite the previous year's successes, 1958 marked the beginning of a period of difficulty for Plymouth, and the auto industry as a whole, due to nation-wide recession and a sudden rise in sales of such lower-priced, small import cars as the Volkswagen Beetle. It wasn't until the 1960 model year that Plymouth came back with its answer to the new small-car demand. Employing careful market research, the company introduced the Valiant, which averaged 27 miles per gallon and featured unibody construction and Chrysler's first electrical alternator. The car's name came from a survey of potential consumers who were given the choices of Chelsea, Columbia, Liberty, Revere, and Valiant.

1960s Downturn

The 1960s proved to be an up and down period for Plymouth, but the Valiant served as an anchor, holding its position as Detroit's best-selling compact through the decade. The entire industry suffered poor sales in 1961, and Plymouth's new line of "unibody" cars—the Savoy, Belvedere, Fury, and Suburban—did particularly poorly. Their styling, which one analyst called "garish," was no competition for that year's more conservatively-styled cars.

At the end of that year, Lynn A. Townsend became president of Chrysler Corporation and instituted an approach which, he told *Business Week* in an apparent response to the less-stylish cars' approach, emphasized stability and consistency. "We call it a Tiffany look around here," he asserted. "High class, good taste, not overbearing, not overdone. Our cars appeal to the great mass of American buyers." However, in 1964 American tastes were leaning toward sporty compact models like the Chevrolet Corvair and Ford's still-legendary Mustang. In response, the company rushed out the Barracuda, a retooled version of the Valiant. Plymouth had greater success in 1965 by introducing a new line of full-size cars, its largest to date: Fury I, Fury II, Fury III, and the Sport Fury. Their popularity, along with the continued strong sales of the Valiant, pushed Plymouth from seventh to fourth place in new car popularity.

Restylings of the popular Fury models in 1971 and 1974 made for good years for the make, but compacts were still Plymouth's top seller. The Valiant continued to dominate the compact market through the early 1970s, until it was phased out in 1977 in favor of the more upscale Volaré. The Volaré, with its roomy interior and conservative styling, sold well from the start. Its appearance was accompanied by an aggressive and memorable advertising campaign which featured Sergio Granchi singing his song of the same name. During this period, the number and range of Plymouth models had shrunk drastically, giving the brand a minimal presence in both the subcompact and full-size markets.

Plymouth was unable to produce a proper response to Detroit's new subcompact models of the early 1970s, including the Ford Maverick and Pinto and AMC's Gremlin. According to *Business Week,* Chrysler Corporation had concluded that it would not be able to make money on small cars and, instead, began importing the British-made Avenger, followed by the Japanese-made Arrow (produced by Mitsubishi Motors before that company began marketing cars in the U.S. under its own name) in order to fit into the niche.

Subcompact Cars

It wasn't until the 1978 model year that Plymouth finally came out with a subcompact car of its own. The introduction of the Plymouth Horizon (and the Omni, its counterpart from the Dodge division of Chrysler), a five-door sedan with a 99.2 inch wheel base, was hailed by *Automotive News* as "a new generation of American-built subcompact cars." The car had been developed in a relatively short period, having made a deal with Volkswagen of West Germany to supply engine blocks and four-speed transaxles for the first model year. The Horizon was, in fact, very similar in styling to the VW Rabbit, but with a quieter ride, roomier interior, and "Americanized" options like AM-FM radio, automatic transmission, and air conditioning. Advertising for the new car, produced by Young & Rubicam of Detroit, stressed the car's safety, handling, and storage space for its size. Less emphasis was placed on fuel efficiency and maneuverability, attributes that Chrysler Corporation felt were a given for small cars.

The Horizon sold well from the beginning. ''But by that point,'' according to *50 Years of American Automobiles,* ''Plymouth was a mere shadow of its former self, down to just Horizons, TC3s, and Volarés. Management tried fostering the illusion that this was still a full-line make by slappng Plymouth nameplates on various captive imports. . . . It was a good move, providing vital sales support at a crucial time, but it only underscored how far a once-prominent marque had fallen.''

Trouble at Chrysler

The mid-1970s proved a difficult time for the auto industry, and Chrysler Corporation, was particularly vulnerable. While the company set sales records in 1972 and 1973, gasoline shortages, inflation, and weakened consumer confidence drove Chrysler into financial crisis as U.S. tastes turned to smaller, fuel-efficient imports. Amid the crisis, John J. Riccardo became chairman of the company in 1975. Three years later he named Lee A. Iacocca president of Chrysler. Iacocca, who eventually replaced Riccardo as chairman, had just been ousted as president of Ford Motor Co. after 32 years with the company.

When Iacocca came on the job, he went to work restructuring the company, firing executives and hiring new ones, many from Ford. In March of 1979 he stunned both Detroit and Madison Avenue by firing the three advertising agencies that had handled Chrysler cars: Young & Rubicam (Plymouth and Chrysler); Ross Roy (Dodge and captive imports); and Batten Barton Durstine and Osborn (corporate). The company retained Kenyon & Eckhardt of Birmingham, Michigan, as its sole agency in what *Automotive News* called ''the largest transaction in advertising history.''

In late 1979, corporate efforts notwithstanding, Chrysler was still in deep trouble. In December of that year, Congress passed the Chrysler Corporation Loan Guarantee Act, which provided the carmaker $1.5 billion in loan guarantees to try and salvage the company. As the company continued to restructure, Iacocca himself began to appear in Chrysler's advertising, and thus became one of the best-known and most recognized business people in the world.

Success in the 1980s

In 1981 Chrysler introduced a new line of ''K-cars,'' which included the Plymouth Reliant, a no-frills sedan starting at $6,300. The Reliant and its sister car, the Dodge Aries, along with the Horizon and Omni, created a level of sales success that allowed Chrysler to pay back its federal loan guarantee in 1983 and return to profitability. The following year, the company scored another hit with the Plymouth Voyager minivan. The Voyager became Chrysler's biggest seller of the decade, generating sales of more than 100,000 vehicles each year. Its car-like ride and maneuverability set it apart from standard vans and harder-to-maneuver competitors.

In the next ten years Chrysler continued to prosper and sales of the Plymouth Reliant and the popular Voyager continued. But the Plymouth line was becoming less distinct from Dodge or Chrysler. In 1984 *Advertising Age* referred to Plymouth as ''the lost car brand.'' That year Kenyon & Eckhardt was at work on the image issue, via the new Caravelle, a ''fancy'' six-passenger K-car, with a new roofline and four (rather than two) headlights. The campaign ''Match it! (if you can)'' was aimed at buyers of the Buick Century and Oldsmobile Ciera, mentioning those General Motors products by name in its advertisements.

The Struggle for Recognition

In 1986 the company again attempted to reposition Plymouth in the market, trying to give it a more upscale image, instead of its appeal, as a Plymouth executive told *Advertising Age,* as a ''cheaper car for older people.'' As many car marketers were looking to do that year, the new positioning was intended to stress ''basic values,'' but also target a youthful and upscale audience, mainly young families. The campaign for the Reliant and Voyager stressed patriotism, aiming to tap into buy-American sentiment, using the copy, ''Plymouth . . . The Pride is Back . . . the best is born in America again.'' The ''Pride'' ads featured a light rock soundtrack and such American themes as the Statue of Liberty, the Flag, cowboys, and boxers. Improving long-neglected brand identification was a slow process, however. Efforts were still underway in 1988, with the Voyager, Reliant, and Plymouth Laser (a joint venture with Mitsubishi Motors), to solve the identification problem.

In 1992, as part of Chrysler Corporation's Project 2000 long-range planning effort, the company seriously considered discontinuing the Plymouth name altogether. The plan was part of an overall consolidation effort, which would eliminate 25 percent of the company's dealers and reduce its three distribution channels to two. The plan was announced to Chrysler network dealers in 1991 but shelved, according to *Automotive News,* because Chrysler feared losing loyal Plymouth buyers, particularly minivan owners. ''Company research indicates,'' according to the newspaper, ''that Plymouth Voyager buyers will balk if the minivan is labeled a Chrysler; they will assume the vehicle carries a higher sticker [price].'' Thus, the company opted to keep Plymouth as a ''value brand'' just as it had started all those years ago, when it became a hot seller during the Great Depression.

Further Reading:

Blonston, Gary L., *Plymouth: Its first 40 Years,* Chrysler Plymouth Division Public Relations Department, Detroit, 1968.

Bohn, Joseph, ''Chrysler ads to stress Dodge and Plymouth,'' *Automotive News,* September 11, 1978; ''2-door Omni-Horizon push mapped,'' *Automotive News,* December 28, 1978.

Connelly, Mary, ''Plymouth to try simple approach,'' *Automotive News,* September 15, 1986; ''Plymouth Lives, Chrysler says,'' *Automotive News,* December 7, 1992.

''C-P leads with new Laser,'' *Automotive News,* September 26, 1983.

50 years of American Automobiles, New York: Beeckman House, 1989.

Gray, Ralph, ''Chrysler differentiating Dodge, Plymouth images,'' *Advertising Age,* September 17, 1979; ''Plymouth saga: Return of the lost brand,'' *Advertising Age,* September 24, 1984.

''How Chrysler fights a skid,'' *Business Week,* April 17, 1971.

Kimes, Beverly Rae, ''Plymouth: Walter Chrysler's Trump Car,'' *Automobile Quarterly,* Summer 1966.

Lapham, Edward, ''Chrysler to reposition Plymouth brand,'' *Automotive News,* September 23, 1985.

Linert, Paul, ''Chrysler taking a major gamble,'' *Automotive News* December 12, 1977.

''New Fury highlights Plymouth Line,'' *Automotive News,* August 23, 1976.

O'Connor, John, ''Chrysler moves to Kenyon & Eckhardt,'' *Advertising Age,* March 5, 1979.

Serafin, Raymond, ''Plymouth survives as a value brand,'' *Advertising Age,* December 7, 1992.

Sommers, Allen, ''Astro minivans are option heaven,'' *Automotive News,* August 19, 1985.

Strnad, Patricia, ''Dodge, Plymouth get new 'spirit,' '' *Advertising Age,* September 26, 1988.

''What's wrong at Chrysler,'' *Business Week,* July 5, 1969.

''What's wrong at Chrysler?,'' *Forbes,* December 1, 1973.

—Martha Schoolman

POLAROID®

Polaroid

The Polaroid Land Instant Camera dazzled the American public when it was introduced in 1947 by the Polaroid Corporation. Using a technique developed by Polaroid's founder, Dr. Edwin H. Land, Polaroid cameras could produce photographs within one minute. During the decades following its introduction, the Polaroid Instant Camera grew to become the best-selling camera in the world. Sales declined during the late 1980s, the result of perceived poor picture quality and expensive film, combined with competition from easy-to-use, inexpensive 35mm cameras. After winning a giant patent infringement lawsuit against Eastman Kodak Comapny in 1991, Polaroid became the sole manufacturer of instant cameras in the world. Instant photography applications span the market from recreational to artistic, commercial, medical, and educational.

Brand Origins

In 1926, while on leave from his undergraduate studies in physics at Harvard University, Edwin H. Land began independent experiments with light polarization. Three years later Land filed a patent for the first synthetic light polarizer, a plastic substance that reduces the glare of sunlight. Potential applications included photographic filters, sunglasses, and glare-reducing airplane windows. After completing his studies at Harvard in 1933, Land incorporated Land-Wheelwright Laboratories with the head of the Harvard Physics Department, George Wheelwright III. Their first sale of Land's polarizers was in 1933 to the Eastman Kodak Company, which used them as components in photographic lens filters.

Land trademarked the term Polaroid in 1936. He later formed the Polaroid Corporation to purchase all the assets of Land-Wheelwright Laboratories. Polaroid introduced a number of scientific and commercial products using the new polarizer, including sunglasses, desk lamps, variable density windows, and military equipment.

The Polaroid Land Instant Camera was by far the greatest commercial success of the new laboratory. Almost unfathomable before its introduction, the Polaroid Land camera delivered completely dry and developed photos within one minute. Land introduced the camera in 1947 at the Optical Society of America. The scientific community was astonished and listed the camera as one of the "ten most outstanding events of the year." By 1948 the Polaroid Corporation had patented 89 different applications in the development of the camera (a move that would prove fortuitous when Kodak entered the one-step photo market in the 1970s) and began contracting to manufacture it for the mass market.

The new camera was introduced to the public in November of 1948 at Jordan Marsh department store in Boston amid much promotional fanfare. Jordan Marsh took out full-page ads in the *Boston Daily Globe, Boston Herald,* and *Boston Post* newspapers. "Imagine! Finished pictures in one minute . . . with this new Polaroid Land Camera!" A newspaper-style column went on to explain the operations of the camera. Demonstration booths were set up in the store, where potential customers could get their picture taken and receive the finished copy within one minute. The camera sold for $89.50.

By 1949, Polaroid had achieved national distribution with about 2,500 dealers across the United States. The camera was advertised through full-page ads in national magazines. Within a year of the camera's introduction, photographic sales (including film) surpassed $5 million and accounted for 80 percent of total Polaroid sales. Camera production was just barely keeping up with demand. Film demands far outpaced production, so much so that Polaroid resorted to restricting film sales to six roles per month to camera owners who received a film reservation book with each camera purchased.

1950s Sales Growth

Camera sales grew tremendously through the 1950s, fueled by heavy national advertising and the continuous introduction of new and improved models. By 1950, Polaroid had produced its one-millionth role of film, and more than 4,000 dealers across the country sold Polaroid cameras, film, and accessories. That decade Polaroid introduced a new line almost every two years: the 1952 Model 110 Land camera called the Pathfinder; the 1954 Speedliner Model 95A and The Highlander; the 1955 Model 700 Land camera; the 1957 Model 80A, 800, and 110A cameras; and the 1960 Model 900 Land camera, the first automatic electric-eye Land camera with a flash. In addition, Polaroid introduced a number of new and improved film versions, from sepia-toned to high resolution black and white.

The 1950s was also a decade of intense advertising. In 1954 Polaroid began advertising its cameras and film live on the *Tonight Show* starring Steve Allen. In the 60-second commercials, Allen would demonstrate the camera and film, making the process famil-

AT A GLANCE

The Polaroid Land brand of instant cameras first introduced in 1947 by Edwin H. Land, founder of the Polaroid Corporation in 1937; Polaroid became a registered trademark in 1936.

Performance: *Market share*—100% of instant camera category in the United States. *Sales*—$2.24 billion worldwide (1993).

Major competitor: Kodak brand cameras (though Kodak does not manufacture an instant camera).

Advertising: *Agency*—BBDO, New York, NY. *Major campaign*—Advertisements for the Captiva model.

Addresses: *Parent company*—Polaroid Corporation, 549 Technology Square, Cambridge, MA 02139; phone: (617) 386-2000.

iar to millions of Americans. Although not all photos were perfect, the live ads helped to support one of Polaroid's key advertising points: "If the picture isn't good, you don't have to wait a week to find out. You can tell right away and have another one sixty seconds later."

By 1956, photographic equipment made up 93 percent of total sales. The one-millionth camera was sold that year. A large percentage of the advertising budget was appropriated to network advertising, although new productions were also introduced nationally through full-page print advertisements. The price of the Model 110A was reduced due to changes in manufacturing, and other prices rose slightly for the first time since 1948. Polaroid expanded into new markets, and by 1958 Polaroid products were available in 45 countries. With $65 million in sales and record revenues of over $10 million, Polaroid, by 1960, became the third-largest photographic corporation, second to Eastman Kodak and General Aniline & Film.

Creative Collaborations

While Polaroid positioned the camera as a simple, fast, and effective means for anyone to obtain good photographs, the corporation also developed strong relationships with prominent artistic photographers. In 1949 Land hired photographer Ansel Adams as a consultant to use Polaroid products and report his findings on any difficulties or flaws the camera might possess. The use of consultants such as artists Paul Caponigro and William Clift added a perspective that Polaroid technicians could not achieve; the use of the consultants also greatly improved Polaroid's image as serious photographic equipment, dispelling any notion that instant pictures were no more than a novelty. Polaroid's policy was often to supply artists with equipment and film, tell them to shoot any photo they pleased, then report any "technical advantages or problems they might find."

During the 1960s Polaroid capitalized on its collaborations with artists, featuring jazz trumpeter Louis Armstrong and photographer Bert Stern in a advertisement for new, high resolution film. The goal was always to "bring the instant photography process more in the public eye." Throughout its history, Polaroid's advertising sought to create a glamorous, and occasionally witty, image of its cameras and film. The employment of artists added a certain cachet to Polaroid's image and was key to Polaroid's success in its heyday.

Market Domination: 1960s

Polaroid Corporation's 1961 sales were just over $100 million, with approximately 96 percent generated by photographic equipment. Polaroid was fast becoming a household word, thanks in part to advertising by agency Doyle Dane Bernbach, which won numerous industry awards for its ad, set in a high school prom, that emphasizes the spontaneity of instant photos. By 1962 more than four million Polaroid cameras had been sold since the brand's introduction. That year, record revenues of $103 million were recorded.

Polaroid achieved another sales coup in 1963 with the debut of its Polacolor instant film that produced color photos in one minute. In conjunction with its new color film, Polaroid spent $5 million in 1963 to introduce the new Automatic 100, a camera that developed both color and black and white film outside the camera. The media blitz included television, outdoor billboard, and poster advertising, as well as full-page ads in major magazines and newspapers across the United States and Canada. Polaroid intended to make the 100 model the basic camera and discontinue production of all other Polaroid models, except for the Professional Model 100B. Fueled by the popularity of the new camera, demands for the color film far exceeded supply in 1963. One year later Polaroid introduced a lower priced version of the 100. The early 1960s were good years for Polaroid. One million cameras sold between 1961 and 1964.

Also in the early 1960s, Polaroid began extensively promoting camera sales in foreign markets. Virtually since their introduction, Polaroid Land cameras were available in Europe, South American, and pockets of Asia. Based on its excellent marketing campaigns, Polaroid received the "E" award from then President John F. Kennedy for excellence in exporting in 1964. That year, Polaroid began manufacturing film in the Netherlands for easy sales in European Common Market. In 1965 Polaroid incorporated subsidiaries in Belgium, Switzerland, and on the Australian continent. International sales had grown to $24 million dollars, approximately ten percent of total U.S. sales.

In 1965 Polaroid introduced Swinger (model 20 Land camera), a light-weight camera that took only wallet-sized black and white photos and sold for a mere $19.95. Sales immediately took off, supported by award-winning advertising that featured a then unknown actress, Ali MacGraw, wearing a bikini and swinging her camera to the rhythms of the catchy Swinger jingle. The ads were so successful that when the camera was introduced in Canada on a Friday, more than 80 percent of the cameras allotted for Canadian sales were sold by Monday. The remaining 20 percent sold out by the end of the week.

U.S. sales in 1965 were $204 million. In 1966 Polaroid began overseas production of the Swinger and also introduced five Electric-Eye 200 Series cameras in all its markets. Sales continued to grow as Polaroid introduced a number of new cameras and improvements through the last half of the decade. In June of 1969, film sales hit their highest mark to date, with more than 51 million units of color film sold that month.

Meeting the Competition: Kodak

By 1976, Polaroid had nearly caught up with Kodak in terms of amateur camera and film sales. Although marketing different products, Kodak and Polaroid viewed each other as rivals virtually since the introduction of Polaroid cameras in the late 1940s. When

Land announced that Polaroid's then new instant photos process was "the only way" to take a photo, Eastman Kodak did not take it lightly. Shortly after Polaroid cameras hit the market, Kodak introduced the Kodak Instamatic, which capitalized on the instant photo concept, but only offered quick-loading film. When Polaroid began discussing pocket-sized instant cameras in the late 1960s, Kodak introduced the Pocket Instamatic.

It was well known to Polaroid officials that Kodak was planning to enter the instant camera market some time in the 1970s. Polaroid continued development of new, improved cameras and in 1972 introduced the SX-70, the "first fully automatic, motorized, folding, single-lens camera, which ejects self-timing, self-developing color prints." The camera debuted via an advertising campaign starring Sir Laurence Olivier—the first commercial ever in which the famous actor agreed to appear.

Polaroid had expected to sell more than one million units of the new camera, but manufacturing snafus slowed production and delayed its nationwide introduction until nine months into the year. Despite the delay, sales were strong: all but 1,000 of its inventory of 461,000 cameras were sold before Christmas of 1973. Industry analysts predicted 1974 sales to total around 1.5 million, however, U.S. sales totaled $487 million and international sales came to $192 million.

Continuing its preparation for Kodak's entry into the instant camera market, Polaroid introduced a series of low-priced cameras in hopes of capturing a greater share of the market before the Kodak debut. Huge advertising campaigns with well-known celebrities such as actor Alan Alda heralded the advent of Electric Zip and Pronto cameras, both priced under $50.

Kodak's camera hit the market in 1976. Polaroid founder Land lightly poked fun at Kodak's instant camera technology during Polaroid's annual shareholders meeting. However, almost immediately, Polaroid filed suit, charging that Kodak infringed on ten of Polaroid's patent rights. This suit dragged on over 15 years, during which time the market for instant cameras changed drastically.

In 1986 Kodak was forced out of the market by a U.S. Appeals Court ruling that Kodak violated seven Polaroid patents. The Appeals court ruling had only a minimal effect on Kodak sales. Instant photography had only accounted for two percent of all Kodak sales from 1976 to 1986. More difficult for Kodak was the 1991 ruling that it must pay Polaroid $925 million in damages.

Instant Camera Market Shrinks

In 1977 Polaroid sales exceeded $1 billion, with more than 90 percent generated by instant cameras and film. Sales stalled, however, in the period from 1978 to 1982, from $1.4 to $1.2 billion. Industry analysts cite an entrenched corporate culture that was unable to keep up with changing markets, stating that Polaroid had "fallen in love with technology" while neglecting the decline of camera sales. Consumer interest in fully automatic 35mm cameras developed by Japanese firms in the 1980s further eroded Polaroid's share of the overall camera market. While Kodak's forced departure assured Polaroid control over the instant camera market in 1986, the market size itself had diminished by 60 percent since 1978. Furthermore, surveys found only 8 to 10 percent of the market had an interest in instant cameras in 1986, compared to a 1976 survey estimating that 42 percent of American households already owned a Polaroid.

Throughout the 1970s and into the 1980s, Polaroid continued its use of well-known actors, such as Candace Bergen, Alan Alda, the Muppets, and Mariette Hartley and James Garner, to star in Polaroid print and television ads. The cleverly written Garner and Hartley ads were so popular that the couple continued on as spokespeople through the early 1980s, even as Polaroid sales declined.

Although Kodak was out of the instant camera market, Polaroid continued its marketing war against its arch rival, introducing the Spectra in 1986. Aimed at capturing a share of the $860 million compact camera market dominated by Kodak, Spectra was Polaroid's most significant new camera product since the SX-70 in 1973.

Spectra was introduced through such intensive advertising that, according to *Marketing News,* "only Americans without TVs have not been exposed to [Spectra's] introductory campaign." Billed as the "first camera of the future," Spectra was said to produce high quality instant photos that rivaled 35mm photos. Advertising was aimed at a "sophisticated upscale audience and people over 40 with large amounts of disposable income."

A disappointing 1.5 million Spectra cameras sold worldwide during the first 18 months of its introduction, leading Polaroid to quickly introduce Impulse, a new, inexpensive camera aimed at attracting young adults from the 35mm point-and-shoot market. But camera buyers had lost their fascination with instant photography, and once again, sales were slow.

After extensive market research (the company conducted more than 15,000 interviews with potential customers), Polaroid developed a compact, autofocus single-lens-reflex camera that would eventually be named Captiva; at first code-named the "Joshua" instant camera system, the product was introduced in Europe under the name Polaroid Vision in 1992, in Japan under the name JoyCam in 1993, and, that same year, in the United States under the Captiva name. The product promised to perform better than company expectations. In Germany, Captiva boosted market share from 11 percent to 15 percent.

Future Predictions

Around 1980 Polaroid Corporation became aware that the consumer instant camera market was shrinking and began focusing its activities on developing high-tech imaging devices for other markets. By 1985, technical and industrial photography accounted for more than 40 percent of total Polaroid sales. The introduction of Spectra was expected to boost consumer camera sales, but sales fell below projections. With the introduction of Captiva in 1993, instant photography accounted for 85 percent of Polaroid sales.

Also in 1993 Polaroid officials determined that if the corporation were to grow, continued development of products outside of the instant photography market was essential. Polaroid divided its operations into three divisions: core photographic imaging, high resolution imaging, and electronic imaging systems. I. MacAlister Booth, chairman and president of Polaroid, told the *Wall Street Journal:* "While we've invested hundreds of millions of dollars in [instant photography] in the past, our plan is to spend tens of millions in the future."

Long-term strategy included nearly doubling sales by the year 2000; to do so, Polaroid officials stated that the company's revenues must grow by an average of seven percent annually. The continued success of Captiva, as well as the development of appealing new imaging devices, will undoubtedly determine Polaroid's future. Based on Polaroid's history of strong U.S. and international marketing strategies, such growth seems within reach.

Further Reading:

Carley, William M., ''Polaroid Seen Wary, Worried as It Girds for Kodak Arrival in Instant-Photo Filed,'' *Wall Street Journal,* April 16, 1976, p. 4.

Harper, Timothy, ''Polaroid Clicks Instantly in Moslem Market,'' *Advertising Age,* January 30, 1986, p. 12.

Higgins, Kevin T., ''Polaroid Stages Marketing Blitz,'' *Marketing News,* June 6, 1986, p. 4.

Jervy, Gay, ''Polaroid Develops Marketing Orientation,'' *Advertising Age,* January 30, 1984, p. 4.

Pereira, Joseph, ''Wall Street Sees a Turnaround Developing at Polaroid,'' *Wall Street Journal,* July 13, 1993.

Phillips, Lisa, ''Specter of Spectra Hangs Over Kodak,'' *Advertising Age,* March 24, 1986, p. 3.

''Polaroid Revenue Set Record in 1962; Profit 2nd Only to 1959 High,'' *Wall Street Journal,* February 13, 1965.

''Polaroid Says Customers Snap Up SX-70 Cameras, Demand Tops Supply,'' *Wall Street Journal,* January 8, 1974.

''Polaroid Says SX-70 Isn't Likely to Show a Profit This Year,'' *Wall Street Journal,* April 23, 1975.

''Polaroid Suit Charges Eastman Kodak's Instant Camera, Film Infringe on Patents,'' *Wall Street Journal,* April 28, 1976, p. 12.

Wurman, Richard Saul, *Polaroid Access: Fifty Years,* Access Press Ltd., 1988.

—Maura Troester

PONTIAC®

PONTIAC.

From "Chief of the Sixes" to "We Are Driving Excitement," the Pontiac Division of General Motors has always stood for automotive performance aimed toward the driver of average income. Apparently it's a positioning that has worked, as Pontiac—whose best known nameplates include Grand Prix, Firebird /Trans Am, and Bonneville—has held an important position among the GM divisions for more than 65 years.

Brand Origins

The origins of Pontiac go back to 1893, according to Thomas E. Bonsall in his book *Pontiac: The Complete History.* It was then that Edward M. Murphy, a manufacturer of horse-drawn buggies, established his new Pontiac Buggy Company in Pontiac, Michigan (about 20 miles north of Detroit). The buggy business had been a profitable one in the past, as Bonsall relates, but as the 20th century loomed, the businessman "read the handwriting on the wall: the horse-drawn buggy was doomed. It was the smelly, noisy unreliable automobile that was going to prevail."

While Murphy wasn't an engineer, he had access to some of the best automotive designers in the country. One of them, A. P. Brush, who worked for Cadillac, had drawn the plans for a two-cylinder car. Cadillac didn't want it, but Murphy did; by 1907, Murphy's Pontiac Buggy Company—now renamed the Oakland Motor Car Company after the county in which Pontiac was located—had taken possession of a 5,000-square-foot carriage plant. The first vehicles were called Oaklands, and sold as part of the General Motors line.

Oakland automobiles sold at increasing rates over the next dozen years, reaching a peak of 52,000 units by 1919, according to Bonsall. Then, "things began to deteriorate," as the author continues. "The nation's economy entered a minor depression [and] Oakland was suffering from internal problems . . . not the least of which was a serious lack of quality control." By the 1920s Oakland's lack of quality had reached the point where production of the car was no longer profitable. Worse, General Motors had no model to compete with Ford's Model T, which at less than $500 was truly a people's car. (GM's lowest-priced make at the time, the Chevrolet 490, began at $795.)

GM began a massive reorganization with the focus being on marketing a full line of automobiles in every price range. Some nameplates—like Scripps-Booth and Sheridan—were canceled, others absorbed. From the ashes of GM's efforts came a new car line concept: a low-priced, six-cylinder vehicle, a "companion" vehicle to the Oakland to be priced somewhere around $800. The task of developing the new make was assigned to the Oakland plant. When general manager A. R. Glancy reported to work on February 1, 1925, as Bonsall relates, the new car was already under development. Bonsall quotes Glancy as recalling, "When I got to the plant I found designs for it hanging on the wall, and over them someone had written 'Pontiac.' " (Not just a tribute to the city that housed the automotive plant, the name *Pontiac* also honors a renowned figure in American history. Chief Pontiac, of the Ottawa nation, had organized a rebellion in 1762 "involving practically every Indian tribe from Lake Superior to the lower Mississippi," according to Bonsall. "Pontiac is considered by historians to have been one of the most important" of all Native American leaders.)

From the beginning, Pontiac models featured advanced styling and six-cylinder performance (hence an early ad campaign, "Chief of the Sixes," as embodied by a portrait rendition of Chief Pontiac himself). For the next several years the plant produced both mid-range Oakland and economy-range Pontiac models. Eventually, the Pontiac cars began to outsell Oakland—and provided keen competition in its price range. "The onset of the Great Depression killed the Oakland in 1931," writes Richard L. Busenkell in *Pontiac since 1945.* "It has often been said that the Pontiac 'stole' sales from the Oakland, and thus precipitated the latter's demise," notes Bonsall. "This is a myth, and deserves to be laid to rest. In fact, quite the opposite was the case. The Oakland had been on GM's list of 'expendables' for years."

Pontiac Weathers the Storm

With such names as the Coupe, the Landau, and the Custom Sedan to entice buyers, Pontiac enjoyed increasing sales throughout the 1920s. The company reached an early sales high of almost 184,000 units in 1928; then came the financial crisis and stock market collapse of late 1929. Pontiac, like virtually all American businesses, had much to lose in the wake of the Depression. Even with cost-cutting in place, Pontiac sales dropped 68 percent between 1929 and 1930.

Coming out of the Depression in 1935, Pontiac entered its tenth year "in splendid shape," according to Bonsall. Economic woes notwithstanding, the company had earned market share and ex-

AT A GLANCE

Pontiac brand of automobile founded in 1893 by Edward M. Murphy in Pontiac, MI, with the establishment of the Pontiac Division; introduced in 1926 as a low-priced companion to the Oakland car line of General Motors Corporation.

Performance: *Sales*—$678,968,000 (1990).

Major competitor: Similarly priced divisions of Ford Motor Co. and Chrysler Corp.; also, Honda and Toyota.

Advertising: *Agency*—D'Arcy Masius Benton & Bowles, Bloomfield Hills, Michigan, since 1926. *Major campaigns*—"We Build Excitement" (1984), "We Are Driving Excitement."

Addresses: *Parent company*—Pontiac Division, One Pontiac Plaza, Pontiac, MI 48340-2952, (810) 857-5000. *Ultimate parent company*—General Motors Corp., New Center Building, Detroit, MI 48226, (313) 556-5000.

panded its line to include a wide variety of six- and eight-cylinder passenger cars. From that point on, Pontiac continued to respond to its customers, offering such highlights as the "silver streak" of chrome that could distinguish a Pontiac model from blocks away; a luxury-sized convertible sedan (now one of the most desirable Pontiac collectors items, according to Bonsall); and, in 1937, its first station wagon. America's involvement in World War II saw Pontiac's main plant given over to the manufacture of war goods. Production of popular models like the Chieftain gave way to Pontiac-produced aircraft torpedoes, tank axles, and truck engine parts.

With Armistice in late 1945 came a new generation of potential customers. Returning soldiers were marrying and moving to the suburbs, sparking a commuting culture that demanded better, sportier, and more attractive cars. Even though supplies like steel and leather (for trim) were still in limited supply, Pontiac closed out the 1940s with the Streamliner sedan and wagon, the Torpedo sedan, and the big Chieftain De Luxe.

Postwar Advances

1950 was a notable year for Pontiac. It introduced the Catalina, a nameplate that would last for three decades. Conceived as a sporty coupe, the Catalina "had the open airy feeling of a convertible," according to Richard L. Busenkell in his book *Pontiac since 1945.* It was an impression reinforced, the author continues, "by several clever touches. A molding running around the roof edge above the glass areas resembled the reinforced edge of a convertible top. A small rectangular corner light was placed in this molding on each side of the car just above the rear seat, while transverse chrome trim strips across the headliner mimicked a convertible's crossbows." One variation on this model, the Super Deluxe Catalina, "was the most luxurious car in America for its price," notes Busenkell. "Top-grain genuine leather covered the seats, with cushions in rust and bolsters in ivory. The rust/ivory motif was carried out on the door panels, instrument panel, and even the steering wheel."

By 1951, the Korean War had left automakers short on supply. But war's end ushered in a new Pontiac model—bigger, more lavish, and more expensive than any Pontiac that had preceded it—the Star Chief. This car line made its 1954 debut as two models, the Deluxe and the Custom. All Star Chief models employed 8-cylinder power, though *Motor Trend* magazine, as quoted in Busenkell's book, noted that it was "not a car with lightning acceleration, it doesn't ride like an easy chair with sponge rubber wheels, and it won't corner like a Ferrari. But people don't buy Pontiacs for . . . those reasons."

Such notices were putting Pontiac in the compromising position of being considered sedate family transportation, when what the division wanted was a more performance-oriented image. Mid-1950s concept cars highlighted sleek little roadsters like the Club De Mer, reminiscent of the imports and—more importantly—rival Chevrolet's much-admired Corvette. The new accent on styling was complemented by an important new engine, the "Strato-Streak" V8, introduced in the 1955 Pontiac lineup.

This engine produced up to 270 horsepower; a more high-performance version reached 317. The Strato-Streak joined other Pontiac powerplants in redefining the division's image; as Busenkell points out, "the *least* powerful engine in 1957 had exactly one hundred *more* horsepower than its *most* powerful engine just three years before!"

Wide-Track Drives Pontiac

Just two years later, the Pontiac name would again become associated with performance: 1959 was the year Wide-Track was introduced. This new chassis design widened the front and rear axle width several inches. This greatly increased a Pontiac's "track," which contributed not only to handling but also to safety: "The glass area was increased enormously," reports Busenkell. "The new 'Vista-Pontiac' windshield alone was no less than 50 percent larger than the previous windshield."

Well-received by critics (*Motor Trend* voted Pontiac "Car of the Year" in 1959) and public alike, Wide-Track helped increase Pontiac market share while solidifying the division's performance image. The Wide-Track Pontiacs remain valuable collectors' items to this day; the city of Pontiac even renamed a major thoroughfare Wide Track Drive in recognition of a design idea that paid off handsomely.

From the chrome strip of the 1940s to the distinctive split grille (which was adopted by autodom's most famous failure—the Ford Edsel), Pontiac always strove to make its models distinctive. And among the more distinctive Pontiacs making its debut in the late 1950s was a nameplate called Bonneville. Sleek, long and V8-powered, Bonneville—touted as "another Pontiac first!" in its print ads, offered sophistication in the face of rising competition. The late 1950s and early 1960s also brought a host of other new names that would become Pontiac standards, like Tempest, LeMans, and Grand Prix.

The Sporty 1960s

Then, in 1964, Pontiac initiated a "sneak attack," as Bonsall writes in his book *Pontiac! They Built Excitement.* The division quietly introduced a sporty small car called the GTO. As Bonsall points out, the GTO was first offered as "an option on the LeMans. . . . [It] was not in the regular Tempest sales catalog; it appeared shortly after the new model announcement." However it was presented, the GTO offered sports car enthusiasts something to get excited about: "a muscular 389 [cubic inch displacement] Pontiac V8 developing 325 horsepower," as Bonsall describes. Celebrated in song—the pop hit "Little GTO" remains an oldies favorite today—the model remained in production until 1973. But a few years before that, in midyear 1967, another all-new Pontiac would assume the mantle of pure Pontiac performance.

Born of a need to compete with the new Ford Mustang (the first of the "pony cars"), Pontiac's Firebird (and its upgrade, Trans Am) quickly caught the eyes of sports car drivers with its aggressive posture and its "Ram Air" air-induction system. Revisions to its appearance led Bonsall to label the 1970 Firebird "undoubtedly among the most beautiful [car bodies] ever to grace America's highways." This sports car, he adds, "seemed to be a piece of rolling sculpture," so perfectly integrated were its components.

The 1970s heralded a new era for Pontiac, and not the least of the changes were directly attributable to the OPEC oil embargo of October 1973. While the product line had been refining its engines for some years to increase efficiency, the oil crisis had one immediate effect—Pontiac sales dropped to the point where the division finished in fifth place in 1974. The emphasis now was on high mileage and fuel economy; Pontiac responded with its smallest car to date, the subcompact Astre, introduced for 1975. Though tight in roominess, the car was still a Pontiac, with available Rally wheels and an optional "luxury" trim package.

By 1976—Pontiac's fiftieth anniversary—the division had another small car to tempt value-conscious drivers. The Sunbird (like its GM "twins" Chevy Monza, Oldsmobile Starfire, and Buick Skyhawk) had a sporty look and an enhanced ride feel over the Astre. One casualty of rising gas prices was the early "demise," as Busenkell puts it, of the Grand Am, then only three model years old. It would return.

Pontiac closed out the decade boasting of "the best year yet" in 1978. First of all, Grand Am was reintroduced to some success. Grand Prix, LeMans, and Firebird also made inroads in popularity. So how to top "the best year yet"? With "our best gets better," the theme for 1979. Among the models introduced that year was a tenth-anniversary Trans Am, resplendent in silver body paint and matching silver leather seats.

A Time for Renewal

The 1970s may have ended well—but the 1980s began on a sour note. Another hike in gas prices affected sales, and one of the victims was Catalina, which looked "incredibly plain" next to the flashy Bonneville, as Bonsall writes. Once Pontiac's best seller, Catalina withered to the point where by 1981 "killing [the model] fell more properly into the category of euthanasia than murder," says Bonsall. "The Bonneville was another story; it was still doing fairly well."

But "fairly well" wasn't good enough to cut it in the 1980s. Pontiac's image as a performance division began to come under scrutiny, while new Japanese imports provided stiff competition for the economy market. Pontiac management responded with intense market research, which resulted in a new "Image Statement" to reflect Pontiac's entire product line: "Pontiac is a car company known for innovative styling and engineering that results in products with outstanding performance and roadability."

In order to make good on that statement, each Pontiac was examined both as an individual car and as a member of the corporate family. "From that analysis," states Bonsall, "the 6000 STE was derived, because the division needed a car in the A-body segment that embodied the new image. The Firebird was due for a complete revision with the 1982 F-body, and that car was considered to be right on target. The Grand Prix was deemed to be close to the mark, but needing work. Everything else was, in [General Manager William E.] Hoglund's words, 'way out in left field.' "

By the 1983 product year, Pontiac's Image Statement had been boiled down to one catchy advertising phrase: "We Build Excitement." Bold words, but in a short time the division would live up to them. Pontiac now produced eight different models, three of them identified only by a number (6000, 2000, and 1000, which would be renamed Sunbird). A year later, one more new model would increase the number to nine. That model: Pontiac's first mid-engine production car, the Fiero.

Fiero's Rise and Fall

The concept for Fiero, after "kicking around Pontiac longer than most people realized," finally saw the light of day in 1984. It would become an object lesson in how marketing can only go so far in assuring a vehicle's success. For the two-seater Fiero, with its low, angular posture and aggressive-looking details, was positioned as something of the workingman's Ferrari. And, initially, the strategy worked: early Fiero sales were more than impressive, reaching more than 100 percent over Pontiac's predictions.

But in time drivers began suspecting that the Fiero's sports-car stance was making promises that the powerplant couldn't keep. A "low-revving, transverse-mounted four-cylinder engine was the only one offered," Bonsall points out, though by 1985 the car would receive a high-output V6. But continuous improvement may have come too late: *Car and Driver,* for one, decided that "the upshot is that the Fiero is not yet ready to take its place among the world's better road cars," as Busenkell's book quotes. (*Road & Track* and *Motor Trend* expressed more enthusiasm, though.) Sales dropped off from the model's big introductory year, and by 1988 the Fiero had left the lineup—one of the best-selling, if shortest-lived, nameplates in Pontiac history.

A New Design for Excitement

By the early 1990s Pontiac was ready for another change. Though the division's cars sold reliably, its better-known names were all several years old. So in 1992, on the heels of Grand Prix's 1989 makeover—which helped the car win the *Motor Trend* domestic Car of the Year award—Pontiac reintroduced Grand Am and Bonneville to great fanfare. Radically redesigned, the two cars now traded in their previous boxy look for a new, round, aerodynamic appearance. Reaction was immediate. Grand Am was now ready to challenge the big-selling Honda Accord with increased horsepower and a sporty look. Bonneville caught the attention of the burgeoning sport-luxury market.

General Motors' consistent top-selling division for years, Pontiac's fortunes rose and fell along with the rest of the American car market during the late 1980s. That era was characterized by a consumer belief that the European and Japanese imports brought greater value for the money. But a consumer turnaround was due by the early 1990s. Vast overall improvements in American workmanship began to turn the tide back toward domestic vehicles. Pontiac contributed to this new era by equipping standard anti-lock brakes in all its models (except Grand Prix, where it was an option) by 1993. Airbags also joined the Pontiac lineup; by 1994 driver or dual airbags were standard in every model except Sunbird. (But the division had bigger plans for Sunbird. The 14-year-old nameplate was slated to be dropped at the end of the 1994 model year, to be replaced by the all-new Sunfire, based in part on a concept car that had been ''wowing 'em'' on the auto-show circuit for the previous four years.)

Marketing and Advertising

Marketing and advertising have always played a big part in Pontiac's success. The division has stood by one advertising agency, D'Arcy Masius Benton & Bowles, for virtually its entire existence. From that ad shop came some well-remembered themes to remind consumers what Pontiac was all about. The early ''Chief of the Sixes'' was just one line that played off the legacy of Chief Pontiac (his image would adorn everything from print ads to hood ornaments). ''We Take the Fun of Driving Seriously'' and ''The Most Beautiful Things on Wheels'' appealed to different target groups. ''We Build Excitement,'' the slogan that heralded Pontiac's new beginning in the 1980s, evolved into ''We Are Driving Excitement.''

Pontiac has successfully employed celebrity spokespeople through the years, beginning with newscaster Lowell Thomas during the 1940s. ''After World War II, the agency used comedian Victor Borge off and on for a number of years, and even retained the Smothers Brothers at the height of their popularity in the 1960s,'' notes Bonsall. ''Golfer Jack Nicklaus [had] a long association with Pontiac . . . while rock singers Hall and Oates were used briefly to represent the Fiero when it first came out.''

Not every spokesperson was right for Pontiac. In particular, Bonsall points to one Natalie Carroll, ''The Firebird Girl,'' who graced giveaway calendars in 1983. That print piece, says Bonsall, ''was exciting in aspects not directly related to Pontiac cars.'' Pontiac management was distinctly unamused, and ordered its agency to concentrate its future creative efforts on the Pontiacs themselves.

In the field of marketing, Pontiac has targeted its youth market by sponsoring ''spring break'' events at Daytona. In late 1993 the division ventured into the realm of interactive marketing by sponsoring the ''TV Car Showroom'' on television's Home Shopping Club. (You couldn't actually buy a car over the air, but you could buy accessories and services related to Pontiac.) Product placement has also brought Pontiac into the public eye. As early as 1955, says Bonsall, the company gained ''celebrated television exposure . . . when the fabulously popular *I Love Lucy* show made extensive use of a Pontiac convertible during Lucy, Ricky, Fred, and Ethel's multiple-episode, cross-country trip to California.'' In later years the most well-known Pontiac ''actor'' was a shining black Trans Am that played the part of KITT, superintelligent crime-fighting vehicle, on the NBC series *Knight Rider.*

And of course, no study of Pontiac marketing would be complete without mention of the division's presence in motorsports. Famed drivers Richard Petty and Rusty Wallace were almost exclusively associated with Pontiac for years. Firebird s and Fiero s, specially modified for racing, have made the NASCAR and IMSA rounds, and other Pontiacs, including Bonneville, have served as pace cars.

Further Reading:

Bonsall, Thomas E., *Pontiac: The Complete History, 1926–1986,* Bookman Publishing, 1986.

Bonsall, *Pontiac: They Built Excitement!,* Stony Run Press, 1991.

Busenkell, Richard L., *Pontiac Since 1945,* Norton, 1989.

PORSCHE®

Porsche automobiles, based on the principle that form follows function, are known more for speed and handling than for aesthetic styling. Their trademark design is a low-slung, aerodynamic body and an air-cooled rear engine. While the company was named after Dr. Ferdinand A. Porsche, one of the world's most renowned automobile designers, the Porsche automobile was named after Porsche's son, Ferry, who introduced the brand in 1948.

Headquartered in Stuttgart, Germany, Porsche AG (full name: Dr. Ing h.c. F. Porsche Aktiengesellschaft) is one of the last independent sports-car makers and a legendary name in automobile road racing, with more than a dozen victories at Le Mans between 1970 and 1987. Its most popular production model is the Type 911, introduced in 1964. Although significantly redesigned over the years, the Porsche 911 was still being sold in the 1990s. The Porsche 911 Turbo, with a 1994 list price of $99,000, is the most expensive Porsche available in the United States. The Porsche 968 Coupe, at $40,000, is the least expensive. Porsche AG sold about 15,000 automobiles in 1993, about 4,000 of them in the United States.

Ferdinand Porsche

Ferdinand Anton Porsche was born in 1875 in Maffersdorf, Bohemia, then part of Austria-Hungary. He was the son of a tinsmith, but he preferred tinkering with electric motors to pursuing his father's craft. As a teenager, he installed a generator in his family's house, making it the first home in Maffersdorf to have electric lights. When he was 18, Porsche went to work for a Vienna company that manufactured electrical equipment. He also took classes at the technical college in Vienna but never formally enrolled.

In 1898 Porsche was hired as a designer by Jacob Lohner & Co, carriage maker to the royal Austrian House of Habsburg, which had begun building automobiles two years earlier. In 1900 the company displayed an "Electric Chaise"—with an innovative drive system identified as "Lohner-Porsche"—at the World Exhibition in Paris. Porsche's design placed electric motors in the hubs of the wheels, improving power transfer and eliminating the need for a transmission.

Porsche left Lohner in 1905 to become technical director for Austro-Daimler, then the largest automobile maker in Austria. Austro-Daimler was licensed to build cars designed by Daimler Motoren A.G. in Stuttgart, Germany. At Austro-Daimler Porsche designed the Maja, a passenger car named for the daughter of a wealthy Austrian, Emil Jellinek. The Maja was a commercial failure. The German Daimler company, however, designed a car named for Jellinek's other daughter, Mercedes, which did become popular. Porsche also designed an airplane engine that Austro-Daimler put into production in 1910, even though there were no airplanes in Austria at the time.

During World War I Porsche designed vehicles for the Austrian military, including a motorized gun carriage for light artillery known as the "Daimler horse." The gun carriage had iron wheels with adjustable steel claws, controlled by the driver, that allowed it to travel through deep mud or snow. In 1916 Porsche received the Officer's Cross from Austrian Emperor Francis Joseph, as well as an honorary doctorate from the technical college in Vienna.

After the war Bohemia became part of Czechoslovakia, and Porsche reluctantly accepted Czech citizenship, which allowed him to retain ownership of the family home and gave him greater freedom to travel. He also continued to work for Austro-Daimler. He advocated building sports cars as the best way to revitalize the company in the postwar economy, and in 1922 he designed the Sascha, which won its class at the Sicilian Targa Florio. The Austro-Daimler board of directors, however, was determined to build luxury automobiles, and Porsche left the company in 1923.

Porsche went to work for Daimler in Germany, where racing was held in higher regard. He was given responsibility for developing a new Mercedes, and in 1924 the Porsche-designed Mercedes SSK won the Targa Florio. The victory earned Porsche his second honorary doctorate, this time from the technical college in Stuttgart.

Porsche spent nearly six years at Daimler and produced more than 60 designs, but a merger in 1926 with the Benz company greatly reduced his influence. Never one to compromise, the 51-year-old Porsche left in 1929 to become chief engineer for the Steyr Motor Works in Austria. Steyr, formed from a dismantled armaments company after World War I, had surpassed Austro-Daimler as Austria's largest car maker by building small cars, an irony that Porsche appreciated. His return to Austria was hailed by the local press: "To know that an engineering genius like Dr. Porsche is back in Austria fills the Austrian motoring public with

AT A GLANCE

Porsche brand of automobile introduced in 1948 by Ferry Porsche, son of Dr. Ferdinand A. Porsche, founder of what would become Dr. Ing h.c. F. Porsche Aktiengesellschaft of Stuttgart, Germany; a legendary name in automobile racing, Porsche won numerous victories at Le Mans between 1979 and 1987; the brand's best-selling production car, introduced in 1964, was the 911.

Performance: *Sales*—$1.6 billion (DM 2.275 billion).

Major competitor: Mazda; also, Nissan (sports car models).

Advertising: *Agency (U.S.)*—Goodby, Berlin and Silverstein, San Francisco, CA.

Addresses: *Parent company*—Porsche AG (Dr. Ing h.c. F. Porsche Aktiengesellschaft), Porschestrasse 42, Stuttgart, Germany; phone: 07-11-827-0. *American subsidiary*—Porsche Cars North America, Inc., 100 West Liberty St., Reno, Nevada 89501; phone: (702) 348-3000; fax: (702) 348-3770.

pride and it was a great deed of the Steyr works to ensure his collaboration.''

Porsche's first design for Steyr was a cabriolet called the Austria, which created a sensation at the Paris automobile show in 1929. A trade paper reported: ''The Austrian automobile industry has successfully and indisputably provided the show with one of the most modern models.'' Porsche's triumph was short-lived, however. Steyr and Austro-Daimler merged in 1930, with management from Austro-Daimler in control. In 1931 Porsche returned to Stuttgart, where he opened his own design firm under the name Dr. ing. h.c. Ferdinand Porsche GmbH., Konstruktionsburo fur Motoren- und Fahrzeugbau. He brought with him nine Austrians—including his son, Ferdinand A. (''Ferry '') Porsche II—to form his design team.

Volkswagen Heritage

Porsche long dreamed of building a small, low-priced vehicle for the average worker, just as Henry Ford had done in the United States. In the early 1930s Porsche was hired by the motorcycle-maker Zundapp Works in Nuremberg to design such a ''Volksauto,'' or ''people's car.'' Only three prototypes were built before the project was abandoned, and Zundapp returned to building motorcycles. The design, however, was resurrected for the Volkswagen (also meaning ''people's car'') that Porsche ostensibly created for the Society of German Automobile Manufacturers, though the project was actually initiated and directed by German chancellor Adolf Hitler, who wanted a low-cost car for the German masses. The first three Volkswagens (later called the Beetle in the United States) were built at Porsche's Stuttgart villa in 1936. In 1937 Daimler-Benz built 30 Volkswagen prototypes, which were test-driven by the German SS to maintain secrecy. Hitler appointed Porsche as a director of the government's new car company, Volkswagenwerk Gmbh, and awarded him the title of professor.

During World War II Porsche designed tanks for the German army. Ironically, the tanks were the first vehicles to carry the Porsche name. Porsche also designed a ''people's tractor,'' another of Hitler's pet projects. When the war ended, Porsche, his son Ferry, and his son-in-law Anton Piech were arrested and questioned about their activities. They were held for several months at an American interrogation center before being released in November 1945. Porsche was then invited to France to discuss the possibility of establishing a Volkswagen factory there. A month into the negotiations, however, he was again arrested and accused of war crimes. The elderly Porsche spent 18 months in prison and was forced to help design the Renault 4CV before he was able to raise one million francs the French were demanding for his release.

When Porsche was released in 1947, he was in poor health. He died in January 1952 after suffering a stroke. At his funeral the West German minister of transport delivered the eulogy: ''We are not only standing at the bier of a great designer, but we are burying with him the heroic epoch of the motor car.''

The Porsche Marque

Despite more than half a century as a design engineer, Ferdinand Porsche never created a car that carried his name. That was left to his son Ferry, who took over management of his father's business after World War II. The younger Porsche would later write: ''Throughout the war I never abandoned the idea of building our sports car, one bearing the Porsche name.'' He achieved that goal in 1948.

The first Porsche was built from spare Volkswagen parts, which were plentiful in postwar Germany. It was an open two-seater with an aluminum body pounded into shape over a wooden form. It was designated the Type 356. Porsche engineering designs were numbered consecutively, beginning with the Type 7 in 1931.

The car was shown for the first time in Geneva in 1949, and received generally good reviews. *Automobil-Revue* wrote: ''It will not be necessary in the future for enthusiastic owners of Volkswagens to tune their cars for extra performance, for the man really able to do this is seeing to it that a special vehicle will soon be available: it is Professor Porsche himself.'' The newspaper *Neue Zeitung* said: ''This is the dream car of old Ferdinand Porsche which now carries his name. All the knowledge of motor engineering that this fortunate man acquired during his life are epitomized in it. . . . The man who manages to unleash the power of this beautiful animal suddenly becomes imbued with a happy feeling whilst realizing that here a genius has brought about a new motoring conception and the vehicle itself has entered into a new era.'' Others, however, were less generous. Bernhard Blank, a Swiss businessman who helped bankroll Porsche, recalled years later: ''I didn't like to drive the bloody things, but they were interesting. And we could make some money.''

In 1950 Porsche calculated that the market for its Type 356 sports cars, which also included coupe and cabriolet models, was no more than 500 worldwide. According to Randy Leffingwell, author of *Porsche Legends,* an ''unmentioned class-consciousness'' also afflicted Porsche: ''It was hinted that if you weren't the offspring of at least a Duke, you needn't ask.'' Reportedly, Porsche even required potential owners to take a driving test because the original Type 356, with a top speed of about 85 m.p.h., was fitted with ordinary Volkswagen brakes. Like the Volkswagen, the engine was also mounted behind the rear axle; the car was considered the best-handling car of its era and therefore was a successful racing vehicle. When production of the Type 356 ended in 1965, more than 76,000 had been sold. The only significant change in styling had come in 1959, when a larger windshield was added and the headlights and bumpers were raised slightly.

The American Market

The United States was the world's largest market for sports cars and played an important role in Porsche's development. Max Hoffmann, an Austrian who operated a Mercedes-Benz dealership in New York, displayed the Porsche 356 in his Park Avenue showroom as early 1950. Hoffmann was the exclusive U.S. importer of Porsche automobiles for several years, and it was Hoffmann who persuaded Porsche to give its cars names as well as numbers. Although the European tradition was to assign a model number, Hoffmann knew that Americans were accustomed to catchy names. When the Porsche 550 was introduced at the Paris car show in 1953, Hoffmann suggested that Porsche name it the "Spyder." The term "spyder" was familiar to Americans as a body type. It was derived from the spindly wooden carriages built in England during the 1860s and had been applied to many open sports cars, including those built by Lancia, Fiat, and Alfa Romeo.

The Porsche 550 Spyder was an open two-seater with a wide collar that enclosed the headrests, giving the car a hunchbacked appearance. It was built so low to the ground that Hans Hermann was able to steer his Spyder beneath a railroad-crossing barrier during a road race in 1954, barely avoiding being hit by an oncoming train. Since his competition had to stop, Hermann easily won his class. A Spyder also won its class at Le Mans in 1955, and in 1956 a Spyder won the Targa Florio, the first overall victory for a Porsche in a major road race.

In 1954, Porsche introduced a car designed specifically for girl-watching in sunny Southern California. The idea came from John von Neumann, a Hollywood car dealer and Hoffmann's West Coast distributor. Von Neumann thought the Porsche 356 was overpriced. He urged Hoffmann to use his influence to convince Porsche to produce a low-cost model. "I pushed Maxie. He had nothing to lose," von Neumann recalled. "I said I wanted a roadster and I wanted it for less than $3,000." What he got was the Porsche Speedster.

The Speedster was based on the Type 356, but it was strictly bare bones. It was an open two-seater with a low-cut, removable windshield and side curtains instead of crank-up windows. "The first time I told [Porsche] about a car without roll-up windows they thought I was nuts," von Neumann said. "Who needs roll-up windows in California." The Speedsters also had a folding top that nearly obscured visibility when it was up and did little to keep out the rain, but von Neumann knew what his customers wanted. "They want to go down Sunset Boulevard with their elbow over the door [so] the girls can see them in the car . . . and they can see the girls on the walks. That I can sell."

The odd-looking Speedster was sometimes compared to a bath-tub with wheels, but von Neumann's "boulevard racer" became one of Porsche's most sought-after cars. It was so popular in the United States that it wasn't available in Europe for the first nine months. Nearly 5,000 were sold in four years. New models of the Speedster were introduced in 1989 and 1994.

Porsche 911 and 914

Porsche unveiled the successor to the Porsche 356 in Frankfurt in 1953. As a prototype, the car was known as the Type 901, but when production began in 1954, it was the Porsche 911. Ferry Porsche was responsible for the engineering, but his son, Ferdinand Alexander ("Butzi") Porsche, designed the body. The streamlined Porsche 911 became Porsche's most popular automobile ever. More than 350,000 Porsche 911s had been sold through 1993. Although there were periodic rumors that Porsche would replace the Type 911 with a new model, the company's 1994 lineup included four versions of the Porsche 911, ranging from the Type 911 Carrera 2 Coupe, with a list price in the United States of nearly $65,000, to the Type 911 Turbo, the company's most powerful production car, with a sticker price of $99,000. The Turbo was road-tested at 174 m.p.h.

Other Porsche 911 models included the Targa convertible, introduced in 1965, which came with a removable hardtop. In 1989 Porsche introduced the Type 911 Carrera 4, its first four-wheel-drive car. One popular feature of the Carrera 4 was a retractable spoiler. The spoiler, mounted just below the rear window, was triggered automatically when the car reached 50 m.p.h. and retracted into the bodywork when the car came to a stop. Racing versions of the Porsche 911—which included Types 935, 936, 956, and 962—dominated automobile endurance racing in the 1970s and 1980s.

In 1969 Porsche and Volkswagen collaborated on the VW-Porsche 914, a mid-engine, two-seat sports car that came with either a Volkswagen or more expensive Porsche engine. The body design was pure Porsche and extremely popular, but the association with Volkswagen hurt Porsche's elitist image. Porsche purchased Volkswagen's interest in the venture in 1973 and discontinued the Type 914 in 1976. More than 150,000 VW-Porsche 914s were sold. The Type 914 was replaced by the Type 924, the first front-engine car built by Porsche. The Porsche 924 began as a design for German car manufacturer Audi, which dropped the project.

Watches and Sunglasses

Since 1978 the Porsche name has also appeared on a variety of consumer products designed by Butzi Porsche. Butzi, who created the Type 911 body style, left Porsche AG in 1972 to form his own design firm in Zell-am-See, Austria. When he was unable to sell some of his more artistic designs to other manufacturers, he founded Porsche Design Produkte GmbH. in 1978 to turn his ideas into products. Hans Peter Porsche joined his brother as business manager.

Among the items to carry the Porsche name were a line of sunglasses with interchangeable lenses, men's titanium wristwatches, leather goods, and headphones that were put on display by the New York Museum of Modern Art. In 1984 Butzi Porsche told *Forbes,* "Every designer is at first happy to work on cars because they are very emotional products. But after a while cars are all the same."

Tarnished Image

The Porsche family withdrew from active management of the Porsche company in 1971 and turned the presidency over to Ernst Fuhrmann. Under Fuhrmann the company broke away from its traditional rear-engine designs to introduce the Type 924 (which began as a Volkswagen design and was built with Audi parts) and the Type 928, which had a top speed of 160 m.p.h.

Neither car, however, found favor with Porsche enthusiasts, and Ferry Porsche was so displeased that he later told *Fortune,* "When I ran the company I did not hesitate to continue using my father's 'signature' in our designs. But others seemed to feel the need to express themselves differently." The 1970s were also a bad time for high-performance "muscle" cars like the Porsche 928 because of the recurring energy crises. Sales plummeted, especially in the all-important U.S. market.

In 1980 Porsche AG replaced Fuhrmann with Peter W. Schultz, a German-born American who had never driven a Porsche. He told *Fortune,* "I was never able to afford one. And people I know who own a Porsche don't toss you the keys and say, 'Go take a spin.' " One of Schultz's first decisions was to scrap plans to race the Porsche 924 at Le Mans in 1981. Entering the Porsche 924 had been a marketing move. Porsche knew the car could never win but hoped that running at Le Mans would boost flagging sales. Schultz, however, wanted to win. Two Porsche Type 936s, which had won at Le Mans in 1976 and 1977, were taken from an in-house museum and outfitted with engines designed for the Indianapolis 500. One of the Type 936s had mechanical problems and finished 13th, but the other took the checkered flag. The victory was Porsche's sixth win at Le Mans. The company would go on to win seven straight at Le Mans; in 1983 Porsche took nine of the top ten places.

Schultz also decided against installing an Audi engine in the Porsche 944. Instead, the Porsche 944 was outfitted with a more powerful Porsche engine, which helped restore the company's cachet with sports-car enthusiasts. Schultz also revitalized the Porsche 911, which Fuhrmann had ignored, by introducing the Cabriolet convertible in 1983. Porsche sales in the United States doubled from about 11,000 cars in 1982 to nearly 22,000 in 1983—about half the company's total sales.

In 1984 Schultz announced "the single most important decision in the company's entire history." Since the late 1960s marketing in the United States had been handled by Volkswagen of America. Most Porsche dealers also sold Volkswagens and Audis, but Schultz decided not to renew the contract with Volkswagen and established a marketing and customer-service organization—Porsche Cars North America, Inc. The move was controversial from the start and nearly turned disastrous when Porsche dealers objected to proposed changes in the way they would be compensated. Millions of dollars in lawsuits were filed before Schultz backed down on the compensation plan.

By 1986 Porsche sales in the United States had increased to more than 30,000 cars—about 60 percent of the company's total. Unfortunately for Schultz, success in the American market eventually proved to be his downfall. Porsche became overly dependent on the U.S. market. When the U.S. economy faltered in the late 1980s, sales plummeted by more than half. The slump was exacerbated by a strong deutsche mark, which devalued U.S. sales.

Schultz attempted to stimulate sales with an entry-level car, the Porsche 924S, priced less than $20,000. Introduced in 1987, the 924S was a commercial failure. Like the original Porsche 924, the Type 924S was underpowered for a Porsche. Sporty cars from mass marketers like Honda and Mazda cost about as much as the Porsche 924S—and were faster.

Brand Outlook

Schultz resigned in late 1987 and was replaced by former chief financial officer Heinz Branitzki, the first nonengineer to head Porsche AG. Branitzki concentrated on rebuilding Porsche's exclusive image by limiting production. He also eliminated the Porsche 924. In 1989 the lowest priced Porsche cost $40,000, double what the Porsche 924 had cost. Sales manager Hans Halbach told *Business Week,* "The entry-level Porsche is now a used car."

Porsche, however, continued to stumble, and Branitzki stepped down in 1990. He was replaced by Arno Bohn. Porsche AG reported losses of DM 65 million for fiscal year 1991-92 on sales of 23,000 automobiles, and losses were expected to exceed DM 250 million in fiscal year 1992-93 on sales of about 17,000 automobiles. Bohn himself was replaced in late 1992 by Wendelin Wiedeking, a member of the Porsche AG board of directors.

While Porsche sold more car in the 1980s than in any other decade (1986 being a banner year), many analysts believed that Porsche AG lost touch with the sports-car market and needed to introduce new luxury models to restore its tarnished image; however, the Porsche 968, introduced in 1992, was another low-end model. New luxury models were reportedly in development for introduction in 1995 or 1996. There was also speculation that Porsche AG would be acquired by a mass-market automobile maker. The Porsche family controlled about 75 percent of the company stock in 1993.

Further Reading:

Blau, John R., "Will the New 968 Solve Porsche's Problems?" *Machine Design,* July 23, 1992, p. 12.

Brady, Rosemary, "What's in a name?" *Forbes,* September 24, 1984, p. 228.

Dornberg, John, "F.A. Porsche: From Wheels to Watches," *ARTnews,* November 1990, p. 89.

Hamilton, Joan O'C., "Race-Car Thrills That the Public Can Buy," *Business Week,* July 22, 1985, p. 103.

Kurylko, Diana T., "Porsche AG Replaces Arno Bohn," *Automotive News,* September 28, 1992, p. 1.

Leffingwell, Randy, *Porsche Legends: Inside History of the Epic Cars,* Oscelola, Wisconsin: Motorbooks International Publishers & Wholesalers, 1993.

Morais, Richard, "What Price Excellence?" *Forbes,* November 17, 1986, p. 234.

"My Other Car Is A . . . ," *The Economist,* February 10, 1990, p. 64.

"Porsche's Detour," *Fortune,* October 24, 1988, p. 8.

"Porsche Gets Set to Go It Alone in the U.S.," *Business Week,* February 27, 1984, p. 46.

"The Racers Edge," *Forbes,* March 9, 1987, p. 8.

Schares, Gail, "Jaguar and Porsche Try to Pull out of the Slow Lane," *Business Week,* December 12, 1988, p. 84.

Taylor, Rich, *Modern Classics: The Great Cars of the Postwar Era,* New York: Charles Scribner's Sons, 1978.

Tinnin, David B., "The American at the Wheel of Porsche," *Fortune,* April 5, 1982, p. 78.

Tinnin, David B., "Porsche's Civil War with Its Dealers," *Fortune,* April 16, 1984, p. 63.

Trachtenberg, Jeffrey, "False Start," *Forbes,* July 1, 1985, p. 120.

Tracy, Eleanor Johnson, "Porsche Is Doing Great—So Changes Course," *Fortune,* March 5, 1984, p. 59.

Von Frankenberg, Richard, *Porsche—the Man and His Cars* (translated by Charles Meisl), Cambridge, Massachusetts: Robert Bentley, 1969.

Von Frankenberg, Richard, with Michael Cotton, *Porsche: Double World Champions 1900–1977,* Somerset, England: The Haynes Publishing Group, 1977.

Vorderman, Don, "Porsche: New Model, New Glory," *Town & Country,* May 1989, p. 176.

—Dean Boyer

PRESTO®

PRESTO®

From its roots as a brand of pressure canners for food storage, the Presto name has come to represent innovation in the field of small electric appliances. The brand has many firsts to its credit: the first electric frying pan, the first steam iron that could use tap water, and the first stainless steel coffee percolator all carried the magical-sounding Presto name.

Brand Origins

The National Pressure Cooker Company's commercial and household canners were offered under the "National" trade name from 1905 to 1939, when the "Presto" brand was introduced. The new trademark captured the speed and convenience of National Pressure Cooker's new saucepan-type pressure cooker, which cooked food 66 percent faster than conventional methods. One observer called the product "the microwave of the 1930s." The Presto pressure cooker also preserved the vitamin and mineral content of foods, a growing concern of American housewives of the 1930s. Within just two years of its introduction, the Presto cooker ranked among the top-selling houseware items in leading stores throughout the country.

Presto household canners enjoyed continued success throughout World War II, as "Victory Gardens" and their companion canning programs proliferated across the United States. Presto pressure cookers would continue to be important products for the brand, which commanded 70 percent of that market through at least 1970. By that time, Presto's only major competitor in this field was Mirro Aluminum Co.

Product Innovations

In the late 1940s, Presto executives realized that freezing was a more convenient method of food storage, and, as more households acquired refrigerators and freezers, would probably supplant canning. They began to look for brand extensions that could use the same basic sales and distribution channels already in place.

Presto moved into the field of small electric appliances with the introduction of a vapor steam iron in 1949. The popular product promised economy and convenience because it used tap water rather than more expensive, store-bought distilled water. The success of Presto's first foray outside cooking and canning convinced the brand's parent to invest more heavily in research and development. It also convinced National to identify itself more closely with its increasingly popular brand, and the company changed its name to National Presto Industries, Inc., in 1953.

During the 1950s, the company's research and development produced several new variations on popular products, including a light-weight, stamped pressure cooker and a new line made of stainless steel pressure cookers. After 1956, Presto's "family" of electric skillets, cookers, and griddles featured a revolutionary "Control Master" heat control that was interchangeable among all the products in the group. This removable electric cord permitted submersion of the disconnected appliances for washing. The feature soon became an industry standard. In 1958, Presto brought out the portable electric appliance industry's first automatic, submersible stainless steel coffee maker. Unlike its "wipe clean" predecessors, Presto's electric percolator featured a fixed brewing temperature and an open spout with no turned edges or crevices to trap bitter coffee oils.

As Presto expanded its line of small household appliances in the 1960s, its innovative products garnered several "Design in Housewares" awards from the National Housewares Manufacturing Association. The brand's automatic can-opener/knife sharpener, cordless electric toothbrush, portable mixer, and loud-ring timer all won awards for their design. Presto brought out its first humidifier in 1963, and led that market by 1970.

Sales of the Presto line of small appliances grew from about $3 million in the late 1940s to $24 million in 1967, to $35 million in 1969. During the late 1960s, the brand's advertising budget ran at about $1 million annually. Most of the ads appeared in women's magazines and featured the theme, "There's more cooking at Presto than pressure cookers." Presto also benefited from cooperative advertising that often offered the branded appliances as premiums.

Niche Products

The small appliances released in the 1960s were mundane in comparison to the ongoing series of "mini-appliances" that Presto pioneered in the 1970s. Early in that decade, Presto launched a cavalcade of convenience appliances (which *Barron's* once dubbed "gizmos") that made many common household tasks more simple, healthy, or even fun. Presto executives, including President Melvin Cohen, recognized the demographic shift toward one- and two-person households, as well as the nation's

AT A GLANCE

Presto brand of small appliances founded by National Pressure Cooker Co. of Eau Claire, Wisconsin; brand name originally National, changed to Presto in 1939; Northwest Steel & Iron Works established in 1905; name changed to National Pressure Cooker Co. in mid-1930s, then to National Presto Industries, Inc. in 1953.

Major competitor: Hamilton Beach; also Black & Decker, Dazey, and West Bend.

Advertising: *Major campaign*—"Salad Shooter helps you everyday."

Addresses: *Parent Company*—National Presto Industries, Inc., 3925 North Hastings Way, Eau Claire, WI 54703; phone: (715) 839-2121; fax: (715) 839-2122.

changing eating habits, which increasingly focused on convenience foods. By the end of the decade, over half of all American households consisted of only one or two people. Unlike many competitors who continued to design appliances for traditional 6-member families, Presto made one- and two-serving models.

Innovation became a cornerstone of the brand's strategy. Instead of concentrating its marketing efforts on commodity appliances like toasters, steam irons, and coffee makers, the brand introduced a succession of niche products that commanded higher profit margins. These relatively low-priced countertop appliances were popular Christmas gift items, so advertising and sales were often concentrated in the fourth quarter. In fact, the fourth quarter usually accounted for two-thirds of annual retail appliance sales.

The PrestoBurger hamburger cooker, introduced in 1974, was promoted with the tag line, "A serving or two in a jiffy or two." It featured a Teflon interior in which the consumer could broil a rare burger in one minute or a well-done patty in three minutes. The appliance won a Pioneer Award from *Appliance Manufacturer* magazine and exploited the seemingly boundless popularity of hamburgers. Over 8.5 million Presto Burger machines were sold in 1976 alone, which helped drive Presto's appliance sales to $98.2 million that year, a 73 percent increase over 1975.

Other fast-food-at-home appliances followed in rapid, logical succession. The FryBaby electric deep fryer was brought to market in 1976. It maintained two cups of oil at an ideal deep-frying temperature to make two servings of food (most likely French fries), and its snap-on lid allowed storage of the oil in the unit. Presto couldn't manufacture them fast enough to keep up with demand. The popularity of the FryBaby led to the introduction of the FryDaddy, a family-size deep fryer, in 1977 and the GranPappy the following year. A *Barron's* analyst called the parade of deep fryers "a curious inversion of the natural order of things." Unlike some of Presto's other products, the FryBaby line endured a competitive assault and joined the brand's class of slow but reliable sellers.

Presto's appliances were popular among the brand's competitors as well as its customers. Rivals came out with imitations, and sometimes outright copies, of Presto's top-selling products. The brand hoped to stay ahead of its competition by blanketing the market with new product introductions, reasoning that it could reap high profit margins until competitors flooded the market with low-priced imitations that eroded earnings. Presto also supported its products with one of the small appliance industry's largest advertising budgets. From 1975 to 1976 the media outlay doubled, to $14 million, and increased another 50 percent, to $20 million, in 1977.

Presto launched 18 new appliances in 1978 alone, including a mini-oven that baked mini-loaves of bread, a small skillet, and the PopCornNow hot air corn popper. PopCornNow popper used hot air, rather than hot oil, "to 'explode' kernels into crisp, plump puffs of popcorn," as Presto literature explained. It became one of that year's few enduring products, as problems with the brand's "shotgun" strategy grew evident. As Presto hurried to bring new products to market before its rivals could discover and exploit them, test marketing was eliminated, making introductions even more of a hit-or-miss proposition than they had been in the past.

A New Strategy

By the last half of the 1980s, Presto had devised a system of introducing a maximum of two new products and three new versions of existing products each year. Rather than race its competitors to market, Presto began to vigorously protect the patents on its products. In 1993, National Presto chairman Melvin Cohen boasted that the company had won every patent infringement case it had ever initiated. Hamilton Beach, for example, was compelled to withdraw from the slicer/shredder market, destroy its inventory, and pay Presto damages. A case against Dazey forced the rival appliance maker to stop selling its deep fryers, which closely resembled Presto's FryBaby line. Black & Decker appealed a 1993 court order to pay Presto $2.3 million in damages. A case pending in June of that year charged West Bend with infringement of Tater Twister patents.

In 1986, Presto brought out the HotTopper, an electric melter/dispenser, with the biggest marketing campaign in the brand's history. The device melted and sprayed butter, maple syrup, barbecue sauce, or any other such topping. Despite its strong support and the introduction of a microwave version in 1988, the HotTopper was discontinued in the early 1990s.

One of Presto's best-performing products of the late 1980s and early 1990s was the Salad Shooter, a hand-held, electric vegetable slicer. Promotional material emphasized the Salad Shooter's ease of use: "Takes the work and mess out of salad making. One ingredient after another shoots right into your salad. There are no extra bowls to clean." Even the gadget itself was easy to clean. The base, with the motor inside, wiped clean, and the parts that actually sliced food were all dishwasher safe. A larger-sized Professional Salad Shooter was subsequently brought out.

Presto's TaterTwister was introduced in 1991. The appliance cut curly potatoes and other vegetables, and enjoyed phenomenal success during the year's fourth quarter. But sales dropped 30 percent in 1992 due to closeouts. No "blockbuster" products were brought out in 1992. The ChipShot electric potato chip maker, introduced in mid-1993, cut thin slices of potato to be deep-fat fried, like conventional potato chips, or microwaved for a low-fat snack. The ChipShot's homemade chips cost one-third as much as commercial chips.

Marketing

Presto's products are distributed through such mass marketers as K Mart, Wal-Mart, and Target. The brand enjoyed a mutually beneficial relationship with these nationwide retailers. However, as the mass marketers consolidated in the 1980s, their buying power and clout grew. The major chains used their buying power to squeeze price concessions out of Presto. In the late 1980s, K Mart and Wal-Mart purchased an average of 27 percent of Presto's total sales. By 1988, these mass retailers had gathered so much marketing clout that Cohen told *Barron's* that "if K Mart and Wal-mart don't take [a Presto appliance], then that's the end of a product." In the early 1990s, Presto's reliance on these giant retailers grew further—by 1993, they accounted for 44 percent of the brand's total annual sales.

Presto was able to maintain its profit margins by backing its newest products with millions of advertising dollars. From 1990 to 1993, the brand's advertising budget averaged about 15 percent of annual sales, whereas many competitors only spent 5 percent to 7 percent. Presto estimated that its ads, most of which aired during the fourth quarter holiday season on network and cable television, reached 98 percent of U.S. households. Because the mass marketers were assured of support, they were eager to carry Presto products.

Performance Appraisal

The Presto brand has been sustained over the decades by sales of its more mundane items. Pressure cookers, frying pans, griddles, deep fryers, and electric cookers accounted for about 42 percent of the company's sales in the late 1980s, and electric kitchen gadgets only brought in approximately 19 percent. The novelty appliances often generated high sales and profits over the short term, but frequently their popularity was short-lived. Presto's most recent focus on careful product releases, strong advertising support, and stringent patent enforcement seemed to result in hardier and longer-lived products.

After surviving over five years of competition, the Salad Shooter appeared to have joined Presto's stable of innovative yet enduring products. However, in 1993, the ChipShot's staying power remained to be seen. The appliance's limited purpose seemed to doom it to the ranks of the PrestoBurger and TaterTwister.

Further Reading:

Brammer, Rhonda, "Gizmo King: And National Presto Is a Veritable Bank, to Boot," *Barron's,* May 10, 1993, p. 14.

Brunelli, Richard, "National Presto Shifts Its Remaining Media Business to SFM from Bozell," *Mediaweek,* March 15, 1993, p. 9.

National Presto Industries, Inc., "Company History," Eau Claire, Wisconsin: National Presto Industries, Inc., 1992.

"National Presto Is Prospering by Thinking Small in Appliances," *Barron's,* August 22, 1977, pp. 30–31.

"Presto Changeo!," *Financial World,* April 15, 1980, pp. 50–51.

"Presto Chango," *Sales Management,* February 1, 1970, pp. 25–27.

Ratliff, Duke, "Bread Machines Boost Sales of Electric Knives," *HFD,* May 3, 1993, p. 121.

Rublin, Lauren R., "Pot Full of Cash," *Barron's,* October 24, 1988, p. 38.

"Tom Swift and His Electric Hamburger Cooker," *Forbes,* October 15, 1977, p. 112.

"What Took the Steam Out of National Presto," *Business Week,* April 3, 1978, pp. 29–30.

—April S. Dougal

PRICE PFISTER®

The Price Pfister brand has existed for the past 84 years, but only recently has its advertising let you know it's the "Pfabulous Pfaucet with the Pfunny Name." Now a Black & Decker product, Price Pfister Faucets are enjoying widespread popularity as a high-tech designer faucet brand.

Brand Origins

Emil Price and William Pfister founded Price Pfister, Inc. in Los Angeles in 1910 originally as a manufacturer of gasoline-powered electrical generators for farmers. By 1912, they diversified and began manufacturing faucets and garden hose valves, and, later, brass plumbing fixtures and fittings for indoor sinks, bathtubs as well as the U.S. military for use during World War I. In 1941, the company was sold to Isadore Familian. The firm contracted with the U.S. government during World War II to manufacture specialty valves and fittings for the military.

Price Pfister constructed its own brass foundry in Pacoima, California in the 1950s. The plant included die casting machinery, stampers, injection molders, automatic screw machines, a machine shop and finishing departments to meet postwar housing boom demands. It was at this time that Price Pfister began specializing in home faucets and fixtures.

Price Pfister operated in virtual anonymity until 1969 when it was purchased by Norris Industries, Inc. of Long Beach, Calif., also a manufacturer of plumbing fixtures, locks, appliances and hardware for individual and industrial use. After a leveraged buyout in 1981, Norris Industries went private and became NI Industries. Price Pfister faucets became a part of Norris' Plumbing Products Group. It was around this time that Price Pfister President Peter Gold, who had started as a salesman in 1956 and was then the senior vice president of the Plumbing and Products Group, offered to buy Price Pfister in another leveraged buyout because he sensed that Norris was about to sell it off for cash to bid on another acquisition.

"I suspected it would be Price Pfister and my suspicions were confirmed," Gold told Peggy Blizzard in *Southern California Business.* "I offered to buy and, of course, their question was, where was I going to get $35 million?" Gold said. "If other people can do a leveraged buyout, why can't I?" Gold succeeded even though the nation was in the midst of a recession and he had to put up $4 million in a cash payment. He joined two other investors to acquire Price Pfister in 1983 and immediately set out to change the company and reposition its faucet brand line for a broader consumer appeal.

In 1988, Price Pfister was sold once more, this time at a price of $215 million to Hartford-based Emhart Corp., a maker of industrial, consumer, and electronic goods. Price Pfister sales seemed to benefit from the move—the firm's 1987 sales of $117 million represented a 100 percent increase in just four years. But in 1989, Black & Decker purchased Emhart and its Price Pfister, Kwikset locks, and True Temper lawn and garden tools brands, for $2.8 billion—nearly doubling in size with the acquisition.

Early Marketing Strategy

The man most responsible for making the Price Pfister a household name—it is the third-leading faucet manufacturer—has been President and CEO Peter S. Gold, who repositioned the line in 1983. Gold aggressively marketed the brand in an effort to create a niche for Price Pfister in a market not widely known for capturing the imaginations of consumers. Price Pfister faucets were known to the construction and plumbing industry, but not the general public. Gold appealed to upscale users and do-it-yourselfers, while staying loyal to the brand's plumbing and contracting market. As the American market was being dominated by expensive, European, decorator fixtures, Gold felt that Price Pfister could match European quality at lower prices—and with 20-year warranties. Gold was instrumental in launching Price Pfister's "Society Finishes" line of European crystal, hardwood, porcelain, polished brass, black nickel and antiquated bronze plumbing fittings.

"We found that we could manufacture and sell decorator faucets at affordable prices, produce them in volume and supply the market on a good basis," Gold told *Industry Week* in 1988. "Consumer acceptance of our 'Society Finishes' line of decorator faucets and fixtures has increased steadily since we introduced these products, which now account for approximately 40 percent of all products sold.

To further distinguish Price Pfister faucets from competing makes, the company developed faucets with signage and hang tags that pointed out specific features like the brand's solid brass construction and genuine crystal handles. And, in addition to company guarantees that ranged from one to 20 years, Price Pfister

AT A GLANCE

Originally founded as Price Pfister, Inc. by Emil Price and William Pfister in Los Angeles, CA, in 1910 as a manufacturer of gasoline-powered electrical generators for farmers; Price Pfister began making faucets, garden hose valves, and brass plumbing fixtures in 1912; Price Pfister, Inc. sold to Isadore Familian in 1941; purchased by Norris Industries of Long Beach, Calif., 1969; firm goes private in a leveraged buyout changing its name to NI Industries in 1981; purchased in a management leveraged buyout headed by President and CEO Peter Gold, 1983; Price Pfister goes public, 1988; Emhart Corporation purchases Price Pfister in 1988 for $215 million; Black & Decker purchases Emhart Corporation and Price Pfister faucets for $2.8 billion in 1989.

Performance: *Market share*—14% in the U.S. faucet market in 1988. *Sales*—$173 million in all plumbing products in 1993.

Major competitor: Delta; also, Peerless, Moen, Hans Groehe, American Standard, Kohler, Chicago Faucets.

Advertising: *Agency*—Eisaman, Johns and Laws, Los Angeles, CA, 1984. *Major campaign*—"The Pfabulous Pfaucet with the Pfunny Name."

Addresses: *Parent company*—Price Pfister, Inc., 13500 Paxton St., Pacoima, CA, 91331; phone: (818) 896-1141; fax: (818) 897-0097. *Ultimate parent company*—Black & Decker Corp., 701 East Joppa Rd., Towson, MD, phone: (301) 583-3900.

also offered consumers decorating tips by providing a toll-free number, brochures, and faucet-care packets at wholesale showrooms, home improvement centers and hardware stores.

Advertising Innovations

Gold also devised the strategy that would get Price Pfister's name known to the public, with the help of the Los Angeles advertising firm Eisaman, Johns & Laws. In 1985, Price Pfister Faucets were advertised in 30-second television spots as "The Pfabulous Pfaucet with the Pfunny Name," in Atlanta and Phoenix test markets. Customers soon were bombarding hardware and plumbing supply stores with requests for that "pfunny pfaucet." Test commercials were expanded the next year and appeared in Dallas, Miami, Tampa, Orlando, and Seattle. In 1987, Price Pfister conducted a virtual advertising blitz on television with commercials on the "Tonight Show," "Good Morning America," "The Today Show," "NBC Nightly News," "Nightline," "The CBS Evening News," and ESPN on cable. Price Pfister officials in 1988 said their after-market accounted for 60 percent of total sales as a result of this successful advertising campaign. Said Gold in *Industry Week:* "The ads have helped tremendously. You can't sell anything if people don't know it's for sale." Despite its purchase by Black & Decker, Price Pfister has wisely been allowed to exploit this classic advertising advantage under its new parent company. In 1994, the brand is still being promoted as the "Pfabulous Pfaucet."

Brand Development

Since 1983, the Price Pfister faucet brand has been developed as a "high fashion" faucet of European quality for the kitchen and bathroom, with an array of decorative levers, towel bars and rings, and matching overflow plates. Price Pfister claims their line of faucet products, available in the United States and Canada, are affordable and competitive with other market leaders, such as Delta, Kohler, American Standard, and Chicago Faucet.

In 1993, Price Pfister also claimed to have developed new ceramic disc valve technology that is the first significant advancement in the faucet category in 40 years. The company claims that ceramic disc valves make its single control faucet the first "truly washerless faucet," even though competitor Delta Faucets (Masco Corp.) claims to have developed the first washerless faucets. Ceramic disc valves are believed to prevent mineral deposits and corrosion that cause other faucets to break down. Price Pfister's new line (guaranteed under a company warranty) ensures quality for at least 80 years. Most other types of faucets use rubber parts that wear out and must be replaced in less than 10 years. The single control faucets feature spray nozzle attachments with 100 percent spray diversion to prevent dribbles. This brand extension is easier for small children to operate and also features a tub/shower attachment that regulates water to prevent scalding. Single control faucets range in price from $75 to $150 in polished chrome, polished brass, white and antique bronze finishes.

Malfunctions

Price Pfister has had to survive a spate of bad publicity and missteps while becoming a more competitive brand in the 1980s and early 1990s. Problems with packaging at one time led to 30 percent of Price Pfister faucets arriving on the job as damaged goods. The culprit was poor cushioning materials that scratched fixture surfaces. Also, boxes were taped shut, preventing easy inspection by contractors and plumbers who bought the faucets directly from the warehouse. Price Pfister resolved the problem by using film laminate sheeting of differing sizes and formations made by Microfoam. Boxes were redesigned to enable all faucet contents to be contained and easily retrieved.

But as the resolution of this problem was saving face for Price Pfister among those in the building trade, another crisis, this one potentially much larger, loomed to threaten the company's credibility and even its livelihood. In early 1993 lab tests found that Price Pfister faucets leaked too much lead into drinking water, leading the California Attorney General to sue the company and 20 other faucet manufacturers whose faucets had also failed the test. Industry experts told the *Los Angeles Times* that overhauling their manufacturing processes to comply with California health standards would cost Price Pfister "tens of millions of dollars." "This could put the plant out of business," said Manuel Barboso, business agent of the Teamster local for Price Pfister, which manufactures in Pacoima, California, near Los Angeles.

According to the suit, Price Pfister faucets leaked the second highest amount of lead (only Chicago Faucets products leaked more) into drinking water—150 times above the limit set by California's Proposition 65 law that bans the discharge of toxic substances in drinking water. The implications were dire for Price Pfister—lead accumulates in the body over time and can cause, among other things, impaired development in children as well as brain damage. But Price Pfister officials doubted the test's findings, claiming their faucets met current federal standards for lead content and that they considered their faucets "very safe." Price Pfister later challenged the lab survey because it only tested one kitchen faucet from each manufacturer and because tests used new faucets, which were likely to leak more lead.

The Plumbing Manufacturers Institute also challenged the state's rulings, calling California's lead law too stringent. Although the Environmental Protection Agency requires that plumbing manufacturers use no more than 8 percent lead in their faucets, there is no federal standard for the amount of lead from faucets that can be leaked into drinking water.

Price Pfister and Chicago Faucet use what some analysts considered an old fashioned sand casting method that requires twice as much lead to make a faucet than modern mold and machining techniques. The extent of the fallout from negative publicity has yet to be determined. Although the *Los Angeles Times* noted that a local plumbing supply store noticed a shift to brands with less lead, major distributors like Home Depot said the average consumer was "far more interested in the design and price of a faucet than how much lead it leaves in water."

Future Growth

Price Pfister has been gaining market share since the early 1980s and stands to gain more, negative publicity notwithstanding. Under Black & Decker, the brand has performed well. A 1993 Morgan Stanley & Co. report stated that Price Pfister showed a 5 percent increase in revenue despite weak wholesale demand in key California markets. Current trends in kitchen and bath plumbing fixtures reveal that American taste for European-styled fittings, polished brass, stainless steel, chrome, and durable decorator finishes is strong. Price Pfister has chosen its markets appropriately and should remain one of the leading faucet manufacturers.

Further Reading:

"Black & Decker to Acquire Emhart, Ending Hostile Bid," *Hardware Age,* May 1989, p. 15.

Blizzard, Peggy, "Price Pfister . . . Pfabulous Pfaucets," *Southern California Business,* March 1988, Sec. 1, p. 7.

Budd, John F., Jr., "Value Needs a Voice," *Industry Week,* May 1, 1989, p. 12.

"Emhart Completes Purchase," *Wall Street Journal,* May 24, 1988, p. 51.

"Emhart May Buy Price Pfister, Inc. for $215 million," *Wall Street Journal,* March 29, 1988, p. 5.

"Emhart Signs Accord to Buy Price Pfister," *Wall Street Journal,* April 12, 1988, p. 62.

Frankenstein, Diane Waxer, and George Frankenstein, *Brandnames: Who Owns What,* Facts on File Publications: New York, 1986.

Hoover, Gary, Alta Campbell, and Patrick J. Spain, *Hoover's Handbook,* The Reference Press, Inc.: Austin, Texas, 1990, p. 129.

Lee, Don, "Price Pfister May Feel Sting of Suit Filed by State," *Los Angeles Times,* Feb. 1, 1993, Part D, p. 2, Col. 3.

Lee, Don, "Price Pfister Under the State's Gun," *Los Angeles Times,* Feb. 9, 1993, Part D, p. 2, Col. 4.

Myers, Janet, "Black & Decker Ups Share in Hardware," *Advertising Age,* July 24, 1989, p. 28.

McClenahen, John S., "Plumbing Success," *Industry Week,* May 16, 1988, p. 32.

Moskowitz, Milton, Robert Levering and Michael Katz, *Everybody's Business,* Doubleday: New York, 1990.

"New Box, Cushioning Help Faucets Arrive Safely," *Packaging,* October 1993, p. 27.

Pierpoint, J. B., "B&D Launching New Power Tool Line to Challenge Japanese Rival," *Daily Record,* April 28, 1993, p. 3, Sec. 1.

"Price Pfister Program Pushes Better Grade of Faucets," *Professional Builder & Remodeler,* Nov. 1, 1991, p. 132.

Shuster, Laurie A., "Selling New Looks in Kitchen and Bath," *Hardware Age,* April 1990, p. 66.

—Evelyn S. Dorman

PRINCE®

Prince Manufacturing, Inc., revolutionized the tennis industry in the mid-1970s with the introduction of its patented oversized racquets. Since then, it has become the top marketer of tennis racquets in the United States and has diversified into several profitable areas, including athletic clothing.

A "Head" Start

The man responsible for revolutionizing the sport and industry of skiing in the United States also played a hand in bringing about a tennis revolution. Before buying into Prince Manufacturing, Howard Head had been esteemed as the inventor of the metal ski. He had also established Head Sports, Inc., as a leading marketer of metal tennis racquets. Prince Manufacturing was primarily known in the tennis world as a maker of ball machines, pneumatic cannons that fired tennis balls over the net.

After joining Prince, Head developed and patented a line of new aluminum racquets. In 1976 Prince debuted the Prince Advantage tennis racquet, which had a hitting surface 50 percent larger (110 square inches) than its contemporaries. The Advantage featured a "sweet spot" (the area on the surface of the racquet head providing maximum hitting power) three and a half times larger than standard racquets without any additional wind resistance. Also, the racquet was completely acceptable to officiating bodies in tennis. In other words, according to Prince advertising, "Without breaking any rules, we broke all the rules." To produce these racquets, Howard Head turned to the same plant he had used to manufacture aluminum racquets for Head Sports: the Maark Corp. in Princeton, New Jersey. Thus, the top two high-end brands were being manufactured in the same place.

The Prince racquet offered similar advantages to those offered by the Head ski. It was easier to use, more forgiving, and gave even experienced players a competitive advantage. At the time of the Prince Advantage's debut in 1976, there were 35 million tennis players in the United States. In 1982, when approximately 1.3 million Prince racquets had been sold, Howard Head estimated that about one fifth of serious tennis players owned a Prince racquet.

The Patent

The company managed to obtain a patent on the product, a crucial marketing step. Howard Head was able to patent racquet faces ranging from 85 to 130 square inches, compared to the industry standard of 75 square inches. He was able to obtain the patent (which expired in 1993) by proving he had created a racquet with unique playing characteristics, stating that he set out to make a more stable racquet. The strings of the Prince racquet were spaced closer together towards the center of the racquet head, unlike most other racquets, whose strings were evenly spaced throughout. More power was a happy coincidence. Also, the racquet was not merely larger; it was proportioned differently. Its length and depth were the same as a conventional racquet, but the hitting face was wider across.

Head also set out to prove to the patent office that the racquet hit balls harder than did conventional racquets. He submitted data to the patent office in which an independent laboratory had fired hundreds of tennis balls at both the Prince racquet and a conventional racquet. The data established that the Prince produced faster rebounds and that its sweet spot was 3.78 times larger than that of a conventional racquet.

The Prince patent only applied to sales in the United States, Canada, Britain, Belgium, Australia, New Zealand, and South Africa. In these areas, Prince enforced the patent vigorously, much to the woe of other manufacturers. In fact, this patent alone was cited as a major cause for Japanese manufacturer Yamaha dropping out of the racquet market in the United States. As one Yamaha official stated, "The more we sold, the more we had to pay in royalties. . . . Obviously they had some very sharp patent lawyers when they brought out the products originally."

However, as Howard Head pointed out in an interview, "the patent doesn't seem to matter that much abroad. Sales are not markedly better in England with protection than Germany without." The nature of oversized racquets—higher string tensions and greater stresses on the frame—demands quality manufacturing, which may have discouraged cheap imitations.

After the Prince oversized racquets gained acceptance, other manufacturers sought their way around the patent by introducing midsized racquets with hitting areas between 75 and 85 square inches. All other manufacturers, in the United States and Europe at least, had to pay licensing fees to Prince if they wished to sell oversized racquets. The list of makers paying such fees included Wilson, but sales of Wilson's oversized racquet did not compare to the original.

AT A GLANCE

Prince tennis racquet patented by Howard Head in 1975; Chesebrough-Pond's acquired Prince Manufacturing for $62.4 million, 1982; Prince later acquired by Edizione Holding S.p.A.

Performance: *Market share*—33% of tennis racquet category. *Sales*—$65.65 million in sporting goods.

Major competitor: Head tennis racquets; also, Wilson and Pro Kennex.

Advertising: *Agency*—Media Buying Service International Inc., New York, NY, 1993—. *Major campaign*—"The sweetest sweet spot in tennis," print campaign for the Extender tennis racquet.

Addresses: *Parent company*—Prince Manufacturing, Inc., Princess Rd., Lawrenceville, NJ 08648-2301; phone (609) 896-2500; fax (609) 895-7092. *Ultimate parent company*—Prince Holdings Inc., P.O. Box 2031, Princeton, NJ 08543-2031; phone (609) 896-2500; fax (609) 895-7092. *Ultimate ultimate parent company*—Edizione Holding S.p.A.

Advertising and the Marketplace

Prince consistently supported its products with advertising, preferring print over television. Features of Prince ads included stinging sign-offs such as, "For people who, given the choice, would rather win than lose." Prince spent about $3 million in 1983 with Waring & LaRosa advertising agency. Advertising grew in importance as the market for tennis grew. In 1973 there were an estimated 27 million players in the United States, spending a total of $500 million on tennis equipment, $100 million of that on balls and racquets; in 1970 only $27.8 million had been spent on tennis balls and racquets.

Endorsements played a role in Prince advertising, but the company typically has not paid the mega-dollars that some other companies have been known to pay. As tennis champions John McEnroe and Bjorn Borg were each commanding $600,000 per year for endorsing racquets, Prince followed a policy of endorsing many college players and younger players, as well as an occasional established professional, such as Gene Mayer, Pam Shriver, and Peter McNamara, whose endorsements were worth $100,000 to $200,000 in 1982. In 1990 teen tennis star Jennifer Capriati signed an endorsement contract with the company.

Performance

The Prince racquet was not as immediately successful as the Head ski had been. Its large face had a tendency to "trampoline" until the company recommended higher string tensions for it—75 pounds per square inch compared to the average 50 pounds. But in 1981 Prince became the best-selling brand of high-end racquet (those costing $50 or more), displacing Head tennis racquets in the process. Prince's share of this category increased from 8.5 percent in 1979 to 30.7 percent in 1981; Head (bought by AMF, Inc., from Howard Head in 1969) saw its share fall from 31.6 percent to 26.3 percent. At the same time, Wilson Sporting Goods fell from 19.2 percent to 10.7 percent of the category. During this period, more than 50 percent of all money spent on tennis racquets was going to Prince Manufacturing. Revenues for Prince were $36 million in 1981.

8.3 million tennis racquets were sold in 1977; sales had fallen to 3.2 million in 1981, perhaps due to the cyclical nature of individual sports. Only 3 million racquets, worth $170 million, were sold in the United States in 1983. As unit sales declined, companies hoped to hold onto dollar volume with high prices. In 1982 the Prince J/R, for children, sold for $45 strung; the basic Prince Classic, which was aluminum, sold for $72 without strings; the Pro sold for $110; the Prince Woodie, which was wood reinforced with graphite, sold for $160; and two graphite models sold for $210 and $295 each. Prince later introduced a boron racquet retailing for approximately $500. In 1984 another material, magnesium, was introduced to Prince racquets, selling for $115. Lower-priced Taiwanese midsized racquets, namely Pro Kennex, hurt Prince's sales in the 1980s, when there were approximately 30 brands on the market.

Diversification and Innovation

Finding tremendous success with tennis racquets, the company introduced tennis clothing and a line of tennis shoes. The clothing, which debuted in the mid-1980s, featured perspiration-absorbing polypropylene linings stitched into the garments. Prince introduced the material, previously used in diapers, to sports fashion. Despite these successful diversifications, the company's annual sales growth at this time—12.8 percent in 1983 compared to an average of 65 percent for the previous ten years—had slowed. Its closest competitor, Head Sports, led the midsized racquet category with its Edge racquet. Prince Manufacturing, Inc., has since diversified into golf, badminton, racquetball, and squash equipment, under brand names such as Ektelon, Langert, and Nitro.

Prince's focus, though, remained on tennis racquets. With a 30 percent share of the high-end tennis racquet market in 1984, the company introduced a number of new and innovative racquets. Prince debuted a new supersize racquet for doubles players, and introduced a line of Series 90 midsized racquets, promising a 38 percent larger sweet spot than Head's Edge racquet. The supersize racquet, made of a magnesium alloy, featured a head size of 125 square inches and a price tag of $125. The Series 90 racquets featured a 90 square inch hitting surface.

In 1987 wide-bodied racquets become the standard, with the introduction of Wilson's Profile; by 1991 the wide-bodied racquets accounted for approximately 90 percent of total racquet sales ($115 million) for the top three makers, Wilson, Prince, and Head. In 1991 Prince introduced its Vortex tennis racquet, which it claimed would adjust its stiffness to the swing of the player. A viscoelastic polymer, reinforced with graphite, gave the racquet this capability by tending to stretch when hit softly and stiffening under high impact. According to the company, these qualities translated to greater touch and control on soft shots and greater power on harder ones. A staggered string pattern also was utilized to provide more control, spin, and stability for off-center shots. The racquet was said to reduce the vibrations reaching a player's arm by 96 percent.

In 1993 Prince introduced its Synergy Extender ($250), an egg-shaped racquet whose strings extended into the handle, giving it a hitting surface of 116 square inches. The following year Prince offered a series of control-oriented racquets. The Precision Spectrum, a medium-flex, wide-bodied racquet retailing for $129, offered a hitting area of 107 square inches and was made from a graphite fiber composite. This racquet was also available in a midsized, 97-square-inch version. The Precision Response was a $169 wide-bodied racquet with an evenly spaced string pattern.

Additional models, the Graphite Extender ($199) and the Extender Thunder ($249), featured an exaggerated egg-shaped hitting area. At 9 1/8 ounce, the Extender Thunder was among the lightest racquets available. With such a history of innovative products, and with a 33 percent market share and almost two decades of success, in 1994 Prince showed no likelihood of relinquishing its position as the top seed among racquet manufacturers.

Further Reading:

''The $4-Billion Market in Fun,'' *Business Week,* February 8, 1969, pp. 82–84.

Beercheck, Richard C., ''Sporting Goods Win with High-Tech Materials,'' *Machine Design,* June 6, 1991, pp. 62–66.

Chirls, Stewart, ''New Racquets Are Fit to Be Tried,'' *Tennis,* March 1994, pp. 64–97.

Dumaine, Brian, ''Prince Gets into Some New Rackets,'' *Fortune,* October 29, 1984, p. 78.

Greising, David, ''Whap! Ace. Point. You Call This Tennis?,'' *Business Week,* September 9, 1991, p. 71.

Harper, Sam, ''Sporting Good Sales Bit [sic] Flabby,'' *Advertising Age,* July 6, 1981, p. 10.

Henry, Lawrence, ''Yamaha Stubs Its Imperial Toe,'' *Industry Week,* April 6, 1992, pp. 29–31.

McQuade, Walter, ''Prince Triumphant,'' *Fortune,* February 22, 1982, pp. 84–90.

Moffatt, Terence, ''The SGB Tennis Market Survey,'' *Sporting Goods Business,* October 1992, p. 40.

''Prince to Promote Its Bigger Racket Via Tennis Books,'' *Advertising Age,* November 3, 1975, p. 35.

Raissman, Robert, ''Bigger Budgets Volley for Bigger Racquets,'' *Advertising Age,* July 25, 1983, pp. 20, 86.

Sloan, Pat, ''Prince Makes a Racquet to Raise Market Share,'' *Advertising Age,* July 25, 1985, p. 20.

Stone, Amey, ''Getting a Grip on High-Tech Tennis,'' *Business Week,* June 7, 1993, p. 118.

''Tennis Market Seen Topping $500 million in '74,'' *Advertising Age,* October 21, 1974, p. 44.

Thomas, Dana L., ''Play's the Thing: There's Profit as Well as Pleasure in All Kinds of Sports,'' *Barron's,* March 27, 1961, p. 3.

Tyler, William, ''Tyler Presents Ten Best Campaigns of 1977: Repetition Spells Success,'' *Advertising Age,* January 16, 1978, pp. 98–101.

Willatt, Norris, ''World of Sports: It Is Growing Bigger and More Sophisticated Every Year,'' *Barron's,* April 2, 1962, pp. 5.

—Frederick C. Ingram

PROCTOR-SILEX®

Proctor-Silex®

Founded in 1929, Proctor-Silex was one of the world's leading brands of small electric appliances. Its parent company, Hamilton Beach/Proctor-Silex, Inc.—owner as well of the Hamilton Beach line of appliances—was the world's largest manufacturer of toasters. Proctor-Silex products were known for their dependability, affordability, and innovative features. In the 1990s they were sold in sleek Euro-style designs.

Brand Origins

The thermostatic electric iron was invented in 1912 by Joe Myers, a 14-year-old boy in Jackson, Michigan. One day he convinced his mother to buy her first electric iron for $2.98. When Myers tinkered with the single-setting iron and added an adjustable-temperature control, he had, in fact, revolutionized the product category. Myers took the new thermostatic electric iron to appliance companies, but each told him the iron could not be produced. Finally, Myers was hired by Liberty Company, a small business located in Cleveland.

Liberty Company displayed its first adjustable-temperature iron in 1926 at the U.S. Sesquicentennial in Philadelphia, where it caught the attention of executives from Proctor and Schwartz Company. Thinking it was an innovative idea and a natural match for the automatic toaster they had just developed, Proctor and Schwartz bought Liberty Company. In 1929 the first Proctor iron and toaster were introduced, heralding a long line of home appliances, many of which used thermostatic controls, such as automatic drip coffeemakers, thermal coffeemakers, irons, toasters, toaster ovens, can openers, popcorn poppers, kettles, coffee mills, and clothes steamers.

Products in the 1990s

Among the many Proctor-Silex appliances during the 1990s were automatic drip coffeemakers, which were featured in the MorningMaker line of Euro-styled, front-reach models. In 1994 Proctor-Silex introduced both thermal carafe and programmable models. The thermal carafe coffeemaker was an 8-cup, automatic drip coffeemaker with automatic shutoff. The product's main feature was its thermal glass-lined carafe capable of keeping coffee hot for up to four hours after brewing. The carafe was portable and could be conveniently transported anywhere, including the workplace. Ian Sole, vice president of marketing for Hamilton Beach/Proctor-Silex, said, "Consumers really appreciate the convenience and portability of thermal carafe coffeemakers. These coffeemakers are a natural fit with lifestyles of the 1990s, similar to the way the break-resistant, lunch box thermos revolutionized school lunches of the 1960s."

The automatic drip programmable coffeemaker, with a 12-cup capacity, was distinguished by its "set-ahead" feature. Using its digital programmable clock, a person could place coffee grounds in the machine at bedtime, set the unit's clock, and wake up the next morning to freshly brewed coffee. Just in case someone overslept past brewing time or forgot to shut the unit off, there was an automatic shutoff feature that turned off the heating element after two hours. The coffeemaker was available in both black and white.

Also popular in the Proctor-Silex line were Ultra-Ease steam irons. In 1994 the company created Ultra-Steam Plus, a new line of larger, full-size irons that were designed to smooth out the toughest wrinkles. The typical steam iron made fabric more pliable, and the pressure of the iron made wrinkles straight. The more steam an iron had, the better the wrinkles were ironed out. Increasing the steam-producing capability of irons, then, would increase the ability to iron out the most stubborn wrinkles. The new Ultra-Ease line had an extralarge soleplate size, along with 53 steam vents that provided effective steam distribution for easy wrinkle removal. For safety the irons automatically shut off after one hour of use, with a convenient reset button if more ironing was needed.

Proctor-Silex was perhaps best known, however, for its line of toasters and toaster ovens, and over the years it has developed new models with unusual features. Introduced in the early 1990s, for example, were its "Bagel Mate" toasters for browning bagels. The increased popularity of bagels, in part as a low-calorie food item, was a major reason for the product's development. In 1994 the company also brought out two new Cool-Touch Extra Wide Slot Toasters—one with two slots and the other with four. The slots were up to 40 percent wider than those on conventional toasters to accomodate hand-sliced bread and large bagels. The Cool Touch feature meant that the exterior of the toaster stayed cool while toasting. One of the most remarkable features was its SmartToast thermostat, which sensed the temperature and moisture level of bread to ensure even and consistent toast color.

AT A GLANCE

Proctor-Silex brand appliances are made by Hamilton Beach/Proctor-Silex, Inc., a company formed in 1990 when Hamilton Beach Co. merged with Proctor-Silex, Inc. The company is a subsidiary of Nacco Industries, Inc. of Cleveland, OH. The Proctor-Silex company began as the Proctor and Schwartz Company, a company that bought The Liberty Company of Cleveland, which had marketed the first adjustable temperature iron known as the Liberty iron. The iron had been developed by 14-year-old Joe Myers, a Jackson, Michigan boy in 1912. In 1929, Proctor and Schwartz introduced the first iron and toaster under the Proctor name.

Performance: *Sales*—$350 million (1992 estimate).

Major competitor: Norelco, Black & Decker, Panasonic, Sunbeam, Braun, Toastmaster, Mr. Coffee.

Advertising: *Agency*—Arian, Lowe & Travis Advertising, Inc., Louisville, KY, 1989—. *Major campaign*—"Our best ideas come from you," print ads placed in bridal magazines and featuring the Proctor-Silex line of toasters.

Addresses: *Parent company*—Hamilton Beach/Proctor-Silex, Inc., 4421 Waterfront Drive, Glen Allen, VA 23060; phone: (804) 273-9777; fax: (804) 527-7230.

Also introduced in 1994 were three "Power Openers," each made especially tall to facilitate easy opening of large cans. It also functioned as a sharpener of knives and scissors.

100 Million Toast Tests

In 1957 Proctor-Silex established a plant in the town of Mount Airy, North Carolina. The town was familiar to television viewers as the hometown of Andy Griffith and the town upon which the fictional Mayberry was based. In 1993 the town decided to honor Proctor-Silex during its 27th Annual Autumn Leaves Festival, the state's largest outdoor festival with more than 250,000 visitors. Mount Airy's Mayor, Maynard Beamer, proclaimed the town the "Toaster Capital of the World," as it was here that Proctor-Silex made its best-selling line of toasters. At a dedication ceremony the mayor unveiled a highway sign declaring the city's new designation. With an almost $20 million payroll, the plant played a major role in the local economy.

The festival coincided with the company's testing of its 100 millionth slice of bread in its toasters. The plant had continually test toasted more than 1,000 loaves of bread daily since 1957 to ensure that each individual toaster toasted perfectly before it was shipped. The toast was then distributed as daily feed to the local livestock. Stephen R. Brian, executive vice president of operations for Hamilton Beach/Proctor-Silex, said, "In commemoration of the 100 millionth slice of bread test toasted in our toasters, we wanted to have a special celebration to thank the city for allowing us to be part of their community for the past 26 years."

Proctor-Silex toasters also received special attention at the January 1994 trade show held by the National Housewares Manufacturing Associations in Chicago. There Piero Biondi, restauranteur and popular host of the radio program "Chef Piero's Food and Wine Show," featured on KIEV-Radio in Burbank, California, performed "gourmet" toaster demonstrations with the Proctor-Silex Extra Side Slot Toaster. Proctor-Silex toasters were also popularly featured in bridal magazines with the tag line "Our best ideas come from you."

Brand Outlook

Future products from Proctor-Silex were expected to reflect the same concern with meeting consumer needs as they have in the past. George C. Nebel, president and chief executive officer at Hamilton Beach/Proctor-Silex, Inc., "Customers continue to invest in the strength of our two brand names and in our products. In turn, we continually invest in service and products to ensure our customers receive the best value for their investments."

Further Reading:

"Brand History," Glen Allen, VA: Hamilton Beach/Proctor-Silex, Inc.

"Proctor-Silex News Releases," Glen Allen VA: Hamilton Beach/Proctor-Silex, 1994.

—Dorothy Kroll

PYREX®

Pyrex is a versatile borosilicate glass dating from 1915 that cooks in the kitchen, experiments in the laboratory, peers into the heavens, and travels in outer space. Originally developed for use in shatterproof railway lanterns, Corning Incorporated successfully positioned Pyrex into laboratory equipment usage and then into the home market. In 1990, Pyrex had 97 percent consumer recognition and 80 percent household penetration.

Battery Jar Baking

Brooklyn Flint Glass Works moved to the village of Corning, New York, in 1868. By the time it incorporated as Corning Glass Works in 1875, it was producing such sophisticated items as thermometer tubing and pharmaceutical ware. The company contributed to the advent of electrical lighting by blowing the first bulbs for Thomas Edison's invention in 1880. The glass works would build a machine four decades later that would produce 15,000 glass bulbs per hour, thus making incandescent light affordable for everyone.

Although Corning Glass Works did not have a research laboratory before the turn of the century, it worked to produce innovative products requiring glass, including thermometer tubing and pharmaceutical glass. The Houghton family, who owned the Glass Works, became particularly interested in problems of railroad signal devices. With the help of scientists at Cornell, Charles Houghton designed and secured the first patents on lenses for the devices as early as 1877. At the turn of the century, the company started work to improve reliability and safety in these devices. Charles's nephew, Arthur Houghton, worked with a scientist from Lederle Laboratories, while his brother, Alanson Houghton, asked that Yale University begin research to perfect true signal colors.

Because of this research project, Corning hired Dr. William Churchill from Yale. He established an optical laboratory at Corning Glass Works in 1904 to design precision optics, while continuing work to develop reliable and consistent colors for signal ware. The work was successful. In 1908, the Railway Signal Association adopted Corning colors as standard for all signal devices.

In 1908 Corning hired Dr. Eugene Sullivan from the U.S. Geological Survey to organize a formal research laboratory, one of the first in all of American industry. The initial assignment for Dr. Sullivan's small staff was to solve another critical railroad safety problem—the shattering of the glass globe of the brakeman's lantern in rain and snow. As a student, Sullivan witnessed German glassmaking experiments that investigated low expansion glasses that were heat resistant. Sullivan and his assistant, William Taylor, expanded on the work of Dr. Otto Schott of Jena Glass Works, who had invented a borosilicate heat resistant glass prior to 1900. They further developed and put into production a new borosilicate composition which had unusual heat resistance. The new CNX (Corning Non-expansion) glass solved the lantern problem and became a registered trademark in 1909. Having been asked to service test the new CNX globes, soon the big railroads wanted to order specially marked lanterns so that trainmen of smaller rail lines would not steal them.

There is more than one version of how Corning transformed the borosilicate glass used in railroad lanterns into Pyrex ovenware. All of the stories include Mrs. Jesse (Becky) Littleton, the wife of Dr. Jesse Littleton, a newly arrived Corning scientist. One of the most told versions appeared as a story in the August 19, 1944, edition of the *Saturday Evening Post.* The story related how Dr. Littleton sawed off the bottom of a glass battery jar made of the new borosilicate composition and took it home with him. The next day he passed a plate of cookies around the research offices. He explained that he had asked his wife to bake a batch of cookies on the battery jar bottom, which measured about two inches high.

Another story comes from the 1919 notes of Dr. Sullivan. According to this version Dr. and Mrs. Littleton had only been in Corning a few weeks when the Guernsey ceramic casserole she recently purchased broke the second time she put it in the oven. She asked her husband whether she could get a glass casserole from the factory to see if it would work better than earthenware. The next day, a lab worker cut the bottoms from two rejected battery jars and took them to Mrs. Littleton, who baked a sponge cake in one of them. Reportedly, the cake baked and browned uniformly and was easily removed from the dish with practically no adhesion.

In 1944 Dr. Churchill disputed the *Post* story that Mrs. Littleton used the battery jar to bake cookies. He recalled that she had noticed an abbreviated battery jar being used to boil water on a visit to the Corning lab. Because her kitchen utensils were still in transit, she asked if she could try one of the jars as a pudding dish. Whatever Becky Littleton made in her battery jar bottom—

AT A GLANCE

Pyrex brand of glass ovenware marketed in 1915 by Corning Glass Works in Corning, New York; provided the mirror for the Hale telescope in California, 1936; measuring cup, number-one selling Pyrex item, redesigned in 1983; company name changed to Corning Incorporated, 1989.

Performance: *Market share*—Top share of the glass bakeware category.

Major competitor: Anchor Hocking.

Advertising: *Agency*—DMB&B, New York, NY, 1983—. *Major campaign*—"Designed for living."

Addresses: *Parent company*—Corning Incorporated, Houghton Park, Corning, NY 14831; phone: (607) 974-9000.

cookies, sponge cake, or pudding—she sparked the idea that glass might suitable as ovenware. Before Corning could use its borosilicate composition to manufacture glass ovenware, however, Dr. Sullivan and William Taylor had to make a crucial modification—the lead ingredient had to be removed. In September of 1915, Sullivan and Taylor applied for a patent for 702EJ, the glass composition used to make the ovenware and chemical ware. By that time Corning's A Factory was already pressing Pyrex ovenware.

Fire-Glass

Even though early Pyrex advertising carried the tagline "Pyrex means 'Fire-glass,' " the word *Pyrex* is not derived from the Greek word *pyr* for fire. Nor is the *rex* in *Pyrex* an allusion to the Latin word for king. Instead, according to one account, the name was selected simply on euphonious grounds. Dr. Churchill suggested the first dish, a pie plate, be called *Pie-Right,* or with an alternate spelling, *Py-rite.* A third suggestion, however, won out— *Py-rex.* In 1939 the company's patent attorney, Vernon Dorsey, would proffer that the Corning employees' ears had already been attuned to the company's previous trademarks, Nonex on the battery jars and CNX on the lantern globes, so Pyrex was easily settled upon.

As a Window Lets In Light

The first order for Pyrex came from Jordan-Marsh in Boston on May 18, 1915. In October of that year, Pyrex expanded its market to San Francisco. Corning launched a nationwide campaign with its first published advertisement for the new product line. The ad used the word "fire-glass" to describe the dozen or so items pictured and included a statement from Mrs. Sarah Tyson Rorer, who was the culinary editor of the *Ladies Home Journal,* principal of the Philadelphia Cooking School, and a cookbook author. Dr. Sullivan wrote in his memoirs that Corning asked her to test Pyrex dishes because she was the leading home economist in the United States. She was reluctant to do the tests because "the idea of putting glass into an oven didn't appeal to her at all." After finally agreeing she stipulated "that she would report the results exactly as she found them." After a long, tense wait, Corning received her enthusiastic report about how a Baked Alaska turned out perfectly in the glass dish. Mrs. Rorer was later hired by Dr. Churchill, then Pyrex sales manager, to travel throughout the United States and Canada generating sales of Pyrex. The Hudson's Bay Co. in Vancouver and Winnipeg was selling the product by April 1916.

Early Pyrex advertisements had tags that educated consumers about the products, for example, "a new material" and "a new way to bake." A September 1916 ad contained the tag "look right through," a picture of a woman, and copy that read: "I cannot see why in creation, you should bake in the dark, as they did in the Ark, when Pyrex permits observation." The same woman also appeared in the December ad with the lead caption "the new gift of science to women. . . . For centuries women have wanted this."

Pyrex advertising emphasized the material's visual and baking qualities until 1917 when someone thought it should also demonstrate its thermal toughness. To prove Pyrex could survive sudden temperature changes, lab technician Evelyn Roberts poured boiling water into a #101 casserole dish buried in a block of ice. The dish did survive, and a March 1918 ad replicated the test on a pie plate. Later, Corning did similar tests on Pyrex's glass-ceramic descendants. As of June 1918, Americans owned some two million pieces of Pyrex.

Pyrex sales reached four-and-a-half million pieces five years after its introduction. The transparency of Pyrex glassware continued to be a selling point. "As a window lets in light . . . " read an ad in the March 1920 *Ladies Home Journal,* which also educated the consumer about the basic physics of how glass works in the cooking process. In addition, Corning published cookbooks with recipes for meals that could be cooked and served in the same dish. According to Jerry Wright of Corning Incorporated, the first cookbook, *Experts Book on Better Baking,* issued in 1924, had "a decidedly aristocratic bearing." This pronouncement was made in light of the fact that a pie plate cost a dollar, a large sum at the time.

Although Corning did not have its own test kitchen until 1929, advertising throughout the 1920s lauded the way Pyrex baked. "For perfect baking . . . no wonder that over 25 million Pyrex dishes are now in use," stated a 1926 ad. Mildred Maddocks of the Good Housekeeping Institute was the first to report that heating food in glass occurred more rapidly than in metal. The fact led to the claims "foods bake better in glass," "for better and faster cooking," and "better baking with less fuel."

During the 1970s, Corning used the tagline "when something gets hot it expands," referring to the brand's popularity and variety of products rather than its physical attributes. Corning continued to advertise Pyrex heavily in national print media until 1987, when other Corning brands took precedence. Hardware and chain stores, though, prominently featured the Pyrex brand in their advertising.

Brand Development

The functionality of Pyrex products kept sales of the brand rising. Dr. Churchill designed bean pots that were on the market in the lean times of the Great Depression. He also designed a hexagonal pie plate, launched in 1917 and produced over a decade. Other early Pyrex designs included a shirred egg dish that became the mushroom dish when topped with its bell cover. The company also launched the Pyrexette set of six scaled down bakeware items that was touted as "the ideal gift for children." As with many Pyrex items, the children's set became prized by collectors who would pay up to $500 for the complete set that originally sold "for only $2 east of the Mississippi." Corning also manufactured a translucent white Pyrex for three years in the early 1920s. In 1927 Corning's new automatic presses began producing new casserole designs that included covers to fit on the rim and, at last, handles which helped homemakers get the hot dishes out of the oven. By this time there were 30 million pieces of Pyrex in American homes.

Several companies in the silver trade developed a niche market based on Pyrex. These companies took various Pyrex dishes and beautified them by mounting the pieces in silver cradles. The trade term for the combinations was ''nickel silver casseroles with Pyrex glass linings.'' In addition, engraving shops around the town of Corning supplied the Pyrex sales division with engraved items that sold for 25 cents to $2 each from the catalog. Pyrex borosilicate glass also has appeared in millions of beverage ware items made for other manufacturers as well as under its own brand. The brand probably reached its zenith in terms of variety of items marketed around 1965-68.

The present design of the Pyrex measuring cup, the number-one selling Pyrex item, came about when a designer discerned what would happen if the handle on the saucepan was allowed to sag after removal from an old mold machine. This post-forming technique was incorporated into the cup's design, which originally had a closed handle. The new cups were also made deeper to minimize boil-over in the microwave oven and included a thumb rest directly on top of the handle bend. The new stackable design of the half-century-old cup retained the pouring lip on top and volume gauge in red on one side. The result of the new design was a 150 percent increase in sales.

Pyrex's functionality extended far beyond the consumer market and accounted for some challenges over the years. The largest reject Corning ever produced was a 200-inch Pyrex disk that is now on display at the Glass Center in Corning, New York. Because Pyrex glass resists temperature changes and mechanical stress and could be ground to super smoothness, scientists chose it for the mirror of the Hale telescope at Mount Palomar in California. The first casting started in 1931 with the molten glass being poured into a complex ceramic mold that gave the disk a ribbed pattern effecting maximum strength at a minimum weight. However, during the casting, the intensely hot glass melted several bolts anchoring mold, causing pieces of core to float to surface. A later casting in 1934 was successful, however. Technicians held the temperature of the glass wheel at 1200 degrees for sixty days, then cooled it over eight months at the rate of barely one degree a day. In 1936, they steel-crated the finished Pyrex disk and shipped it to Mount Palomar to be ground and polished to a concave shape, although World War II interrupted the job. A thin film of aluminum ''steamed'' onto the disk made the glass into the world's largest mirror at the time. The entire process took twenty years and cost $6.55 million. In 1949 Dr. Edwin Hubble became the first astronomer to take photographs on the telescope. In another application, Pyrex has been used in the view ports of all the spacecraft that have gone up since it was installed in the first Mercury space capsule.

For more than 75 years Pyrex has been a well-known brand in the United States. It also is an established brand in other countries. While Corning puts more advertising and marketing energy into its newer, more versatile glass-ceramic brands consumers and scientists alike will still trust the quality of items that carry the Pyrex brand name.

Further Reading:

Ankli, Robert E., ''Corning Incorporated,'' *International Directory of Company Histories,* edited by Adele Hast, Chicago: St. James Press, 1991, pp. 683–85.

The Corning Glass Center, Corning, NY: Corning Glass Works, 1958.

''Corning Updates Name; Corning Glass Works Is Now Corning Inc.,'' *Gifts & Decorative Accessories,* June 1989, p. 10.

Labich, Kenneth and H. John Steinbreder, ''The Innovators; America's Most Imaginative Companies Are Turning New Ideas into Big Dollars,'' *Fortune,* June 6, 1988, p. 50–7.

Pyrex by Corning: A Collector's Guide, Marietta, OH: Antique Publications, 1993.

''Recognition, Not Price, Shapes Brand Popularity,'' *Discount Store News,* October 1, 1990, pp. 70–71.

Sharp, Harold S., *Advertising Slogans of America,* Metuchen, NJ: Scarecrow Press, Inc., 1984.

Additional information was provided by Corning Incorporated, Corning, New York.

—Doris Morris Maxfield

QUASAR®

The Quasar brand has achieved national recognition in a surprisingly short time. First marketed in 1967, within a decade Quasar came to signify quality and excellence. Today Quasar is a leading brand name for televisions, VCRs, camcorders, fax machines, microwave ovens, and other electrical products. Owned by Matsushita Electric Industrial Company, Ltd. of Osaka, Japan, Quasar, along with other Matsushita brands—Panasonic and Technics—is a pacesetter in the highly competitive world of consumer electronic products.

Brand Origins

Quasar was originally conceived by Motorola Company in 1967. The 1960s were a time of great upheaval in the consumer electronics industry in large part because of the advent of the transistor. The transistor supplanted the vacuum tube, until then the only effective means of transmitting and controlling electric current. For nearly 50 years, the clumsy vacuum tube was king in electrical products, leading to the development of radio and eventually, of television. The drawbacks of the vacuum tube, however, were that it used up too much space and energy and gave off unwanted heat. The tiny transistor that supplanted the tube could produce many times the electrical power of a vacuum tube, would use very little power, and emitted virtually no heat.

As far back as 1949, Motorola Company had become the biggest manufacturer of televisions in the United States. These were the huge, bulky sets that contained the indispensable tube that made television—as well as radio—transmission possible. While the transistor was not invented by Motorola, Motorola had the manufacturing capacity to apply the transistor to useful consumer products. By the late 1950s, Motorola was manufacturing transistor radios, the first portable clock radio, small portable TV sets, the first transistor TV set, and finally, the Quasar line of color TV sets, the first transistor color TVs in the world, which came on the market in 1967.

Commercial Success

Motorola had been manufacturing color television sets in 1954 but was forced to discontinue them because of weak market demand and the fact that the majority of TV broadcasting was still done in black and white. In 1963, in partnership with the firm National Video, Motorola once more began producing color television sets. Two years later Motorola claimed ten percent of the color television market of around three million sets, which encouraged the company to develop a distinctive color TV that stood out from the competition.

In 1967 Quasar color TV sets were introduced, the first all-transistor color TVs in the world. Gone was the clumsy rectangular vacuum tube—standard for the industry—which Motorola developed in 1963. The new Quasar TVs were marketed as "easy to repair," a big selling point.

Not surprisingly, Quasar's unique features quickly earned it national recognition. But, while Quasar became famous, times were changing; foreign competition in consumer electronic products had already slashed the number of U.S. television producers from 80 in 1950 to only 18 in 1968 (and to only six by 1980). This was an ominous sign for Quasar's future, despite its initial popularity.

Marketing Strategy

By 1970 Japanese companies had come to dominate the American consumer electronics market, capturing 75 percent. Motorola's Quasar sold well, thanks to effective advertising and good rapport with the company's 90 retail outlets. But even American competitors, giants like RCA and Zenith, were turning out transistor color TVs by then, making the future of Quasar less bright. More importantly, Motorola was turning to the manufacture of semiconductors, or silicon chips. By 1969 its semiconductor business had already outstripped its consumer electronics business. By 1972 Motorola ceased its production of portable and table radios, phonographs, and tape players. Two year later it sold Quasar to the giant Japanese electronics firm Matsushita. Already famous for its Panasonic brand, the Japanese corporation was eager to latch on to a powerful brand that had a wide distribution network.

Matsushita's sales strategy by then was becoming globalized. As far back as 1953, Matsushita had opened a tiny, three-person sales office in New York. By 1959 its American business had grown so much that a wholly owned subsidiary, Matsushita Electric Corporation of America (MECA), was established. Within two years, MECA introduced Panasonic-brand transistor radios in the United States. They became a huge success. This encouraged MECA to establish a high-end audio electronics brand, Technics, in 1973, and a year later, to purchase Quasar. With the last, Matsushita planned to capitalize on the brand's national name

AT A GLANCE

Quasar brand was established by the Motorola Company in 1967. Initially, the Quasar product line consisted of color TV receivers, America's first transistor color TV sets. Quasar was sold to Matsushita Electric Industrial Co., Ltd. in 1974. It would become a leading brand in such diverse product lines as television sets, VCRs, and camcorders, communications products such as telephones and facsimile machines, and microwave ovens and air conditioners. Quasar Company headquarters are in Elgin, IL.

Performance: *Market share*—15% of domestic TV/VCR combo market.

Major competitor: Toshiba.

Advertising: *Agency*—In-house. *Major campaign*—Full-page print ad introducing the Quasar VideoViewer; accompanying text describes the product, attractively displayed in color in center of ad. The slogan reads "Quasar VideoViewer is a superior TV/VCR combo, because it was designed that way." A small photo insert at the lower right depicts "the perfect complement to a Quasar VideoViewer," the Quasar Quarterback Camcorder.

Addresses: *Parent Company*—Quasar Company, 1707 North Randall Rd., Elgin, IL 60123-7847; phone: (708) 468-5600; fax: (708) 468-5656. *Ultimate parent company*—Matsushita Electric Company of America, 1 Panasonic Way, Secaucus, NJ 07094; phone: (201) 348-7000; fax: (201) 392-6007; *Ultimate ultimate parent company*—Matsushita Electric Industrial Co., Ltd.

recognition. It quickly broadened the Quasar product line to include a diverse array of consumer electronic products.

Product Development

Soon after the sale of Quasar to Matsushita, the product line began to diversify: color and projection TVs, video cassette recording equipment and camcorders, portable audio products and home entertainment systems, communications products, microwave ovens, and room air conditioners followed in rapid succession. Such diversification raised the profile of Quasar even higher and established the brand in a number of different industries, instead of just one, television.

Television has undergone fundamental changes over the years. The advent of semiconductors has made smaller, even flatter television sets possible. In 1992, Quasar introduced its "flat screen" TV sets. The trend in recent years to integrate what were separate electronic products into one component is evident also in televisions: separate TV and VCR sets have evolved into TV/VCR combos. Quasar's recent VideoViewer even goes beyond that: not merely a combination of TV and VCR, it integrates the electronic controls and systems and programs everything on screen. Another TV product, the Quasar Model SXW5855, includes an artificial intelligence system that produces high-quality, vivid color to a hitherto unmatched degree. The same is also true of the CinemaVision TV, the 58-inch Quasar model that also features Channel Search for scanning channels or for programming certain channels simultaneously. In addition, 12 to 20 different pictures can be viewed at the same time on the CinemaVision.

Another product line that integrates what formerly were separate product lines is the Quasar "Pax" Machine, which combines a phone (including speaker phone in the top-of-the-line model), fax, and answering machine. Quasar also has begun producing and marketing cordless phones with noise filters and that also utilize a special technology to scramble a user's voice (affording the same protection against eavesdropping offered by corded phones). Microwave ovens in various sizes have also become an important addition to Quasar's product line, as have camcorders, with full color viewing and an industry-leading 100:1 digital zoom with view finder display. The Quasar Model VM538/539 camcorder won the prestigious 1993 Summer International Consumer Electronics Show Innovations award for excellence.

One problem for Quasar in its attempt to create and satisfy new consumer needs is competition from its sister brand, Panasonic. Nonetheless, as with different brands of automobiles manufactured by the same company, Quasar and Panasonic, though similar, do claim customer loyalty and provide the customer with an option.

As part of the giant, multinational Matsushita corporation, Quasar has expanded throughout the United States and Canada. Currently, Quasar is marketed only in these countries, although it probably will expand in the future into Mexican and other Latin American markets.

The Future

At the heart of Quasar's strength as a product line is the strong brand name. Furthermore, its diverse array of products will in the future encompass a broader selection of communications products for the small business office. After undergoing a major pruning of its organization and staff in 1989, Quasar scaled back its bureaucracy and decentralized its operations. The result was a ten percent increase in sales in 1990, a year when other electronics companies were beginning to feel the pinch of the oncoming recession. With a global marketplace and sales strategy and the fall of trade barriers throughout the world—Quasar stands to benefit from the recent passage by Congress of the North American Free Trade Agreement—Quasar's growth in the 21st century seems assured. Still, the problem of differentiating itself from Panasonic, the products of which are virtually identical to Quasar's, remains. There is some possibility that since Panasonic has a greater diversity of products and a greater market, Quasar may be phased out in the future. Though currently, and for the near future, the disappearance of Quasar as a brand appears unlikely.

Further Reading:

Beatty, Gerry, "Quasar: 'Me Too Won't Do,' (Quasar Co. Marketing & Distribution Strategy)," *HFD—The Weekly Home Furnishings Newspaper,* September 23, 1991, p. 164.

"A Cosmic Trip in the Time Machine (Quasar)," *U.S. News & World Report,* December 4, 1989, p. 14.

Greenberg, Manning, "Quasar: Sending Strong Signals: Product Differentiation, Streamlined Operations Revive This Matsushita Division (Company Profile)," *HFD—The Weekly Home Furnishings Newspaper,* March 11, 1991, p. 111.

"Matsushita in America," *Matsushita Electric Corporation in America,* 1993.

"MECA Forms New CE Group (Matsushita Electric Corp. America)," *Television Digest,* December 13, 1993, p. 16.

"Quasar (New Consumer Electronics)," *Television Digest,* June 8, 1992, p. 18.

—Sina Dubovoj

RCA®

The Radio Corporation of America (RCA) was a pioneer in the development of American broadcasting, producing radios and televisions under the RCA brand name and providing programming through its subsidiary, the National Broadcasting Company (NBC). RCA was acquired by the General Electric (GE) in 1985. The company held on to NBC, but disposed of its entire consumer electronics products group, including the GE and RCA product lines, selling them in 1986. RCA, one of the oldest and most popular brands of radios and televisions in the United States, is owned by Thomson S.A., whose U.S. subsidiary is Thomson Consumer Electronics.

Brand Origins

The Radio Corporation of America was established by General Electric in 1919, at the behest of Navy Undersecretary Franklin D. Roosevelt, so that it might acquire the American assets of the British Marconi Wireless Company. By 1921, American Telephone & Telegraph (AT&T) and Westinghouse had purchased large interests in RCA, which operated a growing international and domestic radio network.

RCA began as a marketing concern. Its first products were crystal and tube home radio sets, including the Radiola 1, branded with the RCA name but manufactured by General Electric and Westinghouse. It was David Sarnoff, a Russian immigrant and protege of Guglielmo Marconi, who established RCA as a major brand by creating a nationwide radio network, organized in 1926 as the National Broadcasting Company.

Sarnoff also built RCA into a major brand by marketing components built by the Victor Talking Machine Company under the RCA name. The RCA product family included the Radiotron tube which, because it ran on alternating wall current, eliminated the need for messy acid-core batteries in RCA radios. In 1928, RCA introduced the Photophone process for putting sound on film. But Westinghouse's theater chain adopted a competing system. RCA joined forces with Pathé and Keith-Albee-Orpheum, forming a second theater chain, Radio Keith Orpheum, or RKO.

Sarnoff hoped to market the first multimedia entertainment center by combining an RCA radio with a Victor phonograph. He achieved this in 1929, when RCA purchased the 50 percent of Victor it did not already own from General Electric and Westinghouse for about $4 million. Sarnoff made this acquisition because he feared that GE and Westinghouse would soon be forced to sell their interests in RCA, leaving the company without access to manufacturing facilities. With the addition of Victor and its manufacturing sites in Indiana and New Jersey, the company was renamed RCA Victor.

Through its extensive collection of radio and other patents, RCA held a virtual monopoly on broadcasting and sound systems. AT&T sold out its interest in RCA in 1924. Government antitrust lawyers finally ended RCA's ownership by General Electric and Westinghouse in 1932, but were aided by the fact that the partners were more committed to competition than cooperation.

Early Marketing Strategy

RCA moved its headquarters into a great modern icon, "Radio City" at 30 Rockefeller Center, in 1932. The 70-story building was later christened the RCA Building, and fitted with huge neon RCA letters in 1937. Despite the evaporation of consumer spending during the Depression, Sarnoff invested heavily in radio research and the establishment of new radio stations on the NBC network. In addition to broadcasting, manufacturing, films, and record pressing, RCA branched into marine communications and even established a string of radio schools. Every effort was made to place the RCA name into every aspect of audio and visual entertainment.

Radio benefitted greatly from the Depression. Millions of weary consumers chose broadcast entertainment as a cheap alternative to live entertainment and films. Indeed, RCA brought this entertainment to the nation by broadcasting performances from RKO theaters, concert halls, and hotel ballrooms over NBC. RCA made tremendous amounts of money from its growing radio empire, which included two networks, several stations, factories, laboratories, and international communications. Sarnoff funnelled much of this money back into technological research in an attempt to perfect television.

Sarnoff used the talents of a fellow Russian immigrant, Dr. Vladmir K. Zworykin, who had developed the iconoscope—an early television camera—in 1925. Four years later, Zworykin developed the kinescope picture tube. By 1933, Zworykin had built an all-electronic television set for RCA at the company's Camden, New Jersey, lab.

AT A GLANCE

RCA brand of consumer electronics introduced by Radio Corporation of America, 1922; RCA organized the National Broadcasting Company (NBC), 1926; developed Photophone sound film process and formed RKO, 1928; acquired Victor Talking Machine Company, 1929; in 1933, developed first television, which it demonstrated in 1939; marketed first commercial television set, the Model 630TS, 1946; developed tricolor kinescope color television, 1953; developed 100-percent solid-state television product line, 1974; introduced 4-hour videocassette recorder (VCR), 1977; RCA acquired by General Electric Company, 1985; RCA sold to Thomson Consumer Electronics, 1986.

Major competitor: Philips; also Zenith and Sony.

Advertising: *Agency*—Ammirati & Puris, New York, NY. *Major campaign*—"Changing Entertainment. Again.," featuring live versions of "Nipper" and "Chipper" in skits that emphasize outstanding performance of RCA brand consumer electronic products.

Addresses: *Parent company*—Thomson Consumer Electronics, P.O. Box 1976, Indianapolis, IN 46206-1976; phone: (317) 587-3000.

Sarnoff fought viciously to prevent FM radio, over which RCA held no patents, from sapping profits from RCA's profitable AM broadcast network. He succeeded and, in doing so, gained the funding necessary to develop a practical television. RCA sponsored the world's first television broadcast at the New York World's Fair in 1939. The RCA pavilion was the centerpiece of the exhibition. Working from a speech called "Birth of an Industry," Sarnoff introduced television to the world, and firmly established RCA as the leader in broadcast communications.

Brand Development

Sarnoff settled on a clever but by no means unique marketing technique. He set out to use the NBC network radio network as a marketing tool for RCA products. RCA radios were capable of picking up any station in the frequency range allotted by the government, not just NBC stations. By the same token, radios made by Majestic, Motorola, Zenith, Philco, and others could bring in any radio station, including NBC stations.

The separation of broadcasting and manufacturing units at RCA was so complete that many consumers had no idea the companies were virtually one and the same. But the synergies were obvious. RCA made millions of dollars from its two networks (called the Red and the Blue because of the colored pencils engineers used to map out their coverage), and the NBC radio affiliates.

RCA pressed for the adoption of new radio transmission standards, often with opposition from the rival Columbia Broadcasting System (CBS). At the same time improvements in broadcast technology were implemented, RCA was ready with a new line of compatible products. Such was the case with television. Six companies had televisions on the market in 1939. RCA offered a five-by-nine-inch set selling for $199.50, and a 12-inch tube for $600. But few consumers wanted a television, because the Federal Communications Commission (FCC) had not yet set standards for television broadcasting. Each of the models was designed to a different, competing standard.

RCA's battle for adoption of its own standard was interrupted by World War II, during which all companies geared up for military production. During the war, RCA divested its Blue Network, which was subsequently renamed the American Broadcasting Company. When the war ended in 1945, RCA resumed its push for a 525-line, 30-frame-per-second standard. By this time, RCA's position was strengthened by advances from technologies developed during the war. Zworykin built a more sensitive camera tube and a better picture tube, and established better transmission systems and relay techniques.

Subsidization of RCA's television project was provided again by radio sales, which resumed in November of 1945. Hoping to goad the FCC into choosing its standard, RCA built a television broadcast network linking New York, Washington, Philadelphia, and Schenectady by coaxial cable. The FCC, seeing how well the system operated, selected the RCA standard, which enabled RCA to move directly into production of consumer televisions in 1946. With the NBC television network now nationwide, RCA marketed its famous model 630TS, known as the "Model T" of television. This set, priced at $375, was as large as a dishwasher, but featured only a 10-inch tube. The set was an immediate hit with Depression- and war-weary consumers.

Modern Development

RCA, with substantial interests in television patents, manufacturing, and broadcasting, was in a stronger position than its competitors to develop and advocate new industry standards. The company did not use this fact as a marketing tool, lest it invite antitrust intervention, but it did not need to. RCA led the development of superior technologies for the entire industry, and this greatly enhanced its competitive position in the consumer products industry.

Television was growing faster than radio, a technology that had clearly peaked. As a result, RCA felt little need to protect its position in the radio industry. Competitors rapidly gained advantages in this segment, largely wiping out whatever leads RCA had earned. RCA continued to manufacture radios and phonographs, but branched into other areas that today would be called the "software" side of the industry. That is, RCA maintained a strong presence in radio programming through NBC, and in home entertainment through the sale of record albums pressed under the RCA name.

The next logical step in RCA's business development was the introduction of color television. Again, rivals including CBS attempted to gain FCC approval of color technologies, but these were incompatible with existing black-and-white broadcast systems. Ultimately, the CBS system gained approval. By 1953, however, color television failed to catch on, precisely because the public was unwilling to own two sets, one for black-and-white, and the other for color broadcasts.

RCA undertook the task of developing a broadcast technology that would allow black-and-white sets to take color programming and color sets to accept black-and-white broadcasts. This would enable RCA to gain a reversal of the FCC's approval of the CBS standard. RCA succeeded in 1953 by developing a tricolor kinescope, working on the same principles as black-and-white. The FCC approved the RCA standard in December, and a year later, RCA color televisions went into production.

The company dumped more than $130 million into the color project, an investment that did not produce a profit until 1960. Many programs were switched to color formats, including *Superman, Gunsmoke,* and *Bonanza,* and others came later. By 1966, NBC had switched completely to color programming, followed a year later by ABC and CBS. During the same period, sales in the television industry rose from $200 million in 1962 to more than $3 billion in 1966. RCA took the greatest advantage of this growth.

RCA's strong attention to research and development yielded several new advances that produced terrific, but short-lived, competitive advantages. By 1974, all RCA sets were 100-percent solid state. The only tube in an RCA set was the picture tube. And the company continually improved its picture tube and chassis assemblies, incorporated automatic tuning, remote control, and other features.

Like other manufacturers, RCA maintained a product line dominated by big living room-type sets. This created an opening at the low end of the market for new competitors such as Sony. These companies rapidly gained market share, enabling them to establish American distribution networks and brand-building advertising campaigns and fund technological advances of their own. By the late 1970s, they had advanced to positions of respectability in the wider market.

One area in which RCA failed to take a leadership role was the development of videocassette recorders, or VCRs. Sony and Matsushita battled for acceptance of their VCR formats. When Sony refused to share its technology with other manufacturers, RCA introduced the Matsushita VHS format in 1977 and quickly took the lead in market share from Sony. RCA offered a model that ran at such a low speed that it could accommodate a full four hours of programming, twice that of Sony. RCA also followed the Japanese into video camera technologies, as these graduated from cameras with bulky recorder packs to more compact hand-held models. The first RCA videocam produced black-and-white recordings, but these were quickly supplanted by color models.

Though RCA was originally established to develop long-distance radio systems in the United States, many of the patents it controlled or shared were applicable to production around the world. While RCA sets were sold almost exclusively in the United States, a small number were exported to distributors in Europe and Central and South America, but the company did not actually pursue export marketing due to higher costs of transportation.

Advertising

RCA's first brand logo was a circular emblem containing the three letters, with a lightning bolt connected to the A. This symbol was used exclusively until 1929, when RCA acquired what would become one of the most famous and enduring symbols in American industry. When RCA purchased Victor in 1929, it gained the rights to the image of a befuddled dog staring into the bell of a Victrola. Victor's tagline "His Master's Voice" suggests that even a dog, with super-sensitive ears, cannot discern between a live voice and the excellent sound reproduction of the victrola.

The dog, a black and white fox terrier called "Nipper," was born in England in 1884. He was used as a model for a painting by Francis Barraud, depicting the dog looking into the cone of a cylinder-type phonograph. Barraud later altered the painting to include a disk-model phonograph and sold it to the Gramophone Company. The American rights to the image were acquired by the Consolidated Talking Machine Company (later called Victor) in 1901. At the time RCA acquired Victor, the Nipper was one of the best known images in advertising. The dog and Victrola were subsequently used on every RCA audio product, including phonographs, radios, and record albums, in a somewhat awkward combination with the circular logo.

Another interesting symbol from the early days could only be heard. It was the signature chime used to identify RCA's broadcasting unit. The three musical notes—at the time G, E, and C—were chosen from the initials for RCA's parent, the General Electric Company. The association with GE was terminated in 1930, but the chime survived as a jingle for NBC. The simple tones regained their significance after General Electric acquired RCA and its NBC unit in 1985.

Nipper, RCA's famous canine, has been joined in the brand's advertising by Chipper.

RCA changed its corporate logo in 1968, ending use of the 46-year old circular RCA trademark. The old logo was designed to depict the strange marvel of electricity. But by the 1960s, it was hopelessly outdated. Instead, the company introduced a simple block-lettered "RCA" in bold red, and dropped "Victor" from its corporate name.

Nipper the dog re-emerged in 1977 in advertising for RCA citizens band radios, and was featured on television ads until the national craze for CB radios died out. In 1978, the dog and Victrola symbol were added to service company trucks, shipping cartons, and in promotional literature, and the red block-letter logo was dropped. This use of Nipper proved successful with people who had known and trusted the RCA brand their entire lives.

Many older consumers, intent on purchasing an American-made brand, recognized Nipper and the RCA name from decades past.

In 1990, after RCA became part of Thomson Consumer Electronics, a live Nipper and puppy were used in place of the Nipper caricature. The pair was arranged in front of a television, staring quizzically at the screen. Now, the dogs were unable to tell whether the sound as well as the picture were real. In 1991, Thomson held a nationwide consumer contest to name Nipper's puppy companion, and ultimately settled on the name "Chipper" from more than 85,000 entries. A campaign launched in 1993 featured the two dogs watching television, and used the tagline, "Changing Entertainment. Again."

Performance Evaluation

During the 1980s, RCA shared its leading position in the market with Magnavox (a Philips brand), closely followed by Zenith, and then Sony, Toshiba, JVC, and a number of Japanese brands. RCA encountered tremendous competition from foreign manufacturers whose cost structures were radically lower. This forced RCA to gradually transfer some of its production facilities to countries with low labor costs, while maintaining its Bloomington, Indiana, plant at a high level of production. Despite these competitive pressures, RCA avoided serious deterioration of its leading position in the market. Its product line was pared down considerably, cutting out dozens of non-core products like radios. This enabled RCA to concentrate on its strongest and most profitable product, televisions.

When RCA was acquired by General Electric in 1985, its product line was melded with that of GE, which manufactured its own radios and portable stereos. Television sets for both brands were then produced in Bloomington. But before rationalization of the two product lines could occur, General Electric sold the entire consumer products unit to Thomson S.A.—a French electronics company looking for an easy way into the American market.

As GE brands already occupied the low end of the market, and RCA was a high-quality line, there was little for Thomson to eliminate from either product line. Instead, the company maintained the two product lines, but concentrated on what it considered to be inadequate leveraging of the brand names, inefficient distribution, and ineffective marketing. Through improvements in these areas, Thomson has managed to greatly strengthen RCA's position in the market and build it into a leading franchise.

RCA and GE brand products—TVs, VCRs, camcorders, etc.—are produced by Thomson and marketed through separate retail channels. These products target specific consumer segments and complement, not cannibalize, each other. The RCA brand in particular is prominent on a broad variety of consumer electronics products as well as the United States' first digital satellite receiving system—RCADSS—which will enable consumers to access over 150 TV channels from the nation's first high-power direct broadcast satellite (DBS). As additional new-wave digital products are developed, RCA will continue to be a dominant brand.

Further Reading:

Morgan, Hal, *Symbols of America,* New York: Penguin, 1986.

"No Brand Like an Old Brand," *Forbes,* June 11, 1990, pp. 179–180.

Powers, David Cleary, *Great American Brands,* New York: Fairchild Publications, 1981.

"RCA: Will It Ever Be a Top Performer?," *Business Week,* April 2, 1984, pp. 52–56.

Additional information provided by Thomson Consumer Electronics.

—John Simley

REMINGTON®

REMINGTON®

The second-best-selling men's electric shaver and the top brand of electric shavers for women, Remingtons are known for their dependability, quality, and value. Since their introduction, Remington electric shavers have incorporated technological advances in order to enhance their cutting ability and speed, as well to provide users with greater comfort and flexibility. The first portable shavers for travelers as well as the first shavers to feature rechargeable batteries and replaceable blades were all marketed under the Remington brand name. Consumers learned about the innovations of Remington's shavers through various advertising and marketing strategies, most notably through Remington Products Inc.'s spokesperson and biggest fan—owner Victor K. Kiam II.

Brand Origins

The first Remington electric shaver was introduced in the United States in 1937 by Harry Landsiedel, a vice-president at Remington Rand, Inc. Landsiedel sought to make a safer, simpler, speedier, and more sanitary shaving product. Although several other inventors had worked on the same "dry shaving" concept during the 1920s and 1930s, Landsiedel was the first to meet with success.

From 1937 to 1939 more than 60 other companies entered the potentially lucrative market with dry shavers. But in 1939, Remington achieved a significant boost when its shaver was demonstrated at the New York World's Fair. There thousands of visitors bought their first Remington shaver, and many more people became acquainted with the Remington name. This early version of the Remington shaver was a simple, single-headed product—slow and technically unsophisticated compared to modern electric shavers. However, it represented high quality and reliability for its day, and Remington was on its way to becoming a major player in the market.

Brand Development

In 1940, Remington introduced the first dual volt shaver for use in the home or car, as well as the first shavers designed for women. In 1949, Remington introduced dual-headed shaving. The new shaver doubled the cutting surface and had greater speed than the earlier models, and was the first commercial precursor to modern high speed, multiple-head shavers.

Production of Remington shavers decreased during World War II, as the company retooled its plants for defense work, but by 1945, the shaver again became the company's primary product. During the 1960s, Remington continued to introduce innovative products, marketing the first rechargeable shaver as well as the first replaceable electric shaver blades. In 1977, Remington introduced the Micro Screen shaver, which, into the 1990s, remained the only electric shaver guaranteed to shave as close as a blade.

In 1988, Remington introduced an electric nose and ear hair clipper for men, a concept reportedly inspired by a conversation between Remington's owner, Victor Kiam, and Senator Howard Metzenbaum of Ohio. When Metzenbaum complained to Kiam that electric shavers could not trim hair inside the ear, and the traditional hand-cranked ear hair clipper was awkward and dangerous, Kiam instructed his staff to design a safer electric model. The Remington clipper turned out to be one of the company's hottest items. Remembering Metzenbaum's contribution, Kiam and sent him the very first clipper to roll off the assembly line in Hong Kong, inscribed in gold lettering, "For thought processes and hair growth above the norm."

AT A GLANCE

Remington brand of electric shavers founded in 1937 by Harry Landsiedel, vice-president of Remington Rand, Inc.; as a result of a merger, company name changed to Sperry Rand Corporation, 1955; brand sold in 1979 to Victor K. Kiam II, and became an independent, privately held corporation known as Remington Products, Inc.

Performance: *Market share*—25% of men's shavers category; 35% of women's shavers category. *Sales*—$133 million.

Major competitor: Norelco; also Panasonic and Sanyo.

Advertising: *Agency*—Grey Advertising Inc., New York, NY, 1980—. *Major campaign*—"If you can grow it, we can shave it" and "Hey, Remington, shave this!"

Addresses: *Parent company*—Remington Products Inc., 60 Main St., Bridgeport, CT 06604-5706; phone: (203) 367-4400; fax: (203) 366-6039.

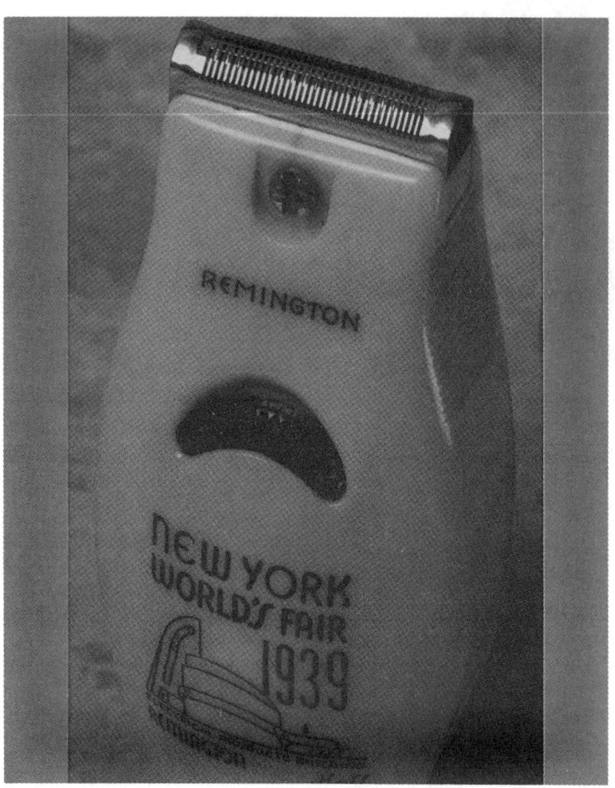

Two years after it was launched, the Remington electric shaver made an appearance at the 1939 World's Fair in New York.

Company Strategies

When the New Orleans-born Kiam bought the Remington brand from the Sperry Rand Corporation in 1979, it faced dwindling market share and declining sales, having lost $30 million over the past three years. Kiam began to restructure, eliminating executive positions, cutting overhead, and cancelling annual price increases and product modifications. Furthermore, all overseas manufacturing was brought back to the United States, where it was concentrated in the company's Connecticut headquarters. On the plant floor, quality circles and 100 percent product inspection were introduced, resulting in a near zero defect rate.

As a result Remington's shavers regained their renown for quality among consumers. In addition, rather than dampening worker morale or enthusiasm, the extensive changes increased worker pride along with product quality. In fact, as of the early 1990s the company was the only leveraged buyout listed in the publication *The 100 Best Companies to Work for in America.*

Advertising Innovations

Remington's owner became the spokesperson for the company soon after he bought it, spending more than $300 million in advertising during a 12-year period. Television viewers became acquainted with Kiam through commercials in which he explained, "I liked the Remington Micro Screen shaver so much, I bought the company." These commercials were broadcast in 15 foreign languages in 31 countries, including Japan.

During the 1980s, Remington's advertising emphasized the product's reliability with the slogan, "Close as a blade or your money back." In 1993, advertising sought to update the product's image, and a new tagline was created to convey the shaver's superior qualities. The commercials opened with a burly, unshaven man offering the challenge, "Hey, Remington, shave this!" At the end of the spot, Kiam appeared to deliver the new tagline, "If you can grow it, we can shave it." The ad was designed to emphasize the success of the shaver's "triple-foil" action on tough beards and in difficult places such as the chin line, the upper lip, and around the ears.

Future Growth

In addition to shavers, the Remington brand name has been extended to other grooming products, such as home haircut kits, moustache and beard trimmers, the nose and ear hair clipper, women's nailcare systems, and nail polish removers. Furthermore the Remington name adorns some small household appliances, including portable air purifiers, swimming pool alarms, clothes shavers, and dryers. In November of 1993, Remington increased its participation in the women's grooming-appliance business by announcing its purchase of Clairol, a maker of such personal care appliances as hair dryers, makeup mirrors, and curling irons. The brand's grooming products are expected to reflect the same level of quality, innovation, and value as its shavers have over the past several decades.

Further Reading:

"A Hair-Razing Passage," *Maclean's,* December 14, 1992, p. 8.

The Remington Products Story, Bridgeport, CT: Remington Products, Inc.

"Remington's Slogan," *Wall Street Journal,* October 28, 1993, p. B12.

"Remington to Buy Hair-Appliance Unit From Bristol-Myers," *Wall Street Journal,* November 3, 1993, p. B10.

—Dorothy Kroll

REVERE WARE®

The Revere Ware line of stainless steel, copper-bottom pots and pans is one of the best known products in housewares in the United States.

Brand Origins

Although Revere Ware is named after Paul Revere, its connection to the American patriot is circuitous. Revere Ware was created by researchers at Revere Copper & Brass, Inc. That company, known for a brief time as the Republic Brass Corporation, was founded in 1928 when six copper and brass companies merged. One of the firms, the Taunton-New Bedford Copper Company, was the successor of Paul Revere and Son, which was founded by Paul Revere in 1801 to make copper sheathing for naval vessels in Canton, Massachusetts. It had existed until 1900, when it merged with two other firms and the Revere name was dropped. Of the five other companies that joined to form Revere Copper & Brass, one was the Rome Manufacturing Company. Based in Rome, New York, it had manufactured housewares since 1892, when it started making tea kettles, and later produced wash boilers and coffee pots.

Revere Copper & Brass, Inc. grew into one of the largest copper fabricators in the United States. Most of the products that the company manufactured were industrial in nature—copper pipes, sheets, tubes, and bars. Given the uncertain nature of copper prices and the fact that the company owned no mines, Revere sought to diversify its operations.

Brand Fills A Niche

In the 1930s much of America's cooking was done in cast-iron skillets. Unfortunately, they were heavy and often difficult to clean. Various manufacturers, including Revere, had tried to come up with alternatives, but there were drawbacks with all of them. In the early 1930s Revere produced solid-copper utensils with chrome-plated linings for a brief period, but when it was discovered that food acids scarred the chromium, this idea was dropped.

In 1932 Revere undertook a research program to study the science of cookware, and it soon discovered that any chrome-plated lining would be affected by food acids on its surface. Revere created a development department to find a metal that had the right qualities for cooking. After testing various metals in different combinations, stainless steel was found to have the preferred qualities. It was strong, durable, and light. It was easy to clean. And it resisted the action of foods on its surface. However, stainless steel did not conduct heat well. By 1936 the decision was made to coat the bottom of the pan with copper. After months of testing, an efficient system was developed to electroplate the copper to stainless steel, allowing heat to be transferred evenly.

Meanwhile, the look and feel of the product was being perfected by design director Archibald Welden. Welden gave the cookware gracefully curved and easy-to-hold handles and knobs made of plastic—a first in the industry. A silversmith's hammer, well worn from use, provided him with the inspiration for the handle's unique shape. Welden also rounded the edges of the cookware, making the product easier to clean.

Revere Ware Copper Clad Stainless Steel Cookware was unveiled at the Housewares Show, in Chicago, in January 1939. Although the 1400 line, as it was (and still is) known, was more expensive than other cookware, it was instantly popular. Demand soon outpaced production capacity.

World War II halted production completely, however. Between 1942 and 1945, the manufacturing facilities turned out cartridge cases, smoke bombs, and rocket cases. At the end of the war, Revere sought to ease back into a peacetime economy. The company built a new plant in Riverside, California, which opened in 1948, and bought a facility in Clinton, Illinois. The plant in Clinton turned out its first piece of Revere Ware, a one quart saucepan, in October 1950. However, production continued to be limited because of the demands on strategic metals by the defense department. Nevertheless, by the end of that year Revere Ware accounted for a tenth of the company's sales and contributed disproportionately to its profits.

With the onset of the Korean War, the company's copper-plating machinery was again put to defense uses. Thus limited, Revere manufactured many stainless-steel items, such as mixing bowls, canisters, utensil racks, and casseroles. Most of these items were eventually discontinued. Through 1956, there was an ever-present backlog of orders for Revere Ware. To capitalize on that popularity, Revere created such spinoff products as Hotel Ware, heavy-duty cookware for industrial use that was introduced in 1954. The line was soon discontinued. The next year Miniature Revere Ware, toy versions of the full size line, was unveiled.

AT A GLANCE

Revere Ware brand of cookware introduced at the Houseware Show in Chicago in 1939 by Revere Copper & Brass, Inc.; Revere Ware, Inc., a subsidiary created in 1986, sold to Corning Glass Works in 1988; Revere Ware Corp. now a wholly owned subsidiary of Corning Consumer Products, Co.

Performance: *Sales*—Approximately $100 million.

Major competitor: Farberware.

Advertising: *Agency*—DMB&B, New York, NY.

Addresses: *Parent company*—Revere Ware Corp., 1000 S. Sherman, Box 250, Clinton, IL, 61727; phone: (217) 935-7200; fax: (217) 935-7399. *Ultimate parent company*—Corning Consumer Products, Inc., Corning, NY, 14831; phone: (607) 974-9000. *Ultimate ultimate parent company*—Corning Inc..

Other product experiments included Copper Maid Cookware, a premium product introduced in 1957 that was copper-clad and stainless steel, but designed differently and with a lighter metal than the 1400 line; it continued for approximately four years. Deluxe Revere Ware Cookware, a line with a different handle and knob design and covers shaped like a Chinese pagoda, was introduced in 1962.

A Long Decline

Starting in 1959 Revere Ware sales began to decline steadily. The Riverside plant closed in 1962. The company continued to try to experiment with different metal and product configurations. In 1964 Revere started lining its copper-clad stainless steel product with Teflon. This was followed by coatings of Permaloc (a Teflon coating with a substrate of metal and ceramic), Teflon II, and later still, Silverstone. None of these proved successful. In 1968 the plant in Rome, New York, discontinued production of the copper-clad stainless steel utensils.

It was not until 1971 that sales began to pick up, hitting a plateau in 1973. The Rome facility started making Revere Ware again in the mid-1970s. Sales then remained fairly constant until the early 1980s.

In 1974 Revere introduced its 7000 line, which was designed just as the original 1400 line but was composed of different metals. It was tri-ply, meaning it was made of two layers of stainless steel around one layer of copper, and proved popular. The 7000 line was still in production in the early 1990s.

In 1980 the company created a wholly owned subsidiary, Revere Copper Products, Inc., to acquire and operate its copper and brass fabricating assets and businesses, including the facilities that produced Revere Ware.

Financial Problems For Parent Company

Revere Ware's parent, Revere Copper & Brass, was experiencing serious financial difficulties by the early 1980s. The company had done well through the 1960s and 1970s with defense contracts fuelled by the Vietnam War. A headlong plunge into aluminum manufacturing in the late 1960s proved to be a disaster for the company, which had lost millions on this experiment by the mid-1970s. Revere Copper & Brass filed for bankruptcy protection in 1982. In July of 1985 a bankruptcy judge approved Revere's reorganization plan and payment schedule to its creditors.

Less than a month later, the Revere Ware brand was put up for sale by its parent company. In 1984 Revere Ware had generated approximately 15 percent of the parent company's $601 million sales, so Revere Copper & Brass reportedly asked for $100 million for this profitable division. Many observers of the industry felt that the asking price was unrealistically high. It was noted that Revere Ware's parent had put off making capital improvements and that a new owner would need to invest heavily to update its machinery.

A Challenge From Imports

Although Revere Copper & Brass had previously been seen as reluctant to sell off its profitable cookware division, the cookware market had changed significantly in the short span of time between 1983 and 1985. A flood of lower-priced imports, mainly from South Korea, over the previous two years had made the market much more competitive. Retailers could not resist stocking the lower-priced products—which realized a higher profit.

In an attempt to face that challenge, Revere Ware in 1986 introduced the 2000 Line—a line of stainless steel cookware with the brazed aluminum bottoms common to imported cookware. It was made in South Korea and assembled in the U.S. This allowed Revere to reduce the prices on all its cookware products and offer retailers the opportunity to lower prices to consumers as well. The line proved popular, and by the end of that year it accounted for 20 percent of Revere Ware's sales. Later that year Revere Ware introduced a line of cutlery manufactured in Japan, with handles based on the classic 1400 line shape. This product was discontinued, however, in 1988.

At about the same time, Revere Copper & Brass announced that it was taking its Revere Ware division off the market. The company noted that "the value placed on Revere Ware . . . was less than the projected value." Cost-cutting measures were also undertaken.

In November of 1986, Revere Copper & Brass created a subsidiary, Revere Ware, Inc., based in Clinton, Illinois, to encompass its consumer-oriented businesses. Besides Revere Ware, these included the company's food-container and packaging business, Revere Foil and Containers, Inc., which served the frozen-food, airline, and food-service industries; and Revere Ware Courtesy Stores, Inc., outlet stores that sold Revere Ware products. This move was seen as part of a strategy to significantly expand its consumer businesses. The Rome facility was closed permanently, and all U.S.-based production was handled at the Clinton plant, where employees agreed to wage concessions. By 1988 it was clear that this restructuring was a success. Record sales and profits prompted Revere Copper & Brass to look again for a buyer for its newly invigorated subsidiary.

Corning Purchases Revere Ware

Revere Copper & Brass sold Revere Ware, Inc. to Corning Glass Works in 1988; the definitive agreement was signed April 28 for a reported $120 million. Corning's well-known glass cookware names—Pyrex, Corning Ware, Visions—were seen as merging nicely with Revere Ware, expanding Corning's cookware offerings and also giving it the ability to penetrate the department stores. Corning had historically been largely limited to distributing its products in the mass merchants. Corning's kitchen pieces were made of glass, and it was thought that Revere Ware's metal cookware would complement them well. "No question about it. We dominate our market, and they dominate theirs. Two premiere brand names are being combined," said Revere Ware president Peter Cameron in *HFD* (Cameron subsequently left the company).

In explaining its move, Corning noted that 65 percent of all cookware was metal, and it was expecting to increase its sales by 10 percent with the purchase of Revere Ware. Industry sources quoted in *HFD* estimated Revere Ware's annual sales to be between $70 and $80 million and experts believed that Corning's resources would allow Revere Ware to expand fully. "Although we were clearly doing very well, with this year being the best year we ever had, it really was a struggle to capitalize and take advantage of the opportunities we saw," Cameron told *HFD* after the purchase by Corning had been announced. "We should now be able to be much more aggressive, for instance, in overseas markets."

Corning worked to place Revere Ware in mass-merchant stores. By 1991, the company claimed to have Revere Ware products distributed in 83 percent of the mass market and that Revere Ware sales made up more than 17 percent of Corning's total mass-merchant cookware sales.

The marriage of Corning and Revere Ware was illustrated in the Vista product line, introduced in 1989. The product's Corning glass cover fit over a copper-clad, stainless steel body with the shape of the classic Revere Ware 1400 line. This product was specifically aimed at the mass merchants.

Revere Ware moved beyond stainless-steel when a line of nonstick skillets was introduced in 1991. Corning hoped to develop a spot at the high end of the mass merchants with the line. Corning research had shown that consumers wanted a nonstick skillet to complement their Revere Ware pieces. According to the company, 25 percent of all households owned Revere's stainless steel cookware. The nonstick pieces were assembled in Illinois from parts manufactured in Hong Kong.

Further Reading:

Bacher, Mary Ann, "Revere Ware May Be Sold," *HFD,* September 2, 1985, p. 1.

Bacher, Mary Ann, and Finkel, Rachel, "Revere, Farber Aim at Importers," *HFD,* November 4, 1985, p. 1.

Bent, Heather, "Revere Regroups with Subsidiary," *HFD,* November 17, 1986, p. 133.

"Chapter 11 for Revere," *Business Week,* November 8, 1982, p. 50.

Cook, James, "Staying on Top," *Forbes,* July 1, 1977, p. 54.

Ellis, Beth R., "Corning Buy Boosts Lines, Distribution," *HFD,* May 9, 1988, p. 1.

"Hot Revere Ware Might Be Sold," *Chicago Tribune,* January 29, 1988, p. 2.

"A Marriage of Ceramic, Metal: Corning to Buy Revere Ware," *Chicago Tribune,* May 1, 1988, p. 7.

Mitchell, Constance, "Corning's Purchase of Revere Expected to Broaden Sales," *Wall Street Journal,* p. 30.

"New Revere Unit Will Encompass Consumer-Oriented Businesses," *American Metal Market,* November 12, 1986.

Rappleyea, Warren, "Corning Glass' Acquisition of Revere Ware Tagged at 120M," *American Metal Market,* May 3, 1988, p. 2.

"Revere's Woes Blamed on Market, Government," *Iron Age,* November 10, 1982, p. 69.

"Revere Ware's Parent Takes Cookware Division Off Block," *HFD,* November 4, 1985.

Weiss, Lisa Casey, "Corning Goes Beyond Stainless," *HFD,* June 17, 1991, p. 69.

—*C. L. Collins*

RICOH®

In the last three decades Ricoh has become one of the most recognizable brand names worldwide for photocopiers and other office machines. In 1962, the Tokyo based Riken Optical Company established its first major, wholly owned subsidiary in the United States, the Ricoh Corporation. So successful were its product lines, in particular its photocopiers, that the parent company in Japan changed its name to Ricoh the following year. Three decades later, Ricoh is among the world's top three brands in digital office machine products, especially photocopiers, fax machines, and computer parts, as well as photographic equipment. In addition, the Ricoh brand name has become known for such innovations as the world's first high-speed office fax machine and multifunctional digital copier, the world's fastest digital full color copier, the world's smallest fax machine, and the world's first integrated office machine, the MF530—which combines fax, photocopying, printing, editing, and scanning functions, plus instantaneous translations of documents from English to Japanese.

Brand Origins

''Ricoh'' became the brand name for a diverse product line that began in Japan in 1936. In that year, the Institute of Physical and Chemical Research in Tokyo had developed a superior photosensitive paper for developing film and proceeded to market it commercially through the Riken Kankoshi Company, founded for that purpose by Mr. Kiyoshi Ichimura. In the coming years, his company would be one of many that would market the inventions of the famous Institute.

Less than two years after the photographic paper came on the market, Ricoh had the largest domestic market share in Japan of photosensitive paper. This encouraged company president Ichimura to think of expanding the product line to include cameras. In 1938, the company changed its name to the Riken Optical Co., Ltd. Two years later it introduced the ''Ricohflex 1,'' a unique twin-lens camera that was the first product to bear the Ricoh brand name.

Commercial Successes

The Second World War devastated Japan's economy as well as halted all production of Ricoh products. Unlike many other companies, Riken Optical was able to reconstitute itself in 1946 under its original founder, Mr. Ichimura, at a time when most pre-war company presidents were prohibited by the American occupation government from resuming their former positions.

The Ricoh camera line was extremely successful. By 1954, sales of the Ricohflex I, II, and III topped those of all other competitors in Japan and was also a big seller abroad—200,000 were sold overseas in one year. Once again, success encouraged the company to expand its product line. Riken's experience with imaging technology led to research on a practical and cost-effective copying machine. This would not be ''xerography,'' or photocopying, which was in its infancy. The complex technology of photocopying was consuming the energy and resources of the Haloid Company in Rochester, New York, which held the patent for the original process, invented by an American in the late 1930s. Nonetheless, business machines were the up and coming products of the future, and in 1955, the ''Ricopy 101'' copier, an attractive, compact mimeograph machine, marked the entrance of Ricoh into the office machine industry, where it would make its greatest mark. This product would be followed in 1960 by the ''Ricoh Offset'' duplicator. In the same year, Sindo Ricoh Co., a wholly owned subsidiary of Riken Optical of Tokyo, was established in South Korea. Riken had become a major player in Japan in copier technology and in photographic equipment.

In 1962, Riken established its biggest and most important subsidiary, Ricoh Industries U.S.A. (later restructured and renamed Ricoh of America, Inc.), in New York. By 1970, this subsidiary's sales topped $1.3 million. But Ricoh had agreed not to sell its copiers in the United States under its own brand name; rather, the company entered into agreements with Savin and Pitney Bowes, two prominent U.S. corporations whose names adorned Ricoh-made machines. Thus, despite its successes in the U.S. market, Ricoh had practically no brand visibility. In 1981, ''Ricoh'' brand products were marketed in the United States.

Early Marketing Strategy

In the years following World War II, Riken Optical's marketing strategy, almost from the outset, was a global one. Beginning with the establishment of its first overseas subsidiary in Korea in 1955, Ricoh went on to establish branches in the United States, Canada, France, the United Kingdom, the Netherlands, and Belgium. In addition, these subsidiary branches were decentralized, with the objective of making them independent members of the Ricoh family of companies. Globalization and product innova-

AT A GLANCE

Ricoh begun in 1936, with the establishment by Mr. Kiyoshi Ichimura of the Riken Kankoshi Company Ltd., a manufacturer of photosensitive paper, in Japan; in 1938, company decided to manufacture cameras, and changed its name to Riken Optical Company; after the war, Riken entered the copier market; company produced Ricoh photocopiers and entered the field of computers; in the 1970s, Ricoh entered the fax machine market; its three major product categories continue to be cameras, fax machines, and copy machines and other electronic products; Ricoh Corporation's U.S. headquarters located in West Caldwell, NJ; parent company, Ricoh Co., Ltd. located in Tokyo, Japan.

Performance: *Market share*—16% of U.S. rewritable optical drive (computer) market (1993). *Sales*—Approximately $9 billion (1993) internationally; approximately $1 billion (1993) in U.S. market.

Major competitor: Xerox; also, Kodak.

Advertising: *Agency*—Gigante Vaz, New York, NY; 1992, *Major campaign*—"The Name to Know."

Addresses: *Parent company*—Ricoh Corporation, 5 Dedrick Place, West Caldwell, NJ 07006; (201) 882-2000; fax: (201) 882-2506. *Ultimate parent company*—Ricoh Company, Ltd.; 15-5, Minami-Aoyama 1-chome, Minato-ku, Tokyo, Japan; phone: 81-3-3479-3111; fax: 81-3-3403-1578.

tion, more than advertising, have made Ricoh an internationally recognized brand name.

The most effective advertising for Ricoh has involved its sponsorship of major sporting events. For instance, the Ricoh Offset duplicator and the Ricoh Auto Shot camera received worldwide recognition from advertising at the Olympic games in Tokyo in 1964. Since then, Ricoh has heavily advertised its product lines at major sporting events, such as the 1992 Olympics, and international trade fairs.

Product Innovation

Ricoh has become a world leader in the office automation equipment industry, producing photocopiers, fax machines, computers and computer parts, while at the same time maintaining its world market dominance in quality cameras and optical equipment. From the mimeograph machine to today's multi-functional copier combining photocopying, editing, printing, faxing, and translation functions, Ricoh has made its mark as a pioneer in the information revolution.

With the success of the Ricopy 101 in 1955, Ricoh was establishing a name for itself in the office copier industry. Another success, the Ricoh Offset duplicator in 1960, was followed five years later by the Ricopy DT1200 "electrostatic" coated paper copier. In 1975, the Ricopy DT1200 plain paper photocopier, the company's first plain paper copier, came on the market.

Ricoh produced the world's first digital copier in 1982. In 1990, Ricoh marketed the Artage 800, the fastest digital full-color copier in the world. By 1991, the world's first multi-functional digital copier arrived, Ricoh's Imagio MF530, with six different functions. This put Ricoh in the forefront of integrated, multifunctional office systems, or "intelligent" office machines that are powered by artificial intelligence built into the system. This is the newest, fastest developing wave in the office machine industry.

Ricoh's success with copiers and cameras encouraged a new product line—printers and computers. The 1976 Ricoh Printer 40, an impact, or daisy-wheel, printer, firmly established Ricoh in the printer market. This had been preceded by Ricoh's entrance into computer manufacturing in 1971 with the Ricom 8, which led in rapid succession to several "new and improved" models over the next two decades. In the early 1980s, after dropping the Savin and Pitney Bowes names from its products, Ricoh came out with its ultra-compact, hand-held business computer, the Ricoh SP25, as well as the Ricoh SP200, a line of desktop computers; in 1991 the company released the Ricoh VC-1, a voice activated PC.

"Intelligent" or "neural" fax machines also have evolved rapidly from the world's first office fax machine—Ricoh's 1973 Rifax 600S—which was also the first fax machine to transmit an international facsimile message in less than a minute. From there, Ricoh developed, according to the 1990 *Guinness Book of World Records,* the world's smallest, lightest fax machine, the portable Ricoh Fax PF-2. In 1994, Ricoh will launch its Intelligent Facsimile System, which combines a multitude of functions, such as laser printing, scanning, and copying. Ricoh fax machines were the first in the world to incorporate both computer and digital copier functions.

International Market

New products emanating from Ricoh's research and development labs have steadily found markets worldwide. Ricoh commands a major share of the U.S. copier market, with strong competition from Kodak and Xerox. With the recent deep recession in the United States, followed by one in western Europe, Ricoh has turned its attention closer to home. Historically, Ricoh has focused on the expansion of its overseas markets rather than the domestic Japanese market. Emerging markets in the 21st century will most likely be China, where Ricoh already has established a subsidiary, and Latin America.

Future Growth

Ricoh's strongest assets are its brand name, product diversity, and reputation for innovation. The $9 billion corporation has been a pacesetter in information technology for over a generation. In the highly competitive office automation industry, Ricoh is one of the big three global manufacturers. Ricoh will most likely take advantage of the North American Free Trade Agreement (NAFTA) to continue its expansion into North American markets. With the fall of trade barriers around the world and free-market economic reforms in China, the world's biggest market, Ricoh should maintain a strong competitive balance for the foreseeable future.

Further Reading:

Annual Report: Ricoh, 1993.

Castro, Janice, "Look Out, Xerox (New Photocopier From Ricoh Translates From English to Japanese)," *Time,* February 1, 1993, p. 15.

Grimes, Brad, "Ricoh Combines Fax Machine, Copier, and Ink Jet Printer," *PC Magazine,* December 21, 1993, p. 70.

Hamilton, David P., "Tired of Shredding? New Ricoh Method Tries Different Tack; Technique Erases the Toner from Photocopy Paper, Making Recycling Easier," *The Wall Street Journal,* August 20, 1993, p. B6(W), p. B2(E).

"Japanese Manufacturers Look to Fast-Growing Asia," *Marketing News,* October 11, 1993, p. 12.

McConville, James A., "Ricoh Joins Portable Fax Ranks: Unveils What is Reportedly the Industry's Smallest, Lightest Unit," *HFD—The Weekly Home Furnishings Newspaper,* October 1, 1990, p. 137.

Okamoto, Akira, "Creative and Innovative Research at Ricoh," *Long Range Planning,* October 1991, p. 9.

"Ricoh Company (Acquires American Office Equipment Company)," *The Wall Street Journal,* March 8, 1993, p. A8(E).

Ricoh 1993 Fact Book, Ricoh Corporation.

Schroeder, Erica, "Ricoh to Offer Its Own Magneto-Optical Drives," *PC Week,* February 8, 1993, p. 24.

Tapellini, Donna, "Incredible Shrinking Fax Machines (From Ricoh Corp.)," *Adweek's Marketing Week,* February 20, 1989, p. 4.

—Sina Dubovoj

ROLLERBLADE®

Rollerblade®

The Rollerblade brand, owned by Minnesota-based Rollerblade, Inc., has been the driving force behind the growth of in-line skating, which in 1993 was the fastest-growing sport in the United States, with more than 12 million participants. Controlling some 50 percent of the market, Rollerblade, introduced in 1980, was for many people synonymous with the sport itself, and this has been both a blessing and a headache for its owners. Since the mid-1980s Rollerblade—like Kleenex, Xerox, and other industry-defining brands—has regularly faced the problem of defending its name, as well as its high-profile, fun, active image, against what one writer called the ''genericization'' of its trademark. As the company regularly pointed out, ''trademarks are proper adjectives'' (as in Rollerblade skates, Problade skates, and Metroblade skates) and not nouns (that is, Rollerblades) and never verbs (for example, rollerblading).

Rollerblade, Inc., a private company headquartered in Minnetonka, a suburb of Minneapolis, was the originator and world leader of the in-line skating industry. Since 1991 it has been 50 percent owned by Italy's largest ski-boot maker, Nordica (which, in turn, was owned by Benetton, the leading European clothes manufacturer). It was at this time that the basic in-line skate patent entered the public domain, resulting in a flurry of upstart products from both new and established manufacturers. The most visible competitor for Rollerblade, Inc., has been First Team Sports, which was also based in Minnesota and was founded by two former Rollerblade employees. First Team came out with their Ultra-Wheels line in 1986, and by 1990 the younger company's share of the market was 22 percent. Although Rollerblade, Inc.'s share was more than double that, gone were the days of complete market dominance. Fortunately, the industry itself was experiencing phenomenal expansion—from 1986 to 1990 wholesale sales of in-line skates increased from $3.5 million to $53 million. By 1993 the estimated industry total was $320 million. Despite the new competition, Rollerblade, Inc., was still the dominant brand and led the way in creative marketing and technological development. With the backing of Nordica, the Rollerblade brand promised to remain at the fore of what looked to be one of the hottest ''life-style'' activities of the 1990s.

The Hockey Connection

Rollerblade skates were first conceived by Scott Olson, a Minnesota high-school hockey Hall of Famer and semipro hockey player. According to a 1985 *Star Tribune* article, Olson was still playing for the Winnipeg Jets in 1978 when he ''happened to see this guy in Minneapolis selling ice skates with wheels on them. The guy was practically giving them away because he couldn't sell any. I bought a pair, and they were fantastic. I just fell in love with them, because it was my dream come true. I could ice skate anywhere I wanted to go.'' By 1980 Olson had negotiated the distribution rights for Canada and the upper Midwest and proceeded to market the in-line roller skates on his own, primarily by wearing them everywhere he went, handing out business cards, and giving sales pitches each time he was stopped. Although the skates were crude, cumbersome, and comparatively slow, Olson was nonetheless impressed with their training possibilities and reasoned that other hockey players would be as well. Distinguished from traditional roller skates by their single line of rollers along a bladelike support system, the skates offered the perfect answer to the problem of off-season training not only for hockey athletes but for any number of sports enthusiasts.

The Los Angeles company that designed and marketed the skates was, in fact, building upon a tradition of invention that has been traced to early eighteenth-century Holland. According to company background information, legend has it that ''a Dutchman attempted to simulate ice skating in the summer by nailing wooden spools to strips of wood, which he attached to the bottoms of his shoes.'' Of course, the actual birth of the in-line skating industry was still nearly three centuries away. Interestingly enough, roller skates themselves were not invented until 1863 and then on American soil. More modern versions of the in-line skate occasionally surfaced but never rose to wide public acceptance.

Although accounts vary somewhat, it is more or less understood that modern-day in-line skating and the Rollerblade brand began simultaneously in 1980, when Olson, aided by his brother Brennan, decided to redesign the flawed L.A. skate. They initially focused on the problems of speed (side-by-side roller skates were still faster) and adaptability (the in-line skate's one-size-only blade restricted easy use by a wide variety of skaters). Olson's solutions were to increase speed by adding a second bearing to each of the wheels and allow for customized blade length by creating a shorter track with adjustable wheel positioning. Terry Fiedler of *Corporate Report Minnesota* writes that Olson hitchhiked to a Chicago trade show, where he attempted to interest one of the L.A. representatives in his new prototype. ''They did not

AT A GLANCE

Rollerblade brand of in-line skates founded in 1980 in Bloomington, Minnesota, by Scott and Brennan Olson; business incorporated in 1982 as Ole's Innovative Sports; company name subsequently changed to North American Training Corporation and then Rollerblade, Inc.; later developers included company owner Robert Naegele, Jr., CEO John Sundet, and marketing executive Mary Horwath.

Performance: *Market share*—50% (estimate) of in-line skating market. *Sales*—$128 million (1992 estimate).

Major competitor: First Team Sports' Ultra-Wheels; also, Bauer Precision brand in-line skates.

Advertising: *Agency*—Carmichael Lynch, 1993—. *Major campaign*—Television spots promoting Rollerblade's Active Brake Technology (ABT), as well as spots targeting children.

Addresses: *Parent company*—Rollerblade, Inc., 5101 Shady Oak Road, Minnetonka, MN 55343; phone: (612) 930-7000; fax: (612) 930-7100.

share his enthusiasm for the skates, and Olson decided to strike out on his own. A patent search discovered that Chicago Rollerskate, at that time the country's largest roller skate manufacturer, had developed a similar design and patented it.''

Chicago Rollerskate had no plans to develop and market its in-line skate, and so Olson, determined to see his dream through, was able to purchase the patent, which had first been issued in the late 1960s. By 1982 he had established a corporation, Ole's Innovative Sports, and was working out of his parents' home in Bloomington, Minnesota, refining and assembling his Rollerblade skates with Brennan, with another brother, Jim, and with a few other assistants. First year sales for the fledgling company exceeded $300,000. According to Rollerblade, Inc., ''Hockey players, who loved the product, were soon turning heads as they glided down Minnesota roads in the summer. Nordic and alpine skiers were also quick to adapt Rollerblade skates to their training regimens.''

Management Woes

In 1983 the company moved to a facility in Eden Prairie near the Minnesota Vikings Training Center while keeping itself focused on boosting sales to the off-season training market. Olson, then just 23, was juggling the roles of company president, public relations manager, advertising director, and chief financial officer. His product now had the appeal and momentum to attract endorsements from National Hockey League players and inquiries from the media, in addition to regular orders from athletes and sporting goods dealers. All seemed to be well, and to ensure that this remained so, Olson hired a longtime friend to oversee the company's finances. The friend proved sorely inadequate to the task. Although the company supposedly showed solid profits in 1984, Fiedler reports that Olson eventually discovered ''vendor bills were going unpaid'' and ''not only was the company not profitable, it was in serious trouble.''

Outside backing was needed to salvage the company and the brand. A successful St. Paul-Minneapolis car dealer, Jack Walser, issued Olson a check for $75,000 and rescued the company from imminent demise. The businessman's initial reaction to the Rollerblade skates, writes Fiedler, was highly favorable. ''I thought the concept was something, really clever. I could see it as a training skate or a recreational skate.'' He also saw the major problems the brand faced in simply surviving in its current atmosphere. In addition to Innovative Sports' poor financial condition, the company was charging too little for its skates and lacked a suitable collections process, he thought.

By 1985 Olson was forced to sell most of his interest in the company for $96,000 plus royalty payments. Olson departed the company the same year and, in 1986, launched a competing business, Innovative Sport Systems, Inc., maker of SwitchIt skates. By October 1987, after more upper management developments, Robert Naegele Jr., president of the Minneapolis investment company Naegele Communications, became the new owner and chief executive officer (CEO) of the original company, renamed Rollerblade, Inc.

''Guerilla Marketing'' and Brand Rebirth

While the company was putting itself back on track financially, it was also rethinking its overall marketing strategy. Beginning in 1984 an emphasis was placed on expanding the in-line skate market both geographically and demographically. Until that time in-line skate buyers were predominantly hockey players, almost exclusively male, and between the ages of 18 and 25. Sales improved as the company broadened its core consumer group to include active males and females between the ages of 18 and 35.

The Macroblade Equipe model of Rollerblade in-line skates.

The key to this change was transforming the Rollerblade corporate image from supplier of training equipment to creator of an exciting new sport. An added catalyst to higher sales came in 1987, when the company began streamlining its skates, dressing them up in neon colors, and more aggressively promoting them to an even broader market—virtually anyone interested in fitness, fun, speed, and outdoor recreation.

Part of the aggressive promotion took the form of covert ''exporting'' of Rollerblade skates to the West Coast. The idea was to give away the latest Rollerblade models to skate-rental shops along such famous Southern California hotspots as Venice Beach, hoping to capitalize on the flair of Californians for starting national trends. The chief architects of this plan, as well as other "guerilla" strategies, were Rollerblade president (and later CEO) John Sundet and promotional director Mary Horwath. In an article for *Working Woman,* Horwath explains that her annual budget then was just $200,000 and that "aggressive, unorthodox strategies that don't cost much money but attract positive publicity quickly" were necessary for the brand's growth.

Giveaways to professional athletes, celebrities, and other high-profile figures were a part of the plan, as were cross-promotional tie-ins. The first such tie-in came about when Minneapolis-based General Mills was formulating a sweepstakes for its Golden Grahams cereal. The cereal maker requested 1,000 pairs of Rollerblade skates for its promotion in return for exposure of the brand on some six million cereal boxes.

Another major tie-in arose when the director of a Swatch-sponsored film on action sports sought an appearance by Rollerblade in-line skaters. According to Horwath, the company's financial obligation for filming and sponsorship rights was minimal in comparison to the benefits of exposure on some 40 campuses nationwide. Soon Rollerblade skates were making regular media splashes and attracting even more lucrative tie-ins, including commercials by Pepsi and Procter & Gamble.

The final step in the rebirth of Rollerblade skates was converting broad public awareness (for example, from tie-ins) into public demand and accelerated sales. To partially achieve this, store displays and accompanying videos were created to inform the consumer of the health and recreational benefits of in-line skating. Because this alone was not likely to overcome buyer sticker shock (Rollerblade models then retailed from $100 to $300 per pair), a major public demonstration and trial-run campaign was launched. Company vans, outfitted with skates and staffed by trained sales and demo personnel, canvassed the country, stopping at public parks, fitness exposition sites, and elsewhere and inviting passersby to test-drive the various Rollerblade models. The campaign was a huge hit and led to an equally successful, ongoing rental program at beach shops, parks, and sporting goods stores. It also inspired the creation of Team Rollerblade, an elite group of in-line skaters whose numerous special promotional appearances have ranged from television commercials for Coors Light, Mountain Dew, and Sunny Delight to performances at the 1992 Winter Olympics and the 1993 Super Bowl.

Still Trailblazing

On April 30, 1991, Rollerblade entered into a 50-50 alliance with Nordica that was considered a prescient move for both companies. By this point the Rollerblade brand had come into its own not only as the undisputed leader of the fast-growing in-line skate industry (which also came into its own in 1991 with the creation of the International In-Line Skating Association) but as one of the hottest product names of the new decade. Although still committed to unusual, attention-grabbing promotions, the company was now beginning to embrace conventional advertising as well. A print campaign that year featured a skater coursing down a mountain highway with the caption: "It's kinda like running a marathon. It's kinda like eating a hot-fudge sundae. Rollerblade."

This dual appeal to fitness and fun has been the mainstay for the skating manufacturer and a powerful inducement to the buying public. Nearly all segments of society, grouped by household income level, geographic region, sex, and age, have shown sizable, annual increases in in-line skating participation since 1989. The one exception, according to a company fact sheet, appeared to be the over-35 crowd, which showed a slight decrease from 1991 to 1992. The largest group of in-line skaters measured by age were 6- to 11-year-olds and then 12- to 17-year-olds, who together formed 65 percent of the market in 1992. Clearly, in-line skating had a future among the young, and Rollerblade, Inc., has endeavored to make it as bright as possible by remaining in the lead in sales, product development, and enhancement of the sport. The company already boasted more than 180 issued and pending patents for its Rollerblade components.

Among these was a new brake system, called Active Brake Technology (ABT), that promised to revolutionize the sport of in-line skating, especially through enhanced safety (prior brake systems were generally considered user-friendly only for those with a high competence level; in addition, quick, effective heel braking for users at all skill levels was always a concern when speeds of 30 m.p.h. or greater were reached). The value of ABT was that it allowed all wheels to remain on the ground; when the skater exerted pressure on the boot cuff, a lever was activated that pressed the brake downward until it made contact with the pavement. ABT was to be released in the spring of 1994 on the Aeroblade ABT skate, the Coolblade ABT skate, and a new line of Bravoblade skates. Jon Lowden wrote that "if the braking system works well, industry insiders say it will be the most important thing to happen to in-line skates since the invention of the skates themselves."

Meanwhile, the Rollerblade name continued to play prominently in the media. In 1992 the *Wall Street Journal* announced that Mattel would launch Baby Rollerblade, "a 15-inch doll that skates on replicas of Rollerblade brand skates and a Rollerblade Barbie and friends line." In 1993 a flurry of tie-ins—including those with Hi-C, Northwest Airlines, and Warner Bros.—were announced in *Advertising Age.* Virtually all that remained for full-scale promotion was a Rollerblade-generated TV commercial, which was completed and released to local Rollerblade distributors in early 1994. Rollerblade brand is the brand that spawned a sport for the 1990s, the brand that defined and continued to define its industry, and the brand that could yet become identified with a global pastime.

Further Reading:

Beran, George, "Rollerblade Inc. on a Roll," *Pioneer Press & Dispatch,* June 19, 1988, pp. 1H, 3H.

"A Business That's on a Roll," *Star Tribune,* November 17, 1985.

"A Craze May Outsprint Its Creator," *New York Times,* August 7, 1990, pp. D1, D6.

Dolliver, Mark, "Rollerblade," *Adweek,* May 10, 1993, p. 42.

Feyder, Susan, "Rollerblade Asks ITC to Enforce Two Patents," *Star Tribune,* February 19, 1993.

Fiedler, Terry, "Rolling with the Punches," *Corporate Report Minnesota,* September 1989, pp. 47–52.

Finn, Michael, "Handling a Hot Trademark: A Company Battles the 'Genericization' of Its Trademark," *Writer's Digest,* September 1992, pp. 52–54.

Goerne, Carrie, "Rollerblade Reminds Everyone That Its Success Is Not Generic," *Marketing News,* March 2, 1992, p. 1.

Gross, David M., "Zipping Along in Asphalt Heaven: An Upstart Minnesota Company, Rollerblade, Streaks to Success," *Time,* August 13, 1990, p. 56.

Horwath, Mary, " 'How I Did It': Guerilla Marketing 101," *Working Woman,* December 1991, pp. 23–24.

Jensen, Jeff, "Rollerblade Teams with Hi-C, Warner in Summer Tie-Ins," *Advertising Age,* June 14, 1993, p. 42.

Kretchmar, Laurie, "Mary L. Horwath," *Fortune,* August 12, 1991, p. 94.

"Mattel Inc.," *Wall Street Journal,* January 28, 1992, p. B6.

Rollerblade, Inc.: Pioneer of the In-Line Skating Industry, Minnetonka, Minnesota: Rollerblade, Inc., 1993.

"Rollerblade Inc. Rolls on Those Using Rollerblade or Even Blade as a Verb," *Wall Street Journal,* January 16, 1992, p. A1.

Schafer, Lee, "It's Not a Fad," *Corporate Report Minnesota,* pp. 31–39.

"Sorry, Roller Skaters, Your Wheels Are Square—It's Time to Lace on a Pair of Blades and Let the Good Times Roll," *People Weekly,* July 23, 1990, pp. 84–85.

Sprout, Alison, "Commuter Skates," *Fortune,* August 24, 1992, p. 99.

Therrien, Lois, "Rollerblade Is Skating in Heavier Traffic," *Business Week,* June 24, 1991, pp. 114–115.

—Jay P. Pederson

ROLLS-ROYCE®

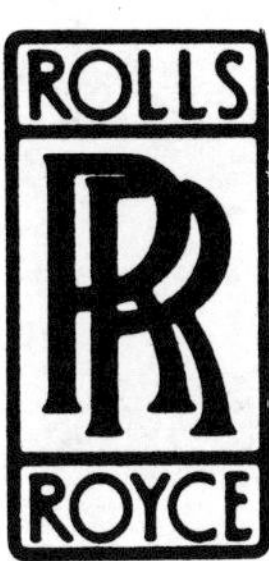

Rolls-Royce—introduced in 1904 as a joint venture between engineer Henry Royce and dealership-owner Charles Rolls—became probably the most famous automobile brand in the world. From handcrafted leather and walnut interiors to "Spirit of Ecstasy" grille mascots, Rolls-Royce automobiles represented the ultimate in motoring elegance. Other automobiles were flashier, faster, or more technologically advanced, but Rolls-Royce automobiles were considered by many to be the final word in overstated luxury. In 1993, Rolls-Royce Motor Cars Ltd. made about 1,300 automobiles. Each took from four to six months to produce.

Sir Henry Royce (1863-1933)

Frederick Henry Royce, born in Lincolnshire, England, in 1863, was the son of a flour-mill operator who died when Henry was nine years old. When he was fourteen, Royce was apprenticed to the Great Northern Railroad at Peterborough, where he worked in the repair shops.

Two years later, he left the railroad and took a job with a tool maker in Leeds, where he began to study electrical engineering. He soon went to work for the Electric Light and Power Company in London, one of the first companies in England to provide electricity for lighting streets and public buildings. After taking classes at Polytechnic Institute in London, Royce was appointed chief engineer at the Lancashire Maxim and Western Electric Company, a subsidiary of Electric Power and Light in Liverpool. But the subsidiary failed in 1883, and the 20-year-old Royce found himself out of work.

The following year, Royce and a friend, A. E. Clairmont, pooled their resources, which amounted to about £70, and formed the electrical engineering firm of F. H. Royce and Company. Their first successful product was an electric doorbell. In 1891, Royce developed a "sparkless" electric dynamo that could be used safely in coal mines and flour mills. In 1894, the company changed its name to Royce Ltd., Electrical and Mechanical Engineers and Manufacturers of Dynamos, Motors and Kindred Articles.

Charles Stewart Rolls (1877-1911)

The Honorable Charles Stewart Rolls was born in 1877, the third son of Lord Llangattock. He studied mechanical engineering at Cambridge University, where he developed an interest in automobiles. In 1896, Rolls purchased a Peugeot in France and brought it to England, where he joined a growing number of motoring enthusiasts who openly challenged the British speed limit of 4 MPH. Rolls became a member of the Self-Propelled Traffic Association, which was successful in getting the speed limit raised to 12 MPH in 1896. The Locomotives on Highways Act also eliminated the requirement that a man precede an automobile on foot waving a red flag!

Rolls, a founding member of the Automobile Club of Great Britain and Ireland, established an automobile dealership, C. S. Rolls & Co., in London in 1903 and began importing automobiles from France and Belgium. The following year, he was joined by Claude Johnson, former secretary of the Automobile Club, who had organized the first automobile exhibit at the Imperial Institute of London in 1896. It was Johnson's ability as a promoter that would make Rolls-Royce one the best known names in the automobile industry.

The Origin of Rolls-Royce

Royce began tinkering with motor cars in 1903, probably with the idea of manufacturing electrical components for the fledgling motor-car industry. He purchased a secondhand Decauville, made in France, which he used as a model in designing and building his own engine and chassis. In the spring of 1904, Royce test drove his own two-cylinder motor car between the shop and his home. A few weeks later, he sent the chassis to a coach builder to be outfitted with a two-seat body. Two other Royce-built cars soon joined the original.

One of the original Royce automobiles was given to Henry Edmunds, a director of Royce Ltd. and a motor car enthusiast. Edmunds recognized the market value of the Royce-built cars, which were much quieter and smoother running than the Decauville. Edmunds arranged a meeting between Royce and Rolls. Later, Johnson also met with Royce, and C. S. Rolls & Co. negotiated an agreement to become the exclusive distributor of Royce-built automobiles. Since Rolls was better known by the motoring public than Royce, the automobile was introduced at the Paris car show in 1904 as the Rolls-Royce.

There were two significant differences between the original Royce cars and the Rolls-Royce unveiled in Paris. Johnson insisted that more attention be given to styling, so the Rolls-Royce featured a finely crafted coach. Royce would later impose strict

AT A GLANCE

Rolls-Royce brand of automobile created in 1904 as a joint marketing venture between Royce Ltd., an electrical and automotive engineering company, and C. S. Rolls and Co., a London automobile dealership; Rolls-Royce Ltd. formed in 1906; company nationalized by British government in 1970; automobile division divested as private company, Rolls-Royce Motors Ltd., in 1973; company acquired by Vickers PLC in 1980.

Performance: *Sales*—1,300 cars (1993).

Major competitor: Mercedes-Benz; also Jaguar and BMW.

Addresses: *Parent company*—Rolls-Royce Motor Cars Ltd., Crewe, Cheshire CWI 3PI England; phone: (270) 255155.

standards on coach builders contracted by the company. The second change was a slightly bowed radiator grille, which overcame the optical illusion that made flat grilles appear to be concave. The classic "Grecian" radiator would become a trademark of Rolls-Royce automobiles. The engine, however, remained the remarkably smooth power plant designed by Royce. Rolls-Royce automobiles were legendary for their ability to be started and driven solely in high gear, which appealed to many from the English leisure class who never bothered to learn the intricacies of shifting gears.

Johnson promoted the Rolls-Royce brand heavily following the Paris car show, taking out full-page ads in *Autocar* and entering two cars in the first Tourist Trophy Race, which would become the most important British road race of the day. After a Rolls-Royce driven by Percy Northey finished second in the 208-mile race on the Isle of Man, C. S. Rolls & Co. began devoting all its efforts to selling Rolls-Royce automobiles. In the summer of 1906, C. S. Rolls & Co. formally merged with the car-making division of Royce Ltd. to form Rolls-Royce Ltd. About 60 Rolls-Royce automobiles were built and sold in 1905 and 1906.

The Silver Ghost

In 1907, Rolls-Royce Ltd. built a six-cylinder motor car with an elegant five-seat, open-touring body that was destined to ensure the company's place in automotive history. To promote the car, Johnson had it painted with aluminum paint and adorned with silver-plated lamps and fittings. He attached a brass plate to the dash with the name "Silver Ghost."

Johnson then set out to prove that the Silver Ghost was fast and reliable, as well as luxurious. In a test supervised by the Royal Automobile Club, the Silver Ghost completed a 15,000-mile journey, which included participating in the Scottish Reliability Test, with only one mechanical glitch—a loose fuel valve that had jiggled closed. The Silver Ghost averaged almost 18 miles per gallon and reached a top speed of 53 MPH. An inspection of the engine afterwards showed almost no wear, and the Silver Ghost was restored to like-new condition for less than £3.

In 1908, Johnson persuaded the Rolls-Royce Ltd. board of directors to adopt a "one model" policy, which allowed the company to concentrate on improving one model at a time. The Silver Ghost became the only Rolls-Royce production model until 1922. When production finally ended in 1925, more than 6,000 Silver Ghosts had been sold. The Silver Ghost became the first Rolls-Royce product to be known as "the best car in the world."

Rolls resigned as managing director of Rolls-Royce Ltd. in April 1910 to devote more time to a new interest—airplanes. He was killed less than three months later when the biplane he was piloting crashed. Ironically, in 1914, Rolls-Royce Ltd. began making airplane engines for the British government, producing 60 percent of all British-built airplane engines used in World War I. During that period, Rolls-Royce Ltd. became as well known for making airplane engines as luxury automobiles.

Royce collapsed from physical exhaustion in 1911 and never fully recovered. He spent the last 20 years of his life in semi-retirement at a villa on the French Riviera, where he continued to review automobile designs. He was knighted in 1931. When Royce died in 1933, Rolls-Royce Ltd. changed the color of its well-known RR grille monogram from red to black.

The Spirit of Ecstasy

The famous Rolls-Royce radiator-cap mascot—The Spirit of Ecstasy—was created in 1911 by Charles Sykes, a sculptor and artist for a trade journal, *Car Illustrated.* He was commissioned by Johnson, who was unhappy with some of the ornaments that owners were affixing to their Rolls-Royce automobiles. Johnson suggested a figure along the lines of a classic Greek statue, but Sykes favored a more fluid sculpture. He called his figurine—a woman in a flowing, wind-swept robe—"The Spirit of Speed." However, a press release written by Johnson renamed the "graceful little goddess" "the Spirit of Ecstasy, who has selected road travel as her supreme delight, and has alighted on the prow of a Rolls-Royce car to revel in the freshness of the air and the musical sound of her fluttering draperies." The statuette, sometimes inaccurately referred to as a winged figure, also became known as "The Flying Lady."

Sykes supervised production of the figurines until 1928, personally inscribing the base of each with his signature. He also created a special figure known as "The Whisperer" for Lord Montagu, who had introduced Sykes to Johnson. In 1933, Sykes sculpted a kneeling figure of a woman in flowing robes that was used on most Rolls-Royce Phantom IIIs, Wraiths, Silver Wraiths, Silver Dawns, and Phantom IVs. The Rolls-Royce automobile used by Queen Elizabeth was adorned with a figure of St. George slaying the dragon that was sculpted by Edward Seago. Over the years, Rolls-Royce figurines have been made of various metal alloys, but never, despite the mythology, of solid silver.

The American Rolls-Royce

After World War I, British car manufacturers began looking to the American market to increase sales. However, import tariffs meant that foreign-built automobiles were more expensive than comparable U.S.-built models. This was especially troublesome for luxury automobiles. To circumvent the tariffs, in 1919 Rolls-Royce Ltd. purchased a vacant factory in Springfield, Massachusetts, and founded Rolls-Royce of America, Inc.

The first Springfield Silver Ghosts were assembled in 1921 from imported parts and were identical to the automobiles built in England except for the wheels and some electrical components. They even had right-side steering wheels and controls. Left-side steering wheels became standard in 1924, and other American influences, such as cylindrical headlights, slowly crept into the styling. The Springfield factory continued to turn out Silver Ghosts even after production ended in England. Consequently, the last Silver Ghost was made in the United States in 1926.

In 1926, the Springfield factory began manufacturing Rolls-Royce Phantoms, the model that replaced the Silver Ghost. However, when the stock market crashed in 1929, the bottom fell out of the market for luxury automobiles. Only 100 Phantoms were manufactured at Springfield in 1930, and production ended altogether in 1931. Limited production resumed in 1933, but Rolls-Royce of America declared bankruptcy in 1934.

A 1928 Springfield Phantom was later featured in the movie *The Great Gatsby,* based on the novel by F. Scott Fitzgerald. In the book, Fitzgerald wrote, "It was a rich cream color, bright with nickel, swollen here and there in its monstrous length with triumphant hat-boxes and supper-boxes and tool-boxes, and terraced with a labyrinth of windshields that mirrored a dozen suns. Sitting down behind many layers of glass in a sort of green leather conservatory, we started to town." During its 16-year existence, Rolls-Royce of America produced 1,701 Silver Ghosts and 1,225 Phantoms.

Postwar Rolls-Royce

The Phantom I was succeeded by the Phantom II in 1929 and the Phantom III—the first and only Rolls-Royce automobile with a V-12 engine—in 1936. Both were classic, oversized Rolls-Royce luxury touring sedans more likely to be driven by chauffeurs than by their owners. Then in 1938, Rolls-Royce Ltd. introduced the Wraith, which showcased Rolls-Royce elegance on a smaller chassis. The Wraith was also the first Rolls-Royce with low-pressure, balloon tires. Unfortunately, fewer than 500 Wraiths were produced before the start of World War II in 1939.

The first postwar automobile from Rolls-Royce was the Bentley Mark VI, a brand name acquired in 1931 when Rolls-Royce Ltd. purchased Bentley Motor Works Ltd. Then in 1947, Rolls-Royce Ltd. introduced the Silver Wraith, the first Rolls-Royce with an all-steel body. Nearly 1,800 Silver Wraiths were produced between 1947 and 1959.

Rolls-Royce Ltd. continued to use "Silver" to designate new models. The Silver Wraith was followed by: the Silver Dawn, 1949-1955; Silver Cloud, 1955-1966; Silver Shadow, 1966-1983; and the Silver Spur and Silver Spirit, introduced in 1980. The Silver Shadow was the first Rolls-Royce with monocoque construction. It was also the first with modern styling, and became the basis for the Corniche convertible, introduced in 1971. Rolls-Royce Ltd. built more than 32,000 Silver Shadows. The company also revived the Phantom designation in 1950, producing 18 Phantom IV limousines for royalty and heads of state between 1950 and 1956. The Phantom V was introduced in 1959, and the Phantom VI in 1968.

Outlook

Entering the 1990s, there were doubts that Rolls-Royce would be able to survive unless the brand was purchased by a much larger auto maker. A lingering recession hit the market for luxury cars hard, especially in the United States and England, and those who could still afford to buy Rolls-Royce automobiles appeared to be shying away from such conspicuous consumption. Even the British trade publication *Car* called the Silver Spirit a "glorious artifact." Sales of Rolls-Royce automobiles slumped 60 percent, from more than 3,300 in 1990 to about 1,300 in 1993.

Rolls-Royce Ltd., however, had weathered difficult times before. In the late 1960s, the company's aero-engine division, which historically contributed more than 80 percent of total revenues, was losing money. In 1970, the British government announced that it was lending Rolls-Royce Ltd. £60 million to keep the company from bankruptcy. Two days later, Rolls-Royce Ltd. was nationalized. *Time* called Rolls-Royce a symbol of "an England that is no more."

In 1973, the government attempted to auction off the motor-car division, but stipulated that the name Rolls-Royce would not be part of the deal unless the winning bid belonged to a British company. There were no foreign bids, and the 10 British bids were rejected as too low. The division was then spun off as a public company, Rolls-Royce Motor Cars Ltd. The company was again facing bankruptcy when it was acquired by Vickers PLC, a British engineering company, in 1980.

Production of Rolls-Royce automobiles fluctuated widely between 1970 and 1990, but unlike some other financially pinched luxury brands, the Rolls-Royce reputation for quality was never tarnished. In the late 1980s, Rolls-Royce Motor Cars Ltd. began focusing on the quality of its cars rather than its elitist image. The company's infrequent advertising began urging American buyers to "Live all you can; it's a mistake not to." Rather than ostentatious status symbols, Rolls-Royce automobiles were positioned as well-deserved rewards for success.

In 1993, CEO Howard Mosher said, "The people who drive these motor cars are the achievers—those who generate the wealth and the jobs in this country. They go the extra mile in their endeavors and it is our mission to produce the world's finest motor cars with every convenience built in to meet their requirements." Those conveniences included: a sentry light, triggered by a sensor mounted under the front bumper, that warned about icy conditions; heated seats made from the hides of cattle raised in electric-fence enclosures to prevent marring by barbed wire; and gloves included with the standard tool kits so drivers would not have to get their hands dirty. Rolls-Royce cars also came with an odometer that registered up to one million miles. According to the company, about two-thirds of the 117,000 Rolls-Royce automobiles made between 1904 and 1994 were still in running condition.

The Rolls-Royce line-up for 1994 included three models available in the United States: the Silver Spur III, with a price of $190,000; the Corniche IV convertible, $269,000; and the Silver Spur Touring Limousine, $337,000. Rolls-Royce Motor Cars also sold six models under the Bentley brand name. Although then-CEO Peter Ward told *Industry Week* in 1988 that the company had automated "the grimy jobs," much of the work making Rolls-Royce automobiles was still done by hand. Each Rolls-Royce automobile took from three to six months to complete.

Further Reading:

Bird, Anthony and Ian Hallows, *The Rolls-Royce Motor-Car and the Bentley since 1931,* New York: St. Martins, 1984.

Fuhrman, Peter, "Live All You Can . . . " *Forbes,* March 5, 1990.

"Has the Flying Lady Lost Her Shine?" *Economist,* February 29, 1992, p. 68.

Harker, Ronald W., *The Engines Were Rolls-Royce,* New York: Macmillan, 1979.

Lamm, John, "Retrospect: 1928 Rolls-Royce Phantom I," *Motor Trend,* April 1974, p. 77.

Moskal, Brian S., "Rolls-Royce: Looking for a Few More Good Millionaires," *Industry Week,* November 21, 1988.

Oliver, Brian, "Rolls-Royce Rides on Reputation, Not Ads," *Advertising Age,* June 16, 1986, p. S30.

Quality Is Timeless, Crewe, England: Rolls-Royce Motor Cars Ltd., undated.

"Rolls-Royce Banks on Bentley," *Marketing,* February 20, 1986, p. 78.

"Rolls-Royce PLC," *International Directory of Company Histories,* volume 7, Detroit: St. James, 1993.

"Rough Ride at Rolls-Royce," *Management Today,* February 1993, p. 38.

—*Dean Boyer*

ROSSIGNOL®

Rossignol, the world's best-selling brand of skis, has long been on the forefront of ski technology and design. Its skis, for example, were used in the Winter Olympics of 1936, the first to include alpine ski events, and they have since remained popular among the world's leading racers. Included in the Rossignol line are a wide range of downhill skis, cross-country skis, monoskis, snowboards, ski boots, ski poles, and accessories.

Skis Rossignol S.A., headquartered in Voiron, France, has been manufacturing skis since 1907. In addition to Rossignol, it owns the popular Dynastar line of skis and the Lange brand of ski boots. Although the company also makes tennis rackets and golf clubs, some 90 percent of its sales came from winter sports equipment. Its major markets are Europe, the United States, and Japan.

Brand Origins

For thousands of years skiing was a means of transportation in snowbound regions, especially Scandinavia, and it also came to be used for hunting and warfare. Not until the 19th century did skiing become a sport, and this took place, not surprisingly, in Norway. Early ski contests featured endurance cross-country races and ski jumps, and with the development of new ski techniques, such as telemark turns, downhill events were also introduced. The skis of this time, made of solid wood, ranged from eight to fourteen feet long, and racers could obtain speeds as high as 80 miles per hour.

The French soon took an interest in sport skiing as well, and among the first to do so was Henry Duhamel, who lived in Grenoble, a town in southeastern France. In 1879 Duhamel began experimenting with a pair of Norwegian skis, but he found them less than suitable for the French Alps, which tended to be both steep and icy. New ski techniques would be developed for these conditions, but not until about 1906 were the first downhill skis manufactured in France. Initially made by the military ski school in Briançon, the early French skis were also made of solid wood, usually ash, pine, or larch, which were chosen for their flexibility and resilience. Meanwhile, in 1907 ski contests were held at Montgenèvre on the Italian border and elsewhere in the French Alps, and with the sudden popularity of the sport, French artisans also began making skis.

One of these craftsmen, Abel Rossignol, was the head of a carpentry workshop in Voiron, a town just northeast of Grenoble, where he was producing wooden articles for the textile industry. In 1907 he decided to introduce his own pair of downhill skis, which were made of solid wood protected with a light-colored varnish. No ordinary skis, they were awarded first prize at a contest sponsored by the Touring Club of France, and in 1911, bolstered by his success, Rossignol established a separate division of his company devoted entirely to the production of skis. Rossignol continued to make solid-wood skis for the next three decades, and production would reach several hundred skis per year.

Product Development

Although alpine skiing was growing in popularity, it did not become an Olympic event until 1936, when the winter games were held at Garmisch-Partenkirchen, Germany. It was there that France emerged as a skiing power, led by Emile Allais, who won the bronze medal in the alpine combined. The following year at the world championships, Allais would do even better, winning the gold medal in all three alpine events and earning the title "champion of the world." All these medals were won on Rossignol skis. During this time Allais was also codifying his own method of ski instruction, published in the book *Ski Français.*

In 1936 Rossignol hired Allais as its technical adviser and official tester, and in this position Allais would help the company design some of the world's most advanced skis. At the time the primary weakness of the company's skis was their solid-wood construction. Although Rossignol had, in fact, made excellent solid-wood skis, there were great problems with quality control. Unless the wood had a uniform grain, for example, the ski would tend to warp during production, and even good solid-wood skis would begin to lose their shape with age. Some of Rossignol's competitors had already found a solution—a laminated, or layered, construction similar to plywood, with wood grains running in different directions—which made a lighter, more durable wooden ski. By using different types of wood and various patterns of lamination, manufacturers could also choose the ski's specific flexibility and resilience. Rossignol would borrow this idea from its competition, but the company's first laminated ski, the Olympic 41, was no mere imitation. Developed in 1941, the ski found great success after World War II, carrying such racers as Henri Oreiller (1948) and Ottmar Schneider (1952) to Olympic victories. The ski's success was also seen at Rossignol's Voiron factory, where production would jump to several thousand skis per year by 1951.

AT A GLANCE

Rossignol brand of ski equipment founded in 1907 in Voiron, France, by Abel Rossignol; his first product was solid-wood skis; Rossignol's first wood-laminated skis developed in 1941; steel skis and fiberglass skis introduced in the early 1960s, cross-country skis in 1971, and ski boots in 1989; public shares of the brand's parent company, Skis Rossignol S.A., first sold in 1971.

Performance: *Market share*—31.1% (first share) of world's ski category; 33% (first share) of ski category in the United States. *Sales*—All products of Skis Rossignol S.A., $335 million (FrF 1.6 billion; 1992-93); alpine skis, $210 million (FrF 1 billion); ski boots, $73 million (FrF 347 million); ski poles, $9 (FrF 44 million); cross-country skis, $7.5 million (FrF 36 million).

Major competitor: For skis: K2; also, Kästle, Elan, Dynastar (owned by Skis Rossignol S.A.), Atomic, Head, and Pre; for boots: Nordica; also, Raichle, Salomon, Lange (owned by Skis Rossignol S.A.), and Tecnica.

Advertising: *Agency*—Weiss, Whitten, Carroll, Stagliano, New York, NY. *Major campaign*—"Sheer Defiance," emphasizing the advanced, high-tech design of its equipment.

Addresses: *Parent company*—Rossignol Ski Company, Inc., P.O. Box 298, Industrial Avenue, Williston, VT 05495; phone: (802) 863-2511; fax: (802) 658-1843. *Ultimate parent company*—Skis Rossignol S.A., 38500 Voiron, France; phone: 011-33-76-66-65-65; fax: 011-33-76-65-67-51.

In 1956 the company finally stopped making wooden articles for the textile industry and focused its full attention on ski equipment.

Although laminated skis were a great improvement over solid wood, there was still much room for improvement. All wooden skis, whether solid wood or laminated, had problems with maintenance and durability. They absorbed water and were easily damaged, and to slide smoothly across the snow, they needed to be regularly waxed. In the 1930s some manufacturers began to experiment with other materials, especially metal. Metal skis would prove to be more durable, more resilient, and faster than wooden skis, but technical problems and then World War II delayed their development until the late 1940s. The first successful metal ski was made by American aviation engineer Howard Head. Using the "sandwich"-type design found on aircraft, Head placed two strips of aluminum (the top and bottom of the ski) around a plywood core, added a plastic bottom, and then attached an exceptionally hard metal edge to improve control. Introduced in the early 1950s, Head skis were an immediate hit, especially among recreational skiers.

Allais, who tested an early pair of Head skis in the United States, was also impressed with their handling in soft snow and powder, but he found them "totally unsuited" for the hard-packed snow of competitive racing. Even so, he brought several pairs of Head skis back to France and began with Rossignol to come up with his own design. One of Rossignol's first metal skis, the Allais 60, would quickly get the world's attention. At the 1960 Winter Olympics, held at Squaw Valley, California, Frenchman Jean Vuarnet won the men's downhill event using the Allais 60, making it the first metal ski to win an Olympic gold medal. According to Emile Allais, the ski's "characteristics, notably its ability to grip [the snow], were much superior to the wood skis still used during this time."

Although immensely successful, the Allais 60 and other metal skis would prove to be merely a transition from wooden skis to those made from fiberglass and other synthetic materials. In fact, Rossignol's first fiberglass ski was introduced in 1960, the same year as the Allais 60, but at the time its production costs were considerably higher. Fiberglass was both lighter and more resilient than metal, and, with the introduction of cheaper production methods, Rossignol and the rest of the industry would fully embrace the fiberglass ski.

Rossignol's first truly successful fiberglass ski was the Strato, introduced in the mid-1960s, which was actually made of a complex layering of various materials. A plastic called acrylonitrile butadien styrene, or simply ABS, formed the top layer and the side walls of the ski. Just below it was a series of fiberglass structural layers, which, in turn, was "sandwiched" around an inner core of laminated wood. On the very bottom, along with the hard steel edges, was a slick layer of polyethylene. The Strato, like previous Rossignol skis, proved popular among world-class racers. At the 1968 Winter Olympics, held in Grenoble (near the Voiron factory), the Strato was worn by five medalists, including Canadian Nancy Greene, winner of the giant slalom. Four years later, at the 1972 games in Sapporo, Japan, American Barbara Cochran won the regular slalom while wearing Rossignol's Strato. By this time the company was also producing skis under the name Dynastar, a brand bought by Rossignol in 1967.

In the early 1970s Rossignol introduced its first skis made without any wood at all. These featured a light density, polyurethane core, which not only was cheaper than wood but also made the ski more comfortable. Rossignol's racing skis, including the

Logos representing two of Rossingnol's most popular lines of ski equipment.

ROC and the ST, were filled with this polyurethane plastic and, as expected, performed exceptionally well in international competition. For example, at the 1976 Olympic games at Innsbruck, Austria, Rossignol's plastic-core skis were worn by six medalists, twice as many at the nearest competing brand. In addition to helping win races, Rossignol's new plastic materials and other technological advancements would help boost sales of its products. In 1972 it had become the world's best-selling brand of ski, a position it would continue to hold into the 1990s.

Over the next two decades Rossignol spent millions of dollars refining the design of its plastic-based skis. Performance and comfort were enhanced, for example, by Rossignol's patented Vibration Absorbing System (VAS), introduced in 1981. Made with an inner layer of steel wire and other material, VAS was designed to reduce only harmful vibration, while preserving vibration that actually improved ski performance and speed. Complementing this system beginning in 1984 was an ''external'' VAS—a light-alloy stress plate attached with ''visco-elastic'' material to the top of Rossignol skis. Another notable improvement was the ''Rossitop,'' introduced in 1992, which was an eight-millimeter-thick layer of transparent plastic that protected the ski's cosmetics.

Diversification

While Rossignol continued to improve its line of downhill skis, it also began to produce other types of ski equipment. Its first major diversification was in 1971, when the company introduced a Rossignol brand of cross-country skis. Manufactured in Sweden, these skis were still made entirely of wood, as were many cross-country skis at the time, but in 1974 the company's Voiron factory began making a fiberglass model. Cross-country skiing grew increasingly popular during the 1970s, and thus, in 1976, Rossignol established a separate cross-country division to oversee the product. This commitment to the sport was seen ten years later, in 1987, when it introduced its ''System Concept'' line of cross-country skis, boots, and bindings, which were specifically designed to work together. That year Rossignol also developed an air-injection method that produced exceptionally lightweight, durable cross-country skis.

Though Rossignol was the world's largest manufacturer of downhill skis, the company did not have its own line of downhill ski boots until 1989, when it purchased Lange, a brand of ski boots since 1965. Rossignol would gain much from Lange's existing research and development program. In the 1980s Lange had been working on a compromise between the two most popular types of ski boots. The first—pioneered in 1965 by Lange's founder, Bob Lange of Dubuque, Iowa—was an all-plastic boot fitted with a series of buckles across the front. Exceptionally stiff, this boot efficiently translated body movement to the ski and was especially popular among competitive racers. The second, introduced in the early 1970s, was an all-plastic rear-entry model, in which the back of the boot hinged off to provide easy access for the foot. The rear-entry boot was more convenient and comfortable than front-buckle models, though some considered its performance inferior. The eventual compromise, introduced in 1989 under both the Lange and Rossignol brand names, was the MID line of ski boots. These were, in fact, front-buckle boots, but a unique hinge system allowed the top to open wider, thus making them easier to put on.

By the early 1990s Rossignol was also making a variety of other ski equipment, including ski poles, monoskis, and snowboards, as well as ski accessories, such as bags, gloves, socks, shirts, sweaters, and hats. A line of Rossignol tennis rackets was introduced in 1977, and in 1990 Rossignol Ski Company, Inc.—the U.S. subsidiary of parent company Skis Rossignol S.A.—purchased Roger Cleveland Golf Company of Paramount, California.

Marketing and Advertising Strategy

As the world's leading producer of skis, Rossignol has enjoyed almost universal brand recognition among skiers. The Rossignol name, prominently marked on all its skis and other ski equipment, could be seen on almost any ski slope around the world. Moreover, many ski shops rented Rossignol skis, thus introducing a large number of potential customers to the Rossignol brand.

Rossignol has done much to cultivate its reputation for high-performance ski equipment, especially through sponsorship of top skiers. The company has long provided equipment to top-ranked athletes, and many have won Olympic and World Cup races on Rossignol skis. In 1968, for example, 55 percent of all Olympic racers wore one of two Rossignol skis, the Strato or the Allais Major, and at the 1972 games Rossignol skis were used by four of the six gold-medal winners of alpine events. Twenty years later, at the 1992 Olympics in Albertville, France, Rossignol skis helped alpine and nordic racers win six gold, seven silver, and three bronze medals. If spectators had forgotten which brand these skiers were using, they were soon reminded in popular skiing magazines. In January of 1994, just before the Winter Olympics in Lillehammer, Norway, Rossignol ran print advertisements in the United States under the tag line ''Sheer Defiance—Rossignol,'' stressing the company's most advanced ski equipment. In one ad the copy read, ''The new 7SK: an evolution in winning. Top American, Canadian and international skiers depend on this ski in world-class slalom competition. . . . [It] slices through snow and grips on ice like no other ski in the world.'' To emphasize the point, the ad featured a picture of Alberto Tomba of Italy—winner of two consecutive Olympic gold medals in the giant slalom—flying though space on a pair of Rossignol 7SK skis. In a different ''Sheer Defiance'' ad it was Olympian Julie Parisien flying through space, this time to promote Rossignol's Course K, ''the boot that defies the rules.''

Brand Outlook

In the mid-1990s Skis Rossignol S.A. was in an enviable market position. Yearly sales of its Rossignol and Dynastar skis together were approaching two million pairs, or about 30 percent of the world's ski category, putting them far ahead of their numerous competitors, such as Head, K2, Elan, Atomic, Salomon, and Pre. The company also had yearly sales of some 800,000 boots (Rossignol and Lange), 80,000 cross-country skis (Rossignol), and 900,000 ski poles (Rossignol, Dynastar, and Kerma).

Heading into the 21st century, Rossignol would continue to face its traditional sales variable—worldwide snow conditions. From 1987 to 1989, for example, poor snowfall in Europe brought declining sales there for Rossignol and other ski brands. Exchange rate fluctuations between the French franc and the currencies of its major markets were also expected to have an impact on the brand's future, as more than 80 percent of all Rossignol's sales were outside of France. The future success of the Rossignol brand, however, was probably most dependent on its ability to maintain a leading role in ski technology and design.

Further Reading:

Bays, Ted, *Nine Thousand Years of Skis: Norwegian Wood to French Plastic,* Ishpeming, Michigan: National Ski Hall of Fame Press, 1980.

Beilinson, Jerry, ''Rossignol: Race Support Pays Off in Olympics,'' *Skiing Trade News,* April 1992, p. 6.

Meader, Cliff, ''Second Year Is First Year for Full Rossi Boot Line,'' *Skiing Trade News,* March 1990, p. 40.

Pachod, Patrick, "Laurent Boix-Vives Discloses Rossignol's Future Path," *Skiing Trade News,* February 1991, p. 19.

"Profit in Current Fiscal Year Is Expected to Nearly Triple [Skis Rossignol SA]," *Wall Street Journal,* January 31, 1994, p. B5A.

Regard sur 50 ans d'innovation dans le ski, Voiron, France: Skis Rossignol S.A., 1993.

"Skis Rossignol—Company Report," *FT Analysis Report,* Thomson Financial Networks Inc., 1993.

Tanler, Bill, "Ski Production Turns to the Fewer, the Bigger," *Skiing Trade News,* October 1993, p. 30.

—Thomas Riggs

RUBBERMAID®

Rubbermaid, a name originally used on a line of household products, was among the best-known brands in the United States. Some 97 percent of all adults had heard of Rubbermaid, with 70 percent having what was called "top of the mind" awareness. In the early 1990s the Rubbermaid logo was found on more than 500 products in 50 different colors in the consumer, commercial, industrial, agricultural, office, marine, automotive accessories, and children's markets. While most of these products were made of plastic, some were made of rubber, just as the original Rubbermaid products were.

The brand's enviable level of consumer awareness was not merely the result of promotional efforts by its parent company, Rubbermaid Incorporated, headquartered in Wooster, Ohio. The company, in fact, had a long-standing commitment to making high-quality products, while at the same time trying to introduce as many products as possible to the market. The company's goal was to double its sales every five years; to help accomplish this objective, the company began to introduce a new product every day of the year.

Brand Origins

In 1920 five individuals founded Wooster Rubber Company in Wooster, Ohio, to manufacture Sunshine brand toy balloons. In the mid-1920s Horatio Ebert and Errett Grable—executives of the Wear Ever Division of Aluminum Company of America—bought Wooster Rubber as a personal investment. By 1928 Wooster Rubber prospered enough that it was able to replace its rented facility with a new factory and office building. Then the Great Depression hit, and sales plummeted.

During the same period, James Caldwell, an employee of Seamless Rubber Company in New Haven, Connecticut, and his wife cast about their kitchen for ideas for household products that could be improved through the use of rubber. They identified 29 products that fit the bill. The first product they designed and manufactured was a red rubber dustpan. It also was the first rubber dustpan ever patented. Although in 1932 their rubber dustpan cost $1.00, compared with 39¢ for a metal one, Caldwell sold nine dustpans after ringing just ten doorbells. Convinced there was a market for rubber products, the Caldwells expanded their line to include a soap dish, sink plug, and drainboard mat. They adopted the brand name Rubbermaid for their enterprise, and the products sold in department stores throughout New England.

Brand Development

Ebert saw Caldwell's rubber products in a department store and thought they would be a good addition to Wooster Rubber Company's line. He eventually worked out an arrangement with Caldwell to combine the Rubbermaid and Wooster Rubber businesses. In July 1934 Wooster Rubber Company started to manufacture rubber houseware products. Under Caldwell's guidance and direction, Rubbermaid items became familiar products in American households. By 1941, 27 of the Caldwells' original 29 product ideas were being sold, and Wooster Rubber's sales reached $685,000. In 1947 the company introduced rubber automobile accessories, including floormats and cupholders.

One reason for Rubbermaid's success was Caldwell's visionary use of national advertising. Beginning in 1938 he placed print ads in national magazines that helped establish Rubbermaid as one of America's best-known and respected brand names. Early ads featured a "maid" using products. Labels with an illustration of a maid and the Rubbermaid trademark identified the household products to buyers.

Wooster Rubber experienced a setback during World War II because the government prohibited civilian use of rubber. It survived by negotiating a subcontract to produce components for self-sealing fuel tanks for military aircraft and by making life jackets and tourniquets. For several months after the war the company manufactured all products in black because there were no coloring agents available.

The Rubbermaid brand went international in 1950 when the company established a Canadian operation to manufacture vinyl-coated wire items. It expanded to a complete line of Rubbermaid products in 1956. (The company entered the European market in 1965.) Wooster Rubber Company introduced its first all-plastic product—the rectangular dishpan—in 1955. Within a year an entire line of all-plastic products was on the market.

In 1957 Wooster Rubber changed its corporate name to Rubbermaid Incorporated to capitalize on the already widely accepted brand name. Its original housewares business would become the Home Products Division, and it would establish other operating companies from a combination of internally developed businesses, acquisitions, and joint ventures. They included Rubbermaid Specialty Products Inc., Rubbermaid Commercial Products Inc., Rub-

AT A GLANCE

Rubbermaid brand of plastic and rubber products founded in 1932 by entrepreneur James Caldwell; brand purchased by Wooster Rubber Company in 1934; company renamed Rubbermaid Incorporated in 1957.

Performance: *Market share*—First share of the plastic housewares category. *Sales*—$1.9 billion (company-wide total).

Major competitor: Tucker; also, Sterilite.

Advertising: *Agency*—DDB Needham, Chicago, IL. *Major campaign*—"Don't you wish everything was made like Rubbermaid," a tag line used in print and broadcast advertising.

Addresses: *Parent company*—Rubbermaid Incorporated, 1147 Akron Rd., P.O. Box 6000, Wooster, OH 44691-6000; phone: (216) 264-6464; fax: (216) 264-5206.

bermaid Office Products Inc., The Little Tikes Company, and the Carver Rubbermaid Group. The first of these expansions beyond consumer goods occurred in 1958, when the company began to produce bathtub mats and doormats for restaurants, hotels, and institutions. By 1974 industrial and commercial products would account for 25 percent of company sales.

A new version of the Rubbermaid logotype, designed to increase readability (it was a heavier weight type and deeper red), went into use in June 1993. The corporate trademark consisted of the word *Rubbermaid* centered in a red panel with the registered mark to the right of the panel. The company's service marks included ''Everything Rubbermaid'' and ''Invincible Customer Service.''

Marketing Wizardry

Jon Berry pegged the company correctly when he wrote in *Adweek's Marketing Week* that Rubbermaid Incorporated was a marketing wizard. That wizardry was by design, and the crux of the design was to introduce a new Rubbermaid product every day. Rubbermaid attached its logo to products in the consumer, commercial, industrial, agricultural, office, marine, automotive accessories, and children's markets. Rubbermaid's marketing secrets included dominating the retail selling space, thinking entrepreneurially, and going overboard on features. It used only high-grade plastics in its products.

Through the years the company used a variety of promotional and advertising schemes. Rubbermaid added the sales party to its marketing efforts in 1969. The party unit had its own line of merchandise, but it was not profitable until 1976 and was discontinued in 1983. In 1971 Rubbermaid entered direct supermarket retail distribution channels.

In 1991 the company established ''Everything Rubbermaid'' departments within retail stores. These departments took all of a store's Rubbermaid household products and placed them in a single location. The result was more impulse purchases of Rubbermaid products and an enhanced brand image. It also contributed to Rubbermaid's $1.6 billion in sales for 1991, an increase of 9 percent over 1990 and of 400 percent over 1981. Within a six-month period in 1992, Rubbermaid installed these departments in approximately 120 stores.

Another way Rubbermaid marketed its brand was to run cross-promotions with companies that already had a strong presence in a market area. For example, because Rubbermaid made plastic fishing boxes, it cosponsored CastingKid and BASS Masters Classic fishing events, which placed the Rubbermaid name and logo on trophies, pennants, and magazines.

Other special promotions focused attention on recycling. Rubbermaid recognized early that recycling was the future of waste disposal and started to use recycled materials in its own products. It also manufactured a line of products to store and take recyclables to a recycling center. To promote its recycling products and to reinforce its long-standing commitment to both recycling and utilizing recycled materials, the company sponsored Earth Day programs. It sent out recycling kits to retailers and educational materials on recycling to public schools. Rubbermaid also used product labels to inform consumers about the environmental benefits of using recycled goods. As a result, the company enjoyed the support of most environmental groups and environmentally conscious consumers for innovating waste disposal.

Besides special promotions, the company emphasized consumer coupon and rebate promotions and advertised the Rubbermaid brand heavily in magazines and on television. Two memorable television commercials featured Rubbermaid storage containers. The ''Squirrel'' commercial shows a squirrel running around looking for a place to store its acorns until it discovers that a Servin' Saver product is the perfect place. The ''Stuff'' spot shows a woman who has accumulated a lot of ''stuff'' during her life. She marries and has two children, and the entire family acquires even more things. With Rubbermaid containers, the family organizes their stuff and then realizes they need more stuff. Among the slogans Rubbermaid used were ''Rubbermaid means better made,'' ''Nothing else stacks up to it,'' and ''Don't you wish everything was made like Rubbermaid.''

A New Product Every Day

Rubbermaid was so successful in making its brand recognized as a household word that consumers thought the company was the No. 2 maker of dishwashing gloves even before it made any. The extent of the brand recognition was not surprising. The company dedicated itself to introducing an average of a new product every day of the year, adding a new market segment every 12 to 18 months, and deriving 30 percent of its sales from products less than five years old. The company depended on new products and new markets for growth because the quality of Rubbermaid products was so high they seldom needed replacing. Another example of the company's market-driven attitude was its devotion to improving products, not just creating new versions of packaging.

Rubbermaid attained its incredible goal of a new product every day through savvy and speedy product development cycles. Relying on demographic and life-style analyses to spot trends, Rubbermaid cranked out new products without market testing. This approach allowed the company to establish the products in their categories before competitors could copy the designs. As of 1992 Rubbermaid Home Products Division alone offered items in 13 product categories: bathware, cleaning, decorative coverings, food storage, food preparation and serving, hardware, home organization, household containers, recycling containers, refuse containers, sinkware, indoor casual furniture, and personal care organization.

Two trends the company spotted and capitalized on were materials recycling and the desire for products in a variety of colors. Rubbermaid became the leading manufacturer of products made from recycled materials and of those used by recyclers. Most of its products contained from 10 to 100 percent recycled post-industrial and post-consumer plastics that ordinarily would have gone into landfills. They all carried a molded-in identification symbol to facilitate recycling efforts. Among the products the company produced for recyclers were containers for storing such recyclable materials as glass jars and old newspapers. It also tapped into "green marketing" when it introduced the environmentally friendly SideKick lunchbox, an insulated cooler that featured three plastic containers for a sandwich, a drink, and one other item, which eliminated the need for plastic bags and, thus, reduced the amount of disposable materials being put into the trash.

Until Rubbermaid started making garbage cans in blue, they came in only green and chocolate. The addition was a good choice; the company sold more blue cans than any other color. The company also was the first to use the colors of brick and teal in post-consumer resins. It introduced the Fun Functional line of brightly colored containers in 1990.

The company's five divisions operated as autonomous companies but shared the common aim of creating products that were "useful, long-lasting, and inexpensive." Rubbermaid changed the name of its Housewares Products Division to Home Products Division to reflect the diversity of products it offered. Those products included step-on wastebaskets; plastic tool boxes; modular storage units; cosmetics organizers; household cleaning utensils; hampers featuring whale, tortoise, and dinosaur shapes; Servin' Saver food containers; Chef kitchen tools; bathroom accessories; and, of course, dustpans.

Rubbermaid Specialty Products Inc., established in 1987, distributed Rubbermaid lawn and garden products, resin casual furniture with designs for indoor-outdoor versatility (including ready-to-assemble furniture, a blow-molded rocking chair, textured marble and color tables, and multiposition and monobloc chairs), and an array of lunch kits and recreational and insulated products. Recreational products included fishing-tackle boxes, sports lockers, and sports-stadium seating. The division also manufactured ActionPacker storage units for highway necessities, DrainTrainer Oil Recycling Containers with lids so the consumer could take used oil to a recycling center, Gas CanTainers with flexible spouts, and other key automotive items.

Rubbermaid Incorporated established Rubbermaid Commercial Products Inc. in 1967. The division was an outgrowth of the company's selling consumer products to institutional markets since the mid-1950s. The division came up with a clear plastic pitcher that looked like glass for use in restaurants. The division also marketed cleaning products with an antimicrobial agent; products to make recycling simple and easy; containers with tops to help avoid messy spills and keep collection areas clean; utility tubs for agricultural applications; rotary brushes; and numerous other specialized products.

After forming Rubbermaid Office Products Inc. in 1990, the company began to distribute Rubbermaid desktop and work-organization products to mass market, warehouse club, and commercial customers. The division also distributed signage and message systems, products that addressed ergonomics and repetitive trauma problems in computer workstations, and modular furniture and workstations.

Power Brand

The Rubbermaid brand name was among the best known and most respected in North America. The company extended that recognition internationally in the 1990s by distributing Rubbermaid products to more than 100 nations, with the objective of having 25 percent of its sales come from markets outside the United States by the year 2000.

Many factors point to the durability of the Rubbermaid brand. Among these was the remarkable level of brand recognition. In the United States 97 percent of all adults knew of the Rubbermaid brand. Moreover, 90 percent of the company's new products succeeded, which was in sharp contrast to the 90 percent failure rate for new consumer products in general. In 1992 Rubbermaid set its 41st consecutive year of sales records and 55th consecutive year of profitable performance; was named for the 8th consecutive year among *Fortune*'s "Top-10 Most Admired Corporations"; and was one of the top-10 consumer goods "Power Brands" in a survey of consumers and retailers (the only top-10 company to improve its ranking).

Rubbermaid Incorporated had a clear mission statement: "Consistently create the best value for customers and consumers: provide highest quality products, reasonably priced; supply a continuous flow of new products; and deliver exceptional service to our customers." The brand's future would greatly depend on the company's ability to carry out these goals.

Further Reading:

"A Whale of an Introduction," *HFD—The Weekly Home Furnishings Newspaper,* September 6, 1993, p. 46.

Akers, Robert, "Shoot Rubbermaid Campaign For DDB Needham," *Back Stage,* February 2, 1990, p. 28.

"As Usual, Rubbermaid Presents What's New," *HFD—The Weekly Home Furnishings Newspaper,* February 24, 1992, p. 80.

Berry, Jon, "The Art of Rubbermaid; and Its Amazing Marketing Wizardry," *Adweek's Marketing Week,* March 16, 1992, pp. 22–25.

Berry, Jon, "46 States. 100,000-plus Little Kids. All Fishing," *Brandweek,* August 16, 1993, p. 13.

Berry, Jon, "Rubbermaid Packs an Ecological Lunch," *Adweek's Marketing Week,* September 9, 1991, p. 10.

Braus, Patricia, "Making Recycling Pay Off," *American Demographics,* October 1992, pp. 506–507.

Braus, Patricia, "Rubbermaid's Recycling Revenue," *American Demographics,* May 1992, p. 53.

Calonius, Erik, "Smart Moves by Quality Champs," *Fortune,* Spring-Summer 1991, pp. 24–29.

Corporate ID Manual: Guidelines for Graphic Standards & Legal Compliance, Wooster, Ohio: Rubbermaid Incorporated, 1993.

"Corporate Profiles: Rubbermaid," *Automotive Marketing,* December 1991, p. 10.

Duff, Mike, "Microwave Cookware Can Heat Up Other Sales," *Supermarket Business,* March 1991, pp. 96–99.

The Early Years of Rubbermaid [typescript], Wooster, Ohio: Rubbermaid Incorporated, n.d.

Lieback, Laura, "New Styles Pop Lid Off Lunch Box Sales," *Discount Store News,* November 16, 1992, p. 48.

Lubove, Seth, "Okay, Call Me a Predator," *Forbes,* February 15, 1993, pp. 150–153.

Mallory, Maria, "A Culture That Just Keeps Dishing Up Success. Profits on Everything But the Kitchen Sink; Rubbermaid's Utilitarian Twist

Has Paid Off in Steady Growth,'' *Business Week Innovation 1989,* June 10, 1989, p. 122.

Mangan, Dan, ''Food Storage Category Grows; Adds Products, Color, Revised Packaging,'' *HFD—The Weekly Home Furnishings Newspaper,* January 20, 1992, pp. 62–65.

Marks, Robert, ''Judgment Day; Will Consumers See Rubbermaid's New RTA as Furniture?,'' *HFD—The Weekly Home Furnishings Newspaper,* June 28, 1993, pp. 15–16.

Moskowitz, Milton, Robert Levering, and Michael Katz, editors, *Everybody's Business: A Field Guide to the 400 Leading Companies in America,* New York: Doubleday, A Currency Book, 1990, p. 147.

''1992 Marketing Achievement Awards; Rubbermaid Breaking All the Molds,'' *Sales & Marketing Management,* August 1992, p. 42.

''Recognition, Not Price, Shapes Brand Popularity,'' *Discount Store News,* October 1, 1990, pp. 70–71.

''Rubbermaid Hopes to Capture Toolbox Market,'' *Discount Store News,* November 5, 1990, p. 34.

Rubbermaid 1992 Annual Report, Wooster, Ohio: Rubbermaid Incorporated, 1993.

Schiller, Zachary, ''At Rubbermaid, Little Things Mean a Lot,'' *Business Week,* November 11, 1991, p. 126.

Sharp, Harold S., *Advertising Slogans of America,* Metuchen, New Jersey: Scarecrow Press, Inc., 1984, p. 407.

Silverstein, Michael J., ''Innovators Have Edge in War of the Brands; How 3 Companies Deter Private Labels,'' *Advertising Age,* August 9, 1993, p. 14.

—Doris Morris Maxfield

SALOMON®

SALOMON®

A brand of skis, poles, boots, bindings, and accessories, Salomon is famous for its exceptional quality and technical advancements. In the mid-1990s it formed the world's best-selling line of winter sports equipment; nearly half of all bindings, for example, carried the Salomon name. Although Salomon products were manufactured in France, that country accounted for less than ten percent of all sales. Japan, where more than a third of its sales took place, was the brand's largest market, followed by the United States (about 25 percent) and the Alpine countries of Germany, Austria, Italy, and Switzerland (together representing about 20 percent). Founded in 1947, Salomon S.A. was headquartered in the city of Annecy in southeastern France. Traditionally a manufacturer of skiing equipment alone, the company purchased the Chicago-based Taylor Made Golf Company in 1985, and by the mid-1990s, Salomon golf equipment provided about one-fourth of the company's total sales.

Brand Origins

By the middle of the twentieth century, Alpine skiing was already a well-established sport in Europe, the United States, and Australia, with inroads into many other parts of the world, including Japan, South America, and the Soviet Union. Resorts providing groomed trails, man-made snow, chair lifts, lodging, and other facilities were making the sport accessible to an increasingly larger number of people.

The sport's growing popularity provided manufacturers with a great financial incentive to improve equipment. While skis were traditionally made of a solid piece of wood (usually ash or hickory) a laminated, or layered, construction began in the 1930s, giving ski makers greater control over the finished product. During this period the problem of "ski edges" was also being confronted. In soft snow, wooden skis were able to dig firmly into a slope, providing enough friction to make a solid turn. In hardpacked snow, however, skiers were not so lucky, and even experts found themselves slipping and sliding down the mountain. The solution—attaching a steel strip along the bottom edge of a ski—was controversial, in part because steel, in addition to cutting into hardpacked snow, could also cut into a skier's leg during a fall. Moreover, steel significantly slowed a ski down, especially on soft, cold snow. Nevertheless, steel edges became a standard part of the modern ski, and, with the help of lamination, ski makers would eventually tuck all but a small bit of the edge inside the ski.

Shortly after World War II the ski industry boomed, and new manufacturers of ski equipment emerged worldwide, particularly in the Alpine regions of Europe. In Annecy, France, François Salomon set up a workshop for making saw blades and ski edges. The workshop, opened in 1947, occupied a 500-square-foot facility in the oldest part of the city. The Salomon ski edges were immediately successful, and sales were steady due to the rising demand for ski equipment. Furthermore, production greatly increased after Salomon's son Georges, then just in his twenties, invented a machine for mass producing ski edges. As a result, the Salomon workshop was able to manufacture some 700 kilometers of ski edges in 1952, the same year it moved into a larger, 2,500-square-foot warehouse on Avenue de Loverchy.

Ski bindings, not ski edges, however, made the Salomon name famous. Until the early 1950s the primary concern among manufacturers of ski bindings was to secure the boot tightly against the ski. A common binding design called the "bear trap," actually locked the boot down to the ski with metal plates. Although the design ensured that the ski could not separate from the boot, it proved unsafe, and broken bones were a common casualty among skiers. In 1940, skier Hjalmar Hvam of Portland, Oregon, introduced an alternative binding, which he developed after fracturing his leg in a skiing accident. Hvam's "Saf-Ski toe irons"—bindings that released under the pressure of a fall—were later followed by other cable systems releasing at both the heel and the toe, doing much to make skiing a safer sport.

In 1952 the Salomon workshop introduced its own ski bindings, combining what it called a "lift" cable heel (allowing the heel to release upward during a fall) and a "skade" release toe (which released from side to side). Some 2,200 of Salomon's bindings were sold in 1952; the following year, the company sold 10,000, nearly all of which were exported to the United States. Exports, in fact, would become Salomon's primary focus. Rising sales, meanwhile, led to increased production throughout the 1950s, and by 1962 the company was again forced to find larger facilities in Annecy, this time at Chemin de la Prairie. Salomon bindings underwent major changes in 1967, when the company introduced heel units that worked without cables. The first two such products, called the "Competition" and "Toutes-Neiges," set the standard on which future Salomon bindings were based. They were also a commercial boon, and by 1972 their sales reached a remarkable one million sets.

AT A GLANCE

Salomon brand of ski equipment founded in 1947 in Annecy, France, by François Salomon, his wife, Jeanne, and his son, Georges; Salomon steel edges for skis introduced in 1947; ski bindings introduced in 1952; skis put on the market in 1990; public shares of the brand's ultimate parent company, Salomon S.A., initially offered in 1983-84.

Performance: *Market share*—20% (top share) of winter sports equipment category; 46% (top share) of Alpine ski bindings category; 25% (second share) of Alpine ski boot category. *Sales*—(All products) $630 million (1992); (Alpine skiing products) $380 mllion; (cross-country skiing products) $46 million; (accessories) $36 million.

Major competitor: (Bindings) Tyrolia, Marker, Look, Ess, and Geze; (boots) Nordica, Raichle, Rossignol, Lange, and Tecnica; (skis) Rossignol, K2, Kästle, Elan, Dynastar, Atomic, and Pre.

Advertising: *Agency*—Kelley & Co., Boston, MA, 1992—. *Major campaign*—Advertisements highlighting the brand's racing performance.

Addresses: *Parent company*—Salomon/North America, Inc., 400 East Main Street, Georgetown, MA 01833; phone: (508) 352-7600; fax: (508) 352-7478. *Ultimate parent company*—Salomon S.A., Siège Social, Metz Tessy., 74996 Annecy Cedex 9, France; phone 011-33-50-65-41-41; fax: 011-33-50-65-42-56 (or 57).

Diversification

In the 1970s, the world's best-selling brand of Alpine ski bindings was extended to a line of ski boots. The traditional leather strap-up boot, which flexed and stretched as the skier moved down the slope, had been replaced by a rigid plastic construction in the late 1950s, providing a more durable and stiffer boot. However, instead of merely imitating the existing selection of ski boots, Salomon financed a research program, which resulted in the introduction of a Salomon ski boot in 1979. The Salomon boot had a unique, patented cable system that firmly held down the heel, ultimately giving a person more control over the skis. A year later Salomon also came out with a Cross Country boot-and-binding system, first marketed in France and Sweden. Salomon boots were immediately praised for their high-quality construction, and by 1982 they had become one of the world's most popular lines.

With its own line of bindings and boots, the company proceeded to focus its attention on skis. Salomon skis were introduced in 1989, after six years and $40 million worth of research. Having a patented "Monocoque," or single shell, construction, the skis were said to be exceptionally quick and responsive. According to Salomon's own advertisements, Monocoque skis had "a uniquely powerful edge grip" and were designed "with an extremely narrow waist . . . remarkably easy to turn and lightning fast edge to edge." Reviewers seemed to agree. In a 1990 issue of *Skiing* magazine, the Salomon 1S—a versatile, high-speed cruising ski—was described as having "very good edge grip" and handling "like a Lear jet."

Advertising and Marketing Strategies

Along with its skis, boots, and bindings, Salomon also sold a line of accessories, including bags, gloves, hats, shirts, and socks, all adorned with the Salomon name. Although such items would amount to only about five percent of total sales, their importance as a marketing tool was considerable. Fashionable accessories reinforced the brand's image as desirable and high-quality.

Athletic sponsorship was also an important marketing tool. In 1992, for example, the company devoted about one percent of its total sales, or about $6 million, to sponsoring skiers at the winter olympics in Albertville, France. Selected athletes were supplied with Salomon equipment, which, the company hoped, would be used to win Olympic events. Much of the payoff would come in later advertisements. A picture of Kerrin Lee-Gartner, the Canadian gold medal winner of the downhill event, was used in a December 1993 Salomon boot ad, which observed that "racers have found a direct connection between power and speed." In another ad for Salomon boots the featured athlete was Ingemar Stenmark, with accompanying text noting that "after 86 World Cup victories of his own [Stenmark] helped . . . come up with a boot that has already won Olympic and World Cup medals." Salomon bindings were also associated with racing. One ad claimed they were "the most successful missile guidance system ever invented. In the battle for racing supremacy, no binding has guided more racers to victory than Salomon." Another contended that Salomon was "the first binding that will absorb everything, but the shock of winning." Salomon skis, of course, also got their share of racing advertisements. Featuring Urs Lehman, the 1993 downhill world champion, one ad boasted, "Next time you're waiting to race, consider this: Every important ski test in the world (not to mention World Cup racing) placed Salomon 9000 Equipe skis at the top. . . . The fastest way to the bottom, and the top."

The company, moreover, publicized its efforts to make Salomon equipment and manufacturing methods environmentally friendly. A Salomon brochure stated, "As a manufacturer that transforms raw materials (mainly plastic), the company is aware that it is partially responsible for exploiting natural resources, producing waste materials and certain types of pollution. Salomon is especially aware that nature is the wonderful domain of sports activities for the skiers, hikers and golfers who buy our products. . . . Therefore, it is as much in our best interest as it is our conviction to preserve this precious 'nature-capital.' " To that end, in 1990 Salomon decided discontinue its use of environmentally harmful chemicals, including CFCs (chlorofluorocarbons), which were used as a foam expanding agent for its Alpine boots. Salomon also began a recycling program, used recycled cardboard for its cardboard boxes, and made its catalogs and brochures from recycled paper.

Brand Outlook

Heading into the twenty-first century, Salomon had a formidable market presence, as well as an enviable reputation for high-quality products and technical advancements. There were no fewer than 16 different kinds of Salomon skis, five variations of poles, 13 models of bindings, and 26 types of boots. Moreover, the number of skiers throughout the world was expected to remain steady at about 50 million, thus providing a predictable market for skiing equipment. In eastern Europe, where Salomon entered into an agreement with the Czech shoe manufacturer Botana, Salomon products were thought to have especially good growth potential.

The market for Salomon products, however, also faced a number of uncertainties. Even with improvements in man-made snow, poor snowfall in a major market could cause a temporary downturn in sales. Furthermore, because Salomon was primarily an export company, sales were also affected by currency fluctuations.

A weak French franc would make Salomon products cheaper abroad, thus improving sales, while a strong franc could have the opposite effect. Nevertheless, diversification has made the brand less susceptible to such variables. And the purchase of Taylor Made Golf Company—providing sales outside the snow dependent ski industry—has brought greater stability to the Salomon brand.

Further Reading:

Glenne, Bard, and Bill Grout, "Salomon's New Skis: A First Look," *Skiing Trade News,* January 1990, p. 15.

Green, Daniel, "Sponsors Vie for Race Stars," *Skiing Trade News,* October 1992, p. 12.

"The Hottest Ride on Snow," *Time,* October 8, 1990, p. 66.

Lloyd, Barbara, "Hiking into the Future with a Lighter Boot," *New York Times,* April 25, 1992, p. 50.

"No Business Like Snow Business," *The Economist,* March 3, 1990, p. 65.

Wallace, Ellen, "The Slopes Are Groomed for Salomon's New Ski," *Business Week,* April 10, 1989, p. 94.

—Thomas Riggs

SAMSONITE®

Samsonite luggage, widely known for its strength and durability, is the top-selling brand of luggage in the world. Its original slogan—"strong enough to stand on"—was coined in 1916 by the Shwayder Trunk Manufacturing Company, a firm that would later be renamed Samsonite. The Shwayder Trunk Manufacturing Company began producing what were commonly known as "suitcases" in 1910 with a meager force of ten employees. Today, the company puts 6,500 employees to work in the manufacture of nearly 60 different models of hardsided and softsided luggage. Since the 1930s, Samsonite also has been a major producer of folding furniture.

Brand Origins

The origins of the Samsonite brand can be traced to the founding of the Shwayder Trunk Manufacturing Company on March 10, 1910. Twenty-eight-year-old Denver native Jesse Shwayder, a former salesman for a trunk company in New York City, launched the firm with an invested capital of $3,500. The fledgling firm began manufacturing trunks and hand luggage in a 50-by-125-foot room of a downtown Denver store with just ten men.

During the early years of the company's existence, Shwayder found the struggle to master the manufacturing business rough going. After the first year's operation, he had lost $2,000 of his original investment. In order to continue, he refinanced with borrowed money. The young entrepreneur persevered and finally prospered. By 1912, the company had outgrown its downtown location and moved to another Denver facility. In 1917 the company moved again, this time to a three-story factory, also in Denver. Over time, Shwayder was joined in the venture by his four brothers—Maurice in 1912, Sol a few years later, and Ben and Mark in 1923. While ten employees produced the trunks and hand luggage, the brothers drummed up sales in Denver and nearby towns.

"Samson," denoting strength, was the first brand name of the Shwayder products. As luggage has traditionally taken a lot of punishment, the Shwayders decided to produce a product that would have a reputation for durability. They also wanted a distinctive luggage that would be easily recognizable as a Shwayder product. In 1916 a picture was taken that for years served as a trademark for the company. It showed Jesse Shwayder, his father, Isaac, and three of his brothers (the weight of these five men representing close to 1,000 pounds) standing on a plank that rested on a Shwayder suitcase. The picture was captioned, "Strong enough to stand on."

Early Marketing Strategies

During the lean years, the company relied primarily on word-of-mouth advertising. "We felt that word-of-mouth advertising had the double advantage of being the cheapest as well as the best form of advertising we could have," Jesse Shwayder recalled in *The Samsonite Story,* a company-produced history. By 1917, the company had launched a direct mail advertising campaign featuring the photo of the Shwayder family standing on the suitcase. The following year, the May Company in Denver devoted an entire window to promoting a new Shwayder case that sold for $4.95. It was shown supporting the weight of a half-ton of sugar.

It wasn't long before the company had again outgrown its production facilities. In 1924 the Shwayders built an 80,000-square-foot factory that produced luggage using assembly line methods. According to the "Samson Luggage Buyers Guide," published in the early 1920s, "Samson builds luggage like Ford builds automobiles. Conveyors, assembling systems and automatic machinery, especially designed for us, enable us to produce quality luggage at prices previously considered impossible." With sales reaching $1 million in 1926, Shwayder executives decided to lease an 85,000-square-foot factory in Ecorse, Michigan, to serve their eastern market.

Advertising Developments

As the company continued to grow, its marketing strategies became increasingly more sophisticated. The Samsonite Classic Attache, introduced in 1962, was the first product to be developed and launched as part of a comprehensive product campaign. The campaign used all the new disciplines of design development, engineering, market research, proven production techniques, expanded distribution, and national advertising. In 1964 the company mounted an extensive display at the Chicago Merchandise Mart, showing for the first time all of the products manufactured by the firm. Samsonite products were then being widely distributed, and the name Samsonite was known throughout the world. The company's name was changed to Samsonite Corporation in 1965.

AT A GLANCE

The Samsonite brand of luggage was introduced in 1939 by Shwayder Brothers Inc. to describe the Samsonite Streamlite luggage line; company had previously used the trade name "Samson"; Samsonite Corporation eventually owned by E-II Holdings, Inc., which reorganized and changed its name to Astrum International Corp.

Performance: *Sales*—$300 million (estimated).

Major competitor: American Tourister (owned by Astrum International); also, Zero Corporation's brand of luggage.

Advertising: *Agency*—Leo Burnett, Chicago, IL.

Addresses: *Parent company*—Samsonite Corporation, 11200 East 45th Ave., Denver, CO 80239-3018; phone: (313) 373-2000. *Ultimate parent company*—Astrum International Corp., 40301 Fisher Island Dr., Fisher Island, FL 33109.

By the early 1070s, Samsonite was conducting an effective advertising, promotion, publicity, and demonstration program. Samsonite's advertising included full-color, full-page ads in a large assortment of national publications and television commercials. Samsonite also made available to dealers a large assortment of advertising, point-of-sale, and promotional materials to coordinate with the national program. In 1993 Samsonite launched an airport promotion to show its luggage line to air travelers. The promotion, created by Leo Burnett USA, Chicago, included a display of 25 luggage items at 7 major airports. The luggage was displayed in 400-square-foot modules located near airline ticket counters or boarding gates. The displays were staffed by Samsonite representatives, with interested customers being referred to retailers in their area.

Brand Development

From the modest production of suitcases and trunks to the manufacture and sale of luggage and folding furniture worldwide, Samsonite has come a long way. The company's first step toward diversification came during the Depression years, when sales dropped drastically. It was then that the Shwayders, like many other manufacturers, started to look for new products to produce. The first of the consumer products other than luggage to be produced were folding card tables, which made their appearance in 1931. The brand name "Samson" was used on these first folding tables to emphasize their strength and durability. With this move toward diversification, the firm's name was changed to Shwayder Brothers Inc. in 1931.

The Denver plant, which was rapidly expanding by the 1930s, was by then the most modern luggage factory in the world. It produced Samson suitcases with such exclusive features as wood frame construction, handles that stayed secure, extra large and sturdy locks, metal drawbolts, rayon linings, hinges riveted to wood, and a one-year guarantee. Samson luggage was made with cowhide, leather, enamel, steel, veneer, and fiber finishes. Samsonhyde, an exclusive Samson product consisting of a vegetable fiber chemically and mechanically treated, was introduced in the early 1930s.

The basic design of the now-classic Samsonite Streamlite luggage line—featuring the tapered-shape case—was introduced in 1939. It was the first time that the word "Samsonite" was used to describe the luggage. At that time, vulcanized fiber covering material was introduced and used together with chrome-tanned "elkhide" leather binding. In the evolution of the Samsonite Streamlite product, the covering material was changed from vulcanized fiber to cellulose acetate, and then to polyvinyl chloride (vinyl).

During World War II most of the Denver plant's production was converted to war materials, including foot lockers, ammunition boxes, incendiary bombs, and hand grenades. The technical knowledge developed under the pressure of war production played a large part in enabling the company to bring out a superior post-war product made with new materials. By 1948, the company was purchasing injection molding presses for plastic parts, replacing rubber with vinyl in the manufacture of "lifetime" handles, replacing leather with vinyl in the luggage bindings, and adapting strong, resilient materials for luggage manufacturing. To spur growth, it was decided to concentrate on luggage production at the Denver plant and furniture production in Detroit.

During the Korean War in the 1950s, the company again went into war production. Throughout the three-year conflict, the Shwayders produced more incendiary bombs than it had during World War II. Luggage production persisted as the decade progressed, though, and a Special Products Division was set up in 1955 to design, manufacture, and market Samsonite cases designed to carry such items as musical instruments and electronic equipment. In 1956, after more than six years of research, the first new luggage product since the introduction of Samsonite Streamlite was designed and introduced. "Ultralite," according to *The Samsonite Story,* was the first luggage to eliminate basic wood box construction and "to use sheets and extrusions of 'jet age' magnesium—the lightest, strongest, structural metal known—combined with injection molded parts of ethyl cellulose." In 1958 Shwayder Brothers introduced Samsonite Silhouette, which has become a luggage industry classic. Composed of new and refined materials, the luggage line was praised for being both lightweight and durable.

To help develop their luggage products, an industrial organization, Design West, Inc., was formed as a subsidiary in 1962. The Samsonite Classic Attache case was introduced that same year and became a big seller. The demand for the product was so great that in 1966 an intermediate-priced Classic Attache was introduced. As the 1970s dawned, Samsonite was firmly established as the world's leading manufacturer of molded luggage and attache cases. From that strong base, the company decided to set its sights on the growing casual luggage market. Samsonite's first entry into this product category—Flee Bags—was an instant success. In 1970 Samsonite opened two "twin" plants—one in Tucson, Arizona, and the other in Nogales, Mexico—that were devoted exclusively to the production and assembly of Softside Casual luggage.

Two years later the company acquired Charles Doppelt and Company, Inc., a Chicago manufacturer of "Dopp-Kitt" leather toiletries kits, leather attaches, and related products. That acquisition helped Samsonite expand even further into the travel and leisure markets. By the mid-1990s, the company was offering an exceptionally wide range of innovative luggage products—both hardsided and softsided. These included: Esteem—The Professional Collection, designed exclusively for women; the Piggyback, a suitcase with a built-in luggage cart; the Ultralite line, which is about one-third lighter than the average structured softside luggage; and the Quantum, an attache with a patented ''smart hinge'' that allows the case to open and close in full-access position both when it is on its side and when it is in an upright position.

International Growth

From the early days of the company, various salespeople had pursued sales opportunities in foreign countries, but Samsonite did not actively enter the international market until the 1950s. The success of Samsonite Silhouette and Samsonite Classic Attache cases helped spur the growth of Samsonite internationally. An Export Sales Department was established in 1956 to handle this growing segment of the business. By that time, Samsonite luggage was already selling well in Canada, and a warehouse had been established in Toronto. One of the first production facilities outside the United States, Samsonite of Canada, Ltd., a wholly owned subsidiary, was put into operation in October of 1956 in Stratford, Ontario.

As export sales into Europe were becoming more significant, Samsonite took steps to reduce ocean freight costs and eliminate duties. Samsonite first endeavored to accomplish this in 1963 by having a contract manufacturer in Holland. Later, permanent manufacturing space was leased in Oudenaarde, Belgium, and an administrative office was set up in Brussels. In 1964 a joint venture, Altro S.A. de C.V., was formed in Mexico. Sales and warehouse facilities also were set up in Switzerland, Germany, France, and Italy in 1965. During the early 1960s Ace Luggage Company Ltd. functioned as a Samsonite distributor. Then, in 1965, arrangements were made for Ace to manufacture Samsonite luggage in Japan under license.

Because of duty considerations, Samsonite of Canada started serving the United Kingdom in 1965, warehousing luggage near the London International Airport. Another Samsonite distributor, Tauro, S.A., in Madrid, Spain, signed a licensing agreement to assemble and manufacture Samsonite luggage from the Spanish market in 1965. Still another distributor, Overseas Corporation, Ltd., in Australia, became a licensee to assemble Samsonite luggage in 1966. To further meet the needs of the European market, Samsonite acquired ODA, a softside luggage plant in Torhout, Belgium, in 1973. Then, in 1984, the company purchased 60 percent of a major Italian luggage company and 100 percent of a major Spanish luggage company. In 1989 Samsonite formed a joint venture in Hungary, acquiring 100 percent of the joint venture two years later. By the 1990s, Samsonite's International Division handled export sales to more than 100 countries and coordinated marketing and plant development on a global basis. The company also was actively pursuing new markets in Eastern Europe.

Performance Appraisal

From a one-room business in downtown Denver with only ten employees in 1910, Samsonite has evolved into a network of 30 manufacturing and distribution centers employing 6,500 individuals. While the early years of the company were lean, the Shwayders had outgrown their original facility by 1912. In 1917 their sales volume was $76,000. By 1924, sales had reached 300,000. Two years later, sales hit the million dollar mark.

Although sales dropped drastically during the Depression, the company quickly rebounded by producing folding card tables to augment sales. In 1946 the Shwayders sold nearly $7 million in luggage, foot lockers, and folding furniture. Two years later company-wide sales volume reached $13 million, the first year to exceed $10 million. By 1991, the company's sales had grown to an estimated $300 million.

Future Growth

As the company has grown, its organizational structure has become more complex. Management has had to become specific in its goal-setting and comprehensive in its planning for future growth. Considering its major areas of recent growth—enlarged production facilities, new product innovations, and expanded international operations—it seems fairly certain that progress will continue to be a part of Samsonite's future. According to the Samsonite Corporation 1992 Annual Report, ''Because of increasing worldwide awareness of the Samsonite brand name and quality image, the company is broadening its horizons to pursue new markets, new production and materials sources and new means of generating revenues to ensure a profitable and bright future.''

Further Reading:

''The Case for Hard-Sided Suitcases,'' *Consumer Reports,* July 1990, pp. 448–53.

''Samsonite Corporation,'' *Advertising Age,* October 18, 1993, p. 34.

The Samsonite Corporation 1992 Annual Report, Denver: The Samsonite Corporation.

The Samsonite Story, Denver: The Samsonite Corporation.

''Service in Business Travel,'' *Fortune,* September 9, 1991, p. 170.

Additional information in the form of press releases and product information obtained from Samsonite Corporation.

—Pam Berry

SANYO®

Sanyo Electric Co., Ltd., is one of the world's largest manufacturers of consumer electronics and home appliances. The brand has earned a reputation for high-tech products at moderate prices. Although the company has consistently incorporated the latest technology in its product lines, with a few exceptions, it has followed the lead of other companies rather than develop its own innovations. That attitude toward research and development changed in the late 1980s when the company began pinning great hopes on its development of alternative energy products, such as its CFC-free air conditioners and its silicon solar cells.

Brand Origins

Toshio Iue founded Sanyo Electric Works in 1947 in Moriguchi, Osaka. Iue had worked at Matsushita Electric Industrial Co. during World War II, helping with the company's military production. After the war, Iue left Matsushita, according to his brother Kaoru, to protect the company and his brother-in-law, the founder of Matsushita, from possible retaliation by the occupying Ally government. The new company began modestly, producing mainly bicycle lamp generators. Iue, however, intended to make the company a major international concern. Thinking of the merchandise he planned to sell across the Pacific, Atlantic, and Indian oceans, Iue named the company Sanyo, which means "three oceans" in Japanese.

Iue quickly expanded Sanyo's product line to include portable radios. The Sanyo radio established the brand with Japanese consumers. By undercutting its competitors' prices, the company developed a strong market for its radios. Sanyo's low-price strategy was helped when the company introduced the first plastic casings for radios in 1952. Iue did not wait long to enter the international market, and he quickly realized his dream of becoming an international force to be reckoned with: by the late 1950s Sanyo led transistor radio exports from Japan.

Japanese consumers created a boom in household appliances in the mid-1950s, much as American consumers did following World War II. Sanyo took advantage of this market explosion by producing in 1953 the first "whirlpool action" washing machines in Japan. Once the company introduced an inexpensive model, Sanyo washing machines held the country's top market share.

Brand Development

Iue continued his program of rapid diversification; by the mid-1950s, Sanyo was selling electric fans, space heaters, and refrigerators. The company soon entered the television market and created its own television division in 1961. By using the same low-price strategy that made their radios so popular, Sanyo became a leading Japanese producer of color televisions. Sanyo introduced rechargeable batteries in 1961 and by the end of the decade was Japan's leading supplier. The company also expanded into other battery types, including fuel cell batteries, a market Sanyo soon dominated.

The company expanded both domestically and internationally in the 1960s. Tokyo Sanyo Electric Co., Ltd., was created in 1959; Sanyo sold 80 percent of its stake to raise money. Two years later Sanyo established a joint venture manufacturer, Sanyo Electric (Hong Kong) Limited, representing the company's first overseas manufacturing. The subsidiary Sanyo Electric, Inc., was founded in the United States the same year. Other subsidiaries followed later in the decade. In 1968 Toshio Iue stepped down as CEO; his brother, Yuro Iue, took his place at the head of the company.

Exports were also strong, although Sanyo's success in the United States caused trouble for the brand both there and at home. The U.S. Treasury filed charges against the company in 1970 for "dumping" color televisions, or selling them far below cost to drive competitors out of business. Many U.S. importers cut back their orders while waiting for a ruling. In addition, when Japanese consumers learned that they were paying up to 25 percent more than their American counterparts for color televisions, they boycotted the Japanese brands, including Sanyo. When combined with a general slowdown in the Japanese economy, these problems spelled trouble for Sanyo. The company's earnings in the second half of 1970 dropped by 17 percent. In response, Sanyo cut its new plant and equipment budget nearly in half and lowered color television prices in Japan by 17 percent.

By 1970 Sanyo had grown to become Japan's second-largest brand of electrical and electronic consumer goods (behind only Matsushita Electric). The company sold 300 different kinds of products, from washing machines to electric sake warmers. However, the company felt its brand recognition was low, both in Japan and overseas. Kaoru Iue, Toshio's brother and Sanyo's president in 1971, told *Business Week,* "In the U.S., people buy quality, but

AT A GLANCE

Sanyo brand of consumer electronics and home appliances founded in 1947 by Toshio Iue in Moriguchi, Japan; company name originally Sanyo Electric Works; incorporated in 1950 as Sanyo Electric Co., Ltd.

Performance: *Sales*—$11 billion.

Advertising: *Agency*—Batey Ads, Los Angeles, for Fisher audio/video products, 1992—. *Major campaign*—Print ads for Fisher CD player, Studio 24 CD changer/management system, using Alice Cooper and the tagline, "Restore Family Harmony."

Major competitor: In consumer electronics, Pioneer; also Sharp and Matsushita. In home appliances, General Electric; also Maytag and Whirlpool.

Addresses: *Parent company*—Sanyo Fisher (USA) Corporation, 21350 Lassen St., Chatsworth, CA 91311; phone: (818) 998-7322; fax: (818) 998-3533. *Ultimate parent company*—Sanyo North America Corp., 666 Fifth Ave., New York, NY 10103; phone: (212) 315-3232; fax: (212) 315-3263. *Ultimate ultimate parent company*—Sanyo Electric Co. Ltd., Japan.

here the brand name is the important thing. We have to build up our image.'' A Tokyo homemaker confirmed Iue's perception of Sanyo's low profile when she said to *Business Week,* ''You never see their ads on TV.''

International Markets

Sanyo also intended to build its brand recognition in the United States. Previously, the company had sold its products through private labels, mostly through Sears, Roebuck & Co. In the early 1970s, Sanyo began selling under its own brand name in the United States. The company broadened its overseas product line, adding cassette and video recorders, washing machines, and vacuum cleaners to its offerings.

In the mid-1970s, the company began to concentrate on its high-tech products rather than its home appliances. Although Sanyo had been exporting color televisions to the United States since 1965, the company emphasized its commitment to selling high-tech products overseas by establishing a manufacturing corporation in the United States in 1976. The next year Sanyo bought control of the U.S. television manufacturer Warwick Electronics Inc. The company added microwave ovens and made the plant ten times as productive. In 1978 Sanyo bought the American electronics company Fisher, but retained that brand name rather than incorporate Fisher electronics into the Sanyo product line.

The company's decision to focus on high-tech products clearly paid off: U.S. sales rose from $71 million in 1972 to $855 million in 1978. The only falter in that rapid growth was caused by Sanyo's decision to enter the new field of video cassette recorders with a line of betamax VCRs. Sales suffered when it became apparent that the VHS format for video cassette recorders had beaten the betamax format to become the industry standard. Quickly changing its product line, Sanyo kept its original misjudgment from greatly affecting its sales growth.

Sanyo's overseas sales continued to grow through the mid-1980s, accounting for the majority of Sanyo's sales. Concentrating on the low end of the electronics market, Sanyo maintained healthy market shares in the United States. With the sharp appreciation in the yen in the mid-1980s, however, growth in exports ended. In response, Sanyo stepped up overseas production and combined the sales and operations of Sanyo and Fisher in the United States. Sales increased slightly, although a recession soon caused further problems. By the early 1990s, the proportion of overseas sales to domestic sales had reversed itself, and Sanyo was selling more in Japan than in the United States.

Brand Renewal

The slowing of the company's exports caused Sanyo to retrench in the mid-1980s. Satoshi Iue, the founder's son, took over the presidency in 1986 when his uncle Kaoru resigned to demonstrate that he took responsibility for several deaths caused by faulty kerosene heaters produced by Sanyo. Within months, Satoshi Iue announced that Sanyo would merge with Tokyo Sanyo Electric Co., in which Sanyo already had a 20 percent stake. The merger would produce cost savings and create economies of scale by allowing the two companies to combine any overlapping product lines, including their video cassette recorders, audio products, and refrigerators. In addition, Tokyo Sanyo revitalized the brand's product line by bringing in such high-growth items as semiconductors and office automation products.

Iue advertised the company's plans for renewal by starring in his own television commercials. With the tagline, ''Now Let's Begin,'' the commercials featured Iue explaining the need for the whole group to pull together. Although Iue considered the reorganization the equivalent of a second founding of Sanyo, he feared making overly drastic changes. The merger created many redundant personnel for whom Iue struggled to find productive positions. He explained to *Business Week,* ''Unlike U.S. companies, we can't dismiss them or lay them off, but we can use their knowledge to create new products.'' In addition, Iue slowly increased offshore production, a change many companies were making in response to the rising yen. Because Japanese workers tended to resent increased overseas manufacturing, Iue decided to increase the percentage gradually.

Energy Research

The oil crisis of the 1970s persuaded Sanyo to begin research on energy-efficient products and alternative energy sources. The company introduced in 1971 an absorption-type chiller that could be used to both heat and cool buildings. In 1974 the company joined MITI's Sunshine Project to develop an experimental solar energy house. Although the general public's interest in alternative energy sources lessened when the energy crisis ended, Sanyo continued its research.

Sanyo began mass producing amorphous silicon solar cells in 1981. Although the noncrystalline cells are less efficient than cells cut from single crystals of silicon, they are much cheaper to produce. Rigid, heavy backings, such as glass, stainless steel, and thick plastic could be coated with the amorphous silicon and used to power electronic goods that did not need a great deal of power. Sanyo popularized rigid solar cells in the 1980s by incorporating them into low-end, mass-marketed consumer products, such as calculators and watches.

Sanyo advanced the technology in the early 1990s by producing a flexible version of its amorphous silicon cells. By coating both sides of a plastic film with silicon and then slipping it between two layers of protective plastic, Sanyo was able to produce a lightweight, flexible solar-cell bank. The cell's efficiency at converting sunlight into electricity was low, requiring large areas to be covered. For example, Sanyo's experimental solar airplane, launched in 1990, had wings that spanned 57.4 feet and were covered with solar cells. The cells generated the 2,000 watts of power needed to operate the 198-pound airplane at 40 to 99 miles per hour. Despite their relative inefficiency, Sanyo was convinced that numerous applications for the cells could be found; it was exploring portable power packs and beach umbrellas, camping tents, and sails that could generate power. By the mid-1990s Sanyo had applied the technology to roofing shingles, solar-collecting windows, and car sunroofs.

Sanyo continued to develop its alternative heating and cooling products. Sanyo absorption coolers, which did not require CFCs to cool the air, garnered greater attention as concern over ozone depletion grew. The company developed a CFC-free refrigerator in the early 1990s. In 1989 the company introduced its Direct Drive Heat Pump, a helium refrigerant heating, cooling, and domestic hot water system. In 1993 Sanyo began selling its solar-powered inverter air conditioner to residential consumers.

After its introduction of rechargeable batteries in 1961, the company went on to develop lithium batteries in 1978. Sanyo licensed that technology to A.G. Batterie of Germany and Mallory and General Electric of the United States. In 1990 the company began production of rechargeable nickel-metal hydride batteries; by 1990 Sanyo was the clear market leader of this popular item. Compared to conventional nickel-cadmium batteries, nickel-metal hydride batteries provide 50 percent more energy output by weight and last longer after recharging. In addition, they do not include cadmium, a toxic heavy metal. Sanyo intended to begin production in the mid-1990s of lithium ion batteries, which are even more powerful than nickel metal hydrides. The company planned on using its advanced batteries in newly designed consumer electronic products.

Future Growth

In the mid-1990s Sanyo rested its hopes on new products that would incorporate its battery and solar cell technology. Sales in the early 1990s had been slipping, and in 1992 Sanyo reported a loss of $11.7 million. A Sanyo director, Yukinori Kuwano, told *Forbes* in 1993, "We are strong in research, but our commercialization and marketing is poor." The low-end strategy the company had followed since its founding was now hurting its sales. Known more for low prices than high quality and slow to bring out new products, Sanyo needed a more compelling image. Overstaffing contributed to Sanyo's problems, but Sanyo held to Japan's strong tradition of lifetime employment. Industry analysts contended that Sanyo would also be well served by focusing its research and development more tightly, using limited funds to develop products that would stand out from the competition. Looking ahead, Sanyo's president, Yasuaki Takano, told *Forbes* in 1993, "It will be very tough for at least the next two years."

Further Reading:

Armstrong, Larry, "Sanyo Tries to Stay One Step Ahead of the Yen," *Business Week,* June 9, 1986, pp. 46–47.

"A Boycott Tunes Down Japan's TV Makers," *Business Week,* March 6, 1971, pp. 41.

Byrne, John A., "At Sanyo's Arkansas Plant the Magic Isn't Working," *Business Week,* July 14, 1986, pp. 51–52.

Eisenstodt, Gale, "Unidentical Twins," *Forbes,* July 5, 1993, p. 42.

"Solar Sells," *Scientific American,* August 1990, p. 103.

—Susan Windisch Brown

SATURN®

General Motors Corp. created the Saturn brand of small cars as a distinctly American import-fighter, an identity each car wore proudly with its very name: the namesake of Saturn is the Saturn rocket, a rocket that symbolically carried the United States ahead of the Soviet Union in the space race. This goal of carrying American automakers ahead of the Japanese in the small-car race was so crucial to General Motors (GM) that it initially promised an investment of $5 billion in the project (later reduced to an estimated $3.5 billion) when it founded the subsidiary, the Saturn Corporation, in 1985. Although GM soon stopped thinking of Saturn as the experiment that would breed success for other GM divisions, the success of Saturn itself did not disappoint: Saturn cars rocketed to third place in the subcompact car market in just three years after their retail introduction in 1990.

This success certainly owed something to Saturn's efforts to create high-quality cars by empowering every employee to be a partner in the constant process of improving production efforts. But absolutely crucial to Saturn's success was its marketing strategy of selling the car through enthusiasm for the company—a strategy masterfully created and conducted by Saturn's ad agency Hal Riney & Partners of San Francisco (hired in 1988). This was an advertising strategy repeatedly summed up by Saturn's understated marketing tag line, "A different kind of company. A different kind of car."

Launching Project Saturn

Project Saturn was born from GM's desperate need in the early 1980s not only to compete with the Japanese and take business away from them but also to overcome its longtime, nearsighted confidence in its ability to succeed through the sheer size of its output. This was a need that was not being fulfilled by GM's numerous attempts to build small cars by shortening its medium car designs, or by collaborating with Japanese car companies. These quick-fix, short-term approaches did not address the serious problem of changing a corporate culture content with the status quo and uninterested in acknowledging, let alone encouraging, any constructive input from its employees: "It wasn't just design, engineering, and manufacturing that needed to change, but the entire business of running the business," said Neil DeKoker, former Saturn director of business systems, in a 1989 *Automotive News* article.

The beginnings of Project Saturn in 1982 were directed by then vice president of the advanced engineering staff, Alex Mair, who wanted to give GM a long-range plan for building leading-edge small cars without Japanese help. It was GM chairman Roger Smith, though, who in 1983 launched Saturn at a press conference as GM's brightest hope for future success. Saturn was to be a laboratory for all GM divisions so that they could develop new management, manufacturing, and marketing techniques devoted to high quality. Smith's grand claims for Saturn made the project—and its status from then on—a closely scrutinized symbol of whether GM was finally heading in the right direction. "The product, the Saturn car, is the least important aspect of the Saturn program," says Phil Fricke, analyst with Goldman, Sachs & Co., in the *Chicago Tribune* in 1985. "I can't emphasize enough that Saturn represents new manufacturing techniques, and whatever GM learns from this small car will be applied throughout the organization in all its cars, big and small." But the question that many skeptical observers were asking was: could GM—a corporation for which Saturn was its first new nameplate since 1918—really pull it off?

Cutting Back the Saturn Vision

As GM's American market share dropped from 44 percent in 1985 to 37 percent in 1988, GM was forced to diminish its goals for the Saturn project, starting by reducing its Saturn budget from $5 billion to $3.5 billion. Saturn was no longer to devote so much of its budget to Smith's vision of Saturn as a laboratory to develop more efficient and higher quality production processes for other GM divisions. As Saturn president Skip LeFauve bluntly explained in a 1988 *Fortune* article, "We're still exploring, but Saturn is no longer an experiment. We're not a laboratory. We're not a social program. We're a business." With this added emphasis on making money, Saturn no longer planned to experiment with leading-edge technology and build a super gas efficient, low-end small car costing $6,000. Instead, Saturn concentrated on building a larger, higher-priced, high-quality, and high-volume car designed to take business away from Japanese top-sellers like the Honda Accord and Toyota Celica, without doing the same damage to GM's other cars. And so, Saturn launched a sedan and a coupe, later adding a wagon in 1993.

AT A GLANCE

The Saturn Project planned by Alex Mair, vice president of advanced engineering staff, and Roger Smith, chairman of General Motors, in Detroit, MI, 1982; General Motors founded the Saturn Corporation as a wholly owned subsidiary in Troy, MI, 1985; Saturn brand was created as a high-quality line of cars that could compete with Japanese small cars on a long-term basis; Saturn automobiles first went on sale in 1990.

Performance: *Market share*—2.69% of 1993 U.S. new-car car category. *Sales*—229,356 cars sold in 1993.

Major competitor: For the sedans (Sl, SL1, and SL2): Honda Civic and Dodge/Plymouth Neon; for the coupes (SC1 and SC2): Toyota Celica and Mitsubishi Eclipse; for the wagons (SW1 and SW2): Toyota Corolla and Ford Escort wagons.

Advertising: *Agency*—Hal Riney & Partners, San Francisco, CA, 1988—. *Major campaign*—TV and print ads selling Saturn's image as a high-quality automaker and automobile, with the tag line, "A different kind of company. A different kind of car."

Addresses: *Parent company*—Saturn Corporation, 1420 Stephenson Highway, P.O. Box 7025, Troy, MI 48007-7025; phone: 1-(800) 522-5000. *Ultimate parent company*—General Motors Corp., 3044 W. Grand Blvd., Detroit, MI 48202; phone: (313) 556-5000.

Marketing Saturn to Import Car Buyers

In order to become an effective import-fighter, Saturn needed to overcome the problem of selling its cars to import car enthusiasts who had no interest in purchasing what they perceived to be lower quality American cars. Enter Hal Riney & Partners of San Francisco, the ad agency responsible for many standout creative ad campaigns, including the famous Bartles & Jaymes wine cooler commercials that "thank you for your support." In 1988 Saturn awarded Hal Riney its $100 million annual advertising account—the largest ever for a new product—giving Riney two years to prepare for Saturn's launch. A surprise choice from more than 50 agencies, Riney was selected by Saturn for several key factors, including Riney's promise of creative and endearing emotional advertising, as well as their location in (and familiarity with) California, where Japanese imports sell better than anywhere else in the country.

Although Saturn began marketing its cars by announcing its goal of beating the Japanese in the small-car race, such an announcement was not in itself enough to excite the consumer who was already quite familiar with the many mediocre attempts of American automakers to enter that race. So, to get import-committed consumers to take Saturn seriously, Saturn's ad agency Hal Riney had to reconcile the extremely tricky set of goals Saturn had set for its image. Riney's dilemma was to make Saturn's American identity a selling point despite two compromising factors: Saturn's parent company was one of these stigmatized American automakers, and Saturn's production philosophy was modeled after Japanese examples.

Riney's resolution to this dilemma is illustrated in part by its simple catch-phrase for Saturn: "A different kind of company. A different kind of car." While clear and concise, the phrase is ambiguous in that it doesn't state what Saturn is different from. If Saturn explicitly said they were different from the Japanese, they would have played the familiar game of domestic/import comparisons that always risked admitting the widespread assumption that the Japanese products were superior. If Saturn explicitly said they were different from the American automakers, they would have either risked appearing "Japanized" or risked being put on the defensive about how they could be different when they were a mere subsidiary of the biggest of the big three, General Motors.

Rather than explicitly insist on the difference from GM, Riney had Saturn take the more subtle approach of trying to distance itself from any stigma GM had among its target consumers, and trying at the same time to reinvest itself with a traditional and popular American image that consumers thought GM had lost. For starters, Saturn ads did not mention the company's affiliation with GM. Riney produced ads that distanced Saturn from the stigma-ridden urban center of American automakers—Detroit—by showing newly hired and hopeful Saturn workers in the act of moving from depressed city scenes to the regenerative and traditionally American rural surroundings of Spring Hill, Tennessee, where the Saturn plant was located.

Although Saturn also needed to establish that it was different from its Japanese counterparts, Riney did not run ads comparing the Saturn car to Japanese cars. And as if not to invite such comparison, Saturn ads barely mentioned the product's features. Instead, the first year of ads that introduced Saturn to American consumers emphasized the rediscovered can-do American values that went into building a quality company and a quality car. To establish this American identity, these ads centered on the same thing as the ads used to establish Saturn's difference from Detroit: Saturn's rural site in Spring Hill, Tennessee. These ads showed pastoral American scenes of farms, front porches, and Little League baseball—images designed to exploit the persistent American faith in its back-to-basics, pioneer spirit. The Saturn employees represented in these ads were no longer the stigmatized lazy assembly-line workers, but rather Spring (Hill)-regenerated automaking "associates" integrally involved in a truly American and democratic effort to build high-quality cars. Since quality was in large part what many American consumers assumed the Japanese accomplished better than the Americans, the ads portrayed Saturn associates telling consumers how everyone on the production end was empowered to constantly help reform and refine the production processes.

Shifting Ad Focus to Customers

After Saturn's first model-year campaign in which its advertising made Saturn employees and dealers its main selling point, Saturn and Hal Riney decided to shift Saturn's marketing focus to the customers of the 1992 model. "The idea now is to build brand equity," stated Thomas Shaver, Saturn's director of consumer marketing, in a 1991 *Advertising Age* article. "Last year, we wanted to tell small-car intenders who and what Saturn is. We've done that." This shift in marketing strategy came after a year in which Saturn lost a higher-than-anticipated $700 million (estimated), contributing to GM's biggest quarterly loss ever—$1.98 billion.

This marketing shift also followed a year in which some industry observers criticized Saturn's first model-year ads, claiming that the ads failed to sell product advantages, being too intent on selling the cars through the company's quality-focused partnership philosophy. Trying to justify its $100 million investment in first model-year ads that didn't even tell consumers what they could expect from the car itself, Patrick Sherwood, Riney's vice president/director of the Saturn account, explained in a 1990 *Automotive News* article that the hope was not so much that Saturn would immediately meet sales volume goals, but that "in a couple of years, people [would] look back and say this is a car company that people like and respect."

So who were the consumers that Riney's ads targeted for the 1992 model year, and how did these ads target them? Saturn found that its cars were attractive to the under-35 generation. This was an important age group to the automobile industry in the early 1990s, not only because it was the consumer group most likely to buy a new car, but also because the group consisted of many first-time buyers, thus allowing the car company that sells to this buyer to gain a long-term brand loyalty. Saturn attracted many from this younger generation of so-called baby busters in part through its soft-sell, no-hassle sales tactics and no-haggle, one-cost pricing. "A lot of Saturn's philosophy and values strike a responsive chord with younger people," said Steve Shannon, Saturn director of consumer marketing, in a 1993 *Advertising Age* article. "They're less inclined to engage in the old shell game of pricing." Given this interest that post-baby boomers showed in Saturn, Hal Riney came up with a network TV spot in which a young first-time car buyer has a no-hassle experience in a Saturn showroom after having just received extensive advice from her father on how to deal with the pushy salesmen he expects she'll encounter.

Banking On Customer Service

This shift in ad focus from the employee's enthusiasm for the company to the customer's proved to be very effective—so much so that Saturn continued to use this customer-focused ad strategy beyond its 1992 model year. "I think the thing that maybe has worked best for us has been the consistency. We've avoided the temptation to say 'gee, it's a new year and let's start all over and have a new ad campaign,'" affirmed Don Hudler, Saturn vice president of sales, service, and marketing, in a 1993 interview for a Saturn news release. It was indeed starting with this 1992 model year of advertising that Saturn began to see several significant signs of its rapidly growing success. These signs of success came in categories that Saturn had already emphasized as keys to the groundwork it wanted to lay for long-term progress: offering devoted customer service at the same time as ensuring that its dealerships could still be highly successful despite the expense of such customer service.

Saturn was well aware that having a solid reputation for excellent customer service was increasingly important for the long-term edge it needed over its top competitors, especially since Saturn had already reached a parity in quality with these top competitors and needed something else to set it apart. Saturn started to build this reputation in spectacular fashion, finishing third on J. D. Power & Associates' 1992 Customer Satisfaction Index, behind number one Lexus and second-place Infiniti, both luxury cars. A year later, in 1993, Saturn proved just how important it considered quality customer service to its long-term success when it ignored pressure by financially troubled GM to reach profitability that year and spent an estimated $8 million to $35 million on an intense customer relations effort during a voluntary recall of 350,000 cars. Jeremy Anwyl, president of Marketec Systems, explained Saturn's logic in a 1993 *Advertising Age* article: "People who have had problems that have been dealt with satisfactorily tend to be even more loyal than customers who haven't had problems."

Of course, the people who dealt directly with the customer during this recall, as with most other car-related services, were the Saturn dealers. Because Saturn couldn't force its dealers to go beyond the call of duty to the customer, the company had to ensure that dealers would be successful enough to avoid their typical parsimony and afford spending the incredible time and money necessary to fulfill Saturn's standard for customer service. Accordingly, Saturn signed up dealers who generally already ranked in the top five percent in customer satisfaction and then gave these dealers franchise agreements allowing them the retailing rights to set up outlets over territories notably larger than the norm. As a result of such retail advantages, Saturn placed first, in 1991, in new-car sales per facility, a distinction that a domestic nameplate had not achieved for 15 years. Saturn was number one again the next year, and dramatically better than the previous year, going from 776 to 1,072 vehicles per dealer outlet, beating out Honda's 654. In fact, Saturn was number one not only in sales per outlet but also in overall value to dealers. J. D. Power & Associates' 1992 Dealer Attitude Study gave Saturn its top-rating for business terms, manufacturer's sales and service support, and vehicle supply. "[Such high ratings] give us confidence that as additional production becomes available we'll continue to be able to build the distribution outlet in the same high quality we've done so far," boasted Don Hudler in a 1993 interview for a Saturn news release.

Increasing Future Competitiveness

So did the recognition Saturn received for its customer service and valuable dealerships translate into high sales? In 1993 Saturn sales were up 17.5 percent, allowing Saturn to take over third place from the Toyota Corolla among best-selling subcompact cars. However, for Saturn to continue to enjoy success, it needed

Three of Saturn's most popular 1994 models.

to improve. Saturn's marketing had a long way to go, for although its award-winning advertising helped bring awareness of the product up to 17 percent in 1993, this percentage was only half of Honda awareness. Moreover, Saturn still needed to work on meeting its goal of taking business away from its import competitors. In 1992 only about 50 percent of those who purchased a Saturn said they would have otherwise bought a Japanese import car, although 73 percent would have bought a non-GM car. Hudler admitted in *Fortune* that "we have failed if 80% of our buyers don't come from the ranks of import owners."

One of the ways in which Saturn planned to grow was to expand its retail locations from the 300 it had at the end of 1993 to ultimately 700 to 800 locations. But if Saturn reached such a size, would it still be able to maintain its image as ''a different kind of company,'' an image that was absolutely fundamental to selling its ''different kind of car''? Saturn was different largely because it was smaller than the mammoth automobile manufacturers; its smaller size allowed it not only to manage a tightly knit partnership philosophy of production and retail, but perhaps more importantly to devote itself to every Saturn customer. Some speculated that Saturn's growing success might eventually undermine the very image that helped achieve that success. Hudler responded to this theory in a 1993 interview for a Saturn news release: ''Obviously, it'll take more management and more people to operate and staff those stores. But, I think if we go about it in the same way, we'll be able to largely retain the same kind of small, family, friendly atmosphere that we have today.''

Further Reading:

Armstrong, Larry, ''If It's Not Japanese, They Wouldn't Bother Kicking the Tires,'' *Business Week,* April 9, 1990, p. 61.

''A Conversation with . . . '' Don Hudler, V.P. of Sales, Service & Marketing, Saturn Corporation, Spring Hill, TN: Saturn Corporation, August 9, 1993.

''A Conversation with . . . '' Skip LeFauve, President, Saturn Corporation, Spring Hill, TN: Saturn Corporation, August 9, 1993.

Customer Satisfaction Is ''The Saturn Difference'' Again in 1994, Spring Hill, TN: Saturn Corporation, August 9, 1993.

Elliott, Stuart, ''Selling Saturn; GM Protecting $3.5B Investment with Down-Home Ads; Campaign Takes Aim at Heartstrings,'' *USA Today,* November 1, 1990, p. 1B.

Important Dates in Saturn History, Spring Hill, TN: Saturn Corporation, 1993.

Keller, Maryann, ''Small Car, Big Strategy: Regaining the Edge,'' *Automotive News,* August 21, 1989, p. 42.

Mateja, James, ''Why Saturn Is So Important to GM,'' *Chicago Tribune,* January 13, 1985, business sec., p. 1.

Oram, Roderick, ''GM Names Saturn Ad Agency,'' *Financial Times,* May 26, 1988, sec. 1, p. 19.

The Power Report on Automotive Marketing, Westlake Village, CA: J. D. Power & Associates, December 1993.

''[An interview with Saturn President] Richard LeFauve; Saturn Corp. Faces a Dilemma: How To Attract Non-GM Buyers While Retaining a GM Identity,'' *Automotive News,* June 26, 1989, p. E20.

Sawyers, Arlena and Lindsay Chappell, ''Storytellers; Early Saturn Ads Shun Cars; Workers Explain Why They Came to Spring Hill,'' *Automotive News,* October 15, 1990, p. 6.

Schlossberg, Howard, *Marketing News TM,* ''Markets Changing as Never Before; Firms Have Tough Choices to Make,'' April 12, 1993, p. 7; ''To Rise to the Top in Satisfaction, It Helps If You've Been Down,'' June 21, 1993, p. 6.

Sederberg, Arelo, ''General Motors Latest Southern California Auto Marketing Campaign Rings of Saturn,'' *Los Angeles Business Journal,* October 1, 1990, p. 29.

Sedgwick, David, *Gannett News Service,* July 13, 1989.

Serafin, Raymond, *Advertising Age,* ''Customers Drive New Saturn Campaign,'' September 16, 1991, p. 6; ''Saturn Recall a Plus for Saturn: Car Marketer Faces Tough Test of Its Customer Service Mission,'' August 16, 1993, p. 4.

Serafin, Raymond and Cleveland Horton, *Advertising Age,* ''Automakers Focus on Service; Customer Care Comes to Forefront of Marketing Efforts,'' July 6, 1992, p. 3; ''X Marks the Spot for Car Marketing; Automakers Push Value Message to Make Good First Impression with Young Generation,'' August 9, 1993, p. 8.

Serafin, Raymond, Gary Levin, Judann Dagnoli, Wayne Walley, Jennifer Pendleton, and Ira Teinowicz, ''Hal Riney vs. Japan; Saturn Ads to Take Risks,'' *Advertising Age,* May 30, 1988, p. 1.

Serafin, Raymond and Patricia Strnad [sic], ''Saturn Will Tout Its People First, Then Its Cars,'' *Automotive News,* August 27, 1990, p. 1.

Serafin, Raymond, Patricia Strnad, and Cleveland Horton, ''Saturn's Ad Approach Wins Dealer Approval,'' *Automotive News,* November 19, 1990, p. 10.

Taylor, Alex III, ''Back to the Future at Saturn,'' *Fortune,* August 1, 1988.

Veverka, Amber, ''Saturn Dawns Through Marketing,'' *Grand Rapids Business Journal,* April 1, 1991, p. 3.

Warner, Fara and Lisa Marie Petersen, ''Blissful Domestic Resurgence: Ford, with Media Spending up $50 Million, Remained the No. 1 Super Brand in the Auto Industry; Supplement: America's Top 2000 Brands,'' *Mediaweek,* October 18, 1993, p. S54.

Wernle, Bradford, ''He's Off!: But Will Auto-Biz Reality Rein in Adman Riney?,'' *Crains Detroit Business,* June 6, 1988, sec. 1, p. 3.

—Jeffrey E. Mash

SCHWINN®

For almost anyone who grew up in the 1950s or 1960s, the name Schwinn might provoke a fond memory of pedaling through suburban streets, negotiating city roads, or just wandering anywhere a bicycle can take you. Though the name is profoundly associated with Baby Boomers on bikes, the Schwinn Bicycle Company, now known as Schwinn Cycling and Fitness, Inc., actually has a history that spans nearly an entire century.

A Family Business

It all began in Chicago in 1895. Ignaz Schwinn, along with partner Adolph Arnold, opened their bicycle business—called Arnold, Schwinn & Company—in a rented downtown building. In its first year, the company produced about 25,000 cycles—an encouraging figure considering the importance of two-wheelers during the pre-automotive era in the United States. But Schwinn wasn't alone in its pursuit of riders. Back then, ''Chicago was the world's bike capital, with about 90 manufacturers,'' noted *Forbes* writer Andrew Tanzer. ''Schwinn is the last [remaining] major one.''

Schwinn is also perhaps the most family-oriented of the big cycling manufacturers. Through the years, four generations of Schwinns have run the business. By 1899 Arnold, Schwinn & Company had earned enough capital to acquire a competitor, March-Davis Bicycle Company. The next year, the company greeted a new century with a new location—a larger facility on Chicago's Northwest Side. Expansion continued into 1901, when the Schwinn business relocated again, this time to a combined corporate headquarters and manufacturing facility on North Kostner Avenue.

From that location came decades of progress and innovation for Schwinn. Some famous early bicycle names of the first part of the century have carried the Schwinn brand: Aerocycle, Cycleplane, and Autocycle—names designed to give an otherworldly feel of flight and speed to the biking experience. In 1938 Schwinn introduced the Paramount models, lightweight bikes that prefigured the performance cycles of today. And in 1963 came one of Schwinn's most fondly remembered names, the Sting-Ray. This sporty-looking model caught the eyes and grabbed the hearts of young riders across the nation.

But model lines weren't Schwinn's only innovation. In the field of technology, the Schwinn Bicycle Company was noted for its functional advancements. According to company records, Schwinn models debuted such design features as the coaster brake, balloon tires, the full-floating saddle and seatpost, the forewheel expander brake, the knee-action spring fork, shoebraking units, and a handlebar-mounted stick-shift gear changer.

Similarly, Schwinn paid attention to the business end of the bike trade, inaugurating a Dealer Authorization Program in 1952 that has grown into more than 1,900 Schwinn authorized dealers in the United States. The Dealer Authorization Program provides Schwinn dealers with bikes and equipment and helps maintain Schwinn's warranty, which is good for the life of the product.

Good Times, Then Bad

The period from the 1950s through the 1970s was a golden age for Schwinn. Back then, ''buying anything but a Schwinn seemed almost un-American,'' as Sandra Atchison put it in a *Business Week* article. Buoyed by a strong dealer network, an easily identifiable name, advertising presence on television, and state-of-the-art design, the company commanded as much as a 25 percent share of the U.S. bicycle market by the '60s. But the tide began to turn in the '80s. Stories of problems in quality and delivery began to surface. ''But more serious was Schwinn's attitude problem,'' noted Atchison, who quoted Scott Sports Group chief executive Tom Stendhal: ''When . . . asked [about] their competition, they said, 'We don't have competition. We're Schwinn.' ''

But competition is exactly what Schwinn was facing. A ''baby bust'' in the latter decades of the twentieth century had lessened the number of children asking for two-wheelers; worse yet, Schwinn missed the mark on a vital new trend: the mountain bike. Introduced to growing acclaim in the early '80s, mountain bikes, with their sturdy, lightweight frames and wide wheels, captured a major share of the total bike market—reportedly as high as 60 percent. But this time, Schwinn was a follower instead of a leader. The company ''never led with innovation in mountain bikes,'' remarked Tanzer. As *Bicycling* editor and publisher J. C. McCullagh elaborated, the company ''had the best bike engineers in the country but it lost its edge because its management didn't respond quickly enough.'' Schwinn, in fact, thought mountain bikes were just a fad. ''They didn't talk to Generation X the way other companies did,'' McCullagh added.

AT A GLANCE

Schwinn brand of bicycles first introduced by Ignaz Schwinn, founder of Arnold, Schwinn & Company, in Chicago, 1895; company later became Schwinn Bicycle Company, then Schwinn Cycling and Fitness, Inc.; remained family-owned and run until 1993, when it was purchased by Scott Sports Group.

Performance: *Market share*—5-7% of bicycle market. *Sales*—About $200 million per year (early 1990s figures).

Major competitor: Trek, Specialized, and Giant; also mass merchandized bike brands Huffy and Murray.

Advertising: *Agency*—Carmichael Lynch, Minneapolis, MN, since 1993. *Major campaign*—"Established 1895. Re-established 1994."

Addresses: *Parent company*—Schwinn Cycling and Fitness, Inc. *Ultimate parent company*—Scott Sports Group, Boulder, CO 80301; phone: (303) 939-0100.

In Tanzer's opinion, Schwinn drove ''another nail in the coffin'' in 1981. When its main-factory workers went on strike in Chicago, ''management panicked. Instead of negotiating a settlement, Schwinn closed the plant'' and sent its engineers to a protege company, the Taiwan-based Giant Manufacturing. In doing so, Schwinn ''handed over everything—technology, engineering, volume—that Giant needed to become a dominant bikemaker,'' noted Tanzer. ''In return, Schwinn imported the bikes and marketed them in the U.S. under the Schwinn name.''

It didn't take long before Giant, with the technological impetus from Schwinn, took off as an independent company, designing and marketing its own line of bikes. By this time, Schwinn had worked on developing its own mountain bikes, but the damage was done. By the early 1990s Schwinn's market share had dropped to about seven percent. With just three years to go until its centennial, the company filed for bankruptcy protection in 1992.

A Bold New Image

Clearly, restructuring was in order. It began with a new owner. In 1993 Schwinn turned over the family business to the Chicago-based investment firm Zell/Chilmark Fund L.P., which acquired the bikemaker for $43 million. Schwinn then became part of the Scott Sports Group, which designs and markets bicycles, accessories, and ski and sports equipment in the United States and Europe. In conjunction with the purchase, Schwinn headquarters were scheduled to move from Chicago to Boulder, Colorado.

Next, Schwinn devoted new attention to its presence in the biking world. The company sponsored a ''three-member professional mountain-bike team that has already caught the attention of enthusiasts,'' according to *Business Week.* Competing at a World Cup event, Schwinn saw its efforts rewarded when a spectator was overheard to remark, ''My God, there goes another Schwinn rider.''

Finally, Schwinn doubled its advertising budget to $10 million, leaning heavily toward enthusiast publications. Its new ad agency, Carmichael-Lynch, launched a series of print ads heavy on imagery and light on detail. A typical ad shows bikers on a forest path. The bikes are not shown close up. The headline waxes poetic: ''You sweat. The air dries you. There is no charge for this service.'' Further copy similarly avoids technical jargon: ''Loyalty is a weld. The more miles, the stronger the weld. Ride a new Schwinn.'' Common to all ads is the company's new slogan: ''Established 1895. Re-established 1994.''

The ads also touch on Schwinn's commitment to producing mountain bikes and city cruisers. One ad, in fact, caused enough controversy to make the Letters page in *Bicycling.* The two-page spread in question shows an urban biker cutting between a school bus and a cab. ''I find this suicide-cyclist image irresponsible,'' one reader told the magazine. ''Nearly as harmful is the 'cars suck' attitude Schwinn encourages.'' But another reader found the Schwinn ad ''wonderful. It raises my spirit to see a major bike manufacturer gearing its products and advertising to the urban commuting market.''

Schwinn in the '90s

Attitude aside, this new positioning—Schwinn as a serious player for serious bikers—has helped the company regain its name in the market. The 1994 Schwinn catalog features a collection of ''sport bikes,'' including the High Timber, High Sierra, Moab, Impact, and Hurricane models, built for cross-country work. For around-town cycling, Schwinn offers such models as the Crisscross. The catalog also highlights Schwinn-branded helmets, gloves, and travel packs.

Expanding on the name it has built through the years, Schwinn has also ventured into the exercise-equipment field. A 1993 Schwinn Fitness catalog, touting ''serious equipment for serious sweat,'' lists such Schwinn-branded items as an AirDyne exercise bike, an electronic treadmill, a ''Bowflex'' resistance-stretcher to work arms and legs, a cross-country ski simulator, and a stair-stepper.

In 1988 the Schwinn name went international. In a worldwide market-expansion move, Schwinn debuted in England, France, Spain, the Netherlands, and other points of Western Europe.

Further Reading:

Atchison, Sandra D., ''Pump, Pump, Pump at Schwinn,'' *Business Week,* August 23, 1993, p. 79.

Bicycling, February 1994, p. 17.

Schwinn Bicycle Company: A History of Quality, Service and Progress, Chicago: Schwinn Bicycle Company, 1993.

Schwinn Fitness, Chicago: Schwinn Cycling and Fitness, Inc., 1993.

Schwinn Sport Bikes: 1994, Chicago: Schwinn Bicycle Company, 1994.

Tanzer, Andrew, ''Bury Thy Teacher,'' *Forbes,* December 21, 1992, p. 90.

—Susan Salter

SCRABBLE®

Scrabble brand crossword game has been one of the world's leading word games for over 40 years. By the 1990s there were an estimated 33 million Scrabble players in the United States and Canada, as well as millions more around the globe. The United States and Canada also had some 200 Scrabble clubs, boasting a membership of more than 10,000 enthusiasts. These impressive statistics could not begin to communicate the passion people have felt for this collection of letter tiles and gridded board. For the more than 6,000 players who competed in tournaments around the world, Scrabble was an obsession that led them to spend hours memorizing lists of all the words beginning with "sea" or ending in "ful." The top-ranked players memorized all 100,000 words in the Official Scrabble Players Dictionary.

This addictive game had humble beginnings in the workshop of an unemployed architect, Alfred M. Butts. Butts began to devise his game in 1931 during the height of the Depression. Initially called Criss-Crosswords, the game was not marketed until 1948, when it was officially renamed Scrabble. James Brunot, a friend of Butts's, was responsible for the initial success of the game, which he produced in a converted little red schoolhouse in Newton, Connecticut. After a slow start, sales of Scrabble took off, and the game became an international fad. Brunot licensed the North American manufacture and marketing of Scrabble to the New York toy company Selchow and Righter, who produced the game until 1986, when the company was bought by Coleco Industries. The Milton Bradley division of Hasbro, Inc., finally acquired the North American rights to Scrabble in 1988, when Coleco declared bankruptcy. The initial success of Scrabble has been maintained throughout the years by a combination of promotion, advertising, and, above all, the sheer enjoyment that people derived from playing this challenging word game.

The Invention of Scrabble

Like many American inventions, Scrabble was the product of the Great Depression. Alfred M. Butts had been a successful architect in the 1920s, but the stock market crash halted virtually all construction, and in 1931 Butts found himself without a job. Butts had always been a game buff, and because he had nothing better to do and money was getting scarce, he decided to try to invent a successful game. According to toy historian Marvin Kaye, Butts did not have a particular idea for a game in mind, but after reviewing his options, he decided that word games were the least represented in the games market. He also felt that the most enjoyable games were those that combined both skill and chance, encouraging repeated play to improve skill without overly discouraging novices who could always rely on the luck of the draw. Butts had always been adept at anagrams, in which letters of words are rearranged to form other words. He thought that the skill involved in working out anagrams combined with an element of luck might produce an interesting game.

Butts began to experiment with his idea. Using architectural blueprint paper as a board, Butts decided that the game should be laid out like a crossword puzzle and that the element of chance would be added by having the players choose their letters at random from a set of letter tiles. Butts realized that he would have to develop a scoring system whereby rarer letters and longer words scored more points. Well trained in minutiae thanks to his architectural background, Butts set out to count the occurrence of letters in typical written English and derive a score for each letter based on the frequency of its occurrence. He chose the front page of the *New York Times* as his sample, reasoning that it contained a wide range of topics and thus possible words. Using this straightforward method, Butts derived the point system and letter distribution now so familiar to millions of Scrabble players. The only letter that received special treatment was "s," which, though occurring frequently in English, was assigned only four tiles to prevent too much pluralization. Butts glued gridded blueprints onto chess boards, hand lettered some ¼-inch plywood for the tiles, and Scrabble (at this point called Criss-Crosswords) was born.

Butts began to play his new game with his wife and friends, modifying rules and scoring slightly in a continual effort to improve his game. One minor improvement that has left a permanent legacy in Scrabble sets came when Butts noticed some wood molding in a lumberyard and realized that it would hold the letter tiles more efficiently than the mah-jongg tile holders he had been using. The odd-looking rounded molding has become an unmistakable symbol of the Scrabble crossword game.

Butts's friends loved playing Criss-Crosswords, but when Butts began to make the rounds of the established game manufacturers, he soon discovered that it was easier to play the game than to sell it. Word games were not popular at that time, the rules were too complex, and it was too highbrow for a general audience. Butts

AT A GLANCE

Scrabble brand of crossword game registered as a trademark in 1948 by Mr. and Mrs. James Brunot of Production and Marketing Company, located in Newtown, Connecticut; the game itself invented in 1931 by a friend, Alfred M. Butts of Poughkeepsie, New York, who called it Criss-Crosswords; American and Canadian marketing and distribution licensed to Selchow and Righter; international marketing licensed in 1953 to the English firm J.W. Spear and Sons PLC; exclusive rights in the United States and Canada bought by Selchow and Righter in 1972; Selchow and Righter bought by Coleco Industries in 1986; in 1988, after Coleco Industries declared bankruptcy, Hasbro Inc. acquired Coleco's assets and assigned Scrabble to its Milton Bradley division.

Major competitor: Other board games, including Parker Brothers' Monopoly and Trivial Pursuit.

Advertising: *Agency*—Griffin Bacal, New York, NY, 1989—. *Major campaign*—"Scrabble, America's Good Time Game," a television commercial featuring a group of friends sitting around a fireplace in a ski lodge and playing Scrabble.

Addresses: *Parent company*—Milton Bradley Company, 443 Shaker Road, East Long Meadow, MA 01028; phone: (413) 525-6411; fax: (413) 525-1767. *Ultimate parent company*—Hasbro Inc., 1027 Newport Avenue, P.O. Box 1059, Pawtucket, RI 02862-1059; phone: (401) 725-TOYS; fax: (401) 727-5544. *Parent company*—J.W. Spear and Sons PLC, Richard House, Enstone Road, Enfield, Middlesex, EN3 7TB England; phone: 81-805-28-48; fax: 81-804-24-26.

received rejection after rejection. Once again busy with his architectural career, Butts put aside his efforts to sell the game. Butts spent the next ten years working as an architect, and Criss-Crosswords was relegated to an after-dinner amusement for his wife and friends.

In 1948 two of these friends, Mr. and Mrs. James Brunot, owners of one of Butts's handmade games, were looking for an opportunity to open a small business that they could run from their country home in Newtown, Connecticut. They asked Butts if they could have the manufacturing rights to Criss-Crosswords, believing that they could manufacture and sell enough games to maintain a steady supplement to their income. Butts readily agreed, and the Brunots formed Production and Marketing Company, which was run out of their Connecticut home. Their first concern was to come up with a unique brand name that would qualify for registration as a trademark. The Brunots and their friends made long lists of possible names to be checked and cleared by their law firm. "Scrabble" was one suggestion with some promise. It was short, memorable, and close enough to the better-known "scramble" to invoke the "mixing" denotation of that word and its dictionary definition—"to scratch or dig frantically with the hands or claws"—which reminded the Brunots of digging into a pile of Scrabble tiles. More importantly, it came back from the lawyers as one of the only names free for trademark purposes. In 1949 "Criss-Crosswords" was rechristened "Scrabble."

Product Performance

The Brunots began to manufacture Scrabble in their home in Connecticut. With the help of some friends, they could turn out twelve games an hour, stamping letters one at a time on wooden tiles. At the rate that orders were coming in, the Brunots did not have to spend more than one hour a day producing the game. Unable to invest any money in advertising, the Brunots had to rely on word of mouth and mail orders to sell the game.

In 1949, the first full year of operation, Production and Marketing Company sold 2,551 games at a loss of $450. James Brunot decided that he could cut expenses by having components of the game made up in full by other manufacturers. Selchow and Righter, one of the most prominent American game manufacturers since 1867, agreed to manufacture the Scrabble boards, and a German firm took on the job of making the tiles. In 1950 Brunot's company moved to an old one-room schoolhouse, where the various components were assembled into games and orders were processed. Word of mouth was slowly spreading Scrabble's reputation. In 1950 sales had increased to 4,800 games, and in 1951 the number of games almost doubled to 9,000. No one could have predicted from these steady but moderate increases what was to happen to Scrabble in 1952.

As reported in Kaye's account of the invention of Scrabble, during the first half of 1952 orders had come in at a steady but unspectacular pace. In June the Brunots, discouraged and thinking about abandoning the enterprise, left for a week's vacation to Kentucky. When they returned they expected to find an accumulation of about 200 orders, but to their surprise the backlog had mounted to an astounding 2,500 requests for Scrabble sets. Thinking that this must be a strange anomaly, the Brunots scrambled to increase production temporarily, but the next week saw a deluge of 3,000 more orders. By the end of 1952 Production and Marketing Company had sold 58,752 Scrabble sets. Unable to meet the demand, the Brunots decided that they would have to take their game to one of the larger game manufacturers. Selchow and Righter was the logical choice since it had already been producing Scrabble boards for the Brunots and therefore knew just how well the game was selling. Selchow and Righter and the Brunot's Production and Marketing Company soon reached a licensing agreement authorizing the giant game company to manufacture and market Scrabble. The Brunot's firm moved to a large warehouse and, employing thirty-four workers, continued to assemble the game as well. In 1954 alone the two Scrabble manufacturers combined to produce 4.5 million Scrabble sets, and still they were obliged to ration the game on a geographic basis because all orders simply could not be met.

It has always been a bit of a mystery why Scrabble sales took off the way they did and when they did. Without advertising or promotions, it is clear that the popularity of Scrabble spread solely by word of mouth, but why the summer of 1952 should have seen a sudden explosion in sales is unclear. One theory is that the owner of Macy's played the game during his summer holidays, raved about it to his friends in the business, and directed his toy department to stock up on the game when he got home. While this certainly might have helped the growing fad, orders had already started to pile up before this incident. It would appear that over the four years since Brunot started marketing Scrabble, word of mouth had spread the popularity of the game to the critical volume needed to create a phenomenon of this scale.

By the mid 1950s Scrabble had reached fad proportions. Celebrities the world over were playing the game. According to Kaye, in Hollywood they had even invented a "dirty word" version of the game. As it turned out, however, Scrabble was much more than a fad. Contrary to everyone's expectations, sales did not drop after a year or two but instead kept steadily rising until Scrabble became one of the most desirable properties in the toy and game industry. In 1972 James Brunot sold the American and Canadian rights to the Scrabble brand to Selchow and Righter, who, until that time, had only had a licensing agreement to produce the game. Scrabble was then the leading word game in the United States and a guaranteed annual profit maker, with sales of about one million games a year. In 1986 Coleco Industries was facing a potential 50 percent drop in sales of their colossal hit Cabbage Patch dolls and were looking for acquisitions that could stabilize their volatile company. Selchow and Righter, with its two game classics, Parcheesi and Scrabble, could provide just that. Coleco used some of the enormous profits they had made on their hit doll to purchase Selchow and Righter. Coleco's monetary troubles were not over, however, and in 1988 it was forced to declare bankruptcy, allowing the giant toy company Hasbro Inc. to acquire its inventory and assets. A Hasbro spokesman, quoted in the *New York Times* at the time of the acquisition, said, "Scrabble is almost like an annuity."

For an annuity, however, Scrabble was not bringing in the kind of returns that Hasbro felt were possible. The beleaguered Coleco Industries had been unable to promote Scrabble, and sales had dropped to a mediocre 500,000 units in 1988, in spite of an overall 14 percent rise in board games sales that year. Hasbro assigned Scrabble to its Milton Bradley division, a well-established game manufacturer that had been acquired by Hasbro in 1984. Milton Bradley began a major advertising and promotional campaign for Scrabble in an attempt to reintroduce the game to American families. This campaign, helped by an overall rise in family board game sales, was a spectacular success. In only one year Scrabble sales more than tripled, soaring to 1.6 million games in 1989. Following this huge increase, sales of the word game continued to rise, albeit at a more moderate pace, into the 1990s.

International Presence

When Scrabble sales took off in the 1950s, it soon became clear that the game was more than just an American phenomenon. Spurred by the international travel of the intellectuals who had started the Scrabble craze, word of the game soon spread to all parts of the English-speaking world. Indian prime minister Jawaharlal Nehru is said to have become a devotee of the game, and British academics, notorious for their love of word games, began not only to play but to write about the game. Feeling that Selchow and Righter did not have the international clout to market Scrabble overseas, Brunot licensed J.W. Spear and Sons PLC to manufacture and distribute the game in all but the American, Canadian, and Australian markets. Scrabble has been distributed by Spear all over Europe and Asia and manufactured in more than a dozen languages and scripts, including Russian, Arabic, and Japanese. The scoring for these non-English versions of the game were, of course, based on the distribution of letters or characters in the respective languages. As reported in the British journal *Accountancy,* a 1988 poll indicated that Scrabble was the most popular board game in the United Kingdom, with 47 percent of households owning a Scrabble set. Although many of these sets had been owned for some time, new sales figures in 1989 indicated that Scrabble, with board and packaging newly redesigned by Spear, was second only to Serif's Trivial Pursuit in units sold. It was clear that Scrabble was still being actively sought after by British families as they continued to discover and rediscover this challenging word game.

Product Development

When Brunot received permission from Butts to market his Criss-Crosswords game in 1948, the rules were quite complex. In order to make the game more marketable, Brunot simplified the playing rules and made some changes in the board layout, including a shift of the first word square from the upper left-hand corner to the middle of the board. The game that would eventually be marketed as Scrabble took on its final form under Brunot's direction. Although spin-offs of the popular game have been introduced, Scrabble itself has resisted change. George Ditomassi, president of Milton Bradley, explained in a 1990 *USA Today* article, "we always get suggestions to change the game but our approach is, if it ain't broke, don't fix it. . . . Scrabble is the only game I know of that becomes a part of people's lives."

Various editions of Scrabble have appeared over the years, including the popular deluxe edition (with a revolving turntable and letter insets), the travel edition (with magnetized pieces), and a senior edition (with 50 percent larger letters). At the height of the Scrabble craze, even a braille edition of the game was produced. In the 1990s high-technology caught up with Scrabble, giving rise to a Scrabble program for personal computers and a Super Scrabble Gameboy for the Nintendo video-game system. A Scrabble game for Juniors, with simple words preprinted on the board, has also been popular in the children's board game market.

Promotion and Advertising

From its inception Scrabble relied heavily on word of mouth to spread its reputation. It was the sheer contagion of playing the game that was responsible for its early spectacular success. As A.H. Malcolm put it in a 1992 *New York Times* article, "playing or watching Scrabble is addictive. . . . Scrabble harnesses the relentless human urge to Kibitz to a board with 225 squares and 100 letter tiles." Selchow and Righter, aware of the ability of Scrabble to sell itself, actively encouraged the formation of Scrabble clubs and tournaments. The National Scrabble Association was formed under its aegis, and it, in turn, oversaw the organization of almost 200 sanctioned Scrabble clubs throughout the United States and Canada. The National Scrabble Association also sponsored local tournaments and a national championship held every two years. By the early 1990s the National Scrabble Association boasted 10,000 members, including 6,000 ranked players who competed in tournament play. Milton Bradley actively supported and promoted the association, providing the prize money and game boards for tournament play. Since 1991 a World Scrabble Championship has been held every two years through the cooperation of Milton Bradley and J.W. Spear and Sons PLC. Tournament players took their game very seriously. Top-ranked Scrabble players spent hundreds of hours memorizing the entire 100,000-word lexicon contained in the Official Scrabble Players Dictionary, published by Merriam-Webster Company. While the $10,000 prize for winning the world championship was nothing to sneeze at, it was clear that Scrabble players competed for the sheer thrill of pushing this 40-year-old board game to its limits.

While the primary promotional tool of Scrabble marketers has been the national association and its member clubs, advertising played a large part in the rebirth of the game in the early 1990s. When Hasbro's Milton Bradley division took over Scrabble in 1988, sales had slumped to a mediocre 500,000 units a year. Working with the ad agency Griffin Bacal, Milton Bradley launched a $1.6 million advertising campaign designed to renew sales of the game. According to a Griffin Bacal spokesperson, the ads were designed to remind consumers of what they liked most about playing Scrabble. Set in a ski lodge, television commercials featured a group of friends gathered around the fireplace playing Scrabble. The wholesome image of Americana was accompanied by a soundtrack of friendly music and a voice-over calling Scrabble "America's good time game." The ads ran in traditional women's time slots, as research indicated that women aged 25 to 49 purchased 90 percent of family games. The campaign, which ran for over four years, was a colossal success, and sales soared to 1.5 million units in 1989.

Brand Outlook

Scrabble has become a classic of the board game industry. Although challenged by electronic games in the early 1980s, sales of family board games subsequently rose steadily as people rediscovered the enjoyment and togetherness that a board game could provide. From the vantage of the mid-1990s, it appeared that Scrabble would remain an asset for its owner well into the 21st century.

Further Reading:

Croft, Martin, "In Pursuit of the Playing Public," *Accountancy,* January 30, 1990, p. 65.

della Cava, Marco R., "Scrabble Pros Wage a War of Words," *USA Today,* August 8, 1990, p. 1D.

Hasbro Inc. Annual Report, Pawtucket, Rhode Island: Hasbro Inc., 1992.

Kaye, Marvin, *The Story of Monopoly, Silly Putty, Bingo, Twister, Scrabble, Frisbee et cetera,* New York: Stein and Day, 1973, pp. 119–128.

Malcolm, Andrew H., "Scrabble's Word Nerds Live for the Perfect Mix," *New York Times,* June 16, 1992.

McGill, Douglas C., "Hasbro to Join Creditors of Coleco in Buyout Bid," *New York Times,* April 20, 1989, p. D2.

North, Sterling, "Fickle Market for Cabbage Patch Kids Pushes Coleco to Diversify Toy Lines," *New England Business,* June 16, 1986, p. 43.

Schewe, Charles, "Effective Communication with Our Aging Population," *Business Horizons,* January/February 1989, pp. 19–25.

Simon, Barry, "Monopoly, Risk and Scrabble Get Windows Treatment," *PC Magazine,* February 9, 1993, p. 516.

Taylor, Michael Ray, "They Have a Way with Words," *Sports Illustrated,* September 23, 1991, pp. 23–24.

—Hilary Gopnik

SEALY®

Posturepedic® Support
Only From Sealy

With annual sales of more than $500 million and 22 percent of the U.S. market, Sealy is the nation's leading brand of bedding. The origins of the Sealy Corporation date back to the late 1800s, when a cotton mill owner first developed a revolutionary new type of mattress. During the next century, Sealy survived turbulent ownership struggles and fierce competition from other bedding manufacturers to become to the largest bedding company in the world.

Brand Origins

It was in the town of Sealy, Texas, in 1881 that a cotton gin and grist mill builder developed a method for compressing long staple cotton fiber into an "air woven" batt. Eventually he devised a new type of mattress from these materials, resulting in a tuftless, resilient mattress. Almost immediately the gentleman began filling orders for this comfortable, cotton-filled mattress.

Within four years, new machinery was developed to mass produce the air-woven mattresses, which were patented in 1889. The new mattress was an instant success and immediately became sought-after by Texans across the state. To accommodate the heavy demand for the mattress, the Sealy-based inventor sold the manufacturing rights to mattress makers in other cities. As the product's fame spread throughout the southwest, people began referring to it as the "mattress from Sealy." Soon, this term was shortened to simply the "Sealy mattress."

In 1906 the inventor sold all of his patents and manufacturing equipment to a large Texas corporation that embraced the "Sealy" trade name. Several years later, the company was sold and all operations relocated to Sugarland, Texas. The new owners recognized the tremendous marketing potential of the Sealy mattress, and they immediately set out to market the brand nationally.

Sealy Goes National

The company's first major move was to purchase advertising space in high-profile national magazines. The effort marked the first time any mattress manufacturer embarked on this high-risk, expensive form of advertising. In 1909 the company registered the Sealy name as a trademark, and by the next year, the demand for Sealy mattresses had outpaced production. It was obvious to the new ownership that a massive expansion was necessary, but the cost of purchasing or building new factories would be too high. Sealy's innovative solution was to establish a licensing program, and by 1924 the company had nearly 30 licensed factories.

In the early 1920s the company decided to exit the bedding industry. One manager disagreed with the move, however. To counter the company's effort, he won the support of the eight strongest licensees and bought the rights to Sealy mattress production. Using royalties each licensee paid on every Sealy mattress sold, national advertising was increased. In 1927 Sealy became the first bedding to be advertised on national radio.

Despite the Great Depression the Sealy brand flourished and even managed a successful introduction of a new product—a button-free innerspring. This marked a turning point in the bedding industry, as springs began to outrank cotton among consumer preferences. In the 1940s doctors began to recommend that patients with back problems sleep on firm mattresses. Sealy recognized a marketing opportunity and developed a specially constructed mattress to satisfy customers who wanted a firm sleeping surface. The company approached orthopedic surgeons for their advice and approval on this new product. The result of this effort was the Orthopedic Firm-O-Rest.

Soon, however, the U.S. Federal Trade Commission (FTC) began to scrutinize companies using the medical term "orthopedic" as part of their brand names. In 1950 the term was finally banned, and the FTC would not allow it to be trademarked. To prevent any damage to the Sealy brand name, the company immediately coined the term "Posturepedic." Advertising also began to include the phrase "No more backache from sleeping on a too soft mattress." The slogan eventually became as much a part of the Sealy marketing strategy as the brand name itself.

Product Innovations

During the 1950s, Sealy forged ahead in product development, as well as in merchandising and advertising. In 1954 the company marked its first move toward international expansion when it added several licensees in Canada. At the time, Sealy was the first U.S. bedding company to move beyond the country's borders. The international expansion and aggressive marketing efforts allowed the Sealy name to grow by leaps and bounds throughout the 1950s. At the end of 1949, the brand's sales were $9 million. Ten years later they had skyrocketed to $48 million.

AT A GLANCE

Sealy brand of bedding founded in 1889 in Sealy, Texas; after changing hands several times, in the early 1920s a Sealy manager established a consortium of licensees to run the company; purchased in 1987 by one of the licensees, The Ohio Mattress Company; in 1990 ownership transferred to banking firm Gibbons, Goodwin, van Amerongen which changed company name to Sealy Corporation; majority of stock acquired by Zell/Chilmark Fund from a First Boston Corporation affiliate in 1993.

Performance: *Market share*—22 percent (top share) of the bedding category. *Sales*—$500 million.

Major competitor: Simmons Beautyrest; also Serta.

Advertising: *Agency*—Leo Burnett, Chicago, IL. *Major campaign*—"Posturepedic Support, Only from Sealy."

Addresses: *Parent company*—Sealy Corporation, 1228 Euclid Avenue, 10th Fl., Cleveland, OH 44115; phone: (216) 522-1310. *Ultimate parent company*—Zell/Chilmark Fund, 2 North Riverside Plaza 1500, Chicago, IL 60606; phone: (312) 984-9711.

At the beginning of the 1950s Sealy brand managers had two major goals: to study and understand the consumer market in addition to defining the brand's market position. Ultimately, the company wanted greater market penetration. Sealy accomplished its first goal when the company commissioned the bedding industry's first consumer motivational study in 1958. This gave the corporate officials a clear understanding of the needs, perceptions, and demographics of the existing consumer market. To achieve its second goal, Sealy hired a high-profile management consulting firm to analyze the company's internal structure. The consulting firm carefully laid out a strategy for Sealy to manage its growth into the next several decades.

During the 1960s Sealy added national television advertisements to its marketing strategy. The 1960s also marked an aggressive campaign to establish dealer support programs. The programs provided retailers with impressive training aids, point-of-sale materials, and "Sleep Centers" within the retail establishments. As a result, the company increased Sealy's visibility on the sale floors immeasurably. In addition, Sealy also continued to increase its international expansion as the company rapidly added new licensees from other countries to its program.

As the company implemented its new marketing policies and added international licensees, Sealy also continued to improve its products. The Posturepedic mattress line underwent the important introduction of the "Posture Grid" torsion bar foundation in 1969. Sealy's customers responded positively to the added feature, and by the end of the 1960s sales of the brand had reached $113 million.

Despite the strong sales levels for the brand, all was not quiet within the Sealy arena. The late 1970s marked the beginning of a 15-year struggle for control within the company. Sealy's consortium of independent licensees was being challenged by one of the members, The Ohio Mattress Company. Although the brand's leaders were embroiled in court battles, the company undertook improvements to its line, including an entirely new Posturepedic sleep system. As a result, Sealy was able to improve its position in the bedding market. To capitalize on Sealy's strong brand name and technical capabilities and diversify its product line, the company formed the Sealy Furniture Division, extending the Sealy development programs to items other that bedding.

New Ownership

In 1987 the legal battle between The Ohio Mattress Company and Sealy's central leadership culminated with a change of ownership. The Ohio Mattress Company purchased Sealy, Inc. and all but one of the nine remaining domestic bedding licensees. The buy-out changed the leadership of the Sealy brand from an association of independent licensees to a single management team. Later that year The Ohio Mattress Company purchased the remaining Sealy stock owned by the single remaining licensee. The stock acquisition made The Ohio Mattress Company, with a 100 percent stake in Sealy, the largest bedding manufacturer in the world.

The Ohio Mattress Company was also in the process of acquiring several of Sealy's competitors, which added to the company's depth and strength in the bedding industry. In 1983 The Ohio Mattress Company purchased Stearns & Foster, one of the nation's oldest and largest manufacturers. Later, it acquired the country's market share leader in the waterbed category, Advanced Sleep Products, and in May of 1984 Lifetime Foam Products, Inc., the largest foam mattress company in the United States, was added to the ranks.

A Leveraged Buy-Out

In November of 1988 The Ohio Mattress Company decided to relinquish ownership of Sealy and announced that the business was for sale. Following a lengthy, extensive competitive bidding process, Sealy ownership was sold to Gibbons, Goodwin, van Amerongen through a leveraged buy-out. In March of 1990, the banking firm changed the company's name from The Ohio Mattress Company to Sealy Corporation.

Still, Sealy's tumultuous ownership problems were not solved. In November of 1991 Sealy Corporation's leaders undertook a dramatic restructuring of the company's debt from the leveraged buy-out. In a debt-for-equity swap, Sealy Corporation gave 93.6 percent of its stock to an affiliate of the First Boston Corporation, an investment banking firm that financed a portion of the earlier buy-out. By February 1993, Sealy's ownership changed hands once again, when a Chicago-based investment fund, Zell/Chilmark, acquired the majority interest in Sealy Corporation from the First Boston Corporation affiliate.

A Focus on Quality

Despite the turbulent ownership questions during the 1980s and early 1990s, Sealy's sales and market share remained strong. By the end of 1992, sales for the brand had reached $500 million, giving the company a 22 percent share of the $2.1 billion bedding industry. Shareholders, competitors, and retailers initially questioned whether Sealy's management team could heal the wounds and retain the brand's superior hold on the industry, but their skepticism gradually faded as Sealy held its ground. In the meantime, Sealy's management team regrouped, focusing its energies and resources on providing the best possible bedding products, while investing heavily in consumer research. As a result, Sealy altered its quality structure. Instead of three different levels of quality in the Posturepedic mattress line, Sealy made the quality features standard for all its mattresses and foundations. As a result of these moves the brand is well positioned to meet the demands of the industry and capitalize on opportunities worldwide. Sealy's management team hopes to maintain its company's industry leadership position in innovative marketing, manufacturing, and technology.

Further Reading:

Boyer, Mike, "Sealy Revamping Premium Mattress," *Cincinnati Enquirer,* May 6, 1993, Sec. B, p. 8.

Mallory, Maria, "Ohio Mattress Gets the Lumps Out at Last," *Business Week,* May 7, 1990, pp. 127–128.

Murphy, H. Lee, "The Sealy Caper: How Cleveland Rival Beat Pritzkers to the Punch," *Crain's Chicago Business,* February 9, 1987, Sec. 1, p. 1.

"Once Upon a Mattress," Cleveland, OH: Sealy Corporation, 1993.

Solomon, Barbara, "Bed Wars: A Sealy Licensee Causes Sleepless Nights," *Management Review,* December 1990, pp. 50–53.

—*Wendy Johnson Bilas*

SEGA®

Sega, a trademark of Japan's Sega Enterprises, Ltd., is the second-best-selling brand of home video game systems and the best-selling brand of advanced game systems in the United States. Sega also manufactures and distributes coin-operated arcade video games. Once a struggling company, Sega is now one of the industry leaders.

Brand Origins

In 1951, Service Games Co., a manufacturer of arcade games and forerunner to Sega Enterprises, was founded in Japan. 14 years later Service Games merged with Rosen Enterprises, Ltd., another Japanese arcade-game company, that had been founded by an American, David Rosen. After the 1965 merger, the company became known as Sega Enterprises, Ltd., with the term "Sega" coined from (Se)rvice (Ga)mes. Sega, a manufacturer, exporter, and importer of mechanical and electronic arcade games, was acquired by U.S.-based Gulf Western, Ltd. in 1969.

Video Games

In 1972 Atari, Inc. introduced Pong, the world's first coin-operated video game. Sega soon followed with several successful arcade video games, including Sega Astron Belt, the first laser disc video game, and SubRoc-3D, the first three-dimensional video game. In 1983 Sega also introduced its first home video game system, the SG-1000, marketed in Japan. However, the Nintendo Co. Ltd. unveiled the popular Famicom system the same year, and the SG-1000 was never successful; the Famicom, renamed the Nintendo Entertainment System for the U.S. market, would become the most successful home video game system in history. In the Western hemisphere, the American market for home video game systems collapsed later that year, and the SG-1000 was never marketed in the United States. In 1984 Gulf Western sold Sega to an investment group led by senior management and CSK, Japan's largest software developer.

In 1985 Nintendo launched the Nintendo Entertainment System in the United States, reviving the American market virtually overnight. After failing in a bid to buy Atari from Warner Communications, Sega formed U.S. subsidiary Sega of America, Inc. and introduced the Sega Master System home video game system in 1986. Unfortunately the Sega Master System suffered the same fate competing against the Nintendo Entertainment System in the United States that the SG-1000 suffered when it went head-to-head with the Famicom in Japan. Nintendo went on to claim nearly 90 percent of the U.S. market, while Sega shared the remainder with the renamed Atari Corporation.

Sega Genesis

Then in 1989 Sega produced the world's first 16-bit home video game system—known as the Sega Mega Drive in Japan and Sega Genesis in the United States—using the same microprocessor that ran early Macintosh computers. The first games developed specifically for Sega Genesis failed to capitalize on the system's enhanced sound and graphics capabilities. Even when the games did make use of the advanced capabilities, the games themselves were often boring. But Sega soon introduced a line of sports games that attracted older video game players. The company also adapted several of its more popular arcade games for the Sega Genesis, such as Altered Beast. Independent companies began developing games for the Sega Genesis, particularly Electronic Arts, which marketed the highly successful John Madden Football and Immortal, a martial-arts game most notable for its graphic depictions of blood and guts. Sega promoted Sega Genesis with the slogan "Sega Genesis does what Nintendon't."

In 1991 Sega also introduced Sonic the Hedgehog, a jaunty, intergalactic cartoon character and a fast-paced video game that captured the imagination of younger players the way Nintendo's Mario had several years earlier. Although still a distant second, Sega had sold more than 1.5 million Sega Genesis video game systems by mid-1991. That September Sega's success forced Nintendo to introduce its own 16-bit video game system, the Super NES, much sooner than originally planned, setting off an advertising war between the two companies. Nintendo spent more than $25 million to launch the Super NES. Meanwhile Sega, whose commercials were even louder and flashier than Nintendo's, advertised heavily on popular youth-oriented shows such as *Beverly Hills 90210* and *The Simpsons.* In one commercial for the Sega Genesis, a young boy was shown resisting the efforts of a pushy adult to sell him a more expensive Super NES.

The advertising battles also spilled over into a war of words between corporate executives. In 1991 Sega's president, Hayao Nakayama told *Forbes,* "I don't like the idea of one company [Nintendo] monopolizing an industry." Hiroshi Yamauchi, president of Nintendo, responded by dismissing Sega's challenge, telling the magazine, "We don't really regard [Sega] as a competitor

AT A GLANCE

Sega brand of video games originated with Service Games Co., which was founded in 1951; company merged with Rosen Enterprises, Ltd., in 1965, forming Sega Enterprises, Ltd.

Performance: *Market share*—1.7% of video game (hardware/software) category (1992). *Sales*—¥347 billion (US$3.15 billion).

Major competitors: Nintendo.

Advertising: *Agency*—Goodby, Berlin and Silverstein, Los Angeles, CA, 1992—. *Major campaign*—"Welcome to the next level."

Addresses: *Parent company*—Sega Enterprises, Ltd., 2-12, Haneda 1-Chome, Ohta-Ku, Tokyo 144, Japan; phone: (03) 3743-7522.

in the United States.'' Despite Yamauchi's claim, the Sega Genesis—with more than 100 available games—outsold the Super NES and its less-than-two dozen games during the 1991 Christmas season. Although Nintendo continued to dominate the total market for home video game systems, Sega was the market leader in advanced 16-bit systems.

Market Innovations

In 1991 Sega presented Game Gear, a hand-held video game system that competed head-on with yet another highly successful Nintendo product, Game Boy, launched two years earlier. Unlike the black-and-white Game Boy, Game Gear featured a color video display and could double as a color television. Commercials showed slow-witted people playing with Nintendo Game Boys while a background voice announced, ''Some people are content to be entertained by simple, one-color electronics. Somehow, these people have just never heard of Game Gear.'' Although Sega sold more than 1.5 million Game Gear systems in 1992, it remained a distant second in the market for hand-held video game systems.

In 1992, Sega introduced the Sega CD, a compact disc system that could be attached to the Sega Genesis to play video games with richer detail and more realistic action. Tom Kalinske, then president of Sega of America, told *Newsweek,* ''CD is far better than anything a game player has seen before.'' Sega sold approximately 1 million Sega CD systems in 1993. Nintendo, which had been expected to launch a CD-based video game system in 1993, instead announced early in 1994, that it would develop a high-capacity game cartridge for its next generation 64-bit game-player. That year Sega planned to introduce Sega VR, a set of ''virtual reality'' goggles for the Sega Genesis. Sega VR would provide a stereoscopic display and come with built-in headphones for stereophonic sound.

Rating Systems

By 1993 parental concern about graphic sex and violence in video games was mounting. Among those games included in the controversy was Mortal Kombat, developed by Acclaim Entertainment Inc. for the Sega Genesis. Sega responded by creating an independent council to evaluate all games and agreed to display the council's rating on game packages. Games were rated ''GA,'' or suitable for general audiences; ''MA-13'' for mature audiences with parental discretion advised; or ''MA-17'' meaning not appropriate for minors. Sega also instituted a toll-free information line for parents wanting more information about the content of specific video games and created the ''Sega Seal of Quality'' to certify that its games did not include any pornographic or anti-religious elements. Regardless, the British Board of Film Classification banned the sale of Night Trap, a Sega CD game in which pajama-clad girls are abducted by zombies, to anyone under 15 because of the sexual content. Night Trap was also the only game among the first 80 considered by Sega's council to earn an MA-17 rating.

Later in 1993, as the U.S. Senate scheduled hearings on sex and violence in video games, several other video game manufacturers, software publishers, and retailers joined with Sega in pledging to develop an industry-wide rating system by the end of 1994. In a press release, Bill White, then vice president of Sega of America, said the company believed a rating system was the best way for ''consumers who are old enough to make their own purchase decisions, and those who need parental assistance, [to] make informed choices.'' Nintendo opposed the rating system though, suggesting it would allow companies to avoid responsibility for the growing sex and violence in video games. Nintendo, whose own version of Mortal Kombat was less graphic, urged video game companies to exercise restraint in the games they licensed or developed.

Outlook

Although Nintendo still dominated the market for home video game systems, Sega established a foothold in the early 1990s by introducing an advanced 16-bit system almost two years ahead of the industry. Sega continued to pressure Nintendo by introducing games that appealed to older players and by introducing more technological advances, including the Sega CD in 1992. By 1994 Sega controlled nearly 15 percent of the total market for video game systems in the United States, but split the market for advanced game systems almost evenly with Nintendo. In the mid-1990s Sega brought together many recognized software developers at the Sega Technical Institute in Redwood City, California, for the purpose of developing original games. Sega also planned to be first to the market with a virtual reality game unit for the general public. In addition, Sega and the Time Warner Entertainment Company were collaborating on The Sega Channel, which would give subscribers access to video games via cable television.

Further Reading:

Brandt, Richard, ''Video Games: Is All That Gore Really Child's Play?,'' *Business Week,* June 14, 1993, p. 38.

Carlton, Jim, ''Sega, Aided by Hedgehog, Is Gaining on Nintendo,'' *The Wall Street Journal,* November 5, 1993, p. B-1.

Dumaine, Brian, ''When Dealy Courts Disaster,'' *Fortune,* December 16, 1991, p. 104.

Eisenstodt, Gale, ''The Charge of the Hedgehog,'' *Forbes,* September 2, 1991, p. 42.

Pollack, Andrew, ''Nintendo's Dominance in Games May Be Waning,'' *New York Times,* April 23, 1993, p. D-1.

Richards, Bill, ''Nintendo, Sega Gear Up to Battle Over Video Game Market Share,'' *The Wall Street Journal,* January 12, 1993, p. B12.

Sheff, David, ''Game Over,'' Random House, New York, 1993.

''Sonic Boom,'' *The Economist,* January 25, 1992, p. 69.

Tetzeli, Rick, ''Videogames: Serious Fun,'' *Fortune,* December 27, 1993.

—Dean Boyer

SHARP®

SHARP®

Sharp brand electronics were intended to enhance the way people live and work by providing greater comfort, convenience, pleasure, and productivity through a broad range of products. The Sharp Corporation, based in Osaka, Japan, produces four major categories of products, which are marketed in the United States by Sharp Electronics Corporation: consumer electronics, information systems, liquid crystal display (LCD) products, and microelectronics.

Audio and video systems sold under the Sharp brand name include compact disc (CD) players, portable mini-disc players, rack systems, LCD products such as SharpVision projection TVs, and portable audio, TV, VCR, and camcorder systems. Home appliances include air conditioners, microwave ovens, and vacuum cleaners. Home office equipment includes calculators, portable electronic typewriters, printers, fax machines, copiers, computers, and word processors. Personal home office products include electronic organizers and personal digital assistants (PDAs).

Sharp Corp. became the world leader in the production of microwave ovens, electronic calculators, and LCDs. Sharp LCD technology was used in the development of many of its own products as well as purchased by other manufacturers. Sharp Corp. also became the U.S. leader in the sale of fax machines and electronic organizers.

Innovative products appearing under the Sharp brand name were the result of the company's aim to create products that no other company offered to consumers. Sharp Corp. created whole products or certain features that excited consumers because they were unique and more convenient or pleasurable. This high level of creativity led to the development of numerous Sharp products that were the first of their type in the world.

For example, the distinction of being the world's first went to the following Sharp brand electronic products: the all-transistor-diode desktop calculator; the electronic calculator with an LCD; the credit-card-sized calculator; the combination personal computer (PC) and TV set; the large-screen projection TV system using LCD technology; the camcorder with a 4-inch color LCD view screen; the turntable in a microwave oven; the dual-swing door refrigerator; the desktop, full-color fax machine; and the laptop computer.

Brand Development

Sharp brand electronics originated in 1925—the year radio broadcasting began in Japan—when founder Tokuji Hayakawa produced Japan's first crystal radio set. Ten years earlier, Hayakawa had invented the first mechanical pencil, which became a commercially successful product under the name Ever-Sharp. Hayakawa sold the rights to this invention and used the proceeds to found a new company, named after the pencil. He incorporated Sharp Corp. in 1935 in Osaka, Japan.

Sharp Corp. remained on the leading edge of technological innovation throughout its history. The company developed an experimental TV in 1951 and began its mass production by 1953. It introduced Sharp brand color TVs in 1960, the same year that color broadcasting began in Japan. In 1962, Sharp Corp. began mass production of its microwave ovens.

Also in 1962, the company created a U.S. subsidiary, Sharp Electronics Corporation, in New York City. Most Sharp consumer electronics products were first introduced in the Japanese market before being transferred to the U.S. subsidiary. By the early 1990s, however, Sharp Electronics marketed some 1,200 products in over 40 product categories.

In 1964, Sharp Corp. made the world's first electronic all-transistor-diode desktop calculator. In 1966, the company introduced the first calculator to use integrated circuits and marketed Japan's first microwave oven with a turntable system.

During the 1970s, several notable achievements took place in Sharp brand calculators, video, audio, and office equipment. Sharp Corp. produced the world's first electronic calculator with an LCD in 1973, followed by a solar-powered calculator in 1976. In 1977, a 5mm-thin, card-sized, sensor-touch, Sharp brand electronic calculator became available. In 1978, Sharp Corp. developed picture-in-picture TV sets. The year 1979 proved to be a busy one, as the company marketed the Sharp brand dual-cassette tape recorder, word processor with pen-based input, pocket-sized electronic translator, and the world's first 1.6mm-thin, credit-card-sized calculator.

The 1980s proved to be just as inventive for Sharp Corp., as it made improvements in some products as well as introduced several totally new products. Sharp brand product introductions for 1980 included calculators and clocks that used voice-synthesis

AT A GLANCE

Sharp brand electronics originated in 1925, when founder Tokuji Hayakawa produced Japan's first crystal radio set; Hayakawa incorporated Sharp Corp. in 1935 in Osaka, Japan; Sharp Corp. was named after the first mechanical pencil, which Hayakawa invented in 1915 and sold under the name Ever-Sharp; Sharp Electronics Corporation was established in New York, NY, in 1962 as the U.S. subsidiary of Sharp Corporation.

Performance: *Market share*—20% (top share) of microwave oven category. *Sales*—(U.S.) $2.4 billion (1992); (worldwide) $13.4 billion (estimate).

Major competitor: Hitachi; also Pioneer, Matsushita, Sanyo, and Sony.

Advertising: *Agency*—Griffin Bacal, New York, NY, 1989—. *Major campaign*—"The winning game plan," a year-long campaign using major sports figures in TV commercials and print ads to promote copier and fax lines.

Addresses: *Parent company*—Sharp Electronics Corporation, Sharp Plaza, Mahwah, NJ, 07430-2135; phone: 201-529-8200; fax: 201-529-8413. *Ultimate parent company*—Sharp Corporation, 22-22 Nagaike-cho, Abeno-ku, Osaka 545 Japan; phone: 81-6-621-1221; fax: 81-6-628-1667.

technology, VCRs with an automatic front-loading system, and integration of a VCR and a TV into a Video-TV. In 1981, product introductions included portable VCRs for camera/TV recording, stereo turntables capable of automatically playing both sides of a disc, and the MZ series of PCs offering system expansion.

In 1982, the company introduced Sharp brand pocket computers using BASIC language, and the world's first combination PC/TV set. In 1985, Sharp Corp. developed the first portable computer, which it originally called a ''lunchbox'' computer but which came to be known as a laptop computer. In the same year, the company developed the Sharp brand word processor with voice and handwritten input, telephone with 100-entry memory, and microwave oven that allowed bar-code input from a special cookbook.

In 1986, Sharp Corp. introduced a combination microwave/toaster oven and a video disc player capable of 3-D image reproduction. The following year, the company introduced the Sharp brand high-definition LCD color TV, electronic organizer with multiple functions, LCD color TV with a thin-film transistor (TFT) drive system, and digital audio tape (DAT) unit capable of digital recording and playback.

Sharp Corp. continued its history of innovation in 1988. Besides introducing a notebook-sized personal computer, the company conducted experimental development of the world's first thin, high-definition, 14-inch, TFT, color LCD TV, which weighed about 4 pounds and measured about one inch from front to back. Using a TFT active matrix system, the display featured enhanced definition, high-contrast, and full color.

Also in 1988, Sharp Corp. originated a new type of product, the electronic organizer, in a line known as the Wizard. The Sharp brand Wizard OZ-7000 included such functions as a calculator, calendar, telephone directory, schedule, and memo pad. Data was typed in with the use of a keyboard and displayed on an LCD screen. Another Sharp brand product introduction in 1988 was a refrigerator with a −55 degrees celsius freezer and interior deodorizing.

In 1989, Sharp Corp. again designed improvements that gave consumers unique ways to use and enjoy ordinary products. For example, the company introduced the Sharp brand LCD projector for displaying TV or video pictures on a large screen for a theater-like experience in the home. Called SharpVision, the system was the world's first large-screen (up to 100 inches) projection system using LCD technology. Further product introductions in 1989 included the world's first dual-swing door refrigerator, and the first cordless phone/answering machine with 100m range.

The 1990s continued the Sharp brand new-product activity of the previous decade, with notable introductions in 1990 including the world's first desktop, full-color fax machine, the world's first fax to incorporate a voice and image memory system using a standard audio cassette, and a home copier/fax machine.

In 1991, Sharp Corp. expanded its line of wall-mounted color LCD TVs to include the world's first 8.6-inch version. Also in this year, fuzzy logic artificial intelligence was incorporated into Sharp brand microwave ovens, washing machines, and vacuum cleaners. Sharp Corp. also marketed an 8.4-inch, color, TFT LCD for notebook computers.

In 1992, Sharp brand product introductions included a cordless pocket telephone that could operate continuously for more than five hours, and the Hi-8mm VL-HL100U ViewCam camcorder. The ViewCam became the world's first camcorder to use a 4-inch, color, LCD view screen rather than the conventional viewfinder. Sharp Corp. thus revolutionized the industry, because the TV screen allowed the user to move around while recording, holding the camcorder at arm's length rather than against the eye. The user simply watched the anti-glare, easy-to-see, color LCD view screen while on the move. The system also doubled as a portable video-cassette viewing system using prerecorded 8 mm movies.

Another product was added to the Sharp line of electronic in 1992, the Wizard OZ-9600 with a 5 1/4-by-3-inch touch-screen. This product was the industry's first hand-held electronic organizer with graphical user interface, infra-red data transmission, an integrated filing system, and touch-screen input technology or stylus. The stylus allowed users to create diagrams, charts and short notes directly on the screen and then save them as files. Add-in cards with customized programs were also available for this series.

Sharp Corp. first offered another product innovation, the PDA, in 1993. The PDA was a variation of the Wizard electronic organizer for people who had no computer knowledge and preferred to use pens rather than keyboards. PDAs were hand-held and also referred to as palmtop computers. The first PDA was the Newton, developed in conjunction with Apple Computer. The device featured a 3-by-5-inch screen, a tablet on which to write, and a pen that attached to the side. It ran on two AAA batteries for up to 100 hours and was designed to link directly to Apple computers. Most palmtops required their own special version of PC programs, which were available on memory cards that slipped into the computer's serial port. Two new Sharp brand audio products were also introduced in 1993—small, light, personal mini-disc players known as the MD-S10 and the MD-D10.

A key to Sharp Corp.'s continued success was its LCD technology. Sharp Corp.'s refinement of LCD displays enabled it not only to become the world leader in LCD production, with an estimated 40 percent market share, but also to use the technology as the base for its development of innovative products. LCDs replaced cathode-ray tubes in TVs and were used as display screens in such items as calculators, electronic organizers, camcorders, color monitors, projection systems, and color notebook computers.

Moreover, Sharp Corp. continually worked to improve the technology, giving it a higher contrast, wider viewing angle, and larger image. The company made Sharp brand LCD monitors from 3 inches to 17 inches, as well as the 4-inch LCD TV. A new series of 8.6-inch, wall-mount, color LCD monitors, known as the Liquid Crystal Museum Series, were also developed.

Advertising Strategies

Sharp Corp. used network TV and print ads to bring specific messages to consumers about particular Sharp products. A commonality during the early 1990s was the use of sports figures as spokespeople. For example, to advertise the new ViewCam, 30-second TV commercials showed hockey star Wayne Gretzky and his two-year-old son roller-skating while using the camcorder. The commercial was part of a $12 million campaign that was intended to show young, active families how easy it was to use the new camcorder.

Sharp Corp. also promoted its copier and fax lines in a $20 million campaign. Commercials aired during TV sports programming and print ads appeared in sports and business publications. The ads featured Chuck Daly, coach of the New Jersey Nets, and Bill Walsh, football coach at Stanford, with the tagline, "The Winning Game Plan."

In addition to traditional advertising and marketing techniques, Sharp Corp. developed several marketing strategies that were as inventive as its products. For example, in 1993 Sharp entered an alliance with AT&T to produce a Wizard pocket organizer that could send and receive messages around the world through AT&T's EasyLink Services. New software allowed users global messaging capabilities simply by plugging the organizer, equipped with a tiny modem, into a telephone jack. The user then dialed a toll-free AT&T number to access information, which was instantly readable on the Wizard's screen. A direct mail campaign promoted the device to corporations, because the main users were expected to be employees who travelled often and needed to check their messages from remote locations.

This global outlook was nothing new for Sharp Corp., which began exporting Hayakawa's Ever-Sharp Pencil in the early part of the twentieth century. By the early 1990s, Sharp Corp. operated 60 overseas facilities in 34 countries around the world. To attain success in each different market, the company analyzed the social environment and consumer demand. Then, Sharp products and manufacturing operations were tailored to fit predetermined needs.

Performance Appraisal

Throughout its history, Sharp Corp. maintained its reputation as a well-managed company that focused on leveraging key technologies to create innovative products. This strategy enabled the company to stay in the black during the recessionary years of the late 1980s and early 1990s, when the consumer electronics industry became saturated with competing products from many companies.

Faced with this crowded marketplace for consumer electronics, Sharp Corp. gradually shifted its focus to industrial electronics. In the early 1990s, an estimated 45 percent of its total sales were in consumer electronics. However, Sharp Corp. continued to provide inventive, exciting products for consumers, many featuring original technology developed by the company. Types of products expected in the future could be in the areas of multimedia systems, mobile telecommunications, and miniature audio discs and cassettes.

Further Reading:

Fitzgerald, Kate, "Sharp's Next Wizard Will Send, Receive Messages," *Advertising Age,* April 26, 1993, p. 39.

"Gretzky and Son in Sharp Ads," *Wall Street Journal,* May 18, 1994, B10.

Johnson, Bradley, "Sharp Backs Viewcam with $12 M," *Advertising Age,* May 24, 1993, p. 39.

Sharp Consolidated Financial Statements, Sharp Corp., 1993.

Sharp, Imagination and Creativity, Sharp Corp., 1993.

Sharp News: Fact Sheet; Sharp's Firsts; LCD Backgrounder; Milestone Moments in Sharp History, Sharp Corp.

"Sharp Puts $20 Million behind New Game Plan," *Brandweek,* January 25, 1993, p. 5.

—Dorothy Kroll

SHERWIN-WILLIAMS®

More than 125 years ago, Sherwin-Williams brand paint pioneered the consumer paint market. The brand's history is a story of ingenuity and teamwork: In the late nineteenth century, Henry Alden Sherwin developed a then-revolutionary product, and Edward Porter Williams came up with the marketing innovation that ensured its success. The introduction of Sherwin-Williams premixed paint changed the paint market in particular by enabling consumers to paint without the aid of a professional and the consumer market in general by inaugurating the ''money-back guarantee'' in America.

The brand's well-known ''Cover the Earth'' logo celebrates its centenary in 2005. Namesake stores, established at the turn of the century, dispensed knowledge as well as paint, and formed the underpinning of the long-running ''Ask Sherwin-Williams'' advertising campaign. Although the Sherwin-Williams brand eventually slipped from its dominance of the consumer paint market, the brand has remained a formidable competitor into the 1990s. In the aggregate, The Sherwin-Williams Company remains the largest supplier of consumer paint in the United States, since it also manufactures and distributes Dutch Boy and other brands.

Brand Origins

Today, paint in its rainbow of computer-matched colors and durable finishes is taken for granted, but in the middle of the nineteenth century, painting was a complicated job. No manufacturer had developed a way to suspend pigments in a solvent so that they would stay mixed for any reasonable length of time. Paint had to be mixed on site, stirred constantly, and used immediately to keep the pigment in suspension. It took a practiced hand to apply this poorly-mixed paint evenly, and if the paint happened to run out before the job was through, very likely the next batch would be inconsistent with the last. Even if someone had developed a way to grind pigments fine enough so that they would stay mixed, there were no resealable containers for paint, meaning it could not be shipped or stored for any length of time. Most early paint manufacturers sold the ingredients for paint—oil, pigments and putty—and customers (primarily professional painters) mixed the coatings themselves.

In 1867, an Ohioan, D. R. Averill, was awarded the first patent for prepared paint and the first trademark for an American product. However, Averill's ''patent paint'' resembled the more familiar patent medicines of the era: it was basically a hoax. His poor-quality premixed paint inspired a hoard of hucksters who weighted their paint cans with stones, diluted their solvents with water, or added chalk to their white paint to make it go farther. Like patent medicines, it was impossible to discover the fraud until the damage was done. ''Patent paint'' gave prepared paint such a bad name that many painters continued to make their own.

Henry A. Sherwin arrived in Cleveland in 1860 at the invitation of an uncle who thought the city offered boundless opportunity for an industrious young man. Working first as a dry goods clerk, then bookkeeper, later in a wholesale grocer, Sherwin saved $2,000, which he invested in a partnership with Truman Dunham & Co. in 1866. He said later in life: ''I quite unexpectedly dropped into the paint business.'' By 1870, the partnership was dissolved, with Dunham and another partner remaining in the linseed oil business and Sherwin concentrating on the paint business with the assistance of two new partners, E.P. Williams and A.T. Osborn.

Sherwin-Williams refused to produce the Averill formula ready-mix paint. In Sherwin's words, it ''made use of a formula which simply could not produce a reputable paint.'' It was always Sherwin's ''endeavor to establish a good reputation by giving good measure and good quality, to avoid every trick that would save a penny at the expense of the other fellow.'' Sherwin handled the technical side of the venture: He sought out the highest quality paint ingredients and sold them to professional painters, with whom he earned a good reputation. He also worked to integrate vertically while formulating a prepared paint, so that Sherwin-Williams & Company would control the quality of its ingredients at every step. Williams focused on the marketing end of the business: he was a Phi Beta Kappan known for his enthusiastic personality and salesmanship.

By 1873, Sherwin-Williams was selling its own products directly to the public. Three years later, Sherwin achieved the breakthrough he had long anticipated. He invented a mill that would grind pigments fine enough to stay suspended in oil. The following year, he developed and patented a reclosable paint can. With these two innovations, Sherwin and Williams launched their first line of prepared paint in 1878.

Early Marketing Strategy

The partners protected their own names and reputations against failure by calling their first product ''Osborn Family Paint.''

AT A GLANCE

Sherwin-Williams brand of paint developed by Henry Alden Sherwin and Edward Porter Williams in Cleveland, Ohio, in 1878 and originally sold as Osborn Family Paints; name changed to Sherwin-Williams Paints in 1880; offered first money-back guarantee in America; first trademark was a chameleon on a paint palette; officially changed to "Cover the Earth" globe in 1905 and registered in 1906; logo changed in 1974 to graphic of "Sherwin-Williams" name; "Cover the Earth" revived in 1980.

Performance: *Market share*—10% of consumer paint market (3rd place, 1991). *Sales*—$2.75 billion.

Major competitor: Glidden; also PPG.

Advertising: *Agency*—CTE Media (in-house), 1993—. *Major campaign*—Uses the slogan, "Ask Sherwin-Williams."

Addresses: *Parent company*—Sherwin-Williams Co., 101 Prospect Avenue NW, Cleveland, Ohio 44115; phone: (216) 566-2000; fax: (216) 566-1832.

Osborn had been a partner in the paint company, and his name was given this dubious honor. Two years of unsuccessful marketing seemed to prove to Sherwin and Williams that their caution was well founded—customers' confidence in prepared paint had been totally eroded by "patent paint."

The partners realized that the only way to market the paint would be to reverse the negative connotations of prepared paint. Williams has been credited with the gimmick they used to do just that. In 1880, they relaunched their product under the Sherwin-Williams name with what has been called the first national, iron-clad, money-back guarantee: "We guarantee that this paint, when properly used, will not crack, flake, or chalk off, and will cover more surface, work better, wear longer, and permanently look better than other paints, including Pure White Lead and Oil. We hereby agree to forfeit the value of the paint and the cost of applying it if in any instance it is not found as above represented." The guarantee gave Sherwin-Williams Paint added value, alleviated customers' concerns about quality, and created a climate of acceptance for the product. The scheme made customers and paint dealers more confident in the product.

Early Trademarks

Sherwin-Williams Paints' first trademark was a chameleon on a painter's palette. The two images emphasized the products' array of colors, but some customers thought the chameleon was a snake. Sherwin-Williams' advertising manager, George W. Ford, adapted the logo of a now-defunct company to the needs of the paint company in the 1890s. He drew a paint can pouring its contents out onto a globe tilted horizontally so that the stream of paint fell directly onto Sherwin-Williams' Cleveland headquarters. Ford and Williams thought the motto, "Cover the Earth" would express corporate confidence, but Sherwin considered the phrase an outrageous exaggeration, because the company had little overseas volume.

The marketing men won—the new logo began to appear on paint labels in 1893, was officially adopted in 1905, and registered in 1895. Sherwin-Williams quickly became the first premixed paint to gain wide public acceptance among the highly fragmented paint market. Sherwin-Williams helped establish Cleveland as one of the United States' primary coatings centers. This status was tied to the establishment of longtime competitor Glidden Varnish Co. in Cleveland in 1895.

Advertising Innovations

Throughout the history of the brand, Sherwin-Williams has concentrated its advertising budget on magazine ads and point-of-purchase displays. Sherwin-Williams embarked on a national advertising campaign at a time when most paint companies concentrated on selling within a city or, at most, a single state. The brand's first magazine ad, in an 1896 edition of *Ladies' Home Journal,* stressed the economy of paint. Sherwin-Williams used the national promotions to expand geographically throughout the Midwest during the last years of the nineteenth century, and, by 1900, the brand led the paint market by a wide margin.

Shortly after the turn of the century, Walter Cottingham became president of the company. He continued the brand's pioneering national advertising, although many paint executives thought the campaign was uneconomical. Cottingham also oversaw the opening of the first Sherwin-Williams store, which offered customers advice on surface preparation, primers, color combinations, brushes, and clean-up materials, as well as the branded paint. Company stores encouraged the growth and development of the do-it-yourself paint market.

Recognizing the popularity of radio, Sherwin-Williams experimented with the media in the 1930s by sponsoring The Metropolitan Auditions of the Air and the Paul Whiteman Show. The brand's favorite and most productive outlet, however, was print. Its advertising budget was almost evenly split between magazine advertising and point-of-purchase displays.

Brand Development

Technological developments and external market forces influenced the targeting and placement of the Sherwin-Williams brand in the 1940s and 1950s. As was the case in many industries, importing restrictions and the shortage of raw materials during World War II encouraged the paint industry to innovate. When the Sherwin-Williams Company developed "KEM-TONE," a one-coat, fast-drying, water-reducible paint for interior use, the company enjoyed rapid growth.

Since household tasks were often divided between men and women according to indoor and outdoor chores, and market research revealed that men usually selected the color and brand of exterior paint, many of the Sherwin-Williams brand paint advertisements began to be aimed at men. Consequently, they were moved from nationally circulated women's magazines to periodicals with a more general circulation. The brand was also promoted through cooperative advertisements in over 175 major metropolitan and nationally circulated newspapers.

Mass discounters started to use paint as a "loss leader" to establish their pricing position and lure customers in the 1950s. Sears, Roebuck and Co. quickly catapulted into the ranks of the top five paint marketers using this method with its private Weatherbeater brand. At the same time, alternative building products, like aluminum siding, redwood, and glass, began a period of intense competition with paint. These two external forces converged with the saturation of the paint market to simultaneously restrict Sherwin-Williams' sales volume and profit margin.

Paint profits dove, and paint manufacturers were forced to re-evaluate their branding positions. Sherwin-Williams had been selling its namesake paints in several markets—mom-and-pop hardware stores, mass merchandisers, independent dealers, and its own outlets. It was not uncommon for Sherwin-Williams paints to be sold at discount prices in one outlet, and premium prices at another.

Company Stores

By 1960, Sherwin-Williams' chain of paint stores had grown to 1,400. During the first half of the decade, the company expanded its namesake chain to about 2,000 stores, which helped boost the brand's volume of sales. Despite intense competition within the paint industry and from other sources, Sherwin-Williams remained the top paint company in the late 1960s, with 15 percent of the U.S. paint market and $282 million in annual sales. PPG and DuPont's Lucite tied for second place with 9 percent, followed by Glidden with 5 percent.

Throughout the 1960s and early 1970s, Sherwin-Williams spent $4 million to $5 million annually on advertising and promotion, continuing to concentrate most of that budget on magazine advertisements.

A new president and chief executive officer, Walter O. Spencer, reorganized the company and its paint marketing in the late 1960s and early 1970s. He discovered that many of the company's stores were devoted to "back door business"—large volume, low margin sales to contractors—virtually ignoring the retail end. Hoping to exploit the do-it-yourself market Sherwin-Williams had pioneered, Spencer transformed some stores into decorating centers; he expanded the product line to included such decorating accessories as carpet, drapes, wallpaper, and furniture. These other products drew customers to the stores and helped distribute profits more evenly throughout the year. Of the three major paint brands, Sherwin-Williams made the most extensive commitment to home decoration. The company opened a 25,000-square-foot "hypermarket" in Charlotte, North Carolina, in 1975. This European-style maze of home decorating vignettes was eight to ten times larger than the average paint store.

Logo Change

CEO Spencer also oversaw a dramatic change in Sherwin-Williams' brand and corporate identification. In November 1974, Sherwin-Williams changed its logo from the decades-old "Cover the Earth" globe to a graphic representation of the company name. The brand's promoters wanted this new trademark to reflect the company's more diversified product line. By this time, the coatings segment accounted for 70 percent (or $562.9 million) of Sherwin-Williams' sales. After more than seventy years of consistent use, the company had hoped to keep some remnant of its "Cover the Earth" logo, which ranked among the ten most recognized trademarks in the world. Three years of research and analysis, however, led the company to introduce its "contemporary graphic logo" in the fall of 1974.

Changing packaging, point-of-purchase signs in 2,000 company stores, and imprints on office supplies cost about $15 million. The repositioning was also supported with a print campaign started in such business publications as *Barron's, Business Week, Fortune,* and *The Wall Street Journal.* The announcement was coordinated to coincide with the release of the company's 1974 annual report and was supported with formal press conferences in Cleveland, Philadelphia, Chicago, Dallas, Atlanta, and Oakland, California (Sherwin-Williams' regional headquarters).

It was also during this time that company management recognized that selling one brand, i.e. the Sherwin-Williams brand, through its company-owned stores, discounters, and specialty paint dealers would continue to create channel conflicts. For this reason in 1975 the company dedicated the Sherwin-Williams brand to its company-owned stores, reserving Kem-Tone and Martin-Senour for the other channels of distribution. The segregation of the paint brands by channel cost the company about 12 million gallons of lost sales in the transition, representing 10 percent to 15 percent of its total paint sales volume at that time. The switch-over heavily impacted company performance in the short term, but was proven correct in the 1980s.

During the late 1970s, however, serious problems within the corporation and the paint industry toppled the Sherwin-Williams brand from its decades of dominance. CEO Spencer had borrowed $100 million to build new company stores and modernize others. The company's debt rose to 40 percent of capital, as margins were squeezed between rising raw materials costs and falling selling prices. The crisis climaxed in 1979 with an $8 million loss and the brand's relinquishment of the top share to Sears, Roebuck & Co.

Sherwin-Williams' directors promoted John G. Breen to the chairmanship in 1979 after Spencer's abrupt resignation. One of the keys to Breen's speedy reorganization was the revival of the popular and well-known "Cover the Earth" logo. Breen, like Spencer before him, tried to shift the Sherwin-Williams stores' primary market from painting contractors to do-it-yourselfers. In 1980, the professionals still accounted for 70 percent of sales in the company's 1,400 stores. Breen's strategy for capturing more of the $40 billion do-it-yourself business was to cut extraneous lines, like furniture and drapes, and to concentrate on complete lines of wallpaper and paint. Breen boosted the advertising budget by 50 percent in 1980, and purchased the Dutch Boy trademark and patents to encourage sales outside company stores.

The purchase of Dutch Boy supported the company's previous move of dedicating the Sherwin-Williams brand only to the Sherwin-Williams paint stores. Kem-Tone and Martin-Senour brands were offered to the mass markets and independent specialty paint stores. Dutch Boy would be offered to lumber and building material stores, which were evolving into the emerging home center retail channel of distribution.

After a long reorganization that reduced the total number of retail paint outlets to 1,367 units by the end of 1982 (from about 2,000 in the mid-1960s), Sherwin-Williams' company stores enjoyed four consecutive years of record profits, from 1980 to 1984. Despite a stagnant economy and a mature paint market, Sherwin-Williams' paint profits increased 22 percent in 1983 alone, from $14 million in 1982 to $29 million in 1983. Once the company stores were back on an even keel, Breen began once again to expand the chain.

International Market

By its very nature, the paint industry has historically been a local business. The weight of prepared paint, coupled with local conditions and tastes, worked against geographic expansion in the business as a whole. However, Sherwin-Williams Paints moved into Cuba, Argentina, Brazil, Mexico, and Europe in the 1920s through the 1940s, but World War II crippled many of the brand's overseas operations. From that time on, international activity was sluggish "because of unsettled political and economic conditions overseas."

Not surprisingly, Sherwin Williams' most successful foreign operations were on the North American continent. By 1975, the company's Canadian subsidiary had 130 branch stores. The Canadian market overall trailed the American business; do-it-yourself painting became popular more slowly there. At that time, Sherwin-Williams also had affiliates, licensees, and sublicensees in 24 countries.

Performance Appraisal

Sherwin-Williams never fully recovered from its late 1970s fall: in the early 1990s, the brand ranked third, with 10 percent of the consumer paint market, behind Glidden, with 13.6 percent, and Sears, Roebuck & Co., with 13.1 percent. The Sherwin-Williams company, however, commanded an additional 6.6 percent of the market through its Dutch Boy brand.

Sherwin-Williams tried to breathe new life into its advertising with an agency switch, from Wyse Advertising of Cleveland to J. Walter Thompson USA, Chicago, in January 1991. The agency tried to capitalize on the brand's popularity with the slower-growth professional market through a 1991 television campaign. Each 30-second ad emphasized that "the pros know" and wrapped up with the long-running "Ask Sherwin-Williams" slogan.

Further Reading:

"At Sherwin-Williams, Change Is More than Logo Deep," *Chemical Week,* January 29, 1975, pp. 34–35.

Barach, Arnold B., *Famous American Trademarks,* Washington, D.C.: Public Affairs Press, 1971.

"Building Downturn Hasn't Hit the Paint Companies," *Financial World,* December 7, 1960, pp. 4, 30.

Cleary, David Powers, *Great American Brands,* New York: Fairchild, 1981.

Cook, Dan, and Marc Frons, "The Tough So-And-So Who Saved Sherwin-Williams," *Business Week,* May 5, 1986, pp. 88–89.

Fitzgerald, Kate, "Flat Paint Sales Spur High-Gloss Ad Plans," *Advertising Age,* May 6, 1991, p. 12.

"Full-Color Ads Jump Sales 62 Percent," *Printers' Ink,* May 6, 1960, pp. 58–59.

Gershman, Michael, *Getting It Right the Second Time,* New York: Addison-Wesley, 1990.

Gordon, Mitchell, "Another Coat," *Barron's,* June 25, 1984, 41–42.

Hassey, Thomas C., "How Sherwin-Williams Changed Its Image," *Public Relations Journal,* July 1975, pp. 9–10, 24.

Maples, Margaret G., "Williams New Logo Aimed at Reflecting Larger Product Line," *Advertising Age,* November 4, 1974, p. 89.

"More Than Just Paint Stores," *Chain Store Age Executive,* November 1976, pp. 32B–33B.

Morgan, Hal, *Symbols of America,* New York: Penguin, 1986.

"The New Gloss at Sherwin-Williams," *Business Week,* July 15, 1967, pp. 154–56, 158.

"S-W Repaints Its Image," *Chemical Week,* May 3, 1978, p. 23.

Teresko, John, "Sherwin-Williams Struggles to Mix a New Color Scheme," *Industry Week,* August 21, 1978, pp. 81–83.

—April S. Dougal

SILLY PUTTY®

Silly Putty is the brand name for a synthetic, rubberlike substance that became a best-selling children's toy and adult novelty. It is sold in small plastic eggs, and according to parent company Binney & Smith, Inc., more than 200 million Silly Putty eggs were sold between 1950, when the product was introduced, and 1994. Binney & Smith, the maker of Crayola crayons, purchased the rights to Silly Putty in 1977.

Physically, Silly Putty behaved as both a liquid and a solid. Like an extremely thick liquid, it had the ability to flow and take the shape of its container. Like a solid, it also could be molded into shapes. Although Silly Putty could be stretched like taffy into a thin thread, it would shatter if struck sharply.

Brand Origins

When Japan cut off the flow of natural rubber from the Far East at the start of World War II, the U.S. government launched a massive effort to develop new sources of synthetic rubber. In 1943 James Gilbert Wright, a chemical engineer at a General Electric Company laboratory in New Haven, Connecticut, was working on the synthetic rubber project when he combined boric acid and a silicone oil. The result was a gooey mass that, much to Wright's delight, bounced when it was dropped on the floor. General Electric sent samples of "bouncing putty" to hundreds of researchers worldwide. Unfortunately, nobody could suggest any practical use for Wright's discovery.

After the war bouncing putty became a popular topic of conversation—and play—at cocktail parties in the New Haven area, which may be how Peter C. L. Hodgson, Sr., was introduced to the substance that would make him a millionaire. The most common story was that Hodgson, an advertising copywriter, attended a cocktail party with Ruth Fallgatter, the owner of a popular New Haven toy store. Hodgson later recalled, "Everybody kept saying there was no earthly use for the stuff. But I watched them as they fooled with it. I couldn't help noticing how people with busy schedules wasted as much as 15 minutes at a shot just fondling and stretching it." In 1950, however, Hodgson also told the *New Yorker* that he was introduced to bouncing putty when a friend left some at his home.

Regardless, Hodgson recognized the potential for bouncing putty as a novelty item. He packed one-ounce blobs of putty in clear, plastic cases (originally designed as woman's compacts) and included a description of the material in a 1949 Christmas catalog he was creating for Fallgatter's Block Shop toy store, which featured novelties and educational toys for New England's academic community. The price was $2. Surprisingly, bouncing putty outsold every other item in the catalog except a 50-cent box of Crayola crayons. Early in 1950 Hodgson purchased a large batch of bouncing putty from General Electric, rented a barn in North Branford, Connecticut, and hired students from nearby Yale University to fill plastic compacts. He also came up with a name, Silly Putty.

Early Marketing

In February Hodgson took Silly Putty to the International Toy Fair in New York and succeeded in attracting the interest of several retail outlets, including Neiman-Marcus department stores and Doubleday bookstores. That spring Hodgson began packing Silly Putty in colorful, pull-apart plastic Easter eggs. He later told interviewers that he "decided to combine [his] putty with Easter and give them both a lift." He shipped the plastic eggs in pasteboard egg cartons just like real eggs. The eggs, with half-ounce chunks of Silly Putty, were priced at $1 each.

Hodgson's big break, however, came in August, when the *New Yorker* ran an article about Silly Putty in the influential "Talk of the Town" column. The *New Yorker* said, "We went into the Doubleday bookshop . . . intending, in our innocence, to buy a book, and found all the clerks busy selling Silly Putty, a gooey, pinkish, repellent-looking commodity that comes in plastic containers the size and shape of eggs." The article quoted the bookstore manager, who explained, "We sell the eggs mostly to men who claim they're buying them for their children. Actually, Silly Putty is a fine toy for adults." The article noted that the manager "compulsively pick[ed] up an egg . . . opened it, took out the putty, rolled it into a sphere, and ricocheted it off an unabridged dictionary."

The *New Yorker* also interviewed Hodgson, who told the magazine that Silly Putty "means five minutes of escape from neurosis. It means not having to worry about [the Korean War] or family difficulties. And it appeals to people of superior intellect; the inherent ridiculousness of the material acts as an emotional release to hard pressed adults." Hodgson also suggested several practical uses for Silly Putty, including as a hand exerciser, a temporary plug for leaks, and the perfect antidote for wobbly

AT A GLANCE

Silly Putty brand of "bouncing putty" founded in 1950 by Peter C. L. Hodgson, Sr., then an advertising copywriter in Connecticut; the product itself, a synthetic, rubberlike substance, was created in 1943 by James Gilbert Wright, a chemical engineer at a General Electric Company laboratory in New Haven, Connecticut; Hodgson's business, Arnold Clark Co., sold Silly Putty as an adult novelty and a children's toy; brand sold to Binney & Smith, Inc., of Easton, Pennsylvania, in 1977.

Performance: *Sales*—$6 million.

Major competitor: None.

Addresses: *Parent company*—Binney & Smith, Inc., 1100 Church Lane, Easton, PA 18044-0431; phone: (215) 253-6271.

furniture. The article explained, "You just stick some of it under the short leg of a jiggly table and there you are." Hodgson, whose Arnold Clark Co. was selling about 10,000 Silly Putty eggs a month before the article, received orders for more than 250,000 soon after the magazine was published.

Milestones

Silly Putty went on to become one of the biggest-selling novelty items of the 1950s, although not without some worrisome moments. In 1951 the Korean War caused the U.S. government to impose restrictions on the use of certain raw materials, including silicone, which nearly forced Silly Putty off the market. Hodgson, however, had stockpiled about 1,500 pounds of bouncing putty, which he parceled out to fill backlogged orders. Production of Silly Putty resumed when the restrictions were lifted in 1952.

Although it started out as a novelty for adults, Silly Putty quickly grew in popularity with children, in large part because of its ability to lift ink images when pressed against comics printed in the newspaper. Once transferred to a flat piece of Silly Putty, the images could be stretched or twisted. By 1955 children between the ages of 6 and 12 had become Silly Putty's biggest market. The popularity among children also brought about a change in the Silly Putty formula. Original Silly Putty would settle into carpets and other fabrics. Although Silly Putty was not sticky, it was almost impossible to remove. The new formula produced a Silly Putty with a harder texture that was less fluid. (The formula was changed again in the late 1970s, again to prevent "puddling.")

To promote Silly Putty, Hodgson threw extravagant parties during the annual toy fairs in New York, renting the ballroom of the Waldorf-Astoria Hotel for an outlandish buffet of exotic foods. Hodgson, who cultivated show-business connections, also provided hard-to-get tickets to the most popular plays on Broadway and rented the famed Sardi's restaurant for dinner afterward. Hodgson launched one of the first television advertising campaigns aimed specifically at children in the mid-1950s, when he began promoting Silly Putty during afternoon programming, which often included the *Howdy Doody* show. To save money, Hodgson would advertise in three local television markets at a time, setting up local warehouse and distribution networks and supplementing the commercials with print advertising. After blanketing a region with advertising for two to three months, Hodgson would move on to a new market. He later purchased network television time, and Silly Putty became a regular sponsor of *Captain Kangaroo* and *CBS Morning News.* More than seven million Silly Putty eggs were sold in 1957—an all-time high.

Silly Putty was demonstrated in 1961 at the U.S. Plastics Expo in Moscow and later became a popular gift for Soviet citizens returning from the United States. When Hodgson died in 1976, Silly Putty, which still sold for $1 an egg, was available in 22 countries. More than five million eggs were sold in 1976, and Hodgson left an estate valued at $143 million.

In 1968 Silly Putty became a footnote in the exploration of space when the product—packaged in eggs made of sterling silver—was carried aboard the Apollo 8 voyage "to help fasten down tools during the weightless period," according to a company fact sheet, as well as "to alleviate boredom." As Hodgson had explained to the *New Yorker,* Silly Putty could be "an emotional release to hard pressed adults." According to Peter C. L. Hodgson, Jr., for several years the Dallas-based Neiman-Marcus department stores had made sterling silver eggs for Hodgson to give to special friends. After the Apollo 8 mission, Neiman-Marcus began including $75 sterling-silver Silly Putty "space eggs" in its Christmas catalog.

Brand Outlook

Sales of Silly Putty dropped off drastically in the late 1970s, in part because of a flurry of imitators, including Nutty Putty, Looney Tunes Putty, Sylvester Putty, Geoffrey Putty, and Goofy Goo. In addition, when Hodgson died in 1976, his estate sold the rights to Silly Putty to Binney & Smith, Inc., the makers of Crayola crayons, which initially did little to promote the brand. Almost a decade later, however, baby boomers led a revival of interest in many of their childhood fads, including Silly Putty, and sales began to grow, doubling from less than two million eggs in the late 1980s to about four million in 1990. *The Philadelphia Inquirer* described the production process as an assembly line "consisting of a converted mortar machine for stirring the putty, a marshmallow machine for cutting it into lumps, and a conveyor belt out of 'I Love Lucy' for packing it into plastic eggs."

In 1990 Silly Putty turned 40 years old, and Binney & Smith celebrated by throwing a party reminiscent of the annual galas staged by Hodgson in the 1950s. The birthday party, held on the opening day of the American International Toy Fair, included a 500-pound "cake" made of Silly Putty, an appearance by Silly Putty artist George Horner (who both sculpted in Silly Putty and painted on Silly Putty "canvases"), and the launch of the first "new" Silly Putty since a glob of goo fell on the floor of Wright's General Electric laboratory in 1943. The *New York Times* reported, "After 40 years of nothing but your basic, bloblike pinkish-beige, Silly Putty is diversifying" with four florescent colors: magenta, orange, green, and yellow. In 1991 Binney & Smith also added "Glow in the Dark" Silly Putty.

In the early 1990s Binney & Smith was producing daily about 12,000 plastic Silly Putty eggs, which were sold primarily through mass merchandisers, such as K Mart, Wal-Mart, and Toys "R" Us. According to Binney & Smith, market research showed that 97 percent of American households recognized the Silly Putty brand name and almost 70 percent had purchased Silly Putty at some time. In a brochure created for the 40th anniversary, Dennis Malloy, then director of new business development, said the "universal awareness and appeal, as well as the positive memories most adults have of playing with Silly Putty as children [means] there is a tremendous opportunity for growth in the Silly Putty business.''

Newer inks and printing processes had put an end to one of Silly Putty's most endearing qualities, the ability to copy newspaper images and then distort them into even more comical creations. Even so, Silly Putty—''the toy with one moving part''—had picked up some more practical uses, including therapeutic stress-relief for people who were quitting smoking, mimicking the earth's crust in seismic experiments, and, since it had the same specific density as human flesh, calibrating medical instruments.

Silly Putty also retained its most basic qualities. As the advertising said, ''Can you bounce like rubber if rolled into a ball? Pull like taffy, yet break into separate pieces? Mold into animals and other shapes? Well . . . Silly Putty can!'' Malloy called Silly Putty the perfect toy: ''To play with Silly Putty you don't need any directions or batteries. There's nothing else like it.''

Further Reading:

''Here to Stay,'' *New Yorker,* August 26, 1950, p. 19.

The History of Silly Putty, Easton, Pennsylvania: Binney & Smith, Inc., 1986.

Matza, Michael, ''Putty Party,'' *The Philadelphia Inquirer,* February 12, 1990, p. 1F.

McFadden, Robert D., ''Peter C.L. Hodgson, Marketer of Silly Putty, Dies at Age 64,'' *The New York Times,* August 7, 1976.

The Silly Putty Story, Easton, Pennsylvania: Binney & Smith, Inc., 1990.

—Dean Boyer

SIMMONS BEAUTYREST®

Simmons Beautyrest brand, produced by the Simmons Company of Atlanta, Georgia, is the third best-selling mattress in the bedding industry. Since its founding in 1870, the Simmons Company has used brand-name recognition, quality assurance, and sophisticated marketing techniques to grow its business. Today, the company employs 2,100 people throughout a network of 17 small, decentralized businesses, each running as a separate profit center with its own management team. According to Chairman and Chief Executive Officer Bob Mangusson, this structure allows the Simmons Company to respond quickly to local customer needs without checking first with a bureaucratic headquarters.

Brand Origins

In 1870, Zalmon G. Simmons started his company in Wisconsin, where he began manufacturing coil springs. An industrious man, Mr. Simmons was an immigrant who arrived in America at the age of 15. He would eventually become the president of the Rock Island Railway Company and the Northwest Telegraphy Company, as well as the mayor of Kenosha, Wisconsin and owner of a country store.

The business was founded when Mr. Simmons purchased a small cheese box factory with nine employees. The company's first product under Simmons' management was a wooden telegraph insulator designed for the Northwest Telegraph Company. When he initially purchased the cheese box company, sleep was the last thing on Simmons' mind, but he entered the bedding business when he accepted a patent for a handmade woven-wire bedspring as payment for a debt incurred at his general store. After enlisting the help of a local inventor, Simmons found a way to automate production of fine, woven-wire bedsprings at a fraction of the normal cost.

In 1884, Simmons incorporated his company under the name Northwestern Wire Mattress Company. By 1889 the company changed its name to the Simmons Manufacturing Company. In the early days, the company's research began with personalized studies that looked for Simmons customers in small-town markets. This strategy proved successful and the company began shipping its metal and brass beds from Kenosha, Wisconsin to all parts of the country between 1890 and 1900. In 1890, Simmons became the largest company of its kind in the world by producing 1,500 woven-wire mattresses daily. By 1900, annual sales of Simmons beds reached $1 million. When Zalmon Simmons died in 1910, the company's annual sales had reached $4 million.

Zalmon Simmons, Jr. took over the leadership of the company upon his father's death. In 1914, the company established its export division, and in 1915, the "Simmons Company" was incorporated in Delaware to succeed the "Simmons Manufacturing Company." In 1918, the company introduced the first modern box spring, and Zalmon Simmons, Jr. recognized the mattress business as a promising opportunity. Like his father, the younger Simmons discovered ways to create manufacturing techniques that enabled the production of high-quality products at lower costs. One of his monumental discoveries was the "Beautyrest" pocket machine, which revolutionized the bedding industry by producing mattresses with independent pocketed coils.

It was during this era that the Simmons Company began expanding into foreign markets. In 1923, the company established its first production facility outside the United States in Monterey, Mexico. Compania Simmons, S.A. was created in 1927 to make and sell Simmons products in Mexico. By 1993, Simmons' international operations consisted of fully licensed "partners" of the Simmons Company who marketed under corporate guidance, taking advantage of regular communications, product updates, and seminars.

The Beautyrest Mattress was introduced to the American marketplace in 1925. Destined to become one of the most recognized brand names in the history of the bedding industry, the name "Beautyrest" was selected from a list of suggestions submitted by company employees. The price of the new mattress was set at a costly $39.50—three to four times what the average customer paid for a mattress—but the Simmons Company believed that aggressive advertising and sales promotions would educate prospective customers on the superior value and comfort of the Beautyrest mattress. The mattress' unique quality rested in its independent pocketed coil construction. This superior structure soon made believers out of thousands of people who purchased the new product in its first several years.

To introduce the new product, Simmons launched one of the most successful advertising and sales promotions campaigns in bedding history. The company used testimonial endorsements from famous Americans like Henry Ford, Thomas Edison, Theodore Roosevelt, and William Howard Taft. Behind this high-

AT A GLANCE

Simmons Beautyrest mattress was introduced by the Simmons Company, founded by Zalmon G. Simmons, in 1925 in Kenosha, WI.

Performance: *Market share*—Approximately 17.1% of bedding category. *Sales*—$350 million.

Major competitors: Sealy and Serta.

Advertising: *Major campaign*—"Nothing energizes your day like a Beautyrest night."

Addresses: *Parent company*—The Simmons Company, One Concourse Parkway, Suite 600, Atlanta, GA 30328-5369; phone: (404) 732-1202.

profile marketing campaign, Simmons' Beautyrest sales jumped to $3 million by 1927 and tripled that total within three years. Because of the record-breaking customer demand, retailers who had never carried the Simmons mattress line began to stock the Beautyrest, and sales continued to soar. When the company introduced its first damask floral cover for the Beautyrest, customers welcomed the attractive cover and enthusiastically purchased the mattress. By 1936, the Simmons Company produced its 2,500,000th Beautyrest mattress at its Elizabeth, New Jersey facility.

The success of the Beautyrest mattress rested in the difference between open coils and Simmons pocketed coils. Ordinary open coils were connected to each other, and they could react to pressure on nearby coils. In the Beautyrest pocketed coil system, however, all coils worked independently. Coils were joined only at carefully designated mid-points, not at the top or bottom. Since these coils all operated independently, they avoided hammocking and firmly supported every inch of a person's body. This innovative and patented system assured complete body support.

The Simmons Company did not rest on its laurels with the success of the Beautyrest. Its marketing techniques became increasingly sophisticated as computerized demographics tracked potential mattress customers based on income, education, location, and needs. Fact-finding surveys and research provided Simmons with vital background information that helped its dealers reach their customers and operate profitable bedding departments.

The company also continued to invest in research and development for new products. In the 1940s, the company introduced the hide-a-bed sofa. In the 1950s, the company created a second revolution in the bedding industry when it created super-sized mattresses. Simmons' king and queen size bedding opened up entirely new markets of opportunity for the company. During the 1970s, Simmons introduced the Maxipedic mattress, the first sleep system on the market with a bedboard built into the box spring. Simmons was also the first manufacturer in the bedding industry to recognize the future growth of the waterbed industry. As a result, the company developed the Beautyrest Feelings Flotation System.

Marketing and Development

By the end of the 1980s, Simmons determined that more than 94 percent of American consumers recognized the Simmons Beautyrest brand name, making it a ''household name'' known throughout the United States. The high-level brand identification made Simmons one of the few companies in the bedding industry with a single corporate identity and identical product standards coast to coast. The company's advertising appeared nationally through the 1980s and 1990s in several media formats that included television, radio, magazines, and newspapers. An extensive co-operative program contributed to dealer efforts in making an impression at the local level. The company employed professionals in the fields of graphics, illustration, copy, print, and broadcast to create attention-getting communications that conveyed the Simmons story and its product benefits.

Since the early days, the Simmons Company supplied its dealers with a wide range of sales aids and point-of-purchase displays that helped them attract customers during the crucial four to six weeks they are in the market. The ''Sleep Gallery Program,'' for example, helped participating Simmons dealers transform ordinary mattress stores into complete environments for sleep and sleep-related products. Sales persons were specially trained to help customers select the best mattresses for their needs. In the Sleep Galleries, customers could test mattresses, ask questions, and receive knowledgeable answers. Throughout the 1980s and 1990s, Simmons continued to invest heavily in Beautyrest brand development. As a result, the company introduced the greatest Beautyrest innovation in sixty years—the Beautyrest ''Contour-Flex'' mattress.

The Contour-Flex construction utilized a unique, ultrasonic bonding process which internally sealed the independently wrapped coils together. This more durable, unitized construction provided superior support and greater sleeping comfort than earlier designs.

Future Growth

Simmons' rate of growth continued to flourish through the 1970s. In 1979, however, the industry's slow average-rate-of-growth and the nation's recession took its toll on the company, and for the first time, Simmons' operating margin fell into the red. At its lowest point, Bob Magnusson was appointed chairman and CEO. Within five years, Magnusson had led the company back to a period of steady growth. Magnusson's success was a result of focusing his attention on improving the company's quality and service. He believed it was crucial to regain the confidence of Simmons' retailers because he understood that store owners and buyers can create a negative image of a company simply by talking amongst themselves.

Under Magnusson's leadership, Simmons developed its seven-point strategy, which bases the company's future on the following points: product superiority, technological leadership, state-of-the-art facilities, the organization of the company, brand-name recognition, selective distribution, and marketing sophistication. By focusing its attention on these seven points, Simmons hoped it could outpace its competition in the slow-growth bedding industry.

Recent signs indicate that the seven-point strategy is working. While the bedding industry has grown an average of 2.56 percent per year, Simmons has experienced a growth rate of 6 percent. To maintain this momentum, Simmons spends $1 million annually on research and development to keep itself ahead of competition. This research includes all product-related research on raw materials, equipment, manufacturing processes, and assembly techniques.

The Simmons manufacturing network actually encompasses 17 small businesses, each running as a separate profit center with its own management team. The individual profit centers function as decentralized organizations and can make decisions quickly without headquarter's permission. As a result, each Simmons functionary is able to respond quickly to its own set of local customer preferences.

Simmons' headquarters operation in Atlanta, Georgia focuses on setting quality standards and raw material specifications as well as conducting research on new products and equipment. They provide purchasing and human resource support, including training and medical insurance. Simmons views this decentralized arrangement as being the best of both worlds: small business flexibility with big business clout.

Simmons' future success also lies in its continued brand-name recognition. While many major brand names have witnessed market-share erosion in recent years, Simmons still believes that its Beautyrest brand name is as valuable as ever. According to the company, consumers are still making buying decisions based on name, even when the price is high—provided the company lives up to its responsibility of offering high-quality products. The company's product-quality and customer-satisfaction ethos, therefore, will continue to guide its operations. Armed with strong brand-name recognition and a history of meeting customers' needs, Simmons expects the Beautyrest mattress to remain a market leader for some time to come.

Further Reading:

Donner, Joanne, ''Behind Simmons' Turnaround,'' *Business Atlanta,* October 1993, p. 16.

The Simmons Company, *Challenger* (newsletter), winter 1993.

The Simmons Company, *Making the Best of a Good Night's Sleep,* Atlanta, GA, 1993.

The Simmons Company, *The Simmons Legacy,* Atlanta, GA.

—Wendy Johnson Bilas

SINGER®

SINGER

The Singer brand of sewing machines, with its original ''Perpendicular Action'' design and sturdy build, is one of the top-selling lines of sewing machines in the United States. For well over 100 years, Singer sewing machines have been offering consumers value, reliability, and durability while keeping up with consumer needs. Hailed by late Nobel Peace Prize winner Mahatma Gandhi as the world's most useful invention, the Singer sewing machine has consistently outstitched and outsold such heavyweight contenders as Kenmore, Elna, Pfaff, and White. Under the ownership of The Singer Co., Inc., a subsidiary of International Semi-Tech Microelectronics, Inc., Singer sewing machines have remained a market share leader due to years of innovative sales strategies and constant product improvement.

Brand Origins

A machinist by profession and a sometime actor, Isaac Merritt Singer, the son of impoverished German immigrants, was in Boston during the summer of 1850 to oversee the sale of a woodcarving machine he invented, and chanced to visit a machine shop where Orson Phelps was trying, unsuccessfully, to manufacture a new sewing machine under license. Studying the malfunctioning of the model in the shop, Singer suggested three major changes: the shuttle should move back and forth in a straight line rather than in a circle; the needle should be straight instead of curved; and the needle should move vertically rather than horizontally.

Phelps was desperate to complete a functioning machine and encouraged Singer to implement his suggestions. In just 11 days, a machine—dubbed ''The Perpendicular Action Belay Stitch Machine'' by Singer—was finally perfected, a machine which would soon be acknowledged as the first genuinely practical sewing machine. To manufacture and market the invention, I. M. Singer and Company was formed in 1851, with Singer as the designer, Phelps as the operator of the machine shop, and George Zieber as the venture capitalist, offering an initial advance of $40.00.

Early Marketing Strategy

Singer drew the job of salesperson, lugging the machine to county fairs and church suppers to exhibit its many capabilities. Soon, garment manufacturers were visiting I. M. Singer and Company and placing sizable orders.

When Elias Howe, Jr., arrived at the machine shop to demand payment of $25,000 for infringement of the Howe patent, Singer decided he needed the services of an attorney and engaged Edward Clark, a junior partner in a prestigious New York City law firm, to tend to the company's legal concerns. In return for his services, Clark received an interest in the Company. While Singer channeled his energies into designing and manufacturing, Clark worked with the lawyers of competing companies to form the Sewing Machine Combination, the first patent pool in the United States, thereby putting to rest the ''sewing machine wars.'' With 24 companies licensed, the sewing machine industry was set to expand.

Clark, turning his attention to marketing, realized that although the sturdy Singer machine was selling extremely well to tailors and garment workers, it was making few inroads into the home sewing market. Moreover, many seamstresses were distrustful, due to earlier, defective models. To dispel distrust, Clark offered to pay $50 for any used machine, without regard to manufacturer, in exchange for a new Singer, thus becoming the originator of the trade-in allowance. As a result of this marketing maneuver, Singer sales tripled during 1856. Theorizing that a homemaker would feel guilty about spending $125 for a Singer sewing machine at a time when the average breadwinner was earning barely $500 a year, Clark introduced the ''Hire-Purchase Plan'' in late 1856 with terms of $5 down and $3 a month, thus pioneering installment selling and doubling Singer's sales during the ensuing year.

First Commercial Success

In order to monitor marketing activity closely, Clark decided not to emulate competitors who sold through wholesalers, jobbers, and retailers. Instead, Clark positioned his own agencies in key markets and his own sales staff in outlying districts. When the Civil War broke out, a war sales tax was levied on manufactured goods. If an article was manufactured from its own raw materials and sold directly to the consumer, the tax was paid once; however, if an article had to pass through a wholesaler and a retailer to reach the consumer, the sales tax was quintupled. Singer seized upon this opportunity to reach more consumers by accelerating the integration of its manufacturing facilities. By 1867, Singer had become almost a total maker-to-user manufacturer.

During the Civil War the value of the dollar depreciated, giving Singer an indelible demonstration of the importance of foreign

AT A GLANCE

Singer brand of sewing machines founded in 1851 in Boston, MA, by Isaac Merritt Singer; patent registered by Isaac Merritt Singer and Orson Phelps, August 12, 1851; I. M. Singer and Company founded in New York by Singer, Phelps, and George Zieber, 1851; company renamed The Singer Manufacturing Company, July 1863; sewing machine division spun off as The Singer Sewing Machine Corporation, July 5, 1986; company and its divisions acquired by International Semi-Tech Microelectronics, Inc., April 15, 1989.

Performance: *Market share*—(All 1992) 50.8% of regular sewing machine category; 38.2% of overlock sewing machine category; 48.3% of aggregate sewing machine category.

Major competitor: Kenmore; also Brother and White.

Advertising: *Major campaign*—"Singer. We make it better."

Addresses: *Parent company*—The Singer Co., Inc., 200 Metroplex Dr., Box 1909, Edison, NJ 08818-1909; phone: (908) 287-0707; fax: (908) 248-9565. *Ultimate parent company*—International Semi-Tech Microelectronics, Inc., 501 Alden Rd., P. O. Box 3009, Markham, Ontario L3R 6G4 Canada; phone: (416) 475-2670; fax: (416) 475-3652. *Ultimate ultimate parent company*—The Singer Company N.V., Chekiang First Bank Bldg., 16th Floor, 60 Gloucester Road, Wanchai, Hong Kong, China.

trade. Because foreign sales entailed no taxation, Singer's revenues from worldwide sales virtually funded production expansion and lowered manufacturing costs. By 1870, Singer sewing machines were selling for $64 each at retail, and Singer became America's most inexpensive and popular brand of sewing machine.

Advertising Innovations

To inform potential consumers of new Singer products and their advantages, Singer became a major advertiser and probably the first company to allocate $1 million a year toward this purpose. Clark became the company's copywriter, producing such print ads as the following: "Why not rent a sewing machine to the housewife and apply the rental fee to the purchase of the machine? Her husband cannot accuse her of running him into debt since he is merely hiring or renting the machine and [is] under no obligation to buy."

Although renting in essence meant buying, the ad represented an clever way of side-stepping the issue of high prices and managed to get the sewing machine into the American home. By offering the wives of teachers, clergymen, and newspaper publishers a 50 percent discount, Clark targeted "influentials" who might consider sewing a character-building activity for women and children. Seamstresses, hired and trained by Clark, demonstrated the machines in the front windows of retail stores, so that female passersby could see just how easy machine sewing could be.

Brand Development and Product Changes

During the Great Depression of the 1930s, which brought with it tighter household budgets and diminished jobs for women—and an attendant revival of home sewing—Singer manufactured new machines, including a portable electric, made of aluminum and weighing only 11 pounds. Also during this time, Singer Sewing Centers offered sewing courses for adults.

During the years following World War II, Singer faced formidable competition when Japanese and European machines, all bearing very attractive price tags, began bombarding the American market. Singer retaliated by revamping its entire product line and by overhauling its production and marketing facilities so that, by the late 1950s, the company had stabilized the foreign threat and had increased its American market share. Offering such improvements as zigzag stitching (in which the needle moves from side to side to create a more durable line of sewing), a slant needle, a pushbutton bobbin, speed basting, and an electric foot control (a vast improvement over the treadle), by the mid-1970s Singer was ready to introduce the world's first electronic sewing machine for the home, the Athena 2000. Boasting an electronic system replacing over 350 mechanical parts, the Athena 2000 empowered the user to sew any of 25 different stitches at the touch of a button.

In 1988, the bobbinless serger, an industrial model sewing machine which could be purchased for the home, showcased three- and four-thread sewing and could make flatlock seams, narrow-rolled hems, and blind hems. The Singer UltraLock Serger, retailing at $619 in 1988 and weighing only 14 pounds,

An early model of the Singer sewing machine.

featured a slotted lower looper judged very easy to thread; a threading chart on the unit regarded as easier to understand than competitors' charts; an easy unit to lubricate (with two oiling points); a one-year warranty on electrical parts; a five-year warranty on mechanical parts; and a unit capable of making a "mock" three-thread flatlock stitch.

The Singer Model #6268, available in 1990, a computer-sized model retailing at $1,749 and weighing only 24 pounds, featured a bobbin that slid in horizontally rather than vertically and was easy to access; easier threading; a foot controller which used air pressure and was connected to the machine with tubing; and less electrical wiring, providing a slight safety advantage. The machine, warranteed for 90 days, boasted a bobbin that wound in place (a convenience when sewing for a long time with the same thread); spacing (ten to 12 millimeters) between the needle tip and the presser foot (thereby mitigating chances of the finger's slipping under the needle accidentally); and a slant needle.

The Singer brand retained its commitment to innovation into the 1990s. The Singer Deluxe Debutante Model #9022, available in 1991, could sew 22 different stitches, including buttonholes, zigzag, rickrack, smocking, monogramming, embroidery, and applique. With an easy threading system, a built-in buttonholer, and horizontal thread delivery, the machine featured a free arm, a front drop-in bobbin, and an automatic bobbin-winder stop. A universal pressure system sewed all fabrics from sheer to heavy seams without adjustments; snap-on pressure feet were quick and easy to change, and an instant or sustained reverse allowed for continuous reverse stitching at the touch of a button. In addition to being sold in Singer Sewing Centers, this model was marketed in consumer electronics outlets such as New York's Trader Horn, because the machine took up relatively little floor space and attracted new customers. Sales were boosted by the recession of the 1990s, when many customers perceived sewing as economical.

International Growth

Singer began marketing its sewing machines internationally in 1853, and by 1861 the company was selling more machines in Europe than in the United States. By 1867, the company was prepared to begin manufacturing operations abroad. Since the 1863 incorporation of the firm as The Singer Sewing Company, Isaac Merritt Singer had been spending most of his time in Europe. When he died in England in 1875, the company was selling nearly as many sewing machines as all other manufacturers combined.

Singer sales staff, inspired by Clark's rhetoric and vision of "the best-known and most widely-used product in the world," lugged their machines everywhere from the Arctic Circle to Equatorial Africa, from South America to the Turkish Empire, and from old Imperial China to Russia, where, at one time, Singer sold more sewing machines than it was selling in any other country in the world, including the United States. Machines were sold to the household market and to a wide variety of businesses, including textile manufacturers, shoemakers, and bookbinderies. Machines reached markets via elephant in Thailand and dog sled in the Arctic Circle. Many salespersons were attacked by mobs, jailed during civil wars, and held hostage by bandits, and some were forced to act as mechanics, collection agents, and sewing teachers.

In Japan, early Singer salesmen encountered a formidable cultural obstacle: Japanese housewives, for centuries, had sewn kimonos loosely by hand with simple basting stitches, all of which they would remove and replace every washday. The early Singer machines, however, produced only short, tight, permanent stitches. Even though Singer met this challenge by developing a new machine that sewed a quarter-inch basting stitch, the Japanese women refused to trust the machine with kimonos. Undaunted, Singer built a sewing school in Tokyo large enough to enroll 1,000 day students and 500 boarders; this sewing school offered, for a modest tuition, a three-year course in how to sew popular Western styles. As a result, Western styles became fashionable in Japan, but the kimono remained stitched only by human hands. Learning from the Japanese experience to respect local customs, Singer thereafter was careful to dress its store mannequins in garments peculiar to the country in which it was selling sewing machines.

Sales staff were provided with instruction books, printed in more than 50 languages, plus some "wordless" books. Singer's motivation for exploring foreign markets was, in part, due to the fact that by the early 1900s, the company considered the American sewing machine market saturated. Ready-to-wear clothing had become part of the American way of life, and over the years increasing numbers of American women were taking jobs outside the home and thus had less time for sewing and other domestic chores. In fact, in 1986, The Singer Sewing Machine Corporation was spun off as a $700 million company by The Singer Company, due to falling American revenues from machines.

The Singer Sewing Machine Corporation was eventually acquired by International Semi-Tech Microelectronics, Inc., in 1989. In 1992 Singer embarked on a new manufacturing venture in Shanghai that amounted to $20 million. In cooperation with the Shanghai Yah Chong Sewing Machine Company, Singer produced multi-function zigzag machines. Since tradition dictated that Chinese women make clothes for themselves and their families, the cooperative venture led to profits for the foreign investor. Semi-Tech's goal was to produce 400,000 sewing machines by 1995.

Performance Appraisal

Since the introduction of the Singer in 1851, the brand name has been recognized for superior home sewing machines. With Clark's insightful understanding of price, perception, and promotion, Singer sewing machines rose above competitors' models to become a powerful worldwide brand in respect of home sewing.

As Singer dominated the global sewing machine market in the second half of the nineteenth century, the countries in which the brand was introduced began copying the models and then manufacturing their own versions, despite Singer's patents and to the company's great detriment. Sales of sewing machines in the United States dropped by 50 percent from 1972 to 1986, primarily because working women simply had no time to sew. In the early 1980s, rival models form Japan, South Korea, and Taiwan precipitated massive company losses. To meet the challenge, Singer set up low-cost manufacturing facilities in South America and Asia and even purchased Singer-branded machines from its major competitors. Nevertheless, Singer was unable to maintain a market share because of lower-priced models, precipitating the acquisition by the Chinese firm International Semi-Tech Microelectronics, Inc. After the announcement of the acquisition, Singer's stock price rose by 20 percent.

In 1993, many Americans still preferred Singer over other lower-priced brands. The machines were built for endurance, and, if not abused, they could last, with only minor repairs, for generations. So sturdily built were the cabinets that housed the early models that these cabinets also doubled as desks or work tables when the machines were not in use. Moreover, the Singer brand name connoted reliability, and the ubiquity of Singer Sewing Centers in urban areas guaranteed the availability of Singer sewing supplies and parts as well as knowledgeable salespeople.

Future Growth

The Singer brand name has succeeded where other machines have failed by emphasizing low prices, innovations, and aggressive marketing. This strategy should serve the brand well into the twenty-first century. Moreover, through its new parent company, International Semi-Tech Microelectronics, Inc., Singer sewing machines were certain to benefit from advanced technology.

Further Reading:

Akijama, Yoshio, "Taiwan-Made Sewing Machines Gaining Market Edge," *Business Japan,* October 1987, p. 195; "Demand Remains

High for Industrial Sewing Machines,'' *Business Japan,* December 1988, p. 45.

Bangsberg, P. T., ''Hong King Firm Hopes to Sew Up Singer Deal,'' *Journal of Commerce,* January 31, 1989, p. 1A; ''Singer Ready to Sew Big Sales in China,'' *Journal of Commerce,* August 17, 1992, p. 5A.

Cleary, David Powers, *Great American Brands,* New York: Fairchild Publications, Inc., 1981, pp. 269–79.

Commins, Kevin, ''Sewing Machine Maker Markets to the World,'' *Journal of Commerce,* June 26, 1990, p. 1A.

Davies, Robert Bruce, *Peacefully Working to Change the World: Singer Machines in Foreign Markets, 1854–1920,* Madison, Wisconsin: Arno Press, 1976.

Edmonds, Marie, ''Sewing Machines Weave into Electronics Stores,'' *HFD—The Weekly Home Furnishings Newspaper,* February 15, 1993, p. 68.

Forman, Ellen, ''Gourmet Stitching: The Sewing Industry Woos the Once-in-a-While Customer,'' *Working Woman,* November 1986, p. 79.

Gershman, Michael, *Getting It Right the Second Time,* New York: Addison-Wesley, 1990, pp. 138–145.

Kasten, Matthew, and Brian Begot, ''Worksavers Showing Up at Bobbin,'' *Daily-News Record,* September 29, 1989, p. 6.

North, Sterling, ''Singer Spins Off Its Homespun Roots for High Tech, Defense Concentration,'' *New England Business,* April 21, 1986, p. 39.

Sekiguchi, Motoi, ''Automated Sewing System Nears Completion,'' *Business Japan,* December 1988, p. 55.

''Sewing Falls While Crafts Rise,'' *Chain Store Age—General Merchandise Trends,* July 1987, p. 41.

''Tough Times for Needle and Thread,'' *Chain Store Age—General Merchandise Trends,* July 1986, p. 38.

The World's Greatest Brands, New York: John Wiley & Sons, Inc., 1991, p. 86.

Yasui, Nobuyuki, ''New Name Reflects Changing Times,'' *Business Japan,* December 1990, p. 51.

—Virginia Barnstorff

SLINKY

According to the old television commercial, "Everyone loves the Slinky." Boasting an 87 percent recognition rate among Americans, the jingle is not far from the truth. Manufactured for nearly 50 years by James Industries Inc. of Hollidaysburg, Pennsylvania, Slinky is a classic American toy. Tens of millions have been sold since the brand's introduction in 1945 and annual sales in the 1980s and 1990s were somewhere in the vicinity of two million units. Yet Slinky is the essence of simplicity: it is merely a spring—no more, no less. Many children over the past 50 years may have imbued their Slinky with lifelike qualities, but Slinky itself has remained ostentatiously plain. The unelaborate spring, made of steel or brightly colored plastic, is probably most famous for its ability to "walk" downstairs, but any child knows that its magic also lies in the organic way it moves from hand to hand or slinks across the floor. Perhaps because of its association with the 1950s baby boom generation, Slinky has become an icon of American popular culture. Among other signs of its success, the toy has been listed in pop culture catalogue advertisements in *Rolling Stone* magazine and has been displayed in the Smithsonian Institution. The physical properties of the spring have been discussed extensively in a variety of scientific journals; Slinky was even taken on the space shuttle Discovery to examine the effect of zero gravity on its ability to walk. But above all, Slinky represents the triumph of the little guy, as its manufacturer steadfastly maintains control of its star product in spite of frequent buyout offers from toy industry giants.

Brand Origins

Anyone who has played with a Slinky knows that of all toys, a Slinky is the antithesis of anything complicated. Yet two years of research and experimentation by a Philadelphia naval engineer named Richard James underlie the ingeniousness of the idea. James never set out to invent toys—the Slinky literally just sprung up at him. After Penn State awarded him a degree in mechanical engineering in 1939, James took a job with the Cramp Shipyard testing the engines of new battleships. Part of these experiments involved measuring small power increments by means of a torsion meter, used to measure the reactive force that an elastic solid—in this instance, a spring—exerts from maintaining its "twisted" structure. One day, during a routine trial of a navy vessel, a sudden lurch of the ship knocked a torsion spring off the table on which James had been working. As James watched the spring bounce back and forth on the floor it occurred to him that a child might enjoy fooling around with a spring like that. James came home that night, his wife, Betty, recalled in a 1984 *Forbes* article, handed her the spring and said "I think there might be a toy in this." He told her that given the right quality of steel and the right tension in the wire he might even be able to get the spring to "walk."

James spent two years experimenting in his spare time before arriving at the perfect tension, wire width, and diameter for his new toy. He gave his wife an important role as well. Betty James spoke about her assignment in a 1993 interview in the *Philadelphia Inquirer:* "I didn't know anything about toys. I really didn't. But he said find a name for it. So I was thinking and I couldn't think of anything. So I got the dictionary and I said, 'I'll try to find a word that depicts the slithering action of it' so that's how 'Slinky' came. It just seemed to depict everything." In 1945 "Slinky" was patented, and James had an order of 400 of the spring toys made up at a local plant. Richard and Betty James then set out to sell their stock.

Sales were very slow. As Betty commented in the same interview, "A Slinky just sitting there on a shelf isn't awfully inspiring, if you think about it. It's kind of like a blob." The Jameses knew they would have to demonstrate their product to get anyone interested, but an unknown naval engineer and his wife had very little pull among the Philadelphia retailers. Finally a reluctant manager of the Gimbel's department store agreed to let them demonstrate their toy spring on one end of a counter in the toy department. That evening was punctuated by the kind of miserable, rainy, November weather that keeps even the heartiest Philadelphians indoors. Betty and Richard agreed that he would go ahead and start the demonstration, and then she and a friend would arrive and each buy one Slinky a piece "to get some enthusiasm going." By the time Betty and her friend appeared, however, a huge crowd had already gathered in the corner where the Slinky was being exhibited. Even more importantly many were holding dollar bills, eager to purchase the novelty item. All 400 Slinkys were sold that night. Betty and her companion never even got a chance to spend their money.

Brand Development

Having confirmed the merchandise's marketability, Gimbel's ordered a shipment of their own; other retail outlets soon followed. With orders teeming, the Jameses scrambled to open a factory capable of producing enough springs to satisfy demand. Calling

AT A GLANCE

Slinky brand of spring toy founded in 1945 by Richard James, of James Industries Inc., Philadelphia, PA.

Performance: *Sales*—$10 million (estimate).

Advertising: *Agency*—Barton and Cureton, Columbia, SC, 1961—. *Major campaign*—"Everyone loves the Slinky."

Addresses: *Parent company*—James Industries Inc., Beaver Street, PO Box 407, Hollidaysburg, PA 16648; phone: (814) 695-5681; fax: (814) 695-5686.

their new single-product company James Industries, they opened a small factory in Germantown, Pennsylvania. For lack of packaging provisions, Richard would bring boxes of the Slinkys home for Betty to wrap in tissue paper. Soon Slinkys were selling in stores across the country, and the Jameses were obliged to move to a larger factory and then, in 1951, to a still larger one in Paoli, Pennsylvania.

If any single factor can account for Slinky's ongoing success story, that factor is Betty James. Though sales were still robust in the late 1950s, James Industries ran into serious difficulties; Richard had become involved with a religious sect to which he began to make large donations out of the family company's assets. Finally, after letting the business run itself into near bankruptcy, Richard ran away to Bolivia, joining a branch of his newly found religion.

Betty was left with a foundering business and six children to raise. In spite of her inexperience running the financial side of the business, Mrs. James moved the Slinky factory to Bellwood, Pennsylvania. There she could be closer to her family. Four years of hard work returned James Industries to a profitable state. As the business began growing again, Betty found her enterprise ready to expand.

The town of Hollidaysburg, Pennsylvania, where the James family was already living, offered her six acres on which to build a new plant in exchange for badly needed jobs. The deal proved to be a good one for the town's citizens. The James Industries factory has remained in the town for some 30 years, manufacturing thousands of Slinkys each day and providing work for hundreds of local workers. James Industries has acquired a number of other small toy companies since moving to Hollidaysburg, but Slinky remains the keystone of the company's success.

The Slinky itself has changed very little through the years. During the early 1960s, concern arose that the metal end of the spring might present a hazard to little fingers and eyes. To remedy this danger, the end was crimped to the second coil; otherwise, today's metal Slinky is exactly the same as the one sold at Gimbel's in 1945. A smaller "Junior" metal Slinky was added to the line in 1950, and in 1979 the plastic Slinky was introduced. Made of brightly colored polystyrene, the newest addition to the family has a larger diameter and is felt to be appropriate for younger children, but Slinky purists note that it lacks the distinctive sound and feel of the original. The plastic Slinky is also now used in Slinky Pull Toys, plastic creatures with Slinkys for bodies, the idea for which came from an independent inventor.

Advertising

Like everything else about Slinky toys, the key to their advertising has been continuity and consistency. Thomas Cureton of the Barton and Cureton agency has handled Slinky ads since 1961, running a continuous series of television commercials. With the exception of a brief foray into animation in the 1960s, the Slinky ads have featured a real Slinky in action, walking down stairs, slinking from hand to hand, in short, performing like a Slinky. The jingle accompanying the commercials ("Everyone loves the Slinky. You ought to have a Slinky.") has been singing the same tune for more than 30 years. This continuity, surprising in the faddish toy industry, has been a deliberate campaign on the part of James Industries to maintain their toy as a "classic," played with by parents and grandparents and now bought for children and grandchildren.

Performance and Competition

Indeed Slinky moved quickly from a popular new toy to a fad, and from a fad to a staple. It is the amazing staying power of Slinky that surprises even Betty James herself. "Every year I think, *this* will be the last—and then it has another cycle. By now, I guess it's here to stay," Mrs. James concluded in a 1987 *Inc.* report. Slinky is one of the very rare breeds of toy that perpetually remains a novelty item. James Industries does not release sales figures, but analysts have estimated annual Slinky sales of nearly 2 million per year for at least the past ten years. Bob Lestochi, secretary-comptroller of James Industries for the past 33 years, admits that Slinky does have its ups and downs, but the overall pattern has been one of increasing sales. Lestochi specifies that Slinky sales are inversely tied to the state of the economy—when times are bad Slinky sales go up.

Slinky's consistently low price has a great deal to do with its increased popularity during periods of economic downturn. Sold for one dollar in 1945, some half century later, in 1994, the retail price finally reached a whopping two dollars. The consumer price index in the same period has risen by more than six times that, meaning with inflation, the price of Slinky has actually dropped approximately two-thirds. Bob Lestochi feels that several factors have contributed to the remarkably stable price. First and foremost has been the product's low mark-up. In an industry known for very high promotion and development costs, and correspondingly high production-to-shelf mark-ups, James Industries has managed to keep costs down. For example, James Industries has no research and development department. Any new products are derived from acquisitions rather than internal development. Management expenditures have also been controlled through very low management to worker ratios. Currently 100 manufacturing employees work around the clock producing Slinkys; in contrast, the management and clerical staff numbers only seven, including company president Betty James.

James Industries' ability to hold the price down has meant not only that sales have remained vigorous, but also that imitators have been given little incentive to copy the popular toy. Copy-cat products—a toy industry plague—normally piggy-back on the original's reputation and promotion and then garner sales by charging a lower price. Imitators have had little room to maneuver around James Industries' mark-up on Slinkys. Some "spring toy" Slinky clones have appeared now and then over the years, but none has managed to damage Slinky's market share.

While the American market constitutes the bulk of Slinky's sales, the toy is also distributed around the world through Century Merchandising in New York. Canadian manufacturing and distribution is licensed to Irwin Toys of Toronto, Canada.

50 years of popularity is a remarkable achievement in a market noted for extremely fickle consumers. At least in part, the Slinky's simple elegance underlies it's phenomenally consistent market value. Slinky's unique combination of nature and mechanics intrigues everyone who's had one. Priced at a mere two dollars, a replacement doesn't require much sacrifice. Slinky's success can also be attributed to the dedication of Betty James and her associates, who have steadfastly refused the proposed deals from giant toy firms. In an industry characterized by centralization and consolidation, James Industries stands out as one of the few small, independent toy manufacturers.

At 75 Mrs. James still manages the company and is in her office every day. She says she will continue to do so as long as she is able. Her eldest son, Tom James, is the sale manager for the company and is the only one of the six children to work at the toy factory.

Further Reading:

Brown, Paul B., "Staying Power," *Forbes,* March 26, 1984, pp. 186, 188.

Cunningham, W. J., "Slinky the Tumbling Spring," *American Scientist,* May/June 1987, pp. 289–90.

Laskas, Jeanne Marie, "This Immortal Coil," *The Philadelphia Inquirer Magazine,* July 11, 1993, pp. 18–20, 32–36.

Mamis, Robert A., "Gross National Products," *Inc.,* April 1987, pp. 46, 48.

Rose, Matthew, "Kitchen Table Startups: Gumby Goes Catalog," *Direct Marketing,* May 1987, pp. 52–56.

—*Hilary Gopnik*

SMITH CORONA®

Smith Corona Corp. is a business machine manufacturer with a record of innovation that is virtually synonymous with the development of the modern typewriter. In 1886 two brothers, Wilbert and Lyman Smith, produced the first typewriter with upper- and lowercase letters, which proved a huge improvement over previous, unwieldy models. In 1916 the siblings helped produce the first commercially successful portable.

Today Smith Corona designs, manufactures, and sells portable and compact electronic typewriters, personal word processors, electronic reference products, related accessories, and customized printed products. The company has a 50 percent share of the U.S. typewriting and word processing market.

Brand Origins

The Smith Corona brand typewriter started out as the Smith typewriter in Syracuse, New York. In the mid-1880s Alexander Brown, an engineer at the L.C. Smith Shotgun Company, asked his employers, Wilbert and Lyman Smith, if they would like to produce a typewriter he had designed. Typewriters were becoming more popular but were hard to use. The first manual was actually patented in 1714. Its inventor, Henry Mill, described it as a device for "impressing letters on paper one after another as in writing."

The Smith brothers' first model, the Smith Premier, produced in 1886, featured two separate keyboards, one each for capital and small letters. The model was a huge success. The Smiths gave up guns in favor of typewriters.

By 1890 the typewriter was no longer considered a novelty. In 1893 the Smiths got together with six other manufacturers to form the Union Typewriter Co., a loose association of leading typewriter manufacturers, including Remington and Monarch. Indeed, there was a great need for manufacturers to join forces—there were 30 different manufacturers and just as many typewriter designs and notions about where the letters should be on the keyboard.

Early typewriters had a big disadvantage: the typists could not see what they were typing. A new model introduced at the turn of the century that allowed the typist to see what was being typed caused disagreement among the members of the Union Typewriter Company. The Smith brothers wanted to construct a similar machine, but the rest of the group did not want to go along. This issue resulted in the Smiths leaving Union Typewriter and joining with two more of their brothers, Hurlbut and Monroe, to found yet another company. In 1903, the Smith brothers embarked on a mission to manufacture the new machine. Their new company was called L.C. Smith & Brothers Typewriter Company. Carl Gabrielson, a Swedish designer, designed the Smiths' visible writing model. It went on the market in 1904.

The new L.C. Smith & Bros. typewriter had a segment shift for capital letters, an interchangeable platen (roller), a built-in tabulator, a two-color ribbon, and ball bearings. The new features became standard throughout the industry. As demand grew, the Smith brothers doubled the size of their plant.

Meanwhile, Benn Conger, a state assemblyman from Groton, New York, and C. F. Brown, a mechanical engineer from Troy, New York, bought the rights to a "folding" visible writing typewriter. It was to become the first really portable typewriter. Conger and Brown formed a new company, the Standard Typewriter Company, and in 1909 they produced their first typewriter. The six-pound machine cost $50 including the carrying case. The carriage could be folded over the keyboard when not in use. After manufacturing another model called the Corona, in 1914 Conger and Brown changed the name of their company to the Corona Typewriter Company. Corona's sales kept growing. The plant was enlarged, and in 1919 the company built a new plant in Cortland, New York.

The move placed the Corona plant near the L.C. Smith plant in upstate New York. The products of the two companies were complementary: Smith made office machines, and Corona made portables. In 1926 Smith & Bros. merged with the Corona Typewriter Company of New York City, linking names and futures. The new corporation had almost 3,000 employees. Business improved after the merger, and the corporation constructed a factory in Toronto in 1929 and moved its headquarters to New York City. Then the stock market crashed. Sales took a dive. By 1932 sales had dropped by two-thirds. To save money, company headquarters were moved back to Syracuse. Business picked up in 1934 after the introduction of Smith Corona's Sterling portable and Super Speed office model. To compete with lightweight foreign machines, Smith Corona introduced the Zephyr in 1938.

War in Europe helped America's typewriter industry. By late 1940, production rocketed to 130,000 typewriters. But when

AT A GLANCE

Smith Corona traces its origins back to Syracuse, NY, in the mid-1880s when two brothers, Wilbert and Lyman Smith, produced their first typewriter. They formed the Union Typewriter Company in 1893 and then, in 1903, formed L.C. Smith & Brothers Typewriter Company In 1926 this company merged with the Corona Typewriter Company. In 1960, Smith Corona Corp. was absorbed by the SCM Corporation. In 1986, Hanson PLC acquired SCM. In 1989, Hanson sold 52 percent of Smith Corona to the public.

Performance: *Market share*—50% of the domestic typewriter and personal word processing market. *Sales*—$309.1 million (1993).

Major competitor: Brother; also Sharp and Panasonic.

Advertising: *Agency*—Rosenfeld, Sirowitz, Humphrey & Strauss, New York, NY. *Major campaign*—"Technology at Your Touch."

Addresses: *Parent company*—Smith Corona Corp., 65 Locust Ave., New Canaan, CT 06840; phone: (203) 972-1471.

America entered the war, production fell again, and the company's factories were used to produce war materials, such as coding and decoding machines, as directed by the War Production Board. After the war, production resumed its prewar levels. Corona "Super 5" portables were introduced in 1949 and soon became the market standard. In 1955 the company produced the first Smith Corona electric office typewriter.

The record of innovation continued. The company introduced the first electric portable typewriter in 1957—the only electric portable available for the next ten years. With the addition of a power carriage in 1960, the portable had all the features of an office typewriter. The first cartridge correction system was developed in 1973, making it possible to change a typewriter ribbon in three minutes. In 1985 the company produced the first electric dictionary for portable typewriters and word processors. Grammar correction systems followed, and in 1989 the company marketed the first laptop personal word processor.

Smith Corona began to diversify its product line in the late 1950s. It purchased Kleinschmidt Laboratories, a company that produced high-speed telecommunications equipment for military and commercial use. In 1958 Smith Corona merged with the Marchant Calculator Company and purchased British Typewriters Ltd. of West Bromwich, England. The English firm was given the job of producing lightweight portables for the European market.

Smith Corona itself was acquired in 1986. Despite the fierce objections of SCM Corporation, by then Smith Corona's parent company, Hanson Industries, the American subsidiary of Hanson PLC, one of Britain's biggest companies, acquired SCM, and Smith Corona was part of the deal. Hanson Industries' chief executive officer was Sir Gordon White, a man known for his penchant for corporate takeovers. Three years after acquiring SCM, he spun off Smith Corona, retaining for Hanson Industries 47.9 percent of the firm's shares and selling the balance on the New York Stock Exchange.

Smith Corona vs. Brother

The 1980s saw a big push for research and redevelopment at Smith Corona and yielded a whole new generation of home and electronic products. But other companies had also been competing for a piece of the American typewriter market. In 1974, Smith Corona filed charges that Brother Industries, Ltd., was "dumping" portable typewriters in the United States.

Citing the Antidumping Act of 1921, Smith Corona filed the first of many complaints with the federal government asserting that Brother Industries was engaging in unfair trade practices and thus hurting Smith Corona's profits. As a result, five years later the United States set an import fee on Brother's typewriters designed to deter Brother from shipping low-cost portables. Nevertheless, Brother's typewriter and word processor sales continued to grow. Smith Corona obtained additional import duties.

The skirmishes between the two companies continued through the 1980s. "Dozens of Washington lawyers earned a good living throughout the 1980s doing little else but filing dumping complaints against Brother and seeking modifications of old anti-dumping orders," wrote Robert B. Reich in the *New Republic.* But Hanson's purchase of Smith Corona changed the terms of the debate. Hanson shifted most of Smith Corona's manufacturing operations to Singapore. Over a million typewriters have been shipped annually to the United States from Singapore ever since. Smith Corona blamed its move to Singapore on Japanese price cutting.

In 1992 Smith Corona transferred operations from its Cortland plant, the last of its American factories, to Mexico. Around the time Smith Corona opened a plant in China, Brother ceased importing its portable typewriters from Japan. Instead, Brother Industries, Ltd. opened a new, American subsidiary, Brother Industries U.S.A., a $13 million typewriter factory in Bartlett, Tennessee. The plant employs roughly 450 Americans and produces 600,000 typewriters a year. Brother claimed that Smith Corona's anti-dumping penalties had forced it to open the American factory. In 1991 Brother charged Smith Corona with dumping Chinese-made automatic and portable typewriters on the American market for as little as $99 each.

In September of 1993 Brother won its anti-dumping case against Smith Corona. The United States International Trade Commission found that Brother Industries U.S.A. had been injured by the cheap Smith Corona imports and that if changes were not made, anti-dumping duties might be levied on Smith Corona's imports. The Department of Commerce had ruled in 1991 that Brother was *not* a U.S. producer and had dropped the case, but the department reopened the issue in 1992 after it was overruled by the U.S. Court of International Trade, which found Brother a U.S. concern. Smith Corona agreed to negotiate with Brother Industries U.S.A. to resolve the trade issues.

Future Predictions

Electric typewriter sales have slackened in recent years—net sales dipped dramatically between 1989 and 1991. Nevertheless, Smith Corona was sounding upbeat and predicted a rebound in 1992. In its annual report for fiscal 1993, Smith Corona acknowledged a net loss of $9 million on net sales of $309.1 million. The previous year, the company had reported a net income of $221 million on net sales of $371.7 million. G. Lee Thompson, Smith Corona's chairman and chief executive officer, ascribed much of the loss to pretax charges associated with relocating manufacturing operations to Mexico. A sluggish domestic economic recovery and a severe international recessionary climate reduced consumer spending in the company's product categories in fiscal 1993, Thompson asserted. He also noted that Smith Corona had been subject to intense price competition. After the Mexican plant becomes fully operational, he said, the company expects an annual pretax savings of approximately $15 million, although in 1994 the company will still be selling products that reflect the higher manufacturing costs incurred in Cortland, New York.

To improve sales, Smith Corona is developing a direct sales organization in Europe. It is also broadening product offerings to take advantage of the company's strong distribution and brand recognition, including launching a new line of compatible ribbons for dot matrix printers and competing brands of typewriters and personal word processors. In 1993 the company announced the inauguration of a new line of laminators, which permanently preserve and protect a variety of materials. Relocating the manufacturing plant, developing new product categories, and developing its international market, chairman Thompson believes, will improve the company's fiscal performance in the coming years.

Further Reading:

''A Brief History: The Typewriter and Smith Corona'' (promotional brochure), New Canaan, CT: Smith Corona Corp.

''Corona's Move,'' *New York Times,* May 28, 1993.

Everybody's Business, New York: Currency, 1991.

Hoover's Handbook, Austin: Reference Press, 1991.

McConville, James A., ''Smith Corona Sees Rebound in 1992 Despite Electronic Typewriter Climate,'' *Home Furnishings Weekly,* November 11, 1991, p. 80.

Reich, Robert B., ''Dumpsters,'' *New Republic,* June 10, 1991, pp. 10–11.

''Ruling in Typewriter Case,'' *New York Times,* September 21, 1993, pp. C18, D20.

''Smith Corona Moving Plant to Mexico,'' *Home Furnishings Weekly,* July 27, 1992, p. 2.

—Margo Nash

SNAPPER®

Snapper Power Equipment has been providing American homeowners with premium quality lawn care equipment since 1950, when it introduced its first walk-behind lawn mower. Snapper is best known for its rear-engine riding mowers; it has sold more of this model of mower than any manufacturer in the industry. Snapper also holds significant market share in the premium quality walk-behind mower segment and competes in the lawn and garden tractor and snow removal markets. The brand experienced over 30 years of nearly continuous growth until an industry recession forced changes in production, design, and marketing. Reconfigured to compete in the 1990s, the Snapper brand stands for quality and performance, qualities highlighted by its promotional slogan, "Anything Less Just Won't Cut It."

Opportunity Knocks

Snapper brand lawn and garden equipment traces its origins to the Southern Saw Works, which was founded in 1890 in East Point, Georgia, to manufacture circular saws for the booming lumber industry of the southeastern United States. Nearly 60 years later, as the saw business declined, the Southern Saw Works looked for a business opportunity that could provide future growth. Though the company's managers knew little about manufacturing lawn mowers, they recognized that the post-World War II boom in suburban housing was creating many new lawns to be mowed. In 1949 they entered the power lawn mower industry and on June 25, 1950, acquired the patents for the "Snappin' Turtle" mowers, then built in Montverde, Florida.

In January of 1951 the Southern Saw Works shipped 16 of its Snappin' Turtle mowers, the first of 3,975 mowers it produced in its first year. The company then employed 11 people working out of a 4,000-square-foot building. By 1954, demand for mowers had grown so steadily that the Southern Saw Works got out of the saw-making business and looked for a potential merger to expand its production facilities. That year they merged with the McDonough Foundry and Machine Company, a McDonough, Georgia, firm that had been making iron castings and textile machinery since 1946. Renamed McDonough Power Equipment, Inc., the company completed construction of its facilities in September of 1956, and manufactured both lawns mowers and textile machinery.

In the early 1960s, McDonough Power Equipment introduced the Snapper Comet, a riding mower with a rear-mounted engine that allowed the operator excellent visibility. Demand for the new product—the first rear-engine riding mower on the market—soon convinced McDonough to dedicate its operations to lawn equipment and expand its manufacturing facilities. The remarkable success of Snapper mowers made McDonough an attractive acquisition, and the company became of subsidiary of Fuqua Industries, Inc., of Atlanta, Georgia, in the fall of 1967. Fuqua, which also manufactured sporting goods, photographic film, and public seating, had a reputation for developing recognizable consumer brands and would provide the backing for years of success for the Snapper brand.

Continuous Growth

Throughout the 1970s Snapper succeeded by producing high-quality rear-engine riding mowers and walk-behind mowers. Consumer demand for Snapper products soon outstripped the production capabilities of the McDonough, Georgia, plant, and in 1975 the company began construction of a new, state-of-the-art manufacturing facility in Forth Worth, Texas. The new facilities gave Snapper over 800,000 square feet of plant space. By 1979, in recognition of the importance of lawn equipment, Fuqua Industries had made McDonough Power Equipment a division of the larger company. Three years later, in 1982, the division was renamed Snapper Power Equipment "to better reflect and associate with the Snapper brand name which had over the years become a household word," according to company documents.

The Snapper brand proved to be a major income producer for Fuqua Industries, accounting for as much as 26 percent of Fuqua's sales and 49 percent of total operating profits in 1983, when the division had sales of $189.9 million. Between 1975, when it expanded production facilities, and 1982, the brand's sales increased at an annual rate of 17 percent, significantly higher than the 6 percent rate for the lawn and garden industry as a whole. With a decade of steadily increasing sales, solid corporate backing, and a strong brand image, Snapper was poised for phenomenal growth in the 1980s.

Snapper Booms

Snapper experienced tremendous growth in the years between 1982 and 1987, both in sales and in the number of products bearing the Snapper brand name. Snapper's sales went from $156.5 million in 1982 to $288 million in 1987, growing almost twice as fast as the industry as a whole. In 1982 Snapper intro-

AT A GLANCE

Snapper brand lawn and garden equipment traces its origins to the Snappin' Turtle walk-behind mower, introduced in 1951 by Southern Saw Works, founded 1890; company changed its name to McDonough Power Equipment, Inc., 1954; Snapper Comet rear-engine riding mower introduced in the early 1960s; McDonough Power Equipment becomes part of Fuqua Industries, Inc., 1968; McDonough Power changed its name to Snapper Power Equipment, 1982; Fuqua Industries, Inc., changed its name to Actava Group; Snapper introduced Ninja mulching technology, 1993.

Performance: *Market share*—10% of walk-behind mower sales; 9% of riding mower sales; 20% of gas snowthrower sales (1992; according to *Appliance Manufacturer.*) *Sales*—$225 million (1993; according to *Appliance Manufacturer*).

Major competitor: Toro, Lawn-Boy, and John Deere.

Advertising: *Agency*—In-house. *Major campaign*—"Snapper: Anything Less Just Won't Cut It."

Addresses: *Parent company*—Snapper Power Equipment, P.O. Box 777, McDonough, GA 30253; phone: (404) 957-9141. *Ultimate parent company*—Actava Group, 4900 Georgia Pacific Center, Atlanta, GA 30303; phone: (404) 658-9000.

duced its new Lawn Tractor, thus rounding out its product line to compete with industry leaders Toro and John Deere. According to company documents, Snapper introduced more products in 1983 than in any year to date, including more lawn tractors, rear tine tillers, and a lightweight snowthrower. In 1985 Snapper added the Snapper String Trimmer, the Blo-N-Vac leaf blower, two electric lawn mowers, and the Pak-N-Sak grass catcher. Snapper's McDonough manufacturing plant churned out a mower every 52 seconds to keep up with demand. In 1987 Snapper sought to transfer its success in the consumer market to commercial applications when it purchased the F. D. Kees Manufacturing Company, a manufacturer of commercial lawn care equipment.

Snapper attributes much of its success in marketing the rapidly growing number of products to its established distribution network. In 1987 Snapper sold its products exclusively to 130 independent distributors in 30 countries who in turn sold to nearly 12,000 authorized dealers. The dealers are provided with training in service and maintenance by Snapper and engage in cooperative marketing arrangements with Snapper, in which the company pays for half of advertising and promotion. In addition to funding local promotions, Snapper spends more than any other lawn equipment manufacturer on television and radio advertising. Snapper doubled its advertising expenditures every year between 1981 and 1986 as it attempted to establish a strong brand identity.

Surviving a Drought

In the summer of 1988, the United States experienced a nearly nationwide drought, and lawn mower sales dried up with American lawns. Declining demand caused by dry weather was exacerbated by the first signs of an economic recession, forcing lawn mower manufacturers to compete for a shrinking sales base. For the first time, manufacturers of high-quality lawn equipment had to compete with lower-priced products sold at mass merchandisers like Wal-Mart, Home Depot, and K-Mart. For Snapper and its competitors, the recession meant surplus inventories and upset distributors. Snapper had failed to react quickly to the decline in sales and was beset by particularly high inventories. As a result, net sales fell 34 percent in two years, from $288 million in 1987 to $191 million in 1989, according to *Adweek Southeast Edition.* During that same period, profits dropped 96 percent, from $59 million to $2.3 million.

Industry sources claimed that Snapper's troubles were due to more than bad weather and increased inventories. "Snapper was the industry leader 15 years ago when it came out with a rear-engine rider," one source told *Adweek Southeast Edition,* "but it hasn't adjusted to the times and hasn't made its equipment more user friendly. They're still good performers, but when you've got companies like Murray and [John] Deere updating each year, it makes Snapper look more out of date."

Snapper's distributors also complained that they were being ill-served by Snapper's advertising strategies. Prior to 1989, distributors had controlled their own promotional efforts, either by hiring their own agencies or using the free service of Snapper's in-house agency, Henco. In return, Snapper matched distributor spending. This arrangement changed in January of 1989, when Snapper hired the J. Walter Thompson agency to handle television, creative, and media buying and asked distributors to contribute a percentage of their profits. Distributors immediately criticized the new arrangement, feeling that they could make better deals on their own and that the national advertising did not suit their local promotional needs. "My area didn't get the coverage it had before," one distributor told *Adweek Southeast Edition;* another added, "They had nice commercials, but they were not effective for my purposes." Snapper dropped J. Walter Thompson on October 15, 1990.

Resurgence

In 1989, in the midst of the worst year in company history, Snapper took steps to reinvent itself for the 1990s. Richard Robinson was named chief executive officer, after which time the company introduced a series of changes designed to bring the company back to profitability. The first step was to correct inventory imbalances. To this end, Snapper cut production and increased promotions to move existing inventory. Snapper also consolidated its manufacturing facilities at its plant in McDonough, a move that was expected to generate annual cost savings of up to $10 million after 1991. Finally, Snapper redesigned and streamlined its product line and mended its relationship with distributors. By 1992, after Robinson was no longer with the company, Snapper posted an operating profit of $17.8 million, reversing the previous year's losses of $50.6 million.

Snapper dealers had good reason to be satisfied with the changes in promotions, which returned much of the control they had lost when Snapper had hired J. Walter Thompson. Under Snapper's new arrangement with the West & Co. agency of Tampa, Florida, the ad agency was responsible for creating advertisements, but dealers retained the freedom to customize their promotional efforts for their particular areas. "West is going to have to earn [the dealers'] trust," one Snapper source told *Adweek Southeast Edition.* "If [the agency] can do that, it'll get some of that media money," which was estimated at $10 to $15 million. Snapper vice-president of marketing Doug Grote told the magazine that West provided "a perfect fit with our overall marketing objective and the sales goals of our dealer network."

In its first advertising campaign, which included four television commercials, 12 radio spots, and newspaper ads, West emphasized the emotional attachment people make with their lawn mower. The ads featured actor Kelsey Grammer, who played pompous psychiatrist Frasier Crane on the popular television series *Cheers*. "I'm often asked about the relative health of investing one's ego into one's yard," Grammer advised in a radio spot. "Invariably I say, 'Look here, good fellow. I'm ok, you're ok and loving your yard's ok. Of course, it is easier when you have a Snapper." Dealers responded favorably to the ads, which were created in response to a survey that showed that consumers had a difficult time differentiating between premium lawn mower brands.

Styling, Performance, and Technology

Snapper's 1994 product line showed the results of renewed emphasis on styling, performance, and technology. Snapper markets two complete lines of walk-behind mowers, the Hi-Vac series and the JetVac series, both promoted for their ability to vacuum up lawn debris, including clippings, leaves, and pine needles, while mowing. The JetVac series, with a deep cast-aluminum chamber and an extra-large discharge opening, is designed especially for mowing in wet conditions or when grass is particularly heavy, and mows with great speed in normal conditions. All but one of the Snapper walk-behind mowers are capable of discharging clippings to the side, bagging clippings with the Kwik-N-Ezy bag kit, or mulching with the patented Ninja mulching system.

Snapper was late in introducing mulching technology for its mowers, but it claims that its Ninja mulching system is the best one available. Mulching mowers work by circulating grass clippings in the sealed cutting chamber where they are cut into fine pieces before they fall to the turf. These clippings provide a biodegradable mulch that is known to enhance the health and beauty of lawns. Snapper's claim to mulching superiority rests on the design of its Ninja blade, which has two cutting surfaces on either end of its blade. The leading blade surface cuts the grass and, with the help of a curved lip, lifts the grass into the path of the trailing blade, which recuts the grass and sends it up into the mowing chamber, where it falls down to be cut again. The "powder-like" mulch then filters down into the turf. Snapper's brochures promote the Ninja by showing the difference in the size of clippings created by it and the "leading competitor's mulching blade." Snapper's April 1993 press release for the Ninja called it "a powerful new tool that promises to revolutionize the way hundreds of thousands of environmentally conscious Americans mow their lawns."

Snapper, which has sold more rear-engine riding mowers than any other manufacturer, continues to market a complete line of dedicated riding mowers. Nine different mowers offer the consumer a range of power from 8- to 16-horsepower, and cutting decks from 25 to 42 inches wide. Each of the mowers is equipped with Snapper's disc power transfer, which avoids the complication of gear boxes and allows for shifting on the go. Most of the rear-engine riders can be equipped with the Ninja mulching system, the Thatcherizer attachment, and a dozer blade for snow removal.

Snapper's line of lawn tractors comes with available power from 12- to 18-horsepower and cutting widths from 30 to 48 inches, with Ninja capability on all but the largest mowing decks. The tractors, which are designed for year-round use, can be fitted with a number of attachments, including a 2-stage snowthrower and a 5-horsepower tiller. In addition to the mowing equipment, Snapper also manufactures nine models of snowthrowers and three models of rear tine tillers. Also available at Snapper dealers are a line of lawn and garden fertilizers. Snapper manufactures its products out of its 900,000-square-feet facilities in McDonough, Georgia, where it employs over 1,200 people.

Fit for the Future

Snapper's entire line of products underwent a facelift in the early 1990s, and the new models looked decidedly modern. The walk-behind models sported swept-back discharge tubes and sleek styling, and the JetVac featured mag-style wheels. The lawn tractors had radically sloped hoods that tapered down to automotive-style headlamps. The television ads for Snapper products boasted of the products' performance, highlighting power, handling, and style. One ad claimed that "a Snapper tractor is like a sports car for your lawn." Snapper's 1994 ads also promoted the products' ease of use, showing women and elderly people talking about how much they enjoy caring for their lawn now that they own a Snapper. The brand's slogan emphasized the high quality of Snapper mowers: "Snapper: Anything Less Just Won't Cut It." Snapper severed its ties with its advertising agency, West & Co., late in 1993.

Snapper began to experience the results of its restructuring and redesign efforts in 1992, when the company posted $248.2 million in sales (nearly $90 million more than 1991) and $17.8 million in profits, and again in 1993, when sales stood at $225 million. In 1992 Snapper maintained a 9 percent share of the U.S. riding mower market (tied for fourth overall and tied for second among premium mower manufacturers), a 10 percent share of the walk-behind mower market (fifth overall and second among premium manufacturers), and a 20 percent share of the gas snowthrower market (tied for second). With a new president and chief executive officer, Jerry J. Schweiner, named in August, 1993, and a new corporate name, Actava Group, Snapper showed every sign of continuing the success that has made it a major player in the U.S. lawn and garden market for over 40 years.

Further Reading:

Fuqua Industries, Inc., *Annual Report,* Atlanta, GA: Fuqua Industries, 1982–1992.

"Market Share," *Appliance Manufacturer,* February 1993, p. 24.

Minardi, Diana, *Adweek Southeast Edition,* "JWT Loses $5-Mil. Snapper Biz," October 15, 1990, p. 1; "A Dry Season for Snapper Power," October 22, 1990, p. 4; "I'm OK, and So Is My Lawn Mower: Snapper Ads Play Up Love Affair with Lawns," April 1, 1991, p. 4.

Osterman, Jim, "Snapper Anchors West's Atlanta Office," *Adweek Southeast Edition,* December 10, 1990, p. 1.

"West Advertising Agency Wins $14 Million Snapper Account," *Tampa Tribune* (Florida), December 8, 1990, p. D1.

Additional information provided by Snapper Power Equipment.

—Tom Pendergast

SONY®

SONY.

The Sony brand, owned by Sony Corporation, is perhaps the world's best-known name in consumer electronics. Sony products can be found in every country in the world, a feat of market dominance achieved in very short time through product quality, competitive pricing, and a talent for anticipating consumer demand. As a result of the company's innovations, Sony is the largest-selling brand of electronics goods in the world, and the Sony name is one of the most respected and valuable trademarks on the market.

Brand Origins

While the Sony brand name emerged in the mid-1950s, its manufacturer's origins date back to 1946, when founder Akio Morita and his partner Masaru Ibuka began manufacturing rice cookers. Spurned from the home appliance market, Morita received a $500 investment from his father, a soy sauce magnate, and began work on a tape recorder.

Morita and Ibuka used an old U.S. Army manual entitled *Nine Hundred and Ninety Nine Uses for the Tape Recorder* as the basis for their first product brochure. The first large order for their tape recorder came from the Tokyo Academy of Art. Shortly after filling the order, however, Morita received a scathing letter from an opera singer at the Academy named Norio Ohga, who criticized the quality of the machine in such precise and instructive terms that Morita was compelled to invite Ohga to meet with the company's engineers. The small company, called Tokyo Tsushin Kogyo (TTK), subsequently turned out a vastly improved machine.

In 1952, Masaru Ibuka read about the invention of the transistor by Bell Labs. Knowing the new device could replace vacuum tubes, Ibuka purchased a manufacturing license with the intention of developing a tiny radio. The first production runs on the radio began in 1954.

Searching for a catchy, internationally marketable name for the product, Morita referred to the Latin language, which he knew to be the basis of all Western languages. He settled on the word *sonus,* meaning sound, which he combined with something a bit more cute, ''sunny,'' producing the word Sony.

Early Marketing Strategy

First, Morita needed a means for introducing the Sony radio to the market. While he had little difficulty gaining access to domestic distribution channels, international sales—from which Morita felt the company could generate the greatest profit—proved more challenging. In this arena, he was compelled to use one of Japan's dozen or so *zaibatsu* conglomerates. However, such companies, including Mitsubishi, Fuji, and Mitsui, among others, dictated terms that would have replaced the Sony brand name with one of their own or demanded too much money for shipping his product.

Morita traveled to the United States, where, he believed, personal disposable incomes were greatest. He made a sales pitch to several large retail firms, but gained interest from only one, Bulova. Asked to quote a unit price for 100,000 Sony radios, Morita constructed an unusual table that showed the price per unit dropping until 40,000 radios. After that, the unit price rose, until the 100,000th radio was nearly as expensive as the first.

Baffled by the schedule, Bulova management asked Morita to explain how price could possibly rise with volume. Morita responded that his factory had an annual production capacity of only 40,000 radios. For orders in excess of this number, he had to include expansion costs in the unit price. However, the sale fell through when Morita was told that the radios would have to carry the Bulova name.

Having failed to sell the product on this trip, Morita appointed American distributor Delmonico International. This company purchased the Sony radio in more manageable quantities and handled all distribution and promotion in America. The arrangement ensured that the radio could be sold under the Sony name and allowed TTK to avoid manufacturing goods under another company's name.

In 1958, with Sony established as a modest but successful international brand, Morita and Ibuka adopted the name for their company. They also decided to economize promotional costs of future products by branding them with the Sony name. The large number of people who were favorably impressed with the Sony radio, they reasoned, would be more inclined to purchase another product carrying the Sony name.

AT A GLANCE

Sony brand of electronics founded in 1958 by Akio Morita and Masaru Ibuka; Sony Corporation of America established in 1960; acquired CBS Records, 1988, and Columbia Pictures, 1989.

Performance: *Sales*—$34.4 billion.

Major competitor: RCA; also Philips and Matsushita's brands of electronics, including Panasonic and Quasar.

Advertising: *Agency*—Leo Burnett, Chicago, 1990—. *Major campaign*—"It's a Sony"; "She got the House, I got the Sony"; "It's Your Life, Isn't it Worth a Sony?"

Addresses: *Parent company*—Sony Corporation, 6-7-35, Kita Shinagawa, Shinagawa-ku, Tokyo 141, Japan; phone: (03) 448-2111.

Brand Development

Sony developed a transistorized black-and-white television set in 1959, and began marketing the product a year later. Due to its compact circuitry, the set was smaller than the models then common in America. It was, however, one of the first models on the market in Japan. While the tiny TV was extremely simple and delivered only a fair reproduction of a signal, it entered a market nearly saturated by American manufacturers of standard living room televisions. Someone wanting a smaller TV for the kitchen, bedroom, or basement opted for a product almost entirely different from that produced by Zenith, Admiral, and RCA.

Sony's modest start in the American television market was extremely important in two ways. First, it established the brand name in the same showrooms as larger sets made by established companies. Second, it provided a steady source of income for company research and new product development.

Sony emerged from its niche in 1965, when a wider line of televisions, including models with larger screens, were introduced. This enabled Sony to build a more upscale image, leaving behind its reputation as an inexpensive Japanese knock-off brand.

During this time, the company expanded its production facilities and distribution channels. With the ability to turn out larger quantities of products, unit costs were driven down. Thus Sony was able to improve the quality of its televisions to better compete with American brands, while still realizing a healthy profit margin. Also during this time, however, market forecasts indicated that sales of black-and-white television sets would slowly stagnate. The fastest growing segment of the market was color models, and it was here that Sony saw its future.

Sony developed a completely unique color system that used one electron gun, rather than three, to project a full spectrum of color. As a result, the system produced a clearer picture by eliminating the need for focus. The system, called "Trinitron," was nothing short of a revolution in television. The company spent large amounts on its development and was forced to gamble even more money simply to bring it to market. But Morita was confident that the Trinitron would sell itself and further boost Sony's reputation into that of a premium manufacturer.

International Growth

In 1960, the same year it entered the TV market, Sony terminated its distribution arrangement with Delmonico International. For greater control over the marketing of Sony products, the Sony Corporation of America was established and gained a listing on the New York Stock Exchange. Sony also established trade offices in Geneva and London. These three offices coordinated the local distribution, advertising, and promotion of Sony products.

The company encountered higher trade restrictions in Europe than in America, primarily because of protectionist legislation and more favorable trade opportunities for companies within the common market. The easiest way around these restrictions would have been to establish a manufacturing facility within the EEC. But there remained restrictions on profit repatriation that destroyed the economic basis for such a move. By contrast, the American market was wide open. There were few, if any, restrictions on what Sony could sell in America, or how much it could charge. The company established a factory at San Diego in 1972, and in Wales in 1974.

Sony avoided culpability in so-called "dumping charges" largely because it operated in the premium sector of the market. Competitors such as Matsushita were routinely challenged for dumping as they tried to recoup economies on huge sales volume. By commodity pricing, Matsushita helped to define the low end of the market, which enhanced Sony's brand differentiation.

In fact, Sony's prices were low precisely because the company's costs were low and because it was able to manufacture and market in such enormous quantities. As domestic competitors lost their own competitive advantages in the American and European markets, Sony emerged with a larger market share in a rapidly growing market.

Turning Point

Sony is notorious for one very expensive mistake it made during the late 1970s. Having already developed a transistorized video tape recorder in 1964—which was marketed to broadcasters and video production houses—Sony introduced a standard called Betamax for home video viewing four years later. With no competition for such a unique product, Sony enjoyed a prolonged monopoly on the system. But by refusing to share the technology with other manufacturers, Sony effectively limited the number of Betamax systems that could enter the market, and the company could only manufacture so many of the devices.

Meanwhile, JVC began developing its own video cassette model, a design incompatible with Betamax called the video home system, or VHS. This design was adopted by JVC's parent company—and Sony's chief competitor—Matsushita, whose brands included Technics, Panasonic, National, and Quasar. Matsushita offered to share the VHS specifications with any manufacturer that asked for them.

Konosuke Matsushita planned to eliminate Sony and its Betamax standard from the market. Facing a market that would soon be flooded with millions of VHS machines, Morita begged Matsushita to abandon VHS and use the admittedly superior Betamax system. However, Matsushita refused, angry at Morita's earlier refusal to share the Betamax design.

A destructive competition ensued, but Sony proved unable to match the combined industrial might of Matsushita and JVC, as well as their licensees: Mitsubishi, Sanyo, Toshiba, NEC, RCA,

General Electric, and Philips. By 1985, the Betamax system was all but dead in America, though still popular in Latin America and Southeast Asia. Rather than shut itself completely out of the home video market, Sony began making VHS models in 1988. The Betamax system, however, remains popular in professional use.

Brand Extensions

Despite the Betamax disaster, Sony remained faithful to its commitment to innovation. Another important product under development in 1979 was inspired by Norio Ohga, the opera singer who had criticized Sony's first tape recorder. Ohga was in the practice of taking opera recordings everywhere he went, listening to the music even in the hallways of the Sony Corporation. In an effort to avoid disrupting others, he used headphones, but complained that the recorder and headphones were cumbersome. Morita, who had already ordered development of tiny high-fidelity headphones, asked his engineers to develop a small tape player with a belt loop. Five months later, the tape machine was paired with the headphones to produce the Sony Walkman.

Morita's detractors claimed the Walkman would flop, as no demand existed for such a novelty item. But Morita was determined to create a market. The most striking thing about the tiny system was its sound quality, and the system provided a sensible alternative to obtrusive portable radios. Through Morita's extraordinary foresight—or luck—the system caught on quickly, inspiring imitation from competitors, including Matsushita.

Later, Sony developed two more rugged versions, the bright yellow Sports Walkman and the khaki-colored Outback Walkman. The Walkman concept itself was later extended to visual entertainment. The Sony Watchman, a line of portable battery-operated televisions, went into distribution in 1985.

During the 1970s, Sony's audio systems graduated from transistor radios to complete lines of home stereo systems, including modular receivers, tape players, and turntables. In the portable market, the Walkman was preceded by a line of "boom boxes" of various sizes that included tape players and AM/FM and shortwave radios.

But the most notable extension of the brand came in 1984 with a revolutionary digital sound technology that Sony developed in collaboration with Philips. Sony pioneered a digital pulse-code technology that could be read from compact disks by lasers developed by Philips. Having learned from the ill-fated Betamax experience the importance of establishing and maintaining a standard, Sony shared its CD technology with the industry. As a result, Sony gave up a monopoly on the system, but relied on its lead in the technology to establish a strong position in the market. The superior sound reproduction of the CD made vinyl records almost completely obsolete by the early 1990s.

Another area in which Sony experienced great success was the video camera. While almost knocked out of the market by its stubborn dedication to the doomed Betamax format, Sony created a third standard specifically for portables. Using a smaller 8-millimeter tape cassette—derived from the Betamax technology—the Sony videocam included a converter that allowed the tape to be used with VHS machines.

Despite the proliferation of new products, Morita considered his company locked in to the hardware side of the electronic entertainment market. New standards, such as the CD, he reasoned, could be more easily supported if the company operated a record company—in effect, a software operation. Sony purchased CBS Records in 1987, and Columbia Pictures in 1989. Soon thereafter, Sony introduced another digital music standard called Minidisc, or MD, supporting its introduction by releasing new recording from CBS in an MD format.

The company also began to establish a high-definition television standard, and embarked on a possibly experimental foray into computer work stations in 1990. While available in Japan, the Sony computer had yet to become available in the United States in 1993. Moreover, the Sony brand name has also been associated with telephone equipment. By producing technologically simple devices, Sony exploited a gap in high-quality telephone equipment that was created when AT&T was forced to convert its rental monopoly into a consumer business.

Advertising

In Sony's first American advertisement, broadcast in 1968, an obese man lay in a hammock, watching the small Sony television perched on his stomach. The entire ad was shot in cross section, and contained no voice over, with the exception of a quick note at the end, added to provide the proper pronunciation of the name Sony. This was the first time anyone in America had ever heard of Sony, and the spot became extremely popular.

Another memorable ad depicted an acrimonious divorce in which the ex-husband took solace in his ex-wife's lopsided court victory. "She got the house . . . " he proudly proclaimed, "but I got the Sony." This marked the end of Sony's brand-focus strategy, and the beginning of product-specific ads. The company no longer needed to raise awareness of the name to drive sales of the products. Instead, it sold the products and let their quality build the Sony identity.

The company's television ads were scaled back during the 1970s, using much more conventional presentations and fact-based sales pitches. The primary selling point for televisions was, of course, the Trinitron system. One campaign that translated well across its entire product line was the "It's a Sony" theme. As if to suggest that no one need question the quality or integrity of its products, Sony ads (primarily those in print) boldly featured the reassuring claim, "It's a Sony." The slogan emphasized the company's 20-year transformation from producing inexpensive televisions to the world's finest electronics goods.

In 1989, Sony began a unique marketing tactic aimed at children. A line of Walkmans for kids was introduced under the name "My First Sony." The product seemed intended to get children to recognize the quality of Sony, 20 years before they would enter the market for stereos, videocams, and big-screen televisions.

Sony's next ad campaign, centered around television sets, portrayed an upper to middle income couple watching their Sony television in front of a beautiful sunset. Appealing to their sense of quality, the voice over stated, "It's your life, isn't it worth a Sony?"

Sony, like other manufacturers, invested heavily in showroom presentation. Reasoning that products are more likely to sell if they look better than other brands on display, Sony layouts emphasize the fact that Sony is not a price-competitive brand, but a feature-rich quality-competitive product.

Performance Evaluation

Sony's formidable reputation in consumer electronics was built not from promotional hype, but from years of technological innovation, facilitated by the company's standing commitment to turn an almost unheard of nine percent of earnings back into research and development. As a result, most of the advances in the world's consumer electronics market were initiated by Sony and adopted or imitated by competitors. Another element of the Sony brand's success is that the name has not been freely extended to non-related products. Rather than producing Sony cameras, vacuum cleaners, or refrigerators, the company has lent the Sony name only to products it can build well and support indefinitely.

Future Growth

Critics found it unlikely that Sony would be able to single-handedly manage a successful introduction of its Minidisc music format, when nearly a billion consumers had just began the expensive transition to the CD. Perhaps a more promising technology is Sony's digital Minidisc system, in general, which, unlike CDs, allows consumers to record from tapes and CDs—with far better sound quality than conventional cassette tapes. In fact, following its acquisition of a recording company and movie studio in the late 1980s, Sony may be expected to build its brand through CDs and videos through the 1990s.

Further Reading:

''Adventures in Wonderland,'' *Barron's,* October 7, 1991, pp. 8–28.

''How Sony Became a Home-Movie Superstar,'' *Business Week,* June 11, 1990, p. 72.

''How Sony Became First with Kids,'' *Adweek's Marketing Week,* November 21, 1988, pp. 58–9.

''How Sony Pulled off a Spectacular Computer Coup,'' *Business Week,* January 15, 1990, pp. 76–7.

Morita, Akio, *Made in Japan, Akio Morita and Sony,* New York: Dutton Press, 1986.

''Sony, Philips Scramble in Format Wars,'' *Adweek's Marketing Week,* February 10, 1992, p. 6.

''When Sony Was an Up and Comer, *Forbes,* October 6, 1986, pp. 98–102.

—John Simley

SPALDING®

SPALDING®

For more than 100 years Spalding sporting goods have excelled amidst the intensely competitive rigors of the sporting goods industry, where continuous product development and high performance standards are the norm. In the process the brand has garnered a reputation for being a relentless innovator, while steadfastly commanding a leadership position in the sporting goods category.

Brand Origins

As a young man, Albert Goodwill Spalding was a pitcher for the relatively unknown Forest City Club of Rockford, Illinois. However, nationally-recognized big city clubs from New York, Cleveland, and Washington D.C. offered him large sums of money to play for their teams. On the advice of his mother, Spalding passed up the offers and completed his studies in bookkeeping at a local college. Over the next five years, Spalding hired on with seven separate firms, all of which went out of business shortly after his arrival. Shaken by the whole experience and questioning whether he was jinxed as a businessman, Spalding went against his mother's wishes and signed with the Boston Red Stockings. He pitched his team to a pennant winning season the very same year.

Spalding pitched for Boston between 1871 and 1875, later joining the Chicago White Sox, where he compiled an eye-opening record of 241 wins against 59 loses. Becoming baseball's first 200-game winner assured Spalding of a spot in the baseball Hall of Fame. In an effort meant to cash in on his status as a national sports hero, Spalding opened a sporting goods store in 1876 in Chicago.

In 1886 Spalding designed and manufactured his own version of a baseball. The following year witnessed, with Albert Spalding's active participation, the formation of the National Baseball League in Louisville, Kentucky. The league's organizers went on record to endorse "the Spalding" as its sole official baseball. In 1901 the newly formed American League followed suit. Not long after the formation of the National League, Spalding introduced what was to become the first Major League baseball glove.

Buoyed by the store's instant success, due in no small measure to the National League endorsement of the "Spalding ball," Spalding moved his operations to Chicopee, Massachusetts, a city then reputed to be the manufacturing hub of the United States. In quick succession Spalding started to broaden the scope of his baseball equipment products, while at the same time venturing into alternative sporting fields. The move was met with critical success based on the brand's growing recognition and association with quality.

Product Development

Spalding's success revolved around two key strategies—the precision manufacturing process put to work in the production of balls and keeping abreast of the latest technologies and material innovations used in the manufacture of custom designed sports gear.

A request from James Naismith, who is credited with inventing the game of basketball, eventually led to the development of the first official Spalding basketball in the early 1890s. During the 1920s Spalding introduced the first basketball without laces, an achievement that was to eventually turn dribbling from a hazard into an art form. In an effort to broaden their sports product line, Spalding was the first U.S. company to manufacture tennis balls and a custom designed tennis racket in the late 1880s.

In 1894 Spalding became the first U.S. sporting goods company to venture into the world of golf when it began to manufacture golf balls and clubs. With the advent of volleyball, Spalding achieved another industry first with the production of its volleyballs. Having gained a reputation for manufacturing balls to a highly-exacting standard, Spalding's reputation spread rapidly. The brand became an early favorite, preferred by numerous professional sporting leagues and associations.

Turning an eye towards sports apparel, in the late 1880s Spalding created a line of baseball clothing, which was soon named to be the official uniforms worn by both American and National League players. In the early 1920s Spalding introduced the first sports shoe with cleats and, a short time later, the first saddle shoe specially designed to offer more lateral support, durability, and comfort.

Production Standards

Until 1977, Spalding received exclusive rights to produce major league baseballs. The construction of each ball typically began with a center of cork tightly wrapped in two layers of soft rubber. It next received four windings of yarn: 121 yards of rough gray wool; 45 yards of fine white wool; 53 yards of fine gray wool;

AT A GLANCE

Spalding brand of sporting goods founded in 1876 by Albert Goodwill Spalding in Chicago, IL; shortly thereafter company was moved to Chicopee, MA; in 1887 National Baseball League named the Spalding baseball its official ball; the American League did the same in 1901; Spalding Sporting Goods eventually merged with Evenflo Products Inc. to become Spalding and Evenflo Companies Inc.

Performance: *Market share*—Number four in the sporting and athletic goods category. *Sales*—$250 million (1992).

Major competitor: Wilson Sporting Goods; also Anthony Industries Inc. and Johnson Worldwide Associates.

Advertising: *Agency*—The Sherry Group, Parsippany, NJ. *Major campaign*—"Total Domination."

Addresses: *Parent company*—Spalding Sports Worldwide, P.O. Box 901, 425 Meadow St., Chicopee, MA 01021; phone: (413) 536-1200; fax: (413) 539-2026. *Ultimate parent company*—Spalding and Evenflo Companies Inc., P.O. Box 30101, Tampa, FL 33630; phone: (818) 887-5200; fax: (818) 887-5208.

and 150 yards of white cotton. The cover was installed by hand, stitched using two needles, each threaded with 88 inches of waxed twine set to make exactly 108 stitches.

In order to pass inspection and receive an "Official" stamp, each baseball had to measure between 9 and 9.25 inches in circumference, weigh between 5 and 5.25 ounces, and have demonstrated initial and rebound velocities. In addition, it had to retain its roundness after being pounded 200 times over its entire surface by a force of 65 pounds and distort less than 0.3 inches upon being compressed between two anvils. Tests of a similar type were performed on Spalding's tennis, basketball, volleyball, golf, and soccer balls before they too could receive the "Official" stamp.

Spalding instituted a Sports Advisory Staff of about 250 athletes contracted to utilize and evaluate the equipment, suggesting improvements if necessary. In other instances, it is not unusual for an athlete to be intimately involved in the design and construction process of new equipment. To supplement the Sports Advisory Staff, Spalding also calls upon top teaching and playing professionals in their respective fields.

Recent product innovations underscore Spalding's commitment to providing high-performance sports products. In 1986 Spalding was making specially-designed baseball gloves for six different player positions. These were available in a series of Professional, Collegiate, Youth and Youngstar levels. Borrowing from the inflatable shoe technology, Spalding introduced its Airflex baseball glove in the 1990s. The glove's construction proved to be more impact resistant than it predecessors. On the basketball front, in March of 1994 Spalding began retailing its Top-Flite 1000 basketball, featuring a new cover made from ZK Composite that replicates leather while providing better grip and durability for outdoor play.

In 1991 Spalding lost its long-held top share of the golf market to Acushnet Titleist. Attempting to recapture the number-one spot, Spalding established a capital investment program of $20 million meant to improve operations at its golf ball factory in Chicopee. By 1992 the fully automated plant was producing near flawless golf balls, right down to the dimples, as programmed by a computerized quality monitor operating along each step in the production process.

In anticipation of beach volleyball's initial entry as an Olympic sport in the 1996 Summer Games, Spalding debuted the AVP Top-Flite 18 volleyball, which was recognized as the official game ball of the Association of Volleyball Professionals. Moving into a non-traditional line of sports products and hoping to capitalize on its name recognition, in 1993 Spalding introduced a line of sport beverages called Spalding Sports Refresher. Fortified with vitamin C, the beverages came packaged in reusable clear plastic sports bottles.

Marketing Strategy

Celebrity endorsements have long appeared on Spalding's products and are a well-known part of the brand's legacy of success. Stemming from Albert Spalding's idea to use "hero authority" to sell his products, the strategy caught on and is regularly used by many industries. In conjunction with this method, Spalding signed on basketball star Shaquille O'Neal in 1993 to endorse their line of basketball products.

In order to market its AVP Top-Flite 18 volleyball, Spalding employed the slogan "Total World Domination." The first phase of the plan involved an education campaign carried out through point-of-purchase displays and information request cards pushing not only the volleyball, but also an entire line of volleyball products. The second phase called for Top-Flite's ads to be placed in popular magazines and sports publications, while phase three provided customers with a five dollar manufacturer's rebate.

The 1993 introduction of the Spalding Sports Refresher beverage targeted teens and adults who participated in athletic activities. The beverage was promoted at such events as 10K runs, beach volleyball tournaments, and triathlons, with retail incentives and sweepstake promotions. The non-carbonated Spalding beverages were not intended to compete with sport drinks like Gatorade, but were promoted as a healthier alternative to the carbonated beverages that appealed to the average consumer.

Future Trends

A number of positive economic trends, along with the favorable resolution of several outstanding industry trade issues, held out promise for the sporting goods industry in general and Spalding in particular. A slowly rebounding economy in the early 1990s meant consumers had more discretionary income to spend on leisure activities. As evidence, retail sporting goods sales rose by more than six percent in the first half of 1993.

A sliding U.S. dollar meant an increase in export trade, an area that Spalding felt represented growth. Indeed, major sporting goods markets, such as Japan, Canada, the United Kingdom, and Germany were forecasted to grow anywhere from 3 to 15 percent by the year 2000. The renewal of the Generalized System of Preferences (GSP) program proved important for sporting goods manufacturers, making it easier to move costly, labor-intensive operations outside of U.S. borders. In addition, the passage of the North American Free Trade Agreement as well as the successful conclusion of the General Agreement on Tariffs and Trade resulted in lower tariffs and stepped-up protection for intellectual property rights applied to patents, copyrights, and trademarks. All of these factors boded well for Spalding's continued growth.

Further Reading:

"All This For A Golf Ball?" *Machine-Design,* December 12, 1991, p.121.

Cleary, David Powers, *Great American Brands,* New York: Fairchild Books, 1987.

Emproto, Robert, "Two Basketball Squads Give Sport Sips a Shot," *Beverage World's Periscope,* August 31, 1993, pp. 16–17.

"Spalding's Factory of the Future," *Golf-Pro Merchandiser,* October 1992, p. 10.

Sprout, Alison L, "Jumbo Golf Balls," *Fortune,* May 17, 1993, p. 89.

"Top-Flite Puts New Spin On Golf Ball War," *USA-Today,* November 22, 1991, p. B1.

"Total World Domination," *Sporting Goods Business,* February 1994, pp. 48–49.

—Daniel E. King

SPECIALIZED® BICYCLES

With the original bicycle produced by Specialized in 1981, American riders were introduced to the first mass-produced, all-terrain bicycle—what has since come to be commonly known as the mountain bike. In less than a decade, the mountain bike became the most popular style of adult bicycle on the market. Before Mike Sinyard, the founder of Specialized, came up with his groundbreaking Stumpjumper, mountain biking was a sport for the brave few experimenting with fat, knobby tires out in the wilderness. Ordinary riders had to be satisfied with the more traditional ten-speed bicycle. Inspired by the ruggedness of his fat-wheeled childhood bicycles and the lightweight ten-speeds popular in the 1970s, Sinyard developed a new type of two-wheeler, originally advertised as "the bike for all reasons."

Brand Origins and Market Conditions

Despite Specialized's huge success on the market in the 1980s and early 1990s, the company had humble beginnings. Founder Mike Sinyard, a business administration student in the 1970s, rediscovered his childhood love for bicycles when he was forced to commute to classes by bike because of car trouble. After graduating from college, he went on a bike trip to Europe, and was introduced to several manufacturers of bicycles and bicycle components in Italy. He struck a deal with some of these companies to distribute their products in the United States, where, at the time, high-end bicycle components were rather scarce.

He started out by distributing bicycle parts to bike shop owners through a hand-written catalog. After initial success, he realized that he did not want to be merely a distributor of foreign-made parts, and decided to begin producing components of his own design. The first item produced by Specialized was a durable, high-performance tire, which was introduced in 1978 under the name Turbo. Following this first success, the company introduced the product that radically changed the bicycle industry and created a huge boom in sales over the next several years. The product was a bicycle named Stumpjumper, launched by Specialized in 1981. The new design merged the rugged, durable characteristics of traditional "balloon tire" bikes with the lightness and agility of a ten-speed bicycle. It was the first mass-produced, all-terrain bicycle (ATB) in the world.

Before the introduction of the mass-produced ATB, the American bicycle market was dominated by European imports, particularly from France and Italy. The mountain bike allowed American bicycle makers to wrest control of the domestic market from foreign competitors. It also allowed them to turn the tables and make significant strides into foreign markets, notably in Europe and Japan. In 1990, American bicycle exports climbed an astonishing 146 percent, and continued to account for 50 percent of the European market in the early 90's.

Brand Development

Ironically, in view of the extraordinary growth in popularity of ATB's in their first decade of existence, leading bicycle manufacturers had initially been skeptical of the new design. In particular, Schwinn, a well-established U.S. bicycle manufacturer, failed to recognize the new trend and continued to produce expensive bicycles incorporating tried and true designs. Specialized was able to capitalize on the reluctance of other manufacturers to invest in the new product, thereby gaining the distinct advantage with consumers that it was the *original* mountain bike manufacturer. More importantly, Specialized came onto the market as a recognized innovator, not just another company that made bikes. However, by the following year other companies recognized the profit potential of the new creation and followed with their own versions of mountain bikes.

Because of founder Mike Sinyard's love of cycling, the drive to innovate came naturally. He made it his practice to regularly ride with his employees on trails in the vicinity of Specialized headquarters in Morgan Hill, California. This first-hand experience of the sport was what allowed him and his team to anticipate new needs and meet them with a steady supply of improved products. As a result of this constant testing, by the company's own racing team as well as its CEO and employees, Specialized bicycles have gradually become more durable, agile, and faster—in short, more fun. But most importantly, because of their enthusiasm for the sport of cycling, Sinyard and his team of designers have remained keenly aware of what other cycling aficionados want.

In addition to bicycles, the Specialized brand includes a wide range of bicycle related products, from parts to accessories, helmets, lights and clothing. Throughout its development, the company has stressed innovation, rider exhilaration, and clever marketing to maintain its cutting-edge image with cycling enthusiasts. But perhaps the best testament to Specialized's contribution to American life is the original-model Stumpjumper bicycle on display at the Smithsonian Institution in Washington, D.C.

Innovation and Competitive Strategy

To cultivate its image as an innovator and to stay on the technological cutting edge of the cycling industry, Specialized has frequently teamed up with technology leaders from other industries. For example, as a result of a partnership with Du Pont, Specialized was able to introduce a three-spoke, drag-reducing wheel. Originally designed for the American Olympic team, the wheel became extremely popular with bicycle racers looking to shave precious seconds off of their times. The new wheel helped to establish the Specialized brand as a leader in high-performance cycling products.

In another collaboration, this time with an aluminum producer, Specialized developed an extremely light bicycle frame. Later, by working with General Electric, the company created a super-strong lightweight helmet. Other Specialized innovations over the years included a self-sealing inner tube designed to eliminate over 90 percent of flat tires, and still more durable, ultra-light bike frames made of carbon and metal composites and other space-age materials. In many cases, Specialized has been able to turn techno-

AT A GLANCE

Specialized brand bicycles were established in 1974 by Mike Sinyard, with the founding of his company, Specialized Bicycle Components; the first bicycle was produced under the Specialized name in 1981.

Performance: *Market share*—6% in world market. *Sales*—$160 million.

Major competitors: Trek, Schwinn, and Raleigh (high-end bicycles); also, Huffy and Murray (mass-merchandised bicycles).

Advertising: *Agency*—Goodby, Berlin & Silverstein, San Francisco, CA, 1989—. *Major campaign*—Print advertising in cycling magazines emphasizing performance and product innovation.

Addresses: *Parent company*—Specialized Bicycle Components, 15130 Concord Circle, Morgan Hill, CA, 95037; phone: (408) 779-6229; fax: (408) 779-7661.

logical wonders into top sellers. In fact, ''Innovate or Die'' is the motto of its research and development group.

Specialized's unwavering pursuit of innovation was also its competitive edge. Sinyard told *The Business Journal:* ''Our competitors didn't understand. Their orientation was: Let's do volume. Ours was: Let's make a difference.'' But it was precisely this proactive approach to innovation that also allowed Specialized to achieve a high volume of sales. Because the company has positioned itself as the industry leader, consumers perceive Specialized products as dependable and up-to-the-minute.

Marketing Strategy

Innovation is also the guiding principle in Specialized's marketing strategy. In any given year, Specialized puts more new products on the market than almost any other bicycle maker, but the company's research and development team does not introduce products blindly. Specialized follows rigorous procedures for determining which products will be successful and for weeding out items that do not sell well. Specialized organizes roundtable discussions with its customers—the independent bicycle dealers who sell Specialized products directly to the consumer. These discussions give Specialized engineers and designers—not just marketing specialists—direct and timely feedback from the customer base. Holding such discussions can be quite costly, but it allows Specialized to immeasurably decrease its R&D expenses and take a certain amount of guesswork out of product design.

Designing top-notch products is crucial to Specialized's strategy of focusing its efforts on the high end of the market. For a brand like Specialized, that market segment is ultimately the most rewarding and profitable. While some of the largest American bicycle makers stress volume sales, Specialized is concerned simultaneously with expanding its customer base and developing serious brand loyalty. Gabe Foo, manager of promotions and PR told *Marketing News:* ''Specialized is still viewed as a higher-end brand of bike, and we want to keep that image of it up with enthusiasts.'' Specialized customers are generally the first to try new cycling products, and the company's strategy is to have those products for them even before they ask. The company's belief is that if they continue to find new products from Specialized season after season, and if those products never fail to enhance the cycling experience, these enthusiasts will become loyal followers, and, in the words of Gabe Foo, ''spokespeople'' for the brand.

To capture the interest of potential buyers, Specialized mixes its primary ''innovator'' message with a healthy dose of pure and uninhibited fun. Their advertising conveys a sense of excitement, speed, and daring. One print advertising campaign depicts members of Specialized's product design team engaged in outrageous feats to test the fruits of their labor—an effective message for a company trying to wed the ideals of high-tech and good times

It also helps that the company owner is a committed cycling enthusiast himself. Mike Sinyard keeps abreast not only of technological developments, but also current cycling issues. Specialized has given away millions of dollars worth of bicycle helmets to promote the all-important issue of cycling safety, and at the same time to develop the brand image. Potential customers can learn about both cycling and Specialized bicycles through literature which the company supplies to retailers. These materials are intended to turn potential customers into discerning enthusiasts who will pass up the lower-end bicycles in favor of Specialized, despite its heftier price tag.

Performance Appraisal

Mountain bikes have traveled from the bottom of the hill in the early 1980s to the height of commanding about two-thirds of the $4 billion U.S. bicycle market in the early 90s. As any new trend, mountain bikes sparked competition, with performance, not price, as the determining factor. Specialized bicycles were at the forefront of this trend. Still, price was a consideration, and in the early 80s Specialized cut the price of a mountain bike in half by taking advantage of lower labor rates in Asian countries. Many other bicycle manufacturers eventually followed suit.

In the ensuing price wars, Specialized was able to grow and increase its market share through progressive design and further focus on product innovation. Thanks to this approach, Specialized has captured 6 percent of the world market, despite the fact that it targets primarily the higher end of that market. In its first years of existence, the company grew very quickly—an average of 30 percent annually. But most of its growth in recent years has been abroad. In 1991 Specialized's European sales nearly doubled, accounting for 40 percent of the company's revenues.

On the domestic side, sales in the early 90s showed much slower growth—only about 4 percent in 1991. This can be partly blamed on the recession of that year, but, despite Specialized's efforts to educate the consumer about quality cycling products, the majority of Americans still shop for bicycles based on price. The lower end of the market is controlled by two giants, Huffy and Murray, who distribute their products through department and discount stores. The trend to move manufacturing to developing countries has also created an avalanche of inexpensive bicycles on the American market. While consumer demand for less expensive bicycles continued throughout the recession, the economic hard times hurt higher-end companies like Specialized. Nevertheless, Specialized was shrewd in focusing its marketing efforts on the more expensive models, and even during the recession the company experienced growth in the $500-and-up bicycle category. As the American economy stabilized in the 90s, higher-end bicycles continued to slowly gain market share.

Future Outlook

Industry experts agree that the biggest challenge to Specialized and other bicycle makers will be changing market conditions. Mountain bikes were the new wave in the 80s; their success was so phenomenal that they became the standard. But while the mountain bike made Specialized, it could also threaten the company in coming years. Manufacturers who were less innovative than Specialized have caught up and have developed ways to produce this standard more cheaply and in greater numbers. These companies, better equipped for volume production and distribution, threaten to erode the market that Specialized has helped to create.

As the market matures, Mike Sinyard and his team of designers will have to work hard to keep the Specialized brand on the cutting edge of the industry. In the early 90s, mountain bikes are everywhere, and the market may be ready for a hot new product. While high-tech components and accessories will continue to bring in a steady stream of customers and provide steady growth, Specialized is unlikely to experience a boom similar to its early popularity without a really inventive new bicycle. Still, Specialized has a proven track record of innovation, and Sinyard told *The Economist* that his research team is hard at work developing the ''bike of the future.''

Further Reading:

Friedman, Dorian, ''Pedaling for Profits,'' *US News and World Report,* August 26/September 2, 1991, p. 49.

Goldman, James S., ''Pedaling Items That Are, Well, Just Bitchin','' *The Business Journal,* April 15, 1991, p. 1.

Greco, Susan, ''Making Customer Roundtables Work,'' *Inc.,* February 1992.

Holzinger, Albert G., ''A Cyclist Who's Riding High,'' *Nation's Business,* August 1992, pp. 16–17.

''Kid's Stuff,'' *The Economist,* June 3, 1989, pp. 69–70.

Miller, Cyndee, ''Popular Bicycles Don't Cost a Fortune—Only $3,000,'' *Marketing News,* July 20, 1992, pp. 2, 14.

''Reinventing the Wheel,'' *The Economist,* August 1, 1992, pp. 61–62.

Savona, Dave, ''Peddling the Best of the US,'' *International Business,* November 1991, pp. 48–52

—Justyna Frank

STAINMASTER®

Stainmaster carpet was introduced in 1986 to instant popularity and proved itself to be one of the most successful new products of the decade. Thanks in part to a massive promotional campaign, it became one of the most recognized brand–name products and has dominated its market since its introduction; it also changed forever the humdrum world of carpet advertising and had a profound effect on the carpet industry as a whole. For Du Pont, the stunningly popular ad campaign proved that the company could successfully and profitably appeal directly to the consumer.

E.I. du Pont de Nemours is known worldwide as a giant of the chemical industry. After its creation in 1802, the company grew into an internationally recognized leader by developing and producing such materials as nylon, Teflon, and Lycra that grew to be a part of the everyday lives of millions of people. However, Du Pont generally did not directly market its goods, as most of Du Pont's customers were manufacturers who made products comprised of Du Pont materials. By the mid-1980s, Du Pont was feeling the pinch as many of its traditional customers were forced to cut costs and purchase less, and Du Pont itself was seriously challenged by competition from foreign suppliers.

Du Pont's Carpet-Fiber Business

Du Pont was organized into various product-line segments, including biomedical products, agricultural and industrial chemicals, and polymer products. Its fiber segment produced materials sold to other industries to process into apparel, home textiles, carpets, and various industrial applications. Before the creation of Stainmaster, Du Pont had developed and manufactured carpet fibers under the Du Pont and Antron brands.

Du Pont and other carpet-fiber producers manufactured the materials from which carpeting was made—mainly nylon, but also polyester and olefin. The carpet fibers were then sent to the carpet mills—most of which made carpeting for several different carpet-fiber producers—where the designs and colors were created. The mills then sent the consumer-ready carpeting to retailers.

Although consumers spent about $15 million annually in the mid-1980s to buy carpeting for their homes, it was often perceived as a commodity product, with little advertising and brand name recognition. When carpet was advertised, it was often badly promoted; as an advertising director for a rival carpet-fiber manufacturer commented in the *Wall Street Journal,* ''When carpet advertising comes on TV, it's so boring that people turn their brains off.'' By the mid-1980s, carpet sales were experiencing little or no growth.

Tom McAndrews, director of the flooring systems division at Du Pont, set about changing the rules. He felt that the carpeting industry was poorly perceived and marketed, therefore losing the battle for consumer's discretionary spending. In 1983, shortly after becoming division head, McAndrews created a task force to ''study the science, if you will, of marketing a flooring product to the American public,'' as he explained in *Across the Board.* The group discovered, among other things, that stain resistance was an important factor in consumer carpet-buying decisions. By 1985 it was concluded that carpet, even already established brands, would benefit from an aggressive advertising campaign. The task force recommended a strategy in which products were marketed at every level of the distribution chain.

For the next 18 months, Du Pont tested the wisdom and efficiency of that strategy by applying it to its established Antron brand. The company hired the advertising agency BBDO to help with its strategic planning, an unusual step for the company. Consumer advertising was increased and the sales force was doubled in size. After testing in a dozen markets, the results proved positive.

Du Pont and others in the carpet-fiber industry had for some years appealed to the consumer preference for stain-resistant carpeting by using fluorocarbon finishes and fiber cross sections that helped mask soil. However, these methods only attacked the problems associated with soiling, and not stains. Materials that stained would be resisted by the fluorocarbon finish, but they would break through and stain the fibers in time. Real stain resistance had not yet been developed, although it was sometimes attributed to carpeting in advertising campaigns.

Stainmaster Is Born

As upper-level management was beginning to reposition Du Pont in the carpet-fiber market, in large part by stressing carpet stain resistance, a research chemist at Du Pont was, coincidentally, testing his own theories on improving that quality. Armand Zinnato had been working on dying nylon carpeting at room temperature; as it was thought that such fibers would stain easily, he looked for ways to block them from absorbing the stain by treating

AT A GLANCE

Stainmaster brand of carpet introduced in 1986 by E.I. du Pont de Nemours & Company in Wilmington, DE.

Performance: *Market share*—Top share of the carpet category.

Major competitor: Allied-Signal's Anso V Worry-Free; also Monsanto's StainBlocker.

Advertising: *Agency*—BBDO, New York, NY, 1986—. *Major campaign*—"Landing."

Addresses: *Parent company*—E.I. du Pont de Nemours & Company, 1007 Market St., Wilmington, DE, 19898; phone: (302) 774-1000.

them after they had been dyed. Zinnato carried on his work in an unofficial capacity, independent of, and unknown to, upper management. By January of 1985 he had proven that materials previously used to improve wash-fastness would also provide stain resistance. Several months later he reviewed his findings with his superiors, who then officially assigned him the task of pursuing his research.

Upper management soon caught wind of Zinnato's work and decided to bring the product into its consumer marketing program, then in its final stages. By the end of the summer, the technology was shifted from the fibers segment to the chemical and pigments division. This was done to hide the company's activities from its competitors and provide a cover for the purchase of large quantities of stain-resistant chemicals as well as to take advantage of that division's experience with stain-fighting chemicals.

While the material was being tested, Du Pont decided upon an aggressive marketing campaign, at least partly to make up for the company's weak patent position. The chemicals that Zinnato had found to be stain resistant had been used extensively in nylon carpets as dye-resist agents, and thus it was felt that Du Pont would not be able to obtain broad patent protection.

In January of 1986 Du Pont sent the fibers for product testing to three mills, which were sworn to secrecy. Soon thereafter, articles appeared in trade publications noting that Monsanto was developing a fiber with improved stain resistance. Tom McAndrews pushed for the Stainmaster, as the carpet had been named, program to be ready six months ahead of schedule. By cutting short the time allotted for test marketing while increasing the number of participating mills to 14, McAndrew was able to hold a press conference to announce the arrival of Stainmaster in August of 1986.

Stainmaster: Ready for Takeoff

Just a few Stainmaster-certified carpet styles were ready in September, when the product was to be unveiled. Carpets not only had to meet weight, density, pile height, and twist-level minimum requirements, they had to be treated with the correct amount of Stainmaster chemicals in order to meet certification requirements. Carpet fibers with higher twist lasted longer, and certain weight and height levels helped reduce crushing—thus the carpets were also especially durable and wear-resistant. The fibers were also treated to reduce static. Mills participating in the Stainmaster program signed agreements that required them to send samples to Du Pont for spot checking. Du Pont supplied the mills with the stain-fighting chemicals as well as the fibers so as to ensure product quality.

Du Pont initially limited the program to two distributors and 1,500 retail outlets. An avalanche of promotional materials was sent to the retailers, including posters, banners, brochures, cards, mobiles, and tags. Photo boards that laid out its television spots were also available. An important merchandising tool was a demonstration unit that allowed customers to test Stainmaster by comparing its stain-resistant qualities against a non-Stainmaster treated tuft of carpeting. Other promotional events were organized, including a "pet parade" in Los Angeles that featured hundreds of animals treading a long length of Stainmaster carpeting.

A Happy "Landing"

Du Pont wanted the television and print advertising to stress the product's quality, durability, and stylishness. As the manager of marketing and communications for Stainmaster pointed out in *Back Stage-SHOOT,* "We had mentioned stain resistance for years. And we didn't want to just say 'new, improved.' We needed breakthrough advertising with a strong, arresting, . . . message." Referring to the Stainmaster television commercials created by BBDO, he stated "they used humor to overcome the fear of staining."

The commercial that took the industry by storm was the 30-second "Landing" spot, which opened the campaign during the major-league baseball playoffs. It featured an impish tot sitting in his high chair, with an airplane-shaped kiddie dish in front of him. As the voiceover clears the plane for takeoff in control-tower fashion, the boy sends his dish airborne, with the inevitable spill landing on Stainmaster carpeting. The spot was an immediate hit. Stainmaster commercials went on to appear during eight of the top ten prime-time television programs.

A commercial more typical of Du Pont advertising, which demonstrated the product and informed the viewer, ran for half of Stainmaster's airtime early on. However, follow-up consumer polling found that "the only spot anyone could remember was "Landing," the marketing and communications manager acknowledged in *Back Stage-SHOOT.* Research found that the young boy appealed to the target audience Du Pont was trying to reach: women 25 to 54 years old (women made or influenced 85 percent of all carpet purchases). Another humorous spot portrayed a woman who tries valiantly to stop a tableful of food from falling on her carpet

The Response Is Immediate

Upon its introduction, Stainmaster was a towering success. Supply failed to meet demand as retailers scrambled for shipments and mills turned out new carpet styles as quickly as they could get the materials from Du Pont. The price of the Stainmaster carpeting for consumers was originally $18 to $20 a square yard. Realizing that competitors were soon to introduce their own lines of stain-resistant carpeting, Du Pont dropped its prices by 15 percent a few months after Stainmaster hit the stores. The price plunge created an even greater shortage of product. By 1988 all of the major carpet mills were producing Stainmaster carpeting.

Fortune magazine listed Stainmaster as the best new product, and the *Wall Street Journal* named its advertising campaign the best of 1987. Stainmaster's introductory commercial, "Landing," won an advertising-industry CLIO award. Du Pont was besieged with queries on the availability of the airplane-shaped dish used in ''Landing''; the dish was specially made for the commercial, but the company contracted out for its production, and within a year over 35,000 dishes were given away with carpet purchases or sold directly.

Carpet sales in the industry as a whole began to climb in 1986. According to the U.S. Department of Commerce, Stainmaster was responsible for 8.5 percent of the growth of the carpeting industry. Du Pont continued to invest heavily in advertising for Stainmaster even after the initial launch. Most of its advertising budget was spent on carpet fibers, and most of that on Stainmaster. In 1988 and 1989 Du Pont spent $34.7 million on its carpet advertising, and $32 million was earmarked for Stainmaster. BBDO continued to use a light touch to sell the brand. Later television spots showed a young couple partaking in a romantic, candlelight dinner. The gentleman accidently upends the table, and Stainmaster carpeting saves the evening.

The Competition

In the mad scramble which followed the launch of Stainmaster, other carpet-fiber producers quickly unveiled their products. Allied-Signal introduced its Anso V Worry-Free fiber in September of 1986. Monsanto also opened its campaign for Wear-Dated carpeting that month. Its television advertising only aired on cable TV, thus avoiding expensive prime-time spots. Late in 1987 Monsanto announced that its Wear-Dated carpeting would be treated with StainBlocker, a stain-resistant chemical that was locked into the fiber. Monsanto later acknowledged that ''consumer surveys show that 92 percent to 95 percent prefer stain resistance that is locked in to that which is added on at the mill.'' Its new StainBlocker was launched in advertising during the Olympics in the summer of 1988.

A late entrant into the market was Amoco subsidiary Amoco Fabrics & Fibers Company, which introduced its Genesis brand of carpet fibers in 1988. Whereas Du Pont, Monsanto, and Allied-Signal all treated nylon carpeting, Genesis made carpets of treated polypropylene. Amoco was hoping to take advantage of the fact that nylon-treated carpets were not impervious to all stains, and that they were especially vulnerable to red wine and hot liquids.

Despite all of the competition, Du Pont enjoyed the position of having been the first to launch its stain-resistant carpet. That, coupled with a memorable advertising campaign, should assure that Stainmaster will continue to be a leader in the market.

Further Reading:

Alsop, Ronald, ''Don Rickles and Devilish Kid Bring Dull Carpet Ads to Life,'' *Wall Street Journal,* July 9, 1987, p. 31.

Brophy, David Bergen, ''Du Pont: The Story Behind Stainmaster,'' *Back Stage-SHOOT,* July 26, 1991, p. 60.

''Carpet Stain Resistance, Guarantees, and Styling,'' *Textile World,* October 1989, p. 65.

Mansfield, Richard G., ''Carpet Fiber Producers Attack Stain Removal,'' *Textile World,* January 1987, p. 75.

Mellow, Craig, ''Successful Products of the Eighties,'' *Across the Board,* November 1988, p. 40.

Quelch, James A., and Paul W. Farris, *Cases in Advertising and Promotion Management,* third ed., Homewood, IL: Irwin, 1991, pp. 41–63.

—C. L. Collins

STANLEY®

One of the best-known trade names in American business, the Stanley name celebrated its sesquicentennial in 1993, having cultivated a worldwide reputation for excellence and achieved total 1992 sales that exceeded $2 billion for the first time. Stanley tools, hardware, and door systems were marketed in 135 countries by the early 1990s. The Stanley Works' roster of consumer and professional brands included: MAC mechanics' tools, Proto, and Bostitch staplers. Stanley is synonymous with do-it-yourself, and its product line includes hand and mechanics' tools, closet systems, automatic doors, paint brushes and applicators, hydraulic tools, pneumatic nailers and staplers, and other specialty hardware products.

Brand Origins

Frederick Trent Stanley founded the Stanley Bolt Manufactory in the small New England town of New Britain, Connecticut, in the first half of the nineteenth century. Born in 1802, Frederick Stanley had worked as a store clerk, made suspenders and door locks, and had even been a traveling hardware salesman in North Carolina and Mississippi. When he returned to New England to start his own business manufacturing wrought iron door bolts, this ''Yankee trader'' continued to sell and install his namesake hardware, thereby establishing quality and customer service as early hallmarks of the brand.

Although the brand's first year of sales amounted to less than $1000, it had an advantage over many of its competitors: automation. One of the region's first steam engines powered the machine that manufactured the factory's bolts and house trimmings. The company grew slowly until the outbreak of the Civil War, when demand for hardware and handtools in the territory west of the Alleghenies blossomed. Sales rose from $53,000 in 1860 to $480,000 by 1872.

In 1852, the company incorporated as The Stanley Works. Two years later, Stanley hired William H. Hart, a 19-year-old ''jack-of-all-trades'' who came up with early display techniques, including neatly labeled telescoping display boxes to replace the anonymous plain paper wrappings Stanley hardware had carried on the store shelf. He also packaged screws and hinges together for added convenience, something that competitors didn't do.

During the 1870s, Hart developed a more attractive finish for Stanley hinges that won industry-wide recognition and helped Stanley pay its first dividend. Putting unheated iron through rollers gave the branded hardware a smooth, bright finish and uniform thickness. Hinges made with this process won a Certificate of Award at the Philadelphia Centennial Exhibition in 1876. Other products from cold-rolled steel included: cabinet hardware, hinges, and, as automobiles proliferated after the turn of the century, garage door hardware.

In 1883, William Hart succeeded Stanley as president. The brand's early heart-shaped logo with the initials ''S.W.'' combined this influential leader's last name with The Stanley Works.

Stanley's long-standing emphasis on quality was formalized with the issue of Standing Order No. 270 in 1906. E. Allen Moore, who later became president of Stanley, advised employees to ''bear in mind that in manufacturing goods in this factory the first requisite is that they shall be manufactured correctly and be first quality in every respect.''

Brand Development

Throughout the first half of the twentieth century, Stanley expanded its market penetration primarily through mergers and acquisitions. The Stanley Works merged with the Stanley Rule & Level Company in 1920, combining two lines of products that had been marketed under the same name by different corporate entities. Stanley Rule & Level had been founded in 1857 by Henry Stanley, a distant cousin and brother-in-law of Frederick T. Stanley. The ''other Stanley'' manufactured carpenter's measuring implements, planers, and wooden toys. During the first two decades of the new century, Stanley Rule & Level had bolstered its product line by purchasing makers of hammers, carpenters squares, and other tools at the rate of nearly one a year. By the time of the merger, Stanley Rule & Level had become one of the world's largest manufacturers of fine-grained boxwood rules, levels, measuring implements, and other woodworking tools.

The two Stanleys' logos were used in tandem from 1920 to about 1936, when Stanley Rule & Level's now-familiar trademark stood alone. The combination of the two Stanley companies reinforced the name for the hard economic times to come. When the Great Depression crippled the construction industry, Stanley sought to expand its market reach with the introduction of portable electric tools. The creation of this division was later called ''the first step in the do-it-yourself revolution'' by the *Magazine of Wall*

AT A GLANCE

Stanley Bolt Manufactory established in New Britain, Connecticut, by Frederick Trent Stanley; incorporated as The Stanley Works in 1852; merged with The Stanley Rule & Level Company in 1920.

Performance: *Sales*—$2.27 billion (1993).

Major competitor: Sears, Roebuck & Co.'s Craftsman; also, True Temper and Vermont American.

Advertising: *Agency*—Ammirati & Puris, New York, NY. *Major campaign*—Slogan, "Stanley helps you do things right."

Addresses: *Parent company*—The Stanley Works, 1000 Stanley Drive, New Britain, CT 06053; phone: (203) 225-5111; fax: (203) 827-5926.

Street. Stanley even came out with a ''Magic Door '' that opened automatically through the use of a beam of light. By 1970, Stanley would be the largest manufacturer of automatic doors.

World War II controls halted the brand's acquisition spree, but Stanley grew and prospered during the postwar building boom, as the middle class fled the cities for the suburbs. ''Rollorama'' coaches and display vans brought 1,300 sample items to hardware dealers in the late 1940s and early 1950s. The brand also pioneered packaging and display methods that were revolutionary, by hardware standards. New merchandising for self-service retail stores included carding—affixing tools and hardware to colorful, descriptive cardboard—and shrink-wrapping. ''Profitool'' pegboard display racks were a practical, yet versatile addition to Stanley's merchandising plan in 1956. Stanley added drapery hardware and aluminum windows and doors to its growing product line during the 1950s. Annual sales topped $100 million in 1959 and surpassed $200 million by 1967, but Stanley had not yet taken full advantage of the market that would make the brand a household name.

Do-It-Yourself Comes of Age

Throughout its over-100 years in business, the Stanley name had been promoted primarily in the professional market—consumer sales constituted only 30 percent of the company's total. During the early 1970s, however, Donald W. Davis, a Harvard Business School graduate who became chairman of Stanley in 1966, noticed that inflation-battered homeowners were beginning to pick up hammers, saws, screwdrivers, and wrenches to do their own repairs and remodeling. The ''do-it-yourself'' phenomenon was sparked by young homeowners who wanted to do things with their hands as well as escape the spiraling charges of professional craftsmen. Davis has been credited with recognizing the do-it-yourself (DIY) movement early in its formation and tying Stanley's fortunes to it. The executive even came up with the slogan that soon permeated marketing: ''Stanley helps you do things right.'' The brand's reputation in the professional tools market was a big asset when the brand began to penetrate the burgeoning DIY market in the 1970s.

Heavy television advertising became a linchpin of Stanley's DIY dominance. Davis initiated an expensive print and television campaign designed both to promote Stanley tools and to indoctrinate new DIY converts. The Stanley advertising budget increased 73 percent from 1976 to 1979 to about $18 million, and rose to $25 million by 1980. Spot television spending alone more than doubled to $5.1 million by 1979. Some ads promoted DIY in general: one in the late 1970s showed a hammer smashing a tennis ball and crowed that the DIY market was 27 times larger than tennis. Other ads touted individual products or projects that required hand tools. One dollhouse plan offer drew over 500,000 requests for instructions.

Davis changed product lines, operations, and marketing to target this growing consumer group. Stanley redesigned hammers, tape rulers, and other tools to fit the lower performance expectations and price point of do-it-yourselfers without sacrificing the brand's long-standing reputation for excellent workmanship. The brand's ''Powerlock '' tape measure set the standard worldwide. Stanley also pared its product lines to concentrate on its strengths. Unable to break Black & Decker's powerful grip on of the power tools industry, Davis abandoned the category: if Stanley couldn't be number one in a particular product line, it would be eliminated.

By 1979, Stanley topped the fast-growing, $22 billion DIY market. Consumer sales constituted 50 percent of Stanley Works sales. The brand spent $100,000 to be named ''official supplier of hand tools'' to the 1980 Winter Olympics in Lake Placid and launched the biggest-ever promotion in the hardware industry with the theme ''You Can Do It America,'' combining Americans' penchants for sports and DIY.

Stanley's strategy for holding its dominant position was to constantly introduce new products and variations of old ones, acquire more shelf space in home centers and hardware stores, and ''hammer home'' the Stanley name. Management invested $5 million to $6 million annually in research and development and began a long-running, profitable relationship with the Public Broadcasting System. Through sponsorship of such how-to and do-it-yourself programs as *This Old House, The New Yankee Workshop,* and *Hometime,* Stanley shored up its reputation for quality and reliability. In the late 1980s, the brand produced a series of seven 45-minute videos starring Dean Johnson and JoAnne Liebler, the hosts of *Hometime.* The how-to tapes detailed repair jobs and featured Stanley tools in use.

International Markets

Stanley products were marketed outside the United States as early as 1870, and the ''Stanley Lady,'' a mythical company representative, offered Australian customers hinges and other products via catalog beginning in 1898. Stanley opened a special export office in 1902 and launched its first foreign manufacturing facility in Ontario, Canada, in 1914. By 1926, there was a Stanley Hardware plant in Germany, and in 1937, Stanley Tools Europe was launched in the United Kingdom. Although a dearth of home ownership in Europe had long stunted the growth of DIY retailing there, home ownership began to rise in the late 1980s.

Stanley expanded into Latin America during the 1960s, primarily through the acquisition of The Collins Company's Brazilian, Mexican, Columbian, and Guatemalan operations. By 1978, about 22 percent of Stanley's annual revenues came from outside North America. The brand is promoted as ''the badge of the professional'' in Latin American markets. The brand established footholds in the Pacific with the creation of The Stanley Works Asia Pacific in Singapore in 1986 and the Stanley Works Japan in 1989.

Future Growth

From 1967 to 1992, retail home improvement sales increased from $17 billion to over $100 billion. This trend promised to continue as low interest rates drew the United States housing market out of recession. There appears to be no end to the do-it-yourself craze. According to a 1993 Leisure Trends study, do-it-yourself projects were one of the top five ways Americans aged 16 and older spent their free time. Industry analysts agreed that the growth in the home-improvement market would continue.

Stanley planned to enjoy the benefits of this ongoing trend by expanding geographically (especially in emerging markets in Asia and Eastern Europe), making strategic acquisitions, introducing new products, and thereby increasing sales and market share.

Further Reading:

Davis, Donald Walter, *The Stanley Works: A 125 Year Beginning,* New York: Princeton University Press, 1969.

Day, J. W., "A Yankee Trader's Dream: The Stanley Works," *Magazine of Wall Street & Business Analyst,* March 14, 1970, pp. 13–15, 38–39.

Fitzgerald, Kate, "Tools Build on Do-It-Yourself," *Advertising Age,* August 22, 1988, p. 24.

Goldman, Tamara, "Nailing Down the Home Improvement Market," *Marketing Communications,* October 1988, pp. 49–52.

Haller, Karl, "Warehouse Stores Lead Home Improvement Push," *Chain Store Age Executive,* August 1993, pp. 25A–27A.

Hussey, Allan F., "Handyman's Friend: Stanley Works Maintains Growth as Toolmaker for Home, Industry," *Barron's,* October 3, 1983.

"The Olympian Sell," *Sales & Marketing Management,* November 12, 1979, pp. 16, 20.

Scott, Jonathan B., *Proud of Our Past: 150 Years of Growth Through Excellence at The Stanley Works.* New Britain, Connecticut: The Stanley Works, 1993.

Spring, Jim, "Seven Days of Play," *American Demographics,* March 1993, pp. 50–53.

"Stanley Works: Capitalizing on the Homeowner Do-It-Yourself Trend," *Business Week,* February 26, 1979, pp. 125–26.

"Stanley Works: Hammering Home a Quality Image," *Dun's Review,* May 1980, pp. 128–29.

—April S. Dougal

STEINWAY®

Brandishing the logo golden lyre above the words "Steinway & Sons" (also in gold), Steinway vertical and grand pianos have been offering expert craftsmanship and unsurpassed tonal quality to musicians for over 140 years. Pianos have evolved from the "gravicembalo col piano e forte" or "harpsichord with soft and loud" of Bartolomeo Christofori of 1709 to the magnificent Steinway & Sons' Concert Grand-Model D of 1993. When radio and television began to usurp the piano as a favorite diversion in America, Steinway pianos, with their unsurpassed quality, exacting detail, and superior resonance, consistently crescendoed over such heavyweight competitors as Chickering & Sons. While Steinway is not the volume leader in piano production—other piano manufacturers such and Yamaha and Kawai have the capacity of producing 200,000 pianos annually, compared to Steinway's 5,000 units—Steinway regards itself as the "quality leader" in the piano industry due to years of astute craftsmanship and constant innovation.

Brand Origins

Heinrich Engelhard Steinweg built his first grand piano in the kitchen of his home in Seesen, Germany, as a wedding present for his bride. In 1849, because the piano business was not flourishing in Germany, Steinweg's son Charles immigrated to the United States. Quickly finding work as a cabinet-maker and enjoying his lifestyle and freedoms, Charles urged his family to join him in the New World. In 1850, Steinweg, his wife, their three daughters, and three of their five sons arrived in New York City to join Charles. (C. F. Theodore, Steinweg's fifth son, remained in Seesen to keep the business running there.)

In America, because discrimination against German immigrants made the Steinwegs feel uncomfortable, the patriarch decided to Anglicize his name to Henry Steinway. After three years of making pianos for other companies, the family started its own business, Steinway & Sons, in America. The company's first piano was sold in that year for $500. (That same piano, in 1993, was on display at The Metropolitan Museum of Art in New York City.) Charles couldn't have picked a better birthplace for the company, for good lumber in America was both cheap and abundant. Although the family encountered cramped working conditions in its rented loft in New York City, the multitalented Steinways interacted well with one another, even in those close quarters. Doretta, the eldest daughter, became an excellent salesperson—sometimes even offering to give free piano lessons to prospective buyers in order to close the sale. Within a year of the founding of the firm, Steinway & Sons moved to a roomier location.

What distinguished the Steinway piano from other pianos of the era was its "overstrung bass" combined with its iron frame. Overstrung square wooden pianos, quite common in that time period, featured bass strings crossing over treble strings; the Steinway grand piano, however, boasted an iron frame, which resonated the tones of the elongated bass strings magnificently. In 1855, Steinway & Sons entered its overstrung square piano at the fair of the American Institute in New York. The piano was awarded the medal for the best semigrand pianoforte at the fair, and Steinway & Sons gained some valuable publicity. By 1859, Steinway & Sons was selling approximately 500 pianos a year.

The overstrung grand piano, as perfected by Henry Steinway, Jr., soon made its influence felt in the musical world. Patented on December 20, 1859, Henry, Jr.'s, overstrung system arranged the bass notes over the middle and upper register strings. Previously, all grand pianos had been straightstrung, with all the strings stretched out in the same direction, parallel to each other. Although square pianos of the day were overstrung, no one had ever applied the concept to grand pianos. Not only did Steinway's new overstrung arrangement improve the sound quality as well as the strength of the notes, it avoided a clutter of strings and made better use of the capacity of the soundboard. Before long, other piano companies began incorporating the overstrung system into their grand pianos. Until Steinway's breakthrough, the firm of Chickering & Sons had enjoyed the number one market share with its 1843-patented full iron frame for flat scale grand pianos. With the development of the overstrung grand piano *and* iron frame, Steinway & Sons quickly became the top seller of grand pianos in the United States. Soon, to accommodate increased demand for the pianos, the company had to move to a more spacious manufacturing facility. The new Steinway factory opened in 1860, and, through the labor of 350 men, was able to produce 1,800 pianos that year. Five years later, the annual piano output soared to 2,200.

Not satisfied with success, the Steinways sought new ways to improve the structure of the grand piano. One of the most important aspects of the piano, from the perspective of its player, was the action, made up of the keyboard and hammer mechanism. In order for the pianist to perform optimally, the keys had to be loose

AT A GLANCE

Steinway brand of pianos founded in New York City in 1853 by Heinrich Engelhard Steinweg (name later Anglicized to Henry Steinway); subsequent developers included his sons C. F. Theodore, Charles, Henry, William, and Albert; "overstrung grand piano" patented on December 20, 1859; company acquired in 1972 by CBS, Inc.; company purchased from CBS in 1985 by Steinway Musical Properties, Inc.; company manufacturers approximately 5,000 pianos annually.

Major competitor: Yamaha; also, Kawai, Chickering & Sons, and Baldwin.

Advertising: *Agency*—In-house. *Major campaign*—"Steinway. The Instrument of the Immortals."

Addresses: *Parent company*—Steinway & Sons, One Steinway Plaza, Long Island City, NY 11105-MMR; phone: (718) 721-2600; fax: (718) 294-7717 and (718) 932-4332. *Ultimate parent company*—Steinway Musical Properties, Inc., 80 South St., #515, Waltham, MA 02154; phone: (617) 894-9770.

enough to be played with minimal effort but, simultaneously, rigid enough to feel comfortable to the fingers. Henry Steinway, Jr., received a patent on May 5, 1857, for an improvement "to obtain a more free and easy movement of the action in repeating." Steinway was granted three more patents by 1862, all relating to the action of the grand piano.

Tragedy hit the family when Henry, Jr., died of tuberculosis in 1865, at the age of 35, and his brother Charles died of typhoid in that same year, at the age of 36, on a visit to their brother C. F. Theodore, in Germany. Charles had helped to establish, organize, and manage the company's new factory. Upon the death of the two brothers and the imminent retirement of the patriarch Henry, Sr., the responsibility of the business fell to another brother, William, who was joined in October 1865 by C. F. Theodore, who, although quite happily living in Germany, had obligingly sold the business there to help his siblings in America. A creative and intelligent man, C. F. Theodore immediately began to channel all his scientific knowledge into the selection of the proper wood, abundant in New York, to manufacture the very best grand pianos.

Early Marketing Strategy

With C. F. Theodore directing his energies into improving the instruments, William was able to concentrate on selling. Perceiving the need to showcase Steinway pianos to the public, William decided to build a music hall in which musicians would give concerts and recitals using Steinway pianos. Steinway Hall opened in New York City in 1867, heralding a new era for American music. William realized that the American people needed and wanted musical education and culture, and he was determined to provide both. Situated in the hub of New York's cultural life, Steinway Hall remained one of New York's leading concert halls for nearly 25 years. Closed in 1890, it was succeeded by the world-famous Carnegie Hall.

William perceived that Steinway grand pianos required an international identity, and so he established a showroom and concert hall in London in 1870. By 1880, Steinway & Sons had begun manufacturing operations in Hamburg, Germany. In order to win respect in the international musical community, Steinway & Sons entered many U.S. and European piano exhibitions. In addition to garnering prizes in London in 1862 and Philadelphia in 1876, Steinway pianos gained lasting international acclaim at the Paris exhibition in 1867, when Steinway & Sons became the first American company to receive the exhibition's prestigious "Grand Gold Medal of Honor" for excellence in manufacturing and engineering. This recognition of Steinway's unique piano-making techniques spurred a revolution in the industry, changing the methods by which pianos were built. Because of the Steinway piano's clearly superior workmanship, it became the piano of choice for many members of foreign royalty and earned the admiration of the world's most respected performing pianists.

Advertising and Promotions

Perhaps the most imaginative of Steinway & Sons' promotions was its Steinway Artists Program, which originated in the latter half of the nineteenth century. Steinway managed the careers of many major international artists, including Anton Rubinstein, Ignace Jan Paderewski, and Sergei Rachmaninoff. Because famed artists preferred the Steinway, the instrument's reputation became inextricably linked with the slogan "The Piano of International Fame." Eventually, the company relinquished its involvement in the management of artists; instead, Steinway Artists were assured of a performance-ready Steinway piano at public concerts anywhere in the United States. In 1993, more than 90 percent of the world's active concert pianists (over 800 artists) bore the title "Steinway Artist." Each owned a Steinway; all chose to perform on a Steinway piano exclusively. None was a paid endorser; all chose to perform publicly on a Steinway because of its unsurpassed sound and unparalleled responsiveness. In addition, because Steinway pianos were ubiquitous at the world's most prestigious music schools—including Juilliard, Yale, and The Curtis Institute of Music, in the United States alone—the artists who graduated from these institutions overwhelmingly chose a Steinway piano for purchase and performance when they began their professional careers.

To reach the masses who had not yet developed an interest in music, Steinway & Sons decided in 1900 to advertise nationally, engaging the services of the N. W. Ayer agency in New York. The first advertising did not sell pianos—it only offered pianos by other manufacturers that the company had received as trade-ins. Not until the fourteenth ad were Steinway pianos actually offered for sale. A 1902 ad proclaimed that His Majesty William Kaiser Wilhelm had purchased a Steinway, tested its merits, and conferred on William Steinway the Order of the Red Eagle. In 1903, fine art began to appear in Steinway ads, to be replaced in 1918 by photographs, in misty focus, of concerts, families, and sweethearts gathered around a Steinway piano. The musician Richard Strauss offered the first published testimonial for Steinway in 1904. In 1920, the slogan "Instrument of the Immortals" was introduced in an ad showcasing the "Old Masters" painting effect; this slogan was to endure in Steinway & Sons' advertising for over 70 years.

Because Steinway & Sons did not care to cheapen its products or use high-pressure salesmanship, in the 1920s, when interest in the family piano yielded to pride in the family car and the piano was supplanted by radio as a family's entertainment, Ayer formulated campaigns that emphasized the importance of musical training in the education of children. A series of four-color double-page ads was launched, with pictures of famous musicians, scenes from operas, and interpretations of famous musical compositions. These advertisements were listed by *The Saturday Evening Post* as the first advertisements of the type ever published. Over the years,

Steinway advertisements have won numerous art awards, including four medals and three honorable mentions in the New York Art Directors' annual exhibitions.

In 1989, Steinway & Sons' retail outlet, Steinway Hall in New York City, launched an inventive direct marketing campaign that won a 1990 Golden Echo Award. Steinway placed 9 advertisements in the *New York Times,* offering such attractions or special offers as slightly used pianos at special prices, festivals, and free books to induce customers to come to Steinway Hall. Ordinarily, Steinway did not use the tactic of price reduction to attract customers; however, the advertisements in this case were deemed amusing and informative while still upholding the image of Steinway Hall.

Between 1853 and 1993, Steinway & Sons crafted a total of 520,000 pianos, compared with the up to 200,000 mass produced annually by some manufacturers. Each piano was serial numbered, and the company maintained records of each sale. In 1903, Steinway & Sons created its first commemorative piano, Serial #100,000, presented it to the American people, and installed it in the White House during the administration of Theodore Roosevelt. Thirty-five years later, Steinway & Sons created its second commemorative instrument, Serial #300,000, which was again presented to the American people and installed in the White House during the administration of Franklin Roosevelt. Number 100,000 was then transferred to the permanent collection of the Smithsonian Institution. To celebrate the 135th anniversary of Steinway & Sons, the company commissioned Wendell Castle, a premier American furniture designer, to create the case for the 500,000th piano. In December 1987, a regular production "Model D" concert grand, in an unfinished case, was shipped from the Steinway & Sons plant to Castle's workshop. The art case, which was unveiled at Carnegie Hall on June 2, 1988, was crafted from rare East Indian ebony and dyed Swiss pear, trimmed with Bubinga wood and Gaboon ebony, and adorned with the hand-etched signatures of over 800 living Steinway Artists. Having an estimated value of $500,000, Serial #500,000 was the most valuable piano ever made. In 1988, this piano began its world tour, which included stops in the United States, Europe, and the Far East.

Product Changes

C. F. Theodore Steinway, an accomplished pianist, had studied acoustics in Germany. Once he arrived at the Steinway factory in America, he began applying his knowledge of acoustics to improving the piano. Following a disciplined scientific approach, he was constantly experimenting. Also, he collaborated with the German physicist and acoustician Hermann von Helmholtz, who first scientifically analyzed overtones and their effect on tonal quality. Between 1860 and 1875, C. F. Theodore personally developed the most significant series of piano inventions ever patented by a single man, inventions that included the upright piano tubular metallic action frame, the grand piano action frame, the double iron frame bridge, the grand piano case design, and the upright piano keybed construction. His scientific approach led him to combine an overstrung scale design with Chickering & Sons' single-piece cast iron plate, resulting in a piano that matched Chickering's in volume but surpassed it in tonal quality because the bridge could be moved to the center of the soundboard for a more even dispersion of sound. In 1875, C. F. Theodore further advanced piano design when he conceived of a one-piece piano rim, made from 20 laminations of veneer, and later designed the machinery to build the rim. Indeed, by the end of the nineteenth century, Steinway & Sons had refined and improved virtually every aspect of the piano.

By 1900, Steinway pianos had incorporated 70 patented components and processes and hundreds of technical construction details. The 1930s saw the introduction of a new Duplex scale, the trademark Accelerated Action (which responded "14 percent faster *fortissimo* and 6 percent faster *pianissimo*"), and the Diaphragmatic soundboard (which tapered gently from the center to the edges to assure freer, more unified vibration for richer, more lasting tonal response). In the 1960s, the Hexagrip pinblock was patented and included in all models to improve tuning characteristics. With this invention, layers of hardrock maple, aligned at 45 to 90 degrees to each other, assured smooth pin movement and precise, longer-lasting tuning.

Twentieth-Century Growth

Steinway pianos have survived bleak economic times. When the Great Depression cut U.S. piano production to under 50,000 units in 1931 from a high of over 280,000 units in 1927, Steinway & Sons stolidly refused to compromise the quality of its products and trademark. Even a $500,000 offer by a home appliance manufacturer for the use of the company name to help sell refrigerators and stoves was firmly resisted. Although by 1940 the piano industry had rebounded, within 6 months of the attack on Pearl Harbor, the manufacturing of all consumer goods, including pianos, was curtailed by the government. However, because of the company's superb skills in laminating large pieces of wood, Steinway & Sons was mandated by the Army Air Corp to build wings and other component parts for its gliders. Also, a limited number of Steinway pianos were produced for use in military bases throughout the world.

By 1950, national advertising had helped sell approximately 250,000 pianos since 1900. Although during some years Steinway produced only 3 to 5 percent of the pianos made in the United States, the company's dollar volume often accounted for 10 to 15 percent of total sales. In 1950, Theodore E. Steinway, then-president of the company, estimated that nearly 25 percent of the 1 million pianos in good condition in the country were Steinways, and 90 percent of all pianos used in concerts were Steinways. In 1989, 5,000 units were sold worldwide, about 50 percent of these to foreign buyers. During the 1991-1992 concert season, 320 of the 355 piano soloists with the 62 major symphony orchestras in the United States and Canada performed exclusively on Steinway pianos.

In 1993, 7 types of grand pianos were available: the Baby Grand-Model S; the Medium Grand-Model M; the Chippendale Grand; the Louis XV Grand; the Living Room Grand; the Music Room Grand-Model B; and the Concert Grand-Model D. Custom-designed art case pianos could be commissioned by customers with highly individualistic tastes. Uprights were available, also. Because the building of each piano entailed such a painstaking selection of materials and such a meticulous manner of assembly, Steinway pianos were, of necessity, expensive. In 1993, the retail price for Steinway grand pianos ranged from approximately $20,000 to $65,000.

Future Directions

"Build to a standard, not a price. Make no compromise in quality. Strive always to improve the instrument." These basic principles, as set forth by founder Henry Steinway, have guided the family since the founding of the company in 1853. With only the finest materials and time-honed skills invested in each instrument, the Steinway piano has earned its reputation as "The Instrument of the Immortals," "The Piano by Which All Others Are Judged," and "The Piano of International Fame."

With 115 patents (the most recent of which was granted in 1993) to the company's credit, Steinway & Sons has done more than any other manufacturer to advance the art of piano making. In the coming years, computer-aided design technologies harnessed to time-honed manual craftsmanship should propel the Steinway piano to new heights of excellence. As the great performer Vladimir Ashkenazy noted, "Steinway is the only piano on which the pianist can do everything he wants and everything he dreams."

Further Reading:

Allen, Frederick, "Where High Tech Does Only the Simplest Jobs," *American Heritage Invention & Technology,* fall 1993.

Alson, Amy, "Returning a Virtuoso Sound; Steinway Seeks Broad Audience, Not Snob Appeal," *Crain's New York Business,* October 6, 1986, p. 1.

Amato, Ivan, "The Finishing Touch: Robots May Lend A Hand in the Making of Steinway Pianos," *Science News,* February 18, 1989, p. 108.

Fostle, D. W., "Henry Z. Steinway: A Grand Tradition," *Audio,* January 1993, p. 52.

Goldstein, Shelly, "There's Nothing Quite as Elegant as a Grand," *MGM Grand,* autumn 1991.

Huffman, Frances, "Play It Again, Henry," *Entrepreneur,* June 1980.

Matusky, Greg, "What We Export Best," *World Trade,* March 1991, p. 81.

McNamara, Victoria, "Piano Players Pull Strings in Race for Endorsements," *Houston Business Journal,* May 28, 1990, p. 1.

"Muted Market," *American Demographics,* November 1986, p. 14.

Myers, William, "Steinway Hits High Note," *Direct Marketing,* January 1989, p. 30.

Rothstein, Edward, "Don't Shoot the Piano Player," *The New Republic,* May 1, 1989, p. 32; "To Make a Piano of Note It Takes More Than Tools," *Smithsonian,* November 1988, p. 142.

Solber, Sara, and Claudia Glenn Dowling, "Ain't It Grand: Steinway & Sons Celebrates 135 Years of Celestial Sound by Building Its 500,00th Classic Piano," *Life,* June 1988, p. 99.

Sommers, Allen, "Value of Steinway Name Estimated to Equal All Its 50-Year Ad Investment," *Advertising Age,* July 24, 1950, p. 46.

Steinway, Theodore E., *People and Pianos, A Century of Service to Music, 1853–1953,* New York: Steinway & Sons, 1953.

"Steinway & Sons' Landmark 500,000th Piano," *Music Trades Magazine,* October 1988.

Steinway & Sons' 140th Anniversary: A Continuing Tradition of Excellence, Long Island City, New York: Steinway & Sons, 1993.

"Steinway & Sons: The Story from Birth to Domination," Long Island City, New York: Steinway & Sons, 1993.

"The Steinway Story," Long Island City, New York: Steinway & Sons, 1993.

Steinway's Living Legacy, Long Island City, New York: Steinway & Sons, 1993.

Stern, Aimee, "Steinway Finds Key to Domestic Market," *Adweek's Marketing Week,* July 18, 1988, p. 50.

Wren, Lisa, "Steinway Way," Fort Worth *Star-Telegram,* May 31, 1989.

—Virginia Barnstorff

STEUBEN®

STEUBEN

The image of Steuben as the most prestigious American crystal of the twentieth century was firmly established in 1947 when both the U.S. Ambassador to London and President Harry S. Truman chose Steuben pieces for their personal and official gifts to Princess Elizabeth of England to commemorate her forthcoming wedding. In Mary Jean Madigan's words, "The royal marriage captured America's imagination . . . [and] in a few short weeks, Steuben's image as a luxury product was immeasurably reinforced—crystal 'fit for the tables of royalty.' " Since that time, each U.S. president has continued the practice of giving Steuben items for their official diplomatic and personal gifts, and the Steuben name has come to be associated with artistic excellence, status, and luxury. Steuben's 1994 catalog summarized the foundation of the brand's reputation for excellence: "Innovative design and flawless craftsmanship have been the foundation of glassmaking at Steuben since its inception. The unique partnership of designer and glassmaker has been a catalyst to design visions that have pushed glassmakers to the edge of creative expression." Steuben's strength is the combination of "age-old methods" with "recent technology" to "fuel an ongoing process of discovery . . . [and] creative visions."

Brand Origins

On March 11, 1903, articles of incorporation were filed in the state of New York for a business to be called Steuben Glass Works. The two partners in the enterprise were Frederick Carder, a well-established, English glass designer and glassworking teacher, and Thomas G. Hawkes, president of the Corning, New York, glass engraving firm Hawkes and Company. For the next 30 years Carder assumed responsibility for all aspects of Steuben Glass production, managerial and artistic. He continued to experiment with Art Nouveau-inspired colored and decorative art glass signed with Steuben's fleur-de-lis trademark, scorning colorless crystal as "the quintessence of vulgarity." In 1904 he patented what was to be his bestseller, an iridescent, gold-toned glass called Aurene. Due to the similarity between Aurene and Tiffany's Favrile, Louis Comfort Tiffany threatened to bring suit, but never followed through.

Enter Corning Glass Works

During World War I, a shortage of lead and coal caused Steuben Glass Works's production of ornamental glass to decrease drastically. Nearby Corning Glass Works, in contrast, continued to operate at full capacity because of increased wartime demands for many of its products, including insulation and optical glass. On January 7, 1918, Corning Glass Works purchased the floundering Steuben Glass Works plant on Erie Avenue, retaining all of its employees. Carder, who was given the title art director and manager, continued to oversee the entire operation, along with John Hostetter from Corning who was appointed assistant manager of the new "Steuben Division."

Corning's acquisition of Steuben allowed Carder a certain amount of freedom from financial pressure and a work environment that fostered his creativity, but Steuben's sales declined throughout the 1920s. In fact several Corning reports from the late 1920s and early 1930s reveal that, except for the year 1926, Steuben ran a yearly deficit. The reports suggested that Carder's refusal to design in the more popular colorless crystal, his unwillingness to delegate managerial responsibilities, and his outmoded marketing and production tactics, in addition to overpriced stock were at fault.

Early Marketing Strategies

One of the trouble spots was undoubtedly Frederick Carder's outdated and inefficient sales and marketing techniques. In the first decade of Steuben's existence, Carder established a force of traveling salesmen to market the products in nationwide retail outlets. He continued this practice in the years following World War I, when he resumed production of creative ornamental glassware. By 1929 Steuben had 3,000 retail accounts throughout the United States, but the same sales staff was responsible for marketing a variety of disparate products, from lighting fixtures and architectural panels to glasses and bowls. Despite this volume and diversity, the company still tried to "cater to individual tastes." Mary Jean Madigan reported the salesmen "would often return to Corning with orders for special variations on stock pieces and for new designs suggested by their clients. These were obligingly turned out by workers in the blowing and finishing rooms, resulting in a growing overstock of unsalable, few-of-a-kind pieces."

In 1932 Steuben's offices, including Carder's studio, were moved to one of Corning's main plants. Despite the efforts of a transition team headed by Steuben Division plant manager John Mackay and design consultant Walter Dorwin Teague, Steuben failed to rally. However, Teague, a highly regarded industrial

AT A GLANCE

Steuben brand of glass and crystal was founded by Frederick Carder and Thomas G. Hawkes, with the incorporation of the Steuben Glass Company in Corning, New York, in 1903; "Aurene" colored glass patented in 1904; acquired by Corning Glass Works in 1918 to become Steuben Division of Corning Glass Works; Arthur Amory Houghton, Jr. became president of Steuben in 1933, with a team composed of architect John Monteith Gates and sculptor Sidney Waugh; Steuben Division reorganized as Steuben Glass, Incorporated in 1933, a wholly owned but administratively and fiscally independent subsidiary of Corning Glass Works; Steuben's first retail outlet opened February 19, 1934; in 1958 Steuben and Corning merged, and Steuben became Steuben Glass, a division of Corning Glass Works; Thomas Scharman Buechner became president in 1973 and Arthur A. Houghton, Jr., became chairman until his death in 1990; Corning Glass Works became Corning Incorporated and Steuben Glass became Steuben in 1989.

Major competitor: Waterford; also Baccarat, Lalique, Orrefors.

Advertising: *Agency*—Steuben Design Communications.

Addresses: *Parent company*—Corning Incorporated, P.O. Box 4000, Corning, NY 14831; phone: (607) 974-4261; fax: (607) 974-8551.

designer, played a pivotal role in the direction of Steuben's future, by suggesting not only a major magazine campaign for Steuben, but art museum exhibitions as well. He was responsible for the first articulation of the firm's purpose in a 1932 memo sent to Corning officials, which evolved into the "Steuben Trilogy." Teague stated: "This is what we have to sell: that delicate excellence possible only when the finest crystal is worked with the ultimate in craftsmanship into designs that come alive with style. . . . Steuben can achieve universal recognition as the ultimate in glass. It can become a demonstration or an advertisement of its owner's good taste and savoir faire. To have Steuben glass in your home and on your table will register you among those who know the right things." The memo clearly established the marketing philosophy—artistic excellence and an appeal to status and luxury—that would guide Steuben under the leadership of Arthur A. Houghton, Jr.

"From Ash Can to Museum"

The years from 1933 to 1972, during which Arthur Amory Houghton, Jr., was in charge of the Steuben Division, were the most experimental and expansive in the brand's history. As a result Steuben established a national and international image for superior artistic quality. In October of 1933 Houghton, great-grandson of the founder of Corning Glass Works, reorganized the Steuben Division into a subsidiary called Steuben Glass, Incorporated, with all of the stock owned by Corning Glass Works. Houghton then hired his support team: architect John Monteith Gates became managing director, and Sidney Waugh, a sculptor, was named designer and artistic consultant. Waugh was charged with designing and marketing the new Steuben products of colorless crystal that were in keeping with trends in design and popular taste. The *New York Times* quoted the company's slogan during the Houghton years as "From ash can to museum in half a generation." In the meantime Frederick Carder returned to his old offices on Erie Avenue, where he continued to work on his own colored crystal designs and architectural panels. He served as an advisor to Steuben until he officially retired in 1959 at the age of 96.

In order to publicize the firm's "new" image, Houghton began a campaign to associate Steuben glass with creative excellence. He arranged the first overseas exhibition of more than 200 pieces of Steuben crystal at the Fine Arts Society Gallery in London from March 20 to April 18, 1935. A preview of selected pieces were shown at the Knoedler and Company art gallery in New York City, and the entire exhibit appeared later that year in several American museums later that year.

Steuben shows continued in 1937 with the architectural exhibition at the Art Gallery of Toronto in Canada; the Corning Glass Works's presentation in the American Pavilion at the 1937 Paris Exposition, where Steuben received a Gold Medal for general excellence; and the Corning Glass Works's display, viewed by nearly three million people, in the Glass Industries Building at the World's Fair held in Flushing Meadow, New York, in 1939 (this exhibit was recreated at the New York store in 1989). Steuben, now recognized worldwide to be preserving an ancient art form, entered the realm of high art when it was the only American glass house invited to the "L'Art due Verre" exhibition at the Louvre in Paris in June of 1951. Other major exhibitions included the 1956 "Asian Artists in Crystal" exhibit at the National Gallery of Art and the Metropolitan Museum of Art, which later toured 16 countries and has been ranked as one of the highest achievements of Steuben's history. The exhibit "Steuben: Seventy Years of Glassmaking" was designed to reaffirm Steuben's established image as the most prestigious American glass. It opened at the Toledo Museum in 1974, traveled to eight other American museums, and then was shown at the Smithsonian for two years.

Steuben Retail Outlets

Another of Houghton's strategies in the rejuvenation of Steuben Glass was the establishment of a self-contained Steuben store that would allow merchandising standards to be set, something that had been impossible to control in the 3,000 different retail outlets carrying Steuben items. The first Steuben retail store, which opened at 748 Fifth Avenue in New York City on February 19, 1934, was designed by John Gates in consultation with his former architectural firm, Charles A. Platt, and decorated by New York interior design firm McMillen, Incorporated. Sales personnel at the gallery (as the stores were often referred to), including three women, were employed for their knowledge of fine art, instead of their knowledge of sales techniques, because their role was to advise and assist customers, not to sell products. In 1937 the New York store moved to its permanent location in the Corning Glass Works new six-story building at the corner of Fifth Avenue and 56th Street. The "House of Glass," designed by Geoffrey Platt and William Platt, was made of Pyrex building blocks. From 1934 to 1937, Steuben retail stores opened across the nation, including such sites as North Michigan Avenue in Chicago and Worth Avenue in Palm Beach. In 1935 the prestigious Boston jewelry store Shreve, Crump and Low began to deal in Steuben glass.

By 1956 Steuben had 19 retail dealers in department stores and specialty shops throughout the United States. Although Steuben had to close almost 20 of its retail stores in 1969, by 1994 it had grown to include galleries in 26 regional locations throughout the United States and six Steuben-owned freestanding stores. In keeping with the association of quality with the Steuben name, the Steuben gallery in The Greenbrier, located in White Sulphur

Springs, West Virginia, won the 1993 International Store Interior Design Award in the category "Smaller Specialty Stores for Hard Goods." The gallery was designed by architect Lee Stout of New York City.

Houghton continued his campaign to associate the Steuben name with the world of art by encouraging international artists to provide designs to be engraved on Steuben crystal for exhibitions in the Fifth Avenue store. In response, Steuben received submissions from such renowned artists as Henri Matisse, Georgia O'Keeffe, Isamu Noguchi, and Salvador Dali, and the resulting exhibit, "Twenty-seven Artists in Crystal," opened at the New York shop on January 10, 1940. The New York Gallery continued to host exhibitions of Steuben designs, including an antique glass collection exhibited from 1941 to 1952, the well-attended "Spring Flower Shows" of 1942 and 1950, and the innovative 1955 "Studies in Crystal" collection that was pivotal in moving Steuben from the production of utilitarian objects into the use of crystal as a medium for artistic sculptural designs.

Steuben has continued to associate retailing with artistic status in the New York gallery with such exhibitions as "Steuben Crystal in Private Collections," a 1961 show viewed by 45,000 people in the first 20 days. One of the most original exhibitions occurred when Houghton invited prominent American poets, including Marianne Moore, Conrad Aiken, Robinson Jeffers, and W. H. Auden to submit original poems which designers used as the basis for crystal sculptures. This blending of the arts culminated in the "Poetry in Crystal" show in 1963, produced in conjunction with the Poetry Society of America. A similar exhibit that revolved around the works of Shakespeare was shown in 1990.

Other Marketing Innovations

Other innovations introduced by Houghton during the 1930s included advertising in major national magazines, beginning with a 1936 full-page ad in the chic *New Yorker* magazine. He also began phasing out the production of colored glass pieces to make room for the simple and elegant clear crystal products that were becoming more popular and sought after. Houghton and his teammates instituted other production and marketing strategies during this time. They modernized the concept of the relationship between the designer and the glass blower by separating the two functions and hiring a staff of designers, primarily young architectural graduates. While the designers worked in the cultural and creatively stimulating atmosphere of New York City, the glassmakers performed their jobs in the town of Corning. In the 1950s, Steuben replaced the decades-old fleur-de-lis logo with the snowflake, representing the purity of the Steuben image and the uniqueness of each individual piece.

In another marketing move, Houghton began distribution of a catalog in 1941. Sensing that customers would associate a high-quality catalog with items of the same caliber, the catalog was used as a selling point for the products. By 1993 Steuben catalogs themselves were competing for artistic design awards, tying that year for the Silver Award in the retail category of the American Catalog Awards. Judges commented on the "superb" creativity, "exquisite" photography, and "scrupulously crafted details," according to *Catalog Age.*

In the aftermath of World War II, European glassmaking houses had either discontinued production or were using obsolete methods and designs. Houghton recognized the possibilities for the brand's growth into international markets and began revamping Steuben's design techniques and marketing strategies to more strongly associate the name Steuben with quality. In his work *Design Policy Within Industry as a Responsibility of High Level Management,* written in 1951, he explained: "At Steuben we began with the realization that good design must be integrated and extended throughout the company's every activity. If we were to convince the public that Steuben represents the very highest level of design in glass, then our advertisements, display rooms, catalogues, booklets, stationery, and packages, all of these auxiliaries must be designed as carefully as the product and must present to the public the same high standard of design as does the glass itself. And in addition, their design must be harmoniously integrated."

Educating the Public

A major Steuben mission has been to educate the public about the history and craft of glassmaking. To this end, Corning opened its Corning Glass Center, which included The Museum of Glass, during 1951, the company's centennial year. Observation galleries and special walkways were integrated into the new Steuben factory so that museum visitors could observe the glassblowing, finishing, and decorating processes. In 1952 the New York store moved a major portion of its antique glass exhibit, collected from countries around the world, to The Museum of Glass.

When former museum director and art scholar Thomas Scharman Buechner succeeded Houghton as president in 1973, Buechner continued educational exhibits by arranging special showings of non-Steuben glass in the New York store, including exhibits of German Blaschka glass, stained-glass window fragments from the Canterbury Cathedral, and Chinese snuff boxes. Buechner's philosophy for Steuben was "We are trying to be a corporation that acts like an artist." One of the most well-received non-Steuben glass exhibits was "Glass Jewelry: 25 Centuries of Style" in 1991.

Technological Innovations and Future Growth

Throughout the century, technological breakthroughs, in addition to design, have contributed to Steuben's image of quality and luxury. In 1932, Corning chemists discovered a process for removing iron impurities to produce a pure optical glass, dubbed "10-M," that was capable of transmitting ultraviolet light instead of absorbing it. In the 1970s Steuben created a press that could mass-produce small designs, allowing for more options in forming glass. It also pioneered an industry first, a melting tank that replaced the traditional ceramic pots and was kept a closely guarded secret for many years. Other design innovations that have allowed for more creative freedom were the creation of a refractive epoxy, the "speed fam," and flexible shaft engraving. As a testament to the Steuben reputation for quality, the firm was chosen by the U.S. government to design the Malcolm Baldrige National Quality Award. Established by a 1987 congressional act, the award is presented annually to those American companies judged to have achieved a standard of excellence in the quality of their products and services.

Although the 1980s brought some major restructuring for Steuben—including reorganization of corporate personnel—in 1992 President Donald M. Rorke reaffirmed Steuben's commitment to produce "the finest crystal the world has ever seen" with a campaign to revitalize the Steuben identity. The brand's image has been enhanced by Rorke's design vision that encompassed not only the pieces themselves, but also the stores and graphics, including Steuben's current logo. In Rorke's words, by ''combining design innovations with masterful artistry, Steuben is recognized worldwide as *the* choice for sophisticated accessories for living and working environments, for those who appreciate quality, value, and contemporary style.''

Further Reading:

''About Steuben,'' New York: Steuben Glass.

Farrar, Estelle Sinclaire, and Jane Shadel Spillman, *The Complete Cut and Engraved Glass of Corning,* New York: Crown, 1971.

Gardner, Paul V., *The Glass of Frederick Carder,* New York: Crown, 1971.

Hays, Lynn, ''Steuben Has Perfected Its Art,'' *Catalog Age,* September 1993, pp. 95–96.

Houghton, Arthur Amory, Jr., *Design Policy Within Industry as a Responsibility of High Level Management,* New York: Steuben Glass, Incorporated, 1951.

James, George, ''Arthur Houghton, Jr., 83, Dies: Led Steuben Glass,'' *New York Times,* April 4, 1990, p. B8.

Madigan, Mary Jean, *Steuben Glass: An American Tradition in Crystal,* New York: Harry N. Abrams, Inc., 1982.

Mallory, Maria, ''Susan King: A Stone Thrower,'' *Business Week,* August 17, 1987.

Reif, Rita, ''Faux Fashion: All That Glitters Here Is Glass,'' *New York Times,* October 13, 1991, sect. 2, p. H33.

Steuben 1994 Catalog, New York: Steuben.

''Steuben Hails Shakespeare,'' *HFD—The Weekly Home Furnishings Newspaper,* September 10, 1990, p. 69.

''Steuben's World's Fair Winners: Firm Recreates Display of Now-Classic Glass Show in '39,'' *HFD—The Weekly Home Furnishings Newspaper,* October 2, 1989, p. 55.

—Mary Katherine Wainwright

SUBARU®

Subaru of America was founded by two entrepreneurs, Harvey Lamm and Malcolm Bricklin, and incorporated in Pennsylvania in 1968 as the exclusive U.S. sales and marketing company for Subaru automobiles, manufactured by the Japanese company Fuji Heavy Industries. Fuji, which was formed by a group of six Japanese companies in 1956, began buying large numbers of shares in Subaru in 1976 in order to protect the newly successful company from a takeover, and ultimately acquired Subaru of America in 1990. Fuji Heavy Industries is currently the seventh-largest manufacturer of transportation equipment in Japan.

Because the company represents a coming together of six companies, it chose the brand name Subaru, the Japanese word for "unite." Likewise, the arrangement of stars found on the car's logo was derived from the constellation Taurus, and each star represents one of the founding partners. Until the Fuji takeover, Subaru of America was unique among import car companies as the only publicly owned one in the United States.

The first car Subaru introduced into the U.S. market was the Subaru 360 mini. Powered by a two-stroke engine and running at an impressive 66.3 miles per gallon, it sold for $1,297. It was nevertheless a failure because *Consumer Reports* pronounced it unsafe for U.S. roads. The bad review sent the young company reeling as Lamm and Bricklin struggled to stay afloat and work with Fuji to modify a car for U.S. requirements.

Rural Marketing

Subaru's first real hold on the U.S. market came through rural buyers in the early 1970s. In 1970, Subaru introduced a front-wheel-drive passenger car called the 1100 Series. While it is now standard in many smaller cars, front-wheel drive wasn't of much interest to American consumers then. That fact, combined with memories of the 360 mini debacle, made for initially sluggish sales nationally. However, in 1972 the New Jersey-based company mounted an extensive reevaluation of its sales and marketing practices and found that rural dealers were showing better results than those in the large metropolitan markets on the East and West coasts.

The company found that in urban markets, where the cars were in direct competition with domestic models, Subaru dealerships could not succeed on the basis of the type of price competition that prevailed in those areas. However, in rural markets, according to Automotive News, "the company was linked up with a different type of dealer. It was a dealer who was an entrepreneur, who put effort into business." Further, in rural markets there wasn't the kind of dealer saturation seen in cities, and consumers were more likely to form loyalties to individual dealers, and also more likely to purchase cars on the advice of other owners.

Based on this evidence, SOA stopped signing metro dealers for the time being and put all of its resources into solidifying relationships with rural dealers. Lamm told *Automotive News* several years later that the extra attention helped raise many dealers' incomes from "just making a living" to levels high enough that the dealers put their earnings back into the dealerships. Meanwhile, as Subaru took this position, many other auto makers were neglecting or ignoring the rural market entirely. The attributes of the 1100 Series, including standard transmissions and improved handling—through front-wheel drive—on rougher rural roads led to a business, according to the company, consisting of 80 percent referrals.

At this point, Subaru was doing business in the United States on a very few models. In 1973 the product line included only three cars, but the company had moved into the top ten of import cars in the country and had begun to show a substantial profit. That same year, Lamm traveled to Japan to discuss further models with Fuji, saying, according to the company, that the U.S. market demanded cars with more style and features. While he was there, Lamm became intrigued by a car used by Japan's rural electric companies that could be converted to four-wheel drive at the flick of a lever. According to *Forbes* magazine, Fuji was preparing to phase out the model for lack of demand when Lamm persuaded the manufacturer to make it available in the United States, thus expanding the brand's appeal to rural buyers.

In the following two years, Subaru continued to solidify its position in the American rural market and began to receive greater recognition within the automotive industry. Already established in the small-car market, Subaru was well positioned to take advantage of the 1970s Arab oil embargo and the attention it focused on fuel efficiency. In 1974 the company launched the Subaru 4WD wagon, the first four-wheel-drive passenger car in America, which incorporated Fuji's driver-activated four-wheel-drive option. In 1975 the company's new Subaru GF model was named *Road Test* magazine's "Import Car of the Year."

AT A GLANCE

Subaru of America was founded in Pennsylvania in 1968 by Harvey Lamm and Malcolm Bricklin as the exclusive sales and marketing company for Subaru automobiles, manufactured in Japan by Fuji Heavy Industries, Ltd. Subaru of America was an independent, publicly traded American company until 1990, when Fuji purchased a majority share.

Performance: *Market share*—Subaru holds approximately 1% of the American auto market, including domestic and imported cars; 25% of all four-wheel-drive passenger cars sold in America are Subarus.

Major competitor: Subaru considers itself a "niche marketer" to consumers of four-wheel-drive vehicles, but its major competitors by size and price of car are Toyota, Nissan, and Honda.

Advertising: *Agency*—Temerlin McClain, Dallas, TX, 1994—.

Addresses: *Parent company*—Subaru of America, Subaru Plaza, P.O. Box 6000, Cherry Hill, NJ 08034-6000; phone (609) 488-3338, fax (609) 488-3274. *Ultimate parent company*—Fuji Heavy Industries Ltd., 1-7-1 Nishi-Shinjuku, Shinjuku-ku, Tokyo 160 Japan; phone (03) 3472111; fax (03) 3472338.

At this point the company was building momentum and 1976, Subaru officials would later say, was "the year in which Subaru of America came of age." At the beginning of the year, it was the country's 12th-largest car importer; by the end of fiscal 1976, Subaru had climbed to number six in that category. The car became the number-one import in Vermont and Maine, and showed especially strong sales performance in the mountainous terrains of New England and the Pacific Northwest. The company's success during this period led it to take another crack at the metropolitan markets, with the help of a new advertising agency: Levine, Huntley, Schmidt, Plapler and Beaver, Inc.

Targeting the Recreational Market

On the advice of the Levine, Huntley agency, the company decided to devote more resources to expanding its market niche from rural buyers to city dwellers fond of outdoor sports. "We felt younger people were the best potential for four-wheel drive," agency president Robert Schmidt told *Forbes.* "The doers, the goers, the hunters, people going to the beach." In order to enhance the appeal to those urban "goers," the company began a partnership with the U.S. Ski Team, whereby the Subaru 4WD station wagon became its official car. The company's approach to the urban markets was still cautious and highly selective. Because referral business remained high for all Subaru cars, the company's advertising focused on brand-name recognition: in 1977, the Levine, Huntley agency unveiled what became the company's long-running advertising theme, "Inexpensive and built to stay that way."

In 1977 Subaru introduced the BRAT, a small, dual-range, four-wheel-drive car with two bucket seats fixed to a pickup-style open-bed back. Among the other car models available at the time, it was outwardly most similar to the Chevrolet El Camino. The BRAT, Harvey Lamm told *Forbes,* was designed by Subaru of America (rather than Fuji) "from the ground up." In an appeal to young buyers who weren't necessarily attracted to the carmaker's staid, functional image, it was targeted for "fun and sun" recreational use. The name of the model was in itself intended to appeal, in a tongue in cheek way, according to the advertising agency, to the "spoiled brat" market. In addition, the warm-weather, outdoor sports image served as a complement to the ski-team tie-in, which appealed mainly to buyers in the snowbelt. The year after it was introduced, the BRAT was presented with an "Excellence in Engineering" award by *Off Road* magazine, which helped shepherd Subaru into the fifth-largest importer position.

By the end of 1978, according to the *Automotive News,* 70 percent of Subaru models were still sold in rural markets, but the company was working to increase its urban presence. In late 1979 (1980 model year) Subaru introduced a dramatically different line of cars with a look designed to appeal more to American tastes than what *Forbes* called the earlier models' "square Japanese look." The new line included a new hatchback model and two different "luxury levels" of existing models designed to appeal to a more upscale urban customer than had been enticed by the more purely functional front- and four-wheel-drive cars that sold so well in the rural markets.

Of the new models, the DL was a front-wheel-drive station wagon with a list price of $5,998, and the GL, the slightly upgraded model, featured four-wheel drive for $350 more. The two smaller cars in the new line, a four-wheel-drive sedan and a four-wheel-drive hatchback, were priced at $4,998 and $4,799 respectively. The latter became the lowest-priced Japanese import available for the next several years. The entire line—with on-demand four-wheel drive available in three of the four models—had found and expanded an unique market niche for itself, which made financial analysts in *Business Week* magazine call Subaru "the only pure play available in small cars" (on the stock market).

By 1980 Subaru had tripled its unit sales over 1975 totals and had positioned itself to overtake Mazda as the number-four Japanese importer in the United States. "Such growth," *Business Week* observed, "enhanced this year [1980] by the introduction of new and sleeker models, has fueled an impressive financial turnaround.

Selling in Metro Markets

Subaru, according to *Advertising Age* magazine, launched a $12 million ad campaign to promote the new cars. The company's advertising agency retained the "inexpensive and built to stay that way" motto and, in the case of the remodeled station wagon, combined it with a television spot that aptly captured the company's aspirations for an expanded sales base that retained rural and recreational buyers at the same time as it appealed to potential urban and suburban drivers. "As first look you might think our Subaru four-wheel-drive wagon is a pretty tame animal. Sleek, handsome, comfortable, well-fed. But flip it from front-wheel drive into four-wheel drive, even up to 50, and you'll unleash a wild and wooly beast that gobbles up hills and claws through curves while barely whetting its small appetite for gas."

In 1981 Subaru formed Subaru Financial Services, Inc. The first of its kind for an import car company, it was created to provide extended service contracts, retail financing and credit insurance, as well as dealer inventory financing. Through that year, according to the company, sales continued to climb—by 23 percent—despite Japan's Ministry of International Trade and Industry agreement to limit the number of cars exported to the United States. The company's earnings would continue to grow between 1980 and 1985 despite such restrictions.

In 1983, Subaru's 15th anniversary, the company sold its one-millionth car in the United States and its sales exceeded $1 billion for the first time. The company became the first carmaker to offer optional four-wheel drive in all models and introduced the first four-wheel drive with an automatic transmission. The same year, "turbo-traction," which is, according to the company, "a unique combination of four-wheel drive and a turbocharged, fuel injected engine, was introduced." The company moved up to number three in the JD Power Customer satisfaction index, and *Forbes* magazine rated Subaru of America fourth out of 1,000 U.S. companies in profitability. In 1984, the J.D. Power survey company ranked Subaru number one in customer satisfaction out of all U.S. and Japanese makes, and second among all domestic and imported brands behind Mercedes-Benz. The number of Subaru vehicles in the United States passed the one million mark.

Company Falters

In 1985 the Subaru wagon became the number-one station wagon model in the United States, with owner registrations higher than any domestically produced model, and 30 percent higher than the next most popular Japanese import. Yet, at the same time that the brand had achieved the height of its market acceptance, the strengthening of the yen relative to the dollar was beginning to wear on the company. The domestic car manufacturers were beginning to recover from their troubles in the late 1970s and early 1980s, and the strong yen forced Fuji to raise prices. In an attempt to limit the effect of the yen on the cars' prices, the company announced a joint venture with Isuzu Motors, another Japanese carmaker, for a production plant in Lafayette, Indiana.

In 1987, the company reported a loss of $30 million to its shareholders, blaming the strong yen, increased importation costs, and a 25 percent increase in the line's retail prices, a change which belied the company's "inexpensive and built to stay that way" slogan. Sales were suffering at a time when larger Japanese importers like Honda, Toyota, and Nissan, faced with the same constraints, had high enough volume to sell cars cheaper than Subaru could. The company responded by introducing two new models: the Justy, a front-wheel-drive minicar powered by a 1.3 liter engine (and targeted to younger buyers with a base price under $6,000); and a performance car, the XT6, a sporty model with a 6-cylinder, 2.7 liter engine.

Also in 1987, the company took over control of three of its regional distributorships. Until then, they had been independently owned and operated and, adding to Subaru's headaches, were said by local dealers to be uncooperative in crucial areas like making replacement parts available to them. Such problems also contributed to lowering the customer satisfaction index, of which Subaru had been so proud.

In 1988 the company reported an even larger loss, $57.9 million, and suspended dividend payments to its shareholders. The loss was blamed on a 13 percent decline in unit sales and a corresponding increase in spending on advertising and rebates in an attempt to increase sales figures. That year, Lamm told the company's shareholders that "the shift in prices has been dramatic and occurred at a time when our subcompact line of cars was nearing the end of its product cycle." Accordingly, as sales continued to decline, Subaru announced an updated line of cars for the 1989 model year. The Justy was made available with a new type of automatic transmission called ECVT (for electronic continuously variable transmission) in which the standard gear system is replaced with a sort of rope-and-pulley system that allows for an almost infinite number of gears to suit any driving conditions. The new model was kept within the under-$8,000 range.

For the next consumer market up, the company repackaged its rather unsuccessful Leone line of subcompact cars under the name Loyale, which included a three-door, a sedan, and a station wagon, and repositioned it to fit in the price range directly above the Justy. In the spring of 1989 Subaru introduced the all-new Legacy, a five-passenger compact car with a 2.2 liter engine, full-time four-wheel drive, four-speed automatic transmission, and ABS anti-lock breaks. The mid-priced sedan and wagon models were marketed in the $11,000-18,000 range.

As the same time as Subaru was announcing these new models, according to the *New York Times,* "the company's three biggest competitors—Toyota, Nissan, and Honda—were trimming the time between model changes and introducing a startling array of sports cars, sedans, and minivans." And the only truly new offering in the Subaru line, the Legacy, was competing with established sellers like the Honda Accord and Toyota's Corolla and Camry models. Unfortunately, Fuji Heavy Industries was having trouble of its own and was to some extent unable to guide Subaru of America.

Communication between the two companies was said to have deteriorated as well. The solution, though it remains to be seen whether it will be the cure, came in 1990. Nissan Motor Company, of Japan, stepped in and bought a 4.51 percent share in Fuji to prevent its faltering further. Fuji, in turn, purchased a majority share, 50.7 percent, in Subaru of America, thus making it a subsidiary.

Company in Transition

Following the takeover, Harvey Lamm quit the company and Takeshi Higurashi assumed the duties of Chairman and Chief Executive Officer. Over the next 18 months the company engaged in a restructuring plan that included changing advertising agencies from Levine, Huntley to Weiden and Kennedy of Portland, Oregon. The company also cut staff by 20 percent, reduced office and administrative expenses by 25 percent, and purchased one of the last of the independently owned distributorships. However, as of 1993, the company's 25th anniversary year, the trouble was still not over. A new subcompact introduced to replace the Loyale, called the Impreza, according to *Automotive News,* arrived about two years after the market needed it and "failed to meet expectations" when it did arrive. At the beginning of 1993, the car sold 3,000 units per month, short of the hoped-for 5,000.

In early 1994, the company changed advertising agencies again, to Temerlin McClain of Dallas, Texas. In the six or so months preceding the change, Subaru seemed to be conspicuously absent from the airwaves as well as from print advertising. Sales difficulties aside, Subarus continue to be recognized for their engineering qualities, but in an era when trade restrictions on Japanese imports have as much support as ever, times may continue to be difficult for the company.

Further Reading:

Bohn, Joseph J., "Success to Shift Subaru Ad Focus," *Automotive News,* September 5, 1977, p. 19.

Chakravarty, Subrata, "Hey! This Is Fun!" *Forbes,* March 17, 1980, p.72.

Fanelli, Louis A., "Subaru Pitching Luxury for '80 Line," *Advertising Age,* November 12, 1979.

Henry, Jim, ''Subaru Sheds Its Hopes for Mass Market,'' *Automotive News,* July 12, 1993, p.1; ''Fuji First: Subaru of America Parent Challenged by U.S. Market,'' *Automotive News,* March 23, 1992.

Johnson, Richard, ''SIA Continues to Hurt Fuji Rebound,'' *Automotive News,* October 14, 1991.

Rescigno, Richard, ''At the Crossroads: Subaru Strives to Get Back Into Gear,'' *Barron's,* March 28, 1988, p. 15.

Russell, John A., ''Subaru Travels Own Path to Success,'' *Automotive News,* February 12, 1979, p. 66; ''Subaru to Offer New Models for 1980,'' *Automotive News,* October 9, 1978, p.44.

Sanger, David E., ''Company Takeover, Tokyo Style,'' *New York Times,* June 27, 1990, p. D1.

''Subaru: The Only Auto Play Left?'' *Business Week,* June 16, 1980, p. 111.

—Martha Schoolman

SUNBEAM®

The Sunbeam brand name is among the most recognized in the U.S. small appliance market and represents a variety of electrical equipment including mixers, toasters, shavers, irons, electric blankets, and heaters. Produced under the auspices of the Sunbeam-Oster Company, Inc., since 1989, the brand continued to garner top domestic market shares for the majority of its products and was a world leader in innovative portable appliance technology.

Brand Origins and Earliest Successes

The founders of the Sunbeam Corporation, John K. Stewart and Thomas J. Clark, established the Chicago Flexible Shaft Company in Dundee, Illinois, in 1897. Initially they produced nonelectrical agricultural tools, such as sheep shearing machines, hand clippers, and flexible shafts used to propel or balance other tools. A few years later, the men set up a factory in Chicago to manufacture the furnaces necessary for producing their clipping and shearing devices. This business expanded to include the production of ''Clark'' carriage heaters and ''Clark'' carbon coal for horse drawn carriages as well as for the new horseless carriages of the day. However, during this time, the business was subject to the seasonal demand for its products, and in 1910 Stewart and Clark decided to embark upon the manufacture and marketing of electric appliances.

That year, the Chicago Flexible Shaft Company introduced the ''Princess'' electric iron. While the company did not invent the electric iron, it foresaw the appliance's popularity and marketability well ahead of its competitors. The iron, which was lightweight and offered superior heating ability, met with success, prompting the company to enlarge its electric appliance business and to adopt the brand name ''Sunbeam'' in its advertisements.

The Sunbeam Mixmaster was one of the company's most successful appliances. Introduced in 1930, the mixer became extremely popular, as it helped decrease the amount of time and effort the consumer spent in the kitchen mixing ingredients by hand. Despite the economic depression of the 1930s, Sunbeam electrical appliances flourished, and the first Sunbeam patented Double automatic Ironmaster Dry Iron was introduced, along with the Sunbeam Shavemaster Shaver, the first pop up electric toaster, and the first automatic electric coffeemaker. During this time, Sunbeam rose to prominence and held the largest share of its market, a position that it maintained into the 1990s.

Product Development

The Chicago Flexible Shaft Company changed its name to the Sunbeam Corporation in 1946, reflecting the importance of its electrical household and personal care appliances. A steady stream of popular innovations ensued, all of which were given the Sunbeam brand name. An automatic Sunbeam Steam Iron and the popular Sunbeam Egg Cooker were introduced in 1950, followed by the Sunbeam Controlled Heat fry pan three years later. In 1955 an electric coffee percolator and the world's first electric blanket were manufactured under the Sunbeam label, as was the Lady Sunbeam Shaver. A deluxe model of the Sunbeam Mixmaster was offered in a variety of colors and featured several new settings, and in 1956, the Controlled Heat Hair Dryer was introduced. In the 1960s, the Sunbeam product line expanded to include the Party Grill, the first cordless hand mixer, the Sunbeam electric Snow Thrower, and the Carousel Rotisserie broiler.

During this time, Sunbeam purchased the John Oster Manufacturing Company, maker of the popular ''Osterizer'' blender, and established it as an important subsidiary. When Sunbeam and Oster were acquired by the Allegheny International Corporation in 1981, the two subsidiaries became AI's most profitable businesses. By then, Sunbeam had added several important product lines, including the floor care and clock divisions.

Manufacture of a steady stream of new products continued on Sunbeam-Oster's assembly lines since the emergence of Sunbeam-Oster as an independent company in 1989. Some of these, such as a unique warming blanket that adjusts heat by sensing the body's temperature, an iron that shuts off automatically, and large print bathroom scales, require high technological proficiency. By the early 1990s, approximately one quarter of company sales derived from its new products.

Advertising and Marketing Strategy

The company's cheerful ''Sunbeam'' name was adopted in all of its advertising—print ads and radio announcements—in 1921. With the emergence of Sunbeam-Oster as an independent company in 1989, a renewed commitment to advertising the famous Sunbeam and Oster brands developed. Year round advertising was extended to television as well as the print media, and the company's advertising budget was increased 20 percent, to $59 million. Furthermore, a renewed effort was made to distribute tradi-

AT A GLANCE

Sunbeam brand of appliances established in 1897 by the Chicago Flexible Shaft Company; company changed its name to Sunbeam Corporation, 1946; company acquired John Oster Manufacturing Company, 1960; company purchased by Allegheny International Corporation, 1981; Allegheny International dissolved, and Sunbeam emerged as the Sunbeam-Oster Company, Inc., 1989.

Performance: *Market share*—40% of domestic mixer market. *Sales*—$500 million.

Major competitor: Hamilton Beach; also Procter/Silex and Black & Decker.

Advertising: *Agency*—In-house. *Major campaign*—"Sunbeam, Made for Life"; print ads for Sunbeam Soft Touch heating pad featuring the tagline "Even Tough Guys Prefer a Soft Touch."

Addresses: *Parent Company*—Sunbeam-Oster Company, Inc., 200 E. Las Olas Blvd., Suite 2100, Fort Lauderdale, FL 33301; phone: (305) 767-2100; fax: (305) 767-2105.

tional as well as new products to large discount stores such as WalMart, K-Mart, Target, Sears, and Best.

International Market

As early as the 1920s, Sunbeam had established wholly owned subsidiaries in Canada and Australia. International expansion was rapid after World War II, with subsidiaries emerging in Puerto Rico, Argentina, Mexico, and Italy. International markets have played an increasingly important role in the fortunes of Sunbeam-Oster. The International Division, established in 1989, accounted for one quarter of company sales in the early 1990s, and while most of these sales are generated in Canada and Latin America, Sunbeam continued efforts to expand in the United Kingdom, the Middle East, Europe, and Japan. In 1993, Sunbeam was the best known American small appliance brand in Great Britain. In Latin America, Sunbeam was the most popular small appliance brand of any nationality, and the company held top market positions in small kitchen appliances in Peru and a leading position, greater than a 60 percent market share, in the same market in Venezuela.

While most of Sunbeam-Oster products are made in the United States, the company developed some manufacturing facilities in Mexico, Venezuela, Peru, and several Central American countries. Sales and distribution of Sunbeam-Oster products in Canada remained extremely strong, with leading market shares in the same product lines as those in the United States, namely heating pads, warming blankets and throws, personal care products, hair clippers, and a variety of small kitchen appliances. Sunbeam-Oster planned to expand its international presence by building on its brand name recognition and marketing worldwide an increasing array of products, including barbecue grills, which had been marketed mainly in the United States and Canada.

The Future

As it approached the twenty-first century, Sunbeam's greatest strength remained its widespread brand name recognition, which became synonymous with quality and durability. Furthermore, its commitment to exploring new product lines was regarded as paramount to its success. With a small, manageable company debt, integrated manufacturing, and a greatly streamlined corporate structure, Sunbeam products were expected to continue to dominate the market for small appliances well into the next century. The Sunbeam brand could also expect to experience greater renown in the international market, particularly in parts of the world where economies were growing and free market economies were still evolving, as in eastern Europe and Russia.

Further Reading:

Allegheny International, A New Global Business Enterprise, New York: Newcomen Society, 1983.

Annual Report: Sunbeam-Oster Co., Fort Lauderdale, Fla.: Sunbeam-Oster Co., 1992.

Farnsworth, Steve, "Sunbeam-Oster Sets Expansion: Company Plots Strategy to Bolster Sales in International Markets," *HDF—The Weekly Home Furnishings Newspaper,* July 6, 1992, p. 61.

"Florida Move for Sunbeam," *New York Times,* October 4, 1993, p. C2, D5.

Purpura, Linda, "Determined to Dominate: Sunbeam-Oster Team Unifies Efforts to Win Market Share Across All Lines," *HDF—The Weekly Home Furnishings Newspaper,* February 15, 1993, p. 49.

Ratliff, Duke, "Sunbeam Oster Shaking Up Massager Field," *HDF—The Weekly Home Furnishings Newspaper,* May 17, 1993, p. 54.

"Sunbeam's Net Rose 71% in 4th Quarter; Overseas Sales Cited," *The Wall Street Journal,* February 4, 1993, p. B4, B6.

—Sina Dubovoj

SUNFISH®

By the early 1980s the Sunfish, which evolved from the Sailfish introduced in the late 1940s, had become the most popular sit-down sailboat in the world. Sunfish sales were almost twice as high as those of its nearest competitor. Although the Sunfish became one of the most familiar images of the second half of the 20th century, hailed by *Fortune* magazine in 1977 as one of the 25 best designed modern products, the little boat was developed not by careful planning, but rather through a series of accidents and streaks of luck. After taking the world by storm, the Sunfish brand changed hands several times. Although the brand has suffered somewhat because of this, its current parent, Sunfish/Laser, Inc., expects the Sunfish will prosper.

Birth of an Idea

The Sunfish was invented by two friends from Waterbury, Connecticut, neither of whom had any formal training in woodworking. However, both Alexander Bryan and Cortland Heyniger enjoyed the craft and knew that one day they wanted to build something. The idea of going into business together dawned on them after both returned from World War II and discovered that the barn which housed their iceboats had burned down. With the money they received from the insurance company, they decided to start their own business, Alcort, Inc. ''Alcort'' was a combination of their first names, which they thought sounded better than ''Cortal.'' Before launching the Sunfish, the partners produced such diverse items as treehouses, iceboats, wooden drawer pulls, ironing boards, baby swings, and toys. They also experimented unsuccessfully with a glider.

The idea for making a sailboat came from an unexpected source. A local Red Cross employee brought some plans, and asked if they could build a small surfboard to be used in lifesaving. He left when the quote he received was too high, but neglected to take his drawings. Bryan and Heyniger, along with an employee named Carl Meinelt, decided to create their first sailboard using those designs.

Brand Origins

According to the founders, that original craft sailed like a log. The designers experimented with different specifications before the boat would sail. They settled on a length of 14 feet, a beam of 36 inches, and a sail shaped as an equilateral triangle. The new craft, named ''Sailfish,'' was still a version of a sailboard. The rider would sit on top with their legs stretched out in front, a position which offered little comfort and even less protection from the spray. Buyers had the option of purchasing a ready-made model, or the somewhat less expensive do-it-yourself kit. The Sailfish arrived on the market in 1947, and after the first year, Alcort had sold about 100 units.

A big publicity boost for the Sailfish came by accident, when an acquaintance who worked for *Life* magazine visited Alcort. She decided to write a story on the little boat, and in 1949 *Life* ran a two-page spread featuring the Sailfish. The response from customers exceeded Bryan and Heyniger's wildest dreams. The partners no longer had to worry about creating demand for their product.

Alcort's business turned around, and the founders no longer had to forego their own paychecks. While they were busy enjoying their new-found success and producing Sailfish by the dozen, Bryan's pregnant wife suggested the craft might be more comfortable if it provided a place for one's feet. The partners took this to heart, and Carl Meinelt set about drawing up suitable plans in the sawdust on the floor. The new spontaneous design included a footwell, which facilitated a more natural sitting position. This feature was incorporated almost immediately, and a few years went by before the designers bothered to create the prints. They named the boat ''Sunfish,'' because of its round and fat contours. The Sunfish logo was created by Heyniger, who traced a nickel on a piece of paper, and added the fins, tail and the eye.

Brand and Product Development

The Sunfish emerged on the scene at just the right time. In the second half of the 1950s, economic prosperity brought Americans plenty of leisure time and discretionary income. Even better, the Sunfish had no direct competition. The craft was the clear leader in mass-produced small sailboats, and Alcort was able to meet the demand with efficient production.

By 1956 Bryan and Heyniger realized that they were not suited to be executives and hired Bruce Connelly to take over administrative and marketing matters. Connelly created a dealer organization, which in the 1980s numbered 700 members, with dealerships in 50 states and around the world. The dealer network provided product information and support to consumers, which lent more credibility to the brand and translated into improved and more efficient sales for the makers of Sunfish.

The Sunfish was always a one-design boat, strictly controlled by the manufacturer. Sailors could do very little by way of expensive add-ons that would make the boat go faster. The design was so simple that it eliminated the need for new sails or hardware every year. Because of its uniform, characteristic shape, the Sunfish became one of the most widely recognized images, inevitably associated with the carefree spirit of summer.

This design evolved slightly over the years, but the first real breakthrough came with the advent of fiberglass. Before 1959 Alcort manufactured all Sunfish boats out of wood. The founders remained skeptical about fiberglass, at least partly because of their love for woodworking, but they had to admit that by molding their boats out of the material would provide more opportunity to expand the company. The fiberglass Sunfish was faster, lighter, and more attractive. Gradually, more modern materials found their way into the Sunfish design. The spruce mast was replaced with aluminum and the cotton sails with Dacron. However, the rudder and dagger board were still made out of mahogany and the tiller out of mahogany-stained ash wood, which proved the most durable.

AT A GLANCE

Sunfish brand of sailboats was originally founded as the Sailfish in 1947 by Alexander Bryan and Cortland Heyniger of Alcort, Inc., in Waterbury, CT; design changes prompted the Sunfish name in the early 1950s; Alcort was sold to American Machine and Foundry Co. in 1969, becoming AMF Alcort; in 1989 Alcort was sold to Pearson Yachts Corp., which created PY Small Boats division to manufacture the Sunfish; in 1991 the Sunfish was purchased by a group of investors organized under the name of Sunfish/Laser, Inc.

Performance: *Sales*—$7.5 million.

Addresses: *Parent company*—Sunfish/Laser, Inc., 200 Highpoint Ave., Portsmouth, RI 02871; phone: (401) 683-5900.

The Sailfish was phased out of production in 1966, followed by the 14-foot Super Sailfish in 1980. In 1969 the founders sold their company to American Machine and Foundry Co. Bryan and Heyniger, along with Carl Meinelt, continued to work there, but the founders soon left the company, while Meinelt remained on board as quality manager.

Market Appeal

Over the years other companies have tried to compete with the Sunfish by offering even less expensive imitations. None of this noticeably affected the success of the Sunfish, which enjoyed the position of having been first on the market. As a one-design, inexpensive, simple-to-operate boat, the Sunfish was a winner in the marketplace. Sailing had always been regarded as a sport for the wealthy, but the Sunfish put it within reach of the average person. As Alexander Bryan put it, "There's something friendly about the appearance of these boats. Something unpretentious."

The Sunfish was so popular, that it soon became a familiar and widely recognized icon, whose image was constantly projected on TV and in print media. The little boat became synonymous with having fun at the beach, appearing in many commercials for other companies and brands, including Air France, Buick, Wamsutta Sheets, and the National Geographic Society. The Sunfish has also appeared on postage stamps for the Bahamas and the island of Montserrat in the British West Indies. In 1977 the craft made *Fortune*'s list of top 25 product designs, one that has been enjoyed by sailing enthusiasts around the world. This was possible because one did not need to be an expert sailor to master the Sunfish. As AMF Alcort's vice president of sales and marketing, Jim Ronshagen, commented in *Sports Illustrated,* "You can race in it, loll in it, let children use it without anxiety. It's just a great product. It's good for everything."

One of those things was racing. Experienced sailors initially perceived the Sunfish as an overrated beach toy. However, the Sunfish class was later officially recognized by the U.S. Yacht Racing Union. As a one-design boat, it did not depend on high-tech additions to make the sailing experience pleasurable. This also made Sunfish racing very different from other sailing competitions, because the Sunfish class was entirely controlled by the manufacturer. Alcort made all decisions regarding the rules, equipment, and techniques designed to make the boat go faster. Many considered the Sunfish the purest form of racing because performance was not determined by high-tech gadgetry.

New Strategic Efforts

After 1989, when Alcort was purchased from AMF by Pearson Yachts, the Sunfish brand suffered serious setbacks. By the late 1980s the Sunfish had lost some its popularity, and Pearson Yachts's unsuccessful attempts to restore the craft to its former glory badly missed the mark. The failing company threatened to take the Sunfish down with it, until it was saved from near bankruptcy in 1991 by a group of investors headed by Peter Johnstone. He hoped that his new company, Sunfish/Laser, Inc., would be able to bolster the craft's image. Johnstone, who was 26 years old when he acquired Sunfish, felt that non-competitive sailors had been largely neglected and that he and his younger management team would be able to assess and fill their needs.

Johnstone's strategy was to increase production efficiency and implement strict quality control standards. Sunfish/Laser moved from the inefficient facility formerly occupied by Pearson Yachts and was able to cut costs through better space management as well as by incorporating employee suggestions for streamlining production. The new company emphasized craftsmanship and the work ethic, utilizing input from employees to develop new quality control guidelines. This enabled the company to overcome problems passed on by Pearson Yachts and boost dealer and consumer confidence in the Sunfish.

Johnstone also emphasized more aggressive marketing, and Sunfish/Laser has taken advantage of the fact that there is little aggressive advertising among other small boat makers. Most of the formal advertising has been in sailing magazines, with the initial emphasis on restoring the brand image among sailing enthusiasts. In addition, by encouraging dealer input, the company has managed to revitalize the relationship with its dealer network. Sunfish/Laser also promotes its boats at regional regattas and has supplied numerous boats for racing events. Johnstone hoped that the revitalized Sunfish/Laser would attract top sailors back to small boats, which he called the purest form of competition. It was expected that the endorsement by top sailors would, in turn, generate renewed interest in small boats among other sailing enthusiasts.

In addition to the Sunfish, the company produces other boats, notably the Laser and the relatively new DaySailer, but plans to remain focused exclusively on the small boat market. The advantage of small boats is their comparatively low price, which can even attract impulse buyers. Johnstone asserted in the *Providence Journal-Bulletin,* "I know the small boats and what the market is out there. It's a mistake to go elsewhere."

Further Reading:

Colt, Tim, "Sunfish/Laser Had a Strong Year and Is Headed for a Second One After Its Rescue by New Owners," *Providence Journal-Bulletin,* June 16, 1992, sec. D, p. 1.

Johnson, William Oscar, "Here She Is, The True Love Boat," *Sports Illustrated,* September 20, 1982, pp. 74–88.

Micheli, Mark, "Peter L. Johnstone: Doing Good Business in Bad Times," *Providence Business News,* June 29, 1992, sec. 1, p. 2.

"PY Small Boats Purchased," *Sail,* August 1991, p. 100.

—Justyna Frank

SUZUKI®

Suzuki is the brand name of three major product lines of the Suzuki Motor Corporation. Best known in the United States and Europe for its line of small, fuel-efficient cars and trucks, Suzuki is also a leading manufacturer of motorcycles and outboard motors. In the American auto market, Suzuki is a leading name in the hybrid utility vehicle market. In Japan, however, Suzuki is known primarily for its line of tiny "midget" cars, designed especially for the congested streets of Japanese urban centers, occupying the market between compact and subcompact.

The company's motorcycle enterprise is run entirely separately from its automotive group. Within Japan, 80 percent of Suzuki's two-wheeled products are mopeds. In America, however, the brand is associated almost exclusively with touring motorcycles. A third franchise, also run independently of other units, is the marine group, which builds a line of boat motors. Based on its expertise with small engines and motors, Suzuki also manufactures generators, water pumps and motorized wheelchairs.

Brand Origins

Suzuki is one of the most popular surnames in Japan. The Suzuki Loom Works was named for its founder, Michio Suzuki. Established in 1909 as a manufacturer of weaving machines, Suzuki supplied equipment to fabric manufacturers throughout Japan. Textile manufacturing was Japan's largest light industry, providing a lucrative market for the Suzuki enterprise. The company built weaving machines exclusively until about 1937, when government militarists initiated a nationwide mobilization for war.

Suzuki, already in the business of equipping other factories, was ordered to convert its production to armaments. The company's location was also a factor in this decision. Based in an obscure town called Hamamatsu, it was far from industrial centers that might become bombing targets. The company turned out a variety of implements, including vehicle parts and mechanized armor, but also continued to build weaving machines, as clothing and other fabrics remained necessities.

The Suzuki factory escaped damage during the war and resumed its textile equipment business virtually without interruption after hostilities ended. But few companies could afford to purchase new looms. Suzuki made a major shift in its business in 1947, when it began to manufacture vehicles, using the experience it had gained during the war.

In 1952 the company developed a simple motorized bicycle, based on a 36cc engine, called the Power Free. By 1954, the company abandoned the loom business entirely and introduced its first line of motorcycles. These products introduced the Suzuki brand name to many in Japan for the first time.

Early Marketing Strategy

As demand evolved from basic transportation to utility vehicles, Suzuki began development of a small sedan called the Suzulight, powered by a 360cc engine, which hit the market in 1955. This was followed in 1958 by another cycle, called the Suzumoped. A year later, the company introduced a small delivery van that was much more practical for small businesses than conventional delivery trucks.

Suzuki's marketing strategy centered on the thousands of tiny but promising businesses whose needs simply were not addressed by other companies. As these companies grew, so would their transportation needs. Suzuki felt that by serving such companies, the brand would command loyalty. It was necessary for Suzuki to expand its product line, however. For those whose needs surpassed the popular delivery van, Suzuki developed a light truck, called the Suzulight Carry FB, introduced in 1961.

In 1962 Suzuki scored a major marketing as well as technological triumph, when one of its motorcycles won the 50cc-class Isle of Man race. The victory established Suzuki as a leading international competitor, and cleared the way for distribution in America beginning in 1964. In another application of its motorcycle engine technology, Suzuki introduced its first outboard motor, the D55, in 1965. Developed specifically for Japanese fishermen, Suzuki outboards were introduced to the U.S. market in 1977, where their price and reliability were major marketing attributes.

Suzuki moved considerably up-market in 1970 by introducing a line of powerful four-stroke engine motorcycles. While leading the market for motorcycles, Suzuki remained a relatively small player in the automobile market. In response, the company leveraged its experience with small engines and its growing reputation for quality by expanding its line of outboard motors and introducing electrical generators.

AT A GLANCE

Suzuki brand of motor vehicles and motors founded initially in 1909 by Michio Suzuki, owner of the Suzuki Loom Works, in Hamamatsu, Japan; moped bicycle developed in 1952; motorcycle introduced in 1954; Suzulight sedan marketed in 1955; U.S. Suzuki Motor Corporation established in 1963; formed marketing alliance with General Motors Corp., 1981.

Major competitor: Mazda (automobiles); Yamaha and Harley-Davidson (motorcycles); Brunswick (outboard motors).

Advertising: *Agency*—Asher/Gould (automobiles), Los Angeles, CA; Lord, Dentsu & Partners (motorcycles), Los Angeles, CA; Bear Advertising (marine). *Major campaign*—"Ask Anyone Who Owns One" (automobiles); "The Ride You've Been Waiting For" (motorcycles).

Addresses: *Parent company*—American Suzuki Motor Corporation, 3251 East Imperial Highway, Brea, CA 92621; phone: (714) 996-7040. *Ultimate parent company*—Suzuki Motor Corporation, 300, Takatsuka-cho, Hamamatsu-shi, Shizuoka-ken 432-91, Japan; phone: (53) 440-2111.

International Growth

Suzuki was led into international markets in the mid 1960s, mainly by its inability to compete more effectively with Toyota, Honda, and Nissan in Japan. Unable to break these companies' grip on the market, or develop a wider product line, Suzuki developed an export strategy targeting Asian markets that were in the same economic condition Japan had been in during the early 1950s.

Suzuki's first export market was Thailand, where Japanese commercial interests had long been established. The company built an assembly plant there in 1967, and subsequently built factories in the Philippines, Indonesia and Taiwan. In these markets, Suzuki gained the same reputation for simple, affordable quality and reliability upon which its domestic franchise had been built. But still lacking the ability to cover a wider scope of the market, Suzuki retained its image as an less sophisticated brand.

More recently, Suzuki has cultivated business in other developing countries with growing populations, including Cambodia, Egypt, Hungary, and China. The company set up a Pakistani production firm in 1982, followed by an operation in India. Suzuki established a partnership in Spain with Land Rover and set up marketing operations in New Zealand and France in 1984.

The company established a plant in the United Kingdom in 1986, producing 15,000 microvans annually, mainly in competition with Bedford and Honda. The company entered into a partnership with the Egyptian firm Modern Motors SAE in order to build compact cars and the Super Carry line of trucks and vans. In 1987 Suzuki licensed Colmotores S.A. to manufacture the Swift/Forsa model in Columbia. In the early 1990s Suzuki, C. Itoh, and Autokonzern RT established a partnership to produce the Suzuki Swift in Hungary.

The keys to Suzuki's success in foreign markets was the quality of its engines and appropriateness of the technology with regard to the market. In addition, Suzuki involves local partners and thereby skirting foreign import restrictions that keep out competitors.

Brand Development

The company moved into the United States in 1963, with the establishment of the U.S. Suzuki Motor Corporation. By the early 1970s, the company was marketing a variety of automobiles, a four-wheel drive FL series sport/utility vehicle, motorcycles, and small engine products. Suzuki cars competed mainly with Volkswagen and Volvo, as they were decidedly more fuel-efficient than gas-guzzling American cars. This was a fortunate attribute because, at that time, the world was gripped by a widespread energy crisis, caused by the 1973 OPEC oil embargo.

Consumers in Japan and in the United States exhibited greater interest in Suzuki automobiles. The cars were simpler and less powerful than competing models from Toyota, Honda, and Nissan, however. Eventually, the crisis that drove such great interest in Suzuki, and which provided a springboard for its entry into the American market, eased off. But the ensuing recession led to a sharp decline in demand. Suzuki's largest franchise, the market for minicars in Japan, declined by more than 65 percent from 1970 to 1974. Most of these reverses were checked by marketing efforts, introduction of improved models, and price adjustments. By 1978, fuel prices were down again and interest in economy cars was waning. But a second energy crisis in 1979 renewed public interest fuel economy.

Advertising

Suzuki's advertising has historically been defined by its place in the market, and for years the cars were marketed primarily on the basis of their fuel efficiency. This created some difficulties during the 1970s, and again in the early 1980s, when consumer interest in fuel economy declined in favor of features and design characteristics. Nevertheless, it provided Suzuki with a unique identity among Japanese brands that still persists. With an average mileage rating of 45.3 miles-per-gallon in 1993, Suzuki automobiles offer greater fuel economy than any other make. Honda is a distant second with 32, while Chrysler imports register 30.1 miles-per-gallon.)

Suzuki advertising has used long employed the tactic of the testimonial. This no-nonsense approach portrays Suzuki owners who make a series of points demonstrating their dedication to the Suzuki brand. The most memorable of these campaigns used the simple tag line, "Ask anyone who owns one." This campaign was designed to appeal to the "everyman," and therefore curiously lacked models or actors. This was particularly so with Suzuki motorcycles, whose appeal transcends age groups, cultures, and even genders. By featuring the product without a model, consumers may more easily picture themselves with the product.

Modern Development

Suzuki entered into a marketing alliance with General Motors in 1981. As part of the deal, GM purchased a 5.2-percent interest in Suzuki, and dovetailed operations with Suzuki and Isuzu Motors, in which it had a 37-percent interest. The three companies established shared facilities and joint marketing agreements.

In 1983, Suzuki introduced its one-liter Swift (Forsa/SA 310), while derivatives were marketed in America as the Chevy Sprint and Geo Metro. This was followed in 1985 by a new sport/utility model called the Samurai. The vehicle was especially popular with young adults who liked the high-riding Samurai because it was rugged, fun to drive, and indicated a livelier lifestyle than conventional sedans. The Samurai was critically reviewed, however, by *Consumer Reports,* which charged that its high center of gravity could cause it to tip over when turning. While corrective measures were taken, Suzuki suffered a devastating blow in the public relations arena.

In 1986 Suzuki opened a joint production facility in Canada with General Motors, called CAMI automotive. This plant commenced operation in 1989, turning out Sprints and Metros and a new Suzuki product, the Sidekick, which was also marketed as the Geo Tracker.

Meanwhile, motorcycle sales, which had declined every year since 1982, mounted a recovery in 1990. In search of a unique product, the company tried to market a rotary-engine model during the 1970s, but the public rebelled against the technology after Mazda, the developer of the engine, suffered a consumer backlash due to mechanical problems. The products that were most responsible for the turnaround were the Katana and Dual Sport motorcycles, popular because they were engineered for off-road riding, but were also street-legal. Solid and reliable, these bikes were affordable and offered challenging levels of performance.

Suzuki also pioneered the market for four-wheel, all-terrain vehicles in 1982. Some years later, competing models with three-wheels were outlawed in the United States after a series of serious accidents. The legislation provided Suzuki with a virtually unchallenged position as competitors scrambled to develop four-wheeled models.

In the automobile market, Suzuki redesigned its troubled Samurai and endeavored to re-establish the vehicle's promising American franchise. Sales of the vehicle, which peaked at 77,000 in 1988, had fallen to less than 4,000 in 1991. Meanwhile, sales of the Sidekick, which shared the same demographic target market and popular appeal as the Samurai, were increasing 20 percent annually, to nearly 20,000 vehicles in 1993.

Still, the Samurai debacle produced a devastating setback for Suzuki, whose total American unit sales had fallen by 63 percent from 1987 to 1993. In 1992 Suzuki suffered further problems in its domestic market. New laws restricted sales of midget cars to people who could prove they had a place to park them. In addition, a strangling recession dried up demand for all cars, including the sub-550cc class midgets made by Suzuki.

Performance Evaluation

Suzuki remains Japan's leading minicar manufacturer, a position it has held for 20 years. In the U.S. market, however, the brand holds only a slight percentage of the market. Losses in the automobile sector, comprising 72 percent of Suzuki's total sales, represent an erosion probably temporary in Suzuki's automotive franchise.

The company's motorcycle division, which contributes 15 percent of Suzuki's total sales, remains an extremely vital enterprise, and is a market where Suzuki enjoys a leading position with Yamaha and Harley-Davidson. Suzuki motorcycles cover the range from 50cc motor scooters to 1100cc touring cycles. The company's leading street racer model is the GSXR-750 which, due to its reputation, affords its owner a favorable racer image. The RF-900, introduced in 1994, is a sport/touring model designed for long-haul riding. Continued growth in the motorcycle franchise has slightly offset earnings losses suffered by the automotive division during the 1990s.

Suzuki's marine products group, comprising only three percent of the company's sales, is a bright spot for the company. Its outboard motors are generally considered to be the highest-quality products in their class. Borrowing liberally from advances in motorcycle engine technology, Suzuki was first to introduce oil injected outboards in 1980, electronic idle speed adjustment in 1985, boron composite-plated cylinders in 1989 and ceramic reinforced pistons in 1990. The company's flagship outboard is the 225 EFI V-6 motor.

Future Predictions

One of the company's greatest assets is its relationship with General Motors. Suzuki might be considered a small car division of GM, having been allowed to operate in segments of the market without competition from other GM units. As part of the teaming strategy, Suzuki will continue to build cars for GM under the Geo nameplate. The company also manufactures parts for Mazda.

While these arrangements will add to Suzuki's business as a kind of original equipment manufacturer, they do little to build equity in the Suzuki brand name. However, they provide Suzuki with valuable experience and a financial safety net that will keep the company strong until it can develop other new models as successful or as promising as its current product line.

Further Reading:

"Suzuki Motor Corporation," *Diamond's Japan Business Directory,* Bristol, PA: Taylor & Francis, 1992, pp. 858–859.

"Suzuki Motor Corporation," *Hoover's Handbook of World Business,* Austin, TX: Reference Press, Inc., 1993, pp. 454–455.

"Suzuki Motor Corporation," *Moody's International Manual,* New York: Moody's Investors Service, Inc., 1993, p. 3093.

Additional information was provided by American Suzuki Motor Corporation.

—*John Simley*

SWISS ARMY® KNIVES

The Swiss Army Knife is more than 100 years old, yet it is one of the world's most endurable brands of pocketknives. Recognized by its red color and silver embossed Swiss cross logo, this multi-blade, multi-tool pocket knife is beloved by millions. So much so that the Victorinox Cutlery Company of Ibach, Switzerland, has not even spent much time or money advertising it, yet the Swiss Army Knife brand line is stronger than ever. Victorinox is the largest industrial enterprise of its kind in the Schwyz district of Switzerland, and it is the largest cutlery manufacturer in Europe. The Swiss Army Knife continues to signify quality, innovation and timelessness well on its way to the 21st century.

Brand Origins

The Elsener family of Ibach, Switzerland, were hatters by profession until one of them switched to a career in cutlery. In 1884 Charles Elsener moved his business to the nearby district of Schwyz, where many farmers were emigrating to other countries. The labor vacuum posed a problem and Elsener soon formed his Swiss Cutlery Guild in 1891 to carve out an economic niche for his fledgling business. He primarily focused his business on reproducing soldier's knives that the Swiss Army had purchased from Solingen in Germany. By October, Elsener had delivered his new pocket knives to the Swiss Army.

In addition to this "Swiss Army Knife," were a line of functional pocket knives: the Student knife, Cadet knife, and Farmer's knife. The Soldier's Knife was useful but heavy, and Elsener modified it in a lighter, more efficient version for army officers. Like the Soldier's knife, the Officer's version had a blade, punch, can opener, and screwdriver. But the Officer's knife contained a second small blade and corkscrew. This "Officer's Knife," with two springs for its six blades, became a registered trademark June 12, 1897, and the official knife of the Swiss Army.

Army officers had to purchase their knives from cutlery shops and soon they began buying Elsener's Officer's Knife in large numbers. The knife's popularity prompted Elsener to add more tools to the multifaceted knife: a wood saw, scissors, bottle opener, small and large screwdrivers, improved can opener, nail file, toothpick, tweezers, metal saw and metal file, fish scaler with hook disgorger and ruler, key ring, magnifying glass, Phillips screwdriver, and much more have been added to the Officer's Knife prototype.

Brand Development

The Officer's Knife—or "Offiziersmesser"—underwent several developments, the most notable being its flagship brand called the Swiss Champ or No. 1.6795. Company records indicate that the Swiss Champ has 30 different features while weighing less than half a pound. The Swiss Army knives were purposely colored red so as to be highly visible when dropped into snow. The New York Museum of Modern Art and Munich's Staatliche Museum fur angewandte Kunst have cited this brand for its superior industrial design. The Swiss Champ is made out of 64 separate parts and takes more than 450 steps to manufacture.

Elsener's knives were popular through the end of the 19th century. Elsener gave his products the "Victoria" trademark after his mother's death in 1909. By 1921, stainless steel was being manufactured and was used extensively in Swiss Army Knife production. The suffix "Inox" was added in 1921 and Victorinox became the official trademark of the knives and Elsener's Ibach-based cutlery company.

Swiss Army knives started penetrating American markets in the European and Pacific theaters during World War II as a staple sold in American PX shops. Americans can probably be credited with calling the knives their current appellation. Americans could not pronounce "Offiziersmesser" and would just ask for that "Swiss Army Knife." The pocketknife was also known in French as the "Couteau Suisse" (Swiss knife) and in Germany and Austria as the "Schweizer Messer." The Swiss Army Knife eventually sold itself on its unique uses. The pocketknife is a virtual one-stop tool for all kinds of uses and a coveted collector's item. Even after 100 years of development, the Original Swiss Army Knife has more than 30 features, including a Swiss watch!

Marketing Strategy

Imitation may be the sincerest form of flattery, but no one could make a pocketknife that surpassed the Swiss Army Knife's innovative design. Many still try to sell imitations, but aficionados say that the logo on a real Swiss Army Knife cannot be duplicated. In fact, depending on who you listen to, the Swiss Cross must either be connected to the gold badge encircling it on the knife or vice versa.

Nonetheless, Elsener's Victorinox Cutlery Corp. claims to be the inventor of the Original Swiss Army Knife, but Wenger,

AT A GLANCE

The Swiss Army Knife was invented by Charles Elsener in Schwyz, Switzerland in 1891. Elsener formed the Swiss Cutlery Guild to produce soldiers's knives that the Swiss Army had previously contracted from Solingen, Germany. Elsener also made refined pocketknives like the Student knife, Cadet knife, and Farmer's knife. Elsener modified his soldier's knife for officers that included a second blade, punch, can opener, screwdriver, and corkscrew. This "Officer's Knife" became a registered trademark June 12, 1897, and the official knife of the Swiss Army; further tools were added to the knife over the next 100 years of its development.

Victorinox becomes the trademark of the Swiss Army Knife brand, 1921, in memory of Elsener's mother Victoria. The "Inox" suffix is added upon the discovery of stainless steel; Swiss Army knives sold to U.S. Armed Forces personnel during World War II; Victorinox Cutlery Corp. and Wenger of Switzerland are the only two companies that can legally manufacture the Original Swiss Army Knife; Forschner Butcher Scale Company formed in 1855; imported butcher knives from Victorinox in 1937; Forschner family sells the company in 1957, after which the company begins importing Swiss Army knives; Louis Marx Jr. buys Forschner for $2 million in 1974; Forschner went public in 1983 and becomes Victorinox's exclusive U.S. distributor under the Victorinox Agreement; Swiss Champ Swiss Army Knife introduced in 1986; Forschner sells Swiss Army brand watches, compasses, and sunglasses in 1989; Super Timer brand Swiss Army Knife with a watch and tools for 31 uses, is introduced in 1992; in 1993, Forschner Group Inc. granted exclusive distributorship rights for Victorinox products in the Caribbean and North America. Forschner also distributes cutlery products under the R.H. Forschner brand for professional use and the Cuisine de France Sabatier brand for consumers. There are more than 40 different models of Swiss Army multiblade pocketknives.

Performance: *Market share*—About 85 to 90% of the U.S. pocketknife category (Victorinox); Wenger has 15% of the U.S. pocketknife market. *Sales*—$250 million from all Swiss Army knives in 1991, American made blades accounted for $120 million according to *Sporting Goods Business;* $10 million in Swiss Army Brand watches in 1991.

Major competitor: Precise Imports Corporation, a U.S. distributor of Swiss Army Knives made by Wenger S.A.; SwissBuck, Cross; Zippo lighters brands of high-quality pocketknives.

Advertising: *Agency*—In-house. *Major campaign—Amazing Games* television campaign on ESPN in the fourth quarter of 1993.

Addresses: *Parent company*—Forschner Group, 151 Long Hill, Shelton, CT 06484; phone: (203) 929-6391. *Ultimate parent company*—Victorinox Cutlery Company, Ibach, Switzerland.

another Swiss company, also makes a Swiss Army Knife that it calls "Genuine." Both companies are the only two companies that can legally manufacture what is now called the Swiss Army Knife according to Swiss judicial orders. Company representatives told *Forbes* that two percent of the company's sales are spent tracking down Swiss Army Knife forgeries. Victorinox swears by its Original Swiss Army Knife that comes with its own life-time guarantee.

Swiss Army knives are sold in the United States through an arrangement between Victorinox and the Forschner Group of Shelton, Connecticut. The Forschner Group was founded as a company in 1855 as a New Britain, Connecticut, maker of butcher scales. The company began importing Victorinox butcher knives in the 1930s, but the butcher scale business was terminated after the Forschner family sold the company in 1957.

It was at this time that Forschner began importing Swiss Army knives to the American market. And by 1974, 20 percent or $800,000 of its $4 million yearly revenues came from Swiss Army knives. Investor Louis Marx, Jr., purchased Forschner for $2 million and soon thereafter, Forschner vigorously marketed the Swiss Army knives in American hunting and camping stores and in specialty stores like Hoffritz. By 1981, Swiss Army Knife sales had reached $11 million. By 1983, Forschner had gone public although Marx had sold his stake in the company.

Advertising Innovations

Devoid of any noticeable advertising in the United States and none in Switzerland, consumers seem to be aware that a Swiss Army Knife is capable of being used for practically anything. Former president George Bush always kept his in his pocket and often gave Swiss Army knives to White House guests. NASA astronauts take one on every shuttle flight because it is good at peeling insulation off of cables in space. ABC television's MacGyver used one on every show to dismantle bombs, cut through ropes, and start his car. Even comedian Jerry Seinfeld said "I never go anywhere without it," and recounted how he had used the knife's tweezers to fix cameras on the set. "It's a rare man who doesn't have at least one Swiss Army Knife story that he is more than ready to tell," Seinfeld explained to Karen J. Benfield in the *Wall Street Journal.*

Swiss Army Knife's mystique is further promoted by its 38-year-old, 200-member fan club, the Swiss Army Knife Society in California. The group publishes the *Crimson Cutter* newsletter, which highlights unique uses of the pocketknife. To wit: one person used his Swiss Army Knife to fish for keys that had fallen into the sewer. He used the knife's can opener attachment to do the trick.

In fact, the blades are so useful that Forschner Group designed a special one for Eli Lilly & Co. that can be used to perform a tracheotomy. Victorinox also makes special Swiss Army Knife orders for other corporate promotions—about $10 million worth. The company was even designing a tool for drug companies that pulled cotton out of pill bottles. More than 90 companies give Victorinox and Forschner all the advertising they need by running their own ads that feature the Swiss Army Knife to link their products with the knife's quality and craftsmanship. Demand in the 1990s outstripped production and forced Victorinox to build another factory. Company documents report that 6.1 million Swiss Army knives are made annually.

New Products

The brand's popularity would almost seem to not warrant augmentation, but Victorinox in 1989 rolled out Swiss Army brand watches, compasses and sunglasses and its first ever national marketing campaign to capitalize on the Swiss Army Knife brand name. Made in Switzerland, the watches retailed for $115 to $695; the sunglasses for $115 (as compared to the pocketknives, which cost from $9 for the simplest one up to $140 for the top-of-the-line model). Industry analysts perceived it as a good move, since Swiss Army Knife sales had increased 4,000 percent from

1974 to 1990 in the United States, reported Fleming Meeks in *Forbes.* The new line generated $2.5 million in sales by the end of 1990; watches alone netted more than $10 million in sales in 1992, up from $4 million in 1991, and have helped boost the company's stock. The new brand extensions were marketed through popular retailers such as Wal-Mart, Macy's, and Kmart.

But the Swiss Army Knife was not to fade into the woodwork. Victorinox introduced two sterling silver versions of the knife brand in elegant gift boxes for $95. Fellow producer Wenger, through its North American importer Price International, had planned to introduce its Swiss Army Knife brand Golf Pro Knife, featuring its own divot repair tool, cleat tightener and club cleaner.

In 1992 Victorinox launched the Super Timer brand Swiss Army Knife with a Swiss quartz watch and 22 tools for 31 uses that include a pen, pliers, and fish scaler. The Super Timer weighs more than the Swiss Army Knife version, which sells for $27. The Super Timer sells for $140. "The thinking was to combine two famous Swiss products in one package," said Forschner Group president Jim Kennedy to the *New York Times.*

International

In 1993, the Forschner Group Inc. was granted exclusive distributorship rights for Victorinox products in the Caribbean and North America. Forschner also distributes cutlery products under the R.H. Forschner brand for professional use and the Cuisine de France Sabatier brand for consumers. There are more than 40 different models of Swiss Army multi-blade pocketknives with up to 32 different implements. These are sold through more than 3,500 retailers and corporate clients that use the knife with a corporate logo for promotions. The Swiss Army orders 30,000 aluminum handled pocketknives each year; half from Victorinox, half from Wenger. The Swiss Army claims the knives are not used as weapons.

Future Growth

The Swiss Army Knife brand line has experienced a doubling of sales from 1990 to 1993 and does not appear to be slowing soon. Company officials project that the brand will remain attractive to cost-conscious consumers who want a brand with established quality. The Forschner Group and Victorinox, however, are not resting on their Swiss Army Knife brand laurels. Despite maintaining a strong consumer loyalty without the benefit of any real advertising, the Forschner Group in 1993 decided on an advertising and marketing blitz to promote the entire Swiss Army Knife brand of products nationwide via aggressive television and print ad campaigns featuring the slogan "Be an Original."

The Swiss Army Knife brands also sponsored the *Amazing Games* series on the ESPN cable network, which featured the first ever television spots for Swiss Army knives and watches. Print advertising was launched in full-page insertions in the *Wall Street Journal, USA Today,* and in major metropolitan newspapers. Retailers also sponsored sweepstakes promotions offering winners trips to Switzerland, Forschner Group products, and other prizes.

"Despite our considerable successes to date, it is important that retailers know we remain committed to expanding our business by helping them to build their sales," CEO and President James Kennedy said, adding "We have one of the strongest brand awareness ratings of any consumer product in the country, and through television we will leverage this strong brand identity and universal appeal to attract millions more Americans to use our products."

Further Reading:

"But Will They Open Cans?" *Time,* September 10, 1990.

Farrell, Scott, "Blade Masters: The 1991 Retail Knife Roundup," *Shooting Industry,* December 1991, p. 76.

Farrell, Scott, "Buck on Buck," *Shooting Industry,* November 1991, p. 20.

"Forschner Adds Exclusive Territories for Swiss Army Knives, Victorinox Watches," *PR Newswire,* Dec. 22, 1993.

Gaffney, Andew, "Swiss, Any Way You Slice It," *Sporting Goods Business,* September 1991, p. 34.

Hamel, J.P., *Forschner Group Company Report,* Alex Brown & Sons, October 22, 1993.

Lloyd, Barbara, "The Swiss Army Knife Just Got Better, with Time," *New York Times,* May 9, 1992, p. 30L.

Marcial, Gene G., "Atten-hut! It's the Swiss Army Watch," *Business Week,* March 23, 1992, p. 80.

Meeks, Fleming, "Blade Runner," *Forbes,* October 15, 1990, p. 164.

Moran, D.S., *Forschner Group Company Report,* A.G. Edwards & Sons, Inc., January 11, 1993.

"New Amazing Sponsor," *Broadcasting & Cable Magazine,* August 30, 1993, p. 34.

Norman, Geoffrey, "Making the Blade," *Forbes,* November 25, 1991, p. F146.

"Precise Providing Swiss Army Program," *Sporting Goods Business,* May, 1991, p. 14.

—Evelyn S. Dorman

TAPPAN®

The Tappan brand name has become synonymous with cooking in the United States, where the brand has been associated with stoves since the 1880s. Tappan also has the distinction of being the first company to introduce a microwave oven for home use. The brand, now produced by the Frigidaire Company, continues to be a leader in this market.

Brand Origins

Tappan's origins can be traced back to 1881, when W. J. (Bill) Tappan began selling cast-iron stoves he made in his Ohio-based foundry. Calling on homes door-to-door in surrounding communities, Tappan received an overwhelmingly positive response from his customers, prompting him to found the Ohio Valley Foundry Company. Mr. Tappan's determination and salesmanship quickly became legendary. He scoured the countryside looking for customers. While his door-to-door prospects were eager to purchase his cast-iron stoves, few had much cash to spare. As a result, many of Mr. Tappan's customers paid him partly in vegetables, grain, and other wares.

In 1891 a solar eclipse took place in the United States and Bill Tappan interpreted it as a propitious sign. That year the Ohio Valley Foundry Company was renamed the Eclipse Company. Soon the Eclipse stove, fired by either wood or coal, was introduced. With its artistically designed floral pattern on the front oven door, the Eclipse quickly became one of the country's best-selling stoves and the center of American family life. Within each home, the family used it for cooking, for heating bath water, and for keeping warm on cold winter nights. By 1920, however, Eclipse switched its operations from cast-iron to sheet steel, patenting an automatic burner lighting device inside the oven and introducing the first "modern" range with rounded corners.

Product Innovation

The onset of World War I presented a challenge to the Eclipse Company's design capabilities. The Army needed a mobile field kitchen the men could use to prepare food at the front lines. Eclipse rose to the occasion by developing a mobile kitchen unit that was far better than its competition. Later Tappan produced an aluminum stove to be used on two Navy dirigibles.

The company continued to forge new paths in the cooking industry, including several range "firsts." The company developed an all-porcelain range in the 1920s, which was available to customers in various fashionable colors; the first completely insulated range ovens were launched in 1925; the first "visualite" see-through oven door window was used in the 1930s; and during the 1940s light-weight, removable oven bottoms, the divided cooking top, a press-toe roll-out broiler, and removable oven rack supports were introduced.

In the early 1940s Eclipse changed its name to the Tappan Stove Company. Until World War II forced the halt of all non-essential consumer goods production, Tappan's sales were consistently above the industry average. This was evidence of the company's continuing advances in engineering and its dedication to salesmanship.

During World War II, the Tappan Stove Company received four Army-Navy "E" awards for excellence in producing a variety of defense materials. The post-war economic boom and the company's aggressive marketing kept its sales levels ahead of the competition. At that time, the company also began to consider new business opportunities. In 1948 Tappan introduced a new line of electric cooking ranges and developed production centers across North America.

Soon after the war, Tappan began to make some acquisitions, including the Gurney Stove Company of Montreal, Canada, and the O'Keefe and Merritt Company in Los Angeles, California. When W. R. Tappan—the son of former General Manager P. R. Tappan—became president, the company undertook the largest expansion program in its history. All existing range production facilities were updated and improved, and the company added several new cooking unit facilities. Tappan also initiated a massive program of diversification by introducing several appliances related to cooking units. The result was a complete all-Tappan consumer kitchen package that included dishwashers, garbage disposals, ventilation hoods for cooking units, refrigerators, cabinets, and the unique "Ultra-flo" automatic push-button water system for kitchen sinks. One product in particular, however, represented success for the Tappan Stove Company and eventually made the brand a household name—the microwave oven.

The Microwave Generation

The history of this revolutionary cooking marvel dates back to the mid-1940s when Percy Spencer—a leader in Raytheon Manu-

AT A GLANCE

Tappan brand of stoves and ovens founded in 1881 by W. J. (Bill) Tappan, founder of the Ohio Valley Foundry Company, in Dublin, OH; name changed to Eclipse Company in 1891; company became Tappan Stove Company in the 1940s; introduced first microwave oven, 1955; Tappan purchased by A.B. Electrolux in 1979; A.B. Electrolux purchased White Consolidated Industries and merged Tappan operations into the WCI Major Appliances Group; WCI Major Appliances Group renamed Frigidaire Company in 1991.

Major competitor: Amana; also General Electric.

Advertising: *Agency*—SBC Public Relations, Westerville, OH. *Major campaign*—"Tappan—for the love of cooking."

Addresses: *Parent company*—Frigidaire Company, 6000 Perimeter Drive, Dublin, OH 43017; phone: (614) 792-4100.

facturing's Power Tube Division—first discovered the relationship between the properties of radar waves and the heat associated with cooking. In 1947 Raytheon announced the invention of the first microwave oven. The company received a patent for its creation two years later, but marketable, consumer-friendly technology lagged far behind the invention itself. Not until the early 1950s did Raytheon produce the first commercially viable microwave oven, which was called the "Radarange." The first Radaranges were placed in refrigerator-sized cabinets and sold in the $2,000 to $3,000 range. At the time, the only markets for the new products were restaurants, railroads, and vending machine companies.

One of the first commercial microwave ovens was installed in the kitchen of a hotel in Washington, D.C. The invention was the subject of many conversations in the area, and the hotel's management proudly led many celebrities back to the kitchen to show off the quick-cooking device. In addition, the main dining room featured several daily entrees that were prepared in the new oven.

Managers at the Tappan Stove Company first heard about the Radarange while building ovens for airplanes, and representatives soon realized that the novel new product had some potential in the Tappan product line. The company began negotiating with Raytheon to allow Tappan to build and market the unit for home use. The two companies finally agreed to a price, and Tappan immediately began experimenting with microwave energy.

Before Tappan could successfully market the microwave oven to consumers, the company needed to overcome several obstacles. In order for the new oven to fit into home kitchens, researchers needed to determine a way to reduce substantially the size of the energy sources required to run it. They also needed to find a method for cooling the high-frequency tubes as well as a way to channel and direct the microwave energy evenly into the food in order to cook it uniformly. Tappan invested a great deal of research capital into this project, but positive results were slow to appear.

Tappan's first commercial microwave oven units had to be connected to both electrical and water lines because the magnetron power unit was water-cooled. With their massive component parts, these units were approximately the size of refrigerators and weighed nearly 750 pounds, despite the fact that the microwave cooking compartment took up only one to two cubic feet.

Microwave cooking still had a long way to go before it was commercially viable. Tappan researchers made a major breakthrough, however, when they developed an air cooling device that eliminated the need to connect the ovens to cumbersome water lines. In addition to the extensive technology research, the company also devoted a great deal of effort to testing recipes. Most successful recipes were the result of seemingly endless trial-and-error attempts.

A Cooking Revolution

The Tappan Stove Company finally introduced the Tappan RL-1 microwave oven in 1955. The announcement took place during a press conference in New York City, and the media heralded this remarkable new cooking unit as "the most revolutionary product developed since the advent of electricity." Many people who read these initial reports were skeptical of the oven's true powers, and most remained unconvinced until they saw the oven operate for themselves. Once they did, customers were amazed at the oven's capabilities.

Tappan's revolutionary new product offered homemakers flexibility and versatility previously unheard of in cooking. Convenience came at a high price, however. The oven had a retail price of $1,200. At 24 inches wide, 24 inches deep and 27 inches high, the first Tappan RL-1 was the size of a single conventional built-in oven with a large oven capacity. In most cases, the microwave was built into a customer's wall, but it was also known as a "stack-on" because it could be placed on a countertop. The unit, then called an "electronic oven," had only two settings—high and low.

The RL-1 operated on the same type of microwave radio technology developed for radar applications during World War II, but the model was guaranteed not to interfere with radios, televisions or other electronic equipment. This policy was still in place in the 1990s under authorization by the Federal Communications Commission. In 1955, first year of production, only 34 units were manufactured. The following year Tappan produced 1,552.

In 1965 Tappan launched its cooking center, which offered the benefits of both a microwave oven and a conventional stove in one unit. In an effort to target the builders market, four years later Tappan introduced the combination unit as a built-in. It was clear that Tappan was at the leading edge of cooking technology. By the early 1990s the microwave oven, along with the Tappan brand, had become an American institution.

Further Reading:

"Microwave Oven Has Revolutionized the Way We Cook Today," Dublin, OH: Tappan Major Appliances.

"Tappan Company Began from a Horse-drawn Wagon," Dublin, OH: Tappan Major Appliances.

"The Tappan Philosophy—Imagination and Innovation," *Harper Gas Service*, September 27, 1973, p. 22.

—Wendy Johnson Bilas

TEENAGE MUTANT NINJA TURTLES®

The Teenage Mutant Ninja Turtles, made by Playmates Toys, Inc., became one of the top three best-selling action figures in toy marketing history only four years after American children first set eyes on them. The four fighting turtles debuted in 1988 and became the hottest toy craze ever, peaking in 1990 with over 60 percent of the action figure market. They began as comic book characters with a small adult cult following, then took off as toy figures backed by a children's comic book and an animated television cartoon. The first film about the quartet, *Teenage Mutant Ninja Turtles: The Movie,* which further fueled the turtle fad, grossed more than $25 million in its first weekend, a record topped only by *Batman.* The Ninja Turtles ultimately appeared on at least six hundred items of turtle paraphernalia, from pajamas to bubble bath to silver coins, and they promoted foods ranging from yogurt and English muffins to vanilla-flavored pizza candy and Teenage Mutant Ninja Turtle pork rinds. Such Ninja Turtle slang phrases as "Cowabunga!" "Hey dudes!" and "Bummer!" infiltrated the vocabulary of the elementary school set. The Ninja Turtle craze struck England, Australia, and New Zealand, as well as non-English speaking countries in Europe and Asia. Though the popularity of the four turtles began to decline in 1991, sales of the figures and accessories still easily surpassed anything else on the market. The staying power of such fad items is always in doubt, yet industry analysts seemed to agree that the turtles' marketers had proved very shrewd, and the Teenage Mutant Ninja Turtles may be headed for classic status.

Brand Origins

The original Teenage Mutant Ninja Turtles were created by two Northampton, Massachusetts, comic book artists. Peter Laird and Kevin Eastman began a comic book series in 1983, which featured four turtles who had been flushed down the New York City sewers as babies. There they fell into a pool of radioactive ooze that caused them to mutate into human-like adolescent creatures. The turtles acquired the names Donatello, Michelangelo, Leonardo, and Raphael, learned a brand of surfer-slang English, and became trained martial arts warriors with an insatiable craving for one food—pizza. Thus the name Teenage Mutant Ninja Turtles. The turtles' adventures were at first confined to Laird and Eastman's black-and-white comic, known to a circle of aficionados that numbered about 150,000.

In 1986 Laird and Eastman met Mark Freedman, who had worked on licensing cartoon figures such as Alvin and the Chipmunks and Hanna-Barbera's Scooby Doo. Freedman was instantly taken with the Ninja Turtles, and he procured exclusive rights to license the turtle quartet. Freedman then shopped the rights around to toy makers, only to be turned down by aghast marketers who found the whole concept of teen warrior turtles too weird, thought the characters were too gross, or thought the name was too long. Only after every other U.S. toy maker had turned him down did Freedman find a taker in Playmates Toys, Inc.

Playmates is based in this country in La Mirada, California, but is owned by a Hong Kong company, Playmates International Holdings, Ltd. Playmates was founded in 1966 by Chan Tai Ho, as a subcontractor to foreign toy producers. The company eventually began subcontracting its own toy designs to makers in China and Macao. Playmates had gradually started making more and more elaborate electronic toys, a path that almost led the company to bankruptcy. When the U.S. branch of Playmates bought the rights to make Ninja Turtle figures, the current president of the company, Thomas Chan, recognized that the Ninja Turtles might take Playmates in a new direction. The plastic action figures were relatively simple, cheap toys, and they had a humor and charm that other boys' action figures like G.I. Joe and He Man lacked. Playmates introduced the new toys at the 1988 New York Toy Fair, where buyers were at first unimpressed.

Meanwhile Mark Freedman had taken his Ninja Turtle rights to long-time friend Tony Marsiglia, the president of the Chicago marketing firm Responsive Marketing Communications, Inc. When Marsiglia learned that Playmates was making the action figures, he agreed to handle all promotion. He loved the combination of turtles and teenagers, and thought the concept would go over big with young boys. Playmates had promoted its new product by paying for the first five installments of a cartoon series on the turtles. The Saturday morning show quickly captured the top ratings in hundreds of markets. Marsiglia's company was soon handling a 100,000-member Ninja Turtle fan club, and licensing turtle hats and patches, to be advertised on the back of Banquet pot pie packages. Retailers could not keep the Ninja Turtle action figures on the shelves, and the licensing of turtle paraphernalia became a frenzy.

Commercial Success

Sales of Teenage Mutant Ninja Turtle action figures and accessories were $23 million in 1988. By 1989, the U.S. total had more than quadrupled, to $115 million. In the next year, Ninja Turtle sales almost quadrupled again, to over $400 million, representing over 60 percent of the toy action figure market. By 1990, more than 90 percent of all American boys aged 3 to 8 owned at least one Ninja Turtle, and the average boy had more than five. In 1991 Playmates set industry records, when it was deemed the most profitable company in toy history. It was also the first toy company ever to net over $100 million in a single year. Playmates so dominated the toy industry that most of the other major companies slumped. Sales of G.I. Joe and Transformers, two best-selling boys' toys, slackened because of the competition with Ninja Turtles, and only companies that had strong lines of girls' toys managed not to be damaged by the growing turtle mania. On the other hand, an ailing Hong Kong stock market rallied significantly in 1990 due in great part to the surging stock of Playmates International Holdings. The *New York Times* jested that the fictional characters had done some real good for once, as Hong Kong economists interpreted Playmates' stellar success as encouragement to all the colony's entrepreneurs.

The release of *Teenage Mutant Ninja Turtles: The Movie* in 1990 gave a big boost to sales of turtle toy and accessories. The

AT A GLANCE

Teenage Mutant Ninja Turtles brand of toy action figure created in 1983 by comic book artists Peter Laird and Kevin Eastman, in Northampton, MA; developed into toy action figures by Playmates Toys, Inc. in 1988; first Ninja Turtle movie released in 1990.

Performance: *Market share*—Approximately 46 percent (top share) of the toy action figure category. *Sales*—$300 million.

Major competitor: G.I. Joe.

Advertising: *Agency*—Sachs-Finley & Co., Los Angeles, CA, 1988—.

Addresses: *Parent company*—Playmates Toys, Inc., 16200 Trojan Way, La Mirada, California, 90638; phone: (714) 739-1929; fax: (714) 739-2912. *Ultimate parent company*—Playmates International Holdings, Ltd., 4F World Finance Center, South Tower, Harbour City, Canton Road, Tsim Sha Tsui, Kowloon, Hong Kong; phone: 7307388; fax: 7352058.

movie was made by an independent production company called New Line Cinema, which had previous success with a series of *Nightmare on Elm Street* films. The movie used actors in radio controlled turtle suits to portray the reptile quartet. The suits, which cost more than $5 million, were designed by Jim Henson, creator of the legendary Muppets. Part of the Ninja Turtles' appeal was the absurdity of turtles performing agile, quick-witted karate moves, and the action-packed movie seemed to bring the creatures' fighting powers to life even better than the animated cartoon. Children flocked to see the film, which eventually grossed $135 million, while its sequel, *The Secret of the Ooze,* grossed $90 million.

Based on this burgeoning popularity, Burger King was selling 200,000 Ninja Turtle cartoon video cassettes a week by April of 1990, and one distributor of movie-related products claimed to send out $100,000 worth of Ninja Turtle goods every day. Ralston-Purina increased production of its marshmallow Teenage Mutant Ninja Turtle cereal, and later came out with a snack food called Turtles Pizza-Crunchabungas. The makers of Hostess Twinkies introduced a green-frosted treat, Teenage Mutant Ninja Turtle snack pies. The turtles advertised for Burger King and Pizza Hut, and the latter spent $20 million promoting a 40-city Teenage Mutant Ninja Turtles rock concert tour. At least 600 Ninja Turtle products were licensed in the United States by 1990, and licensing agent Mark Freedman started to turn down some more outlandish proposals. He refused to let the Ninja Turtles appear on a fishing rod, reasoning that the turtles would not want to catch their friends from the pond. He nixed a Ninja Turtle cologne because it was simply unimaginable. Ninja Turtle condoms did not make it either, though Freedman speculated that this licensing request was not made seriously. All in all hundreds of licensing requests were rejected, while the turtle phenomenon continued to grow around the world.

International Marketing

The Teenage Mutant Ninja Turtle fad landed abroad with tidal wave force. Playmates had expected the craze for turtles to die down in America as it picked up in Europe, but demand for the action figures was still tremendously high in the United States, even as British, Italian, German, Australian, Malaysian, and Japanese youth began to clamor for Leonardo, Donatello, Michelangelo and Raphael. There were not enough figures to go around, however, and a brawl broke out in Portsmouth, England, as 2,000 parents struggled to purchase the 250 Ninja Turtles on sale in that city. Yet keeping supply short was part of Playmates' marketing strategy. The company couldn't possibly provide enough toys to satisfy the public, but it made it a point to ship just enough to keep people wanting. Because parents had to run from store to store looking for the action figures, they eventually tired and bought accessories instead. These included the Brain Sucking Sewer Machines, Flushomatics, and Retromutagen Ooze, or such Ninja Turtle enemy or companion figures as Muckman, Joe Eyeball, and Rat King. Thus the whole Ninja Turtle line prospered, while Playmates continued to ration the action figures. Buyers in England reported receiving only half of what they ordered. Sometimes these were all spoken for by the time they reached the store, and they had to be whisked straight to the stockroom so customers would not see them. Sales of Ninja Turtle products worldwide, including movie tickets, totaled $1 billion wholesale in 1990.

A British company secured the European and South African licensing rights for the turtles, and 80 companies began producing approximately 250 different items. As in the United States, these ranged from coloring books to toiletries to towels, and the turtles promoted their own brands of popcorn and turtle-shaped frozen pizza. Italians and Germans were excited about the Ninja Turtles even without a television cartoon to promote them. In England, a slightly altered version of the American cartoon ran on BBC1. The name was changed to Teenage Mutant Hero Turtles, because executives at the BBC wanted to play down the martial arts aspect of the show. Going further, the BBC edited scenes showing some of the turtles' ninja weapons, and deleted entirely one of the turtles' catch phrases, ''Bummer!''

Not everyone welcomed the American invasion. In 1991 Britain's National Consumer Council claimed that the Hero Turtles show was nothing but an advertisement, and thus violated industry codes on children's programming. Firemen in Leeds, England, had to be rescued from a sewer after they had gone down in search of children playing Ninja Turtles. Many schools in Australia banned the turtle toys from classrooms at the peak of the craze there, blaming the characters for increased school violence. The movie and the television show opened in that country to record audiences, and a community group called the Australian Children's Television Action Committee asserted that there was a direct link between the Ninja Turtles and aggression in school children. A school principal quoted in an August, 1990 *New York Times* article explained that the Ninja Turtles solved problems by force, ''which is incompatible with our aim for a friendly, cooperative and caring school.'' The same claim began to be heard in the United States too. Even in the Ninja Turtles' home state of Massachusetts some schools were banning ''Turtle play,'' and a child psychologist stated in a 1991 *New York Times* feature that ''the Ninja Turtles were not designed for children.''

Performance Appraisal

The Ninja Turtle juggernaut began to slow down in 1991. Nevertheless, U.S. wholesale sales of Ninja Turtle figures and accessories brought Playmates close to $300 million, almost half of the action figure market total of $650 million. The Ninja Turtles were such big business that even as sales declined, they were twice as popular as any other toy for boys. Other toy companies geared up to release what they hoped would be the next big thing.

Playmates itself continued to develop the Ninja Turtle line. Like the makers of the ever popular Barbie doll, Playmates brought out new characters and accessories every year. At the end of 1991 there were 90 versions of the turtles, including military turtles, rock 'n' roll turtles, space turtles, and surfer turtles.

Barbie was an important model for Playmates because she and G.I. Joe were examples of fad toys that had lasted. A more ominous case Playmates' management kept in mind was Worlds of Wonder's Teddy Ruxpin, a talking Teddy Bear that had gone big in the 1980s. When that fad was over, the company went bankrupt. Coleco, the maker of Cabbage Patch Kids, had also gone under when the Cabbage Patch craze died down. Thomas Chan, president of Playmates International, was well aware that his company could have a similar fate. He noted in an interview in *Forbes* magazine in October of 1991 that Coleco and Worlds of Wonder had had thousands of employees and lavish offices that they could not possibly maintain when their products waned. Chan kept Playmates small and spartan. By the end of 1991 he had just 110 employees. Profits were $156 million net, and fixed overhead was only $14 million. The company also cut inventory costs by undersupplying the market. And while continuing to bring out new models of the Ninja Turtles, Playmates also launched new toys that might someday take their place.

In the first four years of the Ninja Turtles' appearance on the action figure market, they broke every kind of toy industry record. The turtles' huge success was not due entirely to their appeal to children, but also to shrewd marketing on the part of Playmates. The building of the Ninja Turtle frenzy was crafted by media exposure, through the television show, the movies, promotional advertising, and the widespread licensing of the figures. Despite the inevitable waning of the boom, Playmates had such a large market share and profit margin that the company could still do well with declining sales. A toy industry analyst quoted in a *Los Angeles Times* article in December of 1991 declared that he had never seen a toy company manage a boom product so well. The challenge for the Ninja Turtles is to maintain a presence on the market even though they are no longer the latest, hottest product. Only a handful of toys, notably Barbie, G.I. Joe, and such cartoon characters as Mickey Mouse and Snoopy have managed to stay in favor with successive waves of children. However, it is still too soon to tell whether the Teenage Mutant Ninja Turtles will return to the sewers or reach classic status.

Further Reading:

Hammer, Joshua, and Annetta Miller, "Ninja Turtle Power," *Newsweek*, April 16, 1990, pp. 60–61.

"Here's Where It Began For Four Ninja Turtles," *New York Times*, July 7, 1991, Section 1, p. 10.

Lazzareschi, Carla, "Rapid-Paced Turtle Sales Starting to Slow Down," *Los Angeles Times*, December 23, 1991, p. D1.

Lipman, Joanne, "Ninja Turtles May Be in Danger of Overexposure by Marketers," *Wall Street Journal*, August 1, 1990, p. B5.

Magiera, Marcy, "Torrid Turtle Race," *Advertising Age*, March 25, 1991, p. 49.

"Ninja Influence on Australian Youth," *New York Times*, August 16, 1990, p. C20.

"Ninja Turtles Abroad," *Wall Street Journal*, July 30, 1990, p. A6.

"Ninja Turtles Invade the Stores With Products From Candy to Surfboards," *Wall Street Journal*, April 26, 1990, p. A1.

Pereira, Joseph, "Hasbro Expects Earnings Drop of Over 50%," *Wall Street Journal*, July 2, 1990, p. B6.

Sterngold, James, "In Hong Kong, A New Confidence," *New York Times*, July 10, 1990, p. D1.

Tanzer, Andrew, "Heroes in a Half Shell," *Forbes*, October 28, 1991, pp. 49–51.

"Tony Marsiglia: Out of His Shell," *Sales & Marketing Management*, August 1990, pp. 28–29.

"Turtle Hero Worship," *Marketing*, June 14, 1990, pp. 28–29.

Warden, John, "NCC Slams Marketing of Turtles Outside ITC Code," *Marketing*, April 18, 1991, p. 7.

—A. Woodward

TEXAS INSTRUMENTS®

Texas Instruments (TI) is one of the world's leading brands of silicon semiconductors. A scientist at Texas Instruments, Inc., in the late 1950s, Jack Kilby, developed the most revolutionary product of the twentieth century: the integrated circuit (IC) on a microchip. Many times more powerful than the recently developed transistor, the microchip enabled computer technology to be born and to evolve swiftly. The IC gave modern electronics the impetus to grow and develop dramatically, to the point where electronics will be the largest industry in the world by the year 2000, worth more than $600 billion. Fortunately for Texas Instruments, it has remained at the forefront of this industry.

Brand Origins

In 1930, when a few brilliant men incorporated Geophysical Service, Inc., in Dallas, they were interested in using a new technology for ferreting out underground oil. However, the high-tech means of finding oil, reflection seismology, bore a resemblance to radar, which was being used to detect submarines and aircraft. This field would become an important sideline for the company during and after World War II and would eventually lead the company to other technologies useful to the military.

After World War II, when the company had changed hands and adopted the name General Instruments, oil exploration became a subsidiary business. The directors of the small, young company made the fateful decision to broaden into the field of electronics. A revolution was underway in electronics because of the development of the transistor by three Americans at Bell Labs in 1951. General Instruments (along with 20 other companies) boldly purchased a manufacturing license from Bell to develop and manufacture the transistor.

The company's entrance into the electronics field was accompanied with a change in name. The Navy, one of General Instruments' clients, had complained that the name of the company sounded too much like the name of another contractor. The prosaic-sounding General Instruments was dropped for the more evocative name of "Texas Instruments"; the company even adopted the state map as its logo. From then on, all of the company's products adopted the brand name "Texas Instruments."

Although research and development at Texas Instruments focused on developing the transistor, TI was also conducting research on the basic element of the transistor, the silicon conductor, which possessed the same ability to amplify and control electrical current as the vacuum tube. Soon TI's scientists had developed a highly refined silicon that was an even better conductor of electricity than the original transistor. This discovery led to the development in the mid-1950s of the transistor radio (manufactured by a customer of TI) and to the company's establishment of a subsidiary in England to manufacture semiconductors for the transistor industry. Only five years after obtaining the right to manufacture transistors, TI was the world leader in the semiconductor business and was transforming itself into a multinational corporation.

Before the invention of the transistor, the vacuum tube was the only effective means of transmitting and controlling electric current. For nearly 50 years, the clumsy vacuum tube was king in electrical products, leading to the development of radio and, eventually, of television. The drawbacks of the vacuum tube, however, were that it used too much energy and gave off unwanted heat. The tiny transistor that supplanted the tube could produce many times the electrical power of a vacuum tube, would use very little power, and emitted no heat.

Texas Instruments' most dramatic and historically significant breakthrough was still to come, however, and was the brainchild of Jack St. Clair Kilby, a young electrical engineer who was hired in the summer of 1958. Experienced in transistor technology, Kilby was not alone in being aware of the drawbacks of the transistor: it was itself a component of an electrical circuit and had to be connected to other components by means of countless wires. Creating these connections was very labor intensive work, as well as expensive. Working alone in his lab one day, Kilby discovered a means of integrating all the individual components of an electrical circuit onto one tiny slice of silicon, creating the world's first silicon chip, or microchip. This "integrated circuit" on a silicon chip, so small that it is barely visible, became so refined that within a few decades a chip could contain hundreds of thousands, even millions, of integrated circuits, the basic components of "artificial intelligence."

Early Marketing Strategy

Skepticism of this simple yet revolutionary device, and of the requisite technology, was almost universal until Kilby, along with a few colleagues, developed practical applications for the IC, or silicon chip. The first and most successful was the hand-held

AT A GLANCE

Texas Instruments brand of electronics founded in 1951, when the 21-year-old Dallas, TX-based company General Instruments decided to change its image and become a high-tech developer and manufacturer of the still-new transistor; company name changed the same year to Texas Instruments, Inc.; in 1958, a TI researcher, Jack St. Clair Kilby, developed the integrated circuit (IC) on a silicon chip, thereby setting in motion a revolution in electronics; in 1967, the company introduced the first hand-held calculator, also co-invented by Kilby, the first of countless commercial products containing silicon chips.

Performance: *Market share*—8% of semiconductor category (1991). *Sales*—$8.5 billion (1993).

Major competitor: NEC; also Toshiba and Samsung.

Advertising: *Agency*—McCann-Erickson, New York, NY, 1989—. *Major campaign*—Full-page magazine ad with close-up photo of latest TI TravelMate 4000E laptop series, accompanied by chart comparing its features with main competitors' laptops. Slogan: "Extending Your Reach With Innovation."

Addresses: *Parent company*—Texas Instruments, Inc., P.O. Box 655474, Dallas, TX 75265; phone: (214) 995-3333; fax: (214) 995-4360.

calculator, introduced in 1967, many times smaller and more powerful than the calculators of that day. Once the calculator proved the practical worth of the silicon chip, marketing it and overcoming the initial skepticism of the military to the new device was not difficult. Prior to the semiconductor's appearance, each B-29 airplane used a thousand vacuums and tens of thousands of connecting devices; it was a cumbersome, expensive, and energy-consuming product. The military and space industries were the first to seize upon this exciting new breakthrough in electronics, which could be applied from radar to ICBMs to the Apollo spacecraft that landed on the moon in 1969.

Soon after the development of the silicon chip, TI began marketing it abroad. By 1967, it had established a branch in Japan, where marketing was extremely difficult because of Japanese distrust of foreign companies and TI's lack of networking experience. TI evolved a successful strategy in Japan by hiring Japanese workers for all of the branch's positions and leaving it up to them to forge relationships with other firms and markets. Japan became one of the largest foreign customers of TI.

Advertising at Texas Instruments grew over the decades; by the early 1990s, it had an enormous advertising budget, in the tens of millions of dollars. Most of that budget was used for full-page magazine ads featuring the latest computers or sponsoring events.

Product Development

Developing and marketing silicon semiconductors became the core business of Texas Instruments. From silicon chips that went into such simple products as hearing aids and hand-held calculators, TI went on to produce highly advanced electronic systems for the defense and space industries. In the 1960s alone, TI developed radar for aircraft and integrated circuits for Minuteman ICBMs, for navigational systems, and for air traffic control radar.

Computers were the logical outgrowth of the development of the silicon chip. Until the silicon chip's appearance in the late 1950s, computers were huge, cumbersome products that lacked versatility and were not always reliable. TI's engineers developed the first computer in 1960 using silicon integrated circuits (microchips); the machine was designed for military rather than civilian use. In 1971, TI would become the first company to invent the single chip microprocessor and single chip microcomputer, which would pave the way for today's desktop and portable computers. Two years later, TI produced the first 4K RAM chip and, a year later, came out with the TMS 1000 microcomputer. A decade and a half later, TI produced the world's first one megabyte memory chip. In 1992, Texas Instruments introduced its TravelMate line of laptops, with all the power, speed, and features of standard desktops: color screen, desktop-sized keyboard, 100 to 200 megabyte hard drive, and four K of random access memory, expandable to twenty. Added features included the built-in 9,600 band fax modem and power-saving components.

Computer manufacture has led Texas Instruments to produce commercial software and to further refine the production of silicon semiconductors. The company pioneered a process known as trenching, which increased memory capacity.

To summarize the most important products developed by Texas Instruments scarcely does justice to the historical significance of the silicon chip, the heart of every present-day electronic device. Kilby's invention made computers possible, as well as digital watches, digital sound systems, in short, virtually all communications networks and systems. The full impact of computers has not yet been felt, but the possibilities are mind boggling, vastly extending mankind's knowledge and capabilities.

International Growth

The development of the integrated circuit in 1958 stimulated the growth and expansion of Texas Instruments, which until then had been a relatively small and unknown company. Thirty years later, TI had transformed itself into a multinational company with subsidiaries and partnerships in 40 nations, employing over 70,000 men and women.

When Texas Instruments established a subsidiary in Bedford, England, in 1956, it became the first U.S. company to establish a subsidiary abroad for the manufacture of semiconductors, the essential component of the transistor. That particular site was chosen because at the time Great Britain had the highest defense budget in Europe outside of the Soviet Union and the military was the biggest customer for the semiconductor, using it in everything from jets to submarines to radar.

The British subsidiary would be only the first step onto the European continent, with expansion rapidly taking place in Italy, the Netherlands, and France. Japan would become a very important springboard to the Asian continent, and, as so many American companies discovered, a tough country in which to establish subsidiaries. A significant problem was the reluctance of Japanese men and women to change jobs, especially for employment in an unknown foreign company. Once TI resolved the personnel problem by the early 1970s, the Japanese market for silicon semiconductors proved to be the most important one outside of the United States. By the late 1970s, several TI factories in Japan were producing the expensive, fragile silicon wafer, or microchip. Until the Japanese began manufacturing their own, TI was the biggest producer of semiconductors in that country. Following TI's inroads into Japan, the company expanded into southeast Asia and India. TI not only manufactures silicon chips but markets them;

foreign sales constitute a over 40 percent of the company's total annual revenues.

The Future

The business operations of Texas Instruments are by no means limited to the manufacture and marketing of semiconductors, but have expanded to embrace the entire spectrum of computer technology—from computers to peripherals to software—including the production of metallurgical materials and defense electronics. It is a company with many historic "firsts" and a far-flung global commercial enterprise. Texas Instruments ranks among the top ten firms in the worldwide semiconductor industry. It has maintained this position despite the reduction in defense spending in the United States and the cutthroat competition at home and abroad.

The computer industry is a volatile one, with companies rising and collapsing in less than a decade. What inspires companies to enter the electronics—especially the computer—business is the insatiable demand for semiconductors and computers in virtually every field of human activity. Texas Instruments remains a U.S. leader in semiconductor manufacture, not only in terms of sales but also in terms of research. Sales of TI semiconductors in 1993 reached the highest level in the company's history. TI has had a head start over other U.S. companies, having established a well-extended network of subsidiaries around the world at a time when most present-day computer companies had not even come into existence. TI also has a wide array of products and is in a position to take advantage of the fall of trade barriers around the world, especially the rise of free market economies in eastern Europe, Russia, and China. There is great demand for semiconductors in the Asia-Pacific region, where TI's presence is strong. In sum, the key to TI's future success appears to be the globalization of its industry.

Further Reading:

Alm, Richard, and Jim Mitchell, "Texas Instruments," four-part series, *Dallas Morning News*, July 26–29, 1987.

Boudette, Neal, "TI Joins List of Vendors with 486 Notebooks," *PC Week*, April 13, 1992, p. 5.

Clifford, Mark, "A New Frontier; US Electronics Firm Expands in Instruments," *Far Eastern Economic Review*, September 17, 1992, p. 62.

Kupfer, Andrew, "The Long Arm of Jerry Junkins," *Fortune*, March 14, 1988.

Morgan, Hal, *Symbols of America*, New York: Penguin, 1986.

Rist, Oliver, "Gateway 2000; Texas Instruments," *PC Magazine*, August, 1993, p. 182.

Robertson, Jack, "20 percent Japan Market Share 'Essential,' TI Chief," *Electronic News*, March 25, 1991, p. 1.

Texas Giants: The New Breed, Austin, Texas: Industrial Commission, 1971.

Texas Instruments Annual Report, Dallas: Texas Instruments, Inc., 1993.

Texas Instruments: Global Growth from Seismology to Space Age Technology, reprint, Dallas: Texas Instruments, Inc., 1971.

"Thirty Years at the Heart of Invention," Dallas: Texas Instruments, 1988.

Zimmerman, Michael R., "TI to Expand TravelMate Line," *PC Week*, October 19, 1992, p. 14.

—Sina Dubovoj

THERMOS®

THERMOS®

The name Thermos is a well-known brand name long associated with vacuum bottles. After four years of litigation with Aladdin Industries, however, a 1962 New Haven, Connecticut, U.S. district court's "genericisation" decision took away American Thermos Products Company, Inc.'s exclusive rights to the word thermos. Although it is still registered as a trademark in more than 80 countries, the loss of rights to the name in the United States means the word thermos has passed into popular and generic usage, available to any and all users. The word thermos, Judge Robert P. Anderson ruled, now appears as a common dictionary entry meaning "vacuum bottle" or any vacuum insulated container. Sidney Diamond, a member of the New York Bar Association writing in *Advertising Age,* observed that the "opinion stands as a case history of what can go wrong with a successful trademark" and noted the similarity of the thermos case with other former trademarks such as aspirin, cellophane, escalator, and shredded wheat.

The Genericisation Decision

Judge Anderson's decision was based on his analysis of Thermos's "advertising program and its policing of improper use" during three different time periods, according to Diamond. Diamond reported that in many ways, during the early days of Thermos advertising (1907 to 1923), Thermos encouraged and contributed to the genericisation of the word thermos by "popularizing the expression 'Thermos bottle,'" even using the statement "Thermos is a household word" in its 1910 catalog. Thermos justified its "careless" marketing approach, however, because of "advantageous free advertising." Judge Anderson summarized the first period analysis with these concluding remarks: "The course of conduct of the plaintiff (American Thermos) from 1907-1923 in its advertising and educational campaigns tended to make 'thermos' a generic term descriptive of the product rather than its origin."

The second period of Judge Anderson's analysis was 1923 to the early 1950s. In a 1923 trademark infringement action against W. T. Grant Co., Thermos was successful, but only because of a technicality: the judge ruled that although it was his opinion that Thermos had become "descriptive" and thus not qualified to be a trademark, W. T. Grant had not acted quickly enough to pursue a defense based on the generic theory. After this case, Diamond reported, Thermos did begin to protest the generic uses of the term thermos, but not do so in a systematic way. Thus, Judge Anderson concluded that during this time period, American Thermos had "failed to use reasonable diligence to rescue 'thermos' from being or becoming a descriptive or generic term."

Beginning in 1954, the third period of Judge Anderson's analysis, American Thermos "put on a determined campaign to educate the public to the trademark significance of 'Thermos,'" and expanded its line of products to include non-vacuum insulated products such as tents, camp stoves, lanterns, and bottle openers. It also increased "policing activities" against infringements on the use of the word. But Judge Anderson concluded that "the plaintiff's extraordinary efforts commencing in the middle of the 1950s and carried on into the time of the trial came too late to keep the word 'thermos' from falling into the public domain; rather it was an effort to pull it back from the public domain—something it could not and did not accomplish."

Diamond stated that Judge Anderson reached a "Solomonic decision" by allowing Aladdin Industries to use thermos in lower case letters following the label "Aladdin" and another brand name, "Aladdin's Huckleberry Hound thermos bottle." Aladdin is also not permitted to label any advertising or marketing material with the words genuine or original or any other such synonym in reference to thermos. American Thermos was still allowed the use of the "logotype version" of capitalized Thermos and retained its registered trademarks.

The appeal was upheld by the U.S. second circuit court of appeals, but in 1964 Judge Anderson had to warn both Thermos and Aladdin to stop distorting the court's decision in their promotional advertising. According to *Advertising Age,* Judge Anderson said that both Aladdin and Thermos "have in advertising and promotional literature so emphasized the portions of the decisions favorable to their own interest, and minimized portions adverse to them, that the actual decision is seriously distorted." Anderson threatened both companies with a $25,000 fine. While he allowed Thermos to continue its "policing" activities, he enjoined the company not to make any references to the case in its letters to potential trademark violators.

Company Origins

The first company to manufacture commercial vacuum flasks was Burger and Aschenbrenner, which founded Thermos GmbH in Germany in 1904. Thermos GmbH adapted for commercial use

AT A GLANCE

Burger and Aschenbrenner company first manufactured vacuum flasks in Germany, 1904; company founded Thermos GmbH; A. E. Gutman obtained U.K. distribution rights, 1905; Thermos trademark registered in England, 1906; Gutman registered Thermos throughout United Kingdom and other parts of world, 1907; William B. Walker formed Thermos Bottle Company of America in Brooklyn, NY, 1913; the Thermos Bottle Company of America bought major shares of Thermos Limited, in the 1920s; King-Seeley acquired American Thermos Products Company, Inc., Thermos Limited, and its subsidiary, Canadian Thermos Products Limited, 1960, to become the King-Seeley Thermos Company; King-Seeley Thermos Company purchased all outstanding shares of Structo Manufacturing Company stock, 1965; Household International bought King-Seeley Thermos Company, 1968; Household International became Household Manufacturing, 1982; King-Seeley Thermos, a division of Household International, acquired the Halsey Taylor Company, 1969; Halsey Taylor and Structo consolidated, 1976; Thermos and Structo merged, 1986, to become The Thermos Company; Thermos/Halsey Taylor was then one division of Household Manufacturing; Halsey Taylor became a division of Scotsman Industries, Inc., 1989; Nippon Sanso, K. K., of Tokyo purchased The Thermos Company (U.S., Canada, and U.K.) from Household Manufacturing International Inc. in August, 1989.

Performance: *Market share*—4% of cooler and jug manufacturers.

Major competitor: Coleman; also, Igloo and Rubbermaid.

Advertising: *Agency*—Golin/Harris Communications.

Addresses: *Parent company*—The Thermos Company, 300 North Martingale Rd., Suite 250, Schaumburg, IL 60173; phone: (708) 240-3200; fax: (708) 240-3211. *Ultimate parent company*—Nippon Sanso K. K. (Japan Oxygen Co., Ltd.), 16-7, Nishi-Shinbashi 1-chrome, Minato-ku, Tokyo, Japan; phone: 03-3581-8401; telex: J24228 NSANSO; fax: 03-3580-9425.

a vacuum flask designed by Sir James Dewar for laboratory use. In 1905 the British firm A. E. Gutman acquired distribution rights, and in 1906 Thermos was registered as a trademark. The next year, Gutman formed Thermos Limited, obtained import rights, and registered the brand name in various countries throughout the United Kingdom and the world. That same year, Thermos Bottle Company of America was founded by William B. Walker in Brooklyn, New York.

What would eventually be known as The Thermos Company is actually a combination of three companies: Thermos Bottle Company of America, Structo Manufacturing Company, and the Halsey Taylor Company. When Thermos Bottle Company of America moved to Norwich, Connecticut, in 1913, the company both pioneered and expanded the vacuum bottle industry. Products included not only the vacuum flask, but also school lunch kits, coffee carafes, and outdoor living products such as chests and jugs. During the 1920s the Thermos Bottle Company of America obtained a major share of the U.K. Thermos organization.

The second company playing a role in Thermos history, Structo, began as an outgrowth of Thompson Manufacturing Company, which began in Freeport, Illinois, in 1907 as a manufacturer of children's toys: steel weaving looms, toy cars and trucks, and steel construction toys (an early version of Erector sets). In 1912 the company changed its name to Structo Manufacturing Company. Structo aided the World War II war effort by manufacturing machine gun water chests, bomb racks, and hand grenade loading fuses, and in 1960 it expanded its product line to include barbecue grills. In 1975 Structo limited its manufactured products to barbecue grills exclusively and has since become a known leader in the industry.

The third company behind Thermos's history is Halsey Taylor. When Halsey Willard Taylor's father died from typhoid fever in Warren, Ohio, Taylor began looking for ways to help prevent the spread of contagious diseases through unsanitary drinking water sources at the Packard Motor Company where his father had been employed. Believing that drinking contaminated water from a common cup was the source of his father's contact with the deadly disease, Taylor invented the "Puritan [Water] Fountain," and founded the Halsey Taylor Company in 1912. His company was revolutionized during World War I when he acquired an army contract to supply sanitary water dispensers to training camps. By that time, he had patented innovations to the original fountain that included a two stream bubbler and lip guard.

Thermos Bottle Company, Structo, and Halsey Taylor all managed to come together through a series of tangled mergers and acquisitions. King-Seeley purchased American Thermos Products Company, Inc. (formerly Thermos Bottle Company of America), Thermos Limited, and its subsidiary, Canadian Thermos Products Limited, in 1960 to form King-Seeley Thermos Company. In 1965 King-Seeley Thermos Company acquired all outstanding shares of Structo stock, and by 1975, the company began producing barbecue grills. In 1968 Household International bought King-Seeley Thermos Company, which became a division of Household International. In 1969 King-Seeley Thermos Company acquired Halsey Taylor, and in 1976 the company consolidated with Structo. Halsey Taylor became part of Scotsman Industries, Inc., in 1988, and The Thermos Company entered into a contract with Scotsman Industries to produce Halsey Taylor drinking fountains and electric water coolers. In 1982 Household International became Household Manufacturing, a name that began replacing the King-Seely Thermos Company name. Thermos and Structo merged in 1986 to become The Thermos Company, a division of Household Manufacturing. In 1989, The Thermos Company became a subsidiary of Nippon Sanso, K. K., of Tokyo, and Halsey Taylor became a division of Scotsman Industries.

1990s and Beyond

At the 1994 International Housewares Show in Chicago, Thermos products maintained a competitive edge. As Vice President of Marketing Shelley Nehrt said, "Thermos brand products are about having fun and entertaining. . . . Whether it's grills, coolers, lunch boxes or vacuum ware, we want our consumers to know they can always count on quality Thermos brand products to make their lives easier and more enjoyable at an appealing price." Specifically showcased at the 1994 show were an old-time favorite, school lunch kits. Thermos's many licenses include Disney's The Little Mermaid, Barney, Barbie, Lamb Chop, The Flintstones, and Looney Tunes; Thermos added innovative design to the lunch kits, as evidenced in The Little Mermaid's shell-shaped kit. In addition, Thermos advertised "something for everyone," with customized variations on the lunch kit designed for the specific needs of various age groups of children, from preschool (ages three to seven) through older children and adults. Because of the popularity with licensed lunch kits, Thermos planned to license other products in the future, including coolers, jugs, travel mugs, and steel vacuum ware.

A new product on the 1994 Chicago show scene was Thermos Nissan Thermal Cookware, which uses vacuum technology to produce what Thermos called the "perfect 'unwatched pot.' " Endorsed by Graham Kerr of PBS's *Graham Kerr's Kitchen,* Thermal Cookware is marketed with Kerr's special recipes developed especially for this product. Kerr said of this new line of Thermos products, "Without question, this is the most significant new cooking idea that is ideally suited to our emerging lifestyle changes. . . . It continues to surprise me with absolute excellence and without fuss or failure . . . truly the 'unwatched pot' that never boils." As The Thermos Company continues to revitalize its existing products and introduce new ones, it seems likely that it will continue to be recognized as a pioneer in contemporary design and superior performance.

Further Reading:

"Ads Twist Ruling on Thermos, Aladdin, King-Seeley Warned," *Advertising Age,* January 13, 1964, p. 16.

"Chronology of Thermos," Schaumburg, IL: The Thermos Company, May 30, 1990.

Diamond, Sidney A., " 'Thermos' Trademark Passes into the Language," *Advertising Age,* August 13, 1962, p. 56.

"Thermos Ad References Restricted," *Editor & Publisher,* January 11, 1964, p. 17.

"Thermos Company History," Schaumburg, IL: The Thermos Company.

"The Thermos Company Offers Lunch Kits for All Ages," Schaumburg, IL: The Thermos Company, January 16, 1994.

"The Thermos Company Rolls Out 1994 Product Line," Schaumburg, IL: The Thermos Company, January 16, 1994.

" 'Thermos' Is Generic Term, Judge Decides," *Advertising Age,* July 2, 1962, p. 2.

" 'Thermos' Is Ruled a Household Word Any Maker Can Use," *New York Times,* June 28, 1962, p. 33.

"Thermos Nissan Blows the Lid Off Cookware with Vacuum Technology," Schaumburg, IL: The Thermos Company, January 16, 1994.

—Mary Katherine Wainwright

THOMASVILLE®

Thomasville®

One of the most unique chairs in the United States sits in the town square in Thomasville, North Carolina, a town known as the "Chair Capital of the South" as early as 1906. "The Big Chair," serving as a "salute to the role furniture has played in the town's well-being," was the 1922 project of Thomasville Chair Company, one of the most enduring and prestigious of the many furniture manufacturers rapidly emerging in North Carolina at the beginning of the 20th century. Originally constructed of enough forest pine to build 100 dining room chairs, "The Big Chair" was 13 feet, 6 inches high. Its seating area of 39 square feet was covered with the largest leather hide available at that time from a Swiss steer. Because of weather erosion, the chair had to be removed in the 1930s, but Thomasville Chair undertook its reconstruction in 1948; the new Duncan Phyfe dining room arm chair was dedicated in 1951, an 18-foot-high, 30-square-foot steel-framed chair built on a limestone base anchored eight feet into the ground, reinforced with concrete piers, and filled with modeling cement. One of its most distinguished visitors to the chair, modeled after a Smithsonian original, was Lyndon Baines Johnson during his whistle stop vice presidential campaign in 1960. Throughout the century, Thomasville Chair Company grew into Thomasville Furniture Industries, Inc., one of the top ten furniture manufacturing companies in the United States with a 27-plant facility that employs over 7,500 employees in four states. Thomasville name has been associated with high quality, stylish furniture marketed toward young, middle-class, married homeowners.

"Chair Capital of the South"

Thomasville Chair Company was begun by G. A. Alison and seven other local businessmen in Thomasville, North Carolina, in 1904; articles of incorporation were filed at Davidson County (North Carolina) Courthouse on February 11, 1905. In 1907 Thomasville Chair was unable to pay its bill for a shipment of lumber to brothers Thomas J. and Charles F. Finch, so the company offered the Finch brothers $2,000 worth of company stock instead. To "protect their investment," the Finches quickly bought up the rest of the company's stock, and Thomas J. Finch took over the company's management, increasing Thomasville Chair's profit during the first year. In 1909, when Thomasville Chair took over the first of its many neighboring lumber and furniture plants, a wagon and a white mule comprised the total transportation department, and chairs sold for $8 to $12 a dozen. Until 1913, chairs were shipped wrapped in newspapers. The town of Thomasville had a competitive edge over other furniture manufacturers springing up in North Carolina because it was serviced by two railroads.

"The Formative Years"

1910 to 1920 have been called the "formative years" for Thomasville because that was when certain procedures were introduced that would make Thomasville a "self-sufficient" plant and insure its future growth. Several plant additions included a central machine shop, a wrapping and upholstery facility (which marked the change from newspaper wrapping to padding), and a veneer factory (the first in the South). In 1914 Thomas Austin Finch replaced his father Thomas J. Finch as company manager and introduced the "Character" line, a label that represented the company's promise of quality. Under the young Finch's leadership, by 1917 company sales reached over $1 million, and Thomasville Chair's reputation for quality furniture, creative and functional design, and innovative manufacturing techniques was firmly established.

Expanded Marketing in the 1920s

By 1923 Thomasville Chair's sales were well over $2 million but were limited to the South because the furniture, although known as "good value," was not considered "stylish" enough for an urban, cosmopolitan market. To reach this new market, Thomasville Chair products were first exhibited at furniture showrooms in New York City and Chicago. (Seventy years later Thomasville was to open its own 2,000-square-foot showroom on Fifth Avenue in New York City "as part of its strategy to create a national presence.")

An appeal to another audience was also created during the post war 1920s when women began to replace men as the major decision makers on consumer goods. In 1925 Finch employed his first designers to shift the emphasis of Thomasville furniture's eye appeal from function to beauty. On February 16, 1925, Thomasville Chair Company incorporated under North Carolina law, and Charles F. Finch sold his shares of company stock to his brother, Thomas J., who became the company's first president. Thomas Austin Finch continued in his role as manager.

AT A GLANCE

Thomasville brand furniture originated with the Thomasville Chair Company, founded by G. A. Alison and others in Thomasville, NC, 1904; company purchased by brothers Thomas J. and Charles F. Finch, 1907; Thomasville Chair merged with B. F. Huntley Furniture Company of Winston-Salem, NC, to become Thomasville Furniture Industries, Inc., 1961; Thomasville first sold public stocks, 1962; stocks first listed on New York Stock Exchange, 1964; company purchased by Armstrong Cork Company, 1968; Armstrong Cork became Armstrong World Industries, Inc., 1980.

Performance: *Market share*—1.8% of furniture retailers. *Sales*—More than $430 million.

Major competitor: Ethan Allen brand furniture; also, Broyhill / Lane furniture and Bassett furniture.

Advertising: *Media Agency*—BBDO, New York, NY. *Brand creative agency*—Long, Haymes, Carr, Lintas.

Addresses: *Parent company*—Thomasville Furniture Industries, Inc., P.O. Box 339, Thomasville, NC 27360; phone: (919) 472-4000. *Ultimate parent company*—Armstrong World Industries, Inc., 313 West Liberty St., Lancaster, PA 17604; phone: (717) 397-0611; fax: (717) 396-2787.

Furniture Industry Firsts

The newly reorganized company moved to the cutting edge of furniture manufacturing during the latter part of the 1920s by introducing many industry firsts. It started a marketing trend by creating the first national 34-person sales force in the furniture industry and also by advertising complete suites of dining room furniture: Thomasville chairs in groupings with tables by St. Johns Table Company of Michigan and buffets by B. F. Huntley Furniture Company of Winston-Salem, North Carolina. Throughout the century Thomasville successfully continued to advertise in collaboration with products from other companies such as Lenox china, Trans-Ocean rugs, and Eastman House Mattresses. In 1992 Thomasville joined forces with Philips Consumer Electronics Company to manufacture and market "home-theaters," entertainment centers that house electronic products in crafted wood cabinets. In 1992 this one product alone accounted for ten percent of Thomasville's sales.

In 1927 the Thomasville image was popularized when Thomasville Chair created another American furniture industry first by manufacturing and marketing its own complete line of dining room suites. A 10-piece set of dining room furniture could be purchased for $94.50. In 1928 Thomasville added bedroom suites. Because of these furniture industry firsts, by the end of the 1920s Thomas Austin Finch had earned a national reputation as an "innovative and progressive manager," instrumental in bringing Thomasville Chair into a "full-service, modern company." When Thomas J. Finch died in 1929, Thomas Austin Finch became Thomasville Chair's second president.

"Tomorrow Is the Thing"

During the depression years, Thomas Austin Finch made some bold decisions. In a 1931 letter to Thomasville employees, Finch described his "credo" for the future. He didn't follow the depression years' solutions adopted by many of his competitors of cutting wages and quality or producing "gaudy, overembellished" borax furniture that flooded the market during the 1930s. Instead, in a bold move, Finch upgraded Thomasville Furniture. He introduced the "Finch Fine Furniture" label in 1932 and hired Radio City Music Hall designer Donald Desky to design new furniture styles. The result was a new furniture line introduced in 1935, American/Modern/Decorative, known as AMODEC, described as "a fresh breath of fashion from a southern manufacturer." AMODEC was introduced by "invitation only" to leading retailers in New York and Chicago. Finch also continued to manufacture furniture even though sales were very low. By storing the pieces in vacant buildings in the town of Thomasville, Finch had a ready inventory when the depression years were over. Thomasville funded its 1930s' expansion by not paying stock dividends and reducing management salaries by 10 percent.

During the 1930s Thomasville Chair continued to earn a unique reputation among southern furniture manufacturers by investing in a massive modernization project. It replaced all wooden buildings with brick, converted steam equipment to electric, and conducted "trade classes" for employees for training in new skills and methods. The 1934 catalog advertised Thomasville's "New Deal Furniture," more than 30 different choices of dining and bedroom furniture. Also in 1934, Thomasville began manufacturing its first upholstered furniture and introduced over 11 different suites composed of two chairs and a sofa. Finch's 1934 message to his employees summarized Thomasville's endeavors during the 1930s and established Thomasville's path for the future: "Yesterday is a thousand years ago—Tomorrow is the thing. Old ideas, old messages, old equipment cannot set the tomorrows that are coming. Let's forget them—look forward—we cannot stand still—we must keep moving—all of us."

Much of Thomasville's technological modernization during these years was the brain child of Thomas Austin Finch's brother, Doak, who joined the company in 1925. After visiting the Ford Motor Company in Detroit, Doak Finch was able to modify the Ford conveyor system to suit furniture manufacturing, thus reducing labor and increasing efficiency. Known as a "mechanical wizard," Doak Finch earned his reputation by urging machinery manufacturers of non-furniture equipment to modify their designs for use in the furniture industry. In addition to the conveyor system, Doak Finch was responsible for automatic nailing machines for furniture and equipping Ford's cab-over-engine trucks with power steering. When Thomas Austin Finch died in 1943, Doak Finch succeeded him as president until 1961.

The Sixties: "Decade of Change"

During the 1950s, the South began to earn a highly regarded reputation for furniture manufacturing, and Thomasville Chair Company opened the largest on-site marketing showroom in 1958. But it was in 1961 that Thomasville Chair began a rapid progress that continued over the next three decades. After merging with B. F. Huntley Furniture Company in 1961, the new Thomasville Furniture Industries, Inc., under the guidance of its new president Tom A. Finch (son of the late Thomas Austin Finch), offered its first public stock in 1962 and was listed on the New York Stock Exchange in 1964. In 1967 Thomasville Furniture was responsible for another industry first: the Environmental Simulation Package Testing Laboratory. In this lab, experiments in the design and construction of cartons helped to reduce expensive damage claims due to packaging and earned the company a reputation as an "industry innovator."

The company's reorganization in 1961 also brought about expanded marketing strategies. In September of 1962 Thomasville Furniture Industries, Inc., first advertised in the national magazines *House and Garden* and *Modern Bride,* and in 1966 Thomasville Furniture was one of the first furniture manufacturers to advertise on national television. Broadcast during the *Today* show, Thomasville's first television commercials were often presented live by Hugh Downs and Frank Blair. In 1988 Thomasville invested an estimated $10 million in a major advertising campaign, becoming the "first full-line furniture marketer to advertise on network TV," according to Pat Sloan in *Advertising Age.* This campaign, which cost more than what the entire furniture industry spent on advertising the previous year, was geared to enhance Thomasville's name brand recognition and bring Thomasville "a larger share of consumers' disposable income," according to company president Frederick B. Starr in 1988.

Thomasville Merges with Armstrong

In order to continue its mission of "complete [consumer] satisfaction," Tom A. Finch announced the merger of Thomasville Furniture with Armstrong Cork Company on July 1, 1968. As a result of the restructuring, several marketing strategies were introduced. At the October, 1973, furniture market, a record-setting number of buyers visited the company's showroom in the town of Thomasville to view all Thomasville furniture products under one roof for the first time. In 1974 the newly opened Appomattox, Virginia, plant introduced a new line of furniture under the name Armstrong Furniture, and in 1977 improved marketing strategies led to the creation of separate sales groups for each line of furniture as a way "to provide better customer service." In 1982 Frederick B. Starr became president and CEO. By that time, Thomasville Furniture Industries, Inc., had grown into one of the country's top ten furniture manufacturing companies with annual sales in excess of $430 million.

The 1980s: Retail Innovations

In the early 1980s Thomasville introduced an innovative concept for the furniture industry with its formation of Thomasville Galleries housed in the stores of independent retailers. Later in the decade, many Galleries converted to Thomasville Home Furnishing stores, retail stores selling Thomasville products exclusively. Both types of sales spaces depended on a unique "partnership" relation between the manufacturer and the retailer. A Gallery is approximately 8,000 square feet of retail showroom within a "multi-line" store used specifically to display Thomasville furniture in settings arranged and accessorized to approximate furnishings in a room in an actual home.

In contrast, the Thomasville Home Furnishing stores are approximately 18,000 square feet of "free-standing" stores that sell only Thomasville furniture. Many Galleries converted to Home Furnishing stores during the late 1980s; as a result, Thomasville has dramatically expanded its line by doubling its bedroom and dining room choices, starting an upholstery division from scratch, purchasing Gordon's table manufacturing company, and adding the Discovery Shop, a boutique within a Gallery or store that showcases an accent furnishings line called "From the Four Corners." First introduced in 1971, From The Four Corners is a collection of accent pieces and accessories selected by buyers on trips around the world. Thomasville also introduced retail sales training sessions to train Thomasville Home Furnishings retailers in marketing, introduce them to advertising strategies, and educate them in the use of consumer education centers that provide potential buyers with such decision-making aids as decorating videos, product literature. and in-store seminars.

Thomasville's president, Frederick B. Starr, explained that the "Thomasville Home Furnishing store concept is in itself a strategic commitment to understanding and satisfying consumers. It enables consumers to make informed buying decisions in an atmosphere that's both friendly and inviting." In 1994 Thomasville was doing business with approximately 500 independent retailers in the United States and Canada and was developing networks with retailers in Japan, Taiwan, and Mexico. By the end of 1994, Thomasville anticipated having as many as 150 separate Home Furnishing stores.

Major Thomasville Furniture styles include 18th-century American and English, country French, contemporary, Shaker, and casual country. The top-selling style for more than 30 years remains the 18th-century Cherry line. By the end of the 1980s, Thomasville had branched into home entertainment furniture and a collection of children's furniture called First Impressions.

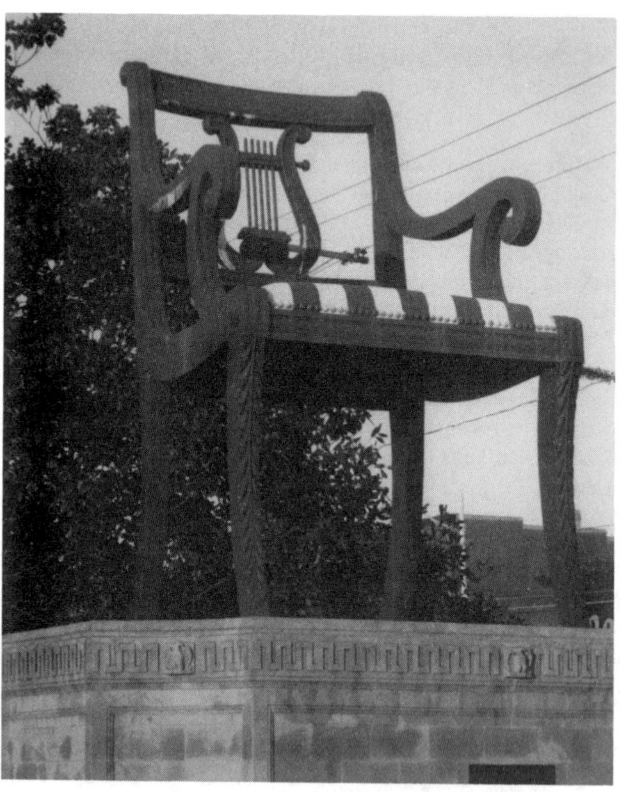

A testimony to the strength of the Thomasville brand, this giant chair sits in the town square of Thomasville, North Carolina.

Thomasville's first licensed home furnishings collection was called "Country Inns and Back Roads," created when Thomasville designers visited country inns across the United States that were recommended by the late Norman Simpson's guide book *Country Inns and Back Roads, North America.* Inspired by their visits, designers created four styles of furniture for the Country Inns and Back Roads collection: American Parlor, Country Cottage, Farm House Basics, and Innkeeper's Classics. Called "nostalgic" and "eclectic," this furniture line offers a wide selection of upholstered "country" looks, including lodge, cabin, cowboy, cottage, or 19th-century parlor, and includes accessories, textiles, window coverings, and lighting.

1992 Advertising Campaign

Thomasville's 1992 North American magazine campaign was the most extensive advertising campaign in the furniture industry as well as the largest investment Thomasville had ever made. Designed by the BBDO advertising firm in New York City and Ian Roberts Advertising of Canada, these advertisements for Thomasville products reached an estimated 130 million consumers in the United States and 8 million in Canada; these consumers represented an estimated 81 percent and 43 percent of the respective target audiences for the two countries. Advertising in such well-known home decorating magazines as *Better Homes & Gardens, House Beautiful, Good Housekeeping, Country Home,* and *Country Living,* Thomasville targets a profile audience comprised of females, married people (82 percent), homeowners (85 percent), and those aged 25 to 55 (70 percent) with an annual household income of $35,000.

Future Growth

Thomasville kicked off its 90th anniversary year in 1994 with a new advertising campaign focused on the message ''The Place to Start is Thomasville.'' *Thomasville Today* stated that the campaign objectives include ensuring that Thomasville is a ''must see'' for target customers; convincing target customers that Thomasville represents the ''very best values''; spotlighting Thomasville's ''unique'' image as ''exceptional examples of fashion, function, comfort, and value''; delivering the ''must see'' message; reaching the ''emotional level'' of target customers; and continuing to ''broaden audience awareness of the Thomasville brand.'' The first national ad to reflect the 1994 campaign strategy was for the Kallista Collection, introduced during the first quarter of 1994 in major monthly home decorating magazines in the United States and Canada. Robert Marks explained that the word Kallista derives from the Greek word kallos, meaning beauty. Thomasville planned to challenge its 1994 competition with a ''promise for the future'': ''to continue to represent quality and value.'' In its breadth of manufacturing and retailing home furnishings, Thomasville has remained on the cutting edge of U.S. furniture makers throughout the century. As it moves into the 21st century, Thomasville has branched out into importing, retailing, ready-to-assemble furnishings, accessories, and electronics, while at the same time maintaining high standards of quality and excellence under a single management entity.

Further Reading:

''The Art and Science of Advertising,'' Thomasville, NC: Thomasville Furnishings, Inc., 1992.

Brin, Geri, and Mary Ann Bacher, ''A Perfect Marriage: Thomasville's Home Theater Combines Exquisite Cabinetry with Philips State-of-the-Art Electronics,'' *HFD—The Weekly Home Furnishings Newspaper,* October 12, 1992, p. 36.

Burgess, John, ''Fighting to Stay Fit,'' *Washington Post,* November 25, 1990, p. H1.

''Furniture Tie-Ins,'' *Television Digest,* October 28, 1991, p. 16.

''Gallery Networks in Front of Revenue Growth Parade,'' *Furniture Today,* Annual Retail Marketing Guide, 1992, p. 62.

Hayes, Mary, ''Furnisher Plans Big Expansion,'' *Business Journal,* September 16, 1991, p. 1.

Hurly, Paul, ''Boosting Sales . . . Electronically,'' *Industry Week,* March 31, 1986, p. 33.

Kelt, Deborah, ''Thomasville Lenox: Double Date,'' *HFD—The Weekly Home Furnishings Newspaper,* April 19, 1993, p. M2.

Marks, Robert, *HFD—The Weekly Home Furnishings Newspaper,* ''Armstrong Seeks Mass Appeal,'' June 7, 1993, p. 18; ''Defining Contemporary,'' May 3, 1993, p. 23; ''Electronics Optional with Thomasville's New Home Theater,'' October 11, 1993, p. 26; ''Thomasville Realigns Unit,'' December 2, 1991, p. 20; ''Thomasville's Country Inns Settings,'' April 19, 1993, p. 24.

McNamara, Michael D., ''Thomasville Program Boosts Eastman House,'' *HFD—The Weekly Home Furnishings Newspaper,* April 22, 1991, p. 30.

''New Management Posts at Henredon, Thomasville Zero in on Consumer Needs,'' *Furniture Today,* January 6, 1992, p. 2.

'''92 Restructuring Cuts Thomasville Profits,'' *Furniture Today,* February 1, 1993, p. 43.

''O'Reilly's Opens Country Inns Shop,'' *Furniture Today,* April 20, 1992, p. 48.

Schancupp, Pam, ''Matching Linen for Restonic, Thomasville Beds,'' *HFD—The Weekly Home Furnishings Newspaper,* May 3, 1993, p. 26.

Schwartz, Donna Boyle, ''Thomasville Tries New York with Showroom,'' *HFD—The Weekly Home Furnishings Newspaper,* October 12, 1992, p. 178.

Seavy, Mark, ''Joining Forces: Electronics and Furniture Industries Find Common Ground in Home-Theater Market,'' *HFD—The Weekly Home Furnishings Newspaper,* October 12, 1992, p. 239.

Sloan, Pat, *Advertising Age,* ''Furniture Maker Builds on TV Ads,'' December 5, 1988, p. 12; ''Furniture Ads Focus on Real Life,'' August 13, 1990, p. 31.

''Thomasville: Furniture Specialists Since 1904,'' Thomasville, NC: Thomasville Furniture Industries, Inc.

''Thomasville Adds 2 Free-Standing Stores, 10 Galleries,'' *Furniture Today,* August 3, 1992, p. 32.

''Thomasville Expanding Country Inns Distribution,'' *Furniture Today,* October 5, 1992, p. 1.

''Thomasville Furniture Industries News,'' Thomasville, NC: Thomasville Furniture Industries, Inc., 1979.

''Thomasville History: Growth to Greatness,'' Thomasville, NC: Thomasville Furniture Industries, Inc.

''Thomasville Home Furnishings: Retailing for the '90s,'' Thomasville, NC: Thomasville Furnishings, Inc.

''Thomasville Marks Opening of 3 Stores, 5 Galleries, 1 Shop,'' *Furniture Today,* August 2, 1993, p. 16.

''Thomasville On Track with Major Revamp of Galleries, Stores,'' *Furniture Today,* January 27, 1992, p. 2.

''Thomasville Sees 50 More Independent Stores in '93,'' *Furniture Today,* December 7, 1992, p. 1.

''Thomasville Strategy Focuses on Consumers,'' *Furniture Today,* January 27, 1992, p. 45.

''Thomasville to Gauge Consumer Satisfaction,'' *Furniture Today,* December 2, 1991, p. 1.

Thomasville Today, Thomasville, NC: Thomasville Furniture Industries, Inc., January-March 1994.

''Thomasville's Operating Profits Quadruple in Quarter,'' *Furniture Today,* February 3, 1993, p. 39.

Van Zante, Shirley, and others, ''5 Great Looks from 5 Great Galleries,'' *Better Homes and Gardens,* November 1988, p. 103.

—Mary Katherine Wainwright

TIFFANY®

TIFFANY & CO.

Tiffany, perhaps more so than any other American brand name, embodies both beauty and grandeur. After more than 150 years, Tiffany still stands for uncommon quality and craftsmanship in silver, in glass, in diamonds—in virtually every medium from which fine gifts and jewelry can be fashioned. In 1988, echoing the comments of Tiffany & Co.'s design director John Loring, Anthony Brandt in *Connoisseur* said, "Tiffany is both a store and a benchmark of American culture. Its jewelry was for decades the standard against which other jewelry was measured. Most sterling-silver baby cups are stamped by machine out of disks of silver. Tiffany still spins them by hand on a lathe. Tiffany bespeaks quality. It is where your family heirlooms—silver candelabra, rococo bread baskets, tea sets, services for thirty—probably came from."

From 1979 to 1984 Tiffany & Co. was under the ownership of Avon Products, Inc.; many feared that the luster of the Tiffany brand would be tarnished by this transition, and indeed the company faltered under Avon ownership. Since 1984, however, Tiffany & Co. has experienced a renaissance that has all but quelled fears of the Tiffany name suffering permanent damage. Always a national and global presence, Tiffany & Co. has in recent years enhanced its profile through an expansion of its retail chain, which now consists of 15 domestic stores as well as retail branches in Toronto, Frankfurt, London, Munich, Zurich, Hong Kong, Singapore, and Taipei, and several boutiques in Japan operated by Mitsukoshi, an upscale department store chain. In addition to fine jewelry and silver, Tiffany & Co.'s offerings include china, crystal, stationery, writing instruments, timepieces, and fragrances. And the list of Tiffany prices is equally extensive, ranging from $15 to more than $500,000.

From Small Shop to World-Class Museum

In the 1992 Tiffany & Co. Annual Report, the glorious and distant past of Tiffany & Co. is frequently linked to its present and future. The message is clear: Tiffany traditions live on. "Years ago, Tiffany & Co. was described as a great museum that 'happened' to sell its exhibits. In fact, the Company has never been passive in its strategies for attracting shoppers. Charles Lewis Tiffany, the Company's founder and one of the 19th century's outstanding merchants and entrepreneurs, had an unerring genius for making news, causing excitement, and capturing the attention of people of taste and discernment. His extraordinary marketing skills set the standard for future generations and brought his small 'Stationery and Fancy Goods' store to the forefront of America's fine retail establishments, with mounting recognition in museums, palaces, homes and businesses the world over."

Charles Lewis Tiffany launched his notions store in New York City in 1837, with the aid of a partner named John P. Young. Four years later a third partner was added, and the enterprise became known as Tiffany, Young, and Ellis. In 1853 the firm was reorganized as Tiffany & Co. During its early years, the Tiffany business, wrote Andrea Gabor in *U.S. New & World Report,* sold "everything from umbrellas to French furniture" and "made simplicity and elegance its hallmark." In 1845 it became one of the first retailers in the country to market its many wares through a catalog.

But already by 1850, the year the company opened its Paris branch, the Tiffany name had become associated with fine gemstones and handcrafted jewelry. In 1951 esteemed American silversmith John C. Moore was brought on board, and one year later the company brought the English sterling standard to the United States, thereafter developing a peerless reputation in silver. After 1868 (a busy year during which the business incorporated as well as opened Tiffany branches in London and Geneva), Tiffany & Co. regularly exhibited and won awards for its silver creations at international expositions; in 1878 a Tiffany & Co. exhibit won a gold medal at the Paris Exposition Universelle. In 1886 the company introduced "The Tiffany Setting," a six-prong setting for diamond solitaires that firmly established Tiffany & Co. leadership in jewelry design and became the utmost in engagement rings. The Tiffany name was further enhanced in 1887 when Charles Tiffany purchased some of the crown jewels of France.

But then as today, the Tiffany name was affined with the distinctive styles of its chief designers, among them rococo revivalists Paulding Farnham and James H. Whitehouse. Through such talents, the company was indeed creating museum-quality exhibits in everything from Greek vases to silverware, all carrying the Tiffany name. However, by far the most important and influential artisan associated with the company during its first century was none other than the founder's son, Louis Comfort Tiffany, who served as Tiffany & Co.'s director of design from 1902 to 1918.

AT A GLANCE

Tiffany brand founded in 1837 by Tiffany & Co. owner Charles Lewis Tiffany; later developers included Tiffany Glass and Decorating Company owner Louis Comfort Tiffany; Tiffany Glass was renamed Tiffany Studios in 1900; Tiffany & Co. bought by Avon Products, Inc., 1979; Avon sold Tiffany & Co. to former Avon president William Chaney and a group of investors, 1984.

Performance: *Sales*—$486 million (total company revenues).

Advertising: *Agency*—McCann-Erickson, 1993—.

Addresses: *Parent company*—Tiffany & Co., 727 Fifth Avenue, New York, NY 10022; phone: (212) 755-8000.

Initially trained as a painter, Louis Tiffany became a member of the National Academy of Design in New York but in 1877 formed his own group, the Society of American Artists, in reaction to the Academy's conservatism. By this same time, Tiffany had already shown a greater inclination toward the decorative arts and interior design and had begun his first experiments in glassmaking. In 1878 he established his own glass factory in Cirona, New York. His Tiffany Glass and Decorating Company made a name for itself during the early 1880s when it was commissioned by President Chester Arthur to redecorate the White House reception rooms.

At the Paris Exhibition of 1889, Tiffany discovered his true genius after witnessing the Art Nouveau glass display of French designer Émile Gallé. During the 1890s Tiffany became a leader of the Art Nouveau movement through his impressionistic stained glass creations, which also drew inspiration from ancient works of glass that had taken on unusual, color-changing characteristics after centuries of chemical changes. His glass was so unique, possessing a mysteriously iridescent quality, that he secured a patent for it under the trade name Favrile in 1894.

Louis Tiffany also distinguished himself in several other mediums, including jewelry design and manufacture. As Janet Zapata wrote, Tiffany did not enter this particular field until 1902. "His lifelong obsession with color led him to gem stones, which offered tones not obtainable in glass, ceramics, and enameled copper, his earlier mediums. His preference was for such opaque or translucent stones as jade, lapis lazuli, turquoise, carnelian, moonstone, and opal. Of these, opals inevitably became one of his favorites, since their constantly changing colors fascinated him." Zapata goes on to speculate that Tiffany & Co.'s resident gem expert, George Frederick Kunz, likely influenced Tiffany in his gem selections. Kunz himself was a great advocate of semi-precious stones and helped keep Tiffany & Co. on the cusp of innovation during this era.

Business as Anything But Usual

"For the first 125 years of its existence," according to the company's 1992 report, "Tiffany's reputation far exceeded its accessibility. Retail sales were largely confined to a single Tiffany & Co. store in New York City." In addition, the company had a potentially self-limiting reputation of catering only to a wealthy clientele. As a 1925 editorial in a New Jersey paper pointed out: "The Universal idea prevalent about Tiffany's is that while it is the finest store ever organized in the world, it is, also, the highest priced. . . . It is this *fear of high prices* that has *scared people away* from Tiffany's. They should swarm the store. . . . A thousand dollars will go further in Tiffany's than a thousand dollars anywhere. So will twenty-five, fifty, or a hundred dollars. . . . So *don't get stage fright* when you pass Tiffany's. Go in! The humble are as welcome as the well-to-do."

Yet the lofty Tiffany reputation, of course, remained the essence of the brand's appeal and the secret to its success. All was remarkably well for Tiffany & Co. until the 1950s, when the business had begun to lose money under president Louis de Bèbian. Anthony Brandt explained that Tiffany & Co. had become "a stuffy outfit" that "paid no attention to new design" and appeared uninterested in internal growth and development. Walter Hoving, a retailing expert, stepped in and rescued the business in 1955. In order to get rid of excess inventory and make way for new designs, he conducted the company's first-ever storewide clearance sale, slashing prices on items by tens of thousands of dollars and making headlines in the process. In another important move, he hired Jean Schlumberger, whose "uniquely lyrical" designs still grace Tiffany & Co. catalogs. During the 1960s under Hoving, Tiffany & Co. returned to profitability and began gradually expanding its retail business, first to San Francisco and then, in the 1970s, to Japan.

In 1979 Avon Products purchased Tiffany & Co., which was still struggling to redefine itself in the modern era, for $104 million. Despite its shortcomings, Tiffany & Co. was a gem of a business, with revenues of $84 million and earnings of $7.3 million. Many industry observers questioned the deal, wondering if Avon's decidedly mass market image and corporate tinkering might dull the Tiffany name. Their skepticism was validated when Tiffany & Co. began losing core customers and posting successive years of losses, despite an infusion of $53 million in Avon capital. By 1984 Tiffany & Co.'s sales had increased to $135 million, but the company had lost $5 million. According to Claire Poole and Jeffrey Trachtenberg in *Forbes:* "The problem was this: Bureaucratic Avon had not appreciated that Tiffany charges high prices because a buyer feels he or she is getting something fairly exclusive. Start selling cheap wineglasses, and watch the aura fade."

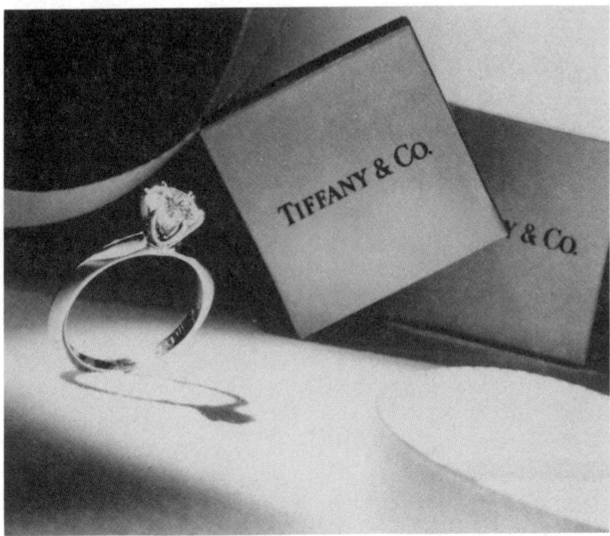

A Tiffany engagement ring with trademark six-prong setting and famous blue box.

Charting a New Course

Tiffany & Co. was due for another transformation and, ironically, a management team headed by former Avon president William Chaney was the answer. This time Tiffany & Co. retooled first by re-attracting its wealthier customers, an elite group that, according to Poole and Trachtenberg, numbers around 5,000. It also elevated the Tiffany name to its former stature by ridding the line of cheaper products. But even this strategy has softened somewhat since the company went public in 1987. As Laura Zinn explained in *Business Week* in 1992: "Part of [Chaney's] approach is to disprove the notion that Tiffany's only provides bibelots for the rich. He is quick to point out that the average Tiffany's transaction is under $200. To get the word out, he has increased Tiffany's ad budget from $6 million in 1986 to $18 million this year, about 3.5% of sales." The Chaney message was borne out in ads that year for Tiffany solitaire engagement rings, which read: "For less than you may have believed, a Tiffany diamond is more than you ever imagined."

Yet there can be no doubt that the air of simplicity and elegance that is Tiffany's hallmark will remain. Simplicity is the unspoken theme of the "Blue Box" advertising campaign, begun in 1987 (and continued through the early 1990s) as the first attempt by the company in its history to unify its numerous product advertisements; the campaign features a series of artwork and photographs of Tiffany & Co.'s best wares, all accompanied by the embossed blue gift box that has become a Tiffany tradition. As for that special Tiffany air of elegance, perhaps Truman Capote in *Breakfast at Tiffany's* said it best: "What I've found does the most good is just to get into a taxi and go to Tiffany's. It calms me down right away, the quietness and proud look of it; nothing very bad could happen to you there, not with those kind men in their nice suits and the lovely smell of silver and alligator wallets."

Further Reading:

Brandt, Anthony, "Tiffany on Top," *Connoisseur,* October 1988, pp. 123–27.

Carpenter, Charles Hope, Jr., and Janet Zapata, *The Silver of Tiffany & Co., 1850–1987,* Boston: Museum of Fine Arts, 1987.

Cropper, Carol M., "Glass Act," *Forbes,* September 13, 1993, pp. 242, 244.

Donegan, Frank, "Tiffany Lamps," *Americana,* May 1988, pp. 16–18.

Gabor, Andrea, " 'My Deah, Have You Heard the News on Fifth Avenue?,' " *U.S. News & World Report,* August 3, 1987, p. 44.

Loring, John, *Tiffany's 150 Years,* Garden City, New York: Doubleday, 1987.

Pulliam, Susan, "Investors' Honeymoon with Tiffany Fades as Some Analysts Give Stock a Cold Shoulder," *Wall Street Journal,* December 22, 1993, p. 2C.

"Tiffany Gift: Breakfast, Lunch, and Dinner for 150 Years," *American Heritage,* September/October 1987, pp. 90–95.

"Tiffany Reports 31 Percent Sales Increase in Holiday Period," Tiffany & Co. News Release, December 27, 1993.

Trachtenberg, Jeffrey A., and Claire Poole, "Bear Hug," *Forbes,* November 16, 1987, pp. 186–87.

Weinstein, Fannie, "Tiffany Times Its Clock Ads Well," *Advertising Age,* March 21, 1988, p. S-4.

Zapata, Janet, "The Opal: Louis Comfort Tiffany's Lens to a World of Color," *Antiques,* September 1993, pp. 318–27.

Zapata, *The Jewelry and Enamels of Louis Comfort Tiffany,* New York: H. N. Abrams, 1993.

Zinn, Laura, and Hiromi Uchida, "Who Said Diamonds Are Forever?," *Business Week,* November 2, 1992, pp. 128–29.

—Jay P. Pederson

TONKA®

Tonka®

Tonka, the standard-bearer of durability in toys, is the number one name in non-powered trucks for kids. In 1986 Tonka dominated the industry with a 75 percent market share. In February of 1993 Tonka was still the leader in the toy truck business, but according to an October 1993 *Forbes* article, SLM International's Buddy L trucks had overtaken Tonka for the number one spot. However, Tonka has proven itself as durable in the market as in the home or sandbox, and regained the top position in the fourth quarter of 1993. So strong is the Tonka brand name that for nearly 30 years it singlehandedly sustained a major manufacturing company. Since 1991 Tonka has served ably as a staple brand in the fold of toys at Hasbro, the world's largest toy company.

Great Beginnings

Lynn E. Baker, Avery F. Crounse, and Alvin F. Tesch founded Mound Metalcraft, Inc., in 1946. A year after its incorporation, the company participated in its first New York Toy Fair, and by 1949 the first toy truck catalog was printed. The manufacturing site was an old school house that overlooked Lake Minnetonka in Mound, Minnesota; the lake was the source of the brand name Tonka, a Sioux word meaning ''great.'' Mound Metalcraft, Inc., became Tonka Toys in 1955. During the remainder of the decade, the company launched major building programs while tripling sales and net worth and increasing profits by tenfold.

In 1961 Tonka Toys went public on the American Stock Exchange. In 1963 Tonka ventured overseas for the first time. And in 1973 Tonka moved to the New York Stock Exchange and opened a year-round New York showroom. Even though sales had reached the $100 million milestone a year later, the company's success story had already taken a U-turn. For the first 20-plus years of its existence, Tonka Corporation flourished with healthy sales and earnings growth each year, all of it fueled by the popularity of Tonka brand trucks. Then, in 1969 and 1970, earnings fell by 35 and 43 percent, respectively. As Dick Youngblood wrote in 1972, Tonka's long-term success with offering a quality product ''virtually left the company unprepared for the toy industry changes beginning in the late 1960s. The toy industry had moved toward a heavy emphasis on marketing and new product development. Tonka's next 20 years included seven years of losses and no period of at least three consecutive years of growth.

Brand Proliferation

Early Tonka marketing focused on maintaining sales of more than one toy per boy (the company's slogan was ''Tonka Trucks for Boys'') and then posting repeat sales each year. To accomplish this, new models were added to the fleet each year. And just as in the American automobile market, the trucks were restyled annually as well. Noted for their durability, Tonka trucks are built of automobile gauge steel and finished with two coats of truck paint. The company diversified the line with the Mini-Tonka, a smaller and less expensive truck. Introduced in 1963, the Mini-Tonka not only helped to target younger children but also helped the company expand to year-round sales. The Mighty-Tonka, a step up in size from the original Tonka, followed in 1965. Both lines enjoyed considerable popularity (the Mighty Tonka Dump, in particular, has survived in the company's words as ''America's Best Selling Truck''). Tiny Tonka was introduced in 1968. By 1970 nearly 100 different Tonka toys and sets had been offered to the consumer.

Tonka's reputation was essential to its marketing plan. The brand name Tonka had proven to be an effective tool in selling the toy trucks to mothers of the company's target-aged boys. Personal interviews with mothers in 1966 showed that ''85 percent of the households interviewed had Tonka toys with an average of 3.2 toys owned per household.'' By 1969 the figures were 91 percent and 5.4 toys, with a quarter of those households having 9 or more of the Tonka toys. Tonka's products were all staple, non-riding transportation toys in a category that accounted for one-fifth of the toy industry sales at that time.

The Tonka vehicles were favorite toys for boys since their introduction, but as Robert J. Flaherty reported in 1980, the company had not come up with a comparable girl's line of basic or staple toys (a partial solution, that of altering the company slogan to ''Tonka Trucks for Boys and Girls,'' had already been tried). Flaherty also noted that just as the Japanese auto industry was encroaching on Detroit, cheaper and more modern-looking toy trucks were capturing some of the market share from Tonka. The company attempted to solve all problems at once in 1978 by introducing a staggering 70 new products. Although many of the products were popular, the production line could not gear up fast enough, and Tonka lost $1.47 per share that year and changed management.

AT A GLANCE

Tonka brand founded in 1946 in Mound, Minnesota, by Mound Metalcraft, Inc. owners Lynn E. Baker, Avery F. Crounse, and Alvin F. Tesch; Mound Metalcraft changed name to Tonka Toys, Inc., 1955, and later to Tonka Corporation; Tonka Corporation acquired by Hasbro, Inc., 1991.

Performance: *Market share*—34% of non-powered toy truck category. *Sales*—$10 million.

Major competitor: SLM International's Buddy L brand trucks.

Advertising: *Agency*—Griffin Bacal. *Major campaign*—"Tonka Tough."

Addresses: *Parent company*—Hasbro, Inc., 1027 Newport Ave., Pawtucket, RI 02862-1059; phone: (401) 727-5000; fax: (401) 727-5779.

Beyond Trucks

In 1982 Tonka's sales fell to a record low of $67 million in spite of holding 45 percent of the toy truck market. "It was becoming obvious that the company couldn't be relying on one traditional product line," said then-president and CEO Stephen Shank in a February, 1986, *Advertising Age* article. Shank decided that Tonka must, for the first time since its founding, develop toy lines in addition to trucks. Former Mattel marketing executives were brought on board and began marketing promotional toys, finding success in 1985 with GoBots and again in 1986 with Pound Puppies.

By this time, a declining interest in toy trucks and a heightened interest in fantasy toys was beginning to dictate the future for Tonka. Older boys were being drawn by toys that had a Saturday morning cartoon tie-in. Five-year-olds were now the average age of boys playing with Tonka trucks. In 1985 Tonka Corporation passed the $200 million sales mark, doubling its pre-GoBots and Pound Puppies sales. But Tonka would need a consistent streak of winners in the promotional toy line to stay profitable. The 1986 Annual Report stated that Tonka nearly doubled its research and development expenditures to $8.3 million or 2.8 percent of revenues. The cost reflected Tonka's recent entry into promotional toys. Advertising expenditures also were increased to $45.7 million, up $5.5 million from the previous year.

Big Debt, Big Problems

Yet, with the higher profit margins from fantasy and promotional toys came increased uncertainty. In October of 1987 Tonka Corporation, trying to move away from its dependence on the volatile trend toys, purchased Kenner Parker. The acquisition catapulted Tonka Corporation from the industry's sixth- to third-largest company. According to Steve Weiner, "Shank had little choice but to buy something like Kenner. One good toy line—in Tonka's case, its tough steel toy vehicles—isn't enough to be consistently profitable in the cyclical toy industry, nor to compete for shelf space." The Kenner purchase also boosted Tonka's international sales, according to an October, 1988, *Business Week* article, rising to 36 from 11 percent of total sales due to Kenner's well established distribution and marketing network. In 1987 Tonka also introduced My First Tonka for preschool children. The line included both vehicles and play sets. Sales that year exceeded $300 million.

By 1989 Tonka's marketing had improved, and the company was beginning to modernize its classic steel truck lines. Tonka was also profitable for the first time in three years with net earnings of $5.7 million on revenues of $870.5 million. Revenues from classic brands brought in 48 percent of the total. But the Kenner Parker purchase had loaded Tonka down with a staggering debt, 86 percent of capital. When the 1990 toy lines failed to produce a hit, operating income plummeted by 60 percent and sales were down 14 percent.

Tonka's next big promotional hit came in 1991 with the Cupcake dolls, but even then some buyers were reluctant to come along. A major retailer was quoted in the April 1991 *Playthings* as saying, "Tonka means trucks, and they've never had a winner in dolls, and we've got plenty of small dolls, so why buy this one?" In a *Forbes* article entitled "Trouble in Toyland," Graham Button anticipated the purchase of Tonka by a toymaker with a stronger financial position, naming Mattel as a possible buyer. In February of 1991 it was not Mattel but Hasbro that signed a merger agreement with Tonka. The final sale price in May of that year was $486 million. The Tonka acquisition boosted Hasbro's sales to $2.1 billion annually, well past Mattel, which had been steadily gaining on the nation's number one toy company.

New Life under Hasbro

According to a July, 1991, *Star Tribune* article, Tonka sales continued to decline after the Hasbro purchase. John O'Neill, Hasbro's chief financial officer, said a decline in sales of Tonka's promotional toys combined with Tonka's difficulty in getting its toys to store shelves accounted for the drop. Getting out its product had been an ongoing problem for the toymaker since it started making promotional toys. In contrast, a July, 1992, *Star Tribune* article reported that the Kenner and Parker Bros. divisions had increased in earnings and revenue for the second quarter of 1992. The 1992 Hasbro Annual Report said the two divisions were "operating extremely effectively." But the report merely said the Tonka brand "has been revitalized and integrated into the Hasbro Toy Division, and now is well positioned for years to come."

In October of 1993 Neil Weinberg reported that SLM International's Buddy L Truck had overtaken Tonka in the marketplace. Over the past year SLM had grabbed 27 percent of the market and $12 million in sales. Matching the Tonka line in quality and price, the plastic Buddy L had the added attraction of a battery-operated light and sound system, complete with idling engine noises and such trucker phrases as "Let's get rolling." When Hasbro announced its new Tonka toy line for 1993, the company said that Tonka was still "the leader in the toy truck business" and had a "bigger-than-ever selection of vehicles for kids of all ages." The Mighty Tonka line was touted as made-in-America and holding a lifetime guarantee. The Mighty Tonka Dump and the other toys of the Mighty Tonka line—the Loader, Backhoe, Crane, Mixer, and Tractor Trailer with Bulldozer—were listed in the $1 to $25 range and targeted for kids three and up. The other 1993 lines included a monster truck, electronic Talk 'N Play Fire Truck, a new toddler vehicle line, GI Joe-inspired military vehicles, sports, adventure, and utility vehicles, the traditional construction vehicles, service vehicles, and the preschool line. Hasbro also announced a move to more contemporary packaging of the Tonka line, but promised to maintain the 40-year tradition of "tough, durable construction and plenty of play value."

The Future

In August of 1993 Mattel, Inc. announced its purchase of Fisher-Price Inc., which according to an August, 1993, *Star Tribune* article would make it the world's biggest toy company. But according to a January, 1994, *Financial World* article, Hasbro is different from its rival Mattel in that it has the "broadest portfolio of toy, game, and puzzle products in the industry." The same article said that company chair and CEO Alan Hassenfeld "boasts that no toy or game makes up more than 5 percent of sales." On the international front, Mattel's European distribution channels are strong but Hasbro, with the purchase of Japan's Nomura Toys and a Southeast Asian toy distributor, sees Asia as its upcoming market. Hassenfeld said, "The disposable incomes and the salary levels have increased far more than anyone expected they would." Perhaps Tonka trucks can move into Asia in the 1990s just as the Japanese toy trucks moved into the United States in the 1970s.

No matter how the toy industry continues to evolve, Tonka has proven that it is a brand that can survive with its reputation intact. Former Tonka chief Russ Wenkstern lamented the purchase of the brand (and company) in 1991, stating that Tonka is "a name that stood for something—for quality and durability." Many industry analysts—as well as young consumers—would argue that is still does. And although Youngblood in his 1991 *Star Tribune* article was pessimistic about the future of the Tonka brand, his words were telling about the brand's ability to persist: "As any parent of the pre-Nintendo, pre-Transformer generation knows, when archeologists a thousand years from now begin sifting through the latter half of the 20th century, they undoubtedly will come up with fleets of small steel trucks, virtually unscathed by time and ready to plow through the nearest sandbox."

Further Reading:

Broderick, Richard, "No Comment from Tonka," *Corporate Report Minnesota,* July 1989, pp. 53–56, 96.

Button, Graham, "Trouble in Toyland," *Forbes,* January 21, 1991, p. 10.

Dahl, Dick, "Raves in Toyland," *Corporate Report Minnesota,* December 1985, pp. 63–66.

Fitzgerald, Kate, "No. 1 Hasbro Buys Tonka," *Advertising Age,* February 4, 1991, p. 6.

Flaherty, Robert J., "Destiny's Toy," *Forbes,* July 7, 1980, pp. 70, 74.

Forkan, James P., "Transformable Toys Take New Twists in '86," *Advertising Age,* February 10, 1986, pp. 3, 80.

Hasbro, Inc. Annual Report, Pawtucket, Rhode Island: Hasbro, Inc., 1992.

"Hasbro's Reduction in Earnings Linked to Tonka Acquisition," *Star Tribune,* July 11, 1991, p. 2D.

Kimelman, John, "No Babe in Toyland," *Financial World,* January 4, 1994, pp. 34–36.

Leibowitz, David S., "Toys in the Cellar," *Financial World,* June 14, 1988, p. 89.

"Mattel to Buy Fisher-Price in $1 Billion Transaction; After Stock Swap, Mattel Will Become the Largest Toy Company in the World," *Star Tribune,* August 20, 1993, p. 3D.

"New Licenses, Categories, and Items Turn Tonka Toward Tomorrow," *Playthings,* March 1984, p. 62.

Ozanian, Michael K., "Tonka: Don't Pass Go," *Financial World,* July 24, 1990, p. 17.

Pereira, Joseph, "Hasbro Agrees to Buy Tonka for $470 Million," *Wall Street Journal,* February 1, 1991, p. A4.

Pitzer, Mary J., "Why Tonka Needs Truckloads of Pay Dirt," *Business Week,* October 24, 1988, pp. 96–97.

Rotenier, Nancy, "Not Toying Around," *Forbes,* January 3, 1994, p. 131.

Stern, Sara E., *Advertising Age,* "Old Standard Now the Tonka the Toy World," February 3, 1986, pp. 4, 43; "Hot Toy Category Has Personality Plush," February 17, 1986, p. 53.

"Success: The Story of Tonka Toys," *Commercial West,* November 12, 1966, pp. 40–41.

Tonka Corporation Annual Reports, Mound, Minnesota: Tonka Corporation, 1968, 1970, 1986, 1987, 1989.

Tonka Corporation Chronology, St. Louis Park, Minnesota: Tonka Corporation, 1991.

"Tonka Expands Truck Line, Broadens Plush and Preschool Lines," *Playthings,* February 1991, p. 92.

"Tonka Rolls Out New Vehicles—and a New Look—for 1993!," Pawtucket, Rhode Island: Hasbro, Inc., 1993.

Verespej, Michael A., "Steve Shank's Secret," *Industry Week,* May 26, 1986, pp. 118–19.

Wanderer, Robert, "Cupcakes Dolls Ride TV Ad Blitz," *Playthings,* April 1991, p. 52.

Wascoe, Dan, Jr., "Rise and Fall of Tonka: Toy Giant Hasbro Is Doing Just Dandy a Year After Gobbling Minnesota Company," *Star Tribune,* April 28, 1992, p. 1D.

Weinberg, Neil, "One Thing Led to Another," *Forbes,* October 25, 1993, pp. 206–07.

Weiner, Steve, "Keep on Truckin'," *Forbes,* October 16, 1989, pp. 220–21.

Youngblood, Dick, *Star Tribune,* "The 'Tonka Touch' Results in Strong Recovery," December 24, 1972, pp. 9–10C; "Sometimes Quality Isn't Enough," February 1, 1991, p. 1D.

—Jay P. Pederson

TORO®

Toro brand products filled almost every niche in the $4.25 billion lawn and garden equipment market in the 1990s. The Toro Company markets a diverse array of lawn and garden equipment, from irrigation systems to hand held electric snow shovels to 20-horsepower Toro Wheel Horse lawn tractors. Long known for their lawn mowers and snowthrowers, Toro expanded its product base in the 1980s to accommodate the needs of a wider variety of homeowners, including the elderly and those who have very small yards to care for. According to the Toro Company's 1993 annual report, the goal of the consumer division is to extend its market leadership from the premium lawn mower market to the medium-price lawn mower market, which could ultimately account for 70 to 80 percent of sales. Sales of Toro brand consumer products totaled $367.9 million in 1993, representing 53.8 percent of corporate sales. The remainder of Toro's sales were accounted for by its irrigation and commercial turf maintenance products. Toro consumer products held no less than the fourth-leading share of every market they entered in 1993.

Brand Origins

The Toro Company traces it origins to the Toro Motor Company, which was founded in 1914 to build engines for the Bull Tractor Company, a farm tractor manufacturer that eventually went bankrupt. Renamed Toro Manufacturing Co. in 1920, the company produced a To-Ro (two-row) cultivator and in 1922 introduced a gang mower unit for golf course fairway maintenance that cut a swath of lawn 12 feet wide. Within three years, Toro Manufacturing had sold turf maintenance equipment to nearly every major golf course in the United States, according to *Appliance Manufacturer.* Toro remained the leading producer of turf maintenance equipment into the 1990s, though competitor John Deere began developing products for this market beginning in 1988. Toro produced its first powered lawn mower for the consumer market in 1939, and followed this twelve years later by introducing its first snow removal equipment. Lawn mowers for professionals and homeowners were Toro's primary products into the early 1970s.

The 1970s saw tremendous growth for the consumer products division of the Toro Company, which was led by David T. McLaughlin. When McLaughlin joined Toro in 1970, the company's sales stood at $57 million; nine years later, Toro sales topped $350 million, largely on the strength of McLaughlin's management of consumer product development and marketing. Much of Toro's growth can be attributed to the boom in sales of Toro snowthrowers, which reached $18 million in 1977 and topped $130 million in 1979. According to *Business Week,* Toro sold out its entire production of snowthrowers between 1977 and 1979, while capturing 50 percent of the market for smaller machines. On the strength of these sales, Toro developed in 1979 what it called an "electric power shovel." The 11-pound snowthrower sold for just $90, and was expected to appeal to people living in areas with relatively light snowfall, consumers who might never consider buying a larger snowthrower. Toro executives predicted that the product could generate $100 million in sales.

Toro's growth relied on more than snowthrowers, however. When an industry wide recession cut into lawn mower sales in the early 1970s, McLaughlin commissioned a marketing study that indicated that "Toro's name recognition among home-product consumers was second only to Hershey's in chocolate," according to *Business Week.* McLaughlin was determined to take advantage of Toro's brand name by introducing a number of new products. The lightweight snowthrower was joined by a light electric grass trimmer, a line of electric chain saws, and a wind-up hose system. "The idea," McLaughlin told *Business Week,* "is to make the Toro name an umbrella under which we can market just about anything." Not surprisingly, the company boosted advertising expenditures to make consumers aware of all the new products. Advertising expenditures for 1978 topped $15 million, twice the previous year's budget.

Distribution also changed as a result of McLaughlin's growth strategy. Toro had long relied on a network of independent distributors who sold both the consumer and professional lawn-care lines, but McLaughlin felt that the company's lower-priced products could best reach the consumer through large chain retailers. According to *Forbes,* Toro's new low-maintenance products allowed the company to "skirt its independent distributors in some cases and sell directly to chains like J. C. Penney and Target, increasing its retail distribution from 10,000 stores to 30,000 stores" between 1976 and 1978. As a result, many independent distributors dropped the Toro brand or refused to service machines that they did not sell.

AT A GLANCE

Toro brand walk-behind lawn mower introduced in 1939 by Toro Manufacturing Corp., which was founded in 1914 as the Toro Motor Co.; Toro brand snowthrower introduced, 1951; Toro Co. acquires Wheel Horse, a manufacturer of lawn tractors, which it markets under the Toro Wheel Horse brand, 1986; Toro Co. acquires Lawn-Boy brand mowers from Outboard Marine Corp., 1989; introduces Recycler mulching technology, 1990.

Performance: *Market share*—14% of riding mower sales (with Lawn-Boy); 15% of walk-behind mower sales (with Lawn-Boy); 25% (leading share) of gas snowthrower sales. *Sales*—$367.9 million.

Major competitor: Snapper; also John Deere.

Advertising: *Agency*—Campbell-Mithun-Esty, Minneapolis, 1982—. *Major campaign*—"Toro: When You Want It Done Right!"

Addresses: *Parent company*—The Toro Company, 8111 Lyndale Avenue South, Bloomington, MN 55420; phone: (612) 888-8100; fax: (612) 887-8258.

Down But Not Out

Toro's fortunes changed dramatically beginning in 1979, as all the factors that had caused growth contributed to the company's three year decline. Light snowfall in the winter of 1979-80 combined with a dry summer of 1980 to decrease sales of Toro's core products. Gambling that the snow would return, Toro continued snowthrower production, only to be faced with a second mild winter in 1980-81. Distributors were furious at being flooded with machines they could not sell, and McLaughlin purged 125 managers as sales plummeted. Contributing to Toro's troubles were a series of new product problems: a garden tiller was recalled, the wind-up hose system developed kinks and had to be redesigned, and Spokane, Washington, targeted as a test city for a new mower-trimmer, was blanketed in the ashes from the eruption of Mount St. Helens. "In the middle of a fiscal year [1981-82] in which Toro's total sales fell a staggering 38 percent—from $400 million to $247 million—McLaughlin resigned to become president of Dartmouth College," noted *Business Week,* which suggested that "Toro came perilously close to going under."

In February 1981, Ken Melrose took on the task of rescuing Toro. According to Robert Magy, writing in the Minneapolis *Corporate Report,* Melrose "began to apply emergency resuscitation efforts. He promptly closed four plants, laid off half the work force, pared back the corporate staff, scaled back production, and reverted to former distribution methods. Gradually, the company's precarious situation improved." Melrose instituted what he called the "Toro Credo," which insisted that every Toro product must be "designed and manufactured as if the maker must personally confront each buyer." Building on Toro's established products and developing and acquiring successful products to expand Toro's line, Melrose brought Toro back to profitability. Between 1983 and 1990, Toro's sales more than tripled, from $240 million to $750 million.

A number of factors accounted for Toro's resurgence in the 1980s. Toro executives recognized that they needed to be less dependent on the sale of equipment that is severely affected by changes in the weather—that is, snowthrowers. The percentage of Toro's sales attributable to snowthrowers dropped from over 40 percent in 1979 to just 7 percent in 1993. Toro also continued to depend on the strength of its commercial market, which tended to counteract cyclical declines in the consumer market. While consumer sales were variable over the years, commercial sales increased steadily, from $121.2 million in 1988 to $204.6 million in 1993.

One of the first things Melrose did when he took over direction of Toro in 1981, wrote Magy, "was to revert to Toro's traditional two-step distribution for all products that require servicing, including all gasoline-powered lawn mowers and snow throwers." Such a system guaranteed that customers received the best possible after-sale service and helped maintain Toro's reputation for quality. Melrose recognized, however, that some of Toro's products could best be marketed through large retail channels. Many of Toro's electric-powered products are sold through mass merchants, home centers, and hardware stores, as is the line of fertilizers, lighting products, and irrigation products. The two-tier marketing strategy is designed to introduce the widest possible number of consumers to the Toro name by providing products for every conceivable lawn and garden need. *Appliance Manufacturer* explained that a young homeowner satisfied with the Toro leaf blower he or she purchased at Kmart would think of Toro first when the time came to buy a large lawn and garden tractor.

Most importantly, however, Toro continued to expand and improve upon the brand image associated with Toro products through acquisition and development. Toro's consumer division achieved sales of $471.6 million in 1990 by building on the strength of its reputation for quality walk-behind mowers, acquiring Lawn-Boy brand mowers, developing riding mowers and lawn tractors via the acquisition of the Wheel Horse brand, and introducing new products for home lawn care. In 1993 walk-behind mowers (both Toro and Lawn-Boy brands) accounted for 35 percent of consumer division sales of $367.9 million, riding mowers and lawn and garden tractors accounted for 22 percent, electric outdoor products accounted for 14 percent, snow products accounted for 7 percent, and other gas products and parts accounted for the remaining 22 percent.

Mature Product Line

According to Magy, "Toro's walk-behind lawn mowers are aimed at the upper end of the residential lawn and garden market." While Toro held approximately 9 to 10 percent of the total walk-behind market in the early 1990s, among premium brands Toro held nearly twice that share, while competing against Honda, John Deere, and Snapper. Toro pioneered mulching technology when it introduced the Recycler mowers in 1990, followed by the Recycler II mowers in 1993. Another technological innovation that distinguished Toro from competitors was the GTS engine, jointly developed by Toro and Briggs & Stratton, which was guaranteed to start on the first or second pull for five years or Toro would fix it for free. Toro marketed 10 walk-behind mowers in the Recycler II and Recycler II Super Pro line and offered a dethatcher attachment, a side discharge kit, a rear bag kit, and a rear-mounted fertilizer application system.

In 1986 the Toro Company acquired Wheel Horse, a manufacturer of lawn tractors based in South Bend, Indiana. According to *Appliance Manufacturer,* "the acquisition of Wheel Horse represented more of an extension than departure. Toro had rear-engine riding mowers in the smaller end of the riding spectrum. Wheel

Horse filled out riders at the other end, offering big, upscale, front-engine lawn and garden tractors.'' All of Toro's riding tractors were then marketed under the Toro Wheel Horse brand name. The line included three rear-engine riding mowers, six yard and garden tractors with 12- to 16-horsepower engines, and six garden tractors ranging from 12- to 20-horsepower and capable of using a wide range of attachment and accessories with the Attach-A-Matic hitch system. Each of the riding tractors could use Toro's Recycler mowers, which were developed for three-blade mowers cutting a 42-inch swath. Toro held 14 percent of the 1992 U.S. riding mower market, according to *Appliance Manufacturer.*

Toro also continued to market a complete line of snowthrowers. Its smallest snowthrower, the electric Power Shovel, could throw a 12-inch swath of snow up to 15 feet; the largest snowthrower, the 11-horsepower walk-behind 1132, was capable of throwing 32-inch swath up to 40 feet and could clear up to 2200 pounds of snow a minute. Commercials promoting the Toro Power Curve Snowthrower pictured a man closing his garage door after clearing his driveway of snow, only to trigger an avalanche of snow from nearby mountains that buries the house. The announcer says ''It's perfect for those times when it really comes down.'' The effect ''is humorously handled,'' noted *Adweek,* ''with surreal yodeling on the soundtrack and a startled deer looking on.''

Toro also marketed a number of products designed to help with yard maintenance, including three gas-powered line trimmers with ergonomically designed handles to alleviate pressure on the user's wrist. Following the 1984 acquisition of Lunalite, Toro marketed a complete line of outdoor lighting products. Toro also converted its recognized expertise in commercial irrigation systems to use in the consumer market, developing easy-to-install irrigation equipment for homeowners accompanied by extensive advisory literature on designing and installing a home irrigation system.

The Greening of a Brand

Many of Toro's technological innovations and brand extensions in the 1990s have been driven by the company's increasing concern with the environment, a concern that reflects the interests of the consumer. Beginning in the late 1980s, U.S. homeowners were made aware that as much as 18 percent of the waste in U.S. landfills came from lawn and garden waste, primarily in the form of grass clippings and leaves. Toro used consumers' increased concern with the environment to develop new products, justify the expense of developing new technologies, and promote a unified brand image. ''We're making Toro a more environmentally responsible company,'' Toro chief executive officer Ken Melrose told *Appliance Manufacturer.* ''We don't want to be known as a lawn-mower company. We want to be known as a company that makes the landscapes clean and green.''

The development of the Recycler and Recycler II mowing systems, which returned finely-chopped grass clippings to the turf where they could biodegrade naturally, was just the first step. Toro also developed its YardCycler composting system, which was capable of converting ''up to 75 30-gallon bags of grass clippings to one bag in a single growing season,'' according to promotional material. Toro also marketed several compost accelerators to speed composting action. In 1992 Toro entered into a joint venture with Bio Huma Netics to develop a line of environmentally sound liquid and dry fertilizers. Marketed under the Toro Nurture trademark, the natural-based products were for use on lawns, flowers, and vegetables. Melrose told *Appliance Manufacturer* that the company would continue its green emphasis: ''We plan to translate environmental pressures into product ideas, using our own Toro engineering as the base for innovation.''

Toro took great care to associate its name with environmentally sound lawn and garden care by promoting its image and educating consumers. The lead slogan for the Toro brand, ''When You Want It Done Right,'' highlighted the technical expertise the company wanted consumers to associate with its mowers and lawn and garden tractors. The Toro Co. spent approximately $10 million advertising the Toro line in 1992. Just as important as advertising was Toro's effort to educate. Toro initiated an Environmental Awareness Program in 20 municipalities across the United States in 1992 which communicated the benefits of composting, recycling, good watering practices, and environmentally responsible fertilizing, according to company literature. In one instance, Toro provided lawn mowers to 25 volunteers who agreed to participate in their ''Don't Bag It'' program. Toro also made available to consumers an extensive array of literature describing the benefits of mulching, recycling, and fertilizing.

Toro's green emphasis positioned the brand for gaining market share in international as well as domestic markets. Toro Ventures International, a subsidiary of the Toro Co., sought to exploit potential overseas markets. With manufacturing facilities in Belgium, Toro hopes to develop its existing European markets. ''Our goal is to capture a 20 percent share of the European premium mower business,'' Melrose told Magy. International sales (including commercial, consumer, and irrigation equipment) grew at a compound annual rate of 27 percent between 1984 and 1989, and stood at $129.4 million in fiscal year 1993.

Toro's plans for continued growth in the 1990s will undoubtedly be helped by a corporate restructuring that began to pay off in 1993. Consolidating manufacturing facilities, trimming overhead, and shrinking employment reduced the consumer division's break-even point by more than 30 percent by the end of 1992, according to *Appliance Manufacturer,* and helped the company realize $13 million in profits in 1993. With continued astute marketing of technically sophisticated and environmentally friendly lawn and garden products, Toro seems well suited to excel in the competitive and mature outdoor power equipment industry.

Further Reading:

Carlson, Scott, ''Toro to Cut Salaried Employees,'' *St. Paul Pioneer Press-Dispatch* (Minnesota), January 22, 1992.

''The Community that Composts Together . . .,'' *Flower & Garden,* December-January 1994, p. 95.

''A Dry Winter Stalls Toro's Growth Plans,'' *Business Week,* March 2, 1981, p. 30.

Kirk, Jim, ''CME May Edge Out Frankenberry if Toro Opts for One Agency,'' *Adweek Midwest Edition,* January 27, 1992, p. 3.

Magy, Robert, ''Toro's Second Season,'' *Corporate Report,* May 1, 1990.

Meeks, Fleming, ''Throwing Away the Crystal Ball,'' *Forbes,* July 22, 1991, p. 60.

Slania, John, ''Toro Grabbing More of the Premium Market,'' *Milwaukee Journal,* October 4, 1989.

''Toro: Coming to Life after Warm Weather Wilted Its Big Plans,'' *Business Week,* October 10, 1983, p. 118.

''The Toro Company,'' *Appliance Manufacturer,* February 1993, pp. T1–T21.

''The Toro Company Annual Report, Bloomington, MN: The Toro Company, 1993.

"Toro Power Curve Snowthrower: Let It Snow," *Adweek Midwest Edition,* February 1, 1993, p. 35.

"The Toro Team Has a Winning Game Plan," *Nation's Business,* August 1979, pp. 45–53.

"Toro! Toro!," *Forbes,* November 27, 1978, p. 102.

"Toro: Transforming Itself to Dominate Home-Care Products," *Business Week,* September 10, 1979, pp. 116–118.

Weinberger, Betsy, "Toro Cuts Deals to Push More Mowers in Stores," *Minneapolis St. Paul Citybusiness,* February 19, 1993.

—Tom Pendergast

TOSHIBA®

TOSHIBA

Often referred to as the "General Electric of Japan," Toshiba's earliest roots extend to the very inception of the electronics and communications industries in Japan. The company we know today as Toshiba is the result of a merger in 1939 of two companies, Tokyo Electric Company, and Shibaura Engineering. The Toshiba Group of companies, Toshiba Corporation of Tokyo, Japan, represents the 24th largest publicly held company and is the third largest electronics manufacturer in the world. On a yearly basis, Toshiba manufactures more than 11 million color picture tubes.

Brand Origins

In 1875, Hisashige Tanaka, an electrical engineer, began producing and refining the technology for telegraph equipment and electrical devices for astronomical observation. He established the Tanaka factory in Tokyo and expanded to manufacture heavy electrical equipment in the 1890s. In 1893, the company was renamed Shibaura Seisakusho (Engineering) Works. Meanwhile, an independent company, Hakunetsu-sha (meaning "white heat"), was formed by Dr. Ichisuke and Dr. Shoichi Miyoshi to manufacture electric light bulbs. This company, incorporated in 1896, became Tokyo Electric Company, Ltd. in 1899 and produced the first incandescent lamps for general lighting purposes in Japan. The company had a significant relationship with Thomas Edison, sharing and consulting on a variety of inventions. By the end of the nineteenth century, Shibaura Engineering was manufacturing hydroelectric generators and electric fans. Tokyo Electric produced coil light bulbs in 1921 and internal frosted bulbs in 1925. Also, Tokyo Electric became the first Japanese company to make X-ray tubes and short and medium wave broadcasting equipment. The 1920s and 30s were periods of growth for both companies and in 1939 they merged into the Tokyo Shibaura Electric Company, Ltd., whose name was shortened and synthesized to become the Toshiba Corporation.

Prior to the 1939 merger, Shibaura Engineering and Tokyo Electric had extensive international operations. The advent of World War II caused a dramatic curtailment of overseas operations, but overseas sales and manufacturing were recommenced in the 1950s. In a landmark event, Toshiba introduced the first Japanese-designed digital computer in 1954. In 1957 the first Toshiba-designed transistor radio appeared in the Japanese market and two years later Toshiba developed the first 16-inch color television set—followed by the first 17-inch set with the Shadow Mask surrounding the screen. Two years later, Toshiba became the first company to develop and introduce the continuous magnetron tube, which now is used in 30 percent of all microwave ovens. In 1960, Toshiba built the first nuclear turbine power plant in Japan.

The intensive technological research continued with the work of Dr. Norikazu Sawazaki on the helical scan recording process, resulting in Japan's first color videotape recorder shown to the public at the Toshiba Science Institute in 1965, and in 1967 Toshiba developed and built Japan's first electronic tuners for television. Two years later, a 110-degree wide deflection color picture tube was developed, the first in the world of its kind.

International Growth

Toshiba's domestic growth was fueled by the company's superb technological innovations; meanwhile, overseas operations grew until 1964, when the first overseas office was opened in New York City. In May of the following year, Toshiba America, Inc., encompassing all American divisions, was established and headquartered in that office. Soon, as new markets opened up, branch offices were opened in Chicago, San Francisco, Hawaii, and Los Angeles.

In every year since 1970 overseas sales accounted for more than 12 percent of consolidated net sales for all Toshiba operations. Steady and continuous growth broadened Toshiba's capabilities and yielded more innovations. The world's first color videophone was developed in 1970 and a Blackstripe picture tube was shown in 1972. In the latter part of the 1970's, interest in microwave technology grew and Toshiba led not only with magnetron tube development, but with large-capacity microwave ovens in 1976 and with full-power (720 watts) microwave ovens in 1977.

Restructuring to Meet Customer Needs

Toshiba's management in the 1970s could see that to better serve customer needs and to respond to rapid changes in the marketplace, separate, independent companies and manufacturing facilities would be needed. Each would be responsible for research, new product design and development, production, and manufacturing, as well as marketing and sales. In August 1978, a new manufacturing facility was opened in Lebanon, Tennessee which specialized in making consumer electronics products. The

AT A GLANCE

Toshiba brand of color televisions developed 1959 (16-inch model), followed by a 17-inch model with a Shadow Mask surrounding the screen; first electronic turner for television developed 1967; first 110-degree wide deflection color picture tube developed 1969; Blackstripe picture tube developed 1972; Toshiba America Consumer Products in Wayne, New Jersey established 1981; Toshiba Westinghouse Electronics Corporation established to produce color picture tubes in 1985 (later became Toshiba Display Devices in 1988); 30-inch and 32-inch color picture tubes developed, 1988; incorporation of Toshiba America Consumer Products, Inc., 1989; currently, color picture tubes manufactured in Horseheads, New York and color television sets and projection television sets assembled in Lebanon, Tennessee.

Performance: *Market share*—5% of color television market (1991). *Sales*—$35,506,639,000 (1992 net operations).

Major competitor: Sony; also, Zenith, RCA (for color televisions only).

Advertising: *Agency*—Calet/Hirsch/Ferrell, 1973—.

Addresses: *Parent company*—Toshiba America Consumer Products, Inc., 82 Totowa Rd., Wayne, NJ 07474; phone: (212) 628-8000. *Ultimate parent company*—Toshiba Corporation, 1-1, Shibaura 1-Chome, Minato-Ku, Tokyo 105-01, Japan; phone: (03) 3457-2104/5; fax: (03) 3456-4776.

plant specialized in color picture tubes, color television sets, projection television sets, and microwave ovens. The facility was expanded in 1980 and again in 1981. Toshiba has established offices and sales subsidiaries as well as manufacturing facilities on five continents in over 120 countries. In the mid-1990s Toshiba television picture tubes were manufactured in New York and assembled as finished sets in Tennessee.

In April, 1989, Toshiba America, Inc. became the holding company for all U.S. operations, with all five divisions reporting to the holding company, yet each consisting of a separate company with its own manufacturing facility. The companies were Toshiba America Consumer Products, Inc. (Wayne, NJ), Toshiba America Information Systems, Inc. (Irvine, CA), Toshiba America Medical Systems, Inc. (Tustin, CA), Toshiba America Electronic Components, Inc. (Irvine, CA) and Toshiba International Corporation (San Francisco, CA). Manufacturing plants can be found in New York, Texas, Tennessee, South Dakota and California. In all, over 8,000 people are employed by Toshiba in the United States.

Advances in Television Technology

In July, 1981 Toshiba America, Inc. restructured its organization into two separate entities. One became the consumer products business sector, incorporated in April, 1989 as Toshiba America Consumer Products, Inc., and the other became the industrial electronics business sector. In 1985, Toshiba began a joint business venture with Westinghouse named Toshiba Electronics Corporation (TWEC) to produce television picture tubes. Toshiba, in the fall of 1988, took over the joint venture and changed the name to Toshiba Display Devices, Inc. (TDD), which became the first facility to produce 30-inch and 32-inch picture tubes in the United States. This division employs over 1,300 people and produces more than 30,000 cathode ray tubes a month. By 1991 the company was producing 35-inch picture tubes.

The key to Toshiba's success in the television market was the development of the FST Supertube, an advanced design specifically made for large-screen televisions. The technology greatly diminishes distortion and signal dispersion common to large-screen tubes. The flatter screen surface deflects light away, resulting in less glare and a wider viewing angle. For picture sharpness and detail, the INVAR Shadow Mask, made with an iron-nickel alloy that can withstand higher operating voltages without warping, was developed. For complete screen image sharpness, an electronic focusing, eight-lens, electron lens is used along with an automatic adjustment device for modulating the speed of the electron gun as it passes from lighter to darker areas of the picture. A digital comb filter is used to enhance horizontal resolution and ensure better color definition. It digitally processes the separation of the luminance and chrominance signals from the input video signal.

Toshiba's color circuitry makes use of a phosphor compound (Maxec) that expands color reproduction by 20 percent and combines the compound with a Blackstripe pattern for accurate contrasts. For example, in darker scenes, some images can disappear into the surroundings, but the Blackstripe pattern and a peak level detector adjust to preserve detail and prevent washout. A popular feature of many television sets is the picture-in-picture (PIP) window feature, which Toshiba has refined with a two-tuner PIP design in selected models. The viewer can watch two different channels at once without additional accessories because two independent tuners are utilized. On-screen displays may be viewed in English, Spanish or French. Every television includes the closed captioning feature.

Toshiba was the first company to use digital sound processing (DSP) in home televisions. This technology—Acoustic Field Simulation—recreates the direct, reflective and reverberated sound patterns of the original locale. The four different environments include stadium, theater, night club, and concert hall. To enhance bass response, dialog and sound effects, Toshiba developed an independent 13-watt amplifier within each set called the Cyclone ABX system. To enhance sound clarity, Toshiba makes use of dbx noise reduction. For a fuller bass response a Sub Bass System was created which extracts key bass frequencies from the audio signal and processes them independently.

Located in Wayne, New Jersey, Toshiba America Consumer Products, Inc. has established an advanced TV technology center with the goal of developing advanced receivers for high-definition network systems (HDTV) that will meet American broadcast standards. Sensitive to America's growing concern with its trade deficit with Japan in the late 1980s and early '90s, Toshiba boasts that 71 percent of the components used in televisions it sells in the United States are American-made—manufactured in the facilities in Horseheads, New York and Lebanon, Tennessee.

Other Electronic Innovations

In the computer and medical device arena, the company developed the world's first 64K CMOS static random access memory (RAM) chip in 1980. The following year saw the development of the world's first X-ray stereoscopic system and in 1982, the highly successful development of the magnetic resonance imaging (MRI) system took place; the MRI is now in use at virtually all important medical research facilities. In the year that followed, another profound medical research device was developed by Toshiba engineers—the first nuclear magnetic resonance CT scanner.

In information system computer technology, Toshiba has contributed such innovations as the first 1-megabyte DRAM chip in 1985; the company followed up with a 4-megabyte DRAM chip in 1986 and 16-megabyte chip in 1989. Toshiba's sales of laptop computers and personal computers took off in 1989, leading the world in market share with more than a million units sold. Also in 1989, Toshiba began selling notebook-sized personal computers, and in 1990 they added high-end models with built-in 16-bit microprocessors and 20-megabyte hard disk drives. In March 1990, because of strong demand from banking institutions and insurance companies, Toshiba began selling the TP 90 host computer series, which provided a modem access to mainframe computers for applications such as transaction processing. The Integrated Communication Systems Division was started in 1989 to strengthen the digital private branch exchange (PBX) developments being pursued. In the office automation equipment business, plain paper copier production was augmented by construction of new facilities in France and California.

Satellite communication application systems are being studied and developed for corporate satellite communication systems. Toshiba is a main contractor in the remote control manipulator of the Japanese Experimental Space Module, which is part of NASA's international space station program. In 1990 Toshiba introduced the first laptop engineering workstation, and its Mobile Communication Systems Division was set up to expand its output of mobile cellular phones and cordless phones. In that same year, Toshiba Electronics Asia, Ltd. was established.

With major overseas sales to Kuwait, India, and Indonesia of thermal power-generating systems, Toshiba increased its sales of heavy electrical apparatus to the global market. In countries with labor shortages and untrained workers, Toshiba's sales of laser machining systems and industrial robots enjoyed solid demand. Worldwide sales of elevators and escalators have also done well. Toshiba has increased sales of washing machines and refrigerators by offering new features and in April, 1991, the company joined into a cooperative agreement to manufacture and market durable appliances with the General Electric Company, thus developing markets for GE, Hotpoint and Creda products in Japan and other Asian countries.

In Japan, Toshiba is accelerating work on the Japan Railway's magnetic levitation train project and is responding to domestic demand for economical electric power supplies by focusing on nuclear power research and advanced fuel-cell technology. In the large-screen market, Toshiba continues to lead the way in color television sales.

Future Growth

The Toshiba family of companies continues to grow through restructure, market growth and advanced planning. Today Toshiba is the third largest electronics manufacturer in the world and has consistently been the recipient of consumer as well as industry praise for its reputation for innovation, quality and reliability. With its eyes on the future, Toshiba continues to make solid technological inroads with pioneering work on very large scale integrated circuits (VLSIC), interactive CATV systems, videotext equipment, interactive mobile electronics, LCD technologies and HDTV. Highly-diversified and with a proven track record as an innovator and manufacturer, Toshiba appears to be well positioned for future success.

Further Reading:

Toshiba America Consumer Products, Inc., Company Materials, Wayne, NJ.

Toshiba Corporation, Company Materials, Tokyo, Japan.

Toshiba Corporation Annual Report 1992, Toshiba Corporation, Tokyo, Japan, 1993.

Moody's Industrial Manual, Moody's Industrial Services, Inc., New York, NY, 1991.

—Victor M. Alfaro

TOYOTA CAMRY®

The Camry brand of Toyota automobiles was launched in the United States in 1983 to replace the Corona, which was the company's family sedan. Camry's roomy interior and smooth-handling, front-wheel drive made it a popular addition to the Toyota line of cars.

Brand Origins

The Camry, introduced more than a decade ago, was designed to be a marriage of economy and style. Economy and value had long been the cornerstone of Toyota's reputation. But with the appearance of Camry, the automaker also began to place greater emphasis on sleek lines and aerodynamic styling. As successive models of Camry revealed, a fuel-efficient engine could be tucked inside a luxurious, roomy body. The first-generation versions of Camry were a four-door sedan and a five-door hatchback with four-cylinder engines. The name Camry was an Anglicized version of the Japanese ''kan-muri,'' which means crown.

Within two years of its U.S. debut, Camry had become a gem for Toyota. It was rated the ''Most Trouble-free Car in America'' by J.D. Power & Associates. By 1986, Camry won another accolade when *Consumers Digest* chose it as a ''best buy.'' The car remained on the magazine's best-buy list from that time on.

Product Changes

Camry was completely redesigned for the 1987 model year. A station wagon replaced the hatchback, and the Camry got a power boost from a new two-liter, Twin-Cam engine. Toyota also introduced the Camry All-Trac, for better traction in bad weather. A year later, Toyota made a V6 engine option available on the Camry. The least expensive version of the Camry cost almost $12,000. In 1986, Toyota broke ground on a production facility, Toyota Motor Manufacturing Inc. (TMM), in Georgetown, Kentucky, with vehicle production beginning in 1988. The majority of Camrys in the early 1990s would be produced at this plant.

Through the end of the '80s, Camry held on to its J.D. Power & Associates rating as the ''Most Trouble-free Compact Car.'' In 1991, the car was ranked in the top ten of the J.D. Power Initial Quality Study.

Brand Development

Although it won a following rapidly, Toyota Camry could not overwhelm its closest competitor, the Honda Accord. By the beginning of the '90s, American car buyers were purchasing 50 percent more Accords than Camrys.

Toyota went back to the drawing board—literally. In 1990, workers at the Georgetown plant began assembling the prototype of a completely redesigned 1992 Camry before the 1991 model had even been built. The '92 redesign was a top-secret undertaking, and a radical departure from the Camrys that were then on the road. According to an article in the *Courier-Journal,* ''from a manufacturing and design standpoint, it will barely resemble today's Camry.'' Although it was customary for Toyota to redesign all models once every four years to keep the look fresh, the new project was closely guarded. The automaker invested $300 million in the changeover.

Yoshi Maatsura, the chief engineer in charge of developing the new Camry, explained that the car would be ''the key player in Toyota's plans for the '90s.'' Those plans included not just improved sales in the U.S. market, but also worldwide. The new Camry, Maatsura said, ''was developed distinct from the Japanese domestic model Camry, a first for Toyota in pursuit of a sedan that would be competitive worldwide.''

By the time of the make-over, Camry was already a crucial part of the Toyota line-up and accounted for 40 percent of U.S. sales. In response to consumers' demands, the new Camry was to be a full seven inches wider, as well as longer and more rounded in its dimensions. Finally, 1992 dawned and the much-anticipated Camry hit the streets. The *Courier-Journal* noted that ''the name remains the same, but the Toyota Camry is really an entirely new car.''

Taking direct aim at both the Accord and the Ford Taurus, Toyota unveiled a Camry that *Business Week* promptly termed a ''bargain luxury car.'' From its practical, square-compact origins, the Camry had become a more elegant, quieter mid–sized sedan. The car boasted 15 percent more interior room, an optional V6 engine and an automatic transmission that shifted unobtrusively. Camry's new stylishness came from the fact that it shared the more expensive Lexus' chassis, engine and suspension. As stan-

AT A GLANCE

Camry brand of Toyota automobiles launched in the United States in 1983 by Toyota Motor Sales, U.S.A. Inc.

Performance: *Market share*—8.5% of the automobile category. *Sales*— 299,737 units (1993).

Major competitor: Honda Accord.

Advertising: *Agency*—Saatchi & Saatchi DFS/Pacific, Torrance, CA, 1984—. *Major campaign*—"Who Could Ask for Anything More?" and "I Love What You Do For Me."

Addresses: *Parent company*—Toyota Motor Sales U.S.A., Inc., 19001 S. Western Ave., Torrance, CA 90509; phone: (310) 618-4000; fax: (310) 618-7800. *Ultimate parent company*—Toyota Motor Corp., 1 Toyota-Cho, Aichi 471, Japan; phone: 565 282121; fax: 565 801116

dard features, Camry offered body-color bumpers and driver's-side airbags.

The upscale look resulted in a significant step away from the low sticker prices consumers had come to associate with Camry. The base price was $14,368, up 10 percent. The most expensive XLE model, which sported alloy wheels, a moonroof, and a power driver's seat, cost more than $20,000. Nevertheless, Toyota had high hopes for the new Camry.

Future Growth

By the mid-1990s, Toyota expected the mid-size segment to grow as car buyers with small families looked for sporty yet comfortable vehicles. The automaker introduced a two-door Camry Coupe available with either a 2.2-liter, four-cylinder engine or a three-liter, aluminum V6 engine. In 1994 both the Coupe and the sedan had five percent more horsepower than previous models and an electronically controlled transmission. A far cry from the angular, plain subcompacts of the '70s and '80s, the midsized Camry of the '90s reflected consumers' fascination with technology and desire for economical, yet attractive, cars.

Further Reading:

Armstrong, Larry, "Oomph, Elegance, Silence: Surprise! It's a Camry," *Business Week,* February 17, 1992, p. 152.

Chappell, Lindsay, "Toyota Boosts U.S. Exports," *Automotive News,* February 10, 1992, p. 2.

Heath, David, "Larger Camry for 1992 May Challenge Accord as Sales Leader in U.S.," *The Courier-Journal,* May 11, 1991, p. B12.

"New for '92: Skylark, Camry, Taurus, Sable," *Automotive News,* September 9, 1991, p. 1.

"Toyota Plant is Gearing up for Redesigned 1992 Camry," *The Courier-Journal,* June 27, 1990, p. B12.

Treece, James, "Toyota's Camry: Made in the USA—Sort Of," *Business Week,* November 22, 1993, p. 6.

Vasilash, Gary. S., "Competing with the World from Kentucky," *Production,* December 1991, pp. 58–61.

"What's Hot: Local Products You Should Watch in the New Year—Toyota Motor Corp.," *The Courier-Journal,* January 12, 1992, p. E2.

White, Joseph B., "Autos: GM Follows Ford by Boosting Car Prices, Creating Big Opportunity for Japanese," *Wall Street Journal,* August 15, 1992, p. B1.

Yeich, Christopher R., "Camry Coupe, a New-Generation Lightweight V6 and Upgraded Safety Features are Toyota's News for '94," *Automotive Industries,* October 1993, pp. 46–47.

—Marinell James

TOYOTA COROLLA®

For more than 25 years, the Toyota Corolla has been one of the best-selling imports in America. Within a few years after Toyota of Japan introduced Corolla to the U.S. market, the subcompact rapidly established a reputation as a well-engineered, virtually trouble-free car.

Brand Origins

Toyota, the world's largest motor manufacturer, introduced the Corolla, a subcompact, two-door sedan, in 1968 as part of a an expansion of the "Crown" and "Corona" model line. The name Corolla refers to the outer crown portion of a flower. The first Corollas had 1.1-liter engines. At that time, the Corolla and its forerunners, the Corona and the Crown, ranged in price from $1,800 to $4,000.

The Corolla had already made its debut in Japan two years earlier. The car was developed after a predecessor, the two-cylinder Publica, flopped. Toyota surveyed car buyers and began design studies for the Corolla in 1963. After rejecting options that included a scaled-down version of the Corona and a simple, boxy design, the manufacturer settled on a look that featured lots of glass and a wide grille.

For Corolla, Toyota developed brand new engineering, which included the creation of a new overhead-valve engine. The automaker also decided, for the first time, to put a four-speed manual transmission in one of its cars.

The initial reception in Japan was lukewarm. Consumers complained about noise and vibrations, and asked for more room. The 1970 Corolla got a new body with more generous proportions as a result.

Shortly after its U.S. introduction, Corolla blossomed into a winner for Toyota. By 1970, the car had become the number-two best-selling import in the United States. Consumers were thrilled with its track record of low maintenance and with its solid, practical design. By 1971, Toyota had developed the Corolla 1600 series in four models.

From the outset, the Corolla was positioned as a family car for the budget-conscious consumer. Marketing strategies emphasized its "value-for-the-money" and its functionality via popular, well-known advertising campaigns such as "You Asked For It, You Got It—Toyota."

Brand Development

The 1970s were good years for the Corolla. The oil embargo and resulting fuel crisis drove American car buyers away from large, domestic "gas guzzlers" and straight to fuel-efficient imports such as the Corolla. From 1974 until 1977, Corolla was the world's best-selling car. It lost market share in 1978 to the Volkswagen Golf, but was back on top again by the end of the decade.

In 1977, Corolla had the lowest price tag in the country and was among the highest rated cars for fuel economy. The two-door model cost about $2,788, and racked up 49 miles per gallon on the highway and 36 in city driving. At that time, Corolla was available with both a 1.2- and 1.6-liter, four-cylinder engine and four-speed manual transmission. The five-millionth Corolla rolled out of the factory in June of 1976.

The Corolla was Toyota's dream car. Of the automaker's 15 lines, Corolla comprised 24.3 percent of production by the end of the '70s. Corolla had even replaced the VW Beetle as the world's top-selling small car. From 1968-78, cumulative Corolla production mushroomed from 100,000 cars to 750,000 annually. The car had been upgraded three times—Toyota made the body larger and wider in response to Western tastes, and offered more powerful engine options.

According to a 1978 article in *Automotive World News,* Toyota's "prosperity and growth during the past decade would not have been possible without the Corolla." The article went on to note that the Corolla's sales record inspired envy on the part of Toyota's archrival, Nissan Motor Co.

A major innovation in the model occurred in 1984, when Toyota turned the Corolla into a modern, front-wheel drive automobile. Buyers had their choice of a four-door sedan, a five-door liftback, or a two-door sport coupe.

Also in 1984, Toyota and General Motors Corp. set out on a joint venture project that eventually became New United Motor Manufacturing Inc. (NUMMI), based in Fremont, Calif. In 1987, NUMMI built the Corolla FX16, its first car for Toyota dealers. Toyota called the FX16 a "high-utility sporty car." It was built on the same frame or platform as the Corolla, but had a zippy, 1.6-liter Twin Cam engine.

AT A GLANCE

Corolla brand of Toyota automobiles introduced in the United States in 1968 by Toyota Motor Sales, U.S.A., Inc.

Performance: *Market share*—9.9% of the automobile category. *Sales*—193,749 vehicles (1993).

Major competitor: Honda Civic.

Advertising: *Agency*—Saatchi & Saatchi DFS/Pacific, Torrance, CA, 1975—. *Major campaign*—"You Asked For It, You Got It," "Oh, What a Feeling," and "Who Could Ask for Anything More?"

Addresses: *Parent company*—Toyota Motor Sales, U.S.A., Inc., 19001 S. Western Ave., Torrance, CA, 90509; phone: (310) 618-4000; fax: (310) 618-7800. *Ultimate parent company*—Toyota Motor Corp., 1 Toyota-Cho, Aichi 471, Japan; phone: 565 282121; fax: 565 801116

For the Corolla's 20th anniversary in the U.S., Toyota introduced an all-new version of the model in 1988. The Corolla styles included four-door sedans and five-door wagons in front-wheel drive and All-Trac versions. The Corolla continued to be Toyota's biggest seller in both the United States and Japan.

In 1988, Toyota opened a plant in Cambridge, Ontario, where Corollas would be manufactured. Sales were still vigorous—Corolla represented 75 percent of Toyota's volume. To maintain its successful track record, Corolla ads during the 20th anniversary year emphasized the car's central selling point—quality. Toyota spent $150 million—75 percent of its advertising budget—on Corolla that year.

Product Changes

As the perennially popular Corolla entered the '90s, it underwent design changes that took it beyond its humble, "econobox" origins. The most obvious change was in styling. The Corollas of the early '90s had sleek, aerodynamic lines, with rounded curves where there had previously been square corners.

In 1993, the Corolla became nearly two inches longer and an inch wider, and was upgraded from a subcompact to a well-equipped compact. A newly designed engine, suspension system, brakes and chassis made for superior driving performance, tighter cornering and better braking. The new Corolla was included in the J.D. Power and Associates 1992 list of the Top 10 trouble-free models.

In its advertising, Toyota not only emphasized Corolla's value, as it always had, but also focused on the improved design. To woo buyers away from its competitor, the Honda Civic, Corolla launched a series of TV spots designed to attract a more upscale, contemporary audience.

The 1993 Corolla models sported such sophisticated safety features as a supplemental restraint system and anti-lock brakes. For the fifth consecutive year, the Corolla made the J.D. Power Top-10 list.

An article in *Autoweek* magazine noted that the Corolla DX, the five-door station wagon in the product line, represented a new class of Corolla: "There's a nimbleness to its pace, even in wagon trim. Its ride, cockpit appointments and noise levels all have benefitted from 'trickle-down' technology from the Lexus division."

Although the new Corolla was still a high-quality car that performed and handled well, one important factor distinguished it from earlier models—price. Thanks to design and engineering innovations, the Corolla moved out of its long-occupied economy niche. *Autoweek* magazine noted that now, "quality comes with a bigger price tag." The wagon's base price, for example, was nearly $13,000. The four-door LE Sedan—which Toyota touted as its most luxurious Corolla—cost $15,200 with a full complement of options.

In the first quarter of 1993, Toyota experienced a sharp decline in sales, while the domestic Big Three—Chrysler, General Motors and Ford—saw increases for the first time in several years. *Fortune* magazine noted that the respective prices of the '93 domestic and Japanese models was an issue. The magazine noted that a Corolla with all options cost $17,200, whereas a comparable Geo Prizm sold for $2,400 less.

In building the 1994 Corolla, Toyota introduced further refinements to the brand. To reduce noise, vibration- and sound-absorbing materials were used, and the engine in all models was set on a liquid-filled mount. In keeping with Corolla's tradition of economy and value, the standard model was still powered by a four-cylinder, 1.6-liter engine.

As Corolla steered its course toward the turn of the century, and consumers continued to shop for stylish, yet fuel-efficient cars, the brand seemed well-positioned to repeat past successes.

Further Reading:

Breese, Kristine Stiven, "Toyota Unveils Bigger Corolla," *Automotive News,* September 7, 1992, p. 26.

Chappell, Lindsay, "Toyota-GM Venture Plans Model Change," *Automotive News,* March 23, 1992, p. 32.

Claes, Cynthia, "Toyota Corolla DX Wagon: Moving Up—and Out of Its Former Niche," *Autoweek,* April 12, 1993, p. 17.

Clark, Laura. "Toyota Ads to Stress Quality in 30th Anniversary Year," *Automotive News,* October 19, 1987, p. 30.

Hill, Carolyn, "Steve Chase and Saatchi/Pacific Drive Toyota Corolla into 1993," *Back Stage-SHOOT,* September 25, 1992, p. 12.

Kahn, Helen. "Corolla Major Factor in GM-Toyota Pricing," *Automotive News,* February 6, 1984, p. 3.

Kiley, David. "Toyota to Roll Out New Corolla," *Adweek,* August 10, 1992, p. 3.

Norbye, Jan P., "Toyota Success Story Detailed," *Automotive World News,* March 27, 1978, p. 14.

Petersen, Lisa Marie, "Toyota's $25 Mil Re-Ups NBC's Seinfeld Comedy Tour," *Brandweek,* March 8, 1993, p. 3.

Rowand, Roger, "Toyota Redesigns Tercel, Camry, Increases Power for Supra Turbo," *Automotive News,* September 15, 1986, p. 34.

Sawyer, Christopher A., "1993 Toyota Corolla," *Automotive Industries,* October 1992, p. 31.

This is Toyota U.S.A., Torrance, CA: Toyota Motor Sales U.S.A., Inc., 1986, pp. 1, 4.

"Toyota Claims Low Price, High MPG," *Automotive News,* December 13, 1976, p. 20.

"Toyota Motor—Corolla and Sprinter Series Boast Full Model Changes," *Business Japan,* vol. 36, no. 9, September 1991, p. 15–17.

"Toyota Unveils Longer, Wider, Costlier Corolla," *Wall Street Journal,* September 3, 1992, p. A4.

Toyota U.S.A.: The First 15 Years, Torrance, CA: Toyota Motor Sales, U.S.A., 1973, pp. 23, 27, 35.

World Guide to Automobile Manufacturers, New York: Facts on File Publications, 1987, pp. 488–490.

Woron, Walt, "Toyota is Conservative in Its Product Approach," *Automotive News,* December 6, 1976, p. 23.

—Marinell James

TREK®

TREK USA

When it began operations in 1975, the Trek Bicycle Corporation consisted of four employees who assembled bicycle frames by hand in a rented warehouse in Waterloo, Wisconsin. Due to innovative manufacturing techniques, product developments, and a continuing commitment to hand–built quality, Trek sales grew steadily throughout the 1980s, at a time when many American bicycle manufacturers were going out of business. By 1993 Trek bicycles had become one of the best-selling brands in the United States, with annual sales of approximately $225 million and nine subsidiaries in Europe and Japan.

Trek has consistently positioned itself as a brand designed for serious bike enthusiasts; it was among the first companies to manufacture mountain bikes during the early 1980s. The Trek line includes Off Road mountain bikes, MultiTrack road/mountain bikes, MetroTrack commuter bicycles, road bikes, and tandems, as well as a full line of bicycling helmets, clothing, gear, and accessories. Trek is a subsidiary of Intrepid Corporation, a privately owned holding company based in Waukesha, Wisconsin, with annual sales of approximately $500 million.

Brand Origin

The first products bearing the Trek name were hand–built framesets assembled in the company's Waterloo warehouse and sold to bicycle dealers across the Midwest. From the beginning, Trek Bicycle Corporation devoted its energies to building a few high-end, high quality products; soon it was producing and selling several models of steel-frame road bicycles. Trek introduced its expensive bicycles at a difficult time in the bicycle industry. Many American manufacturers were being forced out of business due to intense competition from European makers of multi-speed racing and road bikes. Other high-end American manufacturers reorganized into small frame-building shops, selling to a limited number of professional bikers or amateur biking enthusiasts.

Trek sales grew slowly but steadily during this time, supported in large part by a healthy stream of cash from Roth Distribution, which was then its parent company. By 1978 the company had expanded distribution to include California, Colorado, and the New England states. Annual sales of framesets and steel touring bikes totaled 5,000 units.

Building and Marketing a Better Bike

Very early in its history, Trek decided to market its products as serious machinery for serious bikers. Avoiding retail outlets such as hardware, toy, and department stores, Trek sold its products "exclusively through reputable, full-service bicycle shops." The goal: to provide personal service by fitting and customizing bicycles to a customer's interests and usage requirements. In addition, according to a 1984 *Bicycling* article, Trek "benefitted implicitly from 'buy American' enthusiasm, even though the company [did not] emphasize this fact in its marketing. And . . . the product was pretty good and it improved with time."

In 1980 Trek moved its production facilities into a new, automated production plant with state-of-the art tooling machines. Among biking enthusiasts, its reputation as a prestigious product was enhanced by the company's practice of producing only double-butted frames and brazing their steel joints with "fabulously expensive" sliver brazing rods, as opposed to simply welding the joints or brazing them with brass rods like most other frame manufacturers. Sales grew to 15,000 units by 1980, totaling $4 million. Two years later, sales had jumped to 25,000 units, totaling $7 million.

Trek sales continued to increase between 50 and 100 percent annually throughout the 1980s. Shortly after the new facility was built, Trek management began to look into *how* the company would grow. Their attention focused on maintaining "the quality that was critical to Trek's reputation," while increasing production volume and sales.

Production Growth

The key to Trek's successful transition from a small shop to a large producer of quality bicycles lay in a number of technical innovations. Trek's "production method combines a neat mix of machine work where it saves time, and hand labor where it improves the product," noted a *Bicycling* reporter. Streamlining of production gives Trek a competitive edge on labor costs, while its handfinishing of frames enhances the bicycle's image as a high-quality product.

Trek also makes use of "space age" materials such as aluminum and composite in its bike production. Working with members of the aerospace industry, Trek engineers developed a sophisticated process for producing lightweight aluminum frames and

AT A GLANCE

Trek brand of bicycles introduced in 1975 with the founding of Trek Bicycle Corporation in Waterloo, WI; company began as a subsidiary of Roth Distribution, building and selling bicycle framesets and steel road bikes to dealers throughout the Midwest; sales of Trek brand bikes expanded to include Colorado, California, and New England states in 1978; sales expanded across U.S. during 1980s; became wholly owned subsidiary of Intrepid Corp., Waukesha, WI, during 1980s; sales to Europe and Japan began in 1993.

Performance: *Sales*—$225 million.

Major competitor: Specialized; also Huffy, Cannondale, Giant, Schwinn.

Advertising: *Agency*—In-house. *Major campaign*—"Handbuilt in the U.S.A."

Addresses: *Parent company*—Trek Bicycle Corporation, 801 West Madison St., P.O. Box 183, Waterloo, WI 53594; phone: (414) 478-2191; fax: (414) 478-2774. *Ultimate Parent Company*—Intrepid Corp., N14 W23833 Stone Ridge, Waukesha, WI 53188; phone: (414) 523-3000; fax: (414) 523-0700.

rims. In 1985 Trek introduced its first aluminum road bike, the model 2000. The following year, it introduced the 2500, its first carbon composite model.

More important to Trek's growth was its venture into the production of mountain bikes. The first mountain bikes had been created in 1979 by a group of Californians who rebuilt old Schwinn bicycles to make them more suitable for scaling the rough terrain of nearby Mount Tamalpais. Unlike the 10-speed road bikes that dominated the market at that time, mountain bikes had comfortable seats, upright handlebars, fat tires, and wide-ranging gears. Very quickly, mountain biking became a fad that sprouted its own cottage industry. In 1983, after hand building a number of prototypes and custom mountain bikes, Trek introduced its first production mountain bike, the model 850.

By 1984 production topped 45,000 bicycles, totaling $20 million in sales. Trek was one of the world's leading manufacturers of mountain bikes—a quickly growing segment of the industry. In 1986, however, Trek posted a $45 million operating loss, caused by inventory buildup, slow sales, and high development costs. Trek management again reassessed its position in the bicycle market. This time, the company refocused it energies on service, marketing, and distribution. In a five-year period, Trek established distribution centers in California, Wisconsin, and New Jersey; greatly increased the number of Trek dealers across the United States; and opened nine subsidiaries in Europe and Asia.

Sales soared during the next five years, fueled in part by the growing popularity of mountain bikes. By 1990 nearly 45 percent of all bikes sold in the United States were mountain bikes. Mass market manufacturers such as the Huffy Corporation, Murray, and Taiwan's Giant Manufacturing were getting in on the game, driving down prices and threatening to push smaller manufacturers out of the market. Trek was well positioned to respond to these challenges and was also poised to tap into growing foreign markets, having established distributorship in fifteen additional countries.

In the early 1990s, Trek introduced a number of new models, including the MetroTrack commuter bicycle and the lightweight off road OCLV Carbon Composite, as well as a complete line of winter and summer clothing, helmets, biking gear, car carriers, and bags. By 1994 Trek had grown to become one of the largest bicycle manufacturers in the United States, with annual sales of $225 million.

Performance Appraisal and Outlook

Trek's motivating force is the quest to build a better bicycle, a factor that continues to influence its marketing. Nowhere is this more evident than in Trek's catalogs, which resemble cycling magazines. Catalogs contain interviews with Trek employees on bicycle design and production; tips for riding in urban traffic and on winter roads; and glossy photos highlighting the allure of biking. Charts offer further information on the technical details of buying a Trek brand bike, allowing customers to choose a bike suited to their individual riding habits and needs.

Trek sponsors competitive cycling contestants in everything from grass-roots level events to world-class competitions. In addition, it provides a Wrench Force service crew to repair bicycles damaged during more than 70 events nationally. With its bicycles, clothing, and gear, Trek does more than market a product. It markets a lifestyle based on a passion for bicycles. "We're not interested in a one-time sale," Trek declared in its *Trek 1994: Engineering Passion* catalog. "Our long-term goal is to transform you into a real enthusiast. We're riders and racers ourselves. We're here to encourage, explain, demonstrate and generally help you expand your cycling horizons in every way."

Interest in bicycling as a sport, a hobby, and a clean, energy-efficient mode of transportation increased tremendously in the early 1990s. By sharing—and marketing—its passion for biking, Trek grew from a small shop of biking enthusiasts into one of the largest bicycle manufacturers in the United States. With its worldwide distribution and sales channels and growing reputation among the general public, Trek seems well poised to tap into a rapidly growing market.

Further Reading:

Martin, Scott, "Mountain Biking Turns 10," *Bicycling*, October-November 1989, pp. 39–41.

Schubert, John, "Trek Is Going Strong," *Bicycling*, March 1984, pp. 137–40.

Shao, Maria, and others, "Mountain Bikes Just Keep on Climbing," *Business Week*, December 31, 1990, p. 60D.

Trek 1994: Engineering Passion, Waterloo, WI: Trek Bicycle Corporation, 1993.

—*Maura Troester*

TRIVIAL PURSUIT®

Trivial Pursuit, introduced to the board game market in 1983, is one of the truly phenomenal products of the game industry. Against all odds the inventors, two journalists with no experience in the toy or game industry, raised money from barroom friends in order to promote their game, and created the most successful board game of the decade. Although Trivial Pursuit has since lost its position as the best-selling game in the industry, it remains among the top competitors. Licensed to Parker Brothers since 1988, Trivial Pursuit is an example of a simple idea effectively executed. The game took advantage of the varied, often disconnected array of knowledge acquired by baby boomers, and provided the consumer with a vehicle for testing this shared "trivia."

Brand Origins

The story of the invention and licensing of Trivial Pursuit has become almost as much of a legend as the game itself. The Canadian Broadcasting Company has made a movie about the game's inventors, Chris Haney and Scott Abbott, and they have become a symbol of Canadian entrepreneurship. The two men were unlikely candidates for such a role. Haney was a high school dropout who became a photographer and then photo editor of the Montreal English-language newspaper, *The Montreal Gazette*. Abbott was a sports editor for the *Canadian Press* news service. The two men had never had any business training or ambition, and both were known to be unconventional and have quirky senses of humor. Haney and Abbott's friendship had been based, in part, on their shared love of games. Board games, word games, card games—anything that involved friendly competition obsessed them. As they ran out of arenas for competition, the two men began to think about inventing their own game based on the trivia questions that they had traded over the years. The idea of marketing their trivia game commercially developed slowly, but once the decision was reached the two men became consumed with producing and selling their game.

Haney and Abbott recruited Haney's older brother, John, who had some management experience, and his friend Ed Werner, an attorney. The four partners called their new company Horn Abbot Ltd., an amalgam of Chris's nickname, "horn," and Scott's last name minus the final "t." They then set out to raise money to finance an initial production run of their game. The four partners cornered every friend and coworker they could find to show them their hand-lettered board and cards. They sold shares in their company for a thousand dollars apiece, and little by little they managed to convince 34 friends to invest small amounts in the game. Most thought they would never see their money again. Between investors and the total liquidation of all the partners' personal savings, by 1981 Horn Abbot Ltd. had raised enough money for the first prototype production of 1,000 games.

Horn Abbot firmly believed that there was no point in manufacturing the game unless it was done to the highest specifications. They saw the market for their game as young, middle-class professionals whom they believed would only buy a board game if it looked and felt good. Because of the small size of their initial run, however, quality came at the very high price of about $60 a unit. The group began to market the game primarily in the province of Ontario, but were obliged to take heavy losses in order to break into the market. Selling their game at $16 wholesale ($29.95 retail), they sold out the initial run in a matter of months. Convinced that Trivial Pursuit could be a hit, they borrowed heavily to finance a run of 20,000 more games and set out to market their product across Canada and the United States.

Their first stop was the 1982 American International Toy Fair in New York City, the largest and most important venue for introducing new games. To their growing dismay and in spite of good Canadian sales, they were only able to drum up a few hundred orders at the Fair. They were also disappointed in their attempts to secure an American distributor for Trivial Pursuit. The two largest game companies in the United States, Parker Brothers and Milton Bradley, both refused to take on the game. The four partners had mortgaged their houses, used up all their savings, and were heavily in debt with nothing but a few hundred orders to show for it.

The Horn Abbot foursome returned to Canada, discouraged but still convinced that there was a large market out there for Trivial Pursuit if they could only tap into it. Their first real break came when they managed to convince a Canadian toy distributor, Chieftain Products, to take on the game. What had been a trickle of sales soon became a steady stream, and then a torrent. Purely by word of mouth, news of the game spread, and Chieftain began to gear itself up for a minor hit.

In the meantime Horn Abbot was still determined to procure an American distributor for the game. The company approached Selchow and Righter, the 125-year-old game company that had

AT A GLANCE

Trivial Pursuit brand board game invented by Chris Haney and Scott Abbott in Montreal, Canada, 1981; licensed to Selchow and Righter for American manufacture and distribution, 1983; Selchow and Righter, along with Trivial Pursuit, sold to Coleco Industries, 1986; Parker Brothers division of Tonka Corp. acquired license for Trivial Pursuit, 1988; Hasbro Inc. bought Tonka Corp., along with Parker Brothers' Trivial Pursuit game, 1991.

Major competitor: Other popular board games, including, Milton Bradley's Scattergories and Scrabble, and Parker Brother's Monopoly.

Advertising: *Agency*—Grey Advertising, New York, NY, 1991—. *Major campaign*—Celebrities answering Trivial Pursuit questions with tag line: "Is anyone not playing this game?"

Addresses: *Parent company*—Parker Brothers, 50 Dunham Rd., Beverly, MA 01915; phone: (508) 927-7600; fax: (508) 921-3521. *Ultimate parent company*—Hasbro Inc., 1027 Newport Ave., P.O. Box 1059, Pawtucket, RI 02862-1059; phone: (401) 431-TOYS; fax: (401) 727-5544.

been marketing Scrabble for some 30 years. Haney and Abbott felt that Trivial Pursuit had a lot in common with the popular word game. ''In my mind,'' Chris Haney said in a 1984 interview in *Inc.* magazine, ''Scrabble is one of the most dignified games around.'' Still, the first meeting with Selchow and Righter executives on September 22, 1982, was, in Haney's words, like '' 'Saturday Night Live' meets 'The Lawrence Welk Show.' '' In spite of the marked generation gap between the ex-hippies and the staid, conservative Selchow and Righter management, Horn Abbot—with Canadian sales figures in hand—managed to convince the centenarian company that Trivial Pursuit was a valuable commodity. Just how valuable, however, was to be the subject of nail biting negotiations between the two companies to determine royalty fees.

Horn Abbot felt that since it had already invested heavily in the game's development it should be entitled to a higher than average royalty fee, which generally ran at about 5 percent of sales. Partly out of self-confidence and partly out of ignorance, Horn Abbot steadfastly refused to settle for less than an astounding 15.7 percent, according to toy historian Richard Levy. The four partners gambled, not without some trepidation, that Selchow and Righter were already far enough committed to the new game that they would agree to their price. After tense days of negotiation and waiting, Selchow and Righter agreed to take on the game on the inventors' terms. Trivial Pursuit was launched by Selchow and Righter in the United States in 1983 with a $100,000 public relations budget and virtually no advertising. By the end of 1984, 21 million Trivial Pursuit games had been sold, and it is estimated that almost one third of American households owned the blockbuster game.

Brand Development

The very nature of the question and answer format of Trivial Pursuit dictated that additional question cards be made available through the years. Even during 1984, Trivial Pursuit's first full year on the U.S. market, Horn Abbot was preparing another set of 6,000 questions for a second edition of Trivial Pursuit, and Selchow and Righter were introducing Baby Boomer and Young Player's editions of the blockbuster game. By 1985, when sales of the game had begun to fall, add-on question sets with such themes as ''Disney'' and ''Americana'' were bolstering dwindling sales of the board game itself, and further specialty editions, including ''RPM'' and ''Silver Screen,'' had been introduced.

In 1988 Horn Abbot transferred the rights to Trivial Pursuit to Parker Brothers. The new distributors revamped the card set segment by introducing new themes, including ''Family'' and ''TV,'' and adding a Travel Pack collection containing questions and answers about one specific category. In 1993 Parker Brothers introduced a new line of Trivial Pursuit games including an All American Edition and Year in Reviews. These new versions of the game contained only 1,300 questions each, as opposed to the nearly 6,000 questions of the original game. They were designed to create a faster-paced game with a quicker resolution, as people in focus groups had complained that the original game took too long to play. They also included easier, more current questions in an attempt to simplify and de-intellectualize the game. In 1994 the company introduced an edition of the game based on a popular TV version of Trivial Pursuit that ran on the ''Family Channel.''

The All American edition of the popular Trivial Pursuit board game.

Advertising

Although the official Parker Brothers history of Trivial Pursuit attributes the initial success of the game to ''word of mouth,'' Selchow and Righter's advertising budget for the game in 1984 was a hefty $8 million dollars, according to a 1985 article in *Advertising Age.* This included a $100,000 public relations budget to attract media and consumer interest in the game. Ads ran primarily in magazines and featured copy by Jordan, Case and McGrath claiming that ''every American is entitled to life, liberty and the pursuit of trivia'' and calling the game ''the right stuff for the trivia buff.'' When Hasbro bought Parker Brothers in 1991, a new advertising campaign was initiated in an attempt to re-launch the game to American consumers. Produced by Grey Advertising, the 30-second television spots featured celebrities such as Don Adams and De Forrest Kelley answering Trivial Pursuit questions related to the roles for which they were famous. The tag line, ''Is anyone not playing this game?,'' was a clear attempt to revive the fad aura that had surrounded the game in the early 1980s.

International Sales

The phenomenal success of Trivial Pursuit in the American and Canadian markets in 1984 virtually assured some international sales of the game, but Horn Abbot was determined to make as much of the international market as they had of the American one. They founded a sister company, Horn Abbot International, with sole responsibility for international distribution. Through a series of licensing agreements with national games firms, by 1985 Trivial Pursuit was being produced in 14 languages and sold in 17 countries. Teams of writers were hired to adapt each foreign edition to their national markets. They generally kept about one third of the 6,000 questions from the original edition and tailored the remaining 4,000 questions to the specific country in which the edition was to be sold. As discussed in a 1985 article in *International Management,* translation of the game into foreign languages and cultures did not always go smoothly. The team of six writers hired for the Japanese version got badly delayed by their insistence on agreeing on the phrasing for every question. ''It was like a bloody committee,'' said Horn Abbot International's marketing director in the 1985 article. ''Every question had to be approved by committee. If we hadn't put our foot down, it would have taken three years to write the Japanese version.''

Trivial Pursuit was much slower to catch on in the international market than it had been in the United States. In 1985, the first full year of international distribution of the game, only two million units were sold outside North America, compared to 21 million in its first year of American sales. By 1990, however, Trivial Pursuit, marketed by San Serif games, was the best selling game in the United Kingdom. It is credited with revitalizing the adult games industry in that country as it had done some years earlier in the United States. By 1994, Trivial Pursuit was being sold internationally in 19 languages in 33 countries.

Performance

In one brief year, Trivial Pursuit became what can only be described as a phenomenon. In Trivial Pursuit's first full year of sales, about 21 million games were sold totalling $600 million in retail sales. These unbelievable sales figures not only catapulted Trivial Pursuit to the top of the games market, they totally transformed the games category itself. In 1983 total retail sales of all adult games were estimated at only $183 million; by 1984 sales of Trivial Pursuit had quadrupled this figure to $777 million. What's more, adult games, which had previously accounted for only 30 percent of games sales, jumped to more than 50 percent of total sales in the games category. George Ditomassi, then president of competitor Milton Bradley—which had rejected Trivial Pursuit in its infant stages—spoke about the Trivial Pursuit phenomenon in Sydney Stern's *Toyland:* ''The industry was stunned. We would have told you there was no market for that kind of product in that magnitude. . . . It broke all the rules. It had to, to get the kind of numbers it did. Games are primarily played by people twelve years and under, but Trivial Pursuit certainly proved there was one hell of a market for people over twelve, given the right kind of games.''

The huge success of Trivial Pursuit was not all fun and games for its American manufacturer and distributor, Selchow and Righter. With one thousand question cards in each game—all to be printed on in such a specialized way as to get double-coated card stock—the Selchow and Righter manufacturing plant in Holbrook, Long Island, was pushed beyond its capacity. By February of 1984, with Selchow and Righter producing 63,000 Trivial Pursuit games a week, back orders already exceeded one million games. By August, in spite of contracting out to four additional manufacturing firms, 11 million games were on back order, and Selchow and Righter executives were beginning to feel snowed under. ''Believe me, it's no fun,'' the company's vice-president of sales said in a 1984 *Inc.* article on the game. ''I spend the days trying to placate customers. I think our credibility in the marketplace has suffered a great deal this year. On the one hand we are producing a highly desirable item. On the other we are frustrating customers with our uncertainties. . . . Everyone wants it at once. It is just a situation where nerves are frayed and people aren't thinking clearly.''

If Selchow and Righter executives felt overly stressed in 1984, by 1985 they probably would have liked a little of that stress back again. In 1984 Christmas shoppers were waiting in line for hours and spending up to $40.00 for a Trivial Pursuit Genus Edition. By 1985, the game was piling up in warehouses and being discounted in stores across the country. Sales plummeted from the 1984 high of 21 million units to 5.5 million in 1985, and then dropped again in 1986 to only about 3 million games. To make matters worse, after the shortages in 1984, Selchow and Righter had stepped up production of the game, which now gathered dust in the company's warehouses. ''We expected that profit would come down a little each year,'' said Richard Selchow, company president, in a 1986 article in *Forbes,* ''but it came down quicker than I thought it would.'' In spite of the abrupt decline, retail sales of around $125 million still put Trivial Pursuit at the top of the board game category in 1986.

With declining sales of their hit game and no successors to take over the family-run business, Selchow and Righter decided to sell their century-old company. Coleco Industries was looking to acquire new properties after sales of its mega-hit Cabbage Patch Kids had also abruptly dropped. Coleco bought Selchow and Righter in 1986, acquiring rights to Trivial Pursuit in the process. Coleco's new acquisitions did little to help the company out of the deep financial difficulties it had run into. Coleco had little money to put into advertising and promotion, and sales of Trivial Pursuit continued to fall. In 1988, with Coleco near bankruptcy, Horn Abbot declined to renew the firm's license for Trivial Pursuit. The U.S. and Canadian rights to Trivial Pursuit were secured, instead, by the Parker Brothers division of Tonka Corp., one of the largest games distributors in the country. In spite of a re-launching of the game by the experienced games firm, Trivial Pursuit sales failed to rise to anywhere near the levels of the mid 1980s.

One of the great legacies of Trivial Pursuit had been the rebirth of the adult game industry, and that increased competition was eventually to topple Trivial Pursuit from the top position of the category. By 1991, Milton Bradley's hit game Scattergories had secured that position. With new card sets and a strong advertising campaign, however, Trivial Pursuit under Parker Brothers remained one of the top games in the category, maintaining sales of a few million games a year.

Although Parker Brothers has now designated Trivial Pursuit ''a classic'' of the industry, with only ten years under its belt, Trivial Pursuit has a long way to go before it can be classified with such games as the 50-year-old Monopoly or the 35-year-old

Scrabble. The next decade will be the real testing ground for the game's survival. If steady sales can be maintained with the help of new, up-to-date card sets, Trivial Pursuit may well take its place in a volatile industry as the classic, perennial trivia game.

Further Reading:

Arbose, Jules, "Going International: There's Nothing Trivial about This Pursuit," *International Management (Europe Edition),* December 1985, pp. 73–76.

Croft, Martin, "In Pursuit of the Playing Public," *Accountancy,* January 1990, pp. 65–69.

Forkan, James P., "Games Marketers in Pursuit of Trivia Fans," *Advertising Age,* March 26, 1984, p. 52.

Hill, Julie Skur, "Trivia Fans End Board Game Pursuit," *Advertising Age,* December 19, 1985, p. 36.

"Is There Life after Trivial Pursuit?," *Chain Store Age General Merchandise Trends,* February 1985, pp. 113–14.

Lanson, Gerald, "Big Game," *Inc.,* November 1984, pp. 101–11.

Levy, Richard C. and Ronald O. Weingartner, *Inside Santa's Workshop,* New York: Henry Holt and Company, 1990, pp. 23, 69, 79.

Pomice, Eva, "The Up & Comers: Not So Trivial Problems," *Forbes,* April 7, 1986, pp. 82, 84.

"Seeking Board Game Bonanza," *New York Times,* December 30, 1986, pp. D1, D4.

Stern, Sydney and Ted Schoenhaus, *Toyland: The High Stakes Game of the Toy Industry,* Chicago: Contemporary Books, 1990, pp. 123–24, 302.

"Trivial Pursuit Taken from Coleco," *New York Times,* May 21, 1988, p. 19.

—Hilary Gopnik

TUPPERWARE®

Best known as a brand of food-storage containers, Tupperware has been valued for its unique, versatile, high-quality products and lifetime warranty. The warranty was possible because Tupperware adhered to exceptionally high manufacturing standards. It used the best raw materials, the strongest and most uniform molds, and seals that fit and were virtually airtight. The only receipt needed by a customer to receive a replacement was the word *Tupperware* on the product. As a result of this commitment to quality, Tupperware's prices were higher than those of its competitors.

Tupperware products have traditionally been sold at "Tupperware parties"—that is, organized product demonstrations at a person's home. Still common in the 1990s, these occurred at a rate of nearly once every three seconds in one of the 52 countries where Tupperware products were sold. In the United States alone more than 161,000 people gathered each week at such functions. The more than 400 different types of Tupperware food containers, storage containers, toys, and other home accessories were also sold through a mail-order catalog. Although Tupperware was not available in retail stores, the brand's parent company, Tupperware U.S., Inc., had worldwide net sales of $1.1 billion by the early 1990s.

The brand, introduced in 1938, was originally called Tupper and owned by Tupper Plastics Company. In 1951, when the brand became Tupperware, the company also got a new name, Tupperware Home Parties, Inc. Tupperware products were credited with helping to launch the plastics revolution of the 1950s by legitimizing plastic as a material for numerous applications, especially food containers. By the 1990s Tupperware products had become part of American culture and were found in more than 90 percent of all American households.

Brand Origins

Raised on a farm in rural New Hampshire, Earl Silas Tupper first came into contact with plastics when he worked in a Du Pont chemical plant before World War II. He believed that plastic was "the material of the future." Being a self-described "ham inventor and Yankee trader," he formed Tupper Plastics Company in 1938.

During the war Tupper wanted to experiment with plastics, but the government awarded critical materials only to major companies. When he asked his former employer to sell him some leftover material, they gave him a chunk of paraffin-like polyethylene slag.

The slag was a waste product of the oil-refining process. It was black, rock hard, putrid, and almost impossible to work with. Undaunted, the 31-year-old Tupper accepted what he called Poly-T and experimented until he developed a refining process to purify the slag into a tasteless, odorless substance. Tupper also devised an injection-molding machine to form the material into unbreakable, temperature-resistant, shape-retaining plastic, becoming the first person to invent a way to mold Poly-T without cracking or splitting it. One of Tupper's first products was the seven-ounce Bell tumbler, which was described as a perfect remedy for a "thirstquake."

Tupper enjoyed designing products and constantly worked on ideas to use the new material. His ideas would revolutionize the emerging plastics industry. While his plan of plastic shoe heels did not pan out, he would not give up on the notion of using plastic to make food-storage containers, cups, and bowls. He thought these products could help homemakers save money, time, and energy. He introduced Tupper Plastics products in 1945, marketing them in hardware and department stores, as well as by catalog.

Consumers resisted using plastic products. They were used to using glass, metal, and earthenware containers, and plastic had a reputation for being of poor quality. Tupper's products broke down the resistance. His plastics were of high quality, were strong and simple, and had a functional beauty. They also had a benefit that food-storage containers made out of other materials did not have. With their virtually airtight seals, Tupper containers solved the problems of food drying out, wilting, and losing flavor in the refrigerators and freezers more and more households were owning.

The virtually airtight seal, which he modeled after the lid of a paint can, was an innovative coup for Tupper. He discoverd that if the rim of a container flared outward slightly, then a lid molded to the exact dimensions of the container would lock onto it and create a partial vacuum—provided the air inside was "burped" out. When properly sealed, storage containers that were dropped bounced and did not break or spill. He designed the patented seal lids in sizes small enough for pour spouts and large enough for mixing and serving bowls, and he started putting them on his housewares in 1947. According to *Getting It Right the Second*

AT A GLANCE

Tupper brand of plastic products founded in 1938 by Earl Tupper, inventor and founder of Tupper Plastics Company; brand renamed Tupperware in 1951, when the parent company became Tupperware Home Parties; brand and company sold to Rexall Drug Company in 1958; Rexall company renamed Dart Industries, Inc., in 1969; Dart merged with Kraft, Inc., to become Dart and Kraft, Inc., in 1980; company split into Premark International, Inc., which owned Tupperware Home Parties, and Kraft Inc. in 1986; Tupperware U.S., Inc., a Delaware corporation, was formed in 1992, and Tupperware Home Parties ceased to exist.

Performance: *Market share*—60% (first share) of food-storage containers category. *Sales*—$1.1 billion (worldwide net sales).

Major competitor: Rubbermaid.

Addresses: *Parent company*—Tupperware U.S., Inc., a subsidiary of Dart Industries, Inc., P.O. Box 2353, Orlando, FL 32802; 14901 S. Orange Blossom Trail, Orlando, FL 32837; phone: (407) 826-5050; fax: (407) 826-4459. *Ultimate parent company*—Premark International, Inc., 1717 Deerfield Rd., Deerfield, IL 60015; phone (708) 405-6000.

Time, "by 1948, [Tupper's] process [was also] used to make nesting cups for thermos bottles, snack bowls sold with Canada Dry beverages, and 300,000 inexpensive cigarette cases for Camels," as well as "double-walled ice cube containers, poker chips, and bowls with close-fitting caps."

Unique products and the advantages of virtually airtight seals, however, did not bring marketing success to Tupper Plastics Company. Many customers returned the containers because they could not work the seals at home. They complained they did not work like they were shown at the store. The company's fortunes would turn around when Brownie Wise learned how to burp a Tupper seal.

Independent Consultants

During the 1940s and 1950s door-to-door and home demonstrations were popular sales methods welcomed by homemakers. At a home party, direct sellers could show their wares and let partygoers handle them. Some direct sellers discovered Tupper products and bought them through wholesalers to resell to their customers. Earl Tupper heard about their efforts and started to promote home parties as an alternate method of sales. These home demonstrators became the first direct sellers of Tupper products in the late 1940s. Brownie Wise was one of them.

It took Brownie Wise three days to figure out how the seal worked on the Tupper "Wonder Bowl" her friend loaned her. Once she got the lid on, she dropped the bowl on the way to the refrigerator, but it bounced instead of breaking, and the seal held. Already a Stanley Home Products distributor, Wise added Tupper products to round out her line. She realized that when the tricky seals were demonstrated in the low-pressure atmosphere of a home party, homemakers understood the practical application of Tupper products in their homes. The format also kept a potential buyer in and around the products for an average of two hours and lowered their sales resistance.

Before long Wise was selling as much as $1,500 worth of Tupper products a week and had recruited 20 other independent dealers. When she called Tupper in 1949 to complain about late shipments of her wholesale orders, he listened to her complaints, realized she was the perfect salesperson for his products, and put her in charge of a new home-sales program.

Wise gave the company the boost it needed to make its products something few modern households could do without. Because of her energy, creativity, and devotion to the product, Tupper Plastics pulled its products from store shelves and formed Tupperware Home Parties, in April 1951. It was that year that Tupperware became a registered trademark.

There were 200 independent dealers when Wise took over the company's sales system. Three years later there were 9,000. Her dynamic personality was largely responsible for the growth. She imparted her enthusiasm for Tupperware by creating motivational and inspirational messages. She also developed the sales promotions, contests, party games, and format for annual sales conventions. She carried Tupperware product samples every day to show people, as well as a block of Poly-T for the salespeople to rub for good luck.

In addition, Wise set up the sales force structure still in place whereby party hostesses could become independent consultants (dealers), consultants could become managers, and managers could become distributors. The direct-selling system incorporated mentoring, support, recognition, and peer training for the independent Tupperware sales consultants. A career in Tupperware was particularly appealing to homemakers in the 1950s, many of whom never worked before. (It also was a career for men.) Dealers received 35 percent of the gross sales from each party. Home parties produced $25 million in sales in 1954.

By 1958 the Tupperware party was part of American culture, helping new homeowners cope with emerging suburban life. In 1958 Wise left the business and Tupper sold it to Rexall Drug Company for more than $9 million. He moved to Costa Rica, where he died in 1983. Under Rexall sales operations spread in the 1960s throughout western Europe and into four Far East countries and two Latin America countries. (In 1993 international sales accounted for almost 80 percent of the Tupperware brand business.)

Although the Tupperware party was practically a rite of passage for young women, changing life-styles caused Tupperware sales to slide after they peaked in the early 1980s. In response to declining sales, Tupperware began trying a number of new programs to update the image and direct-selling system. These included lead generation advertising, some direct marketing through consultants, catalog changes, and the addition of new party formats.

While independent Tupperware consultants still educated consumers on product benefits, taught their uses, and answered questions, the new party formats accommodated the changing life-styles, market segmentation, and increased time pressures that had become obstacles to customer buying. (Tupperware consultants were as busy as their customers. Approximately half of Tupperware consultants had full-time jobs in addition to demonstrating and selling Tupperware brand products by 1992.) Besides the traditional Tupperware party, consultants offered "Value for Time" classes in microwave cooking, food freezing, and ways to save money and protect the environment; instruction in "Custom Kitchen Planning," using Modular Mates containers to save cabinet space, reduce waste, and save time; "Rush Hour" parties, which allowed customers to shop on their way home from work; "Office" parties at offices, hospitals, day care centers, and factories; and "Stop-N-Shop" opportunities, which gave customers a chance to drop in to talk with the consultant. A direct mail catalog servive for consultants, "Keeping in Touch," was mailed to approximately 750,000 customers in 1993. The service supports consultants' long-standing practice of mailing catalogs to their hostesses, customers, and new prospects. In addition, volunteers could sell a limited edition, fund-raiser line of Tupperware products in exclusive colors to raise money for schools, churches, and other nonprofit organizations.

Another way Tupperware responded to the changing time demands of salespeople and customers was to simplify delivery. The Tupperware Express system required dealers to receive payment along with the orders so products could be shipped directly from the warehouse to the customer. The new plan also positioned Tupperware to compete better with catalog companies for speed and convenience.

The "Tupperized" Kitchen

Patricia Leigh Brown wrote in the *New York Times* that "there was nothing Tupperware couldn't do. It 'provided a soupçon of gay informality' to the table, according to early catalogues. It bounced instead of broke. It was 'insect-tight and feather-light.' It allowed a 'fastidious hostess to express a particular air of intimate hospitality in the translucent tones of her Tupperware.' " The *"Tupperized"* kitchen was well-organized and neat. The variety of containers did away with unsightly open packages and kept food from becoming stale.

Originally Tupperware came in frosted crystal and five pastel colors. Later the plastic bread boxes, cracker crispers, tumblers, salt and pepper shakers, cheese-serving trays, picture frames, mixing bowls, and food containers came in a rainbow of colors. In 1989 the company introduced Fresh-N-Fancy containers in 37 designer colors.

Besides being attuned to color preferences, Tupperware was aware of changing customer needs. Tupperware introduced nonkitchen products, including a traveling desk, drawer organizers, and a plastic carrying case. As more households obtained dishwashers and microwave ovens, Tupperware developed products that could tolerate temperature extremes in these appliances. Almost all products sold since September 1979 were dishwasher safe. For the microwave oven Tupperware created the Reheatables and CrystalWave lines, which could warm up leftovers or cook frozen foods. CrystalWave containers had a vented cap that released steam and prevented messy splattering during microwave reheating, but closed tight when storing food. The containers also had beaded feet on the bottom to promote reheating, see-through windows so the bowl's contents could be determined, and capacities written in Braille for the visually impaired. Two other Tupperware lines were introduced for microwave cooking. The TupperWave Stack Cooker cooked a three-course meal for four in the microwave in 30 minutes without stirring or turning, while Meals in Minutes Microsteamer let cooks prepare a fresh meal for two in ten minutes or less.

Tupperware containers provided positive environmental alternatives to disposable wrap and packaging. These alternatives included the Square-A-Way container to hold a single sandwich, Box Lunch sets, and Lunch 'N Bag sets. Modular Mates containers allowed consumers to buy staples in bulk, to keep them organized and stocked, and to save closet space as well.

Other notable Tupperware products included ceramic-look One Touch serving bowls; nesting Classic Sheer and Pearlescent Sheer bowls; the 32-cup Thatsa bowl; Flavor Savor containers with lift-out trays; Freezer Mates containers with raised feet to freeze foods faster and with the flexibility to pop frozen foods out with a twist; MunchKids children's eating accessories; Exclusive Collection of tableware items, including sugar bowls with trendy black lids in glasslike Ultra Clear; Signature Series containers for storage throughout the house; Kimono-Keepers (for the Japanese market); and Tortilla Keepers (for the Latin American market).

Form Follows Function

Earl Tupper insisted that quality of design and innovation be built into each product. The function and properties of his plastic material defined the form of his strong, spare, product designs, and the resulting innovative shapes earned praise. The 1947 edition of *House Beautiful* called Tupper's products "Fine Art for 39¢." Because of their innovative design, strength, and functional beauty, 15 of the earliest designs were placed in the permanent collection of the Museum of Modern Art and the Smithsonian Institution.

Tupperware's history of form and function did not prevent the brand from developing an image problem as it aged. Although (or because) families handed down Tupperware products and people considered them prized finds at garage sales, they came to be viewed as "something for your grandmother." To overcome this "negative" viewpoint, the company hired designer and Prix de Rome winner Morison Cousins to contemporize and expand the Tupperware product line without abandoning pie wedges and other aspects of its history.

Cousins's updated Tupperware products followed function as well as the popular trend toward rounding and softening the lines of consumer products. He redesigned Tupper's seal, which customers complained was hard to open; removed hard-to-clean ridges and rounded bottoms of One Touch containers; and added large rounded tabs on Wonderlier bowls. Depending on the user's perspective, the new oversized, scallop-shaped tabs on the seals looked like puffy clouds, flower petals, lips, or ears and added whimsy to the food containers.

Like earlier versions, modern Tupperware products earned praise and a place in museums. The Cooper Hewitt, Brooklyn Museum, and Victoria and Albert Museum in London have acquired pieces Cousins designed for the U.S. market for their permanent collections. The double colander, designed in Europe, won a major design award in Germany. Tupperware designers in Europe and the Far East have also produced award-winning designs. The Tupperware 2000 line, designed for the Asia Pacific market, won Japan's Good Design Award.

Brand Outlook

Because Tupperware products faced stiff competition from more accessible brands like Rubbermaid, the company worked to identify the changing needs of its customers and sales force and responded with innovative products and services. Service responses included demonstrations scheduled to accommodate customers' schedules and the introduction of direct-mail catalogs. Tupperware anticipated that revamping its direct-selling methods would reverse the brand's downward domestic-sales trend, which began after sales peaked in the early 1980s.

Drawbacks of the Tupperware direct-selling systems were offset by the company's ability to launch new products rapidly, penetrate the market deeply, gather virtually instant feedback from customers, and respond to the rapidly changing marketplace. In addition, because it was a direct marketer, Tupperware could offer a vast array of products and specialty items, in numerous sizes and colors, that would be too great to display on store shelves. Still, U.S. sales remained less than half of the company's total sales in 1993.

The quality of materials and attention to detail that made Earl Tupper's early pieces so functional and popular continued to be the hallmark of the Tupperware product line in the 1990s. The company set stringent standards for the manufacture of each piece and conducted extensive quality-control testing to reduce the potential for defects in its products. As a result, Tupperware provided a warranty for almost all of its products against chipping, cracking, peeling, and breaking under normal, noncommercial use. The warranty and extensive replacement-parts program made the purchase of a Tupperware product a lifetime investment. It was this product quality that will likely sustain the brand as Tupperware adapts to the new marketplace realities.

Further Reading:

Aaseng, Nathan, *Better Mousetraps: Product Improvements That Led to Success,* Minneapolis: Lerner Publications Company, 1990.

Ballen, Kate, ''Get Ready for Shopping at Work,'' *Fortune,* February 15, 1988, pp. 95–96.

Britt, Bill, ''Tupperware Breaks the Mould,'' *Marketing,* February 15, 1990, p. 1.

Brown, Patricia Leigh, ''At Tupperware, Rethinking the Bowl, Perfecting the Burp,'' *New York Times,* June 10, 1993, p. C1.

Gaffney, Charles, ''Premark Has a Tupperware Party,'' *Financial World,* February 7, 1989, p. 12.

Gershman, Michael, *Getting It Right the Second Time,* New York: Addison-Wesley, 1990, pp. 128–30.

Graham, Judith and Kristine Stiven, ''Filling Down Time for Globe Trotters,'' *Advertising Age,* August 1, 1988, pp. S10–13.

Hall, Lawrie Platt, *Launching the Quiet Revolution: The History of Tupperware*'' [typescript], Orlando, Florida: Tupperware Home Parties, April 1993.

''Now Call It Yupperware (Tupperware Parties Marketed on the Job, at Day-Care Centers, Etc.),'' *Time,* August 1, 1988, p. 43.

Strazewski, Len, ''Tupperware Locks in New Strategy; Uses Direct-Response Campaign, New 'Party' Formats,'' *Advertising Age,* February 8, 1989, p. 30.

Sussman, Vic, ''I Was the Only Virgin at the Party; How a Middle-Aged Man Was Seduced by a Legendary Sales Technique,'' *Sales & Marketing Management,* September 1989, pp. 64–71.

Trachtenberg, Jeffrey A., ''Party Animal,'' *Forbes,* November 16, 1987, pp. 262, 266, 270.

''Tupperware Rolls Out Catalog Nationwide,'' *Catalog Age,* November 1992, p. 27.

Tupperware Today [typescript], Orlando, Florida: Tupperware Home Parties, June 1993.

World's Greatest Brands, New York: Wiley & Sons, 1992, p. 85.

Yawn, David, ''Tupperware Products Travel the World from Huge Plant in Halls, Tenn.,'' *Memphis Business Journal,* January 20, 1992, p. 1.

—Doris Morris Maxfield

TWISTER®

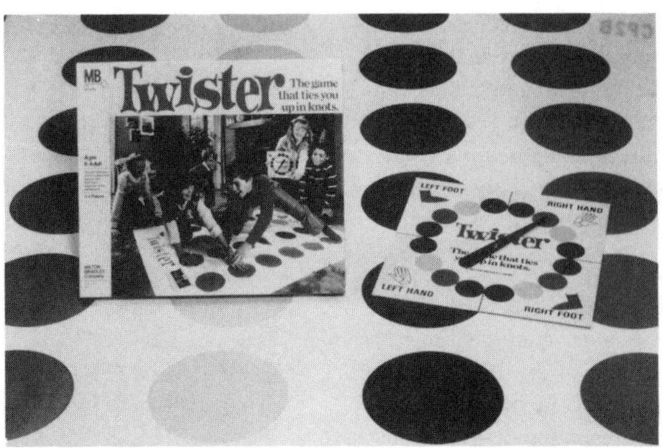

Owned by Milton Bradley Company, Twister has been a popular party game for children, teens, and adults since its introduction in the mid-1960s. It was created by inventor Reyn Guyer of St. Paul, Minnesota, in 1963. By the 1990s Twister was enjoying a resurgence in popularity as baby-boomer parents purchased the toys of their childhood to share with their offspring. Milton Bradley, since 1984 a subsidiary of Hasbro Inc., was also the maker of such standards as ''The Game of Life'' and ''Candyland.''

Origins of the Game

Twister was invented in 1963 by Reyn Guyer (b. 1936), a writer, inventor, musician, and designer in St. Paul, Minnesota, who also created the best-selling Nerf Ball. According to a 1994 interview, Twister grew out of a promotion Guyer was working on for his father's design company. A member of that design team since the mid-1950s, Guyer was working on a project for a line of shoe polishes, the major prop for which was a large floor mat with multicolored circles. Guyer decided to adapt the floor mat to a game, and Twister was born. The game took over a year and several versions to develop. As Guyer pointed out, it was a team effort of several people. The various versions of the game were presented to Milton Bradley, who chose the one still on the market today.

The objective of Twister was to turn one's body into a ''human pretzel'' by first spinning a wheel and then following the instructions (for example, ''left foot on red'' or ''right hand on blue''), all the while maintaining one's balance. In fact, the game was so closely identified with the twisted shape of a pretzel that its original name was going to be Pretzel. Because of minor copyright problems, that name was rejected.

As Guyer pointed out in his 1994 interview, Twister was a unique addition to the game market because it was the first game to use people as game pieces or players. Guyer stated: ''In order for a game to be as huge a success as Twister was, it has to break a few rules. The first rule this game broke was that all games had to use gaming pieces. Until Twister, game players moved gaming pieces around a board. With Twister, the people *were* the gaming pieces, and they moved around the board themselves. And the second rule the game broke was the 'touching taboo' of the 1960s. In the 1960s, people simply didn't usually touch each other the way they had to while playing Twister.'' When two or more people played Twister, though, they usually became hopelessly entangled, often with amusing results. Because of its ''ice-breaking'' potential, Twister became a mainstay at birthday parties, Sweet-16s, and adult ''mixers.''

First Commercial Success

Milton Bradley scored a major marketing coup for Twister in 1964, when the game was played on the popular late-night television program ''The Tonight Show.'' According to Guyer, Eva Gabor persuaded host Johnny Carson to play a round of Twister with her on camera, and the game's popularity soared. Guyer suggested that it may also have been ''Gabor's 'twisting' in a low-cut gown that helped boost the game's ratings.''

During the first few years of Twister's success, a number of similar games were introduced, both by Milton Bradley and by other toy and game manufacturers, but these met with limited success and were discontinued. Given the game's simple concept and its amusing results, however, there was little room for improvement or innovation, and rival toy manufacturers were not able to come up with a serious challenger to Twister, even in the 30 years after its nationwide introduction.

AT A GLANCE

Twister brand of game created in 1963 by inventor Reyn Guyer of St. Paul, Minnesota; purchased by Milton Bradley Company, the game was introduced to the market in the mid-1960s; Milton Bradley became a subsidiary of Hasbro Inc. in 1984; Twister has been a constant success, first with baby boomers and then with their children.

Advertising: *Agency*—Griffin Bacal, New York, NY, 1984/5—.

Addresses: *Parent company*—Milton Bradley Company, 443 Shaker Road, East Longmeadow, MA 01028; phone: (413) 525-6411; fax: (413) 525-4365. *Ultimate parent company*—Hasbro Inc., 1027 Newport Avenue, P.O. Box 1059, Pawtucket, RI 02862-1089; phone: (401) 725-8697; fax: (401) 727-5544.

Media Attention

Twister has been featured in a number of television shows and movies since its debut on NBC television in 1964. According to inventor Guyer, "We used to keep a scrapbook of Twister appearances. Now it's become so popularly used we no longer do it." Among the feature films in which Twister has appeared are the box-office hit *Ghostbusters* and the 1991 teen comedy *Bill and Ted's Bogus Journey,* in which one of the characters plays the game with the Grim Reaper.

The game also remained popular because of its nostalgia factor. A favorite of baby boomers in the 1960s, Twister was later seen by this same group as a game they could play with their own children. Grandparents, too, were buying toys for their grandchildren, and according to Frank Reysen—editor of *Playthings,* a trade magazine for the toy industry—they were likely to buy the same type of toys for their grandchildren that they bought for their own children. According to Reysen, "This trend is contributing to the strength of basic and traditional toys." Twister, Monopoly, Barbie dolls, and other baby-boom favorites fell squarely into this category.

Milton Bradley's advertising agency, New York City-based Griffin Bacal, still featured Twister in television and print ads, even some 30 years after its introduction. Twister had an international following and a secure place in the pantheon of great American games.

Further Reading:

Fashingbauer, Gael, "Inventor with a Twist," *MPLS. St. Paul,* April 1993, pp. 34–35.

Guyer, Reyn, interview with Marcia Mogelonsky, January 1994.

Milton Bradley Company, fact sheets, 1994.

Waldrop, Judith with Marcia Mogelonsky, *The Seasons of Business: The Marketer's Guide to Consumer Behavior,* Ithaca, New York: American Demographics Books, 1992, pp. 100–102.

—Marcia K. Mogelonsky

VOLKSWAGEN BEETLE®

So-called because of its unusual, buglike shape, the Volkswagen Beetle is by far the best-selling car in history, with more than 21 million units sold since 1938. The car's success can be partially explained by its low price, exceptional durability, and distinctive appearance, as well as the elegant but simple design of its rear-mounted, four-cylinder, "air-cooled" engine. In the United States, where it developed an almost cult following, some five million were sold between 1949 and 1979.

The car has had a variety of different names. In 1938 it was called the Kraft durch Freude Wagen, a German phrase meaning Strength through Joy Car. After World War II it was changed to the Type 1 and then to the Volkswagen ("People's Car"). In English-speaking countries it was popularly known as the Beetle, a name officially adopted in 1971, and the Bug, which was never official. Other names existed in non-English-speaking markets. In Germany, for example, it was called the Käfer ("Beetle"); in Mexico, the Volchito; and in Brazil, the Fusca.

Volkswagen AG, founded by the German government in 1938 to produce the Beetle, long manufactured only automobiles powered by air-cooled engines, including several different sedans (the Squareback, Fastback, 411, and 412), the Karmann Ghia (coupé and convertible), commercial vehicles (a pick-up and panel van), and the Station Wagon (a passenger van also known as the Transporter or Microbus, which came in a camper version). In the 1970s, increasingly strict U.S. safety and emissions standards, as well as new competition from inexpensive, higher-powered Japanese cars, led to the phasing out of Volkswagen's air-cooled vehicles in the United States, where the last Beetle sedan was sold in 1977 and the last convertible Beetle two years later. By 1988 the Beetle was manufactured and sold just in Mexico, though in 1993 Beetle production resumed in Brazil. In all other markets Volkswagen sold only its conventional "water-cooled" automobiles, such as the Golf, Fox, Jetta, and Passat, which were technologically far more advanced than the Beetle.

Brand Origins

The Beetle, developed in Germany during the Depression, owes its existence to two men—Ferdinand Porsche, a world-renowned automobile designer, and Nazi leader Adolf Hitler, who was chancellor of Germany from 1933 to 1945 and a car enthusiast. Both men were inspired by Henry Ford's low-cost Model T (1908-27), which gave middle-class Americans their first opportunity to buy an automobile. Porsche, famous for his designs of luxury and race cars, began working on a small, inexpensive car in the 1920s, but the German automobile industry was reluctant to fund such a project, fearing the country's low-paid workers would not be able to afford even the cheapest possible car.

In 1933 Porsche and Hitler began a series of meetings to discuss the design of a new German race car, but their talks soon shifted to ideas about a cheap, reliable automobile, which Hitler called a *volkswagen,* or "people's car," a term he would use repeatedly in later speeches. Impressed by Porsche's past work and ability to discuss technical matters in layman's terms, Hitler offered him state funding to design the people's car, for which Hitler had already set a number of requirements: a seating capacity of two adults and three children, a cruising speed of 62 mph (miles per hour), a fuel efficiency of 33 mpg (miles per gallon), little need for repair or maintenance, and a motor cooled by air circulating in the engine compartment rather than water from a radiator. This "air-cooled" engine was to avoid coolant freeze-up (or boil over), a particular concern in Germany, where most people did not own a garage. Consistent with Porsche's own ideas, the terms were made much more difficult by Hitler's insistence that the price remain under 1,000 Reichmark ($400).

Despite the problem of cost, Porsche signed a contract with the government on June 22, 1934. Given just ten months to deliver the design, Porsche and his staff based their work on another small, inexpensive car, the Type 32, which they designed in 1933 for the German motorcycle company NSU. This car, which never got beyond the prototype stage, was similar to the Beetle in numerous ways, including the unusual, aerodynamic, sloping shape of its front and back ends. Also similar was the rear-mounted, air-cooled, horizontally opposed, flat-four engine (with four horizontal cylinders, grouped in two opposing pairs). Because the engine was one of the most expensive parts of a car, much effort was directed toward reducing costs there, and not until 1935, after numerous failed engine designs, was Porsche able to introduce the first two prototypes (a sedan and convertible). The following year three new prototypes were sent on a virtual non-stop, day-and-night, 30,000-mile test drive through the Black Forest and along the new German autobahn, or superhighway.

Although by now Porsche's deadline had passed, he still had the support of Hitler, and events were beginning to move rapidly.

AT A GLANCE

Volkswagen Beetle brand of car, originally called Kraft durch Freude Wagen ("Strength through Joy Car"), founded in 1938 by Volkswagenwerk GmbH (a company owned by the German government) and designed by Ferdinand Porsche; its factory, damaged by American bombers during World War II, was run by the British military from 1945 to 1949; in 1961, when 60 percent of its shares was placed on the open market, the company was renamed Volkswagen AG; U.S. sales lasted from 1949 to 1979; sales and production of the car, limited to just Mexico beginning in 1988, resumed in Brazil in 1993.

Performance: *Market share*—23% (first share) of the automobile category in Mexico. *Sales*—(in Mexico) 1.7 trillion pesos ($580 million).

Major competitor: (in Brazil) Chevrolet Chevette; also, Fiat Uno Mille; (in Mexico) Nissan Tsuru.

Addresses: *Parent company (Brazil)*—Autolatina Comercio, Negocios e Participacoes Ltda., Caixa Postal 55111, Granja Julieta, CEP 04719, Sao Paulo, S.P. Brazil; phone: 011-55-11-545-9081; fax: 011-55-11-522-0744. *Parent company (Mexico)*—Volkswagen de Mexico S.A. de C.V., Autopista Mexico Puebla Km 116 Apartado Postal 875, 72008, Puebla, Pue, Mexico; phone: 011-52-22-30-87-36; fax: 011-52-22-48-01-01. *Ultimate parent company*—Volkswagen AG, Postfach 3180 Berlinger Ring 2, Wolfsburg, 1, Germany; phone: 011-49-53-61-92-44-88; fax: 011-49-53-61-92-82-82.

By 1938, 30 improved prototypes, now virtually identical to the Beetle, were sent out on a brutal, 50,000-mile test drive conducted by Nazi storm troopers. In May of that year a great ceremony was held in a rural area of north-central Germany to lay the foundation for a new automobile factory. At the ceremony Hitler gave the car its first official name—Kraft durch Freude Wagen ("Strength through Joy Car"), or KdF-Wagen—and plans were made to construct a company town, which came to be called Stadt des KdF-Wagen ("City of the Strength through Joy Car," in 1945 renamed Wolfsburg after a nearby castle). The only way to buy the car was through a savings program requiring the weekly purchase of a 5-Reichmark stamp. Eventually 336,668 Germans would sign up to buy the car, which, despite its official name, would continue to be called the *volkswagen* by the public.

In September 1938 a new government company, Volkswagenwerk GmbH, was formed to oversee the operations, but one year later the German invasion of neighboring Poland would mark the beginning of World War II and the demise of the car-buying plan. The new factory, opened in 1940 and supervised by Porsche, would be used mainly to produce air-cooled military vehicles, as well as parts for airplanes, stoves, mines, and rockets. Among the vehicles built were the Kübelwagen ("bucket car"), a jeep whose body style was similar to the 1970s Volkswagen "Thing"; the Schwimmwagen ("swimming car"), an amphibious jeep equipped with a propeller; and the Kommandeurwagen, a passenger vehicle having the body a KdF-Wagen and a Kübelwagen chassis. Only 630 civilian KdF-Wagens, all painted blue-gray, were manufactured during the war, and all fell into the possession of Nazi officials. Like other German wartime plants, the factory was staffed mostly by a pool of foreign slave labor, but by early 1945 the factory, severely damaged by American bombers, was nearly out of service. After the war the some 280 million Reichmark ($67 million) paid into the saving program was found in a Berlin bank account and confiscated by the Russian government as war reparations.

The British Period, 1945-1949

With Germany defeated and the factory in ruins, there seemed little possibility that production of the KdF-Wagen would be resumed. Germany itself was divided into four occupation zones, held separately by American, British, French, and Russian troops, and the factory, lying in the British territory, seemed destined to be dismantled as reparations. There was even talk of giving the factory to a foreign automobile firm, but none of those that were approached, including the Ford Motor Company, was interested.

The British, however, had taken an interest in the factory for their own use, and after the war's end they sent a group of engineers there to open a repair shop for military vehicles. A KdF-Wagen was soon brought to the attention of Major Ivan Hirst, the British officer in charge of the factory, who was apparently impressed, as he ordered the production of more. With scarce parts and badly damaged facilities, this was a difficult task, and from June through December 1945 only 58 KdF-Wagens were built, although the factory was also able to put out more than 2,000 Kübelwagens, Kommandeurwagens, vans, and trailers. By this point the KdF-Wagen, later the Beetle, was renamed the Type 1.

By January 1946 some 6,000 people, many refugees from the Russian zone, were working at what was now called the Wolfsburg Motor Works, with about half employed to repair the bombed-out facilities. Production of the Type 1 would amount to 10,020 in 1946 and 8,987 in 1947, but during this period the car was not available to the general public, and most went to the occupation forces. This would change as the occupation began to wind down and as the factory came to be seen as a possible engine for the recovery of the German economy. On January 1, 1948, the British selected Heinz Nordhoff, a former manager at the European car company Adam Opel (owned by General Motors), to head the factory. Nordhoff, a German, would guide the company until 1968, and it was his wisdom and dedication, along with Porsche's brilliant design, that would secure the success of this humble little car.

Postwar Growth and Exports

The British, who had done much to rebuild the factory, officially relinquished control of the facilities in late 1949, and subsequently the new German Federal Republic and the state of Lower Saxony became the joint owners. The company name reverted to Volkswagenwerk GmbH, and by now the official name of the car itself had become Volkswagen. Production was also picking up, with 19,244 cars built in 1948, 46,146 in 1949, and 81,979 in 1950. More than 200 dealerships and 200 repair shops were established in West Germany to handle a home market eager for inexpensive cars. Exports began in 1947, when Dutch car dealer Ben Pon brought five Volkswagens to The Netherlands. Foreign sales helped boost yearly production to 279,986 cars in 1955.

In 1960 the government placed on the open market 60 percent of the company's stock, and the company name was changed to Volkswagen AG. The stock would become a good investment, as yearly sales, eventually reaching some 130 countries, would balloon to 838,488 units in 1963; 1,090,865 in 1965; 1,219,314 in 1969; and the peak of 1,291,612 in 1971. The following year the Beetle would surpass the Ford Model T's total production record of 15,007,033. By this time the car had become a virtual legend, especially for its great durability and practical simplicity. The Volkswagen had few "extras," but what it did have was well designed and well built, and every car was meticulously inspected. Also enticing was the price—as low as $1,280 in 1949, $1,565 in 1960, $1,563 in 1965, and $1,839 in 1970. To meet the growing international demand, Volkswagen would begin building factories in other countries, beginning in 1951 in Ireland and South Africa. By the early 1970s the car was being produced in some 20 countries on five continents.

Design Changes

The early postwar Volkswagens were virtually identical to the 1938 KdF-Wagen, and most were even painted the original blue-gray color. They were also problem-ridden, having, Nordhoff said, "more things wrong . . . than a dog has fleas." Changes were soon made, though, especially as the company looked to export its little car. Most important were steps to improve the longevity of the engine, which had a displacement of 1131 cc (cubic centimeters) and a rating of about 25 hp (horsepower), boosted in 1948 to 30 hp. Top speed was just over 60 mph, with fuel efficiency at roughly 34 mpg. Introduced in 1949 was a deluxe, or export, model, which offered numerous upgraded features, including a variety of paint colors, chrome trim, adjustable front seats, and ivory-colored instrument panels. In 1949 the Willem Karmann company of Osnabrüch, Germany, became the sole supplier of Volkswagen convertible bodies, each hand-built and all with four seats. A two-seat convertible by Josef Hebmüller and Son was discontinued after some 700 vehicles were made.

The famous Volkswagen logo.

Although the Volkswagen would look much the same from year to year—a quality later advertised as an advantage—every part except one (the rubber molding under the front hood) would eventually be modified, though within the constraints of Porsche's basic design. In 1950, for example, the car was fitted with hydraulic brakes, which required less maintenance and were easier to apply than its mechanical ones. In 1952 the transmission was "synchronized," allowing the stick shift to move more easily from one gear to another. The engine itself, made of aluminum and magnesium alloys to reduce weight, would be modified numerous times, often to increase power. In 1954 displacement was enlarged to 1192 cc, with a jump in horsepower to 36; seven years later horsepower was again boosted, this time to 40, and an automatic choke was added. Later increases were to 1285 cc, 50 hp, in 1966; 1493 cc, 53 hp, in 1967; and 1585 cc, 57 hp, in 1970; fuel efficiency, however, had dropped to just 25 mpg by 1970. In 1975 the car gained electronic fuel injection and, in California, a catalytic converter (an emissions-control device).

Of the numerous body and interior changes, one of the most noticeable was in the taillights, made of a plastic cover fitted to a metal housing. Beginning about the size and shape of a small Styrofoam cup, they were considerably enlarged in 1962 and again in 1968, with even larger, all plastic taillights introduced in 1973. Its bumpers—until 1967 with "plumbers handles," or additional chrome loops, in the United States—also greatly increased in size. The oval rear window, originally "split" down the middle into two separate glass plates, became a single piece in 1953 and was enlarged periodically for better visibility. The optional sunroof—from 1950 a nearly full-roof opening fitted with a sliding top of cloth or nylon—was much reduced in size in 1964, when it was given a crank-operated steel cover. Among the many unusual features was a reserve fuel tank, discontinued in 1962, when the first gas gauge was installed.

The Super Beetle, sold in the United States from 1971 to 1974, was an upgraded model, with numerous mechanical and body changes, including a 60-horsepower engine. There also was an 85 percent increase in trunk space, created by the larger, bulbous-shaped front hood and the introduction of MacPherson struts, which, because of their placement, allowed the spare tire to lie in a flat, not slanted, position. In 1973 the Super Beetle's traditional flat windshield was replaced by a larger, curved one.

U.S. Sales and Advertising

After World War II a small number of Volkswagens were shipped to the United States by American servicemen, but the first officially imported Volkswagen arrived in New York on January 17, 1949. Brought by Ben Pon, whose Dutch import business was flourishing, the car did not find a receptive audience. The Volkswagen seemed out of place in a U.S. market dominated by large, powerful automobiles, and the American press helped little by choosing to call it "Hitler's car." Only two were sold in the United States in 1949. The following year Max Hoffman, a New York car dealer, agreed to be the car's official importer for the eastern United States, but he treated it as a sidelight to his other, more expensive imported brands, and by 1953, when his contract was revoked, yearly sales had reached only 1,139.

Sales in the United States, where the car was called the Beetle, would surge only after two developments: the establishment in 1955 of the company's U.S. subsidiary, Volkswagen of America, Inc., and the hiring in 1959 of Doyle Dane Bernbach (DDB) Advertising Agency. Volkswagen of America immediately set out to establish a more coordinated approach to sales and service. Dealers were given strict standards to maintain, and all were required to have clean, attractive, similar-looking showrooms. None could operate without a large parts supply and service capacity. In 1955, partially as a result of these efforts, there was a leap in U.S. sales to 32,662, and by 1959 Volkswagen, with nearly 500 dealerships, sold 96,892 Beetles and even had a long waiting list. In 1959 the Beetle accounted for some 20 percent of all U.S. imports and about 2 percent of the entire U.S. car market. U.S.

manufacturers, beginning to take notice, would introduce their own line of small cars, including the Chevrolet Corvair, which also had a rear-mounted, air-cooled engine.

The Beetle's first U.S. advertising campaign, begun in 1959 by DDB, was a sharp departure from the traditional practice of using idealized drawings and slick, generally meaningless copy. By contrast, the Beetle campaign would come to be known for its realistic photographs; its direct, easy-to-read, factual copy, often with a humorous, self-deprecating slant; and, most of all, a sense of honesty. Even perceived shortcomings of the car, especially its unusual shape, were highlighted in advertisements, one of the most famous having the caption "Ugly is only skin-deep." Among its other famous captions were "Lemon," placed under a photograph of a new Beetle, which an inspector had rejected because "the chrome strip on the glove compartment" was blemished; "Mountain Goat," which bragged about the Beetle's excellent handling in rough terrain; and "They said it couldn't be done. It couldn't," commenting on the possibility of fitting basketball star Wilt Chamberlain into the front seat of a Beetle. The DDB ads would win numerous awards and likely pushed even higher the rising curve of U.S. Beetle sales, from 127,159 in 1960 to 232,550 in 1963; 318,563 in 1966; and the 1968 peak of 423,008. So popular was the car that it even had its own Hollywood movie, *The Love Bug,* featuring a Beetle named Herbie, which was the largest grossing film in 1969 and followed by three sequels. The subsequent decline in sales—still 371,097 in 1973 but collapsing to 243,664 the following year, 92,037 in 1975, and 27,009 in 1976—had many causes, including new competition from small, higher-powered Japanese cars. New safety and emissions standards were also becoming difficult to meet within the car's now 40-year-old design. Equally significant was the devaluation of the dollar, causing the U.S. price to jump from $1,999 in 1972 to $3,699 in 1977, the last year the Beetle sedan was sold in the United States. The convertible Beetle, with a total production of some 330,000, was last sold in 1979 at a price of $6,800.

Brand Outlook

The Beetle was phased out in most world markets as the company's production was shifted to a new line of front-engine, water-cooled cars, the most popular being the Golf, until 1984 called the Rabbit in the United States. In Germany, where 6.1 million were sold, Beetle production ended in 1978 and sales in 1985.

By 1980 just seven countries were still manufacturing the Beetle, and yearly production stood at 236,177, dropping to 86,189 in 1985. Venezuela finally quit production in 1981, as did the Philippines in 1982, Brazil in 1986, and Peru, Nigeria, and Uruguay in 1987, leaving just Mexico, which made only 19,008 Beetles during the car's 50th anniversary in 1988. This would prove to be a low point, however, as in 1989 a reduced automobile tax in Mexico lowered the car's price to $5,300, and by 1992 Mexican sales had rebounded to some 100,000 units. That year Mexico had the honor of producing the 21 millionth Beetle, and in 1993, spurred by a similar tax reduction, production resumed in Brazil. These 1990s Beetles were not available in the United States, in part because of the difficulty of meeting U.S. safety standards (beginning in 1993 Mexican Beetles did meet emission standards in 49 U.S. states). Even so, the Beetle began to enjoy a U.S. renaissance in popularity, aided by the large number still on the road, especially outside the rust-belt states. A Beetle in superior condition was often able to command twice its original price, and professionally restored Beetles were available in the early 1990s at a cost of some $6,000 to $9,000. Although not interested in reintroducing the car to its major markets, Volkswagen AG was well aware of the Beetle's enduring popularity in the United States and elsewhere, and in 1993 chairman Ferdinand Piëch, grandson of Ferdinand Porsche, announced plans to build a new "people's car" that would be "the most affordable model in the world."

Further Reading:

"The Bugs from Brazil," *The Economist,* August 21, 1993, p. 54.

Fry, Robin, *The VW Beetle,* North Pomfret, Vermont: David & Charles Inc., 1980.

Kamm, Thomas, "Beetles Could Give Power to the People of Brazil Once Again," *Wall Street Journal,* February 1, 1993, p.1.

Kiefer, Francine, "Volkswagen Considers Exporting Its Popular Bug Back Home to Germany," *Christian Science Monitor,* June 9, 1993, p. 6.

Miller, Krystal, "Ancient Egyptians Weren't Only Ones to Worship Beetles," *Wall Street Journal,* December 27, 1991, p. A1.

Nelson, Walter Henry, *Small Wonder: The Amazing Story of the Volkswagen,* Boston: Little, Brown and Company, 1970.

Prew, Clive, *VW Beetle,* New York: Mallard Press, 1990.

Rowsome, Frank, Jr., *Think Small: The Story of Those Volkswagen Ads,* Brattleboro, Vermont: The Stephen Greene Press, 1970.

Turner, Rik, "Beetle Makes Comeback in Brazil," *Advertising Age,* September 13, 1993, p. 22.

Uhlig, Mark A., "Miss the VW Bug? It Lives Beyond the Rio Grande," *New York Times,* October 20, 1990, p. 2.

Watling, John, "Beetle Has Staying Power in Mexico: VW Refines Design for 21st Century," *Automotive News,* March 9, 1992, p. 34.

—Thomas Riggs

VOLKSWAGEN GOLF®

One of the world's best-selling cars, the Volkswagen Golf, marketed in the United States by Volkswagen of America, Inc., became known for its firm, responsive handling, good gas mileage, and the quality of its "German engineering." It was first sold in Europe in 1974 and a year later exported to the United States. So successful was the early Golf that its front-wheel-drive, hatchback design was copied by many competing automakers. In the United States it was called the Rabbit through 1984. A high-performance version, the GTI, was first sold in the early 1980s.

Total production reached 14 million Golfs by 1993, with some 885,000 sold in 1992 alone. In Germany, its home market, the Golf has consistently been the top-selling car, a position it has held across all of Europe beginning in 1983. Even so, the Golf has experienced diminishing fortunes in the United States, where sales fell from a high of 214,835 in 1979 (when it was still called the Rabbit) to a mere 5,300 (plus 4,059 GTIs) in 1992. The introduction in 1993 of a redesigned model, the Golf III, was expected to improve U.S. sales.

Founded in 1938 in Wolfsburg, Germany, Volkswagen A.G. has become a truly international corporation, with sales in some 190 countries. In the mid-1990s the Volkswagen line included the Golf, Jetta, Passat, Corrado, Fox, and Eurovan. The convertible Golf, or Cabriolet, reintroduced in 1994 as the Cabrio, was crafted by Karmann coachworks of Osnabrück, Germany.

Brand Origins

Much of Volkswagen's history was dominated by a small, oddly shaped car called the Volkswagen Beetle. Nothing else seemed quite like it. The curved, sloping body and circular headlights gave it a buglike appearance. The engine, placed in the back of the car and cooled by circulating air, was noisy but extremely reliable. This cheap little car, in fact, was celebrated for its simple, elegant design. Millions of Beetles were sold across the world, in the process forcing even the big three U.S. automakers to produce smaller and more fuel-efficient cars. By the early 1970s, however, the Beetle's design was seen by many as outdated, and a stronger German mark had boosted the price in its most important export market, the United States.

Moves toward making cars with more a conventional, water-cooled engine (i.e., with a radiator) began as early as 1966, when Volkswagen bought the German car company Auto-Union GmbH, producer of Audi. Seven years later, in 1973, the first water-cooled Volkswagen, the Passat, began to be sold in Europe. Its four-cylinder engine was placed in front, and the car was equipped with front-wheel-drive, giving it better traction. It was exported to the United States the following year under the name Dasher. The sporty Scirocco, Volkswagen's second water-cooled car, was introduced in 1974 (in the United States, 1975) to replace the air-cooled Karmann Ghia.

Also introduced in 1974 was the Golf, which derived its name from the German word *Golfstrom* ("gulfstream"). Although Volkswagen claimed the car would complement, not replace, the aging Beetle, it was clear the Golf would be marketed to the same type of car buyers—those seeking inexpensive, practical transportation. The Golf, however, was a technological leap from the Beetle and had both higher gas mileage (Beetle, 26 mpg; Golf, 38) and greater horsepower (Beetle, 48; Golf, 70). Like all of Volkswagen's new water-cooled cars, the Golf was front-wheel drive, and its lift-up rear door and folding back seat provided ample storage space. In the United States Volkswagen's advertising agency, Doyle Dane Bernbach, chose to rename the car the Rabbit, presumably to make the transition away from the Beetle seem more natural.

Production and Model Changes

Early reviews on the Golf were excellent and may have pushed the Beetle out of Volkswagen's major markets more quickly. It became the best-selling car in Germany the year it was introduced, and the Rabbit was an immediate hit even in the United States, where the Beetle had developed near cult status. Worldwide production of the Golf reached one million on October 27, 1976, just 27 months after it was first manufactured.

The early Golfs had either a 50 or 70 horsepower engine (70 in the United States), with a displacement of 1471 cc (cubic centimeters). Drum brakes were placed all around, and the gas was fed by a two-barrel carburetor. Front suspension was handled by MacPherson struts. A four-speed stick was standard, though customers could opt for automatic transmission. Two- and four-door hatchback models were available. Prices in the United States began at $3,330.

Improvements were quickly made. By 1976 front disc brakes became standard, and engine displacement increased to 1588 cc,

AT A GLANCE

Volkswagen Golf brand of automobile introduced in 1974 by Volkswagen A.G. of Wolfsburg, Germany; first sold in the United States in 1975 under the name Rabbit; two major redesigns were introduced in Europe in 1984 and 1992 (in the United States, 1985 and 1993); U.S. name changed to Golf in 1985.

Performance: *Market share*—1.8% (first share) of the world automobile category; 5.85% (first share) of the European automobile category; less than 1% of the U.S. automobile category. *Sales*—885,781 units.

Major competitor: Dodge Colt; also Ford Escort, Geo Prism, Honda Civic, Mazda Protege, Mazda 323, Mercury Tracer, Nissan Sentra, Toyota Corolla, and Toyota Tercel.

Advertising: *Agency*—DDB Needham, Troy, MI. *Major campaign*—"The most loved cars in the world."

Addresses: *Parent company*—Volkswagen of America, Inc., P.O. Box 3951, Troy, MI 48007; phone: 313-362-6000; fax: 313-362-6047. *Ultimate parent company*—Volkswagen A.G., Postfach 3180 Berlinger Ring 2, Wolfsburg, 1, Germany; phone: 011-49-53-61-92-44-88; fax: 011-49-53-61-92-82-82.

with a boost in horsepower to 71. Deluxe and custom models, which included open-up vent windows, were also offered. In 1977 a fuel-injected engine was introduced, as was the diesel Golf, which got 53 mpg on the highway. The five-speed stick became an option in 1979. While Volkswagen was busy modifying the Golf, sales kept moving along, hitting three million in 1979.

The Beetle convertible, built by Karmann coachworks, slipped out of production on January 10, 1980. Replacing it was the Karmann-built Golf (or Rabbit) convertible, which was sold at nearly twice the cost of the hardtop version. The convertible Golf came with an insulated top (making it a year-round car even in cold climates); a glass back window; an integrated roll bar for safety; and numerous extras, including additional instruments on the dash. It was also fitted with a more powerful engine than found in the regular hardtop model.

By the early 1980s sales were beginning to slow down, for the most part because numerous imitators were absorbing the demand. The Plymouth Horizon, Dodge Omni, Mazda GLC, Ford Fiesta, and Chevrolet Chevette were among the many cars that looked similar to the Golf. Volkswagen, which for years had a line of unusual-looking, air-cooled cars, now faced the task of trying to create its own identity. Equally troubling were reports of quality-control problems, resulting, for example, in faulty valve seals, overheating, and clutch burnout. Referring to such problems in the United States, John Slaven, former Volkswagen marketing director, said, "The Beetle was like an eggbeater that never stopped, and the original Rabbits were not as reliable . . . If American Motors had built the Rabbit, no one would have been surprised. But when VW built it, it was like a family member lying to you." Volkswagen responded to the problems, and subsequent Golfs were seen as more reliable. The sporty GTI Rabbit, introduced in the United States in 1983, also did much to regain consumer enthusiasm. The GTI included a 90-horsepower (1.8 liter) engine, a tuned exhaust, upgraded seats, special instruments on the dash, and wider tires.

Volkswagen introduced a completely redesigned Golf, dubbed the Golf II, in 1984 (in the United States, 1985). Some three inches longer and two inches wider, the new Golf was upgraded from a four- to a five-person car. Its engine was stronger (1786 cc, 85 horsepower), and it had self-adjusting valves, which helped extend engine life. The GTI Golf II was available with either a 102-horsepower or a 123-horsepower (16-valve) engine. With the new design, the Rabbit name was dropped in the United States, where the car was subsequently called the Golf. Although the convertible Golf, renamed the Volkswagen Cabriolet, also had the new engine and other improvements, it kept the original dimensions.

Another major redesign of the car would not occur until the early 1990s, but in Europe this seemed to affect sales little, as the Golf remained the Continent's best-selling car. The Golf was also popular in Mexico and South America, where Volkswagen long maintained automobile plants. In 1988 the ten millionth Golf was produced. Even so, sales lagged in the United States. Volkswagen spent $1.54 billion developing the Golf III, introduced in Europe in 1992 (in the United States, 1993). Among the major changes was improved performance. With a new 2.0 liter, 115-horsepower engine (1984 cc), the Golf III zipped from 0 to 60 mph in just 9.5 seconds. Its styling also became more streamlined. Gone was its traditional boxy look, and the front especially became more rounded. Standard equipment included an anti-theft alarm system, and there was an important new emphasis on safety and environmental concerns. Plastic parts on the Golf were stamped with standardized markings, with the aim of making future recycling of the car easier. Polypropylene, an easily recyclable plastic, was chosen for many parts. No ozone-damaging chlorofluorocarbons (CFCs) were used in the air-conditioning, and brake pads and clutch linings were free of asbestos. Toxic heavy metals were even removed from the paint. The new 16-valve GTI had a rating of 134 horsepower, and an unusual six-cylinder Golf (2792 cc, 174 horsepower), jumped from 0 to 60 in about 7.5 seconds with a top speed of 140 mph. Also introduced was a restyled, more streamlined convertible Golf (Cabriolet), which was renamed Cabrio.

In 1975 Volkswagen introduced the Golf in the United States as the Rabbit.

U.S. Sales and Advertising

Led by the Beetle, Volkswagen long held the distinction of producing the best-selling imported car in the United States. At one time half of all foreign cars sold in the United States were

Volkswagens, and in 1970 the company hit its all-time U.S. sales record of 569,696 vehicles. It was then that Japanese automakers, such as Toyota and Datsun (later Nissan), began to flood the U.S. market with their own cheap, reliable cars. Endowed with an inexpensive, well-trained workforce, the Japanese companies would eat away at Volkswagen's lead, and by 1976 Volkswagen's U.S. sales would reach just 201,670 units, far below Toyota's 356,176 cars and Datsun's 269,489.

The Rabbit provided some stability while Beetle sales tumbled. In 1975, its first year on the market, 96,215 Rabbits were sold in the United States, slightly ahead of the 92,037 Beetles. Rabbit sales then ballooned to 112,056 in 1976; 164,706 in 1977; and 214,835 in 1979. In 1978 Volkswagen began producing Rabbits out of an old Chrysler factory in Westmoreland, Pennsylvania, in part to reduce shipping and labor costs (German autoworkers demanded significantly higher wages than their American counterparts). Quality-control problems plagued Volkswagen, however, and low-priced Japanese cars continued to increase their dominance of the import market in the United States. As early as 1976, J. Stuart Perkins, then president of Volkswagen of America, conceded, "We'll never again have the lowest-priced car on the street."

Adjusting to its new position, Volkswagen attempted a number of marketing and advertising ploys for the Rabbit and Golf. In 1976 some five million former Volkswagen owners were sent a letter about the company's new cars, and European vacations were offered to salesmen who sold the most Volkswagens. By the following year the company had adopted the advertising tag line "Volkswagen does it again"—an attempt, it seemed, to connect the Rabbit with the former success of the Beetle, which disappeared from the U.S. market after 1977 (except for the convertible Beetle, which was last sold in 1979). Volkswagen also emphasized its international presence. One television commercial took place in Kyoto, Japan, where a man speaking Japanese praised the Rabbit's spacious interior and high performance. The announcer then said, "That must be why the Rabbit is the best-selling imported car in Japan." What the commercial failed to reveal was that only 12,468 Rabbits were sold in the heavily protected Japanese market. Because Volkswagen was both importing cars from Germany and producing them in Pennsylvania, it chose not to highlight its German roots or the fact that many Rabbits were American built.

By 1979, when Rabbit sales peaked, Volkswagen took its many imitators head on. With a picture of a Rabbit parked in front of five look-alikes (the Dodge Omni, Plymouth Horizon, Mazda GLC, Ford Fiesta, and Chevrolet Chevette), one print ad pointed out that the Rabbit was "the car everybody's trying to copy." At the same time, a television commercial showed a man putting an expensive painting into his Rabbit. Asked why he owned the car, the man said, "Who would own a copy when he could own the original?" Other ads were even more lighthearted, as, for example, one featuring "Rabbit and Costello" (with an actual customer named Costello). An advertisement for the Rabbit diesel tried to entice customers with the claim, "New York to L.A. for $43."

With sales dwindling to 177,140 in 1980 and 162,445 in 1981, Volkswagen's advertisements took a more serious turn. Ads now focused on the car's technology, and the tag line was changed to "Nothing else is a Volkswagen." A television commercial, for example, highlighted a new dash light that showed when to shift for best gas mileage. During the same period, Volkswagen put out a print ad titled "How the Rabbit Works: The Diesel." Volkswagen's German heritage was also emphasized with the hope of bringing to mind such attributes as quality, performance, and handling. Even so, Rabbit sales continued to fall, from 91,166 in 1982 to 68,362 in 1984, and the redesigned Golf, introduced in 1985, had little effect. By 1987 only 35,635 Golfs were sold (as well as 10,255 GTIs), and the Jetta, called "the Golf with a trunk," had become Volkswagen's best-selling car in the United States. Declining U.S. sales led Volkswagen to abandon its Westmoreland plant in 1988. Later advertisements focusing on the German word *fahrvergnügen* ("driving pleasure") brought renewed visibility but no relief. U.S. sales dropped to just 5,300 Golfs (plus 4,059 GTIs) in 1992. That year, however, Volkswagen was able to sell a record 1.4 million Golfs in its other markets, making it the world's best-selling car.

The Golf III, introduced in the United States in 1993, met with positive reviews. The new six-cylinder engine was especially praised, as was the car's environmentally friendly design and safety features. Backing up the Golf was a new ad campaign, "The most loved cars in the world." Reminiscent of early commercials for the Rabbit, the new spots featured an American tourist in Sweden, Italy, and Japan who learned why people in those countries drove the Golf. Bob Giraldi, director of the commercials, explained, "If safety-conscious people like the Swedes, great drivers like the Italians, or incredibly efficient and orderly people like the Japanese make this particular car their largest import, that has to say something to Americans."

Brand Outlook

In the mid-1990s Volkswagen was the world's fourth-largest automobile company, behind only General Motors, Ford, and Toyota. Its cars were sold in some 190 countries, and the Golf, the world's best-selling automobile, had broad appeal outside of the United States. Despite its success, however, the Golf faced major challenges. Throughout the 1990s trade barriers in Europe were expected to fall, a trend likely to help Japanese car makers, which had long been restrained by European import quotas. One of Volkswagen's most important goals was to lower production costs and thus hold down the price of its cars, including the Golf. In 1993 the price of a Golf started at more than $10,000, placing it far from its origin as a cheap, practical car.

Various explanations were given for the Golf's bleak U.S. sales picture. Some blamed misguided advertising, while others emphasized the numerous management changes at Volkswagen of America. With sales so high in other countries, it was hard to place all the blame on the Golf itself, though past American surveys showed it near the bottom in customer satisfaction. All hope was not lost, however. The introduction of the Golf III—as well as the new Karmann-built Golf, or Cabriolet, convertible—gave Volkswagen another opportunity to prove its long-standing reputation for high-quality, durable cars.

Further Reading:

Chappell, Lindsay, "VW Pins Revival on 3 New Models," *Automotive News,* July 20, 1992, p. 16.

Gray, Ralph, "Fall Ads for '79 Rabbits Won't Emphasize U.S. Origin," *Advertising Age,* July 31, 1978, pp. 2, 60.

Gray, "VW Engineers Push for New Jetta, Golf," *Advertising Age,* October 18, 1984, p. 3.

Markus, Frank, "Volkswagen Golf," *Car and Driver,* December 1991, p. 118.

O'Connor, John J., "VW Ad Plan: A Soft, Thrifty Sell," *Advertising Age,* October 17, 1977, pp. 2, 98.

O'Connor, "VW Battles the Rabbit 'Clones,' " *Advertising Age,* October 16, 1978, pp. 2, 119.

O'Connor, "VW: Let's Get Serious," *Advertising Age,* October 12, 1981, pp. 3, 78.

O'Connor, "VW Says Golf Won't Squash Bug, Will Be Companion," *Advertising Age,* July 8, 1974, pp. 1, 64.

Paul, Rik, "'93 Volkswagen Golf: Can Fahrvergnugen Make a Comeback in the U.S.?" *Motor Trend,* January 1992, pp. 74–75.

Pluenneke, John E., "VW's Golf Is Flunking Its Acid Test in the U.S.," *Business Week,* July 15, 1985, pp. 47–48.

"Rabbit Run, Run, Run," *The Economist,* September 27, 1980, p. 96.

Rechtin, Mark, "Golf Gets V-6 Next Spring," *Automotive News,* July 26, 1993, p 31.

Russell, John, "VW Returns to German Heritage," *Advertising Age,* July 5, 1982, pp. 4, 27.

Rusz, Joe, "Volkswagen Golf and Golf VR6," *Road & Track,* December 1991, pp. 92–94.

Sawyers, Arlena, "Weary Dealers Wait for Golf as VW Suffers," *Automotive News,* November 9, 1992, pp. 1, 62.

Serafin, Raymond, "From Beetle to Bedraggled: Behind VW's Stunning U.S. Decline," *Advertising Age,* September 13, 1993, pp. 16–23.

Templeman, John, "VW's New Boss Has the Beetle in His Blood," *Business Week,* April 13, 1992, p. 56.

Templeman, "What Ended VW's American Dream," *Business Week,* December 7, 1987, p. 63.

Templeman, "What's Bugging Volkswagen," *Business Week,* June 13, 1988, p. 45.

Volkswagen: A Brief Illustrated History, Wolfsburg, Germany: Volkswagenwerk AG, September 1981.

"VW's Third Generation Golf," *Automotive Industries,* October 1991, p. 33.

"Will the Rabbit Save the Beetle ?" *Forbes,* April 15, 1975, p. 40.

—Thomas Riggs

VOLVO®

VOLVO

A line of Swedish-made automobiles, Volvo has been widely recognized as a leader in durability and passenger safety. In 1976, for example, the National Highway Traffic Safety Administration, charged with setting U.S. safety standards, chose the Volvo 240 as the benchmark for testing all other passenger vehicles. In 1992 Volvo was the leading make of automobile in Sweden, with about 23 percent of the market, and was popular throughout Scandinavia. With about 68,000 cars sold in the United States, however, Volvo accounted for just under one percent of the U.S. market. Volvo is also a leading make of trucks and buses worldwide. In North America, relatively few Volvo trucks are sold, but the company does own controlling interest in Volvo GM Heavy Truck Corporation, which sells trucks under the White, Autocar, and GMC names.

Brand Origins

In 1924 Scania Vabis, then Sweden's only car manufacturer, stopped producing automobiles to concentrate on trucks. Soon afterward Svenska Kullagerfarbriken (SKF), a diversified industrial company based in Goteborg, Sweden, began exploring the possibility of filling the void left by Scania Vabis in the domestic market. The highly secret project was assigned to Assar Gabrielsson and Gustaf Larson. Gabrielsson, sales manager for SKF, was the financial planner, while Larson, with a degree from the University of Technology in Stockholm, was the design engineer.

By 1926 Larson, as well as a team of young engineers that worked out of his home in Stockholm, had completed the first designs. SKF then formed a subsidiary, which it named Volvo, and authorized the production of 1,000 vehicles. The company name, which means "I roll" in Latin, came from a discontinued line of ball bearings and was already registered to SKF. The first Volvo, known officially as the OV4 and nicknamed the Jakob, left the factory on April 14, 1927. The car was American in both size and design. It was an open, five-seater with wooden-spoked wheels, a four-cylinder engine, and a top speed of 90 k.p.h. (about 55 m.p.h)—although Volvo recommended a cruising speed of 60 k.p.h. The company also produced a closed model, which proved to be more popular in Sweden's climate.

PV444

Volvo, which became an independent company in 1935, began planning during World War II for an affordable "people's car" that would combine American design with European size. The result was the PV444, which was unveiled in Stockholm in September 1944. It was a closed, four-passenger automobile with the smallest engine Volvo had ever designed. It also came with a price tag of SEK 4,800—the same as the first Volvo had cost 17 years earlier. Interest in the PV444 was so great that Volvo took orders for more than 2,300 cars during the exhibit even though no cars were ready for delivery. In fact, a labor strike and a shortage of steel eventually delayed production for almost three years. By then Volvo had taken orders for nearly 10,000 cars. The cost had also risen to 8,000 kronur.

Various models of the PV444 and the similar PV544, introduced in 1958, remained in production until 1965, with nearly half a million sold. The PV444 was equipped with a laminated "safety glass" windshield in 1949 and was the first Volvo to be exported to the United States in 1956. The PV544 (along with the Volvo P120) was the first production car with factory installed 3-point seat belts in 1959. The 3-point self-adjusting seat belt was patented by a Volvo Engineer, Nils Bohlin. In 1950 Volvo began selling a modified PV444 chassis to carmakers who wanted to build vans or lights trucks. The following year Volvo used the same chassis for the Duett—a vehicle designed for work and leisure. The Volvo Duett would evolve into the popular Volvo station wagon.

U.S. Market

Volvo exported its first automobiles to the United States in 1956—to a less than rousing reception. The styling of the PV444 was reminiscent of the 1940s, and only a few hundred cars were sold during the first couple of years. Volvo, however, developed a marketing strategy around the car's durability—the car built tough enough for the rugged Scandinavian weather and road conditions—and developed a loyal following.

The ruggedness engineered into the Volvo meant that it cost more than the stylish American-made cars, but it lasted longer, which made it less expensive in the long run. In 1991 *Forbes* published an article by a reporter for United Press International whose split-grille 1965 Volvo P122S, a car known in Sweden as the Amazon, had rolled up more than 400,000 miles.

Volvo began to update its image in the 1960s with cars like the stylish P1800, which was driven by Roger Moore in the British television show "The Saint." The P1800 was also the official car

AT A GLANCE

Volvo brand of automobile founded in 1927 by Svenska Kullagerfarbriken (SKF), a diversified industrial company based in Goteborg, Sweden; SKF previously used the brand for a line of ball bearings; SKF's Volvo subsidiary became a separate company, AB Volvo, in 1935.

Performance: *Market share*—23% of Sweden's passenger car category; 0.8% of U.S. passenger car category. *Sales*—SEK 44.6 million (1992).

Major competitor: Mercedes (Daimler-Benz), BMW (Bavarian Motor Works), Saab (Saab-Scania).

Advertising: *Agency*—Messner Vetere Berger McNamee Schmetterer, New York, NY, 1991—. *Major campaign*—"Drive Safely," a campaign begun in 1992 that emphasized the brand's well-established reputation for building safe cars.

Addresses: *Parent company*—AB Volvo, S-405 08, Goteborg, Sweden; phone: 011-46-31-59-0000.

at the 24-hour race at Sebring in 1963 and 1964, but it was the Volvo 144, introduced in 1966, that caught on with U.S. car buyers. The Volvo 144 and the luxury model Volvo 164 met all proposed U.S. safety standards for the 1970s even before they were announced. The Volvos had front-seat belts for all passengers, four-wheel disc brakes, split steering columns, and energy-absorbing crumple zones in both the front and rear.

In 1973 Volvo sold more than 60,000 cars in the United States—not much by Detroit standards but a significant number for a small European company with a total output of about 200,000 cars per year. The United States was Volvo's largest market, even ahead of Sweden. The same year Volvo announced plans to build a factory in Chesapeake, Virginia, that would turn out 100,000 cars per year by 1977.

Had Volvo followed through on its plans, it would have become the first foreign car company to manufacture automobiles in the United States. Instead, Volvo's sales began to fall, in part because of quality problems with the Volvo 240 series introduced in 1974. By 1975 U.S. dealers had a backlog of 32,000 cars they were unable to sell because of bad paint jobs, leaky engines, and even doors that refused to open. Ironically, the Volvo 240 received several awards for design and environmental engineering. In 1976 the National Highway Traffic Safety Administration used the Volvo 240 as the benchmark for automobile safety in the United States. Volvo built its factory in Virginia at a cost of more than $100 million but never manufactured a single automobile there. Instead, the plant was used as a warehouse and preparation center for Volvos exported to the United States.

Volvo rebounded in the late 1970s after Pehr Gyllenhammar, then chief executive officer at AB Volvo, improved production quality. He did this by eliminating the traditional mind-deadening assembly line and replacing it with teams of employees who were regarded as craftsmen. Costs went up, but so did sales, and Volvo regained its reputation for quality. Volvo quit making the Volvo 240 in 1993. More than 2.8 million were sold in 19 years.

Gyllenhammar also brought in Dan Werbin to design an automobile that would appeal specifically to American tastes. Werbin, who had spent four years as Volvo's chief engineer in the United States, set about his task with two basic tenets: U.S. buyers saw Volvo as one step above the Volkswagen Beetle, reliable but dull, and there was a growing market for a value-conscious, upscale family car. In 1982 Volvo introduced the Volvo 760, the first of the Werbin-designed 700 series, which would become a favorite family car for young urban professionals, or "Yuppies," in the 1980s.

Volvo sold more than 100,000 cars in the United States in 1985, making it the best-selling European import. U.S. sales, however, fell to about 68,000 in 1992. That year Volvo sold a total of about 283,000 cars.

U.S. Advertising

In 1986 Volvo Cars of North America added one word to an advertising slogan it had used for years. Instead of "a car to believe in," Volvo became "a car company to believe in." Four years later, the image that Volvo had so carefully crafted came crashing down around a deceptive television commercial. In 1990 Volvo's North American advertising agency, Scali, McCabe & Sloves, re-created an actual "monster truck" exhibition in which an oversized, car-smashing pickup truck had rumbled over a lineup of automobiles, crushing all of them except a Volvo 240 station wagon. The commercial was shot in Texas.

Soon after the commercial began airing, the Texas attorney general's office received a tip that the Volvo had been reinforced with steel supports welded to the inside of the roof. An investigation confirmed the allegations and also revealed that the roofs of the other cars had been intentionally weakened to heighten the visual effect. In a blow to Volvo's credibility, the Texas attorney general announced, "Although Volvo repeatedly touts that a 'Volvo is a car you can believe in,' the same cannot be said of its advertising. The . . . representation is false, misleading and deceptive, and the car-crushing competition was a hoax and a sham."

Volvo immediately killed the television commercial and magazine ads based on the demonstration. From Sweden, Volvo Chairman Pehr Gyllenhammar called the doctored ads "an offense against our company and what we represent, and an insult to all Volvo owners." Although Volvo Cars of North America and the advertising firm both denied knowing that the commercial was rigged, the agency accepted "ultimate responsibility" and resigned the account. Scali, McCabe & Sloves had been Volvo's advertising agency in the United States for 23 years. Blame for the incident was eventually laid at the feet of a film crew that had hired a local welder to do the work. The welder told *Advertising Age* that he was told "to do whatever it took to make a Volvo hold up."

Volvo and the advertising agency each paid $150,000 in fines levied by the Federal Trade Commission (FTC) for deceptive advertising. Volvo also paid more than $300,000 in investigative costs to the Texas attorney general's office. The FTC then took a look at four other Volvo commercials—including an ad in which a heavy truck was balanced on the roof of a Volvo. The investigation revealed that jacks were used to keep the tires from exploding, but there was no structural reinforcement of the Volvo itself.

Volvo continued to stress the structural soundness of its automobiles in its advertising, but it carefully documented all claims. The advertising agency Messner Vetere Berger McNamee Schmetterer created the first post-monster truck commercial for Volvo Cars of North America, which illustrated how the passenger compartment of a Volvo 960 sedan survived a head-on crash into a brick wall. The entire production from setup to cleanup was saved on videotape. The advertising agency also created Volvo's first "infomercial," a 30-minute program shown on cable television stations that went into detail about Volvo's claims about safety and durability.

In 1992 Volvo Cars of North America adopted its first new advertising tag line in 20 years: "Drive Safely." Volvo said the slogan grew from the "realization that Volvo is safety. We are expressing the concept of driving the car." Volvo launched a series of commercials featuring testimonials from people who survived traffic accidents involving Volvos. One controversial commercial compared the damage from similar accidents to a Volvo station wagon and a minivan. Chrysler Corporation, makers of the best-selling minivan in the United States, asked Volvo to pull the ad, which it refused to do.

Volvo 850 GLT

In 1991 Volvo unveiled the 850 GLT, a sports sedan that the company hoped would broaden its appeal with younger and older drivers—those without children. The Volvo 850 still sported a boxy look, although the lines were softened, and came with advanced safety features, such as side-impact protection. Its overall size, however, was smaller than previous sedans, and the handling was more responsive. The *New York Times* reported, "Volvo has wrapped its big news in the same square lines that have typified the Swedish maker's body armor for the past quarter-century, although the suit and its underpinnings represent a billion-dollar development program aimed at creating a sedan with a difference."

Volvo promoted the 850 GLT as a fun car to drive but found it difficult to overcome its own carefully crafted family-car reputation. Robert Austin, then communications director for Volvo Cars of North America, told *Automotive News,* "For the past decade or so, our cars have been nicer to drive and capable of more performance than our image allowed. Driving one [said] 'Married, With Two Kids.' People have even asked us if the kids came with the car in case you didn't have them."

To overcome the safe-but-dull image, Volvo's North American advertising agency, Messner Vetere Berger McNamee Schmetterer, created a series of offbeat commercials. Ron Berger, a partner in the ad agency, explained, "It's very rare that the very thing people think of as a positive becomes something of a barrier. The only way to cut through the strong impression was to attack the image head-on, though tongue in cheek." One commercial opened with a couple driving a tank. An unseen announcer intoned, "Driving a Volvo usually inspires a certain sense of safety." Another commercial showed a box on wheels. The announcer said, "If this is how you think of Volvo, we may have the car to change your thinking."

The Volvo 850 was the first Volvo available in the United States with front-wheel-drive. The Volvo 480ES, a compact built by DAF, a Dutch subsidiary of AB Volvo, had front-wheel-drive, but the car was too expensive to compete in the American market.

Midway through 1992, Volvo introduced the 850 GLE, a more family-oriented version of the Volvo 850 GLT. In 1993 Volvo added the 850 Estate, then the latest in the company's long line of station wagons. An even higher performance turbo version of the 850 was also added as a 1994 model.

Environmental Concept Car

In 1992 Volvo stunned the automobile industry by unveiling a sleek, experimental four-door sedan that it call the Environmental Concept Car, or ECC for short. The ECC, developed at Volvo's Monitoring and Concept Center in Camarillo, California, was powered by a hybrid electric/gas turbine engine. When running on batteries alone, the ECC had a range of about 50 miles and could qualify as a Zero Emission Vehicle under California's strict environmental pollution regulations. With the diesel-fueled gas turbine engine running to recharge, the ECC was classified as an Ultra Low Emission Vehicle—the most pollution-free class for a combustion engine.

The ECC was also designed to be environmentally friendly when it came time to recycle the car. The body was made of aluminum, which could be melted down and used again. All the plastic parts inside the car were designed for easy removal so they, too, could be recycled. Volvo said the ECC could be in production early in the 21st century.

Further Reading:

Berss, Marcia, "The Master Builder," *Forbes,* November 19, 1984, p. 242.

Feast, Richard, "Volvo Steals the Show," *Automotive Industries,* December 1992, p. 35.

Goldman, Kevin, "Volvo Seeks to Soft-Pedal Safety Image," *Wall Street Journal,* March 16, 1993, p. B7.

Gross, Ken, "Sticking with Safety," *Automotive Industries,* March 1992, p. 13.

Henry, Jim, "Volvo Stained by Monster Truck Ad Flap," *Automotive News,* November 12, 1990, p. 1.

Henry, Jim, "Volvo's Fortunes Ride on New 850," *Automotive News,* August 31, 1992, p. 8.

Holusha, John, "At First, the Volvo Wasn't So Popular," *New York Times,* June 23, 1987, p. D5.

"The Immigrants," *Time,* September 24, 1973, p. 112.

Johnson, Richard, "Volvo Aims Its New 800 Series at Mercedes and BMW," *Automotive News,* June 24, 1991, p. 20.

Lohr, Steve, "Volvo Broadens a Sports Marketing Strategy," *New York Times,* September 5, 1988, p. 30.

Magaziner, Ira and Mark Patinkin, *The Silent War,* New York: Random House, 1988.

Moore, Stephen D., "Marriage of Renault, Volvo Isn't All Bliss," *Wall Street Journal,* September 10, 1993, p. B2A.

Mullins, Peter J., "Extra! Extra! Volvo Discovers Front Wheel Drive!" *Automotive Industries,* June 1986, p. 92.

Riding, Alan, "Renault-Volvo Marriage Is On, " *New York Times*, September 7, 1993, p. D1.

Sawyers, Arlena, "Volvo Adopts 'Drive Safely' Tagline," *Automotive News,* October 7, 1991, p. 8.

Sawyers, Arlena, " 'Infomercial' Is Vehicle for Safety Pitch," *Automotive News,* October 7, 1991, p. 8.

Serafin, Raymond, "No More 'Monsters': Volvo Carefully Documents New Advertising," *Advertising Age,* September 23, 1991, p. 1.

Serafin, Raymond and Jennifer Lawrence, "Volvo Parent Seizes Control of Inquiry," *Advertising Age,* November 19, 1990, p. 1.

Schuon, Marshall, "Volvo Aims (Gasp!) at Sports Fans," *New York Times,* March 7, 1993, p. S12.

"A Tough Swede," *Forbes,* June 15, 1971, p. 35.

Volvo Annual Report 1992, Goteborg, Sweden: AB Volvo, 1993.

"Volvo 1927–1993," Goteborg, Sweden: Volvo Car Corporation, 1993.

"Volvo Lowers Its Aim in the U.S. Market," *Business Week,* Sept. 13, 1976, p. 35.

Waterman, Frederick, "The 440,000-Mile Car," *Forbes,* November 25, 1991, p. F120.

Wylie, Kenneth, "Volvo Selling the Company behind the Car," *Advertising Age,* June 16, 1986, p. S-28.

—Dean Boyer

WATERFORD®

WATERFORD CRYSTAL

Waterford brand lead crystal built its reputation for high quality products on a tradition of labor-intensive production processes. The Waterford brand includes stemware, giftware, lamps and lighting fixtures, as well as limited edition master cutter pieces and a small number of eighteenth-century Waterford crystal museum piece reproductions. Waterford Wedgwood PLC is the largest producer of premium lead crystal in the world. Though the Irish company's financial difficulties in the 1980s caused it to lose its leading market position in the United States, its prospects for growth and profit were brighter for the 1990s because of effective cost cutting plans, concentration on markets other than the United States, transfer of some production to other countries, and the profitability of its lower-cost Marquis brand of Waterford crystal. In fact, by 1993 the company had regained its market leadership and posted its first profit in six years.

Reviving a Waterford Tradition

Irishmen Joseph McGrath and Joseph Griffin, founders of the Waterford Glass Co. Ltd., drew inspiration for their company from an older tradition of fine crystal making in Waterford, Ireland. Over one hundred years prior to the 1947 establishment of the Waterford Glass Co. Ltd., George and William Penrose had opened a glasshouse in the town, and the company became famous for deep-cut, geometric designs. The Penroses were forced to close their business in 1851, however, when high British export taxes made it unprofitable. To revive the Penroses' glassblowing tradition, McGrath and Griffin employed Czech craftsmen to imitate their designs. The site chosen for the business was located less than two miles from the original Penrose Waterford Glass House, and the Waterford Glass Co. pledged to maintain the "same dedication to purity of colour, . . . design inspiration, and to the . . . pursuit of the highest quality levels possible." The company's chief designer, Miroslav Havel, researched the old designs and consulted The National Museum of Ireland to make sure the new products' designs followed the established Waterford crystal tradition.

McGrath and Griffin realized that in the postwar era, the United States, rather than the European continent, would be their largest market. Thus Waterford made larger glasses to suit American tastes instead of shipping small European-style sherry glasses. "We didn't know if it was that Americans used ice or just had bigger mouths," a Waterford executive commented in *Forbes.* Waterford's reputation grew quickly, and by the late 1960s it held the largest share of the fine glassware market.

Waterford had built most of its reputation in the United States by the 1980s, but it wished into expand to other markets. To this end, in 1986 Waterford purchased Wedgwood PLC, an English fine china company, and the two firms merged. Although many analysts felt the merger was beneficial to both companies because each could exploit the markets already open to the other, the company divided operations in 1991. Explaining the reason for the split, Waterford Wedgwood USA executive Chris McGillivary pointed out in *HFD* that "specific attention was lost," impeding the brands' ability to grow independently and reach their full potential. Still jointly owned, the companies operated under different boards, with different staff, separate funding, and separate distribution and marketing arms. Only the lighting division remained consolidated, supervised by Waterford because over 90 percent of the companies' combined lighting sales were of Waterford fixtures. Former Wedgwood USA executive Joseph Sardella, Jr., told the Newark, New Jersey *Star-Ledger* that the separation allowed both Waterford and Wedgwood to "have clear identities." Operating alone seemed to pull Waterford out of a sales slump; by the first half of 1993, Waterford reported an 11 percent increase in sales in the United States, according to *Reuter Business Report.* In late 1993, however, the two U.S. subsidiaries became divisions of Waterford Wedgwood USA, Inc.—although separate sales and marketing activities were maintained—under McGillivary, who had become CEO.

Advertising an Exclusive Item

Waterford built its reputation for quality by advertising in upscale magazines like *Gourmet* and the *New Yorker* and limiting distribution to high-end department stores. Most early ads "showed pretty pictures of crystal pieces but were not very informative," according to *Business Week.* Advertisements employed in 1974 added to the air of exclusivity by promoting Waterford crystal as a good investment vehicle. The ads showed a piece of crystal being cut by a craftsman, with copy that read "Now's the time to invest in signed originals by Waterford. There's no more propitious time for you to invest in Waterford. Each piece is a signed work of art, made by hand with heart, as it was two hundred years ago."

AT A GLANCE

Waterford brand of lead crystal introduced in 1947 by Joseph McGrath and Joseph Griffin, founders of Waterford Crystal Co., Ltd., as a revival of an eighteenth-century Waterford, Ireland, crystal-making tradition; in 1986 Waterford purchased Wedgwood PLC, a ceramics and fine china company located in England and formed Waterford Wedgwood PLC; a lower-priced Marquis brand of crystal introduced in 1991 to expand sales.

Performance: *Market share*—33% (top share) of the U.S. premium crystal market ($15 and up); 80% of the higher end of the luxury crystal market ($50 and up). *Sales*—$350 million (all markets).

Major competitor: Baccarat; also the Lenox and Gorham divisions of Brown-Forman Corporation.

Advertising: *Agency*—Altschiller Reitzfeld, New York, NY, 1992—. *Major campaign*—"Worthy of the moment for over two centuries."

Addresses: *Parent company*—Waterford Wedgwood USA, Inc., P.O. Box 1454, Wall, NJ 07719; phone: (908) 919-2112; fax: (908) 938-7768. *Ultimate parent company*—Waterford Wedgwood PLC, Kilbarry, Waterford, Ireland; phone: (51) 73311; fax: (51) 78539.

Demand for the crystal had risen so sharply by 1978 that Waterford cut back on advertising and did not open any new retail accounts for 12 months because it could not increase production enough to meet demand. Nevertheless, Waterford's advertising drew attention—*Advertising Age*'s William D. Tyler named Waterford's ads the best of 1978. That year Waterford asked consumers to send in essays they had written about Waterford crystal. Some of the 50,000 essays received were then used in the company's advertisements. Because many of the entries were in rhyme, the ad's copy posed the question, ''Are Waterford People Poets at Heart?''

From 1972 to 1982, Waterford crystal virtually sold itself. Waterford changed little in its advertising, introduced no new patterns, and expended little energy on its 1,500 U.S. retail accounts, according to *Business Week.* While the fine lead crystal market tripled from 1979 to 1983, however, Waterford's sales increased a mere 20 percent and its share of the stemware category dropped by 5 percent to 25 percent. To recapture its market share, Waterford introduced four new stem patterns, scheduled regular introductions of new patterns, and hired a new ad agency, Ammirati & Puris Inc. of New York, in 1984. In 1989 the company's advertising slogan was ''Steadfast in a world of wavering standards.''

In an effort to make the brand accessible to more people, yet maintain its quality image, Waterford launched a new advertising campaign in 1992. The campaign depicted situations in which the crystal was being used, focusing on the way some moments were made more special with Waterford. The estimated three to four million dollar campaign, created by Altschiller Reitzfeld, employed the slogan ''Worthy of the moment for over two centuries.'' One of the first ads of the campaign pictured a woman and two men enjoying champagne in their Waterford flutes, with the headline ''Officially there are 12 holidays in any given year. Unofficially there is no count.'' A 1993 ad pictured a man showing his child two Waterford candlestick holders with the headline ''If time never stands still, why are there moments that seem to?'' Another 1993 ad showed a woman coyly holding a goblet to her cheek, accompanied by the headline ''Once in a lifetime moments don't just happen once in a lifetime.'' While research indicated the campaign achieved its goals, advertising executive Jonathan Harries noted in *Creativity* that Waterford ads run prior to 1992 were ''as much works of art as the crystal itself.''

Making Craftsmanship Pay

Waterford glass contains the greatest quantity of lead for highest grade crystal, 34 percent. While classic Waterford is completely handmade in Ireland by small production teams of four glassblowers and six cutters, some production of giftware and the lower-priced Marquis line of crystal was contracted out in 1990 to other European companies that sometimes employed machines in the manufacturing process. The teams of craftsmen are paid on a piece-rate basis, so groups agree on a rate of production and work together to meet their goal. ''The rhythm a team establishes is very important,'' stem-maker Gerry Sullivan stated in *International Management.* The teams work hard to achieve high rate of production in order to increase their pay, and working with the same people over long periods of time maximizes efficiency. Therefore, 90 percent of the teams stay intact. ''We have a blower and stem-maker who haven't spoken to each other for 12 years, but you try to separate them, and they will tear your eyes out,'' production manager Colm O'Connell asserted in *International Management.* The entire production process is supervised by former master cutters and blowers, and quality is of such importance, the article went on to point out, that ''four out of every ten glasses produced by the blowers end up being smashed and recycled.''

Waterford employees' skill is expensive. They were the highest paid workers in Ireland in 1987, earning 75 percent more than the Irish industrial average, according to *Accountancy.* Waterford's employees negotiated a lucrative pay scale in 1985, which made their salaries account for 80 percent of the price of their product by 1988. Under the deal, as reported in the *Economist,* wages increased at three times the rate of inflation. When coupled with the drastic devaluation of the U.S. dollar (the currency used to purchase roughly 70 percent of Waterford's output) at that time, the company was becoming unprofitable.

Increasing its prices was not an option for Waterford because consumers were becoming more cost conscious. According to *Business Week,* crystal sales dropped by 11 percent in 1986 and 19 percent in 1987. Moreover, Waterford crystal was already at the top of the premium crystal price scale. ''Consumers are prepared to pay a premium on Waterford, but not a premium on a premium,'' Waterford executive Redmond O'Donoghue commented in *International Management.*

To combat Waterford's high overhead in a shrinking marketplace, the company initiated a cost reduction plan that reduced the workforce of 3,000 by about 750 workers, initiated a new pay schedule, and incorporated diamond cutting wheels and new furnaces to speed production. By 1989, as Waterford executive Patrick Hayes stated in the Baltimore, Maryland *Sun,* ''a production rate equal to 100 percent of the normal, historic rate'' was being achieved due to a work force reduction of 30 percent, coupled with a 20 percent annual cost reduction. Subsequent production efficiencies allowed the work force to be further reduced to 1,400 in 1993. Waterford cut more costs in the 1990s by moving some production to other European countries, where labor costs were ten percent less than those in Ireland. It began marketing German machine-made giftware in 1990, and contracted with companies in Germany, Portugal, and Slovenia in 1991 to produce its lower-priced Marquis brand.

Maintaining Prestige in a Mass Market

In 1978, when demand for Waterford crystal grew faster than supplies could be made available, Waterford decided to expand its market appeal by increasing its capacity for making crystal lamps and lighting fixtures. Throughout the 1960s, lighting products made up only one percent of Waterford's business. But after a limited 1977 advertising campaign sparked consumer interest, Waterford executive Noel Griffin told *Business Week* that "demand [for our lamps] is huge—more than twice what we can supply." Hoping to make lamp production 15 percent of its output, the company embarked on an expansion plan that would increase its total production by 50 percent by 1980. Advertising and distribution plans for the lampmaking business mirrored those used for the crystal. By 1991 the Waterford lighting business included Wedgwood lighting products and consisted of a 32-person sales force. Waterford lighting products sold best in department stores' lighting departments and specialty lighting showrooms, but not as well in furniture, gift, jewelry, or tabletop stores.

Despite the company's historic reliance on the Waterford name to sell its products, the company initiated a new marketing strategy to increase its market share in the 1990s. Adapting itself to consumer tastes, Waterford introduced the lower-priced Marquis brand stemware collection in 1991. The Marquis brand was guided by extensive consumer research, which aided the company in designing patterns and shapes to correspond to the tastes of 90 percent of the premium crystal buyers. The company described Marquis as a "point of entry into the Waterford Crystal lifestyle." Produced in Germany and Slovenia, the Marquis brand was priced between $29.00 and $39.50 per stem, significantly below the stem price of classic Waterford.

Advertising for the Marquis brand catered mostly to the mainstream bridal market. An introductory Marquis advertisement read, "On the occasion of your marriage, Waterford Crystal wishes to make a birth announcement. Introducing Marquis by Waterford Crystal." The ad ran in magazines that catered to young women, including *Vogue, Glamour,* and *Modern Bride.* Marquis brand 1993 ads featured copy typed over a picture of a vase or a glass with the slogan, "Circa now," in contrast to the emphasis on tradition utilized in Waterford advertisements.

The gross margins from sales of the Marquis brand were twice those of the Waterford Crystal line by 1993, and the new brand's sales ranked it fifth in its category. Although the Marquis brand had become very successful, Waterford did not abandon its Waterford line. During the Marquis introduction, Waterford's first gold-banded stemware and 21 giftware items were marketed. In 1992 Waterford held 28 percent of the premium crystal market in the $15 plus segment and 80 percent of the segment starting at $50, according to the *Wall Street Journal.* Figures for the 1993 premium market reached 33 percent (including Marquis).

A Profitable Future

Although Waterford remained dependent on the U.S. market for the majority of its sales in the early 1990s (during this time Waterford exported about 85 percent of its production, 70 percent of which was sold in the United States), plans for sales expansion were focused elsewhere. However, according to *International Management*'s Frederick Studemann, Waterford's plans will not include Europe because many European countries already have well-developed crystal manufacturing, and "Waterford's intricate styles go down poorly with many continental consumers." Instead, the company will focus on the markets of Japan and the United Kingdom, where it can take advantage of the avenues already opened by Wedgwood.

Further Reading:

Arbose, Jules, "Waterford's Contented Craftsmen," *International Management,* November 1976, pp. 36–38.

"Better Times for Waterford Crystal Seen: Waterford Wedgwood Unit Likely to Post '92 Profit after Major Cost Cuts," *Wall Street Journal,* January 24, 1992.

"The Cost of a Craft," *Economist* (Survey), January 16, 1988, p. 20.

"Crystal Clear," *Forbes,* October 15, 1974, p. 81.

Harries, Jonathan, "Waterford Glass: Launches Print Ad for Its Crystal," *Creativity,* November 2, 1992, p. 26C.

Kelly, Matthew, "Preservation Order for a Proud Tradition," *Accountancy,* October 1987, pp. 12–13.

Lappen, Alyssa A., "Table for Two," *Forbes,* December 28, 1987, p. 8.

Maremont, Mark, "Waterford Is Showing a Few Cracks," *Business Week,* February 20, 1989, pp. 61, 65.

Maremont, Mark, and Mark Landler, "Has Waterford Set Loose a Bull in Its Shop?" *Business Week,* November 5, 1990, p. 58.

McQuaid, E. Patrick, "New Leaders Take Over at Ailing Irish Glass Company," *Sun* (Baltimore, MD), April 11, 1989.

Neiss, Doug, "Waterford Wedgwood Divides: Parent Separates Brands to Allow Each to Take Own Direction for Growth," *HFD,* January 2, 1991, p. 124.

O'Connor, Robert, "Waterford's Future in Glassware Now Appears to Be 'Very Delicate,' " *San Diego Union,* May 14, 1989.

Osborne, Judith A., "Breaking Up Tableware Set," *Star-Ledger* (Newark, NJ), July 7, 1991.

Studemann, Frederick, "Mixed Fortunes at Waterford Crystal," *International Management,* May 1993, p. 34.

Tyler, William D., "Tyler Picks the Best of Print Ad Campaigns for '78," *Advertising Age,* December 25, 1978, p. 15.

"Waterford Glass: Reemphasizing Elegance after Diversification," *Business Week,* October 9, 1978, pp. 75–78.

"Waterford's New Chairman Wants Yugoslav Profits from Irish Glass," *Irish Times,* June 22, 1991, p. 13.

"Waterford Wedgwood Back in the Black," *Reuter Business Report,* September 1, 1993.

"What's in an Address," *Economist,* April 14, 1990, p. 72.

Wilson, Andrew, and Amy Dunkin, "Waterford Learns Its Lesson: Snob Appeal Isn't Enough," *Business Week,* December 24, 1984.

Additional information provided by Waterford Wedgwood USA, Inc. of Wall, New Jersey.

—Sara Pendergast

WEDGWOOD®

WEDGWOOD®

Wedgwood ceramics have maintained a prestigious position in international tableware and ornamental ware markets for over 235 years based especially on the English brand's two best known varieties, Queen's Ware, which debuted in 1762, and Jasper ware, introduced in 1773. In 1986 Wedgwood was purchased by Waterford Crystal Ltd.., and their operations were merged with the crystal company's under the name Waterford Wedgwood PLC. After many years of trying to expand sales in the United States, Wedgwood hoped to capitalize on Waterford's established U.S. markets. The early 1990s brought hope for further expansion of the Wedgwood brand as the world recovered from recession and Waterford Wedgwood PLC finished streamlining its operations.

By the 1990s the Wedgwood brand name graced tableware, ornamental ware, and fine bone china. Demand for the brand has made the company one of the largest contributors to the British economy; by the late 1980s it produced as much as one-quarter of the British ceramic tableware industry's output and one-quarter of the industry's exports. Wedgwood's longevity makes Hudson Moore's tribute in *The Old China Book,* as quoted by Elizabeth Baroody in *Antiques & Collecting,* ring true: "In England, there is one name which expresses the greatest heights which English pottery ever reached, and that is, Wedgwood."

Brand Origins

The success of the Wedgwood brand can be traced to Josiah Wedgwood, thirteenth child of a fifth-generation English potter. Wedgwood served his apprenticeship in the family pottery business, initially as a thrower until a bout of small pox damaged his leg and prompted him to begin experimenting with clays and glazes. At the end of his apprenticeship in 1754, Wedgwood became a partner of the well-known English potter Thomas Whieldon, then founded his own pottery business in 1759.

Beginning with his invention of a brilliant green glaze, formula No. 7, Wedgwood produced popular rococo design pottery, such as pitchers in the shape of cauliflowers and pineapples. The majority of Wedgwood's early products were "useful" ware, pottery made for a wide variety of everyday uses. His catalog included egg baskets "to keep boiled Eggs hot in water," strawberry bowls, asparagus pans, jelly molds, and a complete line of dairy equipment, including vases in which cream would ripen for butter making, among other things. However, in 1762 Wedgwood developed the pottery that would establish his reputation—Queen's Ware, the cream-colored earthenware thus named by consent of England's Queen Charlotte.

In 1766 Wedgwood purchased an estate, where he began building a factory. Etruria, as he had named the factory, was completed in 1769, the same year Wedgwood entered into a partnership with his friend Thomas Bentley, a knowledgeable and influential man who had a profound effect on Wedgwood and the success of the business. The partnership ended, however, with Bentley's death in 1780.

The Queen's China

Wedgwood set himself apart from his peers by creating pottery that had "elegance of form," according to *The Story of Wedgwood* author Allison Kelly, who noted that in 1765 a friend of Wedgwood's overheard Lord Gower discuss Wedgwood's pieces, saying "that nothing of the sort could exceed them for a fine glaze." Wedgwood's attention to quality and detail earned his pottery the right to grace royal tables, which in turn established its prestigious image. Queen Charlotte first patronized the company in 1765, and Russian Empress Catherine the Great ordered a service for two dozen in 1770, an order that required 1,244 free-hand paintings of English scenes for the set of 952 pieces.

Not just confined to use by royalty, according to Kelly, Josiah Wedgwood noted in 1767 that "it is really amazing how rapidly the use of [Queen's Ware] has spread over the whole globe, and how universally it is liked." The introduction of Queen's Ware met with great success because the company could produce pottery for every level of consumer spending. He described it as "a species of earthenware for the table, quite new in appearance, covered with a rich and brilliant glaze, bearing sudden alterations of heat and cold, manufactured with ease and expedition, and consequently cheap." The appeal of Queen's Ware spanned continents and centuries; some of the original eighteenth-century Queen's Ware designs, including Plain Traditional, Catherine, Queen's, and Shell Edge, were still being produced in the twentieth century.

By this time Wedgwood was also making "ornamental" ware, including vases, candlesticks, busts, medallions, seals, and small intaglios. Much of the ornamental ware was made from a substance he called Black Basalt, a ceramic colored with water drained from coal mines, which was invented to improve upon

AT A GLANCE

Wedgwood brand of ceramics introduced in 1759 by Josiah Wedgwood in Stoke-on-Trent, Staffordshire, England; developed Queen's Ware, 1762; introduced Jasper ware, 1773; in 1769 Wedgwood became partners with Thomas Bentley and company name was changed to Wedgwood & Bentley; name changed to Wedgwood in 1780, after Bentley's death; name changed to Wedgwood, Sons & Byerley, 1790; name changed to Wedgwood & Son & Byerley, 1793; name changed to Josiah Wedgwood & Sons, 1827; firm changed from a partnership to a limited liability company, Josiah Wedgwood & Sons Ltd., 1895; firm acquired by Waterford Crystal Ltd. in 1986 and formed Waterford Wedgwood PLC.

Major competitor: Royal Doulton; also Royal Worcester.

Advertising: *Agency*—Altschiller Reitzfeld, New York, NY, 1994—. *Major campaign*—"The Great China of Britain."

Addresses: *Parent company*—Waterford Wedgwood USA, Inc., P.O. Box 1454, 1330 Campus Parkway Dr., Wall, NJ 07719-1454; phone: (908) 938-5800; fax: (908) 938-6915; *Ultimate parent company*—Waterford Wedgwood PLC, Kilbarry, Waterford, Ireland; phone: (51) 73311; fax: (51) 78539.

other potters' use of "Egyptian Black" pottery. Although Wedgwood asserted, according to Kelly, that Black Basalt was "sterling and [would] last forever," soon most of the ornamental ware was being crafted from Wedgwood's most prized ceramic—Jasper ware. First produced in 1773, the unglazed vitreous stoneware absorbed color well and was used as a background for white classical reliefs.

Jasper ware became such a distinctive symbol of the Wedgwood brand that *Management Today*'s Geoffrey Whiteley noted in 1983 that "many customers think the company makes nothing else, though it now forms a 'small percentage' of total products." By this time, however, Jasper ware had dropped in popularity in Europe, although it remained a strong seller in North America, Australia, and Britain. Whiteley believed a possible reason for Jasper ware's loss of appeal was the maintenance of its traditional design, one that had not been updated and given a "twentieth-century look." Nevertheless, modern and antique Jasper pieces are considered prized collectibles.

Although Wedgwood faced some economic difficulties during the 1800s, the company not only overcame them, it made progress as well. This period saw advancements in technology and the introduction of bone china. Sales of the china account for most of Wedgwood's export trade.

With Queen's Ware and Jasper ware production as the backbone of the brand, Wedgwood also produced such specialty pieces as pitchers or plates to commemorate historic events. Such pieces include medallions of George Washington during the Revolutionary War and a copy of the Portland Vase—which was originally made for the Barberini family of Italy and later purchased by the Duchess of Portland—that was used to piece together the original when it was smashed by a drunk in 1845. A particularly rare historic piece commemorates a coronation that never took place. It is the plaque designed in 1937 to honor the coronation of Edward VII, who chose to marry the woman he loved rather than ascend to the throne of England.

Managed Quality

In the 1930s, during the Great Depression that saw many other potteries close down, the fifth generation Josiah Wedgwood decided to invest in the company's future. The factory at Etruria, though ahead of its time when first constructed, was becoming obsolete, so property near the town of Barlaston was purchased in order to build a new plant. Construction, begun in 1940, was completed in 1950, just in time for the post-World War II industrial boom and put Wedgwood far ahead of its competitors, who had been damaged by the war. Production at Etruria came to halt not long after it started at Barlaston, the company's showplace. The factory complex has continued its tradition of keeping ahead of the competition by installing the most up-to-date technology available at any given time. Electric furnaces have replaced smokestacks, dry-clay pressing processes remove water from the base material formula, automation for the production of lower-quality hotelware products turn out thousands of plates at a time, and multi-colored transfer prints for fine china and earthenware have replaced some hand-painting.

Advances in technology have allowed Wedgwood to expand its product base by increasing production, thereby keeping the company financially stronger than its competitors. In the late 1960s and early 1970s, Wedgwood used this advantage to acquire other ceramics companies, including Johnson Brothers, makers of utilitarian earthenware table settings. Wedgwood also purchased Coalport, a famous brand of high quality bone china, which surrendered its Hong Kong and Hunting Scene patterns to the Wedgwood brand name. The acquisitions provided Wedgwood with a broad product range that offered something to almost every kind of customer.

Wedgwood's image of quality, established initially with the products themselves, has been reinforced as a direct result of the company's innovative management. Even though there were divisions of labor, relationships between workers and management were characterized by open-communication and trust. Wedgwood was one of the first pottery companies to institute a system of "quality circles," avenues for management and shopworkers to interact and exchange ideas about improving the company. Some innovations that came from these quality circles were machines to open gift boxes in the packing department and a less damaging method of applying identification marks on plates. Also the "Wedgwood Charter," a document written by management and unions, ensures the workers right to know "what makes the company tick, how business is going and what's expected of them," Wedgwood chief executive Sir Arthur Bryan told *Management Today.*

Setting Tables Around the World

In the 1970s, the company's history of capital investment paved the way for the company to react to the recession of the 1980s, when it laid off 4,000 people and increased automation in its plants. Bryan told *Management Today* in 1983 that although the investment plan was designed to help the company expand, it was the means of "keeping us going in the last few, difficult years." In addition, Wedgwood's practice, begun in 1953, of leasing space for "Wedgwood Rooms" in large department stores provided a boost in sales, as did its emphasis on mail order and specialty store markets.

Rationalization of operations continued in 1986, when Wedgwood was purchased by Waterford Crystal, Ltd. in order to "take over place settings all over the world,'' as the *Wall Street Journal* put it, although Wedgwood had already begun expansion into the Middle East and Japan. While Waterford's high overhead costs pulled the profits of the group down, Wedgwood's declining but strong sales made significant contributions to group operating profits throughout the late 1980s. By 1991, however, Wedgwood was functioning as a separate operational division from Waterford. The two companies felt their brands could profit more from separate management and marketing plans. Wedgwood reinvigorated its ''potter's wheel image,'' promoting such aspects of the brand as craftsmanship, tradition, and style.

In the early 1990s, Wedgwood's history as well as its contemporary suitability were featured in an ad campaign emphasizing design coordinates. One ad read, ''Nothing in life matches a pattern by Wedgwood. Except another pattern by Wedgwood. The great china born in the 18th century is eminently suitable to a tradition of the late 20th: the mixing and matching of fine china patterns to create place settings as inspired as what is placed upon them. . . . We think you'll agree that while two patterns of Wedgwood china may be rather easy to match, every one is impossible to equal.'' The 1992 campaign increased sales of the collections with design coordinates, but could not keep china sales volume from dropping 13 percent in a market that had become highly price-driven, however. The advertising agency, Ammirati & Puris of New York, resigned the two million dollar Wedgwood account in 1993.

Although Wedgwood remained profitable in early 1993, unit sales were flat. Waterford Wedgwood PLC chairman Donald P. Brennan told the *Wall Street Journal* that ''the board does not expect any major economic growth in its markets in the near future.'' Later that year it was decided to merge the U.S. Waterford and Wedgwood subsidiaries, though sales and marketing operations would continue to be maintained separately. In that area, based on figures that indicated growth in giftware, Wedgwood had begun to make plans in early 1994 for expanding its share of this market.

Further Reading:

''Ammirati & Puris Drops Waterford Crystal,'' *Adweek* (Eastern Edition), August 12, 1991, p. 41.

Baroody, Elizabeth, ''The Joy of Jasper: Wedgwood's Finest Legacy,'' *Antiques & Collecting,* June 1989, pp. 30–32.

''International Brief—Waterford Wedgwood PLC: Crystal, China Manufacturer Swung into Profit in First Half,'' *Wall Street Journal,* September 2, 1993, sec. A, p. 7.

Kelly, Allison, *The Story of Wedgwood,* London: Faber & Faber, 1975.

Langton, John, ''Reply to Perrow,'' *Administrative Science Quarterly,* June 1985, pp. 284–288.

Neiss, Doug, ''Wedgwood Dinnerware Fills Gamut of Gaps,'' *HFD,* November 4, 1991, p. 68.

Osborne, Judith A., ''Breaking Up Tableware Set,'' *Star-Ledger* (Newark, New Jersey), July 7, 1991.

Perrow, Charles, ''Comment on Langton's 'Ecological Theory of Bureaucracy,' '' *Administrative Science Quarterly,* June 1985, pp. 278–283.

Salmans, Sandra, ''The Worries of Wedgwood,'' *Management Today,* June 1980, pp. 67–73, 163.

Shenker, Israel, ''From the Villages of Stoke-on-Trent, A River of China,'' *Smithsonian,* March 1989, pp. 130–138.

''Waterford Wedgwood Back in the Black,'' *Reuter Business Report,* September 1, 1993.

''Wedgwood Breaks the ICL Tradition,'' *Computing,* November 17, 1988, p. 4.

''Wedgwood to Increase Dartington Output 20 Percent,'' *HFD,* August 12, 1985, p. 49.

Whiteley, Geoffrey, ''Why Wedgwood Wobbled,'' *Management Today,* August 1983, p. 26.

Additional information provided by Waterford Wedgwood USA, Inc.

—*Sara Pendergast*

WESTINGHOUSE®

Owned by the Westinghouse Electric Corporation, the brand name Westinghouse is almost synonymous with electricity. Although George Westinghouse did not invent electricity or the electric light bulb, his contribution to the evolution of this vital source of power was enormous, starting with the development of the first effective alternate current (AC) generator in 1886, capable of transforming direct current (DC) into AC, which assured the transmission of electricity over long distances, and eventually, over the whole world. Shortly thereafter, alternating current fueled the most powerful locomotives of the day, and generated electricity from the majestic Niagara Falls over a wide area. Westinghouse's firm also turned its attention to inventing and manufacturing many useful home appliances, such as the temperature setting electric iron, the electric percolator, the electric waffle iron, the electric fan, and the electric range. This was just the tip of the iceberg for Westinghouse's inexhaustible inventive talents, which made his name a byword for electricity.

Brand Origins

George Westinghouse was born in New York state in 1846. One of ten children, George had plenty of room for his inventiveness in his father's machine shop. He grew up tinkering with machines. After a two-year enlistment in the Union army during the Civil War, the nineteen-year-old enrolled at college, but quickly got bored and left after one semester, never to return to school. (Years later, he happily accepted more than one honorary doctorate.) That same year, 1865, he produced his first major invention, a rotary steam engine.

Between 1865 and the year 1886, when Westinghouse and his associates perfected the AC generator, a number of other significant Westinghouse achievements had made their mark on the world. In 1866, the first steel castings in the United States were manufactured by a small firm that George Westinghouse established, followed by an extremely important invention for the railroad industry, the air brake. With this solution to the perennial problem of railroads of that era—the inability to stop a train automatically—Westinghouse's fame and fortune were established. Though he had had no connection to the railroad industry other than as a passenger, Westinghouse had been so intrigued by the railroad problems of the day that he worked out the solutions on his own time. Westinghouse would apply that same curiosity and ingenuity to the problems encountered at that time with electricity, the late nineteenth century's newest energy source.

By the mid-1880s Thomas Alva Edison had invented the incandescent light bulb, and electricity was being used throughout the country but not very extensively. The problem lay in the impracticality of transmitting electric current over long distances. No solution had been found to that would be both safe and inexpensive.

Several engineers in Europe were tinkering with a generator that could convert the direct current flow of electricity to alternating current, which would give electricity the flexibility to be transmitted over long distances. George Westinghouse, a wealthy businessman by the mid-1880s, bought up the patent rights to these crude generators and, together with his own associates, perfected the AC generator, which dexterously altered the voltage of electricity, depending on distance and other factors. Westinghouse was not merely interested in solving problems intellectually, but in deriving practical uses for them. Consequently, in 1886, he established the Westinghouse Electric & Manufacturing Company in Pittsburgh.

First Commercial Success

The first effective AC generator—which could transform direct current into alternating current by increasing or decreasing the voltage—was not considered at the time to be one of the great discoveries of the nineteenth century. Instead, critics from coast to coast lambasted it as unreliable, unsafe, and even as a people killer. Thomas Edison led the charge against the alternating current system of Westinghouse, in part motivated by professional jealously, but, in public, seemingly motivated by concern over public safety. When Westinghouse advised that AC wires be buried underground instead of strung overhead as were the direct current wires of the day, Edison solemnly declared that the heat generated by these underground wires would burn through the coils and wreck havoc; he went even further and insisted that there was no insulation that could possibly protect the public from the deadly high voltage of alternating currents. Westinghouse's cause also was not helped when, for the first time in history, death row prisoners began to be electrocuted in electric chairs—powered by AC electricity. This seemed to prove the killing potential of "deadly" AC electricity.

AT A GLANCE

Westinghouse brand of electric appliances established in Pittsburgh, PA, in 1886 by George Westinghouse, founder of Westinghouse Electric & Manufacturing Company; company was the first to develop and market alternate current (AC) in the late 1880s, spawning a controversy with the proponents of direct current (DC), developed by Thomas Edison; company was the first to manufacture and mass market electrical appliances, such as lamps, irons, percolators, and electric ranges and the first in the world to invent and manufacture the electric AC transformer, the steam turbine, gas engine generator units, the world's largest telescope, and the atom smasher; company name changed in 1945 to Westinghouse Electric Corporation.

Performance: *Market share*—30% of power generation equipment category (1992). *Sales*—$1.7 billion (1992).

Major competitor: General Electric; also American Brown-Boveri.

Advertising: *Agency*—Ketchum Advertising, Pittsburgh, PA, 1945—. *Major campaign*—Newspaper ad depicting various situations in which "The Best Known Unknown Company in America" has had a decisive impact and featuring the tagline "You can be sure . . . if it's Westinghouse."

Addresses: *Parent company*—Westinghouse Electric Corporation, Gateway Center, Pittsburgh, PA 15222; phone: (412) 244-2000; fax: (412) 642-2466.

However, as history proves, AC won the day, but only through the tireless efforts of George Westinghouse. Given the chance to exhibit his product at the World's Fair, or Columbia Exposition, in Chicago in 1893, he set about creating the most dazzling and popular pavilion in the expo: tens of thousands of electric lights that lit up not only his pavilion but the entire expo at night, powered by AC generators. With no fatalities, injuries, or inconvenience to the thousands of gawkers who viewed the sight—for most, the first ever glimpse of electricity in their lives—this demonstration seemed to lay to rest the dim fears and dire warnings of the imminent dangers of alternating current.

In the six months of the Columbia Expo, the Cataract Construction Company of New York state became completely convinced that alternating current was the most versatile, inexpensive means to harness electricity over long distances. In that time, the company's managers engaged Westinghouse in a project to harness the power of Niagara Falls to produce electrical power. The Westinghouse Electrical & Manufacturing Company set about constructing powerful, 5000 horsepower AC generators to do the job. They were finished in 1895, and the result was the transmission of electric current as far as twenty miles from the Falls, the proof that Westinghouse needed that alternating current was the solution to the problem of electricity's expansion.

Early Marketing Strategy

Westinghouse had no competitors in the early years of the establishment of the Westinghouse Electric & Manufacturing Company, since he was the perfecter and manufacturer of the only effective AC generators in the world at that time. However, Westinghouse had to overcome the general public's misunderstandings about alternating current; he did so by demonstrating the safety and cleanliness of AC at trade shows and at the Columbia Exposition. For the engineering sector of the public, AC generators were explained in trade journals.

Westinghouse's company did not confine itself to the manufacture of generators. In time, hundreds and then thousands of other electrical products would come on the market. Although these were marketed via dealers, Westinghouse did regard a personal trademark as an important asset to his business of selling electrical products. Five years after the Niagara Falls success assured the future of the Westinghouse AC generator, a logo, together with a slogan, were placed on Westinghouse products. The logo appeared as a round black border, within which the words "Westinghouse Electric" were embedded, and in the center of which was displayed the famous slogan of Westinghouse: "The name Westinghouse is a guarantee." The Westinghouse logo evolved several times, resting with the one designed in 1960 by the renowned graphic designer Paul Rand: the underlined letter "W" embedded in a circle. In 1948, a new slogan appeared, "You can be sure . . . if it's Westinghouse," which was still being used in the 1990s.

Advertising

Westinghouse, until his death in 1914, was keenly interested in advertising his inventions and products and did so with a flair. Not only did he strenuously contrive to win a presence at the Columbia Exposition in Chicago in 1893, but he managed to turn his whole pavilion and the entire expo into a miraculous display (for that day and age) of flashing electric lights—a half million of them! This was no ordinary statement, but reflected the imagination and creativity of the genius inventor businessman. In 1905, when the International Railway Congress met in the United States, George Westinghouse personally invited and transported the delegates to East Pittsburgh for a highly successful demonstration of the first ever locomotive powered by alternating current. This got the message across to Europeans as well as Americans. Other technical achievements were advertised and discussed via the trade journals of the day, such as *Electrical Engineering* and *Electrical World.*

Prior to the Second World War, the most popular magazines of the day, such as *The Saturday Evening Post, Ladies Home Journal,* and even *Literary Digest,* advertised the latest Westinghouse appliances. A major advertisement displayed Westinghouse products as an indispensable part of one's 24-hour day, with every hour of the day requiring the use of some Westinghouse product or utility! Then as now, prominent personalities advertised Westinghouse appliances: Miss America in 1926 advertised the Westinghouse automatic electric range, and in the 1930s, Ginger Rogers advertised Westinghouse's 10,000 watt movie lamp. At the 1939 World's Fair in New York, a Westinghouse pavilion was among the most popular. Surprising in that heyday of radio, Westinghouse products were seldom advertised on radio, even though Westinghouse pioneered in the development of radio and owned KDKA radio station. Leery of the tentacles of the newly established Federal Communications Commission, Westinghouse desisted from self-advertising.

The 1939 World's Fair in New York featured a Westinghouse pavilion whose purpose was to advertise (and sell on the premises) its latest electrical appliance: the adjust-o-matic iron. This was the world's first iron that could set different temperatures, and keep them there for as long as the user wanted. Television would be fully utilized as an advertising medium after World War II, with the company even possessing its own TV studio. For years, the beautiful, seductive Betty Furness demonstrated Westinghouse refrigerators and electrical appliances. In 1949, and throughout the decade of the 50s, Westinghouse broadcast "Studio One," a dramatic series that advertised Westinghouse products by the lovely Ms. Furness.

Product Development

An anniversary issue of Westinghouse, commemorating the centennial of the company, noted the striking contrast between the number of Westinghouse products on the market in 1886—13—with the number being produced for the market in 1986—over 4,000. This development probably would have pleased the founder, George Westinghouse, all the more so if the product was in some way mechanical.

Merely listing the number of products and inventions that George Westinghouse created to improve the railroad system would not convey the enormity of his contribution, because any one of these required brilliant intellectual faculties. He is credited with developing the famous air brake, electric locomotives, friction draft gear, and railway signaling and interlocking switches. Westinghouse also turned his attention to creating a system for extracting power from natural gas, and, long before automatic telephone exchanges came into being, Westinghouse had worked out such a system as early as 1880.

Westinghouse's contributions to the development of electricity and electrical products are equally formidable. In addition to the AC transformer generator, in 1900, Westinghouse invented the steam turbine, his second most important and original contribution to the electric power industry. Westinghouse eventually turned to the invention and marketing of useful household items. The innovative electric traveling iron came on the market in 1912, followed by electric sewing machine parts in 1917, and the fully automatic electric range in that same year. Other products already enumerated would make the homemaker's lot notably easier. A new craze in the 1920s, miniature golf, was made possible at night by the world's first floodlights, developed and marketed by Westinghouse. This was followed by circuit breakers and the grid glow tube. In 1912, marine engineering was advanced by the Westinghouse geared turbine drive, installed for the first time on the naval vessel, the USS *Neptune.*

The Depression years saw no abatement in electrical product development. In 1931, Westinghouse entered the important field of x-ray development, followed in the mid-1930s by the production of the world's largest telescope. A harbinger of Westinghouse's future involvement in nuclear energy research was the manufacture in 1937 of the atom smasher. Radar also was an important sideline; a Westinghouse-built radar detected Japanese planes as they zoomed in on Pearl Harbor in 1941.

Westinghouse turned to full-time war production during the Second World War, creating electric torpedoes, water coolers for ships at sea, and guns that fired shells with radar fuses attached, which always found their target. The Westinghouse tank gun stabilizer was also invented, enabling tanks to fire on the mark, regardless of terrain. With the onset of the Cold War, Westinghouse products, services, and inventiveness were called upon frequently. Westinghouse equipped the first atomic powered submarine, the USS *Nautilus,* in 1955, and went on to construct the world's first nuclear power station at Shippingport, Pennsylvania, in 1957. The 1950s also saw Westinghouse develop thermoelectricity (heat from electricity).

Since then, Westinghouse has maintained its leadership role in the development of nuclear energy for commercial use, as well as more traditional electrical energy and products. Most notable have been the 1967 construction in the San Francisco Bay area of the world's first automatic rapid transit system, and, in the 1970s and 1980s, refrigeration units for transportation vehicles. Sophisticated propulsion systems, advanced radar for commercial jets, and power systems and services of all kinds are merely a few of the major research and development areas pioneered by Westinghouse.

International Growth

Westinghouse markets and even manufactures many of its products all over the world (international operations were fully consolidated in 1970). Over half of the world's nuclear plants (excluding those in the former Soviet Union) are Westinghouse built or designed. Yet even on the international scene, it was founder George Westinghouse who paved the way for his future products. From the onset of his career in electricity, he thought globally. In 1903, he established Westinghouse Canada; prior to that, he set up an air brake company in England, followed by similar air brake companies in Germany, France, and Russia. In 1899, the Westinghouse Electric & Manufacturing Company was organized, followed by a French counterpart, which branched into Belgium, Spain, Portugal, Italy, and Holland. Via the global expansion of his company, Westinghouse made a vital contribution to the expansion of his AC system of electrical transmission.

In the early 1990s Westinghouse manufactured its products in eight countries and had already made major inroads into China and eastern Europe, a logical evolution of the major international network established by the founder of Westinghouse. With the fall of communism in eastern Europe and the former Soviet Union and the obsolete state of the power generating systems in those countries, Westinghouse can expect increasing business on the global marketplace, at a time when the U.S. market is declining. The fall of trade barriers and the consequent rise of free markets in Asia also augurs well for the future of Westinghouse products and services.

Further Reading:

Baker, Stephen, "From the Gulf War to the War on Crime," *Business Week,* July 5, 1993, pp. 84–85; "Westinghouse Still Needs to Clean House," *Business Week,* February 8, 1993, p. 24.

Barach, Arnold B., *Famous American Trademarks,* Washington, DC: Public Affairs Press, 1971.

Barron, Lee, *Westinghouse Centennial, 1886–1986,* Barron's, 1985.

Enabnit, Elgin G., "Triumphs of Transmission," *Transmission & Distribution,* September 1988, pp. 82–86.

Holstein, William J., "Going Global," *Business Week,* October 20, 1989, pp. 9–18.

Nulty, "What an Outsider Has to Tackle," *Fortune,* July 26, 1993, p. 102.

Pokrzywinski, J., "Westinghouse Electric—Company Report," Morgan Stanley & Co., Inc., September 3, 1992.

Ruch, Charles, *Centennial Review: 1886–1986,* Pittsburgh: Westinghouse Electrical Corp., 1986.

Schroeder, Michael, "The Decline & Fall of Westinghouse's Paul Lego," *Business Week,* March 8, 1993, pp. 68–70.

Stewart, Thomas A., "Westinghouse Gets Respect at Last," *Fortune,* July 3, 1989, pp. 92–98.

Westinghouse Electric Corporation Annual Report, Pittsburgh: Westinghouse Electric Corp., 1991, 1992.

"The World of Westinghouse," Pittsburgh: Westinghouse Electrical Corp., 1965.

—Sina Dubovoj

WHIRLPOOL®

Whirlpool Corporation is the world's leading manufacturer and marketer of large home appliances. Headquartered in Benton Harbor, Michigan, the company manufactures in 11 nations and markets its products under ten major brand names in more than 120 countries. Although now a world leader, the company had modest beginnings as a family-owned washing machine shop located in a small town on the eastern shore of Lake Michigan. To its founders, Whirlpool's tumultuous early years looked like little more than a bad investment. Little did the entrepreneurs realize, their little company would skyrocket to a multibillion dollar global phenomenon.

Brand Origins

In 1908, 22-year-old Louis Upton took $500—his life's savings at the time—and invested it with his friend E. C. Williams in a business venture to manufacture household equipment. Among the equipment was a manually operated washing machine. When the business venture failed to materialize, Williams was unable to repay his friend in cash and instead offered him the patent to a hand-operated washing machine.

Although discouraged with its bad investment, Upton was unwilling to let the washing machine patent be wasted. He persuaded his uncle in Benton Harbor, Michigan, Emory Upton, a machine-shop operator, to create a crude electric version of the manual machine, "so the women of the country will flock to buy it," according to company records. Two years later, Louis moved to Michigan to team with Emory and later with his younger brother Fred to found Upton Machine Company, a washing machine company. That first year, however, sales of the product were barely profitable. The company brought in a net profit of $150. To make matters worse, the first major customer for the young company soon turned into a competitor and threatened the Uptons' survival.

In 1916, the small company landed its first major deal when Sears, Roebuck & Co., then a mail-order giant, placed its first orders. Upton Machine Company would make two washer models to be sold under the Sears' Allen brand name. Until the 1920s, Sears remained Upton's only customer. Catalog promotion of Sears' Allen washers began slowly and gradually grew through and beyond the World War I era as sales volume grew and new models were added. The Uptons, however, were concerned about being too dependent on their big customer, and as a result, they began to develop and market their own "Upton" washer in the mid-1920s. The two-pronged marketing strategy proved successful as sales grew dramatically. This policy of dual distribution—selling washers through Sears' channels as well as its own—would prove to be the key to the company's future rapid growth. Several other early policies also established enduring traditions for the young company: exceptional attention to quality, fiscal conservatism, and unusual concern for employees' well-being. Despite its phenomenal growth, the company never lost sight of these guiding principles.

Early Growth

Soon, the machine company had outgrown its original manufacturing facilities, and the family built a larger plant with a loan from Sears. Within several years, however, Upton outgrew even this new facility. Searching for ways to increase production, reduce shipping costs, and cut delivery time to the east coast, the Upton family made a decision that would later prove to be a wise one—Upton Machine merged with a competitor, The Nineteen Hundred Washer Company of Binghamton, New York. The new firm, named Nineteen Hundred Corporation, combined the strengths of both companies and offset their weaknesses. Together, they emerged from the Depression era stronger than ever, thanks largely to the company's account with Sears.

With Louis Upton as president, Nineteen Hundred operated plants in Michigan and New York and became the world's leading producer of washing machines in 1941. Behind the Sears name, Nineteen Hundred made several major advances, most notably, its entrance into international markets. Around this time the company also introduced a unique sales education program, thereby initiating another corporate tradition. Under Lou Upton's direction, the company created a program of teaching sales, service, and management personnel how to improve their job performances.

1941's war effort brought new responsibilities to the company. Nineteen Hundred Corporation ceased its normal operations and produced parts and products for the government ranging from gun mounts to bomb parts. When the war ended, Nineteen Hundred refocused its attention on washer production and resumed research on automatic washing machines.

AT A GLANCE

Whirlpool brand of home appliances founded in 1911 in Benton Harbor, MI, by Louis, Fred, and Emory Upton; company name originally Upton Machine Company; merged with Nineteen Hundred Washer Company in 1929 to become Nineteen Hundred Corporation; corporate name changed to Whirlpool Corporation in 1950; renamed Whirlpool-Seeger Corporation in 1955; name changed back to Whirlpool Corporation, 1957.

Performance: *Market share*—Top share of home appliance category. *Sales*—$7.53 billion (1993).

Major competitor: Maytag; also General Electric.

Advertising: *Agency*—D'Arcy Masius Benton & Bowles, New York, NY. *Major campaign*—"How to Make a Home Run."

Addresses: *Parent company*—Whirlpool Corporation, 2000 M-63 North, Benton Harbor, MI 49022; phone: (616) 926-5000; fax: (616) 923-5486.

Whirlpool Brand Is Born

In 1947, Sears introduced Nineteen Hundred's first automatic washer under the Kenmore brand name. Sales soared as the consumer public responded positively to the new contraption. Mindful of its earlier successes with dual distribution, Nineteen Hundred was convinced that strategy could work again. That same year, the smaller firm began to distribute an automatic washer under its own brand name—Whirlpool. The name had been acquired in the merger with Nineteen Hundred, and the company thought it seemed to fit the innovative agitator-type washing machine. To reinforce consumer name recognition, Nineteen Hundred changed its corporate name to Whirlpool Corporation in 1950. The new product was launched with a million-dollar advertising and promotion campaign and the company's first-ever national sales meeting. Again, the two-pronged distribution strategy was a success as sales soared. One year later, the company's founder Louis Upton retired from his day-to-day duties. Under new leadership, Whirlpool began to diversify its product line, adding automatic dryers and acquiring plants in Indiana and Ohio.

Postwar Prosperity

The U.S. economy in the 1950s grew by leaps and bounds, and, with it, Whirlpool prospered. Fueled by rapid technological and social change, demand for Whirlpool products grew faster than its production capabilities, and the company continued to add new facilities throughout the United States. National advertising increased, and Whirlpool expanded its internal sales force. Soon, the ever-expanding dealer network numbered more than 11,000 dealers. Whirlpool also expanded its international business by establishing licensing and distribution agreements throughout Canada, England, and Australia.

The appliance industry was fiercely competitive during this era. Prior to World War II, 26 independent companies manufactured washing machines. After the war, only 8 remained in business. Whirlpool's management team found its dependence on laundry appliances to be unsettling, and they were determined to broaden the company's product line. This strategy, they thought, would work in Whirlpool's favor, since wholesale distributors preferred to carry as many products from a single manufacturer as possible.

Whirlpool's leaders knew that the quickest way to expand the company's product line was through acquisitions and mergers with already-existing brands. Both options worked well for Whirlpool during the 1950s and 1960s. First, the company merged with Seeger Refrigerator Company, thereby providing a quality refrigerator line under the Whirlpool name. The merger also gave Whirlpool control over air conditioning and range product lines previously owned by Radio Corporation of American (RCA). Because of the strength of the RCA name, Whirlpool made a deal with RCA to use its trademark along with the Whirlpool name. The combined brand—RCA Whirlpool—allowed Whirlpool to build public and dealer confidence in its new product ventures. By the end of the 1960s, Whirlpool's product line included refrigerators, freezers, cooking products, air conditioners, vacuum cleaners, and dishwashers, in addition to washers and dryers. In 1968, sales revenues reached $1 billion for the first time, and the press was calling the company "the new giant of the appliance industry."

The 1960s' consumer advocate movement gave rise to new focal points for Whirlpool. Determined to keep production on a level with customer demands, Whirlpool expanded and upgraded its manufacturing facilities and renewed its emphasis on making people and facilities as efficient as possible. The results paid off handsomely; Whirlpool's production grew by 100 percent during this time period when its workforce grew by only 50 percent. Several groundbreaking programs surfaced for Whirlpool in the 1960. A "Warranty Service Central" program provided customers with free warranty service regardless of where or how many times they move during a certain time period. The "Tech-Care Service" enabled franchise companies to provide service on Whirlpool brand appliances. Finally, Whirlpool initiated the toll-free "Whirlpool Cool-Line," a program through which consumers could receive instant information on do-it-yourself installation, repairs, and other related subjects.

During the 1970s, Whirlpool faced its first problematic years since its inception in 1911. Costs of materials, labor, and distribution soared while appliance prices fell behind the national Consumer Price Index. Mass merchandisers put small, specialized appliance dealers out of business. The energy crisis imposed new concerns about energy consumption and waste. Fortunately for Whirlpool, however, the baby boomers were beginning to establish their first households. Whirlpool adhered to its fundamental policies of quality, customer service, and production efficiency. The company also forged strong relationships with the large mass merchandisers of the day and assured itself of solid channels of distribution. Whirlpool intensified its energy conservation programs and increased its appliances' energy efficiency dramatically, lowering its manufacturing-related energy consumption by one-third. The 1970s also ushered in large-scale new product developments, including washers and dryers of increasingly larger capacities and precise control systems, compact appliances, and new textures and materials.

International Expansion

By the 1980s, four major manufacturers produced almost all the 40 million appliances sold in the United States annually. Although Whirlpool faced fewer competitors, those who remained were more sophisticated and powerful than ever. Whirlpool knew what its next move must be: to expand into new international markets. The goal was worldwide leadership in the 190-billion-unit world market. As its international business expanded, the company's success was impacted more by trade barriers and currency exchange rates. Whirlpool entered the decade, however, as the unquestioned leader among home appliance manufacturers.

Whirlpool used the same fundamental strengths to move into global markets as it did to win the domestic market: investing wisely in new markets and maintaining its focus on home appliances. During this time, manufacturers scurried to gain foothold in Europe—the fastest growing of all markets. Whirlpool zeroed in and landed one major deal with the Dutch giant Philips. Together, they formed a joint venture to manufacture and market appliances throughout Europe.

The merger enabled Whirlpool to establish a strong presence in Europe, and as a result, the company became the first global appliance company. By the mid-1990s, major competitors Maytag and General Electric had not yet managed to reach the sales levels of Whirlpool. Unique among competitors, Whirlpool approached Europe as a single market.

By 1993, 40 percent of Whirlpool's sales revenues were overseas, and company officials expect that a majority of sales will be there by the year 2000. Looking ahead, Whirlpool will continue to build on its expertise: major home appliances. By maintaining its core strengths of product focus and efficiency, the company intends to expand its presence throughout western Europe. The company has also pinned great hopes on expanding into the emerging markets of Central and Eastern Europe. By the early 1990s, this region made up 11 percent of the total worldwide appliance market, and as the quality of life improves in that region, Whirlpool expects the appliance market to increase.

In 1993, Whirlpool announced aggressive plans to expand its presence in Asia by establishing Asian headquarters in Tokyo with regional offices in Singapore, Hong Kong, and Tokyo. At the same time, Whirlpool Europe and the North American Appliance Group restructured themselves to improve their positions in the competitive worldwide market.

Listening to Customers

By the end of the 1980s, Whirlpool added another strength to its armory of talents by learning to tap into the minds of its customers. Through massive surveying, Whirlpool learned exactly what customers liked and disliked about their purchases, and they also gained valuable insight into future developments. Each year, Whirlpool mails its "Standardized Appliance Measurement Satisfaction (SAMS)" survey to 180,000 households, asking consumers to rate their appliances' attributes on many different levels. At company headquarters in Benton Harbor, Michigan, Whirlpool hired customer volunteers to play with computer simulations of stove-top and washing machine controls in the company's "Usability Lab." This policy allowed the company to experiment with prototypes, and, as a result, create user-friendly products that hit the market successfully. Throughout the 1980s, Whirlpool also used this customer expertise to differentiate its products and lure buyers from major competitors.

Whirlpool's advertising agency, D'Arcy Masius Benton & Bowles, based in New York City, launched a massive $24.4 million campaign in 1990 using what the company learned in its research. They found, for example, that consumers want worry-free appliances, and they are willing to pay a premium for quality. The campaign heralded the message "Appliances so well built... you don't have to think about them," and it featured appliances disappearing when the user turned away. The campaign helped Whirlpool to weather the poor economy of the early 1990s.

In keeping with its tradition of superior quality, Whirlpool initiated the Worldwide Excellence System in 1991 to combine the best of all corporate total quality management programs with Malcolm Baldridge Award criteria. By doing so, Whirlpool was able to establish a common approach to its quality program in hopes of strengthening customer satisfaction. The results have paid off handsomely. Whirlpool is the unquestioned leader in the world appliance market, commanding a huge share of the U.S. laundry market and ranking high in the refrigerator and dishwasher markets. Where does this leave the giant in future years? Certainly, more mergers and acquisitions lie ahead in Whirlpool's future because, as European president Hank Bowman asserted to *World Trade* magazine, "We'll never be content where we are."

Further Reading:

Cortez, John P., "Appliance Ads Get 'Warm, Fuzzy'," *Advertising Age,* May 3, 1993, p. 44.

Fitzgerald, Kate, "Appliance Ads Try to Put Spin Back into Sales," *Advertising Age,* July 29, 1991, p. 4.

Huffman, Frances, "Spin Doctor," *Entrepreneur,* January 1993, p. 344.

Solo, Sally, "Whirlpool: How to Listen to Consumers," *Fortune,* January 11, 1993, pp. 77–78.

Strnad, Patricia, "Whirlpool Ads Try to Discount Discount Stores," *Advertising Age,* April 8, 1991, p. 12.

Tierney, Robin, "Whirlpool Magic," *World Trade,* May 1993.

Weiner, Steve, "Growing Pains," *Forbes,* October 29, 1991, pp. 40–41.

Whirlpool Corporation, "Whirlpool Corporation 1911–1986: Progressing Toward the 21st Century," Benton Harbor, MI: Whirlpool, 1986.

Woodruff, David, "Whirlpool Goes Off on a World Tour," *Business Week,* June 3, 1991, pp. 99–100.

—Wendy Johnson Bilas

WIFFLE® BALL

WIFFLE® BALL

Wiffle is one of the best known and least advertised brands in the United States. Introduced in 1954, the white, plastic Wiffle balls with their patented oblong holes in one half have been sold for backyard baseball games. The Wiffle Ball Inc. also markets plastic bats, bases, and other toys.

Brand Origins

The first Wiffle balls were created in 1953 by David N. Mullany, for his son, David A. Because of limited space and the possibility of broken windows, the younger Mullany, then 13, and his friends had started playing backyard baseball with a broom stick and a plastic golf ball. However, the elder Mullany, a former semi-pro baseball player, was worried about the wear and tear on his son's arm from trying to put enough spin on the small, plastic golf ball to throw a curve.

The Mullany family lived in Fairfield, Connecticut, and as luck would have it, a nearby cosmetics factory used plastic shells slightly smaller than a baseball to ship bottles of perfume. The elder Mullany obtained a dozen plastic balls, which came in halves, and taped them together for his son to use. He also began experimenting with different patterns of holes cut into the shells with a razor blade to see which would produce the best spin. The design that worked best had eight oblong holes in one half and none in the other. The younger Mullany told the *Wall Street Journal* in 1993: "Dad and I played with it, and it curved better than the real thing. I didn't know the whys of it then and still don't. As long as it works, who cares." In 1985 *Yankee Magazine* described the Wiffle ball as "probably the most unaerodynamic projectile ever conceived; it will dip, rise, twist, wiggle, and do a fair rendition of Chuck Berry's duck strut. . . . Basically, it will do anything but straighten up and fly right."

The younger Mullany named the ball his dad created. "Whiff" was a common euphemism for striking out in baseball, and since the floating, curving plastic balls were so hard to hit, they became known as "Wiffle" balls. Mullany told the *Wall Street Journal,* "When you strike out, you 'whiff'. . . . But neither of us was very good at spelling." The dictionary definition of "whiffle" was appropriate: "to move erratically."

About the time the elder Mullany was carving the first Wiffle balls, the car-polish company that the former pharmaceutical salesman had founded was faltering. Mullany decided to get out of the polish business and begin producing Wiffle balls for a living. He mortgaged his home, patented the design (U.S. Patent #2,776,139), registered the Wiffle trademark, and founded The Wiffle Ball Inc. in February of 1954.

Marketing

To market Wiffle balls, Mullany hired a manufacturer's representative, Saul Mondschein, who achieved his greatest success by bouncing balls off office windows to demonstrate their safety to toy retailers. Wiffle, however, did little advertising. Promotion was almost entirely word-of-mouth, and it took about 18 months for Wiffle balls to become popular. Even after sales began to increase, Wiffle did little consumer advertising. David Mullany, Jr., who succeeded his dad as president, told *Esquire* in 1983: "Not that [advertising] was a bad idea. We just can't afford it. Wiffle balls sell themselves."

Wiffle did produce a commercial in the mid-1960s that featured former New York Yankees pitcher Whitey Ford, and for several years the company printed pictures of Major League ballplayers on Wiffle ball boxes. Among the players whose likenesses appeared on Wiffle boxes were Ford, Eddie Mathews, Jack Jensen, Ted Williams, Pete Rose, Tim McCarver, Rick Suttcliffe, and Thurman Munson. The company, though, stopped using pictures when players began demanding more money. The last Major Leaguer to appear on a Wiffle ball box was Houston Astros pitcher Mike Scott in 1991.

Without advertising, Wiffle was able to hold down the cost of its balls. The first Wiffle balls sold for 49¢ in 1954. In 1994 the same "junior" size Wiffle balls sold for 95¢.

Brand Extensions

In addition to the original Wiffle ball, by 1958 Wiffle had introduced a regulation baseball-sized ball, a softball-sized ball, and a plastic Wiffle bat. Wiffle also sold wooden bats, made from broom handles, until 1972. In 1959 Wiffle introduced a pitching machine, the Wiffle Ball-O-Matic. Rubber bases were added to the Wiffle line in 1980s.

Other Wiffle products included a toy golf set, available from the late 1950s until the early 1970s; plastic golf balls; and a Wiffle Flying Saucer, introduced in 1966. In 1994 the company planned to reintroduce a flying ring that had been sold for a while in the

AT A GLANCE

Wiffle brand name introduced in 1954 by The Wiffle Ball Inc.

Performance: *Sales*— $4.6 million.

Major competitor: None.

Advertising: None.

Addresses: *Parent company*—The Wiffle Ball Inc., 275 Bridgeport Ave., Shelton, CT; phone: (203) 924-4643.

1970s. Wiffle products that were less successful include a plastic football and basketball, and a foam-rubber ball.

Outlook

The Wiffle Ball Inc. remained a family-owned and operated business in 1994, and continued to concentrate on producing millions of Wiffle balls and a few related products. Although the company spends no money for consumer advertising, Wiffle remains one of the most recognized brand names in the United States. *Playboy* magazine once described the Wiffle ball as "an American classic," while *Esquire* called it "a national treasure."

Tony Luccadello, former scout for the Philadelphia Phillies, once recommended that batting coaches use Wiffle balls, tossed from a kneeling position beside the batter, to develop a better swing, and were Wiffle-ball leagues existed throughout the United States—some with their own Wiffle-ball-size stadiums. Wiffle also publishes a set of official rules available upon request at no charge. Most Wiffle balls, however, are sold to kids, and most kids make up their own rules depending on the number of players and the size of the field available.

Other companies marketed competitive products, but strong name recognition, effective design (unchanged in 40 years), and low prices made Wiffle the market leader. Wiffle balls were also almost indestructible, except when gnawed on by a dog, and over the years the Mullanys often hinted at a secret plan to boost sales. As David Mullany, Jr., told *Esquire* in 1983, "If unit sales ever drop all we have to do is put dog food flavoring in the plastic."

Further Reading:

Bucher, Ric, "The Gift of Wiffle," *Yankee Magazine,* October 1985, p. 238.

Klein, Frederick C., "On Sports: Backyard Classic," *Wall Street Journal,* April 16, 1993, p. A13.

Levy, Stephen, "The Wiffle Ball," *Esquire,* August 1983, p. 83.

MacDonald, Dougald [sic], "Wiffle Ball, a 33-Year-Old Institution, Is Still 'Just A Kid's Toy' to Its Maker," *New England Business,* February 17, 1986, p. 29.

Sperry, Benjamin O., "Home Run," *Connecticut's Finest,* autumn 1987, p. 6.

—Dean Boyer

WILSON®

Wilson

The Wilson Sporting Goods brand has prospered throughout the 20th century and is well positioned to do the same in the next, based on the strength of its long-held leading market shares in areas related to golf equipment, tennis and racquetball equipment, and in team sports products such as baseballs and baseball gloves, footballs, and basketballs. Almost since its creation, the Wilson brand has housed an advisory staff of prominent athletes to endorse products, provide recommendations on equipment improvements, and field-test its sporting goods products. The continued presence of the advisory staff, along with a long standing commitment to using state-of-the-art research and development facilities, has helped the brand maintain its position at the innovative forefront of the sporting goods industry. In fact, according to company sources, Wilson was the first brand to utilize the ''computer aided design system'' within the sporting goods industry.

Brand History

Wilson Sporting Goods began in 1913 as the Ashland Manufacturing Company and later became the Thomas E. Wilson Company. The company was principally engaged in the meat packing business, although it also dabbled with apparently unrelated items like violin strings, surgical sutures, and tennis racket strings. The company's first significant leap into the sporting goods industry came in 1923, when it introduced the Gene Sarazen Autograph model of golf clubs. Besides the novelty of using a sport celebrity's endorsement as a marketing device, the clubs were the first of their kind to feature a tapered grip. Embolden by their success, the company began to progressively concentrate entirely on sporting goods. By the end of World War II it had secured leadership positions in golf, tennis, and team sports equipment markets.

In the decades to follow Wilson road the fast-developing U.S. ''Leisure Revolution'' wave to great success. Detecting the same phenomenon starting to gather force in Western Europe, and the United Kingdom in particular, Wilson opened its first overseas plant in Scotland in 1961. In 1970 the majority of Wilson's stock was acquired by PepsiCo, a multi-product company with extensive international operations and a solid financial base that provided Wilson with unprecedented growth opportunities abroad.

On September 16, 1985, WSGC Holdings, Inc., an affiliate of Wesray Capital Corporation, acquired Wilson Sporting Goods as a wholly-owned subsidiary. About three years later, on March 27, 1989, a merger between Holdings and Bogey Acquisition Company was reached. Bogey itself was affiliated with Amer Group Ltd., headquartered in Helsinki, Finland.

The Wilson brand competes in an industry where constant product improvements, new product innovation, and large advertising outlays leading to high brandname visibility set the standards for success. According to company material, Wilson scored an industry first when it ran television commercials for its tennis product line during the 1972 World Championship Tennis tournament, which it co-sponsored. Some 22 years later, in 1994, Wilson committed close to 100 percent of its team sports advertising budget to launch a national print and television campaign to promote its Conform glove, which was proclaimed the official glove of Major League Baseball.

Aggressive marketing, along with a demonstrated customer loyalty, has paid off for Wilson. In 1992, of the top 75 companies active in the sporting and athletic goods industry, Wilson held the number one market share position for the category of total sales with 8.5 percent. Its chief rivals were Anthony Industries Inc., with a 7.0 percent market share, followed by Johnson Worldwide Associates and Spalding & Evenflo Co., Inc., with 4.9 and 4.6 percent market shares, respectively.

Brand Development and Structure

Wilson Sporting Goods manufacturing operations are divided into four separate product line groups: golf equipment, racket equipment, team sports equipment, and other soft goods. Of these, the golf product line was responsible for the greatest percentage of total sales through the late 1980s and into the early 1990s. At the time, Wilson believed it was the largest manufacturer of golf clubs in the world. The ''Staff'' and ''1200 Gear Effect'' golf clubs and the ''Ultra'' and ''Pro'' golf balls were held to be responsible for the greater portion of the brand's professional golf sales, while the ''K-28'', the ''1200 LT'' and the ''Blue Ridge'' golf clubs accounted for the greatest percentage of retail golf club sales. Other Wilson products doing well in this category were golf gloves and bags. Of all the separate product line groups, golf equipment generated the highest gross profit margins, a result attributed to improved manufacturing efficiencies and competitive pricing.

In 1993 Wilson's Humboldt, TN, plant was the recipient of the highly prestigious Shingo Prize for Excellence in Manufacturing.

AT A GLANCE

Began in 1914 as Ashland Manufacturing Company; renamed Thomas E. Wilson Company, active in meat packing business; became an industry leader in sporting goods in 1923; PepsiCo acquires majority stock ownership in 1970; sold to WSGC Holdings Inc., in September, 1985; WSGC Holdings merged with Bogey Acquisition Company, an affiliate of Amer Group Ltd., in 1989.

Performance: *Market share*—8.5% of sporting and athletic goods industry. *Sales*—$460 million (1992).

Major competitors: Anthony Industries Inc., Johnson Worldwide Associates, and Spalding & Evenflo.

Advertising: *Agency*—Bayer Bess Vanderwarker, Chicago, IL.

Addresses: *Parent company*—Wilson Sporting Goods Co., 8700 W. Bryn Mawr, Chicago, IL 60631; phone: (312) 714-6400; fax: (708) 452-3178. *Ultimate parent company*—Amer Group Ltd., Helsinki, Finland.

The plant produced more than 45,000 golf balls daily and was the world's third largest golf ball plant. Production rose by 100 percent per worker over the period of 1985 to 1992—shrinking the production cycle from 10 days in 1987 to just 3 days in 1992.

During the late 1980s, the brand's racket equipment product line included its major tennis products, such as "Wilson Championship" tennis balls and the "Profile", "Pro Staff", "Ultra", "Wilson Ceramic" and "Kramer Staff" tennis rackets. According to Diane Russel of *Sporting Goods Business*, however, the first half of the 1990s witnessed a tennis market that was losing momentum and sales. Wilson hoped to buck the trend with the introduction of its lightweight "ProStaff Lite" 5.8si racket, which weighed a scant 11.4 ounces when strung. The racket was meant to appeal to juniors and other players desiring a lightweight racket with superior performance characteristics. Among other features, the ProStaff Lite was constructed with a dual taper beam with medium flex for long, looplike strokes and fast swing speeds. The brand's other entries featured the "ProStaff Classic" 4.2si and the "Hammer" 6.2si—both designed for full-stroke players desiring fast swing speeds.

In the category of team sports equipment, the Wilson brand held on to market leadership positions in the football, basketball, and baseball market segments. Its leading products included the "A2000" baseball glove, the official "NFL" football, the "1001" collegiate football, and the "Jet" leather basketball. The brand was particularly strong in the football market, which company sources attributed to its long-standing endorsement by the National Football League. The brand is also the officially-endorsed supplier of baseballs to the National Collegiate Athletic Association (NCAA). In 1993, the "Jet" basketball received approval from the International Basketball Federation to be used in international play.

In 1993 Wilson introduced its new "Conform" glove, featuring the patented Dial Fit System (DFS) that customizes the fit of the glove to the players hand. The Conform was available in three different models—an infielder's, pitcher's, and outfielder's glove. The Dial Fit System is meant to mold the glove to the player's hand by adjusting the leather construction after a period of use. The glove received endorsements from the entire 1992 Atlanta Braves pennant-winning staff of starting pitchers.

In the soft goods category, Wilson manufactures a variety of golf clothes sold to professional shops, tennis clothing, and the "ProStaff" tennis shoes sold to professional shops. Uniforms are sold to professional sports teams and other institutional dealers.

Wilson maintains an in-house research and development staff of about thirty professionals. The staff is divided along specific lines, such as research and product concepts, product development, and technical services. Integration of the "computer-aided design" system proved instrumental in shortening product design lead-times by minimizing research costs and development design iterations that used more traditional techniques. It also helped increase quality and performance while permitting more exacting tolerances.

Marketing Structure and Strategies

Wilson actively pursues endorsements by professional athletes as a means to enhance the brand's image and increase product sales. During the 1980s and '90s, Wilson products carried endorsements from over 100 professional athletes, including Ben Crenshaw, Tom Kite, Sam Snead, and Patty Berg in golf: Chris Evert and Jack Kramer in tennis; Joe Montana, Walter Payton, Jim McMahon, and John Elway in football; Michael Jordan and Kevin McHale in basketball; and Roger Clemens and George Brett in baseball. Furthermore, by the early 1990s, Wilson sporting goods were used and promoted by over 1000 golf club professionals and close to 750 tennis club professionals around the world, as well as 100 college coaches. Various other products carry endorsements from the National Football League, the United States Tennis Association, and the National Collegiate Athletic Association.

During the 1970s, Wilson sporting goods were fairly ubiquitous on the "big league" scene. The brand provided the official ball for the National Football League and the National Basketball Association. Most Major League baseball teams wore Wilson uniforms and, as it had done in times past, Wilson provided the official uniforms worn by the United States Olympic teams during the summer games. In tennis, all four finalists playing in the 1971 Men's and Women's U.S. Open at Forest Hills competed with Wilson rackets, including the ultimate winners Stan Smith and Billie Jean King.

Under the direction of its parent company, the Amer Group Ltd., located in Helsinki, Finland, Wilson Sporting Goods has aggressively pursued an international growth strategy that has brought significant profits and positioned the brand for future success. In particular, significant growth has occurred in Japan, the United Kingdom, and Canada, where high-margin products like tennis and golf equipment are big winners.

Wilson divides it customer account base into separate and distinct major trade channels, developing specific marketing and promotional strategies while maintaining separate distribution facilities. In 1988, the brand's major national and regional retail chain customers included Herman's Sporting Goods, Oshman's, K-Mart, Sportmart, Target Stores, and Sears, Roebuck & Co. The brand's 10 largest customers accounted for about 25 percent of its domestic sales.

Wilson maintains a separate sales force for each major trade channel. In particular, the company has a sales group specifically trained to service its professional tennis and golf accounts. Wilson views these efforts as being consistent with their objectives of concentrating on meeting the special needs of professionals. The company justifies the higher customer service expenditure directed at these groups due to the relatively higher profit margins that it makes on the premium priced merchandise sold in professional shops.

Wilson operates on the premise that to sell a large number of products to a knowledgeable customer group requires expertise on the part of its sales force. It believes that such a situation affords it a significant advantage compared to its major competitors, who typically field smaller sales organizations or sell through independent agents. Wilson sales agents are paid on a straight commission basis, and the company boasts that a significant percentage of its sales force remains with the company for a number of years.

In 1988, Wilson's domestic distribution structure consisted of seven sales offices, five professional service centers and three regional distribution centers. In the same year, close to 50 percent of Wilson's golf products were sold to golf professionals who run either on-course or off-course shops. Golf sales to national accounts were responsible for 20 percent of total golf sales while the remainder was made up by other retailers. In general, professional golf products circulate through a network of professional service centers concentrated near key markets. On the other hand, retail golf products move through regional distribution centers.

Nearly 40 percent of all racket products are distributed through Wilson's national retail accounts. The greater bulk was sold to racket sport professional shops, catalog houses, specialty stores, and general retailers. Wilson's tennis balls were typically stored at all regional distribution centers, while limited quantities make their way to various professional service centers.

As for team sports equipment, close to 40 percent was sold to institutional and organizational merchandisers. Another 40 percent was sold to major national retailers, with the balance divided between catalog houses and other retailers. In most instances Wilson's team sports equipment was distributed through its regional distribution centers.

International Growth

Wilson conducts the greater portion of it international transactions through five wholly-owned subsidiary operations in Japan, the United Kingdom, Canada, Germany, and France. It also exports sporting goods to over 100 countries. In 1989, the sales contribution of Wilson's top five foreign subsidiaries accounted for 80 percent of its international sales, with the Japan and U.K. markets leading the way. In any one of the five countries, Wilson can boast of having a strong market position in at least one of its major product lines. Wilson has identified golf and tennis equipment as the principal areas of focus for its international marketing efforts. In 1988, golf clubs and balls, and tennis rackets and balls accounted for about 72 percent of Wilson's total international sales.

Behind only the United States, Japan ranks as the second largest sporting goods market in the world and is a key target market for the Wilson's future international growth. Golf stands as the largest sporting goods category in Japan, and in 1988 Wilson obtained a 5.0 percent share in golf clubs and balls. Wilson also maintained a second-place market share position in the tennis racket and tennis balls product categories.

In 1988, the U.K. market was the most diversified of Wilson's international markets. The brand maintained an established dominant position in the golf equipment market, where it enjoyed the top market share in golf clubs and the third spot in golf balls. Wilson also maintained the second position in sales of both tennis rackets and balls. The brand's high-performance athletic shoes were aimed at exploiting this up-and-coming market. Wilson's London office was home to the brand's entire European operations.

Wilson has also expanded production overseas. In 1989, two-thirds of Wilson's annual revenues were originated from 12 company-owned locations. Eight of these were located in the United States and four abroad. Wilson makes baseballs in Haiti, tennis rackets in St. Vincent, and golf clubs in Canada and Scotland. The remainder of the brand's annual sales were obtained from vendors in North America, Asia, and Europe. Various products like soft goods, shoes, tennis racket parts, baseball gloves, basketballs, and golf club component parts originate from South Korea and Twain.

Future Growth

By 1994, the U.S. economy appeared to be inching its way towards an economic recovery. For the period of 1991-1994, positive growth in the sporting goods industry was assisted by increases in disposable personal income, falling interest rates, and a decline in the ratio of consumer debt-to-income ratio. In the mid 1990s, Wilson ventured into a licensing agreement with Jarold Enterprises Inc., to offer lines of exercise equipment. Jarold's Wilson line featured steppers, treadmills, bikes, skiers, and home gyms of "spa-caliber" quality. The exercise equipment was targeted for mid-level sporting goods distribution.

The long-term decline in the value of the dollar, the removal of tariff barriers due to the passage of the North American Free Trade Agreement, and the successful outcome of the Uruguay Round of the General Agreement on Tariffs and Trade boded well for Wilson's continued growth. Wilson also expected to increase its international market shares redirecting members of its research and development staffs to international markets; offering custom designed products with prices, promotions, and advertising fitted to specific markets; introducing high-performance athletic shoes; and promoting its well-known brand name at major, crowd-drawing sporting events. Plans to increase export sales to certain growth areas, such as Singapore, Hong Kong, Korea, Australia, Taiwan, and Italy were also underway.

Further Reading:

Dutter, Greg, "Wilson, MacGregor License Fitness Gear," *Sporting Goods Business,* March 1992, p. 22.

"Game Plan For '94," *Sporting Goods Business,* February 1994, p. 136.

Hynes, Jaynes, "Talking Tech" *Sportstyle,* August 2, 1993, p. S42.

Losee, Stephanie, "Wilson's Hammer System Racket," *Fortune,* November 19, 1990, p. 138.

Russell, Diane, "Swing Time" *Sporting Goods Business,* February 1994, pp. 140–141.

The Wilson Sporting Goods Company Annual Reports, River Grove, IL: Wilson Sporting Goods Co., 1972, 1987, 1988.

Vasilash, Gary S., "On a Roll At Wilson," *Production,* August 1993, p. 16.

—Daniel E. King

WINNEBAGO®

Once considered the giant of motor home manufacturers, Winnebago now holds the second or third position in the heavily populated recreational vehicle industry. Unlike competitors Fleetwood Enterprises, Coachmen Industries, and Rexhall Industries, Winnebago currently manufactures only motor homes, a highly cyclical segment of the RV industry that has taken a beating from the energy crisis of the 1970s and the Persian Gulf War of 1991. Winnebago offers a variety of motor homes styles and sizes, including the Itasca, Vectra, Elante, and Minni Winnie lines. Winnebagos are sold in the United States, Europe, and Japan.

Brand Origins

In the mid-1950s the farming town of Forest City, Iowa, was suffering an economic depression brought about by technological advancements that left many agricultural workers jobless. The loss of traditional jobs forced young people to leave the area and find work in large cities. Alarmed at the exodus of people from their community, local business people formed the Forest City Industrial Development Commission to bring new industry to the area.

At that time, many Americans were becoming interested in vacationing with travel trailers pulled behind the family car. Seeing potential for growth in the burgeoning trailer industry, John K. Hanson, a local furniture store owner, suggested the manufacturing of trailers to the Industrial Development Commission. In 1957 the Commission voted in favor of Hanson's proposal. Community members invested $50,000 at $100 a share to start up the new corporation under the name Forest City Industries, Inc. Under the start-up plan, Hanson would manage Forest City Industries as a branch manufacturer for Modernistic Industries, Inc., of California, producer of the Aljo brand of travel trailers.

The first Aljo trailer rolled off the line in Forest City in March, 1958. Production was soon halted, however, when several Forest City Industries stockholders broke away and founded their own trailer manufacturing operations. Modernistic threatened to pull out. Hanson offered to purchase Modernistic's share and continue managing the plant as an independent trailer manufacturer under the name Modernistic Industries of Iowa, Inc.

In 1958 Modernistic Industries of Iowa introduced its first trailer, the Winnebago Teepee. It could sleep five comfortably and had cooking and dining facilities, including a propane gas stove, sink, and refrigerator. Hanson had introduced a number of innovations to the Aljo trailer, including lightweight foam cushions for the dinettes, and by March of 1959, the new company had designed five different models in two sizes, with a total of 53 improvements over the old Aljo models. In 1960 Modernistic Industries changed its name to Winnebago Industries, Inc., named after the county of which Forest City was the county seat.

Early Marketing

To market their new trailers, Hanson and other Forest City residents drove across the Midwest on weekends with a Winnebago trailer in tow. The goal was to set up new Winnebago dealerships, sell the trailer in tow as the first of its inventory, and return with a check so Modernistic's payroll for the following week could be met. Hanson also exhibited the new Winnebago line at the 1959 Northwest Sports Show, but sales remained slow. In the fall of 1959 Modernistic began advertising Winnebagos in trade publications, offering free delivery anywhere in the United States. Orders started flowing in, and by the season's end, the company had sold 105 trailers.

Establishing new dealerships were key to the sales of Winnebago trailers. In an effort to attract new dealers, the company instituted Winnebago Dealers Days in 1959, a day-long promotional activity in which Hanson and his wife, Luise, entertained more than 100 potential dealers at the Winnebago factory with tours that allowed them to view models on the assembly line. Other efforts to woo dealers, such as "free vacation deliveries," allowed dealers to try out a Winnebago trailer during their family vacations, then drop it off on the way home. Such generous promotional activities paid off, and by 1962 Winnebago's production capacity was up to 7,800 units a year. By 1963 dealerships had been established across the continental United States.

Technology and Design

"The cheapest way to get things done is to do them yourself" was Hanson's motto. Ever interested in finding industry to support the Forest City community, Hanson made concerted efforts to furnish Winnebago trailers with components manufactured in the region. Unlike most trailer manufacturers at that time, Winnebago incorporated its own subsidiary in 1961 to manufacture upholstered goods for Winnebago products. Named Stitchcraft, the company began in the basement of Hanson's old furniture store and quickly expanded to fill orders for Forest City Industries, Inc.

AT A GLANCE

The Winnebago line of campers and motor homes founded in 1959 by Modernistic Industries of Iowa, Inc., in Forest City, IA; Winnebago became a registered trademark in 1959, Modernistic Industries renamed Winnebago Industries, Inc., in 1960.

Performance: *Market share*—18% of recreational vehicle category.

Major competitor: Coachmen Industries, Inc.'s brand of campers and motor homes.

Advertising: *Agency*—In-house. *Major campaign*—Print ads and radio spots for Winnebago's motor home warranty, as well as for Vectra, Elante, Itasca, Sunrise, Brave, and Minnie Winnie motor homes; also, ads mentioning *Consumers Digest* "Best Buy" awards given to Winnebago.

Addresses: *Parent company*—Winnebago Industries, Inc., Box 152, Forest City, IA 50436; phone: (515) 582-3535; fax: (515) 582-6966.

(the spin-off of Forest City's original trailer manufacturing operations) and more than 70 other trailer manufacturers in the Midwest.

Thermo-Panel, developed by Winnebago in 1964 to cut manufacturing costs, was the advancement that put Winnebago ahead of its competitors. Lighter, stronger, and better insulating than traditional wood and metal components, Thermo-Panel was an aluminum and plywood laminated panel with a polystyrene core. Soon Thermo-Panel replaced all conventional wood construction in Winnebago products. It was an important innovation in the young trailer industry and greatly boosted Winnebago sales. Winnebago was quick to capitalize on its development. Print advertising touted the new components as the ''most important construction in the recreational vehicle industry since the introduction of aluminum skin in the 1930s'' and boasted that it's ''as modern as tomorrow!''

Sales Boom with Motor Homes

By 1966 the Winnebago brand encompassed trailers; pickup campers with sink, cabinets, seats, and bedding; and ''pickup caps,'' smaller units containing windows, doors, and optional bunk beds. ''Pickup campers and other items were going great, but I sensed a market for upgraded products,'' Hanson told *Business Week* in 1970. Using profits from the creation of Thermo-Panel, Winnebago began the development of motor homes, self-contained motorized dwellings with wheel and drive mechanism as part of the whole.

Through the use of the assembly line and other manufacturing innovations, Winnebago could produce a motor home that sold for far less than competitors' models. As Hanson once said, ''We bought the Chevy concept into the motor home market.'' A 19-foot unit that slept four was offered at a sticker price of $6,500, less than half the price of other motor homes at that time.

Within a year of its introduction in 1966, the Winnebago motor home led the industry in sales. In less than six months, Winnebago set up dealer networks across the United States, offering 17-, 19-, and 22-foot models complete with all the comforts of home, such as air conditioning, stoves, and comfortable beds and chairs.

The company decided to specialize in motor homes, a choice that doubled sales and earnings every year from 1966 to 1970. In 1965 total Winnebago sales were $2.5 million. By 1970 they had grown to $50 million, fueled by motor home sales that made up 85 percent of business, according to a 1970 *Business Week* article. Winnebago's annual motor home production was around 10,000. It's market share was 40 percent.

In 1970 Hanson instituted a mobile home rental program in conjunction with United Airlines and Eastern Airlines. Using these airlines, customers would fly to a resort area, and instead of renting a car, they would rent a mobile home. An 18-foot model that slept six rented for $250 a week. Using the slogan ''Fly in and camp out,'' Hanson was betting that half of all mobile homes produced would go to the rental market. Winnebago's future looked bright.

Gasoline Crisis

Motor home sales continued to grow, and by 1973 Winnebago produced 600 motor homes a week. However, just as Winnebago sales were booming, the Arab oil embargo hit and Winnebago was forced to cut output by 25 percent. Sales were still growing—up by 30 percent in the early months of 1973—but the company had optimistically predicted a 50 percent increase for that period. Hanson announced to the *Wall Street Journal* that softening sales ''probably in part reflect consumer uncertainty, weakness of the dollar in world markets, and growing concerns about much-discussed fuel rates.''

Competition, however, might also have caused some of Winnebago's sales erosion. Coachmen Industries, Inc., saw dealer sales rise by 138 percent during the same period. Although Winnebago was the largest of the approximately 800 recreational vehicle producers in the United States, its market share was being chipped away by the entry of big name competitors such as General Motors and White Motor Corp.

In June, Winnebago began factory authorized sales with the hopes of cleaning out excess inventory. But by August the company had received another blow, this time from the Center for Auto Safety, which assailed Winnebago motor homes for ''what appears to be a total lack of crashworthiness.'' Winnebago responded with statistics that the bodily injury rate is far lower in a motor home than in a car, and cited Winnebago's long history of setting industry-wide safety standards. The design of motor homes in general had come under scrutiny by the National Transportation Safety board, which deemed the vehicles ''incapable of maintaining structural integrity in a crash.''

The gasoline crisis worsened in 1974, adversely impacting the recreational vehicle (RV) industry. One of the greatest sales deterrents was that on the average, motor homes only got ten miles per gallon. By January of 1975, 58 percent of RV manufacturing plants had ceased operations, 14 percent of those permanently. Winnebago, being the industry's largest brand name, felt an enormous impact. Production slowed from 600 units before the gasoline crisis to ''practically zero'' in 1974.

In response to its eroding market domination, Winnebago Industries introduced a companion brand to its traditional Winnebago line in November of 1974. Named Itasca, the brand was created to recapture some of Winnebago's dwindling market share. Winnebago also responded by introducing a new line of economy travel trailers, designed for gasoline savings and easy towing, and added the Winnebago name to a line of small commuter busses. Motor homes, however, dominated the Winnebago brand, and tough times in the RV market shook the company. Sales in 1975 were $112 million, and production was about 375 units per week, down from a peak of 600 units per week in 1973.

Winnebago tightened its belt and weathered the crisis. By June of 1976 the economy had improved and sales were on the upswing again. The number of independent Itasca dealers had more than doubled in a year, and Itasca sales were responsible for a large percentage of overall motor home sales. Winnebago stepped up advertising and introduced a new line of mini-motor homes, which captured 10 percent of the mini-motor home market. By 1976, however, Winnebago's share of the motor home market had declined to around 15 percent, down from a high of 40 percent in 1970.

Rocky Roads

By 1977 Winnebago had become the first RV manufacturer to produce 100,000 units; again, though, sales were below projections, and the company was forced to cut output by 17 percent. In 1979 the company once again cut motor home output by 14 percent, due to adverse market conditions brought about by uncertainties over the price of gasoline.

Public interest in motor home vacations was waning. Although camping was up 4 percent at national parks, the percentage of overall mobile home campers at national parks was down 15 percent. In the late 1970s, interest rates rose steadily, making motor homes (which retailed between $27,000 and $90,000) out of the range of many people.

Seeking to immune itself from the pitfalls of the gasoline market, Winnebago introduced an optional liquified propane (LP) gas fuel system on many of its 1979 motor homes. "The dual fuel system—which can also use gasoline—gives the motor home buyer a choice of fuels for traveling without fear of . . . gas rationing," announced Hanson upon its introduction.

But Winnebago was also facing threats from other fronts. "We knew the product was inadequate," Ron Haugen, Winnebago chief executive, told *Forbes* in 1984. The company's basic motor home design had changed little since 1966, and Coachmen Industries and Fleetwood Enterprises had surpassed Winnebago in sales, relegating the one-time giant to third place. Winnebago searched for a growth niche and decided to purse the mileage-conscious market with new, fuel efficient vehicles.

In 1979 the company introduced the economical Warrior and Spectrum lines, designed to get 15 mpg and priced at a reasonable $18,800. Three years later, Winnebago introduced the Winnebago LeSharo/Itasca Phaser line of front-wheel drive, diesel-powered motor homes, intended to provide "the convenience of a car, the roominess of a full-size van and the livability of a motor home." Over 1,500 units were sold in 1983. Industry analysts predicted that Winnebago had a two-year lead on Coachmen and Fleetwood in the new economy niche. 7,800 diesel vehicles were sold between 1983 and 1986, making it the best seller in the downsized motor home category.

Analysis and Future Predictions

Industry analysts agree that management instability at Winnebago Industries hurt the brand. Several times during the 1980s Hanson emerged from retirement to give the company he founded a shot in the arm. By the late 1980s, however, more than 90 percent of Winnebago's efforts were devoted to the production of motor homes. Winnebago's Itasca line was doing extremely well, but the motor home market continued to erratically follow the caprices of the gasoline market.

The Persian Gulf War of 1991 further dampened public interest in motor homes. In 1992 Winnebago introduced an entirely new product line. It reported a net loss of $3.75 million for the first three quarters. But in the fourth quarter, sales picked up by 27 percent and the brand returned to profitability.

Winnebago motor homes remain one of the most respected brands in the field, with a brand recognition level of over 75 percent. Over the years, the motor home industry suffered various economic crises, and Winnebago, being one of the industry's giants, inevitably felt the blows. Due to its constant attention to changing consumer demands, Winnebago has survived when many smaller RV names have not. The brand is a strong contender in a competitive field, and should remain so in the future.

Further Reading:

Brown, Terry P., "In Forest City, Where Winnebago Millionaires Once Abounded, Folks Take Stock Plunge Philosophically," *Wall Street Journal,* July 2, 1973, p. 26.

Dysart, Joe, "Winnebago Returns to Profitability, Debuts '93 Units," *RVBusiness,* August 1992, p. 14.

Gissen, Jay, "Good Times in Forest City," *Forbes,* February 13, 1984, p. 66.

Goldenberg, Sherman, "Downsized-Coach Niche Continues to Shrink," *RVBusiness,* July 1992, p. 14.

Greising, David, "The Unhappy Campers at Winnebago," *Business Week,* May 28, 1980, p. 28.

"Homes for Rent—On Wheels," *Business Week,* February 14, 1970, p. 50.

Mintz, Steven, "Sales and Marketing to the Rescue," *Sales and Marketing Management,* April 4, 1983, p. 35.

"Motor Homes Produced by Winnebago Assailed by Auto Safety Group," *Wall Street Journal,* August 21, 1973, p. 6.

Reiff, Rick, "Bad News, Good Prospects," *Forbes,* October 31 1988, p. 39.

Rescigno, Richard, "Revved Up for Recovery: Recreational-Vehicle Makers Seem Ready to Roll Again," *Barron's,* June 17, 1991, p. 14.

"Winnebago Cuts Output of Motor Homes 25% as Sales Forecast Dips," *Wall Street Journal,* May 7, 1973.

"Winnebago Cutting Motor-Home Output 14%, Workers 8%," *Wall Street Journal,* April 30, 1979.

The Winnebago Story: 1958–1988, Forest City, IA: Winnebago Industries, Inc., 1988.

"Winnebago Trips on Overoptimism," *Business Week,* June 2, 1973, p. 25.

—*Maura Troester*

WORDPERFECT®

WordPerfect®

In the late 1970s, computer science graduate student Bruce Bastian was working on a thesis that used computers to generate three-dimensional graphics of marching-band configurations on a football field. Bastian's work attracted the attention of his faculty adviser at Brigham Young University, Alan C. Ashton, who had designed the outline of a word processing computer program when he was a graduate student in 1969. The two men teamed up and designed the first version of WordPerfect software. WordPerfect Corporation began in 1979 as Satellite Software International (SSI). By the early 1990s the word processing software that they developed had an installed base of more than 15 million users worldwide and existed in 28 languages across 11 operating environments.

From the beginning, the brand was not only synonymous with its company, but was also very closely identified with its founders, Ashton and Bastian. Headquartered in Orem, Utah, the software company gained a reputation for the kind of strength that derived from its conservative but forward-thinking leaders. Actively involved in the Church of Jesus Christ of Latter-day Saints, Bastian and Ashton ran their business with a family-centered attitude. As they grew in reputation and stature, Ashton and Bastian expanded without the benefit of venture capital, and the privately held company came to employ more than 5,000 people in the mid-1990s.

The executives who were brought in largely shared in WordPerfect's vision, and the software reflected their devotion. In January 1994 Ashton and Bastian became co-chairmen of the company's board of directors, focusing on long-term strategic issues. A three-member office of the president was named, including Ad Rietveld, president and CEO; John C. Lewis, executive vice president; and R. Duff Thompson, executive vice president and general counsel.

Matching New Operating Systems

WordPerfect software was able to succeed in the marketplace because company executives stayed abreast of changes in the industry. Ashton's first design differed significantly from the early Wang word processors. WordPerfect's first software was based on the operating system known as DOS, which was the only player in the game for many years. In the 1980s, WordPerfect for DOS was the unchallenged industry leader. When Microsoft Windows entered the scene as a new kind of operating system, WordPerfect executives created a version of their software to run on Windows. But in the time it took them to perfect their new program, Microsoft's word processor, Microsoft Word, had been on the market for two years, and WordPerfect had lost market share.

Many industry leaders did not expect Windows to make such a quick change in the market and gain so many followers. By mid-1993, an estimated one-fifth of all PCs were running Windows. A market research firm, Dataquest Inc., predicted in the trade magazine *PC Week* that Windows-based word processors would increase their market from $315 million in 1991 to $640 million in 1996.

As other operating systems appeared, WordPerfect software was there to work with them. These operating systems, also known as platforms, provided new opportunities for WordPerfect software to branch out and reach more users. WordPerfect's word processor for OS/2 was rated by *PC Magazine* and *Computerworld* as the best word processor available in the format. By the end of 1993, the company discontinued work on a native OS/2 word processor and concentrated on making the Windows version of WordPerfect run well under OS/2. WordPerfect for the Macintosh was created for users of Macintosh and Apple computers. The version was updated in 1993. Apple's System 7 Pro was supported by WordPerfect's Macintosh version too.

Besides the more popular Windows, DOS, Macintosh, and OS/2 platforms, WordPerfect word processing was also available on UNIX, VMS, AS/400, and NEXTSTEP platforms. Its VMS users voted WordPerfect for VMS Systems the Target Award Winner for seven years running, in a competition sponsored by *Digital News and Review*.

Other Products

WordPerfect software began with stunning success in word processing, but soon expanded to include business packages, presentation software, communications software, electronic publishing, and consumer applications. These products included WordPerfect Office; WordPerfect Presentations; database software DataPerfect; LetterPerfect; WordPerfect Works; WordPerfect ClipArt; facsimile software for the fax/modem WP MTEZ/ExpressFax; and specialty products such as grammar checker Grammatik 5; Black's Law Dictionary; and Borland's Electronic Medical Speller.

AT A GLANCE

Precursor of WordPerfect software invented by Brigham Young University professor Alan Conway Ashton, 1977; with his computer science graduate student Bruce Bastian, wrote first version of WordPerfect word processing software, 1979; opened business called Satellite Software International (SSI), 1979; PC version of WordPerfect released, 1982; gradually introduced spreadsheet, database, communications, and other software programs; by 1990s had more than 15 million users.

Performance: *Market share*—60% of word processing software, 16% of business software. *Sales*—$705 million (1993).

Major competitor: Microsoft Word and Lotus Ami Pro for word processing; Microsoft Office and Lotus Smartsuite for business applications; Lotus cc:Mail for workgroup software.

Advertising: *Agency*—Some done in-house; other agencies since 1992 include Merkley Newman Harty, New York, NY; Dahlin Smith White, Salt Lake City, UT; Evans Communications, Salt Lake City, UT; and Hales Allen Inc., Provo, UT. *Major campaigns*—Advertisements in the early 1990s featured the slogans "Beyond Words" and "Dare to Compare."

Addresses: *Parent company*—WordPerfect Corporation, 1555 N. Technology Way, Orem, Utah 84057-2399; phone: (801) 225-5000, fax: (801) 222-5077; *Ultimate parent company*—Novell, Inc., 122 E. 1700 South, Provo UT 84606; phone: (801) 429-7000.

A growth area in the mid-1990s was communications software. WordPerfect's development of E-mail (electronic mail) software was well-received. WordPerfect Office featured E-mail that rivaled Microsoft's Microsoft Mail and Lotus' cc:Mail. WordPerfect's E-mail package could inter-operate across DOS, Macintosh, Windows, and Unix platforms. It was priced at $295 for a server and $495 for a five-user client pack. Known also as workgroup communications, it was the only software to integrate E-mail messages, calendars, task management, and scheduling.

WordPerfect Works included a word processor, a spreadsheet, graphics editor, database, and communications package. WordPerfect also introduced specialty products such as Black's Law Dictionary. When marketed with WordPerfect 6.0, for instance, it increased WordPerfect's appeal to legal professionals. In the early 1990s, WordPerfect acquired Reference Software International, Inc., and integrated its star product, Grammatik 5, into WordPerfect's own software. And, in 1994, WordPerfect released its new telephone interface software and portable document technology. Code named Envoy, "the product enables users to view, annotate, manipulate, and distribute documents without having the application in which those documents were created," WordPerfect press releases noted.

In developing new word processing software, WordPerfect was trying to make new systems customizable by users. OLE, or object linking and embedding technology became very important. With OLE, tools from one Windows application could be shared with other Windows applications. This was especially intriguing given the new popularity of multimedia programs. WordPerfect is also a proponent of the OpenDoc compound document architecture, along with Apple, Taligent, IBM, Xerox, and Novell.

Suites

Increasingly in the mid-1990s, software packages were being sold together in groups of programs known as suites. Microsoft had an advantage over WordPerfect, since it created the Microsoft Office 4.0 suite out of its own programs. WordPerfect teamed up with Borland International Inc. to create an office software suite called Borland Office for Windows, which featured WordPerfect for Windows as its word processor, Borland's Paradox for database management, and Borland's Quattro Pro spreadsheet. Priced at $595, it was competitive with suites from Microsoft and Lotus.

Some industry analysts were pessimistic about the marketability of suites. Many users needed one product almost to the exclusion of others, and some industry experts feared that not enough users needed suites. Some of the issues that arose in the creation of software suites were how to handle customer service, how to sell the package, and how to go about licensing their products. It also became trickier for the companies and industry statisticians to calculate sales of each individual product in the suite.

WordPerfect had worked with Borland earlier in a cross-marketing agreement. Licensed users of WordPerfect 5.1 for Windows could upgrade to WordPerfect 6.0 for Windows and Borland's Quattro Pro for Windows for $150 (The list price of both products, if purchased separately, is $495. They were also given the option to buy a package including Quattro Pro 4.0 for DOS and a Windows spreadsheet for $149.95. Users of competitive word processors could upgrade to WordPerfect for $149. The new suite is owned by Novell, which purchased Quattro Pro from Borland at the same time it signed the definitive merger agreement with WordPerfect.

Customer Service

One of the reasons for the brand's success was the consistently high marks customers gave the company for its support services. A poll by *PC Magazine* in 1992 gave WordPerfect the highest rating for customer service. WordPerfect received a score of above 8.5 on scale of 10, while all other rated software companies scored 7.5 and below. When customers called for toll-free software support, professional disc jockeys played music and talked about WordPerfect software while the call was being forwarded through the waiting queue of callers. WordPerfect's phone switches could handle more than 1,000 calls at a time. Customer service operators created a "hot list" of the most troublesome issues, which were later addressed and corrected. The company saw this as an efficient way to help make their products meet customers' needs.

By the mid-1990s, the company had to adjust to increasing demands on this toll-free system. Because many new software programs had been introduced and each of these needed customer-service representatives who were adequately trained, WordPerfect hired other support companies to assist its own technical support staff. There were complaints by some users of the original DOS-based WordPerfect that toll-free support was not really available since they reached busy signals so often.

Finally a decision was made to charge for support above a specified level. This practice was already widely accepted in the industry. Users said they would be willing to pay for more sophisticated and accessible services. According to Rietveld, this new system did not replace toll-free customer-support, which included free fax-back service as well as SpaceWorks on-line support and a bulletin board service. The fee-based support programs designed for medium- and large-sized organizations included the Platinum support program for $15,000 a year and the Gold support program for a $10,000 annual fee. Platinum support included around-the-clock technical support and a guaranteed response time of four hours. Gold support had an eight-hour guaranteed response time among other benefits. For individual customers wanting to take advantage of fee-based support programs on a per-incident basis, costs range from $2 per minute for desktop applications to $150 per incident for workgroup applications.

Advertising

Manufacturers of WordPerfect software began advertising and marketing slowly, and much of the reputation of WordPerfect word processing software was developed by word-of-mouth. As the climate became increasingly competitive, the corporation began to reach out to professional advertising agencies to assist its in-house advertising staff. Much of the software's advertising and marketing work was still done in-house in the 1990s, but both Utah-based and New York-based advertisers had been hired to create different campaigns to counteract the influence of their competitors. For a few years, Evans Communications of Salt Lake City was the lead agency for creative work on WordPerfect software's account, which was estimated at $ 5.5 million. They were succeeded in 1992 by Doremus and Co., of New York City.

Big changes were seen after Ad Rietveld was brought to the company's Utah headquarters from WordPerfect Europe to be senior vice president of sales and marketing in 1992. He focused on the U.S. market first, and then branched out to look at the international picture. As a member of the seven-member executive committee headed by president and CEO Ashton, Rietveld had a lot of influence in the marketing and sales of WordPerfect software. The company began to use television, direct sales, and sports sponsorships as new advertising media. The flagship word processor was sold in 28 languages in 117 countries, and foreign sales accounted for 40 percent of revenues in 1991. A sweepstakes campaign in the early 1990s emphasized WordPerfect software as the right product no matter the operating system. This 'Freedom of Choice' sweepstakes was part of a new marketing strategy that included corporate acquisitions, joint marketing ventures, and more advertising, public relations, and sales promotions.

Most of the revenue WordPerfect software brought into the company was from word processing, which accounted for an estimated 85 percent of sales by the mid-1990s, but as the company developed other products, advertising for the various software packages increasingly emphasized the non-word-processing software. The slogans "The word processor we developed but you designed" (for WordPerfect) and "E-mail is not enough anymore" (WordPerfect Office) was featured in the early 1990s. WordPerfect Corp, had considered changing its name as a result of the over-identification of the company with its word processor, but they decided it would be a shame to give up that strong brand identification, and have concentrated instead on educating the public about the other software made by WordPerfect.

In the early 1990s, software makers took to television to advertise their products. Microsoft's advertising campaign took direct aim at WordPerfect, comparing the two word processors by name. WordPerfect had three 60-second commercials that aired in early 1993. Created by Doremus and Co., each black-and-white commercial had a lifestyle theme that did not directly refer to its rivals. The scenes took place in offices, and WordPerfect products appeared in color. The aim was to build WordPerfect's image as a developer of high-tech software and to extend brand recognition beyond word processing. The spots emphasized the company's tradition of support and service for customers. Only one of the three commercials was for word processing. The other two featured WordPerfect Presentations workgroup software and WordPerfect Office. The commercials for presentation and communications software were the first TV advertisements in both of those software markets.

This campaign tripled WordPerfect's advertising budget, with an estimated cost of more than $6 million for the television campaign. The heated market share battle involved not only Microsoft, but also Lotus Development. Lotus's word processor Ami Pro was gaining rapidly in the mid-1990s, especially in the Windows environment as people were switching from DOS and shopping around for a new word processor.

Legal Issues

WordPerfect Corp. filed a lawsuit against Microsoft in the fall of 1993. The suit was quickly settled. At issue was a claim that Microsoft was making in advertisements and news releases that its Microsoft Word was the most popular word processing package in the world. Senior vice president for sales and marketing at WordPerfect, Ad Rietveld, was quoted in the *New York Times,* saying, "We take our leadership position seriously and will not allow competitors to make false claims."

The false claims, according to WordPerfect, violated trademark laws. Part of the discrepancy arose from the difficulty of counting the sales of suites. At the time of the lawsuit, Microsoft was selling more than half of its products in suites. It was agreed in the settlement that Microsoft Word could call itself the best selling, and WordPerfect could advertise itself as the most popular and all-time best-selling.

WordPerfect software executives had their hands full trying to police their title. Many software packages used the word "perfect" in their titles or descriptions. Despite the fact that most of these were not word processors, the company felt it was necessary to remind them of WordPerfect's trademark rights. As a result, attorneys for WordPerfect were continuously on the lookout for offenders.

Licensing

Licensing is not only difficult in software suites but also in individual software units. WordPerfect boasts one of the most flexible licensing policies in the industry, especially in the area of concurrent use. The license allows people to use the software on their home or portable computers. Only a few other software vendors allow this, and WordPerfect is the only one to allow this arrangement for networked software.

Earlier licensing arrangements did make accommodations for changing technology. While its Windows version of the word processor was in development, WordPerfect Corp. offered an upgrade policy to existing users. The upgrade policy was a license entitling buyers of the DOS version to run WordPerfect for Windows before the disks and documentation were available. This allowed WordPerfect buyers, especially in business settings, to continue buying WordPerfect for DOS and to upgrade to the Windows version when it was ready.

Rumors surfaced several times in the early 1990s that the brand had become so successful that the company was going to go public. An initial public offering, or IPO, was anticipated in the mid-1990s. WordPerfect Corp., as the largest privately held U.S. software company, was reputedly going to offer 10 million shares on the New York Stock Exchange, priced at $18 to $20 per share. Many industry analysts, therefore, were surprised by the March 21, 1994, announcement that Novell, the leading provider of network operating system software, was merging with and acquiring the WordPerfect Corp. in a stock swap valued at $1.4 billion. Novell also bought Borland International's Quattro Pro spreadsheet operation for $145 million.

Further Reading:

Bridges, Linda, "Where the Big Three are Headed," *PC Week,* April 19, 1993, p. 87.

Brown, Ted Smalley, "Word Processing on OS/2 Takes Shape," *PC Week,* July 12, 1993, p. 37; "WordPerfect to Fix WP 6.0 for DOS Bugs," *PC Week,* August 23, 1993, p. 39.

Clark, Don, "Popularity Contest Leads WordPerfect to Sue Microsoft," *Wall Street Journal,* October 18, 1993, p. B6.

Crowley, Aileen, "Vendors Wage War of Word Processors," *PC Week,* April 19, 1993, p. 87.

"The Datamation 100: North American Profiles," *Datamation,* June 15, 1993, p. 100.

Dubashi, Jagannath, "Customer Service: WordPerfect," *Financial World,* September 29, 1992, p. 58.

Fisher, Lawrence M., "WordPerfect Sues Microsoft in Ad Dispute," *New York Times,* October 16, 1993, p. 41; "Novell to Acquire WordPerfect," *New York Times,* March 22, 1994, p. C1.

Harris, Alison, "The Best Support Money Can Buy," *Service News,* February 1994.

Hoffman, Kurt, "Don't Go with the Flow," *Chilton's Distribution,* October 1992, p. 58.

Horton, Cleveland, "WordPerfect Triples Ad $," *Advertising Age,* December 14, 1992, p. 1.

Lewis, Peter H., "Drawing on Family Values to Fight the Software Wars," *New York Times,* October 3, 1993, Sec. 3, p. 8.

Mendelson, Edward, "Documents Take the Center," *PC Magazine,* November 9, 1993.

"Microsoft and WordPerfect Settle Lawsuit About Ads," *New York Times,* October 20, 1993, p. D4.

Moore, Mark, "WordPerfect Revs Graphics App[lication]," *PC Week,* July 12, 1993, p. 37; "WordPerfect Pay-for-Support Plan OK with Users," *PC Week,* October 25, 1993, p. 18.

Morrissey, Jane, "Borland, WordPerfect Strike a 'Suite' Deal," *PC Week,* April 26, 1993, p. 6.

Rooney, Paula, "Key Exec Resigns in Major Shake-Up at WordPerfect," *PC Week,* March 30, 1992, p. 5; "WordPerfect Acquires Leading Writing Utility," *PC Week,* January 11, 1993, p. 8; "WordPerfect, Borland Will Cross-Market Software Packages," *PC Week,* October 19, 1992, p. 20; "WordPerfect to Rendezvous with Wall Street," *PC Week,* September 21, 1992, p. 1.

Shipley, Chris, "The PC-C Top 100: The Year's Best-Selling Software," *PC-Computing,* January 1992, p. 140.

Singh, Jai, "Word from the WISE: WordPerfect Makes More Than Just WP," *PC Week,* November 16, 1992, p. 217.

Ulanoff, Lance N., "Word Processors," *PC Magazine,* June 16, 1992, p. 298.

—Francine Shonfeld Sherman

XEROX®

XEROX®

Founded in 1959, Xerox was the world's first brand of photocopier. It was developed by The Haloid Company of Rochester, New York, though much of the early research was done by Chester Carlson, who in 1938 invented of a photocopying process known as xerography. So successful was the first Xerox model, the 914, that Haloid became one of the wealthiest American corporations only two years after the product's introduction. In 1961 the company was renamed Xerox Corporation. Xerox would go on to pioneer other major products, such as the first laser printer, but none would compare in significance to the world's first photocopier.

Brand Origins

The world's first photocopier (as opposed to the copying machine, several varieties of which existed long before the Xerox product) was given the brand name Xerox in the 1950s, a shortened form of the word ''xerography.'' This word in turn was ''invented'' or construed by an Ohio State University classics professor in the late 1940s at the request of Battelle Memorial Institute, which was the first to take a serious look at Carlson's invention. Xerography was a combination of two Greek words, ''xeros'' for dry and ''graphein'' for writing, to describe Carlson's process of electrophotography.

The origins of the brand name Xerox came about more than ten years after Carlson's original invention. That discovery occurred in October 1938, when he succeeded in photocopying ''10-22-38 ASTORIA'' from a piece of paper. These barely legible figures had taken the grueling effort of nearly five years of experimentation. It would take another twenty years of hard work to refine Carlson's photocopying process for commercial use.

Carlson's reasons for undertaking such a formidable task, never attempted before, were as complex as he was. Very much a self-made man, he was motivated not only by the intellectual challenge but also out of the desire for more money (though when he finally became a multimillionaire in the 1960s, he gave up most of it to charitable causes). An only child, Carlson became the sole support of his family at age 14 and, by dint of hard work, made his way through junior college, graduating afterward with a B.S. in physics from the California Institute of Technology. His graduation in 1930 coincided with the onset of the Depression. Receiving over eighty job rejections, he finally was hired by Bell Laboratories in New York City, only to be laid off shortly afterward. Desperate, he took on a clerical job offered him by P.R. Mallory & Co. in New York. Much of his daytime work (he studied for a law degree at night) revolved around obtaining copies of documents and drawings. The frustrated Carlson realized how ideal it would be if there were an office machine that could effortlessly copy documents. The only copying machines available in his day required endless carbons with a typewriter, or were slow and inefficient, like the mimeograph machine (invented by Thomas Edison in 1887). High-quality reproductions were possible with the advent in the 1930s of offset printing, but this process took long and was very labor intensive.

Carlson began perusing everything in the New York Public Library connected with imaging, especially the ideas of the Hungarian physicist Paul Selenyi, a specialist in the little-known field of electrostatic images (light striking a photoconductive material and intensifying the electrical conductivity of that material). So intrigued was Carlson with this original approach to light imaging that he began experimenting with this method in the kitchen of his tiny apartment, where he set up a makeshift lab. By 1937 he had worked out the principles of electrophotography and applied for a patent, although he had not managed to get these principles to work.

First Commercial Success

Hiring Otto Kornei, a German refugee physicist as an assistant, Carlson intensified his efforts in a small lab in Astoria, New York. On October 22, 1938, they photocopied (by means of a zinc plate with sulfur coating) a piece of paper on which was written the date and location of the experiment, which became the historic first letters and numbers ever to be ''Xeroxed.'' Crude as this first photocopy was, it opened the door for further improvements.

Despite Carlson's high earnings by then as a patent attorney, the cost of refining his invention and turning it into a useful product was formidable. Company after company rejected Carlson's request for a research contract until he happened one day to present his ideas and the crude photocopying machine to an employee of Battelle Memorial Institute, a nonprofit research organization in Columbus, Ohio. In 1944 the institute, impressed by the possibilities it foresaw in the revolutionary process of electrophotography, signed a royalty contract with Carlson in which it promised to invest $3,000 to develop his process further (it was Battelle that also gave it the name ''xerography''). Shortly

AT A GLANCE

Xerox brand of photocopier introduced in 1959 by The Haloid Company of Rochester, New York; "xerography" (or electrophotograpy), the process that made photocopying by machine possible, invented two decades earlier, in 1938, by Chester Carlson; Haloid bought Carlson's patents in 1955; the first Xerox model, the 914, was the world's first automatic, plain-paper photocopier; company renamed Xerox Corporation in 1961.

Performance: *Market share*—18% of U.S. copier category (1991). *Sales*—$7.5 billion.

Major competitor: Canon, Ricoh, Sharp.

Advertising: *Agency*—Young & Rubicam, New York, NY, 1990—. *Major campaign*—"The Document Company," print ads, aimed at small businesses, giving case histories of how Xerox equipment and services increased office productivity.

Addresses: *Parent company*—Xerox Corporation, 800 Long Ridge Road, P.O. Box 1600, Stamford, CT 06904; phone: (202) 968-3000; fax: (203) 968-4312.

afterward Battelle in turn contracted with The Haloid Company to develop a useful "xerographic" machine.

Haloid at that time was headed by a visionary new president, Joseph C. Wilson. The nondescript firm, a manufacturer of photostatic paper, was eagerly searching for a new product with which to boost its declining sales. Intrigued by xerography, which a Haloid employee had stumbled upon in a scientific journal, the company got in touch with Battelle. By then Battelle researchers had discovered in selenium, a common chemical, a greatly improved photoconductor over sulphur. Battelle officials were happy to find a buyer of a product that they had researched and developed but were not equipped to manufacture. In 1947 Battelle and Haloid signed a contract that gave Haloid a license to manufacture and market a practical xerographic device (and in 1955 Haloid gained full title to the Carlson patents). Two years later Haloid came out with its first Model A xerographic machine, so huge that it could not even fit through an office door and so complicated that it took at least three minutes for a trained attendant to make a copy of anything. The few such models that were manufactured were returned.

It would take another ten years for the first usable office photocopier to appear. Haloid invested every spare penny in developing the machine, to the point that new employees were told to bring their own desks to work with them. The president of the company himself brought along a lunch pail and used orange crates for bookcases. In the end, in 1959, the model 914 was introduced to the world. It, too, was so heavy that it barely fit through an office door, but it was simple, so simple that a child could use it. Moreover, the copies were excellent, requiring only plain paper. While not an overnight success, it would pave the way to the company's fame and fortune.

Early Marketing Strategy

Few offices in 1959 were willing to pay nearly $30,000 for an untried, 650-pound machine, even if it was the world's first automatic, plain-paper copier. There also was notable disaffection in the company over the product's name, which many disliked for its weirdness, meaninglessness, and similarity to the word "zero." Nonetheless, before the 914 saw the light of day, the company's president, Joe Wilson, insisted that this trademark name be adopted, and in 1961 the company changed its name to Xerox Corporation.

It became obvious that people would not be breaking down doors to purchase the enormous 914 photocopier, and there were not enough of them to take to prospective customers to demonstrate (and even had there been, merely transporting the 914s was a logistical nightmare). Hence, a strategy was devised to bring the colossus to the public's attention via canny advertising and a marketing strategy brilliantly suited to the new machines. This strategy consisted not of trying to sell the extremely pricey photocopiers but of leasing them out. A company could order a Xerox photocopier on a fifteen-day trial basis and return it; by far the majority kept the machines, leasing one for a modest monthly sum of less than $100 and a user fee after the minimum monthly number of copies was exceeded (meters monitored the number of copies). This was so practical and affordable that it turned into an unhoped for success, above and beyond the company's wildest dreams. Until well into the 1970s leasing remained the company's main marketing strategy. Thereafter selling photocopiers (which by then were cheaper and far, far smaller and lighter) became the marketing goal.

Advertising

In order to lease, there had to be customers. While it was impractical to tow the cumbersome 914s all over the country for demonstration purposes, the sales men and women devised an advertising ploy that targeted a few highly trafficked areas for displaying the new photocopiers. One of these was the office of Merrill Lynch, situated in New York's Grand Central Station, which drew thousands daily to the Xerox display. The new 914s also received much press coverage. Shortly after the 914 appeared on the market in 1959, *Business Week* featured the machine on its cover.

Television was by far and away the most important medium for advertising the new Xerox machines. Some of the award-winning TV ads emphasized the simplicity of using the new photocopier. In one a child is asked by her father to copy some papers (and she coyly snatches her doll to put on the machine, along with the documents); in another a monkey swings on a rope, snatches some paper from his "boss," photocopies them on a 914, and swings back with the copies. Later, an award-winning series of television commercials centered on a monk, Brother Dominic, who is a scribe in a monastery. In one commercial the monk is asked by his superior to make 500 sets of a document. Downcast at the enormity of the task, Brother Dominic suddenly has the inspiring idea of hopping on a bus, rushing off to a copier store, and breathlessly asking the attendant if he could turn out the required number of copies. By then Xerox copiers were the newer, faster 9200 series, and in virtually no time the monk had the desired number of copies. After he rushes back to his superior with the copies, the older monk exclaims in wonder, "It's a miracle!"

Product Development

The model 914, the world's first ever automatic photocopier, was an enormous success. Four years after its introduction, Xerox Corporation, which had staked everything on its development and marketing, climbed the ranks of the Fortune 500 companies. From an annual sales revenue of only $32 million in 1959, company revenues soared to more than one billion dollars nine years later.

Although Xerox had no competition, there was some anxiety at the company about the potential of wealthier and bigger firms invading the photocopier market (as indeed happened—IBM followed by Kodak). Consequently, Xerox was not content to rest on its laurels. The appearance of the historic 914 was followed by the 813, which was the first true desktop photocopier; thereafter came the 2400 series, which could churn out forty copies per minute.

With the increasing sophistication of the photocopiers produced by Xerox, the monthly lease went up accordingly, greatly increasing the company's revenues. In the 1970s, however, complacency set in, as well as layers of bureaucracy, despite the rise of competition from the Japanese. Unlike American manufacturers, including Xerox, the Japanese emphasized the quality and reliability of their machines, at the time notoriously absent in Xerox photocopiers, which emphasized speed and simplicity of use. The 1970s saw the arrival of the 9200 copier, which could produce 120 copies a minute; the 4000 copier, the first photocopier that could copy on both sides of a page; and another series, the 3100, Xerox's smallest copier.

The 1980s witnessed a major transformation of the Xerox Corporation, which radically downsized and restructured in response to the emergence of the Japanese in the worldwide copier market. Besides sophisticated, high-quality copiers like the 10 Series machines, equipped with tiny microprocessors, and its 5775 digital color copier, Xerox was developing and marketing a whole range of products that justified its slogan, "The Document Company." Among these were the world's first laser printer; Ethernet (developed by the company's research arm), which enabled workstations to communicate among themselves; a computer mouse; and the first graphics-oriented monitor. The company also developed and sold facsimile machines, scanners, and computer software and supplies, as well as support services. Copiers progressively became more multifunctional, and the Docutech Publishing series, which combined copier, scanner, and printer, emphasized the company's leadership role in desktop publishing products. Hence, from catastrophic market share declines in the 1970s, Xerox gradually bounced back and even regained significant market share from its Japanese competitors, remaining the number one U.S. player in the domestic market.

International Growth

Xerox had a global presence as early as 1956, when Haloid formed a joint venture with a British motion-picture firm to establish Rank Xerox Limited, which in 1962 entered into a joint partnership with a Japanese photo-film company to form Fuji Xerox. This marked the beginnings of what would encompass, thanks to intense Japanese competition in the 1970s, a global marketing strategy. Unlike most of its Japanese competitors, Xerox had a marketing presence in more than one hundred countries worldwide and manufacturing centers on four continents; with a global distribution network, Xerox products had penetrated over 130 countries around the world. Unlike most American corporations, Xerox had established a strong and growing presence in eastern Europe and the countries of the former USSR.

Brand Outlook

Of the major U.S manufacturers of copy machines, only Xerox and Kodak retained major market shares in the 1990s, with Japanese companies Canon, Sharp, Ricoh, and Minolta possessing the lion's share of the world market. Xerox was the number two seller of photocopiers in North America, where it had an 18 percent market share (compared with Canon's 27 percent). This was small compared with Xerox's stunning 85 percent market share in 1974, which such Japanese companies as Sharp and Canon eroded to only 10 percent nine years later. Nonetheless, nearly doubling its market share in only a few years since 1985 was a sign of vitality and growth.

While the copier market was mature, it changed constantly—from plain-paper copiers to color copiers to multifunctional copiers—and was far from stagnant. Moreover, approximately one-third of Xerox's multibillion dollar revenue was derived from sales abroad, a percentage that was increasing annually. Coupled with major restructuring and cost-cutting and its global presence in over 130 countries, Xerox would continue to be a major player in the United States and world markets well into the 21st century.

Further Reading:

Buehlmann, David M. and D. Stover, "How Xerox Solves Quality Problems," *Management Accounting (USA),* September 1993, p. 33.

Camp, Robert C., "A Bible for Benchmarking, by Xerox," *Financial Executive,* July-August 1993, p. 23.

DeYoung, H. Garrett, "Back from the Brink: Xerox Redefines Its Notion of Quality," *Electronic Business,* October 16, 1989, p. 50.

Driscoll, Lisa, "The New, New Thinking at Xerox," *Business Week,* June 22, 1992, p. 120.

Flatow, Ira, *They All Laughed: From Light Bulbs to Lasers,* New York: HarperCollins, 1992.

Gabor, Andrea, *The Man Who Discovered Quality: How W. Edwards Deming Brought the Quality Revolution to America, the Stories of Ford, Xerox and GM,* New York: Times/Random House, 1990.

Hage, David, "Xerox Seeks a Green Light for Growth," *US News & World Report,* May 11, 1992, p. 51.

Hamashige, Hope, "Rivalry, Recession Reduce Copier Sales Firms' Ranks, but Xerox Retains Hold on No. 1 Spot by Wide Margin," *Los Angeles Business Journal,* March 22, 1993, p. 23.

Horovitz, Bruce, "Xerox Wants to Portray Unified Global Image (Advertising)," *Los Angeles Times,* July 24, 1990, p. D6.

Jacobson, Gary, and John Hillkirk, *Xerox, American Samurai,* New York: MacMillan, 1986.

Kearns, David T., *Prophets in the Dark: How Xerox Reinvented Itself and Beat Back the Japanese,* New York: Harper Business, 1992.

Lafayette, Jon, "Y&R 'Together' With Xerox," *Advertising Age,* July 30, 1990, p. 4.

LeGallee, Julie, "Copier Technology Improves with New Features and Uses," *The Office,* April 1993, p. 38.

Nevin, Frederick W., "A Corporate Concern for the Environment (Xerox)," *Modern Office Technology,* November 1992, p. 14.

Smith, Douglas K., *Fumbling the Future: How Xerox Invented, Then Ignored the First Personal Computer,* New York: W. Morrow, 1988.

The Story of Xerography, Stamford, Connecticut: Xerox Corporation.

Tilles, Daniel, "Pushing the East European Advertising Envelope," *Adweek Eastern Edition,* October 4, 1993, p. 9.

Vogel, Todd, "At Xerox, They're Shouting 'Once More into the Breach' (Xerox Corp.'s Marketing and Product Development)," *Business Week,* July 23, 1990, p. 62.

Xerox Corporation: Annual Report, 1992.

"Xerox Corp. to Unveil New Photographic Process," *Los Angeles Times,* October 30, 1993, p. D2.

—Sina Dubovoj

YAMAHA®

YAMAHA

The Yamaha brand name means entirely different things to different consumers. Cyclists recognize Yamaha as a motorcycle manufacturer, while sportsmen may know it as a line of outboard motors, snowmobiles, skis or golf equipment. Musicians regard Yamaha as one of the finest names in instruments, while audiophiles associate the name with quality stereo equipment.

For many years Yamaha was simply a brand name affixed to products built by the Nippon Gakki company. But in an effort to better leverage the brand's value, the company adopted Yamaha as its corporate name in 1987. This was a wise choice because while virtually everyone had heard of Yamaha, a not too cumbersome name, very few had ever heard of Nippon Gakki.

Brand Origins

The Yamaha name has its origin with Torakusu Yamaha, a watchmaker who in 1889 established a factory to build organs for primary schools. Yamaha renamed his enterprise the Nippon Gakki (or "Japan Musical Instruments") Company in 1897 and began to also manufacture pianos. The company won widespread recognition for its craftsmanship, and during World War I added harmonicas to its product line.

Based on its woodcarving expertise, Nippon Gakki began crafting aircraft propellers in 1920, a small but important venture because it introduced the company to large industrial combines that built airplanes. In the ensuing years Nippon Gakki endured its founder's death, a major fire, the Great Kanto Earthquake, massive labor trouble, and an appreciating yen. Unable to compete with imported instruments on any basis but price, Yamaha instituted a major quality improvement effort in 1930 and added a pipe organ to its product line in 1932. The company's primary market remained the public school system, which enjoyed tremendous government support during the 1930s.

At the outset of World War II, Yamaha was directed by the government to manufacture steel propellers, fuel tanks, and wing sections for aircraft. This marked an important change in the company's business, enabling it to earn valuable industrial experience that would not have been possible in a peacetime economy. Yamaha survived the war with only one factory intact, but resumed instrument production in November of 1945. With expertise gained during the war, Yamaha began casting its own metal piano frames and horns, and introduced a line of guitars in 1946 and a phonograph a year later. In 1948 the Education Ministry made music instruction mandatory in Japanese schools. This, coupled with the proliferation of Yamaha music schools, provided an enormous new market for Yamaha instruments.

Early Marketing Strategy

By the early 1950s, Nippon Gakki had become the largest instrument manufacturer in Asia and, in terms of sales, one of the largest in the world. In order to secure continued growth, it became necessary for the company to expand into new markets. Nippon Gakki retrieved its wartime metal works from the government in 1954 and began research into metal alloys for electronics and structures, yielding a line of boilers and heating systems for the housing industry. The company produced its first motorcycle—a 125cc model—in 1954, and subsequently established the Yamaha Motor Company to develop other applications for its small engine technologies. Shortly afterward, Yamaha introduced a line of outboard motors, snowmobiles, and golf carts.

Nippon Gakki president Genichi Kawakami launched research into fiber reinforced plastics after a tour of the United States in 1953. This enabled the company to diversify into sailboats in 1960, and later yachts and patrol boats. Seeking other applications for plastics, Nippon Gakki began manufacturing skis, archery equipment, and bathtubs. Despite the diverse nature of Nippon Gakki's expansion, its product lines had one thing in common: with few exceptions, they were all for the leisure and hobby markets. But with every product, the company emphasized manufacturing quality. This was represented in the company's abstract logo, comprised of three tuning forks.

International Growth

Nippon Gakki established its first foreign office in Mexico in 1958. The company manufactured a number of pianos for an American retail chain, and because the most promising market was the United States, Nippon Gakki set up a second office in Los Angeles in 1960. The company repeated its earlier marketing strategy by targeting institutional markets. Its high-quality pianos were priced considerably lower than competing models, enabling the company to win prestige-building contracts with several major school systems. To further drive demand, Nippon Gakki established a string of Yamaha music schools, as it had in Japan.

AT A GLANCE

Established in 1897 as Nippon Gakki Company, an organ manufacturer; pianos added in 1900, harmonicas in 1917, and accordions c. 1930; began war production in 1938, resumed instrument manufacturing after brief hiatus in 1945; guitars added in 1946, phonograph in 1947; music schools established in 1954; first motorcycle produced in 1954, followed by outboard motors, snowmobiles, and golf carts; electone electric organ produced in 1959; fiber reinforced plastic sailboat produced in 1960, followed by sports cars, motorboats, outboard engines, yachts, and patrol boats; wind instruments established in 1965; Yamaha automobile engine marketed in 1966; Concert Grand Piano developed and Yamaha Trail DTI motorcycle introduced in 1967; snowmobiles and stereos added in 1968, golf carts in 1975, and all-terrain vehicles in 1979; integrated circuits and DX-7 synthesizer marketed in 1983.

Major competitors: Suzuki, Outboard Marine, and Brunswick (in sporting equipment); Sony (in electronics); Steinway, Kawai, and Baldwin (in pianos).

Advertising: *Agency*—Saatchi & Saatchi DFS/Pacific (Motorcycles and Snowmobiles); Hoffman York & Compton, Milwaukee (Marine). *Major campaign*—"Yamaha . . . Today is the Day" (motorcycles).

Addresses: *Parent company*—Yamaha Corporation, 10-1, Nakazawa-che, Yamamatsu, Shizuoka 430, Japan, (0534) 60-2141; phone: 534 602850; fax: 534 652-798.

While Yamaha had a burgeoning market for motorcycles in Asia, it was among the first Japanese brands to be widely marketed in the United States. Demand for several models increased after garnering awards at the Tokyo Motor Shows during the 1960s. To better drive demand in overseas markets, Yamaha Motor established sales subsidiaries in the United States in 1977 and in Australia in 1983.

Nippon Gakki remained an aggressive international marketing powerhouse. While virtually all its products were made in Japan, the company established sales subsidiaries throughout Europe and North and South America during the 1970s. To circumvent imminent import controls and reduce transportation expenses, the company opened an electronic keyboard factory in Georgia in 1980. Other similar facilities were established later in the decade, enabling the company to better control inventories and respond to periodic changes in demand. This minimized costs and kept prices below key consumer price points. As a result, people who would otherwise have passed up a Yamaha product purchased it because it was affordable.

Turning to developing markets, Yamaha set up an instrument factory in China in 1989, and stepped up exports to that country during the early 1990s. While vast, the Chinese market is already populated with hundreds of low-end instrument manufacturers. But Yamaha's strategy is not to place a piano in every home, as it had set out to do in Japan, but to gain just a small but still formidable share of the 1.2-billion person market that demands a high-quality instrument.

Brand Development

The company introduced Japan's first electric organ, the Electone, in 1959. This product ushered Nippon Gakki into a new market for electronic instruments and components that would prove valuable in later years.

By seeding the market for interest in its products through its music schools, Nippon Gakki, in effect, created a demand for its pianos. Annual piano production increased from 24,000 in 1960 to 100,000 by 1966. Because widespread musical literacy had been achieved, the company decided to branch into the markets for other instruments. Chairman Genichi Kawakami spearheaded its entry into the market for wind instruments in 1965, including trumpets, trombones, and saxophones. Nippon Gakki began large-scale production of these products and xylophones in 1968. A year later, disgruntled American piano makers launched a costly, but ultimately unsuccessful, battle to assign tariffs against Nippon Gakki and other foreign piano manufacturers.

Building on its experience with the Electone organ, Nippon Gakki attempted to further incorporate integrated circuits into its electronic instruments and stereos, which were introduced in 1968. But it was unable to find a supplier interested in making the small quantity of special components needed by the company. Instead, Nippon Gakki established its own electronics lab in 1971. By entering the electronics market at an early stage, Nippon Gakki reduced its reliance on suppliers such as Toshiba and Fujitsu, which were active in the home audio market. In time, the company's electronic components were used to create digital electronic instruments, such as electric pianos and organs and synthesizers. Nippon Gakki gradually replaced all but a small percentage of its electronics needs with internal production. In 1983, the company began marketing its own circuitry products. The electronics group focused on four markets: integrated circuits and semiconductors, audio/visual equipment, theater acoustics, and Yamaha stereo products.

Advertising

In the American market, Yamaha engages in almost no broadcast advertising. Promotion of the company's products is limited to print ads and point-of-sale displays. These ads, regardless of the product, are not flashy, nor do they appear highly scientific. They are simple information-based ads that efficiently communicate the attributes of the product.

Perhaps due to the nature of the motorcycle buyer, promotion in this area is slightly more energetic in composition. However, no themes have been developed for consistent use. Instead, new campaigns are developed with every new product in the line. This pattern is the same for outboard motor products.

Within the instrument and stereo market, Yamaha excels mainly on its reputation. The company's name is prominently displayed on its keyboards, which may often be seen in the hands of famous musicians. The company's products occupy the high end of the mass-production market, so while they are generally affordable, their price indicates a level of quality above names like Sony and Denon—and their performance bears this out.

In other markets, such as golf and tennis equipment, golf carts, all-terrain vehicles, snowmobiles and the like, Yamaha competes in tight niche markets, where sales volume is more heavily dependent on distribution channels. As a result, promotional campaigns for these products have a very low profile.

Modern Development

The Yamaha Motor division, established in 1955 to seize a stronger position for Yamaha in the small engine products market, absorbed Kitagawa Automobile Industries in 1959. The division introduced a line of motorboats and outboard engines in 1960. Yamaha introduced a sports car in 1964, and continued to build automobiles until 1970, when it was squeezed out of the market by competitors such as Nissan and Suzuki. The company began building yachts in 1965, and began providing automobile engines to the subcontractor market in 1966. The division added a line of snowmobiles in 1968, golf carts in 1975 and all-terrain vehicles in 1979.

The company substantially strengthened its position in the motorcycle market in 1967 when it introduced the Yamaha Trail DTI, a 250cc model that won a prestige-building award at the Tokyo Motor Show. The model inspired greater interest from dealerships, particularly in the Unites States, and established strong distribution channels for subsequent models, including the four-stroke 650cc XSI, introduced in 1970.

The Yamaha Motor division had long trailed Honda in the motorcycle market when, in 1982, it boldly claimed that it would surpass this rival. To gain market share, Yamaha boosted production and cut prices, hoping to make up for slimmer margins with greater volume. Honda defended its position by following suit. In their battle for supremacy, the two companies flooded the North American market with motorcycles, prompting the leading American manufacturer, Harley-Davidson, to press for strict import duties. Ultimately, Yamaha and Honda abandoned their ruthless and loss-making price competition, but with little relief for the beleaguered Harley-Davidson.

Hiroshi Kawakami, a former Sony employee, was named president of Nippon Gakki in 1983. Kawakami boosted the company's audio products division, introducing new lines of stereo equipment, targeted mainly at the high-end audiophile market. But while musical instruments and home electronics accounted for nearly two-thirds of the company's sales, losses in the Yamaha Motor division had a great enough impact on Nippon Gakki to cause severe financial reverses.

Nippon Gakki was by this time wildly diversified into seven separate markets: motorcycles, snowmobiles, outboard motors, electrical components, acoustic products, instruments, and sporting goods. But rather than simplify the company's operations by paring down the number of product lines—to concentrate on more profitable core operations—Kawakami instituted a decentralization.

Research and development yielded a significant new product around this time with the launch of a line of customized chips for CD players, which Nippon Gakki provided for Yamaha's stereo group as well as for competitors. This earned the company a leading position in musical electronics, and yielded the revolutionary DX-7 keyboard. The DX-7 could reproduce any sound, either from a memory cartridge or from a microphone, and was widely used by keyboard players in every musical genre.

In 1987 Kawakami's son Hiroshi took control of the company and eliminated the Nippon Gakki identity in favor of the better known Yamaha name, in the belief that a company involved in so many markets should not have a name like "Japan Musical Instruments"—even if musical instruments comprised the company's strongest product line.

In an effort to boost sales in the marine propulsion market, Yamaha borrowed the example of its music schools. The company sponsored courses on water sports through boating schools in an effort to drive demand for new marine products, such as the Pro V 175 and SWS 225 outboard motors. In 1994 Yamaha introduced a new flagship line of marine engines called the Saltwater Series. Available in five horsepower types, this series of V-6 boat motors contains several features intended specifically to compete with market-leading Suzuki models.

Performance Evaluation

On the surface, the Yamaha brand name appears to have been somewhat haphazardly extended to several lines of unrelated products. In fact, the brand remains limited largely to the high-end, luxury segment of leisure and entertainment products markets. The fact that it appears in so many markets is an indication of how the company has leveraged its experience in one product line to launch others. For example, Yamaha's background in musical instruments provided a segue into electronics, and from there to home stereos and integrated circuit manufacturing. Its metal casting experience earned it a place in motor manufacturing. This led the company into the small automotive market, primarily in sports machinery. This, in turn, ushered Yamaha into sporting goods.

However, Yamaha has recently been stung by setbacks in its core product lines in its key markets. Consumer demand has become saturated as competition has increased, while the Japanese market—which accounts for more than 70 percent of the company's sales—has floundered from a lingering economic recession. Unable to maintain profitability and stem slowing growth rates at Yamaha, Hiroshi Kawakami, Jr. attempted to cut costs by instituting an early retirement program for the company's bloated work force. He was rebuffed by labor unions and forced to resign, ending three generations of leadership by the Kawakami family.

Future Predictions

Hideto Eguchi, who replaced Kawakami in 1992, has concentrated instead on improving product innovation. One example is the Disklavier, an acoustic piano married to a computer, which is capable of precisely regenerating master performances for the student. This has added new strength for Yamaha in a market previously thought to have matured. Another strength is the company's FM synthesis chip, a synthesizer component that emulates the sounds of other instruments. The chip is the heart of the Yamaha YMF262 synthesizer, a popular successor to the DX-7.

But in setting a course for further product development, Eguchi's main task will be to accurately gauge which new products have the greatest market potential and set priorities for their introduction. Clearly, Yamaha's future rests not with its excellent reputation, but in its ability to consistently introduce revolutionary products worthy of its name.

Further Reading:

"Advances in Sound Chips Targeted at Corporate Arena," *PC Week,* July 6, 1992, p. 28.

"Yamaha on its Own Turf," *Boating Industry,* July 1993, p. 42.

"Yamaha Outboards," *Motor Boating & Sailing*, August 1993, p. 22.

"Yamaha's First Century," *Music Trades,* August 1987.

"Yamaha Motor Co., Ltd.," "Yamaha Corporation," *Diamond's Japan Business Directory 1993,* pp. 862–863, 916–917.

"Yamaha Corporation," *Hoover's Handbook of World Business 1993,* pp. 496–497.

"Yamaha: A Century of Excellence: 1887–1987," Yamaha Corp.

—John Smiley

ZENITH®

Prior to the 1970s the American consumer electronics market was dominated by names like General Electric, RCA, Philco, and, prominently, Zenith. In fact, Zenith was a premium brand for more than 40 years when it first met competitors like Sony, Mitsubishi, and Sanyo. Unprepared for an onslaught of cheaper, better-built radios and televisions, Zenith—and the American electronics industry in general—was nearly wiped off the map. By 1990, Zenith was the only remaining American-owned brand still on the market. American brand names had gained notorious, and often well-deserved, reputations for poor quality and shoddy design. To remain in the market against this growing prejudice, Zenith required not only a remake of its public image, but a fundamental re-engineering of its design and marketing operations.

Brand Origins

Zenith was first used as a brand name during the 1920s, after two amateur radio operators, R. H. G. Mathews and Karl Hassel, acquired a license to build radios based on a design patented by Edwin Armstrong. In addition to assembling receivers, the pair set up communication systems for the Nashville, Chattanooga, and St. Louis railroad and the *Chicago Tribune,* operating under the name "Chicago Radio Laboratory." Hassel and Mathews began broadcasting from a cubbyhole at their small factory, hoping that the service would boost radio sales. The call letters of their station were 9ZN. Looking for a snappy brand name, the radio builders used their broadcasting moniker to create the name "Z-Nith."

On New Year's Eve, 1920, Chicago automobile dealer Eugene F. McDonald, Jr., who came to be known at Zenith as "The Commander," noticed several men in a repair garage listening to a music box. McDonald was stunned to learn that this was a radio and that the music was coming through the air from Pittsburgh. Unable to buy a radio, McDonald tried to begin a radio company, but found that Armstrong's licenses had all been sold. He later learned of Hassel and Mathews, and, after purchasing one of their radios, offered to capitalize their fledgling enterprise. However, McDonald considered the Z-Nith name awkward; people were inclined to pronounce it "*zee*-nith." His one condition for backing the company was that its name be changed to Zenith.

Zenith was used not only as a brand name for radios made by the Chicago Radio Laboratory, but as the name of the company's sales and marketing organization. McDonald headed the Zenith Radio Corporation, a marketing organization that absorbed the Chicago Radio Laboratory in 1923.

Brand Development

The Zenith Radio Corporation established a successor to 9ZN, a radio station called WJAZ. This station and a loose band of affiliates introduced the concept of radio advertising, which later included sales pitches for Zenith radios. The company sold WJAZ in 1924, but retained the call letters for a mobile radio station that toured the nation making promotional broadcasts for Zenith Radio Corporation.

By this time, Hassel had invented a tuning device that had nothing to do with Armstrong's patent. The Super-Zenith, as it was called, could be built without the burden of royalty payments. Zenith introduced the first portable radio in 1924. The $200 portable model, revolutionary in its day, was merely installed in a suitcase.

A combination of brand promotion, inventiveness, and high quality standards led to the brand's increasing popularity. McDonald's brilliant marketing ideas helped establish the Zenith brand name. He arranged to have the company's radios taken on Arctic expeditions by Donald MacMillan, and then aired broadcasts to the team that could be heard all over North America. In a demonstration intended to prod the Commerce Department into allowing use of shortwave bands, Zenith radios were used to link expeditions in Tasmania and Greenland. The Zenith name was further enhanced by strict attention to design and manufacturing innovation and product quality. Zenith radios were sturdy, well-built systems that almost never broke down. Gradually, Zenith gained a substantial installed base.

The company made a brief foray into railroad communications, but elected instead to pursue the development of household radio sets. In 1926, Zenith developed a radio that ran on AC wall current, eliminating heavy, messy batteries. A second innovation was the inclusion of a push-button mechanism that automatically tuned the radio to a number of preset stations.

The Great Depression forced Zenith into a drastic retrenchment. The company developed a new line of smaller, less expensive sets to keep production running. Sales, which had reached $1 million in 1929, were decimated. However, after five

AT A GLANCE

Zenith brand of radios and televisions introduced in 1919 as "Z-Nith" by R. H. G. Mathews and Karl Hassel, founders of the Chicago Radio Laboratory; brand name changed to Zenith in 1921; company incorporated as Zenith Radio Corporation in 1923; first experimental television made in 1931; television marketed in 1948; began production of VCRs in 1978 and entered computer market in 1979; ceased radio production in 1982; company name changed in 1984 to Zenith Electronics Corporation; sold computer operations in 1989.

Performance: *Sales*—$1.2 billion.

Major competitor: RCA; also Magnavox and Sony.

Advertising: *Agency*—Foote, Cone & Belding, 1964—. *Major campaign*—"Watch Us."

Addresses: *Parent company*—Zenith Electronics Corporation, 1000 Milwaukee Avenue, Glenview, IL 60025-2493; phone: (708) 391-7000.

years, sales recovered with terrific force, topping $8 million in 1936, and $34 million in 1942.

Despite the tough economic climate, Zenith enhanced its radio designs and developed new products. In 1934, Zenith introduced a car radio with a tuning mechanism that was mounted on the steering wheel. The following year, the company introduced a new line of radios with more precise tuning and large black dials, which could be read from a distance or without glasses. The design was extremely popular, and even inspired imitation from competitors. Zenith built the first radio baby monitor, the "Radio Nurse," in 1937. This enabled parents to hear a baby's crying from another room or floor. The fastest growing product was a line of shortwave receivers with which listeners could hear broadcasts. Zenith gained fame throughout the world for its "TransOceanic" radio.

Extensions

Zenith advocated standards for broadcasting television, a technology first demonstrated in 1926. Zenith opened this new market as it had radio, by establishing its own broadcast station, W9XZV, in 1939. The station was used primarily for testing reception and as an experimental telephone-based pay-per-view system—40 years ahead of its time. Zenith also branched into FM radio, a super-high fidelity system being pioneered by Armstrong. The company set up an FM station, W9XEN, in 1940. Because W9XEN aired classical music, Zenith engineers found it necessary to develop an equally high-fidelity phonograph, leading to commercialization of a tone arm called the Cobra.

All these extensions were interrupted by World War II, during which Zenith converted its operations entirely to military production. The company built radio and radar equipment, frequency meters, and radio bomb fuses. In the process, it developed new manufacturing techniques and better designs. One of the first commercial products to benefit from this work was a hearing aid, introduced in 1943 to enable hearing impaired people to join the war effort in factories.

After the war, Zenith plunged headlong into television, pioneering the use of the UHF band by setting up another station called KS2XBR. In 1947, Zenith restarted its subscription television system, called Phonevision, in the belief that the growing number of broadcasters would so dilute ad revenue that none could remain in business. This never occurred, and the technologically successful system was killed by 20-plus years of lobbying by Hollywood.

Zenith produced its first television set in 1948. It featured a VHF dial and an as yet unused UHF dial. When the FCC opened use of UHF frequencies in 1952, Zeniths were the only sets in use that were capable of pulling in channels on the band. Zenith did pioneering work in color television beginning in the early 1950s, including the first 21-inch three-cathode-ray-gun color picture tube in 1952. The company refused to market the color TV, however, until its size and cost could be reduced. Zenith strengthened its position in home entertainment in 1955, when it introduced an integrated radio, television, and phonograph in a single cherrywood cabinet. Other variations on this design continued well into the 1960s, after the advent of stereo records and FM stereo, a Zenith innovation authorized by the FCC in 1961.

Advertising

At its outset, Zenith's biggest advertising dilemma lay in merchandising. Its radios were tremendously expensive by the standards of the day. With little capital in the early 1920s, the company could not afford newspaper advertising. Instead, Zenith established its own broadcast stations—not to provide endless sales pitches but, with far more foresight, to drive the formation of industry standards and bring greater variety to the airwaves, thus encouraging the purchase of radios.

Zenith began to use print advertising in the late 1920s. In addition to extolling the virtues of the revolutionary radio, the ads boldly splashed the Zenith logo across the ad copy. The name was special in several ways. As a word that began with the letter Z, it was exotic. The sound it represented made people think of the buzz and zap of electricity, which was still a wondrous and modern thing. To drive these points home, the logo's Z was depicted as a giant lightning bolt. Helping matters, Zenith was a common word that described the ultimate in performance, quality, and achievement.

Print ads defined the qualities of the product, and often urged consumers to avoid being saddled with an inferior older model by trading up to a Zenith. In 1927, Zenith ad men created the zippy slogan, "The quality goes in before the name goes on." Battling its image as an expensive product, Zenith employed two unusually pointed taglines, "It costs more, but it *does* more," and "It's built better to last longer."

With the introduction of an FM radio, the company launched an effective point-of-sale effort in which a Zenith radio was tuned in to the company's classical radio station. Passersby were awestruck by the sound quality. With the logo plainly visible, Zenith gained an unshakable reputation for quality that translated to the entire product line.

During the 1950s, the demonstrations were adapted for television consoles that included hi-fi radios and phonographs. By this time, however, the medium of television advertising had opened up. Consumers saw ads for new Zenith televisions on their old Admirals and Quasars. The format of Zenith advertising was typical for the day: The company's products were introduced showroom-style by an attractive housewife who demonstrated all the features of the set. Other ads, ostensibly aimed at men, featured authoritative male voice-overs that spelled out the advantages of the Zenith product. Print ads took a similar tack, while advertising for radio products was drastically reduced.

Despite the advent of mechanically assembled televisions during the 1960s, Zenith televisions were still assembled by hand. This became a great asset to Zenith, whose "Handcrafted Quality" tagline emphasized the painstaking detail and care that went into making each television.

Zenith television advertising was reduced significantly in the late 1980s in the face of mounting losses from enormous competition—primarily from Japanese manufacturers who flooded the market with TVs in an attempt to draw economies from sheer volume. With the formation of a new product line in the early 1990s, Zenith returned to the airwaves with a slightly shocking ad that took a shot, ostensibly, at showroom salesmen. In a scene featuring a Zenith home theater TV system in an elegantly appointed livingroom, a spokeswoman lists the new features people want in a television. "But," she implores, "before someone shows you a TV with some foreign name, ask to see a Zenith." The ad appealed to anti-Japanese sentiment, however latent, and reminded consumers that there was an American alternative to Sony, Mitsubishi, Toshiba, and JVC. However, although Zenith was an American company, its televisions were assembled in Mexico.

A later ad campaign presents a reborn Zenith, with a more modern product line, and uses the tagline, "Watch Us." This simple double entendre asks consumers to expect even greater things from the company and to actually watch a Zenith television. These ads drew heavily upon established equity, while controverting distrust of American brand names.

Brand Development

Television programming grew tremendously during the late 1950s and early 1960s. Network programming offered nightly entertainment, evening news, children's shows, and educational programs. As the medium overtook radio, Zenith seized the lead in television manufacturing. In 1956, the company introduced a revolutionary tuning device that was years ahead of its time, the "Space Command" remote control. This innovation helped Zenith to become the largest manufacturer of televisions in 1959. Two years later, after endless testing, Zenith finally marketed a 10-model line of color televisions, including a 21-inch model.

Zenith offered the highest quality product line then available, successfully translating its venerable name in radios to market leadership in televisions. In 1969, Zenith introduced its "Chromacolor" black matrix color picture tube, which doubled the brightness of color TV and immediately enhanced the Zenith reputation for excellence. In 1972, Zenith put out a 25-inch television that made it the market leader in color models. The company incorporated an extended field electron gun in its projection system in 1976, representing a further improvement in picture reproduction. In 1978, Zenith added a modular chassis, called "System 3," which simplified maintenance and provided even greater miniaturization. Zenith televisions were available in a variety of models, including small, plastic-cased portables, medium size "kitchen" TVs, and larger furniture-type living room sets.

However, while Zenith was selling high-end televisions, the market was being flooded by millions of cheaper sets built in Japan. No longer interested in a piece of furniture with a TV in it, consumers opted for the cheaper set. The Japanese had the advantage of lower wages, factories better oriented for mass-production, and more efficient operations management and distribution. In time, huge sales volumes enabled Japanese manufacturers to introduce larger, more advanced televisions, at last squeezing Zenith and other American manufacturers out of their own market.

While charging its foreign competitors with dumping, Zenith sold its hearing aid operation and moved some of its manufacturing facilities to Mexico and Taiwan. The company also reached an unfortunate agreement to market Sony Betamax video cassette recorders in the United States—two years before Matsushita's VHS system established itself as the standard.

In 1979, the year Zenith lost its number one spot in TV market share to RCA, the company entered the computer industry. It purchased the Heath Company, changed Heath's name to Zenith Data Systems and converted its operations to manufacture computers. Although the extension of the Zenith name and quality process to computers was successful, this market also was facing huge new competition. Zenith's computer business drained funds that could, and probably should, have been used for advertising and promotion. Instead, Zenith adopted a very low profile while its operations were realigned. As a result, some consumers, it seemed, weren't sure whether Zenith was even still in business.

Zenith produced its last radio in 1982, and two years later changed its name from the Zenith Radio Corporation to the Zenith Electronics Corporation. In 1986, the company introduced more new products than ever before, including televisions, cable TV descramblers, computers, and video cassette recorders. With picture technologies reaching maturity, Zenith concentrated on improving television sound and entered a partnership with the audio systems manufacturer Bose. In inventing the "home theater" concept, Zenith established a new market in which it was the leader. In 1987, Zenith introduced a flat tension mask screen that produced clearer, glare-free screens for computer monitors. In 1988, Zenith came out with a Dolby Surround Sound television.

Despite anemic promotional budgets, sales began a small turnaround. Zenith's reputation for engineering excellence remained strong in its institutional efforts to establish new standards for the American television broadcast industry. These efforts, which included a stereo television standard called Multichannel Television Sound, or MTS, helped to keep Zenith on the cutting edge of television technology and a step ahead of its competition.

Zenith sold its computer operations in 1989 to concentrate on building televisions and computer monitors. This decision coincided with another company effort to drive industry standards for High-Definition Television, or HDTV. Zenith initially undertook the project by itself, then in conjunction with AT&T, and later as a leader of the Digital HDTV "Grand Alliance."

Performance Evaluation

Despite the changes Zenith has made to its product line, it has remained absolutely committed to its brand identity. In fact, the company has used the same Zenith logo and "Quality goes in" slogan since they were introduced in 1927. While the famous lightning logo was used in advertising, block letters were used on the company's products for many years until the logo returned to products in the 1980s.

Unlike many consumer products brands, the Zenith name has been defined mostly through a reputation for quality that took years to establish and decades of work to maintain. As a result, the company never attempted to sell a product merely by slapping the Zenith name on it, but by allowing the quality of the product to sell itself, building equity for the Zenith name almost as an afterthought. By preventing a slide in its products quality, the company not only avoided discrediting its brand name, but spared itself the formidable task of rescuing a name the public no longer believed in.

In order to familiarize younger consumers with the Zenith name, the company licenses its name to computers built by Bull, and to SDI Technologies, which manufactures portable stereos, radios, and telephones. With the exception of the computer line, Zenith retains control of the design and promotion of products that carry its name. The arrangement is intended to generate trust in the Zenith name among teenagers for the day when, at an average age of 25, they buy their first television.

In the 1990s, Zenith was rebuilding its market share and preparing for leadership in HDTV. Through its reorganization and strategic partnerships, Zenith stands to regain a leading position in the television market. Having emerged from deep financial trouble with its brand name still favorably regarded, it is unlikely that Zenith will alter its proven identity strategy. The Zenith style is decidedly subtle, understated, and exclusive, giving it great prominence as a premium product.

Further Reading:

Zenith Electronics Corporation, *The Zenith Story,* Glenview, Illinois: Zenith Electronics, 1955.

Zenith Electronics Corporation Annual Reports, Glenview, Illinois: Zenith Electronics, 1990, 1991, 1992.

''Zenith Fact Sheet,'' Glenview, Illinois: Zenith Electronics, 1993.

''Zenith: Highlights of the First 60 Years,'' Glenview, Illinois: Zenith Electronics.

—John Simley

INDEX TO BRAND NAMES

Listings are arranged in alphabetical order under brand name. Brand names appearing in bold type have historical essays on the page numbers appearing in bold. The index is cumulative with volume numbers printed in bold type.

INDEX TO COMPANIES AND PERSONS

Listings are arranged in alphabetical order under the company name; thus Philip Morris Companies Inc. will be found under the letter P. Definite articles (The) that precede the name are ignored for alphabetical purposes. The index is cumulative with volume numbers printed in bold type.

INDEX TO ADVERTISING AGENCIES

Listings are arranged in alphabetical order under the agency name; thus J. Walter Thompson will be found under the letter J. The index is cumulative with volume numbers printed in bold type.

INDEX TO BRAND CATEGORIES

Brand categories are arranged alphabetically; listings beneath each category in turn are arranged alphabetically. This index contains only brand names that have individual historical essays in the series. The index is cumulative with volume numbers following the brand category.

SUN CARE PRODUCTS II

Bain de Soleil
Coppertone
Hawaiian Tropic

TAMPONS

See FEMININE HYGIENE

TEA I

Lipton
Nestea
Salada
Tetley

TELEVISIONS

See ELECTRONICS

TENNIS AND GOLF EQUIPMENT III

Dunlop
Head
Prince
Spalding
Wilson

TIRES III

BFGoodrich
Firestone
Goodyear
Michelin

TISSUE

See FACIAL TISSUE or TOILET TISSUE

TOBACCO I

Benson & Hedges
Camel
Kool
Lucky Strike
Marlboro
Newport
Salem
Virginia Slims
Winston

TOILET TISSUE II

Charmin
Northern
Scott

TOOLS III

Black & Decker
Stanley

TOOTHPASTE II

Aquafresh
Close-Up
Colgate
Crest
Pepsodent

TOWELS III

Fieldcrest
Martex

TOYS AND GAMES III

Atari
Barbie
Cabbage Patch Kids
Duncan Yo-Yo
Etch A Sketch
Fisher-Price
Frisbee
G.I. Joe
Hot Wheels
Hula Hoop
Lego
Lionel
Lincoln Logs
Louisville Slugger
Matchbox
Monopoly
Nerf
Nintendo
Play-Doh
Playskool
Scrabble
Sega
Silly Putty
Slinky
Teenage Mutant Ninja Turtles
Tonka
Trivial Pursuit
Twister
Wiffle Ball

TRUCKS AND OTHER LARGE VEHICLES (also see SPORT-UTILITY VEHICLES) III

Mack Trucks
Winnebago

TYPEWRITERS III

Brother
Olivetti
Smith Corona

UNDERGARMENTS (also see HOSIERY) II

BVD
Calvin Klein
Carter's
Fruit of the Loom
Hanes
Jockey
Maidenform

VACUUM CLEANERS III

Bissell
Black & Decker
Dirt Devil
Eureka
Hoover
Norelco

VEGETABLES

See FRUITS AND VEGETABLES

VITAMINS II

Geritol

WASHERS AND DRYERS

See APPLIANCES

WATCHES AND JEWELRY II (except where indicated)

Citizen
Monet
Rolex
Seiko
Swatch
Tiffany (vol. III)
Timex

WEIGHT LOSS PROGRAMS

Slim-Fast

WINDOWS III

Andersen

WINE AND CHAMPAGNE I

Almaden
Beringer
Dom Pérignon
Gallo
Glen Ellen
Inglenook
Richards Wild Irish Rose
Sutter Home

WRAPS II

Glad
Reynolds Wrap
Saran Wrap

WRITING INSTRUMENTS II

Bic
Crayola
Dixon Ticonderoga
Paper Mate
Parker

NOTES ON CONTRIBUTORS

ALFARO, Victor. Information specialist in the Civil Rights Division of the U.S. Department of Justice. Former editorial assistant in the Economic Studies Program at the Brookings Institution in Washington, D.C.; author of the play *Holy Thursday.*

ARMSTRONG, Robin. Free-lance writer. Contributor to *Contemporary Musicians, Contemporary Black Biography,* and *International Dictionary of Opera.*

AVIZIENIS, Audra. Free-lance writer.

BARNSTORFF, Virginia. Free-lance writer. Special assignment writer and mathematics correlator for Silver Burdett Ginn (Simon & Schuster), 1989–91. Contributing writer, *HSPT Success: Work-A-Text Study Program for Writing,* 1991.

BERRY, Pam. Free-lance writer and editor.

BILAS, Wendy Johnson. Free-lance writer with eight years of professional marketing experience; MBA in marketing, Wake Forest University; director of marketing for the Charlotte Symphony Orchestra.

BOYER, Dean. Former newspaper reporter; free-lance writer in Seattle area.

BROWN, Susan Windisch. Free-lance writer and editor.

COHEN, Kerstan. Financial analyst for Morningstar Incorporated in Chicago, Illinois. French translator; editor for *Letter-Ex* poetry review, Chicago.

COLLINS, Cheryl L. Free-lance writer and researcher.

COVELL, Jeffrey L. Free-lance writer and corporate history contractor.

DORMAN, Evelyn S. Free-lance journalist, public relations consultant, French teacher, tutor, and graduate student. Contributor to *Brides Today,* the *Chicago Sun-Times, Lerner-Pulitzer* newspapers, and St. James Press's *International Directory of Company Histories.*

DOUGAL, April S. Archivist and free-lance writer specializing in business and social history in Cleveland, Ohio.

DUBOVOJ, Sina. History contractor and free-lance writer; adjunct professor of history, Montgomery College, Rockville, Maryland.

FRANCIS, Sean. Graduate student in English at the University of Chicago.

FRANK, Justyna. Free-lance writer and Polish translator. Graduate student at the University of Chicago.

GAREFFA, Peter M. Managing editor, St. James Press.

GOPNIK, Hilary. Free-lance writer.

INGRAM, Frederick. Writer and researcher based in Columbia, South Carolina.

JACOBSON, Robert R. Free-lance writer and musician.

JAMES, Marinell. San Francisco-based writer and editor specializing in business and health-care topics.

JOHNSON, Timothy P. Free-lance writer.

KING, Daniel E. Free-lance writer working on doctorate in economics at the New School for Social Research.

KROLL, Dorothy. Free-lance business writer, journalist, and industry analyst.

MASH, Jeffrey E. Free-lance writer.

MAXFIELD, Doris Morris. Owner of Written Expressions, an editorial services business. Contributor to numerous reference publications; editor of *Online Database Search Services Directory,* 1983–84 and 1988, and of *Charitable Organizations of the U.S.,* 1991–92 and 1992–93.

MCNULTY, Mary. Free-lance writer and editor. Contributor to the *Chicago Tribune* and Press-Republican newspapers. Manager of Publications, American Association of Law Libraries, 1988–93.

MOGELONSKY, Marcia K. Free-lance editor and writer; contributor to *American Demographics,* the *Numbers News, Modern Women,* and other magazines.

NASH, Margo. Free-lance writer specializing in medical topics.

PATTI, Nicholas. Free-lance writer.

PEDERSON, Jay P. Free-lance writer and editor.

PENDERGAST, Sara. Free-lance writer and editor.

PENDERGAST, Tom. Free-lance writer and graduate student in business administration at Purdue University.

RIGGS, Thomas. Free-lance writer and editor.

SALTER, Susan. Writer/contributor to several reference series, including *Contemporary Authors, Newsmakers,* and *Major Authors and Illustrators for Children and Young Adults.*

SARICH, John A. Free-lance writer and editor. Graduate student in economics at the New School for Social Research.

SCHOOLMAN, Martha. Free-lance writer in Chicago.

SHERMAN, Francine Shonfeld. Free-lance writer and editor. Assistant editor, *Compton's Encyclopedia,* 1986–92; contributing editor, *Britannica Book of the Year,* annual.

SIMLEY, John. Economist for Proxy Voter Services in Chicago, Illinois. Former research editor for *International Directory of Company Histories.*

TIVENAN, William. Free-lance writer.

TROESTER, Maura. Chicago-based free-lance writer.

WAINWRIGHT, Mary Katherine. Professor of English at Manatee Community College in Bradenton, Florida.

WALTON, Dorothy. Financial writer for First Analysis Corporation, an investment research firm in Chicago, Illinois. Free-lance writer specializing in business and legislative topics; author of *Mastering the 1993 Tax Act.*

WOODWARD, Angela. Free-lance writer.